Reviewer's Guide for

Addison-Wesley Mathematics
Book 7

The large numbers— 1 , 2 for example—identify eight of the major features of Addison-Wesley Mathematics. Turn to the pages listed below each number to make reviewing easy.

Traditional mathematics applied to the challenges of today

See pages:
T4-T5
55
112-113

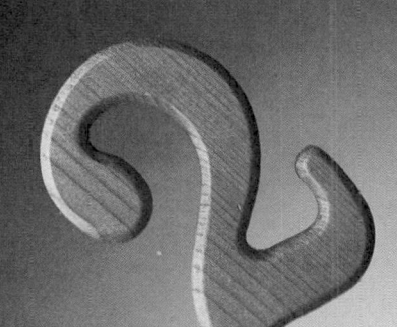

Solid skills development with measurable results

See pages:
T6-T7
61
67
206-207

Problem solving for the decision-makers of the future

See pages:
T8-9   116-117
16-17   362-363
82-83

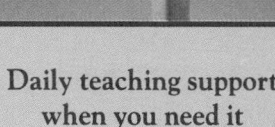

Daily teaching support when you need it

See pages:
T10-11
96-97
142-143
358-359

Resources to meet the challenge of every classroom

See pages:
T12-T13
223A
275B-275C
440-441

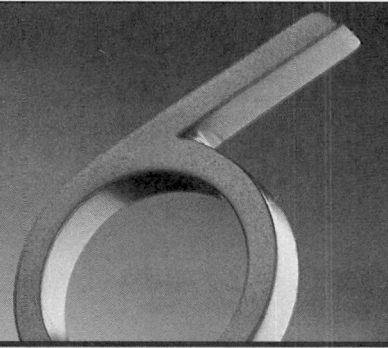

Planning and assessment for simplified management

See pages:
T14-T15
219-221

A flexible teaching package that promotes success

See pages:
T16-T17
367D-367E

A team of math professionals you can trust

See pages:
T18-T19

Addison-Wesley Mathematics K-8 Components

Each one unique and totally integrated
into a complete program

Student Books

Teacher's Editions

Teacher's Resource Books

Practice, Reteaching, Enrichment
   Workbooks
   Duplicator Masters
   Blackline Masters

Cumulative Record Cards K-8

Manipulative Kits

Kindergarten Big Book

Computer Management System

Instructional Software

Answer Booklets

Spanish Editions

and the Addison-Wesley family
of fine mathematics supplements
and teaching source books.

ISBN 0-201-24702-X   CDEFGHIJKL-VH-8987654

Addison-Wesley Mathematics

Teacher's Edition Book 7

Robert E. Eicholz   **Phares G. O'Daffer**   **Charles R. Fleenor**

Randall I. Charles   Sharon Young   Carne S. Barnett

Contents

T4   Program Overview

T20   Scope and Sequence

T26   Objectives for Book 7

1A   Chapter 1 Addition and Subtraction of Whole Numbers

31A   Chapter 2 Addition and Subtraction of Decimals

55A   Chapter 3 Multiplication and Division of Whole Numbers

87A   Chapter 4 Multiplication of Decimals

115A   Chapter 5 Division of Decimals

135A   Chapter 6 Geometry

163A   Chapter 7 Number Theory and Equations

193A   Chapter 8 Addition and Subtraction of Fractions

223A   Chapter 9 Multiplication and Division of Fractions

247A   Chapter 10 Measurement: Metric Units

275A   Chapter 11 Ratio and Proportion

293A   Chapter 12 Percent

321A   Chapter 13 Circles and Cylinders

343A   Chapter 14 Probability, Statistics, and Graphs

367A   Chapter 15 Integers

393A   Chapter 16 Measurement: Customary Units

413   Appendix

440   Materials

441   Long-Range Planning Chart

442   Bibliography

444   Index

449   Acknowledgments

Addison-Wesley Publishing Company

Menlo Park, California   Reading, Massachusetts   London   Amsterdam   Don Mills, Ontario   Sydney

Traditional mathematics . . .

Solid math principles remain the core of professional mathematics instruction. Addison-Wesley puts these basic principles in a format that is clear and easy to follow. But we also recognize that students must go

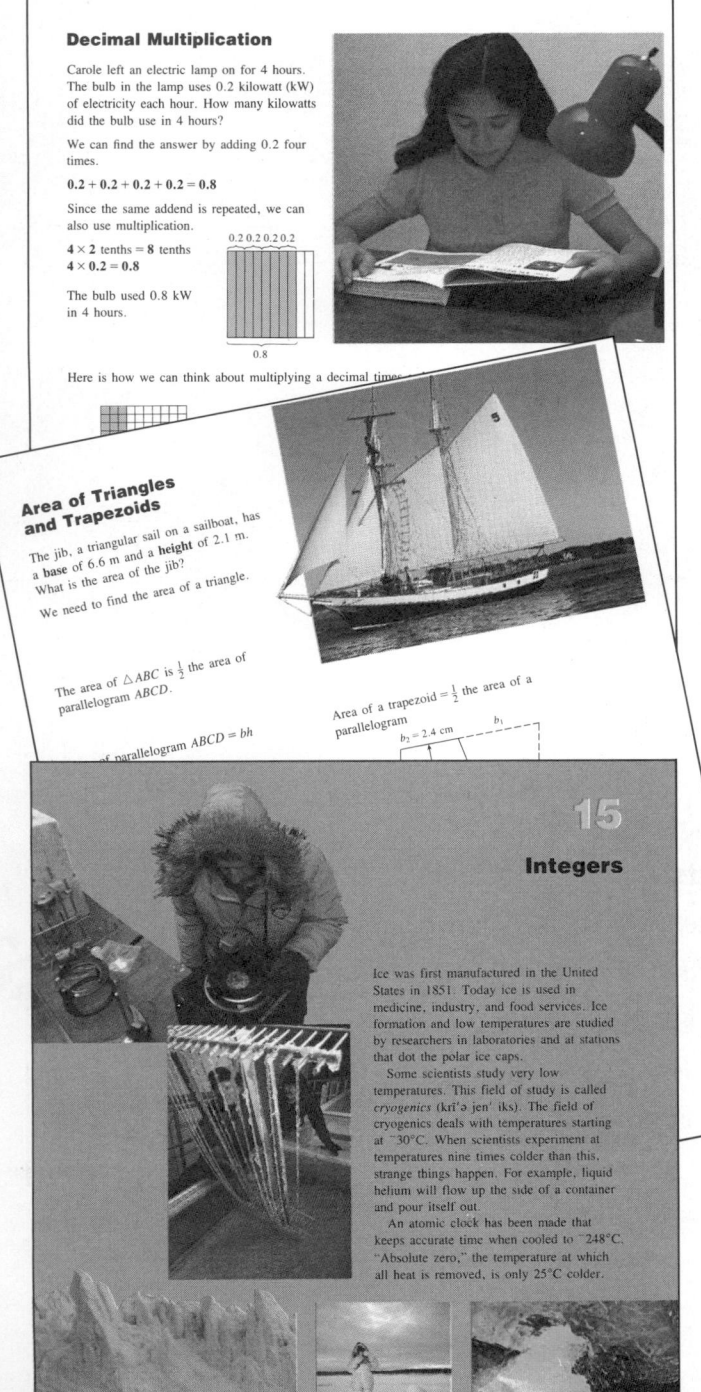

Decimal Multiplication

Carole left an electric lamp on for 4 hours. The bulb in the lamp uses 0.2 kilowatt (kW) of electricity each hour. How many kilowatts did the bulb use in 4 hours?

We can find the answer by adding 0.2 four times.

$$0.2 + 0.2 + 0.2 + 0.2 = 0.8$$

Since the same addend is repeated, we can also use multiplication.

4×2 tenths = **8** tenths
$4 \times 0.2 = 0.8$

The bulb used 0.8 kW in 4 hours.

Here is how we can think about multiplying a decimal time

Area of Triangles and Trapezoids

The jib, a triangular sail on a sailboat, has a **base** of 6.6 m and a **height** of 2.1 m. What is the area of the jib?

We need to find the area of a triangle.

The area of $\triangle ABC$ is $\frac{1}{2}$ the area of parallelogram $ABCD$.

of parallelogram $ABCD = bh$

Area of a trapezoid = $\frac{1}{2}$ the area of a parallelogram
$b_2 = 2.4$ cm

15

Integers

Ice was first manufactured in the United States in 1851. Today ice is used in medicine, industry, and food services. Ice formation and low temperatures are studied by researchers in laboratories and at stations that dot the polar ice caps.

Some scientists study very low temperatures. This field of study is called *cryogenics* (krī'ə jen' iks). The field of cryogenics deals with temperatures starting at ⁻30°C. When scientists experiment at temperatures nine times colder than this, strange things happen. For example, liquid helium will flow up the side of a container and pour itself out.

An atomic clock has been made that keeps accurate time when cooled to ⁻248°C. "Absolute zero," the temperature at which all heat is removed, is only 25°C colder.

Program Overview

The major reason for studying mathematics is to learn how to solve problems. To become effective problem solvers students need to understand *concepts*, know *basic facts*, efficiently use *computational skills*, and select and apply appropriate *problem-solving strategies*. To implement this philosophy Addison-Wesley Mathematics provides a balanced program in each of these areas.

Understanding Concepts

To ensure real understanding of mathematical concepts, teachers are encouraged to use manipulative materials or pictorial models with students whenever appropriate. Understanding of concepts is emphasized through a variety of problem-solving experiences.

Learning Skills

To develop a solid foundation in basic facts and skills students follow an instructional sequence of (1) involvement with *models,* (2) understanding the *fact* or *procedure,* (3) extensive *practice,* and (4) *application* of the skill to problem-solving situations. Mental mathematics and estimation skills are carefully developed and sequenced.

Solving Problems

In Addison-Wesley Mathematics, problem solving is realistic. Students have opportunities to collect data from many different sources and to solve a wide variety of problems. Inherent in the Addision-Wesley Mathematics philosophy is the belief that a student's attitude toward problem solving is extremely important. By choosing problems which come from the real world, by providing understandable techniques for solving problems, and by encouraging students to share their problem solutions with others, positive attitudes are developed and success in problem solving is ensured.

beyond basic skills in order to solve problems in a complex, technological era. It's the successful combination of the traditional and the modern that makes Addison-Wesley *the* math text for today.

What reviewers and users say about Addison–Wesley Mathematics.

- **A complete program**—a balanced development of concepts, facts, computational skills, and problem solving. It is well sequenced. The pace through topics is unhurried, yet all the content is covered.

- **A helpful program**—exceptional opportunities for review and reteaching based on student needs. It provides real help in teaching problem solving. The teachable approach to facts and skills makes learning easy for students.

- **A natural program**—the art and photographs are humanized and interesting to students. Applied problems allow students to make decisions in natural, everyday settings. Problem themes are related to careers and integrated with other subject areas. Students are encouraged to become actively involved with physical models.

- **A sensible program**—solid mathematics for today's needs and for the future. Addison–Wesley Mathematics includes a technology strand, with ample opportunities for students to learn about and use calculators and computers. Calculator exercises are interspersed throughout the program. The development of computer literacy begins with readiness lessons in flowcharting and builds to actual programming in BASIC and logo languages.

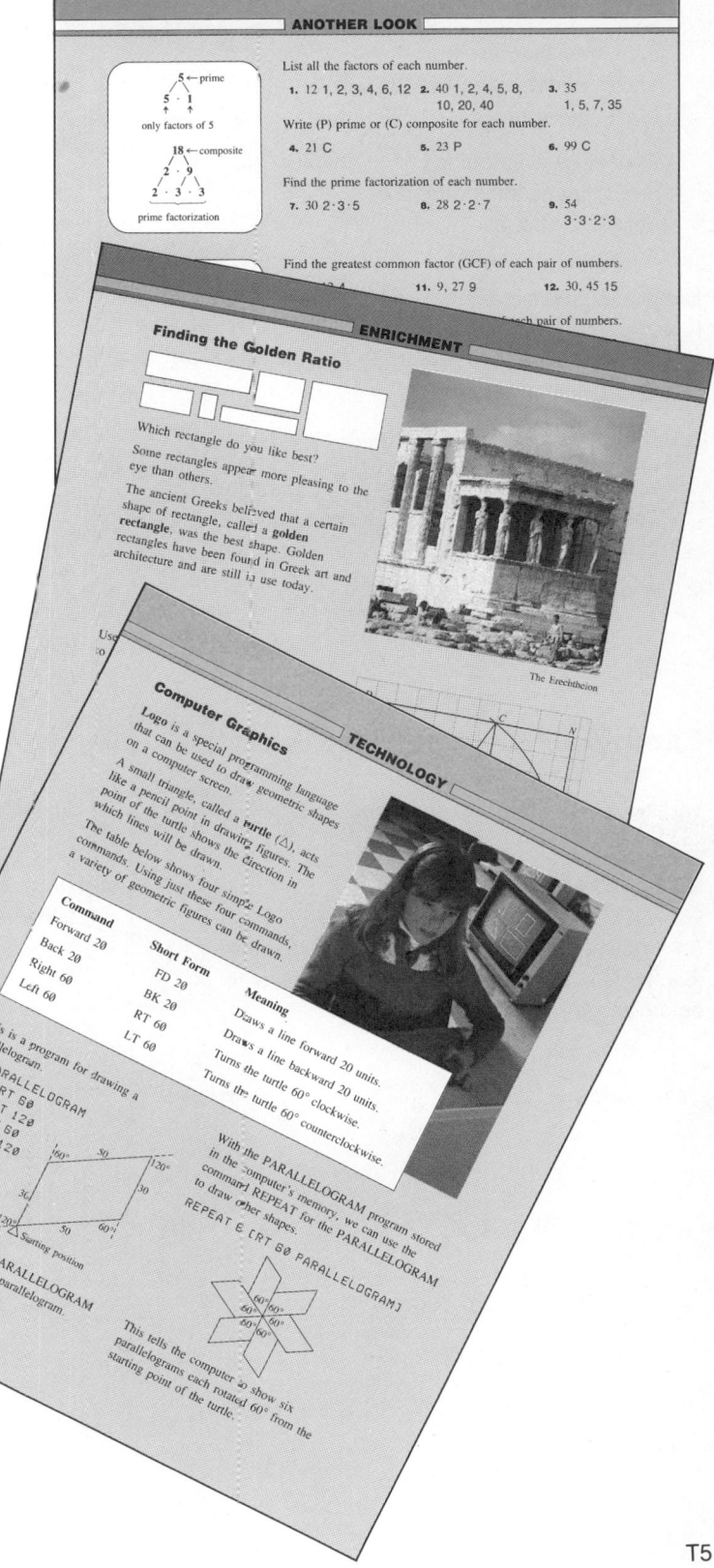

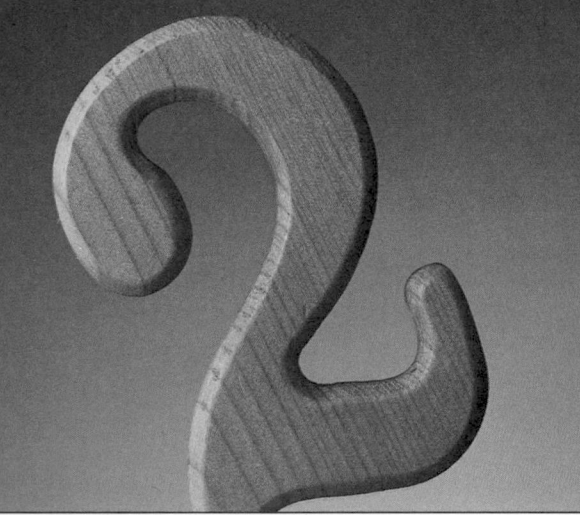

Solid skills development . . .

Through the years, Addison–Wesley has continued to refine its presentation of basic math skills. This new program provides a clear, consistent format for teaching the skills that effectively build your students'

Motivation

- A problem that sets the theme for the lesson and provides a real-life application of the skill to be taught
- Appealing illustrations that involve students' imaginations and bring life and lightness to the page

Development

- Concept statement that suggests a reason for learning the skill
- Instruction boxes that guide students through algorithms
- Think clouds that verbalize the thought process
- Functional color that clarifies development

Examples

Variations of the skill that cover special cases

Diagnosis

An **informal assessment** that enables the teacher to evaluate students' grasp of the skill before assigning the exercises

---

Subtracting Decimals

Using an electronic timer, a tennis serve was clocked at 62.483 meters per second (m/s). A baseball pitch had a speed of 41.556 m/s. How much greater was the speed of the tennis ball?

Since we want to find how much more one number is than another, we subtract.

Decimals can be subtracted just like whole numbers if the decimal points are lined up.

Write the problem with the decimal points in line.	Subtract as with whole numbers.	Place the decimal point in line with the others.
$$\begin{array}{r} 62.483 \\ -41.556 \\ \hline \end{array}$$	$$\begin{array}{r} 114\,7\,13 \\ 62.483 \\ -41.556 \\ \hline 20\ 927 \end{array}$$	$$\begin{array}{r} 114\,7\,13 \\ 62.483 \\ -41.556 \\ \hline 20.927 \end{array}$$

The speed of the tennis ball was 20.927 m/s greater than the speed of the baseball.

Other Examples

$$52 - 37.83$$

$$\begin{array}{r} 52.00 \\ -37.83 \\ \hline 14.17 \end{array}$$ 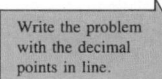 Annex zeros to line up the decimal places.

$$29.196 - 17.4$$

$$\begin{array}{r} 29.196 \\ -17.400 \\ \hline 11.796 \end{array}$$

$$\$25 - \$18.75$$

$$\begin{array}{r} \$25.00 \\ -18.75 \\ \hline \$\ \ 6.25 \end{array}$$

Warm Up

Subtract.

1. $\begin{array}{r}58.42\\-26.65\\\hline 31.77\end{array}$	**2.** $\begin{array}{r}9.27\\-5.969\\\hline 3.301\end{array}$	**3.** $\begin{array}{r}0.8062\\-0.5571\\\hline 0.2491\end{array}$	**4.** $\begin{array}{r}\$601.09\\-233.46\\\hline \$367.63\end{array}$	**5.** $\begin{array}{r}1.213\\-0.944\\\hline 0.269\end{array}$

6. $16 - 2.75$ $13.25

7. $1.8 - 0.635$ 1.165

8. $23.55 - 1.978$ 21.572

9. $32.417 - 29$ 3.417

10. $17 - 0.34$ 16.66

42

T6

. . . with measurable results

proficiency *and* understanding. And, at all levels, motivating illustrations actively involve your students in the learning process.

Subtract.

1. 34.8 − 12.6 = 22.2	**2.** 84.6 − 29.8 = 54.8	**3.** 0.672 − 0.186 = 0.486	**4.** 9.68 − 4.39 = 5.29	**5.** 329.7 − 167.9 = 161.8
6. 17.45 − 8.21 = 9.24	**7.** 5.8623 − 3.4871 = 2.3752	**8.** 56.725 − 38.463 = 18.262	**9.** 19.471 − 7.836 = 11.635	**10.** 40.70 − 26.36 = 14.34
11. 19.01 − 3.98 = 15.03	**12.** 5.63 − 2.48 = 3.15	**13.** 583.6 − 29.9 = 553.7	**14.** 0.697 − 0.248 = 0.449	**15.** 8.721 − 4.83 = 3.891
16. 10.7 − 8.69 = 2.01	**17.** 12.1398 − 8.6476 = 3.4922	**18.** 25.865 − 16.9532 = 8.9118	**19.** 10.07661 − 0.947 = 9.12961	**20.** 2.00075 − 1.29564 = 0.70511
21. $78.02 − 35.43 = $42.59	**22.** $50.06 − 37.69 = $12.37	**23.** $53.40 − 27.86 = $25.54	**24.** $1.00 − 0.69 = $0.31	**25.** $200.00 − 176.29 = $23.71

26. 9.14 − 4.715 4.425   **27.** 29.857 − 16.948 12.909   **28.** 5.76 − 3.042 2.718

29. 2 − 1.675 0.325   **30.** 132.943 − 49.685 133.258   **31.** 9.075 − 4.68 4.395

32. 6.175 − 3.9 2.275   **33.** 0.936 − 0.75 0.186   **34.** 100 − 84.97 15.03

35. A hockey puck had a speed of 44.556 m/s. The pelota, or ball, used in jai alai had a speed of 63.111 m/s. How much slower was the speed of the hockey puck? 18.555 m/s

36. When hit, a golf ball had a speed of 28.361 m/s. After three seconds in the air, the speed dropped to 19.5 m/s. How much slower was the speed after three seconds in the air? 8.861 m/s

THINK MATH

Logical Reasoning

Magic Squares have the same sum in each row, in each column, and in the two diagonals.

Find the missing numbers to make Magic Squares.

9.3

4.96	0.62	3.72
1.86	3.10	4.34
2.48	5.58	1.24

30.6

14.4	1.8	2.7	11.7
4.5	9.9	9.0	7.2
8.1	6.3	5.4	10.8
3.6	12.6	13.5	0.9

More Practice, page 420, Set A   43

81 sets of practice exercises . . .

Practice

• Ample exercises to reinforce learning

• Horizontal and vertical format

• Skillkeepers to help students maintain skills taught previously

SKILLKEEPER

1. 5)48 **2.** 23)5.934 **3.** 13)125.19 **4.** 8)60.4 **5.** 14)2.03

6. 673 ÷ 0.01 **7.** 97.2 ÷ 0.1 **8.** 9,247 ÷ 0.001 **9.** 0.592 ÷ 0.01 **10.** 9.12 ÷ 0.001

11. 0.05)28.15 **12.** 2.3)14.697 **13.** 54)116.532 **14.** 0.36)53.28 **15.** 5.8)3.4162

Application

• Problems that carry through the theme of the page

• Data Hunts in which data is gathered either firsthand or from a variety of sources outside the book

13. DATA HUNT What is the average cost per kilowatt-hour for electricity in your area? Find the amount of a home electric bill for one month. Divide by the number of kilowatt-hours used to find the average cost per kilowatt-hour.

• Data Banks in which data is found in the appendix of the student book

34. DATA BANK What was the time for the winner of the 500-meter speed skating competition in the 1964 Winter Olympics? What was the time as a fraction of a minute? (See page 415.)

• Calculator exercises in which students apply the skills they've learned to the calculator

Extension

Starred problems and Think Math activities challenge students to extend their skills

★ 10. Sylvia can earn up to $2,000 tax-free interest in 1 year. How much principal must she invest at an interest rate of 16% per year in order to earn $2,000 interest?

21. Light from the sun takes about 9,600 seconds to reach the planet Uranus. About how far does light travel from the sun to Uranus? Give both the standard numeral and the scientific notation.

T7

Problem solving . . . .

In Addison–Wesley Mathematics, students become actively involved in problem solving through a variety of real-life situations. The problems encourage students to be decision-makers and apply the techniques they learn

---

PROBLEM SOLVING: Using the 5-Point Checklist

QUESTION
DATA
PLAN
ANSWER
CHECK

To Solve a Problem

1. Understand the QUESTION   4. Find the ANSWER

2. Find the needed DATA   5. CHECK back

3. PLAN what to do

Review the 5-Point Checklist for solving problems. Then study the problem below and its solution.

A tape recording of 42 min used 1,464 ft of tape. How many feet of tape were used to record a song that lasted 14 min?

1. Understand the QUESTION
How many feet of tape are needed for 14 min of taping?

2. Find the needed DATA

minutes	42	14
feet	1,464	?

3. PLAN what to do
Let n = the number of feet of tape needed for 14 min of taping. Write a proportion using the data and n.

$$\frac{42}{1,464} = \frac{14}{n}$$

4. Find the ANSWER

DATA BANK

Whales

Blue Whale
Length 30 m

Gray Whale
Length 15 m

Sei Whale
Length 17 m

Black Right Whale
Length 18 m

Fin Whale
Length 24 m

Sperm Whale
Length 18 m

Killer Whale
Length 9 m

Baird's Beaked Whale
Length 12 m

No. 737 Lowest Annual Temperature of Record—Selected Cities

State	Station	Temp. in degrees C	State	Station	Temp. in degrees C
AL	Mobile	−14	MT	Great Falls	−42
AK	Juneau	−30	NE	Omaha	−30
AZ	Phoenix	−8	NV	Reno	−27
AR	Little Rock	−21	NH	Concord	−38
CA	Sacramento	−7	NJ	Atlantic City	−24
CO	Denver	−34	NM	Albuquerque	−27
CT	Hartford	−32	NY	Albany	−33
DE	Wilmington	−21	NC	Charlotte	−19
DC	Washington	−17	ND	Bismarck	−42
FL	Jacksonville	−11	OH	Cincinnati	−32
GA	Atlanta	−19	OK	Oklahoma City	−20
HI	Honolulu	12	OR	Portland	−19
ID	Boise	−31	PA	Pittsburgh	−28
IL	Peoria	−32	RI	Providence	−25
IN	Indianapolis	−29	SC	Columbia	−16
IA	Des Moines	−31	SD	Sioux Falls	−38
KS	Wichita	−24	TN	Nashville	−26
KY	Louisville	−29	TX	El Paso	−22
LA	New Orleans	−10	UT	Salt Lake City	−34
ME	Portland	−39	VT	Burlington	−34
MD	Baltimore	−22	VA	Richmond	−24
MA	Boston	−24	WA	Spokane	−32
MI	Sault Ste. Marie	−37	WV	Charleston	−24
MN	Duluth	−39	WI	Milwaukee	−31
MS	Jackson	−14	WY	Cheyenne	−37
MO	St. Louis	−26	PR	San Juan	16

Daily Diet of Some Zoo Animals

	Elephant	Giraffe	Gorilla	Hippopotamus
Hay	25 kg	7 kg	—	18 kg
Grain	23 kg	0.5 kg	—	—
Fruit and vegetables	23 kg	—	8 kg	2 kg
Pellets	—	0.5 kg	—	7 kg
Leaves	—	0.5 kg	2 kg	—
Bread	12 kg	—	—	—

416

Problem Solving in Addison–Wesley Mathematics

The foundation of Addison–Wesley Mathematics is a carefully structured and sequenced problem-solving strand. It provides both motivational content and ample opportunity for students to participate in a wide range of problem-solving experiences.

Clear organization and specific instructions for solving problems give the very best help possible for teachers as they work with students in this important task. Strategies and techniques are carefully presented and developed.

The 5-Point Checklist

Throughout the program, sequential instruction in problem solving is based on the following 5-Point Checklist.

5-Point Checklist

1. Understand the *question*.

2. Find the needed *data*.

3. *Plan* what to do.

4. Find the *answer*.

5. *Check back*.

QUESTION
DATA
PLAN
ANSWER
CHECK

Selected problem-solving lessons focus on one step in this checklist while others focus on all five steps. In these lessons, students are given real help in using important ideas under each point of the checklist.

- *Understand the Question*— In the early grades short sentence problems and pictures help students focus on the question. In later grades data or an equation may be given and students are asked to formulate an appropriate question. In all cases, the reading level of the word problems has been analyzed carefully to ensure that it is appropriate for the students at a given grade level.

- *Find the Needed Data*— In addition to the problem-solving lessons which focus on finding data from tables, pictures, advertisements, menus, and so on, other important experiences with data are provided throughout Addison–Wesley Mathematics. Data Bank problems require students to go beyond the text page to collect the needed data from a reference source in the

. . . . for the decision-makers of the future

to their own lives. The clear, efficient organization of the problem-solving program is sequentially consistent from chapter to chapter and from book to book.

Appendix of the textbook. Data Hunt problems encourage students to go outside the textbook to find the needed data from other reference sources or from an experiment conducted by the students.

Integrated into the program are problems with too much data, problems without enough data, and problems in which students must supply data by completing a table, making an organized list, or by other means.

- *Plan What to Do* — Problem-solving lessons which involve using a strategy such as Choose the Operations, Guess and Check, Draw a Picture, or Make a Table, help students learn to plan an approach to solving a problem. A clear understanding of the operations of addition, subtraction, multiplication, and division provides a foundation for the planning phase of problem solving. Problems solved by using one or more operations are given considerable emphasis as students develop their problem solving skills.

- *Find the Answer* — The main reason to develop computational skills is to be able to use them in solving problems. In Addison–Wesley Mathematics, each skill lesson is motivated by a word problem which can be solved using the skill developed in that lesson. After the particular computational skill has been developed and practiced, the students again solve a word problem which involves recognizing and performing the appropriate operation.

- *Check Back* — Selected lessons provide techniques for checking computational procedures and exercises to develop estimation skills. Students are also encouraged to reread the original problem to decide whether or not the answer makes sense.

Problem Solving Strategies

The Addison–Wesley problem-solving program gives considerable attention to the important task of solving nonroutine problems (often called process problems) which are not readily solvable using one or more of the basic operations. After a strategy is developed in a given chapter, "Try This" problems in subsequent chapters give students an opportunity to practice using that strategy. Detailed help, including hints, questions to ask students, problem solutions, and an extension problem, is provided in the Teacher's Edition.

Applied Problem Solving

In each Applied Problem Solving lesson, students are asked to make a decision about a real-life situation given specific information to consider. These special lessons require students to bring together the computational and problem-solving skills they have been learning throughout the program.

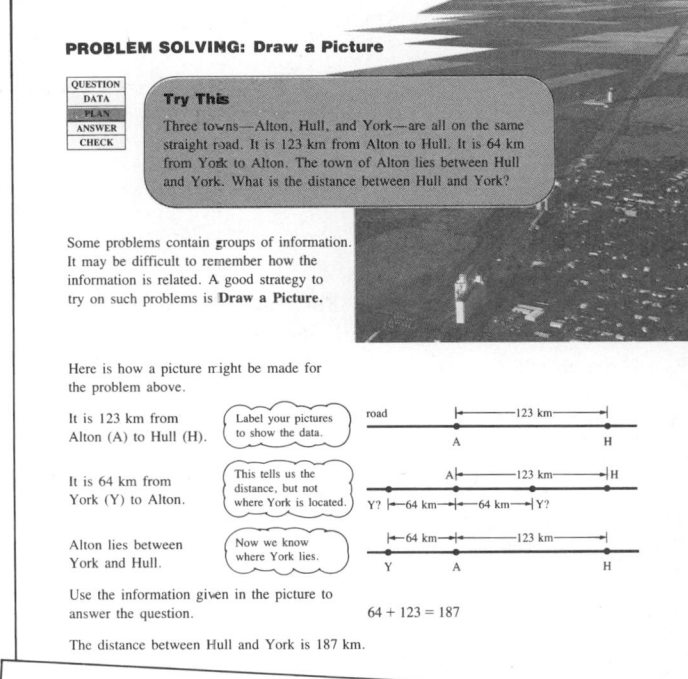

PROBLEM SOLVING: Draw a Picture

QUESTION / DATA / **PLAN** / ANSWER / CHECK

Try This

Three towns—Alton, Hull, and York—are all on the same straight road. It is 123 km from Alton to Hull. It is 64 km from York to Alton. The town of Alton lies between Hull and York. What is the distance between Hull and York?

Some problems contain groups of information. It may be difficult to remember how the information is related. A good strategy to try on such problems is **Draw a Picture.**

Here is how a picture might be made for the problem above.

It is 123 km from Alton (A) to Hull (H). *Label your pictures to show the data.*

It is 64 km from York (Y) to Alton. *This tells us the distance, but not where York is located.*

Alton lies between York and Hull. *Now we know where York lies.*

Use the information given in the picture to answer the question.

$64 + 123 = 187$

The distance between Hull and York is 187 km.

APPLIED PROBLEM SOLVING

QUESTION / DATA / PLAN / ANSWER / CHECK

You have an old TV set and you want to buy a new one. You could try to sell the old set through a newspaper advertisement before you buy a new TV set, or you could trade in your old set on a new set.

Some Things to Consider

- The old TV set is in fairly good condition.
- You want to get a new TV set within two weeks.
- A newspaper advertisement costs $2.75 a day.
- You expect to sell the old set for $50.
- A new TV set costs $389.
- You can trade in your old set on a new set and get $25 off the cost of the new set.

Some Questions to Answer

1. How much money will you have to pay for the new TV set with a trade-in? $364
2. What is the cost of an advertisement for one week? What is the cost of an advertisement for two weeks? $19.25; $38.50
3. If the old TV does not sell after the advertisement runs for two weeks, you must use the old TV as a trade-in. What is the total cost of the new TV set and the advertisement? $402.50
4. How much money must you pay for the new TV set if someone buys the old TV after only one day? $341.75

What Is Your Decision?

How will you plan to use your old TV set to help you buy a new TV set? Answers may vary. If the old set is sold within 9 days, it is better to sell it than to trade it in. To sell the set after 9 days will cost more than to use it for a trade-in.

336

T9

Daily teaching support . . . .

We know that every teacher has an individual style. The organization of the Teacher's Edition makes it quick and easy to locate everything your style demands

Starting the lesson

Quick Review—An optional daily skill maintenance program.

Ideas for Getting Started—Optional activities that introduce or prepare students for the content of the lesson.

Teaching the lesson

All the essentials for teaching the page tinted in yellow for easy access

Clear concise notes that make math easy to teach

Specific questions and step-by-step explanations to lead students through the concepts presented

---

232
Fractions

Quick Review Have students rename each of these fractions.
$16\frac{2}{3}$ $17\frac{1}{3}$ $10\frac{16}{11}$ $11\frac{6}{11}$ $26\frac{49}{49}$ 27 $12\frac{12}{8}$ $13\frac{1}{2}$
$38\frac{17}{9}$ $39\frac{8}{9}$ $14\frac{37}{24}$ $15\frac{13}{24}$ $27\frac{12}{10}$ $28\frac{4}{5}$

Lesson Focus To divide fractions

Ideas for Getting Started

Ask students the following questions to develop an intuitive idea of dividing by fractions. After students answer each question, write the corresponding equation on the chalkboard.

"How many fourths are in one?" $(1 \div \frac{1}{4} = 4)$

"How many halves are in three?" $(3 \div \frac{1}{2} = 6)$

"How many fourths are in one half?" $(\frac{1}{2} \div \frac{1}{4} = 2)$

Using Page 232

Motivational Problem Have students read the introductory problem and restate the question. Ask students to give the data needed to find how long it will take to fill the pool $\frac{9}{10}$ full. Discuss why we can divide to find the answer.

Lesson Development Work through the exercise on the chalkboard and show the steps one at a time. Stress the importance of identifying the divisor and finding the reciprocal of the divisor. Have students check the answer by using multiplication.

Other Examples Have students work through these examples on the chalkboard. Remind students that the whole numbers in the last two examples can be written as fractions with denominators of 1.

Warm Up Use these exercises to diagnose any difficulty students may have with the steps in dividing fractions.

Dividing Fractions

The dolphin tank at a city aquarium was emptied and is to be refilled until it is $\frac{9}{10}$ full. It takes 1 h to fill $\frac{1}{5}$ of the pool. How long will it take to fill the pool $\frac{9}{10}$ full?

We need to find the number of fifths in $\frac{9}{10}$. To do this, we divide $\frac{9}{10}$ by $\frac{1}{5}$.

Dividing by a number gives the same answer as multiplying by the reciprocal of the number.

Look at the divisor. → Find the reciprocal of the divisor. → Multiply the dividend by the reciprocal of the divisor.

$\frac{9}{10} \div \frac{1}{5}$ ← divisor $\frac{5}{1}$ $\frac{9}{10} \times \frac{5}{1} = \frac{9}{2} = 4\frac{1}{2}$ ← quotient
dividend

To check the problem, multiply the quotient by the divisor.

$4\frac{1}{2} \times \frac{1}{5} = \frac{9}{2} \times \frac{1}{5} = \frac{9}{10}$ It checks.

It will take $4\frac{1}{2}$ h to fill the tank $\frac{9}{10}$ full.

Other Examples

$\frac{1}{2} \div \frac{3}{4} = \frac{1}{2} \times \frac{4}{3} = \frac{2}{3}$ $\frac{3}{5} \div 6 = \frac{3}{5} \times \frac{1}{6} = \frac{1}{10}$ $4 \div \frac{3}{8} = \frac{4}{1} \times \frac{8}{3} = \frac{32}{3} = 10\frac{2}{3}$

Warm Up

Find the quotients.

1. $\frac{3}{5} \div \frac{2}{3}$ $\frac{9}{10}$ 2. $\frac{5}{8} \div \frac{1}{6}$ $3\frac{3}{4}$ 3. $\frac{3}{16} \div \frac{1}{4}$ $\frac{3}{4}$ 4. $\frac{7}{10} \div \frac{5}{16}$ $2\frac{6}{25}$

5. $3 \div \frac{1}{2}$ 6   6. $\frac{7}{8} \div \frac{3}{8}$ $2\frac{1}{3}$ 7. $\frac{3}{4} \div \frac{1}{2}$ $1\frac{1}{2}$ 8. $\frac{2}{3} \div 4$ $\frac{1}{6}$

232

Follow Up

Reteaching

Display the following on the chalkboard. Ask students to tell how many sixths are in $1\frac{1}{3}$. (8)

Write the division equation on the chalkboard: $1\frac{1}{3} \div \frac{1}{6} = 8$. Have students check by multiplying. $(\frac{1}{6} \times 8 = 1\frac{1}{3})$ Show that we could write the exercises as $1\frac{1}{3} \times 6 = 8$. Work through other examples in the same way.

Enrichment

Have students match the division to the multiplication exercises and write the correct letter in each blank below.

1. $\frac{3}{4} \div \frac{1}{6}$ A. $\frac{4}{1} \times \frac{3}{2}$
2. $\frac{1}{2} \div \frac{2}{3}$ C. $\frac{3}{4} \times \frac{1}{3}$
3. $\frac{4}{8} \div \frac{1}{2}$ F. $\frac{1}{2} \times \frac{3}{2}$
4. $\frac{1}{9} \div \frac{5}{6}$ I. $\frac{4}{8} \times \frac{2}{1}$
5. $4 \div \frac{2}{3}$ N. $\frac{4}{1} \times \frac{2}{1}$
6. $\frac{4}{6} \div \frac{1}{2}$ O. $\frac{1}{9} \times \frac{6}{5}$
7. $\frac{3}{4} \div 3$ R. $\frac{7}{10} \times \frac{5}{1}$
8. $\frac{7}{10} \div \frac{1}{5}$ T. $\frac{3}{4} \times \frac{6}{1}$

F R A C T I O N   A C T I O N
2 8 5 7 1 3 4 6   5 7 1 3 4 6

for lesson support. The lesson plan is
reliably consistent so you can readily
choose whatever is necessary for
your class.

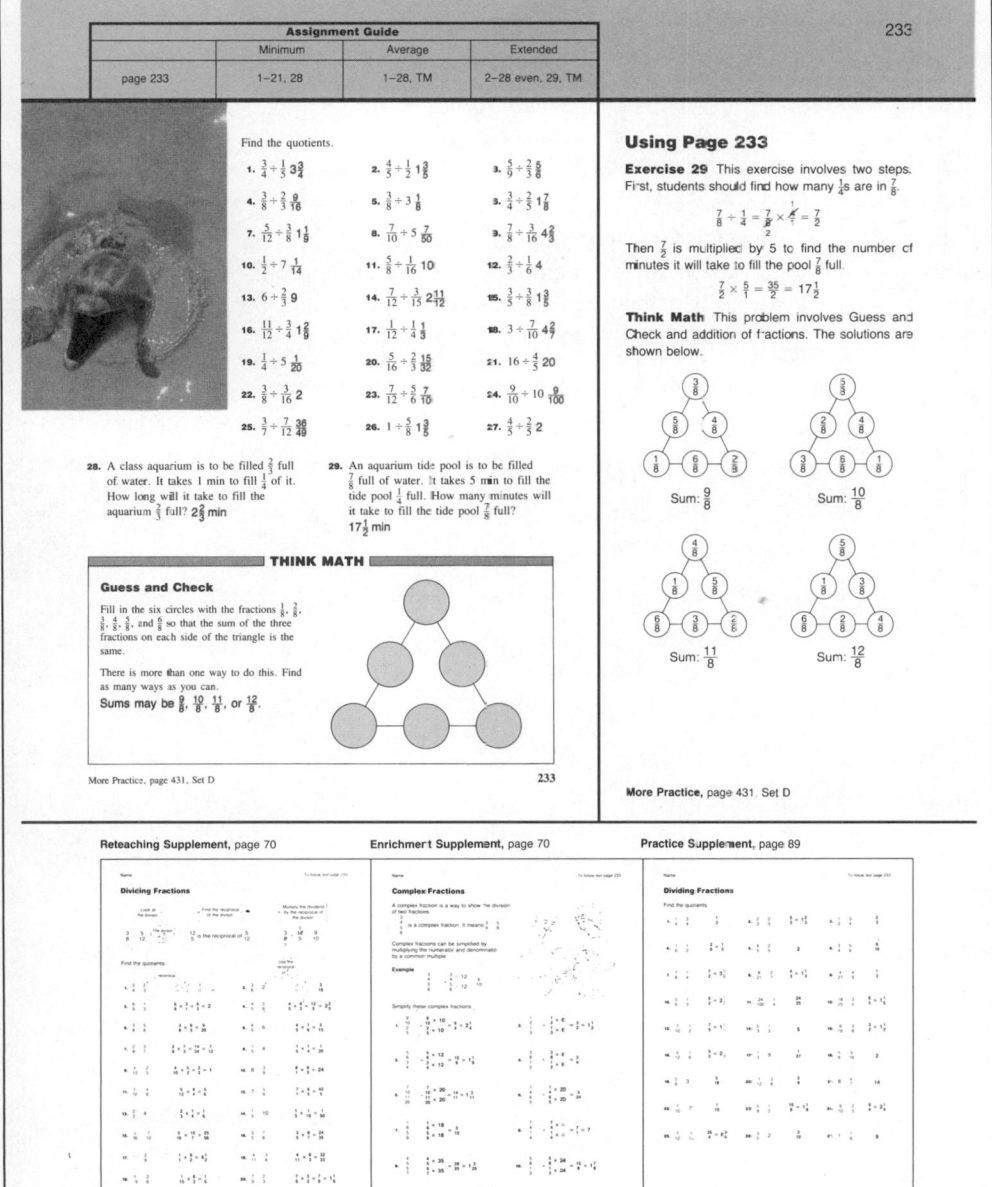

Assigning the exercises

Assignment Guide for individualization in three
ability groups

Teaching notes that alert teachers to special difficulties students may encounter

Meeting individual needs

Follow Up

Reteaching activity—Another way to teach the
concept or skill presented in the lesson—for students who demonstrate misunderstanding

Enrichment activity—To broaden or extend the
skills and concept taught in the lesson

Reteaching, Enrichment, Practice Supplements

- pages reproduced for informed planning
- overprinted answers
- available as workbooks, blackline masters,
  and duplicator masters

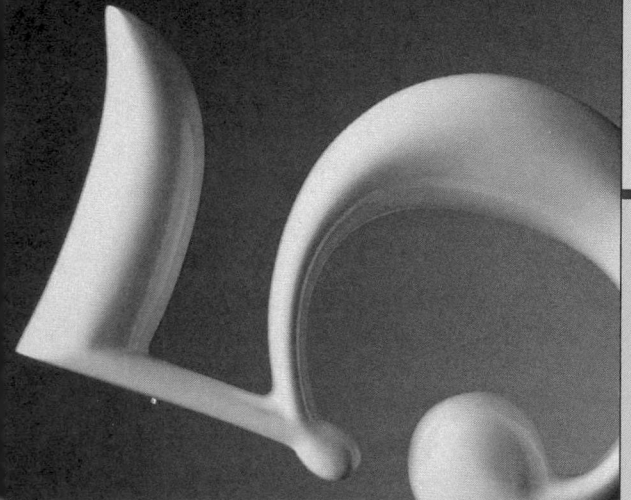

Resources to meet . . .

There are more special features and practical ideas in the Teacher's Edition than any teacher can use. Designed to allow you to find quickly exactly what your needs demand, it frees your valuable time for

Teaching Tips

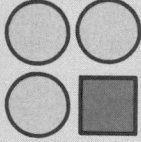 **Error Analysis**

Student errors often fall into predictable patterns that have been observed over and over in classrooms. Once the diagnosis of an error has been made and the cause understood, a program of remediation can be carried out. If the error pattern is caught in its early stages, the errors can be remediated before the pattern is internalized. The Error Analysis section anticipates likely errors related to the content of each chapter and provides the tools to affect change. Two discussions are provided for each error pattern:

- **Diagnosis**
- **Remediation**

 **Problem Solving**

Tips for teaching problem solving contain a large number of classroom-tested techniques for teaching problem solving. The topics selected for this section address five questions teachers ask when building a problem-solving program:

1) How will I provide a classroom environment conducive to problem solving?

2) How can I develop problem-solving skills?

3) What can I do to guide students' work while they solve problems?

4) How can I meet individual needs?

5) How will I evaluate students' problem-solving performance and attitudes?

Background Information

Chapter Overview

Easy to find, understandable information for teaching each key skill or concept (See page 115A.)

- **Objectives**
- **Summary**
- **Mathematical Background**
- **Vocabulary**

Just for Teachers

Interesting facts and information related to the history of mathematics, economics, and current educational theories (See page 84.)

Technology for Teachers

A guide to understanding and teaching the basics of calculator and computer technology (See page 266.)

. . . the challenge of every classroom

working with students. Whatever your classroom needs, it's the problem solver—The Addison–Wesley Teacher's Edition.

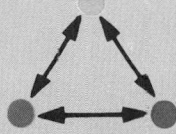

Special Education

This section highlights the special needs of physically-impaired, learning-disabled, mentally-retarded, or behaviorally-disordered learners. These students often lack the information-processing skills of the regular K-8 students and require supplementary activities and special teaching approaches.

The guidelines for working with special students are organized around the triangle model. The corners of this triangle suggest the various levels of abstraction students need in learning mathematics. Specific sides of the triangle may require special emphasis. For example, if a student has verbal and writing deficiencies, the instruction might emphasize the pattern shown on the left below. For the student possessing strong visual and speaking skills, but poor written communication skills, the instructional program might attempt an approach like that shown in the model on the right below.

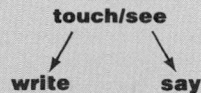

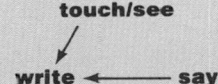

Subject Integration

The themes of the problems in the student book have been carefully selected from a cross section of the curriculum areas in order to provide an integration of mathematics with other subject areas. A list of the themes from the content areas, and from the areas of career and consumer awareness, gives teachers the opportunity to make mathematics part of the total curriculum.

- Science
- Social Studies
- Health
- Fine Arts
- Language Arts
- Physical Education
- Consumer Awareness
- Career Awareness
- Computer Awareness
- History
- Industrial Arts
- Home Economics

Activity Ideas

Activities That Count

A bank of activity ideas and long-range projects adaptable to a variety of skills and appropriate for all ability levels (See page 183.)

- Math Lab
- Game
- Project

Ideas That Work

Practical suggestions for chalkboard activities, manipulative ideas, extensions, and ways to use the calculator in the classroom
(See page 274F.)

- Chalk It Up
- Math for the Gifted
- Special Education
- Calculator Bonus

Quick Review

A 2-minute activity to review and maintain basic skills, intended for use at the beginning of each lesson.
(See page 62.)

Planning and assessment . . .

Only you can accurately evaluate students' progress and diagnose their needs. Addison–Wesley's new program offers a complete range of testing options and an organized class

A comprehensive guide for planning each chapter

Teaching Chapter 1				Meeting Individual Needs						
Objectives	Chapter Content	Pages	TRB Test Items	Lesson Assignments			Follow Up			
				Minimum	Average	Extended	Reteaching	Enrichment	Practice	
	Chapter Opener	1								
1.1 Recall addition and subtraction facts related to sums through 10.	Sums Through 10	2–3	1–8	1–36	1–40	1–40, TM	SE2 Ch 1 RS 1	ES 1	MP 363 PS 1	
	Differences Through 10	4–5		1–36	1–40	1–40, TM	SE2 Ch 1 RS 2	ES 2	MP 363 PS 2	
1.2 Recall addition and subtraction facts related to sums through 18.	Sums Through 18	6–7		1–36, SK	1–36, SK	2–36 even SK	SE2 Ch 3 RS 3	ES 3	MP 364 PS 3	
	Differences Through 18	8–9		1–32	1–32,TM	2–32 even 33–38, TM	SE 2 Ch4 RS 4	ES 4	MP 364 PS4	
	Fact Fa...									

Supplements to fill every need keyed to specific lessons

Clear, concise objectives

Test items correlated to objectives and lessons

Distinct Assignment Guides for 3 ability groups

References to previous student book for reteaching or readiness

Approximately 2,000 additional exercises in the appendix of the student book

Built-in review and individualization at the end of each chapter of the student book

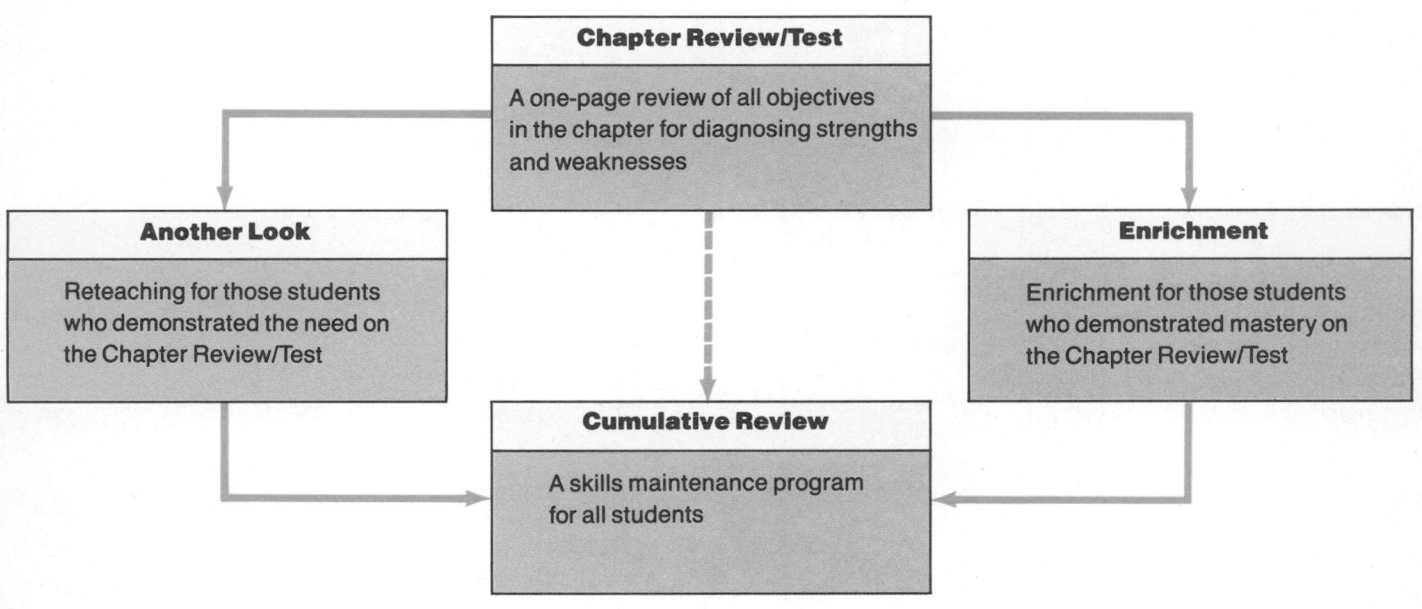

Chapter Review/Test

A one-page review of all objectives in the chapter for diagnosing strengths and weaknesses

Another Look

Reteaching for those students who demonstrated the need on the Chapter Review/Test

Enrichment

Enrichment for those students who demonstrated mastery on the Chapter Review/Test

Cumulative Review

A skills maintenance program for all students

management plan that can help you measure student achievements and direct remedial activities. Efficient management produces lesson-by-lesson accountability.

Fully cross-referenced assessment options

Criterion-referenced chapter tests in two forms:

- Multiple-choice
- Free-response

The items have a one-to-one correspondence in terms of the level of difficulty so you can use them as a pre- and post-test.

Plus, these extra testing materials:

- Basic-Facts Test
- Mid-Year Test
- End-of-Year Test
- Grading Aid
- Answer Sheet

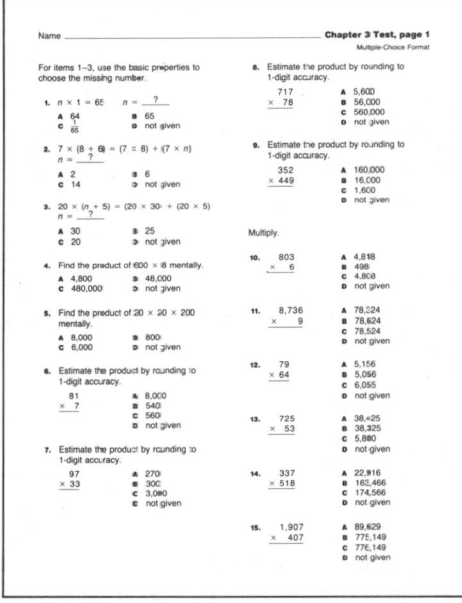

Multiple-Choice Tests

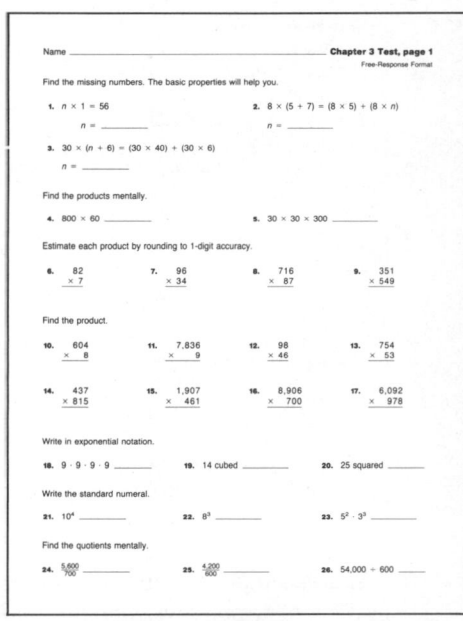

Free-Response Tests

Forms to record test scores and assignments

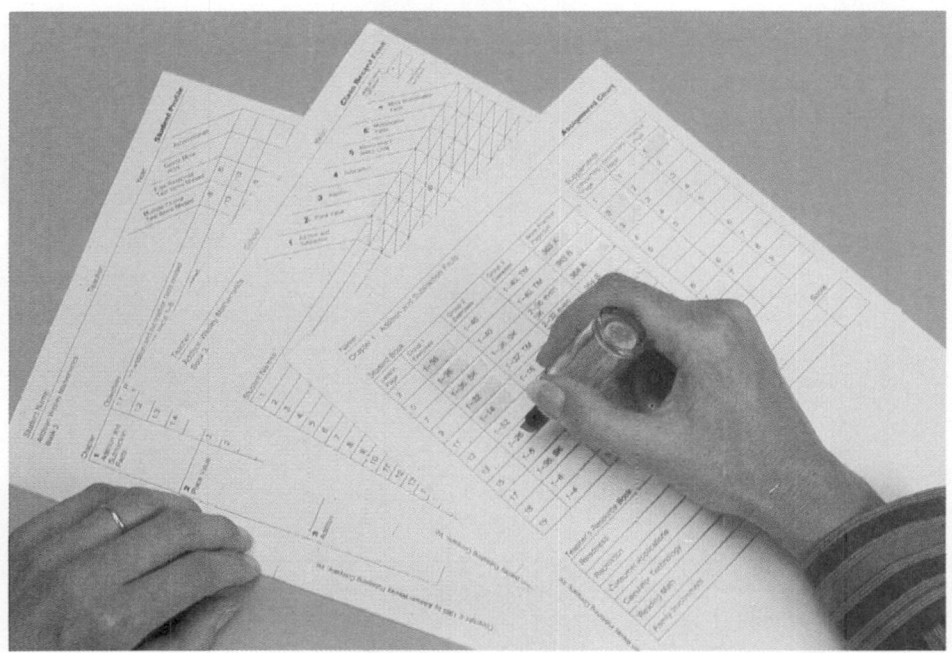

7 A flexible teaching package . . .

The very concept of a Teacher's Resource Book to supplement the math program was created by Addison–Wesley. Our new program has an expanded TRB that includes more sections, more features, and

Readiness

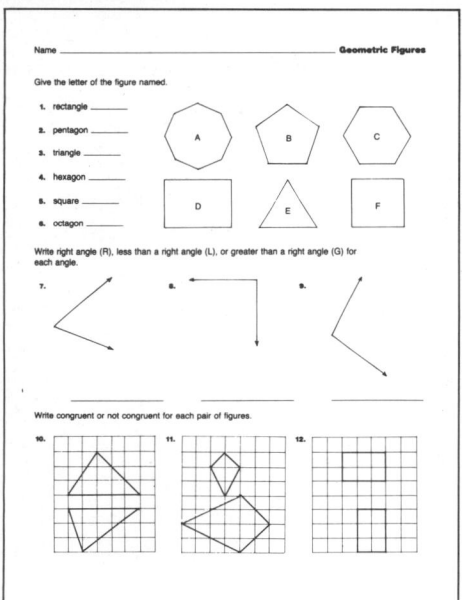

Prepares students for the chapter lessons by presenting and reviewing prerequisite skills and concepts

Activities That Count

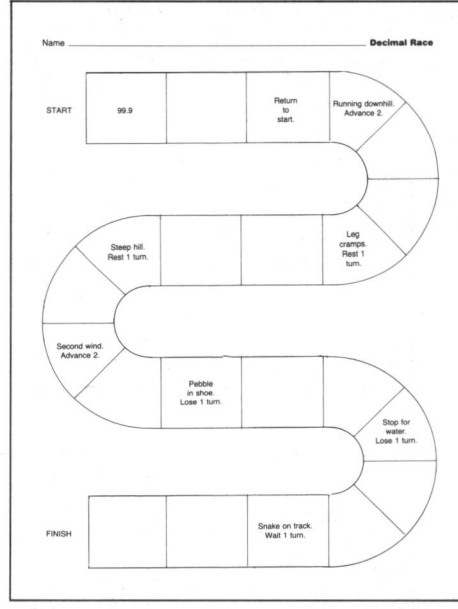

Supports math labs, games, and projects described in the Teacher's Edition

Recreation

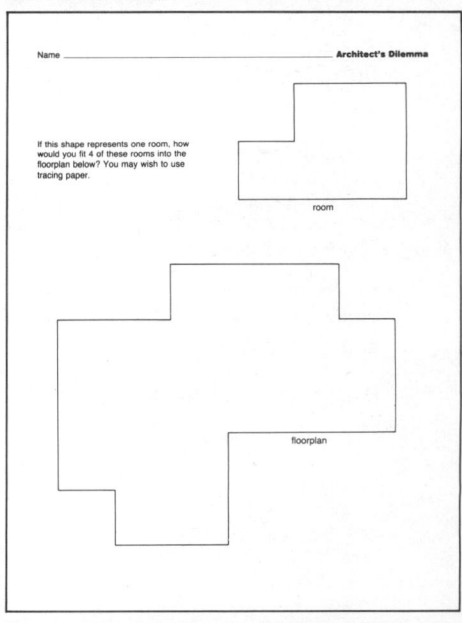

Presents interesting, creative ways of working with numbers, math concepts, and special topics

Calculator Technology

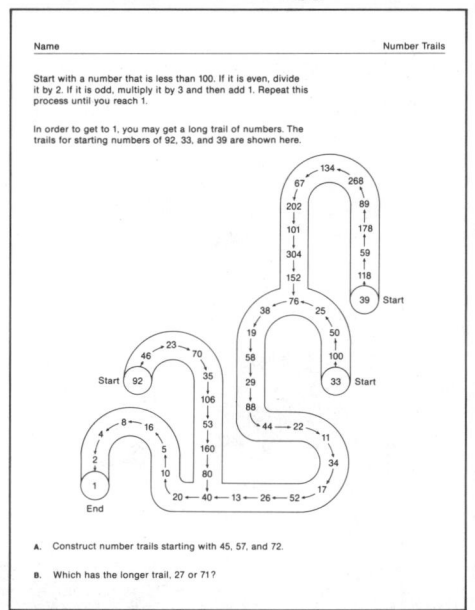

Helps students become comfortable using calculators

Computer Technology

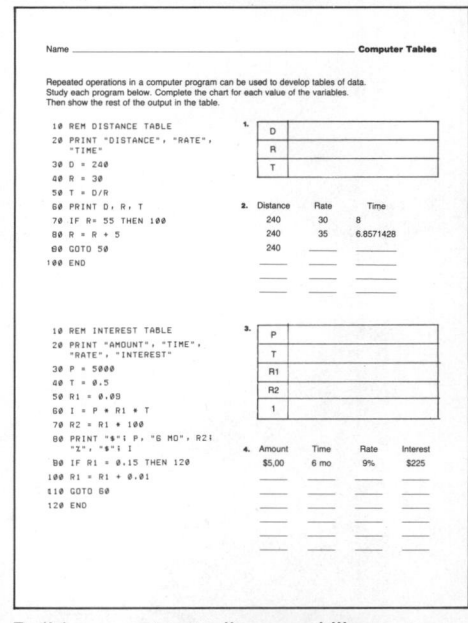

Builds on computer literacy skills introduced in the student book

. . . that promotes success

more teaching aids than ever. This unique, convenient collection of additional materials is completely correlated to the Teacher's Edition. It's designed to encourage students to become successful, independent learners.

Reading Math

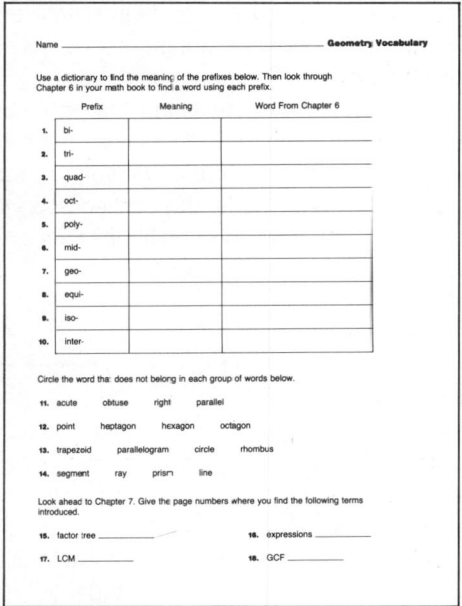

Involves vocabulary, study skills, and reading comprehension in the content area of mathematics

Consumer Applications

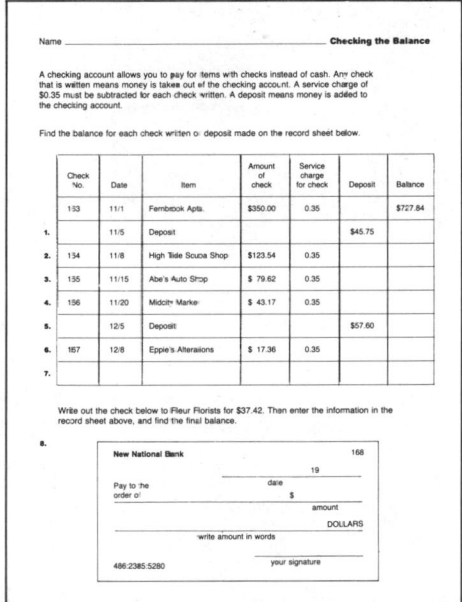

Provides practice with real-life consumer skills such as banking, comparative shopping, taxes, unit pricing, and budgets

Family Involvement

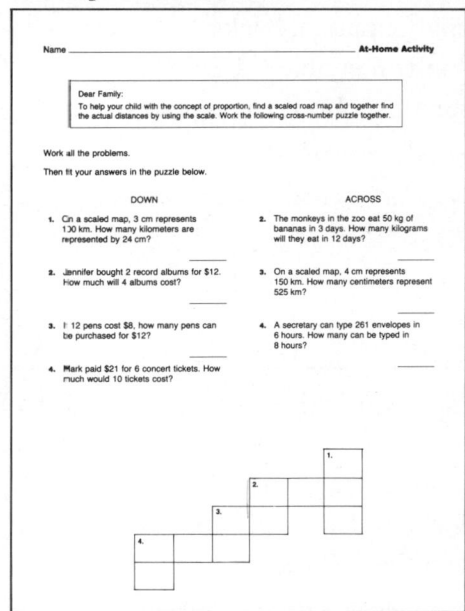

Acquaints parents with the mathematics their children are studying and supports interaction between parents and children

Assessment

- Multiple-Choice Tests
- Free-Response Tests
- Basic-Facts Tests
- Mid-Year Test
- End-of-Year Test

Record Keeping

- Class Record Form
- Student Profile
- Assignment Charts

And, a bulletin board bonus on each TRB divider

Teaching Aids

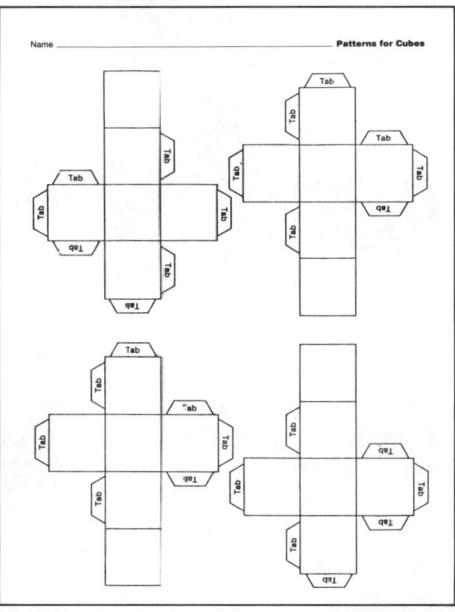

Provides resources for hands-on learning experiences

A team of math professionals.

The authors and consultants bring a broad range of teaching experience and contemporary mathematical application to this new program. Their experiences will save you

"The program provides students with the solid mathematical background and skills that will enable them to face the consumer, technological, and scientific challenges of the future."

Robert E. Eicholz
He has taught at the junior and senior high school levels and has spent 25 years developing mathematics textbooks for teachers and students. He directed the writing team of the Greater Cleveland Mathematics Program K-3, and coauthored *Elementary School Mathematics, Investigating School Mathematics,* and *Mathematics in Our World.* He is often called upon to speak at in-service programs and workshops for mathematics teachers throughout the country.

"Your students will experience a variety of problem situations with an emphasis on real-world applications. Skills are carefully developed so that students will build the repertoire of strategies necessary for creative problem solving."

Phares G. O'Daffer
With teaching experiences at elementary through high school levels, he is now engaged in pre-service and in-service education of elementary mathematics teachers at Illinois State University. He has coordinated the development of a comprehensive mathematics laboratory for teachers and students. He coauthored *Elementary School Mathematics, Investigating School Mathematics,* and *Mathematics in Our World* as well as many other textbooks and journal articles.

"We focus on understanding and careful skill development, with ample practice immediately and at carefully-spaced intervals. Your students will learn mental math and estimation skills that will help them compute quickly, accurately, and properly."

Charles R. Fleenor
His teaching experiences include working with students at the elementary through high school levels. He has conducted many in-service programs for mathematics teachers at all grade levels. The past 15 years he has devoted to developing and writing elementary and junior high school mathematics textbooks including the previous Addison-Wesley series *Investigating School Mathematics* and *Mathematics in Our World.*

Consultants

Martin L. Johnson
With teaching experience at elementary, middle school, and secondary levels, he has published many articles and books on diagnostic and prescriptive mathematics. He teaches mathematics education courses at the University of Maryland.

Carol A. Thornton
After 10 years as an elementary and high school math teacher, she joined the staff of Illinois State University. She has authored many publications relating to mathematics for handicapped or underachieving students.

. . . you can trust

time and make your teaching efficient. With Addison–Wesley Mathematics, you have a distinguished group of colleagues with you in the classroom.

Randall I. Charles

He has teaching experience at all levels including five years as an elementary and junior high school mathematics supervisor. For several years, he was involved in federally-funded problem solving projects for Indiana University and for the West Virginia Department of Education. While at Illinois State University, he has presented in-service programs and authored several publications on the subject of problem solving.

"We give you a flexible teaching package that allows you to teach, test, and manage with ease. You will have the information and materials to select your teaching style to assure success for you and your students."

Sharon Young

Formerly an elementary school teacher in California and New Jersey, she now teaches pre-service and in-service education courses at Louisiana State University. She previously taught mathematics education courses at the University of Colorado and West Virginia University. She has conducted numerous in-service programs and workshops in the United States, Canada, and Europe.

"We provide opportunities to reinforce, reteach, or enrich each lesson. Teaching tips on error analysis, problem solving, and special education allow you to meet all students' needs."

Carne S. Barnett

Her classroom experience includes several years of teaching at the elementary, junior high, and secondary levels. She now instructs and supervises teacher candidates in the Elementary and Secondary Education Departments at the University of California at Berkeley. She is the author of several mathematics education publications.

"Your students will learn to understand the power of calculators and computers. They will be able to read and write simple programs."

John A. Dossey

His teaching background includes experience as a K-12 mathematics coordinator. Now at Illinois State University, he has published many articles and, with Carol Thornton and others, co-authored *Teaching Mathematics to Children with Special Needs*.

Betty C. Lee

As a mathematics demonstration teacher and city-wide teacher consultant, she has planned and conducted in-service mathematics workshops, trained teachers, and developed enrichment materials for the Detroit Board of Education.

Computer Advisors

Bobby Goodson
Sunnyvale, CA

Barbara Peck
New Haven, CT

Connie Beaudry
West Haven, CT

T19

Scope and Sequence

Book 6	Book 7	Book 8
Adding Whole Numbers		
Basic facts, 2-3, 10, 15, 18, 22, 52, 78 Missing addends, 2-3 Addition properties, 3 Mental addition, 32-33, 39 Estimating sums, 32-33 Adding whole numbers, 36-37, 50, 52, 78, 106, 136 Column addition, 38-39	Adding whole numbers, 9, 12-13, 26, 30, 35, 133 Estimating sums, 10-11 Column addition, 12-13, 30, 35* Mental addition, 13* Missing addends, 43 Addition properties, 370	Adding whole numbers, 5, 10-11, 22, 26, 30, 37* Addition properties, 6-7 Estimating sums, 8-9, 11, 19, 26, 30, 231* Column addition, 10-11, 22, 26, 30 Missing addends, 11
Subtracting Whole Numbers		
Basic facts, 2-3, 10, 15, 18, 22, 52, 78 Checking subtraction, 2 Subtraction properties, 3 Mental subtraction, 32-33 Estimating differences, 32-33 Subtracting whole numbers, 40-43, 50, 52, 78, 136 Subtracting across a zero, 42-43	Subtracting whole numbers, 9, 14-15, 26, 30, 35* Estimating differences, 10-11 Mental subtraction, 15*	Subtracting whole numbers, 5, 10-11, 22, 26, 30, 37* Estimating differences, 8-9, 11, 19, 26, 231*
Multiplying Whole Numbers		
Basic facts, 4-5, 10, 15, 18, 22, 52, 78 Multiplication properties, 5, 80 Missing factors, 5 Multiples, 14 Mental multiplication, 80-81, 102, 115, 192 Estimating products, 82-83, 87, 95, 97 Multiplying whole numbers, 84-89, 94-97, 102, 136, 192 Exponential notation, 92-93, 115, Multiplying three numbers, 96, 97* Russian peasant multiplication, 103	Multiplication properties, 56 Mental multiplication, 57, 73, 84, 114, 175* Estimating products, 58-59, 86, 114, 277* Multiplying whole numbers, 15, 19, 39, 60-63, 73, 84, 86, 114, 134 Exponential notation, 66-67, 84, 86, 114, 134, 175* Napier's Rods, 85	Multiplying whole numbers, 5, 16-17, 22, 26, 30, 37, 52 Multiplication properties, 6-7 Mental multiplication, 14 Estimating products, 15, 231* Exponential notation, 60-61, 108, 130, 191, 208-209, 298
Dividing Whole Numbers		
Basic facts, 6-7, 10, 15, 18, 22, 52, 78, 95* Division properties, 7 Mental division, 108-109 Estimating quotients, 110-111, 115* Dividing by a 1-digit number, 112-117, 134, 143, 166, 173, 224 Remainders, 112, 118 Zero in the quotient, 114, 128 Average, 118-119, 134 Dividing by multiples of 10, 120-121, 143, 173, 224 Dividing by a 2-digit number, 122-124, 126-128, 134, 143, 166, 173, 224 Dividing by a 3-digit number, 129, 143	Mental division, 70, 84, 86, 91, 134 Estimating quotients, 71, 277* Dividing whole numbers, 19, 39, 72-76, 84, 86, 91, 134	Dividing whole numbers, 5, 18-19, 22, 26, 30, 37, 52, 83* Mental division, 14 Estimating quotients, 15, 231*
Rounding and Estimation		

Rounding, 30-31, 50, 60-61, 78, 106, 136, 150-151, 166, 325*
Estimating
  sums and differences, 32-34, 62-63, 68, 255*
  products and quotients, 82-83, 87, 95, 97, 110 138-139, 145, 146, 149, 157, 159, 160, 241
  measurement, 171, 178, 180, 182, 191, 292, 396, 398
  time, 185, 283*
  with graphs, 323*
	Rounding, 8-9, 30, 38-39, 52, 54, 86, 118-119
	Estimating
	  sums and differences, 10-11, 26, 30, 44-45, 54, 86
	  products and quotients, 58-59, 71, 86, 90-91, 100-101, 110, 114, 128-129, 132, 134, 162, 192, 222, 277
	  with fractions, 204
	  percent, 299
	  measurement, 249, 335*
		Rounding, 4-5, 9, 26, 30, 36-37, 50, 52
		Estimating
		  sums and differences 8-9, 11, 19, 26, 30, 42-43, 45, 50, 52, 76, 231
		  products and quotients, 15, 57, 69, 74, 108, 114, 128, 130, 154, 214, 231*
		  measurement, 156-157, 160, 162
		  percent, 284-285

Note: Red type indicates that a topic is being introduced for the first time. The page numbers labeled with a * indicate references in Skillkeeper or Think Math activities.

Scope and Sequence

Book 6	Book 7	Book 8

Numbers and Numeration

Whole number place value through hundred billions, 24-27, 43* 50, 59, 78, 136
Expanded notation, 24-27
Comparing and ordering
  whole numbers, 28-29, 50, 78
  decimals, 58-59, 76, 87* 106, 136, 166
  fractions and mixed numbers, 202, 209, 213
  integers, 376, 379* 382, 389* 406
Roman numerals, 47
Decimal place value through hundred-
  thousandths, 54-57, 76, 87* 106, 166
Exponential notation, 92-93, 115*
Scientific notation, 403
Number patterns, 5* 77, 85, 123* 153* 160* 211*
  249, 279* 317, 329* 371* 383
	Whole number place value through hundred trillions, 4-5, 139*
	Comparing and ordering
	  whole numbers, 6-7, 26, 30
	  decimals, 36-37, 52, 54, 86, 240-241
	  fractions, 202-203, 220, 246, 278-279, 290, 292
	  integers, 369, 390, 412
	Ancient numeration systems, 2-3
	Decimal place value through millionths, 32-35, 52, 54, 139*
	Other bases, 55, 339
	Exponential notation, 66-67, 84, 86, 114, 134, 175*
	Scientific notation, 102-103, 110, 114, 162, 192
	Number patterns, 7* 117* 169* 239* 375*
		Whole number place value, 2
		Comparing and ordering
		  whole numbers, 4-5, 26, 30, 52
		  decimals, 34-35, 52, 76, 123*
		  fractions, 82* 83* 85* 90-91, 95* 104, 123* 219* 243, 264
		  integers, 180-181, 240, 298
		Sumarian number system, 27
		Decimal place value through millionths, 32-33, 50
		Exponential notation, 60-61, 108, 130, 191* 208-209, 298
		Scientific notation, 62-63, 108, 130, 209
		Sequences, 153
		Rational and irrational numbers, 388-389
		Number patterns 117* 137* 123* 223* 345

Fractions

Parts of regions or sets, 194-195
Equivalent and lowest-terms fractions, 196-197, 199, 220, 243* 250, 267, 287* 298, 320
Improper fractions and mixed numbers, 200-201
Comparing and ordering fractions and mixed numbers, 202, 209* 213* 241*
Least common denominator, 207, 220
Adding and subtracting fractions and mixed numbers
  like denominators, 204-205, 216, 220, 229*
  unlike denominators, 208-216, 220, 250, 298
Estimating with, 206, 245
Cross products, 213
Finding a fraction of a whole number, 226-227, 248, 276, 281* 320
Multiplying and dividing fractions and mixed numbers, 228-233, 239-243, 248, 276, 281* 287* 320
Reciprocals, 228-229, 231
Mental multiplication, 233*
Fractions and decimals, 236-238, 248, 276, 320
	Fractions, 194-195, 197* 211*
	Equivalent and lowest-terms fractions, 196-199, 209* 220, 246, 274, 292
	Improper fractions and mixed numbers, 200-201, 209* 220, 246, 292
	Comparing and ordering fractions and mixed numbers, 202-203, 220, 246, 278-279, 290, 292
	Cross products, 203*
	Estimating fractions, 204
	Least common denominator, 206, 208
	Adding and subtracting fractions and mixed numbers, 206-215, 220, 229* 230, 233* 246, 292
	Finding a fraction of a whole number, 224-225, 235
	Multiplying and dividing fractions and mixed numbers, 226-230, 232-237, 244, 253* 274, 320
	Reciprocals, 231, 274
	Fractions and decimals, 238-241, 244-245, 274, 320
		Equivalent and lowest-terms fractions, 82-85, 104, 130, 176
		Cross products, 82-83
		Improper fractions and mixed numbers, 86-87, 130, 176
		Least common denominator, 88-89, 154, 176
		Comparing and ordering fractions and mixed numbers, 82* 83* 85* 90-91, 95* 104, 123* 219* 243, 264
		Adding and subtracting fractions and mixed numbers, 92-99, 100-101, 104-105, 111* 124, 130, 154, 176
		Multiplying and dividing fractions and mixed numbers, 110-113, 116-121, 124, 128, 135* 154, 214
		Estimating products, 114, 128, 154, 214
		Reciprocals, 115, 154, 214
		Fractions and decimals, 122-123, 128, 154, 214

Decimals

Decimal place value through hundred- thousandths, 54-57, 76, 87* 106, 166 Comparing and ordering, 58-59, 76, 87* 106, 136 Rounding, 60-61, 76, 106, 150-151, 166 Estimating sums and differences, 62-63, 68 Adding, 64-65, 67* 76, 95* 106, 159* 166 Subtracting, 66-67, 76, 95* 106, 159* 166 Estimating products and quotients, 138-139, 145, 146, 149* 157* 160* Multiplying, 140-145, 159* 160, 164, 183* 192, 250, 309* 337* Mental multiplication and division, 144-145, 152-153, 159* 164, 174, 175* 192, 250 Whole number divisors, 148-151, 153, 160, 173* 183* 192, 205* 250 Decimal divisors, 156-160, 164, 173* 183* 192, 205* Fractions and decimals, 236-238, 248, 276, 320 Mixed decimals, 238, 304-305 Repeating decimals, 249	Decimal place value through millionths, 32-35, 52, 54, 139* Comparing and ordering, 36-37, 52, 54, 86, 240-241 Rounding, 38-39, 52, 54, 86, 118-119 Adding, 40-41, 43* 52, 54, 61* 86 Subtracting, 42-43, 52, 54, 61* 86 Estimating sums and differences, 44-45, 54, 86 Multiplying, 88-89, 92-95, 110, 114, 151* 162, 192 Estimating products, 90-91, 100-101, 110, 114, 162, 192 Zeros in products, 94-95 Mental multiplication, 98-99, 103* 110, 119* 192 Whole number divisors, 116-117, 132, 134, 162, 167* 222 Mental division, 120, 125* 132, 134, 222 Decimal divisors, 124-125, 132, 134, 162, 167* 222 Estimating quotients, 128-129, 132, 134, 162, 222 Repeating and terminating decimals, 240-241	Decimal place value through millionths, 32-33, 50 Comparing and ordering, 34-35, 52, 76, 123* Rounding, 36-37, 50, 64-67 Adding, 38-39, 41* 50-52, 76 Subtracting, 40-41, 44, 50-52, 61* 76 Estimating sums and differences, 42-43, 50, 52, 76 Multiplying, 54-55, 69* 70, 74, 81* 108, 130 Mental multiplication, 56, 108, 157* Estimating products and quotients, 57, 69, 74, 108, 130 Whole number divisors, 64-65, 69* 70, 74, 81* 108 Decimal divisors, 66-67, 69* 70, 74, 81* 108, 130 Mental division, 68, 108, 157* Repeating and terminating decimals, 122-123, 128, 388-389 Nonterminating and nonrepeating decimals, 388-389

Note: Red type indicates that a topic is being introduced for the first time. The page numbers labeled with a * indicate references in Skillkeeper or Think Math activities.

Scope and Sequence

Book 6	Book 7	Book 8

Ratio, Proportion, and Percent

Book 6	Book 7	Book 8
Ratio, 278-279, 296, 303; 320, 364 Equal ratios, 280-281, 296, 303; 320 Cross products, 280-281 Solving proportions, 282-283, 296, 309; 320 Using proportions, 284-285, 288-292 Pi, 297 Ratio and percent, 300-301, 316 Percent, decimals, and fractions, 301-306, 316, 325; 344, 384 Percent of a number, 308-312, 316, 326; 327; 337; 344, 349; 384	Ratio and rate, 276-277, 285; 290 Equal ratios, cross products, 278-279, 290, 366 Solving proportions, 280-281, 286, 290, 366 Golden ratio, 291 Ratio and percent, 294-295, 307* Percent, decimals, and fractions, 296-298, 300-301, 307; 311; 318, 325; 342, 392 Estimating percents, 299 Percent of a number, 302-304, 307; 308-309, 318, 342, 392 Percent one number is of another, 306-309, 318-319, 325; 342, 392 Finding a number when the percent is known, 310-311, 318, 392 Proportion and percent, 314-315 Percent of change, 319	Ratio, equal ratios, cross products, 242-243, 264, 273; 298, 348 Rate, 244-247, 264, 298, 348 Solving proportions, 248-249, 259; 264, 298 Using proportions, 250-259, 264, 298 Compound proportions, 265 Percent, decimals, and fractions, 270-277, 292, 296, 303; 324, 372 Percent of a number, 278-281, 289; 292, 296-297, 324, 372 Percent one number is of another, 282-283, 289; 292, 296, 324, 372 Estimating percents, 284-285, 289; 324, 372 Percent of change, 286 Finding a number when the percent is known, 288-289, 292, 296, 324, 372 Proportion and percent, 293

Number Properties and Number Theory

Book 6	Book 7	Book 8
Order and grouping properties, 3, 5, 80 One and zero properties, 3, 5, 7 Multiplication-addition property, 5 Order of operations, 11, 65* Even and odd numbers, 14, 165 Factors, 15, 113* Prime and composite numbers, 117; 165 Divisibility, 135 Perfect numbers, 165 Greatest common factor, 198-199 Least common multiple, 207 Square and triangular numbers, 29; 221 Square root, 351	Properties of addition and multiplication, 56, 370 Square and triangular numbers, 11; 67 Fibonacci numbers, 27 Palindromic numbers, 65 Order of operations, 75 Casting out nines, 111 Factors, 164-165, 181; 188 Divisibility, 166-167, 382* Prime and composite numbers, 168-169, 181; 188 Prime factorization, 170-171, 174-175, 181; 188, 199; 222, 274 Greatest common factor, 172-173, 188, 189, 198, 199; 222, 274 Abundant numbers, 167* Least common multiple, 174-175, 188, 274	Properties of addition and multiplication, 6, 182-183 Order of operations, 7, 26, 52, 97 Factors, 78-79, 104 Prime and composite numbers, 78-79, 104, 130, 154 Prime factorization, 78-79, 104, 130 Greatest common factor, 80-81, 95; 130 Least common multiple, 88-89, 154, 176 Absolute value, 188, 298 Squares and square roots, 374-378, 383; 392, 412

Integers

Book 6	Book 7	Book 8
Positive and negative, 366-367, 382, 389* Adding, 368-371, 374-375, 382, 389; 406 Subtracting, 372-375, 382, 389; 406 Equations, 372-373, 382-383 Comparing and ordering, 376, 379; 382, 389; 406 Integer coordinates, 378-379	Positive and negative, 368-369, 390, 412 Comparing and ordering, 368-369, 390, 412 Integer properties, 370-371 Adding, 372-375, 377; 383; 390, 412 Subtracting, 376-377, 383; 390, 412 Multiplying, 380-381, 390, 395; 412 Dividing, 382-383, 390, 395; 412 Integer coordinates, 384-385	Positive and negative, 178-179 Comparing and ordering, 180-181, 240, 298 Integer properties, 182-183 Adding, 184-185, 193; 195; 212, 240, 249* Subtracting, 186-187, 195; 212, 240, 249* Multiplying, 190-191, 212, 240, 249* Dividing, 192-193, 212, 240, 249* Integer coordinates, 202-207

Pre-Algebra

Book 6	Book 7	Book 8

	Writing and evaluating expressions, 176-177, 188
	Addition, subtraction, multiplication, and division equations, 178-181, 188, 222, 274, 279*
	Using and writing equations, 182-185
	Graphing equations, 386-387
	Using formulas, 81, 252, 256, 260, 304-305, 322, 324, 328, 330, 338, 398-399
		Evaluating and writing expressions
		  whole number, 132-135, 140-141, 152, 153; 176
		  integer, 194-195
		Addition, subtraction, multiplication, and division equations, 136-137, 142-143, 152, 176, 240, 288-289
		Two-step equations, 144-145, 198-199
		Integer equations, 196-197, 298
		Writing and using equations, 138-139, 146-147, 200-201
		Graphing equations, 204-207, 212
		Using formulas, 148-149, 280, 297, 300-322, 380-385

Note: Red type indicates that a topic is being introduced for the first time. The page numbers labeled with a * indicate references in Skillkeeper or Think Math activities.

Book 6	Book 7	Book 8

Geometry

Book 6

Points, lines, segments, rays, and angles, 252-253
Measuring and drawing angles, 254-255
Perpendicular and parallel lines, 256-257
Triangles: equilateral, isosceles, scalene, acute, right, obtuse, 258-259, 274, 298, 344
Quadrilaterals, 260-261, 274
Other polygons, 262, 274, 298, 344
Circles: center, radius, diameter, chord, central angle, 263, 274, 298, 344
π, 297
Congruent figures, 264-265, 268, 274
Lines of symmetry, 266-267, 274
Graphing congruent and similar figures, 268-269
Drawings and constructions, 255-257, 263, 275
Prism, sphere, cylinder, cone, pyramid, 270-271
Similar figures, 286-287
Translations, 343
Space perception, 19, 265* 271* 331* 387*
Shape perception, 93* 157* 195* 227* 305*

Book 7

Basic geometric figures, 136-137, 192, 246
Angles: acute, right, obtuse, straight, complementary, supplementary, 138-139, 160, 192, 246
Triangles, 140-141, 160, 192, 246
Quadrilaterals, 142-143, 160, 246
Other polygons, 144-145, 192
Circles: center, radius, diameter, chord, central angle, arc, 146-147, 160, 192, 246, 322-325, 329* 331*
Congruent figures, 148-149
Lines of symmetry, 150-151
Polyhedrons, 156-157, 161
Constructions
  perpendicular and parallel lines, 152-153
  segment and angle bisectors, 154-155
Similar figures, 284-285, 290
Cross sections, 334-335
Shape perception, 143* 145* 149* 155* 157* 213* 257*
Space perception, 161, 315*

Book 8

Basic geometric figures, 216-217
Angle measure, 218-219, 223* 238, 324
Lines: parallel, perpendicular, skew, transversal, 220-221, 268, 324
Triangles, 222-223, 238, 268, 324
Other polygons, 224-225, 268, 324
Circles: center, radius, diameter, chord, central angle, arc, secant, tangent, 226-227, 238, 268
Congruent figures: segments, angles, triangles (SSS, SAS, ASA), 228-233, 238, 268, 324
Lines of symmetry, 234-235, 268, 324
Similar triangles, 252-253
Tangent ratio, 258-261, 298, 348
Rule of Pythagoras, 380-385, 392, 397* 412
30°-60° right triangles, 386-387
Ellipse, 409
Constructions, 220-221, 227-233, 239
Space perception, 235* 277* 323, 381*
Shape perception, 39* 87* 89* 129, 159* 221* 227* 253* 409

Graphing, Probability, and Statistics

Book 6

Coordinate graphing, 268-269, 287, 378-379
Bar graphs, 98, 322-323, 330-331, 342, 364
  estimating with, 323*
  double bar graphs, 333
Line graphs, 98, 328-329, 331
Circle graphs, 307, 326-327, 342
Pictographs, 324-325
Making graphs, 323, 325, 327, 329
Evaluating graphs, 330-331
Mean, 151, 332, 342, 357* 364
Median and mode, 334
Probability, prediction, and expected numbers, 336-339, 342, 364

Book 7

Equally likely outcomes, 344-345, 364
Chance and probability, 346-347, 350-351, 353* 364-365, 392
Ordered pairs in probability, 348-351, 364
Prediction, 349*
Frequency, range, and mode, 352-353, 364, 392
Mean and median, 354-355, 364, 373* 392
Bar graphs, 201*
  double bar graphs, 299, 356, 360
  histograms, 356, 360
Circle graphs, 299, 359, 361, 364
Line segment graphs, 357, 361, 378
Pictographs, 358, 392
Making graphs, 356, 357, 358, 359
Coordinate graphing, 385-387
Graphing equations, 386-387

Book 8

Coordinate graphing, 202-203
Graphing equations, 204-207, 212
Latitude and longitude, 213
Counting principle, 326-327, 372
Permutations, 328-329, 372
Combinations, 330-331, 355*
Factorials, 331*
Probability, 332-333, 341* 344, 372
Ordered pairs in probability, 334-335, 344
Prediction, 336-337, 354-355, 370
Odds, 338-339, 344, 372
Dependent and independent events, 340-341
Frequency and range, 350-351, 366, 370
Mean, median, and mode, 352, 361* 366, 370-371, 394, 412
Statistics, 354-355, 362-363, 394
Bar graphs, pictographs, histograms, 356-357, 412
Line segment graphs, 358-359
Circle graphs, 360-361, 370, 375*
Scattergrams, 364-365

Technology

Book 6

Calculator
  using a calculator, 20-21, 383
  multiplying, 27* 85* 95* 97, 145* 317, 383
  adding, 39* 65* 383
  dividing, 117* 123* 129* 139* 151* 153* 157* 160* 305*
  combining operations, 283* 317, 355*
Computer
  binary digits, 51
  giving input, 104-105
  flowcharts, 104-105, 222-223
  decisions in programs, 222-223
  using strings in programs, 318-319
  computer drawings (Logo), 404-405

Book 7

Calculator
  combining operations, 15* 227* 353* 361
  using a calculator, 28-29, 77* 373*
  dividing, 189,
  exponents, 67* 103*
  percent, 303* 307* 311* 319
Computer
  binary place value, 53
  computer operations, 75*
  flowcharts and computer programs, 112-113
  inputs in computer programs, 190-191
  computer decisions, 272-273
  loops in computer programs, 340-341
  computer drawings (Logo), 410-411

Book 8

Calculator
  using a calculator, 28-29
  adding and subtracting fractions, 105
  repeating and nonrepeating decimals, 123* 389*
  integers, 185* 199*
  percent, 275* 277* 283* 287*
  combining operations, 331* 393
Computer
  computer byte code, 75
  programs and flowcharts, 106-107
  FOR-NEXT counting loops, 174-175
  string variables, 266-267
  READ and DATA statements, 346-347
  computer drawings (Logo), 410-411

Note: Red type indicates that a topic is being introduced for the first time. The page numbers labeled with a * indicate references in Skillkeeper or Think Math activities.

Scope and Sequence

Book 6	Book 7	Book 8

Measurement

Book 6

Length
  mm, cm, m, dm, dam, hm, km, 168-177, 190, 197* 224, 276, 328*
  in., ft, yd, mi, 386-389, 399, 402, 406
  computing with customary units, 390
Capacity
  L, mL, kL, 178-179, 190, 224, 276
  fl oz, c, pt, qt, gal, 394-395, 402, 406
Weight
  g, mg, kg, 121* 180-181, 190, 224, 329*
  oz, lb, T, 396-397, 399, 402, 406
Temperature
  Celsius, 182-183, 190
  Fahrenheit, 398, 402
Volume
  cm³, m³, 358-359, 367, 373* 384
  ft³, yd³, 393
Changing metric units, 172-175, 178-180, 190
Scale drawing, 290-292
Perimeter, 346-347, 367, 384, 392, 406
Circumference, 348-349, 384, 406
Area
  of a rectangle, 350-351, 360, 367, 369* 392, 406
  of a triangle, 352, 367, 384
  of a parallelogram, 352*
  of a circle, 354-355, 367, 369* 384
  on a geoboard, 368
Surface area, 356-357, 367, 393
Estimating, 171, 178, 180, 182, 191, 355* 359, 391, 396, 398

Book 7

Length
  mm, cm, dm, m, dam hm, km, 248-251, 261* 270, 292, 320, 342
  in., ft, yd, mi, 394-395, 403* 408, 412
Perimeter, 252-253, 255, 270, 292, 320, 342
Area
  rectangles and parallelograms, 254-255, 270, 320, 396-397, 408, 412
  triangles and trapezoids, 256-257, 270, 292, 301* 342
  circles, 324-327, 329* 331* 338, 366, 396-397, 408
Surface area
  rectangular prisms, 258-259, 320
  cylinders, 328-329, 338, 366
Volume
  prisms, 260-261, 270, 292, 301* 342, 347* 398-399, 408
  cylinders, 330-331, 335* 338, 366, 398-399, 408, 412
  displacement, 271
Capacity
  L, mL, kL, 262-263, 270, 342
  fl oz, c, pt, qt, gal, 400-401, 408, 412
Weight
  mg, g, kg, t, 264-265, 320
  oz, lb, T, 402, 408, 412
Temperature
  Celsius, 266-267
  Fahrenheit, 403, 408, 412
Scale drawings, 286
Circumference, 322-323, 326-327, 331* 338, 366
Estimating, 249, 335*

Book 8

Length
  mm, cm, dm, m, dam, hm, km, 156-159, 160* 172, 214, 268
  in., ft, yd, mi, 396-398, 403* 408
Capacity
  mL, cL, dL, L, daL, hL, kL, 160-161, 169* 172, 214, 268, 318
  fl oz, c, pt, qt, gal, 400-401, 403, 408
Weight
  mg, cg, dg, g, dag, hg, kg, t, 162-163, 169* 172, 214, 268
  oz, lb, T, 403-404, 408
Temperature
  Celsius, 164
  Kelvin, 164, 214
  Fahrenheit, 402
Precision in measurement, 168-169, 268
Scale drawings, 256-257
Perimeter, 300-301, 322, 348, 394
Area
  rectangles and parallelograms, 302-303, 310-311, 322, 348, 394, 398, 408
  triangles and trapezoids, 304-305, 310-311, 315* 322, 348, 394, 408
  circles, 308-311, 322, 348, 394, 398, 408
Circumference, 306-307, 322, 348, 394
Surface area, 312-313
Volume
  prisms and cylinders, 314-315, 318-319, 322, 329* 399, 408
  pyramids and cones, 316-319, 322, 348, 394, 399, 408
Estimating, 156-157, 160, 162

Time and Money

Book 6

Time

Units of time, 184
Adding and subtracting, 185, 190, 205*
Estimating, 185, 283*
Time zones, 186
Elapsed time, 187

Money

Mixed practice, 12, 46, 71-73, 146, 203, 310, 312
Rounding, 30-31, 150-151
Estimating sums and differences, 32-33, 62, 68-69, 255
Adding, 31* 36-39, 50, 52, 64-65, 127* 159
Subtracting, 31* 40-43, 50, 66-67, 122* 136, 159
Making change, 70
Multiplying, 84-85, 127* 141-143, 145
Dividing, 114-117, 126-127, 143* 148-151, 153, 161
Estimating products and quotients, 138-139, 146
Unit price, 161
Simple interest, 310-311, 314
Discount price, 312

Book 7

Time

Adding and subtracting units of time, 18-19, 30
Time zones, 48-49

Money

Adding, 40-41, 54, 61* 297*
Subtracting, 42-43, 54, 61*
Estimating
  sums and differences, 44-45, 54, 86
  products and quotients, 58-59, 90-91, 100-101, 128-129
Mixed practice, 47, 68-69, 96-97, 104-105, 218, 316, 404-405
Multiplying, 93-95, 122-123
Dividing, 118-119
Simple interest, 304-305
Discount and sale price, 312-313
Sales tax, 94-95

Book 8

Time

Units of time, 165, 181* 214, 268
Elapsed time, 166-167, 172-173, 214

Money

Estimating
  sums and differences, 8-9, 11, 19* 26, 42-43, 45, 50, 52
  products and quotients, 57, 69, 108, 114, 285
Adding and subtracting, 10-11, 22, 38-41, 44, 50, 61* 76
Multiplying, 16-17, 22, 54-56, 69* 280-281
Dividing, 18-19, 22, 64-65, 69*
Mixed practice, 20, 45-48, 51, 59, 120-121, 287
Sales tax, 46-47
Unit price, 246-247
Simple interest, 280-281, 287
Discount and sale price, 290-291, 324
Compound interest, 297
Consumer price index, 367

Note: Red type indicates that a topic is being introduced for the first time. The page numbers labeled with a * indicate references in Skillkeeper or Think Math activities.

Book 6	Book 7	Book 8

Problem Solving/Applications

Book 6

Use the checklist, 8-9, 90-91
Understand the question, 12
 question formulation, 12#1-8; 37#30; 39#16; 85#31; 115#35; 143#33; 205#33; 209#31; 231#38; 243#37; 1, 23, 53, 79, 107, 137, 167, 193, 225, 251, 277, 299, 321, 345, 365, 385
Find the data
 graph, 44, 98, 154, 333
 table, 119, 155
 advertisement, 312
 map, 130
 catalog, 203
 plan sheet, 234-235
 picture, 291, 347, 392-393
 reference book, 155, 176-177
 other sources, 13, 35, 72-73, 154-155, 284-285, 374-375
 missing and extra data, 35; 41#25; 125#5, 6; 141#26; 149#35; 154#3; 159#30; 229#41; **DB** 35, 41, 61, 67, 89, 119, 141, 183, 233, 241, 291, 309, 325, 359, 377, 397; **DH** 69, 83, 98, 119, 127, 146, 155, 215, 233, 281, 285, 289, 307, 311, 349, 351, 359, 393, 397, 398, 399
Plan what to do (Strategies)
 Choose the operations, 16, 131, 217; **TT** 34, 35, 44, 45, 46, 69, 99, 131, 187, 245, 311, 359, 377, 393
 Guess and check, 48; **TT** 63, 71, 73, 98, 130, 155, 181, 291, 307, 347, 397; **TM** 11, 25, 27, 39, 67, 97, 141, 185, 231, 367
 Use logical reasoning, 162; **TT** 177, 179, 244, 395; **TM** 3, 33, 37, 41, 59, 89, 121, 139, 149, 209, 215, 289, 379
 Draw a picture, 74; **TT** 83, 91, 125, 293, 313
 Make a list, 132; **TT** 146, 147, 203
 Find a pattern, 77, 221, 246, 249, 317, 383; **TT** 333, 375, 399; **TM** 5, 29, 85, 123, 153, 160, 211, 279, 329, 371
 Make a table, 100; **TT** 111, 119, 161, 217, 285, 335, 351
 Work backward, 188; **TT** 206, 312
 Solve a simpler problem, 218; **TT** 235
Answer and check back, 34, 46, 63, 69, 83, 111, 146, 161, 187, 206, 245, 307, 310-311, 355, 399
Practice and application, 45, 71, 99, 125, 147, 179, 181, 244, 272, 293, 294, 313, 314, 335, 340, 351, 360, 377, 380, 395, 397, 400
Multiple-step problems, 9#4, 8; 16#1, 2; 17#45; 21#7, 8; 34#7, 8; 45#6; 46#2, 5; 49#28; 67#31; 69#3, 8; 71#3, 6-9; 72#4; 73#6, 9; 83#6; 91#6, 8; 98#6; 99#5, 8; 101#38; 111#2, 7; 119#2; 125#7; 130#3, 5; 131#5-7; 146#6; 147#5-7; 154#1, 2, 4; 161#3, 6, 7; 163#36; 179#8; 188#1, 2; 217#4-8; 227#28-30; 229#40; 231#37; 234#4; 235#6; 244#6; 245#7; 247#48; 293#2; 309#34; 312#1-5; 313#6, 7; 314#3; 329#1; 335#4, 5, 8; 340#2-5; 347#3-7; 351#3-5; 355#11; 357#7, 8; 359#4-9; 361#11-13; 377#9; 380#3; 392#5, 6, 8; 393#10, 11, 14, 16, 17; 395#3, 6, 7; 397#2-5; 399#5, 6; 401#28

Book 7

Use the checklist, 16-17, 282-283
Understand the question, 20
 question formulation, 41#39; 207#28; 303#44; 329#19; 347#21; 1, 31, 55, 87, 115, 135, 163, 193, 223, 247, 275, 293, 321, 343, 367, 393
Find the data
 graph, 360-361, 378
 table, 96-97, 105, 122-123, 205, 236-237, 265, 355
 advertisement, 47
 map, 48-49, 286
 missing and extra data, 23; 63#48; 129#14; 277#29; 297#35; 311#31; 373#41; 377#40; 403#10; **DB** 23, 37, 39, 75, 103, 117, 199, 213, 237, 267, 283, 287, 301, 355, 395; **DH** 7, 19, 33, 45, 47, 57, 59, 119, 127, 157, 185, 207, 235, 237, 251, 261, 279, 297, 315, 329, 347, 387, 395
Plan what to do (Strategies)
 Choose the operations, 78-79, 218; **TT** 237, 255, 327, 361, 379
 Guess and check, 24; **TT** 47, 49, 81, 101, 105, 107, 123, 127, 265, 355, 401, 405; **TM** 93, 233, 281, 297, 329, 377, 399
 Use logical reasoning, 242; **TT** 259, 286, 287, 309, 351; **TM** 19, 43, 99, 179, 213, 215, 371, 385
 Draw a picture, 108; **TT** 121, 217, 333, 378
 Make a list, 50; **TT** 69, 79, 305
 Find a pattern, 27, 82; **TT** 97; **TM** 7, 11, 65, 117, 169, 175, 239, 381
 Make a table, 186; **TT** 205, 263
 Work backward, 130; **TT** 185, 267, 283
 Solve a simpler problem, 158; **TT** 183
 Using equations and formulas, 81, 182-185, 305
Answer and check back, 21, 101, 126-127, 287, 404-405
Practice and application, 68-69, 106-107, 121, 217, 255, 259, 263, 267, 268, 288, 308-309, 316, 326-327, 332-333, 336, 350-351, 362, 379, 388, 401, 406
Multiple-step problems, 13#25; 21#3, 4; 41#37; 45#31; 47#3-5, 7; 51#29; 59#37-38; 61#32; 63#48; 65#29; 68#1, 6; 69#8, 10-12; 72#10; 75#27; 77#28; 78#3; 91#31; 95#37; 96#10; 97#7; 101#6-7; 105#8; 109#28, 29, 31; 119#35; 121#3, 8; 123#6, 8, 9; 125#34; 205#6, 9, 11; 211#27; 215#26; 217#4, 5, 7; 225#34; 229#30; 231#20; 233#29; 236#8, 6; 237#9, 11, 15; 253#14, 15; 259#2, 4-8; 261#14; 263#4, 5, 9-12; 265#4, 9; 267#6-7; 283#3, 5, 6, 9, 10; 286#5, 6; 287#2; 295#27; 297#34, 35; 303#42; 305#2, 4-7, 9; 307#22; 309#7, 11, 13; 323#20; 325#17; 326#2, 3; 327#9, 11, 12; 331#7, 8; 333#4, 7-9; 361#19, 20; 375#31; 378#5; 379#1, 3, 7; 395#18; 397#11, 12; 401#5, 12; 402#19, 20; 405#11, 12

Book 8

Use the checklist, 12-13, 138-139
Understand the question, 20
 question formulation, 9#33; 11#28; 65#17; 91#35; 93#29; 95#33; 119#33; 257#9; 1, 31, 53, 77, 109, 131, 155, 177, 215, 241, 269, 299, 325, 349, 373, 395
Find the data
 table, 46-47, 67, 150, 163, 261, 353
 map, 125
 drawing, 254-255, 405
 consumer data, 120-121
 monthly statement, 287
 test scores, 366
 missing and extra data, 23, 58; 63#35; 113#36; 279#41; 283#27; 285#32; 289#26; **DB** 23, 45, 63, 97, 113, 119, 137, 163, 181, 249, 273, 319, 339, 351, 402; **DH** 9, 37, 47, 55, 71, 85, 87, 114, 149, 201, 223, 247, 255, 291, 307, 313, 331, 333, 335, 337, 351, 355, 400
Plan what to do (Strategies)
 Choose the operations; 48; **TT** 58, 59, 101, 167, 291, 311, 319, 366, 367, 385, 401, 404
 Guess and check, 24; **TT** 43, 45, 47, 67, 125, 147, 201, 319, 353, 379; **TM** 83, 187, 193, 203
 Use logical reasoning, 236; **TT** 245, 281, 405; **TM** 9, 85, 183, 191, 363
 Draw a picture, 126, 385; **TT** 139, 255, 261, 385
 Make a list, 72; **TT** 99, 163
 Find a pattern, 210; **TM** 117, 137, 223
 Make a table, **TT** 161, 251, 287; **TM** 341
 Work backward, 102; **TT** 121, 149, 291
 Solve a simpler problem, 170; **TT** 189, 339
 Using equations and formulas, 146-149, 200-201, 250-251, 281; **TM** 141
Answer and check back, 21, 43, 45, 401, 404
Practice and application, 59, 98-99, 101, 161, 167, 189, 245, 262, 291, 294, 310, 319, 320, 339, 342, 367, 368, 379, 390, 406
Multiple-step problems, 5#38; 11#27; 13#4, 8, 10; 17#33; 19#36; 21#7, 9; 25#26; 39#25; 41#32; 43#7, 8; 45#1, 4, 7; 47#10, 13; 55#40, 41; 57#23; 59#6, 7; 95#32; 97#32; 98#1, 2, 4, 5; 99#6, 7, 10-12; 101#7, 10; 111#36; 113#37; 117#32; 120#8; 121#9-11; 159#28; 161#5, 7-9; 167#2, 6; 189#8; 245#11; 271#19; 279#38, 40; 281#5-7; 283#27, 28; 287#7; 291#1-7; 301#14; 307#22; 309#18-20; 310#1, 2; 311#2, 3, 5-8; 313#11; 319#3-6; 379#3; 398#14

TM Think Math
TT Try This
DB Data Bank
DH Data Hunt

Note: Red type indicates that a topic is being introduced for the first time. The page numbers labeled with a * indicate references in Skillkeeper or Think Math activities.

Objectives for Book 7

Chapter 1 Addition and Subtraction of Whole Numbers
1.1 Read and write whole numbers and identify place value in the decimal numeration system.
1.2 Compare, order, and round whole numbers.
1.3 Estimate sums and differences of whole numbers by rounding.
1.4 Add and subtract whole numbers.
1.5 Add and subtract units of time.
1.6 Solve word problems using the 5-Point Checklist and cumulative computational skills.

Chapter 2 Addition and Subtraction of Decimals
2.1 Read and write decimals and identify place value of digits in a decimal.
2.2 Compare, order, and round decimals.
2.3 Add and subtract decimals.
2.4 Estimate sums and differences of decimals by rounding.
2.5 Solve word problems using the 5-Point Checklist and cumulative computational skills.

Chapter 3 Multiplication and Division of Whole Numbers
3.1 Estimate products of whole numbers.
3.2 Find products of whole numbers.
3.3 Write repeated factors and their products using exponential notation.
3.4 Estimate quotients of whole numbers.
3.5 Find quotients and remainders of whole numbers.
3.6 Solve word problems using the 5-Point Checklist and cumulative computational skills.

Chapter 4 Multiplication of Decimals
4.1 Use estimation to find decimal products.
4.2 Find products when the factors are decimals.
4.3 Estimate products when the factors are decimals.
4.4 Use scientific notation to express whole numbers.
4.5 Solve word problems using the 5-Point Checklist and cumulative computational skills.

Chapter 5 Division of Decimals
5.1 Find the quotient of a decimal divided by a whole number.
5.2 Find the quotient when the divisor is a decimal.
5.3 Estimate quotients of decimals.
5.4 Solve word problems using the 5-Point Checklist and cumulative computational skills.

Chapter 6 Geometry
6.1 Identify and write symbols for basic geometric figures and classify angles according to their measure.
6.2 Identify and classify polygons according to the measure of their angles, length of their sides, and number of sides.
6.3 Identify and write symbols for a chord, diameter, radius, central angle, and arc.
6.4 Identify pairs of congruent polygons and lines of symmetry in figures.
6.5 Identify parallel and perpendicular lines and mid-points and perpendicular bisectors of segments.
6.6 Identify basic space figures and count their vertices, faces, and edges.

Chapter 7 Number Theory and Equations
7.1 Find the prime factorization of a composite number.
7.2 Find the greatest common factor or the least common multiple of two numbers.
7.3 Evaluate an expression containing a variable by substituting a number for the variable.
7.4 Solve equations by using addition, subtraction, multiplication, or division.
7.5 Solve word problems using the 5-Point Checklist and cumulative computational skills.

Chapter 8 Addition and Subtraction of Fractions
8.1 Find equivalent and lowest-terms fractions.
8.2 Write a number as an improper fraction or a mixed number.
8.3 Compare fractions and mixed numbers.
8.4 Find the sums and differences of fractions.
8.5 Find the sums and differences of mixed numbers.
8.6 Solve word problems using the 5-Point Checklist and cumulative computational skills.

Chapter 9 Multiplication and Division of Fractions
9.1 Find the products of fractions or mixed numbers.
9.2 Find the reciprocal of a number.
9.3 Find the quotient of fractions or of mixed numbers.
9.4 Compare two fractions by comparing their decimal equivalents.
9.5 Solve word problems using the 5-Point Checklist and cumulative computational skills.

Chapter 10 Measurement: Metric Units
10.1 Express metric units of length in larger or smaller metric units.
10.2 Find the perimeter and area of a simple polygon and the surface area of a rectangular prism.
10.3 Find the volume of a prism.
10.4 Choose appropriate metric units of capacity and weight, and express in larger and smaller units; read Celsius temperatures.
10.5 Solve word problems using the 5-Point Checklist and cumulative computational skills.

Chapter 11 Ratio and Proportion
11.1 Write a ratio as a fraction in lowest terms and use cross products to determine if two ratios are equal.
11.2 Write and solve proportions.
11.3 Use proportions to find the length of a side given a pair of similar figures.
11.4 Solve word problems using the 5-Point Checklist and cumulative computational skills.

Chapter 12 Percent
12.1 Express ratios, fractions, and decimals as percents, and percents as fractions and decimals.
12.2 Find a percent of a number
12.3 Find the percent one number is of another.
12.4 Find a number when a percent of it is known.
12.5 Write and solve a proportion for a percent problem.
12.6 Solve word problems using the 5-Point Checklist and cumulative computational skills.

Chapter 13 Circles and Cylinders
13.1 Find the circumference of a circle.
13.3 Find the area of a circle.
13.3 Find the lateral area and total surface area of a cylinder.
13.4 Find the volume of a cylinder.
13.5 Identify the cross-section view of a space figure.
13.6 Solve word problems using the 5-Point Checklist and cumulative computational skills.

Chapter 14 Probability, Statistics, and Graphs
14.1 Find the probability of a particular outcome given several equally likely outcomes.
14.2 Find the probability of an event when the outcomes are ordered pairs.
14.3 Identify the frequency of an event and find the range, mode, arithmetic mean, and median of a set of numerical data.
14.4 Read, interpret, and make bar graphs, line segment graphs, pictographs, and circle graphs.
14.5 Solve word problems using the 5-Point Checklist and cumulative computational skills.

Chapter 15 Integers
15.1 Read, write, and compare integers.
15.2 Find the sum of two or more integers.
15.3 Find the difference of two integers.
15.4 Find the product of two or more integers and find the quotient of two integers.
15.5 Give integer coordinates of points in a coordinate plane and graph an equation using integer coordinates.
15.6 Solve word problems using the 5-Point Checklist and cumulative computational skills.

Chapter 16 Measurement: Customary Units
16.1 Express customary units of length in larger or smaller customary units, and add and subtract inches, feet, and yards.
16.2 Find the area of a polygon in customary units.
16.3 Find the volume of a rectangular prism and a cylinder in customary units.
16.4 Express customary units of capacity and weight in larger or smaller customary units; estimate customary units of weight and temperature in degrees Fahrenheit.
16.5 Solve word problems using the 5-Point Checklist and cumulative computational skills.

Objectives

1.1 Read and write whole numbers and identify place value in the decimal numeration system.

1.2 Compare, order, and round whole numbers.

1.3 Estimate sums and differences of whole numbers by rounding.

1.4 Add and subtract whole numbers.

1.5 Add and subtract units of time.

1.6 Solve word problems using the 5-Point Checklist and cumulative computational skills.

Summary

The first chapter of this book begins with a lesson on ancient numeration systems. This lesson provides an interesting contrast to the lessons on the decimal numeration system that follow. Since an understanding of place value is necessary for rounding and comparing numbers and for adding and subtracting, place value is emphasized in Chapter 1.

Following a lesson on estimating sums and differences, the addition and subtraction algorithms are reviewed. These algorithms are then applied to practical word problems. Another application of addition and subtraction is presented with units of time.

Mathematical Background

Place value Our decimal numeration system is characterized by these important features:

- It has a base of ten; that is, we group by tens.

- The digits 0, 1, 2, 3, 4, 5, 6, 7, 8, 9 can be used to represent any number.

- The system has place value which means that the number a digit represents depends upon its place in the numeral.

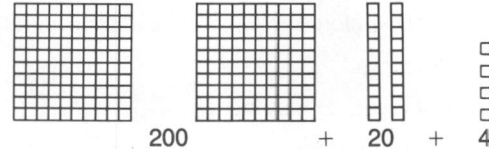

200   +   20   +   4

Thus, in the numeral 224 the 2 on the left represents 2 hundreds while the 2 in the middle represents 2 tens. These ideas are easily extended for larger numbers. In this chapter numbers through trillions are used.

Estimation In teaching estimation it is important to have students round numbers so that they can perform the computation in their heads. The estimation a student makes is partly a function of that student's mental computation ability. For example, in an exercise such as 5,124 + 2,853 some students may choose to round to the nearest thousand while others may decide to round to the nearest hundred.

It is important to remember that there is no such thing as a right or wrong estimate unless the rounding or computing has been done incorrectly. Teachers should determine for themselves a range of acceptable estimates depending on the abilities of their students. With estimation, the process and techniques are just as important as the answer.

Addition and Subtraction Since both addition and subtraction are review topics at this level, the algorithms for these operations are presented with a minimum of explanation. The algorithms may be explained in greater detail by using the basic properties of whole numbers or by using place-value models.

To find the sum of 67 and 54 using the *basic properties* we can follow the steps below.

$67 + 54 = (60 + 7) + (50 + 4)$ Place value definitions

$= (60 + 50) + (7 + 4)$ Commutative and Associative properties

$= (100 + 10) + (10 + 1)$ Adding ones and tens and regrouping

$= 100 + (10 + 10) + 1$ Associative property

$= 100 + 20 + 1 = 121$ Place value definitions

Problem Solving Developing student ability to solve problems is a primary goal of mathematics instruction. To aid students in reaching this goal, a 5-Point Checklist for problem solving is introduced in this chapter and will be reinforced throughout the book.

5-Point Checklist
1. Understand the QUESTION.
2. Find the needed DATA.
3. PLAN what to do.
4. Find the ANSWER.
5. CHECK back.

Each problem-solving lesson will highlight one or more of these five steps—question, data, plan, answer, check—as an important aspect of the problem-solving process. In Chapter 1, the 5-Point Checklist is introduced on page 16, and students are given the opportunity to apply the checklist on page 17. Subsequent lessons focus on the first step, *Understanding the Question* on page 20, and the fourth step, *Answering the Question* on page 21.

A special feature, the Data Hunt, is introduced in Chapter 1. In Data Hunt exercises, pages 7 and 19, students are asked to look outside the book for needed data. On page 23 another feature, the Data Bank, is introduced. For Data Bank exercises, students are directed to the back of the book for data required to solve the problems.

The concluding problem-solving lesson in this chapter introduces a strategy for solving some nonroutine problems. Such problems cannot usually be solved directly by computation. In later mathematics classes students may learn some advanced techniques for solving nonroutine problems. However, at this stage the student may still be able to solve the problem by employing a particular strategy. The strategy of Guess and Check is introduced on page 24. Additional strategies will be introduced in later chapters. These include Make an Organized List, Find a Pattern, Draw a Picture, Work Backward, Solve a Simpler Problem, Make a Table, Choose the Operations, and Use Logical Reasoning. Throughout the book, students will be presented with problems that can be solved by using one or more of these strategies.

Vocabulary

numeral	period	rounding
numeration system	million	estimate
place value	billion	sum
digit	trillion	difference
expanded numeral		

 ## Error Analysis

This chapter reviews the important concepts of place value and Hindu-Arabic numeration. A correct and mature knowledge of these concepts is critical for success in whole number work, particularly the computational algorithms. Error patterns occur both as students develop an understanding of numeration and place value and as they use this knowledge in computation. Some common error patterns are given below.

Error Pattern 1

$$
\begin{array}{r} \overset{1}{2}05 \\ + 978 \\ \hline 1{,}273 \end{array} \qquad
\begin{array}{r} \overset{1}{9}{,}031 \\ + 7{,}695 \\ \hline 17{,}626 \end{array} \qquad
\begin{array}{r} \overset{1}{8}{,}005 \\ + 3{,}776 \\ \hline 12{,}771 \end{array}
$$

Diagnosis The student demonstrates good understanding of basic addition facts, but is unclear about regrouping in an addition situation involving zeros. Instead of adding the regrouped value in a column having zeros, the student "carries" the value to the next nonzero value.

Remediation Begin with examples that do not have zeros, such as 522 + 789. Discuss the steps in the addition algorithm including how regrouping is carried out from ones to tens, and tens to hundreds. Return to an example such as 205 + 978, and focus on the step-by-step addition.

Error Pattern 2

$$
\begin{array}{l} 8 \text{ h } 40 \text{ min} \\ - 6 \text{ h } 35 \text{ min} \\ \hline \end{array} \longrightarrow
\begin{array}{l} \overset{7}{\cancel{8}} \text{ h } \overset{50}{\cancel{40}} \text{ min} \\ - 6 \text{ h } 35 \text{ min} \\ \hline 1 \text{ h } 15 \text{ min} \end{array}
$$

Diagnosis The student has regrouped as in whole number addition, exchanging 1 hour for 10 minutes.

Remediation Discuss grouping by tens and grouping by units of sixty. Review the time relationships used in this example, 60 minutes = 1 hour. Work through additional examples demonstrating how to regroup properly.

Error Pattern 3

$$
\begin{array}{r} \overset{6}{\cancel{9}}\overset{1}{,}\overset{1}{3}\overset{1}{2}4 \\ - 6{,}785 \\ \hline 649 \end{array} \qquad
\begin{array}{r} \overset{2}{\cancel{4}}\overset{1}{3}\overset{1}{4} \\ - 289 \\ \hline 55 \end{array} \qquad
\begin{array}{r} \overset{2}{\cancel{6}}\overset{1}{3}{,}\overset{1}{5}\overset{1}{0}\overset{1}{1} \\ - 13{,}265 \\ \hline 1{,}101{,}346 \end{array}
$$

Diagnosis The student shows a poor understanding of regrouping in subtraction. He or she started with the digit in the highest place value of the minuend and subtracted enough to be able to place a "1" at each digit to the right.

Remediation Begin with 2-digit examples emphasizing the left to right movement. Carefully work through an example showing how to regroup tens as ones, hundreds as tens, etc. Use place-value materials to model the regrouping, if necessary.

 ## Problem Solving

Developing a Positive Classroom Atmosphere

There are four essential ingredients to a successful problem-solving program: 1) the content of the program must be appropriate for students; 2) the problem-solving program must be part of a sound instructional program in all other basic skill areas of mathematics (computational skills, estimation, measurement, and so on); 3) students must have ample opportunity to participate in problem-solving experiences; and 4) the teacher's actions must promote a positive classroom atmosphere related to problem solving.

A successful problem-solving program must have all of the above characteristics. Assistance with the first three is provided by the text. The importance of the teacher in developing a classroom atmosphere that is conducive to problem solving cannot be overemphasized.

There are two ways in which your actions affect the classroom atmosphere. First, your attitude about problem solving will influence your students' attitudes about problem solving. If you demonstrate that problem solving is important, exciting, and fun, most students will develop a similar attitude. Here are some things you can do to promote positive problem-solving attitudes among your students.

- Be enthusiastic about problem solving.

- Encourage students to contribute problems from their personal experiences.

- Personalize problems whenever possible; use students' names in problems, for example.

- Provide the appropriate amount and type of assistance to avoid excessive frustration.

Second, your comments about problem solving communicate to students the types of behaviors you consider to be desirable related to problem solving. Here are some things you can do to promote desirable problem-solving behaviors.

- Recognize and reinforce willingness and perseverance.

- Reward risk takers.

- Encourage students to play hunches.

- Accept unusual solutions.

- Praise students for getting correct solutions but emphasize the selection and use of problem-solving strategies.

- Emphasize persistence rather than speed.

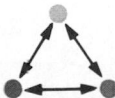 **Special Education**

Presented below are ideas for helping the special students in your class review the whole number concepts and skills of this chapter. Draw from these ideas as you become more aware of the particular learning difficulties your students possess.

The model below presents a framework for helping students with special needs learn mathematics skills and concepts.

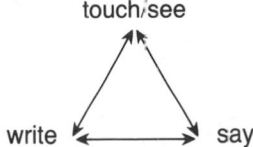

The tips for instruction suggested in this and subsequent Special Education sections focus on various aspects of this model.

Prerequisites First

If you perceive that some students lack prerequisite basic-fact skills, use the basic-facts tests (TRB pp. 89–92) to create a written list of troublesome facts with answers. Then help students systematically master these, a few at a time. Allow students to refer to the list during computation until it is no longer needed.

Visual Guidance

As you review reading and writing larger numbers, help students realize that because they can read and write 1-, 2-, and 3-digit numbers, they can quickly learn to read any larger number. Use a whole number reader as shown below, to help students read numbers within each period and say the period name at the comma.

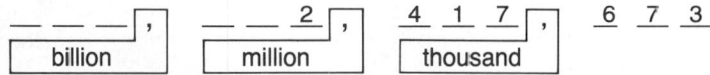

The example of the figure shows 2 million, 417 thousand, 673. Require students themselves to write the billion, million, and thousand labels before beginning. If necessary, a card can be placed over the labels and used to gradually reveal numbers within each period.

Using Color to Cue

Since color perceptions develop early, keep colored chalk at the chalkboard to highlight important points. Sometimes the familiar traffic colors can be used: green for "start working here." For example, use color as in the figure to help students interpret the instruction lines for rounding numbers on page 8. Circle the digit in the place to be rounded. Then mark the digit to its right green, since we start here to make a decision. The green digit tells us what to do with the circled digit. If it is less than 5, the circled digit remains the same; if it is 5 or greater, the circled digit is increased by 1. Make all digits to the right of the circled digit zeros.

$$\rightarrow 6, ②\, 47 \qquad \rightarrow 6, ②\, 00$$

When comparing two numbers, have students vertically align digits with the same place value and underscore in color digits in the first place where they are different.

$$2,1\underline{9}3$$

$$2,1\underline{7}5$$

Some special students will have difficulty discriminating between the > and < signs. Post the symbols on cards of two different colors. Point out that ">" is read "is greater than," and that the open end comes first and is always closest to the greater number, as in 2193 > 2175. If necessary, write the symbol in color to match the backing of the symbol card.

Finger Trace

Students with memory and perception difficulties could be encouraged to finger trace: 1) the digit which initiates the decision making for rounding numbers; 2) the first unlike digits in a pair when comparing or ordering numbers; 3) the > and < symbols, to trigger recognition; 4) the operation sign in written exercises containing a mix of addition and subtraction problems, to focus attention on the procedure to be carried out.

 **Subject Integration**

Subject matter related to other areas of the curriculum has been integrated into the following lessons. This provides an opportunity to highlight the interaction between mathematics and other subjects.

Consumer Awareness Telephone calls, pages 1–15; hunting and fishing licenses, page 30; driver's licenses, page 30

Social Studies River systems, pages 12–13; airport populations, page 21; map reading, page 29

Science Planets, pages 6–7

Health Calories, pages 16–17

History African counting, ancient numerals, page 2; Greek square and triangular numbers, page 11; Fibonacci, page 27

Computer Awareness Data storage, page 23

Career Awareness Retail sales, page 10; time cards, page 18

Management Guide

Teaching Chapter 1				Meeting Individual Needs					
				Lesson Assignments			Follow Up		
Objectives	Chapter Content	Pages	TRB Test Items	Minimum	Average	Extended	Reteaching	Enrichment	Practice
	Chapter Opener	1							
1.1 Read and write whole numbers and identify place value in the decimal numeration system.	Ancient Numeration Systems	2–3	1–3	1–6, 13–30	1–32	2–32 even	SE6 Ch2		PS 1
	Decimal Numeration Systems	4–5	4–7	1–6, 13–30	1–35	1–35 odd	RS 1	ES 1	PS 2
1.2 Compare, order, and round whole numbers.	Comparing and Ordering Whole Numbers	6–7	8–15	1–24, 29–34	1–34	1–33 odd, 34, TM	SE6 Ch 2 RS 2	ES 2	MP 417 PS 3
	Rounding Whole Numbers	8–9	16–18	1–30, SK	1–41, SK	2–40 even, 41–42, SK	SE6 Ch 2 RS 3	ES 3	MP 417 PS 4
1.3 Estimate sums and differences of whole numbers by rounding.	Estimating Sums and Differences	10–11	19–27	1–24	1–26, TM	1–26, TM	SE6 Ch 2 RS 4	ES 4	MP 417 PS 5
1.4 Add and subtract whole numbers.	Adding Whole Numbers	12–13	28–37	1–19, 24	1–25	1–25 odd, TM	SE6 Ch 2 RS 5	ES 5	MP 418 PS 6
	Subtracting Whole Numbers	14–15		1–24, 34, SK	1–30, 34, SK	1–23 odd, 25–35, SK	SE6 Ch 2 RS 6	ES 6	MP 418 PS 7
1.5 Add and subtract units of time.	Adding and Subtracting Units of Time	18–19	38–42		1–17, 19	2–16 even, 17–19, TM	RS 7	ES 7	MP 418 PS 9
1.6 Solve word problems using the 5-Point Checklist and cumulative computational skills.	Problem Solving: The 5-Point Checklist	16–17	43–46	1–6	1–9	1–10	SE6 Ch 2		PS 8
	Problem Solving: Understanding the Question	20		1–4	1–6	1–8	RS 8	ES 8	PS 10
	Problem Solving: Answering the Question	21		1–4	1–6	1–6			
	Problem Solving: Using a Data Bank	23		1–4	1–6	1–6			PS 11
	Skills Practice	22		1–30	1–40	2–46 even			
	Problem Solving: Guess and Check	24							
	Chapter Review/Test	25							
	Another Look/ Enrichment	26–27							
	Technology	28–29							
	Cumulative Review	30							

SE6 Student Edition, Book 6
RS Reteaching Supplement
ES Enrichment Supplement
PS Practice Supplement
MP More Practice
TM Think Math
SK Skillkeeper
TRB Teacher's Resource Book

Masters for use

. . . before Chapter 1

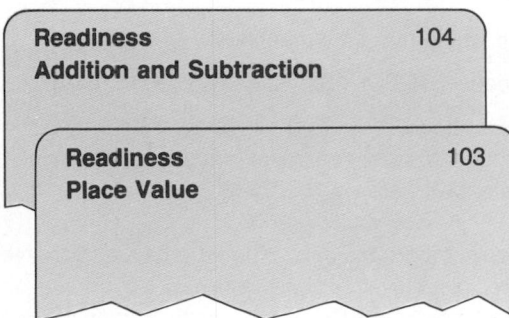

Readiness	104
Addition and Subtraction	

Readiness	103
Place Value	

. . . during Chapter 1

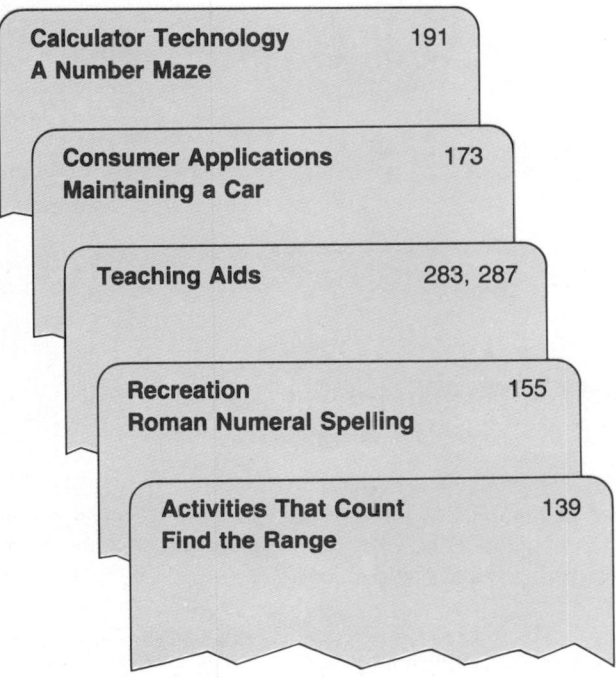

Calculator Technology	191
A Number Maze	

Consumer Applications	173
Maintaining a Car	

Teaching Aids	283, 287

Recreation	155
Roman Numeral Spelling	

Activities That Count	139
Find the Range	

. . . after Chapter 1

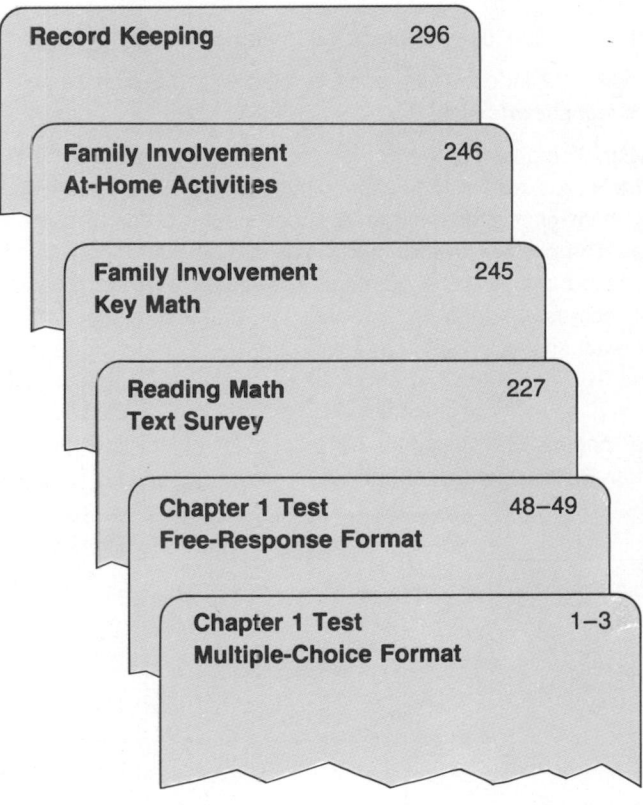

Record Keeping	296

Family Involvement	246
At-Home Activities	

Family Involvement	245
Key Math	

Reading Math	227
Text Survey	

Chapter 1 Test	48–49
Free-Response Format	

Chapter 1 Test	1–3
Multiple-Choice Format	

Supplements

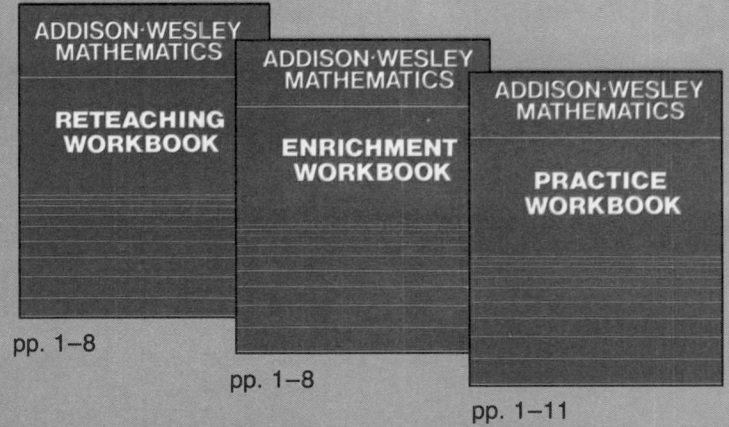

ADDISON·WESLEY MATHEMATICS **RETEACHING WORKBOOK**   pp. 1–8

ADDISON·WESLEY MATHEMATICS **ENRICHMENT WORKBOOK**   pp. 1–8

ADDISON·WESLEY MATHEMATICS **PRACTICE WORKBOOK**   pp. 1–11

Other Addison-Wesley Resources

Books and Kits

The Mad Minute   pp. 151–160
Skillseekers I $\oplus$ 1–10, $\ominus$ 1–12
Baseball: A Game of Numbers   pp. 2–16
Problem-Solving Experiences in Mathematics, Grade 7
  Problems 3, 4, 5, 18, 28, 38, 39, 40, 53, 79, 90, 114,
  129, 144, 149

Technology

Computer Math Activities   Volumes 1–5
Computer Math Games   Volumes 1, 2, 4, 6

Activities That Count

Activities That Count are designed for use throughout this chapter and subsequent chapters. Before beginning Chapter 1, you may wish to review these activities and select the ones you consider appropriate for your class.

Build a Number Game

Purpose To use ideas of place value and compare numbers

Materials 12 index cards, each labeled with a 3-digit number, game sheet shown below

Activity The object of the game is to build the greatest number. After the cards are mixed, each player draws three cards and places them on his or her game sheet in any order to build a number. The players, in turn, read their numbers and then determine which number is the greatest. The player with the greatest number scores a point for that round. The game continues until a player reaches a score of 5 and wins the game. Note that cards such as 014 and 009 could be included, but rules regarding their use would have to be established; for example, a card whose number begins with 0 cannot be placed in the millions period. Variation: Build the smallest number.

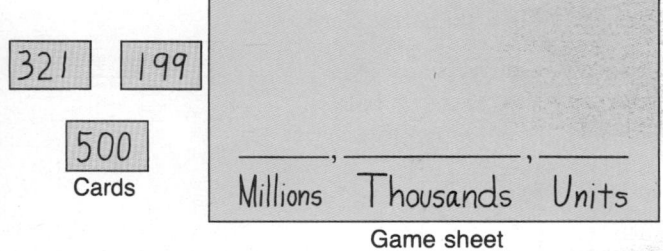

Game sheet

Find the Range Math Lab

Purpose To estimate sums and differences

Materials Activity sheet (TRB p. 139), calculator

Activity Provide students with additional subtraction exercises to write on their activity sheets. Instruct them to estimate the sums and differences and then record the number of the exercise in the space of the range that best fits their estimate. Calculators may be used to check answers. A time limit, according to the abilities of the students, may be used.

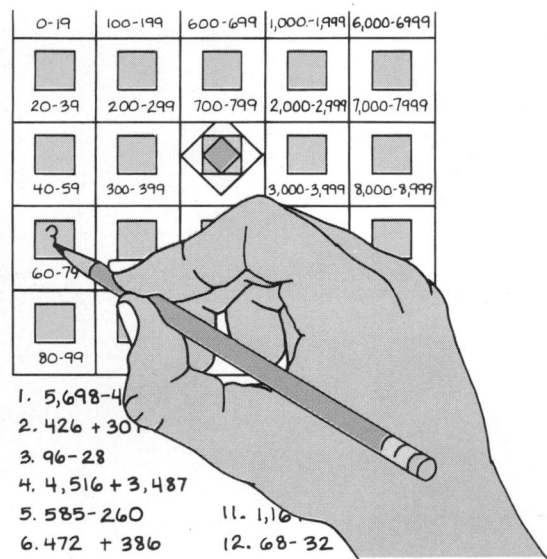

The Dot Connection Game

Purpose To add whole numbers mentally

Materials Dot paper (TRB p. 283)

Activity Students should prepare their game sheets by writing the numbers 1 through 18 within each set of four dots. A portion of the game sheet is shown below.

Each player connects 2 dots at a turn. When 4 dots are connected that form a square, players write their initials in the square and total the number of points. Each player keeps a running total; mental addition is encouraged. The highest score wins.

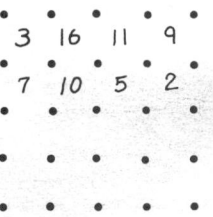

Number Search Project

Purpose To collect and organize data

Activity Ask students to look in newspapers and magazines for examples of numbers in the millions and billions. Make a chart showing the numbers and what each represents, such as people, cars, amounts of money, and so on.

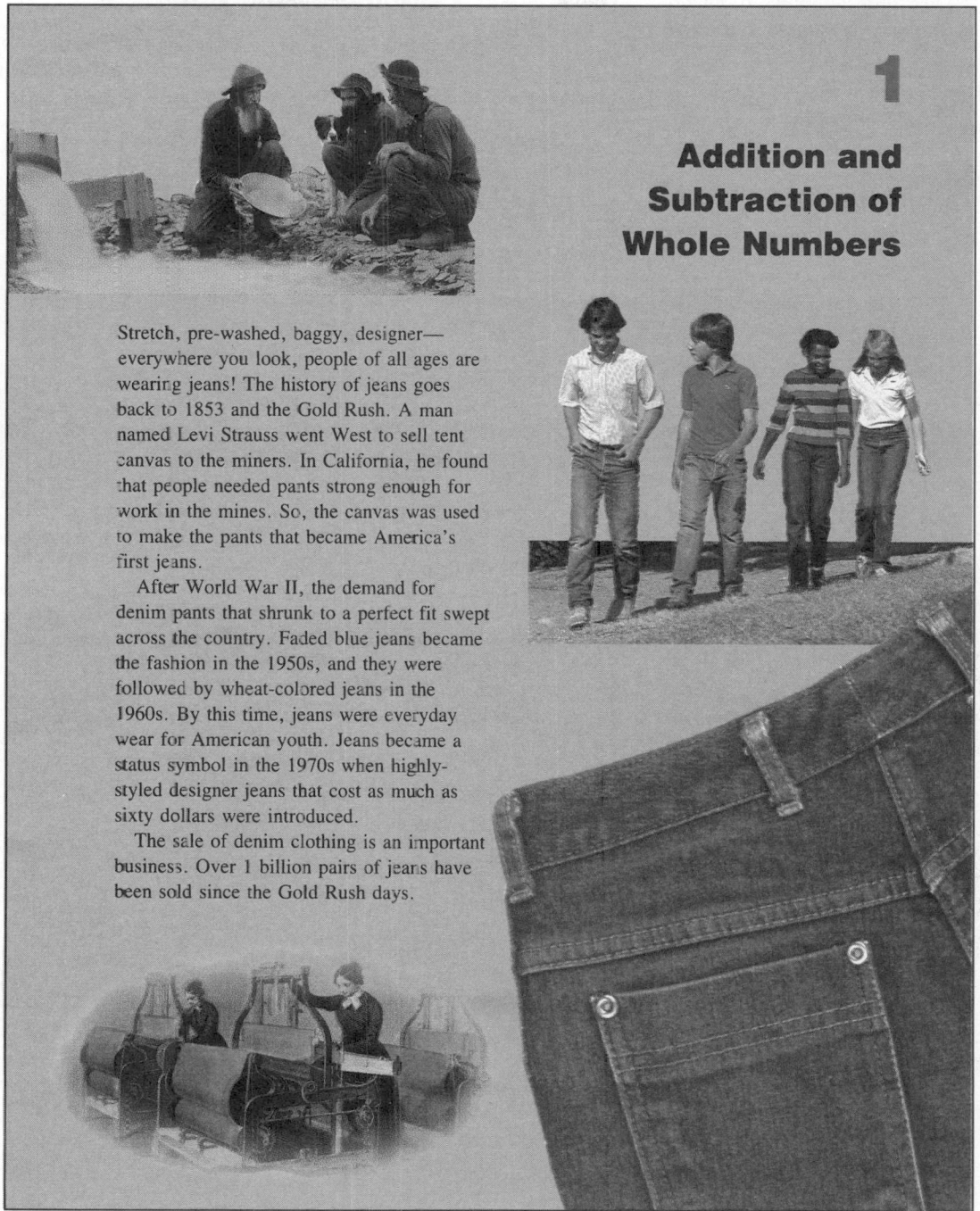

1

Addition and Subtraction of Whole Numbers

Stretch, pre-washed, baggy, designer—everywhere you look, people of all ages are wearing jeans! The history of jeans goes back to 1853 and the Gold Rush. A man named Levi Strauss went West to sell tent canvas to the miners. In California, he found that people needed pants strong enough for work in the mines. So, the canvas was used to make the pants that became America's first jeans.

After World War II, the demand for denim pants that shrunk to a perfect fit swept across the country. Faded blue jeans became the fashion in the 1950s, and they were followed by wheat-colored jeans in the 1960s. By this time, jeans were everyday wear for American youth. Jeans became a status symbol in the 1970s when highly-styled designer jeans that cost as much as sixty dollars were introduced.

The sale of denim clothing is an important business. Over 1 billion pairs of jeans have been sold since the Gold Rush days.

Introducing the Chapter

Discussion One of the topics reviewed in Chapter 1 is numeration systems. Point this out to students so that as they read about the history of jeans, they can note the different ways numbers can be expressed and used. Use this as an opportunity for students to create their own problems using the data in the article.

As you teach this chapter, you may wish to refer back to this page and discuss the Follow-Up Questions. Review the contents of the page before posing the questions.

Follow-Up Questions

After Page 3 In what year did the history of jeans begin? Write that number using Roman numerals. (MDCCCLIII)

After Page 5 How many pairs of jeans have been sold since the Gold Rush days? Write that numeral. (1,000,000,000)

After Page 7 A textile lab conducted tests to determine the durability of various weights and types of denim. The test results show how many times various fabrics were scraped by sandpaper before the fabric wore through: heavyweight cotton/polyester, 2,863; heavyweight cotton, 2,210; middleweight polyester/cotton/nylon, 2,873; and middleweight cotton, 596. Which type of fabric was least durable? (middleweight cotton) Which type was most durable? (middleweight polyester/cotton/nylon)

Quick Review Display the numbers below and have students give the ordinal number for each. Then ask students to give the ordinal number that comes before and after each number displayed.

12   35   159   76   18   63   22   102   49

Lesson Focus To interpret numerals in ancient numeration systems, particularly Roman and Egyptian numerals

Ideas for Getting Started

Display the following:

$$* = 1 \qquad ! = 100$$
$$\$ = 10 \qquad !\$\$\$** = 132$$

Have students study the numeral for 132 and try to discover the rule used to represent the number. Ask for ways to represent 113 (!\$***) and 204 (!!****). Challenge students to use only two characters to show 90 (\$! = 100 − 10). Call on students to write numerals on the chalkboard while the rest of the class identifies the numbers represented.

Using Page 2

Lesson Development Have a student locate Kenya on a map. Then call attention to the method of finger counting used by the Kamba people. Tell students to count with you on their fingers as shown in the pictures. Note that the numbers 1 through 5 are shown with the right hand, and the numbers 6 through 10 are shown using both hands. Select some students to show numbers with their fingers, and let other students name the numbers shown.

Ask students to study the ancient numerals at the bottom of the page. Remind them of the meanings of B.C. and A.D. Tell students that the Eqyptian numeration system was used about 3,700 years ago, the Chinese 2,500 years ago, the Roman 2,000 years ago, and the Mayan 400 years ago. Students should be aware that Chinese—and to a far lesser extent, Roman—numerals are still in use today.

Ask students if they can see a difference between the Mayan numeration system and the other systems. (Mayan system includes zero.) Students may be interested in how the numerals were used in each system to show numbers.

Egyptian: ∩∩∩|||||| 3 tens + 6 ones = 36

Roman: XXXVI   3 tens + 5 + 1 = 36

Chinese: 三   3 ⎫
      十   10 ⎬ 3 × 10 + 6 = 36
      六   6 ⎭

Mayan (base 20): • ← 20
             ☰ ← 16
                 ――
                 36

Ancient Numeration Systems

Mathematics began in early times as counting. Before recorded history, people probably counted on their fingers. The Kamba people of southern Kenya use finger counting today.

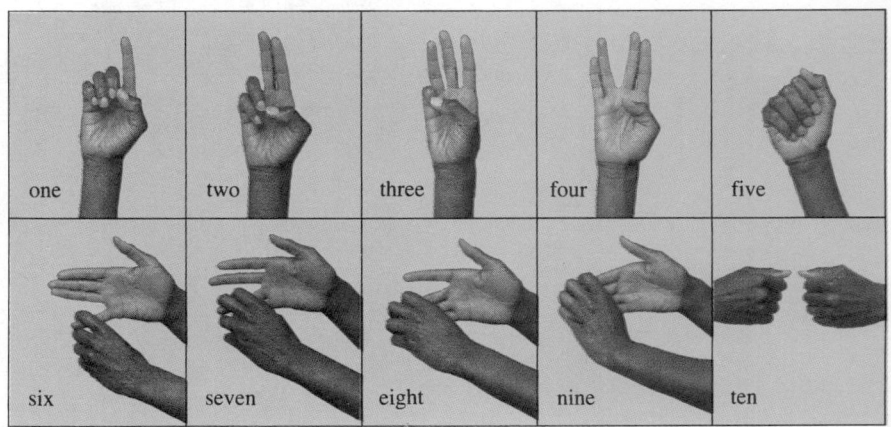

Symbols for numbers, called **numerals,** were invented to keep a record of numbers. Some ancient numerals are shown below.

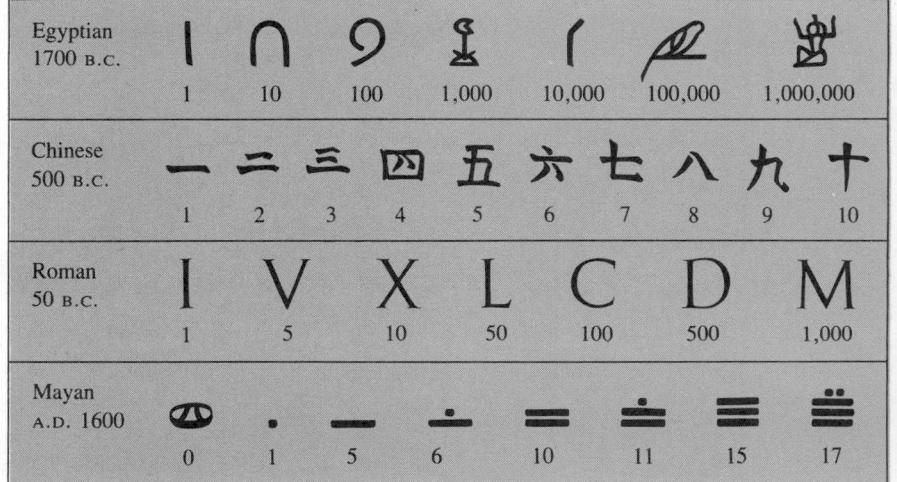

2

Follow Up

Reteaching

Have students find examples in every-day life to show how Roman numerals are used. Examples could include clocks, film credits, cornerstones of buildings, and outlining. To help students read the Roman numerals remind them that when two Roman symbols are placed side by side, we *add* if the smaller number is written on the right.

  50 10 1
   L   X   I   means 50 + 10 + 1

We *subtract* if the smaller number is written on the left.

  100 500
   C   D   means 500 − 100

Enrichment

Write the following exercises on the chalkboard. Have students add or subtract without changing to decimal numerals.

Add.

1. XI + XVI
    XXVII

2. XVII + XVIII
    XXXV

3. CD + M
    MCD

4. LXVII + CLXVI
    CCXXXIII

5. XXXIII − XII
    XXI

6. LX − XX
    XL

7. MXVII − MXI
    VI

8. MDXI − MCX
    CDI

Assignment Guide			
	Minimum	Average	Extended
page 3	1–6, 13–30	1–32	2–32 even

In the Egyptian numeration system, the number for a symbol was found by adding.

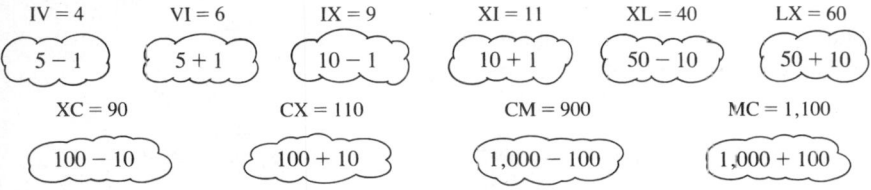

$= 100 + 20 + 4 = 124$

$= 1{,}000 + 200 + 10 + 5 = 1{,}215$

Give the number for each Egyptian numeral.

1. ∩∩∩|||| 34   **2.** 99∩||||||| 216   **3.** ⚚⚚999∩∩|| 2,322

4. ⚚⚚⚚∩∩∩ 3,040   **5.** ⌐⌐⚚999|||| 21,304   **6.** 𓍢𓍢⌐⌐⚚⚚⚚ 223,000

Write the Egyptian numeral for each number.

7. 28 ∩∩||||||||| **8.** 231 99∩∩∩| **9.** 1,416 ⚚9999∩||||||

10. 12,247 ⌐⌐⚚99∩∩∩||||||| **11.** 110,001 𓍢⌐| **12.** 2,204,034 𓍢𓍢𓍢𓍢⚚⚚⚚∩∩||||

The Roman numeration system used both addition and subtraction to find the number for a symbol.

IV = 4	VI = 6	IX = 9	XI = 11	XL = 40	LX = 60
5 − 1	5 + 1	10 − 1	10 + 1	50 − 10	50 + 10

XC = 90	CX = 110	CM = 900	MC = 1,100
100 − 10	100 + 10	1,000 − 100	1,000 + 100

Give the number for each Roman numeral.

13. V 5   **14.** XII 12   **15.** VIII 8

16. LXI 61   **17.** CD 400   **18.** MCLIX 1,159

19. CLXVII 167   **20.** MCCLIX 1,259   **21.** MMDCXCIV 2,694

Write the Roman numeral for each number.

22. 7 VII   **23.** 12 XII   **24.** 20 XX

25. 53 LIII   **26.** 200 CC   **27.** 1,300 MCCC

28. 1,500 MD   **29.** 1,984 MCMLXXXIV   **30.** 3,099 MMMXCIX

31. Write the present year using Roman numerals.

32. Write the year of your birth using Roman numerals.

3

Using Page 3

Exercises 1–32 Before assigning the exercises, discuss the examples of Egyptian numerals and Roman numerals on page 3. Students should note that there are no place-value or zero concepts in either system; this becomes evident when students need to use zero as a placeholder when writing the standard numeral for certain Egyptian or Roman numerals.

As you discuss the Roman numeral examples, point out that:

- Roman numerals are written left to right, using the principle of addition. First write the thousands, then the hundreds, then the tens, and finally the units.

- In Roman numerals, a smaller numeral appearing before a larger numeral indicates the smaller number is subtracted from the larger one. All 4's and 9's use the principle of subtraction. Thus, 4 is written as IV, or 5 minus 1, and 9 is written IX, or 10 minus 1.

Ideas That Work

Math for the Gifted

Use the diagram below to show how the Mayan Indians used place value based on 20.

$6 \times 18 \times 20 = 2{,}160$

$3 \times 20 = 60$

$12 = 12$

$\overline{2{,}232}$

The bottom tier or ones place represents the numbers from 1 to 19. The next tier is the twenties place and represents the number of twenties (or multiples of 20) to 340. Because the Mayans were interested in astronomy and used 360 for the number of days in a year, 18 × 20 was used in the third tier, rather than 20 × 20.

A famous date is represented by this Mayan numeral. What date is it? (1776)

Have students use the chart on page 2 to help them write a decimal numeral for each Mayan numeral shown below.

1. 27   2. 106   3. 1,896

Lesson Focus To review the decimal numeration system and read and write whole numbers

Suggested Materials Three index cards

Ideas for Getting Started

Write the digits 9, 3, and 7 on three index cards. Display the cards so that students see 937. "What is this number?" (Nine hundred thirty-seven) "What does the 9 represent?" (900 or 9 hundreds) "What does the 3 represent?" (30 or 3 tens) "What does the 7 represent?" (7 or 7 ones)

Change the position of the cards to show 793 and ask the same questions about the value of each digit. This demonstration will illustrate the meaning of place value: the *value* of a digit in a numeral depends upon its *place* in the numeral.

Using Page 4

Lesson Development Direct students to the picture of the place-value blocks. Point out that the place-value blocks suggest the expanded numeral 2,000 + 300 + 50 + 6. The standard numeral, 2,356, can be written without actually performing the indicated additions.

Note: In this mathematics series, a comma is used to separate periods, even if the number is a 4-digit numeral. However, some students may be familiar with the use of spaces to separate periods in numerals consisting of five or more digits, and you may wish to allow them to use spaces in their work.

Make a copy of the place-value and period chart on the chalkboard. Review the period names and place-value names with students as they look at the chart. Read the following numbers and have a student write the digits in the appropriate columns:

6,273,149   8,394,748,129   67,000,000

554,607   120,120,012   19,860,000,000

Warm Up Caution students not to use the word "and" when reading whole numbers. The word "and" will be used when reading decimals to denote the place of the decimal point. Thus, 600.27 is read "six hundred and twenty-seven hundredths" while the whole number 627 is read "six hundred twenty-seven."

The Decimal Numeration System

Our system of writing and reading numerals is called a **decimal numeration** system because we group by tens. The prefix **deci** means ten. Some computers may use systems that group by twos, eights, or sixteens.

The decimal numeration system has place value because the value of each digit in a numeral depends upon its place in the numeral.

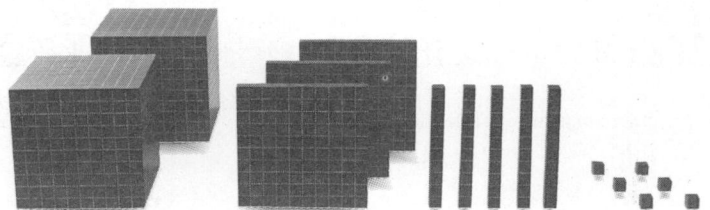

Expanded numeral: **2,000 + 300 + 50 + 6**

Standard numeral: **2,356**

Read: "two thousand, three hundred fifty-six"

The digits for large numbers are usually separated into groups of three called **periods.** We use commas to mark off the periods. This makes the numeral easier to read. The names of the first five periods are shown in the chart below.

Place-value names	hundreds	tens	ones	hundreds	tens	ones	hundreds	tens	ones	hundreds	tens	ones	hundreds	tens	ones
Numeral						2,	7	4	6,	3	8	9,	5	0	1
Period names	Trillions			Billions			Millions			Thousands			Units		

We read 2,746,389,501 as "two billion, seven hundred forty-six million, three hundred eighty-nine thousand, five hundred one."

Warm Up

Read each numeral aloud. See teaching notes.

1. 38,625   2. 1,076   3. 125,744   4. 3,000,000

5. 618,746   6. 84,500,000   7. 185,344,107   8. 100,100

9. 7,000,000,000   10. 55,725,000   11. 40,500,030,100   12. 504,844,623

4

Follow Up

Reteaching

Begin with the number 4 and discuss what it means. Multiply the 4 by 10, $10 \times 4 = 40$. Discuss this value. Point out that the numeral 4 is still involved but found in the tens position. Multiply the 4 by 100, $100 \times 4 = 400$. Discuss the number 400 and what it means.

Write expanded numerals such as 200 + 30 + 5. Have a student recopy in vertical form and add. Discuss the position and place value of each digit in the sum.

Enrichment

Tell students that in addition to the periods shown, there are larger periods such as quadrillions, quintillions, sextillions, and so on. Have students make a place-value chart through sextillions and use it to write the following numerals in words.

1. 15,000,000,000,000,000,000
   fifteen quintillion

2. 7,000,000,000,000,000
   seven quadrillion

3. 30,000,000,000,000,000,000,000
   thirty sextillion

4. 216,000,000,000,000
   two hundred sixteen trillion

Assignment Guide			
	Minimum	Average	Extended
page 5	1–6, 13–30	1–35	1–35 odd

Give the place value of each underlined digit.

Example: 6,739   Answer: 700

1. 5,349 40
2. 25,339 5,000
3. 167,923 60,000
4. 16,894 6,000
5. 376,518 300,000
6. 750,100,570 50,000,000
7. 6,235,000 6,000,000
8. 87,367,950 80,000,000
9. 39,799,947,499 30,000,000,000

Write the numeral.

10. three thousand, two hundred forty-seven 3,247
11. eighteen million, five hundred twenty-three thousand, one hundred twenty 18,523,120
12. seven hundred seventy-five thousand, sixty-six 775,066
13. eleven thousand, eleven 11,011
14. five billion, nine hundred million 5,900,000,000
15. two hundred seventeen million, eighty-four thousand, two hundred thirty-nine 217,084,239

Write each standard numeral in words.

16. 47,200 forty-seven thousand, two hundred
17. 42,591 forty-two thousand, five hundred ninety-one
18. 2,763 two thousand, seven hundred sixty-three
19. 500,065 five hundred thousand, sixty-five
20. 3,575,000 three million, five hundred seventy-five thousand
21. 6,280,000,000 six billion, two hundred eighty million

Write an expanded numeral for each standard numeral.

22. 6,723 6,000 + 700 + 20 + 3
23. 50,468 50,000 + 400 + 60 + 8
24. 487,083 400,000 + 80,000 + 7,000 + 80 + 3
25. 17,609,203 10,000,000 + 7,000,000 + 600,000 + 9,000 + 200 + 3
26. 34,589,403 30,000,000 + 4,000,000 + 500,000 + 80,000 + 9,000 + 400 + 3
27. 200,042,000,892 200,000,000,000 + 40,000,000 + 2,000,000 + 800 + 90 + 2

Write a standard numeral for each expanded numeral.

28. 4,000 + 300 + 50 + 7 4,357
29. 5,000 + 400 + 60 + 1 5,461
30. 20,000 + 7,000 + 900 + 60 + 2 27,962
31. 300,000 + 5,000 + 2 305,002
32. 7,000,000 + 60,000 + 2,000 + 80 7,062,080
33. 4,000,000 + 700 + 9 4,000,709
34. 8,000,000 + 300,000 + 500 + 4 8,300,504
35. 8,000,000,000 + 500,000 + 1,000 8,000,501,000

5

Reteaching Supplement, page 1

Enrichment Supplement, page 1

Practice Supplement, page 2

6
Numeration

Quick Review Have students round each time below to the nearest hour, half hour, and quarter hour.

	3:16	7:08	1:38	10:50	12:01
4:59	11:26	5:44	12:47	9:20	2:37

Lesson Focus To compare two whole numbers using the symbols of inequality (> and <) and to order whole numbers

Ideas for Getting Started

Display the following:

Airline distances from New York City	
Atlanta	1,203 kilometers (km)
San Francisco	4,139 km
Seattle	3,984 km
Montreal	533 km

"What city is closest to New York City?" (Montreal) "Which city is farthest from New York?" (San Francisco)

Ask a student to arrange the cities in order from closest to farthest from New York City and to explain his or her thinking process.

Using page 6

Motivational Problem Have students read the problem at the top of the page. "The question asks which distance is greater. What two distances are we talking about?" (Between Saturn and Dione, and between Earth and its moon.) "What numbers are we being asked to compare?" (378,000 and 384,500)

Lesson Development Have students work through the steps in the instruction boxes. Point out that since the digits in the hundred-thousands place are the same, we go on to compare the digits in the ten-thousands place. Here the digits are different, and as 8 is greater than 7, the number 384,500 is greater than 378,000.

Discuss the correct use of the symbols > and <. Ask students for their methods of remembering how to use the symbols. Anticipate responses such as, "The point is always toward the smaller number," or "The open part of the symbol is always next to the larger number."

Other Examples Call students' attention to this feature. The purpose of these examples is two-fold: 1) to present additional examples similar to those in the motivational problem, and 2) to show variations that require adaptations of the algorithm. For instance, the first and third examples reflect the steps described in the instruction lines. The second example shows that when one number has more digits than the other, it can be identified as greater without going through the steps.

Warm Up Answers **5.** 2,664; 2,763; 2,876; 2,918
6. 363,719; 365,035; 367,738; 368,904
7. 7,482,630; 7,482,649; 7,484,119; 7,500,000
8. 38,746,239; 93,647,149; 438,927,988; 3,742,811,266

Comparing and Ordering Whole Numbers

The planet Saturn has nine moons. One of its moons, Dione, is 378,000 kilometers (km) from Saturn. The average distance between Earth and its moon is 384,500 km. Which distance is greater?

To compare two numbers, we compare digits in the same places of the two numbers.

Start at the left and compare the digits in the same place.	Compare the digits in the first place where they are different.	The numbers compare the same way the digits compare.
384,500 378,000	384,500 378,000	384,500 > 378,000 *is greater than*
	8 is greater than 7.	378,000 < 384,500 *is less than*

The distance between Earth and its moon is greater.

Other Examples

$73,629 < 73,820$ $103,483 > 98,734$ $2,754,366 > 1,754,636$
  $6 < 8$ 6 digits 5 digits $2 > 1$

Warm Up

Which number is greater?   Which number is smaller?

1. 54,291,733   **2.** (13,992,248)   **3.** (1,071,429)   **4.** 966,773
(59,066,927)   13,920,929   1,073,934   (966,769)

List the numbers in order from least to greatest. See teaching notes.

5. 2,763	**6.** 368,904	**7.** 7,482,649	**8.** 38,746,239
2,918	363,719	7,500,000	3,742,811,266
2,664	365,035	7,482,630	438,927,988
2,876	367,738	7,484,119	93,647,149

6

Follow Up

Reteaching

Write these numbers on the chalkboard: 53,720 and 53,927. Then write the numbers in expanded form for comparison: 50,000 + 3,000 + 700 + 20 + 0 and 50,000 + 3,000 + 900 + 20 + 7. Have students begin at the left and compare the numbers until they find the first place where they differ, 700 and 900. Since 900 > 700, 53,927 is greater than 53,720. Give students other examples and have them work through these steps to compare the numbers.

Enrichment

Have students order the numbers in exercise 1 from least to greatest, and in exercise 2 from greatest to least.

1. a) 161 29 341
       29 161 341
   b) 587 1,002 99 742
       99 587 742 1,002
   c) 1,717 9,123 2,319 1,711
       1,711 1,717 2,319 9,123
2. a) 81 18 716
       716 81 18
   b) 409 94 881 2,001
       2,001 881 409 94
   c) 12,345 13,245 23,145 21,435
       23,145 21,435 13,245 12,345

Assignment Guide	Minimum	Average	Extended
page 7	1–24, 29–34	1–34	1–33 odd, 34, TM

Write > or < for each ⬤.

1. 1,875 ⬤ 1,862 >

2. 2,193 ⬤ 2,175 >

3. 6,470 ⬤ 6,490 <

4. 92,364 ⬤ 92,634 <

5. 26,083 ⬤ 29,095 <

6. 186,025 ⬤ 188,012 <

7. 3,004,700 ⬤ 3,004,693 >

8. 7,000,000 ⬤ 700,000 >

9. 867,010 ⬤ 867,001 >

10. 666,675 ⬤ 666,667 >

11. 90,004,063 ⬤ 90,004,036 >

12. 999,000,000 ⬤ 1,000,000,000 <

Give the number that is 1 more.

13. 99 100

14. 329 330

15. 1,999 2,000

16. 400,342 400,343

17. 9,999 10,000

18. 399,999,999 400,000,000

Give the number that is 1 less.

19. 400 399

20. 1,000 999

21. 3,800 3,799

22. 2,780,780 2,780,779

23. 51,000,000 50,999,999

24. 1,000,000,000 999,999,999

Give the number.

25. 100 more than 1,000 1,100

26. 1,000 less than 100,000 99,000

27. 10 more than 99 109

28. 1 more than 999,999 1,000,000

Write the numbers in order from least to greatest.

29. 25 13 245 13; 25; 245

30. 1,400 1,329 1,321 1,321; 1,329; 1,400

31. 18,908 17,809 17,909 17,809; 17,909; 18,908

32. 14,874,000 14,874 148,740,000 14,874; 14,874,000; 148,740,000

33. Neptune's moon, Triton, is 354,000 km from its planet. Our moon is 384,500 km from Earth. Which distance is less? Use > or < to compare the numbers. Triton to Neptune; 354,000 < 384,500

34. **DATA HUNT** What are the four largest moons of Jupiter? Give their names and list their distances from Jupiter in order from nearest to farthest. Io, 422,000 km; Europa, 671,000 km; Ganymede, 1,070,000 km; Callisto, 1,885,000 km

━━━ **THINK MATH** ━━━

See teaching notes.
Digit Patterns

How many digits would you use if you wrote all of the whole numbers from 1 through 1,000?

More Practice, page 417, Set A

Using Page 7

Exercises 1–33 These exercises provide students with practice in comparing numbers using the symbols > and < and with counting and ordering. Exercises 13–28 could be assigned as oral practice.

Data Hunt Most real-world problems require the problem solver to obtain the data needed to solve the problem. For this reason, Data Hunt problems such as exercise 34 are presented throughout this book. To solve these problems, students need to obtain the data from encyclopedias, almanacs, or other sources outside this textbook. Sometimes the data may be gathered through measurements or experiments. Please note that in all these cases, the data may vary depending upon the sources used.

If references are not readily available, supply students with the data and have them order the moons from nearest to farthest.

Think Math To solve the nonroutine problem, students must understand that the numbers from 1 to 1,000 are 1-, 2-, 3-, and 4-digit numbers.

Numbers	Digits
1–9	9 (9 1-digit numbers)
10–99	180 (90 2-digit numbers)
100–999	2,700 (900 3-digit numbers)
1,000	4 (1 4-digit number)
	2,893

More Practice, page 417, Set A

Reteaching Supplement, page 2

Name _____ To follow text page 7

Comparing and Ordering Whole Numbers

Start at the left and compare the digits in the same place.	→	Compare the digits in the first place where they are different.	→	The numbers compare the same way the digits compare.
23,782 23,762		23,782 23,762		8 and 6 (8 is greater than 6.)
(Ten thousands, thousands, and hundreds are the same.)		(Tens are different.)		23,782 is greater than 23,762.

Write the symbol > (is greater than) or < (is less than) for each ◯.

Remember: The number with more digits is greater.

1. 64,403 < 64,579   (64,403 / 64,579 / 4 < 5)

2. 42,352 > 9,827

3. 3,275 > 3,257

4. 5,432 < 5,632

5. 62,543 > 62,452

6. 93,644 < 96,344

7. 28,531 > 27,432

8. 40,000 < 4,000,000

9. 777,832 > 777,723

10. 8,432,200 > 8,340,200

11. 99,340 < 1,000,340

12. 75,392 > 75,390

Write the numeral.

13. 10 less than 999 989

14. 100 more than 10,000 10,100

15. 1 less than 1,000 999

16. 1,000 more than 80,000 81,000

17. 10 more than 9,000 9,010

18. 1 less than 9,999 9,998

Enrichment Supplement, page 2

Name _____ To follow text page 7

Rearrange the Digits

Use the digits given to write 4-digit numbers that will make each statement true. Answers may vary. Some possible answers are given.

1. Use 2, 3, 8, and 9.   2,398 > 2,389

2. Use 4, 6, 8, and 9.   9,846 < 9,864

3. Use 3, 5, 7, and 9.   5,735 < 9,753

4. Use 1, 4, 8, and 0.   8,410 > 8,401

Rearrange the digits in each of the numbers below to form the greatest number possible.

5. 5,378 8,753

6. 20,406 64,200

7. 875,902 987,520

8. 43,201 43,210

9. 1,929 9,921

10. 468,590 986,540

You can write many different 5-digit numbers using the digits 3, 4, 5, 6, and 7. Write the least 5-digit number you can without repeating digits. Then write in order from least to greatest the next eight 5-digit numbers.

11. 34,567

12. 34,576

13. 34,657

14. 34,675

15. 34,756

16. 34,765

17. 43,567

18. 43,576

19. 43,657

Practice Supplement, page 3

Name _____ To follow text page 7

Comparing and Ordering Whole Numbers

Write > or < between each pair of numbers.

1. 2,496 > 2,473

2. 7,489 < 7,498

3. 3,290 > 3,240

4. 83,621 > 83,261

5. 54,092 < 58,085

6. 432,017 > 430,079

7. 385,200 < 385,020

8. 428,761 > 428,716

9. 7,008,200 > 7,008,195

10. 2,000,000 > 200,000

11. 3,000,000,000 > 300,000,000

12. 74,000,068 > 47,000,068

Write the number.

13. 1 more than 39 40

14. 1 more than 499 500

15. 1 more than 6,999 7,000

16. 1 more than 799,999 800,000

17. 1 less than 500 499

18. 1 less than 3,000 2,999

19. 1 less than 4,200,000 4,199,999

20. 1 less than 6,000,000,000 5,999,999,999

21. 10 more than 319 329

22. 100 more than 7,000 7,100

23. 1,000 less than 90,000 89,000

24. 100 less than 4,000 3,900

Write the numbers in order from least to greatest.

25. 17 436 89 17 89 436

26. 2,918 2,981 2,819 2,819 2,918 2,981

27. 56,382 65,382 56,832 56,382 56,832 65,382

28. 3,590,071 5,903,071 5,309,071 3,590,071 5,309,071 5,903,071

Quick Review Have students give two addition and two subtraction equations for each fact family below.

7, 8, 15   4, 6, 10   5, 9, 14   1, 2, 3   3, 9, 12   6, 7, 13

Lesson Focus To round whole numbers to a specified place

Suggested Materials Newspapers

Ideas for Getting Started

Show the class some numbers in a daily newspaper. Ask students whether the numbers represent exact or approximate quantities. For example, "38,000,000 Shares of Stock Traded" indicates an approximate quantity, while "12,473 Ticketholders at a Baseball Game" indicates an exact quantity.

Next display the following sets of three numbers.

1. 30   38   40
2. 210   212   230
3. 1,900   1,993   2,000
4. 40,000   45,000   50,000

Point out that the second number in each set is between the other two numbers. "Which of the other two numbers is closer to the middle number in each set?" Note that 45,000 is half-way between 40,000 and 50,000. Emphasize that in such cases, it is customary to round up—that is, to 50,000.

Using Page 8

Lesson Development Discuss with students whether the number 64,752 in the problem at the top of the page is an exact or approximate number. (exact)

Point out that the number line illustrates the fact that 64,752 is closer to 65,000 than to 64,000. Work through the steps for rounding 64,752 to the nearest thousand. Then discuss how to round 64,752 to the nearest hundred and to the nearest ten.

Other Examples Display a copy of the instruction lines and use the numbers in the examples to further illustrate the procedure for rounding. For example, as the class rounds 396 to the nearest ten, ask questions such as these: "To which place are we rounding?" (tens) "What is the digit to the right of that place?" (6) "Is that number 5 or more?" (yes) "Do we keep 9 the same or add 1 to it?" (add 1 to it) "What is 396 rounded to the nearest ten?" (400)

Warm Up If students experience difficulty with these exercises, show them how to use number lines to round numbers.

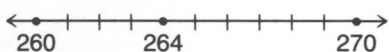

264 is closer to 260 than it is to 270, so 264 rounded to the nearest ten is 260.

Rounding Whole Numbers

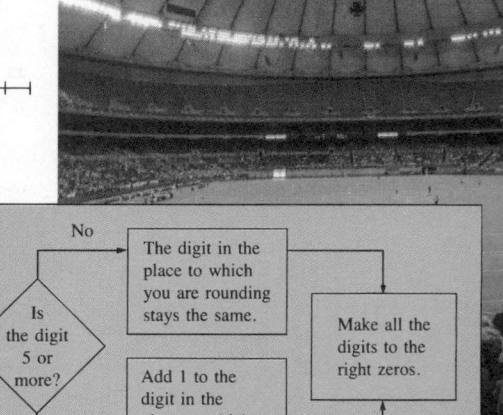

The Seattle Kingdome has 64,752 seats. A ticket agency wants to know the approximate number of seats.

To find the approximate number, we round. What is 64,752 rounded to the nearest thousand?

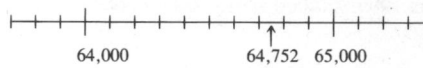

64,000   64,752 65,000

64,752 is closer to 65,000 than to 64,000.

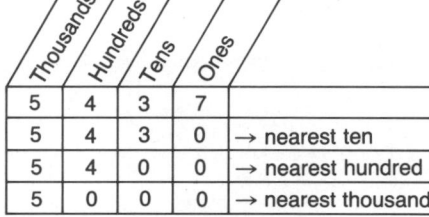

64,752 **rounded to the nearest thousand** is 65,000.

Other Examples

396 rounded to the nearest **ten** is **400.**

839 rounded to the nearest **hundred** is **800.**

64,752 rounded to the nearest **ten thousand** is **60,000.**

39,684,922 rounded to the nearest **million** is **40,000,000.**

Warm Up

Round to the nearest ten; to the nearest hundred.

1. 264
260; 300

2. 2,055
2,060; 2,100

3. 6,247
6,250; 6,200

4. 781
780; 800

Round to the nearest ten thousand; to the nearest million.

5. 752,293
750,000;
1,000,000

6. 1,234,809
1,230,000;
1,000,000

7. 29,792,874
29,790,000;
30,000,000

8. 34,419,369
34,420,000;
34,000,000

8

Follow Up

Reteaching

Use a chart like the one shown below to focus on rounding to a specific place.

Thousands	Hundreds	Tens	Ones	
5	4	3	7	
5	4	3	0	→ nearest ten
5	4	0	0	→ nearest hundred
5	0	0	0	→ nearest thousand

Discuss the procedure for rounding 5,437 to the nearest ten, nearest hundred, and nearest thousand. Have students make charts and work through other examples in the same way.

Enrichment

Write the following numbers on the chalkboard and have students round them to the specified place, indicating if the number is rounded up (↑) or down (↓).

Round to the nearest hundred:

1. 1,576   ↑   **1,600**
2. 12,147   ↓   **12,100**
3. 486,321   ↓   **486,300**
4. 2,146,476   ↑   **2,146,500**

Round to the nearest million:

1. 27,792,874   ↑   **28,000,000**
2. 33,964,321   ↑   **34,000,000**
3. 76,123,865   ↓   **76,000,000**
4. 84,364,198   ↓   **84,000,000**

Assignment Guide			
	Minimum	Average	Extended
page 9	1–30, SK	1–41, SK	2–40 even, 41–42, SK

Round to the nearest hundred.

1. 742 700	**2.** 2,375 2,400	**3.** 18,492 18,500	**4.** 350 400	**5.** 2,550 2,600
6. 5,641 5,600	**7.** 37,719 37,700	**8.** 614,189,960 614,190,000	**9.** 663,097,985 663,098,000	**10.** 126,855 126,900

Round to the nearest thousand.

11. 6,239 6,000	**12.** 8,574 9,000	**13.** 10,807 11,000	**14.** 74,682 75,000	**15.** 19,854 20,000
16. 8,500 9,000	**17.** 7,449 7,000	**18.** 998,998,992 998,999,000	**19.** 1,817,296 1,817,000	**20.** 225,500 226,000

Round to the nearest ten thousand.

21. 28,847 30,000	**22.** 59,163 60,000	**23.** 417,900 420,000	**24.** 96,432 100,000	**25.** 94,432 90,000
26. 109,955 110,000	**27.** 81,957 80,000	**28.** 509,867 510,000	**29.** 862,385 860,000	**30.** 547,658 550,000

Round to the nearest million.

31. 1,654,821 2,000,000	**32.** 9,946,275 10,000,000	**33.** 1,284,715 1,000,000	**34.** 5,555,187 6,000,000	**35.** 3,982,133 4,000,000
36. 508,837 1,000,000	**37.** 15,897,446 16,000,000	**38.** 967,681,000 968,000,000	**39.** 34,767,100 35,000,000	**40.** 5,555,555 6,000,000

41. The Atlanta-Fulton County Stadium has a seating capacity of 60,489. What is the seating capacity rounded to the nearest hundred? 60,500

42. The Milwaukee County Stadium has a seating capacity of 55,958. Is the seating capacity 55,900, 56,000, or 55,960 when rounded to the nearest hundred? 56,000

SKILLKEEPER

1. 7 + 5 = 12	**2.** 13 − 6 = 7	**3.** 9 + 7 = 16	**4.** 17 − 8 = 9	**5.** 5 + 9 = 14	**6.** 9 + 4 = 13
7. 11 − 2 = 9	**8.** 8 + 1 = 9	**9.** 9 + 9 = 18	**10.** 17 − 9 = 8	**11.** 8 + 7 = 15	**12.** 10 − 7 = 3
13. 6 + 7 = 13	**14.** 9 + 8 = 17	**15.** 6 + 6 = 12	**16.** 11 − 6 = 5	**17.** 7 + 3 = 10	**18.** 4 + 8 = 12
19. 12 − 8 = 4	**20.** 5 + 6 = 11	**21.** 12 − 9 = 3	**22.** 5 + 8 = 13	**23.** 18 − 9 = 9	**24.** 9 + 7 = 16

More Practice, page 417, Set B

Using Page 9

Exercises 1–42 Note that exercises 8, 9, 15, 24, 32, and 42 require regrouping when rounding to the place specified. For example, when rounding 663,097,985 to the nearest hundred (exercise 9), we need to add 1 to the 9 in the hundreds place. The 10 hundreds can be regrouped to 1 thousand, increasing the digit in the thousands place to 8.

Skillkeeper The purpose of the Skillkeeper exercises is to provide regular review and maintenance of computational skills. These exercises should be assigned to all students. Addition and subtraction facts were introduced and reviewed in previous grade levels.

More Practice, page 417, Set B

Reteaching Supplement, page 3

Name _____   To follow text page 9

Rounding Whole Numbers

Rounding to the nearest 10 | Rounding to the nearest 100 | Rounding to the nearest 1,000

283 →Round down→ 280 (< 5)
2,467 →Round up→ 2,470 (> 5)
435 →Round up→ 440 (= 5)

534 →Round down→ 500 (< 5)
6,784 →Round up→ 6,800 (> 5)
653 →Round up→ 700 (= 5)

8,245 →Round down→ 8,000 (< 5)
14,924 →Round up→ 15,000 (> 5)
6,528 →Round up→ 7,000 (= 5)

Round to the nearest ten.
1. 354   350
2. 634   630
3. 943   940
4. 9,248   9,250
5. 1,282   1,280
6. 15,267   15,270

Round to the nearest hundred.
7. 731   700
8. 566   600
9. 784   800
10. 5,985   6,000
11. 2,743   2,700
12. 13,431   13,400

Round to the nearest thousand.
13. 3,642   4,000
14. 8,231   8,000
15. 7,524   8,000
16. 11,529   12,000
17. 55,738   56,000
18. 48,215   48,000

Round to the nearest ten thousand.
19. 52,800   50,000
20. 546,932   550,000
21. 398,544   400,000
22. 878,450   880,000

Enrichment Supplement, page 3

Name _____   To follow text page 9

Round Up or Down

These numbers are the least and greatest numbers that round to the same number. In the blank, write the number to which they round.

1. 225   230   234
2. 3,650   3,700   3,749
3. 4,500   5,000   5,499
4. 20,150   20,200   20,249
5. 550   600   649
6. 32,850   32,900   32,949
7. 6,425   6,430   6,434
8. 786,050   786,100   786,149
9. 786,500   787,000   787,499
10. 5,955   5,960   5,964
11. 18,050   18,100   18,149
12. 24,500   25,000   25,499

These numbers are rounded to the nearest **thousand**. Write the least and greatest number that would round to the given number.

13. 1,500   2,000   2,499
14. 500   1,000   1,499
15. 22,500   23,000   23,499
16. 9,500   10,000   10,499

Practice Supplement, page 4

Name _____   To follow text page 9

Rounding Whole Numbers

Round to the nearest ten.
1. 847   850
2. 6,283   6,280
3. 37   40
4. 187   190
5. 23,757   23,760
6. 1,908   1,910
7. 299   300
8. 775   780
9. 2,996   3,000

Round to the nearest hundred.
10. 875   900
11. 2,649   2,600
12. 72,663   72,700
13. 9,747   9,700
14. 336   300
15. 126,754   126,800
16. 15,608   15,600
17. 557   600
18. 78,149   78,100

Round to the nearest thousand.
19. 3,218   3,000
20. 6,747   7,000
21. 19,570   20,000
22. 1,876   2,000
23. 7,496   7,000
24. 77,519   78,000
25. 60,903   61,000
26. 66,619   67,000
27. 29,751   30,000

Round to the nearest ten thousand.
28. 73,428   80,000
29. 59,162   60,000
30. 93,798   90,000
31. 413,306   420,000
32. 271,850   270,000
33. 354,542   350,000
34. 883,841   880,000
35. 728,005   730,000
36. 506,607   510,000

Round to the nearest million.
37. 2,463,111   2,000,000
38. 5,934,012   6,000,000
39. 84,398,826   84,000,000
40. 77,096,614   77,000,000
41. 325,688,125   326,000,000
42. 547,899,008   548,000,000

Quick Review Call out basic facts in rapid succession and have students give the sums, differences, products, or quotients.

4 × 5	9 − 3	21 ÷ 7	42 ÷ 6	6 + 4	17 − 8	3 × 9	40 ÷ 5
8 × 4	16 ÷ 4	11 − 4	8 − 4	27 ÷ 3	8 + 9	1 × 5	6 × 0

Lesson Focus To estimate sums and differences of whole numbers

Ideas for Getting Started

Conduct an oral drill in which students mentally find sums and differences of multiples of 10, 100, and 1,000. Present sequences of problems like those below.

1. 50 + 30   500 + 300   5,000 + 3,000
2. 80 − 20   800 − 200   8,000 − 2,000
3. 60 + 110   600 + 1,100   6,000 + 11,000
4. 200 − 90   2,000 − 900   20,000 − 9,000

Using Page 10

Lesson Development After students have read the problem at the top of the page, ask: "How can you tell, without adding, that 695 is not a reasonable answer for 376 + 519?" (One number is more than 500 and the other is more than 300, so the sum should be more than 800.)

Tell students that even when they use a calculator, it is important to make an estimate of an answer. This helps them detect large errors that may be made through misuse or a malfunction of the calculator.

Discuss with students that when we make estimates, we often do this in our heads. To make estimates, we try to round the numbers so that it is possible to do the calculations mentally.

Use the example of 2,261 − 914 to show how estimates may vary depending upon to which place —hundreds or thousands—the numbers are rounded.

Warm Up As students work on these problems, observe to see whether some students might be finding the exact sums or differences and then rounding the exact answer to get an estimate. This practice should be discouraged. However, there are occasions when it is helpful to find the exact sum or difference and compare it with an estimate in order to check the closeness of the estimate.

Estimating Sums and Differences

Tim Griffin manages a large record store. On Friday the store sold 376 records. On Saturday, 519 records were sold. Tim uses a calculator to add the two numbers.

First try   Second try

Which sum seems more reasonable? We can make an **estimate** of the sum by rounding each addend to the nearest hundred.

376 + 519   400 + 500 = 900
   estimate

The estimate 900 is close to 895, so 895 seems more reasonable.

Estimates may vary because of the way the numbers are rounded.

Estimate the difference. 2,261 − 914

Round to the nearest thousand.

2,261 − 914   2,000 − 1,000 = 1,000
   estimate

Round to the nearest hundred.

2,261 − 914   2,300 − 900 = 1,400
   estimate

Warm Up

Estimate each sum or difference by rounding to the nearest ten.

1. 79 + 17
100

2. 64 − 29
30

3. 119 + 72
190

4. 209 − 87
120

Estimate each sum or difference by rounding to the nearest hundred.

5. 278 + 415
700

6. 930 − 666
200

7. 2,311 + 892
3,200

8. 1,747 − 1,288
400

Estimate each sum or difference by rounding to the nearest thousand.

9. 2,774 + 1,828
5,000

10. 6,105 − 1,978
4,000

11. 4,915 − 3,282
2,000

12. 12,835 + 5,166
18,000

Follow Up

Reteaching

Use examples in which rounding is helpful in forming an estimate. Word problems can be used to provide motivation. For example, "A computer cost $995 and a disk drive $495. How much will the two cost if bought together?" First, ask students for their rounded numbers; then ask for their estimates.

995 ⟶ 1000
495 ⟶ 500
       1500

Enrichment

Write the following problems on the chalkboard. Answers may vary.

1.   123
     + 487

2.   3,452
     + 4,189

3.   9,767
     + 6,152

4.   16,599
     − 28,658

5.   532
     − 120

6.   6,460
     − 4,201

Have students estimate the sums or differences by rounding to the nearest 10, 100, or 1,000. Without copying the problems or making pencil and paper computations, students should simply write their estimates beside each exercise. If calculators are available, they can use them to check the reasonableness of their answers.

Assignment Guide			
	Minimum	Average	Extended
page 11	1–24	1–26, TM	1–26, TM

Answers may vary. See teaching notes.

Estimate each sum by rounding.

1. 89 + 33 120

2. 76 + 82 + 39 200

3. 214 + 388 + 115 700

4. 772 + 226 1,000

5. 1,296 + 1,825 3,000

6. 2,775 + 3,148 6,000

7. 3,280 + 1,790 5,000

8. 813 + 629 1,400

9. 2,372 + 5,127 7,000

10. 6,904,381 + 7,870,468 15,000,000

11. 336,639 + 290,714 600,000

12. 334,441 + 206,027 500,000

Estimate each difference by rounding.

13. 81 − 37 40

14. 72 − 38 30

15. 627 − 196 400

16. 915 − 388 500

17. 707 − 185 500

18. 914 − 299 600

19. 7,124 − 1,958 5,000

20. 9,213 − 5,838 3,000

21. 5,856 − 2,935 3,000

22. 6,274,399 − 3,812,939 2,000,000

23. 883,270 − 264,449 600,000

24. 530,627 − 218,963 300,000

25. A record store sold 83 rock records, 71 country-western records, 38 classical records, and 66 other kinds of records in one day. Estimate the total number of records sold. 260

26. Estimate how much less the January sales were than the December sales. $8,000

Spinner Record Store

December sales	$19,714
January sales	$12,048
February sales	$13,541

THINK MATH

Number Patterns

1   3   6   10

The ancient Greeks called numbers like 1, 3, 6, and 10 **triangular numbers.**

1   4   9   16

Numbers like 1, 4, 9, and 16 are called **square numbers.**

List all the triangular numbers up to 100. 1, 3, 6, 10, 15, 21, 28, 36, 45, 55, 66, 78, 91
List all the square numbers up to 100. 1, 4, 9, 16, 25, 36, 49, 64, 81, 100
Choose a triangular number. Add it to the next larger triangular number. What do you notice about the sum? square number

Try this again with any triangular number.

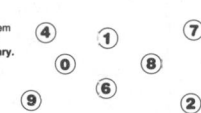

More Practice, page 417, Set C

Using Page 11

Exercises 1–26 Note that no rounding instructions are given for these exercises. This allows the student to make the decision regarding the kind of rounded numbers to use in making an estimate. In general, encourage students to round the numbers so that the estimates for the sums and differences can be easily found mentally. For further discussion of estimation, refer to the Chapter Overview.

The answers supplied here are suggested answers, and students may arrive at other estimates depending upon the rounding used. Therefore, it is important to establish parameters for acceptable estimates. If a student's estimate departs radically from that range, that may indicate that the student is having problems rounding or computing correctly.

If students have difficulty estimating when no rounding instructions are given, specify a place to round to as you work through several more examples with them.

Think Math By examining differences between the numbers in each sequence, we see that triangular numbers can be written as the sum of consecutive whole numbers.

1 ⌣ 3 ⌣ 6 ⌣ 10 ⌣ 15 . . .
　2　　3　　4　　5

Also, square numbers can be written as the sum of consecutive odd numbers.

1 ⌣ 4 ⌣ 9 ⌣ 16 ⌣ 25 . . .
　3　　5　　7　　9

The last part of this Think Math illustrates the fact that the sum of any two consecutive triangular numbers is a square number.

More Practice, page 417, Set C

Reteaching Supplement, page 4

Name _____   To follow text page 11

Estimating Sums and Differences

Estimate the sum of 2,746 and 5,295.

$$2,746 \xrightarrow{\text{rounds to}} 3,000$$
$$+\ 5,295 \xrightarrow{\text{rounds to}} +\ 5,000$$
$$8,000$$

2,746 + 5,295 is about 8,000.

Estimate the difference between 738 and 587.

$$738 \xrightarrow{\text{rounds to}} 700$$
$$-\ 587 \xrightarrow{\text{rounds to}} -\ 600$$
$$100$$

738 − 587 is about 100.

Estimate each sum or difference by rounding.

1. 564 → 600   2. 66 → 70   3. 3,264 → 3,000
   − 382 → 400   − 16 → 20   + 968 → + 1,000
        200   50   4,000

4. 69 → 70   5. 81 → 80   6. 41 → 40
   + 43 → 40   + 92 → 90   − 17 → 20
       110   170   20

7. 678 → 700   8. 784 → 800   9. 523 → 500
   − 534 → 500   − 193 → 200   + 817 → + 800
        200   600   1,300

10. 6,745 → 7,000   11. 8,354 → 8,000   12. 7,057 → 7,000
    + 1,210 → 1,000   + 8,002 → 8,000   − 2,455 → 2,000
         8,000   16,000   5,000

13. 22,195 → 20,000   14. 64,708 → 60,000   15. 22,899 → 20,000
    + 49,264 → 50,000   − 14,264 → 10,000   + 52,674 → 50,000
          70,000   50,000   70,000

16. 54,624 → 50,000   17. 94,696 → 95,000   18. 69,483 → 69,000
    − 18,635 → 20,000   + 3,159 → 3,000   − 4,281 → 4,000
          30,000   98,000   65,000

19. 56,294 − 4,765
     56,000
    − 5,000
     51,000

20. 16,182 − 6,054
     16,000
    − 6,000
     10,000

Enrichment Supplement, page 4

Name _____   To follow text page 11

Rounding and Estimation

Write one digit in each ◯ to make each problem correct. Use a different digit for each ◯ in the problem. Then add or subtract. Answers will vary. Some possible answers are given.

④ ① ⑦
⓪ ⑧
⑨ ⑥
②

1. ② ⑧ Rounds to → 30   2. ④ ⑦ Rounds to → 50
   + ① ⑨ Rounds to → 20   − ① ② Rounds to → 10
      4 7   50   3 5   40

3. ④ ⑨ ⑦ Rounds to → 500   4. ⑦ ④ ⑥ Rounds to → 750
   − ⑧ ② Rounds to → 80   + ① ⑨ ⑥ Rounds to → 200
      4 1 5   420   9 4 4   950

5. Write the two 2-digit numbers that give the greatest sum possible. Then estimate the sum by rounding to the nearest ten.

   ⑨ ⑦ ——→ 100
  + ⑧ ⑥ —— − 90
     1 8 3   190

6. Write the two 2-digit numbers that give the least difference possible. Then estimate the difference by rounding to the nearest ten.

   ② ⓪ —— 20
  − ① ④ — − 10
     8 6   10

7. Write the two 3-digit numbers that give the greatest difference possible. Estimate the difference by rounding to the nearest ten.

   ⑨ ④ ⑥ —— 950
  − ⓪ ⑦ ② — − 870
     7 4   80

8. Write the two 3-digit numbers that give the least sum possible. Estimate the sum by rounding to the nearest hundred.

   ① ④ ⑦ —— 100
  + ② ⓪ ⑥ — + 200
     3 5 3   300

Practice Supplement, page 5

Name _____   To follow text page 11

Estimating Sums and Differences

Estimate each sum or difference by rounding to the nearest ten.

1. 86 + 24 110
2. 37 + 93 130
3. 48 + 29 80
4. 221 + 19 240
5. 164 + 76 240
6. 149 + 152 300
7. 78 − 49 30
8. 95 − 28 70
9. 8 − 22 60
10. 143 − 82 60
11. 259 − 175 80
12. 304 − 101 200

Estimate each sum or difference by rounding to the nearest hundred.

13. 104 + 295 400
14. 156 + 244 400
15. 563 + 711 1,300
16. 3,240 + 1,806 5,000
17. 868 + 2,437 3,300
18. 3,569 + 738 4,300
19. 366 − 215 200
20. 941 − 387 500
21. 677 − 293 400
22. 1,486 − 955 500
23. 7,430 − 2,251 5,100
24. 3,659 − 872 2,800

Estimate each sum or difference by rounding to the nearest thousand.

25. 2,651 + 1,179 4,000
26. 3,835 + 1,177 5,000
27. 5,118 + 874 6,000
28. 2,737 + 8,463 11,000
29. 5,216 + 6,666 12,000
30. 14,342 + 1,979 16,000
31. 4,516 − 3,382 2,000
32. 9,415 − 7,775 1,000
33. 4,628 − 1,395 4,000
34. 2,747 − 798 2,000
35. 8,273 − 4,685 3,000
36. 19,431 − 12,118 7,000

Quick Review Conduct an oral drill where students mentally find sums of three or more 1-digit addends.

3 + 4 + 5 **12**   8 + 8 + 9 **25**   2 + 7 + 6 + 9 **24**   6 + 4 + 6 **16**

7 + 8 + 5 **20**   1 + 5 + 7 **13**   3 + 2 + 7 + 3 **15**

Lesson Focus To add whole numbers

Suggested Materials Place-value models

Ideas for Getting Started

Display problems like those below.

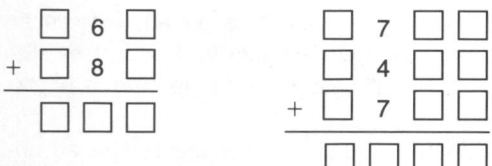

Direct students to the first problem. "Why could the tens digit in the sum be either 4 or 5?" (If the sum of the ones is less than 10, the tens digit will be 4; if greater than 10, it will be 5.) "Could the tens digit in the sum ever be 6?" (No, the most we could be adding in the ones place is 9 + 9, where only 1 ten would have to be regrouped.)

Direct students to the second problem. "Why could the hundreds digit in the sum be either 8, 9, or 0? Could the hundreds digit in the sum be 1?" (No, the most we could regroup is 2 hundreds.)

Using Page 12

Motivational Problem Read the introductory problem with students. "What are we asked to find?" (length of the river system) "What data does the problem provide?" (This river system is the longest in the United States and the third longest in the world.) "What data does the map provide?" (where the rivers flow, how they link up, the length of each segment) "What data do we need to find the total length of the system?" (Red Rock to Missouri, 246 mi; Missouri to Mississippi, 2,315 mi; Mississippi to Gulf of Mexico, 1,180 mi) "How would we use this data to find the total?" (add)

Lesson Development Show how to find the answer by following the steps outlined. Explain the regrouping from the ones place to the tens and from the tens place to the hundreds. Then have students check the reasonableness of the answer by making an estimate of the sum using rounded numbers.

Other Examples Point out the importance of aligning the digits properly. Then have students work through these examples.

Warm Up Watch for students having difficulty with basic addition facts or with regrouping. For students having trouble with memorization of the basic facts, plan additional drill. If regrouping is a problem, use place-value models to show the regrouping process.

Adding Whole Numbers

The Mississippi-Missouri-Red Rock river system is the longest in the United States and the third longest in the world. What is the total length of the system?

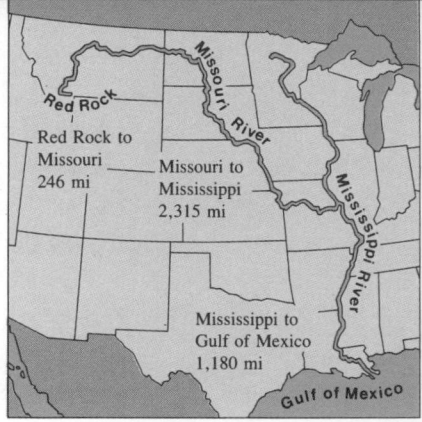

To find the total of the numbers, we add.

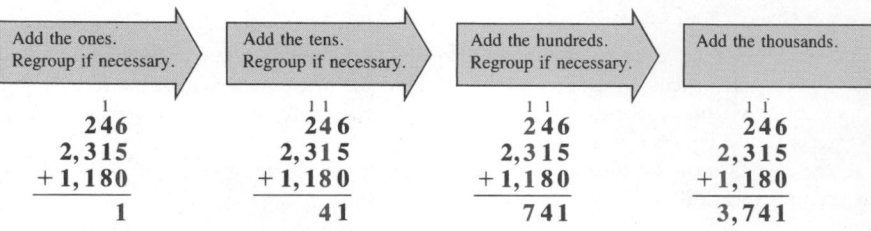

Add the ones. Regroup if necessary.	Add the tens. Regroup if necessary.	Add the hundreds. Regroup if necessary.	Add the thousands.
1 246 2,315 + 1,180 —— 1	1 1 246 2,315 + 1,180 —— 41	1 1 246 2,315 + 1,180 —— 741	1 1 246 2,315 + 1,180 —— 3,741

The total length of the system is 3,741 miles (mi).

Other Examples

```
       235         2 2              1 1 1 1    1
     + 963       2,839           20,348,209
     ——————        748            1,461,601
     1,198      + 1,507       +     500,268
                ———————        ——————————————
                  5,094          22,310,078
```

Warm Up

Find the sums.

1. 282 + 355 —— 637	2. 817 + 629 —— 1,446	3. 8,809 + 6,477 —— 15,286	4. 22,746 + 19,815 —— 42,561	5. 6,384 + 5,616 —— 12,000
6. 14,392,406 + 2,690,000 ———— 17,082,406	7. 5,714 6,073 + 9,215 —— 21,002	8. 862 749 688 + 977 —— 3,276	9. 4,378 925 2,833 + 95 —— 8,231	10. 31,428 66,773 90,306 + 42,177 —— 230,684

12

Follow Up

Reteaching

To review the addition of whole numbers, use a pocket chart and model the addition algorithm. Illustrate problems with no regrouping and with regrouping, such as 463 + 251. Make certain students understand the place value of each pocket as you discuss each step in the algorithm.

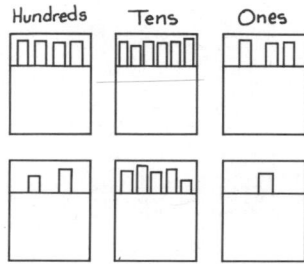

Enrichment

Write the following on the chalkboard.

9	3	6
1	4	7
2	5	8
3	6	9
+ 4	7	1

2, 1 8 1

The arrangement of the digits beginning at the top of a column is such that the next digit below is always one more, unless the upper digit is a 9. Have students fill in the correct digits. One solution is shown.

Add.

1. 83 + 74 157	**2.** 619 + 352 971	**3.** 884 + 776 1,660	**4.** 375 + 275 650	**5.** 8,141 + 3,776 11,917

6. 23,548 + 66,395 = 89,943

7. 9,337 + 6,129 = 15,466

8. 7,075 + 6,848 = 13,923

9. 30,542 + 75,598 = 106,140

10. 8,627,150 + 7,490,980 = 16,118,130

11. 11,324 + 1,776 + 22,974 = 36,074

12. 10,854 + 12,321 + 13,664 = 36,839

13. 97,291 + 829 + 1,089 = 99,209

14. 3,581,380 + 6,287,402 + 5,749,015 + 1,255,102 = 16,872,899

15. 62,847,421 + 59,417,342 + 88,093,106 + 52,898,830 = 263,256,699

Find the sums.

16. 247 + 129 + 547 923

17. 7,140 + 8,337 + 2,950 18,427

18. 853 + 94 + 119 + 87 1,153

19. 7,075 + 3,834 + 2,966 13,875

20. 14,562,000 + 13,013,691 27,575,691

21. 2,716,593 + 36,829,720 39,546,313

22. 1,822,745 + 19,091 + 33,706 1,875,542

23. 57,626 + 84,188 + 93,727,013 93,868,827

24. The Arkansas River and the Colorado River are each 1,450 mi in length. The Columbia River is 1,214 mi long. What is the total length of these rivers?
4,114 mi

25. The Allegheny River is 325 mi long. The Ohio River is 656 mi longer than the Allegheny River. What is the combined length of the two rivers?
1,306 mi

THINK MATH

Mental Math

You can find the sum of this column of numbers mentally. Follow the arrow to add the tens, then the ones, of each number. The sum is 119.

$$2\ \ 6$$
$$3\ \ 8$$
$$+ 5\ \ 5$$

20 + 6 = 26
26 + 30 = 56
56 + 8 = 64
64 + 50 = 114
114 + 5 = 119

Find the sums using mental addition.

1. 32 15 + 43 90	**2.** 47 26 + 35 108	**3.** 19 66 + 49 134	**4.** 62 84 27 + 23 196	**5.** 33 46 81 + 25 185

More Practice, page 418, Set A

13

Using Page 13

Exercises 1–25 Encourage students to use estimation as a check of their computation. Remind students that when they copy exercises 16–23 in vertical form, they need to be careful that the ones, tens, hundreds, and so on are aligned properly for accurate addition.

Think Math These mental addition exercises require good understanding of addition as well as skill in remembering partial sums. Encourage students to think only of the partial sums as they work through each exercise. For example, when adding the numbers in the first exercise (32 + 15 + 43), students should think, "32, 42, 47, 87, 90. The sum is 90."

Some students may develop their own strategies. For the path shown below, the partial sums would be 32, 37, 47, 87, 90.

$$32$$
$$15$$
$$+ 43$$

More Practice, page 418, Set A

Reteaching Supplement, page 5

Enrichment Supplement, page 5

Practice Supplement, page 6

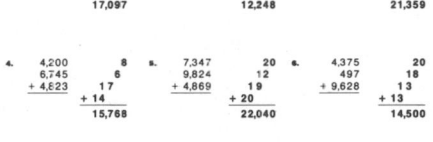

Lesson Focus To subtract whole numbers

Ideas for Getting Started

Provide students with regrouping exercises like the ones below.

Show 10 more ones

Example: 4$\cancel{62}$ ⁵¹²

227
803
5,000

Show 10 more tens

Example: $\cancel{6}$26 ⁴¹²

700
3,000
6,045

Using Page 14

Motivational Problem After students read the problem at the top of the page, ask the following questions. "Does the question indicate that there are more or less telephone calls per person per year in Norway compared to the United States?" (more) "Look at the table. How many calls are made per person per year in Norway?" (2,641) "In the United States?" (1,092) "How can we find how many more calls are made per person per year in Norway?" (subtract)

Lesson Development On the chalkboard, work through the steps shown to find the answer. Discuss the necessity of regrouping to get more ones and regrouping to get more tens. Ask why regrouping to get more hundreds is not necessary. Then ask a student to explain why we can check a subtraction problem by using addition. Have that student show that $1,092 + 1,549 = 2,641$ is a check of $2,641 - 1,092 = 1,549$.

Other Examples Work through these exercises orally or have selected students work through them at the chalkboard. Prior to performing the indicated subtraction, have students determine a reasonable answer by making an estimate of the difference using rounded numbers. Then subtract and compare the answer to the estimate. Note that the last two examples involve subtracting across zeros. Discuss these cases in detail, as this type of problem is difficult for some students.

Warm Up Use these exercises to help you assess your students' skill with subtraction. Observe students carefully to detect whether any of them are showing errors consistently in the areas of basic facts or regrouping. Another commonly found error pattern is subtracting the smaller digit from the larger digit without regard to which number is the minuend and which is the subtrahend.

Subtracting Whole Numbers

Throughout the world, people use the telephone many times during a year. How many more telephone calls per person per year are made in Norway than in the United States?

To find out how much more one number is than another, we subtract.

Telephone Calls Per Person Per Year	
Norway	2,641
Sweden	2,302
Finland	1,493
United States	1,092
Switzerland	886
Canada	825

Subtract the ones. Regroup if necessary.	Subtract the tens. Regroup if necessary.	Subtract the hundreds. Regroup if necessary.	Subtract the thousands.

$$\begin{array}{r} \scriptstyle 3\ 11 \\ 2,6\cancel{4}\cancel{1} \\ -1,092 \\ \hline 9 \end{array} \qquad \begin{array}{r} \scriptstyle 5\ 13\,11 \\ 2,\cancel{6}\cancel{4}\cancel{1} \\ -1,092 \\ \hline 49 \end{array} \qquad \begin{array}{r} \scriptstyle 5\ 13\,11 \\ 2,\cancel{6}\cancel{4}\cancel{1} \\ -1,092 \\ \hline 549 \end{array} \qquad \begin{array}{r} \scriptstyle 5\ 13\,11 \\ 2,\cancel{6}\cancel{4}\cancel{1} \\ -1,092 \\ \hline 1,549 \end{array}$$

Not enough ones. Regroup 1 ten for 10 ones.

Not enough tens. Regroup 1 hundred for 10 tens.

There are 1,549 more telephone calls made per person per year in Norway.

Check: 　$\begin{array}{r} 1,092 \\ +1,549 \\ \hline 2,641 \end{array}$ 　It checks.

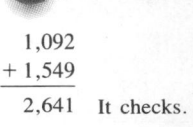

Other Examples

$$\begin{array}{r} \scriptstyle 6\ 14\ 14 \\ \cancel{7}\cancel{5}\cancel{4} \\ -695 \\ \hline 59 \end{array} \qquad \begin{array}{r} \scriptstyle \ \ 10 \\ \scriptstyle 7\ \cancel{8}\ 13 \\ 8,\cancel{1}\cancel{3}4 \\ -672 \\ \hline 7,462 \end{array} \qquad \begin{array}{r} \scriptstyle 8\ 9\ 10 \\ \cancel{9}\cancel{0}\cancel{0} \\ -127 \\ \hline 773 \end{array} \qquad \begin{array}{r} \scriptstyle 6\ 9\ 9\ 14 \\ \cancel{7},\cancel{0}\cancel{0}\cancel{4},764 \\ -3,268,352 \\ \hline 3,736,412 \end{array}$$

Warm Up

Subtract. Check your answers.

1.	$\begin{array}{r} 636 \\ -318 \\ \hline 318 \end{array}$	**2.**	$\begin{array}{r} 7,129 \\ -4,572 \\ \hline 2,557 \end{array}$	**3.**	$\begin{array}{r} 1,278 \\ -844 \\ \hline 434 \end{array}$	**4.**	$\begin{array}{r} 2,713 \\ -1,957 \\ \hline 756 \end{array}$
5.	$\begin{array}{r} 600 \\ -375 \\ \hline 225 \end{array}$	**6.**	$\begin{array}{r} 1,014 \\ -769 \\ \hline 245 \end{array}$	**7.**	$\begin{array}{r} 1,200,618 \\ -351,509 \\ \hline 849,109 \end{array}$	**8.**	$\begin{array}{r} 10,000,352 \\ -8,472,163 \\ \hline 1,528,189 \end{array}$

14

Follow Up

Reteaching

Use a pocket chart and paper strips, as illustrated on page 12, to demonstrate the subtraction algorithm. As you go through each step, ask questions such as "Can we subtract?" and "What must be regrouped?" Stress the place value of each pocket.

Enrichment

Write the following puzzle on the chalkboard. Have students fill in the missing numbers.

6,007	−	1,078	=	4,929
−		−		−
2,541	−	360	=	2,181
=		=		=
3,466	−	718	=	2,748

Assignment Guide			
	Minimum	Average	Extended
page 15	1–24, 34, SK	1–30, 34, SK	1–23 odd, 25–35, SK

Using Page 15

Exercises 1–24 Have students check their answers by using addition or estimation. If calculators are available, they could be used to check answers. Again, remind students to be careful to align the digits properly when copying exercises 16–24 into vertical form.

Exercises 25–33 Work through a few exercises with the students to refamiliarize them with the procedure of performing operations within the parentheses first. Point out that the order of operations can affect the result. For instance, $8 - (3 + 2) = 3$, while $(8 - 3) + 2 = 7$.

Skillkeeper Multiplication and division facts were introduced in previous grade levels.

Subtract.

1.
```
  73
- 28
-----
  45
```
2.
```
  305
-  82
-----
  223
```
3.
```
  482
-  96
-----
  386
```
4.
```
  6,208
- 4,796
-------
  1,412
```
5.
```
  4,816
- 2,379
-------
  2,437
```
6.
```
  3,500
- 1,765
-------
  1,735
```
7.
```
  5,600
- 2,349
-------
  3,251
```
8.
```
  2,714
- 1,376
-------
    838
```
9.
```
  18,401,783
-    301,641
-----------
  18,100,142
```
10.
```
  17,105
-  3,440
-------
  13,665
```
11.
```
  27,000
- 13,427
-------
  13,573
```
12.
```
  16,243
-  5,685
-------
  10,558
```
13.
```
  75,346
- 31,976
-------
  43,870
```
14.
```
  9,000,188
- 6,385,029
---------
  2,615,159
```
15.
```
  86,683
-  4,974
-------
  81,709
```

16. $315 - 96$ 219
17. $800 - 355$ 445
18. $2,117 - 854$ 1,263
19. $704 - 227$ 477
20. $1,259 - 877$ 382
21. $6,006 - 3,727$ 2,279
22. $8,396 - 5,227$ 3,169
23. $26,105 - 19,704$ 6,401
24. $30,000,000 - 712,982$ 29,287,018

Add or subtract. Do the operations inside the parentheses first.

25. $(827 - 454) + 197$ 570
26. $683 + (1,027 - 366)$ 1,344
27. $700 - (847 - 689)$ 542
28. $2,346 - (548 + 727)$ 1,071
29. $9,005 - (7,213 - 69)$ 1,861
30. $88,176 - (954 - 778)$ 88,000
31. $2,818 + (6,274 - 2,818)$ 6,274
32. $(72,421 - 628) - 33,249$ 38,544
33. $72,421 - (29,628 + 3,249)$ 39,544

34. How many more telephone calls per person per year are made in the United States than in Canada? Use the table on page 14. 267

35. There are about 185,200,000 telephones in use in North America. South America has about 16,900,000 telephones in use. How many fewer telephones are in use in South America? 168,300,000

SKILLKEEPER

1. 3×7 21
2. $40 \div 5$ 8
3. 8×4 32
4. $48 \div 6$ 8
5. 9×5 45
6. 7×7 49
7. $18 \div 2$ 9
8. $36 \div 9$ 4
9. 6×9 54
10. $27 \div 3$ 9
11. 9×3 27
12. 6×6 36
13. $42 \div 6$ 7
14. 8×7 56
15. $0 \div 7$ 0
16. $32 \div 8$ 4
17. $81 \div 9$ 9
18. 1×9 9
19. 3×8 24
20. $20 \div 4$ 5
21. $56 \div 7$ 8
22. $4 \div 1$ 4
23. 6×4 24
24. 9×7 63
25. 7×4 28
26. $72 \div 9$ 8
27. 0×8 0
28. $18 \div 6$ 3
29. 9×6 54
30. $63 \div 7$ 9

More Practice, page 418, Set B

15

More Practice, page 418, Set B

Reteaching Supplement, page 6

Name _____ To follow text page 15

Subtracting Whole Numbers

Enrichment Supplement, page 6

Name _____ To follow text page 15

Missing Digits in Addition and Subtraction

Practice Supplement, page 7

Name _____ To follow text page 15

Subtracting Whole Numbers

Quick Review Have students give the correct symbol (>, <, =) for each statement.

$9 + 7 \boxed{=} 8 + 8$ $6 \times 5 \boxed{>} 7 \times 4$ $27 \div 3 \boxed{>} 15 - 7$

$12 - 5 \boxed{<} 11 - 2$ $56 \div 7 \boxed{=} 40 \div 5$ $13 - 7 \boxed{<} 12 - 5$

Lesson Focus To solve word problems using the 5-Point Checklist

Ideas for Getting Started

Display questions like those below. Substitute the names of some of your students to create more interest.

1. How much taller is Michelle than Diane?
2. What is the total weight of Jack and Fred?
3. Who lives closer to school, Otis or Sonya? How much closer?

For each question ask, "What data or numbers do we need to know to answer the question?" and "What should we plan to do to find the answer?"

Using Page 16

Lesson Development Have students study the 5-Point Checklist. Explain that these 5 points are not rules for solving word problems—they are points that will give the students a systematic plan to use when trying to solve word problems. Then use the problem at the top of the page to illustrate the use of the 5 points. Stress these ideas:

1. In order to *understand the question,* students must read the problem carefully. The question asks students to find something, but they should be aware that it may not always be phrased in a question format.

2. The *data* for a problem may be listed separately (as in the motivational problem at the top of the page), it may be included in the statement of the problem, or it may have to be obtained from sources outside the problem.

3. The *plan* usually involves the decision to use one or more mathematical operations to solve the problem. Some problems, however, do not require the use of a mathematical operation.

4. To *find the answer,* we usually need to do some calculating. The answer should be the answer to the question in the problem. For example, the answer to the motivational problem is "425 calories," not just the number 425.

5. *Check back* involves such things as estimating the answer, rechecking computation, and/or rereading the problem to see whether the answer seems reasonable.

Exercises 1–2 Have students solve the two problems at the bottom of the page. Discuss how they used the 5-Point Checklist to solve the problems.

PROBLEM SOLVING: The 5-Point Checklist

| QUESTION |
| DATA |
| PLAN |
| ANSWER |
| CHECK |

To Solve a Problem

1. Understand the QUESTION
2. Find the needed DATA
3. PLAN what to do
4. Find the ANSWER
5. CHECK back

These 5 points give an organized way of solving problems. Follow them to solve this problem.

Ralph Martin decided to count the calories in his meals. What is the total calorie count in his breakfast?

1. **Understand the QUESTION**
   You are asked to find the number of calories in the breakfast.

2. **Find the needed DATA**
   This is the number of calories in each item of food: 90; 115; 160; and 60.

3. **PLAN what to do**
   Since you are asked to find the total, you must add.

4. **Find the ANSWER**
   Do the computation.
   The breakfast has 425 calories.

$$\begin{array}{r} 90 \\ 115 \\ 160 \\ + \ 60 \\ \hline 425 \end{array}$$

5. **CHECK back**
   See if your answer is reasonable.
   Estimate or check your computation.

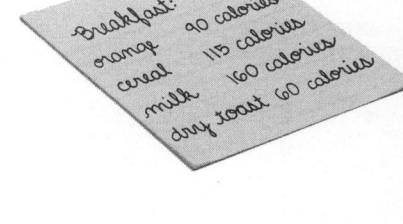

Breakfast:
orange 90 calories
cereal 115 calories
milk 160 calories
dry toast 60 calories

Solve. Use the 5-Point Checklist.

1. Ralph wants to compare the number of calories in the milk and the cereal. How many more calories are in the milk than in the cereal? 45

2. One morning Ralph ate a scrambled egg (95 calories) instead of cereal and milk. How many calories were in this breakfast? 245

16

Follow Up

Reteaching

Ask for a volunteer to make up a word problem. Write the problem on the chalkboard. Discuss each step in the 5-Point Checklist as you work through the problem with students. Have them record the information on Problem-Solving worksheets (TRB p. 287). Allow time for discussion at each step.

Enrichment

Have students answer the following questions.

1. Which of the following amounts could be paid with three different coins?
   a. 30¢   b. 15¢   c. 27¢   d. 36¢
   d. 1 quarter, 1 dime, 1 penny

2. Which of the following amounts could be paid with four different coins?
   a. 66¢   b. 20¢   c. 26¢   d. 31¢
   a. 1 half dollar, 1 dime, 1 nickel, 1 penny

Breakfast

	Calories
Tomato juice	45
1 scrambled egg	95
Dry toast	60
Cocoa	220

Lunch

	Calories
Soup	85
Sandwich	280
Fruit gelatin	110
Carrot cake	180

Dinner

	Calories
Chicken slices	200
Green beans	80
Salad	65
Milk	160
Frozen yogurt	225

Solve.

1. What is the total number of calories in the lunch menu? 655

2. What is the total number of calories in the dinner menu? 730

3. What is the total number of calories for all three meals? 1,805

4. For lunch Van Thu ate everything but carrot cake. How many calories were in her lunch? 475

5. How many more calories are in a serving of cocoa than in a serving of tomato juice? 175

6. Janet Goodwing is trying to gain weight. For lunch she had 2 sandwiches, soup, and carrot cake. How many calories were in her lunch? 825

7. Frank Federico wanted to eat meals that did not total more than 1,850 calories per day. He counted the calories one day and found that they totaled 2,210. How many more calories than 1,850 is this? 360

8. How many calories are in a dinner of chicken slices, green beans, and salad? 345

9. What would be the total calories in the lunch if milk were substituted for carrot cake? 635

★ 10. Jason Johnson ate all but one of the lunch items. The total number of calories for his lunch was 545. What item on the lunch menu did he not eat? fruit gelatin

17

Using Page 17

Exercises 1–10 Before assigning the problems, point out that most of the data needed to solve the problems is provided in the three menus at the top of the page.

When discussing solutions to the problem, note that different plans to solve a given problem may be used by different students. For example, in exercise 4, some students may plan to add everything in the luncheon menu other than carrot cake. Other students may plan to subtract the number of calories in the carrot cake from the total number of calories in the lunch, which was found as an answer to exercise 1. Point out that different plans may be used to solve problems; however, some plans may be more efficient than others.

Note that exercise 10 is a starred problem because it requires more sophisticated skill with problem solving.

The 5-Point Checklist gives students a practical guide for solving problems of all types.

Ideas That Work

Special Education

Have students form groups of five to discuss the problems on page 17. Each student in a group should select one of the steps in the 5-Point Checklist and explain to the others his or her thinking process in that step for the problem(s) assigned their working group.

Let students with abstract reasoning, reading, or memory difficulty make the first selection. The goal is to provide as many successful experiences as possible to promote better attitudes toward problem solving, and greater achievement. It is good to publicly reinforce what students can do best. As special students become more confident, they can give others first choice, then move on to select different steps in the Checklist to describe. If time allows, group sessions could be treated as practice periods during which students use input from others in the group to refine their descriptions before presenting them to the entire class.

Practice Supplement, page 8

Name _____   To follow text page 17

Problem Solving: The 5-Point Checklist

Breakfast	Calories	Lunch	Calories	Dinner	Calories
orange juice	110	green salad	160	fish	170
yogurt and fruit	215	soup	95	peas	110
raisin muffin	145	carrot juice	150	rice	75
hard boiled egg	80	almonds	215	fruit salad	120

Solve.

1. What is the total number of calories on the breakfast menu? 550

2. What is the total number of calories on the lunch menu? 620

3. What is the total number of calories on the dinner menu? 475

4. For lunch Bill ate everything on the lunch menu and an extra glass of carrot juice. How many calories were in his lunch? 770

5. For breakfast Sally ate everything but the hard boiled egg. How many calories were in her breakfast? 470

6. What is the total number of calories for all three meals? 1,645

7. How many more calories are there in a green salad than in soup? 65

8. How many more calories are there in almonds than in carrot juice? 65

9. How many more calories does the lunch menu have than the dinner menu? 145

10. What would be the total number of calories in the dinner menu if a green salad were substituted for the fruit salad? 515

Quick Review Have students give at least two different combinations of coins that represent each amount below. Example: 12¢ 1 dime, 2 pennies; 2 nickels, 2 pennies.

37¢   72¢   20¢   55¢   93¢   41¢   65¢

Lesson Focus To add and subtract hours and minutes and find elapsed time

Ideas for Getting Started

Review the notation for recording time in hours and minutes and the meaning of a.m. and p.m. Then give the following practice in regrouping minutes to hours and minutes and vice versa.

Express in hours and minutes	Express in minutes
80 min (1 h 20 min)	1 h 10 min (70 min)
66 min (1 h 6 min)	1 h 25 min (85 min)
120 min (2 h)	2 h (120 min)
75 min (1 h 15 min)	1 h 55 min (115 min)

Using Page 18

Motivational Problem Ask students to read the problem at the top of the page. "We are being asked to find how many hours and minutes Jenny works in her part time job. What time does she start?" (4:45 p.m.) "What time does she stop?" (8:15 p.m.) "What can we do to find how many hours and minutes Jenny works?" (subtract the starting time from the stopping time)

Lesson Development Remind students that 4:45 p.m. means 4 hours and 45 minutes after noon, and that 8:15 p.m. means 8 hours and 15 minutes after noon. Since 45 minutes cannot be subtracted from 15 minutes, regrouping is necessary. Point out that 7 hours 75 minutes is the same as 8 hours 15 minutes. Then demonstrate how to subtract the minutes and the hours. The answer could be checked by counting forward 3 hours and 30 minutes from the starting time.

Other Examples In the first example, we add minutes to minutes and hours to hours, which will give us 5 h 85 min. Minutes over 60 are usually regrouped to hours and minutes, so 5 h 85 min becomes 5 h plus 1 h 25 min, or 6 h 25 min.

The second example focuses on finding elapsed time when one time is a.m. and the other is p.m. This kind of problem must be solved in three steps: 1) finding the number of hours and minutes from the first time to noon (or midnight), 2) finding the time from noon (or midnight) to the second time, and 3) adding the two elapsed times.

Warm Up Exercise 4 requires that we regroup 8 h 45 min to 7 h 105 min. Students should be aware that they are to apply the regular subtraction algorithm for subtracting across a middle zero to subtract 59 min from 105 min.

Adding and Subtracting Units of Time

Jenny works part time after school. She works from 4:45 p.m. to 8:15 p.m. How many hours (h) and minutes (min) does she work?

To find the time she works, we can subtract the starting time from the stopping time.

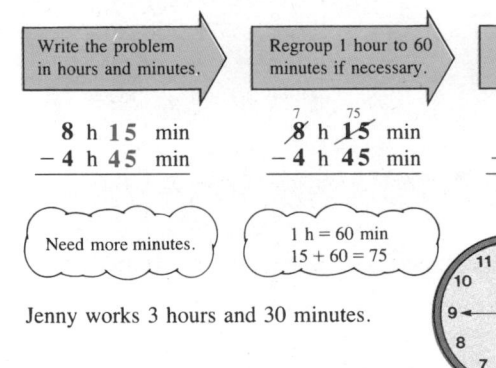

Write the problem in hours and minutes.	Regroup 1 hour to 60 minutes if necessary.	Subtract the minutes. Subtract the hours.
8 h 15 min − 4 h 45 min	7 75 8 h 15 min − 4 h 45 min	7 75 8 h 15 min − 4 h 45 min 3 h 30 min
Need more minutes.	*1 h = 60 min* *15 + 60 = 75*	

Jenny works 3 hours and 30 minutes.

Other Examples

Add 3 h 30 min and 2 h 55 min.

3 h 30 min
+ 2 h 55 min
5 h 85 min = 6 h 25 min

85 min = 1 h 25 min

How many hours and minutes is it from 8:15 a.m. to 2:50 p.m.?

From 8:15 a.m. to noon	12 h − 8 h 15 min	= =	11 h 60 min − 8 h 15 min 3 h 45 min
From noon to 2:50 p.m.		Total =	+ 2 h 50 min 5 h 95 min or 6 h 35 min

Warm Up

Add or subtract the hours and minutes.

1. 3 h 20 min
   + 4 h 35 min
   7 h 55 min

2. 11 h 25 min
   − 7 h 19 min
   4 h 6 min

3. 7 h 37 min
   + 8 h 46 min
   16 h 23 min

4. 8 h 45 min
   − 6 h 59 min
   1 h 46 min

5. How many hours and minutes is it from 9:10 a.m. to 2:25 p.m.? 5 h 15 min

6. How many hours and minutes is it from 10:35 p.m. to 7:45 a.m.? 9 h 10 min

18

Follow Up

Reteaching

Use an example to show how to regroup minutes to hours and minutes. Explain that since 60 min = 1 h and 95 min > 60 min, we subtract. (95 − 60 = 35)

95 min = 1 h 35 min

Next work through an example regrouping hours to minutes.

4 h 17 min = (3 h + 1 h) + 17 min
= 3 h + (60 min + 17 min)
= 3 h 77 min

Enrichment

Provide students with the following jogging record and have them find the total time spent jogging.

Week 1	8 h 15 min
Week 2	8 h 35 min
Week 3	9 h
Week 4	9 h 5 min
Week 5	9 h 10 min
Week 6	9 h 25 min
Week 7	9 h 30 min
Week 8	7 h 27 min
Week 9	7 h 24 min
Week 10	10 h

85 h 171 min = 87 h, 51 min

Find the total hours and minutes.

1. 1 h 25 min
    + 3 h 35 min
    —————
    5 h

2. 4 h 17 min
    + 6 h 54 min
    —————
    11 h 11 min

3. 8 h 42 min
    3 h 9 min
    + 2 h 26 min
    —————
    14 h 17 min

4. 2 h 45 min
    5 h 17 min
    + 4 h 28 min
    —————
    12 h 30 min

Find the differences in hours and minutes.

5. 6 h 47 min
    − 3 h 39 min
    —————
    3 h 8 min

6. 8 h 10 min
    − 4 h 20 min
    —————
    3 h 50 min

7. 5 h 15 min
    − 1 h 28 min
    —————
    3 h 47 min

8. 10 h
    − 5 h 39 min
    —————
    4 h 21 min

Find the number of hours and minutes between the two times.

9. From 6:50 a.m. to 11:30 a.m. 4 h 40 min

10. From 2:30 p.m. to 10:55 p.m. 8 h 25 min

11. From 9:15 a.m. to 3:15 p.m. 6 h

12. From 8:05 a.m. to 3:15 p.m. 7 h 10 min

13. From midnight to 6:27 a.m. 6 h 27 min

14. From 1:25 p.m. to 12:10 a.m. 10 h 45 min

15. From 6:35 a.m. to 2:10 p.m. 7 h 35 min

16. From 5:09 a.m. to 1:37 p.m. 8 h 28 min

17. One day Jenny went to work at 3:25 p.m. She worked until 6:10 p.m. How many hours and minutes did she work? 2 h 45 min

18. A store is open for business from 8:00 a.m. to 5:30 p.m., Monday through Friday. On Saturday it is open from 8:00 a.m. to noon. How many hours and minutes is the store open during one week? 51 h 30 min

19. DATA HUNT What time does your school start? What time do you get out of school? How many hours and minutes are you in school each week?

THINK MATH

Mental Math

You can do subtraction exercises like 1,000 − 299 in your head.

Think: **1,000 − 300** is **700.**

I subtracted 1 too many, so I must add 1 back.

700 + 1 = 701   **1,000 − 299 = 701**

Solve mentally.

1. 600 − 399 201
2. 700 − 198 502
3. 5,000 − 1,999 3,001
4. 2,000 − 299 1,701
5. 362 − 99 263
6. 1,500 − 499 1,001
7. 875 − 199 676
8. 1,750 − 49 1,701
9. 162 − 63 99
10. 375 − 76 299

More Practice, page 418, Set C

19

Using Page 19

Exercises 3–4 Point out that when adding more than two addends, the procedure is the same: add the minutes and then the hours, and regroup the total if necessary.

Exercises 9–16 Caution students to note whether the times given in each exercise involve a.m. or p.m.

Data Hunt Note that answers will vary, depending upon the hours your school observes.

Think Math These exercises involve the ability to round numbers, calculate, and reason logically. The process used in the mental procedure suggested can be justified algebraically.

$$1,000 - 299 = 1,000 - (300 - 1)$$
$$= (1,000 - 300) + 1$$
$$= 700 + 1$$
$$= 701$$

This analysis, however, need not be presented to the students.

More Practice, page 418, Set C

Reteaching Supplement, page 7

Enrichment Supplement, page 7

Practice Supplement, page 9

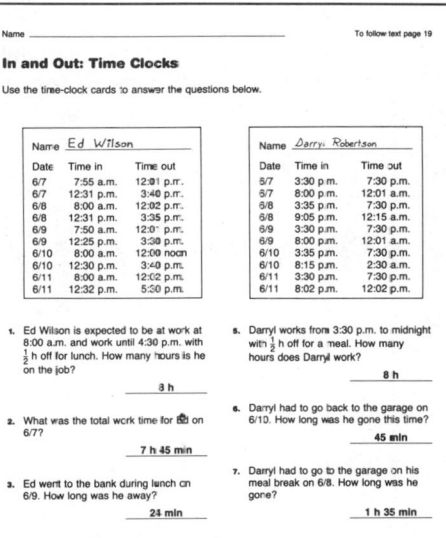

Applications

Quick Review Have students tell whether each time below refers to a.m. or p.m.
2 h 36 min after noon **p.m.** 7 h 3 min before noon **a.m.**
4 h 17 min after midnight **a.m.** 17 h after midnight **p.m.**

Lesson Focus To solve word problems focusing on understanding the question; to solve word problems focusing on answering the question

Ideas for Getting Started

To stimulate interest in word problems, play "What's the Question" with students. Write these answers on the chalkboard:

1. The answer is 4 books.
2. The answer is 20 km.
3. The answer is 36 points.
4. The answer is 2 sweatshirts.
5. The answer is 57 doors.

Call on students to quickly invent a problem for each answer. The problems that students create may be light-hearted or humorous, but they should be such that the question and the data fit the answer.

Using Page 20

Lesson Development Have students read the material at the top of the page. The problem-solving logo will remind students of the 5-Point Checklist. Point out that problems on this page emphasize the first step of the checklist: understanding the question.

Exercises 1–8 Before assigning the exercises, tell students that the question in each problem is missing. They are to write a reasonable question for the data that is given and solve the problem. Discuss the idea that some questions are unreasonable for the data. For example, an unreasonable question for the data in exercise 1 is "What is the combined height of Brian and Maxine?" Even though this question could be answered, the answer would be of little practical value or interest.

After students have completed the assignment, check their questions and answers. Note that the question, and thus the answers, will vary. Select several student-created questions and discuss with the class the reasonableness of each question.

PROBLEM SOLVING: Understanding the Question

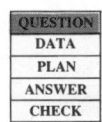

| QUESTION |
| DATA |
| PLAN |
| ANSWER |
| CHECK |

To solve any problem, you must know what it is you are trying to find. The question always asks you to find something.

Make up a question about the information given in each group of sentences below. Find the answer to each question.

1. Brian is in the 7th grade and is 157 centimeters (cm) tall. His sister Maxine is a 9th grader and is 171 cm tall.

2. Roberta has saved $57 to buy a new bicycle. The model she would like to buy costs $139.

3. Lamont got 27 people to sign for his walk in a charity "Walk-a-thon." Louise got 32 people to sign for her, and Heather got 39 people to sign.

4. Libby has 87¢ but spends 69¢ for a ballpoint pen for school. Later on, Libby earns 50¢ more.

5. Arianna put 23 new stamps in her collection. She counted all her stamps and found that she had collected 207 stamps.

6. Carl wants to put up 3 shelves, each 118 cm long. He has one piece of wood that is 360 cm long.

7. Ed Johnson was on a business trip 425 km away from his home city of Daviston. He started driving home at 2:00 p.m. At 5:15 p.m. he passed a highway sign that read, "Daviston 139 km."

8. Elvia starts school at 8:05 a.m. School ends at 3:50 p.m.

See teaching notes.

20

Follow Up

Reteaching

Write this statement on the chalkboard: In 3 days of vacation driving, the Isenharts drove 425, 513, and 402 kilometers.

Ask students to write a question to complete a word problem. Encourage a variety of questions. Discuss each question and what it asks students to find. Have students find the answer to each question.

Enrichment

Using each of the digits 0 through 9 only once, have students write additional problems which have two three-digit addends and a four-digit sum. **Answers will vary. Some possible answers are:**

$$579 + 483 = 1{,}062$$
$$859 + 743 = 1{,}602$$
$$589 + 473 = 1{,}062$$
$$857 + 349 = 1{,}206$$

Assignment Guide

	Minimum	Average	Extended
page 20	1–4	1–6	1–8
page 21	1–4	1–6	1–6

PROBLEM SOLVING: Answering the Question

QUESTION
DATA
PLAN
ANSWER
CHECK

You can write a short sentence that answers the question in a problem.

Airport Code Letters

CLE Hopkins Field, Cleveland
DFW Dallas-Ft. Worth
ATL Atlanta
JFK Kennedy, New York
SFO San Francisco
MIA Miami
DCA National, Washington, D.C.
IAD Dulles, Washington, D.C.
LAX Los Angeles
LGA LaGuardia, New York
ORD O'Hare Field, Chicago

JFK had 22,545,000 passengers in one year. LGA had 15,087,000 passengers. ATL had 29,977,000 passengers that year.

How many more passengers did the two New York airports have together than the Atlanta airport?

JFK	22,545,000	Total	37,632,000
LGA	+ 15,087,000	ATL	− 29,977,000
Total	37,632,000		7,655,000

The New York airports had 7,655,000 more passengers.

Do the computation to solve the problems.
Write a short sentence that answers each question.

1. SFO had 20,249,000 passengers in one year. DFW had 2,931,000 fewer passengers than SFO that year. How many passengers did DFW have? DFW had 17,318,000 passengers.

2. IAD had 2,300,000 passengers in a year, and DCA had 14,200,000 passengers the same year. The total for the two Washington, D.C. airports is about the same as the number of passengers for MIA. About how many passengers did MIA have? MIA had about 16,500,000 passengers.

3. JFK had 22,545,000 passengers. ORD had 852,000 less than double this number. How many passengers did ORD have? ORD had 44,238,000 passengers.

4. DCA had double the number of passengers of CLE. CLE had 7,100,000 passengers. What was the total number of passengers for the two airports? The total number of passengers was 21,300,000.

5. MIA had 16,500,000 passengers. LGA had 15,087,000 passengers. How many fewer passengers did LGA have? LGA had 1,413,000 fewer passengers.

6. The number of passengers for three busy airports are given below.
   ORD 44,238,000
   ATL 29,977,000
   LAX 28,361,000
   What is the total number of passengers for the three airports? The total number of passengers is 102,576,000.

21

Using Page 21

Lesson Development Before going through the example, direct students' attention to the chart at the top of the page showing the code letters for airports. Ask them if they can give the code letters of some airports not listed. Other codes include:

MCI	Kansas City
IAH	Houston
SEA	Seattle-Tacoma
TPA	Tampa-St. Petersburg/Clearwater
PHL	Philadelphia

The problems on this page focus on another part of the 5-Point Checklist: find the answer. Read the example problem with students. Have them restate the question and give the data. Point out that the plan involves the use of two operations.

On the chalkboard, work through finding the answer. After the computation is performed, notice with the students that the answer is written in a sentence. Stress that the answer is more than just a number. It is a short sentence or phrase that answers the question in the problem. Note: While answers in sentences help students determine whether or not their results are reasonable, they are not expected to write answers in full sentences in the following lessons. However, you may request students to do this on occasion to make sure they understand what the problem asks them to find.

Reteaching Supplement, page 8

Name _____   To follow text page 20

Problem Solving: Understanding the Question

Peg worked at the computer 35 minutes yesterday and 20 minutes today.

Sample Question 1
How much longer did she work at the computer yesterday? (35 − 20 = 15)
15 minutes

Sample Question 2
What is the total time she worked at the computer? (35 + 20 = 55)
55 minutes

Make up a question that can be answered from the information in each problem. Then find the answer to your question. **Answers may vary. Samples are given.**

1. On Monday Pete sold 15 tickets to the play, on Tuesday he sold 23 tickets, and on Wednesday he sold 19 tickets.
Question: How many tickets did he sell in all?
Answer: 57

2. The Tigers scored 28 points during the first half of the basketball game and 36 points during the second half.
Question: How many points did they score in all?
Answer: 64

3. Gina called her grandparents long distance on their anniversary. She talked from 7:28 p.m. until 7:45 p.m.
Question: How long did the phone call last?
Answer: 17 min

4. Terry earned $85 his first week at work. He saved $37 of his earnings.
Question: How much did he spend?
Answer: $48

5. Carol needs 2 lengths of rope each 264 cm long. She found a piece of rope in the garage 550 cm long.
Question: Can she cut the pieces she needs from it?
Answer: Yes. (264 × 2 = 528)

6. A logging truck left camp at 1:25 p.m. and arrived at the sawmill at 3:10 p.m.
Question: How long did the trip take?
Answer: 1 h 45 min

Enrichment Supplement, page 8

Name _____   To follow text page 20

Grow Up

Read each problem below. Decide which questions can be answered with the data given. Write the answers. Where there is not enough data, tell what else you need to know in order to answer the question. Then make up the data and find the answer. **Answers will vary where student supplies data.**

1. If you multiply my age by 6 and add 28, you get 100. How old am I?
12

2. My brother and I were born on the same day, but I am 2 years older than he. On our last birthday, we each had a cake with a number of candles equal to our age. In all, there were 26 candles used. How old are we?
14 and 12

3. Nina is older than Ted. Ted is 5 years older than Sue Ann. What is the difference in the ages of the oldest and the youngest?
You need to know how much older Nina is than Ted.

4.
12 plates   25 plates   28 plates
You need to buy some paper plates for a birthday party. How many of each package should you buy to have the least number of extra paper plates?
You need to know how many people are coming to the party.

5. Five years from now, I will be 15 years old. In what year was I born?
10 years ago
(Student may give data based on current year.)

6. Choose a friend. Which of you is older? How many minutes older?
Answers will vary.

Practice Supplement, page 10

Name _____   To follow text page 20

Problem Solving: Understanding the Question

Make up a question about the information in each problem below. Find the answer to your question. **Answers will vary. Samples are given.**

1. Andrew needs $225 to go to summer camp. He has $138.
How much more money does Andrew need? $87

2. It takes Norma 23 minutes to get to school. It takes Cindy 19 minutes.
How much longer does it take Norma to get to school? 4 min

3. Gira practiced her violin for 35 minutes on Monday, 45 minutes on Tuesday, and 30 minutes on Wednesday.
How long did she practice in all? 1 h 50 min

4. Sandy had 95¢. He bought a postcard for 25¢. Then he found 10¢ on the sidewalk.
How much money did he have then? 80¢

5. The home team scored 58 points. The visiting team scored 75 points.
How many more points did the visiting team score? 17

6. Ms. Sanchez left home at 9:07. She got to work at 9:28.
How much did it take her to get to work? 21 min

7. Mr. Glenn planted 42 tomato plants, 16 squash plants, and 58 pea plants.
How many plants did he plant in all? 116

8. It is 186 km from Westport to Lawrence. It is 394 km from Westport to North Beach.
How much farther is it from Westport to North Beach? 208 km

9. Amy arrived at school at 8:35 a.m. She left school at 3:10 p.m.
How long was she at school? 6 h 35 min

10. Bobby earned $45. He spent $28 on a basketball.
How much money did he have left? $17

Quick Review Conduct an oral drill on basic multiplication and division facts by posing questions like these:
"Factor 6, product 42. What's the other factor?"
"Dividend 32, divisor 8. What's the quotient?"

Lesson Focus To practice finding sums and differences of whole numbers; to use data from a Data Bank to solve word problems

Ideas for Getting Started

To introduce the Data Bank lesson on page 23 display the following table on the chalkboard.

October Weather Report

City	Average High Temp. (F)°	Average Low Temp. (F)°	Rain Days
Atlanta	72°	52°	6
Boston	64°	47°	9
Chicago	65°	45°	8
Denver	66°	37°	5
Honolulu	82°	72°	13
Los Angeles	78°	59°	2
Miami	84°	71°	15
Washington, DC	69°	49°	12

After students examine the table, have them answer questions such as these: "What is the average high temperature for October in Miami?" (84°) "What is Boston's average low temperature in October?" (47°) "In what cities can you expect to have more than 10 rainy days during October?" (Honolulu, Miami, and Washington, DC)

Using Page 22

Exercises 1–46 You may wish to select specific types of problems that have caused students difficulty and work through them as a class activity before making the assignment for this page.

Assign the exercises on page 22 according to the needs and abilities of the students. If you have students who are clearly competent in one of these skills, you may wish to omit those exercises from the assignment for those students.

Skills Practice

Add.

| 1. | 374 + 259 = 633 | 2. | 658 + 467 = 1,125 | 3. | 889 + 602 = 1,491 | 4. | 406 + 394 = 800 | 5. | 5,253 + 8,957 = 14,210 |

| 6. | 4,675 + 9,326 = 14,001 | 7. | 27,982 + 90,635 = 118,617 | 8. | 3,044,689 + 9,276,042 = 12,320,731 | 9. | 7,813,621 + 6,782,394 = 14,596,015 | 10. | 14,962,153 + 15,347,964 = 30,310,117 |

| 11. | 2,603 84 + 575 = 3,262 | 12. | 13,909 6,724 + 10,688 = 31,321 | 13. | 683,011 1,429 + 3,462,914 = 4,147,354 | 14. | 74,991,620 31,374,826 + 80,367,555 = 186,734,001 | 15. | 93,286,523 81,103,675 + 44,632,193 = 219,022,391 |

Subtract.

| 16. | 39,451 − 2,301 = 37,150 | 17. | 622,210 − 3,101 = 619,109 | 18. | 70,398 − 62,179 = 8,219 | 19. | 96,457 − 18,368 = 78,089 | 20. | 427,561 − 238,462 = 189,099 |

| 21. | 358,200 − 269,147 = 89,053 | 22. | 721,165 − 630,476 = 90,689 | 23. | 365,926 − 70,977 = 294,949 | 24. | 62,100 − 3,172 = 58,928 | 25. | 4,983,576 − 1,897,649 = 3,085,927 |

| 26. | 23,078,210 − 4,556,701 = 18,521,509 | 27. | 80,031,001 − 37,741,269 = 42,289,732 | 28. | 92,613,172 − 37,985,275 = 54,627,897 | 29. | 9,300,010 − 4,768,201 = 4,531,809 | 30. | 101,000,101 − 33,918,652 = 67,081,449 |

Add or subtract.

| 31. | 42,760,130 979,893 + 4,250,618 = 47,990,641 | 32. | 22,009,876 1,998,032 + 460,171 = 24,468,079 | 33. | 65,532,988 10,738,642 + 9,473,590 = 85,745,220 | 34. | 8,643,201 − 7,896,469 = 746,732 | 35. | 5,551,328 − 3,875,219 = 1,676,109 |

| 36. | 33,761,002 − 32,694,554 = 1,066,448 | 37. | 56,439,802 − 50,429,809 = 6,009,993 | 38. | 85,770,341 − 29,872,403 = 55,897,938 | 39. | 1,632,104 7,522,462 8,196,344 + 3,010,257 = 20,361,167 | 40. | 23,501,269 7,116,330 11,408,791 + 986,032 = 43,012,422 |

41. 36,029,410 + 59,983,570
96,012,980

42. 6,103,451 − 6,004,988
98,463

43. 25,003,681 − 24,855,392
148,289

44. 947,305 + 956,895
22 1,904,200

45. 7,000,931 − 6,989,744
11,187

46. 7,116,330 + 177,033
7,293,363

Follow Up

Reteaching

Work with students individually or in small groups to determine their particular difficulties. Prescribe activities that will correct these deficiencies. For example, assign basic-facts drill for students who are missing basic facts. If students are having difficulty with the algorithms, have them talk through the steps of their work with you.

Enrichment

Display the following on the chalkboard.

WRONG
+ WRONG
RIGHT

Explain to students that each different letter represents a different digit from 1 through 9, (0 is not used). Challenge them to find the digits so that the addition problem will work correctly.

There are several solutions. Two appear below.

12,734
+ 12,734
25,468

25,938
+ 25,938
51,876

Assignment Guide			
	Minimum	Average	Extended
page 22	1–30	1–40	2–46 even
page 23	1–4	1–6	

PROBLEM SOLVING: Using a Data Bank

QUESTION
DATA
PLAN
ANSWER
CHECK

A **data bank** is any source of information or **data.**

Modern microcomputers and computers can be used for storing and retrieving data. Large amounts of data can be stored on magnetic discs. The computer can quickly retrieve data. It can also direct a printer to print any stored data.

Information can be passed from one computer to another over telephone lines.

Thus, great amounts of data stored in a central library, or **data bank,** can be retrieved and used by people all over the world.

On pages 413–416, a data bank has been printed for your use. You will find Data Bank problems throughout this book that ask you to go to the data bank to find the information you need.

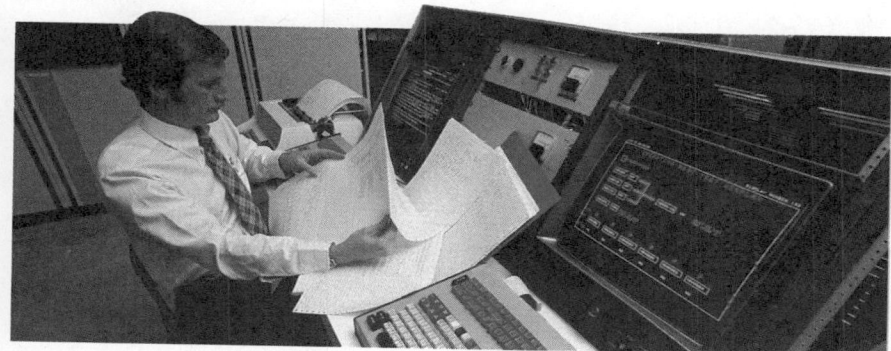

Use the Data Bank on page 413 to find the answers to these questions.

1. An advertising manager of a company wants to contact each AM radio station in the state of Colorado. How many stations must be contacted? 72

2. A company wishes to advertise a new product on TV stations in Ohio, Indiana, and Michigan. What is the total number of TV stations in these states? 68

3. Which state is listed as not having a TV station? Delaware

4. Which five states have the most TV stations? List the states and the number of TV stations from largest to smallest. Texas, 58; California, 54; Florida, 31; New York, 30; Pennsylvania, 27

5. Which state has more FM radio stations, New York or Pennsylvania? How many more? Pennsylvania; 5

6. What is the number of AM, FM, and TV stations in your home state? See appropriate state; page 413.

23

Using Page 23

Lesson Development Have students read through the material at the top of the page. Encourage them to share with the class any experiences they may have had with computers and stored data. Then have students turn to the beginning of the Data Bank on page 413. Tell them they will need to refer to this section for information to solve the Data Bank problems that appear throughout the text.

Discuss the nature of real-life problems—in order to solve these problems, it is often necessary to obtain data from outside sources. Ask students to name sources that might be used to solve math problems that occur in daily life. (maps, encyclopedias, graphs, tables)

Exercises 1–6 Work through exercise 1 as a class activity. "What data is needed to solve exercise 1?" (the number of AM radio stations in Colorado) "Refer to the table on page 413. What does it show?" (the number of radio stations in each state) "Locate this information for the state of Colorado and answer the question in exercise 1." In exercise 6, answers will vary depending on your home state.

Ideas That Work

Special Education

To reinforce the computational practice, have students form groups of 2 or 3 to play "Rank-a-Blank."

Students will need a game sheet as shown, their math book, index cards labeled with numbers of exercises from page 22, and an answer key or calculator.

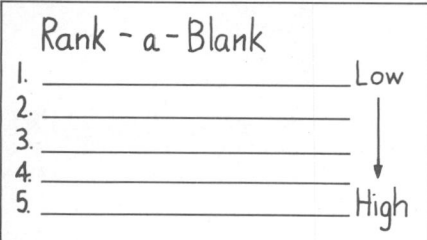

Students should mix the cards, place them in a pile, and take turns turning over the top card. At "go" all players copy the problem indicated by the top card, work it, then check answers with others. Calculators or answer keys can be used to settle differences. (A graded assignment sheet could be used as a key.) When correct, players write the answer on one blank of their game sheet. The goal is to write answers low to high, so sometimes players might have to pass and not record an answer. The first player to correctly rank five answers wins the round.

Practice Supplement, page 11

Name _____   To follow text page 23

Problem Solving: Using a Data Bank

Data Bank	
Aircraft	Maximum Seating Capacity
DC-10	380
L1011	400
727	189
747	550
757	233
767	289

Use the data bank to answer these questions.

1. A DC-10 had 311 passengers on board. How many empty seats were there? 69

2. How many more seats are there on a 747 than on a 727? 361

3. Which three planes have the most seats? List the maximum seating capacities in order from largest to smallest. 747, 550; L1011, 400; DC-10, 380

4. Which planes have a seating capacity of fewer than 250 passengers? 757, 727

5. How many fewer seats are there on a 757 than on a 767? 56

6. Which planes have a seating capacity of more than 350 passengers? DC-10, L1011, 747

7. 248 people want seats on a 757 going to New York. How many people will not get seats? 15

8. 487 people want to go on a tour. Which plane should they charter? 747

9. How many empty seats will there be on the tour if 487 people go? 63

10. What is the difference in seating capacity between the largest and the smallest plane? 361

Lesson Focus
To guess and check as a strategy for solving nonroutine word problems

Ideas for Getting Started

Play "Guess My Numbers" with the students. Display the following problem on the chalkboard.

The sum of my numbers is 24.
One number is double the other number.
Can you guess my numbers? (8 and 16)

After most students appear to have found the numbers, ask them to tell what their guesses were, and to explain how they used the given information to check their guesses. Then ask whether their next guess was larger or smaller, and to explain why.

Present another problem and repeat the questions.

The sum of my numbers is 21.
One number is 5 more than the other.
Can you guess my numbers? (8 and 13)

As a long-term project, begin a problem-solving bulletin board. As you teach each of the 9 strategies presented in Book 7, add the name of the newly-introduced strategy to the bulletin board. Students can refer to the bulletin board when they are trying to think of a strategy that can help them solve a nonroutine problem.

Using Page 24

Motivational Problem After students read the Try This problem at the top of the page, ask them to restate the question. Then ask, "How many buttons does Kris have?" (13 more than Gary) "What other data is given in the problem?" (Kris and Gary together have 125 buttons.) Point out that in some problems we may not be able to decide on a plan that will give the answer to the problem directly.

Lesson Development Go through the example solution with the students, emphasizing that our plan or strategy is to try to guess the number of buttons Gary has and then check to see if our guess is correct. Explain that we call this strategy Guess and Check. Discuss how to tell when guesses are too large or too small. Emphasize that part of the check means rereading the problem to make certain that the answer makes sense.

Exercises 1–2 Remind students to use the 5-Point Checklist to help them solve these problems. Have them try to use the plan or strategy of Guess and Check. Discuss students' solutions, calling attention to the idea of guess, check, guess, check, and so on.

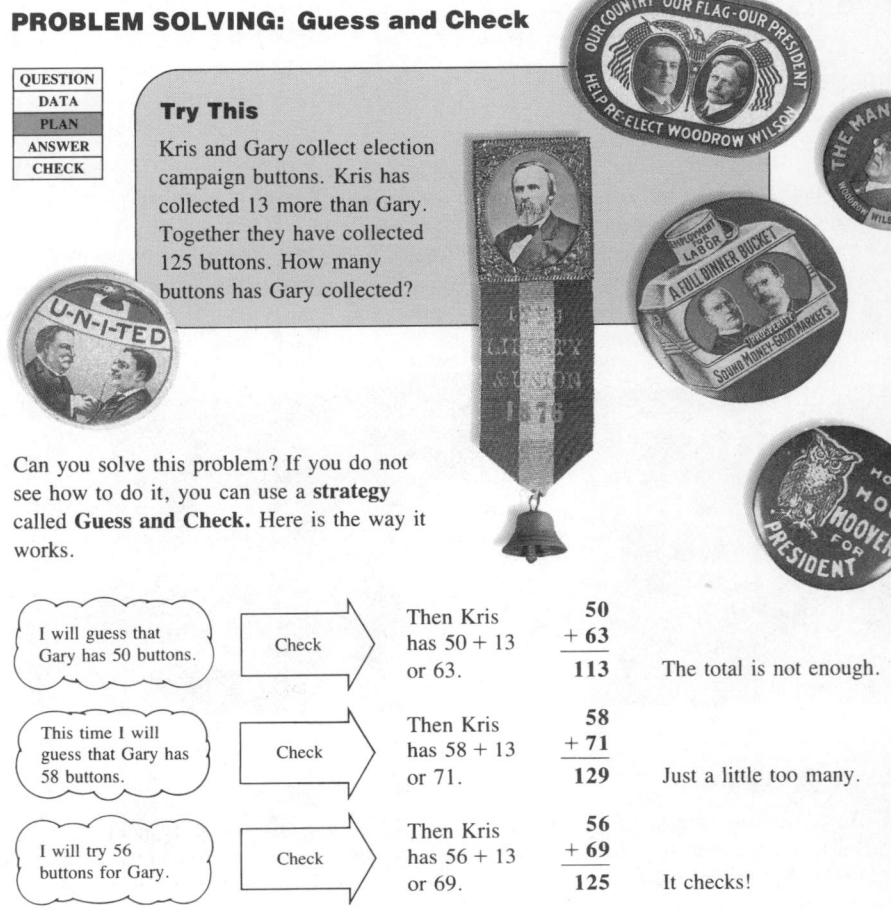

PROBLEM SOLVING: Guess and Check

QUESTION
DATA
PLAN
ANSWER
CHECK

Try This

Kris and Gary collect election campaign buttons. Kris has collected 13 more than Gary. Together they have collected 125 buttons. How many buttons has Gary collected?

Can you solve this problem? If you do not see how to do it, you can use a **strategy** called **Guess and Check.** Here is the way it works.

I will guess that Gary has 50 buttons.	→ Check →	Then Kris has 50 + 13 or 63.	$\begin{array}{r} 50 \\ + 63 \\ \hline 113 \end{array}$	The total is not enough.
This time I will guess that Gary has 58 buttons.	→ Check →	Then Kris has 58 + 13 or 71.	$\begin{array}{r} 58 \\ + 71 \\ \hline 129 \end{array}$	Just a little too many.
I will try 56 buttons for Gary.	→ Check →	Then Kris has 56 + 13 or 69.	$\begin{array}{r} 56 \\ + 69 \\ \hline 125 \end{array}$	It checks!

Gary has collected 56 buttons.

Solve.

1. In an election campaign button collection, there are 15 more modern buttons than old-time buttons. There are 121 buttons all together. How many old-time buttons are there? 53

2. Lakisha and Jay have a total of 210 stamps in their stamp collections. Lakisha has 24 fewer stamps than Jay. How many stamps are there in Jay's collection? 117

24

Strategy Test Item

Optional Problem If you wish to assess students' ability to apply the strategy called Guess and Check introduced in this chapter, provide them with the problem below.

> Bob and Ron have a total of 360 stamps in their stamp collection. Bob has collected 50 more stamps than Ron. How many stamps has Bob collected?

Solution

Guess: Bob (205) Ron (155)
Check: 205 + 155 = 360
Bob has collected 205 stamps.

CHAPTER REVIEW/TEST

Write the numeral.

1. four thousand, six hundred seventeen 4,617

2. seventeen thousand, nine hundred forty-three 17,943

3. three hundred five million, sixty-three thousand 305,063,000

4. forty-eight billion 48,000,000,000

Write > or < for each ●.

5. 9,673 ● 9,681 <   **6.** 16,279 ● 15,729 <   **7.** 315,073 ● 314,073 >

Estimate each sum or difference by rounding to the nearest hundred.

8. 673 − 420 300   **9.** 2,628 + 1,233 3,800   **10.** 49,986 − 1,200 48,800

Estimate each sum or difference by rounding to the nearest thousand.

11. 8,709 − 1,397 8,000   **12.** 4,378 + 2,691 7,000   **13.** 69,284 − 28,748 40,000

Find the sums or differences.

14.	**15.**	**16.**	**17.**	**18.**
278	3,851	1,391	12,800	8,748
+ 753	− 1,627	+ 429	− 490	+ 7,284
1,031	2,224	1,820	12,310	16,032

19.	**20.**	**21.**	**22.**	**23.**
36,869	43,076	65,135	54,172,000	9,000,846
+ 5,295	− 41,582	+ 67,040	− 27,358,000	− 2,637,797
42,164	1,494	132,175	26,814,000	6,363,049

Find the sums or differences in hours and minutes.

24.	**25.**	**26.**	**27.**	**28.**
3 h 15 min	8 h 53 min	9 h 27 min	2 h 40 min	6 h 10 min
+ 4 h 24 min	− 3 h 35 min	+ 8 h 45 min	+ 3 h 25 min	− 3 h 30 min
7 h 39 min	5 h 18 min	18 h 12 min	6 h 5 min	2 h 40 min

29. What is the total number of calories in the lunch? 435

Lunch	
salad	115 calories
sandwich	235 calories
juice	85 calories

30. There are about 3,712,407 telephones in use in Mexico. There are about 5,583,330 telephones in use in Australia. How many more telephones are in use in Australia than in Mexico? 1,870,923

25

Using Page 25

The exercises in the Chapter Review/Test emphasize the major concepts and skills presented in this chapter. These exercises may be used as a review assignment or as a test, depending upon your needs.

Item Analysis The table below correlates the Chapter Review/Test items with objectives and with the student text pages on which the concepts or skills were taught. Please note that items 24–28 are derived from a lesson for which no minimum assignment was suggested in the Assignment Guide. Only those students who were assigned this lesson should be expected to complete the corresponding Chapter Review/Test items.

Items	Objectives	Related Text Pages
1–4	1.1	2–5
5–7	1.2	6–9
8–13	1.3	10–11
14–23	1.4	12–15, 22
24–28	1.5	18–19
29–30	1.6	16–17, 20–21, 23

Assessment Options

If you use the Chapter Review/Test as a review assignment, you may wish to use the free-response test or the multiple-choice test to evaluate mastery of the chapter objectives. The items on these tests have a one-to-one correspondence in terms of content and level of difficulty. A correlation of test items to objectives and student text pages is provided in the Management Guide for Chapter 1. Note: Items 38 through 40 are derived from a lesson for which no minimum assignment was suggested in the Assignment Guide.

Multiple-Choice Test, TRB pages 1–3
Free-Response Test, TRB pages 48–49

TRB Options

The following blackline masters are available for use with this chapter. If you have not already assigned these materials, you may wish to use them to close the chapter.

Recreation, TRB page 155
Consumer Applications, TRB page 173
Calculator Technology, TRB page 191
Reading Math, TRB page 227
Family Involvement, TRB pages 245–246

Using Page 26

The exercises on this page are intended for those students who experienced difficulty with the Chapter Review/Test on page 25. Should students require reteaching of these key concepts and skills, please refer to the teaching notes below. Otherwise, the Another Look exercises can be assigned as independent work, with students using the accompanying sample problems and hints as guides.

Exercises 1–4 This skill was originally taught on pages 6–7. Direct students' attention to the display box at the top of the page. Explain that since the digits in the thousands place are the same, we go on to compare the digits in the hundreds place. Since 6 is greater than 4, the number 3,652 is greater than 3,462.

Exercises 5–10 This skill was originally taught on pages 8–9. Have students examine the display box on the left. Ask questions such as these: "To which place are we rounding?" (hundreds place) "What is the digit to the right of that place?" (3) "Is that number 5 or more?" (no) "Do we keep 9 the same or add one to it?" (same) "What is 7,931 rounded to the nearest hundred? (7,900)

Exercises 11–16 This skill was originally taught on pages 10–11. On the chalkboard, work through the example in the display box. Point out that two steps are involved in making estimates of sums and differences: **1)** rounding the numbers and, **2)** performing the mental calculations.

Exercises 17–22 This skill was originally taught on pages 12–13. Use the example in the display box to reteach addition of whole numbers. Remind students to be careful to align the digits properly when copying the exercises.

Exercises 23–28 This skill was originally taught on pages 14–15. Work through the example with students, emphasizing the regrouping. Remind students to check their answers by using addition.

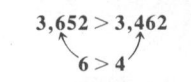

ANOTHER LOOK

$3,652 > 3,462$
$6 > 4$

Write $>$ or $<$ for each ⬤.

1. 2,942 ⬤ 3,942 $<$
2. 64,827 ⬤ 68,427 $<$
3. 903,414 ⬤ 930,414 $<$
4. 862,374 ⬤ 862,574 $<$

Round to the nearest hundred.

$7,931 \rightarrow 7,900$
less than 5 hundreds

Round to the nearest hundred.

5. 2,381 2,400
6. 64,729 64,700
7. 128,552 128,600

Round to the nearest thousand.

8. 7,726 8,000
9. 59,607 60,000
10. 554,398 554,000

Round to the nearest ten.

$64 \rightarrow 60$
$29 \rightarrow 30$
$+ 18 \rightarrow + 20$
110 estimate

Estimate each sum or difference by rounding.   Answers may vary.

11.	29 39 + 42 110	12.	389 − 115 300	13.	6,388 − 4,426 2,000
14.	227 519 + 194 900	15.	3,096 + 4,779 8,000	16.	51,628 − 19,742 30,000

1 1
6 3 8
+ 3 7 6
1,0 1 4

Find the sums.

17.	394 + 762 1,156	18.	1,809 + 2,776 4,585	19.	231,792 + 469,347 701,139
20.	35 76 + 42 153	21.	129 317 + 662 1,108	22.	1,247 3,374 + 2,908 7,529

Check.
5 9 13
6̶ 0̶ 3̶   417
− 1 8 6   + 186
4 1 7   603

Find the differences.

23.	836 − 782 54	24.	6,021 − 4,227 1,794	25.	8,004 − 5,176 2,828
26.	23,719 − 16,446 7,273	27.	936,042 − 666,781 269,261	28.	809,107 − 365,386 443,721

26

Just for Teachers

Calendars

For thousands of years, civilization measured time by observing the sun, moon, and stars. They were able to determine a yearly cycle. Seasonal events like floods, cold, or drought were predicted by the appearance of particular constellations in certain places in the night sky. The ancient Egyptians, whose lives and occupations depended upon the Nile, developed the most accurate calendar in antiquity: 365 days, also divided into the three seasons of the Nile's annual cycle.

The Romans at one time used a calendar of 10 lunar months that ignored more than 60 days. Obviously impractical, this calendar was modified by the addition of two lunar months. Every other year a kind of "leap month" was added. Julius Caesar finally arranged for an Alexandrian scholar to devise a more accurate calendar. The Julian calendar, which was based on the Egyptian model, was used throughout the

---

ENRICHMENT

Discovering a Pattern

The numbers in the sequence below are called **Fibonacci numbers.** Fibonacci was the nickname of the medieval mathematician Leonardo of Pisa (c. 1170–1250).

1, 1, 2, 3, 5, 8, 13...

Can you guess what the next few numbers would be? Write down your guesses before going on. Study the pattern below.

$1 + 1 = 2$ $1 + 2 = 3$ $2 + 3 = 5$

$3 + 5 = 8$ $5 + 8 = 13$ $8 + 13 = ?$

$13 + ? = ?$ $8 + 13 = 21$ $13 + 21 = 34$

Continue this pattern to find more numbers in the Fibonacci sequence.

Try these problems.

1. List the first 30 numbers in the Fibonacci sequence.

2. Study the pattern below.

$$1 + 1 = \ 3 - 1 = \ 2$$
$$1 + 1 + 2 = \ 5 - 1 = \ 4$$
$$1 + 1 + 2 + 3 = \ 8 - 1 = \ 7$$
$$1 + 1 + 2 + 3 + 5 = 13 - 1 = 12$$

Write the next three rows in this pattern.

3. Use the pattern shown in problem 2 to give the sum of the first ten numbers in the Fibonacci sequence without actually adding the numbers. 143

4. Find the sum of the first 30 numbers in the Fibonacci sequence. 2,178,308

1; 1; 2; 3; 5; 8; 13; 21; 34; 55; 89; 144; 233; 377; 610; 987; 1,597; 2,584; 4,181; 6,765; 10,946; 7,711; 28,657; 46,368; 75,025; 121,393; 196,418; 317,811; 514,229; 832,040

$1 + 1 + 2 + 3 + 5 + 8 = 21 - 1 = 20$
$1 + 1 + 2 + 3 + 5 + 8 + 13 = 34 - 1 = 33$
$1 + 1 + 2 + 3 + 5 + 8 + 13 + 21 = 55 - 1 = 54$

Biologists find patterns which show Fibonacci numbers in nature.

Using Page 27

This page is intended for those students who successfully completed the Chapter Review/Test on page 25. You may wish to assign this page as independent work while you use the Another Look exercises to reteach the basic concepts and skills of this chapter. Or, you may decide that all students would benefit from exposure to this Enrichment Activity.

Lesson Development Have students read the paragraph at the top of the page and direct attention to the number sequence below. After students discern the pattern ask them to state the rule used to form the Fibonacci sequence. (The sum of any two successive numbers in the sequence, is the next number in the sequence.) Explain to students that numbers in the Fibonacci sequence can be found in patterns in nature. The figure at the bottom of the page illustrates opposing spirals, such as those found in the center of the sunflower. Eight spirals can be traced in the clockwise direction and five spirals can be traced in the countercockwise direction.

Exercises 1–4 In exercise 1, the numbers grow large quickly so you might encourage students with calculators to use them. The pattern of the equations in exercise 2 shows that the sum of the first n numbers in the Fibonacci sequence is 1 less than the $(n + 2)$th number in the sequence. This result can be used to answer exercises 3 and 4. Hence, the sum of the first 10 numbers is $144 - 1 = 143$, and the sum of the first 30 numbers is $2,178,309 - 1 = 2,178,308$. Students can use their calculators to check these answers.

---

western world for centuries. Nevertheless, it was $11\frac{1}{4}$ minutes per year too long. It was not until 1582 that this was corrected. Pope Gregory XIII dropped 10 days from the calendar.

The Gregorian calendar used today still exceeds a year by 26 seconds. The earth requires 365 days, 5 hours, 48 minutes, and 46 seconds to circle the sun. The moon takes about 29 days and 12 hours to circle the earth once, and does this a little more than 12 (12.37) times per year. Even these times are not unvarying. Astronomers have observed periods in which the earth arbitrarily sped up or slowed down by some fraction of a second.

Lesson Focus To use the calculator's memory to store a number and recall it for later use

Suggested Materials Calculators with memory, owner's manual for each calculator, if available

Ideas for Getting Started

Have students choose a 4-digit number, write it on paper and enter it on their calculators. Then tell students to multiply that number by 5; add 500; divide by 20; and finally multiply by 4. Ask if the number displayed is greater than or less than their original number (greater than). Ask how much greater (100).

Next ask students to choose a new 4-digit number. Tell them to store it in the memory of their calculator. They should check the calculator's owners manual to find out which keys to use for memory and memory recall. Often the memory key is M+ and memory recall is MR. After students enter the new 4-digit number, they should press the memory key to store a copy of it. Tell students once again to multiply the number by 5, add 500, divide by 20, and multiply by 4. Ask them to compare the result to the original number stored in memory. (The result is 100 more than the original number.) Point out that arithmetic operations do not affect the stored number.

Using Page 28

Lesson Development Explain to students that a calculator can save a copy of a number in its memory. Guide students through the examples on the page. Tell students to enter 39,483 and then press the memory key." Explain that the number is now stored in memory. Some calculators display an M or a dot to show that a number is stored. Next, tell students to press c to clear the display, and then press MR (or an equivalent key depending on the brand of calculator) to recall the number. "What number is displayed?" (39,483) "Did clearing the number from the display erase it from memory?" (no) "To erase the memory, press MC (memory clear) as shown in the example." The number can also be erased from memory by turning off the calculator.

Guide students through the second example in the same way.

Using a Calculator

Some calculators have memories. A number can be stored in the memory of a calculator and used at a later time.

Store, recall, and clear a number. Use 39,483.

Enter	Press	Display	Comments
39483	M+	M 39483.	The number is stored.
	C	M 0.	The display is cleared.
	MR	M 39483.	The number is recalled.
	MC	39483.	The calculator memory is cleared.

Store the number 4,186 and use the memory of the calculator to solve this exercise.

$$\frac{3 \times 4,186 \times 4,186 + 4,186}{4,186}$$

Enter	Press	Display	Comments
4186	M+	M 4186.	4,186 is stored.
3	× MR	M 4186.	$3 \times 4,186$
	× MR	M 4186.	$12,558 \times 4,186$
	+ MR	M 4186.	$52,567,788 + 4,186$
	÷ MR	M 4186.	$52,571,974 \div 4,186$
	=	M 12559.	The answer is 12,559.

28

Technology for Teachers

Calculators operate in various ways. It is important for you and your students to become familiar with how your calculators operate. In some lessons, you may wish to modify the approach to take into account the features of your specific model. All calculators have memory registers to store numbers and arithmetic operations, and to accumulate results. Many calculators also have at least one user-accessible memory that can store numbers for you to use later. If a calculator has more than one of these memory registers, you must indicate the "address" or number of the memory location you want to use. Each memory register can store only one number at a time. The number stored is the one most recently entered in that specific location. When a number is recalled from memory, it is copied into another calculator location to be used in calculations. Most calculators use either arithmetic or algebraic logic. A calculator using arithmetic logic performs operations in the order in which the numeral and symbols are entered. A calculator with an algebraic logical system performs operations in the same order used in mathematics. For example, if 5 + 2 × 3 = is entered, a calculator with arithmetic logic will add 5 + 2 = 7, and then multiply 7 × 3 = 21. A calculator with algebraic logic will multiply 2 × 3 = 6, and then add 5 + 6 = 11.

Store 45,788 in the memory of the calculator. Add 45,788 to each number.

1. 56,845 102,633   **2.** 123,377 169,165   **3.** 60,583 106,371   **4.** 987,445 1,033,233

Store 3,094 in the memory of the calculator. Subtract 3,094 from each number.

5. 4,096 1,002   **6.** 27,999 24,905   **7.** 5,000 1,906   **8.** 400,004 396,910

Solve.

9. $(482 \times 492) + 482$ 237,626   **10.** $(11,284 \div 1,612) + 1,612 + 1,612$ 3,231

11. $\dfrac{(1,788 \times 1,788) + 1,788}{1,788}$ 1,789   **12.** $\dfrac{(3 \times 2,491) + 2,491 + 2,491}{5}$ 2,491

Use the map to solve the problems below.

Automobile Touring Distances Between Some Western Cities

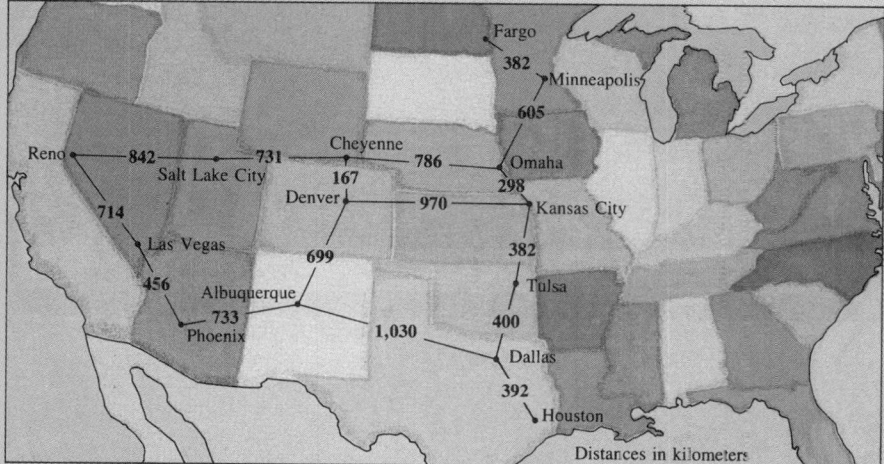

Distances in kilometers

13. How much greater is the distance from Minneapolis to Reno than the distance from Fargo to Houston? Hint: Find the distance from Fargo to Houston first and store it in the memory of the calculator. 505 km

14. How much greater is the distance of a journey from Reno to Cheyenne and Phoenix and on to Reno than the round trip from Omaha by way of Cheyenne, Albuquerque, Dallas, and Kansas City? 580 km

29

Using Page 29

Exercises 1—4 You may wish to have students estimate answers to check the reasonableness of the sum found on the calculator. If the answer on the calculator does not make sense, they should redo the problem.

Exercises 5—8 Remind students that the order in subtraction is important. They must enter the number given in the problem first and then subtract 3,094.

Exercises 9—12 In these exercises, students must decide which numbers to store in the calculator's memory. Numbers that appear more than once should be stored.

Exercises 13—14 Discuss finding distances on the map. The numbers between the cities give the distances in kilometers. Tell students to write the problems on paper before entering the numbers on the calculator. In exercise 13, find the distance from Fargo to Houston.

382 + 605 + 298 + 382 + 400 + 392 = 2,459

Next, store this result in memory, and find the distance from Minneapolis to Reno.

605 + 786 + 731 + 842 = 2,964

Then, find the difference by pressing [−] [MR] [=].

To find how much greater the round trip from Reno is in exercise 14, find the length of the round trip from Omaha.

786 + 167 + 699 + 1,030 + 400 + 382 + 298 = 3,762

Next store this distance in memory, and find the length of the trip from Reno.

842 + 731 + 167 + 699 + 733 + 456 + 714 = 4,342

Then subtract by pressing [−] [MR] [=].

Using Page 30

The exercises on the page provide practice for maintaining cumulative skills. The emphasis in this Cumulative Review is on place value (Chapter 1), adding and subtracting whole numbers (Chapter 1), and problem solving (Chapter 1).

Item Analysis The table below correlates the Cumulative Review items with objectives and with the student book pages on which the concepts or skills were taught.

Items	Objectives	Related Text Pages
1–2	1.1	2–5
3–4	1.2	6–9
5–6	1.3	10–11
7–12	1.4	2–15, 22
13–14	1.5	16–17, 20–21, 23

CUMULATIVE REVIEW

1. What is each group of three digits in a numeral called?

   Ⓐ a period   **B** a comma
   c a unit   **D** not given

2. What is the numeral for twenty thousand, eighty-six?

   A 2,086   Ⓑ 20,086
   c 20,860   **D** not given

3. Which is correct?

   A $2,748 < 2,497$ Ⓑ $27,500 > 25,709$
   c $83,409 < 81,999$ **D** not given

4. Round 386,729 to the nearest thousand.

   Ⓐ 387,000   **B** 390,000
   c 400,000   **D** not given

5. Estimate the sum. $38 + 42$

   A 70   Ⓑ 80
   c 90   **D** not given

6. Estimate the difference. $640 - 281$

   A 200   **B** 900
   c 400   Ⓓ not given

Find the sums.

7.   838
      576
   + 647
        A 2,051
        B 1,961
        Ⓒ 2,061
        D not given

8.   9,275
      1,866
      4,773
   + 8,495
        A 2,249
        Ⓑ 24,409
        c 21,049
        D not given

Find the differences.

9.   1,608
   −   923
        Ⓐ 685
        B 785
        c 325
        D not given

10.   6,100
    − 2,738
         A 4,638
         B 3,462
         c 4,662
         Ⓓ not given

11. Add.

       6,245,621
    + 4,952,912
         A 10,198,533
         B 11,197,533
         Ⓒ 11,198,533
         D not given

12. Subtract.

       10,655,961
    −   9,296,523
         A 1,369,448
         Ⓑ 1,359,438
         c 1,459,448
         D not given

13. During one year, a state issued 719,000 fishing licenses and 423,000 hunting licenses. What is the total number of licenses?

    Ⓐ 1,142,000   **B** 1,132,000
    c 11,420,000   **D** not given

14. A state issued 483,000 driver's licenses and 315,000 learner's permits. How many more driver's licenses were issued than learner's permits?

    A 68,000   **B** 172,000
    Ⓒ 168,000   **D** not given

Objectives

2.1 Read and write decimals and identify place value of digits in a decimal.

2.2 Compare, order, and round decimals.

2.3 Add and subtract decimals.

2.4 Estimate sums and differences of decimals by rounding.

2.5 Solve word problems using the 5-Point Checklist and cumulative computational skills.

Summary

The material in this chapter parallels the material in Chapter 1. The first lessons deal with decimal concepts of place value, rounding, and comparison. Place value for decimals is presented as an extension of place value for whole numbers. Decimals are presented without relating them to fractions at this time. This approach is sometimes called a fraction-free development of decimals.

The algorithms for adding and subtracting decimals are taught as simple extensions of the algorithms for adding and subtracting whole numbers. Lessons on rounding and comparing decimals prepare students for work in estimating sums and differences using decimals. Problem solving is extended to include addition and subtraction of decimals.

Mathematical Background

Place Value To help students understand place value for decimals, physical models such as the ones below are used.

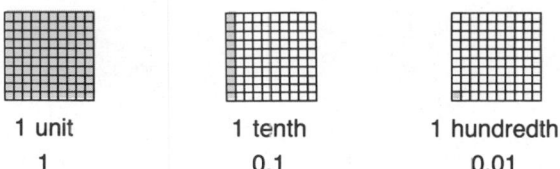

1 unit	1 tenth	1 hundredth
1	0.1	0.01

We can think of dividing the small square representing 1 hundredth into 10 equal parts. Each tenth of the 1 hundredth square would be 1 thousandth. In this manner, we can think of extending the place value chart to the right of the units place to include decimals.

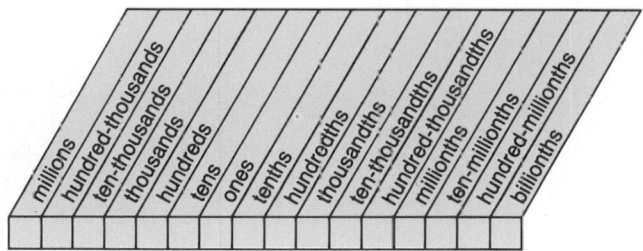

A thorough understanding of place value will help students round and compare decimals, as well as prepare them for estimation and computation with decimals.

Addition and Subtraction of Decimals Most students can understand that the computational algorithms for addition and subtraction of decimals are extensions of the algorithms used for addition and subtraction of whole numbers. However, some students may benefit from looking at place-value models of addition and subtraction of decimals. Use the sum of 1.6 plus 0.5 as an example. Combining 6 tenths and 5 tenths, we have 11 tenths or 1 unit and 1 tenth. Adding the 2 units gives us the sum of 2.1.

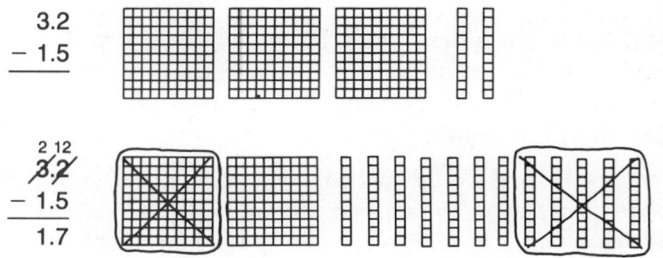

$$\begin{array}{r} 1.6 \\ + 0.5 \\ \hline 2.1 \end{array}$$

Subtraction can be modeled in a similar fashion. We use 3.2 minus 1.5 as an example. Since 5 tenths cannot be subtracted from 2 tenths, we trade 1 unit for 10 tenths which gives us 12 tenths. Subtracting 5 tenths from 12 tenths leaves 7 tenths. Next we subtract the units. There is 1 unit left so the difference is 1.7.

$$\begin{array}{r} 3.2 \\ - 1.5 \end{array}$$

$$\begin{array}{r} \overset{2\ 12}{\cancel{3.2}} \\ - 1.5 \\ \hline 1.7 \end{array}$$

Problem Solving Problem solving in this chapter is extended to include addition and subtraction of decimals as well as whole numbers. On page 47, students will solve problems that use data from advertisements. Problems involving time zones are featured on pages 48–49. Emphasis upon the various parts of the 5-Point Checklist should be made as these problem-solving lessons are taught. A new problem-solving strategy, Make an Organized List, is introduced on page 50.

Vocabulary

decimal	hundredths	1-digit accuracy
decimal point	thousandths	
tenths	millionths	

Teaching Tips

 ## Error Analysis

This chapter deals with decimal concepts and operations with decimals. A solid understanding of place value and the Hindu-Arabic numeration system as it applies to whole numbers is basic for the development of concepts of tenths, hundredths, and thousandths. Hopefully this can be seen as an extension of the numeration system previously studied.

Decimal operations parallel those of whole numbers. Very often, many of the same errors are found in the computational work. Some common errors using decimals are listed below.

Error Pattern 1

0.3	0.4	0.9	0.7
+ 0.9	+ 0.7	+ 0.9	+ 0.8
.12	.11	.18	.15

Diagnosis The student added correctly but placed the decimal point incorrectly. The decimal point has been placed to the left of all digits in the answer, just as they appear in the addends.

Remediation Review the rules for regrouping hundredths to tenths, tenths to ones, and ones to tens. For example, 13 tenths can be exchanged for 1 unit and 3 tenths. Use place-value models to show the regrouping if necessary.

Error Pattern 2

3.69	5.32	7.18
− 2.8	− 4.3	− 3.5
1.1	1.9	4.3

Diagnosis The student does not annex a zero in the hundredths place in the subtrahend before subtracting. Places are therefore not aligned properly and the student subtracts the tenths place from the hundredths place.

Remediation Have the students use graph paper to help line up the places correctly, annexing zeros as needed. Go through the steps in the algorithm, emphasizing that hundredths are subtracted from hundredths, tenths are subtracted from tenths, and so on.

	3	.	6	9
−	2	.	8	0

Error Pattern 3

0.5 < 0.256   0.2 < 0.18   0.7 < 0.302

Diagnosis The student has compared the decimals by counting the number of decimal places; the decimal with the greater number of places is thought to be the greater decimal.

Remediation Have the student annex zeros to make the decimals have the same number of decimal places. Go through the steps in the procedure of comparing decimals. Point out that we begin at the left and compare each digit. The first place having different digits is used to select the larger decimal.

 ## Problem Solving

Using the 5-Point Checklist

Throughout the Addison-Wesley math program, a 5-step plan is presented in the text as a guide for solving problems. The five steps are: 1) Understand the *Question*, 2) Find the needed *Data*, 3) *Plan* what to do, 4) Find the *Answer*, and 5) *Check* back. This plan is intended to guide a student's thinking by drawing attention to the key actions that need to be taken and the key decisions that must be made when solving problems. Successful problem solving is not guaranteed by the use of this plan. It provides a useful framework for attacking problems and for discussing problems and their solutions. You should also recognize the cyclic nature of the plan. For example, if students are nearing the answer but reach an impasse, encourage them to return to an earlier step in order to continue their work toward a solution.

Many teachers find it helpful to make a bulletin-board display using the checklist theme. Students can then refer to this guide in solving problems on their own. Or, the bulletin-board display can be used as the focal point of a class discussion of a problem. Here is a sample bulletin-board display.

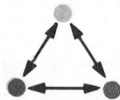

Special Education

The special students in your class may benefit from your use of the following ideas in presenting the decimal concepts and skills of the chapter.

Use Color to Cue

Color can be used as a visual cue for those with memory or auditory problems. If carefully presented, color can help most other students as well, particularly those who are strong visual learners. Two important uses of color for special students occur in early work with decimals.

- Visually emphasizing the "th" sound for ten<u>ths</u>, hundred<u>ths</u>, and other decimal names.

0.7
seven ten<u>ths</u>

- Cueing students to say the correct decimal name by visually associating the number of zeros and the number of decimal places, as in the following diagrams.

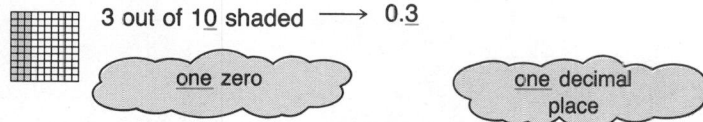

3 out of 1<u>0</u> shaded ⟶ 0.<u>3</u>

<u>one</u> zero   <u>one</u> decimal place

"When you see or write one decimal place, say tenths."

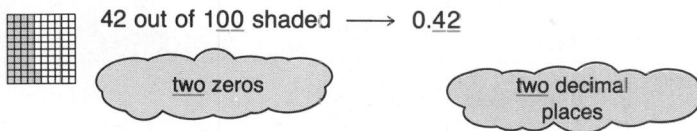

42 out of 1<u>00</u> shaded ⟶ 0.<u>42</u>

<u>two</u> zeros   <u>two</u> decimal places

"When you see or write two decimal places, say hundredths."

Color cueing can also be used when comparing or rounding decimals, in a manner similar to that suggested in the Chapter 1 Teaching Tips for whole numbers.

Visual/Auditory Reinforcement

Provide a deck of cards like those shown and a calculator. Students, working independently or in pairs, draw the cards one at a time and punch the number into the calculator. Then they can compare the visual calculator display with the decimal written on the back of the card. Encourage students to keep a record of the number of correct answers for a given time period and to work to improve that record at another time.

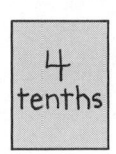
4
tenths

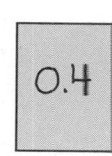
0.4

Draw a card   Punch to show   Turn card to check

A variation of this activity can be used to build auditory memory and association skills. Read (or have the student read) the cards into a tape recorder. Then, at playback, the student listens, punches the number heard, and then uses the card deck to check.

Finger Trace

If necessary, have students finger trace as suggested in the Chapter 1 Teaching Tips. Finger tracing will help students round and compare decimals, eliminate confusion over the > and < symbols, and focus on the correct operation in exercises of mixed addition and subtraction.

Cross Out Means 10

If students are still struggling with column addition, allow them to use the following cross-out technique. As shown, they add down a column until a 2-digit sum is reached (4 + 9 = 13). The last digit, 9, is crossed out to represent 10 (of the 13). The student mentally retains the 3 and adds it to 8, with the cross-out idea being repeated. When a column is added, the number of cross outs is the number regrouped. If students reverse digits or have trouble remembering, they can write each digit that is retained, as in the second figure.

$$\begin{array}{r} \overset{2}{} \\ 0.64 \\ 0.59 \\ +\,0.88 \\ \hline 1 \end{array} \qquad \begin{array}{r} \overset{2}{} \\ 0.64 \\ 0.59\,3 \\ +\,0.88 \\ \hline \end{array}$$

Special Help for Subtraction

Some special students may still have difficulty with subtraction involving minuends similar to the one shown. Have students shade squares to show, for example, that 0.2 = 0.20; then encourage them to annex the 0 in the minuend before computing problems of this type.

$$\begin{array}{r} 84.2 \\ -\ 6.27 \end{array} \longrightarrow \begin{array}{r} 84.20 \\ -\ 6.27 \end{array}$$

Subject Integration

Subject matter related to other areas of the curriculum has been integrated into the following lessons. This provides an opportunity to highlight the interaction between mathematics and other subjects.

Consumer Awareness Advertisements, page 47
Science Genetics, electron microscope, pages 34–35; astronomy, pages 38–39
Social Studies Foreign currency, pages 40–41
History Typography, page 31
Physical Education Basketball, pages 36–37; tennis, baseball, hockey, golf, pages 42–43

Teaching Chapter 2				Meeting Individual Needs					
Objectives	Chapter Content	Pages	TRB Test Items	Lesson Assignments			Follow Up		
				Minimum	Average	Extended	Reteaching	Enrichment	Practice
	Chapter Opener	31							
2.1 Read and write decimals and identify place value of digits in a decimal.	Tenths and Hundredths	32–33	1–4	1–20	1–20, 22	1–22	SE6 Ch 3		PS 12
	Decimal Place Value	34–35	5–8	1–18, SK	1–21, SK	1–22, SK	SE6 Ch 3 RS 9	ES 9	PS 13
2.2 Compare, order, and round decimals.	Comparing and Ordering Decimals	36–37	9–16	1–29	1–32, TM	2–28 even, 29–32 TM	SE6 Ch 3 RS 10	ES 10	MP 419 PS 14
	Rounding Decimals	38–39	17–19	1–41, SK	1–41 44, SK	1–43 odd, 44, SK	SE6 Ch 3 RS 11	ES 11	MP 419 PS 15
2.3 Add and subtract decimals.	Adding Decimals	40–41	20–29	1–30	1–36	1–35 odd, 36–39	SE6 Ch 3 RS 12	ES 12	MP 419 PS 16
	Subtracting Decimals	42–43		1–30	1–35, TM	1–35 odd, 36, TM	SE6 Ch 3 RS 13	ES 13	MP 420 PS 17
2.4 Estimate sums and differences of decimals by rounding.	Estimating Sums and Differences with Decimals	44–45	30–37	1–20, 32	1–30, 32	2–30 even, 31–32	SE6 Ch 3 RS 14	ES 14	MP 420 PS 18
	Skills Practice	46		1–35	1–45	1–45 odd			
2.5 Solve word problems using the 5-Point Checklist and cumulative computational skills.	Problem Solving: Using Data from an Advertisement	47	38–42	1–6	1–9	1–10	SE6 Ch 12 RS 15	ES 15	PS 19
	Problem Solving: Using Data from a Map	48–49		1–10		1–2, 7–15			PS 20
	Problem Solving: Make an Organized List	50							
	Chapter Review/Test	51							
	Another Look/ Enrichment	52–53							
	Cumulative Review	54							

SE6 Student Edition, Book 6
RS Reteaching Supplement
ES Enrichment Supplement
PS Practice Supplement
MP More Practice
TM Think Math
SK Skillkeeper
TRB Teacher's Resource Book

Masters for use

. . . before Chapter 2

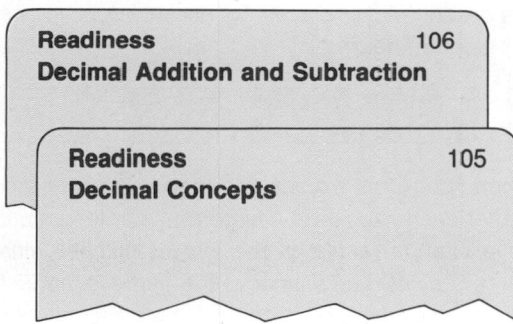

Readiness	106
Decimal Addition and Subtraction	

Readiness	105
Decimal Concepts	

. . . during Chapter 2

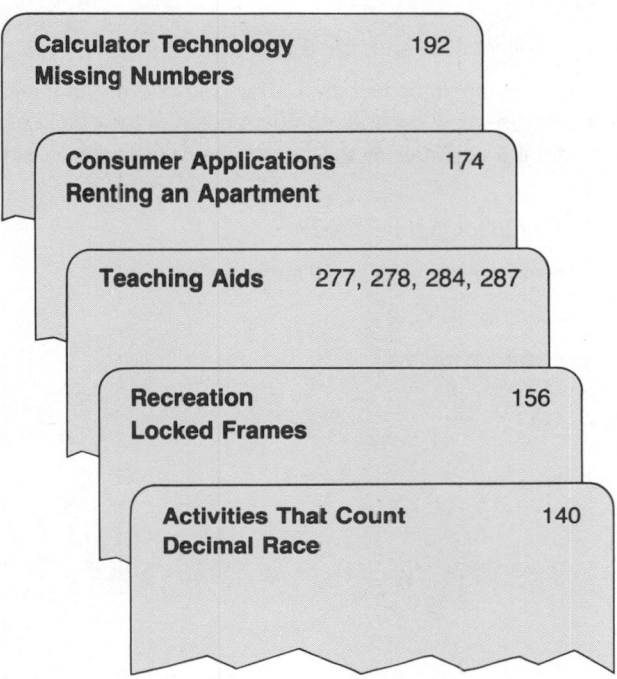

Calculator Technology	192
Missing Numbers	

Consumer Applications	174
Renting an Apartment	

Teaching Aids	277, 278, 284, 287

Recreation	156
Locked Frames	

Activities That Count	140
Decimal Race	

. . . after Chapter 2

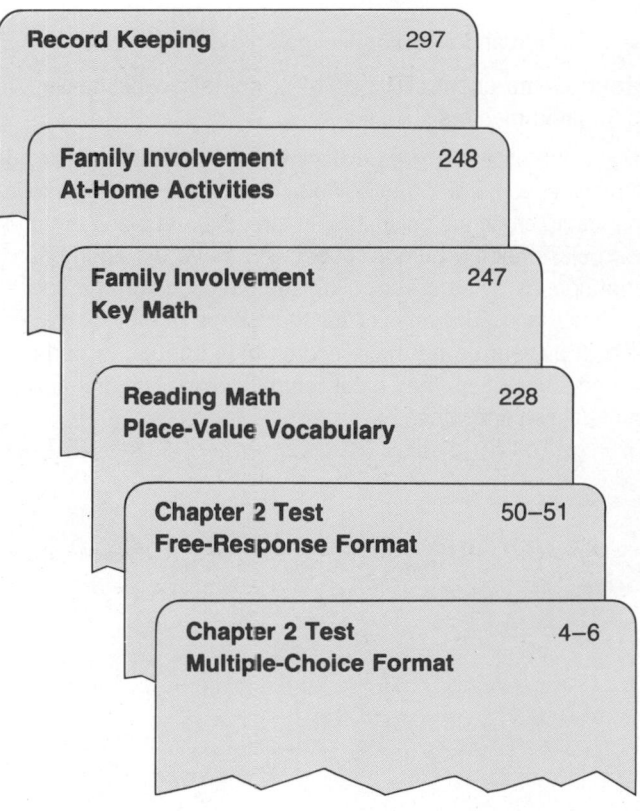

Record Keeping	297

Family Involvement	248
At-Home Activities	

Family Involvement	247
Key Math	

Reading Math	228
Place-Value Vocabulary	

Chapter 2 Test	50–51
Free-Response Format	

Chapter 2 Test	4–6
Multiple-Choice Format	

Supplements

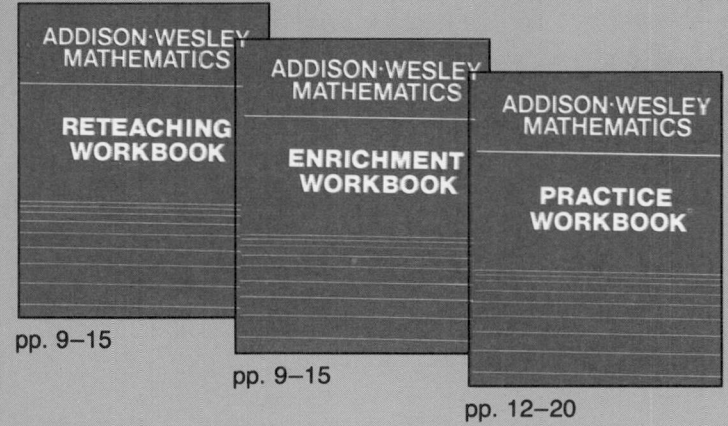

ADDISON·WESLEY MATHEMATICS
RETEACHING WORKBOOK
pp. 9–15

ADDISON·WESLEY MATHEMATICS
ENRICHMENT WORKBOOK
pp. 9–15

ADDISON·WESLEY MATHEMATICS
PRACTICE WORKBOOK
pp. 12–20

Other Addison-Wesley Resources

Books and Kits

Skillseekers III ⊕ 1–3, ⊖ 4–6

General Mathematics: Making Practice Fun 5A, 5B, 7, 11, 12B

Arithmetic Primer pp. 222–231, 270–272

Problem-Solving Experiences in Mathematics, Grade 7
Problems 2, 8, 13, 14, ⁻5, 47, 48, 49, 50, 68, 73, 83, 93, 99, 103, 108, 120, 125

Technology

Computer Math Activities Volumes 1–5
Computer Math Games Volumes 1, 2, 4, 6

Activities That Count are designed for use throughout this chapter and subsequent chapters. Before beginning Chapter 2, you may wish to review these activities and select the ones you consider appropriate for your class.

Decimal Race   Game

Purpose   To add and subtract decimals

Materials   Game sheet (TRB p. 140), number cube labeled 1 through 6, game markers

Activity   Have students write a decimal and a symbol (+ or −) in each blank space of the game sheet. The object of the game is to be the first to cross the finish line. In turn, players place a game marker on start, roll the number cube, and move the appropriate number of spaces. They are to follow the directions on the space on which they land. The answer for that space is their score for the round. If players do not have scores high enough to perform an indicated subtraction, they must return to start. The first player to cross the finish line wins.

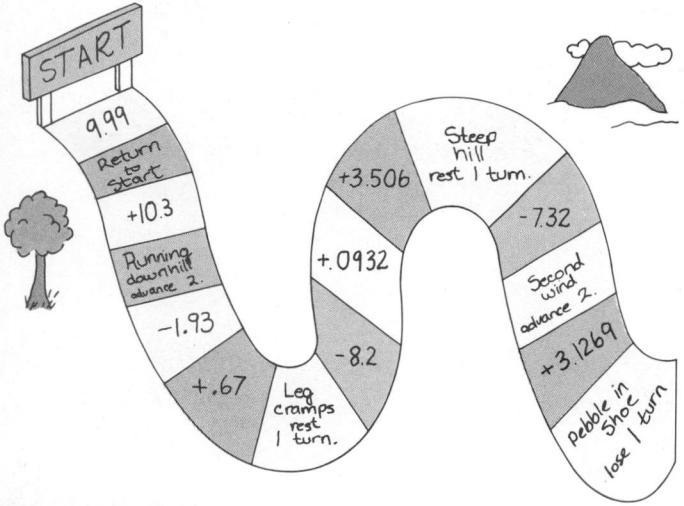

Block Patterns   Math Lab

Purpose   To use logical reasoning and space perception

Materials   Cube pattern (TRB p. 278)

Activity   Have students letter the faces of four cube patterns exactly as shown. Then have them cut out the patterns and fold and tape the edges together to form cubes. Next, students should try and stack the four cubes so that **1)** the word MATH appears on one side of the stack, **2)** the other three sides each form a 3 or 4 letter word, and **3)** all four sides together spell out a sentence.

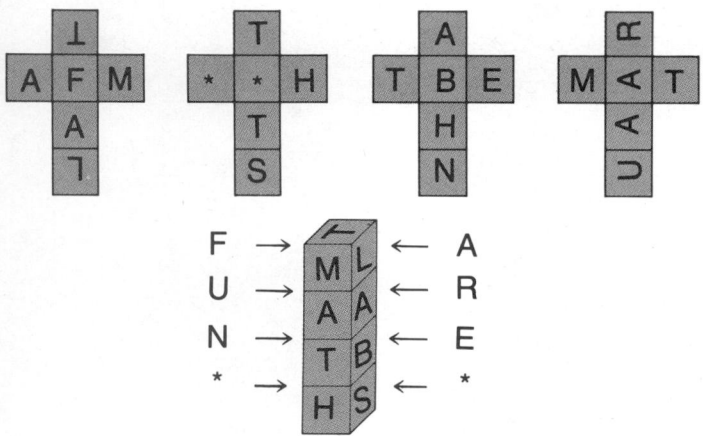

Digit Exchange   Game

Purpose   To use place value ideas and compare numbers

Materials   10 index cards, labeled 0 through 9, a marker to represent a decimal point

Activity   After mixing the cards, the first player places five of them in a row. The second player places the decimal point in one of 4 positions, as illustrated below:

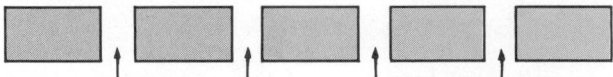

The two players then take turns exchanging the positions of any two digits so that after each exchange a larger number is formed. The player whose exchange results in the largest number wins the round and scores a point. The winner of the game is the first player to score 10.

Decimal Data   Project

Purpose   To collect data and round decimals

Activity   Have students collect data related to one of the topics below. Ask them to show decimal numbers given in their sources, and then round the decimals to the nearest whole number, tenth, or hundredth.

- Rainfall records for a state or city
- Record times or distances for Olympic events
- Speed records for aircraft
- Density of various metals

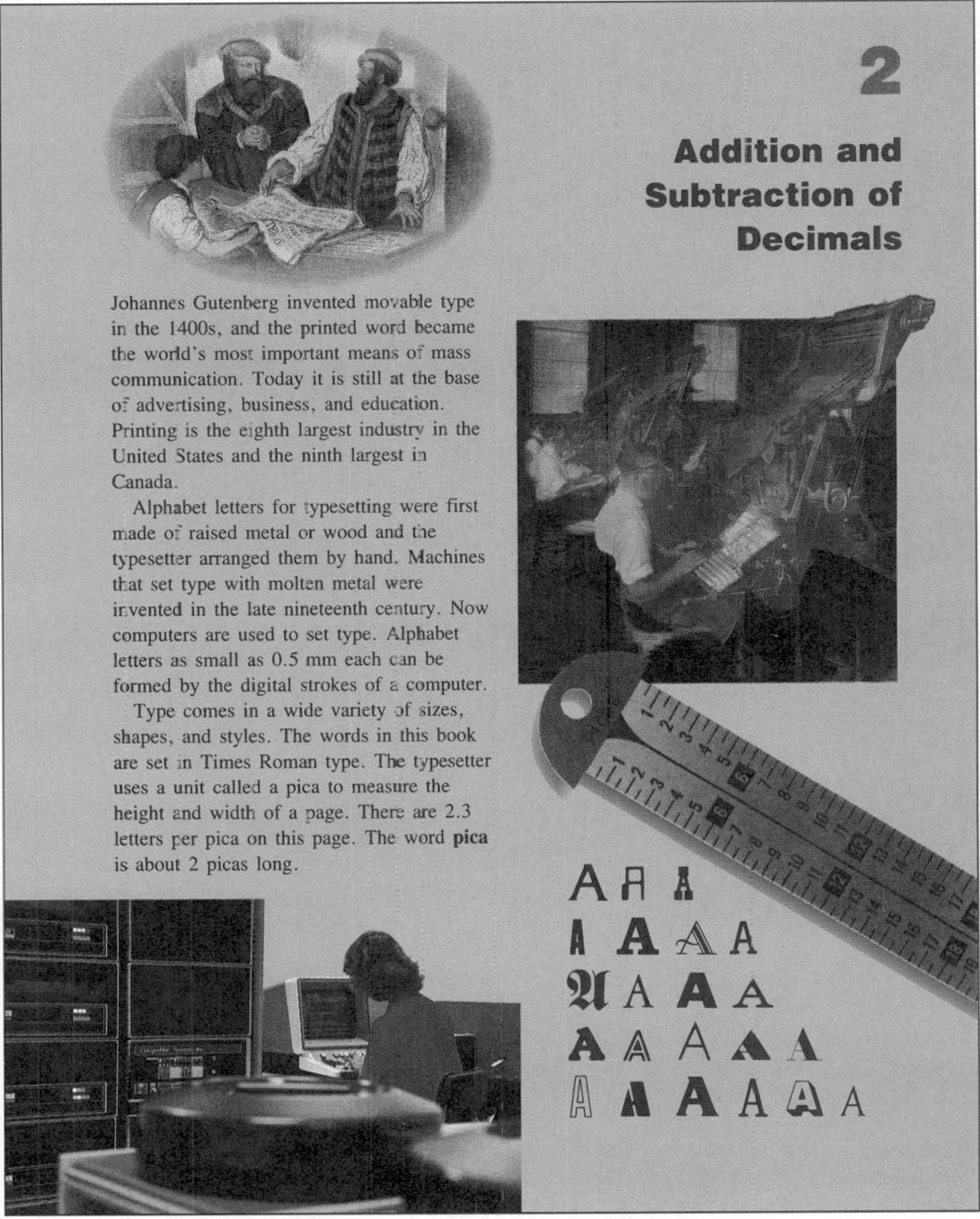

2

Addition and Subtraction of Decimals

Johannes Gutenberg invented movable type in the 1400s, and the printed word became the world's most important means of mass communication. Today it is still at the base of advertising, business, and education. Printing is the eighth largest industry in the United States and the ninth largest in Canada.

Alphabet letters for typesetting were first made of raised metal or wood and the typesetter arranged them by hand. Machines that set type with molten metal were invented in the late nineteenth century. Now computers are used to set type. Alphabet letters as small as 0.5 mm each can be formed by the digital strokes of a computer.

Type comes in a wide variety of sizes, shapes, and styles. The words in this book are set in Times Roman type. The typesetter uses a unit called a pica to measure the height and width of a page. There are 2.3 letters per pica on this page. The word **pica** is about 2 picas long.

Introducing the Chapter

Discussion After students have had an opportunity to examine the pictures and read the accompanying material, discuss some of the data that is given. "About how many years ago did Gutenberg invent movable type?" (500) "When were machines that set type with molten metal invented?" (late nineteenth century) "About how many years ago was that?" (100) "What is the unit used by the typesetter to measure the height and width of a page?" (pica) This is an opportunity for students to create their own questions based on the data in the article.

As you teach the chapter, you may wish to refer back to this page and discuss the questions below. Review the contents of the article briefly before posing the questions.

Follow-Up Questions

After Page 35 Very small alphabet letters can be formed by the digital strokes of a computer. What size are these small letters? (five tenths mm or zero point five mm) How many letters per pica are on page 31? (two and three tenths or two point three)

After Page 39 In the type used for the chapter title, there are 1.56 letters per pica. What is this number rounded to the nearest tenth? (1.6)

After Page 43 How many more letters per pica are in the text than in the chapter title? (0.71)

After Page 45 A typesetter today can earn $12.50 per hour. In 1930, a typesetter earned about $1.20 per hour. Estimate how much more per hour a typesetter earns today.

Quick Review Have students supply numbers that meet these requirements:
6-digit number with 3 thousands and 4 tens
8-digit number with 7 millions, 6 hundred thousands, 5 hundreds
5-digit number with 2 ten thousands, 9 ones.

Lesson Focus To read and write decimals in tenths and hundredths

Suggested Materials Centimeter graph paper (TRB p. 284)

Ideas for Getting Started

Draw two squares on the chalkboard or overhead projector as shown below.

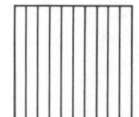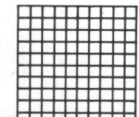

Elicit from students that the square on the left is divided into 10 equal parts, or tenths, and the square on the right is divided into 100 equal parts, or hundredths. Point out that each square is one unit. Ask students which is greater, 1 tenth or 1 hundredth?

Shade in parts of the squares and have students tell which part of each unit square is shaded. For each example, write the word name and the decimal on the chalkboard.

1 tenth—0.1	12 hundredths—0.12
1 hundredth—0.01	6 tenths—0.6
3 tenths—0.3	25 hundredths—0.25

Use the last example to show that 0.25 means 2 tenths + 5 hundredths or 0.2 + 0.05.

Ask students to outline some 10 by 10 squares on their graph paper. Then read aloud these decimals and have students shade in the appropriate part of a square.

0.4	0.23	0.07	0.5
0.63	0.9	0.75	0.99

Using Page 32

Lesson Development After students read the material at the top of the page, discuss the models showing tenths and hundredths of a unit. Point out that when writing decimals for numbers less than 1, we place a 0 in the ones place. This helps alert us to the location of the decimal point. If the decimal 0.45 were written as .45, the decimal point could be overlooked and the number thought to be the whole number 45.

In discussing the models representing 1.2 and 2.54, stress the use of *and* to communicate the location of the decimal point. Direct the students' attention to the squares showing 0.4 and 0.40 at the bottom of the page. "What part of the tenths square is shaded?" (0.4) "What part of the hundredths square is shaded?" (0.40) "Which is greater, 0.4 or 0.40?" (They are equal). Explain that decimals such as 0.4 and 0.40 are equivalent since they represent the same part of a unit square.

Tenths and Hundredths

There is often a need for numbers other than whole numbers. The newspaper headlines show some numbers that are called **decimals**.

10 equal parts	100 equal parts
3 parts shaded	3 parts shaded
3 **tenths** shaded	3 **hundredths** shaded
0.3 shaded	0.03 shaded

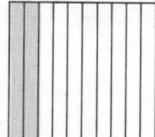  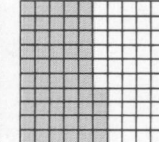

1 and 2 tenths shaded
1.2 shaded

2 and 54 hundredths shaded
2.54 shaded

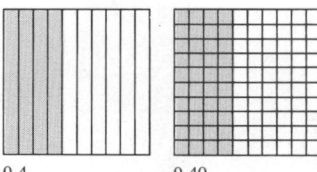 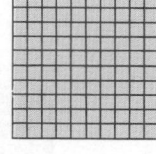

0.4   0.40

The same part is shaded.
0.4 = 0.40

100 hundredths shaded
10 tenths shaded
1 whole unit shaded
1.00 = 1.0 = 1

32

Follow Up

Reteaching

Use place-value models to illustrate decimals. Name the hundred-square as the unit. Then each ten-stick becomes 1 tenth and each unit-cube becomes 1 hundredth. Place 5 ten-sticks on the desk and ask how many tenths there are. Write 0.5 on the chalkboard. Continue representing decimals using the ten-sticks and unit-cubes. Have students practice both reading and writing tenths and hundredths.

Enrichment

Display these sequences on the chalkboard and have students write the next four decimals in each sequence.

1. 0.01, 0.02, 0.03, 0.04, . . .
   0.05, 0.06, 0.07, 0.08
2. 0.6, 0.7, 0.8, 0.9, . . .
   1.0, 1.1, 1.2, 1.3
3. 0.03, 0.13, 0.23, 0.33, . . .
   0.43, 0.53, 0.63, 0.73
4. 1.14, 1.16, 1.18, 1.20, . . .
   1.22, 1.24, 1.26, 1.28
5. 0.05. 0.10, 0.15, 0.20, . . .
   0.25, 0.30, 0.35, 0.40
6. 0.77, 0.83, 0.89, 0.95, . . .
   1.01, 1.07, 1.13, 1.19

Assignment Guide			
	Minimum	Average	Extended
page 33	1–20	1–20, 22	1–22

Write a decimal for the part shaded.

1.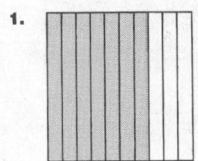
0.7

2.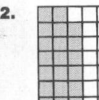
0.29

3.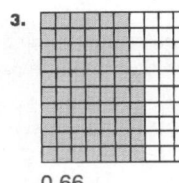
0.66

4.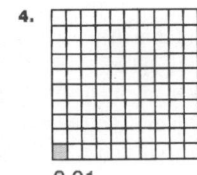
0.01

5.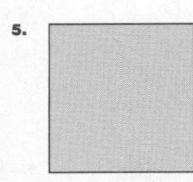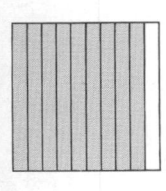
1.9

6.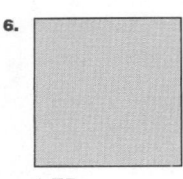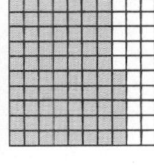
1.75

Write the decimal.

7. 3 and 5 tenths 3.5

8. 16 and 52 hundredths 16.52

9. 2 tenths 0.2

10. 3 and 16 hundredths 3.16

11. 90 hundredths 0.90

12. 47 hundredths 0.47

13. 10 and 7 hundredths 10.07

14. 15 and 5 tenths 15.5

15. 2 and 21 hundredths 2.21

16. 2 hundredths 0.02

17. 32 and 2 hundredths 32.02

18. 32 hundredths 0.32

19. How many tenths are shaded? 0.2
How many hundredths are shaded? 0.20

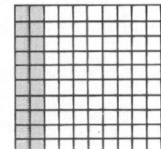

20. What part is shaded? 0.67
What part is not shaded? 0.33

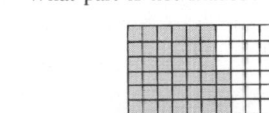

★ **21.** What part is shaded? Write the decimal.
0.42

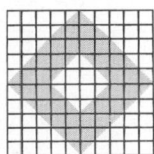

22. **DATA HUNT** What part of the letters used in printing newspaper or magazine articles are vowels? To find out, count off 100 letters in a newspaper or magazine. Count the number of vowels in the 100 letters. Write your answer as a decimal. Answers will vary. See teaching notes.

33

Using Page 33

Exercise 21 This exercise involves counting squares and half-squares. A useful strategy in this problem is to count the unshaded squares and subtract from 100. The 4 unshaded corners together make 50 small squares. The small unshaded square in the center is 8 squares, giving us a total of 58 squares. Since 100 − 58 = 42, 0.42 of the unit square is shaded.

Data Hunt Most of the student samples for this Data Hunt will fall between 0.35 and 0.40. Students who find significant variations from this range may have some interesting words in their selections.

Ideas That Work

Special Education

Let students form groups of 2 or 3 and work on the "Draw and Shade" activity. They will need graph paper (TRB p. 284), 20 index cards labeled with tenths and hundredths as shown below, and an envelope for the cards. Students should outline 10 by 10 squares on the graph paper.

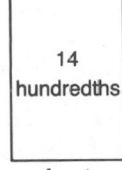
14 hundredths
front

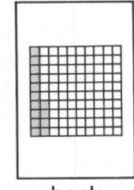
back

The cards should be mixed and placed in the envelope. One student draws a card, shows it, and reads it aloud. Players shade parts of a square to illustrate the decimal named, and then turn the card over to check.
Variations:

- Draw a card and write the decimal.

- Use the back side of the cards first. Draw a card and write the decimal.

- Use the back side of the cards first. Draw a card and name aloud the decimal.

Practice Supplement, page 12

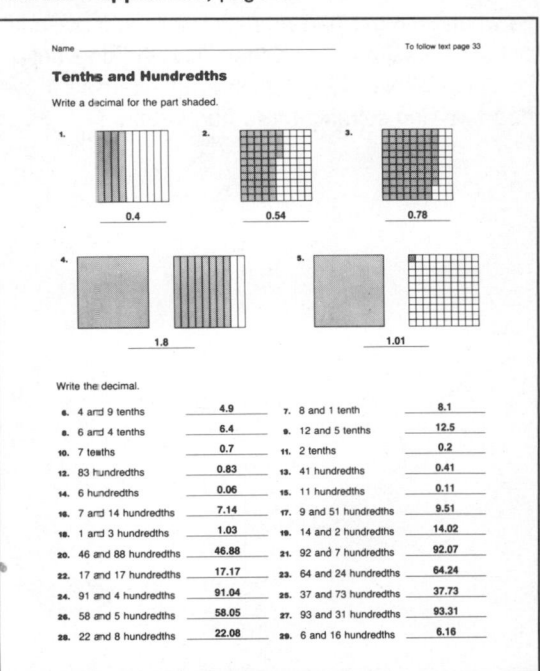

Quick Review Have students arrange each expanded numeral below in proper order and then write the standard numeral.

5 + 20,000 + 40 **20,045**   400 + 70,000 + 60 + 8,000 + 1 **78,461**

70 + 30,000 + 4,000,000 + 9 **4,030,079**   300 + 90,000 + 10 **90,310**

Lesson Focus To read and write decimals through millionths

Ideas for Getting Started

Display this place-value chart on the chalkboard.

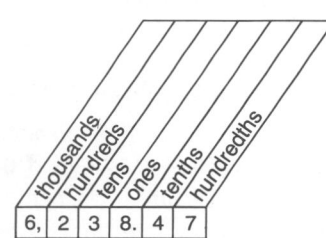

Have students give the place value of each digit in the decimal. Then read the following numbers and have selected students write the digits in the appropriate columns.

1.3   12.47   152.8   0.53   1,247.2   347.63

Tell students that today they will learn how the place-value system can be extended to places beyond hundredths.

Using Page 34

Lesson Development Ask students to read the material at the top of the page and study the place-value chart below. Point out that each place in a decimal is ten times the place to its right and one tenth as large as the place to its left.

Explain that it is common practice in reading or checking decimal numerals to simply read each digit and use the word "point" for the decimal point. Thus, "three point zero six" means 3.06.

Warm Up To help students read the decimals, give the following instructions: For decimals less than 1, read as for whole numbers and then attach the place value name of the last decimal place. For example, in exercise 2 we read "six thousand one hundred twenty-eight ten-thousandths."

For decimals involving whole number parts, read the whole number part as usual, followed by "and" for the decimal point, and then read the decimal as explained above. For example, in exercise 1 we read "two and seventy-three hundredths."

Decimal Place Value

Martin Thomas is a genetic scientist. With the aid of an electron microscope, Martin can see parts of cells magnified thousands of times. The ribosome particle found in a cell is 0.000002 cm in diameter.

To read this number, we can extend the idea of place value to decimals. Each place in the decimal is 10 times the place to its right.

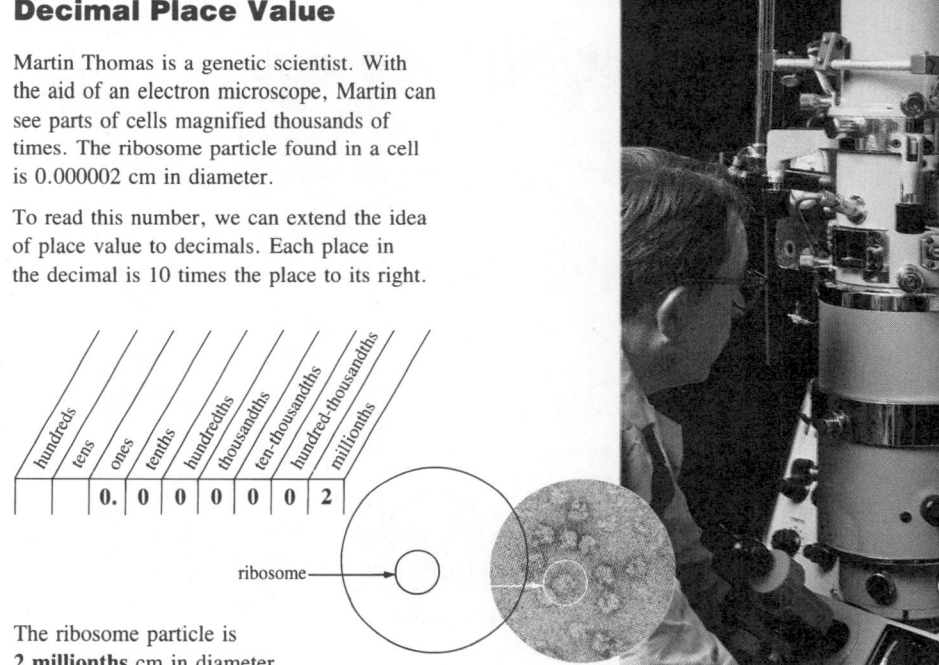

ribosome

The ribosome particle is **2 millionths** cm in diameter.

Decimal numeral: 36.284

Read: "thirty-six **and** two hundred eighty-four **thousandths**"

We do not always have to use place-value names. We can read each digit and read the decimal as **point**.

6.9547 "six **point** nine five four seven"

0.0339 "zero **point** zero three three nine"

Other Examples

5.2840   five **and** two thousand, eight hundred forty **ten-thousandths**

0.0100   one hundred **ten-thousandths**

0.03912   three thousand, nine hundred twelve **hundred-thousandths**

100.010   one hundred **and** ten **thousandths**

Warm Up

Read both ways. See teaching notes.

1. 2.73   2. 0.6128   3. 19.73764   4. 0.08395

5. 0.0650   6. 37.037   7. 243.010   8. 0.000093

34

Follow Up

Reteaching

Display a place-value chart (TRB p. 277) on the chalkboard or the overhead projector. Write a whole number such as 327 in the chart. Point out that the last digit to the right is in the ones place; hence, the number will be named as ones.

Next use the example of 0.32. Notice with students the place value of the 2, the last digit to the right. It is in the hundredths place, so 0.32 is read as hundredths. Continue using other examples.

Enrichment

Have students write each of the following decimals in words.

213.659   **two hundred thirteen and six hundred fifty-nine thousandths**

0.4985   **four thousand nine hundred eighty-five ten-thousandths**

0.0013   **thirteen ten-thousandths**

18.2597   **eighteen and two thousand five hundred ninety-seven ten-thousandths**

Assignment Guide			
	Minimum	Average	Extended
page 35	1–18, SK	1–21, SK	1–22, SK

Write the decimal.

1. sixteen and four hundred twenty-five thousandths 16.425

2. three thousand, sixty-six ten-thousandths 0.3066

3. fifty-two thousand, eight hundred nine hundred-thousandths 0.52809

4. fourteen ten-thousandths 0.0014

5. sixty-three thousand, four hundred twelve hundred-thousandths 0.63412

6. one hundred ninety-five millionths 0.000195

7. eighteen point four six two seven 18.4627

8. one thousand, twenty-seven and eight hundredths 1,027.08

9. eight hundred one and one hundred eight thousandths 801.108

10. sixty-five hundred-thousandths 0.00065

11. nine hundred forty-one ten-thousandths 0.0941

12. seventy millionths 0.000070

Give the place value of each underlined digit.

Example: 2.13<u>5</u>6   Answer: 0.005

13. 6.2<u>7</u> 0.07   **14.** 0.<u>7</u>14 0.7   **15.** 0.187<u>5</u> 0.0005   **16.** 5.6<u>9</u>2 0.09

17. 23.09<u>1</u> 0.001   **18.** <u>2</u>84.7 200   **19.** 0.000019<u>6</u> 0.000009   **20.** 3.3458<u>7</u> 0.00007

21. The human eye can see particles that are about one ten-thousandth of a meter in diameter. Write this number as a decimal. 0.0001

★ **22.** A field ion microscope can magnify a million times so that an atom that is twenty-seven billionths of a centimeter in diameter can be seen. Write this number as a decimal. 0.000000027

SKILLKEEPER

1. 629 + 597 1,226	**2.** 804 − 369 435	**3.** 567 827 + 904 2,298	**4.** 2,663 6,801 + 5,353 14,817	**5.** 54,683 95,347 + 38,845 188,875
6. 742 − 356 386	**7.** 9,304 − 4,665 4,639	**8.** 2,384 + 6,388 8,772	**9.** 23,000 − 18,374 4,626	**10.** 512,508 − 129,742 382,766

35

Using Page 35

Exercises 13–20 Students have had practice reading the place value of a digit at the end of a number. These exercises now ask them to give the value of the indicated digit in a number. Before assigning exercises 13–20, make certain students understand the example. "In what place is the digit 5?" (thousandths place) "What does the 5 represent?" (5 thousandths or 0.005)

Exercise 22 In order to answer exercise 22, students will need to extend the idea of place value to include billionths.

Skillkeeper This skill was originally taught in Chapter 1.

Reteaching Supplement, page 9   **Enrichment Supplement,** page 9   **Practice Supplement,** page 13

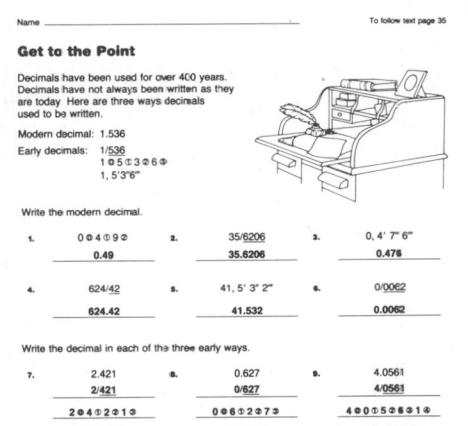

Lesson Focus To compare two decimals using the symbols of inequality (> and <) and to order decimals

Ideas for Getting Started

Write these pairs of numbers on the chalkboard. Have students choose the correct symbol, > or <, to complete each statement.

2,704 ◯ 2,905   101,011 ◯ 101,101
38,369 ◯ 38,254   67,499 ◯ 68,949

Using Page 36

Motivational Problem Have students read the problem at the top of the page. "The problem asks which team made the greater part of their shots. What part of their shots did the Cougars make?" (0.322) "What part of their shots did the Lions make?" (0.325) Explain that since the question asks us which team made the greater part of its shots, our plan is to compare the decimals.

Lesson Development On the chalkboard, work through each step shown in the instruction lines. "How many tenths are in each decimal?" (3) "How many hundredths are in each decimal?" (2) "How many thousandths are in each decimal?" (2 and 5) Explain to students that in this case the number of thousandths tells which number is greater. Since 5 > 2, 0.325 > 0.322. Hence, the Lions made the greater part of their shots.

Other Examples Call attention to the second example of 0.273 and 0.27. Point out that when decimals do not have the same number of places, we can *annex,* or add, zeros to the right of the last decimal place. In this case, the two decimals will have the same number of places after we annex one zero to 0.27, giving us 0.270. Comparing the digits in the thousandths place, we have 3 > 0. Therefore, 0.273 > 0.270.

Warm Up In exercises 1–4, have selected students write the comparison of the number pairs on the chalkboard, using the symbols > and <. Use exercises 5–8 as an oral class activity.

Comparing and Ordering Decimals

The Cougars made 0.322 of their shots in a basketball game. The Lions made 0.325 of their shots. Which team made the greater part of their shots?

To compare the decimals, follow the steps below.

Start at the left and compare the digits in the same place.	Compare the digits in the first place where they are different.	The numbers compare the same way the digits compare.

0.322   0.322   0.325 > 0.322
0.325   0.325

5 > 2

The Lions made the greater part of their shots.

Other Examples

1.07 < 1.6   0.273 > 0.27   26.3175 < 26.3775
  0 < 6   3 > 0   1 < 7

Warm Up

Write > or < for each ●.

1. 2.736 ● 2.716 **>**   2. 0.660 ● 0.693 **<**   3. 0.007 ● 0.070 **<**   4. 24.95 ● 23.95 **>**

Give the decimals in order from least to greatest.

5. 0.068 0.065   6. 3.155 3.15   7. 0.0084 0.0084   8. 5.7762 5.7759
   0.065 0.068   3.182 3.155   0.0089 0.0089   5.7759 5.7762
   0.605 0.605   3.15 3.182   0.0189 0.0189   5.7852 5.7852

36

Follow Up

Reteaching

Write 0.26 and 0.29 on the chalkboard. Use place-value models to represent these amounts, again using the hundred-square as the unit. Start with the tenths and compare. Each of the decimals has a 2, so move to the hundredths. Since 9 > 6, 0.29 > 0.26. Represent other decimals with the models and compare them in the same way.

Enrichment

Write the following pairs of decimals on the chalkboard. Have students write three decimals between each pair. These three decimals should have the same number of decimal places as the given pair.

0.4 and 0.8   **0.5, 0.6, 0.7**

6.09 and 6.13   **6.10, 6.11, 6.12**

0.71 and 0.75   **0.72, 0.73, 0.74**

25.62 and 25.66   **25.63, 25.64, 25.65**

0.20 and 0.24   **0.21, 0.22, 0.23**

10.6 and 11.0   **10.7, 10.8, 10.9**

Assignment Guide

	Minimum	Average	Extended
page 37	1–29	1–32, TM	2–28 even, 29–32, TM

Write >, =, or < for each ◐.

1. 0.83 ◐ 0.87 <
2. 0.4 ◐ 0.2 >
3. 0.715 ◐ 0.725 <
4. 2.73 ◐ 2.92 <
5. 0.667 ◐ 0.677 <
6. 0.35 ◐ 0.350 =
7. 0.04 ◐ 0.40 <
8. 12.46 ◐ 12.046 >
9. 6.46 ◐ 6.5 <
10. 2.1 ◐ 2.100 =
11. 0.0628 ◐ 0.06281 <
12. 0.014 ◐ 0.140 <
13. 0.2678 ◐ 0.2695 <
14. 0.5 ◐ 0.55 <
15. 3 ◐ 3.00 =
16. 0.99 ◐ 1.00 <
17. 0.009 ◐ 0.01 <
18. 634.275 ◐ 634.268 >

Which decimal is greatest?

19. 0.086
    0.083
    0.806
20. 5.143
    5.185
    5.147
21. 9.35
    9.3
    0.93
22. 0.0084
    0.0089
    0.0189

Write each set of decimals in order from least to greatest.

23. 0.72   0.67   0.79
    0.67;   0.72;   0.79
24. 0.628   0.678   0.648
    0.628;   0.648;   0.678
25. 0.043   0 34   0.24
    0.043;   0.24;   0.34
26. 0.09   0.009   0.9
    0.009;   0.09;   0.9
27. 2.73   2.39   2,180
    2.180;   2.39;   2.73
28. 0.4348   0 3448   0.4483
    0.3448; 0.4348; 0.4483

29. Jones of the Cougars made 0.723 of his free throws. McAllen of the Lions made 0.698 of his free throws. Which player made the greater part of his free throws? Jones; 0.723

30. Desterman of the Lions made 0.4 of his field goal attempts. Garcia made 0.524, and Shane made 0.50. Which player made the greatest part of his field goal attempts? Garcia; 0.524

31. Make your calculator display the smallest possible decimal, greater than 0, in the ordinary decimal notation. Write the word name for this decimal. Answers may vary. See teaching notes.

32. DATA BANK (Use the Data Bank on page 415.) Which professional basketball player made the greater part of his free throws, Rick Barry or Bill Sharman? Compare the decimals. Use > or <. Rick Barry; 0.899 > 0.884

▌ THINK MATH ▐

Calculator Puzzle

How does William earn his living? Find the answers on a calculator. Turn the calculator upside down to read the words. Bills sells shoe soles.

			255	
2,139			827	19,742
1,982	100,000		974	28,887
+ 3,597	− 42,265		+ 989	+ 5,076
7718	57735		3045	53705

More Practice, page 419, Set A

37

Using Page 37

Exercises 23–28 For these exercises, students may simply list the numbers from least to greatest. Or, they could use the symbol for less than (<) to show the ordering. In exercise 19, for example, the order can be shown as 0.083 < 0.086 < 0.806. This *compound inequality* is read, "0.083 is less than 0.086 and 0.086 is less than 0.806."

Exercise 31 This exercise, as well as others that will appear throughout Book 7, can be done quite readily with a calculator. If the number of available calculators is limited, you might set up two or three calculator centers and let students take turns using them to work the exercises.

Data Bank Remind students of the Data Bank in Chapter 1. "What data is needed to answer exercise 32?" (the part of his total free throws that Rick Barry made and the part of his total free throws that Bill Sharman made) Have students find the appropriate table on page 415. Discuss the information given in each column. Point out that the column labeled Percent gives the decimal value of free throws made.

More Practice, page 419, Set A

Reteaching Supplement, page 10

Enrichment Supplement, page 10

Practice Supplement, page 14

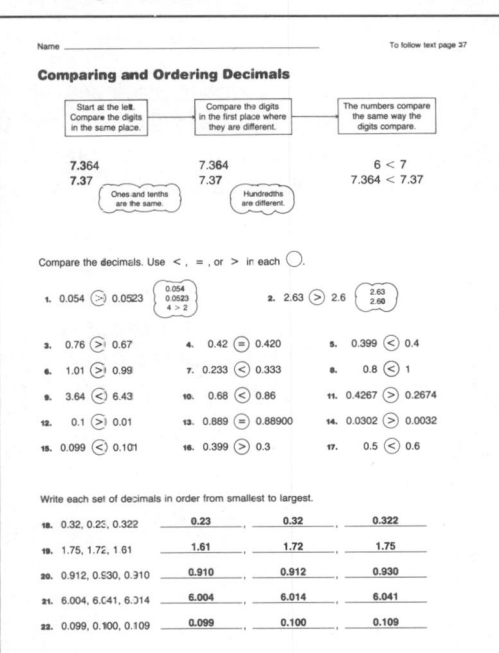

Quick Review Have students identify the place to which each number was rounded. Example: 40,551 → 40,600 hundreds
374 → 370 **tens**   95,251 → 95,000 **thousands**   17,607 → 17,610 **tens**
607,607 → 607,610 **tens**   4,290,376 → 4,300,000 **hundred thousands**

Lesson Focus To round decimals to a specified place

Ideas for Getting Started

Since identification of places is necessary in rounding decimals, review the names of places with students. Write the number below on the chalkboard. As you point to each digit, have students name its place.

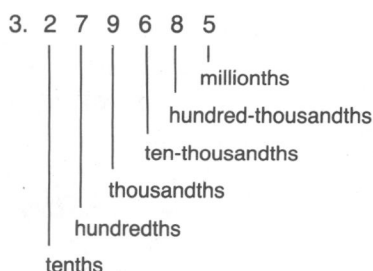

3. 2 7 9 6 8 5

| millionths
| hundred-thousandths
| ten-thousandths
| thousandths
| hundredths
| tenths

Using Page 38

Motivational Problem After students read the introductory problem, ask them to give the meaning of *astronomical unit.* Then have students restate the question and identify the data in the problem.

Lesson Development On the chalkboard, work through the procedure for rounding 0.387 to the nearest tenth as shown in the example. Point out that the method for rounding decimals is essentially the same as that for rounding whole numbers. "What digit do we need to consider to round 0.387 to the nearest tenth?" (the digit in the hundredths place which is 8) "Is that digit 5 or more?" (yes) "Do we keep 3 the same or add 1 to it?" (add 1 to it) "What is 0.387 rounded to the nearest tenth?" (0.4) Explain to the students that we drop all digits to the right of the tenths place. Zeros are not added.

Other Examples As you go through these examples, ask students to name the place to which we are rounding, the digit in that place, the digit to the right of the rounding place, and if that digit is 5 or more.

Point out to students that in rounding 3.4196 to the nearest thousandth, 6 is more than 5 so we increase the thousandths digit by 1. Notice that this digit is 9. When we increase 9 by 1, we get 10 so the 1 in the hundredths place must be increased to 2. Explain that since the zero is in the place to which we have rounded, it should not be dropped.

Direct students' attention to the example of rounding to 1-digit accuracy. Tell students that in order to estimate, we usually round numbers to 1-digit accuracy so that it is easy to do mental computation for the estimates.

Warm Up Watch for errors that involve rounding to the wrong place and double rounding, such as rounding 8.449 to 8.45 and then rounding 8.45 to 8.5.

Rounding Decimals

Astronomers call the distance from Earth to the sun 1 **astronomical unit.** They use this unit to measure the distance other planets are from the sun. The planet Mercury is 0.387 astronomical units from the sun. What is this number rounded to the nearest tenth?

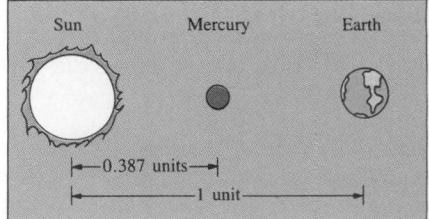

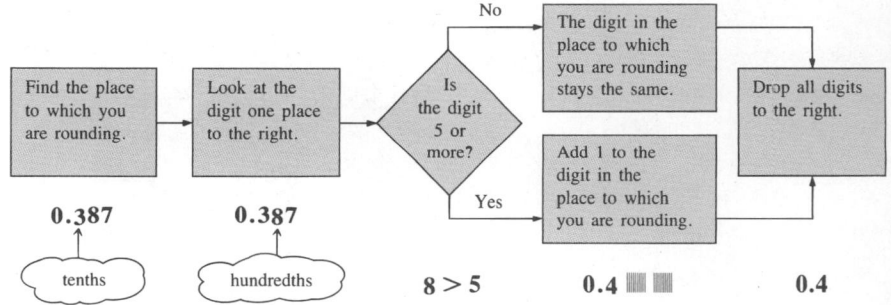

0.387 rounded to the nearest tenth is 0.4.

Other Examples

Decimal	Nearest tenth	Nearest hundredth	Nearest thousandth	Nearest whole number
3.4196	3.4	3.42	3.420	3
16.9635	17.0	16.96	16.964	17
0.70692	0.7	0.71	0.707	1

Sometimes we round numbers to **1-digit accuracy.** Working from left to right, round to the first place that is not 0.

Number	1-digit Accuracy
8.632	9
27.48	30
0.07712	0.08

Warm Up

Round to the nearest tenth.

1. 7.864 7.9   **2.** 12.072 12.1

Round to the nearest hundredth.

3. 0.695 0.70   **4.** 0.0372 0.04

Round to the nearest thousandth.

5. 0.4563 0.456   **6.** 2.9996 3.000

Round to 1-digit accuracy.

7. 0.7719 0.8   **8.** 35.8 40

38

Follow Up

Reteaching

Use a place-value chart (TRB p. 277) to reteach rounding to various places. Go through each step in the instruction boxes as you discuss the examples.

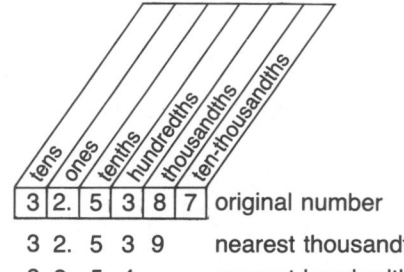

3 2. 5 3 9   nearest thousandth
3 2. 5 4   nearest hundredth
3 2. 5   nearest tenth
3 3   nearest whole number

Enrichment

Write these rounded decimals on the chalkboard and have students find the least and the greatest three-place decimal that will round to each.

1. 1.31	**1.305, 1.314**
2. 4.62	**4.615, 4.624**
3. 0.77	**0.765, 0.774**
4. 2.08	**2.075, 2.084**
5. 0.95	**0.945, 0.954**
6. 0.01	**0.005, 0.014**

Assignment Guide			
	Minimum	Average	Extended
page 39	1–41, SK	1–41, 44, SK	1–43 odd, 44, SK

Round to the nearest tenth.

1. 3.728 **3.7** 2. 6.922 **6.9** 3. 0.5514 **0.6** 4. 16.362 **16.4**

5. 0.4935 **0.5** 6. 8.4809 **8.5** 7. 12.082 **12.1** 8. 0.1482 **0.1**

Round to the nearest hundredth.

9. 23.028 **23.03** 10. 3.4857 **3.49** 11. 0.5538 **0.55** 12. 0.29721 **0.30**

13. 0.4350 **0.44** 14. 1.9967 **2.00** 15. 0.07296 **0.07** 16. 148.6464 **148.65**

Round to the nearest thousandth.

17. 0.38824 **0.388** 18. 10.7066 **10.707** 19. 5.031532 **5.032** 20. 0.00848 **0.008**

21. 12.43309 **12.433** 22. 0.129852 **0.130** 23. 0.70950 **0.710** 24. 0.010762 **0.011**

Round to the nearest whole number.

25. 42.66 **43** 26. 6.3994 **6** 27. 18.55 **19** 28. 382.089 **382**

29. 1,278.5 **1,279** 30. 469.883 **470** 31. 8.4589 **8** 32. 23,507.664 **23,508**

Round to 1-digit accuracy.

33. 72.48 **70** 34. 8.68 **9** 35. 0.742 **0.7** 36. 0.0695 **0.07**

37. 69.814 **70** 38. 0.00522 **0.005** 39. 0.1875 **0.2** 40. 0.9628 **1**

41. Mars is 1.524 astronomical units from the sun. Round the number to the nearest tenth. **1.5**

42. Saturn is 9.539 astronomical units from the sun. Round the number to the nearest hundredth. **9.54**

43. Astronomers have measured the length of one year on Earth as 365.25636 days. Round the number of days to the nearest hundredth and to the nearest whole number. **365.26; 365**

44. **DATA BANK** Is Uranus or Neptune farther from the sun? Round the two distances in astronomical units to the nearest tenth. (See page 415.) **Neptune; 19.2; 30.0**

SKILLKEEPER

1. 7 × 8 **56** 2. 18 ÷ 3 **6** 3. 27 ÷ 9 **3** 4. 6 × 5 **30** 5. 9 × 8 **72**

6. 45 ÷ 5 **9** 7. 5 × 9 **45** 8. 6 × 6 **36** 9. 48 ÷ 6 **8** 10. 8 × 8 **64**

11. 64 ÷ 8 **8** 12. 42 ÷ 7 **6** 13. 3 × 8 **24** 14. 32 ÷ 4 **8** 15. 54 ÷ 6 **9**

16. 7 × 6 **42** 17. 7 × 7 **49** 18. 49 ÷ 7 **7** 19. 4 × 8 **32** 20. 40 ÷ 8 **5**

More Practice, page 419, Set B

39

Using Page 39

Data Bank Have students identify the data needed to solve the problem. Caution them to think carefully about what is asked so that they use the appropriate data from the table.

Skillkeeper Multiplication and division facts were introduced in previous grade levels.

More Practice, page 419, Set B

Reteaching Supplement, page 11

Name _____ To follow text page 39

Rounding Decimals

Rounding to the nearest tenth
tenths 4.26 Round up. → 4.3 > 5

Rounding to the nearest hundredth
hundredths 5.431 Round down. → 5.43 < 5

Rounding to the nearest thousandth
thousandths 3.5425 Round up. → 3.543 > 5

Rounding to the nearest whole number
whole number 17.34 Round down. → 17 < 5

Round to the nearest tenth.
1. 8.639 **8.6** Check here 2. 47.52 **47.5** 3. 7.85 **7.9**
4. 0.423 **0.4** 5. 0.39 **0.4** 6. 27.257 **27.3**

Round to the nearest hundredth.
7. 67.141 **67.14** 8. 36.439 **86.44** 9. 3.692 **3.69**
10. 0.914 **0.91** 11. 2.5553 **2.56** 12. 0.3632 **0.36**

Round to the nearest thousandth.
13. 9.6324 **9.632** 14. 5.4376 **5.438** 15. 57.3123 **57.312**
16. 2.2745 **2.275** 17. 3.5291 **8.529** 18. 0.8713 **0.871**

Round to the nearest whole number
19. 27.42 **27** 20. 63.1 **63** 21. 18.285 **18**
22. 184.5 **185** 23. 73.28 **73** 24. 534.295 **534**

Round to 1-digit accuracy.
25. 0.08814 **0.09** 26. 13.43 **10** 27. 7.841 **8**
28. 0.5337 **0.5** 29. 0.9614 **1** 30. 0.1763 **0.2**

Enrichment Supplement, page 11

Name _____ To follow text page 39

Calculator Rounding

Round each number to the decimal place indicated. Enter the rounded number in your calculator. Push ⊞ . Then enter the next rounded number. Continue doing this for each number in the group. Push ⊟ after you have entered the last rounded number. Then turn your calculator upside down. If you have rounded correctly, your calculator should show the check word given below each problem.

Round to the nearest tenth.
1. 21.04 **21.0** + 2. 50.27 **50.3** +
   7.25 **7.3** +   28.96 **29.0** +
   12.08 **12.1** +   81.44 **81.4** +
   11.54 **11.5** +   76.88 **76.9** +
   39.86 **39.9** =   113.13 **113.1** =
   Total: **91.8**   Total: **350.7**
   Check word: BIG   Check word: LOSE

Round to the nearest hundredth.
3. 683.156 **683.16** + 4. 84.418 **84.42** +
   952.239 **952.24** +   139.183 **139.18** +
   2,306.749 **2,306.75** +   265.474 **265.47** +
   971.599 **971.60** =   88.278 **88.28** =
   Total: **4,913.75**   Total: **577.35**
   Check word: SLEIGH   Check word: SELLS

Round to the nearest thousandth.
5. 0.2627 **0.263** + 6. 427.9927 **427.993** +
   0.9263 **0.926** +   68.4523 **68.452** +
   1.4214 **1.421** +   47,029.0358 **47,029.036** +
   0.4349 **0.435** =   7,847.5644 **7,847.564** =
   Total: **3.045**   Total: **55,373.045**
   Check word: SHOE   Check word: SHOELESS

Practice Supplement, page 15

Name _____ To follow text page 39

Rounding Decimals

Round to the nearest whole number.
1. 3.4 **3** 2. 16.8 **17** 3. 23.37 **23**
4. 2.904 **3** 5. 246.17 **246** 6. 5.0774 **5**
7. 7.5 **8** 8. 72.42 **72** 9. 109.58 **110**
10. 23.35 **24** 11. 7.733 **8** 12. 20.64 **21**

Round to the nearest tenth.
13. 3.29 **3.3** 14. 17.44 **17.4** 15. 38.068 **38.1**
16. 9.65 **9.7** 17. 129.31 **129.3** 18. 0.669 **0.7**
19. 0.174 **0.2** 20. 9.705 **9.7** 21. 50.6363 **50.6**
22. 10.055 **10.1** 23. 0.085 **0.1** 24. 7.983 **8.0**

Round to the nearest hundredth.
25. 3.748 **3.75** 26. 0.666 **0.67** 27. 8.125 **8.13**
28. 0.933 **0.93** 29. 82.408 **82.41** 30. 0.7466 **0.75**
31. 0.085 **0.09** 32. 9.465 **9.47** 33. 0.3315 **0.33**
34. 0.7565 **0.76** 35. 62.1675 **62.17** 36. 0.0986 **0.10**

Round to the nearest thousandth.
37. 0.7183 **0.718** 38. 1.9486 **1.949** 39. 3.0661 **3.066**
40. 0.0335 **0.034** 41. 8.9397 **8.940** 42. 55.0816 **55.082**
43. 0.00744 **0.007** 44. 2.1308 **2.131** 45. 0.5055 **0.506**

Round to 1-digit accuracy.
46. 63.29 **60** 47. 0.56 **0.6** 48. 39.46 **40**
49. 0.379 **0.4** 50. 0.085 **0.09** 51. 6.952 **7**
52. 0.1984 **0.2** 53. 3.3091 **3** 54. 0.0087 **0.009**

Decimals

Quick Review For each pair of numbers, have students estimate the sum and the difference by rounding to the nearest thousand.

7,983 and 3,398	11,000, 5,000	$74,683 and $4,811	$80,000, $70,000
61,846 and 9,734	72,000, 52,000	$19,790 and $11,214	$31,000, $9,000

Lesson Focus To add decimals

Ideas for Getting Started

Write this matching quiz on the chalkboard.

1. 0.2 + 0.3	**a)** 0.05
2. 0.02 + 0.3	**b)** 0.23
3. 0.2 + 0.03	**c)** 0.32
4. 0.02 + 0.03	**d)** 0.5

Have students match the sums to the exercises. (1-d, 2-c, 3-b, 4-a) Then use the chalkboard or overhead projector to illustrate each sum with a unit square divided into hundredths as shown in the example below.

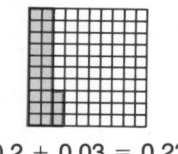

0.2 + 0.03 = 0.23

Using Page 40

Motivational Problem The question asks us to find a total value in U.S. dollars. What total does this refer to? (the total of 1 British pound note, 1 German mark, and 1 Greek drachma) "Where can we find the necessary data?" (in the chart) Explain to students that since we are looking for the total amount, our plan is to add.

Lesson Development Have students study each step in the procedure for adding decimals. Point out that after aligning the decimal points in the addends, adding decimals is the same as adding whole numbers. Notice with students that since our total, 2.1632, is in dollars, we need to round to the nearest hundredth or cent. The total value to the nearest cent is $2.16.

Other Examples The first example illustrates adding "ragged decimals." Explain to students that we can make all decimals have the same number of decimal places if we *annex* zeros. This helps us keep the decimal points aligned properly. Point out that this procedure is unnecessary when calculators are used for adding decimals.

Warm Up Watch for students who forget to annex zeros in exercises involving "ragged decimals," and therefore fail to line up the decimal points correctly. In exercise 6, remind students that the decimal point follows a whole number and that zeros can be added to the right of the decimal point.

Adding Decimals

Jason visited some European countries. He has 1 British pound note, 1 German mark, and 1 Greek drachma. What is their total value in U.S. dollars?

Since we want to find the total amount, we can add.

Decimals can be added just like whole numbers if the decimal points are lined up.

Country	Unit of money	Value in U.S. dollars*
Germany	deutsche mark (DM)	0.4075
Great Britain	pound (£)	1.7412
Greece	drachma (Dr)	0.0145
*Values in a recent year		

Write the problem with the decimal points in line. → Add as with whole numbers. → Place the decimal point in line with the others.

```
  0.4075          0.4075          0.4075
  1.7412          1.7412          1.7412
+ 0.0145        + 0.0145        + 0.0145
                   2 1632          2 1632
```

The total value is $2.1632 or $2.16, rounded to the nearest hundredth (cent).

Other Examples

3.6 + 1.28 + 9

```
  3.60
  1.28      Annex zeros
+ 9.00      to line up the
 13.88      decimal places.
```

12.795 + 0.693 + 5.759

```
  12.795
   0.693
+  5.759
  19.247
```

Neuschwanstein, West Germany

Warm Up

Add.

1. 32.8 + 27.4 = 60.2	**2.** 0.26 + 0.58 = 0.84	**3.** 1.385 + 2.776 = 4.161	**4.** 0.96 + 1.488 = 2.448	**5.** 0.72595 + 0.68867 = 1.41462

6. 12.4 + 6 + 8.49 = 26.89

7. $25 + $3.98 + $0.65 = $29.63

8. 9.5 + 0.772 + 0.9 = 11.172

Follow Up

Reteaching

Begin with an example such as 0.32 + 0.26. Illustrate the addition algorithm with place-value models, emphasizing that when decimals are added, tenths are added to tenths, hundredths are added to hundredths, and so on. Now use examples such as 0.376 + 0.498 and go through the algorithm, regrouping as needed.

Enrichment

Have students give the missing digits.

```
  [3]9.37          57.4[4]
    .8[6]            2.[3]7
   1.09              .63
+ 4[3].85         +8[1].28
 85.[1]7          [1][4]1.72
```

```
  5.373[7]          .03[4]7
 [7].1059           .8524
  .[7]006           .001[7]
+ .0069          + .0[7]35
[1]3.1[8][7]1       .[9]623
```

Assignment Guide			
	Minimum	Average	Extended
page 41	1–30	1–36	1–35 odd, 36–39

Add.

1.	5.94 + 6.87 ‾‾‾ 12.81	**2.**	0.467 + 5.39 ‾‾‾ 5.857	**3.**	6.875 − 27.436 ‾‾‾ 34.311	**4.**	0.087 + 9.689 ‾‾‾ 9.776	**5.**	2.043 + 0.857 ‾‾‾ 2.900
6.	4.6817 + 9.3548 ‾‾‾ 14.0365	**7.**	59.634 + 24.86 ‾‾‾ 84.494	**8.**	7.492 + 0.685 ‾‾‾ 8.177	**9.**	59.379 + 86.458 ‾‾‾ 145.837	**10.**	33.286 + 77.975 ‾‾‾ 111.261
11.	4.96 8.75 + 7.68 ‾‾‾ 21.39	**12.**	6.597 8.68 + 3.046 ‾‾‾ 18.323	**13.**	0.798 0.697 + 0.483 ‾‾‾ 1.978	**14.**	54.967 38.482 + 9.768 ‾‾‾ 103.217	**15.**	0.63497 0.57218 + 0.84956 ‾‾‾ 2.05671
16.	25.63 13.8 + 9.09 ‾‾‾ 48.52	**17.**	$8.47 1.96 + 0.78 ‾‾‾ $11.21	**18.**	$15.84 19.36 + 23.99 ‾‾‾ $59.19	**19.**	0.681 0.883 + 0.393 ‾‾‾ 1.957	**20.**	$349.50 277.54 + 194.85 ‾‾‾ $821.89
21.	0.3 7.92 + 26.0 ‾‾‾ 34.22	**22.**	$ 9.57 10.35 + 16.80 ‾‾‾ $36.72	**23.**	$0.92 0.34 + 1.87 ‾‾‾ $3.13	**24.**	0.3806 0.4009 + 0.5760 ‾‾‾ 1.3575	**25.**	$688.23 492.32 + 711.96 ‾‾‾ $1,892.51

26. 4.56 + 9.4 + 3.768 17.728

27. 0.975 + 4.38 + 6 11.355

28. 497.6 + 0.786 + 4.975 503.361

29. 74.96 + 3.875 + 0.684 79.519

30. 27.0 + 19.0 + 0.28 46.28

31. 342.5 + 57.5 + 0.24 400.24

32. 0.101 + 10.01 + 0.001 10.112

33. 37.6 + 67.3 + 84.9 189.8

34. $27.56 + $9.34 + $16 $52.90

35. $97.99 + $7.06 + $12.79 $117.84

Use the table on page 40 to do problems 36 and 37.

36. How much are 2 German marks, 1 British pound, and 2 Greek drachmas worth in U.S. dollars? $2.5852

37. Erik has 3 German marks and 2 British pounds. Does he have money that is worth as much as $5.00 in U.S. money? How much is Erik's money worth? no; $4.7049

38. Lucy exchanged $3.00 in U.S. money for Greek drachmas. She got 68.7156 drachmas for each dollar. To the nearest hundredth, how many drachmas did she get? 206.15 drachmas

39. Use the information in the table on page 40 to write your own problem. Solve the problem.

More Practice, page 419, Set C

Using Page 41

Exercises 1–35 Note that some of these exercises deal with the addition of money. Adding money in dollars and cents is simply an exercise in adding numbers in hundredths.

Exercises 36–38 These problems can be solved using repeated addition.

More Practice, page 419, Set C

Reteaching Supplement, page 12

Name _____   To follow text page 41

Adding Decimals

Add: 4.53 + 21.6 + 13.14

Write the problem with the decimal points in line. → Add as with whole numbers. → Place the decimal point in line with the others.

```
 4.53                    1              1
21.60   Annex a zero    4.53          4.53
+13.14  to help line   21.60         21.60
        up the decimals +13.14       +13.14
                        39 27        39.27
```

Find the sums.

1.	3.667 2.410 + 5.230 11.207	2.	0.24 7.57 + 16.34 24.15	3.	2.64 1.70 + 13.20 17.54
4.	6.973 + 8.746 15.719	5.	1.505 + 7.588 9.093	6.	0.649 + 8.716 9.365	7.	6.752 + 9.837 16.589
8.	4.522 + 3.63 8.152	9.	7.759 + 2.84 10.599	10.	6.96 + 5.087 12.047	11.	5.176 + 1.29 6.466
12.	4.343 9.409 + 0.518 14.270	13.	7.657 1.794 + 2.813 12.264	14.	9.92 6.075 + 8.18 24.175	15.	8.276 5.39 + 3.486 17.152
16.	5.867 + 9.48 + 1.09 5.867 9.480 + 1.090 16.437	17.	0.798 + 56.47 + 9.36 0.798 56.47 + 9.36 66.628	18.	4.07 + 3.281 + 5.009 4.07 3.281 + 5.009 12.360

Enrichment Supplement, page 12

Name _____   To follow text page 41

Buying a Stereo

Pretend that you have $1,000 to spend for a turntable, a receiver, two matching speakers, and a tape deck. Choose each item from those you see and find the total amount. If your total is greater than $1,000, try again. If your total is less than $1,000, change one or more of your selections to get closer to $1,000.

Turntables: $189.95, $154.75, $219.95, $89.95 each
Receivers: $409.95, $195.95, $399.95
Tape Decks: $239.95, $129.95, $79.95
Speakers: $189.95 each, pair $300.00

Choices	Prices	Prices	Prices	Prices	Prices
Turntables					
Receivers					
Speakers					
Tape Decks					
Totals					

Answers will vary. The most expensive equipment is $1,247.85 and the least expensive is $660.75.

Practice Supplement, page 16

Name _____   To follow text page 41

Adding Decimals

Add.

1.	1.89 2.47 + 6.03 10.39	2.	9.06 1.77 + 4.29 15.12	3.	5.17 12.83 + 6.42 24.42	4.	123.4 276.5 + 92.8 492.7	5.	0.129 0.377 + 0.643 1.149
6.	12.95 1.6 − 3.48 18.03	7.	8.3 0.92 + 2.755 11.975	8.	0.97 0.48 + 0.55 2.00	9.	0.5 0.55 + 0.555 1.605	10.	7.218 3.464 + 9.309 19.991
11.	5.2796 + 3.8422 9.1218	12.	1.671 + 3.859 5.530	13.	0.05822 + 3.17055 3.22877	14.	4.829 + 12.517 17.346	15.	9.214 + 3.778 12.992
16.	$44.86 3.21 + 19.88 $67.95	17.	$51.17 74.12 + 6.99 $132.28	18.	$82.32 5.09 + 17.76 $105.17	19.	$11.98 2.44 + 33.81 $48.23	20.	$ 2.01 10.28 + 16.61 $28.90

21.	1.35 + 5.4 + 13 1.35 5.4 + 13. 19.75	22.	0.46 + 3.2 0.46 + 3.2 3.66
23.	21.8 + 3 + 5.11 21.8 3. + 5.11 29.91	24.	14.5 + 3.217 14.5 + 3.217 17.717
25.	$0.31 + $0.70 + $0.78 $0.31 0.70 + 0.78 $1.79	26.	$8.23 + $6.34 + $2.20 $ 8.23 6.34 + 2.20 $16.77

Quick Review Read aloud the numbers below and have students write the standard numeral for each.

38,462	2,407	504,004	842,630,800	60,606
179,111	26,010	7,391,745	82,500,017	14,073,000

Lesson Focus To subtract decimals

Ideas for Getting Started

Write this subtraction problem on the chalkboard and represent the minuend with place-value models.

2.2 − 0.75

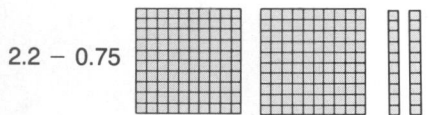

"To subtract 0.75 from 2.2 we must take away 5 hundredths. What must be traded in order to take away 5 hundredths?" (trade 1 tenth for 10 hundredths) Explain that we take away, 5 hundredths, leaving 2 units, 1 tenth, and 5 hundredths.

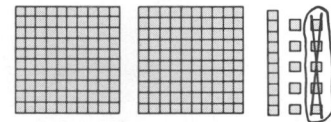

"What must be traded in order to subtract 7 tenths?" (trade 1 unit for 10 tenths) Point out that after we take away 7 tenths, the remaining pieces show 1.45.

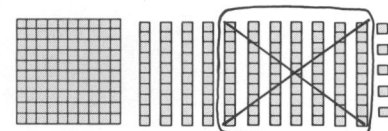

Ask a student to write the problem on the chalkboard in vertical form and check by adding.

Using Page 42

Motivational Problem "The question indicates that the speed of the tennis ball is the greater of two speeds. What other speed is involved?" (the speed of a baseball pitch) "What data is needed to answer the question?" (speed of the tennis serve, 62.483 m/s and speed of the baseball pitch, 41.556 m/s) "Since we want to find out how much more one number is than another, what is our plan? (subtract)

Lesson Development On the chalkboard, go through the steps for subtracting decimals as shown in the instruction boxes. Point out that just as in addition of decimals, we must keep the decimal points in a line. Have students check the reasonableness of the answer, 20.927 m/s, by using estimation. Then show another check using addition: 20.927 + 41.556 = 62.483.

Other Examples The first example shows the annexing of zeros in the minuend to aid in aligning decimal points. The second example shows the annexing of zeros in the subtrahend. The third example illustrates subtracting using money notation.

Subtracting Decimals

Using an electronic timer, a tennis serve was clocked at 62.483 meters per second (m/s). A baseball pitch had a speed of 41.556 m/s. How much greater was the speed of the tennis ball?

Since we want to find how much more one number is than another, we subtract.

Decimals can be subtracted just like whole numbers if the decimal points are lined up.

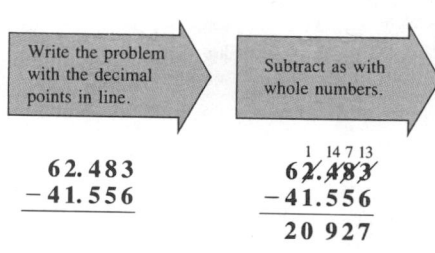

Write the problem with the decimal points in line.	Subtract as with whole numbers.	Place the decimal point in line with the others.

$$\begin{array}{r} 62.483 \\ -41.556 \\ \hline \end{array}$$

$$\begin{array}{r} {\scriptstyle 1\ 14\ 7\ 13} \\ 6\!\!\!\!/2.\!\!\!\!/4\!\!\!\!/8\!\!\!\!/3 \\ -41.556 \\ \hline 20\ 927 \end{array}$$

$$\begin{array}{r} {\scriptstyle 1\ 14\ 7\ 13} \\ 6\!\!\!\!/2.\!\!\!\!/4\!\!\!\!/8\!\!\!\!/3 \\ -41.556 \\ \hline 20.927 \end{array}$$

The speed of the tennis ball was 20.927 m/s greater than the speed of the baseball.

Other Examples

52 − 37.83

$$\begin{array}{r} 52.00 \\ -37.83 \\ \hline 14.17 \end{array}$$ Annex zeros to line up the decimal places.

29.196 − 17.4

$$\begin{array}{r} 29.196 \\ -17.400 \\ \hline 11.796 \end{array}$$

$25 − $18.75

$$\begin{array}{r} \$25.00 \\ -18.75 \\ \hline \$\ 6.25 \end{array}$$

Warm Up

Subtract.

1.	2.	3.	4.	5.
$\begin{array}{r} 58.42 \\ -26.65 \\ \hline 31.77 \end{array}$	$\begin{array}{r} 9.27 \\ -5.969 \\ \hline 3.301 \end{array}$	$\begin{array}{r} 0.8062 \\ -0.5571 \\ \hline 0.2491 \end{array}$	$\begin{array}{r} \$601.09 \\ -233.46 \\ \hline \$367.63 \end{array}$	$\begin{array}{r} 1.213 \\ -0.944 \\ \hline 0.269 \end{array}$

6. $16 − $2.75
$13.25

7. 1.8 − 0.635
1.165

8. 23.55 − 1.978
21.572

9. 32.417 − 29
3.417

10. 17 − 0.34
16.66

42

Follow Up

Reteaching

Use place-value models to illustrate the subtraction algorithm as shown below.

$$\begin{array}{r} 0.32 \\ -0.17 \\ \hline \end{array}$$

$$\begin{array}{r} 0.\overset{2}{\cancel{3}}\overset{12}{\cancel{2}} \\ -0.17 \\ \hline 5 \end{array}$$

$$\begin{array}{r} 0.\overset{2}{\cancel{3}}\overset{12}{\cancel{2}} \\ -0.17 \\ \hline 0.15 \end{array}$$

The difference is 0.15.

Enrichment

Display the following table and have students copy it.

Amount	1¢	5¢	10¢	25¢	$1	$5	$10
$5.46	4			2	4		1
$12.38	2		1	2	2	1	
$3.21	4			3	1	1	1

Present students with this problem:

A customer makes a purchase with a twenty-dollar bill. What change should be given for each amount listed?

Have students complete the table, using the smallest possible number of coins and bills.

Assignment Guide

	Minimum	Average	Extended
page 43	1–30	1–35, TM	1–35 odd, 36, TM

Subtract.

1. 34.8 − 12.6 = 22.2	2. 84.6 − 29.8 = 54.8	3. 0.672 − 0.186 = 0.486	4. 9.68 − 4.39 = 5.29	5. 329.7 − 167.9 = 161.8
6. 17.45 − 8.21 = 9.24	7. 5.8623 − 3.4871 = 2.3752	8. 56.725 − 38.463 = 18.262	9. 19.471 − 7.836 = 11.635	10. 40.70 − 26.36 = 14.34
11. 19.01 − 3.98 = 15.03	12. 5.63 − 2.48 = 3.15	13. 583.6 − 29.9 = 553.7	14. 0.697 − 0.248 = 0.449	15. 8.721 − 4.83 = 3.891
16. 10.7 − 8.69 = 2.01	17. 12.1398 − 8.6476 = 3.4922	18. 25.865 − 16.9532 = 8.9118	19. 10.07661 − 0.947 = 9.12961	20. 2.00075 − 1.29564 = 0.70511
21. $78.02 − 35.43 = $42.59	22. $50.06 − 37.69 = $12.37	23. $53.40 − 27.86 = $25.54	24. $1.00 − 0.69 = $0.31	25. $200.00 − 176.29 = $23.71

26. 9.14 − 4.715 4.425
27. 29.857 − 16.948 12.909
28. 5.76 − 3.042 2.718
29. 2 − 1.675 0.325
30. 182.943 − 49.685 133.258
31. 9.075 − 4.68 4.395
32. 6.175 − 3.9 2.275
33. 0.936 − 0.75 0.186
34. 100 − 84.97 15.03

35. A hockey puck had a speed of 44.556 m/s. The pelota, or ball, used in jai alai had a speed of 63.111 m/s. How much slower was the speed of the hockey puck? 18.555 m/s

36. When hit, a golf ball had a speed of 28.361 m/s. After three seconds in the air, the speed dropped to 19.5 m/s. How much slower was the speed after three seconds in the air? 8.861 m/s

THINK MATH

Logical Reasoning

Magic Squares have the same sum in each row, in each column, and in the two diagonals.

Find the missing numbers to make Magic Squares.

9.3

4.96	0.62	3.72
1.86	3.10	4.34
2.48	5.58	1.24

30.6

14.4	1.8	2.7	11.7
4.5	9.9	9.0	7.2
8.1	6.3	5.4	10.8
3.6	12.6	13.5	0.9

More Practice, page 420, Set A

43

Using Page 43

Exercises 26–34 Make certain that in recopying these exercises, students align decimal points properly, annexing zeros as needed.

Think Math If students have difficulty with this problem, ask "What is the magic sum for the square?" Then ask students what they must do to find another number, and what the next number is that they can find in the square.

More Practice, page 420, Set A

Quick Review Display the numbers below. Point to different combinations of two numbers and have students tell which number is greater.

| 136,427 | 1,364,672 | 136,489 | 1,728,411 |

1,389,654   136,399   1,711,411

Lesson Focus To estimate sums and differences of decimals

Ideas for Getting Started

Ask students to round the following numbers to the nearest tenth.

23.77   10.628   32.85   6.727

Then have students round these numbers to the nearest dollar.

$12.48 $3.79 $27.50 $130.30

Point out that rounding money is a common but special application of rounding.

Using Page 44

Motivational Problem Have students read the introductory problem and tell what the question asks us to find. Then ask them to identify the data in the problem. Explain that our plan is to round each amount and do the addition mentally to find an estimate of the total.

Lesson Development On the chalkboard, work through each step of the example problem. Then have students find the exact sum of the four items ($14.58), and compare it to the estimate of $15. Discuss whether or not Hal's estimate is reasonable.

Other Examples In the first two examples, the decimal point and the two zeros to the right have been dropped. Generally, when rounding decimals, including the special case of money, we drop the zeros to the right of the rounding place.

Warm Up Check to see if anyone is finding the sum or difference first, and then rounding. Discuss with students how they rounded the numbers in each exercise to arrive at their estimates. Calculators could be used to check the reasonableness of the estimates.

Estimating Sums and Differences with Decimals

Hal needs to buy four items at the grocery store. He estimates the total cost by rounding each amount to the nearest dollar. What is his estimate?

$$
\begin{array}{rcr}
\$1.89 & \to & \$\ 2 \\
5.95 & \to & 6 \\
2.68 & \to & 3 \\
+4.06 & \to & +\ 4 \\
\hline
& & \$15
\end{array}
$$

His estimate is 15 dollars.

Other Examples

Estimate $62.95 − $37.36.
Round to the nearest ten dollars.

$$
\begin{array}{rcr}
\$62.95 & \to & \$60 \\
-37.36 & \to & -40 \\
\hline
& & \$20
\end{array}
$$

Estimate $219.75 + $376.47.
Round to the nearest hundred dollars.

$$
\begin{array}{rcr}
\$219.75 & \to & \$200 \\
+376.47 & \to & +400 \\
\hline
& & \$600
\end{array}
$$

When estimating sums or differences with decimals, round each decimal to the same place.

Estimate 0.614 + 0.78

$$
\begin{array}{rcr}
0.614 & \to & 0.6 \\
+0.78 & \to & +0.8 \\
\hline
& & 1.4
\end{array}
$$

Estimate 0.07339 − 0.0492

$$
\begin{array}{rcr}
0.07339 & \to & 0.07 \\
-0.0492 & \to & -0.05 \\
\hline
& & 0.02
\end{array}
$$

Warm Up

Estimate each sum or difference by rounding. Estimates may vary.

1. $1.87	2. $88.19	3. $709.48	4. 0.0808
+ 2.98	− 39.75	− 285.50	− 0.047
$5	$50	$400	0.03
5. $0.89	6. 0.822	7. 0.6261	8. 0.0122
0.62	0.466	− 0.1984	0.0638
+ 0.49	+ 0.317	0.4	+ 0.0771
$2	1.6		0.15

44

Follow Up

Reteaching

Have the students round these numbers to 1-digit accuracy and use the rounded numbers to estimate the sums and differences.

1. 9.75	2. $50.00
+ 2.33	− 28.76
12	$20
3. $72.36	4. 4,828
− 18.22	− 2,157
$50	3,000
5. 0.812	6. 0.937
+ 0.745	− 0.251
1.5	0.6

Enrichment

Display the following on the chalkboard and ask students if each total can be paid with $100. Have them decide without adding. Next have them find the totals and determine how much change should be given.

1. $11.98	2. $12.95	3. $14.45
24.23	4.98	9.98
4.89	15.25	24.69
13.16	2.49	25.08
32.49	31.18	12.39
2.54	4.85	12.25
$89.29	$71.70	$98.84

Change:

| $10.71 | $28.30 | $1.16 |

Estimate each sum or difference by rounding to the nearest dollar.

1. $1.88
3.14
+ 2.75
$8

2. $8.25
− 6.99
$1

3. $5.75
6.22
+ 4.05
$16

4. $9.09
− 2.89
$6

5. $8.50
2.45
+ 7.27
$18

Estimate each sum or difference by rounding to the nearest ten dollars.

6. $23.14
+ 58.85
$80

7. $91.45
− 56.50
$30

8. $49.99
27.75
+ 33.69
$110

9. $77.25
− 19.37
$60

10. $83.12
33.98
+ 47.45
$160

Estimate each sum or difference by rounding to the nearest hundred dollars.

11. $719.09
− 195.24
$500

12. $209.17
131.45
+ 377.66
$700

13. $518.35
− 195.00
$300

14. $903.29
− 419.83
$500

15. $606.99
478.10
+ 825.50
$1,900

Estimate each sum or difference by rounding. Estimates may vary.

16. 0.313
0.251
+ 0.482
1.1

17. 0.74
− 0.198
0.5

18. 0.0612
0.017
+ 0.05422
0.13

19. 0.4841
− 0.29
0.2

20. 5.059
3.8
+ 2.1774
11

21. 0.2884 + 0.442 0.7

22. 0.6923 − 0.3117 0.4

23. 0.89 + 0.78 + 0.43 2.1

24. 3.04 + 2.95 + 6.16 12

25. 0.071 − 0.0477 0.02

26. 29.124 − 18.88 10

27. 0.175 + 0.388 + 0.89 1.5

28. 609.4 − 189.29 400

29. 0.0072 − 0.0039 0.003

30. Jessica needs to buy grocery items that cost $2.77, $2.19, $1.68, $3.55, and $1.95. She estimates the total by rounding to the nearest dollar. What is her estimate? $13

31. Anthony bought grocery items that cost $1.89, $2.09, $1.19, and $3.84. He paid with a $20 bill. Estimate how much change he should get back. $11

32. DATA HUNT What is the estimate of the cost of eight grocery items? Find and list the prices of the items. Estimate the total cost. Find the exact total.

More Practice, page 420, Set B

45

Using Page 45

Exercises 16–29 While estimates may vary, the answers given for these exercises are based on rounding to 1-digit accuracy.

Data Hunt Students who work the Data Hunt will need to collect advertisements containing the prices of various grocery items. As an alternative, you may wish to post the following data on a bulletin board or the chalkboard for their use.

Cheese	$1.38	Paper Towels	$0.89
Milk	$1.05	Peanut Butter	$2.15
Eggs	$0.89	Applesauce	$0.59
Hamburgers	$2.33	Bread	$0.89
Cereal	$1.89	Frozen Peas	$1.58
Detergent	$2.45	Lettuce	$0.69
Cat Food	$0.67	Cauliflower	$0.89
Bleach	$1.35	Potatoes	$1.66
Sugar	$2.75	Oranges	$1.10

More Practice, page 420, Set B

Reteaching Supplement, page 14

Name _____   To follow text page 45

Estimating Sums and Differences with Decimals

To estimate the total, round each price, then add.

Round to the nearest whole dollar

$4.87 → $5
0.75 → 1
+ 3.19 → 3
$9 Estimate

To estimate the difference, round each price, then subtract.

Round to the nearest ten dollars.

$26.84 → $30
− 15.21 → 20
$10 Estimate

First estimate, then find the exact sum or difference. One appropriate estimate is given for each.

1. Exact Estimate
$0.74 → $0.70
0.29 → 0.30
+ 0.19 → 0.20
$1.22 $1.20

2. Exact Estimate
$72.15 → $70
28.59 → 30
+ 40.88 → 40
$141.62 140

3. Exact Estimate
0.85 → 0.90
− 0.33 → 0.30
0.52 0.60

4. Exact Estimate
$5.97 → $6
6.37 → 6
+ 2.88 → 3
$15.22 $15

5. Exact Estimate
0.72 → 0.70
0.38 → 0.40
0.61 → 0.60
+ 0.29 → 0.30
2.00 2

6. Exact Estimate
$160.90 → $160
277.42 → 280
+ 424.50 → 420
$862.82 $860

7. Exact Estimate
$127.25 → $100
223.40 → 200
+ 471.31 → 500
$821.96 $800

8. Exact Estimate
$75.30 → $75
24.15 → 24
+ 96.24 → 96
$195.69 $195

9. Exact Estimate
$354.20 → $350
423.98 → 420
+ 764.32 → 760
$1,542.50 $1,530

10. Exact Estimate
0.77 → 0.80
− 0.23 → 0.20
0.54 0.60

11. Exact Estimate
$58.48 → $58
− 19.06 → 19
$39.42 $39

12. Exact Estimate
0.419 → 0.420
− 0.198 → 0.200
0.221 0.220

13. $69.33 − $48.75
Exact Estimate
$69.33 → $69
48.75 → 49
$20.58 $20

14. $72.45 − $68.31
Exact Estimate
$72.45 → $72
− 68.31 → 68
$ 4.14 $ 4

Enrichment Supplement, page 14

Name _____   To follow text page 45

Bargain Shopping

Cheap Eats
Paper towels 99¢
Biscuit mix 89¢
Butter $1.90
Oranges 36¢
Milk $1.02
Flour $1.47
Bread 98¢ SPECIAL!
Eggs 95¢

Buy More
Milk $1.05 SPECIAL!
Oranges 41¢
Bread 94¢
Butter $1.95
Biscuit mix 77¢
Eggs 90¢
Flour $1.56
Paper towels $1.06

Shop 'n Spend
Butter $2.07
Bread 98¢ SPECIAL!
Eggs 83¢
Flour $1.41
Biscuit mix 95¢
Oranges 32¢
Paper towels 99¢
Milk $1.01

Estimate the answers to the problems below by rounding the prices to the nearest ten cents.

1. You want to buy milk, bread, and oranges. Where will you find the best bargain?
Shop 'n Spend

2. You want to buy bread, oranges, butter, and paper towels. Where will you find the best bargain?
Cheap Eats

3. You bought eggs, butter, and oranges at one of the stores and spent about $3.20. Where did you shop?
Shop 'n Spend

4. You want to buy biscuit mix, eggs, flour, and milk. Where will you find the best bargain?
Shop 'n Spend

5. You want to buy biscuit mix, eggs, and bread. Where will you find the best bargain?
Buy More

6. You bought all the things listed at one of the stores. You spent about $8.70. Where did you shop?
Cheap Eats

Practice Supplement, page 18

Name _____   To follow text page 45

Estimating Sums and Differences with Decimals

Estimate each sum or difference by rounding to the nearest dollar.

1. $6.41
3.07
+ 2.59
$6
+ 3
$12

2. $0.88
2.68
+ 2.72
$1
+ 3
$8

3. $4.34
4.36
+ 0.95
$4
3
+ 1
$8

4. $9.82
− 5.77
$10
$ 4

5. $7.24
− 3.15
$7
− 3
$4

6. $8.81
− 2.56
$9
− 3
$6

Estimate each sum or difference by rounding to the nearest ten dollars.

7. $17.75
42.60
+ 33.21
$ 20
40
+ 40
$100

8. $49.09
32.18
+ 57.77
$ 50
30
+ 60
$140

9. $38.72
42.68
+ 61.33
$ 40
40
+ 60
$140

10. $59.18
− 32.02
$60
− 30
$30

11. $93.35
− 41.14
$90
− 40
$50

12. $57.79
− 19.66
$60
− 20
$40

Estimate each sum or difference by rounding to the nearest hundred dollars.

13. $351.62
488.19
+ 210.10
$ 400
500
+ 200
$1,100

14. $638.14
172.15
+ 511.89
$ 600
200
+ 500
$1,300

15. $216.19
349.27
+ 655.32
$ 200
300
+ 700
$1,200

16. $823.10
− 2.576
$800
− 200
$600

17. $591.29
− 358.77
$600
− 400
$200

18. $772.27
− 184.33
$800
− 200
$600

46
Decimals

8

88

Quick Review	Have students find the sums and differences.			
$126 + 884 = $1,010	$16,135 − 8,757 = $7,378	$20,004 − 13,716 = $6,288	$834 − 703 = $131	$13,472 + 6,189 = $19,661

Lesson Focus To practice finding sums and differences of decimals; to solve word problems using addition and subtraction of decimals or a combination of these operations

Suggested Materials Newspaper advertisements

Ideas for Getting started

To introduce the problem-solving lesson on page 47, distribute advertisements to members of the class. While students work at the chalkboard, ask them to choose two items they would like to buy, and to find the total cost of the items. Then ask students to select a pair of items and find the difference in the prices. Finally, ask students to estimate the total of 3 items in the advertisement.

Using Page 46

Exercises 1–45 You may wish to select specific types of problems that have caused students difficulty and work through them as a class activity before making the assignment for this page.

Assign exercises according to the needs and abilities of the students. If you have students who are clearly competent in one of these skills, you may wish to omit those exercises.

Skills Practice

Add.

1. 27.30 + 84.97 = 112.27
2. 8.092 + 13.645 = 21.737
3. 0.039 + 8.966 = 9.005
4. 95.842 + 68.731 = 164.573
5. 49.051 + 0.998 = 50.049

6. 9.87 + 3.05 + 6.21 = 19.13
7. 24.09 + 26.1 + 84.3 = 134.49
8. $36.95 + 54.60 + 0.38 = $91.93
9. $13.56 + 88.17 + 26.63 = $128.36
10. 57.167 + 0.4 + 3.6 = 61.167

11. 0.82971 + 0.67553 + 0.48401 = 1.98925
12. $833.96 + 917.42 + 1,000.63 = $2,752.01
13. $268.71 + 350.28 + 140.93 = $759.92
14. 1.01365 + 208.45 + 2.369 = 211.83265
15. 0.2873 + 0.396 + 0.5439 = 1.2272

Subtract.

16. 79.1 − 30.2 = 48.9
17. 63.4 − 54.7 = 8.7
18. 0.4812 − 0.3945 = 0.0867
19. 83.52 − 29.17 = 54.35
20. $50.37 − 48.99 = $1.38

21. 0.6213 − 0.6139 = 0.0074
22. $94.60 − 83.75 = $10.85
23. 3.0 − 1.54 = 1.46
24. 56.48 − 49.0 = 7.48
25. $418.63 − 379.56 = $39.07

26. $7,000.03 − 6,521.04 = $478.99
27. 84.1 − 6.25 = 77.85
28. 0.53 − 0.52999 = 0.00001
29. 4.0007 − 3.4695 = 0.5312
30. $2,987.30 − 2,986.49 = $0.81

Add or subtract.

31. 32.0 + 51.167 = 83.167
32. 0.032917 + 0.094655 = 0.127572
33. 55.0 − 44.41 = 10.59
34. $99.99 + 90.05 = $190.04
35. 0.9826 − 0.9817 = 0.0009

36. 861.95 + 23.1 + 367.02 = 1,252.07
37. 56.0128 − 55.6437 = 0.3691
38. 577,102 − 465,391.5 = 111,710.5
39. 457.92 − 412.99 = 44.93
40. 0.000051 − 0.0000483 = 0.0000027
41. 9,623.47 − 8,847.89 = 775.58
42. 33,015.6 + 24,782.5 + 101,621.9 = 159,420.0
43. 0.0257 + 0.026931 + 0.03804 = 0.090671
44. 13,279.84 + 62,943.10 + 70,062.48 = 146,285.42
45. 592.43 + 1,167.05 + 43.29 = 1,802.77

Follow Up

Reteaching

Divide students into teams for a computational competition. Call on a student from each team to work one of the exercises on page 46 at the chalkboard while other members of the team check his or her work. The first team to finish the exercise correctly is awarded one of the letters in W I N N E R S. Continue until one team receives all seven of the letters and wins the competition.

Enrichment

Tell students they have $250 to buy items from mail-order catalogues. Selections made from the catalog should be listed by item and cost. The total cost of all items should also be recorded. Students should compute the amount of money left after the purchase is made.

Challenge students to try and list the greatest number of items possible, without exceeding the $250 limit.

Assignment Guide

	Minimum	Average	Extended
page 46	1–35	1–45	1–45 odd
page 47	1–6	1–9	1–10

PROBLEM SOLVING: Using Data from an Advertisement

QUESTION
DATA
PLAN
ANSWER
CHECK

Hair dryer $9.99

Bracelet $3.88

Electronic game $8.75

T-shirt $6.95

Duffel bag $13.95

Belt $3.75

Socks $1.29

Poster $4.99

SALE!

Solve.

1. Terry bought a hair dryer and 2 bracelets. What was the total cost? **$17.75**

2. Sharma bought a duffel bag. She paid for it with a $20 bill. How much money did she get back? **$6.05**

3. Larry wants to buy a pair of socks and a belt. He only has $5.00. Does he have enough money? Find the difference. **no; $0.04**

4. Carlos had $25.00. He bought 2 electronic games. How much money did he have left after paying for the games? **$7.50**

5. Luann bought a hair dryer, a poster, and a belt. She paid for her purchases with 2 ten-dollar bills. How much change should she get back? **$1.27**

6. The duffel bag usually sells for $18.50. How much less is the price in the advertisement? **$4.55**

7. Dustin bought a duffel bag and a belt. Jason bought a hair dryer and an electronic game. How much more did Jason spend than Dustin? **$1.04**

8. Estimate the total cost of all the articles in the advertisement. Find the exact total. Compare your estimate with the exact total. **$54; $53.55**

9. **DATA HUNT** How much would it cost to buy four articles of clothing? List the articles with the prices and find the total.

10. **Try This** Julie and Margaret went shopping. Margaret spent $2.50 more than Julie. Together they spent a total of $28.60. How much did Julie spend? Hint: Guess and check. **$13.05**

Using Page 47

Lesson Development Use the first two problems as sample problems and work through them with the class. Stress the 5 points of the problem-solving checklist as you discuss each problem. Observe with students that the data is obtained from the advertisement.

Exercises 1–8 Note that several of the problems involve more than one operation.

Data Hunt Students can collect data for this problem from advertisements they find outside the classroom. Or, advertisements from newspapers or catalogs can be posted on a bulletin board for use with the Data Hunt.

Try This A possible strategy, Guess and Check, was taught on page 24.

Discussion "What does the question ask us to find?" (how much Julie spent) "Who spent more money, Julie or Margaret?" (Margaret) "How much more?" (S2.50) "What other data is given in the problem?" (Together they spent $28.60.) "If we cannot find the answer directly by using addition or subtraction, what strategy could we use?" (Guess and Check) Ask students to guess how much Julie spent. Then have them find the amount spent by Margaret and check by adding. Continue in this way until the answer is found.

Solution Guess: Julie ($13.05) Margaret ($15.55)
Check: $13.05 + 15.55 = $28.60
Julie spent $13.05.

Reteaching Supplement, page 15

Name _____ To follow text page 47

Problem Solving: Using Data from an Advertisement

Printing calculator $59.75

Wallet calculator $9.59

Business calculator $18.99

Solar-powered calculator $13.29

Electronic time/pen $12.57

Calculator pen $16.95

Calculator watch $49.99

Calculator watch (with alarm) $54.59

Solve.

1. Ernie bought a solar-powered calculator and an electronic time pen. What was the total cost?
To find the total add the cost of each item. **$25.86**

2. The usual cost of the printing calculator is $66.99. How much is saved by buying it on sale?
To find the difference, subtract. **$7.24**

3. Steve saved $4.99 by buying the business calculator on sale. How much was the calculator before it went on sale? **$23.98**

4. Karen wants to buy a wallet calculator and an electronic time pen. She has $20. How much more money does she need? **$2.16**

5. How much more does the calculator watch with an alarm cost than the watch without an alarm? **$4.60**

6. David bought a business calculator. He paid for it with a $20 bill. How much money should he get back? **$1.01**

7. Betty bought two solar-powered calculators. She paid for them with two $20 bills. How much money did she get back? **$13.42**

8. Robert bought a wallet calculator and a calculator watch with an alarm. Dean bought a business calculator and an electronic time pen. How much more did Robert spend than Dean? **$32.62**

Enrichment Supplement, page 15

Name _____ To follow text page 47

Oops! That Can't Be!

Each of these problems contains an error. Describe what "can't be" in each problem.

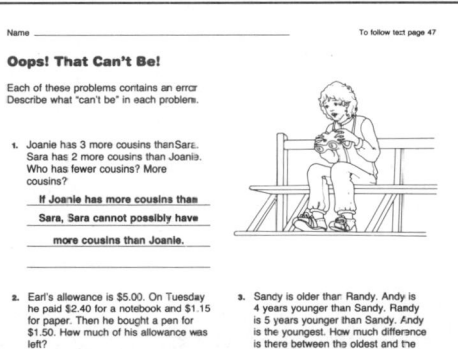

1. Joanie has 3 more cousins than Sara. Sara has 2 more cousins than Joanie. Who has fewer cousins? More cousins?
If Joanie has more cousins than Sara, Sara cannot possibly have more cousins than Joanie.

2. Earl's allowance is $5.00. On Tuesday he paid $2.40 for a notebook and $1.15 for paper. Then he bought a pen for $1.50. How much of his allowance was left?
Earl had only $1.45 left after buying the notebook and paper. He could not have bought the pen.

3. Sandy is older than Randy. Andy is 4 years younger than Sandy. Randy is 5 years younger than Sandy. Andy is the youngest. How much difference is there between the oldest and the youngest?
Andy can't be the youngest. If he's 4 years younger than Sandy and Randy is 5 years younger than Sandy.

4. Harry worked in a grocery store on September 7 and every seventh day of the month after that. He worked in a movie theater on September 9 and every ninth day after that. On which dates in September did Harry work at both places?
Harry couldn't have worked in both places on the same day since 7 and 9 have no common multiple under 63.

Practice Supplement, page 19

Name _____ To follow text page 47

Problem Solving: Using Data from an Advertisement

Film $2.89

Camera strap $7.66

Photo album $4.78

Camera case $19.99

Flash cubes $2.79 per package

SALE today

Solve.

1. Gail bought 2 rolls of film and a package of flash cubes. What was the total cost? **$10.57**

2. Lee bought a camera strap. He paid for it with a $10 bill. How much money did he get back? **$2.34**

3. Sarah wants to buy a photo album and a roll of film. She has $10. Does she have enough money? Find the difference. **Yes $1.33**

4. The camera case usually sells for $21.95. How much less is the price in the advertisement? **$4.96**

5. Sam bought a roll of film, a photo album, and a camera strap. How much did he spend? **$16.33**

6. Duke bought a camera case and a roll of film. Donna bought a camera strap and 2 photo albums. Who spent more money? How much more? **Duke $6.66**

7. Alice bought a camera strap and a photo album. How much change did she get from $20? **$7.56**

8. A photo album usually sells for $6.29. How much less is the price in the advertisement? **$1.51**

Quick Review "How many seconds in a minute?" **60**   "Minutes in an hour?" **60**
"Hours in a day?" **24**   "Days in a week?" **7**   "Months in a year?" **12**
"Days in a year that's not a leap year?" **365**   "Days in a leap year?" **366**

Lesson Focus To solve word problems related to time zones

Suggested Materials Wall map of the United States

Ideas for Getting Started

Before discussing the different time zones, give students practice adding and subtracting hours. "If it is 2:00 a.m., what time will it be in 4 hours?" (6:00 a.m.) "If it is 11:00 p.m., what time will it be in 3 hours?" (2:00 a.m.) "If it is 1:00 p.m., what time was it 3 hours ago?" (10:00 a.m.)

Tape string across the wall map to show the various time zones as indicated on the map on page 48. Call on students to locate cities you name and give the time zone—EST, CST, MST, or PST—for that city. Then ask, "When it is noon in New York, what time is it in Chicago?" (11:00 a.m.) "When it is 6:00 a.m. in Los Angeles, what time is it in Miami, Florida?" (9:00 a.m.) "What time is it in Cincinnati when it is 9:30 p.m. in Phoenix?" (7:30 p.m.) "When it is 3:00 p.m. in Minneapolis, what is the local time?"

Using Page 48

Lesson Development Have students read the sample problem and state the question in their own words. "What data is given in the statement of the problem?" (Carol telephones from Seattle at 6:00 p.m. PST, Chicago is on CST) "What data must be obtained from the map?" (CST is 2 hours ahead of PST.) "What should we plan to do to find the answer?" (Since CST is 2 hours ahead of PST, we must add.) Have students check to see if the answer is reasonable. "Does it make sense for it to be 8:00 p.m. in Chicago and 6:00 p.m. in Seattle?"

PROBLEM SOLVING: Using Data from a Map

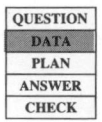

There are 24 time zones around the world. Standard time begins in Greenwich, England, and time zones are one hour apart. The map below shows four standard time zones, Eastern Standard Time (EST), Central Standard Time (CST), Mountain Standard Time (MST), and Pacific Standard Time (PST).

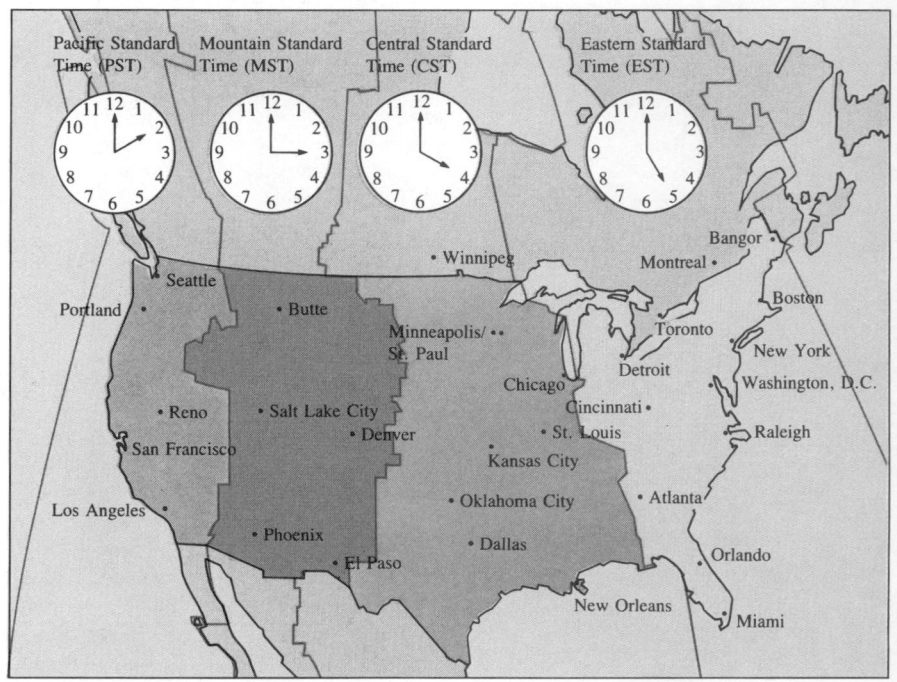

Carol Franklin lives in Seattle. At 6:00 p.m. (PST) she telephones her mother in Chicago. What is the time (CST) in Chicago?

The map shows that it is 2 hours later in Chicago than in Seattle. Therefore, the time is 8:00 p.m. (CST).

Solve.

1. It is 2:00 p.m. (CST) in Oklahoma City. What time (MST) is it in Phoenix?
   48 1:00 p.m.

2. What is the time (EST) in Cincinnati when it is midnight (PST) in Portland?
   3:00 a.m.

Follow Up

Reteaching

Have students use the map on page 48 to answer these questions.

1. In what time zone is
   a) St. Louis? b) Miami? c) Reno?
      CST   **EST**   **PST**

2. How many hours difference between
   a) CST and PST? **2**
   b) MST and EST? **2**
   c) EST and PST? **3**
   d) CST and EST? **1**

3. When it is 3:00 p.m. in Chicago, what time is it in
   a) Seattle? b) Boston? c) Dallas?
      1:00 p.m.   4:00 p.m.   3:00 p.m.

Enrichment

Display the following and have students answer the questions.

9:00 a.m.   12:00 noon   5:00 p.m.

San Francisco   New York   London

1. What time is it in London when it is 10:00 a.m. in New York? **3:00 p.m.**

2. When it is noon in San Francisco, what time is it in London? **8:00 p.m.**

3. A flight from San Francisco to London takes about 11 h. If you leave San Francisco at 8:00 a.m. on Wednesday, when will you arrive in London? **3:00 a.m. Thursday**

Assignment Guide			
	Minimum	Average	Extended
page 48–49		1–10	1–2, 7–15

3. It is 7:00 a.m. (CST) in Minneapolis. What time (PST) is it in San Francisco? 5:00 a.m.

4. What time is it in Miami when it is 11:00 a.m. (MST) in Salt Lake City? 1:00 p.m.

5. It is 8:45 a.m. in Detroit. What time is it in Montreal? 8:45 a.m.

6. It is 1:00 p.m. in Washington, D.C. What is the time in Los Angeles? 10:00 a.m.

7. Rosana lives in Atlanta. At 10:15 a.m. (EST), she called a friend in Los Angeles. What was the time (PST) in Los Angeles? 7:15 a.m.

8. Roger lives in Orlando. He called a friend in Chicago at 8:30 p.m. (EST). What was the time in Chicago? 7:30 p.m.

9. Mrs. Wood has to make a business call to San Francisco from her office in New York City. She wants to make her call at 10:00 a.m. (PST) in San Francisco. What time (EST) should she make her call from New York? 1:00 p.m.

10. Estelle lives in Reno. Her mother lives in Boston. Estelle calls her mother at 9:25 p.m. (PST). What time (EST) is it in Boston? 12:25 a.m.

11. Larry lives in Denver. His brother Barry lives in Raleigh. Larry called Barry at 6:52 p.m. (MST). They talked on the telephone for 15 minutes. What time (EST) was it when Barry hung up the telephone in Raleigh? 9:07 p.m.

12. A nonstop flight from Denver to San Francisco left Denver at 10:00 a.m. (MST). It arrived in San Francisco at 11:30 a.m. (PST). How long was the flying time? 2 h 30 min

13. The flying time for a nonstop trip from Atlanta to Seattle is 5 hours and 3 minutes. If a flight from Atlanta arrived in Seattle at 6:15 p.m. (PST), what time did the plane leave Atlanta? 4:12 p.m.

14. A nonstop flight from Los Angeles to Chicago takes 3 hours and 50 minutes. What is the latest time (PST) you could leave Los Angeles to arrive in Chicago no later than noon (CST)? 6:10 a.m.

15. **Try This** Mary talked for several minutes on the telephone. Her sister Michelle made another call that was 9 minutes longer than Mary's call. Their father told them, "You girls have been using the telephone for 55 minutes." How long was Mary's call? 23 min

Using Page 49

Try This A possible strategy, Guess and Check, was taught on page 24.

Discussion "What are we asked to find?" (the length of Mary's call) Elicit from students the data given in the problem. "Who talked longer, Mary or Michelle?" (Michelle) "How much longer?" (9 min) "What was the total amount of time the telephone was in use?" (55 min) Have students guess and check, recording their information on the chalkboard.

Solution Guess: Mary (23 min) Michelle (32 min)
Check: 23 + 32 = 55
Mary used the telephone 23 minutes.

Ideas That Work

Chalk It Up

Display the diagram and exercises shown below. Challenge students to discover the code and find the indicated sums and differences. Give this example: ┐ + ┌ 0.67 + 12.4 = 13.07.

3.27	21	0.003
425.6	0.09	5.192
0.67	7.23	12.4

1. □ − └ 0.09 − 0.003 = 0.087
2. ┘ + ⊐ + ⊓ 3.27 + 452.6 + 7.23 = 463.10
3. ⊏ − ┘ 5.192 − 3.27 = 1.922
4. └ + ⊓ 0.003 + 7.23 = 7.233
5. ⊔ − ┌ 21 − 12.4 = 8.6
6. ┌ + ⊏ 12.4 + 5.192 = 17.592

Practice Supplement, page 20

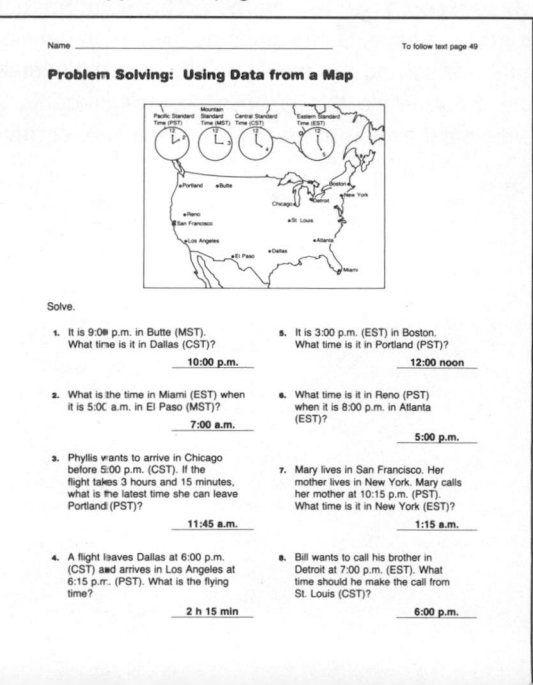

Name ____________ To follow text page 49

Problem Solving: Using Data from a Map

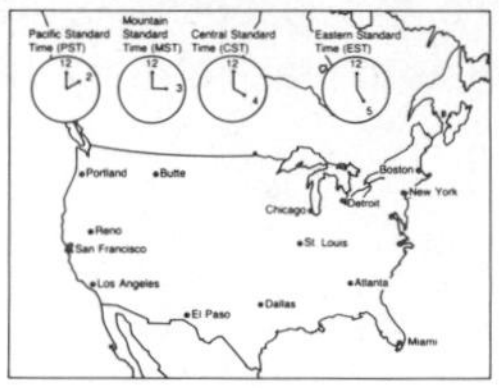

Solve.

1. It is 9:00 p.m. in Butte (MST). What time is it in Dallas (CST)? **10:00 p.m.**
2. What is the time in Miami (EST) when it is 5:00 a.m. in El Paso (MST)? **7:00 a.m.**
3. Phyllis wants to arrive in Chicago before 5:00 p.m. (CST). If the flight takes 3 hours and 15 minutes, what is the latest time she can leave Portland (PST)? **11:45 a.m.**
4. A flight leaves Dallas at 6:00 p.m. (CST) and arrives in Los Angeles at 6:15 p.m. (PST). What is the flying time? **2 h 15 min**
5. It is 3:00 p.m. (EST) in Boston. What time is it in Portland (PST)? **12:00 noon**
6. What time is it in Reno (PST) when it is 8:00 p.m. in Atlanta (EST)? **5:00 p.m.**
7. Mary lives in San Francisco. Her mother lives in New York. Mary calls her mother at 10:15 p.m. (PST). What time is it in New York (EST)? **1:15 a.m.**
8. Bill wants to call his brother in Detroit at 7:00 p.m. (EST). What time should he make the call from St. Louis (CST)? **6:00 p.m.**

Lesson Focus
To make an organized list as a strategy for solving nonroutine word problems

Ideas for Getting Started

Write the names of 5 students on slips of paper. Fold the slips and place them in a box and mix them. Have a student draw 3 slips from the box and write the names on the chalkboard. "How many different groups of 3 students could we draw from 5 students?" Some students may guess 5 × 3 or 15 groups. Do not tell the students whether their guesses are correct or incorrect, but tell them that today they will learn a strategy which will help them check these guesses.

Using Page 50

Motivational Problem Have students read the Try This problem at the top of the page. "What does the question ask us to find?" (the number of different groups of three that can be formed using 5 names) "Name one such group." (Julia, Frank, Beth) "Is the group of Julia, Frank, and Beth different from the group of Beth, Frank, and Julia?" (No, they are the same.) Explain that we can use the strategy, Make an Organized List, to solve the problem.

Lesson Development Add the strategy, Make an Organized List, to the problem-solving bulletin board display described on page 24. Have students study the list on page 50. Note that using the first letter of each name makes the list simpler. Call attention to the heading of each column and elicit from the students the system used to organize the list.

Discuss how the problem can be checked. Note that Julia was listed in 6 of the groups. "In how many groups was Frank listed?" (6) "Is each student in the same number of groups?" (yes, each student is in 6)

Exercises 1–2 Assign the problems at the bottom of the page. Some students may try to develop rules for solving the problem without actually making a list. While this is possible, ask students to write out their lists to make certain they are correct.

PROBLEM SOLVING: Make an Organized List

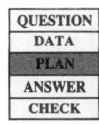

QUESTION
DATA
PLAN
ANSWER
CHECK

Try This

Julia, Frank, Beth, Eduardo, and Linda were students suggested to the principal to serve on the honors committee. The principal put the five names into a hat and drew out three of them. Using the five names, how many different groups of three can be drawn from the hat?

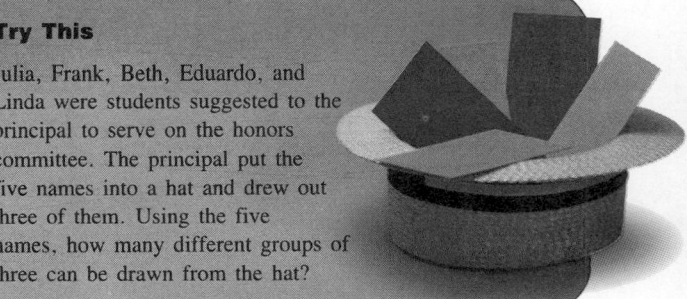

In some problems you must find the number of different ways something can be done. To help you do this, try the strategy **Make an Organized List.** Here is a way the problem might be solved using this strategy.

To make the list simpler, use only the first letter of each person's name.

All groups of three with Julia as one of the members	All remaining groups with Frank as a member	Remaining group with Beth as a member
JFB JBE JEL JFE JBL JFL	FBE FEL FBL	BEL

There are ten different groups of three names that can be drawn from the hat.

Solve.

1. At the cafeteria there are three choices of sandwiches: hamburger, tuna salad, or peanut butter and jelly. There are three choices of drinks: milk, cocoa, or fruit juice. How many combinations of one sandwich and one drink are possible? 9

2. Ettalene saw the word STOP on a sign. She wondered how many different combinations could be made using the four letters in the word. How many combinations are possible? 24

50

Strategy Test Item

Optional Problem If you wish to assess students' ability to apply the strategy called Make an Organized List introduced in this chapter, provide them with the problem below.

Brian paid 90¢ for an ice cream cone. He paid with a nickel (N), dime (D), quarter (Q), and a half-dollar (H). He handed out the coins one at a time. How many different ways could he have handed them out?

Solution

NDQH	DQHN	QHND	HNDQ
NDHQ	DQNH	QHDN	HNQD
NQDH	DHQN	QNHD	HDNQ
NQHD	DHNQ	QNDH	HDQN
NHQD	DNHQ	QDHN	HQND
NHDQ	DNQH	QDNH	HQDN

He could have handed out the coins 24 different ways.

▌ CHAPTER REVIEW/TEST ▐

Write a decimal for the part that is shaded.

1. 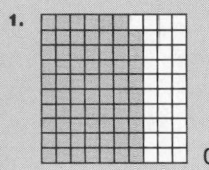 0.69

2. 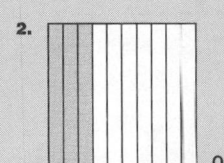 0.3

3. 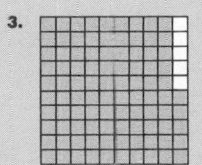 0.95

Write the decimal.

4. two hundred fifty-four thousandths 0.254   **5.** twenty-four and sixty-eight thousandths 24.068

Write > or < for each ⬤.

6. 20.347 ⬤ 23.047 <   **7.** 7.42 ⬤ 7.22 >   **8.** 0.8 ⬤ 0.09 >

9. Round 23.456 to the nearest tenth. 23.5   **10.** Round 0.7435 to the nearest hundredth. 0.74   **11.** Round 0.334725 to the nearest thousandth. 0.335

Round to 1-digit accuracy.

12. 3,816 4,000   **13.** 0.7628 0.8   **14.** 0.0462 0.05

Add or subtract.

15. 23.7
   + 14.9
   ——
   38.6

16. 9.6
   − 1.88
   ——
   7.72

17. 69.1
   − 33.8
   ——
   35.3

18. $24.95
   + 72.56
   ——
   $97.51

19. $100.00
   − 83.47
   ——
   $16.53

20. 2.15 + 4.9 7.05   **21.** 0.937 − 0.85 0.087   **22.** 12.59 + 71.556 84.146

Estimate each sum or difference by rounding to the nearest tenth.

23. $0.79
   0.87
   0.33
   + 0.48
   ——
   $2.50

24. $79.89
   − 49.99
   ——
   $29.90

25. 0.56
   0.34
   + 0.88
   ——
   1.8

26. 0.625
   0.292
   + 3.567
   ——
   4.5

27. 8.952
   − 0.628
   ——
   8.4

28. The height of the Columbia is 17.89 m. The height of a pilot is 1.83 m. What is the difference in the heights? 16.06 m

29. Leon bought running shoes for $23.95 and socks for $2.95. He paid for them with a $20 bill and a $10 bill. How much money should he get back? $3.10

51

Using Page 51

The exercises in the Chapter Review/Test emphasize the major concepts and skills presented in this chapter. These exercises may be used as a review assignment or as a test, depending upon your needs.

Item Analysis The table below correlates the Chapter Review/Test items with objectives and with the student text pages on which the concepts or skills were taught.

Items	Objectives	Related Text Pages
1–5	2.1	32–35
6–14	2.2	36–39
15–22	2.3	40–43, 46
23–27	2.4	44–45
28–29	2.5	47

Assessment Options

If you use the Chapter Review/Test as a review assignment, you may wish to use the free-response tests or the multiple-choice test to evaluate mastery of the chapter objectives. The items on these tests have a one-to-one correspondence in terms of content and level of difficulty. A correlation of test items to objectives and student text pages is provided in the Management Guide for Chapter 2.

Multiple-Choice Test, TRB pages 4–6
Free-Response Test, TRB pages 50–51

Teacher's Resource Book Options

The following blackline masters are available for use with this chapter. If you have not already assigned these materials, you may wish to use them to close the chapter.

Recreation, TRB page 156
Family Involvement, TRB pages 247–248
Reading Math, TRB page 228
Consumer Applications, TRB page 174
Calculator Technology, TRB page 192

Using page 52

The exercises on this page are intended for those students who experienced difficulty with the Chapter Review/Test on page 51. Should students require reteaching of these key concepts and skills, please refer to the teaching notes below. Otherwise, the Another Look exercises can be assigned as independent work, with students using the accompanying sample problems and hints as guides.

Exercises 1–5 This skill was originally taught on pages 32–35. Have students examine the example at the left. Note that the unit square at the top is divided into tenths. The illustration shows 10 tenths and 1 tenth or 1.1. The square at the bottom is divided into 100 parts, so each part represents 1 hundredth or 0.01.

Exercises 6–7 This skill was originally taught on pages 36–37. Go through the example on the left. Remind students that in comparing two numbers, they should start at the left and compare digits in the same place. "How many ones are in each decimal?" (1 and 0). Explain that since 1 > 0, 1.1 > 0.01.

Exercises 8–11 This skill was originally taught on pages 38–39. Have students examine the second display box. "To what place are we rounding?" (hundredths) "What is the digit to the right?" (8) Since 8 is more than 5, we increase the hundredths place by 1. "What is 1.818 rounded to the nearest hundredth?" (1.82)

Exercises 12–17 This skill was originally taught on pages 40–41. On the chalkboard, work through the example in the display box. Stress the necessity of lining up the decimal points. Point out that we can annex a zero to 16.4 to make the numbers have the same number of decimal places. Show students that we add as with whole numbers and then place a decimal point in line with the others.

Exercises 18–23 This skill was originally taught on pages 42–43. Remind students to line up the decimal points, annexing zeros to help keep the decimals aligned properly. Emphasize that the decimal point in the answer should be placed in line with the others.

ANOTHER LOOK

1.1 = one and one tenth

0.01 = one hundredth

1.1 > 0.01

Write a decimal for the part that is shaded.

1. 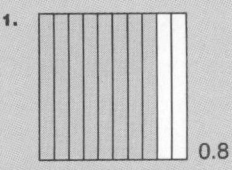 0.8

2. 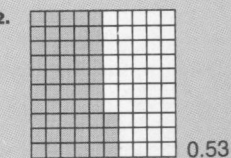 0.53

Write the decimal.

3. twenty-five and four tenths 25.4

4. eighteen thousandths 0.018

5. nine thousand, six hundred fourteen ten-thousandths 0.9614

Write > or < for each ⬤.

6. 0.3 ⬤ 0.4 <

7. 2.8 ⬤ 0.03 >

Round to the
nearest hundredth.

1.818 ← 5 or more
       hundredths
Round up to 1.82.

Round to the nearest hundredth.

8. 23.4872 23.49

9. 0.7539 0.75

Round to the nearest thousandth.

10. 5.3557 5.356

11. 0.6295 0.630

Line up decimal points.
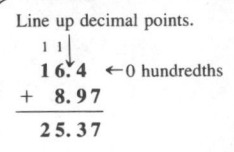
16.4 ← 0 hundredths
+ 8.97
25.37

Add.

12.   7.68
  + 3.89
  11.57
	13. 0.8276
	  + 0.5775
	  1.4051
		14. $25.75
		  32.95
		  + 18.47
		  $77.17

15. 3.89 + 0.618
4.508

16. 26.4 + 9.88
36.28

17. 0.0526 + 0.09
0.1426

6.8 − 1.33
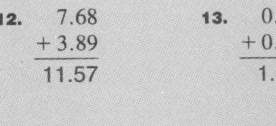
6.80 ← 0 in the
− 1.33   hundredths
5.47   place

Subtract.

18.   8.34
  − 3.18
  5.16
	19. 16.05
	  − 9.77
	  6.28
		20. 0.703
		  − 0.096
		  0.607

21. 12.4 − 9.86
2.54

22. 3.17 − 0.5
2.67

23. 0.9572 − 0.83
0.1272

52

Just for Teachers

Sophie Germain

Throughout history, a woman who pursued a career in mathematics had to overcome the prejudices of her society. Women who succeeded were often helped by a supportive family, but this was not always the case. Sophie Germain, born in Paris in 1776, had parents who believed rigorous study was a dangerous strain on a woman's health.

Germain, however, had great mathematical talent and determination to learn. During the turmoil of the French Revolution, she spent many hours in her family's library studying mathematics. Against parental restraints and without a tutor, Sophie Germain taught herself mathematics, including differential calculus.

During the late 1700s, promising French mathematicians and scientists studied at the newly founded Ecole Polytechnique. Women were not admitted there, but Germain managed to obtain lecture notes for some of the courses. Using a masculine pen name, she submitted an end-of-term paper to Joseph Louis Lagrange who was doing work in the relatively new field of calculus. Lagrange was astounded when he

Using Page 53

This page is intended for those students who successfully completed the Chapter Review/Test on page 51. You may wish to assign this page as independent work while you use Another Look exercises to reteach the basic concepts and skills of the chapter. Or you may decide that all students would benefit from exposure to this Enrichment activity.

Lesson Development Determine if students have had any previous experience with binary numerals. Explain that in base ten we group by tens. In the binary system we group by twos. Use sets of dots to illustrate numerals in base ten and in base two.

Base Ten	Base Two
1 ten and 1 one	1 two and 1 one
11	11

Call attention to the base-two place-value chart on the page. Go through the example showing how this chart can be used to change the binary numeral, 111011, to the base-ten numeral, 59.

Display the table showing base-ten numerals and binary numerals. The first example involves changing a base-ten numeral to a binary numeral. The numeral 10 must be written in terms of groups of 8, 4, 2, and 1. Base-two place values are subtracted until 0 or 1 is reached. "What is the greatest base-two place value that is less than 10?" (8) "Subtract to see how much is left."

```
  10
-  8    one group of 8            1 __ __ __
   2    2 is less than 4
        so there are no
        groups of 4              1  0 __ __
-  2    one group of 2           1  0  1 __
   0    0 is less than
        1 so there are
        no ones                  1  0  1  0
```

"What is the binary numeral for 10?" (1010)

Direct students' attention to the next line in the table. "You can find the base-ten numeral by adding the values of the digits in each place. What is the base-ten numeral?" (49) Have students complete the rest of the table on their own.

Place Value

Computers and calculators often use a numeration system based on two instead of ten. A base-two system uses only two digits: 0 and 1. Base-two numerals are called **binary** numerals.

Base-Ten Numerals

0	1	2	3	4	5	6	7	8	...

Binary Numerals

0	1	10	11	100	101	110	111	1000	...

To find a base-ten numeral for a binary numeral such as 111011, we can use a place-value chart.

Add the values of the digits in each place.

The base-ten numeral for the binary numeral 111011 would be 59.

Copy and complete the table.

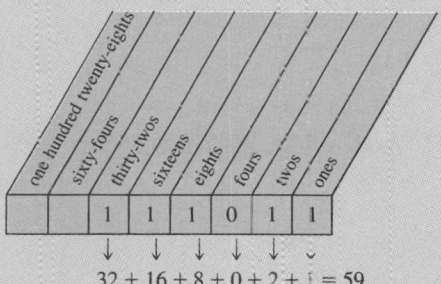

one hundred twenty-eights	sixty-fours	thirty-twos	sixteens	eights	fours	twos	ones
		1	1	1	0	1	1

$$32 + 16 + 8 + 0 + 2 + 1 = 59$$

Base-Ten Numeral   **Binary Numeral**

Base-Ten Numeral	128s	64s	32s	16s	8s	4s	2s	1s
10				1	0	1	0
49			1	1	0	0	0	1
17				1	0	0	0	1
104		1	1	0	1	0	0	0
185	1	0	1	1	1	0	0	1

Give the base-ten numeral for each binary numeral.

1. 110 6   **2.** 1111 15   **3.** 11 3   **4.** 11001 25

5. 11111 31   **6.** 100000 32   **7.** 1000000 64   **8.** 1000001 65

Give the binary numeral for each base-ten numeral.

9. 12 1100   **10.** 16 10000   **11.** 20 10100   **12.** 30 11110

13. 193 11000001   **14.** 70 1000110   **15.** 128 10000000   **16.** 250 11111010

---

discovered "M. LeBlanc" to be female. Because he thought Germain was talented and persevering, he introduced her to important mathematicians and scientists. Her correspondence with them furthered her education.

Germain continued to be concerned that her work would not be taken seriously because she was a woman. When she wrote to mathematician Carl Friedrich Gauss in 1801 about her research on number theory, she again signed herself "M. LeBlanc." Gauss later recommended Germain for an honorary doctorate from the University of Gottingen. She died just before she was to receive it.

Sophie Germain's work won numerous prizes, most importantly the French Academy's grand prize in 1816 for her paper—submitted under her own name—analyzing mathematical laws concerning vibrations of elastic surfaces. Both mathematicians and physicists have recognized the lasting value of her research on number theory, acoustics, and elasticity as well as her personal courage and determination.

Using Page 54

The exercises on the page provide practice for maintaining cumulative skills. The emphasis in this Cumulative Review is on place value of whole numbers (Chapter 1) and decimals (Chapter 2).

Item Analysis The table below correlates the Cumulative Review items with objectives and with the student book pages on which the concepts or skills were taught.

Items	Objectives	Related Text Pages
1	1.1	2–5
2	2.1	32–35
3, 5	2.2	36–39
4	1.2	6–9
6, 9	1.4	12–15, 22
7–8, 10–11	2.3	40–43, 46
12	2.4	44–45
13–14	2.5	47

CUMULATIVE REVIEW

1. Which digit in 246,789 is in the ten thousands place?

   A 2   **(B)** 4
   C 6   **D** not given

2. What is the decimal for ninety and forty-eight thousandths?

   A 90,048   **B** 90.0048
   (C) 90.048   **D** not given

3. Which is correct?

   A $0.07 > 0.7$ **(B)** $0.07 < 0.7$
   C $0.07 = 0.7$ **D** not given

4. Round 62,299 to the nearest hundred.

   (A) 62,300   **B** 62,000
   C 60,000   **D** not given

5. Round 195.975 to the nearest hundredth.

   A 200   **(B)** 195.98
   C 195.97   **D** not given

Find the sums.

6. $838 + 576 + 647$

   A 2,051   **(B)** 2,061
   C 1,961   **D** not given

7. $16.98 + $23.44 + 17.66

   A $57.98   **B** $56.08
   (C) $58.08   **D** not given

8. $2.37 + 6.48 + 9.29 + 0.65$

   A 18.80   **(B)** 18.79
   C 19.79   **D** not given

Find the differences.

9. $2,304 - 876$

   (A) 1,428   **B** 1,438
   C 1,528   **D** not given

10. $500 - 39.47

   A $34.47   **B** $539.47
   C $570.53   **(D)** not given

11. $56.39 - 2.968$

   A 53.438   **(B)** 53.422
   C 26.71   **D** not given

12. Estimate by rounding.

   $12.95 - 7.87

   (A) $5   **B** $4
   C $6   **D** not given

13. Jacklyn bought a dress that cost $49.75. The sales tax was $2.99. What was the total cost?

   A $46.76   **(B)** $52.74
   C $51.64   **D** not given

14. A baseball was pitched at a speed of 38.555 m/s. A tennis ball was hit at a speed of 56.5 m/s. How much faster was the speed of the tennis ball?

   A 22.055 m/s   **B** 27.945 m/s
   (C) 17.945 m/s   **D** not given

Multiplication and Division of Whole Numbers

Objectives

3.1 Estimate products of whole numbers.
3.2 Find products of whole numbers.
3.3 Write repeated factors and their products using exponential notation.
3.4 Estimate quotients of whole numbers.
3.5 Find quotients and remainders of whole numbers.
3.6 Solve word problems using the 5-Point Checklist and cumulative computational skills.

Summary

In this chapter students review multiplication of whole numbers using 1-, 2-, and 3-digit multipliers. Exponents and exponential notation are introduced. Division of whole numbers with 1-, 2-, and 3-digit divisors is reviewed and the method of short division is developed. Special products and special quotients are presented as prerequisite skills for estimation of products and quotients using rounded numbers. Problem solving is extended to include the operations of multiplication and division as well as addition and subtraction.

Mathematical Background

Multiplication The usual algorithm used for multiplying two whole numbers can be justified by use of the distributive property of multiplication with respect to addition. This principle states that for all numbers a, b, and c, $a \cdot (b + c) = (a \cdot b) + (a \cdot c)$.

The principle can be applied to a problem like $62 \cdot 37$ as follows:

$$62 \cdot 37 = 62 \cdot (30 + 7)$$
$$= (62 \cdot 30) + (62 \cdot 7)$$
$$= 1,860 + 434$$
$$= 2,294$$

The same ideas are used in the standard multiplication algorithm, but in a shorter form. For example:

$$
\begin{array}{r}
62 \\
\times\ 37 \\
\hline
434 \quad \leftarrow 62 \cdot 7 \\
1860 \quad \leftarrow 62 \cdot 30 \\
\hline
2,294 \quad \leftarrow 62 \cdot 37
\end{array}
$$

Exponents If the same addend is repeated we can use multiplication. If the same factor is repeated we can use exponents.

$$5 \times 5 \times 5 \times 5 \times 5 \times 5 \times 5 = 5^7$$

The repeated factor is the base and the number of times the factor is repeated is the exponent. The number represented by the base with its exponent is called a power of the base. Thus 5^7 is the seventh power of five, or five to the seventh power. Bases which have exponents of 1 or 0 may need special explanation. If n is any nonzero number,

$$n^1 = n \text{ and } n^0 = 1.$$

These special cases can be made plausible to students by observing some patterns that occur when powers with the same base are divided.

$$\frac{2^4}{2^2} = \frac{2 \times 2 \times 2 \times 2}{2 \times 2} = 2^{4-2} = 2^2,$$
$$\frac{2^4}{2^3} = \frac{2 \times 2 \times 2 \times 2}{2 \times 2 \times 2} = 2^{4-3} = 2^1 = 2$$
$$\frac{2^4}{2^4} = \frac{2 \times 2 \times 2 \times 2}{2 \times 2 \times 2 \times 2} = 2^{4-4} = 2^0 = 1$$

In the last example, a number is divided by itself which gives a quotient of 1. But the subtraction pattern of the exponents gives a zero exponent. Since this relation is true for any base, we can conclude that any number, except zero, to the zero power is 1.

Division While the basic concept of division involves its relationship to multiplication, the division algorithm is based upon the relationship between division and subtraction. To find $1,482 \div 43$, one could repeatedly subtract 43 from 1,482 keeping track of the number of 43s subtracted. Eventually we could count the number of 43s in 1,482. The subtraction process would be faster if we subtracted multiples of 43 in the early stages.

$$
\begin{array}{r}
1,482 \\
-\quad 430 \leftarrow \text{ten 43s} \\
\hline
1,052
\end{array}
\qquad
\begin{array}{r}
1,052 \\
-\quad 430 \leftarrow \text{ten 43s} \\
\hline
622
\end{array}
\qquad
\begin{array}{r}
622 \\
-\quad 430 \leftarrow \text{ten 43s} \\
\hline
192
\end{array}
$$

$$
\begin{array}{r}
192 \\
-\quad 86 \leftarrow \text{two 43s} \\
\hline
106
\end{array}
\qquad
\begin{array}{r}
106 \\
-\quad 86 \leftarrow \text{two 43s} \\
\hline
20
\end{array}
$$

After the last subtraction, less than 43 remains. We subtracted 34 forty-threes with a remainder of 20.

The standard division algorithm provides a short, convenient way of performing the repeated subtractions.

$$
\begin{array}{r}
34 \text{ R } 20 \\
43\overline{)1,482} \\
1290 \quad \longleftarrow 30 \times 43 \\
\hline
192 \\
172 \quad \longleftarrow 4 \times 43 \\
\hline
20
\end{array}
$$

Problem Solving Problem-solving skills are extended in this chapter to include problems involving multiplication and division as well as using addition and subtraction of whole numbers and decimals developed in the previous chapter. On pages 68 and 69, the focus of the problem set is using the 5-Point Checklist. The problem-solving lesson on pages 78 and 79 is concerned with choosing the correct operation. On page 81, students will use a formula to solve problems. A new problem-solving strategy, Find a Pattern, is introduced on page 82. Later chapters will feature Try This problems that can be solved using this strategy.

Vocabulary

associative	base	dividend
commutative	exponent	divisor
distributive	exponential notation	quotient
factor	power	remainder
product	square	formula
multiple	cube	pattern

Teaching Tips

 ## Error Analysis

This chapter reviews and extends the operations of whole number multiplication and division. Exponents and exponential notation are introduced. Many student errors are associated with the content in this chapter. Some of them are listed below.

Error Pattern 1

$$\begin{array}{r} \overset{3}{36} \\ \times\ 25 \\ \hline 180 \\ 92 \\ \hline 1{,}100 \end{array} \qquad \begin{array}{r} \overset{6}{47} \\ \times\ 59 \\ \hline 423 \\ 265 \\ \hline 3{,}073 \end{array} \qquad \begin{array}{r} \overset{1}{58} \\ \times\ 92 \\ \hline 116 \\ 462 \\ \hline 4{,}736 \end{array}$$

Diagnosis The student multiplied by the ones correctly, but when multiplying by the tens he or she failed to regroup properly. The number saved in the fist step was used as the regrouped value.

Remediation Have the student do the example in two parts; that is, for 36×25, multiply 36×5 and then 32×20. Review the algorithm and the reason for "saving" the number that is regrouped. Go back to the vertical algorithm and instruct students to mark through the number saved in the first step before multiplying by the tens.

Error Pattern 2

$$\begin{array}{r} 65\ \text{R5} \\ 6\overline{)3{,}635} \\ 36 \\ \hline 35 \\ 30 \\ \hline 5 \end{array} \qquad \begin{array}{r} 42\ \text{R7} \\ 8\overline{)3{,}223} \\ 32 \\ \hline 23 \\ 16 \\ \hline 7 \end{array} \qquad \begin{array}{r} 25\ \text{R34} \\ 37\overline{)7{,}619} \\ 74 \\ \hline 219 \\ 185 \\ \hline 34 \end{array}$$

Diagnosis The student failed to place a zero in the quotient in the appropriate place. The next digits in the quotient are written without regard to place value.

Remediation Work through each step in the division algorithm with an example such as $8\overline{)3{,}223}$. After dividing 32 by 8 and bringing down the tens digit, ask "Can we divide 2 by 8?" Since the answer is no, we place a zero in the quotient. Emphasize this point in the algorithm. Continue to use other examples to illustrate this step.

Error Pattern 3

$$10^4 = 4 \times 10 \qquad 8^3 = 3 \times 8 \qquad 2^4 = 4 \times 2$$

Diagnosis The student has interpreted the exponent as a factor and not as an indication of how many times the base is used as a factor.

Remediation Develop the concept of exponent by using a discovery approach.

$$10 \times 10 = 10^2$$
$$10 \times 10 \times 10 = 10^3$$
$$10 \times 10 \times 10 \times 10 = 10^4$$

Ask students to generalize about what the exponent indicates.

 ## Problem Solving

Helping Students Understand Problems

In teaching problem solving, one of the most critical moments is when a student says, "I don't know what to do." Because of a need to say something, we often respond with "Try again," or we tell the student exactly how to proceed to find the answer. In both cases, we have not taken a very positive step toward improving the student's ability to understand that problem in particular, or math problems in general.

There are many factors that influence the degree to which a student understands math problems. Among these are the student's abilities in the areas of reading, memory, and logical thinking, the number of problem-solving experiences the student has previously had, and the degree to which the student experiences anxiety to perform well. If a student has difficulty with a given problem, there are several techniques you can introduce to facilitate understanding.

One of the most powerful ways to help a student understand a problem is to give hints by asking leading questions that focus the student's attention on the relevant data in the problem or on the question being asked. The teaching notes for the Try This problems in this problem-solving program exemplify this approach. Below is a sample problem and four discussion questions or hints to help students understand it.

> **PROBLEM:** Six children came to a birthday party. Each child shook hands one time with each other child. How many handshakes were exchanged?

Discussion "How many children came to the party?" (6) " What were the children doing?" (shaking hands) "If Bill shook Mary's hand, would he shake her hand again?" (no) "If Bill shook Mary's hand, is that one handshake or two?" (1)

Here are some other ideas for helping students improve their abilities to understand problems

- Have students explain the problem in their own words.
- Remind students of a similar problem.
- Help students replace larger numbers with smaller numbers.
- Have students use a colored marker to highlight important phrases and data.
- Tell students to list the data needed to solve the problem.
- Help students draw a picture or use objects to show the action in the problem.
- Help students act out the problem.
- Remove the numbers from the problem and discuss the action in the problem.
- Discuss key words as *potential* key words—that is, for a particular problem, discuss whether a key word suggests the correct operation or whether it is misleading. (Note: Do not teach students to rely on key words.)

Improving a student's ablity to understand problems is a task not easily or quickly accomplished. However, it is something that can be achieved through hard work by student and teacher over a period of time.

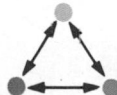 **Special Education**

The suggestions in this section will help you plan multiplication and division activities for the special students in your class. Many of the ideas are directed to learning approaches which can be incorporated into the lessons in this chapter to meet special needs of students. Others focus on ways to handle common problems experienced by special students.

Visual-Kinesthetic Cues to Mental Math

Encourage students to color underscore or finger trace over digits which are keys to the patterns in special products and quotients. Doing so often helps them understand and retain the ideas being presented. In follow-up exercises like the one shown below, it may be necessary to allow students to write the exercise before giving the estimated product. As students become more confident, they will be able to think rather than write the rounded factors they use to derive an estimated product.

Given: 69   Student writes: 70
          × 8   × 8

Do It - Show It

As you review whole number multiplication, require students to use visuals to actively interpret the instruction boxes shown on pages 60 and 62. This will be necessary to correct misconceptions and to insure retention of correct procedures.

Allow students to combine and regroup place-value models step by step as they complete several written problems. Graph paper (TRB p. 284) can be used to illustrate the multiplication of selected problems as shown. Have students state that they add the results of the two small multiplications to find the total, in this case 24 × 28.

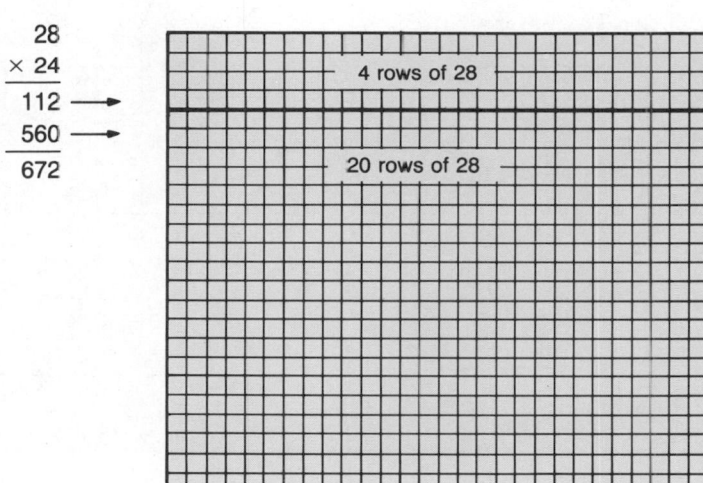

```
  28
× 24
 112  →
 560  →
 672
```

Look Ahead

When multiplying by a 1-digit factor, have students cross out each digit they regroup as they use it. This will later avoid confusion with 2-digit factors when two or more regrouped digits are visually present.

```
  224          26
×   3        × 67
 672          182
             1560
            1,742
```

Oral Guidance

The language of sharing should prove useful for reviewing the long division procedures of this chapter. Reference to money, as illustrated below, often helps special students relate to and remember the basic steps for division.

Students can interpret division examples as money to be shared with a given number of people. For example, in the exercise 2,674 ÷ 23, point out that there are not enough thousand dollar bills to share, but there are enough hundreds. Carry through with the idea of sharing money, following the basic steps summarized on page 74, until the division is complete.

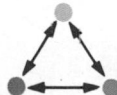 **Subject Integration**

Subject matter related to other areas of the curriculum has been integrated into the following lessons. This provides an opportunity to highlight the interaction between mathematics and other subjects.

Consumer Awareness Estimation of grocery costs, pages 58–59; automobile costs, pages 68–69

Fine Arts Musical instruments, pages 60–61

Science Applications of computers and office machines, page 55; vibration and musical instruments, pages 60–61; crystal growth, page 66; glide ratio, pages 78–79

Social Studies Population density, pages 64–65

History Napier's Rods, page 85

Physical Education Baseball, pages 74–75

Health Calories, pages 76–77

Computer Awareness Applications of computers, page 55; computer languages, page 67

Management Guide

Objectives	Chapter Content	Pages	TRB Test Items	Minimum	Average	Extended	Reteaching	Enrichment	Practice
	Teaching Chapter 3			**Meeting Individual Needs**					
				Lesson Assignments			**Follow Up**		
	Chapter Opener	55							
3.1 Estimate products of whole numbers.	Basic Properties of Multiplication	56	1–3	1–11	1–14	1–14	SE6 Ch4		
	Special Products: Mental Math	57	4–5	1–30, 40	1–40	1–39 odd, 40–43	RS 16	ES 16	PS 21
	Estimating Products	58–59	6–9	1–36	1–36, 39	1–35 odd, 36–39	SE6 Ch 4 RS 17	ES 17	MP 420 PS 22
3.2 Find products of whole numbers.	Multiplying by a 1-digit Factor	60–61	10–11	1–15, 21–31, SK	1–31, SK	1–31 odd, 32, SK	SE6 Ch 4 RS 18	ES 18	MP 421 PS 23
	Multiplying by a 2-digit Factor	62–63	12–13	1–20, 31–47	1–47	1–47 odd, 48	SE6 Ch 4 RS 19	ES 19	MP 421 PS 24
	Multiplying by Larger Factors	64–65	14–17	1–23	1–28, TM	2–28 even, 29, TM	SE6 Ch 4 RS 20	ES 20	MP 421 PS 25
3.3 Write repeated factors and their products using exponential notation.	Exponential Notation	66–67	18–23	1–30	1–36, 38	1–37 odd, 38, TM	SE6 Ch 4 RS 21	ES 21	MP 422 PS 26
3.4 Estimate quotients of whole numbers.	Special Quotients: Mental Math	70	24–26	1–20	1–28	1–28			
	Estimating Quotients	71	27–29	1–20	1–28	2–32 even,	SE6 Ch 5 RS 22	ES 22	MP 422 PS 28
3.5 Find quotients and remainders of whole numbers.	Dividing by a 1-digit Divisor	72	30–32	1–9	1–10	1–10	SE6 Ch 5 RS 23	ES 23	PS 29
	Short Division	73	33–35	1–10, SK	1–15, SK	1–15, SK			MP 423
	Dividing by a 2-digit Divisor	74–75		1–20, 25	1–25, 28	1–25 odd, 26–28, TM	SE6 Ch 5 RS 24	ES 24	MP 423 PS 30
	Using Larger Divisors	76–77			1–27	1–27 odd, 28, TM	SE6 Ch 5 RS 25	ES 25	MP 423 PS 31
3.6 Solve word problems using the 5-Point Checklist and cumulative computational skills.	Problem Solving: Practice	68–69		1–10	1–11, 15	5–15			PS 27
	Problem Solving: Choosing the Operation	78–79	36–40	1–7	1–7, 10	3–10	SE6 Ch 5 RS 26	ES 26	PS 32
	Problem Solving: Using a Formula	81		1–4	1–5	1–6			PS 33
	Skills Practice	80		1–32	1–40	1–47 odd			
	Problem Solving: Finding a Pattern	82							
	Chapter Review/Test	83							
	Another Look/ Enrichment	84–85							
	Cumulative Review	86							

SE6 Student Edition, Book 6
RS Reteaching Supplement
ES Enrichment Supplement
PS Practice Supplement
MP More Practice
TM Think Math
SK Skillkeeper
TRB Teacher's Resource Book

Masters for use

. . . before Chapter 3

| Readiness Rounding Numbers | 108 |
| Readiness Multiplication and Division | 107 |

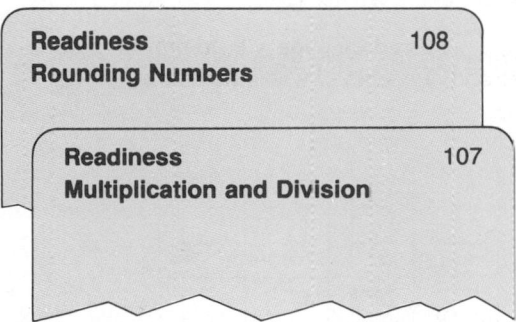

. . . during Chapter 3

Calculator Technology Number Trails	193
Consumer Applications Checking the Balance	175
Teaching Aids	284, 287
Recreation Repeating Tile Designs	157
Activities That Count Quintet	141

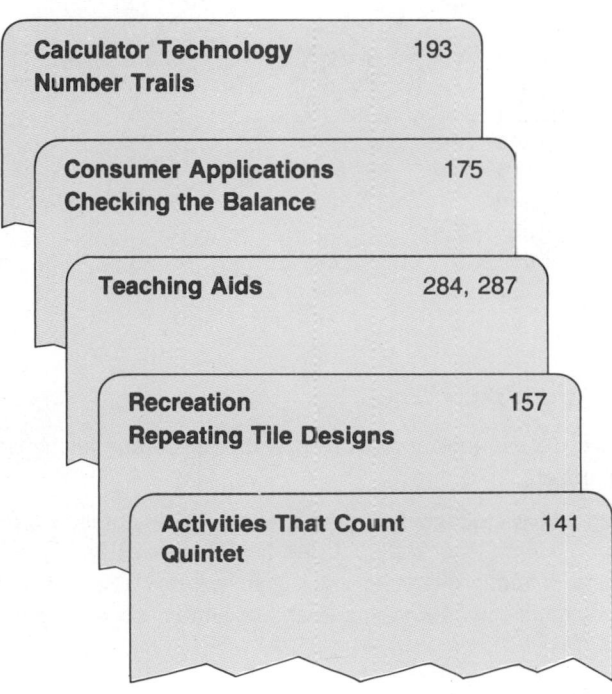

. . . after Chapter 3

Record Keeping	298
Family Involvement At-Home Activities	250
Family Involvement Key Math	249
Reading Math Operations	229
Chapter 3 Test Free-Response Format	52–53
Chapter 3 Test Multiple-Choice Format	7–9

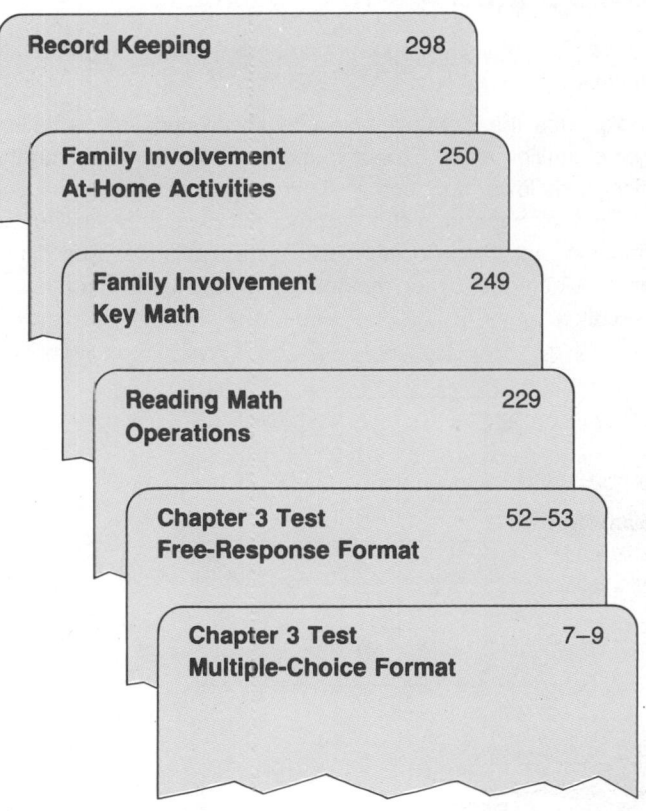

Supplements

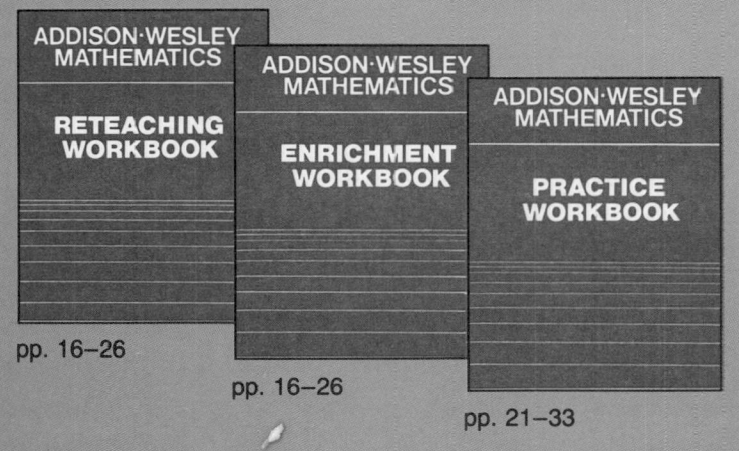

ADDISON·WESLEY MATHEMATICS
RETEACHING WORKBOOK
pp. 16–26

ADDISON·WESLEY MATHEMATICS
ENRICHMENT WORKBOOK
pp. 16–26

ADDISON·WESLEY MATHEMATICS
PRACTICE WORKBOOK
pp. 21–33

Other Addison-Wesley Resources

Books and Kits

A New Twist   pp. 9, 11, 35, 67, 75

Baseball: A Game of Numbers   pp. 17–22

The Mad Minute   pp. 161–170

Problem-Solving Experiences in Mathematics, Grade 7
   Problems 3, 12, 17, 18 23, 28, 29, 30, 33, 38, 53, 58, 64,
   65, 88, 89, 100, 104, 112, 115, 123, 130, 150

Technology

Computer Math Activities   Volumes 1–5

Computer Math Games   Volumes 1–4, 6

Activities That Count

Activities That Count are designed for use throughout this chapter and subsequent chapters. Before beginning Chapter 3, you may wish to review these activities and select the ones you consider appropriate for your class.

Lattice Multiplication Math Lab

Purpose To multiply whole numbers using an alternate algorithm

Activity Use the example below to show students the lattice method of multiplication. Explain that after multiplying, we start the addition in the lower right corner. Then have students copy lattice frames on their paper and choose other numbers to multiply using this method. Ask them to think about the similarities and differences between the usual method of multiplication and lattice multiplication.

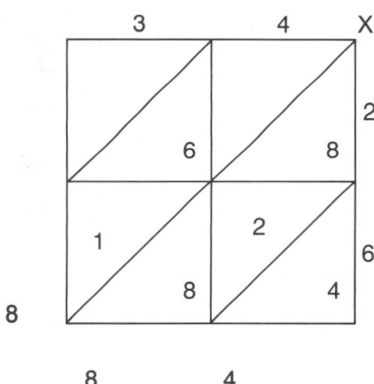

Find the Range Math Lab

Adapt this activity, described on page 1 F, to provide practice estimating products and quotients of whole numbers.

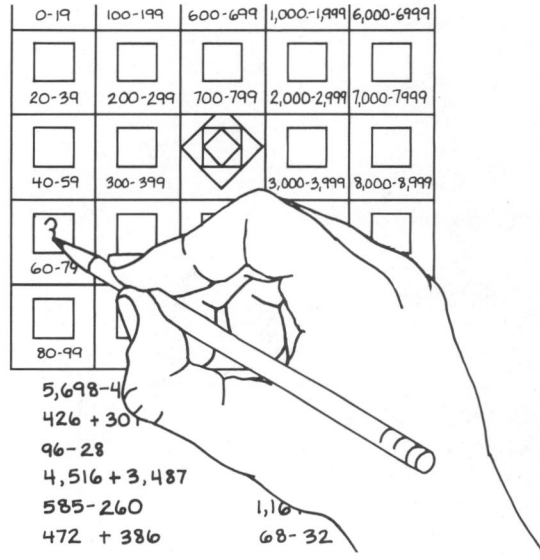

Quintet Game

Purpose To find products of whole numbers

Materials Index cards numbered 17, 58, 212, 781, 947, 1,000, and 2,055, game board (TRB p. 141)

Activity Cut out game boards and distribute a different board to each player in a group. In turn, players draw 2 cards, find the product of the two numbers, and cover the product on their game boards. Cards must be shuffled after each draw. The winner is the first player to cover 5 squares in a straight line vertically, horizontally, or diagonally.

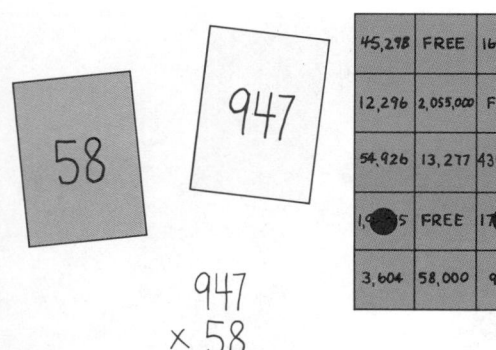

Touchdown Project

Purpose To use logical reasoning and practice operations with whole numbers

Activity Have students find seasonal summaries of their favorite football teams. After they find the final scores of each game, have them determine whether it is possible to tell from the score how many touchdowns were made and how many scores are multiples of 7.

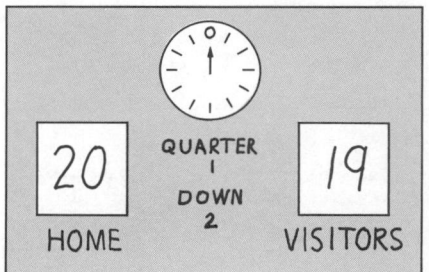

Realistic art and story themes put the mathematics into meaningful and relevant settings.

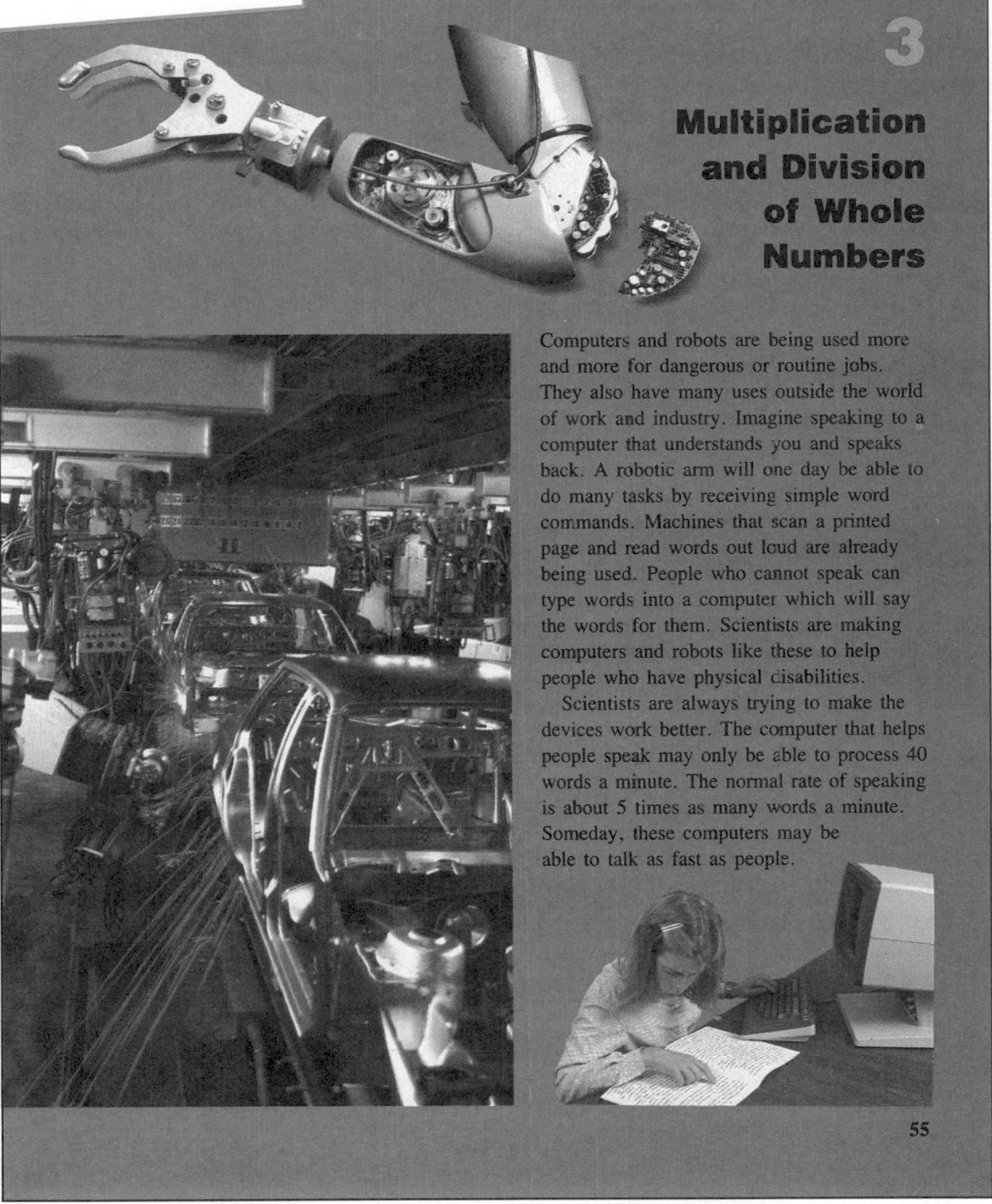

3

Multiplication and Division of Whole Numbers

Computers and robots are being used more and more for dangerous or routine jobs. They also have many uses outside the world of work and industry. Imagine speaking to a computer that understands you and speaks back. A robotic arm will one day be able to do many tasks by receiving simple word commands. Machines that scan a printed page and read words out loud are already being used. People who cannot speak can type words into a computer which will say the words for them. Scientists are making computers and robots like these to help people who have physical disabilities.

Scientists are always trying to make the devices work better. The computer that helps people speak may only be able to process 40 words a minute. The normal rate of speaking is about 5 times as many words a minute. Someday, these computers may be able to talk as fast as people.

Introducing the Chapter

Discussion Have students read about the applications of computers and other machines. Discuss some of the advances made possible through technology. This is an opportunity for students to create their own questions based on the data in the article.

As you teach the chapter, refer back to this page and discuss the questions below. Review the contents of the article briefly before posing the questions.

Follow Up Questions

After Page 57 How many words per minute is the normal rate of speech? (200) One machine can recognize 20 spoken words. Another machine has a "vocabulary" of 50 times as many words, but the chance of making errors is greater. How many words can the second machine recognize? (1,000)

After Page 70 A reading machine can scan a printed page and read out loud at four different speeds: 60, 100, 180, and 300 words per minute. How many times faster is the highest speed than the lowest speed? (5) How many times faster is the second highest speed than the lowest speed? (3)

Number Properties

Quick Review As you read aloud each number below, have students identify how many zeros are in the number.

3,000	40	10,000	700,000	800	720,000
10	40,000	17,200	222,000	2,000	450

Lesson Focus To identify the basic properties of multiplication; to multiply numbers by multiples of 10, 100, and 1,000

Ideas for Getting Started

Ask students to solve this riddle: "I'm thinking of a number. When you multiply it times 8, the product is 8. What is my number?" (1) Have each of two students suggest a number. Write the numbers on the chalkboard, find the product, and ask, "Can you multiply these numbers in a different order and get a different product?" (No) Ask each of three students to suggest a number. As the numbers are given, multiply the first two, then the third, and ask, "Could you give me these numbers in a different order so that the product would be different?" (No)

Next write these multiplication exercises on the chalkboard.

1	10	100	1,000
× 7	× 7	× 7	× 7

Have volunteers give the answers 7, 70, 700, and 7,000. Then ask students to formulate a rule for multiplying by 10, 100, and 1,000 by looking at these examples.

Using Page 56

Lesson Development Remind students that the *commutative* property deals with order. The *associative* property deals with grouping three or more factors. Explain that since multiplication, like addition, is both commutative and associative, we can change both the order and the grouping without changing the product. As a consequence, we often omit parentheses when showing multiplication with 3 or more factors. Point out to students that 0 is the *identity element* for addition since $n + 0 = n$. In the same way, 1 is the identity element for multiplication since $n \cdot 1 = n$ for every number n. The *distributive* property ties together the operations of addition and multiplication. Illustrate to students its use in the multiplication algorithm.

$$
\begin{array}{r}
576 \\
\times \quad 3 \\
\hline
18 \longleftarrow 3 \times 6 \\
210 \longleftarrow 3 \times 70 \\
1500 \longleftarrow 3 \times 500 \\
\hline
1,728
\end{array}
$$

Exercises 1–14 Use the problems as class exercises or assign them as independent work. Make certain students see how the properties can help them find the missing numbers in exercises 7–14.

Basic Properties of Multiplication

The Commutative Property
For every pair of numbers *a* and *b*,
$a \times b = b \times a$
Changing the order of factors does not change the product.

Example: $23 \times 35 = 35 \times 23$

The Associative Property
For any three numbers, *a*, *b*, and *c*,
$(a \times b) \times c = a \times (b \times c)$
Changing the grouping of factors does not change the product.

Example: $4 \times (2 \times 10) = (4 \times 2) \times 10$

The Property of One
For every number *n*,
$n \times 1 = n$
Any number times 1 is equal to the number.

Example: $32 \times 1 = 32$

The Distributive Property
For any numbers *a*, *b*, and *c*,
$a \times (b + c) = (a \times b) + (a \times c)$
Multiplying a sum by a number is the same as multiplying each addend by the number and then adding the products.

Example: $3 \times (40 + 2) = (3 \times 40) + (3 \times 2)$

The basic properties can be used to explain the rules we use to multiply numbers.

Since both the order and grouping of factors can be changed without changing the product, we can arrange three or more factors any way we choose.

$$
\begin{aligned}
2 \times (3 \times 4) &= 3 \times (2 \times 4) \\
&= (4 \times 2) \times 3 \\
&= (2 \times 3) \times 4
\end{aligned}
$$

Name the property used.

1. $35 \times 1 = 35$ Property of One
2. $276 \times 809 = 809 \times 276$ Commutative
3. $(5 \times 2) + (5 \times 8) = 5 \times (2 + 8)$ Distributive
4. $(6 \times 5) \times 2 = 6 \times (5 \times 2)$ Associative
5. $3,357 \times 1 = 3,357$ Property of One
6. $(8 \times 4) + (8 \times 6) = 8 \times 10$ Distributive

Find the missing numbers. The basic properties will help you.

7. $27 \times 26 = n \times 27$ 26
8. $9 \times (8 \times 2) = 9 \times (n \times 8)$ 2
9. $18 \times n = 18$ 1
10. $n \times 6 = 6 \times 23$ 23
11. $5 \times (9 + 3) = (n \times 9) + (5 \times 3)$ 5
12. $6 \times (7 + 4) = (6 \times 7) + (6 \times n)$ 4
13. $20 \times (n + 5) = (20 \times 30) + (20 \times 5)$ 30
14. $n \times 1 = 47$ 47

56

Follow Up

Reteaching

Use familiar words related to the names of the properties to help students distinguish between them. Suggest that commute means to move from one place to another, associate means to group together, and distribute means to spread out or allot to several.

Write the following series of exercises on the chalkboard. Call on students to give the products.

6×7	6×70	6×700	$6 \times 7,000$
2×5	2×50	2×500	$2 \times 5,000$
3×9	30×9	300×9	$3,000 \times 9$
8×4	80×4	800×4	$8,000 \times 4$

Enrichment

Give students multiplication problems and have them apply the distributive property, using graph paper (TRB p. 284) and colored pencils.

Example: $3 \times 6 = 18$

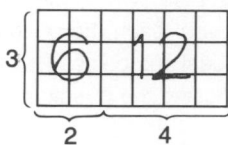

$(3 \times 2) + (3 \times 4) = 3 \times (2 + 4)$

1. $3 \times 7 = 21$
2. $2 \times 5 = 10$
3. $4 \times 4 = 16$
4. $5 \times 6 = 30$

Assignment Guide	Minimum	Average	Extended
page 56	1–11	1–14	1–14
page 57	1–30,40	1–40	1–39 odd, 40–43

Special Products: Mental Math

The patterns below show multiplication of numbers by 10, 100, and 1,000.

$8 \times 10 = 80$ $35 \times 10 = 350$ $167 \times 10 = 1,670$
$8 \times 100 = 800$ $35 \times 100 = 3,500$ $167 \times 100 = 16,700$
$8 \times 1,000 = 8,000$ $35 \times 1,000 = 35,000$ $167 \times 1,000 = 167,000$

When factors are multiples of 10, 100, or 1,000, the products can be found without using paper and a pencil. Study the patterns below.

$30 \times 2 = 60$ $20 \times 4 = 80$ $700 \times 8 = 5,600$
$300 \times 2 = 600$ $20 \times 40 = 800$ $700 \times 80 = 56,000$
$3,000 \times 2 = 6,000$ $20 \times 400 = 8,000$ $700 \times 800 = 560,000$

Write the products only.

1. 7×10 70
2. 9×10 90
3. 4×100 400
4. 100×10 1,000
5. 36×10 360
6. 74×10 740
7. 86×100 8,600
8. 254×100 25,400
9. 40×10 400
10. $87 \times 1,000$ 87,000
11. 7×50 350
12. 20×9 180
13. 40×80 3,200
14. $8 \times 6,000$ 48,000
15. 80×90 7,200
16. $9 \times 3,000$ 27,000
17. 20×300 6,000
18. 50×60 3,000
19. $4,000 \times 3$ 12,000
20. 700×10 7,000
21. 70×70 4,900
22. 600×40 24,000
23. $9,000 \times 6$ 54,000
24. $4,000 \times 40$ 160,000
25. 80×300 24,000
26. $6 \times 7,000$ 42,000
27. 60×90 5,400
28. 400×100 40,000
29. 70×500 35,000
30. $6,000 \times 70$ 420,000

Find the products mentally.

31. $8 \times 10 \times 4$ 320
32. $50 \times 100 \times 6$ 30,000
33. $8 \times 7 \times 100$ 5,600
34. $40 \times 20 \times 10$ 8,000
35. $60 \times 30 \times 100$ 180,000
36. $2,000 \times 3 \times 10$ 60,000
37. $9 \times 1,000 \times 3$ 27,000
38. $20 \times 20 \times 20$ 8,000
39. $10 \times 100 \times 1,000$ 1,000,000

40. There are 60 seconds in 1 minute and 60 minutes in 1 hour. How many seconds are there in 1 hour? 3,600 s

41. There are 1,000 m in 1 km. How many centimeters are there in 10 km? 1,000,000 cm

42. Have you lived 1 billion seconds? Estimate how old a person is who has lived 1 billion seconds. 30-32 years old

43. **DATA HUNT** What is your weight in kilograms? What is your weight in grams? (There are 1,000 grams in 1 kilogram.)

57

Using Page 57

Lesson Development Discuss the examples of multiplying by 10, 100, and 1,000 at the top of the page. Be sure that all students understand the rules for finding the products by annexing 1, 2, or 3 zeros to the digits of the other factor.

On the chalkboard work through the other examples. Elicit from students the relationship between the number of zeros in the factors and the number of zeros in the product.

Exercise 41 This exercise suggests a good physical example of the number 1,000,000. Some students may have run in a 10 km race. Tell them that this race could be called a "1 million centimeter" race.

Exercise 42 Students must use this data:

1 minute = 60 seconds
1 hour = 60 minutes
1 day = 24 hours
1 year = 365 days (approximately)

A person reading this on his or her 13th birthday has lived $13 \times 365 \times 24 \times 60 \times 60$ seconds. The product of these numbers is larger than the capacity of most calculators. However, using the ideas of this lesson, we can find the product of $13 \times 365 \times 24 \times 6 \times 6$ and annex 2 zeros to get 409,968,000 seconds.

Reteaching Supplement, page 16   Enrichment Supplement, page 16   Practice Supplement, page 21

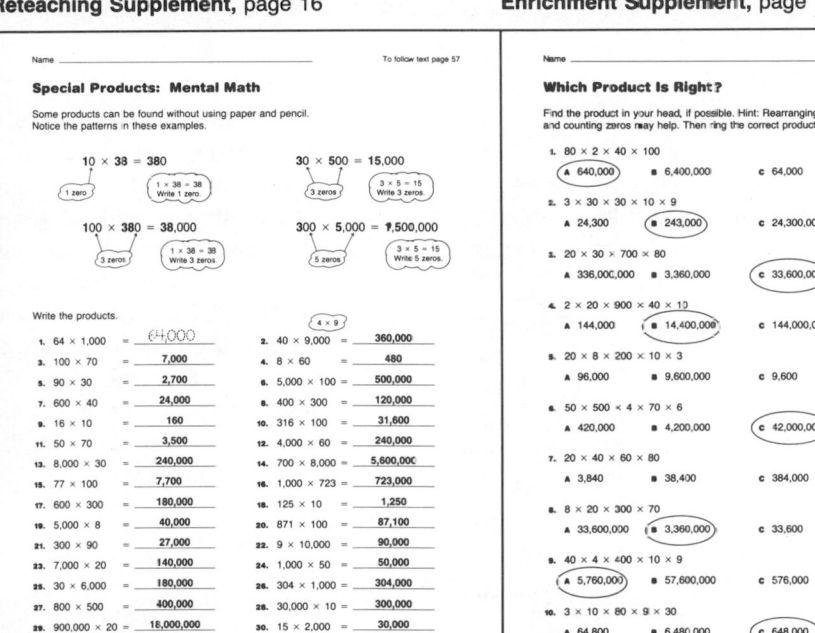

Quick Review Have students mentally find products of three factors.

$2 \times 3 \times 4\ 24$	$5 \times 1 \times 7\ 35$	$0 \times 8 \times 9\ 0$
$3 \times 2 \times 5\ 30$	$2 \times 4 \times 5\ 40$	$3 \times 3 \times 3\ 27$
$2 \times 2 \times 2\ 8$	$1 \times 9 \times 9\ 81$	$2 \times 3 \times 9\ 54$

Lesson Focus To estimate the product of two whole numbers

Ideas for Getting Started

Rounding and performing mental calculations are two important phases in estimating. To prepare students for this lesson, have them round these numbers to 1-digit accuracy.

89   172   53   906   29   317   480   19

Then have students find these products mentally.

20 × 40   8 × 200   50 × 60   700 × 90
30 × 70   600 × 400   10 × 300   80 × 90

Using Page 58

Lesson Development Have students read the problem at the top of the page. Discuss how the numbers are rounded to 1-digit accuracy, or in this case to the nearest ten, to estimate the product. Remind students that they should multiply 50 × 30 in their heads. Point out that the estimate is not the exact product.

Other Examples Work through the other examples with students. In the first example, point out that we can tell the exact product will be larger than the estimate because one factor was rounded down. In the second example, the exact product would be smaller because each factor was rounded up. In the third example, it is difficult to decide because one factor was rounded up and the other rounded down.

Warm Up Use exercises 1–4 as an oral class activity. Have students tell what rounding they did to estimate each product. Then assign exercises 5–12 as independent work.

Estimating Products

Gail Cooper finds cat food on sale. She wants to estimate the cost of a case of 48 cans of cat food.

Estimate 48 × 33¢ by rounding each factor to 1-digit accuracy.

$$48 \times 33¢$$
$$\downarrow \quad \downarrow$$
$$50 \times 30¢ = 1,500¢ = \$15.00$$

The case of 48 cans will cost about $15.00.

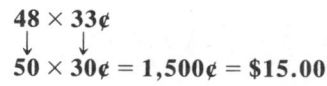

Cat Food Sale
33¢ a can

Other Examples

$418 \rightarrow 400$	$691 \rightarrow 700$	$174 \rightarrow 200$
$\times\ 8 \rightarrow \times\ 8$	$\times\ 49 \rightarrow \times\ 50$	$\times 327 \rightarrow \times 300$
$3,200$	$35,000$	$60,000$

Warm Up

Choose the best estimate of each product.

1. 93 × 7	**2.** 69¢ × 83	**3.** 519 × 37	**4.** 284 × 196
A 1,000	**A** 480¢	**(A)** 20,000	**A** 6,000
B 700	**B** 560¢	**B** 2,000	**(B)** 60,000
(C) 630	**C** $48.00	**C** 24,000	**C** 40,000
D 6,300	**(D)** $56.00	**D** 15,000	**D** 4,000

Estimate each product by rounding to 1-digit accuracy.

5. 87 × 6 = 540	**6.** 237 × 9 = 1,800	**7.** 53 × 79 = 4,000	**8.** 779 × 62 = 48,000
9. 208 × 57 = 12,000	**10.** 819 × 206 = 160,000	**11.** 984 × 327 = 300,000	**12.** 119 × 784 = 80,000

58

Follow Up

Reteaching

Work through an example with students to review estimating products. Show how to use the number line to help in rounding numbers. In the exercises below, have students select the number that is the best estimate.

1. 74 × 5	350 **400** 450	**2.** 32 × 57	1,500 **1,800** 2,400
3. 275 × 4	120 800 **1,200**	**4.** 612 × 75	4,200 42,000 **48,000**
5. 46 × 23	800 **1,000** 10,000	**6.** 374 × 52	2,000 **20,000** 15,000

Enrichment

Have students form groups of 3 and write 25 2-digit and 3-digit numbers on a sheet of paper. In turn, students name product goals. After a goal is given, each of the players selects two numbers from their paper whose product is close to the goal. The players can then multiply their numbers on the calculator to see who is closest to the goal. The player whose factors have a product closest to the goal wins a point. The first player to score 10 points wins.

Assignment Guide			
	Minimum	Average	Extended
page 59	1–36	1–36, 39	1–35 odd, 36–39

Estimate each product by rounding to 1-digit accuracy.

1.
$$\begin{array}{r} 69 \\ \times\ 8 \\ \hline 560 \end{array}$$

2.
$$\begin{array}{r} 23 \\ \times\ 37 \\ \hline 800 \end{array}$$

3.
$$\begin{array}{r} 209 \\ \times\ 33 \\ \hline 6{,}000 \end{array}$$

4.
$$\begin{array}{r} 73 \\ \times\ 18 \\ \hline 1{,}400 \end{array}$$

5.
$$\begin{array}{r} 425 \\ \times\ 67 \\ \hline 28{,}000 \end{array}$$

6.
$$\begin{array}{r} 63 \\ \times\ 7 \\ \hline 420 \end{array}$$

7.
$$\begin{array}{r} 39 \\ \times\ 9 \\ \hline 360 \end{array}$$

8.
$$\begin{array}{r} 83 \\ \times\ 6 \\ \hline 480 \end{array}$$

9.
$$\begin{array}{r} 389 \\ \times\ 3 \\ \hline 1{,}200 \end{array}$$

10.
$$\begin{array}{r} 5{,}089 \\ \times\ 6 \\ \hline 30{,}000 \end{array}$$

11.
$$\begin{array}{r} 84 \\ \times\ 27 \\ \hline 2{,}400 \end{array}$$

12.
$$\begin{array}{r} 63 \\ \times\ 41 \\ \hline 2{,}400 \end{array}$$

13.
$$\begin{array}{r} 47 \\ \times\ 18 \\ \hline 1{,}000 \end{array}$$

14.
$$\begin{array}{r} 38 \\ \times\ 82 \\ \hline 3{,}200 \end{array}$$

15.
$$\begin{array}{r} 43 \\ \times\ 17 \\ \hline 800 \end{array}$$

16.
$$\begin{array}{r} 51 \\ \times\ 69 \\ \hline 3{,}500 \end{array}$$

17.
$$\begin{array}{r} 34 \\ \times\ 68 \\ \hline 2{,}100 \end{array}$$

18.
$$\begin{array}{r} 67 \\ \times\ 23 \\ \hline 1{,}400 \end{array}$$

19.
$$\begin{array}{r} 78 \\ \times\ 19 \\ \hline 1{,}600 \end{array}$$

20.
$$\begin{array}{r} 38 \\ \times\ 43 \\ \hline 1{,}600 \end{array}$$

21.
$$\begin{array}{r} 521 \\ \times\ 11 \\ \hline 5{,}000 \end{array}$$

22.
$$\begin{array}{r} 588 \\ \times\ 61 \\ \hline 36{,}000 \end{array}$$

23.
$$\begin{array}{r} 709 \\ \times\ 67 \\ \hline 49{,}000 \end{array}$$

24.
$$\begin{array}{r} 892 \\ \times\ 77 \\ \hline 72{,}000 \end{array}$$

25.
$$\begin{array}{r} 475 \\ \times\ 83 \\ \hline 40{,}000 \end{array}$$

26. 95×25
3,000

27. 36×69
2,800

28. 72×66
4,900

29. 22×87
1,800

30. 47×95
5,000

31. 722×128
70,000

32. 643×315
180,000

33. 296×504
150,000

34. 726×194
140,000

35. 814×578
480,000

36. Estimate the cost of 6 boxes. $4.80

37. Estimate the change from $5 if Gina buys 12 cans of dog food. $0.20

★ **38.** Estimate the total. $9.70

39. DATA HUNT Find the cost of a grocery item in an advertisement. How much would 36 of that item cost? Make an estimate.

SALES RECEIPT			
6	Cat toys at	48¢ each	?
5	Dog bones at	83¢ each	?
3	Bird seed bells at	92¢ each	?
		Total	?

More Practice, page 420, Set C

Using Page 59

Exercise 38 This exercise involves two operations. Students must estimate the products, and then they must find the sum of the estimates.

Data Hunt Students who work the Data Hunt will need a grocery store advertisement. You may wish to post one on a bulletin board for them to use.

More Practice, page 420 Set C

Reteaching Supplement, page 17

Estimating Products

To estimate the product of **37 × 684**:

Round each factor to 1-digit accuracy.

$$\begin{array}{r} 684 \\ \times\ 37 \end{array} \xrightarrow{\text{rounds to}} \begin{array}{r} 700 \\ \times\ 40 \\ \hline 28{,}000 \end{array}$$

Multiply the rounded numbers.

$4 \times 7 = 28$ Write 3 zeros.

Estimate each product.

1. $43 \to 40$, $\times 16 \to \times 20$ = 800
2. $578 \to 600$, $\times 3 \to \times 3$ = 1,800
3. $208 \to 200$, $\times 350 \to \times 400$ = 80,000

4. $39 \to 40$, $\times 4 \to \times 4$ = 160
5. $523 \to 500$, $\times 6 \to \times 6$ = 3,000
6. $74 \to 70$, $\times 8 \to \times 8$ = 560
7. $967 \to 1,000$, $\times 33 \to \times 30$ = 30,000

8. $72 \to 70$, $\times 55 \to \times 60$ = 4,200
9. $87 \to 90$, $\times 63 \to \times 60$ = 5,400
10. $99 \to 100$, $\times 50 \to \times 50$ = 5,000
11. $68 \to 70$, $\times 32 \to \times 30$ = 2,100

12. $375 \to 400$, $\times 42 \to \times 40$ = 16,000
13. $98 \to 100$, $\times 73 \to \times 70$ = 7,000
14. $280 \to 300$, $\times 64 \to \times 60$ = 18,000
15. $31 \to 30$, $\times 29 \to \times 30$ = 900

16. $862 \to 900$, $\times 53 \to \times 50$ = 45,000
17. $74 \to 70$, $\times 32 \to \times 30$ = 2,100
18. $97 \to 100$, $\times 61 \to \times 60$ = 6,000
19. $348 \to 300$, $\times 52 \to \times 50$ = 15,000

20. 782×695 → $800 \times 700 = 560,000$
21. 254×963 → $300 \times 1,000 = 300,000$
22. 807×72 → $800 \times 70 = 56,000$

Enrichment Supplement, page 17

Mystery Factors

Use estimation to find which two factors on the chalkboard would produce the given product. Check your work by using a calculator to find the product.

246	426	527	910
475	105	574	875
	172	98	634	584
217	250	304	722

1. $\underline{426} \times \underline{574} = 244{,}524$
2. $\underline{394} \times \underline{634} = 249{,}796$
3. $\underline{584} \times \underline{475} = 277{,}400$
4. $\underline{246} \times \underline{105} = 25{,}830$
5. $\underline{327} \times \underline{875} = 286{,}125$
6. $\underline{172} \times \underline{98} = 16{,}856$
7. $\underline{250} \times \underline{722} = 180{,}500$
8. $\underline{810} \times \underline{217} = 175{,}770$

Make up two factors whose estimated product is approximately (≈) the given number. Each factor must have at least two digits. Use a calculator to find the actual product of your factors.

Compare the product of your factors to the given one. Then find the difference. Compare your results with a friend.
Answers will vary.
Some possible answers are given.

		Product of your factors	Difference
9. $\underline{225} \times \underline{255} \approx 57{,}352$			
10. $\underline{376} \times \underline{500} \approx 188{,}250$			
11. $\underline{706} \times \underline{800} \approx 565{,}152$			
12. $\underline{425} \times \underline{742} \approx 315{,}456$			

Practice Supplement, page 22

Estimating Products

Estimate each problem by rounding to 1-digit accuracy.

1. $\begin{array}{r} 58 \\ \times\ 7 \end{array}$ → $\begin{array}{r} 60 \\ \times\ 7 \\ \hline 420 \end{array}$
2. $\begin{array}{r} 92 \\ \times\ 3 \end{array}$ → $\begin{array}{r} 90 \\ \times\ 3 \\ \hline 270 \end{array}$
3. $\begin{array}{r} 77 \\ \times\ 7 \end{array}$ → $\begin{array}{r} 80 \\ \times\ 7 \\ \hline 560 \end{array}$

4. $\begin{array}{r} 19 \\ \times\ 32 \end{array}$ → $\begin{array}{r} 20 \\ \times\ 30 \\ \hline 600 \end{array}$
5. $\begin{array}{r} 88 \\ \times\ 24 \end{array}$ → $\begin{array}{r} 90 \\ \times\ 20 \\ \hline 1{,}800 \end{array}$
6. $\begin{array}{r} 53 \\ \times\ 77 \end{array}$ → $\begin{array}{r} 50 \\ \times\ 80 \\ \hline 4{,}000 \end{array}$

7. $\begin{array}{r} 219 \\ \times\ 4 \end{array}$ → $\begin{array}{r} 200 \\ \times\ 4 \\ \hline 800 \end{array}$
8. $\begin{array}{r} 883 \\ \times\ 7 \end{array}$ → $\begin{array}{r} 900 \\ \times\ 7 \\ \hline 6{,}300 \end{array}$
9. $\begin{array}{r} 315 \\ \times\ 6 \end{array}$ → $\begin{array}{r} 300 \\ \times\ 6 \\ \hline 1{,}800 \end{array}$

10. $\begin{array}{r} 199 \\ \times\ 31 \end{array}$ → $\begin{array}{r} 100 \\ \times\ 30 \\ \hline 3{,}000 \end{array}$
11. $\begin{array}{r} 211 \\ \times\ 84 \end{array}$ → $\begin{array}{r} 200 \\ \times\ 80 \\ \hline 16{,}000 \end{array}$
12. $\begin{array}{r} 693 \\ \times\ 18 \end{array}$ → $\begin{array}{r} 700 \\ \times\ 20 \\ \hline 14{,}000 \end{array}$

13. $\begin{array}{r} 8{,}141 \\ \times\ 3 \end{array}$ → $\begin{array}{r} 8{,}000 \\ \times\ 3 \\ \hline 24{,}000 \end{array}$
14. $\begin{array}{r} 7{,}042 \\ \times\ 9 \end{array}$ → $\begin{array}{r} 7{,}000 \\ \times\ 9 \\ \hline 63{,}000 \end{array}$
15. $\begin{array}{r} 1{,}964 \\ \times\ 6 \end{array}$ → $\begin{array}{r} 2{,}000 \\ \times\ 6 \\ \hline 12{,}000 \end{array}$

16. $\begin{array}{r} 509 \\ \times\ 67 \end{array}$ → $\begin{array}{r} 500 \\ \times\ 70 \\ \hline 35{,}000 \end{array}$
17. $\begin{array}{r} 884 \\ \times\ 73 \end{array}$ → $\begin{array}{r} 900 \\ \times\ 70 \\ \hline 63{,}000 \end{array}$
18. $\begin{array}{r} 415 \\ \times\ 99 \end{array}$ → $\begin{array}{r} 400 \\ \times\ 100 \\ \hline 40{,}000 \end{array}$

19. $\begin{array}{r} 311 \\ \times\ 201 \end{array}$ → $\begin{array}{r} 300 \\ \times\ 200 \\ \hline 60{,}000 \end{array}$
20. $\begin{array}{r} 777 \\ \times\ 119 \end{array}$ → $\begin{array}{r} 800 \\ \times\ 100 \\ \hline 80{,}000 \end{array}$
21. $\begin{array}{r} 184 \\ \times\ 196 \end{array}$ → $\begin{array}{r} 200 \\ \times\ 200 \\ \hline 40{,}000 \end{array}$

22. 88×23
$90 \times 20 = 1,800$
23. 52×17
$50 \times 20 = 1,000$
24. 18×19
$20 \times 20 = 400$

25. 48×61
$50 \times 60 = 3,000$
26. 32×56
$30 \times 60 = 1,800$
27. 81×14
$80 \times 10 = 800$

28. 248×312
$200 \times 300 = 60,000$
29. 206×155
$200 \times 200 = 40,000$
30. 325×812
$300 \times 800 = 240,000$

Quick Review Have students perform the calculations mentally.

Quick Review Have students perform the calculations mentally.

$(7 \times 5) + 3$ 38	$(5 \times 4) + 9$ 29	$(9 \times 9) + 9$ 90
$(3 \times 3) + 7$ 16	$(8 \times 6) + 7$ 55	$(2 \times 4) + 5$ 13
$(0 \times 6) + 8$ 8	$(9 \times 1) + 8$ 17	$(7 \times 7) + 7$ 56

Lesson Focus To multiply by a 1-digit number

Ideas for Getting Started

Write these addition exercises on the chalkboard.

$7 + 7 + 7 + 7 + 7 + 7 + 7 + 7$

$28 + 28 + 28 + 28 + 28$

$219 + 219 + 219 + 219 + 219 + 219$

"Can you think of a shorter way to find these sums?" In each case, there is a repeated addend so we can use multiplication.

Review with students the meaning of factors and product.

$$8 \times 5 = 40$$
$$\uparrow \quad \uparrow \quad \quad \uparrow$$
$$\text{Factors} \quad \text{Product}$$

Using Page 60

Motivational Problem Have students read the problem. "What does the question ask us to find?" (the number of times the string will vibrate in 4 seconds) "What data is needed to solve the problem?" (the number of times the string vibrates in 1 second, which is 256) Explain that since the string vibrates the same number of times each second, we can multiply to solve the problem.

Lesson Development On the chalkboard, go through the steps in the algorithm shown in the instruction lines. Explain the regrouping necessary at each stage. Then show a check of the problem by repeated addition:

$256 + 256 + 256 + 256 = 1,024.$

Warm Up Watch for students who reverse the digit to be saved with the digit to be multiplied, as shown in the example below.

$$
\begin{array}{r}
4 \\
27 \\
\times \ 6 \\
\hline
262
\end{array}
$$

Multiplying by a 1-digit Factor

Jamie likes to play the guitar. When she plucks the middle C string on her guitar, the string vibrates 256 times in 1 second. How many times will the string vibrate in 4 seconds?

Since the same number is repeated, we can use multiplication.

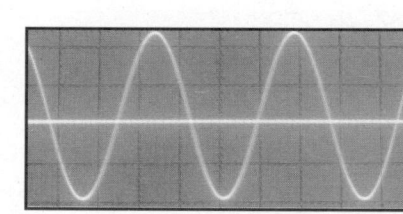

Multiply the ones. Regroup if necessary.	Multiply the tens. Add and regroup if necessary.	Multiply the hundreds. Add if necessary.
$\begin{array}{r} 2 \\ 25\,6 \\ \times \quad 4 \\ \hline 4 \end{array}$	$\begin{array}{r} 2\ 2 \\ 25\,6 \\ \times \quad 4 \\ \hline 24 \end{array}$	$\begin{array}{r} 2\ 2 \\ 25\,6 \leftarrow \text{factor} \\ \times \quad 4 \leftarrow \text{factor} \\ \hline 1,024 \leftarrow \text{product} \end{array}$

The string will vibrate 1,024 times in 4 seconds.

Other Examples

$\begin{array}{r} 7 \\ 59 \\ \times\ 8 \\ \hline 472 \end{array}$	$\begin{array}{r} 4 \\ 380 \\ \times\ 6 \\ \hline 2,280 \end{array}$	$\begin{array}{r} 2\ 6\ 4 \\ 3,275 \\ \times\quad 9 \\ \hline 29,475 \end{array}$	$\begin{array}{r} 4 \\ 307 \\ \times\ 6 \\ \hline 1,842 \end{array}$

Warm Up

Multiply.

1. $\begin{array}{r} 23 \\ \times\ 6 \\ \hline 138 \end{array}$	2. $\begin{array}{r} 79 \\ \times\ 8 \\ \hline 632 \end{array}$	3. $\begin{array}{r} 80 \\ \times\ 5 \\ \hline 400 \end{array}$	4. $\begin{array}{r} 239 \\ \times\ 9 \\ \hline 2,151 \end{array}$	5. $\begin{array}{r} 826 \\ \times\ 4 \\ \hline 3,304 \end{array}$
6. $\begin{array}{r} 367 \\ \times\ 9 \\ \hline 3,303 \end{array}$	7. $\begin{array}{r} 1,293 \\ \times\quad 7 \\ \hline 9,051 \end{array}$	8. $\begin{array}{r} 5,276 \\ \times\quad 3 \\ \hline 15,828 \end{array}$	9. $\begin{array}{r} 3,737 \\ \times\quad 7 \\ \hline 26,159 \end{array}$	10. $\begin{array}{r} 8,309 \\ \times\quad 8 \\ \hline 66,472 \end{array}$

60

Follow Up

Reteaching

Illustrate how the multiplication algorithm is carried out, using the sequence shown below.

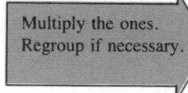

$$
\begin{array}{r} 136 \\ \times\ 4 \\ \hline \end{array} \longrightarrow
\qquad
\begin{array}{r} 100 + 30 + 6 \\ \times\ 4 \\ \hline \end{array} \longrightarrow
$$

$$
\begin{array}{r} 100 + 30 + 6 \\ \times\qquad\quad 4 \\ \hline 400 + 120 + 24 \end{array} \longrightarrow
\qquad
\begin{array}{r} 1\ 2 \\ 136 \\ \times\ 4 \\ \hline 544 \end{array}
$$

Have students work through some exercises following this example.

Enrichment

Challenge students to find these products and break the code.

$\begin{array}{r} 131,702 \\ \times\qquad 5 \\ \hline 658,510 \\ \text{ROBOTS} \end{array}$	$\begin{array}{r} 467 \\ \times\ 1 \\ \hline 467 \\ \text{ARE} \end{array}$	$\begin{array}{r} 13 \\ \times\ 3 \\ \hline 39 \\ \text{IN} \end{array}$

A	B	E	I	N	O	R	T	S
4	8	7	3	9	5	6	1	0

Then have students write some multiplication problems and devise their own codes. Present these to the rest of the class.

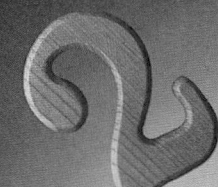

Multiply.

1.	62 × 5 = 310	**2.**	37 × 7 = 259	**3.**	95 × 8 = 760	**4.**	53 × 9 = 477	**5.**	85 × 6 = 510
6.	224 × 6 = 1,344	**7.**	380 × 9 = 3,420	**8.**	604 × 8 = 4,832	**9.**	375 × 5 = 1,875	**10.**	642 × 9 = 5,778
11.	3,247 × 2 = 6,494	**12.**	26,093 × 4 = 104,372	**13.**	15,776 × 7 = 110,432	**14.**	8,200 × 9 = 73,800	**15.**	3,006 × 8 = 24,048
16.	5,881 × 3 = 17,643	**17.**	3,948 × 5 = 19,740	**18.**	6,275 × 6 = 37,650	**19.**	36,344 × 4 = 145,376	**20.**	8,826 × 7 = 61,782

21. 854 × 9 = 7,686 **22.** 64 × 7 = 448 **23.** 1,024 × 8 = 8,192 **24.** 7,142 × 4 = 28,568 **25.** 8,166 × 9 = 73,494

26. 952 × 7 = 6,664 **27.** 7,965 × 8 = 63,720 **28.** 654 × 3 = 1,962 **29.** 52,560 × 6 = 315,360 **30.** 2,927 × 4 = 11,708

31. The lowest note on a piano is made by a string vibrating 27 times a second. How many times will the string vibrate in 3 seconds? 81

32. The highest note on a piano is made by a string vibrating 3,473 more times per second than the string for the lowest note. How many vibrations will it make in 6 seconds? 21,000

SKILLKEEPER

1.	5.36 + 2.77 = 8.13	**2.**	8.1 − 0.20 = 7.90	**3.**	29.564 + 1.6 = 31.164	**4.**	0.567 + 6.439 = 7.006
5.	23.544 − 17.256 = 6.288	**6.**	7.629 − 3.542 = 4.087	**7.**	678.35 + 9.706 = 688.056	**8.**	0.766 − 0.379 = 0.387
9.	$51.97 − 0.79 = $51.18	**10.**	$0.98 + 0.29 = $1.27	**11.**	$5,979.60 − 2,596.70 = $3,382.90	**12.**	$288.00 + 199.00 = $487.00
13.	$905.20 + 617.90 = $1,523.10	**14.**	$5.67 − 2.39 = $3.28	**15.**	$0.75 + 0.38 = $1.13	**16.**	$6,095.77 − 5,966.98 = $128.79

More Practice, page 421, Set A

Using Page 61

Exercises 1–32 Encourage students to check their answers by estimation. In exercises 14 and 15, be sure students do not skip over the second zero in the top factor.

Skillkeeper These skills were originally taught in Chapter 2.

Skillkeepers provide practice and review of basic skills at spaced intervals throughout the book.

More Practice, page 421, Set A

Reteaching Supplement, page 18

Enrichment Supplement, page 18

Practice Supplement, page 23

Multiplication

Quick Review Display the numbers below. Point to different combinations of three numbers and have students order from least to greatest.

899,789	91,560	899,780	89,780
890,634	99,736	899,790	90,422

Lesson Focus To multiply by a 2-digit number

Ideas for Getting Started

Have students find the products of 3 × 42 and 10 × 42. (126 and 420) "What is the sum of the two products?" (546) "How many 42s are in this sum?" (3 + 10 or 13) Tell students that we could find 13 × 42 by this method, but we combine the 2 multiplications and the addition in the usual multiplication algorithm.

$$
\begin{array}{r}
42 \\
\times\ 13 \\
\hline
126 \leftarrow\quad 3 \times 42 \\
420 \leftarrow\quad 10 \times 42 \\
\hline
546
\end{array}
$$

Using Page 62

Motivational Problem Have students read the introductory problem and state the question in their own words. "What data do we need to solve the problem?" (There are 24 rows of tiles and 28 tiles in each row.) "Why can we plan to use multiplication to find the answer?" (because each row has the same number of tiles)

Lesson Development On the chalkboard, work through the problem explaining each step and the regrouping that is necessary. Notice with students that the digits "saved" are no longer written. When multiplying 28 by the ones digit, we write the 2 in the ones place and remember the 3 tens. Then we multiply 4 × 2 and add the 3 for a total of 11. Some students may have been taught to write the digits saved in the regrouping process. Encourage them to do both the multiplying and adding in their heads.

Have students check the reasonableness of the product of 28 × 24 by rounding each factor and estimating the product.

Other Examples Call attention to the second example. When we multiply by a multiple of 10, we write 0 in the ones place, and then multiply by the number of tens.

Warm Up If some students do write the digits saved, be sure that they mark them out before they multiply by the tens. Otherwise, the likelihood of errors will increase.

$$
\begin{array}{r}
{}^{3}\\
28 \\
\times\ 24 \\
\hline
112
\end{array}
\qquad
\begin{array}{r}
{}^{1}\\
\cancel{28} \\
\times\ 24 \\
\hline
112 \\
560 \\
\hline
672
\end{array}
$$

Multiplying by a 2-digit Factor

To cover a floor, it will take 24 rows of tiles. Each row will have 28 tiles. How many tiles will it take to cover the floor?

Since each row has the same number of tiles, we multiply.

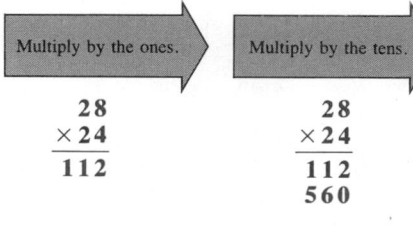

Multiply by the ones.	Multiply by the tens.	Add the products.
$\begin{array}{r}28\\ \times 24\\ \hline 112\end{array}$	$\begin{array}{r}28\\ \times 24\\ \hline 112\\ 560\end{array}$	$\begin{array}{r}28\\ \times 24\\ \hline 112\\ 560\\ \hline 672\end{array}$

It will take 672 tiles to cover the floor.

Other Examples

$$
\begin{array}{r}
257 \\
\times\ 38 \\
\hline
2056 \\
7710 \\
\hline
9{,}766
\end{array}
\qquad
\begin{array}{r}
523 \\
\times\ 70 \\
\hline
36{,}610
\end{array}
\qquad
\begin{array}{r}
4{,}078 \\
\times\ 59 \\
\hline
36702 \\
203900 \\
\hline
240{,}602
\end{array}
$$

Warm Up

Multiply.

1. $\begin{array}{r}72\\ \times 46\\ \hline 3{,}312\end{array}$	**2.** $\begin{array}{r}67\\ \times 76\\ \hline 5{,}092\end{array}$	**3.** $\begin{array}{r}94\\ \times 73\\ \hline 6{,}862\end{array}$	**4.** $\begin{array}{r}59\\ \times 60\\ \hline 3{,}540\end{array}$	**5.** $\begin{array}{r}80\\ \times 52\\ \hline 4{,}160\end{array}$
6. $\begin{array}{r}163\\ \times 42\\ \hline 6{,}846\end{array}$	**7.** $\begin{array}{r}309\\ \times 75\\ \hline 23{,}175\end{array}$	**8.** $\begin{array}{r}1{,}824\\ \times 56\\ \hline 102{,}144\end{array}$	**9.** $\begin{array}{r}5{,}227\\ \times 43\\ \hline 224{,}761\end{array}$	**10.** $\begin{array}{r}9{,}561\\ \times 84\\ \hline 803{,}124\end{array}$

62

Follow Up

Reteaching

Write the following exercises on the chalkboard. Have students identify the two factors in each partial product, and then write the total product.

Example:
$$
\begin{array}{rl}
35 & \\
\times\ 24 & \\
\hline
20 & 4 \times 5 \\
120 & 4 \times 30 \\
100 & 20 \times 5 \\
600 & 20 \times 30 \\
\hline
840 &
\end{array}
$$

$$
\begin{array}{r}
76 \\
\times\ 51
\end{array}
\qquad
\begin{array}{r}
49 \\
\times\ 31
\end{array}
\qquad
\begin{array}{r}
27 \\
\times\ 86
\end{array}
\qquad
\begin{array}{r}
63 \\
\times\ 95
\end{array}
$$

Enrichment

Have students complete the following exercises by filling in the correct digits.

1.
$$
\begin{array}{r}
\boxed{7}\,1 \\
\times\ 5\,4 \\
\hline
2\,8\,\boxed{4} \\
\boxed{3}\,\boxed{5}\,\boxed{5}\,0 \\
\hline
3{,}\boxed{8}\,3\,4
\end{array}
$$

2.
$$
\begin{array}{r}
9\,9 \\
\times\ \boxed{2}\,\boxed{3} \\
\hline
2\,\boxed{9}\,\boxed{7} \\
\boxed{1}\,9\,8\,0 \\
\hline
2{,}\boxed{2}\,\boxed{7}\,0
\end{array}
$$

3.
$$
\begin{array}{r}
\boxed{3}\,\boxed{5}\,\boxed{9} \\
\times\ 7\,7 \\
\hline
2\,\boxed{5}\,1\,\boxed{3} \\
2\,\boxed{5}\,1\,\boxed{3}\,0 \\
\hline
2\,7{,}\,6\,\boxed{4}\,\boxed{3}
\end{array}
$$

Assignment Guide

page 63	Minimum	Average	Extended
	1–20, 31–47	1–47	1–47 odd, 48

Multiply.

1. 25 ×43 = 1,075	**2.** 63 ×82 = 5,166	**3.** 79 ×37 = 2,923	**4.** 68 ×87 = 5,916	**5.** 94 ×69 = 6,486
6. 772 ×37 = 28,564	**7.** 306 ×48 = 14,688	**8.** 529 ×87 = 46,023	**9.** 623 ×92 = 57,316	**10.** 375 ×64 = 24,000
11. 990 ×81 = 80,190	**12.** 403 ×94 = 37,882	**13.** 924 ×98 = 90,552	**14.** 965 ×19 = 18,335	**15.** 665 ×38 = 25,270
16. 2,137 ×58 = 123,946	**17.** 5,074 ×83 = 421,142	**18.** 9,544 ×97 = 925,768	**19.** 6,626 ×49 = 324,674	**20.** 7,189 ×81 = 582,309
21. 8,064 ×53 = 427,392	**22.** 7,009 ×47 = 329,423	**23.** 1,398 ×45 = 62,910	**24.** 7,799 ×86 = 670,714	**25.** 5,238 ×42 = 219,996
26. 6,078 ×39 = 237,042	**27.** 3,009 ×74 = 222,666	**28.** 9,849 ×76 = 748,524	**29.** 4,396 ×17 = 74,732	**30.** 7,468 ×84 = 627,312

31. 17×12 = 204
32. 42×38 = 1,596
33. 24×18 = 432
34. 56×62 = 3,472
35. 129×31 = 3,999
36. 248×72 = 17,856
37. 365×98 = 35,770
38. 279×84 = 23,436
39. 824×76 = 62,624
40. 747×39 = 29,133
41. $9,055 \times 99$ = 896,445
42. $8,630 \times 70$ = 604,100
43. $8,296 \times 57$ = 472,872
44. $56,296 \times 18$ = 1,013,328
45. $20,304 \times 56$ = 1,137,024
46. $36,068 \times 77$ = 2,777,236

47. Lisa is covering a rectangular table with small square tiles. It will take 32 rows of tiles with 48 tiles in each row. How many tiles are needed to cover the table? 1,536

48. A classroom floor is covered with square tiles. There are 14 blue tiles and 15 white tiles in each row. There are 23 rows of tiles. How many tiles are on the floor? 667

More Practice, page 421, Set B

63

Using Page 63

Exercises 1–46 Work individually or in small groups with any students having difficulty with these exercises. Determine whether the difficulty is with weakness in multiplication facts or in understanding the steps in the algorithm. Some students may need extra practice with the basic facts, while others may need help in using the algorithm correctly.

More Practice, page 421, Set B

Reteaching Supplement, page 19

Enrichment Supplement, page 19

Practice Supplement, page 24

Multiplication

Lesson Focus To multiply by a 3-digit number

Ideas for Getting Started

Present the following exercises as an oral drill.

8 times 3 plus 4	9 times 7 plus 5
6 times 6 plus 7	3 times 9 plus 2
7 times 7 plus 4	5 times 3 plus 8
4 times 9 plus 4	8 times 4 plus 6

Then use the following exercises to review multiplying by 2-digit factors.

29	691	329	880	706
× 37	× 58	× 50	× 64	× 47

Using Page 64

Motivational Problem "What question is asked in the problem?" (What is the total population of Carroll County?) "What is the needed data?" (There are 798 people per square mile and 572 square miles in Carroll County.) Explain that each square mile has 798 people, so we multiply to find the total population.

Lesson Development On the chalkboard, go through the steps in the instruction boxes. Point out to students that this algorithm is a simple extension of multiplying by a 2-digit number.

Show how to check the answer by estimating the product, using 800 × 600 = 480,000. Notice with students that since we rounded both factors up, our estimate should be greater than the actual product.

Other Examples These examples can be used to illustrate some special cases involving zeros in the partial products. If your students indent the partial products correctly and do not write the extra zeros, allow them to continue this practice. The last two examples show that certain zeros are necessary in the partial products.

Warm Up Have students check some of their answers by estimating the products. Students who make alignment errors should write the zero in the partial product.

Multiplying by Larger Factors

Carroll County has 798 people per square mile (mi²) and an area of 572 mi².
What is the total population of Carroll County?

Since the number of people is given for each square mile, we multiply to find the total number of people.

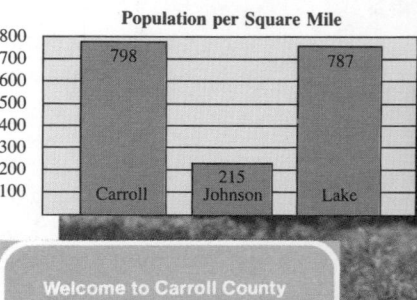

Population per Square Mile

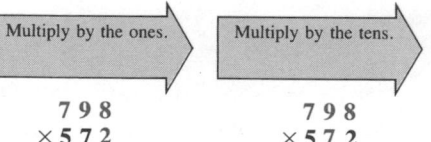

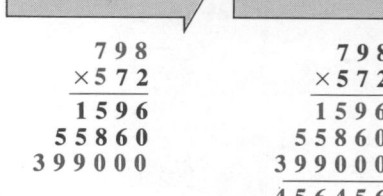

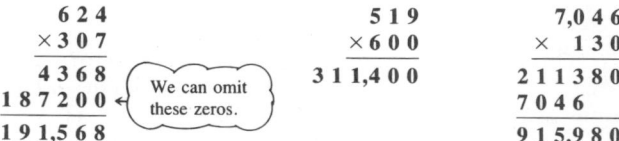

Multiply by the ones.	Multiply by the tens.	Multiply by the hundreds.	Add the products.
798 ×572 — 1596	798 ×572 — 1596 55860	798 ×572 — 1596 55860 399000	798 ×572 — 1596 55860 399000 — 456,456

The total population of Carroll County is 456,456.

Other Examples

$$\begin{array}{r} 624 \\ \times 307 \\ \hline 4368 \\ 187200 \\ \hline 191,568 \end{array}$$ ← We can omit these zeros.

$$\begin{array}{r} 519 \\ \times 600 \\ \hline 311,400 \end{array}$$

$$\begin{array}{r} 7,046 \\ \times\ 130 \\ \hline 211380 \\ 7046 \\ \hline 915,980 \end{array}$$

Warm Up

Multiply.

1. 225 × 164 — 36,900	**2.** 818 × 376 — 307,568	**3.** 807 × 209 — 168,663	**4.** 1,255 × 800 — 1,004,000
5. 628 × 350 — 219,800	**6.** 1,829 × 607 — 1,110,203	**7.** 3,009 × 850 — 2,557,650	**8.** 9,132 × 278 — 2,538,696

64

Follow Up

Reteaching

Write an example such as 369 × 5,324 on the chalkboard. Focus on how the distributive property is used.

5,324	5,324	5,324
× 300	× 60	× 9
1,597,200	319,440	47,916

Now write the exercise in vertical form and solve, showing all partial products.

$$\begin{array}{r} 5,324 \\ \times\ 369 \\ \hline 47916 \\ 319440 \\ 1597200 \\ \hline 1,964,556 \end{array}$$

Enrichment

Have students find the products in exercises 1–3. Then have them guess the products in exercises 4 and 5 and check by multiplying.

1. 12,345,679 ×　　　 9 — 111,111,111	**2.** 12,345,679 ×　　　 18 — 222,222,222
3. 12,345,679 ×　　　 27 — 333,333,333	**4.** 12,345,679 ×　　　 36 — 444,444,444
5. 12,345,679 ×　　　 45 — 555,555,555	

Multiply.

1.	375	**2.**	432	**3.**	842	**4.**	828	**5.**	783
	$\times\,267$		$\times\,357$		$\times\,109$		$\times\,839$		$\times\,497$
	100,125		154,224		91,778		694,692		389,151
6.	260	**7.**	907	**8.**	834	**9.**	777	**10.**	509
	$\times\,195$		$\times\,226$		$\times\,506$		$\times\,296$		$\times\,386$
	50,700		204,982		422,004		229,992		196,474
11.	419	**12.**	923	**13.**	622	**14.**	8,139	**15.**	9,067
	$\times\,700$		$\times\,850$		$\times\,266$		$\times\,\ 116$		$\times\,\ 340$
	293,300		784,550		165,452		944,124		3,082,780

16. 213×819 174,447
17. 297×664 197,208
18. $1,365 \times 745$ 1,016,925
19. $8,281 \times 706$ 5,846,386
20. $2,684 \times 804$ 2,157,936
21. $52,609 \times 905$ 47,611,145

Multiply.

22. $23 \times 37 \times 84$ 71,484
23. $27,469 \times 129$ 3,543,501
24. $(9 \times 8 \times 7) - (6 \times 5 \times 4)$ 384
25. $(120 \times 119 \times 118) - (117 \times 116)$ 1,671,468
26. $(100 \times 100) - (99 \times 99)$ 199
27. $(1,000 \times 1,000) - (999 \times 999)$ 1,999

28. Jackson County has an area of 510 mi^2. The population density is 1,164 people per square mile. What is the population of the county? 593,640

29. Oakvale County has an area of $1,147 \text{ mi}^2$. The population density is 780 people per square mile. The population of the county is how many less than 1 million? 105,340

THINK MATH

Finding Patterns

Palindromic numbers are numbers that remain unchanged when their digits are written in reverse order.

These are examples of palindromic numbers.

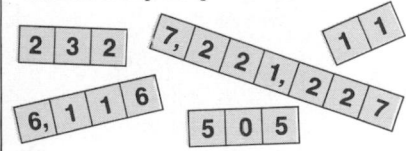

2 3 2   7, 2 2 1, 2 2 7   1 1
6, 1 1 6   5 0 5

Find the smallest multiple of 13 that is a palindromic number. You may want to use a calculator. $38 \times 13 = 494$

What is the second smallest multiple of 13 that is a palindromic number?
$45 \times 13 = 585$
List all the palindromic multiples of 13 that are less than 1,000. Can you see a pattern in these numbers? See teaching notes.

More Practice, page 421, Set C

Using Page 65

Exercises 22–27 These exercises provide good opportunities for calculator use. Exercises 24–27 require 2 operations, multiplication and then subtraction. If a student's calculator does not have the parentheses keys, the memory of the calculator will be helpful in these exercises. For example, to solve exercise 24, find the product of $6 \times 5 \times 4$ and store it in memory. Then find the product of $9 \times 8 \times 7$ and press [−] [MR] [=] to find the answer.

Exercises 28–29 Explain that *population density* means the average number of people living in each square mile.

Think Math This problem involves an understanding of the definition of palindrome, multiples of 13, and patterns. Many calculators have constant adders so that multiples of 13 are easily found. Enter 13 and then press [+] and [=]. Each time [=] is pressed, 13 is added and the next multiple of 13 is displayed. In this case, 494 is the first multiple of 13 that is a palindrome. Thereafter, each 7th multiple of 13 is another palindrome. Thus, each successive palindrome is 91 more than the previous one. The palindromic multiples of 13 that are less than 1,000 are 494, 585, 676, 767, 858, and 949.

More Practice, page 421, Set C

Reteaching Supplement, page 20

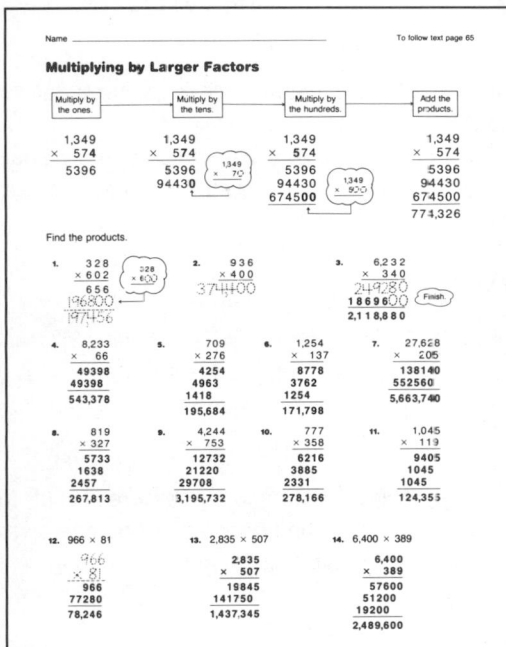

Enrichment Supplement, page 20

Practice Supplement, page 25

Multiplication

Quick Review Read aloud the numbers below and have students give the number that is 1 less and the number that is 1 more.

999   60,000   68,729   877,942   76,500   412

399,990   5,010   33,000   16,420   14,080

Lesson Focus To write repeated factors in exponential notation and to find the number for a power in exponential notation

Ideas for Getting Started

Write the following equations on the chalkboard.

$2 \times 2 =$ $10 \times 10 =$
$2 \times 2 \times 2 =$ $10 \times 10 \times 10 =$
$2 \times 2 \times 2 \times 2 =$ $10 \times 10 \times 10 \times 10 =$

Call for each product to complete the equations. Then ask students how many times 2 is a factor of 4 (2), of 8 (3), and of 16 (4). For the next series, ask how many times 10 is a factor of 100 (2), of 1,000 (3), and of 10,000 (4). Introduce the term *repeated factor*.

Using Page 66

Motivational Problem Read with students the material at the top of the page. Point out that on each surface, 5 new surfaces will form. On each of the new surfaces, 5 more surfaces will form. The early growth of crystals will continue in this way. Explain that the term *exponential* describes this pattern of repeating the same factor.

Have students identify the question in the problem and the needed data. Ask them to tell the operation we will use to solve the problem.

Lesson Development Point out to students the notation used for repeated factors. Introduce the terms *base* and *exponent*. Discuss reading numbers written in exponential notation as shown in the chart. Many students may feel that 5^0 should be equal to zero instead of 1. This can be explained with the following sequence.

$5 \cdot 5 = 5^2$ $5 \cdot 5 \cdot 5 = 5^3$
$5^1 \cdot 5^1 = 5^{1+1}$ $5^2 \cdot 5^1 = 5^{2+1}$

$5 \cdot 5 \cdot 5 \cdot 5 = 5^4$ $5 \cdot 5 \cdot 5 \cdot 5 \cdot 5 = 5^5$
$5^2 \cdot 5^2 = 5^{2+2}$ $5^3 \cdot 5^2 = 5^{3+2}$

Now write:

$$5^2 \cdot 5^0 = 5^{2+0}$$
$$(5 \cdot 5) \cdot ? = 5^2$$

Explain that in order for the pattern of addition of exponents to hold, we must agree that $5^0 = 1$. In general, $n^0 = 1$, if $n \neq 0$.

Other Examples In the example of $4 \cdot 10^2$, point out that we find the second power of 10 before we multiply. In general, exponentiation is performed before arithmetic operations.

Warm Up In exercises 11–15, watch for students who interpret the exponent as a factor.

Exponential Notation

Crystals grow by adding new layers of their own substance on exposed geometric surfaces. The early growth is **exponential**.

On a unit with 5 surfaces for growth, 5 new units will form. How many surfaces for growth will there be in 4 generations of growth?

When the same factor is repeated, we can use **exponential notation.**

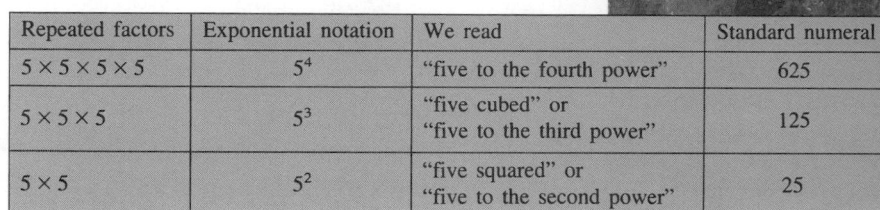

$$\underbrace{5 \times 5 \times 5 \times 5}_{\text{Repeated Factors}} = 5^{4}\quad\substack{\longleftarrow\text{Exponent}\\ \longleftarrow\text{Base}}$$

Repeated factors	Exponential notation	We read	Standard numeral
$5 \times 5 \times 5 \times 5$	5^4	"five to the fourth power"	625
$5 \times 5 \times 5$	5^3	"five cubed" or "five to the third power"	125
5×5	5^2	"five squared" or "five to the second power"	25

There will be 625 surfaces for growth.

The exponents 0 and 1 have special meanings. $5^0 = 1$ and $5^1 = 5$.

Other Examples

A centered dot can be used instead of an $\times$ for multiplication.

$7 \cdot 7 \cdot 7 = 7^3 = 343$ $10 \cdot 10 \cdot 10 \cdot 10 = 10^4 = 10,000$ $4^1 = 4$
$4 \cdot 10^2 = 4 \cdot (10 \cdot 10) = 400$ $3 \cdot 2^5 = 3 \cdot (2 \cdot 2 \cdot 2 \cdot 2 \cdot 2) = 3 \cdot 32 = 96$ $6^0 = 1$

Warm Up

Read. State which number is the **base** and which is the **exponent.**

1. 2^5 2 base, 5 exponent
2. 4^7 4 base, 7 exponent
3. 5^3 5 base, 3 exponent
4. 9^2 9 base, 2 exponent
5. 6^4 6 base, 4 exponent

Give in exponential notation.

6. $8 \cdot 8 \cdot 8$ 8^3
7. 3 squared 3^2
8. 10 cubed 10^3
9. $5 \cdot 5 \cdot 5 \cdot 5 \cdot 5$ 5^5
10. $3 \cdot 3$ 3^2

Give the standard numeral.

11. 6^2 36
12. 2^4 16
13. 3^3 27
14. $8 \cdot 10^3$ 8,000
15. $5 \cdot 2^2$ 20

66

Follow Up

Reteaching

Explain to students that the use of exponents is a shortcut. The exponent tells us how many times a number is used as a factor. For example, 2^4 is a short way of writing $2 \cdot 2 \cdot 2 \cdot 2$. Do not let students think that 2^4 means $2 \cdot 4$.

Review the terms base, exponent, and power. Have students write the following expressions using exponents.

1. $4 \cdot 4 \cdot 4$ 4^3
2. $7 \cdot 7 \cdot 7 \cdot 7$ 7^4
3. $6 \cdot 6$ 6^2
4. $5 \cdot 5 \cdot 5 \cdot 5 \cdot 5$ 5^6
5. $7 \cdot 7 \cdot 7$ 7^3
6. $8 \cdot 8 \cdot 8 \cdot 8 \cdot 8$ 8^5

Enrichment

Have students make a table of the powers of 2^1 through 2^{12}.
Write the exercises below on the chalkboard and have students use the table to rewrite them with exponents.

Example: $8 \cdot 16 = 128$ $2^3 \cdot 2^4 = 2^7$
1. $32 \cdot 64 = 2048$ $2^5 \cdot 2^6 = 2^{11}$
2. $4 \cdot 1024 = 4096$ $2^2 \cdot 2^{10} = 2^{12}$
3. $2048 \div 256 = 8$ $2^{11} \div 2^8 = 2^3$
4. $512 \div 16 = 32$ $2^9 \div 2^4 = 2^5$
5. $4096 \div 512 = 8$ $2^{12} \div 2^9 = 2^3$

Ask students to generalize about the products and quotients of numbers written in exponential notation.

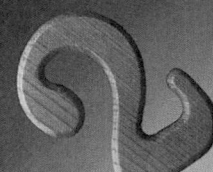

Write in exponential notation.

1. $2 \cdot 2 \cdot 2 \cdot 2$ 2^4
2. $8 \cdot 8 \cdot 8 \cdot 8$ 8^4
3. $10 \cdot 10$ 10^2
4. $3 \cdot 3 \cdot 3 \cdot 3 \cdot 3$ 3^5
5. $9 \cdot 9 \cdot 9 \cdot 9 \cdot 9 \cdot 9$ 9^6
6. $5 \cdot 5 \cdot 5$ 5^3
7. 4 squared 4^2
8. 3 to the fourth power 3^4
9. 12 cubed 12^3
10. 2 to the tenth power 2^{10}
11. 25 squared 25^2
12. 7 to the seventh power 7^7
13. 100 cubed 100^3
14. 10 to the sixth power 10^6
15. 3 to the first power 3^1

Write the standard numeral.

16. 6^2 36
17. 2^3 8
18. 9^2 81
19. 5^1 5
20. 10^2 100
21. 4^3 64
22. 5^4 625
23. 10^3 1,000
24. 2^5 32
25. 12^2 144
26. 3^0 1
27. 2^7 128
28. 3^5 243
29. 8^2 64
30. 10^6 1,000,000

Find the products.

31. $5 \cdot 10^2$ 500
32. $4 \cdot 5^2$ 100
33. $3 \cdot 2^3$ 24
34. $2 \cdot 7^2$ 98
35. $9 \cdot 10^4$ 90,000
36. $6 \cdot 10^6$ 6,000,000

37. What is 7^3 written as a standard numeral? 343
38. What is the missing exponent in $3^{\blacksquare} = 43,046,721$? Hint: 3 is the repeated factor. 16

THINK MATH

Computer Exponents

Many computer languages use an upward arrow (↑) to show exponents.

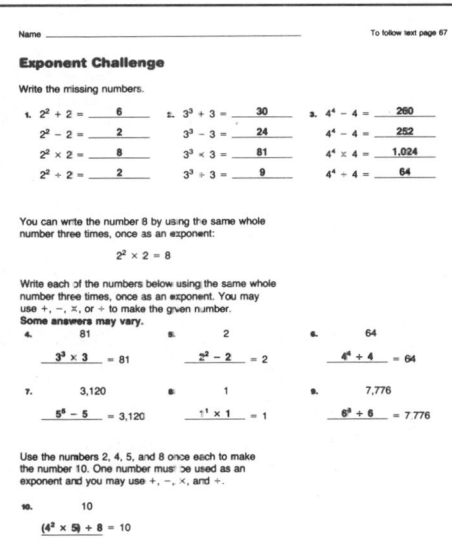

2 ↑ 3 MEANS 2^3 OR 8.

3 ↑ 2 MEANS 3^2 OR 9.

Write in the usual exponential notation. Then write the standard numeral.

1. 3 ↑ 4 3^4; 81
2. 2 ↑ 5 2^5; 32
3. 5 ↑ 2 5^2; 25
4. 10 ↑ 3 10^3; 1,000
5. 7 ↑ 2 7^2; 49
6. 5 ↑ 3 5^3; 125
7. 10 ↑ 4 10^4; 10,000
8. 12 ↑ 2 12^2; 144
9. 8 ↑ 3 8^3; 512
10. 4 ↑ 4 4^4; 256
11. 100 ↑ 2 100^2; 10,000
12. 2 ^ 10 2^{10}; 1,024

More Practice, page 422, Set A

67

Using Page 67

Exercise 38 This exercise suggests the use of a calculator. Some calculators have an exponential key, y^x. Using this key, the student can guess to find the missing exponent by following these steps:

1. Enter 3
2. Press y^x
3. Enter a guess

If students do not have calculators with an exponential key, they must count the number of times 3 is repeated as a factor to give the power.

Think Math The arrow notation used by many microcomputers is introduced here. This may be review for some students who are familiar with computer language. Explain that the order in which the symbols are written is important. Show that 2 ↑ 5 ≠ 5 ↑ 2.

You may wish to point out that another symbol, ∧, is sometimes used for exponentiation.

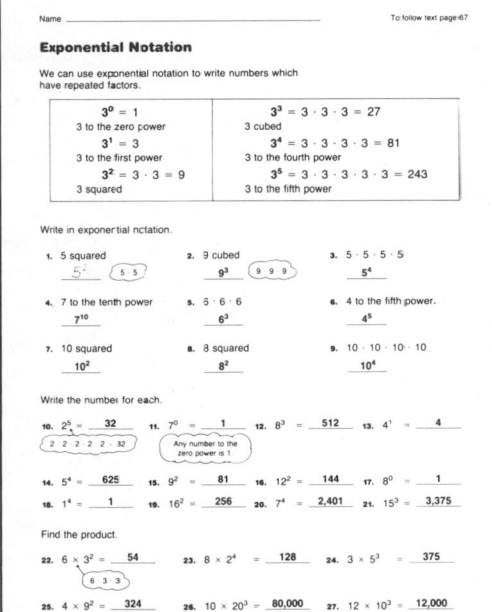

Think Math activities provide interesting extensions of the lesson content—with no teacher planning necessary.

More Practice, page 422, Set A

Reteaching Supplement, page 21

Name _____   To follow text page 67

Exponential Notation

We can use exponential notation to write numbers which have repeated factors.

$3^0 = 1$ 3 to the zero power	$3^3 = 3 \cdot 3 \cdot 3 = 27$ 3 cubed
$3^1 = 3$ 3 to the first power	$3^4 = 3 \cdot 3 \cdot 3 \cdot 3 = 81$ 3 to the fourth power
$3^2 = 3 \cdot 3 = 9$ 3 squared	$3^5 = 3 \cdot 3 \cdot 3 \cdot 3 \cdot 3 = 243$ 3 to the fifth power

Write in exponential notation.

1. 5 squared 5^2 (5 5)
2. 9 cubed 9^3 (9 9 9)
3. $5 \cdot 5 \cdot 5 \cdot 5$ 5^4
4. 7 to the tenth power 7^{10}
5. $6 \cdot 6 \cdot 6$ 6^3
6. 4 to the fifth power. 4^5
7. 10 squared 10^2
8. 8 squared 8^2
9. $10 \cdot 10 \cdot 10 \cdot 10$ 10^4

Write the number for each.

10. $2^5 =$ 32 $2 \cdot 2 \cdot 2 \cdot 2 \cdot 2 = 32$
11. $7^0 =$ 1 Any number to the zero power is 1
12. $8^3 =$ 512
13. $4^1 =$ 4
14. $5^4 =$ 625
15. $9^2 =$ 81
16. $12^2 =$ 144
17. $8^0 =$ 1
18. $1^4 =$ 1
19. $16^2 =$ 256
20. $7^4 =$ 2,401
21. $15^3 =$ 3,375

Find the product.

22. $6 \times 3^2 =$ 54 (6 3 3)
23. $8 \times 2^4 =$ 128
24. $3 \times 5^3 =$ 375
25. $4 \times 9^2 =$ 324
26. $10 \times 20^3 =$ 80,000
27. $12 \times 10^3 =$ 12,000

Enrichment Supplement, page 21

Name _____   To follow text page 67

Exponent Challenge

Write the missing numbers.

1. $2^2 + 2 =$ 6
   $2^2 - 2 =$ 2
   $2^2 \times 2 =$ 8
   $2^2 \div 2 =$ 2
2. $3^3 + 3 =$ 30
   $3^3 - 3 =$ 24
   $3^3 \times 3 =$ 81
   $3^3 \div 3 =$ 9
3. $4^4 - 4 =$ 260
   $4^4 - 4 =$ 252
   $4^4 \times 4 =$ 1,024
   $4^4 \div 4 =$ 64

You can write the number 8 by using the same whole number three times, once as an exponent:

$$2^2 \times 2 = 8$$

Write each of the numbers below using the same whole number three times, once as an exponent. You may use +, −, ×, or ÷ to make the given number. **Some answers may vary.**

4. 81 $3^3 \times 3 = 81$
5. 2 $2^2 - 2 = 2$
6. 64 $4^4 + 4 = 64$
7. 3,120 $5^5 - 5 = 3,120$
8. 1 $1^1 \times 1 = 1$
9. 7,776 $6^6 \div 6 = 7,776$

Use the numbers 2, 4, 5, and 8 once each to make the number 10. One number must be used as an exponent and you may use +, −, ×, and ÷.

10. 10 $(4^2 \times 5) \div 8 = 10$

Practice Supplement, page 26

Name _____   To follow text page 67

Exponential Notation

Write in exponential notation.

1. $3 \cdot 3 \cdot 3 \cdot 3 =$ 3^4
2. $2 \cdot 2 \cdot 2 \cdot 2 \cdot 2 \cdot 2 =$ 2^6
3. $8 \cdot 8 \cdot 8 =$ 8^3
4. $10 \cdot 10 \cdot 10 \cdot 10 \cdot 10 =$ 10^5
5. $6 \cdot 6 =$ 6^2
6. $5 \cdot 5 \cdot 5 \cdot 5 \cdot 5 \cdot 5 =$ 5^7
7. $23 \cdot 23 =$ 23^2
8. $11 \cdot 11 \cdot 11 =$ 11^3
9. $9 \cdot 9 \cdot 9 =$ 9^3
10. $7 \cdot 7 \cdot 7 \cdot 7 \cdot 7 \cdot 7 \cdot 7 =$ 7^7
11. 6 to the fourth power 6^4
12. 10 cubed 10^3
13. 5 to the sixth power 5^6
14. 9 to the seventh power 9^7
15. 12 squared 12^2
16. 7 to the first power 7^1 or 7

Find the products.

17. $5^2 =$ $5 \cdot 5 = 25$
18. $100^3 =$ $100 \cdot 100 \cdot 100 = 1,000,000$
19. $7^3 =$ $7 \cdot 7 \cdot 7 = 343$
20. $6^4 =$ $6 \cdot 6 \cdot 6 \cdot 6 = 1,296$
21. $12^2 =$ $12 \cdot 12 = 144$
22. $10^5 =$ $10 \cdot 10 \cdot 10 \cdot 10 \cdot 10 = 100,000$
23. $11^3 =$ $11 \cdot 11 \cdot 11 = 1,331$
24. $5^5 =$ $5 \cdot 5 \cdot 5 \cdot 5 \cdot 5 = 3,125$
25. $25^2 =$ $25 \cdot 25 = 625$
26. $3^6 =$ $3 \cdot 3 \cdot 3 \cdot 3 \cdot 3 \cdot 3 = 729$
27. $8^3 =$ $8 \cdot 8 \cdot 8 = 512$
28. $9^4 =$ $9 \cdot 9 \cdot 9 \cdot 9 = 6,561$
29. $2^4 =$ $2 \cdot 2 \cdot 2 \cdot 2 = 16$
30. $2^8 =$ $2 \cdot 2 \cdot 2 \cdot 2 \cdot 2 \cdot 2 \cdot 2 \cdot 2 = 256$

Applications

Quick Review Display the amounts of money shown below and have students write each amount in words. Example: $3.04 three dollars and four cents.

| $7.64 | $0.72 | $9.05 | $3.33 | $1.11 |
| $4.40 | $11.16 | $10.00 | $12.90 | $4.68 |

Lesson Focus To use the 5-Point Checklist to solve problems involving addition, subtraction, and/or multiplication with whole numbers or decimals

Ideas for Getting Started

Discuss some of the things that make up the cost of operating an automobile. Besides the obvious costs of gasoline and oil, students should name such things as tire replacement, repairs, insurance, cleaning costs, auto license fees, and the loss of value of a car as it grows older.

Using Page 68

Lesson Development Work through the first problem as a class activity. Call on volunteers to discuss each step in the 5-Point Checklist. Then assign the remaining problems as independent work.

Exercises 1–6 You may wish to provide an opportunity for students to check and discuss their work on this page before proceeding to the problems on page 69. Note that exercises 2–5 are one-step problems, involving subtraction or multiplication. Exercise 6 is a two-step problem involving first subtraction and then addition.

PROBLEM SOLVING: Practice

QUESTION
DATA
PLAN
ANSWER
CHECK

Solve.

1. Amber spends about $3 a day to drive to work. Three people want to ride with her, and the 3 passengers will divide the driving costs equally. What will it cost each of the 3 passengers to ride with Amber for 5 working days? $5

2. Carl Fleetwing pays $645 a year for car insurance. If he joins a car pool, his insurance will be reduced by $78 a year. How much will Carl then pay a year for insurance? $567

3. Sara James has a new car. She estimates that it will cost about 25¢ per kilometer to drive her car. How much will it cost to drive 20,000 km? $5,000.00

4. Scott Whitson has a car that costs 15¢ per kilometer to drive. How much will it cost Scott if he drives 20,000 km the first year he has the car? $3,000.00

5. Connie pays about $2,000 a year for gasoline, oil, and tolls when she drives to work alone. If she rides in a company van, she will pay $1,200 a year. How much can she save a year by riding in the van? $800

6. Joe spent $56 for gasoline in November. In December he cut his gasoline bill by $15. How much did Joe spend for gasoline for the two months? $97

68

Follow Up

Reteaching

Have students analyze each problem in the lesson by listing the information for Question, Data, Plan, Answer, and Check on the Problem-Solving Worksheet (TRB p. 287).

Example: (Problem 2)

Question: How much will Carl pay a year for insurance?

Data: $645 per year; reduced by $78

Plan: Subtract

Answer: 645 − 78 = 567

Check: 567 + 78 = 645

Enrichment

Present students with the following problem.

A grandfather counted his change and found that he had 100 coins which he was going to give to his grandaughter to save. The value of the 100 coins is $5.00. There are no nickels. What coins did the grandfather have? **60 pennies, 39 dimes, and 1 half dollar**

Assignment Guide			
	Minimum	Average	Extended
page 68–69	1–10	1–11, 15	5–15

69

7. Leslie Farmer pays $6 per day to ride a commuter train. What will it cost her to ride the train for 23 days? **$138**

8. Kaye Werner's budget for car expense is $25.00 per week. One week she buys gasoline twice. The two tanks cost $11.46 and $9.29. She also buys one can of oil for $1.75. How much is left in her budget for car expense that week? **$2.50**

9. Donna McCormick pays $387 for automobile insurance every six months. If she pays for insurance once a year, she will save $24. What is the total cost of the insurance if she pays once a year? **$750**

10. Susan Martinez budgeted $1,500 for car expense during one year. Her expenses were as follows: January through March, $387; April through June, $411; July through September, $435; October through December, $328. How much more or less than $1,500 were her expenses? **$61 more**

11. The cost of crossing a toll bridge is 75¢. Jill Fox paid $12 for a book of 20 tickets to cross the bridge. How much will she save? **$3.00**

12. A book of 20 tickets for crossing a bridge costs 60¢ a ticket. When Walt Swanson turned in a book with 7 unused tickets, he got a refund of $1.75. How much did he lose on the 7 unused tickets? **$2.45**

13. When Mr. Banks drives alone, he leaves home at 8:15 a.m. and gets to work at 8:55 a.m. If he joins a car pool, it will take him 20 minutes longer to get to work. What time must he leave home to get to work at 8:55 a.m.? **7:55 a.m.**

★ 14. Mr. Kent has savings between $8,500 and $9,500. He wants to buy a car that costs between $6,900 and $7,300. If he pays cash for the car, what is the least amount and the greatest amount that could be left in his savings account? **between $1,200 and $2,600**

15. Try This Four cars—one red, one yellow, one green, and one black—arrive at a toll booth. How many different ways can they line up to pass through the toll area? Hint: Make an organized list. **24**

69

Using Page 69

Exercises 8–14 Each of these exercises is a two-step problem involving addition, subtraction, and/or multiplication.

Try This A possible strategy, Make an Organized List, was taught on page 50.

Discussion "What is the question in the problem?" (How many different ways can the cars line up?) "What are the facts or data given in the problem?" (four cars arrive at a toll booth; the cars are red, yellow, green, and black) The hint suggests making an organized list. Have students use the letters R, Y, G, B to identify the four cars by color.

Solution

RYGB	YGBR	GBRY	BRYG
RYBG	YGRB	GBYR	BRGY
RGBY	YRBG	GYRB	BYRG
RGYB	YRGB	GYBR	BYGR
RBGY	YBRG	GRYB	BGRY
RBYG	YBGR	GRBY	BGYR

There are 24 different ways of lining up for the toll booth.

Ideas That Work

Special Education

Even after analyzing examples similar to the problems of these pages, learning-disabled students and slower learners in the class may have difficulty deciding what needs to be done to solve a problem. The 2-step examples included in these exercises may cause particular difficulty. Provide additional help for this lesson by letting students work in pairs for the following activity. Instruct students to follow these steps.

1. Use your math book or your own completed paper for the problem on pages 68 and 69, and mark the 2-step problems you find.

2. Then write the steps for solving each problem on strips of paper, one step to a strip. Place the problem number on the back of each strip.

Problem 12	Find 7 × 60¢

Subtract $1.75 from 7 × 60¢

3. Place the strips for each problem in a pile so the problem number shows. Take turns choosing a problem, reading it from the math book, telling what should be done, and rearranging the strips in the correct sequence to check.

Quick Review Read the following aloud and have students write the number for each. Use both "and" and "point" to designate placement of the decimal point.

0.06   0.0007   588.01   16.30   2,803.0104   10,001.101   48,0100

Lesson Focus To find quotients related to products involving multiples of 10, 100, and 1,000; to estimate quotients

Ideas for Getting Started

Review some special products. Use the following.

| 5 × 60 | 8 × 30 | 9 × 70 | 6 × 80 |
| 60 × 30 | 70 × 50 | 80 × 40 | 30 × 90 |

For each multiplication exercise above, ask students to state or write two division statements. For 5 × 60 = 300, we have 300 ÷ 5 = 60 and 300 ÷ 60 = 5.

Using Page 70

Lesson Development Ask students to work these exercises:

$$30\overline{)360} \qquad 3\overline{)36}$$
$$50\overline{)150} \qquad 5\overline{)15}$$
$$80\overline{)2400} \qquad 8\overline{)240}$$

Afterward, elicit from students the idea that when the dividend and the divisor are both divided by the same number, the quotient will be the same.

Discuss the examples shown at the top of the page and the shortcut shown below. Point out how we can check division by using multiplication.

Other Examples Have students state the corresponding multiplication equation for each division equation.

Exercises 1–28 These exercises can be assigned as oral or written practice. Encourage students to avoid pencil and paper calculating as much as possible.

Special Quotients: Mental Math

When we know special products, we can use them to find some special quotients.

300 ÷ 10 = 30 because 30 × 10 = 300

1,200 ÷ 100 = 12 because 12 × 100 = 1,200

6,000 ÷ 1,000 = 6 because 6 × 1,000 = 6,000

800 ÷ 40 = 20 because 20 × 40 = 800

4,000 ÷ 50 = 80 because 80 × 50 = 4,000

We can use a shortcut to find some quotients.

$$200 \div 50 = \frac{200}{50} = \frac{20}{5} = 4 \qquad\qquad 15{,}000 \div 300 = \frac{15{,}000}{300} = \frac{150}{3} = 50$$

Divide each number by 10.   This bar means divide.   Divide each number by 100.

Check: 4 × 50 = 200   Check: 50 × 300 = 15,000

Other Examples

$$1{,}800 \div 100 = \frac{1{,}800}{100} = 18 \qquad\qquad 30{,}000 \div 50 = \frac{30{,}000}{50} = 600$$

Find the quotients mentally.

1. $\frac{2{,}000}{500}$ 4
2. $\frac{900}{300}$ 3
3. $\frac{36{,}000}{4{,}000}$ 9
4. $\frac{21{,}000}{700}$ 30

5. 1,600 ÷ 40 40
6. 8,000 ÷ 400 20
7. 2,800 ÷ 70 40
8. 15,000 ÷ 3,000 5

9. 60,000 ÷ 20 3,000
10. 1,200 ÷ 300 4
11. 2,800 ÷ 70 40
12. 1,300 ÷ 100 13

13. 29,000 ÷ 100 290
14. 1,900 ÷ 10 190
15. 14,000 ÷ 20 700
16. 900,000 ÷ 300 3,000

17. 240 ÷ 60 4
18. 1,500 ÷ 300 5
19. 800 ÷ 40 20
20. 350 ÷ 70 5

21. 600 ÷ 10 60
22. 900 ÷ 30 30
23. 1,200 ÷ 600 2
24. 4,200 ÷ 600 7

25. 4,000 ÷ 50 80
26. 6,300 ÷ 900 7
27. 7,200 ÷ 800 9
28. 60,000 ÷ 2,000 30

70

Follow Up

Reteaching

Provide students with examples that demonstrate patterns when multiplying and dividing by multiples of 10.

Number	×10	×100	÷10	÷100
300	3,000	30,000	30	3
2,000				
15,000				
700				
1,000				

Help students discover relationships such as:

- When multiplying by 100, add 2 zeros.

- When dividing by 10, mark off 1 zero.

Enrichment

Write the following numbers on the chalkboard.

6   30   40   400
   600   800   1,200   2,400
16,000   24,000

Have students write as many division equations as possible, using only these numbers.

$$\frac{24{,}000}{800} = 30 \qquad \frac{16{,}000}{400} = 40 \qquad \frac{1{,}200}{40} = 30$$

$$\frac{24{,}000}{600} = 40 \qquad \frac{2{,}400}{400} = 6$$

Assignment Guide			
	Minimum	Average	Extended
page 70	1–20	1–28	1–28
page 71	1–20	1–28	2–32, even

Estimating Quotients

We can use special quotients for estimation.

To estimate quotients, we round each number to 1-digit accuracy.

Estimate $2{,}163 \div 39$.

$$\frac{2{,}163 \rightarrow}{39 \rightarrow} \; \frac{2{,}000}{40} = \frac{200}{4} = 50$$

The estimated quotient is 50.

Other Examples

$39{,}419 \div 523$

$$\frac{39{,}419 \rightarrow}{523 \rightarrow} \; \frac{40{,}000}{500} = \frac{400}{5} = 80$$

$321\overline{)936}$

$$\frac{936 \rightarrow}{321 \rightarrow} \; \frac{900}{300} = \frac{9}{3} = 3$$

Estimate each quotient by rounding to 1-digit accuracy.

1. $1{,}927 \div 41$
50
2. $629 \div 19$
30
3. $4{,}214 \div 53$
80
4. $31{,}427 \div 620$
50

5. $1{,}999 \div 49$
40
6. $390 \div 81$
5
7. $33{,}747 \div 6{,}419$
5
8. $78{,}109 \div 427$
200

9. $409 \div 21$
20
10. $622 \div 32$
20
11. $1{,}877 \div 37$
50
12. $899 \div 28$
30

13. $2{,}774 \div 58$
50
14. $788 \div 38$
20
15. $3{,}919 \div 83$
50
16. $6{,}077 \div 29$
200

17. $\frac{5{,}166}{493}$ 10
18. $\frac{3{,}792}{77}$ 50
19. $\frac{2{,}919}{309}$ 10
20. $\frac{7{,}935}{412}$ 20

21. $\frac{8{,}283}{396}$ 20
22. $\frac{5{,}877}{1{,}939}$ 3
23. $\frac{38{,}717}{5{,}062}$ 8
24. $\frac{9{,}273}{319}$ 30

25. $71\overline{)719}$ 10
26. $607\overline{)2{,}888}$ 5
27. $795\overline{)41{,}266}$ 50
28. $5{,}776\overline{)27{,}509}$ 5

29. $25\overline{)857}$ 30
30. $432\overline{)7{,}754}$ 20
31. $519\overline{)24{,}562}$ 40
32. $8{,}252\overline{)81{,}652}$ 10

More Practice, page 422, Set B

71

Using Page 71

Lesson Development Review the meaning of rounding to 1-digit accuracy. Work through the example at the top of the page, noting how the rounding is done before making the estimate.

Other Examples Notice with students that we have three ways to indicate division: $a \div b$, $b\overline{)a}$, and $\frac{a}{b}$.

Exercises 1–32 Discuss with students how they rounded the numbers and what shortcuts were taken before arriving at their estimates.

More Practice, page 422, Set B

Quick Review Read these problems aloud and have students find the differences mentally.

| 37 − 32 | 49 −45 | 50 − 42 | 83 − 81 | 68 − 64 | 23 −16 |
| 79 − 72 | 33 − 27 | 55 − 49 | 70 − 64 | 45 − 36 | 20 − 14 |

Lesson Focus To find the quotient and remainder when dividing by a 1-digit divisor; to find the quotient and remainder using short division

Ideas For Getting Started

Present students with the following situation. "Four young students collected $52 for aluminum cans and soft drink bottles. They wished to divide the money equally but no one knew how to divide. How could they figure out how much each one was to receive?"

Draw a picture of 5 ten-dollar bills and 2 one-dollar bills on the chalkboard. From the picture show that each of the four students could get 1 ten-dollar bill. There would be 1 ten and 2 ones left. Explain that we could trade the 1 extra ten for 10 ones making 12 ones in all. Then each person could take exactly 3 ones for a total of $13. Follow the model with an illustration on the chalkboard of 4)52 using the long division algorithm.

Using Page 72

Motivational Problem "What does the question ask us to find?" (the number of kilograms of aluminum that each person collected) "What is the data in the problem?" (Four students collected a total of 138 kg of aluminum.) Point out that we know the total kilograms and the number of persons. Since we want to find how many kilograms for each person, we should plan to divide.

Lesson Development On the chalkboard, work through the steps in the algorithm. Emphasize that in each step of dividing we multiply, subtract, and compare. The partial remainder must be less than the divisor. Show the check for division by multiplying. Emphasize the terms divisor, quotient, dividend, and remainder.

Other Examples The first example illustrates a remainder of 0. The second example involves a middle zero in the quotient. Omission of this zero is a source of error for some students. The third example illustrates a ones digit of zero. Some students may forget to write this zero so it is another source of error.

Dividing by a 1-digit Divisor

Four students are collecting aluminum cans. They collected 138 kg of aluminum. If the weight is divided equally, how many kilograms is this for each person?

To find the number of kilograms for each person, we divide.

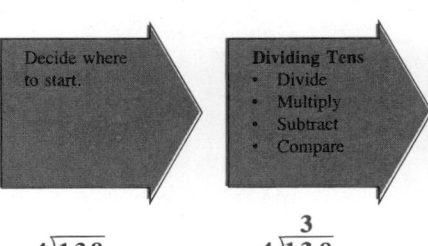

| Decide where to start. | Dividing Tens • Divide • Multiply • Subtract • Compare | Dividing Ones • Bring down • Divide • Multiply • Subtract • Compare |

```
                3              34 R2
   4)138       4)138          4)138       Check:    34  ← quotient
               12             12                   ×  4  ← divisor
  4>1  Not enough   1         18                    136
       hundreds.              16                  +   2  ← remainder
  4<13 Divide the tens.        2                    138  ← dividend
```

The students collected 34 kg of aluminum per person and 2 kg extra.

Other Examples

```
    163          240 R 2        308 R 5
 3)489        9)2,162        6)1,853
   3             18             18
   18            36             053
   18            36             48
   09            02              5
    9             0
    0             2
```

Find the quotients and remainders.

```
      147              201 R2              293 R4             3,522 R1
1. 6)882          2. 4)806           3. 6)1,762          4. 2)7,045
      402 R3             591              608 R3              567 R2
5. 7)2,817        6. 3)1,773          7. 4)2,435          8. 8)4,538
```

9. James, Diane, and Sandy collected 74 kg of aluminum cans. How many kilograms is this per person?

72   24 kg per person, remainder 2 kg

10. Laurie collected 147 bottles for a refund of 60¢ a carton. How many cartons of 6 bottles were there? 24 cartons, remainder 3 bottles

More Practice, page 422, Set C

Follow Up

Reteaching

Illustrate the division algorithm with place-value models. Write each step on the chalkboard as you progress. Use the example of dividing 87 by 3. Show 87 as 8 ten-sticks and 7 unit-cubes. Ask students if 8 ten-sticks can be shared equally among 3 people. "How many for each person?" (2) "How many left?" (2)

Explain that we can trade the 2 ten-sticks for 20 unit-cubes and combine them with the 7 unit-cubes. Then have students share 27 unit-cubes among 3 people. "How many unit-cubes for each person?" (9) Next discuss the exercise without models.

Enrichment

Put the following illustration on the chalkboard:

Using five of the digits, 1 through 9, have students make the greatest and then the least quotient. Each square must be replaced with a digit and no digit can be used more than once.

```
                        9,876
greatest quotient    1)9,876

                        137 R1
least quotient       9)1,234
```

Assignment Guide			
	Minimum	Average	Extended
page 72	1–9	1–10	1–10
page 73	1–10, SK	1–15, SK	1–15, SK

Short Division

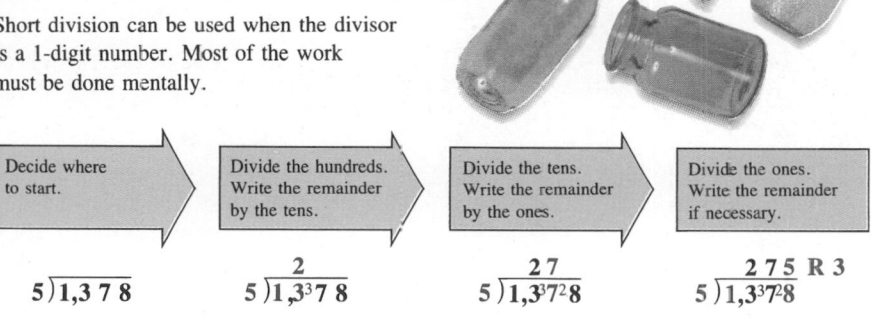

Five classes collected 1,378 kg of glass for the Martin Luther King, Jr. Middle School. How many kilograms was this per class?

Since we want to find the number of kilograms per class, we divide.

Short division can be used when the divisor is a 1-digit number. Most of the work must be done mentally.

Decide where to start.	→	Divide the hundreds. Write the remainder by the tens.	→	Divide the tens. Write the remainder by the ones.	→	Divide the ones. Write the remainder if necessary.

$$5\overline{)1,3\ 7\ 8}$$
$$\overset{2}{5\overline{)1,3^3 7\ 8}}$$
$$\overset{2\ 7}{5\overline{)1,3^3 7^2 8}}$$
$$\overset{2\ 7\ 5\ \text{R}\ 3}{5\overline{)1,3^3 7^2 8}}$$

$13 \div 5 = 2$ with R3 $37 \div 5 = 7$ with R2 $28 \div 5 = 5$ with R3

Each class collected about 276 kg of glass.

Find the quotients and remainders. Use the short division method.

1. $6\overline{)316}$ 52 R4
2. $4\overline{)2,055}$ 513 R3
3. $3\overline{)155}$ 51 R2
4. $8\overline{)393}$ 49 R1
5. $6\overline{)902}$ 150 R2
6. $4\overline{)842}$ 210 R2
7. $8\overline{)9,728}$ 1,216
8. $2\overline{)3,825}$ 1,912 R1
9. $5\overline{)8,215}$ 1,643
10. $3\overline{)1,520}$ 506 R2
11. $9\overline{)4,623}$ 513 R6
12. $6\overline{)3,290}$ 548 R2
13. $7\overline{)2,828}$ 404
14. $3\overline{)9,531}$ 3,177
15. $5\overline{)1,023}$ 204 R3

SKILLKEEPER

1. 3×7 21
2. 3×70 210
3. 3×700 2,100
4. 30×70 2,100
5. 30×700 21,000
6. 4×80 320
7. 40×80 3,200
8. 400×8 3,200
9. $4,000 \times 8$ 32,000
10. 400×80 32,000
11. 9×6 54
12. 9×60 540
13. 90×60 5,400
14. 900×6 5,400
15. $9,000 \times 6$ 54,000
16. 7×8 56
17. 70×8 560
18. 7×80 560
19. 70×80 5,600
20. 700×8 5,600

More Practice, page 423, Set A

73

Using Page 73

Motivational Problem Have students read the introductory problem and identify the question and data in the problem. "Why can we use division to solve the problem?" (because we want to find the number of kilograms for each class)

Lesson Development On the chalkboard, first find the quotient using the algorithm on the previous page, and then show the short division algorithm.

$$\begin{array}{r} 275 \text{ R3} \\ 5\overline{)1,378} \\ 1\ 0 \\ \hline ③7 \\ 35 \\ \hline ②8 \\ 25 \\ \hline 3 \end{array}$$

$$\overset{2\ 7\ 5\ \text{R3}}{5\overline{)1,3^3 ⑦^2 ⑧}}$$

Point out that the corresponding circled digits in each algorithm represent the same number. The 3 represents 3 hundreds which is regrouped with 7 tens to form 37 tens. The 2 represents 2 tens regrouped with 8 ones to form 28 ones. Have students check the answer by multiplying.

Skillkeeper This Skillkeeper reviews material taught in this chapter.

More Practice, page 422, Set C
More Practice, page 423, Set A

Reteaching Supplement, page 23

Enrichment Supplement, page 23

Practice Supplement, page 29

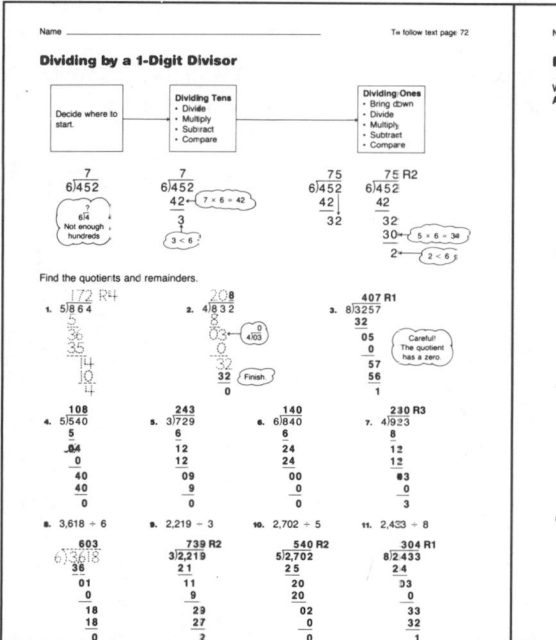

Ideas for Getting Started

Lesson Focus To find the quotient and remainder when dividing by a 2-digit divisor

Use these exercises to review with students the standard algorithm for 1-digit division.

8)132   9)629   7)1,233   6)2,407

5)3,316   4)828   3)1,137   9)2,144

Point out that we are going to review division with divisors of more than one digit. The process is the same, but in multiplying to find the partial products we will have a 2-digit factor.

Using page 74

Motivational Problem Have students read the problem, restate the question, and identify the data. Explain that since we want to know the number of games pitched each year, we should plan to divide.

Lesson Development On the chalkboard, work through the steps of the algorithm. Explain that since there are not enough hundreds to divide by 18, we look at the tens. The 4 hundreds and 2 tens are 42 tens which can be divided by 18. Point out that in the second step we round 18 to 20 and use the tens digit of the divisor and the hundreds digit of the dividend to estimate the first digit of the quotient. Be sure to emphasize that the quotient is multiplied by 18, not the rounded divisor of 20. Emphasize also that we multiply, subtract, and compare in each step.

Show the check of the quotient and remainder by multiplying and adding. Notice with students that the answer is over 23 games each year because there is a remainder.

Other Examples In the third example there is a middle zero in the quotient. Stress the importance of writing this zero when we see that 12 tens cannot be divided by 57. Many students may understand that the zero product (0 × 57) can be omitted and the 5 "brought down" as shown below.

```
        402 R11
57)22,925
    22 8
    ─────
      125
      114
      ───
       11
```

Warm Up If students have difficulty estimating the first digit of the quotient have them list the multiples of the divisor.

Make certain students multiply, subtract, and compare at each step.

Dividing by a 2-digit Divisor

Bob Feller pitched 428 major league baseball games over a period of 18 years. About how many games did he pitch each year?

Divide the number of games pitched by the number of years.

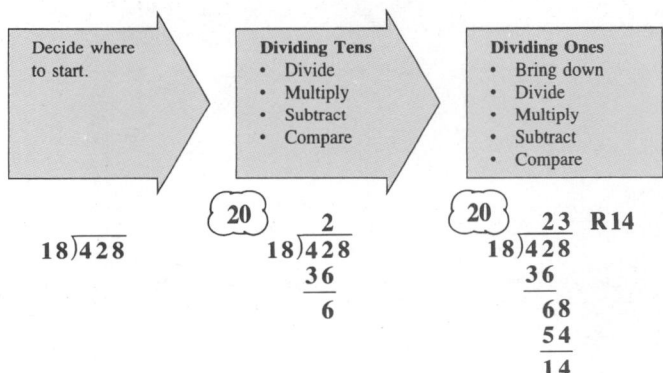

Bob Feller pitched over 23 games each year.

Other Examples

```
(60)    7 R 40       (90)    32 R 4      (60)    402 R 11
63)481              89)2,852            57)22,925
   441                 267                228
   ───                 ───                ───
    40                 182                 12
                       178                  0
                       ───                125
                         4                114
                                          ───
                                           11
```

Warm Up

Divide. Check your answers.

		24 R28			20 R24			12 R35			24 R10			17 R14
1.	32)796		2.	48)984		3.	54)683		4.	35)850		5.	35)507		

		50 R38			67 R6			27 R42			34 R30			60 R8
6.	45)2,288		7.	51)3,423		8.	68)1,878		9.	75)2,580		10.	24)1,448		

Follow Up

Reteaching

Review rounding to the nearest 10 as a prerequisite skill for 2-digit division. Write some division exercises on the chalkboard and focus on determining the first digit in the quotient.

Can 8 be divided by 27?

Can 83 be divided by 27?

27)836

Round 27 to the nearest ten and estimate the number of 30s in 83. Emphasize that we multiply 2 times 27, not 2 times the rounded number. Try other examples, discussing the important first phase of dividing.

Enrichment

Provide students with the following problems. Have them find the missing digits.

```
       ⊡ 7 7                  5 7 ⊡
28)4,9 6 ⊡          6 ⊡)3 5,6 7 4
   ⊡ 8                   3 1 0
   2 1 ⊡                 ⊡ 6 7
   ⊡ 9 6                 4 3 4
   ⊡ 0 ⊡                 3 3 4
   ⊡ 9 ⊡                 ⊡ 1 0
     6                   2 4
```

Find the quotients and remainders.

1. 36)876 **24 R12**
2. 52)970 **18 R34**
3. 34)673 **19 R27**
4. 83)3,735 **45**

5. 47)1,268 **26 R46**
6. 74)4,626 **62 R38**
7. 25)5,049 **201 R24**
8. 72)3,603 **50 R3**

9. 84)5,265 **62 R57**
10. 25)2,274 **90 R24**
11. 16)5,401 **337 R9**
12. 63)2,520 **40**

13. 49)2,819 **57 R26**
14. 81)4,006 **49 R37**
15. 88)929 **10 R49**
16. 65)1,581 **24 R21**

17. 25,740 ÷ 45 **572**
18. 21,633 ÷ 93 **232 R57**
19. 13,398 ÷ 29 **462**
20. 7,255 ÷ 15 **483 R10**

21. 17,360 ÷ 57 **304 R32**
22. 38,019 ÷ 70 **543 R9**
23. 27,676 ÷ 68 **407**
24. 43,800 ÷ 72 **608 R24**

25. Cy Young pitched in 826 major league games over a period of 22 years. About how many games did Cy Young pitch each year? **over 37**

26.

Pitcher	Winning Games	Years
Bob Feller	266	18

How many games did he win per year? **over 14**

★ 27. Red Ruffing pitched for 22 years. If he had pitched 14 more games, he would have pitched 23 games a year. How many games did Ruffing pitch? **492**

28. **DATA BANK** Who pitched more games per year, Warren Spahn or Grover Alexander? (See page 414.) **Warren Spahn; over 35**

■ THINK MATH ■

Computer Operations

The tables show the symbols and order of operations for many computer languages.

Symbol	Operation
+	Addition
−	Subtraction
*	Multiplication
/	Division
↑	Exponentiation

Order of operations
1. Operations within parentheses
2. Exponentiation
3. Multiplication and division
4. Addition and subtraction

What number would a computer print for each of these?

1. 9 * 2 − 5 **13**
2. 20/4 + 7 **12**
3. 6 * 3 − (8 + 4) **6**
4. 5 ↑ 2 * 4 **100**

5. 10 + 5 * 2 **20**
6. (10 + 5) * 3 **45**
7. 18/6 + 42/7 **9**
8. 2 ^ 3 + 3 ↑ 2 **17**

9. 9 ↑ 2/9 − 9 **0**
10. 15 − (24 − 16) **7**
11. 4 * 4 − 4 ↑ 2 **0**
12. (9 * 4)/3 − 8 **4**

More Practice, page 423, Set B

Using Page 75

Exercises 25–26 These exercises ask students to find about how many games were averaged each year. In exercise 25, the quotient is 37 with a remainder of 12. Remind students that the remainder indicates over 37 games were pitched.

Data Bank After reading the problem, have the students locate the appropriate table on page 414. "What data does the table give us?" (the number of years in each player's career and the number of games pitched) "The problem asks us who pitched more games per year. How can we find the number of games each player pitched per year?" (divide the total number of games pitched by the number of years) Have students complete the problem on their own.

Think Math The problems in Think Math will be review for any student familiar with computer symbols and language. If a microcomputer is available in your school, you might illustrate these problems on the computer.

More Practice, page 423, Set B

Reteaching Supplement, page 24

Enrichment Supplement, page 24

Practice Supplement, page 30

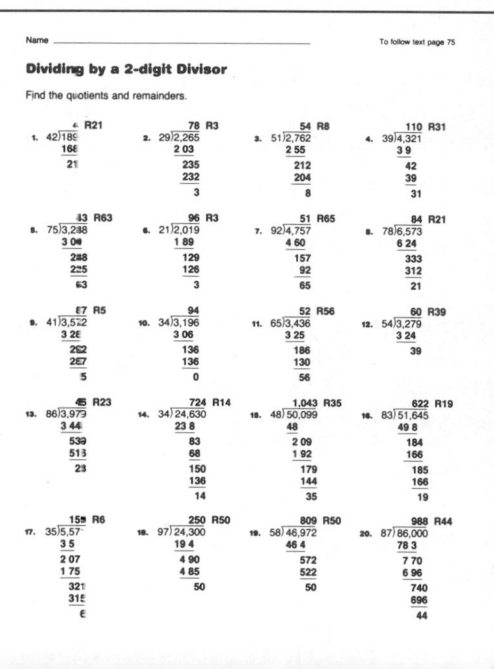

Quick Review Display the numbers below. Point to digits and have students give the period name and place value of each digit. Example: 4,366 units, 60

4,839,377   15,945,263,187   72,388,265,123,741

Lesson Focus To find the quotient and remainder when dividing by a 3-digit divisor

Ideas for Getting Started

To prepare students for this lesson, have them round each number to the nearest 100.

289   417   706   861   922

132   177   529   392   650

Next have them find these products mentally.

300 × 7   700 × 8   200 × 3   400 × 6

500 × 3   800 × 4   900 × 3   800 × 7

Review the division algorithm for 2-digit divisors. Use these examples.

$28\overline{)1,275}$ We think 12 ÷ 3

$92\overline{)3,944}$ We think 39 ÷ 9

$46\overline{)2,775}$ We think 27 ÷ 5

Using Page 76

Motivational Problem "What does the question ask us to find?" (the number of calories in each serving of butter) "What data is given in the problem?" (There are 204 servings of butter in each kilogram and 1 kg contains 7,142 calories.) "What should we plan to do to solve the problem?" (divide the total number of calories by the number of servings)

Lesson Development Work through the steps of the algorithm on the chalkboard. To help students know where to start, show the exercise in the steps below.

$204\overline{)7}$ "Can 7 be divided by 204?" (No)

$204\overline{)71}$ "Can 71 be divided by 204?" (No)

$204\overline{)714}$ "Can 714 be divided by 204?" (Yes)

Tell students that to estimate the first digit of the quotient, we round 204 to 200 and use only the hundreds digit, 2. Explain that since 7 ÷ 2 is about 3, the first digit of the quotient should be 3. Then we multiply, subtract, and compare the remainder with the divisor. Point out that we repeat the process for the next digit in the quotient.

Have students check by multiplying the divisor times the quotient and adding the remainder.

Other Examples Give special attention to the second and third examples in which zeros occur in the quotients. This is a common source of error in dividing.

Warm Up Some students may have difficulty mentally multiplying a digit in the quotient times a 3-digit divisor. Allow these students to write the vertical multiplication.

Using Larger Divisors

A restaurant serves butter in small pats. There are about 204 servings of butter in 1 kg of butter. Each kilogram of butter contains about 7,142 calories. How many calories are in each serving of butter?

Since we want to find the number of calories in each serving, we divide.

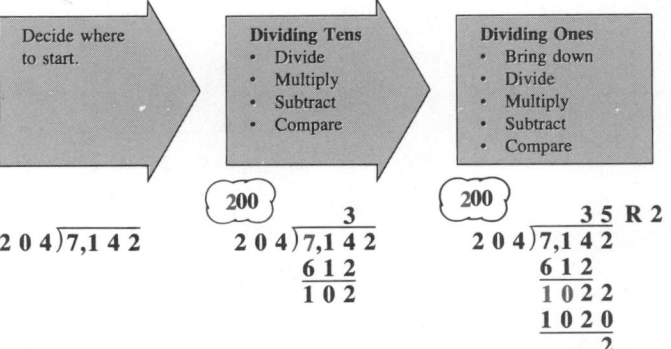

Decide where to start.

Dividing Tens
• Divide
• Multiply
• Subtract
• Compare

Dividing Ones
• Bring down
• Divide
• Multiply
• Subtract
• Compare

$$204\overline{)7,142}$$

$$\begin{array}{r} 3 \\ 204\overline{)7,142} \\ \underline{6\,1\,2} \\ 1\,0\,2 \end{array}$$

$$\begin{array}{r} 3\,5 \text{ R }2 \\ 204\overline{)7,142} \\ \underline{6\,1\,2} \\ 1\,0\,2\,2 \\ \underline{1\,0\,2\,0} \\ 2 \end{array}$$

Each serving of butter has about 35 calories.

Other Examples

$$\begin{array}{r} 5\,6 \text{ R }60 \\ 129\overline{)7,284} \\ \underline{6\,4\,5} \\ 8\,3\,4 \\ \underline{7\,7\,4} \\ 6\,0 \end{array}$$

$$\begin{array}{r} 8\,0 \text{ R }35 \\ 392\overline{)31,395} \\ \underline{3\,1\,3\,6} \\ 3\,5 \\ \underline{0} \\ 3\,5 \end{array}$$

$$\begin{array}{r} 2\,0\,7 \text{ R }83 \\ 482\overline{)99,857} \\ \underline{9\,6\,4} \\ 3\,4\,5 \\ \underline{0} \\ 3\,4\,5\,7 \\ \underline{3\,3\,7\,4} \\ 8\,3 \end{array}$$

Warm Up

Divide.

1. $316\overline{)8,286}$ 26 R70

2. $547\overline{)21,898}$ 40 R18

3. $793\overline{)27,467}$ 34 R505

4. $987\overline{)641,228}$ 649 R665

76

Follow Up

Reteaching

Have students work division exercises at the chalkboard so that you can observe their work as they proceed through each step. In this way you can diagnose difficulties and help them correct their errors as they occur.

Enrichment

Have students solve each exercise below and check their division using a calculator.

1. $318\overline{)16,941}$ 53 R87

2. $596\overline{)147,212}$ 247

3. $278\overline{)85,193}$ 306 R125

4. $421\overline{)26,145}$ 62 R43

Students can check either by multiplying the divisor and quotient and adding the remainder, or by doing the division and using the calculator memory to find the remainder (TM, p. 77).

Assignment Guide			
	Minimum	Average	Extended
page 77	1–20	1–27	1–27 odd, 28, TM

Find the quotients and remainders.

1. $294\overline{)6,428}$ 21 R254
2. $727\overline{)12,955}$ 17 R596
3. $509\overline{)8,143}$ 15 R508
4. $419\overline{)9,207}$ 21 R408

5. $633\overline{)53,229}$ 84 R57
6. $711\overline{)27,542}$ 38 R524
7. $385\overline{)36,397}$ 94 R207
8. $528\overline{)19,636}$ 37 R100

9. $166\overline{)6,569}$ 39 R95
10. $977\overline{)297,008}$ 304
11. $402\overline{)153,929}$ 382 R365
12. $849\overline{)648,342}$ 763 R555

13. $26,145 \div 421$ 62 R43
14. $10,267 \div 295$ 34 R237
15. $43,324 \div 682$ 63 R358
16. $43,932 \div 523$ 84

17. $335,345 \div 775$ 432 R545
18. $139,461 \div 198$ 704 R69
19. $350,208 \div 912$ 384
20. $516,883 \div 824$ 627 R235

Estimate each quotient by rounding to 1-digit accuracy. Then find the exact quotients.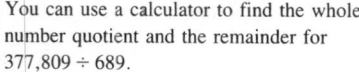

21. $6,358,842 \div 8,334$ 750; 763
22. $4,598,979 \div 5,093$ 1,000; 903
23. $947,947 \div 1,001$ 900; 947

24. $34,864,545 \div 62,819$ 500; 555
25. $49,946,395 \div 50,707$ 1,000; 985
26. $39,978,001 \div 19,999$ 2,000; 1,999

27. A loaf of bread has 1,680 calories. There are 24 slices of bread in the loaf. How many calories are in each slice? 70

28. A slice of wheat bread has 80 calories. One pat of butter has 35 calories. If 2 pats of butter are spread on each slice of bread, how many slices of buttered bread equal 1,500 calories? 10

THINK MATH

Calculator Division

You can use a calculator to find the whole-number quotient and the remainder for $377,809 \div 689$.

Study the method below. Follow the steps and use a calculator to do exercises 13–20 on this page.

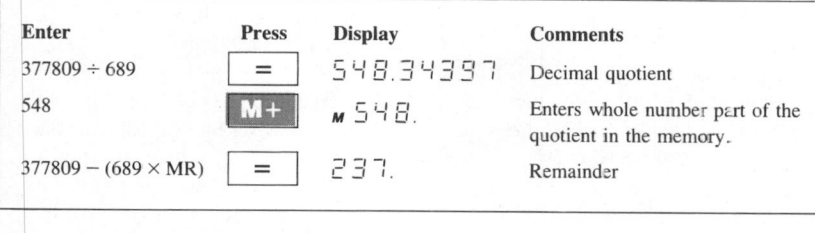

Enter	Press	Display	Comments
$377809 \div 689$	=	548.34397	Decimal quotient
548	M+	M 548.	Enters whole number part of the quotient in the memory.
$377809 - (689 \times MR)$	=	237.	Remainder

Solution: $377,809 \div 689 = 548$ R237

More Practice, page 423, Set C

Using Page 77

Exercises 21–26 These exercises provide opportunities for calculator use in checking estimates. To help students estimate quotients when dividing with large numbers, work through exercise 21:

$$6,358,842 \div 8,334$$

$6,000,000 \div 8,000$	Rounded numbers
$6,000 \div 8$	Each number divided by 1,000
About 700	Estimate

Think Math This problem gives a method of finding whole-number quotients and the remainder when dividing with a calculator. The steps shown assume that the calculator has a memory key and parentheses keys. If these features are not on the calculators available, the method shown can be modified and used with simpler calculators. Without a memory or parentheses keys the problem could be worked out as follows.

$$377,809 \div 689 = 548.34397$$

548 is the whole number quotient.

$$548 \times 689 = 377,572$$

Write the product above on paper.

$$377,809 - 377,572 = 237$$

237 is the remainder

More Practice, page 423, Set C

Reteaching Supplement, page 25

Enrichment Supplement, page 25

Practice Supplement, page 31

Quick Review Have students round each decimal to the nearest tenth, hundredth, thousandth, and whole number.

4.62746 14.6; 14.63; 14.627; 15   9.5134 9.5; 9.51; 9.513; 10
35.47983 35.4; 35.48; 35.480; 35   99.4799 99.5; 99.480; 100

Lesson Focus To solve word problems involving subtraction, multiplication, and division

Ideas for Getting Started

Write these problems on the chalkboard.

1. Jack traveled at 60 mi an hour on a freeway. He traveled 3 hours. How far did he go?

2. Mary went 132 mi in 3 hours. About how far did she go in 1 hour?

3. Carl had to travel a distance of 350 mi. After traveling 183 mi he stopped to fill up his car with gas. How much farther does he have to go?

4. Lena traveled 206 mi in the morning. Then she drove 185 mi more in the afternoon. What was the total distance she traveled that day?

Ask students to tell what operation they would plan to use to solve the problems. Discuss how they made the choice of operation.

Using Page 78

Lesson Development Have students read the material at the top of the page. Make certain they understand the meaning of the term *glide ratio*. Ask them to think about a paper airplane or glider which glides 16 ft while falling 4 ft to the floor. Explain that the glide ratio is:

$\frac{d}{a} = \frac{16}{4}$ $a = 4$ ft

$= 4$

$d = 16$ ft

"How far would the glider travel if gliding from an altitude of 3 ft." (Since $\frac{d}{3} = 4$, we multiply to find d; $3 \times 4 = 12$) "How much altitude will it lose in a glide that is 20 ft?" (Since $\frac{20}{a} = 4$, we divide to find a; $20 \div 4 = 5$)

PROBLEM SOLVING: Choosing the Operation

QUESTION
DATA
PLAN
ANSWER
CHECK

Wayne Burgess owns a glider school and trains people to fly gliders. Gliders are aircraft that have no engines. They are used mostly for recreational flying.

One of the most important features of a glider is its glide ratio. This is the distance the glider will fly forward while it is losing 1 unit in altitude.

What is the glide ratio of a glider that can fly 2,500 feet (ft) forward while losing 100 ft in altitude? The ratio will help us choose the operation to solve the problem.

$$\frac{2,500}{100} = 2,500 \div 100 = 25$$

The glide ratio is 25. The glider can fly 25 ft while losing 1 ft in altitude. Some gliders have glide ratios of more than 40.

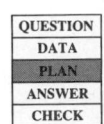

Glide ratio = distance ÷ altitude = $\frac{d}{a}$

Choose the operation to solve these problems.

1. A glider moves forward 12,600 ft while losing 360 ft in altitude. What is the glide ratio for this glider? 35

2. A glider has a glide ratio of 35. How far forward will it fly while losing 150 ft in altitude? 5,250 ft

3. The glide ratio of a glider is 25. It is at an altitude of 3,200 ft. How far will it glide forward while it drops in altitude to 2,500 ft? 17,500 ft

4. A glider has a glide ratio of 28. How much altitude will it lose in a glide that is 2,520 ft long? 90 ft

5. A glider has long, narrow wings. One glider has wings 810 in. long. The wings are 30 times as long as they are wide. How wide are the wings? 27 in.

6. A glider flew 159 mi in 3 hours. How many miles per hour (mph) did the glider fly? 53 mph

7. A record altitude of 46,266 ft for a glider was set by Paul Bikle in 1961. Commercial jet airliners fly at about 35,250 ft. How much higher is the glider's record altitude? 11,016 ft

78

Follow Up

Reteaching

Elicit from students the meaning of each operation. For example, addition is the operation that will find a total whenever the parts (addends) are known.

Have the students write word problems with no questions. Share these with the class and ask for volunteers to complete the problems with questions that involve each operation.

Enrichment

Have students write word problems that involve various operations. Each problem should be solved by the writer. Students can exchange papers and solve each others problems. If the two students do not agree upon the solution to a given problem, they should attempt to find the errors together.

Using Page 79

Try This A possible strategy, Make an Organized List, was taught on page 50.

Discussion "What are we asked to find?" (the number of different seat selections) "What data are we given? Where is it found?" (The chart tells us we have a choice of aisle, middle, or window; of first class or coach; of smoking or nonsmoking; of right or left aisle.) "What is one seating plan you could choose?" (aisle, first class, smoking, right)

Solution

AFSR	MSFR	WFSR
AFSL	MFSL	WFSL
AFNR	MFNR	WFNR
AFNL	MFNL	WFNL
ACSR	MCSR	WCSR
ACSL	MCSL	WCSL
ACNR	MCNR	WCNR
ACNL	MCNL	WCNL

There are 24 different choices.

Extension Marion, Larry, and Helen have 3 seats together. One is a window seat, one a middle seat, and the other an aisle seat. If they can sit in any one of the three seats, how many different seating arrangements could they have? (6)

8. In 1972 Hans Werner Grosse made a long-distance flight of 907.7 mi in a glider. In 1977 Karl Striedieck made a flight of 1,016 mi. How much farther was Striedieck's flight? **108.3 mi**

9. The record speed for a short glider race was 102.74 mph. The record speed for a race ten times as long was 54.78 mph. How much faster was the speed in the shorter race? **47.96 mph**

10. Try This When you travel by air, you select your seating by making different choices. How many different selections of seating are possible using the four choices below? **24**

> **Universal Airlines Seating**
> 1. Aisle, middle, or window (A,M,W)
> 2. First class or coach (F,C)
> 3. Smoking or nonsmoking (S,NS)
> 4. Right or left aisle (R,L)

Reteaching Supplement, page 26

Name _____ To follow text page 79

Problem Solving: Choosing the Operation

Problem: An airline pilot flies ▢▢ hours per month. How many hours does she fly in ▢▢ months?

The numbers in the problem have been covered. Even though you cannot see the numbers, you should be able to decide which operation

Since the pilot flies the same number of hours each month, you *multiply*.

+ − × ÷

could be used to solve the problem.

Ring the operation that you would use to solve the problem.

1. Last month an airline handled ▢▢ luggage pieces. The month before, ▢▢ pieces were handled. How many more pieces were handled last month than this month?
+ − (Find the difference) ÷

2. Toni is a flight attendant. She earns ▢▢ per month. How much does she earn in a year?
+ − (×) ÷

3. ▢▢ round-trip tickets cost ▢▢. How much does one round-trip ticket cost?
+ − × (÷)

4. Trudy paid ▢▢ dollars for her plane ticket, ▢▢ dollars for her hotel, and ▢▢ dollars for her rental car. What was the total cost?
(+) − × ÷

5. Judd has been flying for ▢▢ years. He was ▢▢ years old when he started. How old is Judd now?
(+) − × ÷

6. Meg has worked at the airport for ▢▢ years. Gary has worked there for ▢▢ years. How much longer has Gary worked at the airport than Meg?
+ (−) × ÷

7. Each of the ▢▢ meals on the flight costs ▢▢. What is the total cost of the meals served?
+ − × (÷)

8. A plane flew ▢▢ round trips to the same city for a total of ▢▢ km. How many kilometers are in one round trip?
+ − × ÷

Enrichment Supplement, page 26

Name _____ To follow text page 79

Orient Tours

Pretend that you are a travel agent. Answer the questions below about Orient Tours. **Estimate** to find the answers.

ORIENT TOURS		
26 days	$2,790	plus round-trip air fare
22 days	$2,390	plus round-trip air fare
18 days	$1,495	plus round-trip air fare
15 days	$ 875	plus round-trip air fare

Round-trip air fares
▶ from New York $1,196
▶ from San Francisco $972

1. About how much difference is there between air fare from New York and air fare from San Francisco for 4 people? **$800**

2. You sold 2 tours for a total of about $4,800 not including air fare. For how many days were these tours? **22 days**

3. The total cost of Mr. Lau's trip to the Far East including air fare from San Francisco was a little less than $2,500. How long was he gone? **18 days**

4. A group of 4 tourists spent about $3,500 (without air fare) for their vacation in China. How long were they gone? **15 days**

5. Mr. and Mrs. Kahn spent about $8,000 for their trip including air fare from New York. How long were they gone? **26 days**

6. A business club decided to save some money by taking the 13-day tour rather than the 22-day tour. About how much did each club member save? **$900**

7. How much more would it cost for 2 people to take the 26-day trip rather than the 22-day trip? **$800**

8. An advertising agency wants to offer a tour of the Far East for 2 people as first prize in a contest. If they have $5,000 to spend for the trip packages including air fare from San Francisco, which trip for 2 should they offer? **18 days**

Practice Supplement, page 32

Name _____ To follow text page 79

Problem Solving: Choosing the Operation

Solve each problem.

1. Ms. Ramos earns $24,180 a year. How much does she earn each month? (12 months in a year) **$2,015**

2. How many pieces of yarn 92 cm long can be cut from a piece 1,950 cm long? **21**

3. What is the total cost of 4 books at $14 each and 3 books at $12 each? **$92**

4. When Jae had her car repaired the parts cost $12.95, the labor cost $24.00, and the tax was $0.84. What was the total bill? **$37.79**

5. The distance around the earth is about 40,000 km. If you were to travel around the world in 80 days, about how many kilometers would you have to average each day? **500 km**

6. Carl earns $35 a day. How much does he earn in 15 days? **$525**

7. Round-trip plane tickets cost $1,240. What is the cost of 5 round-trip tickets? **$6,200**

8. Mr. Linden has $1,260 to buy lamps for his store. How many lamps can he buy if each lamp costs $86? **14**

9. Larry spent $11.95 for a shirt and $3.75 for school supplies. How much change did he receive from $20.00? **$4.30**

10. Susan bought a record for $3.98 and some film for $2.15. The sales tax was $0.40. How much change should she get back from $10? **$3.47**

Multiplication and Division

Quick Review Display the numbers below. For each number, ask students to identify which digit is in the tens, hundredths, thousandths, ones, thousands, and hundreds places.

2,490.381   5,267.914   14,862.037   8,392.4075

Lesson Focus To practice finding products and quotients of whole numbers; to solve word problems using a formula

Ideas for Getting Started

To introduce using a formula, display the following on the chalkboard or overhead projector.

$$w = \frac{P}{2} - l$$

Perimeter is the distance around the figure.

Explain that when certain kinds of problems must be solved repeatedly, we often use a formula to help us find the answer. Tell students the formula given above will help us compute the width of a rectangle when the perimeter, (P), and length, (l), are known. Show students how to find the width when

$P = 40$ cm and $l = 12$ cm.

Substitute: $w = \dfrac{40}{2} - 12$

Compute: $w = 20 - 12$

$w = 8$

Notice with students that 40 must be divided by 2 before 12 is subtracted. Point out that we can check by adding: $8 + 12 + 8 + 12 = 40$. Have students find w when $P = 312$ m and $l = 79$ m. ($w = 77$ m)

Using Page 80

Exercises 1–48 You may wish to display various problems chosen from this page and have selected students work the problems at the chalkboard, while other students check the work at their desks. Continue to emphasize the importance of checking the reasonableness of answers.

Assign these problems as needed for strengthening skills in multiplication and division of whole numbers.

Skills Practice

Multiply.

1. 376 × 4 = 1,504	**2.** 8,097 × 9 = 72,873	**3.** 71,549 × 8 = 572,392	**4.** 60,526 × 7 = 423,682	**5.** 21,009 × 5 = 105,045
6. 598 × 43 = 25,714	**7.** 614 × 57 = 34,998	**8.** 72,885 × 68 = 4,956,180	**9.** 94,301 × 92 = 8,675,692	**10.** 10,653 × 48 = 511,344
11. 924 × 375 = 346,500	**12.** 618 × 593 = 366,474	**13.** 23,110 × 406 = 9,382,660	**14.** 57,291 × 813 = 46,577,583	**15.** 28,962 × 489 = 14,162,418
16. 312 × 784 = 244,608	**17.** 2,197 × 356 = 782,132	**18.** 3,091 × 424 = 1,310,584	**19.** 87,135 × 1,099 = 95,761,365	**20.** 26,290 × 1,847 = 48,557,630

Divide.

21. $5\overline{)9,173}$ = 1,834 R3   **22.** $7\overline{)2,682}$ = 383 R1   **23.** $8\overline{)510,329}$ = 63,791 R1   **24.** $6\overline{)749,141}$ = 124,856 R5

25. $73\overline{)45,016}$ = 616 R48   **26.** $92\overline{)305,729}$ = 3,323 R13   **27.** $56\overline{)9,410,321}$ = 168,041 R25   **28.** $81\overline{)7,648,113}$ = 94,421 R12

29. $113\overline{)75,043}$ = 664 R11   **30.** $702\overline{)94,680}$ = 134 R612   **31.** $255\overline{)107,332}$ = 420 R232   **32.** $648\overline{)386,190}$ = 595 R630

33. $811\overline{)63,172}$ = 77 R725   **34.** $304\overline{)40,879}$ = 134 R143   **35.** $582\overline{)951,632}$ = 1,635 R62   **36.** $375\overline{)154,875}$ = 413

Multiply or divide.

37. 6,821 × 754 = 5,143,034   **38.** 9,763 × 1,340 = 13,082,420   **39.** $491\overline{)60,152}$ = 122 R250   **40.** $387\overline{)92,610}$ = 239 R117

41. 8,762 ÷ 523 = 16 R394   **42.** 112,764 ÷ 109 = 1,034 R58   **43.** 2,413 × 8,760 = 21,137,880   **44.** 6,243 × 7,095 = 44,294,085

45. 4,991 × 3,714 = 18,536,574   **46.** 5,261 × 2,788 = 14,667,668   **47.** 294,344 ÷ 660 = 445 R644   **48.** 829,726 ÷ 741 = 1,119 R547

80

Follow Up

Reteaching

Present the instruction boxes below for the typing speed formula.

Example: Problem 1

List the value of each letter → Substitute the numbers for letters

$W = 380$
$e = 7$
$n = 5$

$s = \dfrac{380 - (10 \cdot 7)}{5}$

Multiply $10 \cdot e$ → Subtract from W → Divide by n

$s = \dfrac{380 - 70}{5}$ $s = \dfrac{310}{5}$ $s = 62$

Enrichment

Explain that we can use the formula below to find any triangular number:

$$\frac{n^2 + n}{2}$$

For example, to find the fifth triangular number we substitute 5 for n.

$$\frac{5^2 + 5}{2} = \frac{25 + 5}{2}$$

$$= \frac{30}{2}$$

$$= 15$$

Have students find the seventh, eighth, and ninth triangular numbers. **28, 36, 45**

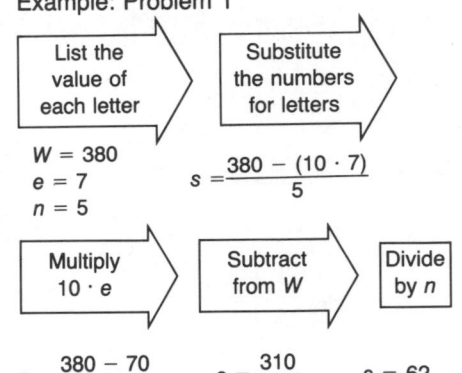

Applications

PROBLEM SOLVING: Using a Formula

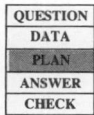

QUESTION
DATA
PLAN
ANSWER
CHECK

Ronald typed 285 words in 5 minutes. He made 6 errors. For each error made, 10 words are subtracted from the total. What is his typing speed?

The formula for finding typing speed is

$$S = \frac{W - (10 \cdot e)}{n}$$

Each letter represents a number.

S = typing speed e = number of errors
W = number of words n = number of minutes

Step 1: List the value for each letter in the formula.

$W = 285$ $e = 6$ $n = 5$

Step 2: Substitute the numbers for the letters in the formula.

$$S = \frac{285 - (10 \cdot 6)}{5}$$ ← Remember, this bar means divide.

Step 3: Perform the operations in the formula.

$$S = \frac{285 - 60}{5} = \frac{225}{5} = 45$$

Ronald's typing speed is 45 words per minute.

Use the formula to find these typing speeds.

1. Dave typed 380 words in 5 minutes with 7 errors. **62 words per minute**

2. Lamar typed 886 words in 9 minutes. He made 13 errors. **84 words per minute**

3. A legal secretary typed 2,450 words in 20 minutes with 17 errors. **114 words per minute**

4. Vicky typed 554 words in 12 minutes and made 11 errors. **37 words per minute**

5. **DATA HUNT** What is your typing speed? Have another person watch the time while you type for 5 minutes. Use the formula to find your speed.

6. **Try This** Ann typed 5 more words per minute than Jeff. Together they typed 73 words in one minute. How many words did each person type in one minute? **Jeff 34, Ann 39**

81

Using Page 81

Lesson Development On the chalkboard, work through the example problem. Remind students to first do the multiplication inside the parentheses, then the subtraction, and then the division.

Data Hunt Have students try this problem if a typewriter is available. As an alternative, have students time a typist in your school office for 2 or 3 minutes and use the resulting data to compute the typing speed.

Try This A possible strategy, Guess and Check, was taught on page 24.

Discussion "What are we asked to find in the problem?" (the number of words each person typed in one minute) "What data is given?" (Ann typed 5 more words per minute than Jeff; together they typed 73 words per minute.) "What plan should we try to use for the problem?" (Guess and Check)

Call on students to make guesses and show the checks on the chalkboard. After each incorrect guess, discuss how to use the information in the check to improve the next guess.

Solution

Guess: Ann (39)   Jeff (34)
Check: 39 + 34 = 73

Ann typed 39 words per minute and Jeff typed 34 words per minute.

Extension Jason typed twice as many words as Rene in a minute. Marie typed as many words a minute as Jason and Rene together. If Marie's typing speed was 72 words a minute, how many words a minute did Jason type? How many did Rene type? (Rene 24, Jason 48)

Ideas that Work

Special Education

Ideas like the following will help you provide special help to students having difficulty with long division.

• Encourage students to think about sharing as they work with long division. An exercise may be interpreted as dollars to be shared.

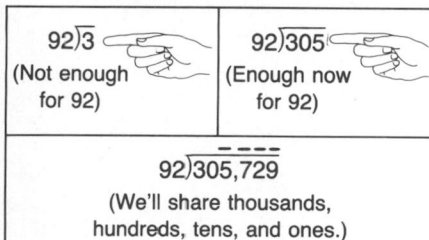

$92\overline{)3}$ (Not enough for 92)	$92\overline{)305}$ (Enough now for 92)

$92\overline{)305{,}729}$
(We'll share thousands, hundreds, tens, and ones.)

• Before dividing suggest that students determine where the quotient digits will occur. Systematically uncovering and marking digits as shown often helps. The marking aids alignment and visually confronts students if they omit a middle or terminal zero in a quotient.

• Provide isolated practice on troublesome steps: 1) rounding the divisor; 2) multiplying "sideways", 3) determining whether a quotient digit is too large or too small, and 4) multiplying or estimating to check an answer.

Practice Supplement, page 33

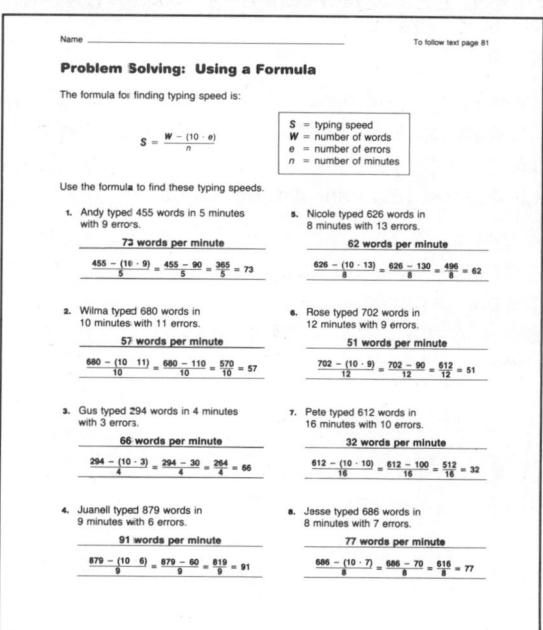

Strategies

Lesson Focus
To find a pattern as a strategy for solving nonroutine word problems

Ideas for Getting Started

Tell students that there is a pattern for each of the following sequences of numbers. Have them try to find the pattern and give the next four numbers in the sequence.

1. 1, 4, 7, 10, 13, . . . (Numbers increase by 3)

2. 5, 10, 20, 40, 80, . . . (Numbers double)

3. 1, 4, 9, 16, 25, . . . (Numbers are successive squares)

Have students create some number patterns and put them on the chalkboard to see if other students can discover the patterns.

Using Page 82

Motivational Problem Have students read the Try This problem at the top of the page. "What is the question in the problem?" (How many members are in the fan club by Saturday?) "Bill starts the club on Sunday. How many members join on Monday?" (2) "How many people join on Tuesday?" (4) "What do the new members do the day after they join?" (each gets 2 more people to join the club)

Lesson Development Ask students to complete the table started for the problem. Ask them if they see a pattern for the way the membership grows. (the number of new members doubles each day) Make certain students understand that to find the total number of members on a given day, the total from the previous day is added to the number of new members on the given day. By completing the table, some students will discover that the total number of members each day is one less than twice the new members. Have students reread the problem to check that the pattern discovered fits the facts and is reasonable. Add the strategy Find a Pattern to the problem-solving bulletin board display described on page 24.

Exercise 1 The pattern in this problem involves increasing amounts each year. By completing the table through year 18, the answers for the 12th year and the 18th year can be found.

Exercise 2 The pattern in this problem is that the bamboo shoot grows 1 cm more each day than it did on the previous day. Students can extend the pattern in the table to 14 days to find the total height of 119 cm.

These special lessons introduce strategies for solving word problems. The strategies are then practiced in Try This problems in Problem Solving lessons throughout the book.

PROBLEM SOLVING: Find a Pattern

| QUESTION |
| DATA |
| PLAN |
| ANSWER |
| CHECK |

Try This

On Sunday, Bill decides to start a soccer team fan club. On Monday, Bill gets 2 friends to join the fan club. Each of the 2 friends gets 2 more people to join the club on Tuesday. New members each get 2 more people to join the club the day after they join. This goes on all week. How many people, including Bill, are members of the fan club by the end of Saturday?

Some problems seem difficult because they are long and complicated. To solve these problems, you may need to use the strategy **Find a Pattern**. To solve the above problem, find the pattern.

What is the pattern for the new members? The numbers double or multiply by 2.

Is there a pattern for the total members? number $\times 2 - 1$

The solution for the problem is given below.

There are 127 members of the club by the end of Saturday.

	New members	Total members
Sunday	1	1
Monday	2	3
Tuesday	4	7
Wednesday	8	15
Thursday	16	31
Friday	32	63
Saturday	64	127

Solve.

1. Kristy's parents put $100 in a savings account on Kristy's first birthday. Each year on her birthday they put in $200 more than on her last birthday. What will the total be when she is 12 years old? What will the total be when she is 18 years old? $14,400; $32,400

Year	1	2	3
Amount	$100	$300	$500
Total	$100	$400	$

2. A bamboo shoot is 2 cm high on the first day, 5 cm high on the second day, 9 cm high on the third day, 14 cm high on the fourth day, and so on. If this growth pattern continues, how high will the bamboo shoot be at the end of two weeks? 119 cm

Day	1	2	3	4	5
Height in centimeters	2	5	9	14	

82

Strategy Test Item

Optional Problem If you wish to assess students' ability to apply the strategy called Find a Pattern, introduced in this chapter, provide them with the following problem.

Jones bought some stock for $1,000. Each week the stock increased in value as shown below.

Week	0	1	2	3	4	. . .
Value	$1,000	$1,025	$1,075	$1,150	$1,250	. . .

What will the stock be worth at the end of 7 weeks if the pattern continues?

Solution

Week	5	6	7
Value	$1,375	$1,525	$1,700

At the end of 7 weeks the value of the stock is $1,700.

CHAPTER REVIEW/TEST

Estimate each product by rounding to 1-digit accuracy.

1. 42×68
2,800

2. 53×79
4,000

3. 216×61
12,000

4. 45×96
5,000

Find the products mentally.

5. 4×90 360

6. $8 \times 3,000$ 24,000

7. 700×80 56,000

8. 60×30 1,800

Find the products.

9. $\begin{array}{r} 67 \\ \times\ 3 \\ \hline 201 \end{array}$

10. $\begin{array}{r} 39 \\ \times\ 6 \\ \hline 234 \end{array}$

11. $\begin{array}{r} 283 \\ \times\ 9 \\ \hline 2,547 \end{array}$

12. $\begin{array}{r} 1,406 \\ \times\ 4 \\ \hline 5,624 \end{array}$

13. $\begin{array}{r} 27 \\ \times 58 \\ \hline 1,566 \end{array}$

14. $\begin{array}{r} 682 \\ \times\ 93 \\ \hline 63,426 \end{array}$

15. $\begin{array}{r} 428 \\ \times 336 \\ \hline 143,808 \end{array}$

16. $\begin{array}{r} 237 \\ \times 496 \\ \hline 117,552 \end{array}$

Write in exponential notation.

17. 7 squared 7^2

18. 2 to the sixth power 2^6

19. $4 \cdot 4 \cdot 4 \cdot 4 \cdot 4$ 4^5

Write the standard numeral.

20. 3^3 27

21. 5^2 25

22. $3^2 \cdot 2^3$ 72

Estimate each quotient by rounding to 1-digit accuracy.

23. $4,177 \div 439$ 10

24. $5,972 \div 298$ 20

25. $3,879 \div 78$ 50

26. $4,392 \div 52$ 80

Find the quotients and remainders.

27. $6\overline{)259}$ 43 R1

28. $82\overline{)1,095}$ 13 R29

29. $47\overline{)3,166}$ 67 R17

30. $91\overline{)5,880}$ 64 R56

31. $66\overline{)12,445}$ 188 R37

32. $29\overline{)82,821}$ 2,855 R26

33. $187\overline{)37,629}$ 201 R42

34. $433\overline{)18,109}$ 41 R356

35. There are 24 hours in one day. How many hours are there in one year of 365 days? 8,760

36. A loaf of raisin bread has 3,630 calories. There are 22 slices in the loaf. How many calories are there in each slice? 165

83

Using Page 83

The exercises in the Chapter Review/Test emphasize the major concepts and skills presented in this chapter. These exercises may be used as a review assignment or as a test, depending upon your needs.

Item Analysis The table below correlates the Chapter Review/Test items with objectives and with the student text pages on which the concepts or skills were taught. Please note that items 33 and 34 are derived from a lesson from which no "Minimum" assignment was suggested in the Assignment Guide. Only those students who were assigned this lesson should be expected to complete the corresponding Chapter Review/Test items.

Items	Objectives	Related Text Pages
1–8	3.1	57–59
9–16	3.2	60–65
17–22	3.3	66–67
23–26	3.4	70–71
27–34	3.5	72–77
35–36	3.6	68–69, 78–79, 81

Assessment Options

If you use the Chapter Review/Test as a review assignment, you may wish to use the free-response test or the multiple-choice test to evaluate mastery of the chapter objectives. The items on these tests have a one-to-one correspondence in terms of content and level of difficulty. A correlation of test items to objectives and student text pages is provided in the Management Guide for Chapter 3.

Multiple-Choice Test, TRB pages 7–9
Free-Response Test, TRB p. 52–53

TRB Options

The following blackline masters are available for use with this chapter. If you have not already assigned these materials, you may wish to use them to close the chapter.

Recreation, TRB page 157
Consumer Application, TRB page 175
Calculator Technology, TRB page 193
Reading Math, TRB page 229
Family Involvement, TRB pages 249–250

Reteaching

Using Page 84

The exercises on this page are intended for those students who experienced difficulty with the Chapter Review/Test on page 83. Should students require reteaching of these key concepts and skills, please refer to the teaching notes below. Otherwise, the Another Look exercises can be assigned as independent work, with students using the accompanying sample problems and hints as guides.

Exercises 1–6 This skill was originally taught on page 57. Have students study the example at the top of the page. Point out the relationship between the number of zeros in the factors and the number of zeros in the product.

Exercises 7–15 This skill was originally taught on pages 60–65. On the chalkboard, work through the example in the second display box. Discuss each step and the regrouping that is necessary. As a check, have students round the factors to 1-digit accuracy and estimate the product.

Exercises 16–19 This skill was originally taught on pages 66–67. Direct students' attention to the example on the left. Explain that we can use exponential notation to show 2 as a factor 4 times. Ask students to name the base and the exponent and then give the fourth power of 2.

Exercises 20–25 This skill was originally taught on page 70. Work through the examples with students. Review the shortcut of dividing each number by 10, as in $\frac{1,60\emptyset}{8\emptyset} = \frac{160}{8} = 20$. Point out how we can use multiplication to check division.

Exercises 26–34 This skill was originally taught on pages 72–77. Use the example at the left to show on the chalkboard the steps in the algorithm. "Can 2 be divided by 62?" (No) "Can 21 be divided by 62?" (No) "Can 217 be divided by 62?" (Yes) Remind students that to estimate the first digit of the quotient, we round 62 to 60 and use only the tens digit, 6. Explain that $21 \div 6$ is about 3, so the first digit in the quotient should be 3. Point out that the next step is to multiply, subtract, and compare the partial remainder with the divisor. Repeat the process for the next digit in the quotient.

ANOTHER LOOK

2 zeros

$$30 \times 40 = 1,200$$
$$3 \times 4 = 12$$

$$
\begin{array}{r}
2\,7\,6 \\
\times\ \ 3\,4 \\
\hline
1\,1\,0\,4 \leftarrow 4 \times 276 \\
8\,2\,8\,0 \leftarrow 30 \times 276 \\
\hline
9,3\,8\,4 \leftarrow 34 \times 276
\end{array}
$$

---

2 as a factor 4 times

$$2 \cdot 2 \cdot 2 \cdot 2 = 2^4 = 16$$

2 to the fourth power

$1,600 \div 80 = 20$
because $20 \times 80 = 1,600$
$3,500 \div 7 = 500$
because $7 \times 500 = 3,500$

60

$$
\begin{array}{r}
3\,5\ \text{R}\,7 \\
6\,2\,)\overline{2,1\,7\,7} \\
1\,8\,6 \\
\hline
3\,1\,7 \\
3\,1\,0 \\
\hline
7
\end{array}
\qquad
\begin{array}{r}
6\,2 \\
\times\ \ 3 \\
\hline
1\,8\,6
\end{array}
\quad
\begin{array}{r}
6\,2 \\
\times\ \ 5 \\
\hline
3\,1\,0
\end{array}
$$

84

Find the products mentally.

1. 7×30 210
2. 80×20 1,600
3. 400×3 1,200
4. $2,000 \times 9$ 18,000
5. 60×50 3,000
6. 700×60 42,000

Multiply.

7.
$$
\begin{array}{r}
27 \\
\times\ \ 8 \\
\hline
216
\end{array}
$$
8.
$$
\begin{array}{r}
126 \\
\times\ \ 7 \\
\hline
882
\end{array}
$$
9.
$$
\begin{array}{r}
4,073 \\
\times\ \ \ \ \ 5 \\
\hline
20,365
\end{array}
$$
10.
$$
\begin{array}{r}
34 \\
\times\ 29 \\
\hline
986
\end{array}
$$
11.
$$
\begin{array}{r}
82 \\
\times\ 67 \\
\hline
5,494
\end{array}
$$
12.
$$
\begin{array}{r}
259 \\
\times\ \ 83 \\
\hline
21,497
\end{array}
$$
13.
$$
\begin{array}{r}
213 \\
\times\ 175 \\
\hline
37,275
\end{array}
$$
14.
$$
\begin{array}{r}
1,918 \\
\times\ \ \ 207 \\
\hline
397,026
\end{array}
$$
15.
$$
\begin{array}{r}
5,217 \\
\times\ \ \ 468 \\
\hline
2,441,556
\end{array}
$$

Write in exponential notation.

16. $3 \cdot 3 \cdot 3 \cdot 3 \cdot 3$ 3^5
17. 8 squared 8^2
18. 10 to the fifth power 10^5
19. 7 cubed 7^3

Find the quotients mentally.

20. $800 \div 4$ 200
21. $2,500 \div 50$ 50
22. $9,000 \div 3$ 3,000
23. $6,400 \div 8$ 800
24. $20,000 \div 40$ 500
25. $5,600 \div 70$ 80

Find the quotients and remainders.

26. 7 R3 $7)\overline{52}$
27. 26 R3 $9)\overline{237}$
28. 128 R2 $8)\overline{1,026}$
29. 27 R17 $21)\overline{584}$
30. 23 R22 $69)\overline{1,609}$
31. 45 R33 $53)\overline{2,418}$
32. 217 R57 $70)\overline{15,247}$
33. 330 R4 $13)\overline{4,294}$
34. 142 R1 $89)\overline{12,649}$

Just for Teachers

Historical Methods of Multiplication

The operation of multiplication has been performed in various ways since civilization began to use numerals to count livestock, measure acreage, and record the movement of time. The abacus usually served as the principal computing tool of cultures. The arithmetical operations performed on it have evolved with time.

The ancient Egyptians were accomplished astronomers and engineers, but they used only the operations of addition and subtraction. More complex operations were carried out by repeated use of these concepts.

The Greeks were more abstract than practical. They devised a system using letters of their alphabet which differs from our own to stand for various numbers: The first nine letters were 1–9, the next nine letters 10–90, the last nine stood for 100–900. (Greater numbers were expressed using the letters with a slash.) This notation completely removed the operational significance from the numeric symbol. Tables had to

ENRICHMENT

History of Mathematics

A simple calculator that could be used to multiply any number by a 1-digit number was invented by the Scottish mathematician John Napier (1550–1617). Napier's calculator is called **Napier's Rods** or **Napier's Bones.** It may have been given the name Napier's Bones because some were made of bone.

Here is the way to use Napier's Bones to find 849 × 7.

Place the strips headed 8, 4, and 9 side by side. Place the index beside the three strips. Use the numbers that are opposite 7 on the index. Start at the right and add diagonally to find the product.

849 × 7 = 5, 9 4 3

Make a copy of the ten strips of Napier's Bones. Use them to find these products.

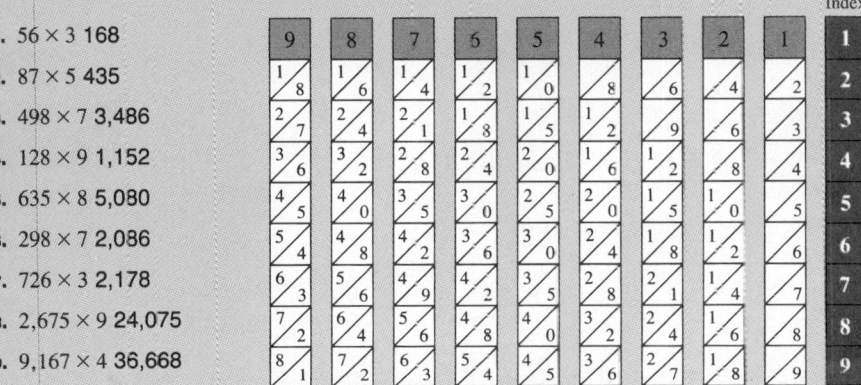

1. 56 × 3 168
2. 87 × 5 435
3. 498 × 7 3,486
4. 128 × 9 1,152
5. 635 × 8 5,080
6. 298 × 7 2,086
7. 726 × 3 2,178
8. 2,675 × 9 24,075
9. 9,167 × 4 36,668

85

be consulted both before and after numbers were multiplied. The multiplication tables of the Greeks were extensive, the basic one involving three sets of nine rows and nine columns. Each step required use of the abacus. The tables, if not memorized, would have to be consulted to determine just how many abacus beads each of these letters represented.

The use of only ten symbols in positional notation to express any number developed in India about 400 or 500 A.D. This system greatly simplified the operations of arithmetic and allowed computation without the abacus. Only one table of ten rows and ten columns had to be memorized to perform multiplication on any two numbers.

Using Page 85

This page is intended for those students who successfully completed the Chapter Review/Test on page 83. You may wish to assign this page as independent work while you use Another Look exercises to reteach the basic concepts and skills of the chapter. Or, you may decide that all students would benefit from exposure to this Enrichment activity.

Lesson Development Discuss the way to use Napier's Bones to find 849 × 7. Point out that Napier's Bones enable a person to multiply without knowing basic multiplication facts. Finding products with the bones involves only addition facts.

Have students make the ten strips of Napier's Bones. Students could make a zero strip in addition to the ones shown.

You may wish to show students how to use the rods for multipliers that are 2-digit numbers. To multiply 849 × 27, place the strips headed 8, 4, and 9 side by side, and place the index beside the three strips. Use the numbers that are opposite the 2 on the index, as well as those opposite the 7.

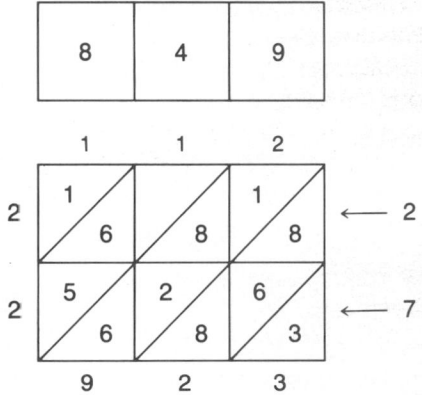

Add the numbers diagonally and regroup to the next diagonal columns if necessary.

849 × 27 = 22,923

Review

Using Page 86

The exercises on the page provide practice for maintaining cumulative skills. The emphasis in this Cumulative Review is on estimating and finding sums and differences of decimals (Chapter 2), and estimating and finding products and quotients of whole numbers (Chapter 3).

Item Analysis The table below correlates the Cumulative Review items with objectives and with the student book pages on which the concepts or skills were taught.

Items	Objectives	Related Text Pages
1–2	2.2	36–39
3–4	2.3	40–43
5	3.2	60–65
6	3.5	72–77
7–8	2.4	44–45
9–10	3.5	72–77
11	3.1	57–59
12	3.3	66–67
13	2.5	47
14	3.6	47, 66–69, 78–79, 81

CUMULATIVE REVIEW

1. Which number is largest?

Ⓐ 0.48　　　B 0.40
C 0.4　　　D not given

2. Round 0.9567 to the nearest thousandth.

A 0.956　　　Ⓑ 0.957
C 0.96　　　D not given

3. Find the sum.

$$\begin{array}{r} 27.2 \\ 61.6 \\ + 99 \end{array}$$
A 18.78　　　Ⓑ 187.8
C 188.70　　　D not given

4. Find the difference.

$$\begin{array}{r} 123.4 \\ - 87.63 \end{array}$$
A 36.77　　　B 35.71
Ⓒ 35.77　　　D not given

5. Multiply.

$$\begin{array}{r} 722 \\ \times 39 \end{array}$$
Ⓐ 28,158　　　B 8,564
C 28,058　　　D not given

6. Find the quotient.

$88\overline{)9,255}$
A 15 R10　　　Ⓑ 105 R15
C 105　　　D not given

7. Estimate the difference.

$$\begin{array}{r} \$92.68 \\ - 29.05 \end{array}$$
A $70　　　B $66
Ⓒ $60　　　D not given

8. Estimate the sum by rounding each number to 1-digit accuracy.

59¢ + 83¢ + 39¢ + 42¢

Ⓐ $2.20　　　B $25.00
C $2.00　　　D not given

9. Divide.

72,000 ÷ 9　　A 800　　　B 80
　　　　C 900　　　Ⓓ not given

10. Find the quotient.

$9\overline{)3,847}$　　Ⓐ 427 R4　　　B 427
　　　　C 427 R3　　　D not given

11. Choose the best estimate.

$$\begin{array}{r} 276 \\ \times 54 \end{array}$$
A 10,000　　　Ⓑ 15,000
C 1,500　　　D not given

12. Find the product.

$3^3 \cdot 8^2$　　Ⓐ 576　　　B 432
　　　　C 1,296　　　D not given

13. One year, the cost of automobile insurance was $279.14. The next year the cost was $323.70. How much was the increase?

Ⓐ $44.56　　　B $54.56
C $44.66　　　D not given

14. Clara typed 340 words in 5 minutes with 12 errors. What was her typing speed? Use this formula.

$$S = \frac{W - (10 \cdot e)}{n}$$

A 49 words per minute
B 57 words per minute
Ⓒ 44 words per minute
D not given

Objectives

4.1 Use estimation to find decimal products.

4.2 Find products when the factors are decimals.

4.3 Estimate products when the factors are decimals.

4.4 Use scientific notation to express whole numbers.

4.5 Solve word problems using the 5-Point Checklist and cumulative computational skills.

Summary

This chapter reviews and extends the students' experiences in multiplication with decimals. The important strand of estimation continues with work in multiplying decimals and the special powers of ten, namely 10, 100, 1,000, 0.1, 0.01, and 0.001. In addition to the special products, estimating products by rounding factors is extended to include decimal factors. Scientific notation for large numbers, an application of exponents, is introduced in Chapter 4. Finally, problem solving, using all previous operations plus the decimal multiplication of this chapter, is presented in a variety of situations.

Mathematical Background

Multiplication of Decimals The introductory lesson of this chapter is largely conceptual. Simple models show that multiplication of a decimal by a whole number can be thought of as repeated addition of the same decimal addend. Models for multiplying tenths times tenths, and tenths times hundredths, are also presented.

Estimation of products helps in formulating and justifying the rule for placing the decimal point in a product. Using rounded factors, we find that $20 \times 10 = 200$. Therefore, the answer to the exercise below must be 219.996 and we see that the answer is a three-place decimal.

$$
\begin{array}{r}
22.68 \quad \leftarrow \text{ two-place decimal} \\
\times \quad 9.7 \quad \leftarrow \text{ one-place decimal} \\
\hline
219.996 \quad \leftarrow \text{ three-place decimal}
\end{array}
$$

The algorithm for multiplying decimals is essentially the same as for multiplying whole numbers. The only new concept is the placement of the decimal point in the product. The algorithm for multiplying with decimals involves two steps: 1) Multiply the two numbers as if they were both whole numbers, and 2) place a decimal point so that the product has the same number of decimal places as the sum of the decimal places in the factors.

Scientific Notation Scientific notation is used in reporting very large numbers such as astronomical measurements or very small positive numbers such as those used by a microbiologist or a genetic scientist.

A number is written in scientific notation if it is written as the product of a number from 1 to 10 (excluding 10) and a power of 10. Thus if k is such that $1 \leq k < 10$ and $N = k \times 10^e$, then N is written in scientific notation. If the exponent e is positive, then N is greater than 1. If the exponent is negative, then N is between 0 and 1. In this chapter only positive exponents are used. Hence,

scientific notation is used only to express large numbers.

The rules for writing a number in scientific notation are based upon the fact that multiplying or dividing a number by a power of ten has the effect of shifting the decimal point in the number. Thus in the equation $2.5 \times 10^6 = 2,500,000$, the decimal shifts 6 places to the right.

Problem Solving In this chapter problem solving involves multiplying with decimals as well as using operations with numbers developed in earlier chapters. Problems with multiple-step solutions appear throughout the chapter. On pages 96 and 97, the problem-solving lesson deals with finding the cost of local and long distance telephone calls by using a rate table. On page 101, students use estimation to solve problems. Finding the cost of running a classified advertisement is the focus of the lesson on page 105. Problems about diving scores provide experience in multiple-step problems on pages 106 and 107

A new problem-solving strategy, called Draw a Picture, is introduced on page 108. This strategy is useful in many routine and nonroutine problems and will be used in problems in later chapters of the book.

Vocabulary

scientific notation

Teaching Tips

 **Error Analysis**

This chapter deals with multiplication of decimals. Many student errors result from a misunderstanding of whole number multiplication and how to place the decimal point in the product.

Error Pattern 1

5.36	5.6	93.26
× 0.26	× 0.8	× 0.33
3216	44.8	27978
1072		27978
139.36		3,077.58

Diagnosis The student multiplied correctly but did not place the decimal point correctly in the answer. The student has attempted to line up the decimal points as in addition or subtraction.

Remediation Begin with factors having one decimal place. Show how to find the product of an example such as 1.3×2.8, using estimation to place the decimal point in the product. Since $1 \times 3 = 3$, the decimal point must be placed so that the product is close to 3 (3.64).

Review the rule for placing the decimal point in a product and apply it to factors with more than one decimal place.

Error Pattern 2

$54,000 = 5.4 \times 10^5$

$8,690,000 = 8.69 \times 10^7$

$271,000,000 = 2.71 \times 10^9$

Diagnosis The student has counted the number of digits in the standard numeral to determine the exponent, instead of counting the number of places the decimal point has been shifted.

Remediation Review the meaning of scientific notation. Emphasize that it is simply a way of rewriting the number. The number itself does not change. When we multiply by the power of ten, the product should be the original number.

Review special products and multiplying by 10^1, 10^2, 10^3, and so on. Stress that the exponent tells us the number of places the decimal point shifts to the right.

Error Pattern 3

0.63	0.67	0.59
× 0.32	× 0.05	× 0.07
126	0.335	0.413
189		
0.2016		

Diagnosis The student multiplied correctly but when a zero was needed in the product, the decimal point was placed incorrectly.

Remediation Begin with an example such as 0.3×0.3. Show that 3 tenths times 3 tenths is 9 hundredths, 0.09. We must write a zero in the product so that the 9 is in the hundredths place.

Remind students of the rule for placing the decimal point in the product. Stress that in some cases we must write zeros in the product in order to have the correct number of decimal places.

 **Problem Solving**

Evaluating Problem-Solving Performance—Part 1

As problem-solving experiences play a greater role in your mathematics program, the evaluation of these experiences becomes more important. The best way to evaluate problem-solving performance is through a one-to-one interview either while the student is solving a problem or immediately after the problem is solved. Unfortunately, this type of interview takes more time than is available to most teachers.

There are, however, two evaluation techniques that do not require much time: 1) analyzing a student's written work, and 2) observing while a student solves problems in a whole-class setting. When used jointly, those techniques can provide valuable information about each student's problem-solving performance. A scheme for analyzing a student's written work and a sample problem are given below. Guidelines for observing students are presented in the Teaching Tips for Chapter 7.

A Scoring Scheme for Written Work

Understanding the problem

    0—Complete misinterpretation of the problem

    1—Misinterpretation of part of the problem

    2—Complete understanding of the problem

Choosing and implementing a solution strategy

    0—No attempt or a totally inappropriate strategy

    1—Misinterpretation of part of the problem

    2—Complete understanding of the problem

Answering the problem

    0—No answer or a wrong answer based on an inappropriate solution strategy

    1—Copying error, computational error, partial answer for a problem with multiple answers, or an answer labeled incorrectly

    2—Correct solution

> A well is 10 meters deep. A frog climbs up 5 meters during the day but slips back 4 meters during the night. If the frog starts at the bottom of the well, how many days does it take the frog to reach the top?

According to the scoring scheme, the following examples of solutions to the problem might be scored as shown below:

Student A

Solution:

```
      5 meters
    − 4 meters
      1 meter  gained each day
```

It takes 10 days for the frog to reach the top.

Score: 1, 1, 0

Student B

Solution:

```
    5 meters each day
   10 meters in all
```

It takes 2 days for the frog to reach the top.

Score: 1, 0, 0

Student C

Solution:

```
      5 meters
    − 4 meters
      1 meter  gained each day
```

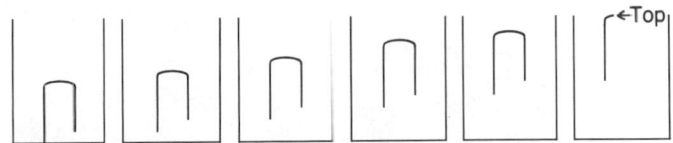

It takes 6 days for the frog to reach the top.

Score: 2, 2, 2

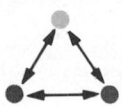 # Special Education

The focus of this chapter is on multiplication of decimals and related topics. The following suggestions highlight special approaches and techniques which may be necessary for helping learning-disabled students master ideas being presented.

Oral and Visual Guidance

Careful teacher questioning and visual prompting can lead students themselves to understand and describe the procedure for placing the decimal point in decimal multiplication. This approach actively involves the students and will be necessary for many to retain the procedure. As you check the problems on pages 90 through 91, retain a list of several examples on the chalkboard. For each problem ask students to tell 1) the number of decimal places in the exercise and 2) the number of decimal places in the product.

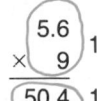 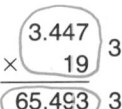 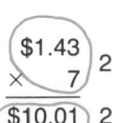

Use colored chalk to draw the circles as you ask the questions and then record student answers. Have them describe the pattern that there is the same number of decimal places in the product as in the problem. Check that this pattern holds for other examples before turning to the summary of this idea on page 92.

"One Step" for Practice

As a follow-up to the above, provide exercises in which students do just the one step of placing the decimal point in otherwise completed multiplication problems. Practice of this type reinforces what is new in decimal multiplication—placing the decimal point. Students already are familiar with the general computational procedure from work with whole numbers.

Oral Expression

As often as possible have students describe or justify orally what they are doing. This increases their retention of the ideas being discussed. On page 98, for example, students can note how multiplying by any number greater than 1 shifts the decimal point to the right, that is, gives a greater number. Multiplying by any number less than 1 shifts the decimal point to the left, giving a smaller number.

Visual Prompt

Until comfortable with an idea, many special students may find it necessary to write out rather than just think of the intermediate steps. Keep this in mind throughout the chapter when directions require students to estimate. Students will independently drop the written step when they feel they no longer need it.

```
Given      9.1    Child writes      9
         × 3.8                    × 4
```

Color Coding and Block-Out Cues

During early work with scientific notation, it often helps students to highlight the digits to be used.

$$6{,}2\underline{4}0{,}0\,0\,0 = \underline{6}.\underline{2}\,\underline{4} \times 10^6$$

Color coding in this manner helps minimize the chance of losing the place or misperceiving the numbers read.

Some students need to use a card, as shown, to block out part of the number field while counting digits. The students move the card, digit by digit, as they count.

35,400,000 → 3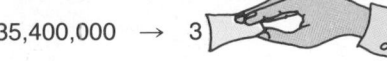

 # Subject Integration

Subject matter related to other areas of the curriculum has been integrated into the following lessons. This provides an opportunity to highlight the interaction between mathematics and other subjects.

Science Planets, page 87; electricity and kilowatt hours, page 88; thunder and the speed of sound, page 100; speed of light, pages 102–103

Social Studies Maps, pages 92–93

Industrial Arts Machine tools, pages 98–99

Consumer Awareness Sales tax, pages 94–95; telephone rates, pages 96–97; cost of classified advertisements, page 104

Physical Education Diving scores, pages 106–107

Career Awareness Cartography, page 92

Management Guide

Teaching Chapter 4				Meeting Individual Needs					
Objectives	**Chapter Content**	**Pages**	**TRB Test Items**	Lesson Assignments			Follow Up		
				Minimum	Average	Extended	Reteaching	Enrichment	Practice
	Chapter Opener	87							
4.1 Use estimation to find decimal products.	Decimal Multiplication Concepts	88–89	1–4	1–18	1–24	1–24	RS 27	ES 27	PS 34
	Finding Products Using Estimation	90–91	5–8	1–24 30, SK	1–30, SK	2–30, even 31, SK	SE6 Ch 6		PS 35
4.2 Finding products when the factors are decimals.	Multiplying Decimals	92–93	9–13	1–29 36–39	1–38, TM	2–38, even 39, TM	SE6 Ch 6 RS 28	ES 28	MP 424 PS 36
	Zeros in Products	94–95	14–16	1–20, 36	1–36	2–36, even 37	RS 29	ES 29	MP 424 PS 37
	Multiplying Decimals: Mental Math	98–99	17–22	1–61	1–61	1–61, odd 62, TM	RS 30	ES 30	PS 39
4.3 Estimate products when the factors are decimals.	Estimating Products Using Decimals	100	23–26	1–20	1–25	1–25, odd	SE6 Ch 6 RS 31	ES 31	MP 424 PS 40
4.4 Using scientific notation to express whole numbers.	Scientific Notation	102–103	27–32	1–19, SK	1–19, 22 SK	1–22, SK	RS 32	ES 32	MP 424 PS 41
	Skills Practice	104		1–30	1–40	1–45, odd			
4.5 Solve word problems using the 5-Point Checklist and cumulative computational skills.	Problem Solving: Using Data from a Table	96–97	33–37	1–6 / 1–6	1–9 / 1–8	1–10 / 1–9			PS 38
	Problem Solving: Using Estimation	101		1–6	1–8	1–10			
	Problem Solving: Using Data from a Table	105		1–6	1–8	1–8	RS 33	ES 33	PS 42
	Problem Solving: Practice	106–107		1–8	1–10	1–11, odd			PS 43
	Problem Solving: Draw a Picture	108							
	Chapter Review/Test	109							
	Another Look/ Enrichment	110–111							
	Technology	112–113							
	Cumulative Review	114							

SE6 Student Edition, Book 6
RS Reteaching Supplement
ES Enrichment Supplement
PS Practice Supplement
MP More Practice
TM Think Math
SK Skillkeeper
TRB Teacher's Resource Book

Masters for use

. . . before Chapter 4

| Readiness Multiplication with Money | 110 |
| Readiness Decimal Multiplication | 109 |

. . . during Chapter 4

Calculator Technology Decimal Detective	194
Consumer Applications Airline Fares*	176
Teaching Aids	278, 284, 285
Recreation Map Puzzle	158
Activities That Count Checks and Balances	142

. . . after Chapter 4

Record Keeping	299
Family Involvement At-Home Activities	252
Family Involvement Key Math	251
Reading Math Vocabulary	230
Computer Technology Scientific Notation	209
Computer Technology Basic Variables	210
Computer Technology Humans or Machines	211
Chapter 4 Test Free-Response Format	54–55
Chapter 4 Test Multiple-Choice Format	10–12

Supplements

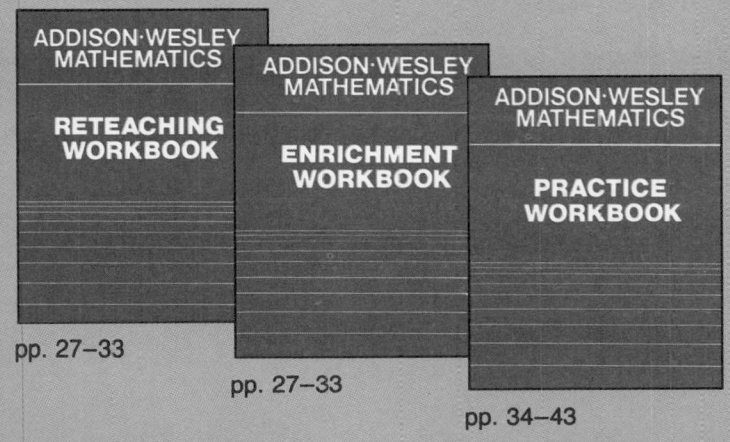

ADDISON-WESLEY MATHEMATICS
RETEACHING WORKBOOK
pp. 27–33

ADDISON-WESLEY MATHEMATICS
ENRICHMENT WORKBOOK
pp. 27–33

ADDISON-WESLEY MATHEMATICS
PRACTICE WORKBOOK
pp. 34–43

Other Addison-Wesley Resources

Books and Kits

Skillseekers III $\div$ 12–18

General Mathematics: Making Practice Fun 19A, B, 21

The Arithmetic Primer pp. 231–235

Problem-Solving Experiences in Mathematics, Grade 7
Problems 9, 10, 44, 45, 75, 94, 139, 140, 144, 149

Technology

Computer Math Activities Volumes 1–5

Computer Math Games Volumes 1, 2, 6

Activities That Count

Activities That Count are designed for use throughout this chapter and subsequent chapters. Before beginning Chapter 4, you may wish to review these activities and select the ones you consider appropriate for your class.

Missing Factor   Game

Purpose   To use estimation to find the missing factor

Materials   Game sheet as pictured below

Missing Factor

1. $52.4 \times$ _____ $= 361.56$ 2. _____ $\times 0.24 = 22.32$

1st player: $52.4 \times 7.2 = 377.28$
2nd player: $52.4 \times 5.1 = 282.96$
3rd player: $52.4 \times 6.9 = 361.56$

3. $1.7 \times$ _____ $= 890.8$ 4. _____ $\times 9.5 = 60.8$
5. _____ $\times 84 = 18.48$ 6. $587 \times$ _____ $= 228.93$

Tiebreaker $3.12 \times$ _____ $= 17.94$

Activity   The object of this game is to complete the equation with the missing factor. The first player guesses the first missing factor. That player then finds the product of the given factor and the guessed factor. This information is recorded under the appropriate problem on the game sheet. The next player uses that information to make a guess. For example, if the product was too high, a smaller factor should be guessed. Play continues until one player guesses the correct factor. That player scores 1 point. The next player in turn then makes the first guess on the next problem.

   Play continues until all problems have been used. The player with the highest score is the winner. If there is a tie, the tiebreaker problem is used. Only those players involved in the tie participate in the tiebreaker.

Checks and Balances   Math Lab

Purpose   To add, subtract, and multiply amounts of money

Materials   Game board (TRB p. 142), number cube labeled 1 through 6 (TRB p. 278), game marker for each person

Activity   The player begins on START and rolls the number cube to determine the number of spaces to move the marker. Each time the marker lands on a space, the transaction must be recorded on the form on the gamesheet. The final balance should be reported when the student lands on or passes STOP.

Scientific Notation   Project

Purpose   To write large numbers in scientific notation

Activity   Have students collect data related to one of the topics below and write the large numbers given in their sources in scientific notation.

- Distances of planets from the sun
- Mass of planets
- Size of stars

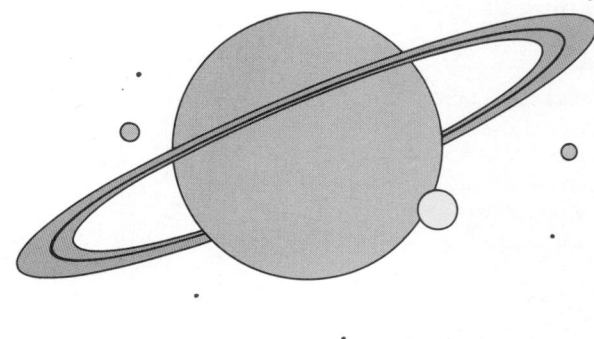

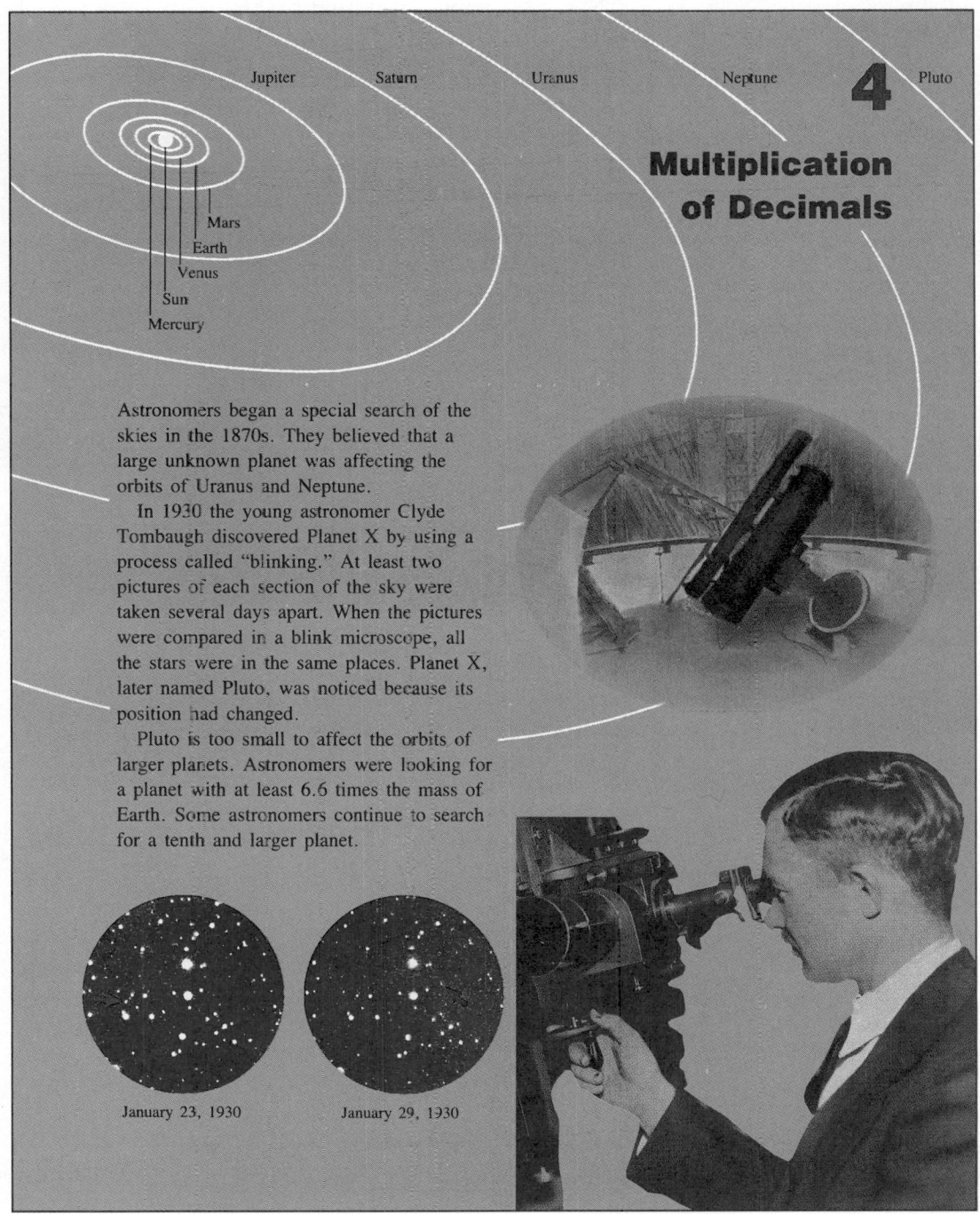

Jupiter   Saturn   Uranus   Neptune   Pluto

Mars
Earth
Venus
Sun
Mercury

4

Multiplication of Decimals

Astronomers began a special search of the skies in the 1870s. They believed that a large unknown planet was affecting the orbits of Uranus and Neptune.

In 1930 the young astronomer Clyde Tombaugh discovered Planet X by using a process called "blinking." At least two pictures of each section of the sky were taken several days apart. When the pictures were compared in a blink microscope, all the stars were in the same places. Planet X, later named Pluto, was noticed because its position had changed.

Pluto is too small to affect the orbits of larger planets. Astronomers were looking for a planet with at least 6.6 times the mass of Earth. Some astronomers continue to search for a tenth and larger planet.

January 23, 1930   January 29, 1930

Introducing the Chapter

Discussion Have students read about the discovery of Pluto and examine the accompanying pictures. Encourage discussion and comments. This is an opportunity for students to create their own questions based on the data in the article. As you teach the chapter you may wish to refer back to this page and discuss the questions below.

Follow-Up Questions

After Page 93 While asteroids may be about 2.5 astronomical units from the sun, Pluto's average distance is about 15.76 times as far. What is Pluto's average distance from the sun? (39.4 astronomical units)

After Page 99 Mercury's average distance from the sun is 0.01 of Pluto's average distance. Find Mercury's average distance from the sun. (0.394 astronomical units)

After Page 103 An astronomical unit is about 1.495×10^8 km. Write the standard numeral for this number. (149,500,000 km) The mass of Pluto is estimated to be approximately 13,200,000,000,000,000,000 metric tons. Write this number in scientific notation. (1.32×10^{19})

Quick Review Display the following and have students identify which are incorrect.

$36,491 > 36,487$ $6,576.884 < 6,576.304$ incorrect $301,890 < 301,900$

$99.817 > 99.917$ incorrect $139,481 < 139,399$ incorrect $6.389 > 16.211$

Lesson Focus To review basic concepts related to multiplication of decimals

Suggested Materials Graph paper (TRB p. 285)

Ideas for Getting Started

Display a 10 by 10 grid on the chalkboard or overhead projector. Have a student shade 0.2 or 2 rows of the square. Ask a second student to shade in 3 times as much as 0.2. The student should shade in 0.6 of the square. Show that we can think of 0.6 as 0.2 + 0.2 + 0.2 or 3 × 0.2.

Call on a student to shade in 0.09 of the square or 9 small squares. Ask a second student to shade in 4 times as much of the square. Then discuss the fact that 4 × 0.09 = 0.36.

Using Page 88

Motivational Problem Read the introductory problem with students. "What does the question ask us to find?" (the number of kilowatts used in 4 hours) Point out that kilowatts are a measure of the amount of electricity. "What is the data in the problem?" (The lamp used 0.2 kilowatts each hour for 4 hours.)

Lesson Development Explain that we can find the answer by addition in this simple case, but since the addend 0.2 is repeated 4 times, it is the same as multiplying 0.2 by 4. Stress that when a whole number is multiplied by tenths, the product will be a number in tenths.

Decimal Multiplication

Carole left an electric lamp on for 4 hours. The bulb in the lamp uses 0.2 kilowatt (kW) of electricity each hour. How many kilowatts did the bulb use in 4 hours?

We can find the answer by adding 0.2 four times.

$$0.2 + 0.2 + 0.2 + 0.2 = 0.8$$

Since the same addend is repeated, we can also use multiplication.

4×2 tenths $= 8$ tenths
$4 \times 0.2 = 0.8$

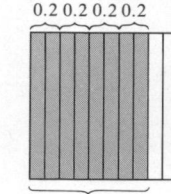
0.2 0.2 0.2 0.2

The bulb used 0.8 kW in 4 hours.

0.8

Here is how we can think about multiplying a decimal times a decimal.

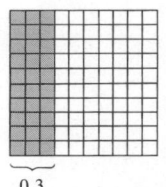
0.3

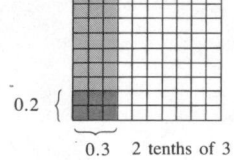
0.2 {
0.3   2 tenths of 3 tenths

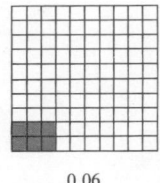
0.06

2 tenths $\times$ 3 tenths $=$ 6 hundredths
$0.2 \times 0.3 = 0.06$

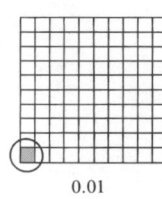
0.01

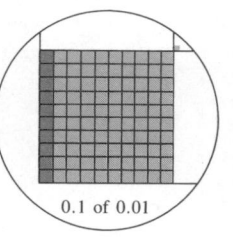
0.1 of 0.01

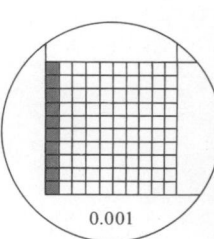
0.001

1 tenth $\times$ 1 hundredth $=$ 1 thousandth
$0.1 \times 0.01 = 0.001$

88

Follow Up

Reteaching

Use place-value models to help students understand decimal multiplication. Name the hundred-square as 1 unit and the ten-stick as 1 tenth. Show examples such as these using the models.

3 sets of 2 tenths
"What is 3 times 2 tenths?" (6 tenths)
"Write the multiplication equation."
(3 × 0.2 = 0.6)

3 sets of 4 tenths
"What is 3 times 4 tenths?" (12 tenths)
Point out that 12 tenths may be regrouped as 1 unit and 2 tenths. Ask students to write the multiplication equation. (3 × 0.4 = 1.2)

Enrichment

Let a group of students work together to make an instructional bulletin board entitled "Decimal Multiplication." Students can shade 10 by 10 grids on graph paper (TRB p. 285) to illustrate problems such as 0.3 × 0.2 = 0.06. Have them write the corresponding equation under each grid.

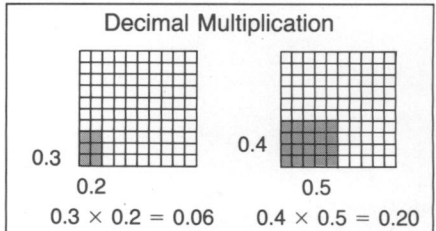
Decimal Multiplication

0.3
0.2
0.3 × 0.2 = 0.06

0.4
0.5
0.4 × 0.5 = 0.20

Assignment Guide

	Minimum	Average	Extended
page 89	1–18	1–24	1–24

Find the sums and the products.

1. 0.3 + 0.3 + 0.3 0.9
3 × 0.3 0.9

2. 0.6 + 0.6 + 0.6 + 0.6 2.4
4 × 0.6 2.4

3. 0.07 + 0.07 0.14
2 × 0.07 0.14

4. 0.012 + 0.012 + 0.012 0.036
3 × 0.012 0.036

5. 0.5 + 0.5 + 0.5 + 0.5 2.0
4 × 0.5 2.0

6. 0.09 + 0.09 + 0.09 + 0.09 + 0.09 0.45
5 × 0.09 0.45

Write a multiplication statement for each figure.

7.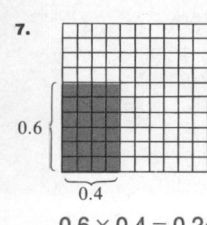
0.6
0.4
0.6 × 0.4 = 0.24

8.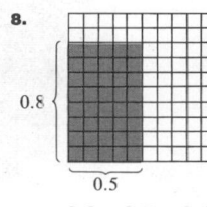
0.8
0.5
0.8 × 0.5 = 0.40

9.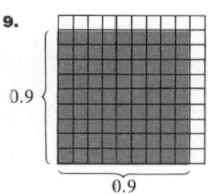
0.9
0.9
0.9 × 0.9 = 0.81

10.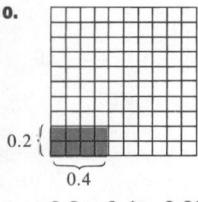
0.2
0.4
0.2 × 0.4 = 0.08

11.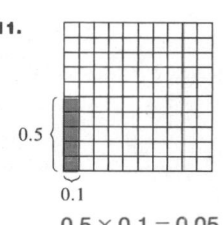
0.5
0.1
0.5 × 0.1 = 0.05

12.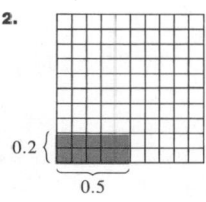
0.2
0.5
0.2 × 0.5 = 0.10

13.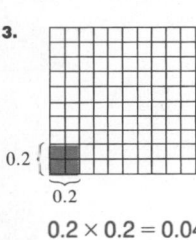
0.2
0.2
0.2 × 0.2 = 0.04

14.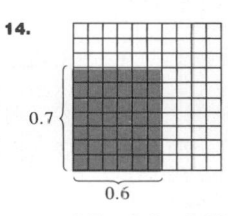
0.7
0.6
0.7 × 0.6 = 0.42

15.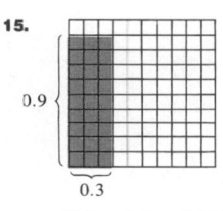
0.9
0.3
0.9 × 0.3 = 0.27

Multiply.

16. 2 × 0.7 1.4

17. 3 × 0.4 1.2

18. 4 × 0.04 0.16

19. 4 × 0.07 0.28

20. 6 × 0.009 0.054

21. 8 × 0.07 0.56

22. 0.3 × 0.02 0.006

23. 0.5 × 0.09 0.045

24. 0.1 × 0.01 0.001

89

Using Page 89

Exercises 1–6 These exercises illustrate how repeated decimal addends can be thought of as multiplying a whole number times a decimal.

Exercises 7–15 These exercises visually reinforce the multiplication of tenths times tenths.

Exercises 16–24 Use a 10 by 10 grid to illustrate some of these exercises. Avoid giving rules for these exercises at this stage.

Reteaching Supplement, page 27

Enrichment Supplement, page 27

Practice Supplement, page 34

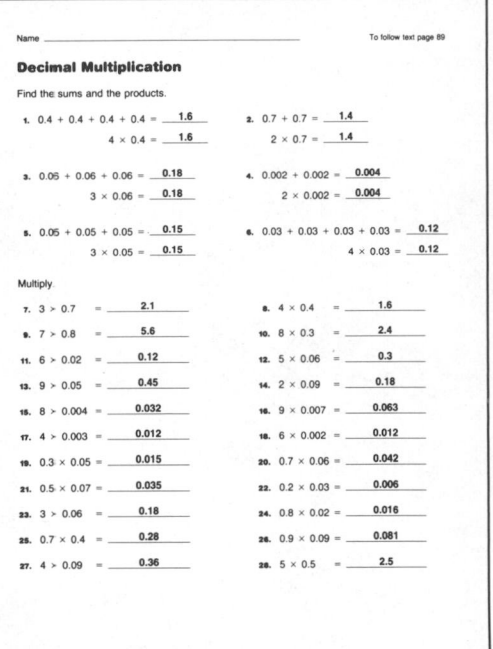

Lesson Focus To find the product of a whole number times a decimal using estimation

Ideas for Getting Started

To prepare students for the estimation in this lesson have them round these numbers to 1-digit accuracy.

3.8	7.1	10.5	6.75	23.27
$2.67	$8.50	$12.40	$16.39	$29.99

Using Page 90

Motivational Problem Have students read the problem at the top of the page. "What does the problem ask us to find?" (the weight of 8 quarters) "What data do we need to solve the problem?" (1 quarter weighs 5.6 g) "How can we find the total weight?" (multiply)

Lesson Development Explain to students that we can round 5.6 to 6 and multiply to estimate the total weight as 48 g. This estimate helps us place the decimal point in the product. "If we know the digits in the product are 448, where will we place the decimal point in order to have a number close to our estimate?" (44.8)

Other Examples These examples show that when a decimal and a whole number are multiplied, the product will have the same number of decimal places as the decimal factor. The second example shows that multiplication of money expressed in dollars and cents notation is the same as multiplying a decimal in hundredths by a whole number.

Warm Up Work through the first few exercises orally. Have students round the factors to 1-digit accuracy and then estimate the product. In the first exercise, 6 × 9 = 54. Therefore, the decimal point must be placed so that the product is close to 54 (56.7).

Finding Products Using Estimation

Charles has 8 quarters. He puts 1 quarter on a balance scale and finds that it weighs 5.6 grams (g). What is the total weight of 8 quarters?

To find the total weight, we can multiply.

Use an estimate to help place the decimal point in the product.

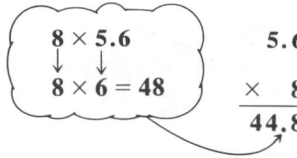

$$\begin{array}{r} 5.6 \\ \times\ 8 \\ \hline 44.8 \end{array}$$

The 8 quarters have a total weight of 44.8 g.

Other Examples

64 × 1.8	5 × $3.96	23 × 6.025
Estimate: 60 × 2 = 120	Estimate: 5 × $4 = $20	Estimate: 20 × 6 = 120

$$\begin{array}{r} 1.8 \\ \times\ 6\,4 \\ \hline 7\,2 \\ 1\,0\,8 \\ \hline 1\,1\,5.2 \end{array}$$

$$\begin{array}{r} \$\,3.9\,6 \\ \times\ \ \ 5 \\ \hline \$\,1\,9.8\,0 \end{array}$$

$$\begin{array}{r} 6.0\,2\,5 \\ \times\ \ \ 2\,3 \\ \hline 1\,8\,0\,7\,5 \\ 1\,2\,0\,5\,0 \\ \hline 1\,3\,8.5\,7\,5 \end{array}$$

Warm Up

Use estimation to place the decimal point in each product.

1. 6.3 × 9 = 567
   56.7

2. 7 × 7.186 = 50302
   50.302

3. 6 × $19.75 = $11850
   $118.50

4. $2.35
   × 29
   ———
   $6815 **$68.15**

5. 32.41
   × 7
   ———
   22687 **226.87**

6. 5.784
   × 31
   ———
   179304 **179.304**

Find the products. Use estimation to place the decimal point.

7. 6.19
   × 8
   ———
   49.52

8. $2.04
   × 57
   ———
   $116.28

9. 9.306
   × 12
   ———
   111.672

10. 87.3
    × 44
    ———
    3,841.2

90

Follow Up

Reteaching

Provide students with exercises like the following. Have them round the factors to 1-digit accuracy, estimate the product, and place the decimal point in the answer.

$$6.34 \times 7 = 44.38$$
$$\downarrow \qquad \downarrow \qquad \uparrow$$
$$\underline{6} \times \underline{7} = \underline{42}$$
rounded factors   estimate

$$5.3 \times 62 = 328.6$$
$$\downarrow \qquad \downarrow \qquad \uparrow$$
$$\underline{5} \times \underline{60} = \underline{300}$$
rounded factors   estimate

Enrichment

Display the following on the chalkboard:

Estimates

1. 2.35 × 1.7	A. 24	**1B**
2. 88.9 × 9.3	B. 4	**2E**
3. 72 × 2.8	C. 72	**3F**
4. 6.23 × 4.1	D. 480	**4A**
5. 57.4 ×8.3	E. 810	**5D**
6. 9.16 × 8.41	F. 210	**6C**

Have students match the problems with the estimated products, rounding to 1-digit accuracy. Then have them find the exact product for each problem using a calculator.

Assignment Guide			
	Minimum	Average	Extended
page 91	1–4, 30, SK	1–30 SK	2–30 even, 31, SK

Use estimation to choose each product.

1. 5×6.28 A 3.140 Ⓑ 31.40 c 314.0

2. 8×92.7 Ⓐ 741.6 B 74.16 c 7,416

3. $28 \times \$6.35$ A \$17.78 Ⓑ \$177.80 c \$1,778.00

4. $8 \times \$27.95$ A \$2,236.00 B \$22,360.00 Ⓒ \$223.60

5. 72×9.44 A 67,968 B 67.968 Ⓒ 679.68

6. 39×1.897 A 7.3983 B 739.83 Ⓒ 73.983

7. 11×119.4 Ⓐ 1,313.4 B 131.34 c 13,134

8. 42×0.996 A 0.41832 B 4.1832 Ⓒ 41.832

9. 9.7×140 Ⓐ 1,358.0 B 13.580 c 135.80

Find the products. Use estimation to place the decimal point.

10. $\begin{array}{r} 3.4 \\ \times\ 8 \\ \hline 27.2 \end{array}$

11. $\begin{array}{r} 1.9 \\ \times\ 5 \\ \hline 9.5 \end{array}$

12. $\begin{array}{r} 7.2 \\ \times\ 7 \\ \hline 50.4 \end{array}$

13. $\begin{array}{r} 5.6 \\ \times\ 9 \\ \hline 50.4 \end{array}$

14. $\begin{array}{r} 8.8 \\ \times\ 6 \\ \hline 52.8 \end{array}$

15. $\begin{array}{r} \$1.43 \\ \times\ 7 \\ \hline \$10.01 \end{array}$

16. $\begin{array}{r} \$6.09 \\ \times\ 13 \\ \hline \$79.17 \end{array}$

17. $\begin{array}{r} \$12.79 \\ \times\ 42 \\ \hline \$537.18 \end{array}$

18. $\begin{array}{r} \$63.18 \\ \times\ 28 \\ \hline \$1,769.04 \end{array}$

19. $\begin{array}{r} \$83.41 \\ \times\ 76 \\ \hline \$6,339.16 \end{array}$

20. 2.9×34 98.6

21. 6.8×90 612.0

22. 8.5×54 459.0

23. 6.7×75 502.5

24. 9.8×47 460.6

25. 59×32.4 1,911.6

26. 86×8.08 694.88

27. 63×72.5 4,567.5

28. 19×3.447 65.493

29. 68×3.108 211.344

30. One nickel weighs about 5.2 g. What is the weight of a roll of 40 nickels? **208.0 g**

31. One quarter weighs about 5.6 g. One nickel weighs 5.2 g. What is the total weight of 5 nickels and 5 quarters? **54.0 g**

SKILLKEEPER

1. $320 \div 10$ **32**
2. $600 \div 100$ **6**
3. $10,000 \div 1,000$ **10**
4. $55,000 \div 10$ **5,600**
5. $850,000 \div 1,000$ **850**
6. $25,000 \div 100$ **250**
7. $9,000 \div 10$ **900**
8. $7,200 \div 100$ **72**
9. $41\overline{)25,720}$ **627 R13**
10. $93\overline{)21,633}$ **232 R57**
11. $29\overline{)13,398}$ **462**
12. $15\overline{)7,255}$ **483 R10**
13. $57\overline{)17,360}$ **304 R32**
14. $70\overline{)38,019}$ **543 R9**
15. $68\overline{)27,676}$ **407**
16. $72\overline{)43,800}$ **608 R24**

Using Page 91

Exercises 1–30 Encourage students to think about the estimate they make for each product and decide whether their estimate is larger or smaller than the actual product. For exercise 1, an estimate of 5×6 or 30 for 5×6.28 would be smaller than the actual product. An estimate of 5×7 or 35 would be larger than the actual product, so we would expect the product to be between 30 and 35. Since the computed product is 31.40, the answer is reasonable.

Exercise 31 This problem may be solved using either of these techniques: 1) Find the sum of the weight of 1 nickel and 1 quarter.

$$5.6 \text{ g} + 5.2 \text{ g} = 10.8 \text{ g}$$

Since there are 5 pairs of 1 nickel and 1 quarter we can multiply.

$$10.8 \times 5 - 54.0 \text{ g}$$

2) Find the weight of 5 nickels and 5 quarters.

$$5 \times 5.6 = 28.0 \text{ g}$$
$$5 \times 5.2 = 26.0 \text{ g}$$

Then find the sum of the weights.

$$28.0 \text{ g} + 26.0 \text{ g} = 54.0 \text{ g}$$

Skillkeeper This Skillkeeper reviews material taught in this chapter.

Ideas That Work

Special Education

To reinforce the work of pages 90 and 91, let students play "Over or Under" in groups of two or three. Each group will need a coin and index cards labeled 1 through 30.

Students should take turns being dealer. The dealer mixes the cards and gives three to each player. The remaining cards go in a pile, top card face up. This card is the target card. The numbers on the cards tell which problems on page 91 to use. The dealer writes the problem for the target card on a piece of paper, answers the problem, and places the paper so all can see. Players then write the problems for their three cards, multiply and estimate to place the decimal point. The dealer then flips the coin. For heads, players earn 1 point for each correct answer *over* the product for the target card. For tails, players earn 1 point for each correct answer *under* the target card product. Players earn 2 points if an answer equals the target card product.

The winner is the player with the most points at the end of time allowed for play.

Practice Supplement, page 35

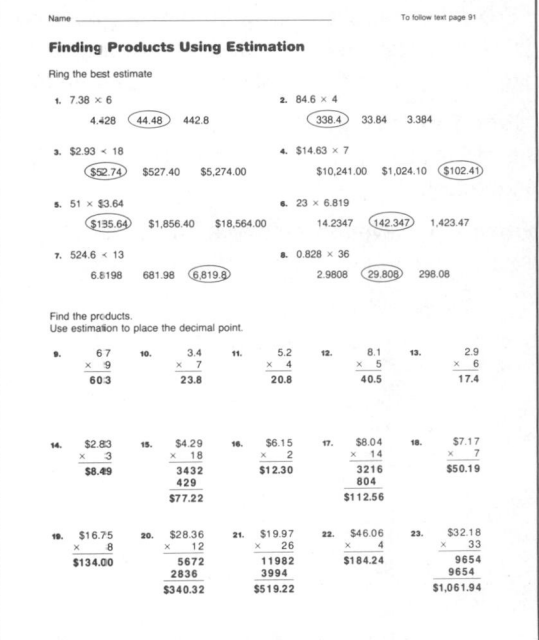

Lesson Focus To multiply two decimals using the standard multiplication algorithm

Ideas for Getting Started

Write these problems on the chalkboard. Tell students that the answers are correct but the decimal point has been omitted. Have them estimate the product and place the decimal point in the given product in the correct position according to their estimate.

24.7	84	9.37
× 3.9	× 8.1	× 6.85
9663	6804	641845
(96.63)	(680.4)	(64.1845)

Show that when the decimal point is placed according to the estimate, the product has as many decimal places as the sum of the places in the two factors.

Using Page 92

Motivational Problem Call on a student to read the problem at the top of the page. Discuss the work of cartographers or map makers. A career in cartography is only one of many careers that requires an understanding and use of mathematics.

Have a student tell what the question asks us to find. (the distance represented by 3.7 cm) "What data are we given in the problem?" (1 cm represents a distance of 25.4 km) "How can we find what distance 2 cm represents?" (2 × 25.4 km) "What distance does 3 cm represent?" (3 × 25.4 km = 76.2 km) Point out that our plan will be to multiply to find the distance for 3.7 cm.

Lesson Development On the chalkboard, work through the steps shown to find the answer. Notice with students that we multiply as with whole numbers. Discuss the rule for placing the decimal point. "What is the sum of the decimal places in the factors?" (2) "How many decimal places are in the product?" (2)

Show that the estimate of the answer does two things. It verifies that our answer is reasonable and that the decimal point has been placed correctly.

Other Examples Work through the examples, stressing the rule for placing the decimal point in the product.

Warm Up Have students give an estimate of the products before multiplying in these exercises.

Multiplying Decimals

Myra Bailey is a cartographer, or map maker. She is working on a map that uses 1 cm to represent an actual distance of 25.4 km. What distance would 3.7 cm represent?

Since each centimeter on the map represents the same distance, we multiply.

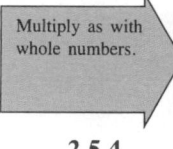

Multiply as with whole numbers.	Write the product so it has the same number of decimal places as the sum of the decimal places in the factors.

```
  2 5.4                    2 5.4  ← 1 decimal place
×   3.7                  ×   3.7  ← 1 decimal place
  1 7 7 8                  1 7 7 8
  7 6 2                    7 6 2      Tenths × tenths
  9 3 9 8                  9 3.9 8  ← 2 decimal places   equals hundredths.
```

The distance represented is 93.98 km.
Use an estimate to check. 25 × 4 = 100
The estimate and product are close.

Other Examples

```
  0.3 3  ← 2 decimal places      4 1.3 7  ← 2 decimal places      0.6 5 9  ← 3 decimal places
×   6.5  ← 1 decimal place     ×     1 2  ← 0 decimal places    ×     0.8  ← 1 decimal place
  1 6 5                          8 2 7 4                          0.5 2 7 2  ← 4 decimal places
  1 9 8                          4 1 3 7
  2.1 4 5  ← 3 decimal places    4 9 6.4 4  ← 2 decimal places
```

Warm Up

Find the products.

1. 2.9 × 6.4 **18.56**	2. 38.7 × 0.26 **10.062**	3. 5.123 × 0.85 **4.35455**	4. 27.8 × 0.07 **1.946**
5. 0.86 × 0.74 **0.6364**	6. 3.125 × 9 **28.125**	7. 125 × 0.008 **1.000**	8. 5.2^2 **27.04**

92

Follow Up

Reteaching

Have students give the number of decimal places for each ☐ and place the decimal point in the product.

```
 27.8  ← 1  decimal place
× 0.42  ← 2  decimal places
  556
 1112
 11.676  ← 3  decimal places

  1.859  ← 3  decimal places
× 0.92  ← 2  decimal places
 3718
16731
 1.71028  ← 5  decimal places
```

Enrichment

Have students give the missing digits.

```
1.     8 . 8              2.      0 . 7 2
    ×    3 . 7               ×      9 . 9
       6 1 6                     6 4 8
     2 6 4                     6 4 8
    3 2 . 5 6                7 . 1 2 8

3.       6 . 7            4.       1 . 4 6
    ×      4 . 9               ×      5 . 5
        6 0 3                     7 3 0
      2 6 8                     7 3 0
     3 2 . 8 3                8 . 0 3 0
```

Assignment Guide			
	Minimum	Average	Extended
page 93	1–29, 36–38	1–38, TM	2–38 even, 39, TM

Find the products.

1.
$$3.9 \times 0.8 = 3.12$$

2.
$$6.8 \times 0.37 = 2.516$$

3.
$$0.715 \times 3.8 = 2.7170$$

4.
$$0.89 \times 0.89 = 0.7921$$

5.
$$42.8 \times 0.06 = 2.568$$

6.
$$72.5 \times 4.7 = 340.75$$

7.
$$0.813 \times 6.9 = 5.6097$$

8.
$$8,000 \times 0.52 = 4,160.00$$

9.
$$3.14 \times 19 = 59.66$$

10.
$$9.075 \times 3.7 = 33.5775$$

11.
$$8.54 \times 6.9 = 58.926$$

12.
$$9.033 \times 0.8 = 7.2264$$

13.
$$257.2 \times 0.45 = 115.740$$

14.
$$0.33 \times 8.4 = 2.772$$

15.
$$10.09 \times 8.6 = 86.774$$

16.
$$\$23.75 \times 6 = \$142.50$$

17.
$$\$415.95 \times 3 = \$1,247.85$$

18.
$$\$0.75 \times 15 = \$11.25$$

19.
$$\$18.95 \times 5 = \$94.75$$

20.
$$\$1.33 \times 128 = \$170.24$$

21.
$$34.90 \times 1.05 = 36.6450$$

22.
$$87.50 \times 1.25 = 109.3750$$

23.
$$6,740 \times 0.16 = 1,078.40$$

24.
$$172.75 \times 0.09 = 15.5475$$

25.
$$62.44 \times 12 = 749.28$$

26. 7.1×19.76 140.296

27. 0.67×600 402.00

28. 56×0.938 52.528

29. 0.93×2.31 2.1483

30. 0.5×3.51 1.755

31. 14×0.55 7.70

32. 0.99×4.56 4.5144

33. 1.06×2.66 2.8196

34. 8.4^2 70.56

35. 0.68^2 0.4624

36. 36.8^2 1,354.24

37. 3.03^2 9.1809

38. On a map, 1 cm represents 38.5 km. What distance would 6.3 cm represent?
242.55 km

39. On a map, 3 cm represents 282 km. What distance would 0.7 cm represent?
65.8 km

▰ THINK MATH ▰

Number Puzzle

Which rings on the dart board must be hit to score exactly 99 points with 6 darts?
$(3 \cdot 17) + (3 \cdot 16) = 99$
Which rings on the dart board must be hit to score 100 points with 6 darts?
$(4 \cdot 17) + (2 \cdot 16) = 100$

16 17 23 24 39 40

More Practice, page 424, Set A

Using Page 93

Exercises 34–37 These exercises are given in exponential notation. Remind students that 8.4^2 means 8.4×8.4.

Exercise 39 This is a two-step problem. First, the distance represented by 1 cm is found by dividing 282 km by 3. Then the quotient, 94 km, is multiplied by 0.7.

Think Math This problem involves addition skills, the Guess and Check strategy, and logical reasoning. Since $16 + 17 = 33$ and $3 \times 33 = 99$, we see that 3 darts on the 16 ring and 3 darts on the 17 ring would give a total of $48 + 51 = 99$ points. The only way to score exactly 100 points with 6 darts is to hit 17 with 4 darts and 16 with 2 darts.

$$(4 \times 17) + (2 \times 16) = 68 + 32 = 100$$

More Practice, page 424, Set A

Reteaching Supplement, page 28

Name _____ To follow text page 93

Multiplying Decimals

Multiply as for whole numbers. → Write the product so that it has the same number of decimal places at the sum of the decimal places as the factors.

$$\begin{array}{r} 43.6 \\ \times 0.18 \\ \hline 3488 \\ 4360 \\ \hline 7848 \end{array}$$

$$\begin{array}{r} 43.6 \leftarrow 1\ place \\ \times 0.18 \leftarrow 2\ places \\ \hline 3488 \\ 4360 \quad (2+1=3) \\ \hline 7.848 \leftarrow 3\ places \end{array}$$

Find the products.

1. $7.469 \leftarrow 3\ places$
$\times \quad 3.3 \leftarrow 1\ place$
22407
224070
24.6477 (3 + 1 places)

2. $0.543 \leftarrow 3\ places$
$\times \quad 5.7 \leftarrow 1\ place$
3801
27150 (Finish.)
3.0951

3. 16.4
$\times 6.8$
1312
9840
111.52

4. 32.6
$\times 0.9$
29.34

5. 1.75
$\times 15$
875
1750
26.25

6. 142
$\times 2.5$
710
2840
355.0

7. 12.75
$\times 0.8$
10.200

8. 3.5
$\times 4.5$
175
1400
15.75

9. 266
$\times 1.8$
2128
2660
478.8

10. 55.3
$\times 2.9$
4977
11060
160.37

11. 12.8
$\times 3.7$
896
3840
47.36

12. 2.166×0.83
2166
$\times 0.83$
6498
17328
1797.78

13. 19.46×0.18
19.46
$\times 0.18$
15568
1946
3.5028

14. 774.3×8.2
774.3
$\times 8.2$
15486
61944
6,349.26

Enrichment Supplement, page 28

Name _____ To follow text page 93

What's Wrong?

Pretend that you are a math teacher. One of your students, B. Fuddled, missed every problem on this paper. Describe the error in each problem. Then rework the problem correctly.

1.
$$\begin{array}{r} 482.4 \\ 16.28 \\ + 3.729 \\ \hline 10.181 \end{array} \qquad \begin{array}{r} 482.4 \\ 16.28 \\ 3.729 \\ \hline 502.409 \end{array}$$
Error: Student didn't align the decimal points.

2.
$$\begin{array}{r} 0.9 \\ \times 0.8 \\ \hline 1.7 \end{array} \qquad \begin{array}{r} 0.9 \\ \times 0.8 \\ \hline 0.72 \end{array}$$
Error: Student added instead of multiplying.

3.
$$\begin{array}{r} 60.03 \\ - 27.48 \\ \hline 33.65 \end{array} \qquad \begin{array}{r} 60.03 \\ - 27.48 \\ \hline 32.55 \end{array}$$
Error: Student didn't rename correctly.

4.
$$\begin{array}{r} 34.94 \\ + 264.2 \\ \hline 6.136 \end{array} \qquad \begin{array}{r} 34.94 \\ + 264.2 \\ \hline 299.14 \end{array}$$
Error: Student didn't align the decimal points.

5.
$$\begin{array}{r} 0.168 \\ \times 4.29 \\ \hline 1512 \\ 336 \\ 672 \\ \hline 7.2072 \end{array} \qquad \begin{array}{r} 0.168 \\ \times 4.29 \\ \hline 1512 \\ 336 \\ 672 \\ \hline 0.72072 \end{array}$$
Error: Student didn't put the decimal point in the right place in the answer.

6.
$$\begin{array}{r} 2.742 \\ \times 28.6 \\ \hline 16452 \\ 21936 \\ 5484 \\ \hline 581.9812 \end{array} \qquad \begin{array}{r} 2.742 \\ \times 28.6 \\ \hline 16452 \\ 21936 \\ 5484 \\ \hline 78.4212 \end{array}$$
Error: Student didn't write the third product in the right place.

7.
$$\begin{array}{r} 83.72 \\ - 67.59 \\ \hline 24.27 \end{array} \qquad \begin{array}{r} 83.72 \\ - 67.59 \\ \hline 16.13 \end{array}$$
Error: Student always subtracted the smaller number from the larger.

8.
$$\begin{array}{r} 3.1 \\ \times 7.2 \\ \hline 62 \\ 217 \\ \hline 223.2 \end{array} \qquad \begin{array}{r} 3.1 \\ \times 7.2 \\ \hline 62 \\ 217 \\ \hline 22.32 \end{array}$$
Error: Student didn't put decimal point in the right place in the answer.

Practice Supplement, page 36

Name _____ To follow text page 93

Multiplying Decimals

Find the products.

1.
$$3.4 \times 7 = 23.8$$

2.
$$0.82 \times 4 = 3.28$$

3.
$$4.07 \times 6 = 24.42$$

4.
$$66.7 \times 3 = 200.1$$

5.
$$21.6 \times 4 = 86.4$$

6.
$$7.39 \times 0.6 = 4.434$$

7.
$$53.7 \times 0.9 = 48.33$$

8.
$$64.2 \times 0.7 = 44.94$$

9.
$$5.96 \times 0.6 = 3.576$$

10.
$$47.6 \times 0.7 = 33.32$$

11.
$$55 \times 3.1 = \begin{array}{r} 55 \\ 165 \\ \hline 170.5 \end{array}$$

12.
$$11.3 \times 6.2 = \begin{array}{r} 226 \\ 678 \\ \hline 70.06 \end{array}$$

13.
$$6.8 \times 13 = \begin{array}{r} 204 \\ 68 \\ \hline 88.4 \end{array}$$

14.
$$8.7 \times 2.3 = \begin{array}{r} 261 \\ 174 \\ \hline 20.01 \end{array}$$

15.
$$340 \times 8.2 = \begin{array}{r} 680 \\ 2720 \\ \hline 2,788.0 \end{array}$$

16.
$$40.2 \times 3.3 = \begin{array}{r} 1206 \\ 1206 \\ \hline 132.66 \end{array}$$

17.
$$3.26 \times 27 = \begin{array}{r} 2282 \\ 652 \\ \hline 88.02 \end{array}$$

18.
$$1.12 \times 8.5 = \begin{array}{r} 560 \\ 896 \\ \hline 9.520 \end{array}$$

19.
$$0.69 \times 0.29 = \begin{array}{r} 621 \\ 138 \\ \hline 0.2001 \end{array}$$

20.
$$9.31 \times 3.1 = \begin{array}{r} 931 \\ 2793 \\ \hline 28.861 \end{array}$$

21.
$$78.7 \times 0.04 = 3.148$$

22.
$$1.11 \times 0.61 = \begin{array}{r} 111 \\ 666 \\ \hline 0.6771 \end{array}$$

23.
$$0.303 \times 2.3 = \begin{array}{r} 909 \\ 606 \\ \hline 0.6969 \end{array}$$

24.
$$6.67 \times 0.03 = 20.01$$

25.
$$15.3 \times 0.82 = \begin{array}{r} 306 \\ 1224 \\ \hline 12.546 \end{array}$$

26.
$$\$89.15 \times 7 = \$624.05$$

27.
$$\$0.77 \times 19 = \begin{array}{r} 693 \\ 77 \\ \hline \$14.63 \end{array}$$

28.
$$\$34.41 \times 5 = \$172.05$$

29.
$$\$59.82 \times 16 = \begin{array}{r} 35892 \\ 5982 \\ \hline \$957.12 \end{array}$$

30.
$$\$2.22 \times 177 = \begin{array}{r} 1554 \\ 1554 \\ 222 \\ \hline \$392.94 \end{array}$$

Lesson Focus To multiply two decimals having a product in which a zero must be added to place the decimal point

Ideas for Getting Started

Ask students to find the product of 85 × 23. (1,955) Then write these exercises on the chalkboard.

$$\begin{array}{ccc} 8.5 & 0.85 & 0.85 \\ \times\ 0.23 & \times\ 0.23 & \times\ 0.023 \end{array}$$

Have students write the products for the three exercises using the fact that 85 × 23 = 1,955.

The first two exercises should be easy but the third presents a problem. We must place a decimal in 1955 so that a 5-place decimal results. The only way we can do this is to write a zero to the left of the digit 1, which gives us 0.01955.

Using Page 94

Motivational Problem Have students read the problem at the top of the page. Most localities have sales tax. Ask students if they know what the local or state sales tax is. The tax is often expressed as a rate in percent, but it is not necessary to teach percent in this lesson. You may want to point out that a sales tax which is 0.06 of the cost of an article means that a tax of 6¢ on each dollar must be paid.

Lesson Development On the chalkboard work through the steps for multiplying $0.79 by 0.06. Observe with students that both factors are 2-place decimals. Then ask how many decimal places are in the product. Explain that a zero must be written in the tenths place in order to have a 4-place decimal.

Notice with students that the question asks for the sales tax to the nearest cent, so the product must be rounded to the nearest hundredth of a dollar. Point out to students that a check of the answer might be as follows. If the pen had cost $1.00, the sales tax would have been 6¢. Since 79¢ is a little less than $1.00, 5¢ for the sales tax seems about right.

Other Examples Have selected students show how to find the products in these examples.

Warm Up Use these exercises to check if students are placing the decimal points in the products correctly. Watch for these errors:

$$\begin{array}{l} 0.76 \\ \times\ 0.09 \\ \hline 0.684 \quad \text{no zero in tenths place} \end{array}$$

$$\begin{array}{l} 0.76 \\ \times\ 0.09 \\ \hline 0.6840 \quad \text{zero in wrong place} \end{array}$$

Zeros in Products

Maria wants to buy a notebook that costs $0.79. The sales tax is 0.06 of the cost. To the nearest cent, what is the sales tax on the notebook?

Since we want to find 0.06 of the cost, we multiply.

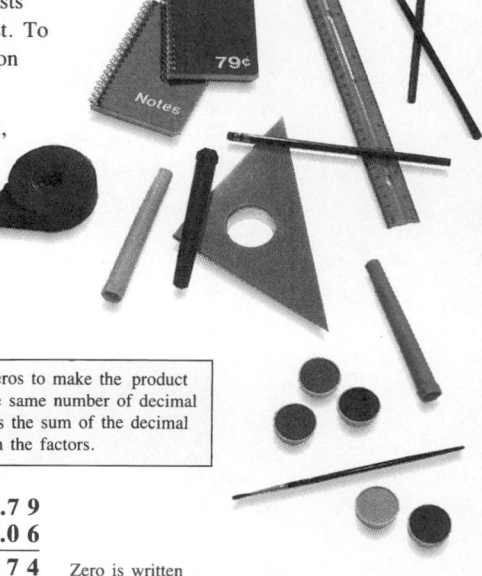

Multiply as with whole numbers.	→	Write zeros to make the product have the same number of decimal places as the sum of the decimal places in the factors.

$$\begin{array}{ll} \$\,0.7\,9 & \leftarrow\ 2\ \text{decimal places} \\ \times\,0.0\,6 & \leftarrow\ 2\ \text{decimal places} \\ \hline 4\,7\,4 & \leftarrow\ \text{Must have} \\ & \quad 4\ \text{decimal places}. \end{array}$$

$$\begin{array}{l} \$\,0.7\,9 \\ \times\,0.0\,6 \\ \hline \$\,0.0\,4\,7\,4 \quad \text{Zero is written to make 4 decimal places.} \end{array}$$

$0.0474 rounded to the nearest cent, or hundredth of a dollar, is $0.05. The sales tax is 5 cents.

Other Examples

$$\begin{array}{l} 0.0\,6 \leftarrow 2\ \text{places} \\ \times\,0.0\,9 \leftarrow 2\ \text{places} \\ \hline 0.0\,0\,5\,4 \leftarrow 4\ \text{places} \end{array}$$

$$\begin{array}{l} 3\,8\,4 \leftarrow 0\ \text{places} \\ \times\,0.0\,0\,0\,2\,4 \leftarrow 5\ \text{places} \\ \hline 1\,5\,3\,6 \\ 7\,6\,8 \\ \hline 0.0\,9\,2\,1\,6 \leftarrow 5\ \text{places} \end{array}$$

$$\begin{array}{l} 0.0\,1\,3 \leftarrow 3\ \text{places} \\ \times\ \ 0.2\,5 \leftarrow 2\ \text{places} \\ \hline 6\,5 \\ 2\,6 \\ \hline 0.0\,0\,3\,2\,5 \leftarrow 5\ \text{places} \end{array}$$

Warm Up

Give the number of decimal places in each product. Find the products.

1. 0.76 × 0.09	**2.** 0.033 × 0.17	**3.** 0.028 × 0.035	**4.** 0.019 × 0.6	**5.** 0.35 × 0.041
4; 0.0684	5; 0.00561	6; 0.000980	4; 0.0114	5; 0.01435

94

Follow Up

Reteaching

Provide students with exercises like the following. Have them give the number for each □ and write the decimal point in the proper place, adding zeros as necessary.

$$\begin{array}{ll} 0.031 & \leftarrow \boxed{3}\ \text{decimal places} \\ \times\ \ \ 0.2 & \leftarrow \boxed{1}\ \text{decimal places} \\ \hline \mathbf{0.00}62 & \leftarrow \boxed{4}\ \text{decimal places} \end{array}$$

$$\begin{array}{ll} 0.417 & \leftarrow \boxed{3}\ \text{decimal places} \\ \times\ \ \ 0.03 & \leftarrow \boxed{2}\ \text{decimal places} \\ \hline \mathbf{0.01}251 & \leftarrow \boxed{5}\ \text{decimal places} \end{array}$$

$$\begin{array}{ll} 0.012 & \leftarrow \boxed{3}\ \text{decimal places} \\ \times\ \ \ 0.08 & \leftarrow \boxed{2}\ \text{decimal places} \\ \hline \mathbf{0.000}96 & \leftarrow \boxed{5}\ \text{decimal places} \end{array}$$

Enrichment

Ask students to use decimals to illustrate the multiplication properties given on page 56.

Example: The Associative Property

$$(2.1 \times 0.4) \times 1.5 = 2.1 \times (0.4 \times 1.5)$$
$$0.84 \times 1.5 = 2.1 \times 0.60$$
$$1.260 = 1.260$$

Find the products.

1.
$$\begin{array}{r} 0.05 \\ \times\ 0.7 \\ \hline 0.035 \end{array}$$

2.
$$\begin{array}{r} 1.7 \\ \times 0.0008 \\ \hline 0.00136 \end{array}$$

3.
$$\begin{array}{r} 0.0024 \\ \times\ \ 0.04 \\ \hline 0.000096 \end{array}$$

4.
$$\begin{array}{r} 68 \\ \times 0.0006 \\ \hline 0.0408 \end{array}$$

5.
$$\begin{array}{r} 0.47 \\ \times 0.001 \\ \hline 0.00047 \end{array}$$

6.
$$\begin{array}{r} 0.71 \\ \times 0.09 \\ \hline 0.0639 \end{array}$$

7.
$$\begin{array}{r} 0.028 \\ \times\ 0.05 \\ \hline 0.00140 \end{array}$$

8.
$$\begin{array}{r} 3.2 \\ \times 0.07 \\ \hline 0.224 \end{array}$$

9.
$$\begin{array}{r} 0.0086 \\ \times\ \ 0.8 \\ \hline 0.00688 \end{array}$$

10.
$$\begin{array}{r} 0.27 \\ \times 0.04 \\ \hline 0.0108 \end{array}$$

11.
$$\begin{array}{r} 0.36 \\ \times 0.13 \\ \hline 0.0468 \end{array}$$

12.
$$\begin{array}{r} 2.7 \\ \times 0.025 \\ \hline 0.0675 \end{array}$$

13.
$$\begin{array}{r} 0.51 \\ \times 0.028 \\ \hline 0.01428 \end{array}$$

14.
$$\begin{array}{r} 14.6 \\ \times 0.04 \\ \hline 0.584 \end{array}$$

15.
$$\begin{array}{r} 0.079 \\ \times 0.034 \\ \hline 0.002686 \end{array}$$

16.
$$\begin{array}{r} 1.025 \\ \times 0.066 \\ \hline 0.067650 \end{array}$$

17.
$$\begin{array}{r} 3.94 \\ \times 0.059 \\ \hline 0.23246 \end{array}$$

18.
$$\begin{array}{r} 6.01 \\ \times 0.78 \\ \hline 4.6878 \end{array}$$

19.
$$\begin{array}{r} 0.034 \\ \times 0.062 \\ \hline 0.002108 \end{array}$$

20.
$$\begin{array}{r} 463 \\ \times 0.0096 \\ \hline 4.4448 \end{array}$$

21.
$$\begin{array}{r} 0.0742 \\ \times\ \ \ \ 67 \\ \hline 4.9714 \end{array}$$

22.
$$\begin{array}{r} 8.72 \\ \times 0.053 \\ \hline 0.46216 \end{array}$$

23.
$$\begin{array}{r} 0.918 \\ \times 0.422 \\ \hline 0.387396 \end{array}$$

24.
$$\begin{array}{r} 12.15 \\ \times 0.013 \\ \hline 0.15795 \end{array}$$

25.
$$\begin{array}{r} 9.49 \\ \times 0.0038 \\ \hline 0.036062 \end{array}$$

Find the products. Round the answers to the nearest cent.

26.
$$\begin{array}{r} \$2.84 \\ \times 0.08 \\ \hline \end{array}$$
$0.2272; $0.23

27.
$$\begin{array}{r} \$45.99 \\ \times\ 0.06 \\ \hline \end{array}$$
$2.7594; $2.76

28.
$$\begin{array}{r} \$0.95 \\ \times 1.04 \\ \hline \end{array}$$
$0.9880; $0.99

29.
$$\begin{array}{r} \$235.50 \\ \times\ \ 0.04 \\ \hline \end{array}$$
$9.4200; $9.42

30.
$$\begin{array}{r} \$80.00 \\ \times 0.035 \\ \hline \end{array}$$
$2.80000; $2.80

31.
$$\begin{array}{r} \$59.95 \\ \times\ 0.05 \\ \hline \end{array}$$
$2.9975; $3.00

32.
$$\begin{array}{r} \$147.90 \\ \times\ \ 0.13 \\ \hline \end{array}$$
$19.2270; $19.23

33.
$$\begin{array}{r} \$4.95 \\ \times 0.03 \\ \hline \end{array}$$
$0.1485; $0.15

34.
$$\begin{array}{r} \$0.67 \\ \times 0.50 \\ \hline \end{array}$$
$0.3350; $0.34

35.
$$\begin{array}{r} \$9.99 \\ \times 0.45 \\ \hline \end{array}$$
$4.4955; $4.50

36. A package of notebook paper costs $1.33. The sales tax is 0.06 of the cost. What is the amount of sales tax, rounded to the nearest cent? $0.08 or 8¢

37. A ballpoint pen costs $0.69. The sales tax is 0.06 of the cost. What is the sales tax, rounded to the nearest cent? What is the total cost of the pen, including sales tax? $0.04; $0.73

More Practice, page 424, Set B

Using Page 95

Exercises 26–36 These exercises are 2-step problems. After the product is found, it must be rounded to the nearest hundredth of a dollar or nearest cent. Make certain students understand that factors, such as 0.08 in exercise 26, are not dollar amounts.

After students have completed the exercises, you might suggest that they use a calculator to check their answers, reworking any problem that does not check.

Exercise 37 This problem has two questions. Be sure students answer both of them.

More Practice, page 424, Set B

Reteaching Supplement, page 29

Name _____   To follow text page 95

Zeros in Products

Multiply as with whole numbers. | Write zeros to make the product have the same number of decimal places as the sum of the places in the factors.

$$\begin{array}{r} 0.345 \\ \times\ 0.03 \\ \hline 1035 \end{array}$$
0.345 ← 3 places
0.03 ← 2 places
Need 5 places. Write a zero, then the decimal point
0.01035 ← 5 places

Find the products.

1. 0.0033 ← 4 places
× 4.5 ← 1 place
165
132
0.014485
Need 5 places. Write a zero, then the decimal point

2. 0.008 ← 3 places
× 0.4 ← 1 place
0.0032 ← Need 4 places

3. 0.135
× 0.63
405
810
0.08505

4.
$$\begin{array}{r} 0.3 \\ \times 0.2 \\ \hline 0.06 \end{array}$$

5.
$$\begin{array}{r} 0.03 \\ \times\ 0.8 \\ \hline 0.024 \end{array}$$

6.
$$\begin{array}{r} 0.07 \\ \times 0.09 \\ \hline 0.0063 \end{array}$$

7.
$$\begin{array}{r} 0.11 \\ \times 0.5 \\ \hline 0.055 \end{array}$$

8.
$$\begin{array}{r} 0.08 \\ \times 0.08 \\ \hline 0.0064 \end{array}$$

9.
$$\begin{array}{r} 0.127 \\ \times\ 0.5 \\ \hline 0.0635 \end{array}$$

10.
$$\begin{array}{r} 0.048 \\ \times\ 0.7 \\ \hline 0.0336 \end{array}$$

11.
$$\begin{array}{r} 0.209 \\ \times 0.09 \\ \hline 0.01881 \end{array}$$

12.
$$\begin{array}{r} 0.026 \\ \times 0.014 \\ \hline 104 \\ 260 \\ \hline 0.000364 \end{array}$$

13.
$$\begin{array}{r} 0.015 \\ \times 0.25 \\ \hline 75 \\ 300 \\ \hline 0.00375 \end{array}$$

14.
$$\begin{array}{r} 0.25 \\ \times 0.33 \\ \hline 75 \\ 750 \\ \hline 0.0825 \end{array}$$

15.
$$\begin{array}{r} 0.043 \\ \times\ 1.2 \\ \hline 86 \\ 430 \\ \hline 0.0516 \end{array}$$

16. 21.6 × 0.0095
216
× 0.0095
1080
1944
0.20520

17. 0.716 × 0.13
3.716
× 0.13
2148
716
0.09308

18. 4.28 × 0.0076
4.28
× 0.0076
2568
2996
0.032528

Enrichment Supplement, page 29

Name _____   To follow text page 95

Decimal Points in the Factors

The factors in the problems below are incomplete. Rewrite the factors so that the given products are correct. Show two ways to do this for each problem. Hint: The sum of decimal places in the factors should equal the number of decimal places in the product. **Answers will vary. Some possible answers are given.**

Example

$$\begin{array}{r} 7 \\ \times 8 \\ \hline 0.0056 \end{array} \longrightarrow \begin{array}{r} 0.07 \\ \times 0.08 \\ \hline 0.0056 \end{array} \quad \begin{array}{r} 0.007 \\ \times\ 0.8 \\ \hline 0.0056 \end{array}$$

1.
$$\begin{array}{r} 9 \\ \times 3 \\ \hline 0.027 \end{array} \longrightarrow \begin{array}{r} 0.9 \\ \times 0.03 \\ \hline 0.027 \end{array} \quad \begin{array}{r} 0.009 \\ \times\ 3 \\ \hline 0.027 \end{array}$$

2.
$$\begin{array}{r} 12 \\ \times 4 \\ \hline 0.048 \end{array} \longrightarrow \begin{array}{r} 0.12 \\ \times 0.4 \\ \hline 0.048 \end{array} \quad \begin{array}{r} 0.012 \\ \times\ 4 \\ \hline 0.048 \end{array}$$

3.
$$\begin{array}{r} 23 \\ \times 6 \\ \hline 0.00138 \end{array} \longrightarrow \begin{array}{r} 0.023 \\ \times 0.06 \\ \hline 0.00138 \end{array} \quad \begin{array}{r} 0.23 \\ \times 0.006 \\ \hline 0.00138 \end{array}$$

4.
$$\begin{array}{r} 8 \\ \times 9 \\ \hline 0.72 \end{array} \longrightarrow \begin{array}{r} 0.8 \\ \times 0.9 \\ \hline 0.72 \end{array} \quad \begin{array}{r} 0.08 \\ \times\ 9 \\ \hline 0.72 \end{array}$$

5.
$$\begin{array}{r} 44 \\ \times 5 \\ \hline 0.0220 \end{array} \longrightarrow \begin{array}{r} 0.044 \\ \times\ 0.5 \\ \hline 0.0220 \end{array} \quad \begin{array}{r} 0.44 \\ \times 0.05 \\ \hline 0.0220 \end{array}$$

6.
$$\begin{array}{r} 16 \\ \times 32 \\ \hline 0.00512 \end{array} \longrightarrow \begin{array}{r} 0.016 \\ \times 0.32 \\ \hline 0.00512 \end{array} \quad \begin{array}{r} 1.6 \\ \times 0.0032 \\ \hline 0.00512 \end{array}$$

7.
$$\begin{array}{r} 127 \\ \times 96 \\ \hline 1.2192 \end{array} \longrightarrow \begin{array}{r} 1.27 \\ \times 0.96 \\ \hline 1.2192 \end{array} \quad \begin{array}{r} 0.127 \\ \times\ 9.6 \\ \hline 1.2192 \end{array}$$

8.
$$\begin{array}{r} 437 \\ \times 28 \\ \hline 0.012236 \end{array} \longrightarrow \begin{array}{r} 0.437 \\ \times 0.028 \\ \hline 0.012236 \end{array} \quad \begin{array}{r} 4.37 \\ \times 0.0028 \\ \hline 0.012236 \end{array}$$

Practice Supplement, page 37

Name _____   To follow text page 95

Zeros in Products

Find the products.

1.
$$\begin{array}{r} 0.5 \\ \times 0.4 \\ \hline 0.20 \end{array}$$

2.
$$\begin{array}{r} 0.09 \\ \times\ 0.7 \\ \hline 0.063 \end{array}$$

3.
$$\begin{array}{r} 0.13 \\ \times 0.06 \\ \hline 0.0078 \end{array}$$

4.
$$\begin{array}{r} 7.9 \\ \times 0.08 \\ \hline 0.632 \end{array}$$

5.
$$\begin{array}{r} 0.36 \\ \times 0.007 \\ \hline 0.00252 \end{array}$$

6.
$$\begin{array}{r} 0.75 \\ \times 0.06 \\ \hline 0.0450 \end{array}$$

7.
$$\begin{array}{r} 0.083 \\ \times\ 0.62 \\ \hline 166 \\ 498 \\ \hline 0.05146 \end{array}$$

8.
$$\begin{array}{r} 0.48 \\ \times 0.33 \\ \hline 144 \\ 144 \\ \hline 0.1584 \end{array}$$

9.
$$\begin{array}{r} 0.082 \\ \times\ 7.5 \\ \hline 410 \\ 574 \\ \hline 0.6150 \end{array}$$

10.
$$\begin{array}{r} 0.125 \\ \times 0.046 \\ \hline 750 \\ 500 \\ \hline 0.005750 \end{array}$$

11.
$$\begin{array}{r} 1.72 \\ \times 0.057 \\ \hline 1204 \\ 860 \\ \hline 0.09804 \end{array}$$

12.
$$\begin{array}{r} 3.9 \\ \times 0.0026 \\ \hline 234 \\ 78 \\ \hline 0.01014 \end{array}$$

13.
$$\begin{array}{r} 0.96 \\ \times 0.057 \\ \hline 672 \\ 480 \\ \hline 0.05472 \end{array}$$

14.
$$\begin{array}{r} 0.0043 \\ \times\ 7.1 \\ \hline 43 \\ 301 \\ \hline 0.03053 \end{array}$$

15.
$$\begin{array}{r} 0.075 \\ \times 0.008 \\ \hline 0.000600 \end{array}$$

16.
$$\begin{array}{r} 0.206 \\ \times 0.075 \\ \hline 1030 \\ 1442 \\ \hline 0.015450 \end{array}$$

17.
$$\begin{array}{r} 0.0038 \\ \times\ 0.072 \\ \hline 76 \\ 256 \\ \hline 0.0002736 \end{array}$$

18.
$$\begin{array}{r} 0.919 \\ \times 0.0084 \\ \hline 3676 \\ 7352 \\ \hline 0.0077196 \end{array}$$

19.
$$\begin{array}{r} 0.0628 \\ \times\ \ 1.37 \\ \hline 4396 \\ 1884 \\ 628 \\ \hline 0.086036 \end{array}$$

20.
$$\begin{array}{r} 0.746 \\ \times 0.0352 \\ \hline 1492 \\ 3730 \\ 2238 \\ \hline 0.0262592 \end{array}$$

Find the products. Round the answers to the nearest cent.

21.
$$\begin{array}{r} \$9.28 \\ \times 0.06 \\ \hline \end{array}$$
$0.5568 = $0.56

22.
$$\begin{array}{r} \$23.77 \\ \times\ 0.05 \\ \hline \end{array}$$
$1.1885 = $1.19

23.
$$\begin{array}{r} \$47.49 \\ \times\ 0.08 \\ \hline \end{array}$$
$3.7992 = $3.80

24.
$$\begin{array}{r} \$16.67 \\ \times\ 0.07 \\ \hline \end{array}$$
$1.1669 = $1.17

25.
$$\begin{array}{r} \$82.85 \\ \times\ 0.18 \\ \hline 66280 \\ 8285 \\ \hline \end{array}$$
$14.9130 = $14.91

26.
$$\begin{array}{r} \$150.00 \\ \times\ \ 0.27 \\ \hline 105000 \\ 30000 \\ \hline \end{array}$$
$40.5000 = $40.50

27.
$$\begin{array}{r} \$38.87 \\ \times 0.065 \\ \hline 19435 \\ 23322 \\ \hline \end{array}$$
$2.52655 = $2.53

28.
$$\begin{array}{r} \$337.68 \\ \times\ \ 0.015 \\ \hline 168840 \\ 33768 \\ \hline \end{array}$$
$5.06520 = $5.07

Quick Review Display the following groups of digits. Focus on one group at a time and position the decimal point in different places. Have students read the number each time you place the decimal point.

3 5 7 4 0   1 7 3 5   9 3 1 0 4 7   8 0 0 1 0

Lesson Focus To solve 2-step word problems using data from a table

Suggested Materials Telephone book

Ideas for Getting Started

To create interest in this lesson, ask students to give their home telephone number including the area code. It is likely that everyone will have the same area code, but the first three digits of their telephone numbers, the prefix numbers, may be different. Each telephone number has a local number which is different from any other number having the same area code and prefix number.

Use a telephone book to point out the rate tables, area codes, and prefix numbers for different localities.

Using Page 96

Lesson Development Have students read the material at the top of the page. Write the telephone number, 415-755-4806, on the chalkboard. "What is the area code?" (415) "What is the prefix number?" (755) Point out that we are asked to find the cost of a 4-minute call to a number with a 755 prefix. Have students find this prefix number in the table. "What is the cost for the first minute?" ($0.19) "What is the cost for each additional minute?" ($0.12) Work through the 2-step solution to find the answer. Then give these additional examples.

- Find the cost of an 8-minute call to 415-772-1359. ($1.13)
- Find the cost of a 15-minute call to 415-747-2938. ($0.94)

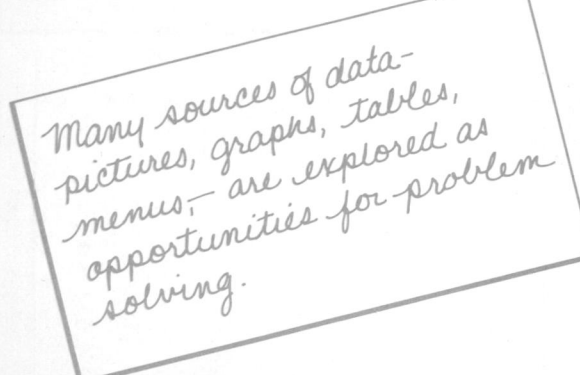

Many sources of data — pictures, graphs, tables, menus — are explored as opportunities for problem solving.

PROBLEM SOLVING: Using Data from a Table

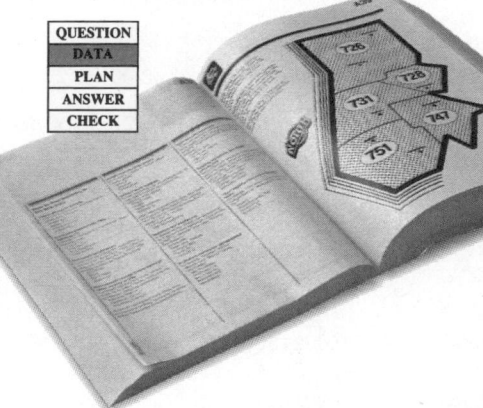

QUESTION
DATA
PLAN
ANSWER
CHECK

| | Telephone Rates | |
Prefix	First minute	Each additional minute
726	$0.13	$0.08
728	0.19	0.12
731	0.22	0.13
747	0.10	0.06
751	0.22	0.13
755	0.19	0.12
756	0.19	0.12
761	0.19	0.12
762	0.22	0.13
768	0.22	0.13
769	0.22	0.13
771	0.22	0.13
772	0.22	0.13
775	0.22	0.13
781	0.22	0.13

Telephone numbers are usually 10-digit numbers.

311 - 555 - 2368
↑   ↑   ↑
area code   prefix   local number

A telephone directory gives tables of rates for making calls to nearby areas.

What would be the cost of making a 4-minute call to a number with a 755 prefix?

The rate for the first minute is $0.19. Each additional minute costs $0.12.

$$\begin{array}{r} \$\,0.1\,2 \\ \times \qquad 3 \\ \hline 0.3\,6 \\ +\,0.1\,9 \\ \hline \$\,0.5\,5 \end{array}$$
← Rate for additional minutes
← Additional minutes
← Rate for first minute
← Cost of a 4-minute call

Find the cost of each call.

1. a 5-minute call to 756 prefix $0.67

2. an 8-minute call to 726 prefix $0.69

3. a 10-minute call to 772 prefix $1.39

4. a 3-minute call to 751 prefix $0.48

5. a 20-minute call to 747 prefix $1.24

6. a 30-minute call to 771 prefix $3.99

7. a 9-minute call to 761 prefix $1.15

8. a 11-minute call to 781 prefix $1.52

9. a 43-minute call to 775 prefix $5.68

10. Which telephone call costs more, a 7-minute call to a number with a 756 prefix, or a 6-minute call to a number with a 731 prefix? How much more does it cost? 7-minute call to 756 prefix; $0.04 or 4¢

96

Follow Up

Reteaching

Some students may simply multiply the total number of minutes of the call times the rate for each minute. Explain that the cost of the first minute is more than the cost of additional minutes, so it must be considered separately.

Have students give the following information for each problem.

Example: Problem 1

Total time of call: 5 min
Number of additional minutes: 4 min
Rate for additional minutes: $0.12
Cost for additional minutes: $0.48
Rate for first minute: $0.19
Cost of call: $0.48 + $0.19 = $0.67

Enrichment

Provide students with the following information:

Parking Rates	
First hour	$1.00
Each additional hour	0.50
Maximum per day	6.00

Have students find the amount charged for parking for each time below.

1 hour	$1.00
2 hours	$1.50
4 hours	$2.50
6 hours	$3.50
10 hours	$5.50
12 hours	$6.00

Long distance calls may be dial-direct or operator-assisted.
The table below shows long distance rates from a city in California.

Cost of a 6-minute dial-direct call to Phoenix:

$$\$0.50 + (3 \times 0.34) = \$0.50 + 1.02 = \$1.52$$

Cost of a 4-minute operator-assisted call to Phoenix:

$$\$2.05 + 0.34 = \$2.39$$

Weekday Long Distance Rates

To	Dial-direct		Operator-assisted	
	First 3 minutes	Each additional minute	First 3 minutes	Each additional minute
Phoenix	$0.50	$0.34	$2.05	$0.34
Denver	0.52	0.36	2.15	0.36
Washington, D.C.	0.54	0.38	2.25	0.38
Miami	0.54	0.38	2.25	0.38
Honolulu	0.65	0.48	2.55	0.52
Chicago	0.52	0.36	2.15	0.36
Reno	0.44	0.30	1.85	0.30
New York	0.54	0.38	2.25	0.38
Seattle	0.50	0.34	2.05	0.34

Find the cost of each long distance call.

1. a 5-minute dial-direct call to Washington, D.C. **$1.30**

2. a 6-minute operator-assisted call to Denver **$3.23**

3. an 8-minute dial-direct call to Seattle **$2.20**

4. a 7-minute operator-assisted call to Reno **$3.05**

5. a 12-minute dial-direct call to Honolulu **$4.97**

6. a 15-minute operator-assisted call to Miami **$6.81**

7. How much more does a 5-minute operator-assisted call to Denver cost than a dial-direct call of the same length of time? **$1.63**

8. How much would it cost for a 1-hour call to Chicago using the direct-dial method? **$21.04**

9. **Try This** A long distance call costs $3.77. The costs for the first 4 minutes are shown in the table. How long was the telephone call? Hint: Find a pattern to complete the table. **10 minutes**

Minutes	1	2	3	4
Total cost	$0.53	$0.89	$1.25	$1.61

See teaching notes.

97

Using Page 97

Lesson Development Work through the first example with students using the dial-direct portion of the table. "What is the cost of the first 3 minutes of a dial-direct call to Phoenix?" ($0.50) "How much is each additional minute?" ($0.34) Explain that there are 3 additional minutes so we multiply 3 × $0.34 and add the product to the cost of the first 3 minutes.

Go through the second example that uses the operator-assisted portion of the table. Call attention to the savings when using the direct-dial method. Point out that telephone companies have many other special rates for evenings and holidays.

Try This A possible strategy, Find a Pattern, was taught on page 82.

Discussion "What does the question ask us to find?" (the length of the telephone call) "What data is given in the problem?" (the call cost $3.77) Have students study the table and elicit from them that each additional minute costs $0.36. "What can you do to find the number of minutes of the call?" (Add $0.36 for each additional minute and complete the table to $3.77.)

Solution

5	6	7	8	9	10
$1.97	$2.33	$2.69	$3.05	$3.41	$3.77

The telephone call was 10 minutes long.

Extension A dial-direct call cost $0.55 for 1 minute, $0.90 for 2 minutes, $1.25 for 3 minutes, $1.60 for 4 minutes, and so on. How long could the call be if the cost were $10.00? (28 minutes)

Ideas That Work

Calculator Bonus

Present students with this problem.

A farmer agreed to sell 16 small pigs, using either of these contracts.

Contract A: $25 per pig

Contract B: 1¢ for the first pig, 2¢ for the second, 4¢ for the third, 8¢ for the fourth, and so on, doubling the number of cents each time.

Which contract would you choose if you wanted to buy the pigs? How much would you save or lose by your choice?

Contract A $400.
Contract B $655.35
Contract A would save $255.35

Try This teaching notes give real help in reviewing strategies.

Practice Supplement, page 38

Name _____ To follow text page 97

Problem Solving: Using Data from a Table

Weekday Long Distance Rates

To	Dial-direct		Operator-assisted	
	First 3 minutes	Each additional minute	First 3 minutes	Each additional minute
Phoenix	$0.50	$0.34	$2.05	$0.34
Denver	0.52	0.36	2.15	0.36
Washington, D.C.	0.54	0.38	2.25	0.38
Miami	0.54	0.38	2.25	0.38
Honolulu	0.65	0.48	2.55	0.52
Chicago	0.52	0.36	2.15	0.36
Reno	0.44	0.30	1.85	0.30
New York	0.54	0.38	2.25	0.38
Seattle	0.50	0.34	2.05	0.34

The table shows long distance rates from a city in California.
Find the cost of each long-distance call.

1. A 7-minute, dial-direct call to Honolulu. **$2.57**

$0.48
× 4
$1.92

$1.92
+ 0.65
$2.57

2. A 13-minute, operator-assisted call to Chicago. **$5.75**

$0.36
× 10
$3.60

$3.60
+ 2.15
$5.75

3. A 10-minute, dial-direct call to Seattle. **$2.88**

$0.34
× 7
$2.38

$2.38
+ 0.50
$2.88

4. A 15-minute, operator-assisted call to Denver. **$6.47**

$0.36
× 12
72
36
$4.32

$4.32
+ 2.15
$6.47

5. An 11-minute, operator-assisted call to New York. **$5.29**

$0.38
× 8
$3.04

$3.04
+ 2.25
$5.29

6. How much more does a 9-minute, operator-assisted call to Phoenix cost than a dial-direct call of the same length? **$1.55**

$0.34
× 6
$2.04

$2.04
+ 0.50
$2.54

$2.04
+ 2.05
$4.09

$4.09
− 2.54
$1.55

7. How much more does a 20-minute, operator-assisted call to Reno cost than a dial-direct call of the same length? **$1.41**

$0.30
× 17
210
30
$5.10

$5.10
+ 0.44
$5.54

$5.10
+ 1.85
$6.95

$6.95
− 5.54
$1.41

Decimals

Lesson Focus To multiply by 1,000, 100, 10, 0.1, 0.01, and 0.001 using a shortcut

Suggested Materials Meter stick

Ideas for Getting Started

Review the relationship between the metric units.

1 m = 0.1 dm	10 dm = 1 m
1 m = 0.01 cm	100 cm = 1 m
1 m = 0.001 mm	1,000 mm = 1 m

Show students each of these units on the meter stick.

Review multiplying whole numbers by 10, 100, 1,000, and 10,000. Have students find the following products.

7 × 10	16 × 10	253 × 10
7 × 100	16 × 100	253 × 100
7 × 1,000	16 × 1,000	253 × 1,000
7 × 10,000	16 × 10,000	253 × 10,000

Using Page 98

Motivational Problem Have students read the introductory problem. Ask them to restate the question in their own words and identify the data in the problem. Explain that since 1 m contains 10 dm, we need to multiply to express the measurement in decimeters. There are 100 cm in 1 m and 1,000 mm in 1 m, so we multiply by 100 to change m to cm and by 1,000 to change m to mm.

Lesson Development Direct students' attention to the example exercises showing the shortcuts for multiplying decimals by 10, 100, and 1,000. Point out the relationship between the number of zeros in the factor and the number of places the decimal point shifts to the right in the product.

Call attention to the second shortcut showing how to multiply by 0.1, 0.01, and 0.001. Ask students to tell the relationship between the number of decimal places in the factor and the number of places the decimal point shifts to the left in the product. Students should be able to find these answers mentally instead of using the multiplication algorithm.

Other Examples Make certain students understand that zero must be placed correctly in some products. In the first example, a zero must be written in the ones place. In the last example, a zero must be written in the tenths place.

Warm Up Watch for students who multiply by 10, 100, and 1,000 as with whole numbers and add zeros instead of shifting the decimal point.

Wrong: 6.25 × 10 = 6.250

Wrong: 6.25 × 100 = 6.2500

Multiplying Decimals: Mental Math

A machinist is making two holes in a machine part. The blueprint shows that the centers of the holes are to be 0.613 m apart. What is this distance in decimeters, centimeters, and millimeters?

To change the number of meters to decimeters (dm), centimeters (cm), and millimeters (mm), we multiply by 10, 100, and 1,000.

Study the shortcuts below.

$0.613 \times 10 = 6.13$ $0.613 \times 100 = 61.3$ $0.613 \times 1,000 = 613.$

shift 1 place right shift 2 places right shift 3 places right

The centers of the holes should be 6.13 dm, 61.3 cm, or 613 mm apart.

We can also multiply decimals by 0.1, 0.01, and 0.001 mentally.

$543.8 \times 0.1 = 54.38$ $543.8 \times 0.01 = 5.438$ $543.8 \times 0.001 = 0.5438$

shift 1 place left shift 2 places left shift 3 places left

Other Examples

$3.5 \times 100 = 350$ $0.075 \times 1,000 = 75$ $18.26 \times 1,000 = 18,260$

$0.87 \times 0.1 = 0.087$ $65 \times 0.01 = 0.65$ $12.7 \times 0.001 = 0.0127$

Warm Up

Multiply each number by 10, 100, and 1,000.

1. 6.25 62.5; 625; 6,250 **2.** 0.8 8; 80; 800 **3.** 0.235 2.35; 23.5; 235 **4.** 0.047 0.47; 4.7; 47 **5.** 9.8 98; 980; 9,800

Multiply each number by 0.1, 0.01, and 0.001.

6. 31.4 3.14; 0.314; 0.0314 **7.** 190 19; 1.9; 0.19 **8.** 5.2 0.52; 0.052; 0.0052 **9.** 200 20; 2; 0.2 **10.** 0.88 0.088; 0.0088; 0.00088

98

Follow Up

Reteaching

Use the following exercises to help students discover the short cut to be used when multiplying by 10, 100, 1,000, 0.1, 0.01, 0.001. Have them complete the chart and then describe the way the decimal point is placed in the product.

Number	Multiply by	Product
32.46	1,000	32,460
32.46	100	3,246
32.46	10	324.6
32.46	1	32.46
32.46	0.1	3.246
32.46	0.01	0.3246
32.46	0.001	0.03246

Enrichment

Display the following diagram on the chalkboard. Have students work downward and write the final product in the square at the bottom of the diagram.

7.3	0.04
× 0.1	× 10
× 10	× 0.1
× 0.01	× 1,000
× 10	× 0.01
× 100	× 10
730	4

Assignment Guide			
	Minimum	Average	Extended
page 99	1–61	1–61	1–61 odd, 62, TM

Multiply each number by 10.

1. 2.71 27.1   **2.** 0.86 8.6   **3.** 31.42 314.2   **4.** 0.081 0.81   **5.** 9.4 94

6. 0.006 0.06   **7.** 21.79 217.9   **8.** 0.728 7.28   **9.** 746.2 7,462   **10.** 1.014 10.14

Multiply each number by 100.

11. 7.476 747.6   **12.** 0.913 91.3   **13.** 82.47 8,247   **14.** 0.0077 0.77   **15.** 9.2 920

16. 0.083 8.3   **17.** 0.0009 0.09   **18.** 1.5 150   **19.** 16.56 1,656   **20.** 8.728 872.8

Multiply each number by 1,000.

21. 3.142 3,142   **22.** 0.9163 916.3   **23.** 12.75 12,750   **24.** 0.0048 4.8   **25.** 17.8 17,800

26. 0.72 720   **27.** 3.14 3,140   **28.** 0.0046 4.6   **29.** 0.255 255   **30.** 1.427 1,427

Multiply each number by 0.1.

31. 2.87 0.287   **32.** 34.5 3.45   **33.** 726 72.6   **34.** 0.9 0.09   **35.** 62.75 6.275

36. 0.04 0.004   **37.** 142.5 14.25   **38.** 6,276 627.6   **39.** 0.007 0.0007   **40.** 8.044 0.8044

Multiply each number by 0.01.

41. 175.6 1.756   **42.** 9.7 0.097   **43.** 23.6 0.236   **44.** 0.5 0.005   **45.** 276.97 2.7697

46. 0.78 0.0078   **47.** 0.043 0.00043   **48.** 200 2   **49.** 2,746.1 27.461   **50.** 847.3 8.473

Multiply each number by 0.001.

51. 7,468.3 7.4683   **52.** 29,744 29.744   **53.** 59.7 0.0597   **54.** 6.28 0.00628   **55.** 0.97 0.00097

56. 47.63 0.04763   **57.** 5,094 5.094   **58.** 927.5 0.9275   **59.** 3,000 3   **60.** 679.24 0.67924

61. A machine part is made from a piece of metal 0.76 cm long. What is the length of metal needed to make 10 parts? 7.6 cm

62. A steel bar 2.38 cm thick had 0.01 of the thickness ground off. How thick is the bar now? 2.3562 cm (0.0238 cm ground off)

■ THINK MATH ■

Logical Reasoning

How can a 3-minute egg timer and a 5-minute egg timer be used together to time exactly 7 minutes of cooking? **See teaching notes.**

Using Page 99

Exercises 1–30 Emphasize that multiplying by 10, 100, and 1,000 shifts the decimal point in the product 1, 2, or 3 places to the right. Note that we may have to add zeros in some products.

Exercises 31–60 Stress that multiplying by 0.1, 0.01, 0.001 shifts the decimal to the left. Zeros may have to be added to place the decimal point in some products.

Exercise 62 This is a 2-step problem. First, we multiply, 2.38 cm × 0.01 = 0.0238 cm. Then we subtract, 2.38 cm − 0.0238 cm = 2.3562 cm.

Think Math The solution to the Think Math uses the Guess and Check strategy and logical reasoning. The key to the problem lies in realizing that there is a 2-minute difference between the 3-minute and 5-minute times. If both timers are started together, there will be 2 minutes left on the 5-minute timer when the 3-minute timer runs out. The remaining 2 minutes plus another 5 minutes with the 5-minute timer will give a total of 7 minutes.

Reteaching Supplement, page 30

Enrichment Supplement, page 30

Practice Supplement, page 39

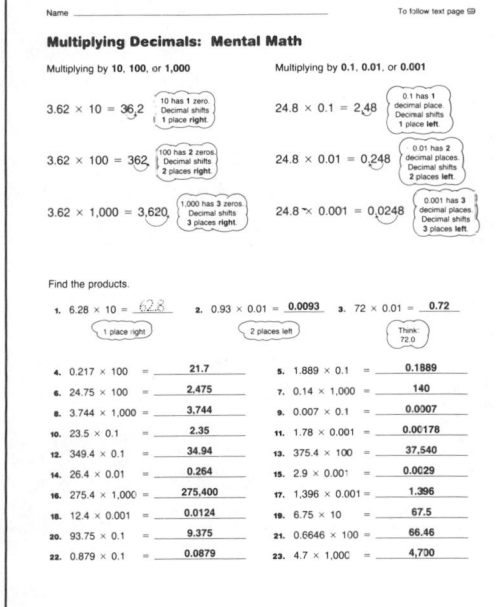

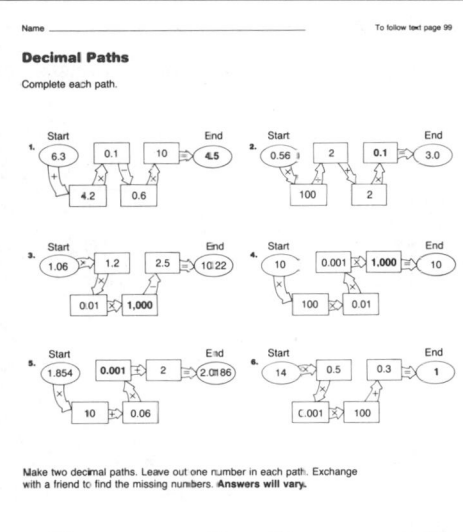

Estimation

Quick Review Display numbers below. Randomly point to digits and have students give the place value of those digits. Example: 3<u>6</u>2 → 60

7,324,643	8,888	623,547,937
593,711	12,832	14,865,394	4,356,092

Lesson Focus To estimate products with decimal factors; to solve word problems involving estimation

Ideas for Getting Started

To prepare students for this lesson, write these exercises on the chalkboard or overhead projector. Have students round each number to 1-digit accuracy.

6.809	36.1	0.927	0.0664
389.4	0.866	0.0989	0.9665

Then have students find these products mentally.

6 × 0.4	0.8 × 0.7	20 × 0.5
0.4 × 0.03	0.8 × 0.9	0.09 × 6
30 × 0.08	0.05 × 0.2	

Using Page 100

Motivational Problem Ask students to read the problem and restate the question in their own words. Have them give the data in the problem and tell how it is related. Make certain students know that the sound of the thunder from the lightning travels 0.33 km in 1 second.

Help students understand that we can multiply to find the distance. A picture like the one below will reinforce this idea.

```
      1 second    2 seconds    3 seconds
   |-----------|-----------|-----------|----->
   ← 0.33 km → ← 0.33 km → ← 0.33 km →
```

Lesson Development On the chalkboard, go through the steps of making an estimate. Explain that to estimate the product, we round each factor to 1-digit accuracy and then multiply.

Other Examples Work through these examples as a class activity to ensure students understand how to estimate products.

Exercises 1–25 For the answers given, factors were rounded to 1-digit accuracy.

Estimating Products Using Decimals

Melissa sees a flash of lightning. She hears the thunder from the lightning 4.8 seconds later. If sound travels 0.33 km in 1 second, about how far away is the flash of lightning?

Since the distance is the same each second, we can multiply.

To make an estimate of the product, we round each number to 1-digit accuracy.

$$
\begin{array}{rcr}
0.3\,3 & \to & 0.3 \\
\times\ 4.8 & \to & \times\ \ 5 \\
\hline
& & 1.5
\end{array}
$$

The lightning is about 1.5 km away.

Other Examples

$$
\begin{array}{rcr}
6.8\,2 & \to & 7 \\
\times 2.3\,5 & \to & \times\,2 \\
\hline
& & 1\,4
\end{array}
\qquad
\begin{array}{rcr}
\$2\,9.4\,3 & \to & \$\ \ 3\,0 \\
\times 0.0\,8\,2 & \to & \times 0.0\,8 \\
\hline
& & \$\,2.4\,0
\end{array}
\qquad
\begin{array}{rcr}
0.5\,9 & \to & 0.6 \\
\times 0.7\,2 & \to & \times 0.7 \\
\hline
& & 0.4\,2
\end{array}
$$

Estimate each product.

1. 9.1 ×3.8 = 36	**2.** 6.27 ×0.73 = 4.2	**3.** 0.413 ×0.609 = 0.24	**4.** 29.3 × 8.8 = 270	**5.** 7.26 ×0.05 = 0.35
6. 0.36 × 5.2 = 2.0 or 2	**7.** 31.6 ×57.4 = 1,800	**8.** 9.95 ×3.87 = 40	**9.** 0.772 ×0.619 = 0.48	**10.** 42.7 × 8.5 = 360
11. 1.74 × 6.6 = 14	**12.** 34.5 ×0.19 = 6.0 or 6	**13.** 2.7 ×3.2 = 9	**14.** 209 × 3.1 = 600	**15.** 28.6 ×0.77 = 24.0 or 24

Estimate each amount of money.

16. $2.98 ×3.75 = $12	**17.** $10.25 × 0.58 = $6	**18.** $43.45 × 0.18 = $8	**19.** $19.09 × 0.04 = $0.80	**20.** $0.92 ×0.75 = $0.72
21. $39.95 × 0.06 = $2.40	**22.** $62.42 × 8.16 = $480	**23.** $295.98 × 0.028 = $9.00	**24.** $22.75 × 0.05 = $1.00	**25.** $548.73 × 0.67 = $350

More Practice, page 424, Set C

Follow Up

Reteaching

Write the following exercises on the chalkboard.

$$
\begin{array}{rcl}
9.17 & 9 \\
\times 0.89 & 0.9 \\
\hline
& 8.1
\end{array}
\qquad
\begin{array}{rcl}
54.7 & 50 \\
\times 0.32 & 0.3 \\
\hline
& 15.0
\end{array}
$$

$$
\begin{array}{rcl}
3.8 & 4 \\
\times 7.5 & 8 \\
\hline
& 32
\end{array}
\qquad
\begin{array}{rcl}
\$6.95 & \$7 \\
\times 0.37 & 0.4 \\
\hline
& \$2.8
\end{array}
$$

Ask a student to go to the chalkboard, point to each factor, and call on a volunteer to round factors to 1-digit accuracy. Then have the student write the rounded factors on the chalkboard and estimate the product.

Enrichment

Provide students with the following equations. Have them find the missing factors.

1. 0.3 × <u>100</u> = 30
2. 25 × <u>0.001</u> = 0.025
3. 6 × <u>0.1</u> = 0.6
4. 0.7 × <u>20</u> = 14
5. 50 × <u>0.02</u> = 1.00
6. 5 × <u>0.0005</u> = 0.0025
7. 0.9 × <u>30</u> = 27
8. 8 × <u>0.004</u> = 0.032
9. 90 × <u>0.003</u> = 0.27
10. 80 × <u>0.03</u> = 2.4

Assignment Guide			
	Minimum	Average	Extended
page 100	1–20	1–25	1–25 odd
page 101	1–6	1–8	1–10

PROBLEM SOLVING: Using Estimation

QUESTION
DATA
PLAN
ANSWER
CHECK

1. Jackie's paycheck for a week of work is $289.67. Estimate how much Jackie will earn in a year of 52 weeks. $15,000

2. Armando found gasoline that costs $0.399 per liter (L). He bought 29.9 L of gasoline. What is an estimate of the cost of the gasoline? $12

3. A warehouse worker is checking an order for 10,000 advertising brochures which are packed in boxes with 335 to a box. What is an estimate of the number of boxes of brochures? 33

4. There are 1,287 registered voters in precinct 23. In the last election, 0.52 of those registered voted. Estimate the number of people who voted in the last election. 500

5. Harry took 314 strides to cross the courtyard. Each of his strides is 0.69 m long. What is Harry's estimate of the distance across the courtyard? 210 m

6. Brian bought 2 shirts that cost $18.95 each, and 3 pairs of socks for $2.25 each. What is an estimate of the amount that Brian spent? $46

7. Leslie has $831.66 in her checking account. She must write a check for $89.75 and another check for $62.50. What is an estimate of the amount Leslie will have left in her account? $650

8. Shirley Pierson wants to buy a new car that costs $6,893. The sales tax on the car is 0.0625 of the cost of the car. What is an estimate of the sales tax? $420

9. At Willow Junior High School, the enrollment is 595 students. The secretary used a calculator to compute that 0.0303 of the students were absent one day. Estimate the number of students that were absent. 18

10. **Try This** One month Hannah and Larry Brown earned a total of $4,000. Hannah earned $600 more than Larry. What did each person earn? Hannah, $2,300; Larry $1,700

101

Using Page 101

Exercises 1–9 Students should be able to work these problems independently. Remind students that estimates should be made by using the data rounded to 1-digit accuracy.

After students have solved the problems using estimation, have them compare some of the estimates with the actual answers, using the numbers of the problems.

Try This A possible strategy, Guess and Check, was taught on page 24.

Discussion "What does the question ask us to find?" (the amount each person earned) "How much money did Hannah and Larry Brown earn together?" ($4,000) "Who earned more?" (Hannah) "How much more?" ($600) "Can you guess how much Larry earns?"

Solution
Guess: Larry ($1,700) Hannah ($2,300)
Check: $1,700 + $2,300 = $4,000
Larry earns $1,700 a month and Hannah earns $2,300 a month.

Extension The president of a company has a yearly salary that is $9,000 more than that of a vice president. The president and vice president have a combined yearly salary of $141,000. What is the yearly salary of the president? What is the yearly salary of the vice president? (president: $75,000; vice president: $66,000)

More Practice, page 424, Set C

Reteaching Supplement, page 31

Enrichment Supplement, page 31

Practice Supplement, page 40

Quick Review Read aloud the exercises below and have students estimate the products or quotients by rounding to 1-digit accuracy.

36×41 **1,600** $541 \div 96$ **5** $172 \div 43$ **5** 731×47 **350,000**
$971 \div 23$ **50** 520×48 **250,000** 76×82 **6,400** $306 \div 52$ **6**

Lesson Focus To write whole numbers in scientific notation and to write standard numerals for numbers expressed in scientific notation

Suggested Materials Calculator with scientific notation capability

Ideas for Getting Started

Have students find these products.

3.2×10^3 0.7×10^4 29×10^5

Elicit from students the relationship between the exponent in the power of ten and the number of places the decimal point shifts to the right in the product.

On the chalkboard write the multiplication problem $600,000 \times 4,000$. Ask a student to find the product by the usual method. Have a second student use the calculator to find the product. Have both students record their answers on the chalkboard.

Standard numeral	Calculator
2,400,000,000	$2.40 \quad 09$

Explain to students that the calculator answer means 2.40×10^9. Since multiplying a number by 10^9 moves the decimal 9 places to the right, the two answers are the same.

$$2.40 \times 10^9 = 2,400,000,000$$

Using Page 102

Motivational Problem After students read the problem at the top of the page, have them identify the question and the data in the problem. Then ask students to tell which operation to use to find the answer.

Lesson Development Explain that the calculator answer means 1.5×10^8. Multiplying by 10^8 shifts the decimal point 8 places to the right. Hence, $1.5 \times 10^8 = 150,000,000$.

Be sure students understand that scientific notation does not change the number. Point out that writing a number in scientific notation is equivalent to dividing and then multiplying by the same number.

$$150,000,000 = (150,000,000 \div 10^8) \times 10^8$$
$$= 1.5 \times 10^8$$

Other Examples The last three examples show how to write numbers in scientific notation. Stress that the decimal factor is always a number between 1 and 10, so the decimal point is written to the right of the first nonzero digit.

Scientific Notation

Light from the sun, traveling 300,000 km each second, takes 500 seconds to reach the earth. How many kilometers does the light travel?

Since the distance is the same for each second, we can multiply using a calculator or a pencil and paper.

scientific notation

$1.5 \quad 08$ means 1.5×10^8

↑ a number from 1 to 10   ↑ a power of 10

$1.5 \times 10^8 = 150,000,000$

shift decimal 8 places

The light travels 150,000,000 km.

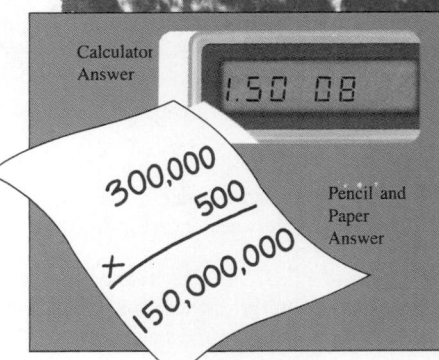

Other Examples

$2.4 \times 10^6 = 2,400,000$ (6 places) $8.06 \times 10^4 = 80,600$ (4 places) $7 \times 10^7 = 70,000,000$ (7 places)

$5,040,000 = 5.04 \times 10^6$ (6 places) $300 = 3 \times 10^2$ (2 places) $639,000 = 6.39 \times 10^5$ (5 places)

Warm Up

Give the missing exponent.

1. $5,000 = 5.0 \times 10^{\blacksquare}$
3

2. $45 = 4.5 \times 10^{\blacksquare}$
1

3. $27,500,000,000 = 2.75 \times 10^{\blacksquare}$
10

Give the missing factor.

4. $9,600 = \blacksquare \times 10^3$
9.6

5. $271,000,000 = \blacksquare \times 10^8$
2.71

6. $68,000,000 = \blacksquare \times 10^7$
6.8

Write the standard numeral.

7. 6.3×10^6
102 6,300,000

8. 1.9×10^{12}
1,900,000,000,000

9. 3.11×10^9
3,110,000,000

Follow Up

Reteaching

Explain that scientific notation is useful when working with large numbers. Discuss how to write numbers in scientific notation and how to interpret them. Write 536,000 on the chalkboard. Observe with students the location of the decimal point: 536,000↓ Then write 53,600.0 and compare it with 536,000. Point out that if 53,600.0 is multiplied by 10, it will be the same as 536,000. Continue in this way using 5,360.00, 536.000, and so on. Show that writing a number in scientific notation does not make the number larger or smaller. It is simply a way of rewriting it.

Enrichment

Have students write the standard numeral for each of the following. Then have them check their answers with a calculator.

1. 5×10^6 5,000,000
2. 4×10^3 4,000
4. 8×10^2 800
7. 61×10^5 6,100,000
8. 32×10^4 320,000
3. 7×10^8 700,000,000
6. 98×10^7 980,000,000

Assignment Guide			
	Minimum	Average	Extended
page 103	1–19, SK	1–19, 22, SK	1–22, SK

Write in scientific notation.

1. 25,000 2.5×10^4

2. 580,000,000 5.8×10^8

3. 610,000,000,000 6.1×10^{11}

4. 300,000 3.0×10^5

5. 11,000,000,000 1.1×10^{10}

6. 2,400 2.4×10^3

7.
6.7×10^6

8.
5.9×10^5

9.
2.0×10^6

Write the standard numeral.

10. 3.2×10^5 320,000

11. 6.5×10^8 650,000,000

12. 8.9×10^3 8,900

13. 3.09×10^5 3,090,000

14. 1.86×10^7 18,600,000

15. 6.75×10^{10} 67,500,000,000

16.
36,000,000

17.
4,660,000,000

18.
13,700,000,000

19. The planet Saturn is about 1.43×10^9 km from the sun. Write the standard numeral for this number. 1,430,000,000

20. Jupiter is about 778,000,000 km from the sun. Write the distance in scientific notation. 7.78×10^8

21. Light from the sun takes about 9,600 seconds to reach the planet Uranus. About how far does light travel from the sun to Uranus? Give both the standard numeral and the scientific notation. 2,880,000,000 km or 2.88×10^9

22. DATA BANK Find the distance from the sun to the planet Neptune. About how many seconds would it take light from the sun to reach Neptune? (See page 415.) 15,000 seconds

SKILLKEEPER

1. 5.6×0.1
0.56

2. 98×0.1
9.8

3. $8,769 \times 0.1$
876.9

4. 4.78×10
47.8

5. 0.359×10
3.59

6. 7.254×100
725.4

7. 6.50×0.01
0.0650

8. 45.9×0.01
0.459

9. 0.005×0.01
0.00005

10. 2.729×100
272.9

11. 0.77×0.001
0.00077

12. 7.007×0.001
0.007007

13. $956.4 \times 1,000$
956,400

14. 5.6×0.001
0.0056

15. $99.99 \times 1,000$
99,990

16. 0.0947×0.001
0.0000947

17. 0.52×10
5.2

18. 62.51×0.01
0.6251

19. $2.3 \times 1,000$
2,300

20. $9,675 \times 0.001$
9.675

21. 0.257×0.1
0.0257

22. 585.6×10
5,856

23. 0.06×0.001
0.00006

24. $7,952 \times 0.01$
79.52

More Practice, page 424, Set D

Using Page 103

Exercises 16–18 Note that these exercises use calculator numerals in scientific notation.

Exercise 21 A calculator may be used for this exercise. Keep in mind that some 4-function calculators may not have scientific notation capabilities.

Data Bank Students may round their answers to the nearest second.

Skillkeeper This Skillkeeper reviews material that is taught in this chapter.

More Practice, page 424, Set D

Reteaching Supplement, page 32

Enrichment Supplement, page 32

Practice Supplement, page 41

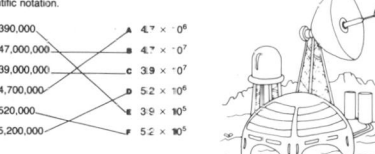

Quick Review Conduct an oral drill on special products and quotients.

30 × 100 **3,000**	250 ÷ 50 **5**	81,000 ÷ 900 **90**	500 × 70 **35,000**
320,000 ÷ 400 **800**	6,000 × 60 **360,000**		40 × 1,000 **40,000**
720,000 ÷ 800 **900**	7,000 × 40 **280,000**		479,000 ÷ 1,000 **479**

Lesson Focus To practice multiplying decimals; to solve word problems using data from a table

Suggested Materials Classified advertisement sections of newspapers

Ideas for Getting Started

To introduce the problem-solving lesson on page 105, display the advertisement section of the newspaper. Explain that classified advertisements are sometimes called classified ads or Want Ads. Find the rate schedule for the classified ads in your newspapers and write some of the rates on the chalkboard. There is a wide variety of payment plans for classified advertisements. Have students compute the cost of a 4-line advertisement using the rate table for your newspaper.

Using Page 104

Exercises 1–46 You may wish to choose various problems from this page for selected students to work at the chalkboard. Assign these problems as needed for strengthening skills in decimal multiplication. Have students use estimation to check some of the answers.

Skills Practice

Multiply.

1. 3.4 × 7.8 = 26.52	**2.** 5.7 × 0.03 = 0.171	**3.** 4.2 × 9.1 = 38.22	**4.** 0.65 × 1.6 = 1.040	**5.** 0.95 × 0.08 = 0.076
6. $1.03 × 29 = $29.87	**7.** $8.46 × 13 = $109.98	**8.** $3.52 × 40 = $140.80	**9.** $6.93 × 57 = $395.01	**10.** $4.75 × 16 = $76.00
11. 11.83 × 0.02 = 0.2366	**12.** 26.72 × 0.57 = 15.2304	**13.** 72.04 × 0.36 = 25.9344	**14.** 31.90 × 0.25 = 7.975	**15.** 68.53 × 0.18 = 12.3354
16. 0.09 × 0.03 = 0.0027	**17.** 0.013 × 0.07 = 0.00091	**18.** 0.006 × 0.104 = 0.000624	**19.** 0.092 × 0.017 = 0.001564	**20.** 3.4 × 0.0052 = 0.01768
21. 1.092 × 0.57 = 0.62244	**22.** 22.01 × 1.1 = 24.211	**23.** 65.1 × 0.09 = 5.859	**24.** 83.45 × 0.13 = 10.8485	**25.** 70.01 × 0.045 = 3.15045
26. 6.58 × 0.46 = 3.0268	**27.** 88.9 × 0.62 = 55.118	**28.** 4.06 × 0.39 = 1.5834	**29.** 25.3 × 5.7 = 144.21	**30.** 0.689 × 4.2 = 2.8938
31. 0.622 × 0.23 = 0.14306	**32.** 39.4 × 3.11 = 122.534	**33.** 4.27 × 0.381 = 1.62687	**34.** 0.575 × 4.14 = 2.3805	**35.** 0.361 × 0.084 = 0.030324

Multiply. Round to the nearest cent.

36. $23.04 × 1.15 = $26.496 ($26.50)	**37.** $62.15 × 3.39 = $210.6885 ($210.69)	**38.** $48.25 × 6.20 = $299.15	**39.** $39.31 × 7.45 = $292.8595 ($292.86)	**40.** $81.24 × 10.05 = $816.462 ($816.46)

Find the products.

41. 36.01 × 23.5 = 846.235

42. 0.654 × 3.91 = 2.55714

43. 783.1 × 0.0072 = 5.63832

44. 92.3 × 40.01 = 3,692.923

45. 86.33 × 0.9271 = 80.036543

46. 0.018 × 0.907 = 0.016326

104

Follow Up

Reteaching

Each problem on page 104 involves more than one step. Some students may simply multiply the charge per line times the number of days. If students leave out one of the steps, have them write the following at the top of their papers.

$$\text{Cost per line} \times \text{Number of lines} \times \text{Number of days}$$

Enrichment

Ask students to write their own advertisements and specify the number of days they should run. Then have them use the table on page 105 to find the total cost for each.

Assignment Guide			
	Minimum	Average	Extended
page 104	1–30	1–40	1–45 odd
page 105	1–6	1–8	1–8

PROBLEM SOLVING: Using Data from a Table

QUESTION
DATA
PLAN
ANSWER
CHECK

Gloria Rodriguez works in the classified advertising department of a daily newspaper. She must compute the cost of advertisements.

What is the cost of running a 4-line advertisement for 5 days?

$ 1.9 6 ← Cost per line per day
× 4 ← Number of lines
$ 7.8 4
× 5 ← Number of days
$ 39.2 0 ← Total cost

The Daily News

Classified Advertisement Rates (Minimum 2 lines)	
Consecutive day insertions	Charge per line per day
12 or more days	$1.08
9 days	1.34
7 days	1.66
6 days	1.93
4–5 days	1.96
1–3 days	2.61

Find the total cost for each advertisement.

1. **Cat Lost** Reward. Long hair, white with orange polka-dots. Declawed but dangerous. Answers to the name of Gwendolyn or Sid.

Insert for 3 days $23.49

2. **Labrador Lost** Female, with 3 puppies and 2 kittens pretending to be puppies. Reward: 50¢ plus 2 puppies and 1 kitten.

Insert for 9 days $36.18

3. **Terrier Found** Looking for owner of funny-looking pink dog found underneath bed. Will not come out and refuses to eat. Owner please call Sherlock Bones to claim.

Insert for 7 days $46.48

4. **Goofy Dog** found. Small collie with limp; missing upper fang. Call Pearl at 999-9999.

Insert for 2 days $10.44

5. **Black Cat** found. At the top of my tulip tree; won't come down. Owner please claim. Bring ladder, fire truck, or trampoline.

Insert for 15 days $48.60

6. **Goldfish Found** in supermarket parking lot. Owner please claim before my cat does.

Insert for 12 days $25.92

7. Which costs more, a 3-line advertisement for 3 days or a 2-line advertisement for 5 days? 3-line advertisement for 3 days

8. Mr. Craney wrote a 5-line advertisement to run for 4 days. Gloria helped him shorten his advertisement to 3 lines. How much will Mr. Craney save? $15.68

9. **Try This** The total cost of two advertisements was $113. One advertisement cost $18 less than the other. What was the cost of each advertisement? $47.50; $65.50

105

Using Page 105

Lesson Development Call on a student to read the problem at the top of the page. "What does the question ask us to find?" (the cost of running a 4-line advertisement) "How many days will the advertisement run?" (5) "Which rate in the table should be used?" ($1.96) Make certain students understand that since each line costs the same, we can multiply by the number of lines to find the cost of the advertisement. Then the product must be multiplied by the number of days the advertisement will run to find the total cost.

Exercises 1–7 The students should use the rate table at the top of the page.

Try This A possible strategy, Guess and Check, was taught on page 24.

Discussion "What does the question ask us to find?" (the cost of each advertisement) "What data is given in the problem?" (the total cost is $113, one advertisement costs $18 less than the other) Have students guess and check to solve the problem.

Solution

Guess: Ad #1 ($65.50)   Ad #2 ($47.50)

Check: $65.50 + $47.50 = $113.00
One advertisement cost $65.50 and the other cost $47.50.

Reteaching Supplement, page 33   **Enrichment Supplement,** page 33   **Practice Supplement,** page 42

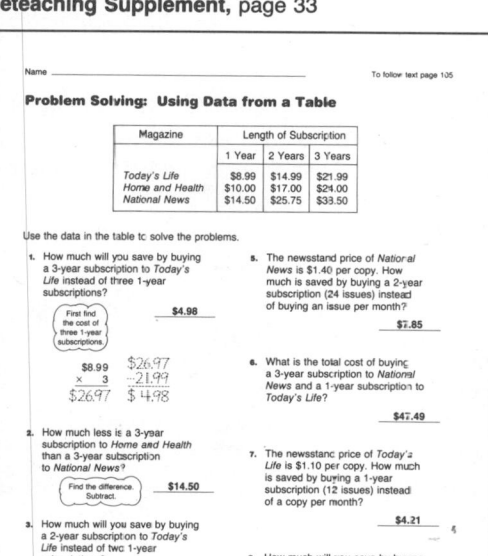

Quick Review Conduct an oral drill where students provide the standard numeral for numbers expressed in exponential notation.

10^2 2^3 3^2 7^2 3^3 10^4 5^2 4^2

9^2 6^2 10^3 2^2 8^2 3^1 10^5 2^5

Lesson Focus To solve multiple-step word problems

Ideas for Getting Started

To create interest in the lesson, ask students if they have ever watched competitive diving contests in person or on television. Perhaps some students have participated in such contests. Ask if anyone knows the names of some particular kinds of dives or how diving performances are rated.

Using Page 106

Lesson Development Have students read through the material at the top of the page. Explain that the degree of difficulty of a dive varies with the kind of dive performed. Relatively simple dives have degrees of difficulty between 1 and 2. Harder dives have degrees of difficulty that are between 3 and 4.

Discuss the way dives are scored. Work through the example with the class. Each of the dives on this page has five judges' ratings.

PROBLEM SOLVING: Practice

QUESTION	Dive	Difficulty	Ratings	Score
DATA				
PLAN	1	1.6	8.5; 9.0; 8.5; 9.0; 7.5	68.00
ANSWER				
CHECK				

Mimi is on the school diving team. She enters the springboard diving competition which is judged by experts. There are from three to seven judges who rate the dives from 0 to 10. Each dive is assigned a number called the **degree of difficulty.**

Mimi completed her first dive. Here is the way her score was computed.

Score = degree of difficulty × (sum of
         judges' ratings)
      = 1.6 × (8.5 + 9.0 + 8.5 + 9.0 + 7.5)
      = 1.6 × 42.5 = 68.00

Mimi's score was 68.00.

Find the score for each dive.

1. Forward $1\frac{1}{2}$-somersault, tuck position
   Degree of difficulty: 1.5
   Judges' ratings: 7.0; 7.5; 7.5; 7.0; 8.0
   55.50
2. Back $2\frac{1}{2}$-somersault, pike position
   Degree of difficulty: 3.0
   Judges' ratings: 6.5; 6.5; 7.0; 6.5; 6.0
   97.50
3. Reverse, layout position
   Degree of difficulty: 2.0
   Judges' ratings: 8.0; 8.5; 8.5; 8.0; 9.0
   84.00

4. Reverse $2\frac{1}{2}$-somersault, tuck position
   Degree of difficulty: 2.8
   Judges' ratings: 7.5; 7.5; 7.0; 7.0; 7.0
   100.80
5. Inward double somersault, pike position
   Degree of difficulty: 2.6
   Judges' ratings: 7.5; 7.5; 8.5; 8.0; 8.0
   102.70
6. Forward $2\frac{1}{2}$-somersault, 2 twists, free position
   Degree of difficulty: 3.2
   Judges' ratings: 6.5; 7.0; 6.0; 7.0; 7.5
   108.80

106

Follow Up

Reteaching

Have students follow these steps to solve the problems.

Find the sum of the judges' ratings	→	Multiply the sum times the degree of difficulty

In the first step, ask students to check to see that the decimal points are properly aligned and that the addition is correct. In the second step, have them use estimation to check their multiplication and determine if the decimal point is placed correctly in the product.

Enrichment

Have students find the product of the factors along each branch of the path. Then ask them to find the difference of the products.

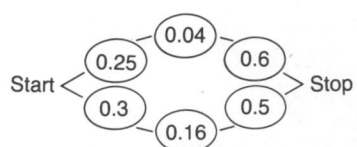

0.25 × 0.04 × 0.6 = 0.00600   0.0240
0.3 × 0.16 × 0.5 = 0.0240   − 0.0060
                                _____
                                 0.0180

Find the score for each dive and the total for each diver.

7.

Dive	Difficulty	Ratings	Score
1	2.2	7.0; 7.0; 6.5; 7.5	▨
2	1.7	8.5; 8.0; 8.5; 7.5	▨
3	2.5	6.0; 6.0; 6.0; 6.5	▨
4	1.9	7.0; 7.5; 8.5; 8.0	▨
		Total	▨

Diver:
C. Williams
61.60
55.25
61.25
58.90
237.00

8.

Dive	Difficulty	Ratings	Score
1	1.8	9.0; 9.0; 8.5; 8.5	▨
2	1.7	7.0; 7.0; 7.0; 7.0	▨
3	2.4	6.5; 7.0; 6.5; 7.0	▨
4	2.8	5.5; 6.0; 6.0; 6.5	▨
		Total	▨

Diver:
J. Montez
63.00
47.60
64.80
67.20
242.60

9.

Dive	Difficulty	Ratings	Score
1	1.4	8.0; 8.5; 8.0; 9.0	▨
2	2.1	6.5; 6.5; 7.0; 6.5	▨
3	2.3	7.0; 6.5; 8.0; 7.5	▨
4	3.3	5.5; 6.0; 6.0; 5.5	▨
		Total	▨

Diver:
L. Freel
46.90
55.65
66.70
75.90
245.15

10.

Dive	Difficulty	Ratings	Score
1	2.5	6.0; 6.0; 5.5; 6.5	▨
2	2.4	9.0; 9.5; 8.5; 9.0	▨
3	2.8	8.0; 7.5; 7.0; 7.0	▨
4	3.0	6.5; 6.5; 6.5; 6.0	▨
		Total	▨

Diver:
M. Kennard
60.00
86.40
82.60
76.50
305.50

11. Try This After completing three dives, Nadine
has a total score of 201 points. The score for
her second dive is 2 points more than for her
first dive. The score for her third dive is
2 points more than for her second dive. What
is her score for each of the three dives?
65, 67, 69

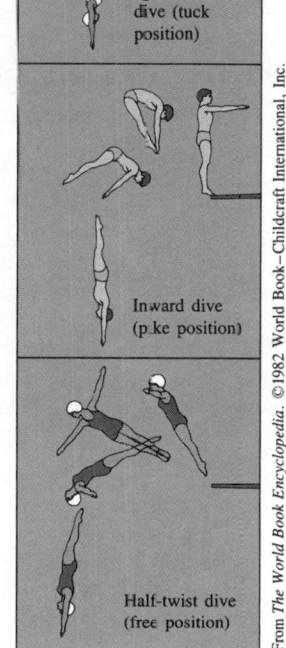

Forward dive
(layout position)

Forward
$1\frac{1}{2}$-somersault
dive (tuck
position)

Inward dive
(pike position)

Half-twist dive
(free position)

From *The World Book Encyclopedia.* ©1982 World Book–Childcraft International, Inc.

107

Using Page 107

Exercises 7–10 These problems deal with the
total scores for four dives by each diver.

Try This A possible strategy, Guess and Check,
was taught on page 24.

Discussion "What does the question ask us to
find?" (the score for each of Nadine's three dives)
"How are the scores of the dives related?" (the
score of each dive is 2 points more than the one
before) "What is the total score for the three
dives?" (201 points) "What strategy can we use to
solve the problem?" (Guess and Check) After students find the answer, have them reread the problem to see if the scores make sense. "Is each
score 2 points higher than the one before it? Is the
total 21?"

Solution

Guess: Dives (65, 67, 69)

Check: 65 + 67 + 69 = 201

Nadine's scores for the dives were 65, 67, and 69.

Ideas That Work

Math for the Gifted

Number theory is a source of many interesting problems. Challenge your students with the following:

1. The year 1936 was a perfect square.
   Find the number whose square is
   1936. What is the next year that will
   be a perfect square?
   44, 2025

2. An *automorph* is a number whose
   digits reappear at the end of its
   square.
   Examples $1^2 = \underline{1}$ $6^2 = 3\underline{6}$
               $5^2 = 2\underline{5}$ $25^2 = 6\underline{25}$

   Find all other automorphs that are
   less than 100. **$76^2 = 5\underline{976}$**

3. The number 85 can be expressed as
   the sum of two squares in two distinct
   ways:
   $85 = 2^2 + 9^2$ $85 = 6^2 + 7^2$

   What is the smallest whole number
   that can be expressed as the sum of
   two squares in two distinct ways?

   $65 = 8^2 + 1^2$ $65 = 7^2 + 4^2$

Practice Supplement, page 43

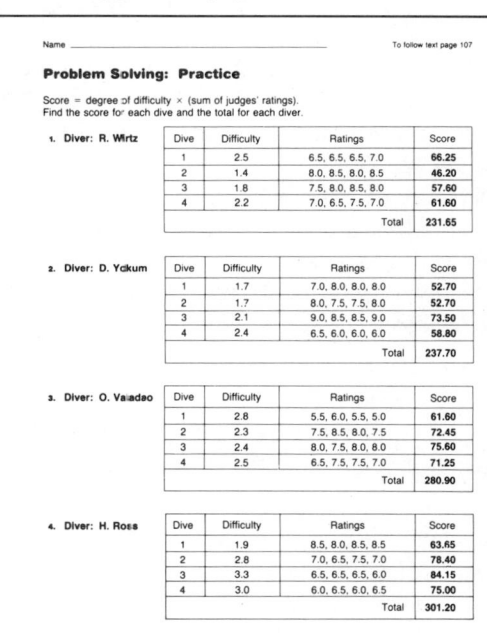

Lesson Focus To draw a picture as a strategy for solving nonroutine word problems

Ideas for Getting Started

Tell students that you are going to write some facts on the chalkboard. Students are to draw a picture or diagram that will illustrate these facts. "Two towns, A and B, lie on a straight road 100 km apart. A third town, C, is on the same road, 50 km from A."

```
        A ←—— 100 km ——→ B
├————————•———————————————•————————
C                 C
```

C can be in either of two places.

"After driving 30 km from A toward B, you are 80 km from C."

```
C  50 km  A ←—— 100 km ——→ B
├———•—————•———————————————•————————
↑
C must be here.
```

"How far is it from C to B? Use the picture to see what to do." (50 km + 100 km = 150 km)

Using Page 108

Motivational Problem Read the Try This problem at the top of the page. "What does the question ask us to find?" (the distance between Hull and York) "Identify the data in the problem." (Alton, Hull, and York are on the same straight road. It is 123 km from Alton to Hull and 64 km from York to Alton. Alton is between Hull and York.) Explain that we will need to add or subtract to solve the problem but we must decide which operation to use. The strategy, Draw a Picture, will help us. Add this strategy to the problem-solving bulletin board display described on page 24.

Lesson Development Work through the solution to the Try This problem with the class. Explain to students that a good plan is to read each part of the problem carefully, and then draw and label a picture that shows the data given. It is sometimes necessary to change our picture to make the data fit.

Point out that when the picture has been drawn to fit all the facts and data, it is usually a simple matter to decide what to do to find the answer. In this case we can add 123 and 64 to find the distance between Hull and York.

Exercises 1–2 Have students try the two problems at the bottom of the page. Ask selected students to put their pictures on the chalkboard and explain their solutions to the class.

PROBLEM SOLVING: Draw a Picture

| QUESTION |
| DATA |
| **PLAN** |
| ANSWER |
| CHECK |

Try This

Three towns—Alton, Hull, and York—are all on the same straight road. It is 123 km from Alton to Hull. It is 64 km from York to Alton. The town of Alton lies between Hull and York. What is the distance between Hull and York?

Some problems contain groups of information. It may be difficult to remember how the information is related. A good strategy to try on such problems is **Draw a Picture.**

Here is how a picture might be made for the problem above.

It is 123 km from Alton (A) to Hull (H).
(Label your pictures to show the data.)

It is 64 km from York (Y) to Alton.
(This tells us the distance, but not where York is located.)

Alton lies between York and Hull.
(Now we know where York lies.)

Use the information given in the picture to answer the question.

$$64 + 123 = 187$$

The distance between Hull and York is 187 km.

Solve.

1. Three towns—Adding, Plus, and Minus—are on one straight road. It is 186 km from Adding to Plus. It is 57 km from Minus to Plus. Minus is between Adding and Plus. What is the distance between Adding and Minus?
   108 **129 km**

2. The combined height of Jack and Bob is 340 cm. This is 158 cm more than Al's height. Al is 8 cm taller than Jack. How tall is Bob? **166 cm**

Strategy Test Item

Optional Problem If you wish to assess students' ability to apply the strategy called Draw a Picture introduced in this chapter, provide them with the problem below.

> Towns Buford, Medina, and Wells lie on one straight road. It is 88 km from Buford to Medina and it is 54 km from Medina to Wells. Wells is between Buford and Medina. How far is it from Buford to Wells?

Solution

```
B ←——————— 88 km ———————→ M
        W ←——— 54 km ———→
```

$$88 \text{ km} - 54 \text{ km} = 34 \text{ km}$$

It is 34 km from Buford to Wells.

Find the products.

1.	3.8	2.	0.92	3.	6.3	4.	0.007
	×0.7		× 8		×7.5		× 6.8
	2.66		7.36		47.25		0.0476

5.	0.722	6.	$21.24	7.	$18.50	8.	3.125
	× 0.04		× 24		× 0.06		× 10.4
	0.02888		$509.76		$1.11		32.5000

9.	0.05	10.	0.012	11.	420	12.	0.059
	×0.07		× 0.13		×.015		×0.027
	0.0035		0.00156		6.300		0.001593

13. 10×7.295 **72.95**   14. $1,000 \times 8.34$ **8,340**   15. 100×12.729 **1,272.9**

16. 0.1×62.8 **6.28**   17. 0.01×534 **5.34**   18. 0.001×72.9 **0.0729**

19. $0.001 \times 8,647.7$ **8.6477**   20. 0.001×38.9 **0.0389**   21. 0.001×0.883 **0.000833**

Estimate each product.

22.	19.42	23.	3.842	24.	0.72
	× 0.7		× 5.41		×0.96
	14.0		20		0.7

Write the standard numeral.

25. 6.4×10^5
640,000

26. 8.1×10^8
810,000,000

27. 3.03×10^4
30,300

28. A local call costs $0.13 for the first minute, plus $0.08 for each additional minute. What is the cost of a 10-minute call? **$0.85**

29. A long distance telephone call costs $2.04 for the first 3 minutes, plus $0.34 for each additional minute. What is the cost of a 12-minute call? **$5.10**

30. Oranges cost $0.44 each. How much would 10 oranges cost? **$4.40**

31. For a 4-line advertisement, a newspaper charges $1.46 per line for each day. What is the cost to run the advertisement for 5 days? **$29.20**

Using Page 109

The exercises in the Chapter Review/Test emphasize the major concepts and skills presented in this chapter. These exercises may be used as a review assignment or as a test, depending upon your needs.

Item Analysis The table below correlates the Chapter Review/Test items with objectives and with the student text pages on which the concepts or skills were taught.

Items	Objectives	Related Text Pages
1–12	4.1–4.2	88–95,104
13–21	4.1–4.2	98–99
22–24	4.3	100–101
25–27	4.4	102–103
28–31	4.5	96–97,101,105,106–107

Assessment Options

If you use the Chapter Review/Test as a review assignment, you may wish to use the free-response test or the multiple-choice test to evaluate mastery of the chapter objectives. The items on these tests have a one-to-one correspondence in terms of content and level of difficulty. A correlation of test items to objectives and student text pages is provided in the Management Guide for Chapter 4.

Multiple-Choice Test, TRB pages 10–12
Free-Response Test, TRB pages 54–55

Teacher's Resource Book Options

The following blackline masters are available for use with the chapter. If you have not already assigned these materials, you may wish to use them to close the chapter.

Recreation, TRB page 158
Consumer Applications, TRB page 176
Calculator Technology, TRB page 194
Computer Technology, TRB pages 209–211
Reading Math, TRB page 230
Family Involvement, TRB pages 251–252

Reteaching

Using Page 110

The exercises on this page are intended for those students who experienced difficulty with the Chapter Review/Test on page 109. Should students require reteaching of these key concepts and skills, please refer to the teaching notes below. Otherwise, the Another Look exercises can be assigned as independent work, with students using the accompanying sample problems and hints as guides.

Exercises 1–12 This skill was originally taught on pages 88–95. Discuss the first example in the display box. Observe with students that we multiply as with whole numbers. Then elicit from students the rule for placing the decimal point in the product.

Direct students' attention to the second example in the display box at the top of the page. On the chalkboard, work through each step in the problem. Stress that zeros must be placed correctly in the product. In this case, we write zeros in the tenths place and hundredths place.

Exercises 13–20 This skill was originally taught on pages 98–99. Discuss the examples in the second display box. Remind students that when we multiply by 10, 100, or 1,000, the decimal point shifts 1, 2, or 3 places to the right. When we multiply by 0.1, 0.01, or 0.001, the decimal point shifts 1, 2, or 3 places to the left.

Exercises 21–28 This skill was originally taught on page 100. Work through the example with students. Emphasize rounding to 1-digit accuracy and placing the decimal point correctly in the product.

$$2.74 \leftarrow 2 \text{ decimal places}$$
$$\times \ 0.8 \leftarrow 1 \text{ decimal place}$$
$$2.192 \leftarrow 3 \text{ decimal places}$$

$$0.13 \leftarrow 2 \text{ decimal places}$$
$$\times 0.06 \leftarrow 2 \text{ decimal places}$$
$$0.0078 \leftarrow 4 \text{ decimal places}$$
Add 2 zeros to make 4 decimal places.

Find the products.

1.	12.8	**2.**	0.72	**3.**	2.038	
	× 6		× 9		× 25	
	76.8		6.48		50.950	

4.	4.7	**5.**	0.84	**6.**	0.825	
	×0.5		× 0.9		× 0.03	
	2.35		0.756		0.02475	

7.	0.42	**8.**	1.09	**9.**	0.043	
	×0.03		×0.07		× 0.15	
	0.0126		0.0763		0.00645	

10.	0.234	**11.**	0.0006	**12.**	10.45	
	×0.008		× 0.28		× 6.28	
	0.001872		0.000168		65.6260	

$$10 \times 0.46 = 4.6$$
$$100 \times 3.142 = 314.2$$
$$0.01 \times 6,285 = 62.85$$
$$0.001 \times 9,000 = 9.000$$

Find the products mentally.

13. 100×6.428 642.8   **14.** 10×0.762 7.62

15. $1,000 \times 3.1416$ 3,141.6   **16.** 0.1×22.7 2.27

17. $0.001 \times 7,200$ 7.2   **18.** 0.01×62.57 0.6257

19. 100×0.67 67   **20.** 0.001×16.5 0.0165

Estimate.

$$0.92 \times 0.48$$

Round to 1-digit accuracy.

$$0.9 \times 0.5 = 0.45$$

Estimate the products.

21. 9×8.89 81   **22.** 0.72×0.88 0.63

23. 59.25×8.09 480   **24.** $17 \times \$2.12$ \$40

25. $8 \times \$0.92$ \$7.20   **26.** $115 \times \$3.09$ \$300

27. 19.4×5.7 120   **28.** 0.27×0.04 0.012

Just for Teachers

Time

Aristotle said, "Time is the number of motion." Time has always been fundamental to the development and application of mathematics.

Egyptians relied upon sundials, which measured shadows, and water clocks, which measured the flow of water out of a vessel. The water clocks were divided into 12 equal parts. The ancient Romans noted sunrise and sunset. Later in the civilization they also noted noon. At the beginning of the Christian era, Romans began dividing the time of daylight into five periods. The Christian church named 7 hours of prayer, beginning at 6 a.m. and marking only periods of daylight. The length of the hour varied with the season. The winter hours were shorter than the summer hours, because there was less daylight during the winter.

ENRICHMENT

Number Theory

Casting Out Nines is an old method of checking computation. To cast out nines from a number, you can use either of these methods.

Add the digits of the number. Add the digits of the sum until you get a single digit. If the single digit is 9, cast it out to get 0.

Look for the digits in the number that have a total of 9. Cast out these digits. Add the other digits to get a single-digit sum.

$$2,749 \rightarrow 2+7+4+9 = 22 \rightarrow 2+2 = 4 \qquad \cancel{2}\ \cancel{7}\ 4\ \cancel{9} \rightarrow 4$$

$$30,213 \rightarrow 3+0+2+1+3 = 9 \rightarrow 0 \qquad \cancel{3}\ 0\ \cancel{2}\ \cancel{1}\ \cancel{3} \rightarrow 0$$

You can use the digits you get by casting out nines to check your computation.

Multiplication

$$
\begin{array}{r}
259 \rightarrow 7 \\
\times\ 65 \rightarrow 2 \\
\hline
1295 \\
1554 \\
\hline
16,835 \rightarrow 5
\end{array}
\qquad
\begin{array}{l}
7 \\
\times 2 \\
\hline
14 \rightarrow 5 \\
\\
5 \text{ and } 5 \\
\text{It checks.}
\end{array}
$$

Division

$$
\begin{array}{r}
13 \rightarrow 4 \qquad\quad 8 \leftarrow \text{divisor} \\
8 \leftarrow 296\overline{)3,849} \rightarrow 6 \quad \times 4 \leftarrow \text{quotient} \\
296 \qquad\qquad\quad \hline 32 \\
\hline 889 \qquad\qquad +1 \leftarrow \text{remainder} \\
888 \qquad\qquad \hline 33 \rightarrow 6 \text{ dividend} \\
\hline 1 \rightarrow 1 \qquad\qquad \text{It checks.}
\end{array}
$$

Which answers are correct? Check by casting out nines.

1.
$$
\begin{array}{r}
728 \quad 8 \\
\times\ 86 \quad \times 5 \\
\hline
4368 \quad 40 \rightarrow 4 \\
5824 \\
\hline
62,508 \quad 3
\end{array}
$$

2.
$$
\begin{array}{r}
819 \quad 0 \\
\times\ 69 \quad \times 6 \\
\hline
7371 \quad 0 \\
4914 \\
\hline
56,511 \quad 0
\end{array}
$$

③.
$$
\begin{array}{r}
215 \text{ R29} \\
32\overline{)6,909} \rightarrow 6 \\
64 \\
\hline
50 \qquad 8 \\
32 \qquad \times 5 \\
\hline
189 \quad 40 \rightarrow 4 \\
160 \qquad\quad +2 \\
\hline
29 \qquad\quad 6
\end{array}
$$

4.
$$
\begin{array}{r}
139 \text{ R402} \\
619\overline{)84,443} \rightarrow 5 \\
61\ 9 \\
\hline
23\ 54 \qquad 4 \\
18\ 57 \qquad \times 7 \\
\hline
5\ 973 \quad 28 \rightarrow 1 \\
5\ 571 \qquad\quad +6 \\
\hline
402 \qquad\quad 7
\end{array}
$$

Find the products and quotients. Check by casting out nines.

5.
$$
\begin{array}{r}
237 \quad 3 \\
\times\ 29 \quad \times 2 \\
\hline
6,873 \quad 6
\end{array}
$$

6.
$$
\begin{array}{r}
564 \quad 6 \\
\times\ 57 \quad \times 3 \\
\hline
32,148 \quad 18 \rightarrow 0
\end{array}
$$

7.
$$
\begin{array}{r}
2,618 \quad 8 \\
\times\ 93 \quad \times 3 \\
\hline
243,474 \quad 24 \rightarrow 6
\end{array}
$$

8.
$$
\begin{array}{r}
9,356 \quad 5 \\
\times\ 247 \quad \times 4 \\
\hline
2,310,932 \quad 20 \rightarrow 2
\end{array}
$$

9.
$$
\begin{array}{r}
51 \text{ R42} \\
57\overline{)2,949} \\
(3 \times 6)+6 \rightarrow 6
\end{array}
$$

10.
$$
\begin{array}{r}
442 \text{ R69} \\
86\overline{)38,081} \\
(5 \times 1)+6 \rightarrow 2
\end{array}
$$

11.
$$
\begin{array}{r}
37 \text{ R2} \\
566\overline{)20,944} \\
(8 \times 1)+2 \rightarrow 1
\end{array}
$$

12.
$$
\begin{array}{r}
120 \text{ R506} \\
777\overline{)93,746} \\
(3 \times 3)+2 \rightarrow 2
\end{array}
$$

111

Mechanical clocks appeared in the 13th century. Refined over the next 400 years, clocks became important in commerce and science, as well as religion. An hour was eventually redefined as $\frac{1}{24}$th of the 360° revolution of the earth. In recent times, the definition of a "second" has been debated. It was once considered as $\frac{1}{86,400}$ of a "mean solar day," but it has been noted that a mean solar day is a rather elusive concept. Thus, a second was pinned down to a fraction of a particular year: $\frac{1}{31,556,925.975}$ of the year 1900.

Even without Einstein's research, it is clear that time is relative and inextricably bound to space, matter, and motion. However precisely we attempt to "keep" time, the words of Aristotle remain valid.

Ideas for Getting Started

Display the following on the chalkboard or overhead projector. Explain that this is a diagram of instructions called a flowchart. Each figure in a flowchart indicates the type of step. The starting and ending points are shown with an oval shape. The rectangles contain instructions to be followed. A parallelogram shows incoming (input) or outgoing (output) information. Have students follow the flow lines and give the output. (20)

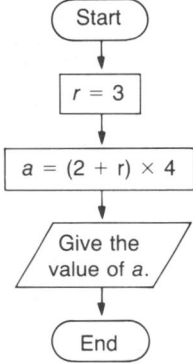

Using Page 112

Lesson Development After students read the material at the top of the page, direct their attention to the box showing mathematical symbols used in the BASIC language. Explain that the computer cannot use symbols with more than one meaning, so substitutes are necessary for some of our mathematical symbols.

Have students study the flowchart. Then work through the program with students. Point out that each statement is preceded by a number, called a line number, indicating the order in which the instructions are to be performed. Programmers usually number the lines by tens to leave room for the addition of lines if they are necessary later.

Explain that the variables in computer programs name locations in a computer's memory. The values assigned to variables are stored in the computer and can be used later in the program. Line 40 tells the computer to print the contents of memory locations A, B, and C. Note that the statement in line 50 was continued to the next line because of lack of space in the text. If this program were entered into a computer, statement 50 should appear in one line. The command RUN is not part of the program itself but instructs the computer to execute the program in memory.

Technology lessons are optional. They require no special teacher expertise.

Computer Programs and Flowcharts

Computers must be given a precise set of instructions called a **program** to accomplish any task. These instructions must be written in a special language that the computer understands. We are going to use a language called **BASIC** (Beginners' All-Purpose Symbolic Instruction Code).

Flowcharts are sometimes used to plan computer programs. Study the example below.

Mathematical Symbol	BASIC
$3 + 4$	$3 + 4$
$12 - 9$	$12 - 9$
25×17	$25 * 17$
$63 \div 7$	$63 / 7$
$3(9 + 4)$	$3 * (9 + 4)$
2^5	$2 \uparrow 5$ or $2 ** 5$
0 (zero)	$\emptyset$

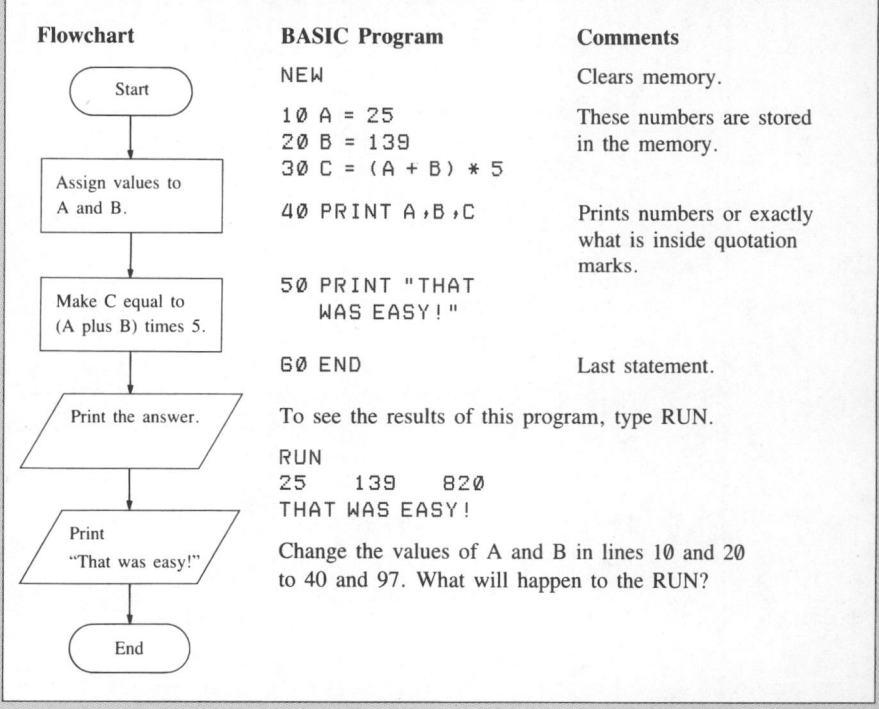

Flowchart	BASIC Program	Comments
	NEW	Clears memory.
	10 A = 25	These numbers are stored
	20 B = 139	in the memory.
	30 C = (A + B) * 5	
	40 PRINT A,B,C	Prints numbers or exactly what is inside quotation marks.
	50 PRINT "THAT WAS EASY!"	
	60 END	Last statement.

To see the results of this program, type RUN.

```
RUN
25    139    820
THAT WAS EASY!
```

Change the values of A and B in lines 10 and 20 to 40 and 97. What will happen to the RUN?

Technology for Teachers

A computer language is a tool used to control the power of a computer. It is a systematized set of instructions that conveys information to a computer. BASIC is one of the most commonly used languages used on microcomputers. Like other programming languages, BASIC is composed of units, called commands and statements, that resemble words. A command is equivalent to a complex set of detailed instructions as illustrated by the following PRINT statements.

Statement	Instruction
PRINT 3 * 5	Display the result of the operation, 3×5.
PRINT A + 5	Add 5 to the contents in memory location A and display the result.
PRINT A ; " TO THE SECOND POWER IS ";A ↑ 2	Display the contents in memory location A. In the next space, display information in the quotation marks. Then use the contents of memory location A to find A^2 and display the result in the next space

Write the RUN for each program.

1. ```
10 M = 100
20 T = 4
30 S = M/T
40 PRINT M,T,S
50 END
RUN   100   4   25
```

2. ```
10 A = 48
20 B = 72
30 C = (A + B)/12
40 D = A + B/12
50 PRINT A,B,C,D
60 END
RUN   48   72   10   54
```

3. ```
10 K = 5
20 Z = 2
30 M = K↑Z
40 Q = Z↑K
50 PRINT K,Z,M,Q
60 END
RUN   5   2   25   32
```

4. ```
10 A = 10
20 B = 70
30 PRINT A + B,B - A
40 PRINT A * B,B/A
50 PRINT A↑3,B↑2
60 END
RUN   80        60
      70         7
    1000      4900
```

5. ```
10 A = 10
20 PRINT A;" TO THE SECOND
   POWER IS ";A↑2
30 PRINT A;" TO THE THIRD
   POWER IS ";A↑3
40 PRINT A;" TO THE FOURTH
   POWER IS ";A↑4
50 END
RUN
10 TO THE SECOND POWER IS 100
10 TO THE THIRD POWER IS 1000
10 TO THE FOURTH POWER IS 10000
```

6. ```
10 A = 35
20 B = 12
30 PRINT A;" TIMES ";B;
   " EQUALS ";A*B
40 END
RUN   35 TIMES 12 EQUALS 420
```

7. Assign different values to the variables in exercises 1–6. Give each new RUN. Answers will vary.

8. Make a flow chart for your own program. Then write the program and show the RUN. Answers will vary.

Rick Rasay checks a computer program.

113

In computer language, a single punctuation mark may represent a set of instructions. Commas in PRINT statements tell the computer to leave space between numbers or letters in the output and display them in predetermined columns. The output screen (or paper if a printer is used) is divided into fields, or zones, usually 14 spaces wide. The PRINT statement, "PRINT M, T, S," instructs the computer to print the contents of M in the first zone, the contents of T in the second zone, and the contents of S in the third zone. If semicolons are used, space between items is eliminated.

Computers languages have a very precisely defined structure, known as syntax. Misspelled words or misplaced punctuation marks will not be understood by the computer. One of the benefits of learning a language like BASIC is that students learn very quickly the need for precision in writing and entering their information into the computer.

Using Page 113

Exercises 1–8 Students may either enter these programs on a microcomputer or play the role of the computer themselves and determine the results of each RUN. If students are typing the programs on a computer, be sure and remind them to press the RETURN or ENTER key at the end of each line. This puts the line of instructions into the computer's memory.

In exercise 4, expressions are used in PRINT statements. The computer evaluates the expression and prints the result when the PRINT statements are executed. Exercises 5 and 6 show that the two kinds of output — numbers and messages in quotations marks — can be used in one PRINT statement. The semicolon is used to separate items. Some computers do not require the use of the semicolon; others use other symbols.

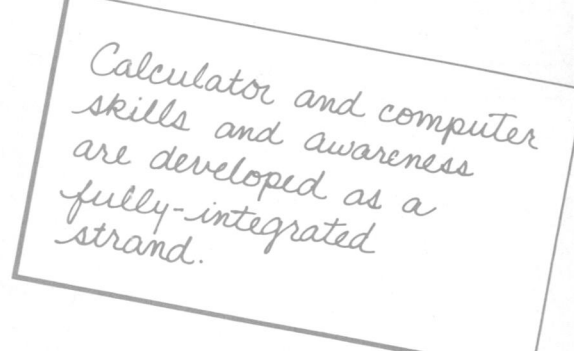
Calculator and computer skills and awareness are developed as a fully-integrated strand.

Review

Using Page 114

The exercises on the page provide practice for maintaining cumulative skills. The emphasis in this Cumulative Review is on estimating products and quotients of whole numbers (Chapter 3), multiplying and dividing whole numbers (Chapter 3), multiplying decimals (Chapter 4), and problem solving (Chapter 4).

Item Analysis The table below correlates the Cumulative Review items with objectives and with the student book pages on which the concepts or skills were taught.

Items	Objectives	Related Text Pages
1	3.2	60–65
2	3.5	72–77
3, 5	3.4	70–71
4	3.1	57–59
6–7	4.2	88–95,104
8	3.3	66–67
9	4.3	100
10–12	4.2	98–99
13	3.6	68–69,78–79
14	4.5	96–97,101,105,106–107

CUMULATIVE REVIEW

1. Multiply.
 529
 × 705
 A 372,845 **B** 372,945 c 39,675 D not given

2. Find the quotient.
 56)9,124
 A 162 R20 B 16 R52 **C** 162 R52 D not given

3. Estimate the quotient by rounding each number to 1-digit accuracy.
 $98,759 \div 988$
 A 90 B 1,000 **C** 100 D not given

4. Choose the best estimate.
 609×25
 A 18,000 B 1,800 c 180,000 D not given

5. Find the quotient.
 $64,000 \div 800$
 A 9,000 B 8,000 c 800 **D** not given

Multiply.

6. 2.76 × 9.3
 A 25.668 B 286.68 c 28.668 D not given

7. 0.057 × 0.95
 A 0.05515 **B** 0.05415 c 0.5415 D not given

8. $7^2 \cdot 9^5$
 A 35,721 **B** 2,893,401 c 413,349 D not given

9. Estimate the product by rounding each number to 1-digit accuracy.
 0.129×0.62
 A 0.6 **B** 0.06 c 6.0 D not given

10. Find the product.
 912.47×100
 A 91.247 B 9,124.7 **C** 91,247 D not given

11. Multiply.
 0.545×0.001
 A 0.000545 B 545 c 0.00545 D not given

12. Find the product.
 6.59 × 0.1
 A 6,590 B 65.90 **C** 0.659 D not given

13. Each row of chairs in a large room has 27 chairs. There are 18 rows of chairs. How many chairs are there all together?
 A 45 **B** 486 c 288 D not given

14. A 7-minute telephone call costs $0.54 for the first minute and $0.38 for each additional minute. What is the total cost of the call?
 A $0.92 B $3.62 **C** $2.82 D not given

Objectives

5.1 Find the quotient of a decimal divided by a whole number.

5.2 Find the quotient when the divisor is a decimal.

5.3 Estimate quotients of decimals.

5.4 Solve word problems using the 5-Point Checklist and cumulative computational skills.

Summary

The primary emphasis in this chapter is on dividing decimals. It is likely that students will need considerable practice in developing skills with the division algorithm as it applies to decimals. In addition to developing skill with the division algorithm, the chapter extends the estimation and problem-solving strands to include division of decimals.

Mathematical Background

Division of a Decimal by a Whole Number The division algorithm for decimals is essentially the same as division with whole numbers. The new feature is developing a set of rules for placement of the decimal point in the quotient. To develop the needed rules, decimals are first divided by whole numbers. In this case, the decimal point in the quotient is placed directly above the decimal point in the dividend.

$$
\begin{array}{r}
0\,.\,3 \\
8\,\overline{)2\,\uparrow\,4}
\end{array}
\qquad 0.3 \times 8 = 2.4
$$

Division of a decimal by a whole number can be explained with place-value models. To find the quotient of $4.35 \div 3$, we show 4 units, 3 tenths, and 5 hundredths and separate the models into 3 groups.

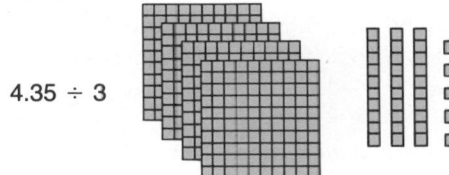

$4.35 \div 3$

Divide the units. There is 1 unit in each of 3 groups with 1 unit left. Trade the 1 unit for 10 tenths and combine with the 3 tenths to give 13 tenths.

Divide the tenths. There are 4 tenths in each group with 1 tenth left. The 1 tenth is traded for 10 hundredths and combined with the 5 hundredths to give 15 hundredths.

Divide the hundredths. There are 5 hundredths in each group with no hundredths left.

$$
\begin{array}{r}
1.45 \\
3\,\overline{)4.35} \\
\underline{3} \\
1\,3 \\
\underline{1\,2} \\
15 \\
\underline{15} \\
0
\end{array}
$$

Division of a Decimal by a Decimal To divide a decimal by a decimal we change the form of the problem so that the divisor is a whole number. This is done by multiplying the divisor by a power of ten and multiplying the dividend by the same power of ten. Thus, to find $3.5\overline{)7}$ we think of multiplying both numbers by 10 so that the problem is changed to $35\overline{)70}$, a problem that we know how to do. One should observe that we could multiply 3.5 and 7 by any convenient number that would make the divisor a whole number. For example, we could use 2 as a factor in the same problem.

$$
3.5 \times 2\,\overline{)7 \times 2} \qquad 7\,\overline{)\overset{2}{14}}
$$

However, if the multiplier is a power of 10, we can use a short cut to multiply and shift the decimal points in the divisor and dividend.

$$
3.5_{\curvearrowright}\,\overline{)7.0_{\curvearrowright}}^{\;2.}
$$

In division with decimals, we continue dividing past the decimal point instead of writing a remainder. This often results in repeating decimals, rather than terminating decimals. In this chapter, emphasis is not on repeating decimals but on rounding decimal quotients to an appropriate place.

Problem Solving A variety of problem-solving sets are presented in this chapter. Many of the problems are multiple-step problems. In a problem-solving practice lesson on page 121, students apply previously learned skills using addition, subtraction, multiplication, and division. On pages 122 and 123 a set of problems using data from a water rate table gives the students experience in solving consumer-oriented problems. The idea of average or arithmetic mean of a list of numbers is review and word problems about averages are presented on pages 126 and 127.

A new strategy for nonroutine problems, Work Backward, is taught on page 130. This strategy will be used in Try This problems in later chapters of the book.

Vocabulary

average   inverse operation

Teaching Tips

Error Analysis

The division algorithm involves knowledge of addition, subtraction, and multiplication. A lack of understanding of any of these operations could result in error patterns in division. Of course, error patterns will also occur if the student has inadequate knowledge of the basic concept of division or the division algorithm. Teachers must study each student's work in detail to diagnose the cause of errors. Some commonly occuring errors are given below.

Error Pattern 1

$$
\begin{array}{r}
6.5 \\
6{\overline{)36.5}} \\
36 \\
\hline
5
\end{array}
\qquad
\begin{array}{r}
6.6 \\
7{\overline{)42.6}} \\
42 \\
\hline
6
\end{array}
\qquad
\begin{array}{r}
9.3 \\
9{\overline{)81.3}} \\
81 \\
\hline
3
\end{array}
$$

Diagnosis The student has started to divide correctly; however, when the value to be divided is smaller than the divisor, the smaller value is placed in the quotient.

Remediation To remediate this error, concentrate on review of the division algorithm. Explain that once the decimal point is placed in the quotient, division with decimals is the same as division with whole numbers. Emphasize when to place a zero in the quotient.

Error Pattern 2

$$
\begin{array}{r}
1.74 \\
0.5{\overline{)87.3}} \\
5 \\
\hline
37 \\
35 \\
\hline
23 \\
20 \\
\hline
3
\end{array}
\qquad
\begin{array}{r}
.159 \\
0.6{\overline{)9.54}} \\
6 \\
\hline
35 \\
30 \\
\hline
54 \\
54 \\
\hline
0
\end{array}
$$

Diagnosis The student has divided correctly but the decimal point is placed incorrectly in the quotient. The student has used the total number of decimal places in the divisor and dividend to determine the position of the decimal point in the quotient.

Remediation Have the student check the division by multiplying. Since $0.5 \times 1.74 = 0.870$, not 87.3, the check indicates something is incorrect in the process being used.

Review the idea of multiplying the divisor and dividend by the same number. Show that the quotient is not changed.

$$\frac{0.8}{2} = 0.4 \qquad \frac{8}{20} = 0.4 \qquad \frac{80}{200} = 0.4$$

Explain that if we multiply by a multiple of 10 we can change the form of the problem and make the divisor a whole number.

Have the student work some division problems by following these steps.

First: Make the divisor a whole number by thinking of multiplication and moving the decimal point.

$$0.5{\overline{)87.3}}$$

Second: Move the decimal point in the dividend the same number of places.

$$0.5{\overline{)87.3}}$$

Third: Place the decimal point in the quotient.

$$0.5{\overline{)87.3}}$$

Fourth: Divide as with whole numbers.

Error Pattern 3

$$3.2 \div 10 = 32$$
$$3.2 \div 100 = 320$$
$$3.2 \div 1,000 = 3,200$$
$$3.2 \div 10,000 = 32,000$$

Diagnosis The student has moved the decimal point to the right instead of to the left. Dividing by a multiple of 10 has been confused with multiplying by a multiple of 10.

Remediation Use the standard division algorithm with the same problems and compare the quotient and dividend.

$$
\begin{array}{r}
0.32 \\
10{\overline{)3.20}} \\
3\,0 \\
\hline
20 \\
20 \\
\hline
\end{array}
\qquad
3.2 \xrightarrow[\text{by 10}]{\text{divide}} 0.32
$$

$$
\begin{array}{r}
.032 \\
100{\overline{)3.200}} \\
3\,00 \\
\hline
200 \\
200 \\
\hline
\end{array}
\qquad
3.2 \xrightarrow[\text{by 100}]{\text{divide}} 0.032
$$

Continue with other examples until the relationship is clear.

Problem Solving

Using Hints To Help Develop Solution Strategies

You may be able to recall a time in a math class when you were working on a problem, got stuck, asked for help, and were given a hint. Often, the hint was just what was needed to get you started toward finding a solution. Sometimes, however, the hint was of absolutely no help. It may have actually been confusing since it suggested an approach different from the idea you had for solving the problem.

Giving hints is a necessary part of teaching problem solving. Because each student reacts differently to a hint, selecting appropriate hints and deciding when to use them are two of the most difficult tasks in teaching problem solving. There are no rules or signals from the students that will assure you of the right hint to use or the right time to use it. The best way to improve one's skills selecting and using hints is through experience teaching problem-solving. Here are a few guidelines to help decide when to use a hint.

- The student's work on a particular problem is based on a misconception or misunderstanding.

- The student is ignoring or overlooking important information.

- The student has thought of a good strategy but needs your help to use it effectively.

- It seems appropriate to suggest that the student give more serious thought to using one or more strategies.

- You feel that the student will become completely frustrated unless you give some assistance.

There are three general categories of hints: 1) hints to help students understand a problem, 2) hints to help students develop a solution strategy, and 3) hints to help students accurately carry out or evaluate a particular solution strategy.

In the Teaching Tips for problem solving in Chapter 3, page 56C, a problem is presented with examples of discussion questions and hints to help students understand the problem. Here is the same problem with examples of hints to help students develop a solution strategy.

> Six children came to a birthday party. Each child shook hands one time with every other child. How many handshakes were exchanged?

Discussion "Write the names of 6 children and show me with whom the first child would shake hands." Or, "Draw a picture of 6 children. Show who would shake hands." Or, "If you were the first child, with how many people would you shake hands?"

Discussion questions are provided in the Teacher's Edition for each nonroutine problem; however, hints to help students carry out a particular solution strategy cannot be identified prior to the lesson. As you observe and question students while they solve problems, your comments should be related to the particular way the student is solving the problem. Studying these example hints will help you to decide the appropriate hints as you work with the students.

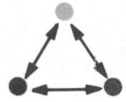 ## Special Education

Most special students in your class will need the chance to actively participate in the lessons throughout this chapter if they are to learn and retain the ideas being presented. Suggestions for this purpose are given below.

Different Approaches

Generally it is best for the activities suggested below to precede an analysis of the procedures to be used. If students have reasoning difficulties, it is helpful to do the following.

- Discuss the textbook instruction lines or summary statement in conjunction with several examples.

- Have the students copy the instruction lines onto index cards for ready reference.

- Have students use the procedure to work a number of problems until they become familiar with the general procedure.

- Discuss the answers with students and help them to realize that the answers are reasonable.

Before having the students attempt to memorize the procedures to follow, use the activity suggestions.

Verbal, Manipulative, Visual Guidance for Division

The language of sharing proves useful for helping students understand the procedure for dividing a decimal by a whole number. Allow students to share money or graph paper pieces while working exercises like those in the figure. Retain a list of these

exercises on the chalkboard to use as a basis for discussion. Students can be visually cued, as shown, to note how the decimal point in the quotient is directly above the one in the dividend.

Share the ones, then the tenths, then the hundredths

Visual, Verbal, Kinesthetic Reinforcement

Some students will see a pattern better if they also can hear it and feel it. In the development of the short cut for dividing by powers of 10, use the idea shown in the figure so students can better associate the number of zeros in the power of 10 with the number of decimal place shifts. In the example there are two visual, two verbal, and two motor inputs in each instance. A similar approach can help students see the pattern for multiplying by powers of 10.

Touching each zero. "One, *two* zeros."

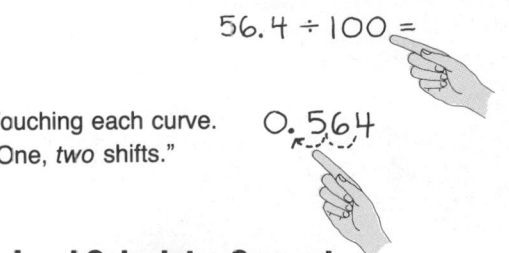

Touching each curve. "One, *two* shifts."

Oral and Calculator Support

To divide by a decimal, we change the problem to an equivalent exercise. The language of sharing is useful to help students intuitively see the need for this change. The instruction lines on page 124 show how to make the needed change, not only to the divisor but to the dividend as well.

It may be helpful to allow the students to use a calculator to divide pairs of exercises, like 0.25)6 and 25)600 to emphasize that both exercises have the same answer. A calculator could also be used to show that it is not enough to change the divisor to a whole number. The dividend must be changed accordingly for the answer to be the same.

 ## Subject Integration

Subject matter related to other areas of the curriculum has been integrated into the following lessons. This provides an opportunity to highlight the interaction between the mathematics and other subjects.

Consumer Awareness Film costs, pages 118–119; water costs, page 128; water conservation, pages 122–123
Fine Arts Sculpture, page 115
History Karl Friedrick Gauss, page 133
Home Economics Party Preparation, page 124
Physical Education Racing, page 120–121
Science Zoo, pages 116–117

Management Guide

Teaching Chapter 5				Meeting Individual Needs					
Objectives	Chapter Content	Pages	TRB Test Items	Lesson Assignments			Follow Up		
				Minimum	Average	Extended	Reteaching	Enrichment	Practice
	Chapter Opener	115							
5.1 Find the quotient of a decimal divided by a whole number.	Dividing a Decimal by a Whole Number	116–117	1–3	1–31	1–33	1–33 odd, TM	SE6 Ch 6 RS 34	ES 34	MP 425 PS 44
	Rounding Decimal Quotients	118–119	4–11	1–33, SK	1–34, 36, SK	1–35 odd, 36, SK	SE6 Ch 6 RS 35	ES 35	MP 425 PS 45
	Dividing Decimals: Mental Math	120		1–10	1–10	1–10	SE6 Ch 6 RS 36	ES 36	PS 46
5.2 Find the quotient when the divisor is a decimal.	Dividing by a Decimal	124–125	12–16	1–33, SK	1–34, SK	1–33 odd, 34–35 SK	SE6 Ch 6 RS 37	ES 37	MP 425 PS 48
5.3 Estimate quotients of decimals.	Estimating Quotients with Decimals	129	17–21	1–9, 13	1– 13	1– 13 odd, 14	SE6 Ch 6 RS 39	ES 39	MP 425 PS 50
5.4 Solve word problems using the 5-Point Checklist and cumulative computational skills.	Problem Solving: Practice	121	22–25	1–7	1–9	1–10			
	Problem Solving: Using Data from a Table	122–123		1–4 / 1–4	1–4 / 1–7, 10	1–4 / 4–10			PS 47
	Problem Solving: Finding Averages	126–127		1–7	1–7, 10, 11	4–11	RS 38	ES 38	PS 49
	Skills Practice	128		1–32	1–40	1–47 odd			
	Problem Solving: Working Backward	130							
	Chapter Review/Test	131							
	Another Look/ Enrichment	132–133							
	Cumulative Review	134							

SE6 Student Edition, Book 6
RS   Reteaching Supplement
ES   Enrichment Supplement
PS   Practice Supplement
MP   More Practice
TM   Think Math
SK   Skillkeeper
TRB Teacher's Resource Book

Masters for use

. . . before Chapter 5

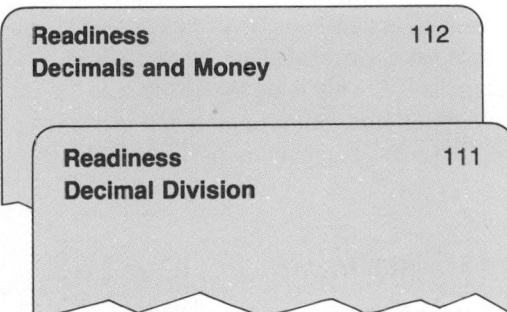

Readiness Decimals and Money	112
Readiness Decimal Division	111

. . . during Chapter 5

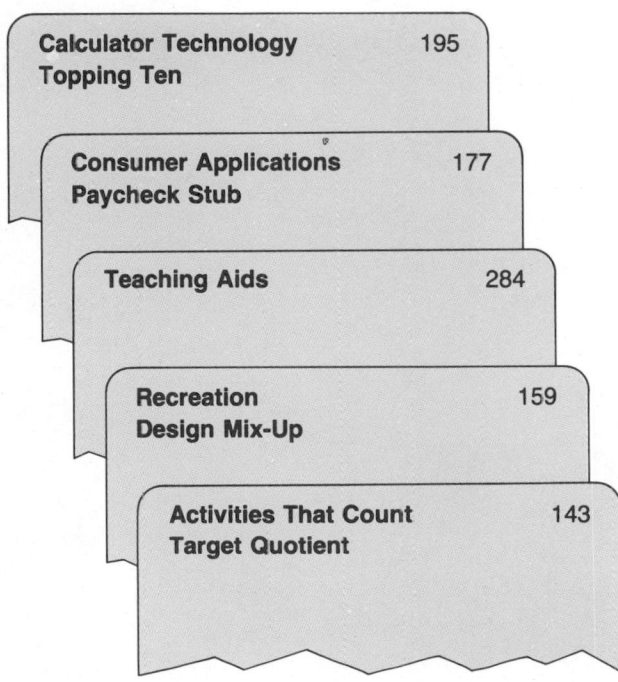

Calculator Technology Topping Ten	195
Consumer Applications Paycheck Stub	177
Teaching Aids	284
Recreation Design Mix-Up	159
Activities That Count Target Quotient	143

. . . after Chapter 5

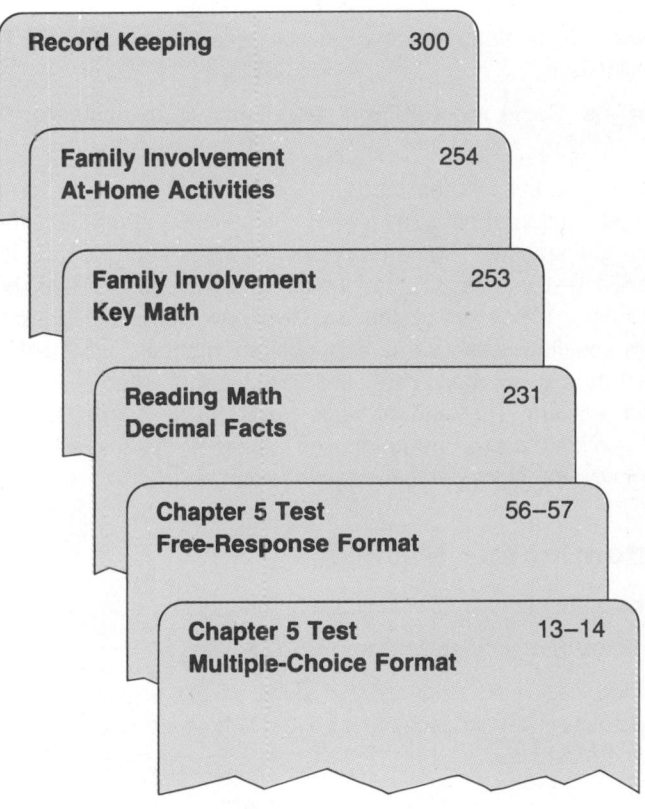

Record Keeping	300
Family Involvement At-Home Activities	254
Family Involvement Key Math	253
Reading Math Decimal Facts	231
Chapter 5 Test Free-Response Format	56–57
Chapter 5 Test Multiple-Choice Format	13–14

Supplements

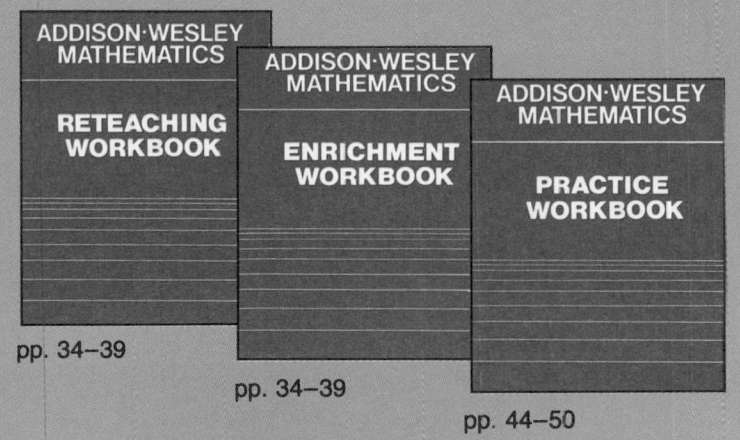

ADDISON·WESLEY
MATHEMATICS

**RETEACHING
WORKBOOK**

pp. 34–39

ADDISON·WESLEY
MATHEMATICS

**ENRICHMENT
WORKBOOK**

pp. 34–39

ADDISON·WESLEY
MATHEMATICS

**PRACTICE
WORKBOOK**

pp. 44–50

Other Addison-Wesley Resources

Books and Kits

Skillseekers III ÷, 12–18
Baseball: A Game of Numbers pp. 23–36, 53–58
General Mathematics: Making Practice Fun 25A, B, 27A, B
The Arithmetic Primer pp. 236–238, 273–274
Problem-Solving Experiences in Mathematics, Grade 7
Problems 3, 8, 24, 25, 27, 48, 59, 60, 63, 67, 78, 83, 85, 98, 103, 124, 135, 147

Technology

Computer Math Activities Volumes 1–5
Computer Math Games Volumes 1, 2, 6

Activities That Count

Activities That Count are designed for use throughout this chapter and subsequent chapters. Before beginning Chapter 5, you may wish to review these activities and select the ones you consider appropriate for your class.

Target Quotient   Game

Purpose   To reinforce place-value concepts and practice dividing decimals

Materials   Game sheet (TRB p. 143), index cards numbered 0 to 9

Activity   Players mix the cards and draw two of them to form the target quotient. Each player should record the target quotient on their game sheet. The cards are mixed again and one card is drawn. Each player records that number in any of the six places of the diagram. Cards are mixed and two new cards are drawn. Players continue in the same way until six numbers have been drawn. When all six spaces are filled, the students are to solve the division problem. The student whose quotient is nearest to the target quotient scores one point. The winner of the game is the student with the highest score after five rounds.

Pentominoes   Math Lab

Purpose   To use spatial visualization and logical reasoning

Materials   Scissors, graph paper (TRB p. 284)

Activity   Explain to students that polyominoes are formed by placing squares next to each other so that they share sides. These are some examples.

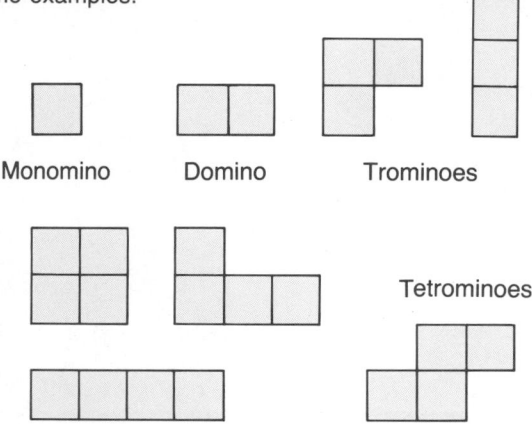

Monomino   Domino   Trominoes

Tetrominoes

Have students cut five paper squares the same size and arrange them to form a pentomino. Challenge them to form as many as they can, drawing a picture of each on the graph paper.

Unit Pricing Project

Purpose   To use division in practical applications

Activity   Have students visit stores and record the prices and amounts of various items. Encourage them to concentrate on collecting data that will enable them to compare unit prices for the same item packaged in different sizes. Such items as boxes of soap or cereal, canned or frozen fruits or vegetables, and packages of rice or flour are usually available in several sizes and thus would provide suitable data. Ask students to use the data they collect to compute unit prices and make appropriate comparisons. You might also wish to ask the students to make charts to display their findings.

Decimal Race   Game

Adapt the activity described on page 30 F for adding, subtracting, multiplying, and dividing decimals.

5

Division of Decimals

When you see a large bronze sculpture, you might not realize that a sculptor starts by making a small clay model. Larger models that may be 0.9 m high and 2.70 m high are then made.

The models are sent to a foundry where the founder uses them to make a full-size hollow wax model. The sculptor works with the wax model before it is filled and coated with plaster. This lump of plaster is baked for three days. The wax melts at 63°C and runs out. Bronze, heated to 1,100°C, is poured into the space where the wax used to be. When the plaster is chipped away, only the hardened bronze sculpture is left. The sculptor applies the final finishing touches to the surface.

Introducing the Chapter

Discussion After students have had an opportunity to examine the photographs and read the accompanying material, ask if they have had experience modeling or casting figures. Then discuss some of the data that is given. "The melting point of wax is about 63°C whereas bronze must be heated to approximately 1,100°C in order to be poured. How many times hotter is the melting point of bronze than of wax?" (over 17)

As you teach the chapter you may wish to refer back to this page and discuss the questions below. This is an opportunity for students to create their own questions based on the data in the article.

Follow-Up Questions

After Page 119 A bronze sculpture weighs 250.8 kg which is 8 times the weight of a clay model. What is the weight of the clay model to the nearest kilogram? (31 kg)

After Page 125 A small clay model measures 0.27 m high, while the finished bronze sculpture is 1.75 m high. How many times taller is the bronze sculpture? Round the answer to the nearest tenth. (6.5) Bronze is a combination of copper and tin. Modern bronze can be made of about 0.85 copper and 0.15 tin. How many times more copper than tin is this? Round the answer to the nearest hundredth. (5.67)

After Page 128 A model is 0.42 m high, a sculpture is 2.55 m high. Estimate how many times taller the sculpture is. (6)

Decimals

Quick Review Display the numbers below. Point to digits and have students give the place value of those digits. Example: 26.37<u>4</u>   0.004

268.3374   7,174.85656   6,211,867.492   2.57362

Lesson Focus To divide a decimal by a whole number

Ideas for Getting Started

Write these problems on the chalkboard or overhead projector.

$3\overline{)240}$ $3\overline{)24.0}$ $3\overline{)2.40}$

Have students find the quotients for the first two exercises. (80 and 8.0) Then ask students to estimate the quotient for the third problem. Since $3 \times 0.8 = 2.4$, the quotient must be 0.80 or 0.8. Point out that the only difference in the quotients for the three problems is the position of the decimal point.

Work through some other examples of division with whole number, 1-digit divisors.

$3\overline{)153}$ $3\overline{)15.3}$ $3\overline{)1.53}$

Using Page 116

Motivational Problem Have students read the problem at the top of the page. "What does the question ask us to find?" (the number of kilograms of biscuits the bear was fed each day) "What is the data in the problem?" (The bear was fed 28.25 kilograms of biscuits in 5 days.) Explain that because the bear eats about the same amount each day for 5 days, we divide the total weight of the biscuits by 5.

Lesson Development On the chalkboard, work through the steps shown to find the answer. Stress the fact that the division process is exactly the same as for whole numbers. The only new feature is determining the position of the decimal point in the quotient.

Show a division check multiplying 5×5.65 to get 28.25. This will help to strengthen the confidence of the student in the rules used for placing the decimal point in the quotient.

Other Examples The first example shows a middle zero in the quotient. Point out that if this zero were omitted, the student might get 2.6 as the quotient. The check $2.6 \times 24 = 62.4$ would show there must be an error in the division. The second example shows the case where a zero must be placed in the tenths place. Show that if the zero were omitted, the check would detect the error since $4 \times 0.54 = 2.16$ instead of the correct dividend 0.216.

Warm Up Have students try these exercises at their seats or at the chalkboard. Check to see that they are correctly placing the decimal point in the quotient.

The Data Bank—a unique Addison-Wesley feature—helps students learn to use sources of data.

Dividing a Decimal by a Whole Number

The Alaskan brown bear at the Cumberland Zoo is fed 28.25 kilograms (kg) of special biscuits in 5 days. How many kilograms of biscuits is the bear fed each day?

Since we want to find the amount of kilograms fed each day, we divide.

Divide the whole number part. → Place the decimal point. Divide the tenths. → Divide the hundredths.

$$\begin{array}{r} 5 \\ 5\overline{)28.25} \\ 25 \\ \hline 3 \end{array}$$
3 and 2 tenths → 32 tenths

$$\begin{array}{r} 5.6 \\ 5\overline{)28.25} \\ 25 \\ \hline 32 \\ 30 \\ \hline 2 \end{array}$$
2 tenths and 5 hundredths → 25 hundredths

$$\begin{array}{r} 5.65 \\ 5\overline{)28.25} \\ 25 \\ \hline 32 \\ 30 \\ \hline 25 \\ 25 \\ \hline 0 \end{array}$$

Check:
$$\begin{array}{r} 5.65 \\ \times\ \ 5 \\ \hline 28.25 \end{array}$$

The bear is fed 5.65 kg of biscuits each day.

Other Examples

When dividing a decimal by a whole number, place the decimal point in the quotient directly above the decimal point in the dividend.

$$\begin{array}{r} 2.06 \\ 24\overline{)49.44} \\ 48 \\ \hline 144 \\ 144 \\ \hline 0 \end{array}$$

Zeros show not enough ones or tenths. Divide the hundredths.

$$\begin{array}{r} 0.054 \\ 4\overline{)0.216} \\ 20 \\ \hline 16 \\ 16 \\ \hline 0 \end{array}$$

Warm Up

Find the quotients. Check by multiplying.

1. $32\overline{)18.24}$ → 0.57
2. $9\overline{)0.504}$ → 0.056
3. $7\overline{)26.74}$ → 3.82
4. $19\overline{)77.33}$ → 4.07

Follow Up

Reteaching

Illustrate dividing a decimal by a whole number by using place-value models. In the example $3\overline{)7.2}$, use 7 hundred-squares to show 7 units and 2 ten-sticks to show 2 tenths. As you work through the example, write the steps on the chalkboard.

Ask students to divide the units equally among 3 groups. There will be 1 unit remaining. Trade the 1 unit for 10 tenths. Ask students to divide the 12 tenths equally among 3 groups. The division is completed. The quotient is 2.4. Discuss the division exercise by working through it without the place-value models.

Enrichment

Have the students find the missing digits.

$$\begin{array}{r} 5.\boxed{8} \\ \boxed{4}\overline{)2\boxed{3}.2} \\ 20 \\ \hline 3\boxed{2} \\ \boxed{3}\boxed{2} \\ \hline 0 \end{array}$$

$$\begin{array}{r} 3.82 \\ 8\overline{)3\boxed{0}.\boxed{5}\boxed{6}} \\ \boxed{2}\boxed{4} \\ \hline \boxed{6}\boxed{5} \\ \boxed{6}\boxed{4} \\ \hline \boxed{1}\boxed{6} \\ \boxed{1}\boxed{6} \\ \hline 0 \end{array}$$

Find the quotients.

1. $\dfrac{3.27}{2\overline{)6.54}}$
2. $\dfrac{2.9}{7\overline{)20.3}}$
3. $\dfrac{5.3}{8\overline{)42.4}}$
4. $\dfrac{7.4}{9\overline{)66.6}}$
5. $\dfrac{3.4}{8\overline{)27.2}}$

6. $\dfrac{3.41}{5\overline{)17.05}}$
7. $\dfrac{57.2}{6\overline{)343.2}}$
8. $\dfrac{7.28}{4\overline{)29.12}}$
9. $\dfrac{32.49}{7\overline{)227.43}}$
10. $\dfrac{6.53}{5\overline{)32.65}}$

11. $\dfrac{1.19}{9\overline{)10.71}}$
12. $\dfrac{0.09}{6\overline{)0.54}}$
13. $\dfrac{0.34}{8\overline{)2.72}}$
14. $\dfrac{0.037}{4\overline{)0.148}}$
15. $\dfrac{0.33}{5\overline{)1.65}}$

16. $\dfrac{0.486}{3\overline{)1.458}}$
17. $\dfrac{6.4}{42\overline{)268.8}}$
18. $\dfrac{3.5}{71\overline{)248.5}}$
19. $\dfrac{3.24}{78\overline{)252.72}}$
20. $\dfrac{4.9}{52\overline{)254.8}}$

21. $\dfrac{3.25}{85\overline{)276.25}}$
22. $\dfrac{3.07}{29\overline{)89.03}}$
23. $\dfrac{5.7}{91\overline{)518.7}}$
24. $\dfrac{0.039}{18\overline{)0.702}}$
25. $\dfrac{0.016}{73\overline{)1.168}}$

26. $15.96 \div 57$
0.28
27. $76.14 \div 81$
0.94
28. $34.65 \div 45$
0.77
29. $2.07 \div 9$
0.23
30. $197.6 \div 52$
3.8

31. An animal trainer at the zoo feeds 6 sea lions a total of 59.76 kg of mackerel each day. How many kilograms does each sea lion get? **9.96 kg**

32. Three pairs of hornbills are fed 1.32 kg of soaked raisins as part of their daily diet. How much is fed to each hornbill? **0.22 kg**

33. **DATA BANK** If 6 giraffes were fed a total of 3.0 kg of grain per day, would this be about the right amount for each giraffe? (See page 416.) **yes**

THINK MATH

Finding Patterns

How many different squares can you count in each figure?

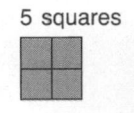

Continue the pattern with a 4×4 square and a 5×5 square.
$1^2 + 2^2 + 3^2 + 4^2 + 5^2 = 55$
How many different squares are in an 8×8 checkerboard? **204**

1 square   5 squares   14 squares   30 squares

1^2

$1^2 + 2^2 = 5$

$1^2 + 2^2 + 3^2 = 14$

?

$1^2 + 2^2 + 3^2 + 4^2 = 30$

More Practice, page 425, Set A

117

Using Page 117

Exercises 1–33 All the exercises have zero remainders. Ask students to estimate the answers before dividing. Direct them to check some of their answers by multiplying divisor times quotient.

After completing the exercises, some students might check their answers with a calculator, either by direct division or by multiplying divisor times the computed quotient.

Data Bank Each giraffe eats about 0.5 kilograms of grain per day. This is the amount indicated in the table on page 416.

Think Math Some students may need some help in seeing the relationship between the number of different squares and the squares of the whole numbers. For the 3×3 square, show the following pattern:

Number of 3×3 squares $= 1 = 1^2$
Number of 2×2 squares $= 4 = 2^2$
Number of 1×1 squares $= 9 = 3^2$
       Total squares $= 14 = 1^2 + 2^2 + 3^2$
Continuing this pattern we have:

$4 \times 4 \rightarrow 1^2 + 2^2 + 3^2 + 4^2 = 30$
$5 \times 5 \rightarrow 1^2 + 2^2 + \ldots + 5^2 = 55$
$6 \times 6 \rightarrow 1^2 + 2^2 + \ldots + 6^2 = 91$
$7 \times 7 \rightarrow 1^2 + 2^2 + \ldots + 7^2 = 140$
$8 \times 8 \rightarrow 1^2 + 2^2 + \ldots + 8^2 = 204$

More Practice, page 425, Set A

Reteaching Supplement, page 34

Enrichment Supplement, page 34

Practice Supplement, page 44

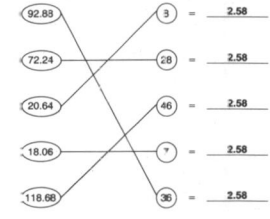

Quick Review Have students write each of the following, first in exponential notation and then as a standard numeral.

$3 \times 3 \times 3 \times 3$ 3^4, 81　　$6 \times 6 \times 6$ 6^3, 216　　$9 \times 9 \times 9 \times 9$ 9^3, 729
$4 \times 4 \times 4 \times 4 \times 4$ 4^5, 1,024　　$8 \times 8 \times 8 \times 8$ 8^4, 4,096

Lesson Focus To round a quotient to a specified place when dividing a decimal by a whole number

Ideas for Getting Started

Use these exercises to prepare students for this lesson. Have them round each number to the nearest tenth and the nearest hundredth.

0.9374	6.084	9.216
17.8449	0.725	0.0666

Have students round each of these amounts to the nearest cent or hundredth of a dollar.

$1.289　　$0.666　　$27.4226　　$0.195

Using Page 118

Motivational Problem After students have read the problem at the top of the page ask, "What data is given in the problem?" (The film has 36 exposures and costs $4.89.) Explain that since we know the total cost of the film and want to find the cost of each exposure, we can divide the cost by the number of exposures.

Lesson Development On the chalkboard, go through the steps shown in the instruction boxes. Show that in order to find the answer to the nearest cent, we must carry out the division to thousandths of a dollar. To do this a zero must be placed in the thousandths place in the dividend. After completing the division, round the 3-place decimal to the nearest hundredth of a dollar or to the nearest cent.

Point out that if multiplication is used as a check, we must be careful to decide what decimal part is the remainder. Since 30 is aligned under the hundredths and thousandths places, it must be interpreted as 0.030. The check can then be made as usual.

```
   $0.135
 ×     36
------------
      810
     405
------------
   $4.860
 + 0.030
------------
   $4.890
```

Other Examples Both examples involve adding zeros to the dividend in order to carry out the division to the required number of decimal places.

Warm Up Check to see that students are adding zeros to the dividends as needed.

Rounding Decimal Quotients

James Tong buys a roll of camera film with 36 exposures for $4.89. What is the cost (to the nearest cent) of each exposure?

To find the cost (to the nearest cent) of each exposure, we divide and round the quotient to the nearest hundredth of a dollar.

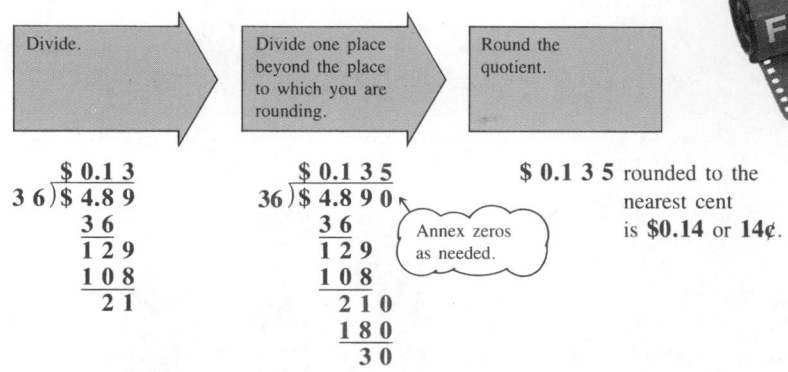

Divide. → Divide one place beyond the place to which you are rounding. → Round the quotient.

```
    $ 0.1 3
36)$ 4.8 9
     3 6
    -----
     1 2 9
     1 0 8
     -----
       2 1
```

```
    $ 0.1 3 5
36)$ 4.8 9 0
     3 6
    -----
     1 2 9
     1 0 8
     -----
       2 1 0
       1 8 0
       -----
         3 0
```
Annex zeros as needed.

$ 0.1 3 5 rounded to the nearest cent is **$0.14** or **14¢**.

Each exposure will cost 14¢.

Other Examples

```
      7.4 4  → 7.4 (nearest tenth)
29)2 1 6.0 0
   2 0 3
   -----
     1 3 0
     1 1 6
     -----
       1 4 0
       1 1 6
       -----
         2 4
```
Divide to the hundredths place.

```
      0.2 1 7 3  → 0.2 1 7 (nearest thousandth)
23)5.0 0 0
   4 6
   -----
     4 0
     2 3
   -----
     1 7 0
     1 6 1
   -----
       9 0
       6 9
   -----
       2 1
```
Divide to the ten-thousandths place.

Warm Up

Find the quotients to the nearest thousandth.

1. 9 ÷ 23　　　　**2.** 43.00 ÷ 17　　　　**3.** 28.6 ÷ 7
　　0.3913 (0.391)　　　　2.5294 (2.529)　　　　4.0857 (4.086)

Find the quotients to the nearest cent.

　　　　$1.971　　　　　　$2.247　　　　　　$1.554
4. 7)$13.80 ($1.97)　**5.** 15)$33.71 ($2.25)　**6.** 34)$52.86 ($1.55)

118

Follow Up

Reteaching

Write the following problems on the chalkboard.

```
  0.666       0.375       0.222
6)4.000     8)3.000     9)2.000
```

Ask students to round the quotients to the nearest tenth and nearest hundredth. Emphasize that if we are rounding to the nearest tenth, we look at the hundredths place, and if rounding to the nearest hundredth, we look at the thousandths place.

Enrichment

Write the following on the chalkboard.

24 ÷ 19	**1.2631578**	**1.3**	**1.26**
51 ÷ 13	**3.9230769**	**3.9**	**3.92**
36 ÷ 7	**5.1428571**	**5.1**	**5.14**
73 ÷ 21	**3.4761904**	**3.5**	**3.48**
67 ÷ 12	**5.5833333**	**5.6**	**5.58**
94 ÷ 19	**4.9473684**	**4.9**	**4.95**
9 ÷ 71	**0.1267605**	**0.1**	**0.13**
7 ÷ 26	**0.2692307**	**0.3**	**0.27**

Have students use calculators to find the quotients. The quotient on the display should be recorded and then rounded to the nearest tenth and nearest hundredth.

Find the quotients to the nearest tenth.

1. $6\overline{)20}$ 3.33 (3.3)   **2.** $9\overline{)14}$ 1.55 (1.6)   **3.** $3\overline{)14}$ 4.66 (4.7)   **4.** $7\overline{)12}$ 1.71 (1.7)

5. $14\overline{)26}$ 1.85 (1.9)   **6.** $12\overline{)75}$ 6.25 (6.3)   **7.** $15\overline{)32}$ 2.13 (2.1)   **8.** $13\overline{)37.2}$ 2.86 (2.9)

9. $23\overline{)62.8}$ 2.73 (2.7)   **10.** $56\overline{)375}$ 6.69 (6.7)   **11.** $42\overline{)74}$ 1.76 (1.8)   **12.** $35\overline{)37}$ 1.05 (1.1)

Find the quotients to the nearest thousandth.

13. $7\overline{)9.2}$ 1.3142 (1.314)   **14.** $3\overline{)7.1}$ 2.3666 (2.367)   **15.** $6\overline{)8}$ 1.3333 (1.333)   **16.** $9\overline{)17}$ 1.8888 (1.889)

17. $12\overline{)4.1}$ 0.3416 (0.342)   **18.** $17\overline{)13}$ 0.7647 (0.765)   **19.** $18\overline{)19.2}$ 1.0666 (1.067)   **20.** $19\overline{)21}$ 1.1052 (1.105)

21. $34\overline{)21.4}$ 0.6294 (0.629)   **22.** $28\overline{)35.4}$ 1.2642 (1.264)   **23.** $47\overline{)26}$ 0.5531 (0.553)   **24.** $52\overline{)38}$ 0.7307 (0.731)

Find the quotients to the nearest cent.

25. $6\overline{)\$24.80}$ \$4.133 (\$4.13)   **26.** $18\overline{)\$15.75}$ \$0.875 (\$0.88)   **27.** $64\overline{)\$172.96}$ \$2.702 (\$2.70)   **28.** $36\overline{)\$53.88}$ \$1.496 (\$1.50)

29. $72\overline{)\$50.00}$ \$0.694 (\$0.69)   **30.** $120\overline{)\$97.75}$ \$0.814 (\$0.81)   **31.** $54\overline{)\$19.63}$ \$0.363 (\$0.36)   **32.** $250\overline{)\$688.76}$ \$2.755 (\$2.76)

33. Film with 24 exposures costs \$3.89. What is the cost (to the nearest cent) of each exposure? \$0.16

34. One dozen rolls of film costs \$42.65. What is the cost (to the nearest cent) of each roll? \$3.55

35. A roll of home movie film costs \$7.10. The roll has a total of 3,240 frames. What is the cost (to the nearest cent) of 10 frames? \$0.02

36. DATA HUNT Find the cost of developing a roll of color print film. What is the cost (to the nearest cent) of each print?

SKILLKEEPER

1. 9.7×10
97

2. 0.35×100
35

3. 12.67×100
1,267

4. 0.004×10
0.04

5. 5.5×100
550

6. 0.056×100
5.6

7. $15.7 \times 1,000$
15,700

8. 0.0009×10
0.009

9. 10.73×10
107.3

10. $0.47 \times 1,000$
470

11. 0.423×0.1
0.0423

12. 123×0.001
0.123

13. 5.98×0.1
0.598

14. 2.3×0.001
0.0023

15. 2.734×0.1
0.2734

16. 593.7×0.01
5.937

17. 12.9×0.001
0.0129

18. 0.062×0.1
0.0062

19. 5.6×0.01
0.056

20. 3.35×0.01
0.0335

More Practice, page 425, Set B   **119**

Using Page 119

Exercises 1–34 You might allow students to use calculators to find the quotients and then round to the specified place on their own. Or you may wish to have them use calculators to check their answers. This will give them additional practice in rounding decimals.

Exercise 35 Calculators could be used for this problem. Two ways of solving the problem are shown below.

$(\$7.10 \div 3,240) \times 10 = \$0.0219135$

$\$7.10 \div (3,240 \div 10) = \$0.0219135$

To the nearest cent, the cost of 10 frames is \$0.02.

Skillkeeper This skill was originally taught in Chapter 4.

More Practice, page 425, Set B

Reteaching Supplement, page 35

Enrichment Supplement, page 35

Practice Supplement, page 45

Quick Review Display the Roman numerals below. Have students give the number for each.

XXIII 23   LIV̆ 54   XVII 17   MMCCV 2,205
CCIX 209   CMI 901   DXX 520   XLIII 43

Lesson Focus To divide a decimal by 10, 100, or 1,000; to solve 1- and 2-step word problems using a variety of operations

Ideas for Getting Started

Write these division equations on the chalkboard.

$$8,000 \div 10 = 800$$
$$8,000 \div 100 = 80$$
$$8,000 \div 1,000 = 8$$

Show that the three quotients could be written as 800.0, 80.00, and 8.000 so that dividing 8,000 by 10, 100, or 1,000 has the effect of moving the decimal point 1, 2, or 3 places to the left.

Using Page 120

Motivational Problem To stimulate interest in the problem at the top of the page, ask students if any among them has participated in a 10-km race. If someone has, ask the approximate time it took to run the race and use that time instead of the time given in the problem.

Read the introductory problem with students and have them identify the question and the data. Explain that our plan is to divide the time for the 10 km race by 10 to get the time for 1 km.

Lesson Development Work through the usual division algorithm. Then show that we could use the shortcut of moving the decimal point 1 place to the left in 56.4 to get the quotient 5.64. Also show the shortcut to divide by 100 and 1,000, shifting the decimal point 2 or 3 places to the left.

Other Examples Work through these examples with the class. Point out that in some exercises zeros must be written in the quotient to place the decimal point correctly.

Exercises 1–10 Students should be able to find the quotients in these exercises mentally.

Dividing Decimals: Mental Math

Lele ran a 10-kilometer race in 56.4 minutes (min). At this rate, how long did it take her to run 1 km?

Since we know the time for 10 km, we divide to find the time for 1 km.

```
        5.6 4
  1 0 )5 6.4 0
        5 0
          6 4
          6 0
            4 0
            4 0
             0
```

It took Lele 5.64 min to run 1 km.

Study the division pattern. Look for a shortcut for dividing a decimal by 10, 100, or 1,000.

$56.4 \div 10 \quad = 5.64$ shift 1 place left
$56.4 \div 100 \quad = 0.564$ shift 2 places left
$56.4 \div 1,000 = 0.0564$ shift 3 places left

Other Examples

$1,950 \div 10 \quad = 195.0$	$32.6 \div 10 \quad = 3.26$	$0.25 \div 10 \quad = 0.025$
$1,950 \div 100 \quad = 19.50$	$32.6 \div 100 \quad = 0.326$	$0.25 \div 100 \quad = 0.0025$
$1,950 \div 1,000 = 1.950$	$32.6 \div 1,000 = 0.0326$	$0.25 \div 1,000 = 0.00025$

Find the quotients mentally. Write only the answers.

Divide each number by 100.

1. 0.7	**2.** 52.95	**3.** 2,372	**4.** 0.045	**5.** 1,875
0.007	0.5295	23.72	0.00045	18.75

Divide each number by 1,000.

6. 31,682	**7.** 5,746	**8.** 397	**9.** 4,280	**10.** 127
31.682	5.746	0.397	4.28	0.127

120

Follow Up

Reteaching

Associate division of decimals by multiples of 10 with multiplication ideas. Have students complete the following. Discuss what happens to the decimal point in each example.

Number	Product
3.6 × 10	36
5.678 × 100	567.8
25.73 × 1,000	25,730

Number	Quotient
3.6 ÷ 10	0.36
5.678 ÷ 100	0.05678
25.73 ÷ 1,000	0.02573

Enrichment

Have students find the missing number in each equation.

1. $\boxed{256} \div 100 = 2.56$
2. $1.9 \times \boxed{1,000} = 1,900$
3. $\boxed{0.35} \div 10 = 0.035$
4. $4.2 \times 100 = \boxed{420}$
5. $\boxed{63.7} \div 1,000 = 0.0637$
6. $57 \div \boxed{100} = 0.57$
7. $0.99 \times 10 = \boxed{9.9}$
8. $\boxed{0.2} \div 100 = 0.002$
9. $0.536 \times \boxed{100} = 53.6$
10. $24 \div 1,000 = \boxed{0.024}$

Assignment Guide			
	Minimum	Average	Extended
page 120	1–10	1–10	1–10
page 121	1–7	1–9	1–10

PROBLEM SOLVING: Practice

QUESTION
DATA
PLAN
ANSWER
CHECK

Solve.

1. Ned can walk 10 km in 95 min. How many minutes will it take him to walk 1 km? 9.5 min

2. The winner of a 10-kilometer roller-skating race had a time of 21.87 min. About how many minutes did it take the winner to skate 1 km? 2.187 min

3. Karen ran 100 m in 13.2 seconds (s). Her time was 1.3 s slower for the second 100 m. What was her total time for running the 200 m? 27.7 s

4. In a 15-kilometer cross-country ski race, one skier skied the first 5 km in 17.4 min. At this rate, how long would it take that person to ski the 15 km? 52.2 min

5. In a 1,000-meter speed-skating race, the winning time was 1 min 19.32 s. How many seconds did it take the winner to skate 1 m? Round your answer to the nearest hundredth of a second. 0.08 s

6. An airplane flew 1,000 km in 62 min. At this rate, how many seconds did it take the airplane to fly 1 km? 3.72 s

7. In a 100-meter butterfly-stroke swimming race, the winning time was 60.56 s. The second place time was 61.03 s. How much slower was the second place time? 0.47 s

8. In a 1,500-meter race, a runner runs the first 1,000 m in 2.9 min. At this rate, how long will it take the runner to run the 1,500 m? 4.35 min

9. A car traveled 100 km in 68 min. How long did it take the car to travel 1 km? How many seconds is this time? 0.68 min; 40.8 s

10. **Try This** May, Carrie, Wilma, and Leslie are the first four finishers in a 10-kilometer run. May ran the race in 43.56 min. Carrie was 1.09 min faster than Leslie. Wilma was 2.35 min slower than Leslie. May was 0.65 min behind Leslie. What was the order of the finish? Hint: Draw a picture. Carrie 1st, Leslie 2nd, May 3rd, Wilma 4th

121

Using Page 121

Exercises 1–9 Problem 9 has two questions. Make certain students answer both of them. Be alert to the fact that students may use different methods to solve some problems. For example, in exercise 8 a student might reason that the 1,500-m race is 1.5 times as long as 1,000 m because $1,500 \div 1,000 = 1.5$. Multiplying 1.5×2.9 min gives the answer of 4.35 min.

Another way to solve the problem is to think 2.9 min for 1,000 m. There are 500 m left so it will take 2.9 min ÷ 2 for the rest of the race.

$$2.9 \text{ min} \div 2 = 1.45 \text{ min}$$
$$2.9 \text{ min} + 1.45 \text{ min} = 4.35 \text{ min}$$

Try This A possible strategy, Draw a Picture, was taught on page 108.

Discussion "What does order of finish mean?" (who came in first, second, third, and fourth) Ask students to list the data for the problem.

Call attention to the hint we are given. Have students explain how to draw the picture to show the relationship between the numbers given in the problem.

Solution

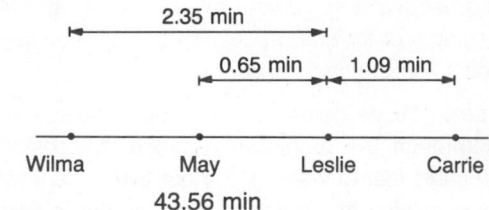

Carrie was first, Leslie was second, May was third, and Wilma was fourth.

Reteaching Supplement, page 36

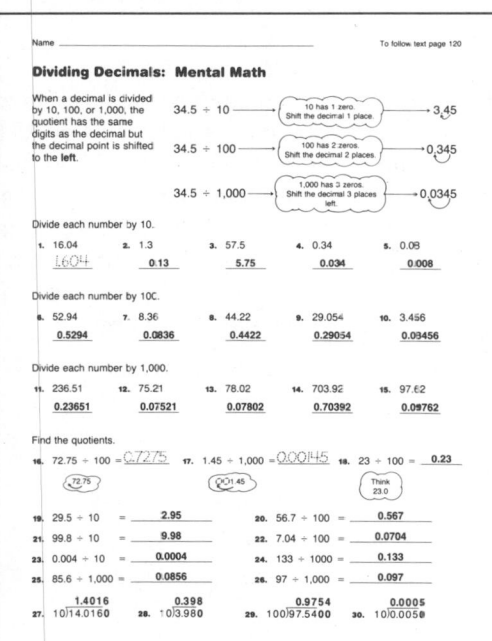

Enrichment Supplement, page 36

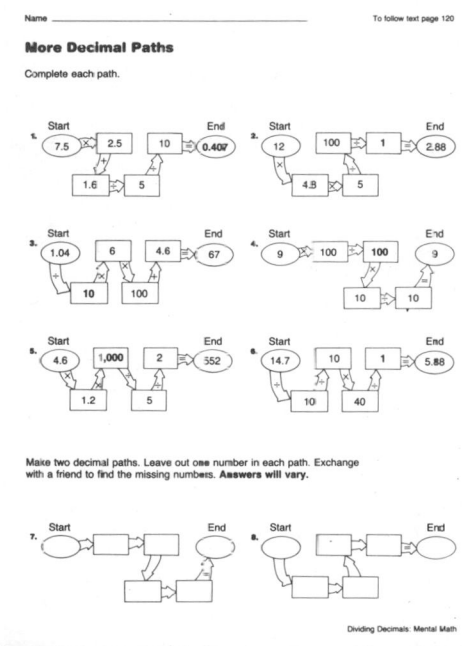

Practice Supplement, page 46

Quick Review Display the numbers below. Randomly point to combinations of any two numbers as factors and have students tell how many decimal places should be in each product.

0.346   0.92   42.617   0.0013   74   8.26   9.7138   1.0001

Lesson Focus To solve word problems using data from a table

Ideas for Getting Started

The table used in this lesson gives the water rate per 100 cubic feet. To prepare students for the lesson, review dividing numbers by 10, 100, and 1,000 with emphasis on dividing by 100. Write the following numbers on the chalkboard or overhead projector. Have students divide each number by 100.

850   2,700   37,500   90,000

6,570   140,000   200,000   319,000

Using Page 122

Motivational Problem Discuss the rate table at the top of the page. "What is the rate or cost per 100 cubic feet for 2,500 cubic feet of water?" ($0.365) Repeat this question with different amounts of water. Have students read the problem and restate the question in their own words. Then ask, "What data is given in the problem? (The Jessel family used 6,400 cubic feet of water.) "What data is needed to solve the problem?" (the rate per 100 cubic feet for 6,400 cubic feet of water) Have students use the chart to find the rate.

Lesson Development On the chalkboard, work through the problem of finding the cost of 6,400 cubic feet of water. Point out there are three steps in solving this problem. First, students must decide which rate applies. Second, find the number of hundreds of cubic feet. Third, multiply the hundreds of cubic feet by the appropriate rate.

Exercises 1—4 Work through these problems as a class activity. Have students compare the costs of the amounts of water in the exercises.

PROBLEM SOLVING: Using Data from a Table

| QUESTION |
| DATA |
| PLAN |
| ANSWER |
| CHECK |

To encourage people to conserve water, the Sunnyside City Council approved new water rates.

The more water a customer uses, the higher the water rate is.

During the month of May, the Jessel family used 6,400 cubic feet (ft³) of water. What is the cost of this amount of water?

Sunnyside Water Rates

Cubic feet (ft³) of water	Rate per 100 ft³
0–600	$0.300
601–2,000	0.350
2,001–5,000	0.365
5,001–50,000	0.375
50,001–125,000	0.385
125,001–250,000	0.395
250,001 and above	0.405

To solve the problem, you must use several steps.

Find the correct rate from the table.	6,400 falls between 5,001 and 50,000. The rate for this amount is $0.375 per 100 ft³.
Find the number of hundreds of cubic feet of water used.	6,400 ÷ 100 = 64
Multiply this amount by the rate.	64 × $0.375 = $24.00

The cost of the water is $24.00.

Use the rate table to find the cost of each amount of water. Round to the nearest cent.

1. 500 ft³ $1.50

2. 1,500 ft³ $5.25

3. 3,750 ft³ $13.69

4. 63,880 ft³ $245.94

122

Follow Up

Reteaching

Focus on solving problems that involve multiplying and dividing by multiples of 10. Generate data from sources such as food sold in 100 pound bags and football fields being 100 yards long.

Ask questions involving both multiplication and division.

Enrichment

Tell students that three cars get the following mileage (mi per gal): Car A, 15 mpg; Car B, 30 mpg; Car C, 40 mpg. Using the mileage chart in a road atlas, have students find the number of gallons of gasoline, to the nearest tenth, needed for each trip. Answers may vary depending on the source used.

1. Car A, Boston to Chicago
   1,034 mi., 68.9 gal.

2. Car B, San Francisco to Detroit
   2,546 mi., 84.9 gal.

3. Car C, Atlanta to New York
   876 mi., 21.9 gal.

Use the water rate table on page 122 to solve these problems. Round your answers to the nearest cent when necessary.

1. The Ahmeds used 4,950 ft³ of water one month. What is the cost of this amount of water? $18.07

2. Mrs. Wagner used only 780 ft³ of water in a month. What was her water bill for the month? $2.73

3. The Custom Manufacturing Company uses water to make its products. During the month of June, the company used 329,000 ft³ of water. What was the cost of this amount of water? $1,332.45

4. The Cardillas used 4,560 ft³ of water in July. During August, they watered the lawn and garden heavily and used 7,380 ft³. How much more was their water bill in August than in July? $11.04

5. The Chesters used 2,100 ft³ of water in May, 3,200 ft³ in June, and 4,800 ft³ in July. What rate did they pay for the water each month? What is the total number of cubic feet used? $0.365 per 100 ft³; 10,100 ft³

6. What was the Chester's total water bill for the months of May, June, and July? (See problem 5.) $36.87

7. The Rockwell household paid a total of $306.00 for water in one year. What was the cost of water per month? $25.50

8. The Morgans were averaging 7,600 ft³ of water use per month. They started being more careful and cut their use of water by 0.35 of this amount. How much water did they now use a month? What was the cost of this amount of water? 4,940 ft³; $18.03

9. The Universal Company was using 450,000 ft³ of water per month. By using conservation methods, they reduced the amount of water used per month to 375,000 ft³. How much money did the company save on water per month? $303.75

10. **Try This** Kelly MacGregor paid $6.30 for water for one month. What amount of water did she use during the month? Hint: Use the rate table to guess and check. 1,800 ft³

123

Using Page 123

Exercises 1–9 You may wish to allow students to use calculators to solve these problems.

Try This A possible strategy, Guess and Check, was taught on page 24.

Discussion "What does the problem ask you to find?" (the amount of water Kelly MacGregor used during one month) "What data is given in the problem?" (she paid $6.30) "Where is additional data found?" (in the table on page 122) Explain that we do not know the amount of water used, but we can guess and then use the rate table to check our guess. "What would be a good first guess?"

Solution   Guess: 1,800 cubic feet
          Check: 1,800 ÷ 100 = 18
                 18 × $0.35 = $6.30
Kelly MacGregor used 1,800 cubic feet of water.

Ideas That Work

Calculator Bonus

Display the following on the chalkboard.

$$\frac{10^1 - 7}{3} = 1$$

$$\frac{10^2 - 7}{3} = 31$$

$$\frac{10^3 - 7}{3} = 331$$

$$\frac{10^4 - 7}{3} = 3,331$$

Ask students to find the quotients. Then have them extend this pattern.

$$\frac{10^5 - 7}{3} = 33,331$$

$$\frac{10^6 - 7}{3} = 333,331$$

$$\frac{10^7 - 7}{3} = 3,333,331$$

Practice Supplement page 47

Name _____   To follow text page 123

Problem Solving: Using Data from a Table

Sunnyside Water Rates

Units of water	Rate per 100 units
0-600	$0.300
601-2,000	0.350
2,001-5,000	0.365
5,001-50,000	0.375
50,001-125,000	0.385
125,001-250,000	0.395
250,001 and above	0.405

Use the water-rate table to solve each problem. Round your answers to the nearest cent when necessary.

1. Find the cost of 700 units of water. $2.45

2. Find the cost of 25,000 units of water. $93.75

3. Find the cost of 80,250 units of water. $308.96

4. Find the cost of 215,500 units of water. $851.23

5. Find the cost of 265,375 units of water. $1,074.77

6. The Franklins used 5,250 units of water one month. What was the cost of their water? $19.69

7. The Lius used 2,640 units of water in a month. What was their water bill that month? $9.64

8. The Marques family used 3,720 units of water in April and 5,380 units in May. How much more was their water bill in May? $6.60

9. The Howes were averaging 8,400 units of water use per month. By conserving, they cut their use by 0.25 of this amount. How much water did they now use a month?   6,300 units
What was the cost of the water? $23.63

10. The National Company was using 600,000 units of water per month. By conserving, they reduced the amount of water used to 470,000 units per month. How many fewer units were they using?   130,000 units
How much money did the company save on water per month? $526.50

Quick Review Have students identify what power of ten they would have to multiply each number by to make it a whole number.

| 3.6 **10** | 46.2 **10** | 6.931 **1,000** | 0.97 **100** | 0.0001 **10,000** |
| 897.78 **100** | 5.375 **1,000** | 0.070 **1,000** | 67.9 **10** | 43.88 **100** |

Lesson Focus To divide a decimal by a decimal

Ideas for Getting Started

Write these problems on the chalkboard.

2)8   20)80   200)800   2,000)8,000

Have students find that each problem has a quotient of 4. Point out that the divisor and dividend in each problem were multiplied by the same number, namely 10, 100, or 1,000. This multiplication did not change the quotient.

Using Page 124

Motivational Problem After students read the problem at the top of the page, ask them to restate the question in their own words. Then ask, "In order to find the number of servings in 6 L of punch, what data is needed?" (the size of each serving) "What data is given?" (the serving cups hold 0.25 L) Explain that our plan is to divide. "Do we want to find how many 6s are in 0.25 or how many times 0.25 is contained in 6?" (how many times 0.25 is in 6)

Lesson Development Show the steps for dividing 0.25)6. Stress the fact that students have already learned how to divide when the divisor is a whole number. We can change the divisor of 0.25 to 25 by multiplying by 100. If the dividend is also multiplied by 100, the quotient will not change. On the chalkboard, complete the division process to find the quotient of 24.

Tell students to use the original divisor and dividend in checking the problem. By doing this, errors in shifting the decimal point in either divisor or dividend will be detected.

Other Examples Work through the examples with students. These exercises also involve rounding the quotient to a given place.

Warm Up Remind students that they may need to annex zeros in the dividend. Check to make sure they divide one place beyond the place to which they are rounding.

Dividing by a Decimal

Paper cups that will hold 0.25 liters (L) of liquid will be used for a club party. How many servings this size are there in 6 L of fruit punch?

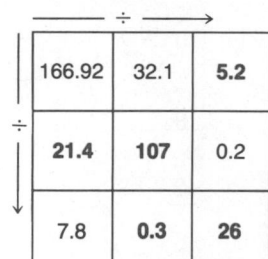

Since each serving will be the same amount, we divide the total amount of punch by the amount in one serving.

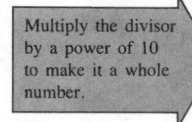

| Multiply the divisor by a power of 10 to make it a whole number. | Multiply the dividend by the same power of 10. | Divide. |

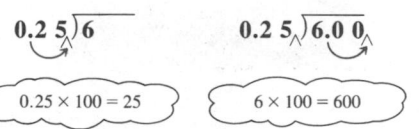

0.2 5)6

$0.25 \times 100 = 25$

0.2 5)6.0 0

$6 \times 100 = 600$

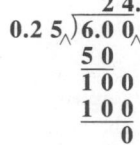

```
      2 4.        Check:     24
0.2 5)6.0 0               × 0.25
      5 0                   120
      1 0 0                  48
      1 0 0                 6.00
          0
```

There are 24 servings of fruit punch.

Other Examples

```
       2.8 5  →  2.9 (nearest tenth)
0.7)2.0 0 0
    1 4
      6 0
      5 6
        4 0
        3 5
          5
```

Multiply divisor and dividend by 10.

```
         0.0 3 7  →  0.0 4 (nearest hundredth)
4.8)0.1 7 8 0
    1 4 4
      3 4 0
      3 3 6
          4
```

Multiply divisor and dividend by 10.

Warm Up

Find the quotients to the nearest tenth.

1. 3.8)53.7   (14.1)   [14.13]
2. 0.42)1.848   [4.4]
3. 0.039)0.814 (20.9)   [20.87]

Find the quotients to the nearest hundredth.

4. 0.47)1.92 (4.09)   [4.085]
5. 7.6)913 (120.13)   [120.131]
6. 0.082)0.1487 (1.81) [1.813]

124

Follow Up

Reteaching

Provide students with the following exercises. Include the correct digits in each quotient. Have students complete the exercise by placing the decimal point in the quotient.

1. 5)17.35   [3.47]
2. 0.8)2.7 2   [3.4]
3. 5.4)3 3.6 4 2   [6.2 3]
4. 2.41)154.24   [64.]
5. 0.71)2.4 8 5   [3.5]
6. 28)181.44   [6.48]
7. 6.2)148.8   [24.]
8. 3.02)70.66 8   [23.40]

Enrichment

Display the following on the chalkboard. Have students complete the division and fill in the empty boxes.

÷ →		
166.92	32.1	**5.2**
21.4	**107**	0.2
7.8	**0.3**	**26**

(÷ down arrow on left side)

Challenge students to make up puzzles of their own to share with other members of the class. Multiplication as well as division can be used.

Assignment Guide			
	Minimum	Average	Extended
page 125	1–33, SK	1–34, SK	1–33 odd, 34, 35, SK

Find the quotients to the nearest tenth.

1. 0.6)1.7 — 2.83 (2.8)
2. 0.9)7 — 7.77 (7.8)
3. 0.4)1.9 — 4.75 (4.8)
4. 0.7)1.35 — 1.92 (1.9)
5. 3.6)23.74 — 6.59 (6.6)
6. 1.6)130 — 81.25 (81.3)
7. 0.82)2.795 — 3.40 (3.4)
8. 1.5)50 — 33.33 (33.3)
9. 2.8)130 — 46.42 (46.4)
10. 0.75)3.882 — 5.17 (5.2)
11. 0.94)1.875 — 1.99 (2.0)
12. 6.9)123.4 — 17.88 (17.9)

Find the quotients to the nearest hundredth.

13. 6.1)32.46 — 5.321 (5.32)
14. 6.8)0.75 — 0.110 (0.11)
15. 7.3)38.42 — 5.263 (5.26)
16. 0.54)2.793 — 5.172 (5.17)
17. 0.048)0.702 — 14.625 (14.63)
18. 9.8)103.6 — 10.571 (10.57)
19. 0.17)0.132 — 0.776 (0.78)
20. 0.9)7 — 7.777 (7.78)
21. 2.6)5.84 — 2.246 2.25
22. 0.59)0.3954 — 0.670 (0.67)
23. 7.2)26.48 — 3.677 (3.68)
24. 0.11)0.4184 — 3.803 (3.80)

Find the quotients to the nearest thousandth.

25. 0.36)5 — 13.8888 (13.889)
26. 4.5)8.924 — 1.9831 (1.983)
27. 8.1)580 — 71.6049 (71.605)
28. 0.9)1.4 — 1.5555 (1.556)
29. 0.67)0.384 — 0.5731 (0.573)
30. 0.052)0.159 — 3.0576 (3.058)
31. 2.8)120 — 42.8571 (42.857)
32. 1.6)0.9284 — 0.5802 (0.580)

33. How many 0.27-liter servings are there in 3.78 L of milk? 14

34. How much money would be earned by selling 7.5 L of apple juice if each serving of 0.3 L costs 25¢? $6.25

35. Which division problem at the right has a quotient different from the others? Try to decide without dividing. Then check your answer.

A 0.68)17.68 — 26
B 6.8)176.8 — 26
C 0.068)1.768 — 26
D 68)0.1768 — 0.0026

Using Page 125

Exercises 1–33 Students should be able to work the exercises on this page without additional instruction. However, you should observe closely any students who may have difficulty.

Exercise 34 This is a 2-step problem. First, divide 7.5 L by 0.3 L to find the number of servings.

$$7.5 \text{ L} \div 0.3 \text{ L} = 25$$

Then multiply the number of servings by $0.25.

$$25 \times \$0.25 = \$6.25$$

Exercise 35 The concept developed in this lesson can be used to solve exercise 35. If the divisor and dividend of a division problem are each multiplied by the same power of ten to make the divisor a whole number, the quotient is not changed. In problems A, B, and C, if the divisor is changed to 68, the dividend is changed to 1,768. Hence the quotients are the same for these problems. But in problem D, the divisor is already 68 and the dividend is not 1,768. Therefore, the quotient in this problem will be different.

Skillkeeper This Skillkeeper reviews material taught in this Chapter.

SKILLKEEPER

1. 0.09 ÷ 10
0.009
2. 56,600 ÷ 1,000
56.60
3. 29.62 ÷ 100
0.2962
4. 576.3 ÷ 10
57.63
5. 2.65 ÷ 100
0.0265
6. 0.596 ÷ 10
0.0596
7. 634.22 ÷ 100
6.3422
8. 9,270 ÷ 1,000
9.27
9. 7,954 ÷ 1,000
7.954
10. 0.6 ÷ 100
0.006
11. 93.54 ÷ 10
9.354
12. 256 ÷ 100
2.56

More Practice, page 425, Set C

More Practice, page 425, Set C

Reteaching Supplement, page 37

Enrichment Supplement, page 37

Practice Supplement, page 48

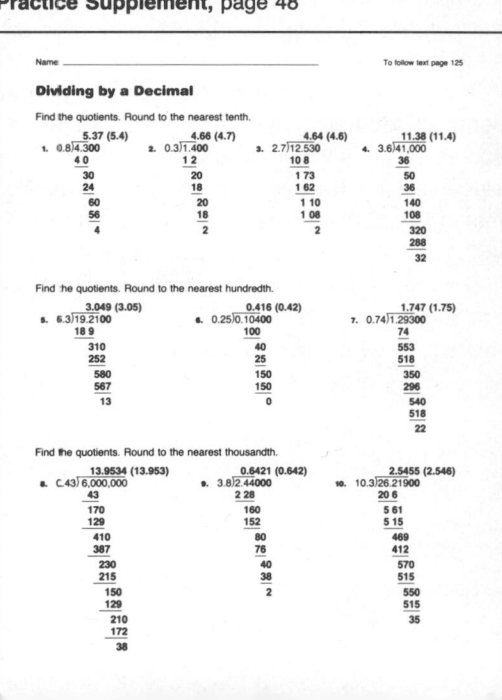

Quick Review Read each of the following and have students supply the missing operation sign.

$2 \underline{\times} 3 = 6$ $18 \underline{-} 9 = 9$ $6 \underline{+} 7 = 13$ $5 \underline{\times} 5 = 25$ $32 \underline{\div} 4 = 8$

$72 \underline{\div} 9 = 82$ $11 \underline{-} 2 = 9$ $5 \underline{+} 4 = 9$ $7 \underline{\times} 2 = 14$ $3 \underline{\times} 3 = 9$

Lesson Focus To solve word problems involving averages or arithmetic means

Ideas for Getting Started

Most students will be familiar with the concept of the average of a list of numbers, but a review of this idea will be helpful. Write these numbers on the chalkboard.

2   10   9   9   12   6

Have students find the sum of the 6 numbers. Then ask, "What single number could replace each of the 6 numbers and give the same sum?" (8) Help students to see that this number is easily found by dividing the sum by 6 since 6 numbers were added. Show the results with a diagram like the one below.

$2 + 10 + 9 + 9 + 12 + 6 = 48$

$48 \div 6 = 8$

$8 + 8 + 8 + 8 + 8 + 8 = 48$

We say that 8 is the average or arithmetic mean of 2, 10, 9, 9, 12 and 6.

Using Page 126

Motivational Problem Have students tell what the introductory problem asks us to find. Discuss the meaning of *average* daily attendance. Explain that we will use data from the table at the top of the page to solve the problem.

Lesson Development On the chalkboard, work through finding the average daily attendance. Stress that there are two steps in finding the average of a list of numbers. First we find the sum of the numbers, and then we divide by how many numbers in the list. Call attention to the quotient and point out that statistics sometimes give information about decimal parts of people! Discuss the fact that it is reasonable to round the average to the nearest whole number since we are reporting the average number of students attending school each day.

The second example problem on the page presents an interesting application of averages to test scores. After working through this example with students ask if Katy could score enough on the fifth test to have an average of 92. Show that $5 \times 92 = 460$, so Katy would have to score $460 - 351$ or 109 on the fifth test. Explain that since test scores are usually based on 100 points or 100 percent, an average of 92 cannot be attained.

PROBLEM SOLVING: Finding Averages

| QUESTION |
| DATA |
| PLAN |
| ANSWER |
| CHECK |

What is the average daily attendance at Jefferson School?

Jefferson School Daily Attendance Form	
Day	Attendance
Monday	372
Tuesday	384
Wednesday	378
Thursday	390
Friday	388

The **average** of a list of numbers is the sum of the numbers divided by how many numbers there are in the list.

$$
\begin{array}{r}
372 \\
384 \\
378 \\
390 \\
+388 \\
\hline
1,912
\end{array}
$$
← total attendance

$$
\begin{array}{r}
382.4 \\
5\overline{)1,912.0} \\
\end{array}
$$
← average daily attendance

The average daily attendance was 382.4, or about 382 students per day.

What score must Katy make on the fifth test in order to raise her test score average to 90?

Katy's scores must total 450 to average 90 on the five tests ($5 \times 90 = 450$). The total for the first four tests is 351. Therefore, Katy must score 99 ($450 - 351$) on the fifth test.

Katy's Test Scores	
Test	Score
1	84
2	92
3	86
4	89
5	?

Solve.

1. The daily attendance for one week at Creekside School was 273, 252, 269, 271, and 265. What was the average daily attendance? 266

126

2. Reggie's weekly math test scores for one month were 85, 82, 90, and 67. What was his average score for the month? 81

Follow Up

Reteaching

Pose questions to students to develop the concept of average. For example, ask "What is an average person?" Elicit from students the idea that average means typical or representative.

Have students find the average of each list of numbers given below.

1. 7, 4, 3, 6 **5**
2. 23, 19, 17, 21, 20 **20**
3. 9.2, 6.3, 2.5 **6.0**
4. 0.9, 0.7, 1.2, 3.0 **1.45**
5. 12.7, 21.3, 15.2, 16.8, 15.5 **16.3**

Enrichment

Have students collect data about their favorite basketball teams. Then have them use the data to answer questions like the following.

1. What is the average height of the players on the team?
2. How many points did one player average during five games?
3. What was the team's average score for three games?

Display the data and results on a bulletin board.

Assignment Guide			
	Minimum	Average	Extended
page 126–127	1–7	1–7, 10, 11	4–11

3. What is the average price of soap powder? **91¢**

4. Find the average height to the nearest whole inch (in.). **61 in.**

Name	Height (in.)
Carla	60
Charlie	58
Ross	64
Laverne	63
Mark	62
Jose	60
Ken	59

5. Find the average gasoline price to the nearest tenth of a cent. **138.2¢**

Station	Price per Gallon
A	140.9¢
B	139.9¢
C	138.0¢
D	136.7¢
E	135.4¢

6. Find the test score averages to the nearest whole number. Who has the higher average? **Leona**

Name	Test Scores				Average	
Leona K.	78	87	84	90	▦	85
Pete R.	80	80	85	86	▦	83

7. Find the average weight to the nearest pound (lb). **105 lb**

Name	Weight (lb)
Michel	115
Nancy	94
Polly	120
Matt	98
Bev	95
Dave	109
Kathy	101

8. Raoul had scores of 93, 88, and 92 on his first three tests. What is his average test score? **91**

9. Raoul is going to take a fourth test. What is the lowest score he could make on the fourth test and have an average of 90? (Use the data in problem 8.) **87**

10. DATA HUNT Find the height of eight of your classmates. What is the average height?

11. Try This

Lennie: "What were your last two test scores?"

Minnie: "I raised my test score on the last test by 12. That made a total of 170 for the two tests."

What was Minnie's score on each test? **79, 91**

127

Using Page 127

Exercise 9 To average 90 on four tests, Raoul would have to score a total of 4 × 90 = 360. The total for the first three scores is 272, so he must make 360 − 273, or 87 on the fourth test.

Data Hunt This problem could be extended so that the average height for all students in the class is found. Have students write the name of the person or persons they think are nearest to the average height before finding the average. Calculators could be used for this problem.

Try This A possible strategy, Guess and Check, was taught on page 24.

Discussion "What are we asked to find in this problem?" (Minnie's scores on the two tests) "What facts are given in the problem?" (she scored 12 more on the second test, the total for the two tests is 170) "What strategy could be used on the problem?" (Guess and Check)

Solution

Guess: First test (79)   Second test (91)

Check: 79 + 91 = 170

The test scores were 79 and 91.

Reteaching Supplement, page 38

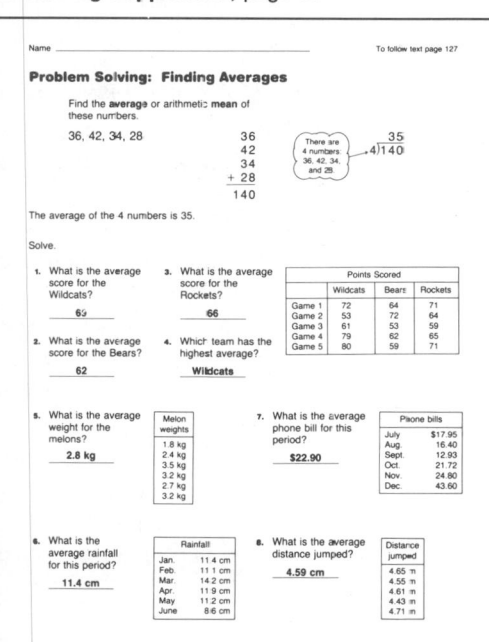

Enrichment Supplement, page 38

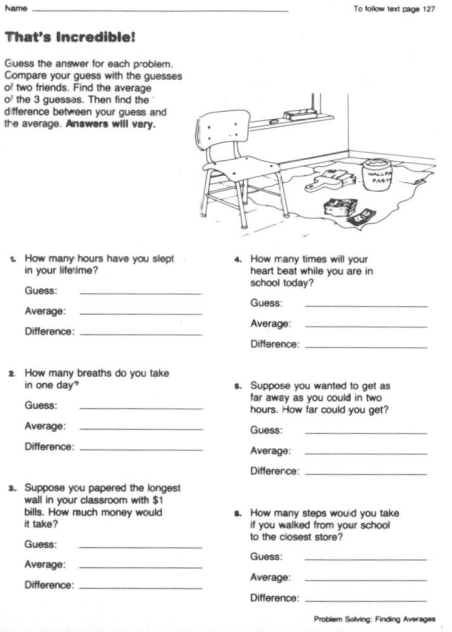

Practice Supplement, page 49

Decimals

Quick Review Display the exercises below. Have students estimate the products.

4.86 × 7.8 **40**	0.76 × 5.2 **4.0**	31.4 × 0.062 **1.80**
29.7 × 9.2 **270**	48 × 8.1 **400**	7.3 × 65.2 **490**

Lesson Focus To practice dividing decimals; to estimate a quotient when dividing a decimal by a decimal

Ideas for Getting Started

To review placing decimal points in quotients, have the students work these exercises.

8)0.4	0.8)0.4	80)4	8)0.4
6)3.0	0.6)30	0.6)0.3	60)3.0

Using Page 128

Exercises 1–40 Assign these problems as needed for strengthening skills in dividing decimals. As students do the problems, watch closely for those having difficulty. Work with these students individually or in small groups to diagnose and remediate errors. (See Teaching Tips on p. 114 B for a discussion of error patterns in division of decimals.)

Skills Practice

Find the quotients to the nearest tenth.

1.   36.77 / 0.9)33.1 (36.8)
2.   13.33 / 0.6)8 (13.3)
3.   5.6 / 0.5)2.8
4.   1.43 / 0.3)0.43 (1.4)

5.   25.29 / 3.3)83.46 (25.3)
6.   1.3 / 0.97)1.261
7.   13.28 / 6.4)85.03 (13.3)
8.   0.629 / 7.3)4.594 (0.63)

9.   3.51 (3.5) / 0.28)0.9832
10.   12.90 (12.9) / 3.11)40.126
11.   63.14 (63.1) / 1.01)63.781
12.   0.011 / 4.51)0.0532 (0.01)

13.   12.46 (12.5) / 6.43)80.137
14.   840.79 (840.8) / 1.03)866.02
15.   198.83 (198.8) / 0.055)10.936
16.   0.09 / 0.247)0.0226 (0.1)

Find the quotients to the nearest hundredth.

17.   438.265 (438.27) / 0.2)87.653
18.   0.491 (0.49) / 6.7)3.2951
19.   82.732 (82.73) / 8.1)670.13
20.   37.855 / 0.01)0.37855 (37.86)

21.   15.580 (15.58) / 0.056)0.8725
22.   0.006 (0.01) / 39.1)0.2643
23.   0.020 (0.02) / 4.55)0.0952
24.   0.337 / 86.1)29.031 (0.34)

25. $73.981 ($73.98) / 1.6)$118.37
26. $8.609 ($8.61) / 3.2)$27.55
27. $1.703 ($1.70) / 64.1)$109.20
28. $4.854 / 55.3)$268.43 ($4.85)

29. $28.862 ($28.86) / 15.8)$456.02
30. $3.134 ($3.13) / 3.72)$11.66
31. $94.111 ($94.11) / 0.09)$8.47
32. $1.351 / 43.5)$58.78 ($1.35)

Find the quotients to the nearest thousandth.

33.   0.0156 (0.016) / 2.48)0.0389
34.   1.0791 (1.079) / 0.091)0.0982
35.   0.0834 (0.083) / 65.3)5.451
36.   31.7673 / 1.01)32.085 (31.767)

37. 82 ÷ 0.815 / 100.6134 (100.613)
38. 11.01 ÷ 3.06 / 3.5980 (3.598)
39. 37 ÷ 22.9 / 1.6157 (1.616)
40. 0.042 ÷ 65.1 / 0.0006 (0.001)

41. 0.001 ÷ 0.093 / 0.0107 (0.011)
42. 8.6921 ÷ 47.3 / 0.1837 (0.184)
43. 0.1825 ÷ 0.071 / 2.5704 (2.570)
44. 0.6 ÷ 63.72 / 0.0094 (0.009)

45. 0.55 ÷ 33.49 / 0.0164 (0.016)
46. 8.6392 ÷ 0.092 / 93.9043 (93.904)
47. 4.71 ÷ 0.4713 / 9.9936 (9.994)
48. 0.009 ÷ 3.9 / 0.0023 (0.002)

Follow Up

Reteaching

Discuss each step in estimating the quotient by using an example. Ask students to rewrite the problem after rounding the divisor and dividend to 1-digit accuracy. Next, have students think of multiplying the divisor and dividend by the same multiple of 10. Then ask them to place the decimal point and estimate the first digit in the quotient.

0.57)3.296   0.6)3.0

5.
0.6)3.0   0.6)3.0

Enrichment

Have students solve these problems.

1. Joanna bought 41.5 L of gasoline at 36¢ a liter. Estimate the cost of the gasoline. **$16.00**

2. Abe ran 1,500 m in 4.66 min. Estimate the number of meters per minute that he ran. **300 m/min**

3. Bananas cost 89¢ per kilogram. About how many kilograms of bananas can be bought for $5.00? **5 kg**

4. Crystal had $50.00. She bought items that cost $14.98, $6.50, $8.87, and $3.19. Estimate the amount of money she had after paying for the items. **$16**

Assignment Guide			
	Minimum	Average	Extended
page 128	1–32	1–40	1–47 odd
page 129	1–9, 13	1–13	1–13 odd, 14

Estimating Quotients with Decimals

It takes 21.9 L of purified water to fill Helen's aquarium. The water costs $3.69. What is the estimated cost of 1 L of water?

To find the estimated cost of 1 L, we round each number to 1-digit accuracy and divide the cost by the number of liters.

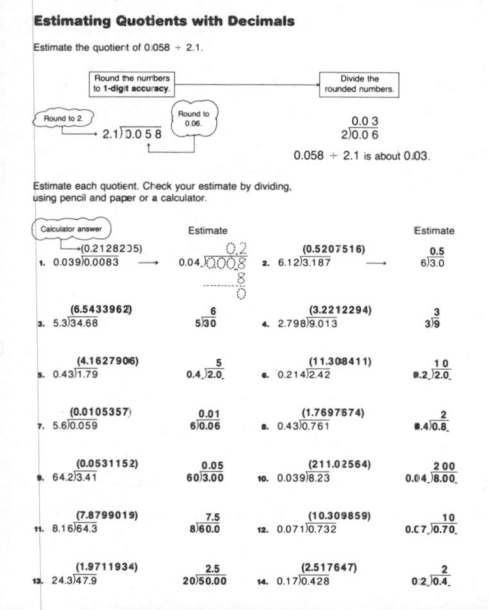

Problem	Estimate
$21.9\overline{)\$3.69}$	$\overset{\$0.20}{20\overline{)\$4.00}}$

The estimated cost of the water is $0.20 per liter.

Other Examples

Problem	Estimate	Problem	Estimate
$0.838\overline{)2.755} \rightarrow 0.8\overline{)3.0}^{\ 3.}$		$4.12\overline{)0.866} \rightarrow 4\overline{)0.9}^{\ 0.2}$	

Estimate each quotient.

1. $3.56\overline{)16.86}^{\ 5}$

2. $0.818\overline{)1.731}^{\ 2}$

3. $6.8\overline{)0.5214}^{\ 0.07}$

4. $0.077\overline{)0.1913}^{\ 2}$

5. $37.4\overline{)5.817}^{\ 0.1}$

6. $9.93\overline{)68.09}^{\ 7}$

7. $0.188\overline{)4.26}^{\ 20}$

8. $28.144\overline{)609.85}^{\ 20}$

9. $0.54\overline{)10.37}^{\ 20}$

10. $6.5\overline{)0.1954}^{\ 0.03}$

11. $0.68\overline{)0.2546}^{\ 0.4}$

12. $0.032\overline{)9.1}^{\ 300}$

13. Robert filled his aquarium with 38.6 L of purified water. He paid $7.56 for the water. Estimate the cost of 1 L of water. What was the actual cost per liter? $0.20; $0.195

14. Mary bought 21.0 L of water and a filter for her aquarium. The total cost was $12.25. The filter cost $1.95. Estimate the cost of the water per liter. Find the actual cost. $0.50; $0.490

More Practice, page 425, Set D

Using Page 129

Motivational Problem Have students read the problem at the top of the page. Ask them to restate the question and tell what data is needed to solve the problem.

Lesson Development Discuss each step in finding the estimated cost of 1 L of water. Show how to round the numbers to 1-digit accuracy and estimate the first non-zero digit in the quotient.

Other Examples Work through the other examples with students. Point out that after the numbers are rounded in the first example, we must shift the decimal points in the divisor and dividend in order to make the estimate.

Exercises 1–12 If necessary, students can write the division problems with the rounded numbers before they make their estimates.

Exercises 13–14 These problems ask for both an estimate and the exact quotient. Make certain both answers are given.

More Practice, page 425, Set D

Reteaching Supplement, page 39

Estimating Quotients with Decimals

Estimate the quotient of 0.058 ÷ 2.1.

Enrichment Supplement, page 39

Which One Is Reasonable?

Practice Supplement, page 50

Estimating Quotients with Decimals

Lesson Focus
To work backward as a strategy for solving nonroutine word problems

Ideas for Getting Started

Play the game of "Find My Number" with students. Give these problems:

"If you add 25 to my number you get 42. Find my number." (17)

"If you multiply my number by 7 you get 91. Find my number." (13)

"If you divide my number by 6 you get 12. Find my number." (72)

"If you subtract 9 from my number you get 19. Find my number." (28)

Help students understand that in each case, we can do the opposite or inverse operation to find the number.

Extend the game to 2 operations, but keep the numbers small and the game moving rapidly.

"If you add 2 to my number and multiply by 2, you get 10. Find my number." (3)

"If you divide my number by 5 and add 1, you get 3. Find my number." (10)

Explain that these problems can be solved by thinking about the operations in the reverse order and using the opposite operation.

Using Page 130

Motivational Problem Have students read the Try This problem. "What does the question ask us to find?" (the year the girl was born) Ask students for the data in the problem. Explain that when we start with an unknown number, perform several operations, and know the result, the unknown number can be found by working backward. Have a volunteer add the strategy, Work Backward, to the problem-solving bulletin board display.

Lesson Development On the chalkboard, draw the diagram showing the order of operations in the statement of the problem. Explain that by taking the opposite of what the diagram shows starting with 59, we can get back to the starting number or birth year. Write out the second flow chart on the chalkboard and compute the birth year according to the steps shown in the chart.

Exercises 1–2 Have students work these problems on their own. The solutions are shown below.
Exercise 1:

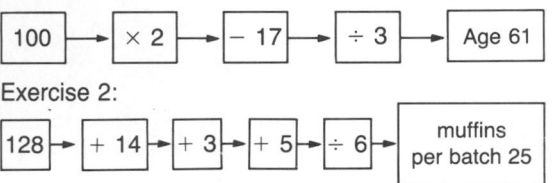
100 → × 2 → − 17 → ÷ 3 → Age 61

Exercise 2:

128 → + 14 → + 3 → + 5 → ÷ 6 → muffins per batch 25

PROBLEM SOLVING: Work Backward

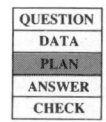

| QUESTION |
| DATA |
| **PLAN** |
| ANSWER |
| CHECK |

Try This

A girl in Colonial Williamsburg said, "I divided the number for my birth year by 2, subtracted 365, and divided that answer by 9. The result was 59. In what year was I born?"

Some problems start with an unknown number. Several operations are performed, and you are told the final result. To find the starting number you can use the strategy called **Work Backward**. Here is a way to use this strategy to solve the problem above.

Show the steps of the problem in the order given.

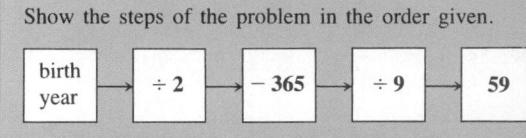
birth year → ÷ 2 → − 365 → ÷ 9 → 59

Work backward by using the numbers in opposite order and use opposite or **inverse** operations.

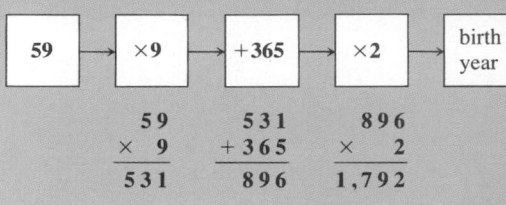
59 → ×9 → +365 → ×2 → birth year

$$\begin{array}{r} 59 \\ \times\ 9 \\ \hline 531 \end{array} \qquad \begin{array}{r} 531 \\ +365 \\ \hline 896 \end{array} \qquad \begin{array}{r} 896 \\ \times\ \ 2 \\ \hline 1{,}792 \end{array}$$

The girl was born in 1792.

Solve.

1. Ted's grandfather said, "If you multiply my age by 3, then add 17 to that answer, then divide by 2 you will get exactly 100." How old is Ted's grandfather? 61

2. Mavis Dean baked 6 batches of corn muffins. She gave 5 muffins to a friend, she ate 3 muffins, and she put 14 muffins in the freezer. There were 128 muffins left. How many muffins were in each batch? 25

130

Strategy Test Item

Optional Problem If you wish to assess students' ability to apply the strategy called Work Backward introduced in this chapter, provide them with the problem below.

> Tiffany said, "If you multiply my age by 6, subtract 2, and divide by 25, you get my younger brother's age which is 4." What is Tiffany's age?

Solution

4 → × 25 → + 2 → ÷ 6 → 17

$$\begin{array}{cc} 25 & 100 \\ \times\ 4 & +\ \ 2 \\ \hline 100 & 102 \end{array} \qquad 102 \div 6 = 17$$

Tiffany's age is 17.

CHAPTER REVIEW/TEST

Find the quotients.

1. $6\overline{)15.6}$ → 2.6

2. $4\overline{)15.04}$ → 3.76

3. $21\overline{)134.4}$ → 6.4

4. $56\overline{)2,027.2}$ → 36.2

Find the quotients to the nearest tenth.

5. $4\overline{)17.1}$ (4.3) → 4.27

6. $5\overline{)12.3}$ (2.5) → 2.46

7. $20\overline{)43}$ (2.2) → 2.15

8. $16\overline{)34.02}$ (2.1) → 2.12

Divide.

9. $26.4 \div 10$
2.64

10. $648.3 \div 1,000$
0.6483

11. $2.73 \div 100$
0.0273

12. $47 \div 1,000$
0.047

Find the quotients to the nearest hundredth.

13. $0.31\overline{)0.6}$ (1.94) → 1.935

14. $4.25\overline{)18.52}$ (4.36) → 4.357

15. $14.2\overline{)351}$ (24.72) → 24.718

16. $29.5\overline{)226.8}$ (7.69) → 7.688

17. $25\overline{)\$181.28}$ ($7.25) → $7.251

18. $5\overline{)\$34.92}$ ($6.98) → $6.984

19. $251\overline{)\$1,396.88}$ ($5.57) → $5.565

20. $14\overline{)\$0.19}$ ($0.01) → $0.013

Find the quotients to the nearest thousandth.

21. $17\overline{)44.82}$ (2.636) → 2.6364

22. $3.6\overline{)46.7}$ (12.972) → 12.9722

23. $0.06\overline{)4.451}$ (74.183) → 74.1833

24. $0.23\overline{)251}$ (1,091.304) → 1,091.3043

Estimate each quotient.

25. $0.4\overline{)18.32}$ → 50.

26. $3.1\overline{)0.58}$ → 0.2

27. $2.381\overline{)18.592}$ → 10.

28. $0.63\overline{)0.3441}$ → 0.5

29. Clifford bought 15 oranges for $1.38. What was the cost (to the nearest cent) of each orange? $0.09

30. Jan bought a can of 3 tennis balls for $2.59. What was the cost (to the nearest cent) of each ball? $0.86

31. Find the average test score. 89

Name	Test Scores
Kaye	79
Reed	85
Hector	96
Dotty	95
Jeff	89
Liz	90

Using Page 131

The exercises in the Chapter Review/Test emphasize the major concepts and skills presented in this chapter. These exercises may be used as a review assignment or as a test, depending upon your needs.

Item Analysis The table below correlates the Chapter Review/Test items with objectives and with the student text pages on which the concepts or skills were taught.

Items	Objectives	Related Text Pages
1–12	5.1	116–120
13–16	5.2	124–125, 129
17–21	5.1	116–120
22–24	5.2	124–125, 129
25–28	5.3	128
29–31	5.4	121–123, 126–127

Assessment Options

If you use the Chapter Review/Test as a review assignment, you may wish to use the free-response test or the multiple-choice test to evaluate mastery of the chapter objectives. The items on these tests have a one-to-one correspondence in terms of content and level of difficulty. A correlation of test items to objectives and student text pages is provided in the Management Guide for Chapter 5.

Multiple-Choice Test, TRB pages 13–14
Free-Response Test, TRB pages 56–57

TRB Options

The following blackline masters are available for use with this chapter. If you have not already assigned these materials, you may wish to use them to close the chapter.

Recreation, TRB page 159
Calculator Technology, TRB page 195
Reading Math, TRB page 231
Family Involvement, TRB pages 253–254

Reteaching

Using Page 132

The exercises on this page are intended for those students who experienced difficulty with the Chapter Review/ Test on page 131. Should students require reteaching of these key concepts and skills, please refer to the teaching notes below. Otherwise, the Another Look exercises can be assigned as independent work, with students using the accompanying sample problems and hints as guides.

Exercises 1–3 This skill was originally taught on pages 116–117. Call students' attention to the display box at the top of the page. Work through the example on the chalkboard, discussing each step. Note that once the decimal point is placed in the answer the division process is the same as for whole numbers.

Exercises 4–9 This skill was originally taught on pages 118–119. Emphasize that to round to the nearest tenth we need to find the quotient to the hundredths place. Then have students talk through each step as they work the example on the chalkboard. Note that in some division problems, as in exercise 4, we need to write a zero in the hundredths place of the dividend in order to find the quotient to the tenths place.

Exercises 10–12 This skill was originally taught on page 120. Have students examine the example in the display box. Ask them to describe the shortcut for dividing by 10, 100, and 1,000. Remind students that in some cases it is necessary to write zeros in the quotient in order to place the decimal point correctly.

Exercises 13–24 This skill was originally taught on pages 124–125. Work through the example in the display box with students. Stress that we need to multiply the divisor and the dividend by the same power of 10 so the quotient does not change. We then divide as with whole numbers, carrying out the division to one place beyond the place to which we round.

Exercises 25–27 This skill was originally taught on page 129. Have students explain how to round the divisor and dividend in the example to 1-digit accuracy. Then ask them to estimate the first digit in the quotient.

ANOTHER LOOK

$$\begin{array}{r} 0\,.\,18 \\ 21\overline{)3\uparrow78} \end{array}$$ whole number divisor

Find the quotients.

1. $25\overline{)60}$ (2.4)

2. $8\overline{)7.2}$ (0.9)

3. $7\overline{)0.126}$ (0.018)

To round to the nearest tenth, find the quotient to the hundredths place.
$$\begin{array}{r} 0.16 \to 0.2 \\ 21\overline{)3.48} \end{array}$$

Find the quotients to the nearest tenth.

4. $8\overline{)23.0}$ (2.9)

5. $16\overline{)27.8}$ (1.7)

6. $25\overline{)42.4}$ (1.7)

7. $12\overline{)54.9}$ (4.6)

8. $29\overline{)1.972}$ (0.1)

9. $54\overline{)95.8}$ (1.8)

$$12.8 \div 10 = 1.28$$
1 zero → shift 1 place

Divide each number by 10, 100, and 1,000.

10. 7.2 0.72; 0.072; 0.0072

11. 0.16 0.016; 0.0016; 0.00016

12. 0.48 0.048; 0.0048; 0.00048

Make the divisor a whole number.
$$6.2\overline{)17.4\,81}$$
×10   ×10

Find the quotients to the nearest hundredth.

13. $0.4\overline{)0.3519}$ (0.88)

14. $5.6\overline{)29.34}$ (5.24)

15. $2.3\overline{)4.0}$ (1.74)

16. $0.86\overline{)1.208}$ (1.40)

17. $0.69\overline{)0.748}$ (1.08)

18. $0.079\overline{)0.334}$ (4.23)

Find the quotients to the nearest thousandth.

19. $7.4\overline{)5}$ (0.676)

20. $3.6\overline{)46.7}$ (12.972)

21. $0.03\overline{)0.1723}$ (5.743)

22. $0.024\overline{)0.76}$ (31.667)

23. $57\overline{)9.385}$ (0.165)

24. $0.26\overline{)0.755}$ (2.904)

$$0.43\overline{)0.76}$$
$$\begin{array}{r} 2. \leftarrow \text{estimate} \\ 0.4\overline{)0.8} \end{array}$$

Estimate each quotient.

25. $0.2\overline{)5.61}$ (30.)

26. $0.29\overline{)0.0893}$ (0.3)

27. $1.5\overline{)0.8}$ (0.4)

Just for Teachers

Math Avoidance and Math Anxiety

A disparity in mathematical performance between males and females traditionally appears in junior high school. Four years later, boys significantly outperform girls in the mathematics portion of college entrance exams.

Because females begin to exhibit poorer performance in math about the time of puberty, it is logical to examine possible connections to other factors occuring at the same time—hormonal changes, for instance. Linking math performance to hormones does not, however, explain why some women excel at mathematics and some men fail.

Tradition has held that boys are expected to do better in mathematics than girls. Like many commonly-held notions, the expectation turns into a self-fulfilling prophecy. Research has shown that males are not genetically more intelligent than females.

Undoubtedly there are individuals—both male and female—who begin to suffer from math anxiety because of inability to understand a particular concept. The student

Using Page 133

This page is intended for those students who successfully completed the Chapter Review/Test on page 131. You may wish to assign this page as independent work while you use the Another Look exercises to reteach the basic concepts and skills of the chapter. Or, you may decide that all students would benefit from exposure to this Enrichment activity.

Lesson Development Have students read the story about Gauss. On the chalkboard, find the sum of the numbers from 1 to 10 using the method shown. Be certain students understand that the sum obtained by reversing the addends and adding these to the original series is just twice the required sum. Then dividing by 2 will give the required sum.

Explain that not every addend need be written. In finding the sum of the numbers from 1 to 100, we write only enough sums to see the pattern.

$$\begin{array}{r} 1 + \quad 2 + \quad 3 + ... + \quad 99 + 100 \\ 100 + \quad 99 + \quad 98 + ... + \quad 2 + \quad 1 \\ \hline 101 + 101 + 101 + ... + 101 + 101 = 100 \times 101 \end{array}$$

The 100 addends of 101 must be divided by 2.

$$\frac{100 \times 101}{2} = 5,050$$

The sum of the whole numbers from 1 to 100 is 5,050.

You may wish to challenge students with these additional problems.

1. Find the sum of the whole numbers from 1 to 1,000. (500,500)

2. Find the sum: $5 + 10 + 15 + 20 + ... + 490 + 495 + 500.$ (25,250)

3. If you could earn $1 the first day, $2 the second day, $3 the third day and so on, how much would you earn in a year? ($66,795)

ENRICHMENT

History of Mathematics

Karl Friedrich Gauss was a famous German mathematician. When Gauss was a young student, his mathematics teacher gave him the task of adding all the whole numbers from 1 to 100. Gauss surprised his teacher by using a shortcut to quickly find the sum.

Karl Friedrich Gauss
German, 1777–1855

To see how Gauss might have discovered a shortcut, examine this simpler problem.

What is the sum of all the whole numbers from 1 to 10?

Suppose we reverse the order of the addends and add the pairs of numbers vertically.

$$\begin{array}{r} 1 + \ 2 + \ 3 + \ 4 + \ 5 + \ 6 + \ 7 + \ 8 + \ 9 + 10 \\ 10 + \ 9 + \ 8 + \ 7 + \ 6 + \ 5 + \ 4 + \ 3 + \ 2 + \ 1 \\ \hline 11 + 11 + 11 + 11 + 11 + 11 + 11 + 11 + 11 + 11 = 10 \times 11 \end{array}$$

The product of 10×11 is twice the sum we are seeking, because each number from 1 to 10 has been added twice. Therefore, the correct sum is

$$\frac{10 \times 11}{2} = \frac{110}{2} = 55$$

Use the shortcut to find these sums.

1. The sum of the whole numbers from 1–15. $(15 \times 16) \div 2 = 120$

2. The sum of the whole numbers from 1–20. $(20 \times 21) \div 2 = 210$

3. The sum of the odd numbers from 1–19. $(10 \times 20) \div 2 = 100$

4. The sum of the whole numbers from 1–100. $(100 \times 101) \div 2 = 5,050$

5. The sum of the odd numbers from 1–99. $(50 \times 100) \div 2 = 2,500$

6. The sum of the even numbers from 2–100. $(50 \times 102) \div 2 = 2,550$

133

---

must be encouraged to apply more effort and concentration, and not be afraid to ask questions. Asking a question involves a risk of appearing too smart as well as too stupid.

Until research proves some biological basis for the disparity in math performance between the sexes, it must be assumed that the difference lies in attitude and experience, the two most important components of success in any field. The willingness to take risks, to have confidence in one's intuition, and the ability to see oneself as a whole person rather than as feminine or masculine have been shown to be significant factors in superior performance in mathematics. Encouraging these attitudes in girls will help to involve them in the many dimensions of mathematics and to eliminate math avoidance and math anxiety.

Review

Using Page 134

The exercises on the page provide practice for maintaining cumulative skills. The emphasis in this Cumulative Review is on multiplication and division of whole numbers (Chapter 3) and division of decimals (Chapter 5).

Item Analysis The table below correlates the Cumulative Review items with objectives and with the student book pages on which the concepts or skills were taught.

Items	Objectives	Related Text Pages
1	3.2	60–65
2	3.3	66–67
3–4	3.5	72–77
5	3.1	56–59
6	5.1	116–120
7	3.4	70–71
8–9	5.2	124–125
10	5.1	116–120
11	3.5	72–77
12	3.2	60–65
13	3.6	68–69, 78–79, 81
14	5.4	121–123, 126–127

CUMULATIVE REVIEW

1. Find the product.

$\begin{array}{r} 218 \\ \times\ 59 \end{array}$
- **A** 15,142
- **B** 15,042
- **C** 12,862
- **D** not given

2. Multiply.

$6^2 \cdot 5^3$
- **A** 4,500
- **B** 3,750
- **C** 7,500
- **D** not given

3. Find the quotient.

$37)\overline{35,742}$
- **A** 966
- **B** 836
- **C** 976
- **D** not given

4. Find the quotient and remainder.

$76)\overline{2,749}$
- **A** 36 R13
- **B** 37 R37
- **C** 37 R47
- **D** not given

5. Estimate the product by rounding to 1-digit accuracy.

427×85
- **A** 32,000
- **B** 37,800
- **C** 36,000
- **D** not given

6. Divide.

$24)\overline{4.212}$
- **A** 0.1756
- **B** 0.2755
- **C** 0.1766
- **D** not given

7. Estimate the quotient by rounding to 1-digit accuracy.

$3,200 \div 262$
- **A** 16
- **B** 10
- **C** 15
- **D** not given

8. Find the quotient.

$0.18)\overline{4.212}$
- **A** 0.234
- **B** 23.4
- **C** 2.34
- **D** not given

9. Divide. Round to the nearest hundredth.

$9.5)\overline{0.654}$
- **A** 0.068
- **B** 0.060
- **C** 0.069
- **D** not given

10. Divide.

$7.596 \div 100$
- **A** 75.96
- **B** 759.6
- **C** 7,596
- **D** not given

11. Find the quotient.

$5,956 \div 1,000$
- **A** 5.956
- **B** 59.56
- **C** 0.5956
- **D** not given

12. Find the product.

$2,597 \times 808$
- **A** 2,098,376
- **B** 209,837
- **C** 2,020,000
- **D** not given

13. Alex collects 884 golf balls at the driving range. He places the same number of golf balls in 17 baskets. How many golf balls are in each basket?
- **A** 52
- **B** 42
- **C** 53
- **D** not given

14. Five students in Miss Marshall's class have scores of 154, 162, 152, 149, and 158. What is the average score?
- **A** 152
- **B** 155
- **C** 158
- **D** not given

Objectives

6.1 Identify and write symbols for basic geometric figures and classify angles according to their measure.

6.2 Identify and classify polygons according to the measure of their angles, length of their sides, and number of sides.

6.3 Identify and write symbols for a chord, diameter, radius, central angle, and arc.

6.4 Identify pairs of congruent polygons and lines of symmetry in figures.

6.5 Identify parallel and perpendicular lines and midpoints and perpendicular bisectors of segments.

6.6 Identify basic space figures and count their vertices, faces, and edges.

Summary

This chapter reviews and extends the geometric experiences that students may have had at earlier grade levels. The vocabulary list for this chapter is lengthy because of the number of geometric figures and geometric relations that are covered. Ways to classify angles and triangles are presented. Students learn about special kinds of quadrilaterals, and about polygons and circles. Congruent figures are reviewed, and figures with lines of symmetry are explored. In one lesson, simple space figures such as prisms, pyramids, cylinders, cones, and spheres are introduced.

Mathematical Background

Basic Geometric Figures In formal geometry courses, point, line, and plane are "undefined terms." Certain assumptions or postulates are made concerning these terms and from these assumptions some conclusions are drawn. The approach in this chapter is quite informal. Intuitive descriptions, rather than formal definitions, are made regarding points and lines. Since most intuitive understanding of geometry comes from the real world, basic geometric figures are related to those things that are familiar to the student in everyday living. Thus a telephone line suggests a geometric line, a pencil point suggests a geometric point, and a flat table top suggests a part of a plane. A laser beam suggests a ray, and the hands of a clock suggest an angle. The lessons on angles deal with classification of angles as acute, right, straight, or obtuse and with a review of degree measure of angles. Supplementary and complementary angles are introduced in this chapter. A pair of supplementary angles have measures which total 180 degrees. A pair of complementary angles have measures which total 90 degrees.

Polygons and Circles A triangle is the simplest polygon. Triangles are classified by the lengths of their sides or by the kinds of angles. Equilateral, isosceles, and scalene triangles have respectively all sides of equal length, two sides of equal length and no two sides with equal length. If all angles have the same measure, the triangle is equilateral. A triangle with three acute angles

is acute; a triangle with one obtuse angle is obtuse; a triangle with one right angle is a right triangle. An important property of every triangle is that the sum of the measures of the three angles is 180 degrees. Polygons are named according to the number of their sides. Quadrilaterals have 4 sides, pentagons 5 sides, hexagons 6 sides, and so on. Regular polygons have all sides the same length and all angles the same measure.

  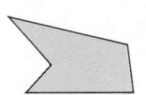

Regular polygon   Convex polygon   Concave polygon

The only kind of polygons studied in this chapter are convex polygons. All of the interior angles of a convex polygon are less than a straight angle. In contrast, some polygons are concave, as in the figure above.

A circle is the set of all points in a plane at a fixed distance from one point, called the center. Several important terms related to circles are given in this chapter. Circumference and area of circles will be covered in a later chapter.

Space Figures Prisms and cylinders are two of the most familiar geometric space figures. A box is a model of a rectangular prism; the familiar vegetable or fruit can is a model for a cylinder. Other space figures are pyramids, cones and spheres. A polyhedron is a space figure with faces that are polygonal regions. If all the polygonal regions are congruent and the polyhedral angles at each vertex are congruent, the polyhedron is a regular polyhedron. There are exactly 5 different kinds of regular polyhedrons.

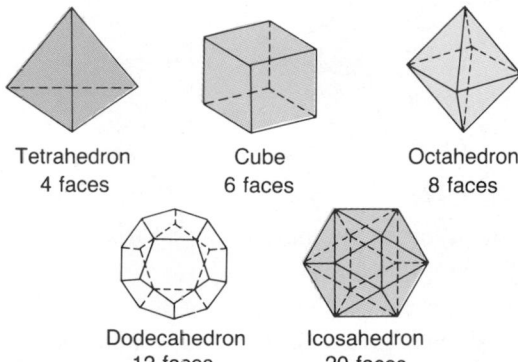

Tetrahedron   Cube   Octahedron
4 faces   6 faces   8 faces

Dodecahedron   Icosahedron
12 faces   20 faces

Vocabulary

point	supplementary	polygon	central angle
line	complementary	pentagon	arc
plane	triangle	hexagon	congruent
ray	scalene	heptagon	symmetry
segment	isosceles	octagon	perpendicular
parallel	equilateral	nonagon	bisector
vertex	quadrilateral	decagon	midpoint
protractor	trapezoid	regular	prism
degrees	parallelogram	circle	pyramid
acute	rhombus	chord	cylinder
obtuse	rectangle	diameter	face
right angle	square	radius	edge

Error Analysis

This chapter deals with basic concepts of geometry. Students are asked to classify angles and triangles, to identify special kinds of quadrilaterals and space figures, and to make constructions with ruler and compass. Many errors made with the content of this chapter will reflect a poor understanding of basic concepts, such as angle, line, line segment, radius, chord, and arc and/or a lack of skill in classifying based on similarities.

Error Pattern 1

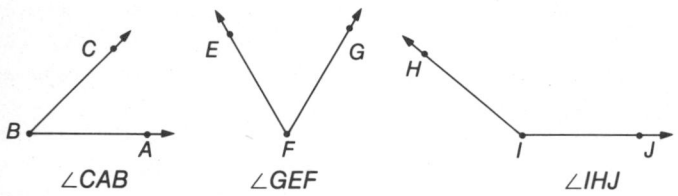

| ∠CAB | ∠GEF | ∠IHJ |

Diagnosis The student does not use the conventional procedure for naming angles. The letter that names the vertex has not been written as the middle letter in naming the angle.

Remediation Show examples of angles on the chalkboard and review how to name an angle with letters. Explain that an angle with vertex *B* can be named ∠*ABC* or ∠*CBA*. Stress that the letter representing the vertex is the middle letter of the named angle.

Error Pattern 2

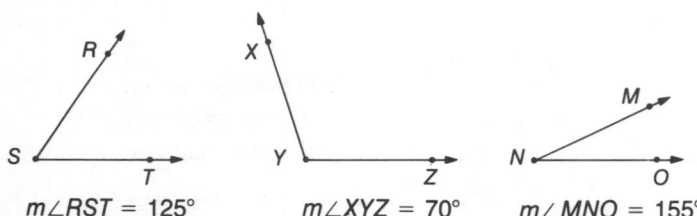

| m∠RST = 125° | m∠XYZ = 70° | m∠MNO = 155° |

Diagnosis In measuring the angles, the student has used the wrong scale on the protractor.

Remediation Discuss the meaning of the measure of an angle. Point out that the measure is the number of degrees inside or in the interior of the angle. Review how to use a protractor. Emphasize that the measure of an angle must be read from the scale that has the 0° mark on the one side of the angle.

Error Pattern 3

Measure of the angle	Measure of the complementary angle
45°	45°
86°	94°
33°	147°
80°	100°

Diagnosis The student has confused the meaning of complementary angle with that of supplementary angle. For a given angle measure, he or she may find either.

Remediation The definition of complementary and supplementary angles must be reviewed. Discuss angle measure and the angles of 90 degrees and 180 degrees. Carefully review addition and subtraction of angle measure. Use examples to illustrate complementary and supplementary angles.

 ## Problem Solving

Helping Students Check Back

Question, Data, Plan, Answer, Check—each of these steps is very important in the problem-solving process. Many students have difficulty understanding problems and in selecting and carrying out solution strategies. Because of this, there is a tendency to emphasize the first four of these steps during instruction and to play down the importance of checking back. No problem-solving session is complete, however, unless the check-back stage is included.

The purpose of the check-back stage of problem solving is for students to evaluate their work on a particular problem. To help students check back, here are four teaching actions you can use.

- Have students check whether all the relevant information was used. Two common errors made by elementary school students are 1) forgetting to use a necessary piece of data, and 2) neglecting a condition stated in the problem. Students who have committed these types of errors will often detect their errors when they are asked to check back.

- Have students check the reasonableness of their answers. Students should be required to estimate answers to problems whenever possible. Estimating answers and comparing estimates to exact answers verifies whether correct solution strategies were selected and whether computational work was performed with reasonable accuracy.

- Have students check their computation. Students should always be required to check for and, if necessary, correct any computational errors.

- Have students write their answers in complete sentences. This action encourages students to relate the numerical part of a solution to the story setting. Also, it helps students determine whether they have indeed answered the question asked in the problem.

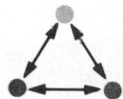 **Special Education**

The focus of the chapter is on the development of basic geometry concepts. The applications of geometric ideas in everyday life need to be emphasized for special needs students in your classroom. The location of this chapter provides you with an opportunity to continue strengthening the computation skills of your special needs students and for narrowing the gap that separates them from some of their classmates. In teaching the chapter's contents, the following ideas may help your special students.

Multisensory Concept Development

The chapter contains a large amount of concept-related vocabulary for students to master. This can be a difficult task for students whose reading, verbal, or listening skills are weak. To counterbalance this, attack the problem with an approach which uses students' stronger avenues of learning. One method of developing the concepts is having students pantomime the various ideas and asking other students to guess the concept. The target concept could be drawn from a deck of cards listing the topics covered to that time.

A second method is to photograph local scenes where real life models of the concepts are displayed. These pictures can then be shown in class and the models for the concepts discussed. The importance of the recognition of street sign shapes and use of geometric ideas in blueprints can be stressed. An example of one such scene is shown below.

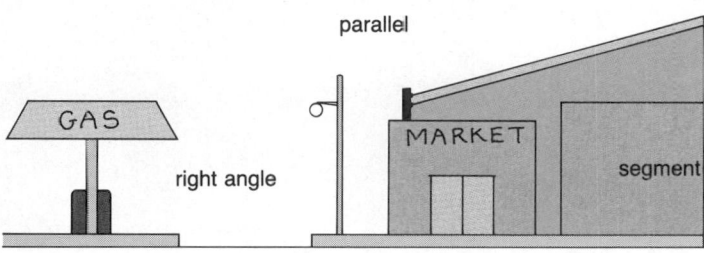

A third method of developing understanding and recognition skills is useful in teaching the space figures introduced on pages 156 and 157. Use models of the shapes along with a blindfold. Special students can be blindfolded and then handed a model of one of the solid shapes. Using only the sense of touch, students should be encouraged to name the shape. Such an activity stresses the importance of likenesses and differences. Here the notions of edges, corners, angles between faces, and related ideas take on greater importance.

Building Prerequisite Skills

The work on circles and angle measurement needs careful development for later applications in measurement and in circle graph construction. In working with the circle, special emphasis needs to be placed on the concepts of diameter, radius, and central angle. The first two of these are needed in discussing circumference and area, the latter in interpreting and constructing circle graphs. In order to construct circle graphs, students must be able to use a protractor. This skill can be fostered by starting with a paper protractor as shown in the figure, where the folded lines are developed by continual bisections of the original straight angle. The development of these markings through paper folding and the writing of angle measures helps students learn to estimate and test the reasonableness of statements concerning angle measure.

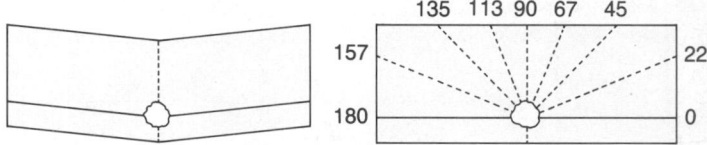

 **Subject Integration**

Subject matter related to other areas of the curriculum has been integrated into the following lessons. This provides an opportunity to highlight the integration between mathematics and other subjects.

Science Helicopter, page 35; diatoms, page 140; constellation Pegasus, page 142; honeybee cells, page 144
Social Studies Chinese bi, page 146
Computer Awareness Computer graphics, page 148
Physical Education Hockey, page 150
Career Awareness Railroad engineers, page 158

Management Guide

Teaching Chapter 6				Meeting Individual Needs					
Objectives	Chapter Content	Pages	TRB Test Items	Lesson Assignments			Follow Up		
				Minimum	Average	Extended	Reteaching	Enrichment	Practice
	Chapter Opener	135							
6.1 Identify and write symbols for basic geometric figures and classify angles according to their measure.	Basic Geometric Figures	136–137	1–4	1–12	1–12	1–12	SE6 Ch 10 RS 40	ES 40	PS 51
	Angles	138–139	5–11	1–11 17–26, SK	1–31, SK	1–31, odd SK	SE6 Ch 10 RS 41	ES 41	PS 52
6.2 Identify and classify polygons according to the measure of their angles, length of their sides, and number of their sides.	Triangles	140–141	12–23	1–12	1–16	1–19	SE6 Ch 10 RS 42	ES 42	PS 53
	Quadrilaterals	142–143		1–9	1–11	1–11, TM	SE6 Ch 10 RS 43	ES 43	PS 54
	Polygons	144–145		1–10	1–11, TM	1–12, TM	SE6 Ch 10 RS 44	ES 44	PS 55
6.3 Identify and write symbols for a chord, diameter, radius, central angle and arc.	Circles	146–147	24–28	1–12	1–16	1–16	SE6 Ch 10 RS 45	ES 45	PS 56
6.4 Identify pairs of congruent polygons and lines of symmetry in figures.	Congruent Figures	148–149	29–30	1–13	1–16, TM	1–16, TM	SE6 Ch 10		PS 57
	Lines of Symmetry	150–151	31–32	1–9, SK	1–14, SK	1–15, SK	RS 46	ES 46	PS 58
6.5 Identify parallel and perpendicular lines and mid-points and perpendicular bisections of segments.	Constructing Parallel Lines and Perpendicular Lines	152–153	33–34		1–6	1–8			PS 59
	Bisecting Segments and Angles	154–155			1–8	1–10, TM			PS 60
6.6 Identify basic space figures and count their vertices, faces and edges.	Space Figures	156–157	35–40	1–9	1–14	1–14, TM	SE6 Ch 10 RS 47	ES 47	PS 61
	Problem Solving: Solve a Simpler Problem	158							
	Chapter Review/Test	159							
	Another Look/ Enrichment	160–161							
	Cumulative Review	162							

SE6 Student Edition, Book 6
RS Reteaching Supplement
ES Enrichment Supplement
PS Practice Supplement
MP More Practice
TM Think Math
SK Skillkeeper
TRB Teacher's Resource Book

Masters for use

. . . before Chapter 6

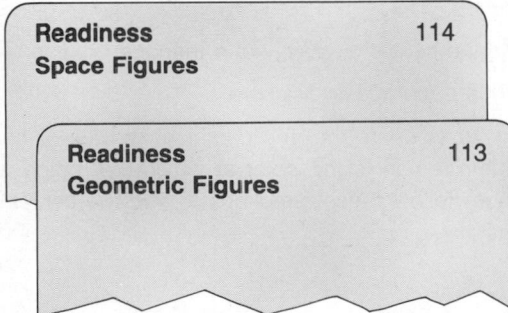

| Readiness Space Figures | 114 |
| Readiness Geometric Figures | 113 |

. . . during Chapter 6

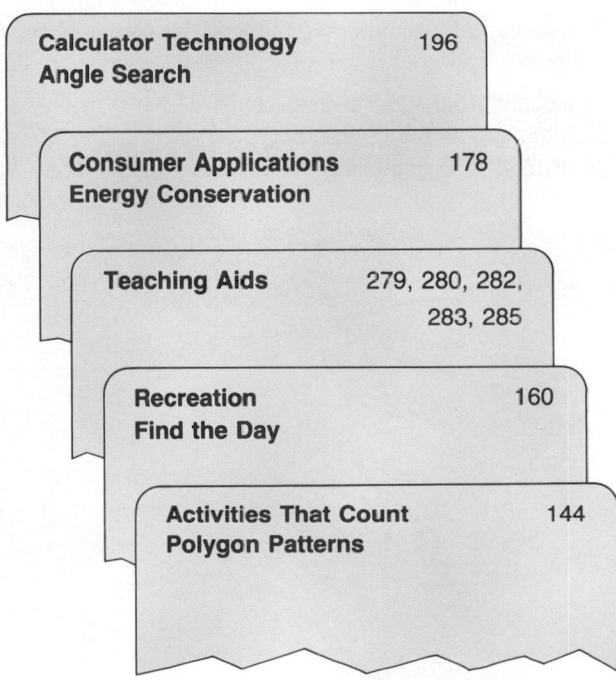

Calculator Technology Angle Search	196
Consumer Applications Energy Conservation	178
Teaching Aids	279, 280, 282, 283, 285
Recreation Find the Day	160
Activities That Count Polygon Patterns	144

. . . after Chapter 6

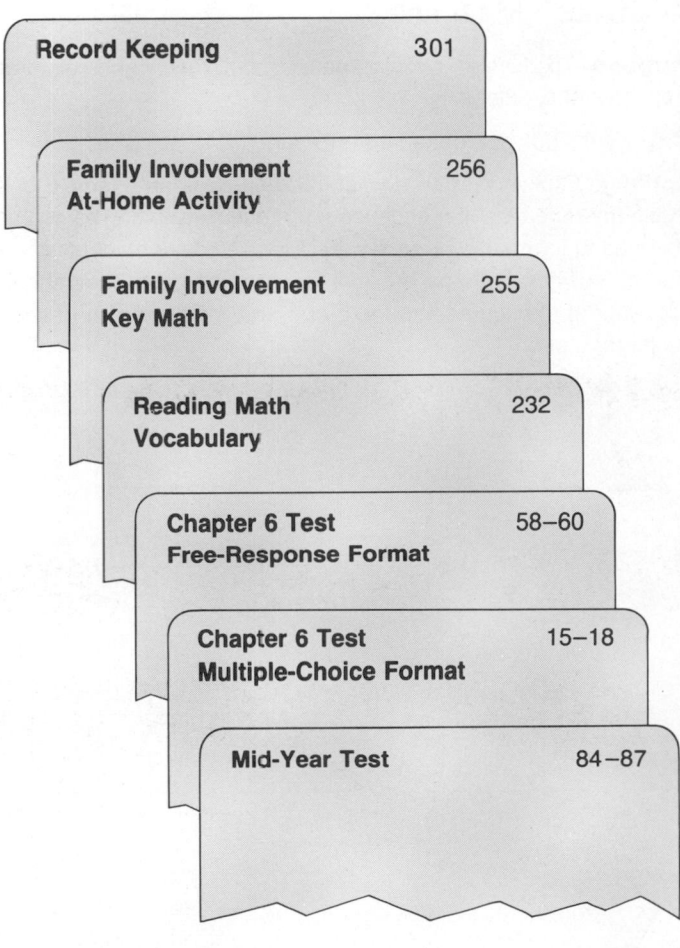

Record Keeping	301
Family Involvement At-Home Activity	256
Family Involvement Key Math	255
Reading Math Vocabulary	232
Chapter 6 Test Free-Response Format	58–60
Chapter 6 Test Multiple-Choice Format	15–18
Mid-Year Test	84–87

Supplements

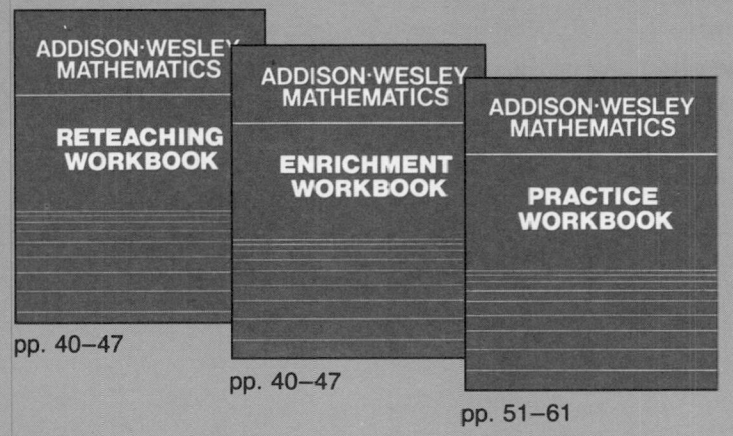

ADDISON-WESLEY MATHEMATICS
RETEACHING WORKBOOK
pp. 40–47

ADDISON-WESLEY MATHEMATICS
ENRICHMENT WORKBOOK
pp. 40–47

ADDISON-WESLEY MATHEMATICS
PRACTICE WORKBOOK
pp. 51–61

Other Addison-Wesley Resources

Books and Kits

Dice and Dots   pp. 39–42, 49–53
A New Twist   pp. 21, 27, 87
General Mathematics: Making Practice Fun   67A, 67 B

Technology

Computer Math Activities   Volumes 2, 3, 5

Activities That Count

Activities That Count are designed for use throughout this chapter and subsequent chapters. Before beginning Chapter 6, you may wish to review these activities and select the ones you consider appropriate for your class.

Reptiles Math Lab

Purpose To develop skill in spatial visualization and reinforce properties of polygons

Materials Polygon patterns (TRB page 144), scissors

Activity Explain that an equilateral triangle is an example of a reptile (for repeating tile) because four equilateral triangles can be arranged to form a larger equilateral triangle. Have students show that the polygon patterns are reptiles. In each case, they should trace four of the figures, cut them out, and arrange them to show the larger figure.

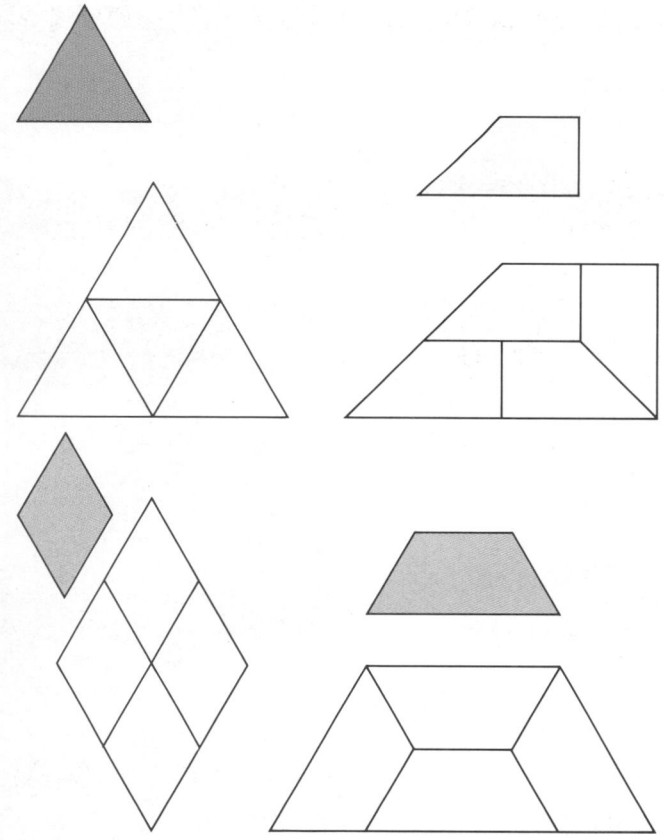

Unlucky 13 Game

Purpose To use logical reasoning

Materials 13 counters

Activity Place the 13 counters in a row. At each turn, a player may choose to take one, two, or three counters. The player who is forced to take the last counter loses the game. To help students develop some strategies, pose these questions: 1) If there are 3 counters left and it is your turn, will you win or lose? 2) If there are 4 counters left and it is your turn, will you win or lose? 3) If there are 5 counters left and it is your turn, will you win or lose? Encourage students to make an organized list of the possibilities to help answer these questions.

Center of Gravity Math Lab

Purpose To find the center of gravity of a triangular region

Materials Tagboard, compass, scissors

Activity Explain to students that the center of gravity, or *centroid,* of a geometric region is the point at which the region will balance. Have them follow these directions to find the center of gravity of a triangular region.

1. Draw a triangle.
2. Use a compass and straightedge to construct the perpendicular bisector of each side.
3. Connect the midpoint of each side to the opposite vertex of the triangle.
4. The intersection of the three segments is the center of gravity of the region.

Instruct students to make a pinhole at the center of gravity and balance the triangle on the tip of a pencil.

Variation: Instead of constructing the bisectors of the sides with compass and straightedge, have students use rulers to measure the sides of the triangle to find the midpoints.

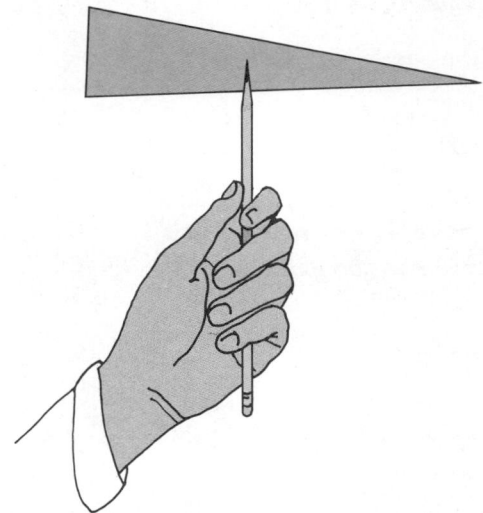

Geometry Collage Project

Purpose To recognize geometric shapes in pictures

Activity Have the students cut out pictures of geometric shapes from magazines and paste them on colored paper to make a collage. Make a bulletin board display with them.

6

Geometry

A helicopter can fly up, down, sideways, forward, and backward. Long blades spinning above the helicopter body form the rotor disc. The main rotor disc on a traffic helicopter has a diameter of 10.16 meters.

To fly up, the left hand is used to pull up on the "collective stick." This is a lever which changes the angle of the blades. Once the helicopter is up in the air, the right hand moves another lever called the "cyclic stick." This changes the angle of the rotor disc. As the rotor disc tilts forward, the helicopter will fly forward.

At the age of 16, you could get a student pilot's license and find out firsthand how a helicopter flies.

Up

Hovering

Down

Introducing the Chapter

Discussion After students have had an opportunity to read the article and look at the accompanying pictures, ask if any of them have seen or been in a helicopter. Encourage them to share their experiences with the class.

As you teach the chapter you may wish to refer back to this page and discuss the questions below. This is an opportunity for students to create their own questions based on the data in the article.

Follow-Up Questions

After Page 139 When a helicopter is at rest the blades form a straight angle. When it is hovering, the blades rise up slightly. Is the resulting angle formed by the blades acute, obtuse, or right? (obtuse) The angle at which all the blades are tilted when the helicopter is going straight up is usually between 3° and 14°. To see how much the blades might tilt, use your protractor to draw an angle of 14°.

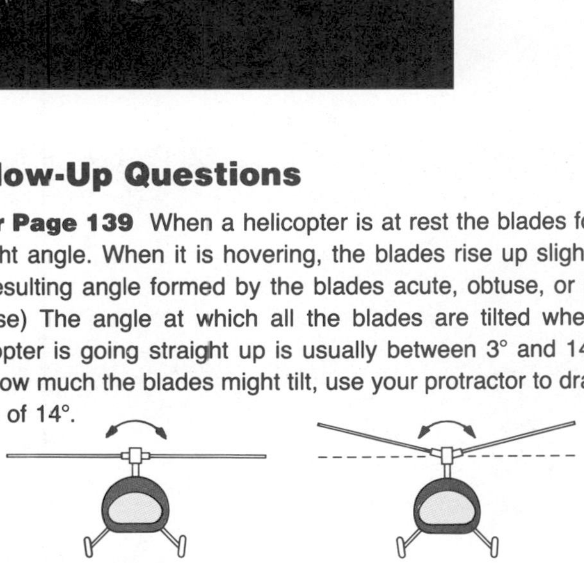

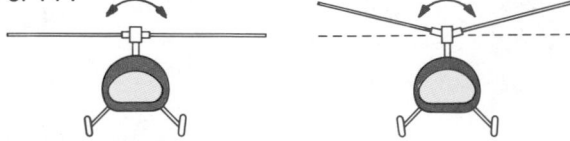

After Page 146 The radius of the rotor disc on a traffic helicopter is the approximate length of the blades. What is the radius of the rotor disc? (5.08 meters)

Quick Review Have students write each number in words.

38,462.040	842,637,800.007	33.00006
26,000.39	500,004.2068	16.2000

Lesson Focus To identify and write symbols naming points, lines, segments, rays, planes, parallel lines, and intersecting lines

Suggested Materials Meter sticks or rulers, string, tagboard

Ideas for Getting Started

Ask students to name geometric figures suggested by objects in the room. Expect responses such as squares, rectangles, circles, cubes, and triangles. Bring out other ideas such as a point suggested by a pencil tip, a plane suggested by a desktop, and a line suggested by the intersection of two walls.

Using Page 136

Lesson Development After students read the material at the top of the page, have them examine the accompanying pictures. Ask them if the pictures remind them of geometric figures and to name the shapes they see.

As you discuss each of the geometric figures on the page, show a physical model of the figure. Use a meter stick or piece of string stretched taut between two points to illustrate a segment. To illustrate a ray, have a student hold one end of a long piece of string fixed while another student walks away holding the string straight and continuing on in the same direction. Two rulers can be used to show intersecting and parallel lines. Place a piece of tagboard over the rulers to illustrate that two intersecting lines are always *coplanar,* that is, they lie in the same plane. You can show that two lines do not necessarily have to be in the same plane by holding two rulers at right angles, one slightly below the other. The mathematical term that describes these lines is *skew.*

Basic Geometric Figures

Everywhere we look we see objects that remind us of different geometric figures or shapes.

Points, **lines**, and **planes** are the simplest geometric figures.

We think of a **point** as a position in space with no length, width, or thickness.

$P.$

Point *P*: *P*

We think of a **line** as a straight path of points.

Line *RS*: $\overleftrightarrow{RS}$ or $\overleftrightarrow{SR}$

We think of a **plane** as a flat surface.

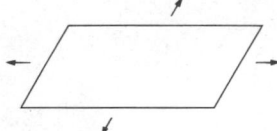

A **segment** is two points on a line and all the points on the line between them.

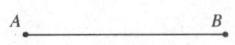

Segment *AB*: $\overline{AB}$ or $\overline{BA}$

A **ray** is the part of a line that has one endpoint and extends endlessly in one direction.

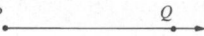

Ray *PQ*: $\overrightarrow{PQ}$

In the same plane, two lines are either **parallel** or they **intersect**. Parallel lines do not meet.

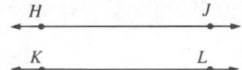

Line *HJ* is parallel to line *KL*. $\overleftrightarrow{HJ} \parallel \overleftrightarrow{KL}$

Intersecting lines meet at one point.

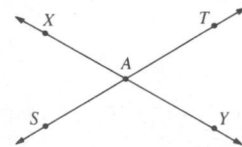

Lines *XY* and *ST* intersect at point *A*.

Follow Up

Reteaching

Write the words point, line, plane, line segment, ray, parallel lines, and intersecting lines on index cards. Write the definitions of each term on another set of index cards. Mix the word and definition cards together and distribute to students. Begin by asking a student to write on the chalkboard the word that appears on his or her card. Whoever has the matching definition should then give the definition and find an example of an object in the room that suggests this concept. After the definition and example are given, discuss the concept with students.

Enrichment

Have students use line segments to make a geometric design on graph paper (TRB p. 285). Once the design is established, have them duplicate the design in the other squares and shade the designs as desired with colored pencils. Below are some design examples.

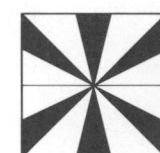 

Assignment Guide			
	Minimum	Average	Extended
page 137	1–12	1–12	1–12

Using Page 137

Exercises 1–2 Be certain students understand that certain geometric figures can be named in different ways. For example, the segment in exercise 1 can be named either $\overline{MN}$ or $\overline{NM}$. In exercise 3, students should see that $\overrightarrow{PO}$ is not the same as $\overrightarrow{OP}$ because they have different endpoints and point in different directions.

All possible answers for exercises 5–8 are not shown since each segment has two names.

Draw a picture of each geometric figure. Write the symbol for the picture.

1. Segment *MN* 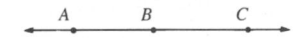 ; $\overline{MN}$

2. Point *Z*   *Z* • ; *Z*

3. Ray *OP* O 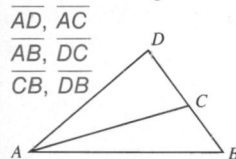 ; $\overrightarrow{OP}$

4. Line *TR*   *T*____*R* ; $\overleftrightarrow{TR}$

5. Use the three points to name three different segments. $\overline{AC}, \overline{AB}, \overline{BC}$

    A   *B*   *C*

6. Use the four points to name six different segments. $\overline{RS}, \overline{RT}, \overline{RU}, \overline{ST}, \overline{SU}, \overline{TU}$

    R   *S*   *T*   *U*

7. Name all the segments shown in the figure.
$\overline{AD}, \overline{AC}$
$\overline{AB}, \overline{DC}$
$\overline{CB}, \overline{DB}$

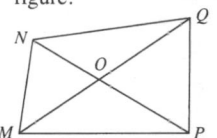

8. Name ten different segments shown in the figure.

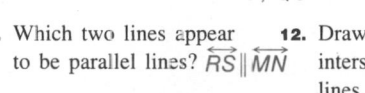

$\overline{NQ}, \overline{NO}$
$\overline{NP}, \overline{NM}$
$\overline{MO}, \overline{MQ}$
$\overline{MP}, \overline{PQ}$
$\overline{PO}, \overline{QO}$

9. Name all the rays shown in the figure. $\overrightarrow{OZ}, \overrightarrow{OY}, \overrightarrow{OX}$

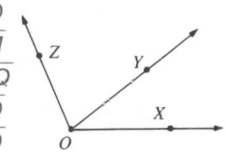

10. Use points *A* and *B* to name two rays. $\overrightarrow{AB}, \overrightarrow{BA}$

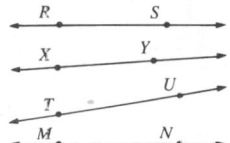

11. Which two lines appear to be parallel lines? $\overleftrightarrow{RS} \parallel \overleftrightarrow{MN}$

12. Draw a picture of a line intersecting two parallel lines.

137

Reteaching Supplement, page 40

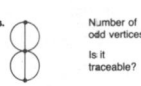

Name _____ To follow text page 137

Basic Geometric Figures

Ideas from Geometry

This is **point** *A*.
• *A*

This is **line** *AB*.
We write $\overleftrightarrow{AB}$.
(Arrows on both ends)

This is **segment** *AB*.
We write $\overline{AB}$.
(It stops at *A* and *B*.)

This is **ray** *AB*.
We write $\overrightarrow{AB}$.
(Arrow on one end)

These lines **intersect** at point *B*.

These lines are **parallel**.
They do not meet.

This is a **plane**.
An endless surface

1. Draw line *RS*.

2. Draw point *T*.
• *T*

3. Draw ray *EF*.

4. Draw line segment *CD*.

5. Draw two lines, *GH* and *KL*, that are parallel.

6. Draw two line segments that intersect at *P*.

7. List the 5 segments shown in the figure.
$\overline{MN}, \overline{NO}, \overline{OP}, \overline{PM}, \overline{NP}$

8. List the rays shown in the figure.
$\overrightarrow{UR}, \overrightarrow{US}, \overrightarrow{UT}$

9. Which lines appear to be parallel?
$\overleftrightarrow{CD}$ and $\overleftrightarrow{GH}$

Enrichment Supplement, page 40

Name _____ To follow text page 137

Networks

This figure is a **network**. It is **traceable** because you can draw it without lifting your pencil from the paper and without retracing any line.

The points *A*, *B*, *C*, and *D* are ports of intersection. They are called the **vertices of the network**. *A* and *D* are **even** vertices because you can enter or leave by an even number of paths (2). *B* and *C* are **odd** vertices because you can enter or leave by an odd number of paths (3).

Try to trace each network. Give the number of odd vertices and tell if the network is traceable.

1. Number of odd vertices: **2**   Is it traceable? **yes**

2. Number of odd vertices: **4**   Is it traceable? **no**

3. Number of odd vertices: **0**   Is it traceable? **yes**

4. Number of odd vertices: **0**   Is it traceable? **yes**

5. Number of odd vertices: **0**   Is it traceable? **yes**

6. Number of odd vertices: **2**   Is it traceable? **yes**

7. When is a figure traceable?
when the number of odd vertices is 0 or 2

Practice Supplement, page 51

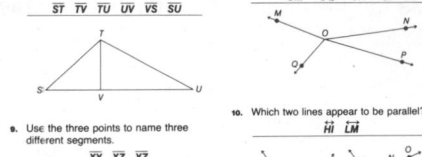

Name _____ To follow text page 137

Basic Geometric Figures

Draw a picture. Write the symbol.

1. Draw segment *AB*.
*A*____*B* $\overline{AB}$

2. Draw point *X*.
• *X*

3. Draw ray *OT*.
*O*____*T* $\overrightarrow{OT}$

4. Draw line *YZ*.
*Y*____*Z* $\overleftrightarrow{YZ}$

5. Draw two lines, *CD* and *EF*, that are parallel.
*C*____*D*
*E*____*F* $\overleftrightarrow{CD} \parallel \overleftrightarrow{EF}$

6. Draw two lines that intersect at point *S*.

Use the figures to find the answers.

7. Name the six segments shown in the figure.
$\overline{ST}\ \overline{TV}\ \overline{TU}\ \overline{UV}\ \overline{VS}\ \overline{SU}$

8. Name the four rays shown in the figure.
$\overrightarrow{OM}\ \overrightarrow{OQ}\ \overrightarrow{ON}\ \overrightarrow{OP}$

9. Use the three points to name three different segments.
$\overline{XY}\ \overline{XZ}\ \overline{YZ}$

10. Which two lines appear to be parallel?
$\overleftrightarrow{HI}\ \overleftrightarrow{LM}$

Lesson Focus To measure angles in using protractors and to classify angles according to their measure

Suggested Materials Chalkboard protractor and student protractors (TRB p. 280)

Ideas for Getting Started

Spend some time showing students how protractors are used. Draw several angles on the chalkboard or overhead projector. Have selected students use the protractor to measure the angles. Watch for these errors:

- Vertex of angle is not aligned with the center point of the protractor.

- Side of the angle improperly aligned with the protractor.

- If protractor has double scales, the wrong scale is used.

Using Page 138

Lesson Development Discuss the notation used for naming angles. Stress that the vertex letter is written in the middle of the other two letters when the three-letter notation is used.

On the chalkboard, illustrate the four kinds of angles: acute, right, obtuse, and straight. Point out that the symbol ⌐ is used to denote a right angle. Show that angles can have different orientations.

Explain that complementary and supplementary angles as defined do not have to be adjacent although they may be. Display the diagram below.

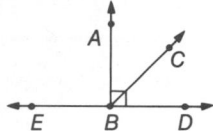

Elicit from students that $\angle ABC$ and $\angle CBD$ are complementary and $\angle EBC$ and $\angle CBD$ are supplementary. "How can you find the measure of an angle which is supplementary to an angle whose measure is 62°?" (180° − 62° = 118°) "How can you find the measure of an angle which is complementary to an angle whose measure is 27°?" (90° − 27° = 63°)

Call attention to the notation for the measure of angle A, $m\angle A$. Note that the symbol $\angle A$ represents the figure while the symbol $m\angle A$ represents the number of degrees in the measure of the angle.

Angles

An angle is two rays from the same endpoint or **vertex**. The rays are the sides of the angle.

We can use a **protractor** to find the **measure** of an angle in **degrees**.

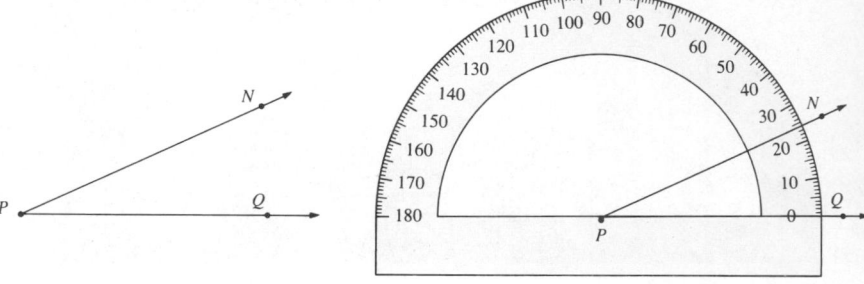

Angle NPQ or angle QPN or angle P
$\angle NPQ$ $\angle QPN$ $\angle P$

The measure of $\angle NPQ$ is 24 degrees.
$m\angle NPQ = 24°$

Angles are named according to their measures.

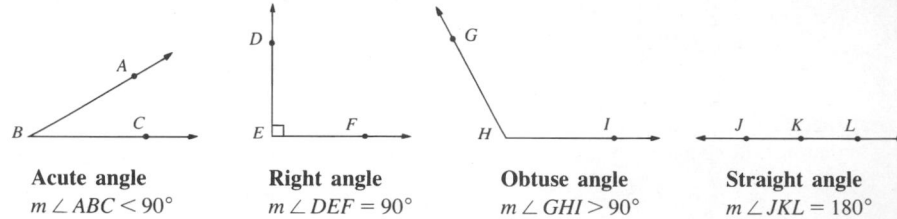

Acute angle	**Right angle**	**Obtuse angle**	**Straight angle**
$m\angle ABC < 90°$	$m\angle DEF = 90°$	$m\angle GHI > 90°$	$m\angle JKL = 180°$

Two angles are **complementary** if their measures have a sum of 90°.

Two angles are **supplementary** if their measures have a sum of 180°.

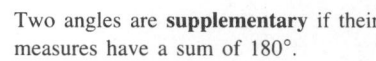
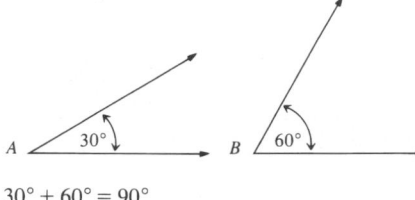

$30° + 60° = 90°$
$\angle A$ and $\angle B$ are complementary angles.

$135° + 45° = 180°$
$\angle C$ and $\angle D$ are supplementary angles.

138

Follow Up

Reteaching

Have each student draw an angle on a sheet of paper. Then ask students to exchange papers and measure the angle on the paper. If students have difficulty, work with them individually or in small groups and show how the protractor is used to measure angles.

Discuss the meaning of complementary and supplementary angles. Write various angle measures on index cards. Include their complements and supplements. Have students try to match an angle with its complement or supplement.

Enrichment

Display the figure below on the chalkboard.

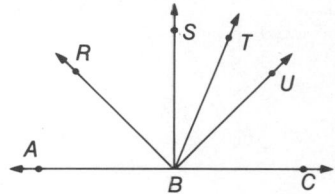

Have students name as many angles as possible.

$\angle ABR$ $\angle RBS$ $\angle SBT$ $\angle TBU$ $\angle UBC$
$\angle ABS$ $\angle RBT$ $\angle SBU$ $\angle TBC$
$\angle ABT$ $\angle RBU$ $\angle SBC$
$\angle ABU$ $\angle RBC$
$\angle ABC$

Assignment Guide

page 139	Minimum	Average	Extended
	1–11, 17–26, SK	1–31, SK	1–31 odd, SK

Give the measure of each angle.
State if the angle is **right**, **acute**,
obtuse, or **straight**.

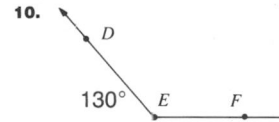

1. ∠BAC
25°; acute

2. ∠BAD
62°; acute

3. ∠BAE
90°; right

4. ∠BAF
135°; obtuse

5. ∠BAG
155°; obtuse

6. ∠BAH
180°; straight

7. ∠EAF
45°; acute

8. ∠GAH
25°; acute

Estimate the measure of each angle. Then measure the angle
with a protractor. Estimates will vary.

9.

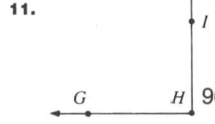
B ∠50° C

10.
130°

11.
90°

Give the measure of angles that are complementary to angles
having the measures below.

12. 40° 50°   **13.** 75° 15°   **14.** 12° 78°   **15.** 32° 58°   **16.** 80° 10°

17. 29° 61°   **18.** 66° 24°   **19.** 45° 45°   **20.** 88° 2°   **21.** 11° 79°

Give the measure of angles that are supplementary to angles
having the measures below.

22. 50° 130°   **23.** 120° 60°   **24.** 80° 100°   **25.** 135° 45°   **26.** 90° 90°

27. 65° 115°   **28.** 148° 32°   **29.** 106° 74°   **30.** 177° 3°   **31.** 33° 147°

SKILLKEEPER

Give the place value of each underlined digit.

1. 7<u>5</u>9 50	**2.** 6,<u>7</u>78 700	**3.** 1<u>5</u>,952 5,000	**4.** <u>7</u>5,912 70,000	**5.** 9,6<u>2</u>7 20
6. 6.9<u>2</u> 0.02	**7.** 0.5<u>1</u>9 0.01	**8.** 7.9<u>6</u>5 0.9	**9.** 15.6<u>2</u> 0.02	**10.** 0.21<u>5</u> 0.005
11. 3.596<u>7</u> 0.0007	**12.** 72.3<u>2</u> 0.02	**13.** <u>7</u>92.8 700	**14.** 0.6<u>2</u>1 0.6	**15.** 7.95<u>8</u> 0.008

139

Using Page 139

Exercises 9–11 Before assigning these exercises, discuss ways to estimate angle measures. As a guideline, have students think about how each angle compares to a right angle. In exercise 9, the measure of ∠A is a little more than half of 90°, while in exercise 10, the measure of ∠E is slightly less than one and a half times 90°. Students should recognize the angle in exercise 11 as a right angle.

After estimating the measure of each angle, students are asked to find the measure with a protractor. Students often have difficulty using a protractor to measure angles given in their texts. The protractor may cover part of the angle or the rays pictured may not be long enough to reach the calibration on the protractor. Show students how to use the edges of a piece of paper or an index card to extend the rays to the calibration marks.

Skillkeeper These skills were originally taught in Chapters 1 and 2.

Reteaching Supplement, page 41

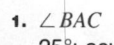

Enrichment Supplement, page 41

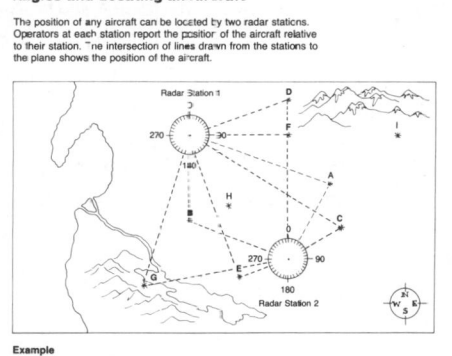

Practice Supplement, page 52

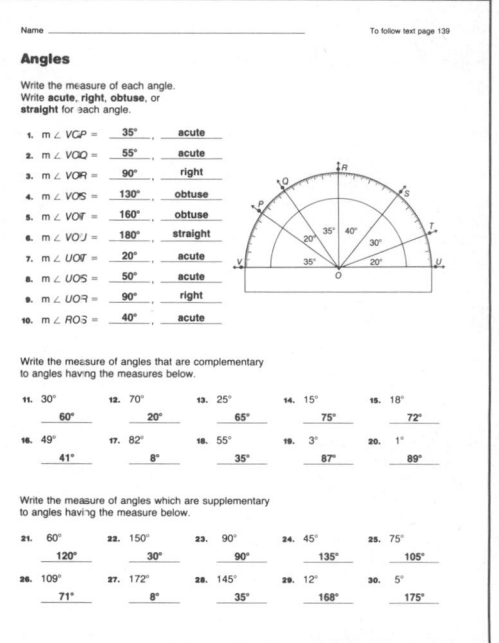

Quick Review Have students give the missing addends.

$35 + \underline{37} = 72$ $\underline{34} + 64 = 98$ $61 + \underline{23} = 84$

$\underline{6} + 39 = 45$ $56 + \underline{15} = 71$ $\underline{61} + 33 = 94$

Lesson Focus To identify triangles according to the measure of their angles or sides and to find the measure of one angle of a triangle when the measures of the other two angles are known

Ideas for Getting Started

Mark three points *X, Y,* and *Z* on the chalkboard. "How many different segments are determined by these three points?" (three) Draw the segments and identify the figure formed by the three segments as triangle *XYZ.* Write the symbol △*XYZ* on the chalkboard. Explain that we can write the three letters in any order to name the triangle.

Ask selected students to name the sides and angles of the triangle and write the symbol for each on the chalkboard.

Using Page 140

Lesson Development Have students read the material at the top of the page and look at the accompanying photograph. Explain that diatoms are one-celled plants, a type of algae. Some species are food for small sea animals, which, in turn, are eaten by fish. Most of the fish of the world would die if there were no diatoms.

Discuss the two ways of describing or classifying triangles, according to their angles and according to their sides. Point out that all equilateral triangles are isosceles since equilateral triangles have at least two sides of the same length, but not all isosceles triangles are equilateral.

Demonstrate that the sum of the measures of the three angles of a triangle is 180°. The picture at the bottom of the page suggests a way this can be done. Cut out a paper triangle, tear off two angles, and place the three angles side by side to form a straight angle. Another demonstration is to draw several differently shaped triangles on the chalkboard. Have students measure the angles of each triangle and then find the sum. The sum of the angles should be 180°; however, small errors in measurement are likely to occur making the sums slightly more or less than 180°.

Triangles

Some diatoms are shaped like **triangles**. Triangle *ABC* (△ *ABC*) has three **sides**, three **vertices**, and three **angles**. The sides are $\overline{AB}$, $\overline{AC}$, and $\overline{BC}$. The vertices are points *A*, *B*, and *C*. The angles are ∠*A*, ∠*B*, and ∠*C*.

Triangles are named according to the measures of their angles or the lengths of their sides.

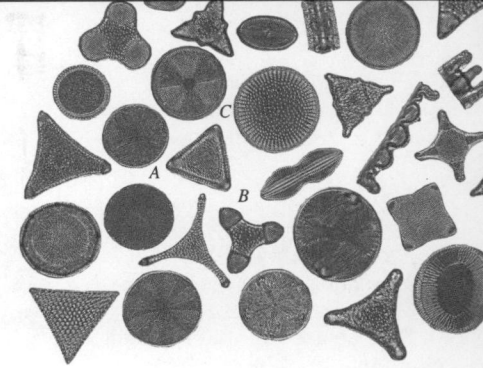

Light micrograph of diatoms

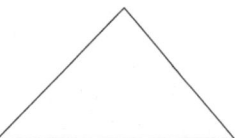 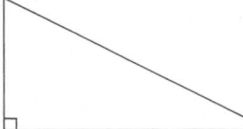 

Acute triangle
All angles measure less than 90°.

Right triangle
One angle measures 90°.

Obtuse triangle
The measure of one angle is greater than 90°.

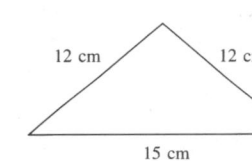 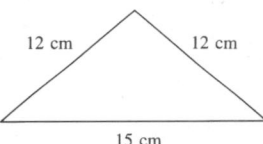 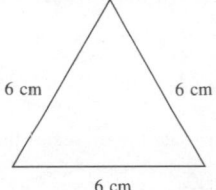

Scalene triangle
All three sides have different lengths.

Isosceles triangle
At least two sides have the same length.

Equilateral triangle
All three sides have the same length.

The sum of the measure of the angles of any triangle is 180°.

In △*ABC*, $m\angle A = 58°$ and $m\angle C = 30°$. What is the measure of the third angle?

$m\angle A + m\angle C = 58° + 30° = 88°$

$m\angle B = 180° - 88° = 92°$

$m\angle A + m\angle B + m\angle C = 180°$

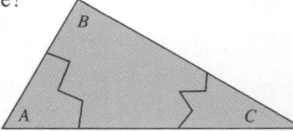 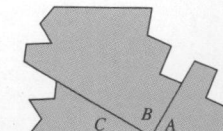

140

Follow Up

Reteaching

Discuss angle measure and draw a triangle having all angles with measures less than 90°. Name this triangle acute. Continue in the same way, naming right and obtuse triangles. Have students draw triangles of different shapes and sizes. Ask them to determine the measure of each angle in the triangle and decide if the triangle is acute, right, or obtuse. Then have them find the sum of the measures of the angles in each triangle.

Enrichment

Have students draw triangles, using rulers and protractors (TRB p. 280), which fit these descriptions.

1. right and isosceles
2. obtuse and scalene
3. acute and scalene
4. acute and isosceles
5. obtuse and isosceles
6. right and scalene

Name each triangle according to the measure of its angles.

1. 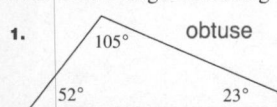 obtuse
2. 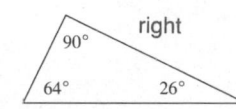 right
3. acute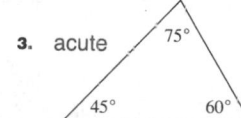

Name each triangle according to the length of its sides.

4. isosceles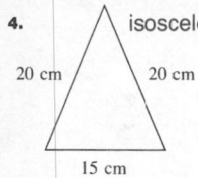
5. scalene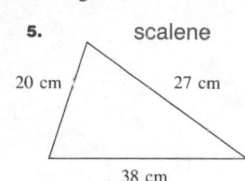
6. 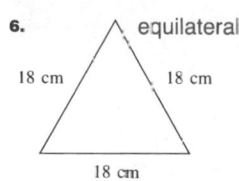 equilateral

Give two names for each triangle.

7. 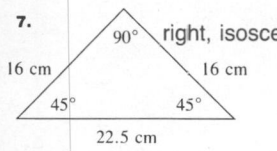 right, isosceles
8. right, scalene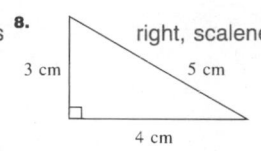
9. obtuse, isosceles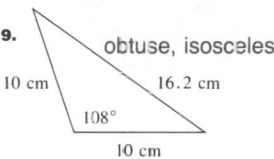

Find the measure of the third angle in each triangle.

10.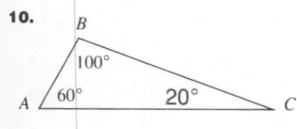
11.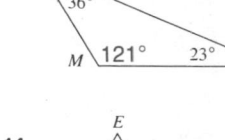
12.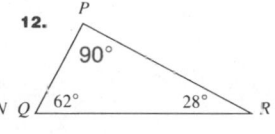

13.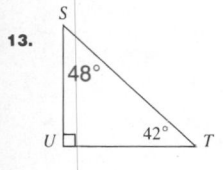
14.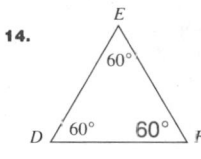
15.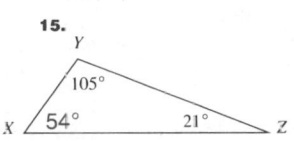

16. The measures of the angles of a triangle are 28°, 37°, and 115°. Is the triangle acute, right, or obtuse? obtuse

17. The measures of two angles of a triangle are 67° and 72°. Is the triangle acute, right, or obtuse? acute

18. Can a triangle have two obtuse angles? Explain your answer. No, the sides would not meet. The sum of the angles would be greater than 180°.

19. Can a triangle have one right angle and one obtuse angle? Explain your answer. No, the sides would not meet. The sum of the angles would be greater than 180°. 141

Using Page 141

Exercises 10–15 Some students may use their protractors to find the measure of the third angle in each triangle. Remind them that the sum of the three angles in any triangle is 180°, so they can use addition and subtraction to find the missing measure. Write an equation for one of the problems on the chalkboard. For example, in exercise 10 the measure of angle C is 180° − (100° + 60°) = 20°.

Exercises 18–19 Have students use their protractors to draw figures that illustrate their answers.

Exercise 18:

Exercise 19:

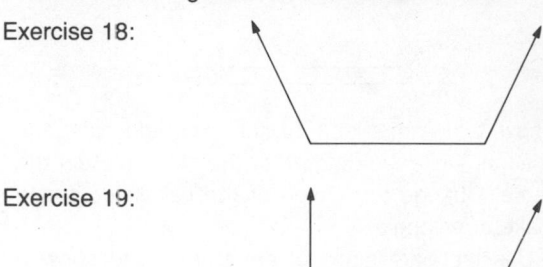

Reteaching Supplement, page 42

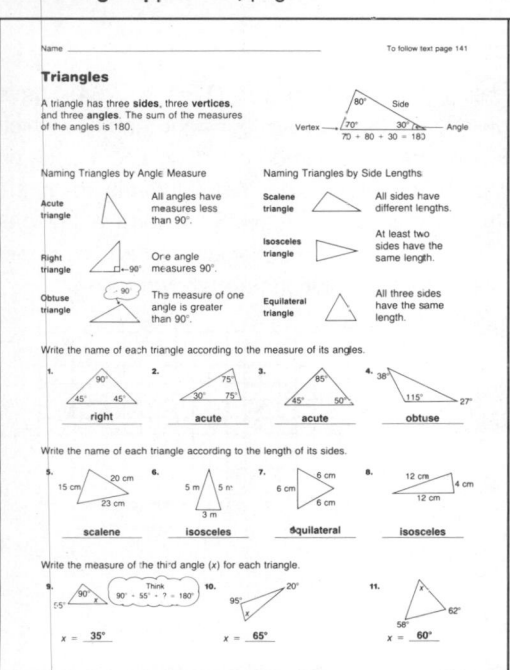

Enrichment Supplement, page 42

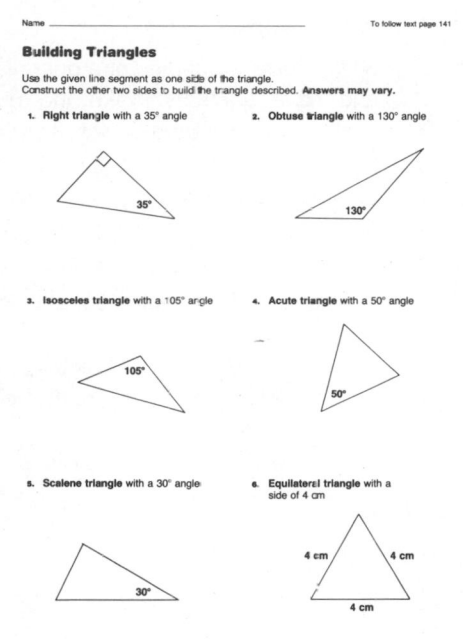

Practice Supplement, page 53

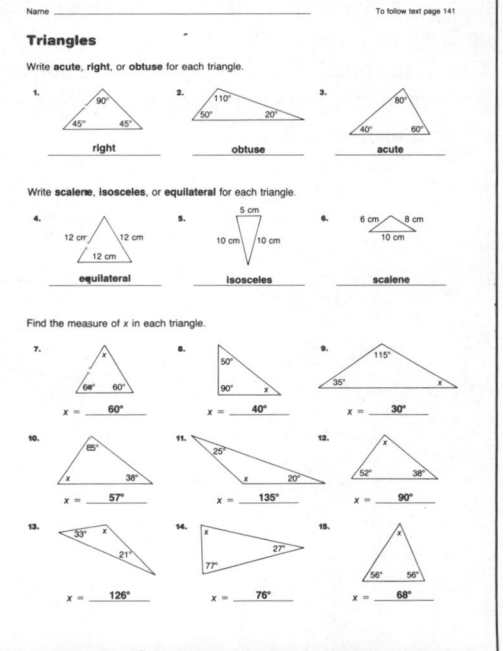

Lesson Focus To identify special quadrilaterals and to find the measure of one angle of a quadrilateral when the measures of the other three angles are known

Suggested Materials Tagboard strips, paper fasteners

Ideas for Getting Started

Make a parallelogram with tagboard strips and paper fasteners.

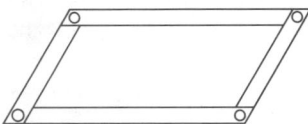

Show that the shape of the parallelogram can change, while the lengths of the sides remain the same. Change the shape of the parallelogram to make a rectangle.

Use tagboard strips of equal length to show a rhombus. Change the shape of the rhombus to make a square.

Using Page 142

Lesson Development Discuss the definitions of the special quadrilaterals and the relationships between them. The diagram below may prove helpful in illustrating these relationships.

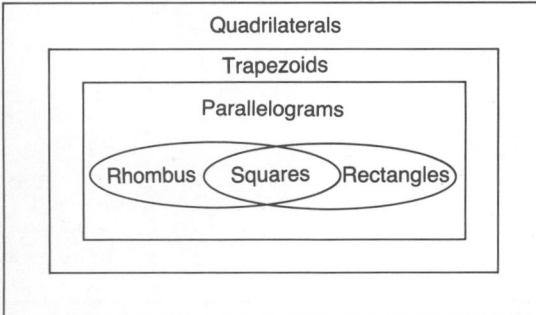

The figure shows that parallelograms are a kind of trapezoid. It also shows that every square is both a rhombus and a rectangle.

Direct students' attention to the quadrilateral at the bottom of the page and discuss why the sum of the four angles is 360°.

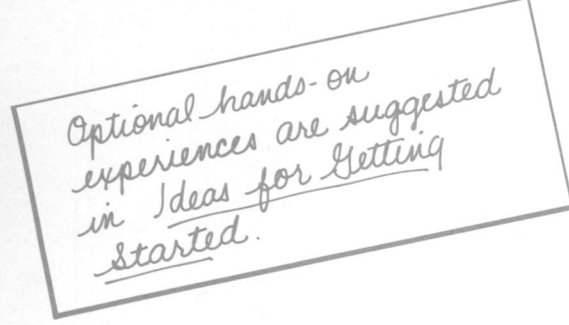

Optional hands-on experiences are suggested in Ideas for Getting Started.

Quadrilaterals

Quadrilaterals have four sides and four angles.

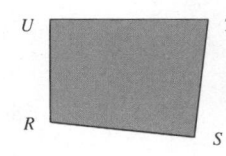

Quadrilateral *RSTU*
Sides: $\overline{RS}$, $\overline{ST}$, $\overline{TU}$, $\overline{UR}$
Angles: $\angle R$, $\angle S$, $\angle T$, $\angle U$

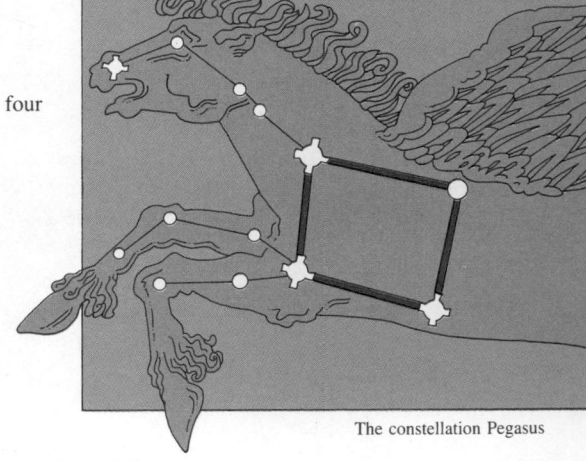

The constellation Pegasus

Some special kinds of quadrilaterals are shown below.

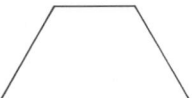

Trapezoid
A quadrilateral with a pair of parallel sides

Parallelogram
A quadrilateral with both pairs of opposite sides parallel

Rhombus
A parallelogram with all sides the same length

Rectangle
A parallelogram with four right angles

Square
A rectangle with all sides the same length

$\overline{AC}$ is a **diagonal** of quadrilateral *ABCD*. This diagonal divides the quadrilateral into two triangles.

The sum of the measures of the angles in each triangle is 180°.

Therefore, the sum of the measures of the four angles of any quadrilateral is 360°.

142

$m \angle A + m \angle B + m \angle C + m \angle D = 360°$

Follow Up

Reteaching

Name some properties of a quadrilateral and have students make the quadrilateral on a geoboard or dot paper (TRB p. 283). Ask students to give the name of each figure. For example, ask students to make:

- A quadrilateral having four equal sides and four equal angles (square)
- A quadrilateral with opposite sides parallel and four right angles (rectangle)
- A quadrilateral with two sides parallel (trapezoid)

Enrichment

On graph paper (TRB p. 284), have students make four right triangles which have 3 units on one side and 4 units on the other side. Ask students to fit the four pieces together to form a triangle, rectangle, parallelogram, and trapezoid. Some solutions are shown below.

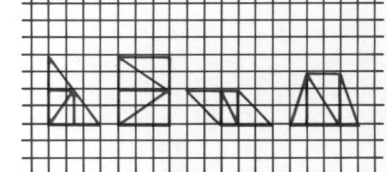

4

Name the kind of quadrilateral shown.

1.

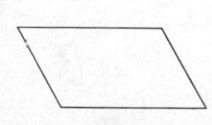

parallelogram

2.

6 cm

6 cm

6 cm

6 cm

rhombus

3.

trapezoid

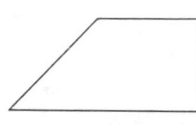

Find the measure of the fourth angle in each quadrilateral.

4.

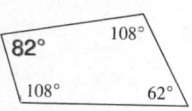

82° 108°

108° 62°

5.

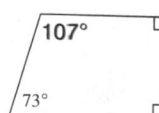

107°

73°

6.

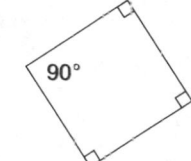

90°

7.

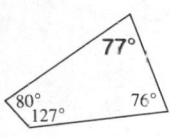

77°

80° 76°

127°

8.

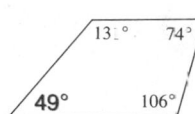

13_° 74°

49° 106°

9.

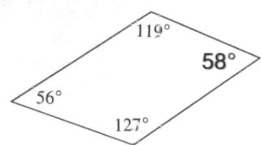

119°

58°

56°

127°

10. What is the measure of ∠C of a quadrilateral *ABCD* when *m* ∠ *A* = 70°, *m* ∠ *B* = 107°, and *m* ∠ *D* = 80°? **103°**

11. Draw a parallelogram that has a right angle. What kind of figure will result? **rectangle or square**

■ **THINK MATH** ■

Shape Perception

Draw a large quadrilateral *ABCD*. Measure each side and mark the middle points *M*, *N*, *O*, and *P*.

Draw a quadrilateral *MNOP*. It should be a parallelogram.

Cut off the four triangles in the figure. Try to place the four triangles so that they will exactly cover quadrilateral *MNOP*.

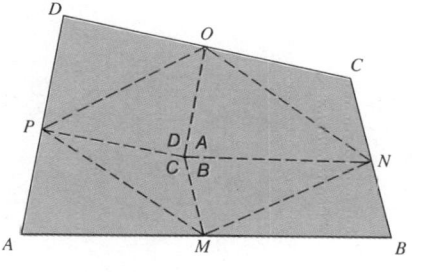

143

Using Page 143

Think Math This problem involves geometric relationships and spatial perception. Have students make a large copy of a quadrilateral. Regardless of its shape, the figure formed by joining the consecutive midpoints of the sides will be a parallelogram. The parallelogram can be covered by the four triangles without turning over any of the pieces.

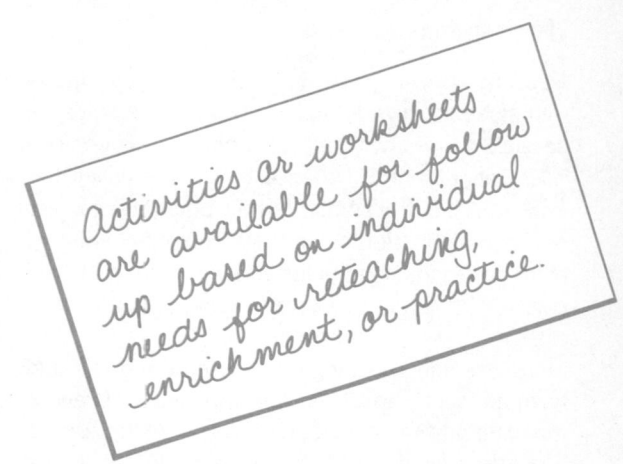

Activities or worksheets are available for follow up based on individual needs for reteaching, enrichment, or practice.

Reteaching Supplement, page 43

Enrichment Supplement, page 43

Practice Supplement, page 54

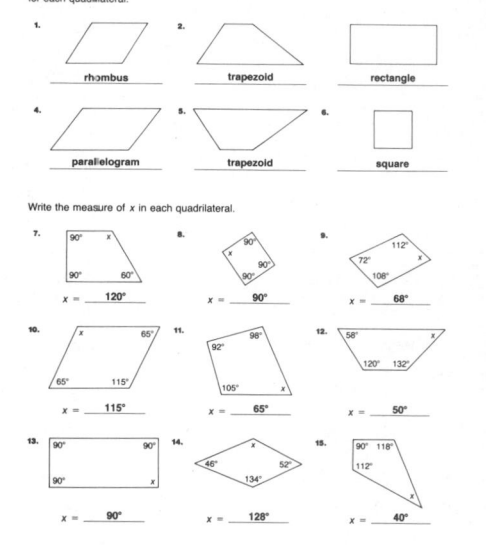

Quick Review Have students give the missing factor.
$7,000 = \underline{7} \times 10^3$ $267,000 = \underline{2.67} \times 10^5$ $139 = \underline{1.39} \times 10^2$
$4,280,000 = \underline{4.28} \times 10^6$ $50,600 = \underline{5.06} \times 10^4$ $4,530 = \underline{4.53} \times 10^3$

Lesson Focus To identify polygons according to the number of sides

Ideas for Getting Started

Write the word *polygon* on the chalkboard. Ask students for the meaning of the prefix "poly." If no one volunteers the meaning of "many" or "much", have a student find the prefix in the dictionary. Also have someone look up the suffix "gon," which refers to an angle. Explain that a polygon is a figure of many angles. Since an angle has 2 sides, polygons are also figures with many sides.

On the chalkboard, draw some figures that are polygons and some figures that are not polygons. Explain that polygons have segments as sides, are closed, and have sides that do not cross.

Not Polygons   Polygons

Using Page 144

Lesson Development In discussing polygons with students, give as many physical examples as possible for the polygons of 5 or more sides. The U.S. Department of Defense building is called the Pentagon. Floor tiles and honeycombs are regular hexagons, and stop signs have octagonal shapes. Mathematicians use the terms 15-gon, 20-gon, and *n*-gon to refer to polygons having 15, 20, or *n* sides.

Discuss the meaning of the term regular and have students examine the examples. Draw a rhombus on the chalkboard. "Is a rhombus always a regular polygon?" (No, because all angles do not have the same measure.)

Exercises 1–8 Use these as oral exercises. Have students state if the polygon is regular.

Polygons

Honeybees build six-sided cells for storage. A geometric figure having many sides that are segments is a **polygon**.

Polygons are named according to the number of sides they have.

Polygon	Number of sides	Name
	3	triangle
	4	quadrilateral
	5	pentagon
	6	hexagon

Polygon	Number of sides	Name
	7	heptagon
	8	octagon
	9	nonagon
	10	decagon

Polygons with all sides the same length and all angles having the same measure are called **regular polygons**.

      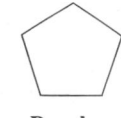      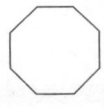

Equilateral triangle   **Square**   **Regular pentagon**   **Regular hexagon**   **Regular octagon**

Name each polygon.

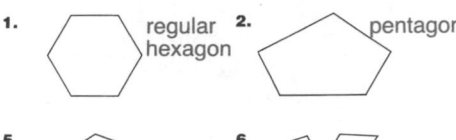

1. regular hexagon   2. pentagon   3. quadrilateral   4. triangle

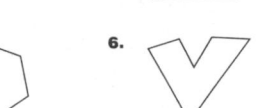

5. heptagon   6. hexagon   7. decagon   8. octagon

144

Follow Up

Reteaching

Have students use geoboards or dot paper (TRB P. 283) to make figures having different numbers of sides. Give the condition that the figure must be closed and that sides cannot cross. After the figures are made, have students describe their figures. Discuss and name each polygon.

Enrichment

Have students cut out Tangram pattern pieces (TRB p. 279). There are 13 different convex polygons that can be formed by using all seven Tangram pieces.

Challenge students to find as many of the 13 polygons as possible.

There is one square, one rectangle, two trapezoids, one general quadrilateral, two pentagons, and four hexagons.

Use the drawing at the right for exercises 1–4.

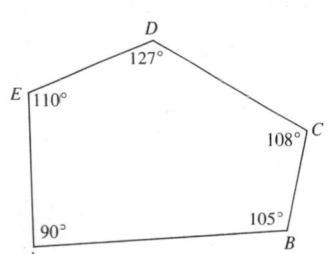

1. Name polygon *ABCDE*. pentagon

2. Name each side of the polygon.
$\overline{AB}, \overline{BC}, \overline{CD}, \overline{DE}, \overline{EA}$

3. Give the measure of each angle of the polygon. $m\angle A = 90°$, $m\angle B = 105°$, $m\angle C = 108°$, $m\angle D = 127°$, $m\angle E = 110°$

4. What is the sum of the angles of the polygon? 540°

Name each polygon. State if it is regular.

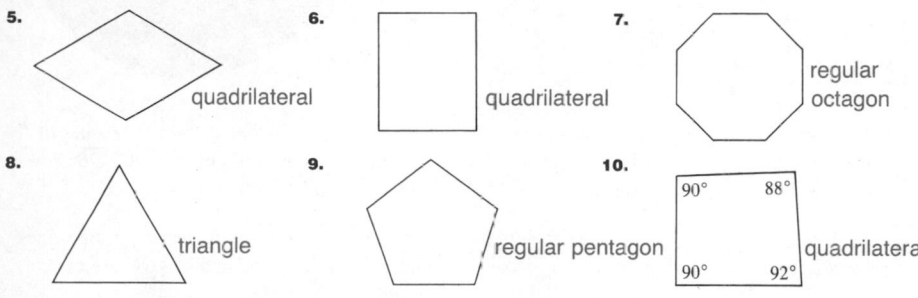

5. quadrilateral

6. quadrilateral

7. regular octagon

8. triangle

9. regular pentagon

10. quadrilateral

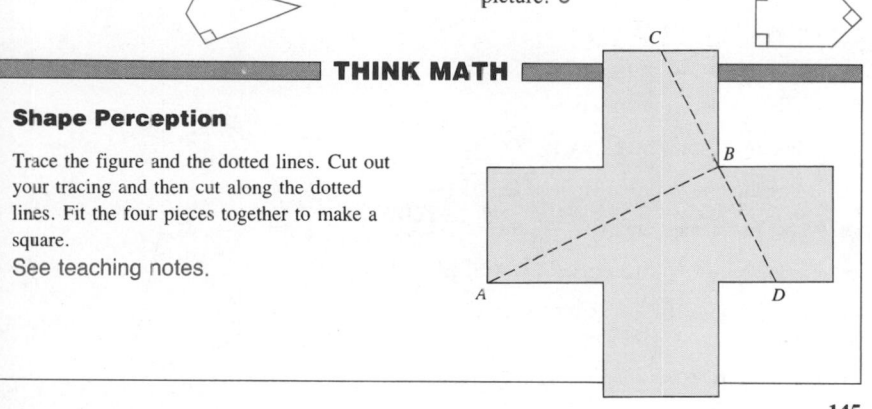

★ 11. Can a quadrilateral have two right angles and no parallel sides? Draw a picture. yes

★ 12. What is the greatest number of right angles possible in a pentagon? Draw a picture. 3

━━━━━ **THINK MATH** ━━━━━

Shape Perception

Trace the figure and the dotted lines. Cut out your tracing and then cut along the dotted lines. Fit the four pieces together to make a square.

See teaching notes.

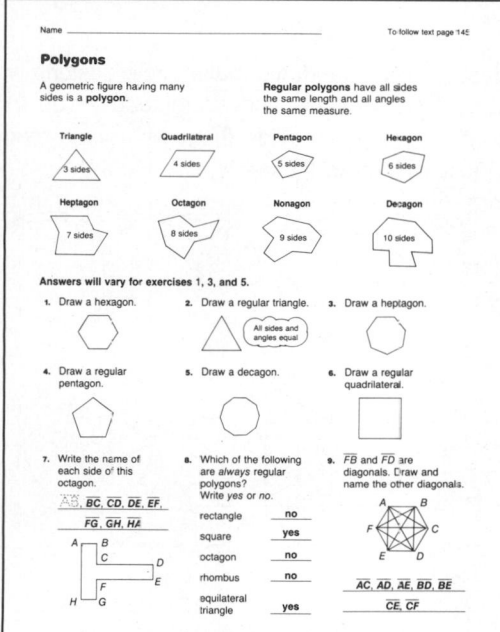

Using Page 145

Exercise 4 Students will find that the sum of the angles of a pentagon is 540°. This is true of any pentagon because a pentagon can be partitioned into 3 triangles, each having an angle sum of 180°.

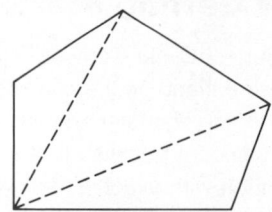

In general, the sum of the angles of any polygon is $(n - 2) \times 180$, where *n* is the number of sides.

Think Math This problem involves spatial perception and understanding the properties of a square. It would be helpful for students to draw the pattern of the cross on graph paper. Note that *C* and *D* are midpoints of two sides of the cross.

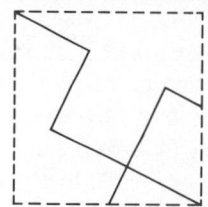

After students have solved the problem, challenge them to make some other shapes with the 4 pieces.

Reteaching Supplement, page 44

Enrichment Supplement, page 44

Practice Supplement, page 55

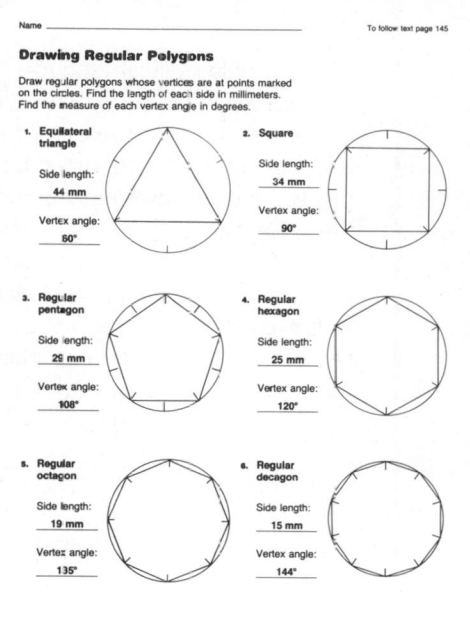

Quick Review Have students multiply to check which of the following quotients are incorrect.

52 R4	38 R6 **incorrect**	304 R2 **incorrect**	215 R6
6)316	7)2,162	5)1,524	7)1,511

Lesson Focus To identify the diameter, radius, central angles, chords, and arcs in a circle

Suggested Materials Chalkboard compass and student compasses

Ideas for Getting Started

Conduct a "Perfect Circle Contest." Have selected students draw freehand on the chalkboard the best circle they can. The diameter should be at least 30 cm. Ask each student to estimate the center of the circle and mark it with a dot. Then have the class vote on the best circle. Discuss why it was chosen. Some students may say it is the "roundest." Show that we might check the drawing by sketching radii from the center and measuring these radii to see if they are all about the same length. Relate the activity to the definition of a circle given in the student book.

Using Page 146

Lesson Development Call students' attention to the art at the top of the page. The jade *bi* was carved by an unknown Chinese artist. It dates from the Chou dynasty (400–200 B.C.).

Discuss the geometric terms defined on the page. The words diameter and radius will be review for most students. Elicit from students the relationships between the radius and diameter of a circle.

Explain that there are two ways the term radius is used in mathematics. It can refer to a segment from the center of the circle to a point on a circle, or it can refer to the length of the segment. "A circle with a radius of 6 cm" means "a circle with a radius of length 6 cm."

Give students several examples of central angles, chords, and arcs. Only *minor arcs,* that is, arcs less than a semi-circle, are discussed here.

Exercises 1–8 These exercises will strengthen students' understanding of the concepts presented on this page. In exercises 2–6, the order the points are given may be reversed.

Circles

In the Chinese jade disk, called a *bi*, there are shapes that remind us of circles.

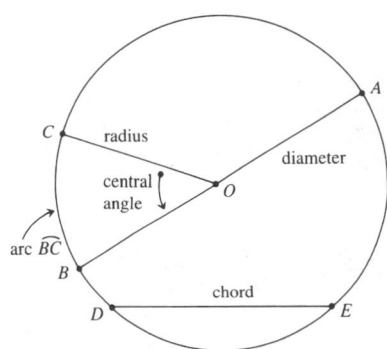

A **circle** is all the points in a plane that are the same distance from one point called the **center**. Point O is the center of circle O.

A **chord** is a segment with its endpoints on the circle. $\overline{AB}$ and $\overline{DE}$ are chords.

A **diameter** is a chord that passes through the center of the circle. $\overline{AB}$ is a diameter.

A **radius** is a segment from the center of the circle to a point on a circle. $\overline{OC}$, $\overline{OB}$, and $\overline{OA}$ are radii.

A **central angle** has its vertex at the center of a circle. $\angle BOC$ and $\angle AOC$ are central angles.

An **arc** is a part of a circle. $\overset{\frown}{BC}$ or $\overset{\frown}{CB}$ is the shorter arc with endpoints B and C.

Use circle Q for exercises 1–8.

1. Name the center of the circle. **point Q**

2. Name a diameter of the circle. **$\overline{YW}$**

3. Name two chords of the circle. **$\overline{YX}$, $\overline{WX}$**

4. Name three radii of the circle. **$\overline{ZQ}$, $\overline{YQ}$, $\overline{WQ}$**

5. Name two central angles of the circle. **$\angle ZQW$, $\angle ZQY$**

6. Name four arcs of the circle. **$\overset{\frown}{YX}$, $\overset{\frown}{XW}$, $\overset{\frown}{WZ}$, $\overset{\frown}{ZY}$**

7. If the length of $\overline{QZ}$ is 1.8 cm, what is the length of $\overline{WY}$? **3.6 cm**

8. If $m \angle ZQY = 85°$, what is $m \angle ZQW$? **95°**

146

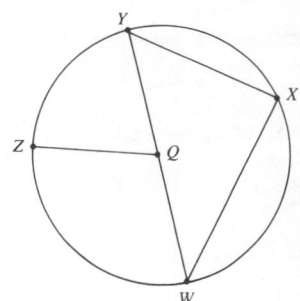

Follow Up

Reteaching

Discuss objects that suggest circles, such as coins, plates, windows, wheels, and so on. Draw a circle on the board and identify related terms, such as the center, radius, diameter, and chord. Point out that the diameter and radius are line segments. Use different colors of chalk to highlight radii and diameters. Define central angle and arc of a circle. Discuss the notation for describing arcs. For example, $\overset{\frown}{CB}$ means arc CB.

Enrichment

Have students make circle designs with a compass and straightedge. You may wish to provide them with some examples like these:

Assignment Guide			
	Minimum	Average	Extended
page 146–147	1–12	1–16	1–16

Follow the directions and answer the questions. Drawings may vary for exercises 9–14.

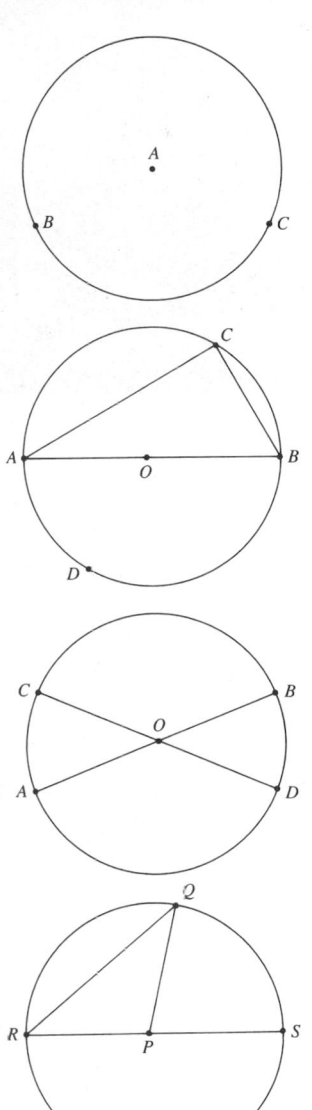

9. Draw a circle with center point *A*. Draw any two radii, $\overline{AB}$ and $\overline{AC}$. Draw chord $\overline{BC}$. What kind of triangle is △*ABC*? **isosceles**

10. Draw a circle with center *O*. Draw diameter $\overline{AB}$ and mark any point *C* on the circle. Draw $\overline{AC}$ and $\overline{BC}$. What is the measure of ∠*ACB*? **90°**

11. Use the same circle as in exercise 10. Mark another point *D* on the circle. Draw $\overline{AD}$ and $\overline{BD}$. What is the measure of ∠*ADB*? **90°**

12. What is the measure of an angle whose vertex is on a circle and whose sides pass through the endpoints of a diameter of the circle? **90°**

13. Draw a circle with center *O*. Draw diameters $\overline{AB}$ and $\overline{CD}$. Draw chords $\overline{AD}$, $\overline{DB}$, $\overline{BC}$, and $\overline{AC}$. What kind of quadrilateral is polygon *ADBC*? **rectangle**

14. Draw a circle with center *P*. Draw a diameter $\overline{RS}$. Mark a point *Q* on the circle. Draw $\overline{PQ}$ and $\overline{RQ}$. What is the measure of the central ∠*QPS*? **Answers will vary.**
What is the measure of ∠*QRS*? **Answers will vary.**
How do the measures of these two angles compare in size? **∠*QRS* is one half ∠*QPS*.**

15. Name the angle that is supplementary to ∠*RPQ*. **∠*QPS***

16. Give the measure of ∠*RPS*. **180°**

147

Using Page 147

Exercises 9–16 Students will need a compass and straightedge for these exercises. Protractors will be needed for exercises 10, 11, and 14. In exercise 14, the measurements for ∠*QPS* and ∠*QRS* may vary if students make their own drawings. However, all should agree that *m*∠*QPS* is twice *m*∠*QRS*.

Reteaching Supplement, page 45

Circles

A circle is all the points in a plane that are the same distance from one point called the center.

These geometric ideas are shown in the figure.

Diameter $\overline{BC}$
Radius $\overline{AD}$ or $\overline{AC}$ or $\overline{AB}$
Chord $\overline{EF}$
Arc DC, BC, BD
Central Angle ∠CAD, ∠BAD
Center point A

1. Write a name for each part of the figure shown.

Center **point R**
Radius **$\overline{RT}$, $\overline{RS}$, or $\overline{RU}$**
Longest Chord **$\overline{US}$**
Diameter **$\overline{US}$**
Central Angle **∠TRU, ∠TRS**

2. Draw a circle with center *P*. Draw diameter $\overline{MN}$ and mark any point Q on the circle. Draw $\overline{MQ}$ and $\overline{NQ}$. What kind of triangle is △MQN? **right triangle**

3. Draw a circle with a central angle named ∠DEF. What is the name of the arc cut off by the central angle? **DF**

4. Draw a circle with a diameter $\overline{JK}$, a chord $\overline{JL}$, and a chord $\overline{LK}$. What polygon did you make? **triangle**

Enrichment Supplement, page 45

Drawing Circles

Circles and One Point

1. How many circles can have point P as a center? **an unlimited number**
Draw two of them. **Circles will vary.**

2. How many different circles can pass through point R (R is not the center)? **an unlimited number**
Draw two of them.

Circles and Two Points

3. How many circles can be drawn that go through both points S and T? **an unlimited number**
Draw two of them.

4. Describe how to find the center of a circle with diameter $\overline{ST}$. **Draw line $\overline{ST}$. Find the midpoint of $\overline{ST}$. That is the center of the circle.**

Practice Supplement, page 56

Circles

Use circle O for numbers 1 through 7.

1. Name the center of the circle. **O**
2. Name a diameter. **$\overline{AC}$**
3. Name two chords. **$\overline{AB}$, $\overline{ED}$**
4. Name three radii. **$\overline{OC}$, $\overline{OB}$, or $\overline{OA}$**
5. Name two central angles. **∠AOB, ∠BOC**
6. Name five arcs. **$\overline{AB}$, $\overline{BC}$, $\overline{CD}$, $\overline{DE}$, $\overline{AE}$**

7. If the length of $\overline{OA}$ is 2.4 cm, what is the length of $\overline{AC}$? **4.8 cm**

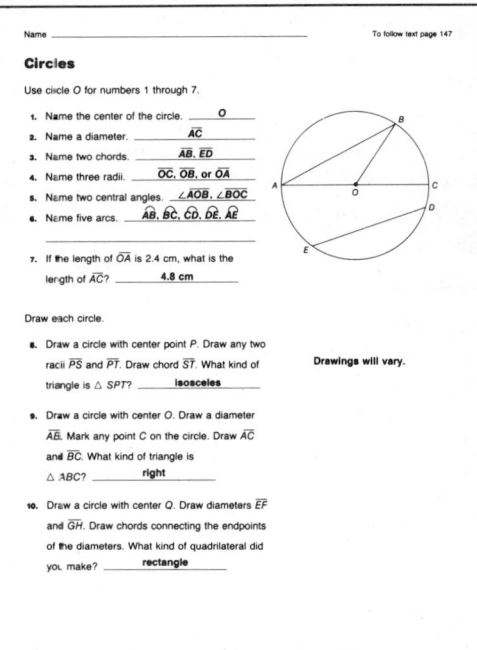

Draw each circle.

8. Draw a circle with center point P. Draw any two radii $\overline{PS}$ and $\overline{PT}$. Draw chord $\overline{ST}$. What kind of triangle is △ SPT? **isosceles** **Drawings will vary.**

9. Draw a circle with center O. Draw a diameter $\overline{AB}$. Mark any point C on the circle. Draw $\overline{AC}$ and $\overline{BC}$. What kind of triangle is △ ABC? **right**

10. Draw a circle with center O. Draw diameters $\overline{EF}$ and $\overline{GH}$. Draw chords connecting the endpoints of the diameters. What kind of quadrilateral did you make? **rectangle**

Lesson Focus To identify congruent pairs of segments, angles, and triangles

Ideas for Getting Started

Fold a sheet of paper in half. Draw a picture of a simple polygon on one half of the paper. Then cut out the polygon through both sheets of paper producing two regions that have the same size and shape. Use these regions to introduce the idea of congruent figures. Point out that if two figures are congruent, we can think of placing one figure on top of the other so that all the points of one figure match all of the points of the other.

Using Page 148

Lesson Development The definition of congruent segments and congruent angles is given in terms of their measures. Tell students that if two polygons are congruent, both the corresponding sides and the corresponding angles are congruent. Display these polygons on the chalkboard and explain why each pair is not congruent.

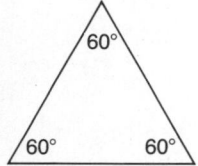 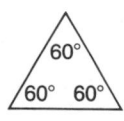

The two equilateral triangles are not congruent because matching sides are not congruent.

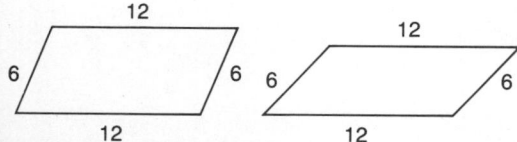

The two parallelograms are not congruent because matching angles are not congruent.

Stress that the order in which we write the vertices shows how the sides and angles of polygons are matched. In the example found on this page, $\triangle ABC \cong \triangle EDF$. Point out that the matching vertices are $A \leftrightarrow E$, $B \leftrightarrow D$, and $C \leftrightarrow F$, and that the same matching is shown by writing $\triangle BCA \cong \triangle DFE$. Explain that it would be incorrect to write $\triangle ABC \cong \triangle DEF$ because the matching angles and matching sides indicated by this notation are not congruent.

Exercise 1 You may wish to have students compare measures of the segments by using the edge of a paper and marking off the length of each.

Congruent Figures

Two geometric figures are **congruent** to each other if they have the same size and shape.

Two segments are congruent to each other if they have the same length.

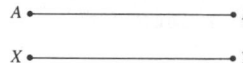

$\overline{AB}$ is **congruent** to $\overline{XY}$.
$\overline{AB} \cong \overline{XY}$

Two angles are congruent if they have the same measure.

$m \angle P = 37°$ $m \angle Q = 37°$
$\angle P$ is congruent to $\angle Q$.
$\angle P \cong \angle Q$

Two polygons are congruent if their vertices can be matched so that the matching sides are congruent and the matching angles are congruent.
    Vertices A, B, and C can be matched to vertices E, D, and F so that

$\angle A \cong \angle E$	$\overline{AB} \cong \overline{ED}$
$\angle B \cong \angle D$	$\overline{BC} \cong \overline{DF}$
$\angle C \cong \angle F$	$\overline{CA} \cong \overline{FE}$

$\triangle ABC$ is congruent to $\triangle EDF$.
$\triangle ABC \cong \triangle EDF$

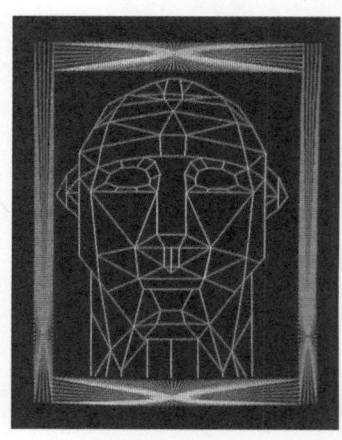
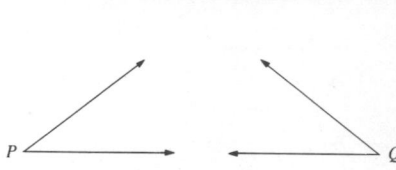
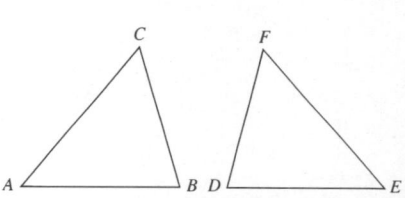

1. Which pair of segments is congruent? $\overline{CD} \cong \overline{GH}$

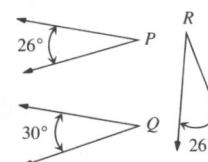

2. Which pair of angles is congruent? $\angle P \cong \angle R$

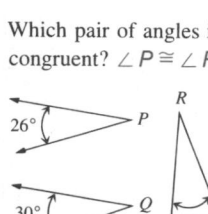

3. Which pair of triangles is congruent? $\triangle XYZ \cong \triangle JLK$

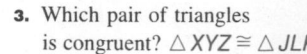
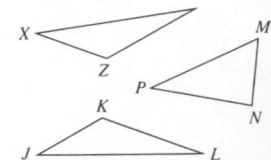

Follow Up

Reteaching

Have students draw a triangle on their paper. Then ask them to use another sheet of paper and trace the triangle. Discuss how the traced figure and the original are the same. If sides are the same length and angles are the same measure, the figures are congruent.
    Repeat the activity with other figures. Have students label the figures and indicate matching parts.

Enrichment

Have students use Tangram puzzle pieces (TRB p. 279) to make a triangle congruent to one of the large triangles in the puzzle. Ask them how many different ways this can be done. There are four possibilities, including the other large triangle.

Each pair of triangles is congruent. List the pairs of congruent angles and pairs of congruent sides.

4.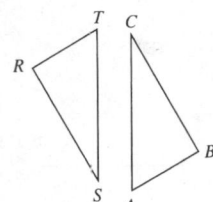

$\angle X \cong \angle G$
$\angle V \cong \angle E$
$\angle W \cong \angle F$
$\overline{VX} \cong \overline{EG}$
$\overline{XW} \cong \overline{GF}$
$\overline{WV} \cong \overline{FE}$

5.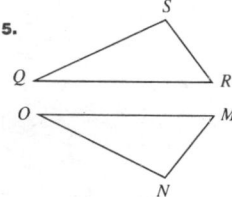

$\angle Q \cong \angle O$
$\angle S \cong \angle N$
$\angle R \cong \angle M$
$\overline{QS} \cong \overline{ON}$
$\overline{SR} \cong \overline{NM}$
$\overline{RQ} \cong \overline{MO}$

6.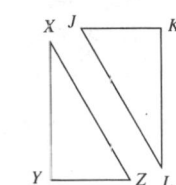

$\angle T \cong \angle A$
$\angle S \cong \angle C$
$\angle R \cong \angle B$
$\overline{RT} \cong \overline{BA}$
$\overline{TS} \cong \overline{AC}$
$\overline{SR} \cong \overline{CB}$

7.

$\angle X \cong \angle L$
$\angle Y \cong \angle K$
$\angle Z \cong \angle J$
$\overline{XY} \cong \overline{LK}$
$\overline{YZ} \cong \overline{KJ}$
$\overline{ZX} \cong \overline{JL}$

Use $\triangle ABC$ and $\triangle TRS$ for exercises 8–16. $\triangle ABC \cong \triangle TRS$

8. $\angle A \cong \blacksquare \angle T$

9. $\angle B \cong \blacksquare \angle R$

10. $\angle C \cong \blacksquare \angle S$

11. $\overline{AB} \cong \blacksquare \overline{RT}$

12. $\overline{AC} \cong \blacksquare \overline{ST}$

13. $\overline{BC} \cong \blacksquare \overline{RS}$

14. What is the length of $\overline{RT}$? **5 cm**

15. What is the measure of $\angle S$? **90°**

16. What is the length of $\overline{ST}$? **4 cm**

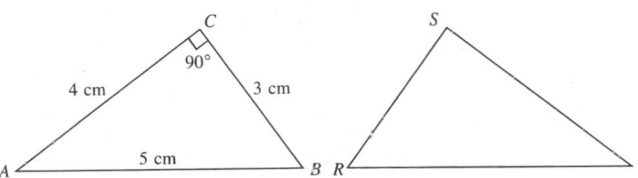

┃ **THINK MATH** ┃

Shape Perception

How many pairs of congruent triangles can you find in this picture? **7**

Name the pairs you find.
See teaching notes.

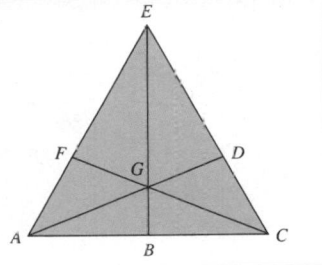

149

Using Page 149

Exercises 4–16 In exercise 5, students may need to imagine that $\triangle OMN$ is flipped to make it seem congruent to $\triangle QRS$. In exercises 6 and 7, one of the triangles can be rotated to make the pairing of congruent parts easier to see. Exercises 14, 15, and 16 rely upon the definitions of congruent segments and angles. When two segments or two angles are congruent, they have the same measure.

Think Math This problem relies upon an understanding of congruent triangles, the ability to perceive overlapping triangles, and the strategy of Making an Organized List. The overlapping pairs of congruent triangles are the most difficult for students to see. Make isolated drawings of these triangles to help the students visualize them.

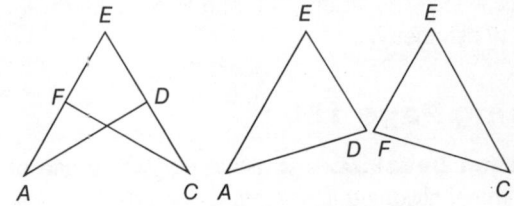

There are 7 pairs of congruent triangles.

$\triangle ABG \cong \triangle CBG$
$\triangle AGF \cong \triangle CGD$
$\triangle FGE \cong \triangle DGE$
$\triangle ACD \cong \triangle CAF$
$\triangle ADE \cong \triangle CFE$
$\triangle AGE \cong \triangle CGE$
$\triangle ABE \cong \triangle CBE$

Ideas That Work

Special Education

The idea of congruence of segments, angles, and polygons can be reinforced with "Make a Match." In this game, students complete pairs of cards that contain congruent figures. All cards, including a joker, are distributed. Players match any pairs in hand. Then the first player draws from the player at the right and may continue to draw as long as each card results in a match. When a card is drawn that does not match, it is the next player's turn. The player left with the joker loses.

Figures on the cards should have different orientations so that students will apply the concepts of congruence.

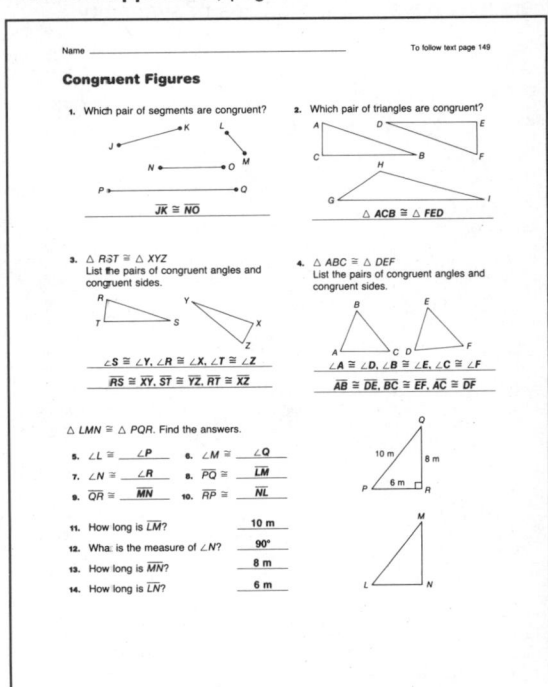

Lesson Focus To recognize and find lines of symmetry in geometric figures

Ideas for Getting Started

Draw these 4 letters on the chalkboard or overhead projector.

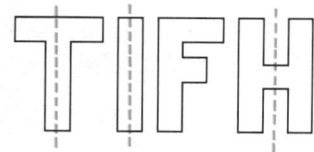

Tell students that all of the letters except one have a common geometric property. Challenge students to try and find the one letter that does not belong with the others. If no one can find the letter, suggest that it is F. Then show that each of the other letters can be divided into 2 matching parts by a vertical line. The letters T, I, and H have a vertical line of symmetry.

Using Page 150

Lesson Development Point out that a line of symmetry divides a figure into 2 congruent halves. The two halves would fit exactly, one on top of the other, if we could fold the figure on its line of symmetry. Show how to make a figure with a line of symmetry by folding a piece of paper and cutting out a region, starting and ending on the fold line.

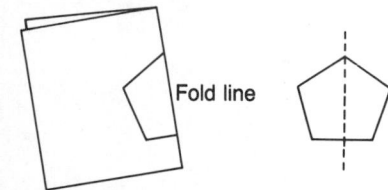
Fold line

The fold line is the line of symmetry.

Exercises 1—9 Work through these exercises as an oral class activity. They illustrate that some figures may have no lines of symmetry, while others may have 1 or more lines of symmetry.

Lines of Symmetry

Think of folding the picture of the hockey rink on the red line or centerline. The two halves of the rink will match.

The red line is a **line of symmetry** of the rink.

Some geometric figures have lines of symmetry.

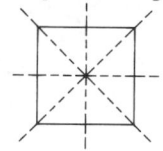 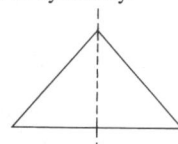 

Square
four lines of symmetry

Isosceles triangle
one line of symmetry

Parallelogram
no lines of symmetry

Think of folding each figure on the dotted line.
Is the dotted line a line of symmetry?

1. yes

2. yes

3. no

4. yes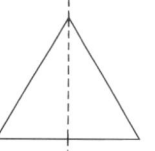

5. yes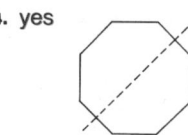

6. no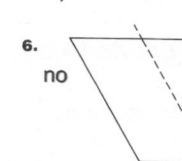

7. yes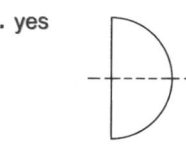

8. no

9. no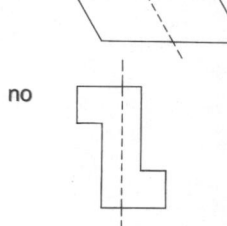

150

Follow Up

Reteaching

Explain to students that figures have a line of symmetry if they can be folded so that the two halves match. For example, if you fold a hexagon as shown, the two parts match and the fold line is a line of symmetry.

Line of symmetry

Have students cut out paper models of the figures on page 151 and find the lines of symmetry by folding.

Enrichment

Challenge students to find all the letters of the alphabet that have lines of symmetry. Ask them to draw the letters and the symmetry lines.

Vertical lines of symmetry:

A H I M O T U V W X Y

Horizontal lines of symmetry:

B C D E H I O X

Assignment Guide			
	Minimum	Average	Extended
page 151	1–9, SK	1–14, SK	1–15, SK

Draw each figure on graph paper. Draw all lines of symmetry.

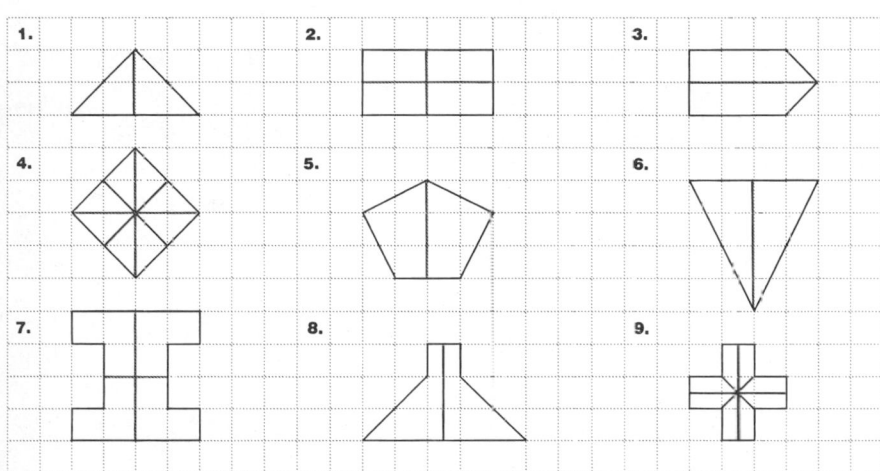

How many lines of symmetry does each polygon have?

10. **11.** **12.** **13.**

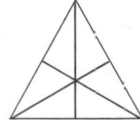 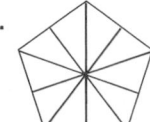 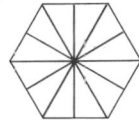 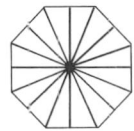

Equilateral triangle 3   Regular pentagon 5   Regular hexagon 6   Regular octagon 8

14. How many lines of symmetry does a regular decagon have? 10

15. What is true of any one of the lines of symmetry of a circle? It is a diameter.

SKILLKEEPER

1.	2.	3.	4.	5.
9.7 × 7	0.35 × 3	12.67 × 19	0.004 × 67	5.05 × 92
67.9	1.05	240.73	0.268	464.60
6. 0.56 × 0.5	**7.** 5.7 × 0.20	**8.** 0.0009 × 0.8	**9.** 10.73 × 0.5	**10.** 0.47 × 0.7
0.28	1.14	0.00072	5.365	0.329
11. 0.423 × 0.015	**12.** 0.598 × 5.6	**13.** 3.8 × 0.05	**14.** 12.34 × 6.2	**15.** 2.724 × 0.16
0.006345	3.3488	0.19	76.508	0.43584

Using Page 151

Exercises 1–9 Graph paper is recommended for these exercises. It will help students to draw the figures symmetrically and find the lines of symmetry.

Skillkeeper This skill was originally taught in Chapter 4.

Reteaching Supplement, page 46

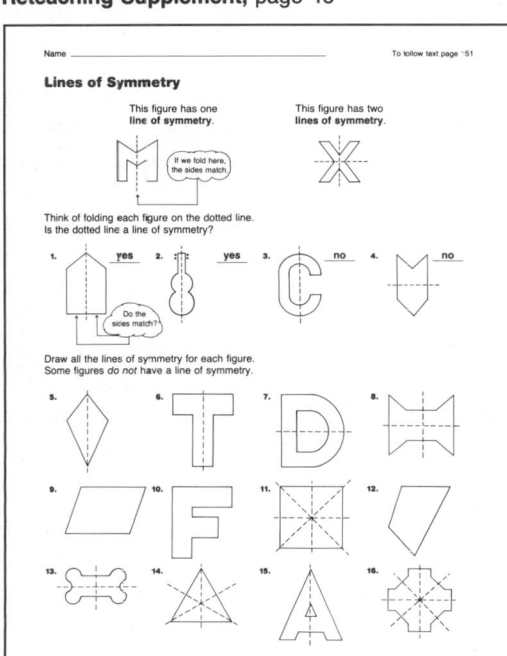

Enrichment Supplement, page 46

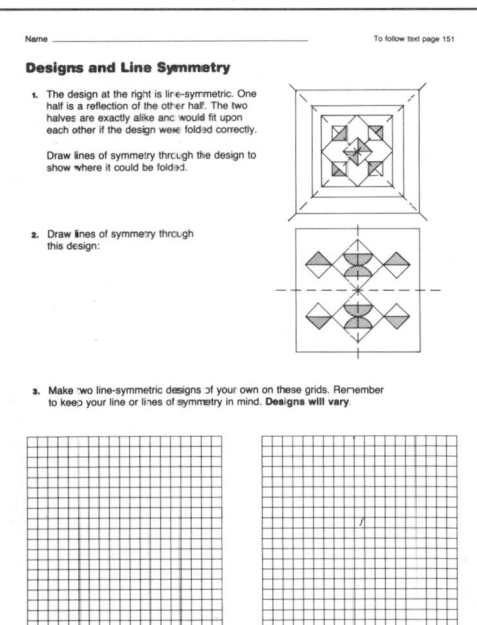

Practice Supplement, page 58

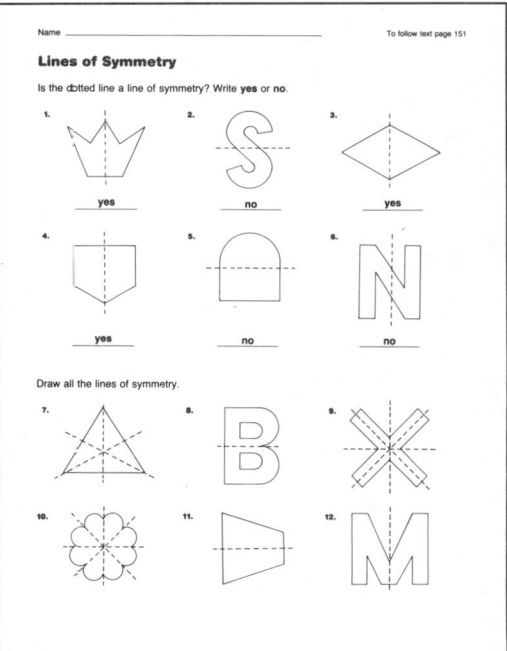

Quick Review Have students estimate the products by rounding to 1-digit accuracy.

| 17.4 × 0.2 **4.0** | 0.97 × 0.72 **0.7** | 0.62 × 0.37 **0.24** |
| 8.4 × 0.62 **4.8** | 39.3 × 2.7 **120** | 642.37 × 0.34 **180.0** |

Lesson Focus To use a straightedge and compass to construct two perpendicular lines and two parallel lines

Suggested Materials Chalkboard compass and student compasses

Ideas for Getting Started

Discuss the use and care of a compass. Suggest that students use several sheets of paper under their working paper in order to prevent damage of the desk top and to stop the compass from slipping. Tell students that slanting the compass in the direction that the drawing point is moving helps to make the drawing smoother and keeps the center point fixed.

Using Page 152

Lesson Development The symbols ⊥ for perpendicular and ∥ for parallel may be new to some students. Notice with students that in the examples at the top of the page, lower-case letters are used to denote lines rather than naming 2 points on each line.

On the chalkboard, show the steps for each construction. Use the techniques for teaching constructions that work best for you. One useful method is to have students construct each step as they follow your step-by-step demonstration.

Constructing Parallel Lines and Perpendicular Lines

Two lines in the same plane that do not intersect are **parallel lines**.

Two lines that intersect to form right angles are **perpendicular lines**.

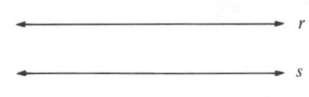

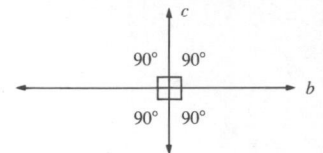

Line r is parallel to line s.
We write: $r \parallel s$

Lines b and c are perpendicular lines.
We write: $b \perp c$

Construct a line perpendicular to a line through a point on the line.

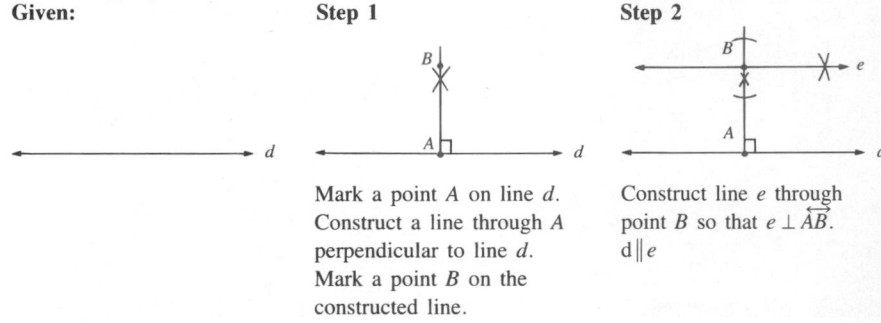

Given: | **Step 1** | **Step 2** | **Step 3**

Draw arcs with center at P. Label points A and B.

Open compass wider and draw arcs with centers A and B. Label the point of intersection C.

Draw $\overleftrightarrow{CP}$. $\overleftrightarrow{CP} \perp f$ at point P.

Construct a line parallel to a given line.

Given: | **Step 1** | **Step 2**

Mark a point A on line d. Construct a line through A perpendicular to line d. Mark a point B on the constructed line.

Construct line e through point B so that $e \perp \overleftrightarrow{AB}$. $d \parallel e$

152

Follow Up

Reteaching

Discuss with students models for parallel lines, such as railroad tracks and yellow lines on highways. Use the example of highway intersections to discuss lines that intersect. Ask students for other examples.

Draw a map of your community. Have students identify both parallel and perpendicular lines.

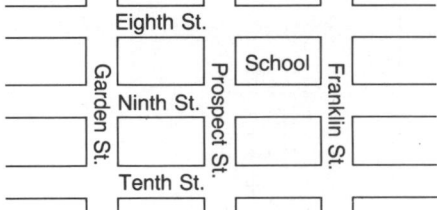

Enrichment

Have students use a ruler and compass to construct parallel and perpendicular lines to form individual patterns, such as those used in wrapping paper, placemats, or fabrics. By using the colored pencils to draw line segments or to shade regions, the design can be made more attractive. Have students cut out the completed design and paste it on colored paper. When laminated, they can be used for placemats or bulletin board displays.

Assignment Guide			
	Minimum	Average	Extended
page 153		1–6	1–8

1. Draw a line *t* and mark a point *R* on the line. Construct a line *m* through *R* perpendicular to *t*.

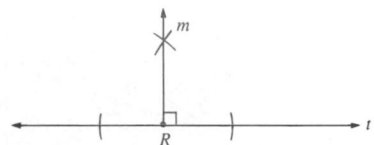

2. Draw any line *m*. Construct a line *a* parallel to *m*.

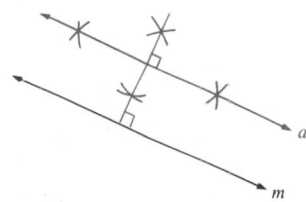

3. Draw two lines, each perpendicular to $\overleftrightarrow{AB}$, one through *A* and the other through *B*. How are the two constructed lines related? $\overleftrightarrow{A} \parallel \overleftrightarrow{B}$

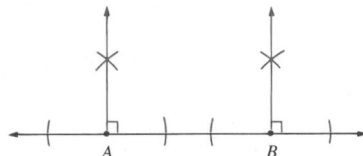

4. Draw any line *s*. Construct two lines each parallel to *s* and on opposite sides of *s*.

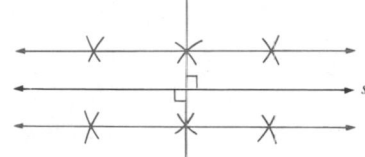

5. Use a ruler and a compass to construct a square.

Students' constructions should closely resemble these drawings.

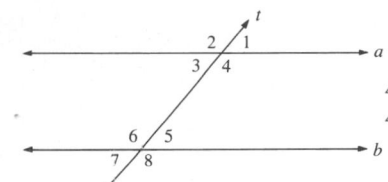

6. Construct a trapezoid that has two right angles.

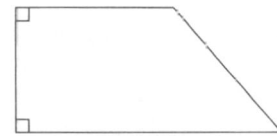

7. Lines *a* and *b* are parallel. Line *t* intersects *a* and *b*. Which numbered angles appear to be congruent angles?

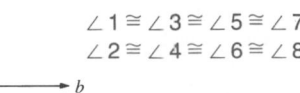

8. Using the figure for exercise 7, suppose the measure of ∠1 = 50°. What is the measure of each of the other numbered angles in the figure? ∠2 = 130°; ∠3 = 50°; ∠4 = 130°; ∠5 = 50°; ∠6 = 130°; ∠7 = 50°; ∠8 = 130°

∠1 ≅ ∠3 ≅ ∠5 ≅ ∠7; ∠2 ≅ ∠4 ≅ ∠6 ≅ ∠8

Using Page 153

Exercise 5 The ruler is to be used as a straight-edge and not to measure. You may need to show students how to use their compass to copy a segment.

Ideas That Work

Chalk It Up

Display this figure on the chalkboard.

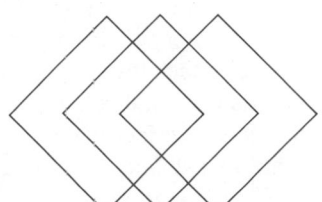

Direct students to start at any point and draw the figure without crossing any lines, retracing any lines, or lifting their pencils from the paper.

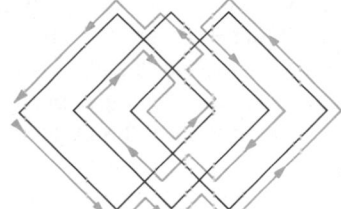

Practice Supplement, page 59

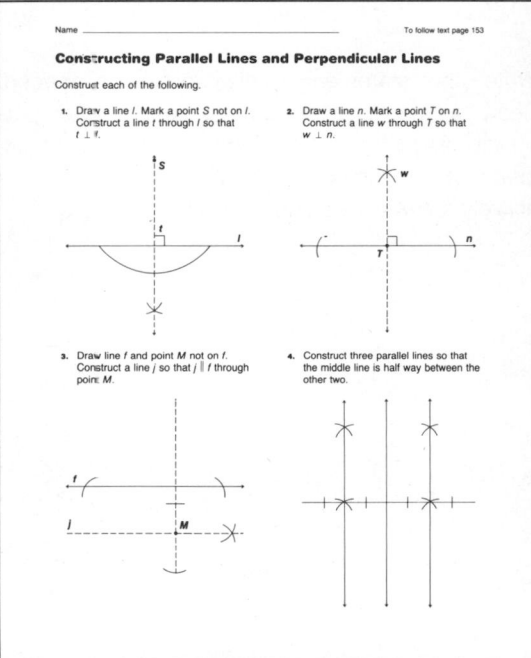

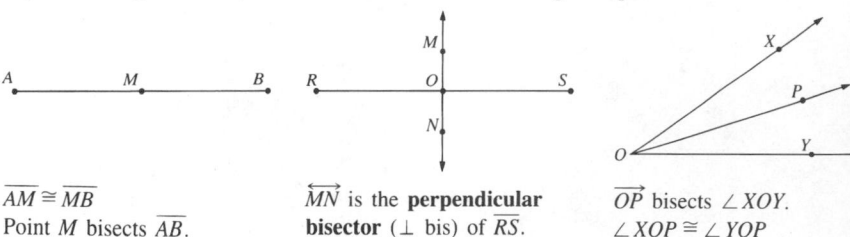
Quick Review Have students use the basic properties of multiplication to find the missing numbers.

$154 \times n = 154$ **1** $42 \times n = 23 \times 42$ **23** $n \times 1 = 78$ **78**

$6 \times (5 \times 9) = (6 \times n) + (6 \times 9)$ **5** $n \times (5 + 3) = (2 \times 5) + (2 \times 3)$ **2**

Lesson Focus To bisect a segment and construct the perpendicular bisector of a segment with a straightedge and compass

Suggested Materials Compass, ruler for use as a straightedge

Ideas for Getting Started

Have students draw and label segment $\overline{AB}$ on their papers. "Without using your ruler, compass, or any other equipment, can you find a way of locating the *middle point* or *midpoint* of $\overline{AB}$?" After students have had an opportunity to try and locate the midpoint, discuss the methods they used. Point out that the midpoint can be located by folding the paper so that points A and B fall on each other. The midpoint is at the intersection of the fold line and $\overline{AB}$.

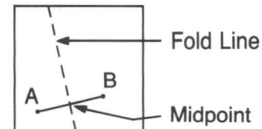

Explain that the fold line is perpendicular to the segment at its midpoint. Therefore, it is the *perpendicular bisector* of the segment. Notice with students that the fold line is a line of symmetry of the segment.

Using Page 154

Lesson Development Write the following statement on the chalkboard to emphasize the meaning and notation for perpendicular bisector.

$\overleftrightarrow{AB}$ is the $\perp$ bis of $\overline{XY}$ at P

Have students sketch (not construct) a drawing for the statement.

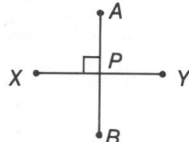

Write other statements similar to this as needed. Show a step-by-step construction of the perpendicular bisectors of a segment on the chalkboard or overhead projector. Have students actively follow the construction at their desks.

Bisecting Segments and Angles

A geometric figure is **bisected** if it is divided into two congruent parts.

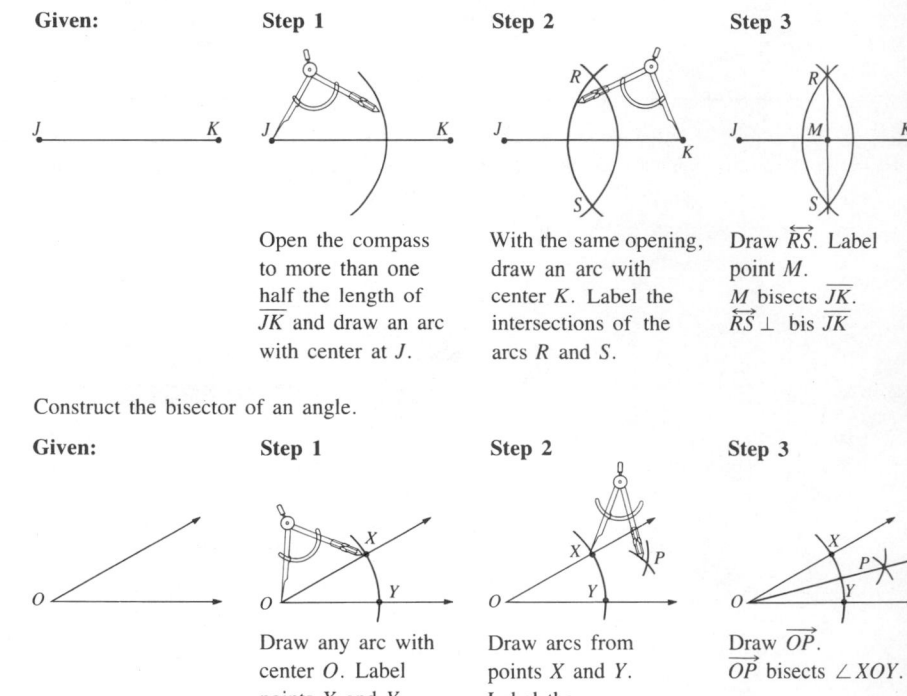

$\overline{AM} \cong \overline{MB}$
Point M bisects $\overline{AB}$.

$\overleftrightarrow{MN}$ is the **perpendicular bisector** ($\perp$ bis) of $\overline{RS}$. Point O is the **midpoint**. $\overline{RO} \cong \overline{OS}$ and $\overleftrightarrow{MN} \perp \overline{RS}$.

$\overrightarrow{OP}$ bisects $\angle XOY$. $\angle XOP \cong \angle YOP$

Construct the perpendicular bisector of a segment.

Given: | **Step 1** | **Step 2** | **Step 3**

Open the compass to more than one half the length of $\overline{JK}$ and draw an arc with center at J.

With the same opening, draw an arc with center K. Label the intersections of the arcs R and S.

Draw $\overleftrightarrow{RS}$. Label point M. M bisects $\overline{JK}$. $\overleftrightarrow{RS} \perp$ bis $\overline{JK}$

Construct the bisector of an angle.

Given: | **Step 1** | **Step 2** | **Step 3**

Draw any arc with center O. Label points X and Y.

Draw arcs from points X and Y. Label the intersection P.

Draw $\overrightarrow{OP}$. $\overrightarrow{OP}$ bisects $\angle XOY$.

154

Follow Up

Reteaching

Direct students to draw an angle and construct the angle bisector using compass and ruler. If students have difficulty with the construction, work through each step with them individually or in small groups. Then have them trace the angle and trace the ray that bisects the angle. Next they should fold the paper at the ray. The two halves of the angle should match.

Have students construct the perpendicular bisector of a segment, and repeat the activity.

Enrichment

Direct students to draw any triangle. Have them use a compass and ruler to construct the perpendicular bisector of each side. Connect the points that bisect the sides so that the original triangle is divided into four triangles.

"Are the four triangles congruent?" (yes). Tracing paper can be used to check. "Are the four triangles congruent regardless of the shape of the triangle you draw?" (yes)

Assignment Guide			
	Minimum	Average	Extended
page 155		1–8	1–10, TM

1. Draw $\overline{XY}$. Then bisect $\overline{XY}$ using a ruler and a compass.

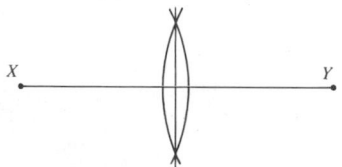

2. Draw $\overline{MN}$. Then construct the perpendicular bisector of $\overline{MN}$.

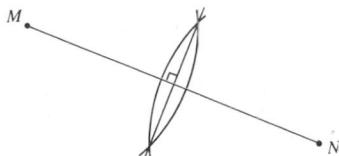

3. Draw acute $\angle G$. Then bisect $\angle G$ with a ruler and a compass.

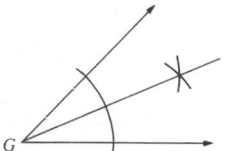

4. Draw obtuse $\angle H$. Then bisect it.

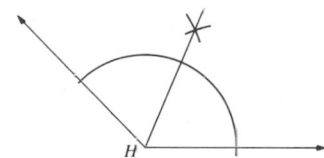

5. Draw any segment. Divide the segment into four congruent parts by bisecting the segment, then bisecting each half.

6. Draw any angle. Divide the angle into four congruent angles by bisecting the angle repeatedly.

7. Draw $\triangle XYZ$. Construct the perpendicular bisectors of each of the three sides of the triangle.

8. Draw $\triangle RST$. Bisect each angle of the triangle.

Students' constructions should closely match what is asked for in exercises 5–8.

9. Point K is the midpoint of $\overline{HG}$. $\overline{HG}$ is 3.2 cm long. What is the length of $\overline{HK}$?
1.6 cm

10. The measure of $\angle BAC$ is 78°. $\overrightarrow{AP}$ is the bisector of the angle. What is the measure of $\angle BAP$? 39°

▌THINK MATH▐

Shape Perception

Follow the steps below to draw the shape of an egg.

1. Draw a circle with $\overline{AB} \perp \overline{CD}$.
2. Extend chords $\overline{AC}$ and $\overline{BC}$ as shown.
3. Draw $\overset{\frown}{BF}$ with center at A. Draw $\overset{\frown}{AE}$ with center at B.
4. Draw $\overset{\frown}{EF}$ with center at C.
5. Shade in the egg-shaped region.

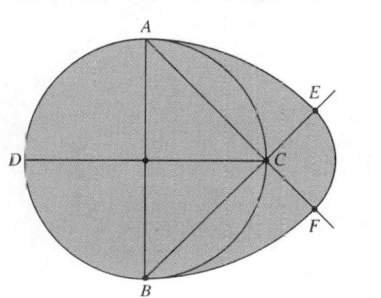

155

Using Page 155

Exercises 1 and 3 The ruler is to be used as a straightedge and not to measure in these exercises.

Exercises 7–8 In each exercise, the three bisectors intersect in one point.

Exercises 9–10 Have students draw a figure for these problems if they have difficulty visualizing the relationships between segments or angles.

Think Math This problem provides an interesting extension of the construction ideas of the lesson.

Ideas That Work

Special Education

For some physically handicapped students or children with poor motor skills, the work with straightedge and compass required in the constructions may be virtually impossible. These problems can be bypassed by using a piece of tinted plastic for the constructions. This method makes use of line reflections to accomplish the standard constructions. A student needs to learn to look through the plastic and trace to carry out the constructions. One construction is shown below. Other constructions can be found in *Geometry: An Investigative Approach*, O'Daffer and Clemens, Reading, MA: Addison-Wesley, 1976.

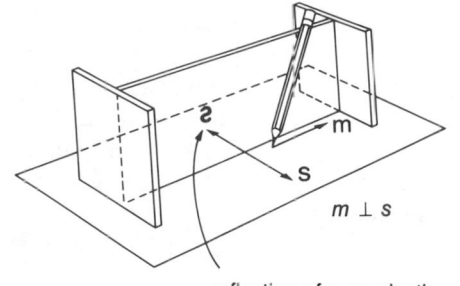

reflection of s on plastic

To construct line m perpendicular to a given line s, place the plastic so that the reflection of line s falls on line s. Draw line m.

Practice Supplement, page 60

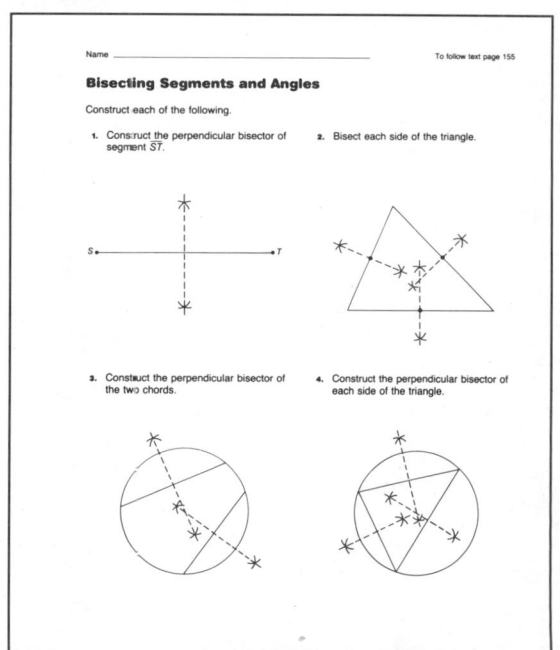

Geometry

Lesson Focus To identify prisms, pyramids, cylinders, cones, and spheres and to count the faces, edges, and vertices of various space figures

Suggested Materials Models of as many space figures as possible

Ideas for Getting Started

Show a model of a cube. Point out that each face is a square. "How many faces does the cube have?" (6) "How many segments or edges does it have?" (12) "How many corners or vertices does it have?" (8) Repeat this for other kinds of space figures. Display models of cylinders, cones, and spheres. Use informal descriptions of these figures rather than precise mathematical definitions.

Using Page 156

Lesson Development Have students study the space figures shown on the page. Some students may have difficulty visualizing the 3-dimensional figures. Explain that the dashed lines are hidden edges on the figures. Keep the models in view and have students compare them with the pictures as an aid in visualizing the figures.

Students should understand that prisms and pyramids are named according to the names of their bases, which are polygonal regions. A polygonal region is a polygon and its interior. In a rectangular prism, any face can be considered to be the base.

Space Figures

Geometric figures whose points do not all lie in the same plane are called **space figures**.

A **prism** has two bases which lie in parallel planes. The bases are polygonal regions. The other faces are regions formed by parallelograms.

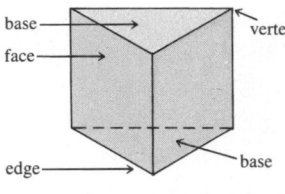
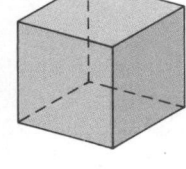
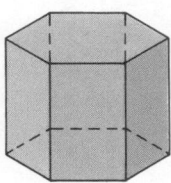

Triangular prism   **Cube**   **Hexagonal prism**

A **pyramid** has one base which is a polygonal region. The other faces of a pyramid are triangular regions.

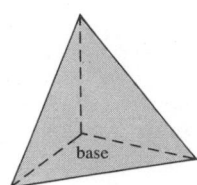
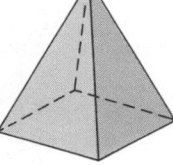
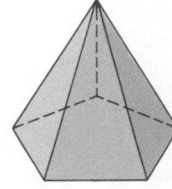
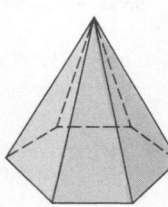

Triangular pyramid   **Rectangular pyramid**   **Pentagonal pyramid**   **Hexagonal pyramid**

Other Space Figures

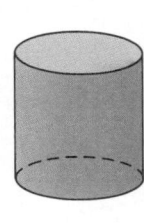
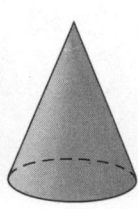

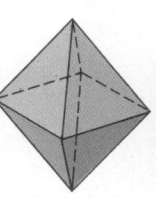
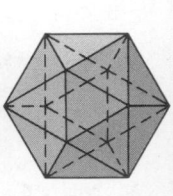

Cylinder   **Cone**   **Sphere**   **Octahedron**   **Icosahedron**

156

Follow Up

Reteaching

Use polyhedron models to help students understand the ideas of face, edge, and vertex. If students have difficulty counting faces, edges, or vertices, suggest that two or more students work together and place their fingers on each part in question. Then they can simply count the fingers.

Enrichment

Present the following problem to students: Suppose a bug is at point *A*. What is the shortest path it can crawl in order to get to point *B*? Draw this path.

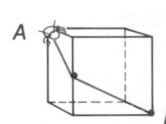
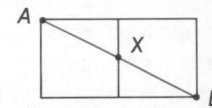

When the left side and front of the cube are spread flat, they form a rectangle. Thus the path from *A* to *X* to *B* will be the shortest distance.

Assignment Guide			
	Minimum	Average	Extended
page 157	1–9	1–14	1–14, TM

Give the number of vertices (*V*), faces (*F*), and edges (*E*) of each figure.

1.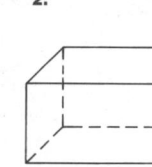

V 6, *F* 5, *E* 9

2.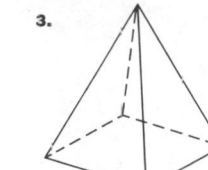

V 8, *F* 6, *E* 12

3.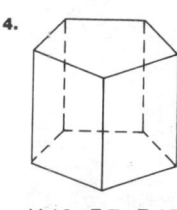

V 5, *F* 5, *E* 8

4.

V 10, *F* 7, *E* 15

5.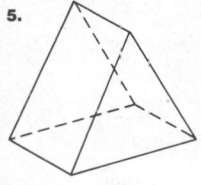

V 6, *F* 5, *E* 9

6.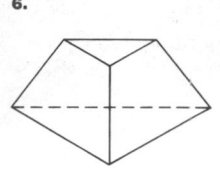

V 6, *F* 5, *E* 9

7.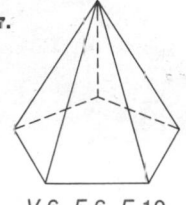

V 6, *F* 6, *E* 10

8.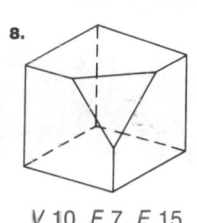

V 10, *F* 7, *E* 15

9. Use your answers for the numbers of vertices, faces, and edges in exercises 1–8 to show that *V* + *F* − *E* = 2. See teaching notes .

10. DATA HUNT How many vertices, faces, and edges does a dodecahedron have?
V 20, *F* 12, *E* 30

Name the space figure that would be formed if each of the patterns were folded on the dashed lines.

11.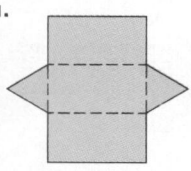

triangular prism

12.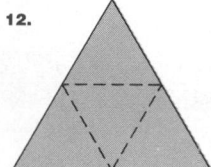

triangular pyramid

13.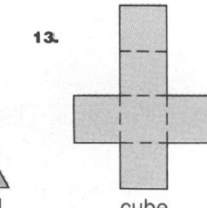

cube

14.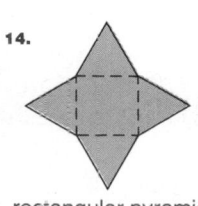

rectangular pyramid

╞══ **THINK MATH** ══╡

Shape Perception

In what ways is this odd-shaped space figure like a cube? It has the same number of faces (6), vertices (8), and edges (12).

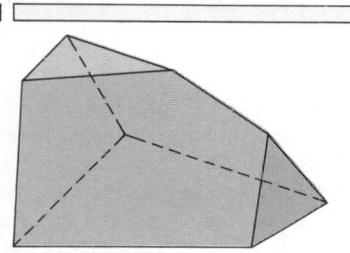

157

Using Page 157

Exercise 9 The formula *V* + *F* − *E* = 2 was proved by the great Swiss mathematician Leonhard Euler (1707–1783).

Data Hunt A dodecahedron has twelve faces, each a regular pentagon.

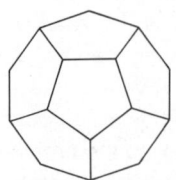

Exercises 11–14 If time permits, have students draw the patterns shown and make models of the space figures.

Think Math This problem involves spatial perception and the relationships *V* + *F* − *E* = 2 .

Reteaching Supplement, page 47

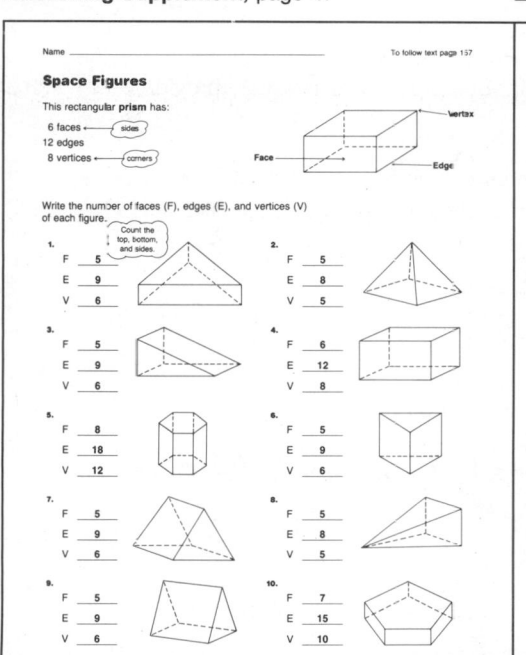

Enrichment Supplement, page 47

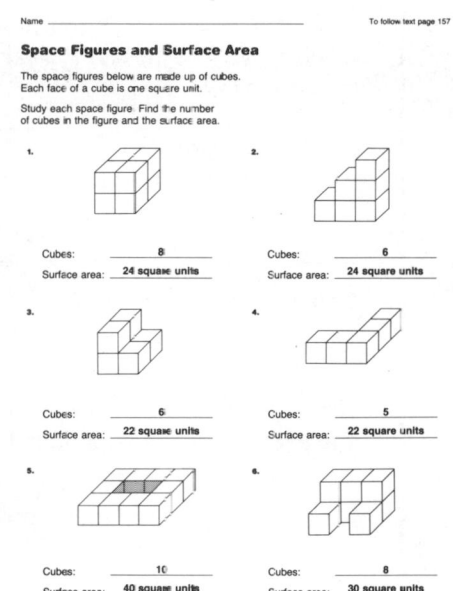

Practice Supplement, page 61

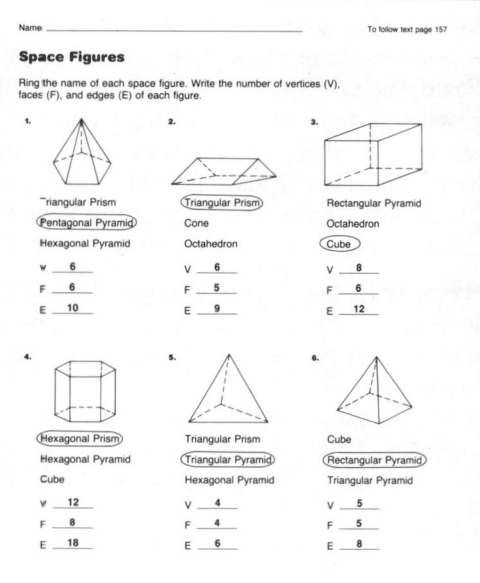

Lesson Focus To simplify the problem as a strategy to solve nonroutine word problems

Ideas for Getting Started

Write the following problem on the chalkboard or overhead projector.

In a city with a population of 93,384, 1 out of every 4 persons is 18 years of age or younger. Among these young people, 1 out of every 6 is under the age of 6 years. How many people are in the age group of 6 years through 18 years old?

After students read the problem ask, "How many of you do not see immediately how to solve the problem?" In all likelihood, several students will admit they do not. Write this simplified version of a similar problem on the chalkboard: In a room of 24 people, 1 out of 4 of them are 18 years or younger. Among these young people 1 out of 6 is under the age of 6. How many of the people are in the age group of 6 through 18 years old?

Work through the solution of the simplified problem with students.

24 ÷ 4 = 6 people 18 years and under
6 ÷ 6 = 1 person under 6 years
6 − 1 = 5 people from 6 through 18 years

Now show that the more difficult problem can be worked by exactly the same steps. (19,455 people from 6 through 18 years)

Using Page 158

Motivational Problem Have students read the Try This problem at the top of the page. "What does the question ask us to find?" (the distance Howard traveled when Sully has traveled 1,020 km farther than Howard) "What data is given in the problem?" (Sully averages 388 km a day and Howard averages 320 km a day.) Tell students that to solve this problem it may help to think of a simpler problem that is similar to the given problem.

Lesson Development Add the strategy Solve a Simpler Problem to your problem-solving bulletin board display. Have students compare the simpler problem to the original Try This problem. On the chalkboard, write out the steps for solving the simpler problem. Then show that the answer for the original problem can be found by following the same steps that solved the simpler problem.

Exercises 1–2 Have students work the problems at the bottom of the page using the new strategy. In working these multiple-step problems be certain that students identify in words each intermediate answer obtained rather than just doing the arithmetic.

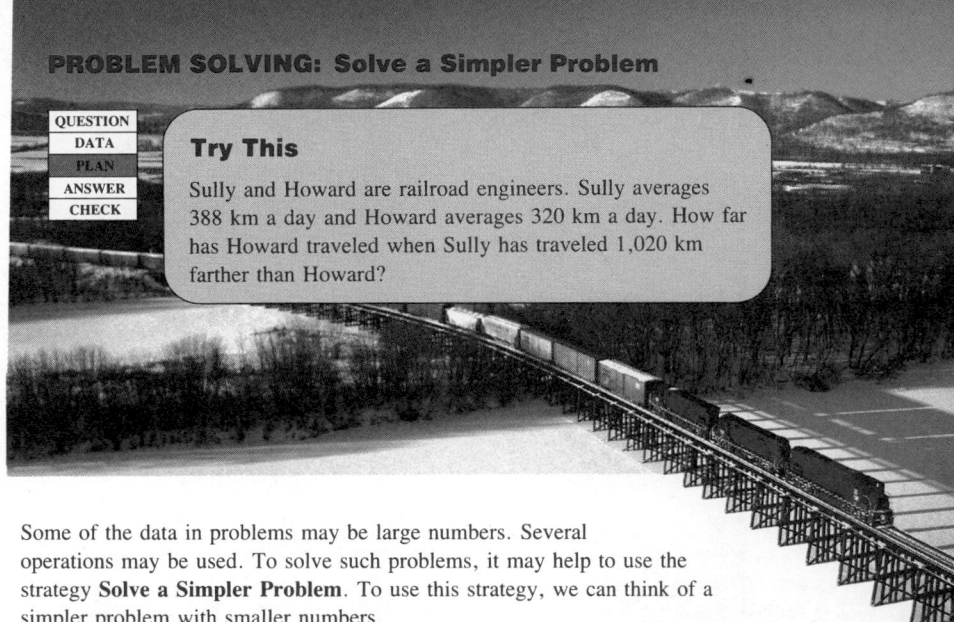

PROBLEM SOLVING: Solve a Simpler Problem

QUESTION
DATA
PLAN
ANSWER
CHECK

Try This

Sully and Howard are railroad engineers. Sully averages 388 km a day and Howard averages 320 km a day. How far has Howard traveled when Sully has traveled 1,020 km farther than Howard?

Some of the data in problems may be large numbers. Several operations may be used. To solve such problems, it may help to use the strategy **Solve a Simpler Problem**. To use this strategy, we can think of a simpler problem with smaller numbers.

Sully averages 10 km a day and Howard averages 8 km a day. How far has Howard traveled when Sully has traveled 20 km farther than Howard?	$10 - 8 = 2$ $20 \div 2 = 10$ $10 \times 8 = 80$	Sully travels 2 km a day farther. In 10 days, he will have traveled 20 km more than Howard. Howard will have traveled 80 km in this number of days.

Now use the same steps to solve the harder problem.

$388 - 320 = 68$	Sully travels 68 km a day farther.
$1,020 \div 68 = 15$	In 15 days, Sully will have traveled 1,020 km more than Howard.
$15 \times 320 = 4,800$	Howard will have traveled 4,800 km during this time.

Solve.

1. In a city of 45,300, a survey found that 0.14 of the people listened to radio station KXYU. The survey also found that 1 out of every 6 listeners tuned in to both the morning and the evening news broadcast. How many people in the city listen to both morning and evening news from KXYU? 1,057

2. There were 16,780 cars parked in a stadium parking lot. The average number of people per car was 1.5. How many fewer cars would have been used if there were 2.5 people per car? 6,712

158

Strategy Test Item

Optional Problem If you wish to assess students' ability to apply the strategy called Solve a Simpler Problem introduced in this chapter, provide them with the problem below.

> Bountiful Boutique had 47 dresses with a price of $79.95. Only 12 of the dresses were sold at this price. The rest were reduced in price by $24.96 and sold. What was the total amount received from the sale of the dresses?

Solution

$12 \times \$79.95 = \$959.40$
$(47 - 12) \times (\$79.95 - \$24.96) = \$1,924.65$
$\$959.40 + \$1,924.65 = \$2,884.05.$
The total amount received from the sale of the dresses was $2,884.05.

CHAPTER REVIEW/TEST

Write the symbol for each figure.

1. 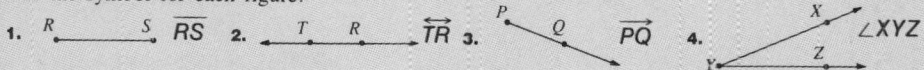 $\overline{RS}$ 2. $\overrightarrow{TR}$ 3. $\overrightarrow{PQ}$ 4. $\angle XYZ$

5. What kind of angle is $\angle ABC$? **obtuse**

6. What kind of angle is $\angle BAC$? **acute**

7. Give the measure of the angle that is supplementary to $\angle ABC$. **120°**

8. Give two names for $\triangle ABC$. **scalene, obtuse**

9. Find the measure of $\angle ACB$. **20°**

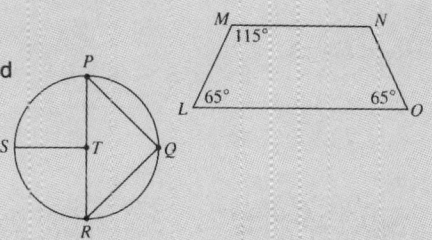

10. What kind of quadrilateral is figure $LMNO$? **trapezoid**

11. Find the measure of $\angle MNO$. **115°**

12. Name the center of the circle. **point T**

13. Name two chords of the circle. $\overline{RQ}$, $\overline{PQ}$

14. Name two central angles of the circle. $\angle STP$, $\angle STR$

15. Which pair of triangles is congruent? $\triangle LMN \cong \triangle PQR$

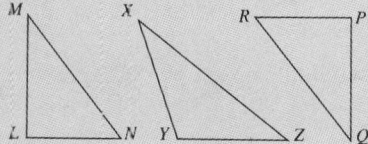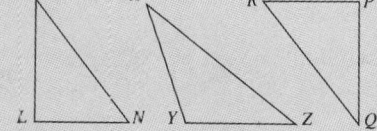

16. Name the polygon. Give the number of lines of symmetry. **regular hexagon; 6**

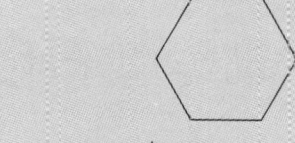

17. Name the line perpendicular to $\overleftrightarrow{AB}$. **t**

18. Name the line parallel to $\overleftrightarrow{CD}$. $\overleftrightarrow{AB}$

19. Give the measure of $\angle XMD$. **90°**

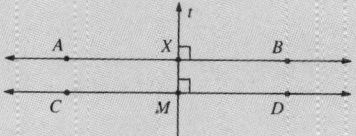

Name each space figure. Show that $V + F - E = 2$ for each.

20.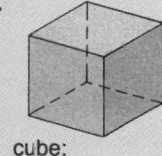
cube;
$8 + 6 - 12 = 2$

21.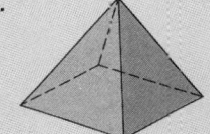
rectangular pyramid;
$5 + 5 - 8 = 2$

22.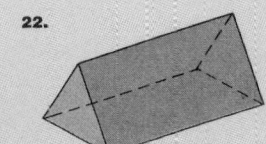
triangular prism;
$6 + 5 - 9 = 2$

159

Using Page 159

The exercises in the Chapter Review/Test emphasize the major concepts and skills presented in this chapter. These exercises may be used as a review assignment or as a test, depending upon your needs.

Item Analysis The table below correlates the Chapter Review/Test items with objectives and with the student text pages on which the concepts or skills were taught.

Items	Objectives	Related Text Pages
1–7	6.1	136–139
8–11	6.2	140–145
12–14	6.3	146–147
15–16	6.4	148–151
17–19	6.5	152–155
20–22	6.6	156–157

Assessment Options

If you use the Chapter Review/Test as a review assignment, you may wish to use the free-response test or the multiple-choice test to evaluate mastery of the chapter objectives. The items on these tests have a one-to-one correspondence in terms of content and level of difficulty. A correlation of test items to objectives and student text pages is provided in the Management Guide for Chapter 6. Note: Items 00-00 are derived from lessons for which no minimum assignment was suggested in the Assignment Guide.

Multiple-Choice Test, TRB pages 15–18
Free-Response Test, TRB pages 58–60

TRB Options

The following blackline masters are available for use with this chapter. If you have not already assigned these materials, you may wish to use them to close the chapter.

Recreation, TRB page 160
Consumer Applications, TRB page 178
Calculator Technology, TRB page 196
Reading Math, TRB page 232
Family Involvement, TRB pages 255–256

Using Page 160

The exercises on this page are intended for those students who experienced difficulty with the Chapter Review/Test on page 159. Should students require reteaching of these key concepts and skills, please refer to the teaching notes below. Otherwise, the Another Look exercises can be assigned as independent work, with students using the accompanying sample problems and hints as guides.

Exercises 1–2 This skill was originally taught on pages 138–139. Review with students the meaning of the terms right, acute, and obtuse. Have them examine the examples in the display box. Point out that an acute angle is less than a "square corner," while an obtuse angle is greater than a square corner.

Exercises 3–7 This skill was originally taught on pages 140–141. Direct students' attention to the display box. Use the examples to show that triangles can be classified by the measures of their angles and by the length of their sides. Remind students that the sum of the measures of the angles in a triangle is 180°.

Exercises 8–9 This skill was originally taught on pages 142–143. On the chalkboard, show examples of a trapezoid, parallelogram, rhombus, rectangle, and square. Ask students to describe each quadrilateral by telling about the sides and angles.

Exercises 10–13 This skill was originally taught on pages 146–147. Have students study the figure and terms in the display box. Then ask them to describe a radius, diameter, chord, and central angle. Make certain they understand that a chord is a segment with its endpoints on the circle, a diameter is a special kind of chord, and a central angle has its vertex at the center of a circle.

Exercises 14–15 This skill was originally taught on pages 156–157. Use a physical model of a space figure to illustrate the meaning of face, vertex, and edge. Then direct students' attention to the display box and have them study the drawing.

ANOTHER LOOK

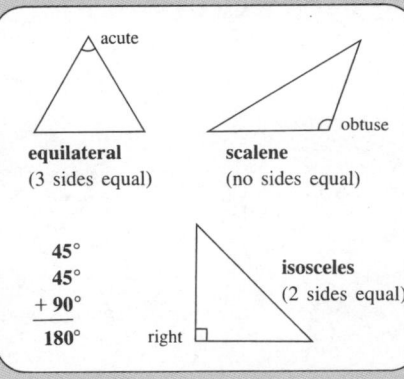

equilateral (3 sides equal) scalene (no sides equal)

45° 45° + 90° = 180° right

isosceles (2 sides equal)

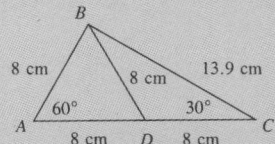

1. Is ∠BAD right, acute, or obtuse? **acute**

2. Is ∠BDC right, acute, or obtuse? **obtuse**

3. What kind of triangle is △ABD? **equilateral**

4. What kind of triangle is △BDC? **obtuse, isosceles**

5. What kind of triangle is △ABC? **right, scalene**

6. Give the measure of ∠ABC. **90°**

7. Give the measure of ∠ADC. **180°**

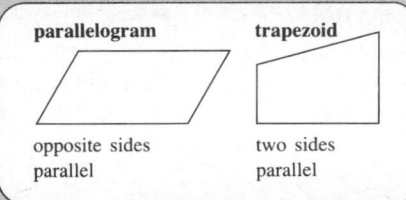

parallelogram   **trapezoid**

opposite sides parallel   two sides parallel

Name each quadrilateral.

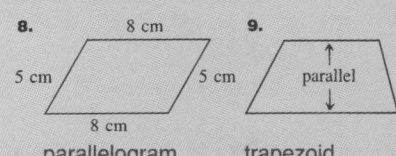

8. **parallelogram**   9. **trapezoid**

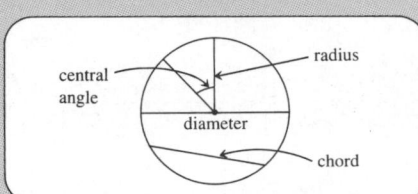

central angle   radius   diameter   chord

10. Name a radius of circle O. **ON, OP, or OQ**

11. Name a diameter. **PN**

12. Name a chord. **LM**

13. Name a central angle. **∠POQ, ∠NOQ, or ∠PON**

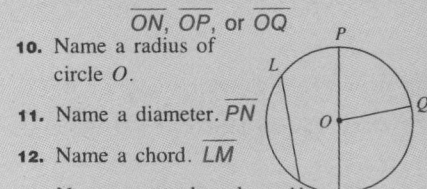

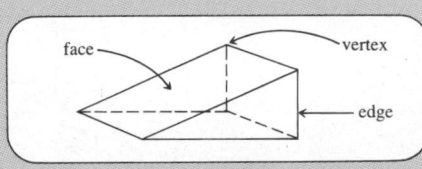

face   vertex   edge

14. Name six vertices. **T, U, V, W, X, Y**

15. Name nine edges. **TV, VU, UT, UW, WX, XY, YW, VX, TY**

160

Just for Teachers

Topology

Mathematics is the language of size, order, and shape, serving as both a scientific tool and an artistic reflection. The vocabulary and grammatical rules have been fashioned over time by the interaction of use, need, logic, and the ever-present human determination to *understand*. Every language has different forms of expression and exploration; mathematics is expressed in geometry, calculus, symbolic logic, and everyday arithmetic.

The ancient Greeks in 500 B.C. first perceived that mathematics could be studied as an art aside from its practical applications. The Greeks wanted to know why certain mathematical formulas worked. There were some concepts, such as irrational numbers, that they found difficult to incorporate into their philosophical and arithmetical structures. Partly because of this difficulty, the Greeks studied *shapes* and their properties, or geometry.

Twenty-five hundred years later, mathematics encompasses many sub-fields. One of the branches is topology, a new study of shapes and their properties. Topology is

ENRICHMENT

Space Perception

There are five **regular polyhedrons** or solids. The faces of regular polyhedrons are congruent regular polygonal regions. These five regular polyhedrons are sometimes called the **Platonic solids**. They are named after Plato, one of the Greeks who studied them. The Greeks appear to have discovered that each regular polyhedron could be drawn inside a sphere.

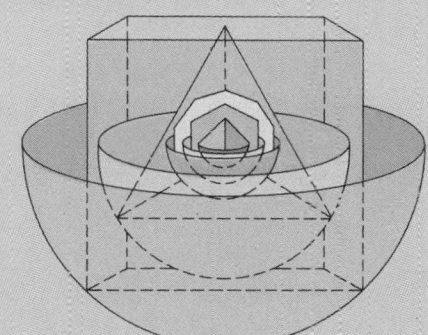

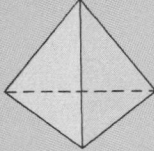
Tetrahedron

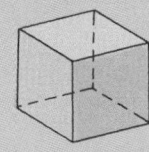
Cube

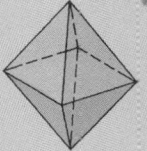
Octahedron

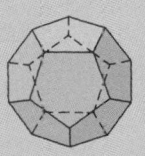
Dodecahedron

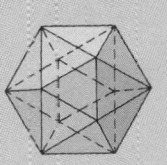
Icosahedron

Make a larger pattern for each polyhedron on lightweight posterboard. Cut out the patterns and tape the edges together to form models of the polyhedrons.

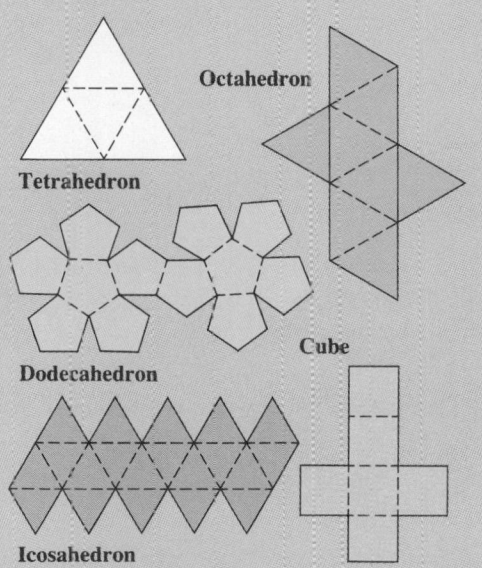

Octahedron

Tetrahedron

Dodecahedron

Cube

Icosahedron

Use your models to complete the table for the number of vertices (*V*), faces (*F*), and edges (*E*).

Polyhedron	V	F	E	$V + F - E$
Tetrahedron	4	4	6	2
Cube	8	6	12	2
Octahedron	10	8	16	2
Dodecahedron	20	12	30	2
Icosahedron	12	20	30	2

161

Using Page 161

This page is intended for those students who successfully completed the Chapter/Review Test on page 159. You may wish to assign this page as independent work while you use Another Look exercises to reteach the basic concepts and skills of the chapter. Or, you may decide that all students would benefit from exposure to this Enrichment activity.

Lesson Development If possible provide students with copies of each of the patterns of the 5 polyhedrons. If students make their own patterns, have them use isometric dot paper (TRB p. 282) to make the tetrahedron, octahedron, and icosahedron. The pattern of the dodecahedron is the most difficult due to the difficulty of constructing a regular pentagon. If students make their own pattern, suggest that they make one regular pentagon and use it as a pattern for all the faces. Each angle of the pentagon should have a measure of 108°.

sometimes called rubber-sheet geometry. Imagine that figures are made of elastic and in moving can be stretched, twisted, and pulled. Topology is concerned with properties of figures that do not change under elastic motions.

One of the most fascinating of the topologist's objects, a Möbius strip, is a piece of paper with only one side, first conceived by Augustus Ferdinand Möbius (1790–1868), German mathematician and astronomer. Constructing a Möbius strip is easy—give a strip of paper a half twist and then tape the edges together. Several activities will reveal its curious characteristics: 1) try to color each "side" a different color—the colors will meet; 2) try to cut it in half lengthwise—one two-sided strip will result; 3) try to cut it in thirds lengthwise—the two cuts will join to make one continuous cut resulting in two intertwined strips, one being a two-sided loop, the other a new Möbius strip.

Using Page 162

The exercises on the page provide practice for maintaining cumulative skills. The emphasis in this Cumulative Review is on decimal multiplication (Chapter 4) and decimal division (Chapter 5).

Item Analysis The table below correlates the Cumulative Review items with objectives and with the student book pages on which the concepts or skills were taught.

Items	Objectives	Related Text Pages
1–2	4.2	92–95, 98–99
3	4.3	100
4–6	4.2	42–95, 98–99
7–8	5.1	116–120
9	3.5	72–77
10–11	5.2	124–125
12	5.3	128
13	4.5	96–97,101,105,106–107
14	5.4	121–123, 126–127

CUMULATIVE REVIEW

Find the products.

1. 7.29
    × 63
    A 45.927 **B** 459.27
    C 459.37 **D** not given

2. 0.56
    × 8.4
    A 4.604 **B** 46.04
    C 4.704 **D** not given

3. Estimate the product.

   $52.63 × 3.2$

   A $150 **B** $200
   C $15.60 **D** not given

Multiply.

4. $0.627 × 100$

   A 6.27 **B** 62.7
   C 627 **D** not given

5. $73.29 × 0.001$

   A 7.329 **B** 7,329
   C 732.9 **D** not given

6. $954.62
    ×   8
    A $7,637.12 **B** $763.69
    C $7,636.96 **D** not given

7. Divide.

   $8)\overline{0.056}$ **A** 0.07 **B** 7
   C 0.007 **D** not given

Find the quotients. Round to the nearest hundredth.

8. $12)\overline{\$15.75}$ **A** $1.31 **B** $1.312
   C $1.32 **D** not given

9. $56)\overline{376}$ **A** 6 **B** 6.72
   C 6.714 **D** not given

Find the quotients. Round to the nearest thousandth.

10. $0.59)\overline{17.3}$ **A** 0.293 **B** 29.322
    C 2.932 **D** not given

11. $2.83)\overline{977.6}$ **A** 34.544 **B** 345.441
    C 345.442 **D** not given

12. Estimate the quotient.

    $3.2)\overline{0.57}$ **A** 0.1 **B** 20
    C 0.2 **D** not given

13. A record album costs $8.99. The sales tax is 0.06 of the cost. What is the total cost of the record album?

    A $9.05 **B** $9.53
    C $9.52 **D** not given

14. Purified water costs $9.35 for 21.5 L. What is the cost (to the nearest cent) per liter?

    A $0.43 **B** $0.40
    C $0.434 **D** not given

Objectives

7.1 Find the prime factorization of a composite number.

7.2 Find the greatest common factor or the least common multiple of two numbers.

7.3 Evaluate an expression containing a variable by substituting a number for the variable.

7.4 Solve equations by using addition, subtraction, multiplication, or division.

7.5 Solve word problems using the 5-Point Checklist and cumulative computational skills.

Summary

The first half of this chapter reviews the idea of factors of numbers, prime and composite numbers, the greatest common factor (GCF) of two numbers, the least common multiple (LCM) of two numbers, and simple divisibility rules for dividing by 2, 3, 5, 9, or 10. This block of content is sometimes called number theory. The remaining part of the chapter introduces expressions with variables and then develops 1-step solutions of equations by performing the same operation on each side of the equation.

Several of the topics developed in this chapter will have important applications in later chapters, particularly GCF, LCM, and equations.

In addition, problem solving is extended to include writing and solving an equation for a word problem.

Mathematical Background

Number Theory Number theory is concerned with the set of whole numbers (0, 1, 2, 3, 4, . . .). The set of whole numbers has many interesting and useful subsets, such as odd numbers, and factors and multiples of a given number. The idea of a factor of a number is important. If a, b, and c are whole numbers and $a \cdot b = c$, then a and b are factors of c. If a number c has exactly 2 different factors, it is a prime number. Numbers greater than 1 with more than 2 factors are composite numbers. Every composite number can be expressed uniquely as the product of prime numbers. This statement is called the Fundamental Theorem of Arithmetic. The prime factorization of 10,164 is $2^2 \cdot 3 \cdot 7 \cdot 11^2$. Except for the order of the primes in the product, the factorization of 10,164 is uniquely expressed.

The concepts of least common multiple of two numbers and greatest common factor of two numbers have immediate application in work with fractional numbers in the following chapters.

Equations Variables are introduced as letters that are replaced by numbers. To evaluate an expression containing a variable, we replace the variable with a specified number and then perform the operation in the expression. In this chapter, only simple expressions involving one operation are introduced.

Equations are presented using a balance scale as a model. This particular model for equations is easy for students to understand. The balance point or the fulcrum corresponds to the equals sign in the equation. In order to keep the balance, we must do the same things to both sides of the equation.

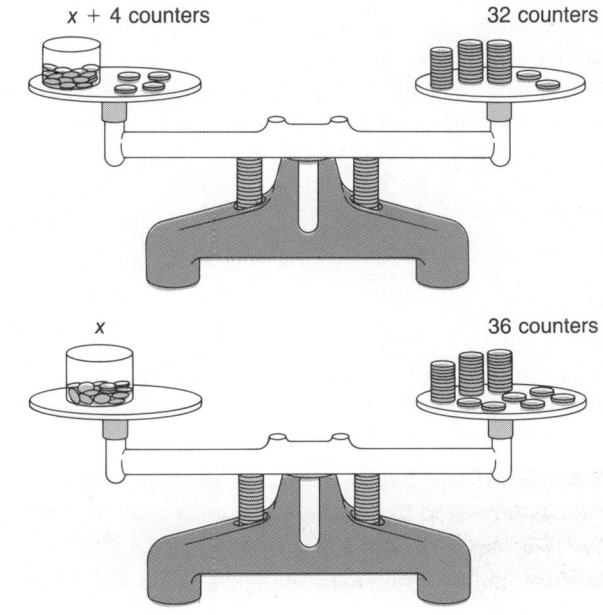

Technically, to solve an equation means to find all the replacements for the variable which will form a true statement. Given the equation $\frac{n}{8} = 17$, we perform the following steps:

$$8 \cdot \frac{n}{8} = 17 \cdot 8 \quad \text{Multiply both sides by 8}$$
$$n = 136 \quad \text{Simplify}$$

We have not yet found the solution. What we have found is that no number other than 136 can be a solution. To show that 136 is a solution, we should substitute it in $\frac{n}{8} = 17$, which gives the true statement $\frac{136}{8} = 17$. Hence, 136 is the only solution.

Problem Solving Two lessons on problem solving in this chapter extend problem solving to include writing and solving equations for word problems. On pages 182–183, the lesson provides a choice of equations and the student must select the right equation for the problem. The second set of problems, on pages 184–185, gives students the opportunity to write and solve an equation for a problem. Since all equations, at this time, are simple 1-step equations, a high percent of student success with the problems should be expected. By moving slowly with these pre-algebra ideas, most students will not be overwhelmed and discouraged in their efforts. The final problem-solving lesson on page 186 introduces the strategy Make a Table.

Vocabulary

divisible	factor tree	variable
prime number	greatest common factor	expression
composite number	relatively prime	equation
prime factorization	least common multiple	

Teaching Tips

Error Analysis

This chapter introduces the content called number theory. The concepts involved are critical for advanced mathematics because students move beyond mere algorithmic thinking. The foundation is laid for work in algebra with the introduction of the concept of variable and writing and solving equations.

Error patterns may be found related to any of the concepts covered in this chapter. A few common error patterns are listed below.

Error Pattern 1

Number	Factors
6	2, 3
8	2, 4
12	2, 3, 4, 6

Diagnosis The student has not included 1 and the number itself. All other factors are listed.

Remediation Begin by discussing the concept of factors. Point out that factors exist in pairs. Use an example such as finding the factors of 6. Ask the student what number times 1 equals 6. Then write 1 and 6 on the chalkboard. Continue in this way until all factors are listed.

Error Pattern 2

$$30 = 2 \cdot 3 \cdot 5 \qquad\qquad 63 = 3 \cdot 3 \cdot 7$$
$$42 = 2 \cdot 3 \cdot 7 \qquad\qquad 70 = 2 \cdot 5 \cdot 7$$
$$GCF = 2 \cdot 2 \cdot 3 \cdot 3 = 36 \qquad GCF = 7 \cdot 7 = 49$$

Diagnosis The student gave the prime factorization correctly but used common factors twice, one from each number, to form the greatest common factor. For example, since 2 and 3 are prime factors of both 30 and 42, $2 \cdot 2 \cdot 3 \cdot 3$ was used in the GCF.

Remediation Discuss the meaning of greatest common factor. Begin with the idea of common factor. Explain that if a factor is a common factor of two numbers, it is a factor of each number. A factor of 42 is 2, but $2 \cdot 2$ or 4 is not a factor. Stress that the only factors in the GCF are factors of each given number.

Error Pattern 3

$$t - 4 = 11 \qquad\qquad h - 9 = 27$$
$$t - 4 + 4 = 11 \qquad h - 9 + 9 = 27$$
$$t = 11 \qquad\qquad\quad h = 27$$

Diagnosis The student added a number to the left side of the equation to get the variable by itself. The same number was not added to the right side of the equation.

Remediation Begin with whole number sentences, such as $15 + 36 = 51$. Subtract 36 from each side of the equation and point out that the two sides are still equal. Next use an addition equation such $n + 5 = 30$. Show that we can get n by itself if we subtract 5 from the left side of the equation. Explain that if we subtract 5 from the left side, we must also subtract 5 from the right side in order for both sides to remain equal.

Error Pattern 4

$$12k = 144 \qquad\qquad 3n = 30$$
$$\frac{12k}{12k} = \frac{144}{12k} \qquad\qquad \frac{3n}{3n} = \frac{30}{3n}$$
$$1 = \frac{144}{12k} \qquad\qquad 1 = \frac{30}{3n}$$

Diagnosis The student has divided each side of the equation by the same value but has used both the whole number and the variable.

Remediation Review how to solve equations using division. Use an example such as $7 \times 5 \div 5$ to show that multiplying by a number and then dividing by the same number leaves the number unchanged. Emphasize that we do not multiply or divide by the variable.

Problem Solving

Evaluating Problem-Solving Performance—Part 2

A complete and accurate evaluation of students' problem-solving performances cannot be achieved if evaluation techniques are limited to the point system described in Chapter 4, page 86. Many of the goals in teaching problem solving involve students' attitudes toward problem solving, their methods of understanding problems, choosing and implementing solution strategies, and checking solutions. Goals like these cannot be accurately assessed only by examining students' written work for problems. While your students are involved in solving problems, observe and question them about their work. Informal evaluative comments can be made directly to them at that time, or observations can be recorded and shared later, at a parent or child conference, for example. Here is a checklist that can be used to summarize and report your observations.

Problem-Solving Observation Checklist

Name _____ Date _____

	Always	Sometimes	Never
shows a willingness to try	___	___	___
demonstrates self-confidence	___	___	___
approaches problems systematically (question—data—plan—answer—check)	___	___	___
selects appropriate solution strategies	___	___	___
tries different strategies when stuck	___	___	___

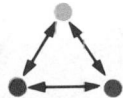 **Special Education**

The topics of number theory and solving simple equations play important roles in helping students model and solve problems.

Providing Structure

Finding the prime factorization of a number is a difficult task for students with special needs. The factorization method shown below can help them structure their work. This method can be augmented with a list of primes less than 50 on a chart posted at the front of the room. To use this method, students must check to see if the number is divisible by 2, the smallest prime. If it is, they divide by 2 and write the quotient (150) above the number (300). They must then check to see if the quotient is again divisible by 2. If it is not, they go on to check the next larger prime (3). Since 3 divides 75, we write the quotient 25 above the 75 and check to see if 3 will divide 25. Since it does not, we continue to divide by the next larger prime, 5. The process continues until the quotient reaches 1. At this point, the numbers in the left hand column are the prime factors of the original number. In this example, $300 = 2 \cdot 2 \cdot 3 \cdot 5 \cdot 5$.

	1
5	5
5	25
3	75
2	150
2	300

Primes Less than 50				
2	3	5	7	11
13	17	19	23	29
31	37	41	43	47

Creating Concrete Models

The concepts of greatest common factor and least common multiple can be given concrete representation through a simple card game activity. Using index cards and two different colored marking pens, make a set of cards for each color with six 3s, four 5s, three 7s, and two each of 11, 13, 17, and 19. These cards can then be used to find the greatest common factor.

Suppose we want to find the greatest common factor of 90 and 105. We first need to find the prime factorizations of both numbers: $90 = 2 \cdot 3 \cdot 3 \cdot 5$ and $105 = 3 \cdot 5 \cdot 7$. Laying out the prime factor cards for 90, using one of the colors, we obtain the cards shown in the top row below. We then lay out the factor cards for 105 using cards of the second color. In doing so, we place any factor cards we can on top of another one for the same number as shown. The common prime factors for the two numbers are quickly seen to be 3 and 5. Their product gives the greatest common factor.

90 = $\boxed{2}$ $\boxed{3}$ $\boxed{3}$ $\boxed{5}$ GCF = $3 \cdot 5$

105 = $\boxed{3}$ $\boxed{5}$ $\boxed{7}$ LCM = $2 \cdot 3 \cdot 3 \cdot 5 \cdot 7$

The card display also gives us the least common multiple of the two numbers. Since the doubling up of common factors removes the duplication of factors, the product of the number on the top card of each pile gives the least common multiple. In the above display for 90 and 105, we have $2 \cdot 3 \cdot 3 \cdot 5 \cdot 7$ or 630. Thus the least common multiple of 90 and 105 is 630.

Developing Strategies for Equation Solving

The steps in solving an equation can be stressed by having students think about the problem $x + 7 = 16$ as "What number plus 7 equals 16?" This quickly gives the answer of 9. This verbal pattern also suggests that we need subtraction to solve the equation. In the equation $3s = 27$ we need to ask, "What number multiplied by 3 gives 27?" This should trigger the idea of dividing in order to obtain the solution of 9.

Subject Integration

Fine Arts Record albums, page 163
Career Awareness Paper route, pages 166–167; packing boxes, page 182; salaries, page 186
Computer Awareness Computer screen, page 168
Home Economics Cutting material, pages 172–173
Physical Education Ice skating, page 174
Social Studies Mountain heights, page 184

Teaching Chapter 7				Meeting Individual Needs					
				Lesson Assignments			Follow Up		
Objectives	Chapter Content	Pages	TRB Test Items	Minimum	Average	Extended	Reteaching	Enrichment	Practice
	Chapter Opener	163							
7.1 Find the prime factorization of a composite number.	Factors	164–165	1–4	1–36	1–38	1–35 odd, 37–46	RS 48	ES 48	PS 62
	Divisibility Rules	166–167	5–6		1–42	1–41 odd, 42, TM			PS 63
	Prime and Composite Numbers	168–169	7–10	1–28	1–30, 33	1–27 odd, 28–33, TM	RS 49	ES 49	MP 426 PS 64
	Prime Factorization	170–171	11–13	1–24	1–25, 27–30	1–25 odd, 26–30	RS 50	ES 50	MP 426 PS 65
7.2 Find the greatest common factor or the least common multiple of two numbers.	Greatest Common Factor	172–173	14–16	1–12, 25–33, SK	1–35, SK	1–33 odd, 34, SK	SE6 Ch 8 RS 51	ES 51	MP 426 PS 66
	Least Common Multiple	174–175	17–19	1–24	1–30	9–31, TM	SE6 Ch 8 RS 52	ES 52	MP 426 PS 67
7.3 Evaluate an expression containing a variable by substituting a number for the variable.	Variables and Expressions	176–177	20–28	1–27	1–35, TM	1–15 odd, 16–35, TM	RS 53	ES 53	MP 427 PS 68
7.4 Solve equations by using addition, subtraction, multiplication, or division.	Addition and Subtraction: Equations	178–179	29–32	1–24	1–39	1–39 odd, TM	RS 54	ES 54	MP 427 PS 69
	Multiplication and Division: Equations	180–181	33–36	1–24, SK	1–39, SK	1–39 odd, SK	RS 55	ES 55	MP 427 PS 70
7.5 Solve word problems using the 5-Point Checklist and cumulative computational skills.	Problem Solving: Choosing the Right Equation	182–183	37–40	1–8	1–9, 12	1–12			PS 71
	Problem Solving: Writing and Solving an Equation	184–185		1–6	1–7, 9	1–10	RS 56	ES 56	PS 72
	Problem Solving: Make a Table	186							
	Chapter Review/Test	187							
	Another Look/ Enrichment	188–189							
	Technology	190–191							
	Cumulative Review	192							

SE6	Student Edition, Book 6
RS	Reteaching Supplement
ES	Enrichment Supplement
PS	Practice Supplement
MP	More Practice
TM	Think Math
SK	Skillkeeper
TRB	Teacher's Resource Book

Masters for use

. . . before Chapter 7

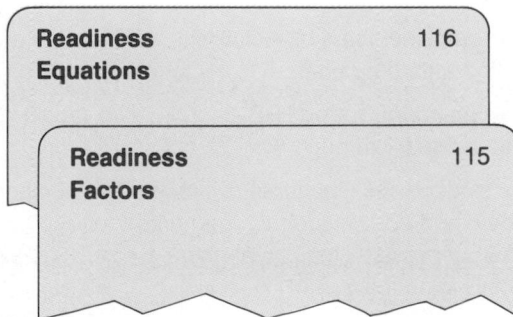

Readiness Equations	116
Readiness Factors	115

. . . during Chapter 7

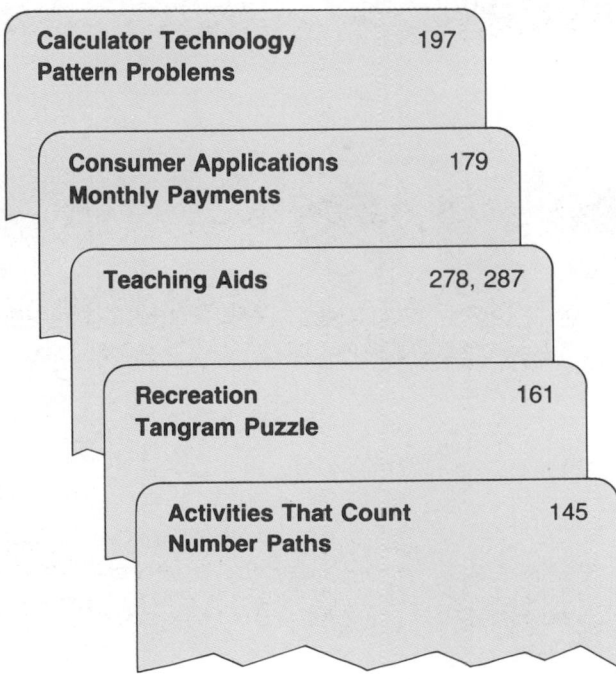

Calculator Technology Pattern Problems	197
Consumer Applications Monthly Payments	179
Teaching Aids	278, 287
Recreation Tangram Puzzle	161
Activities That Count Number Paths	145

. . . after Chapter 7

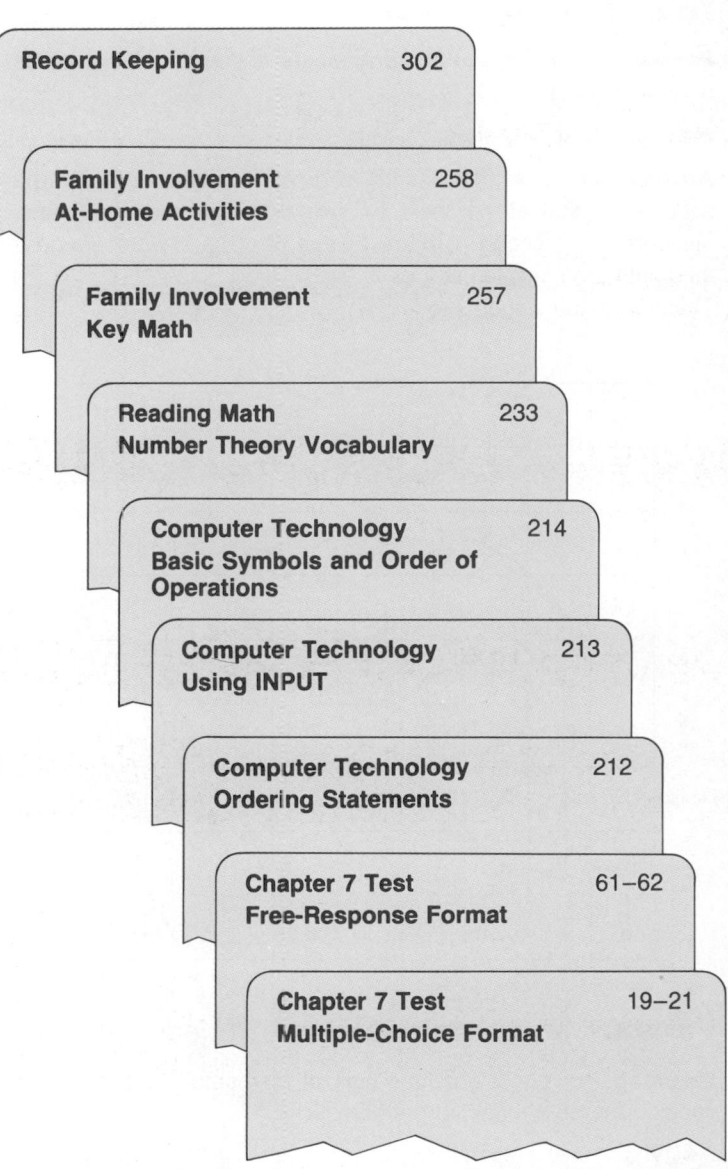

Record Keeping	302
Family Involvement At-Home Activities	258
Family Involvement Key Math	257
Reading Math Number Theory Vocabulary	233
Computer Technology Basic Symbols and Order of Operations	214
Computer Technology Using INPUT	213
Computer Technology Ordering Statements	212
Chapter 7 Test Free-Response Format	61–62
Chapter 7 Test Multiple-Choice Format	19–21

Supplements

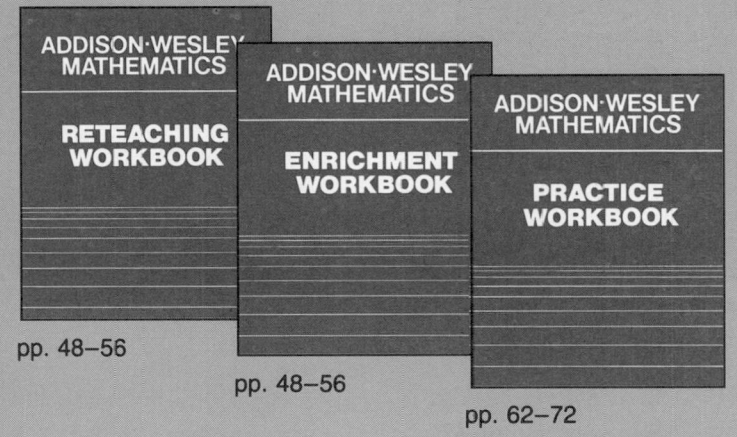

ADDISON-WESLEY MATHEMATICS
RETEACHING WORKBOOK
pp. 48–56

ADDISON-WESLEY MATHEMATICS
ENRICHMENT WORKBOOK
pp. 48–56

ADDISON-WESLEY MATHEMATICS
PRACTICE WORKBOOK
pp. 62–72

Other Addison-Wesley Resources

Books and Kits

A New Twist pp. 25, 37, 41, 43, 45

Arithmetic Primer pp. 124–127, 129–133

Basic and the Personal Computer pp. 27–36

Problem-Solving Experiences in Mathematics, Grade 7
   Problems 19, 20, 54, 55, 65, 74, 84, 105, 119, 140, 145, 150

Technology

Computer Math Activities Volume 5

Activities That Count

Activities That Count are designed for use throughout this chapter and subsequent chapters. Before beginning Chapter 7, you may wish to review these activities and select the ones you consider appropriate for your class.

Number Paths Math Lab

Purpose To recognize prime numbers and factors or multiples of a given number

Materials Activity sheet (TRB p. 145)

Activity Have students find 3 different paths through the squares so that all numbers on one path are prime numbers, numbers on a second path are factors of 60, and numbers on a third path are multiples of 2 or 7.
Then challenge students to find a new path using their own rules.

16	6	4	91	2	61	67	59	0
7	10	3	11	35	10	100	1	19
21	5	12	30	12	29	57	91	2
92	18	13	1	51	17	39	53	47
42	57	14	4	15	20	37	85	21
23	81	19	55	21	71	3	29	40
77	43	97	18	75	63	5	45	13
6	88	10	1	14	60	32	20	31
7	39	105	35	55	39	4	8	2

Famous Mathematicians Project

Purpose To read about the lives of mathematicians and their contributions to the field of mathematics

Activity Have students read about some of the famous mathematicians of the past and write or give an oral report to the class. Suggest that students try to find what main contributions to mathematics were made as well as some interesting things about the mathematicians' lives.

Agnesi	Euclid	Euler
Fermat	Gauss	Germain
Hypatia	Kovalevskaya	Pascal
Somerville		

Prime Number Game

Purpose To form prime numbers by multiplying two numbers and adding or subtracting a third number

Materials Three number cubes (TRB p. 278), two labeled 4 through 9 and one labeled 1 through 6

Activity In turn, students toss the three cubes, multiply numbers on two of the cubes, and add or subtract the number on the third cube. If a prime number results, the player score 1 point. The first player to get 5 points wins the game.

$(4 \times 4) - 9 = 7$ prime

No prime is possible.

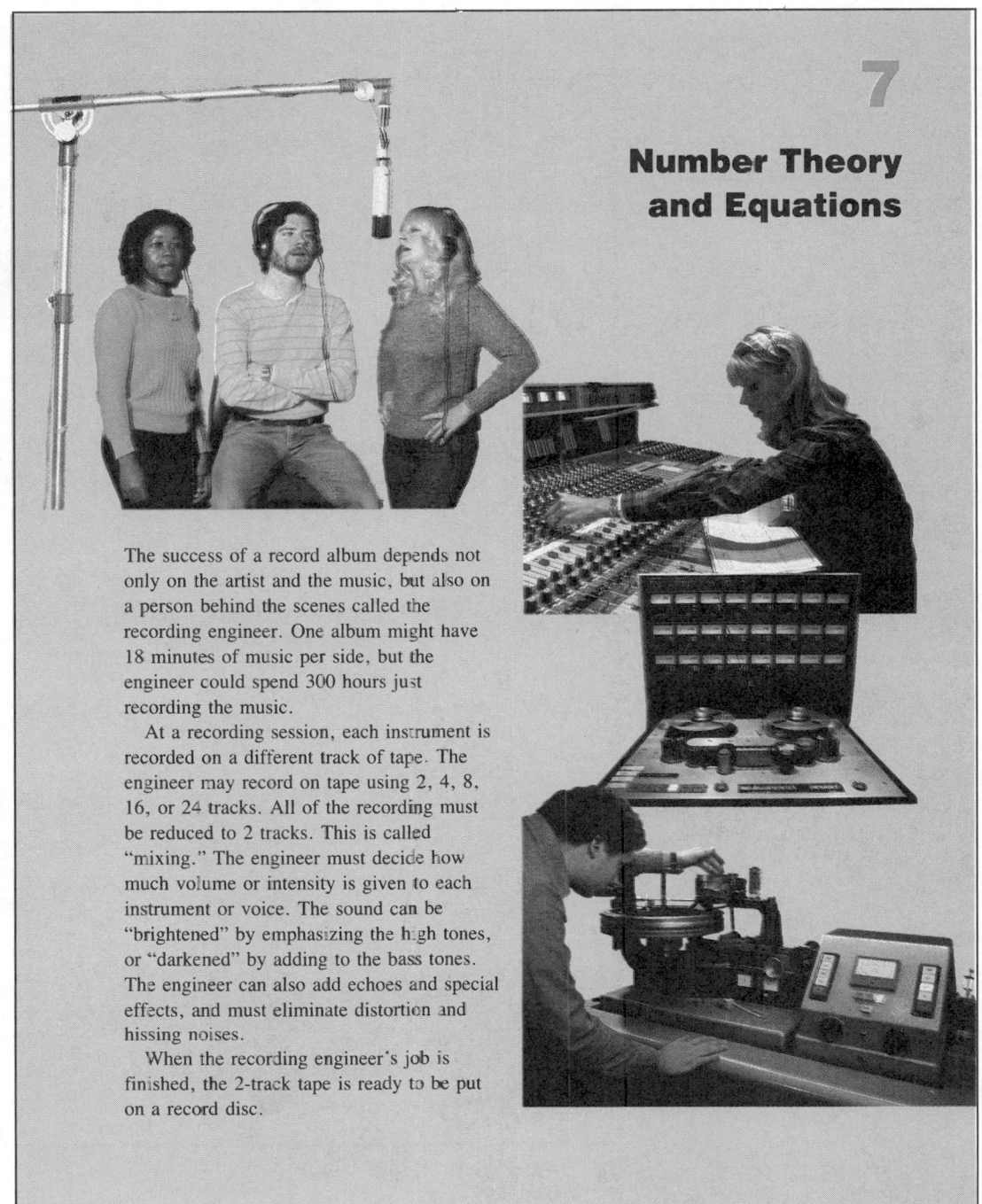

7

Number Theory and Equations

The success of a record album depends not only on the artist and the music, but also on a person behind the scenes called the recording engineer. One album might have 18 minutes of music per side, but the engineer could spend 300 hours just recording the music.

At a recording session, each instrument is recorded on a different track of tape. The engineer may record on tape using 2, 4, 8, 16, or 24 tracks. All of the recording must be reduced to 2 tracks. This is called "mixing." The engineer must decide how much volume or intensity is given to each instrument or voice. The sound can be "brightened" by emphasizing the high tones, or "darkened" by adding to the bass tones. The engineer can also add echoes and special effects, and must eliminate distortion and hissing noises.

When the recording engineer's job is finished, the 2-track tape is ready to be put on a record disc.

Introducing the Chapter

Discussion Have students read about the recording engineer and examine the accompanying photographs. Encourage discussion about recording studios and the given data. This is an opportunity for students to create their own problems based on the data in the article.

As you teach the chapter, you may wish to refer back to this page and discuss the questions below. Review the contents of the article briefly before posing the questions.

Follow-Up Questions

After Page 176 A rock group is charged $125 per hour of studio recording time. Let h = the number of recording hours. Then $125h$ = the total amount charged. Complete the chart to find the cost in dollars for 7, 12, and 100 hours of recording time.

h	$125h$
7	(875)
12	(1,500)
100	(12,500)

After Page 184 Write and solve an equation for the following problem. If tape speed is 15 inches per second and music has been recorded on 30,000 inches of tape, how many seconds of music were recorded? ($15n = 30,000$, $n = 2,000$)

Number Theory

Quick Review Read aloud the amounts of money shown below and have students write each amount in dollar and cent notation.

| $72.36 | $2,600.74 | $0.06 | $1,730.02 | $83.91 |
| $12.00 | $17,003.14 | $3.82 | $505.50 | $6.08 |

Lesson Focus To determine if one number is a factor of another and to list all the factors of a number

Ideas for Getting Started

Review the relationships between multiplication and division and the terms factor and product. Write 7 · 4 = 28 on the chalkboard. "What do we call the numbers 7 and 4?" (factors) "What do we call the number 28?" (product) "What two division facts can you write using the numbers 7, 4, and 28?" (28 ÷ 7 = 4 and 28 ÷ 4 = 7)

Using Page 164

Lesson Development Have students read the material at the top of the page. Point out that for small numbers, thinking of multiplication facts helps us list the factors. Ask students to name all the factors of two numbers such as 8 and 9. (8: 1, 2, 4, 8 and 9: 1, 3, 9)

Discuss the meaning of *divisible*. Explain that one number is divisible by another if the quotient is a whole number and there is no remainder. A number is divisible by its factors.

"Division by 0 is undefined" is another way to say division by zero is impossible. To reinforce that we cannot divide by 0, show that there is no way to find the quotient of 5 ÷ 0. Write the following on the chalkboard.

$$0\overline{)5} \rightarrow 0 \times \underline{\hspace{1cm}} = 5$$

Ask students for the missing number. Explain that since there is no number times 0 that gives a product of 5, we cannot divide by 0.

Other Examples Discuss the way division can be used to find factors of larger numbers. Work through these examples with students.

Factors

Which number has more factors, 36 or 40?

36 has 9 factors:
1, 2, 3, 4, 6, 9, 12, 18, and 36.

40 has 8 factors:
1, 2, 4, 5, 8, 10, 20, and 40.

36 has more factors.

Factors of 36	Factors of 40
1 × 36	1 × 40
2 × 18	2 × 20
3 × 12	4 × 10
4 × 9	5 × 8
6 × 6	

Any whole number, except 0, is divisible by each of its factors.

$40 \div 1 = 40$	$40 \div 2 = 20$	$40 \div 4 = 10$	$40 \div 5 = 8$
$40 \div 8 = 5$	$40 \div 10 = 4$	$40 \div 20 = 2$	$40 \div 40 = 1$

Zero is not a factor of any whole number except 0, but every whole number is a factor of 0.

$$0 \times 0 = 0 \qquad 1 \times 0 = 0 \qquad 2 \times 0 = 0 \qquad 3 \times 0 = 0 \ldots$$

We cannot divide any number by 0.

Other Examples

We can divide to find a factor of a number.

Is 8 a factor of 158?

$$8\overline{)158} \quad \underset{}{19} \text{ R6}$$

The remainder is not 0.
8 is not a factor of 158.

Is 7 a factor of 105?

$$7\overline{)105} \quad \underset{}{15} \text{ R0}$$

The remainder is 0.
7 and 15 are factors of 105.

Warm Up

List all the factors of each number.

1. 10
   1, 2, 5, 10
2. 12
   1, 2, 3, 4, 6, 12
3. 16
   1, 2, 4, 8, 16
4. 11
   1, 11

Use division to decide if the first number is a factor of the second number.

5. 8 and 232
   yes; 8 × 29
6. 16 and 500
   no
7. 23 and 529
   yes; 23 × 23
8. 54 and 324
   yes; 6 × 54

164

Follow Up

Reteaching

Illustrate the factors of a number with arrays. Use an example, such as 12. With counters, or dots on the chalkboard, form the following arrays to show all factors of 12.

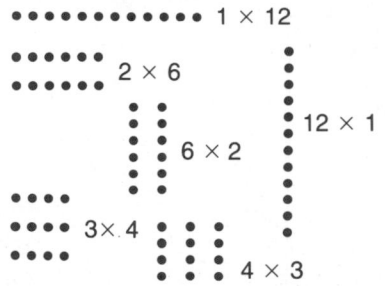

Have students summarize the findings.

Enrichment

Ask students to list all factors for the numbers 2 through 36. Have them name all numbers with an odd number of factors and tell what these numbers have in common.

Numbers with an odd number of factors: 4, 9, 16, 25, 36. Each number is the square of a number, or a *perfect square*.

Assignment Guide			
	Minimum	Average	Extended
page 165	1–36	1–38	1–35 odd, 37–46

List all the factors of each number.

1.
28
1×28
2×14
4×7

1, 2, 4, 7, 14, 28

2.
51
1×51
3×17

1, 3, 17, 51

3.
92
1×92
2×46
4×23

1, 2, 4, 23, 46, 92

4.
54
1×54
2×27
3×18
6×9

1, 2, 3, 6, 9, 18, 27, 54

5. 20
1, 2, 4, 5, 10, 20

6. 24
1, 2, 3, 4, 6, 8, 12,

7. 15
1, 3, 5, 15

8. 17
1, 17

9. 18
1, 2, 3, 6, 9, 18

10. 33
1, 3, 11, 33
24

11. 1
1

12. 80 1, 2, 4, 5, 8, 10,
16, 20, 40, 80

13. 100 1, 2, 4, 5, 10,
20, 25, 50, 100

14. 56
1, 2, 7, 8, 28, 56

15. 45
1, 3, 5, 9, 15, 45

16. 68 1, 2, 4,
17, 34, 68

17. 75
1, 3, 5, 15, 25, 75

18. 84 1, 2, 3, 4, 6, 7,
12, 14, 21, 28, 42, 84

19. 72 1, 2, 3, 4, 6, 8,
9, 12, 18, 24, 36, 72

20. 120 1, 2, 3, 4, 5,
6, 8, 10, 12, 15,
20, 24, 30,
40, 60, 120

Use division to decide if the first number is a factor of the second number.

21. 6 and 108
yes; 6×18

22. 7 and 162
no

23. 3 and 111
yes; 3×37

24. 4 and 138
no

25. 13 and 741
yes; 13×57

26. 18 and 666
yes; 18×37

27. 29 and 1,769
yes; 29×61

28. 25 and 525
yes; 25×21

29. 14 and 520
no

30. 31 and 967
no

31. 23 and 1,541
yes; 23×67

32. 42 and 2,142
yes; 42×51

33. 55 and 1,785
no

34. 120 and 600
yes; 120×5

35. 39 and 1,521
yes; 39×39

36. 231 and 28,413
yes; 231×123

37. What is the smallest whole number with exactly two different factors? 2; 1, 2

38. Which number is a factor of any even number? 2

39. What is the smallest whole number with exactly three different factors? 4; 1, 2, 4

40. What is the smallest whole number with exactly four different factors?
6; 1, 2, 3, 6

Divide to decide if the first number is a factor of the second number.

41. 2,769 and 994,071 yes; $2,769 \times 359$

42. 3,427 and 23,396,129 yes; $3,427 \times 6,827$

43. 9,683 and 33,803,357 no

44. 47,287 and 13,902,378 yes; $47,287 \times 294$

45. 64,543 and 13,560,885 no

46. 15,625 and 1,000,000 yes; $15,625 \times 64$

Using Page 165

Exercises 1–40 Have students work the assigned exercises independently. Note that exercise 38 gives a definition of even number.

Exercises 41–46 Calculators can be used for these exercises.

Reteaching Supplement, page 48

Name _____   To follow text page 165

Factors

Find the factors of 16.

Remember: The **factors** of a number are all the whole numbers that divide it evenly.

1 and 16 are factors.	2 and 8 are factors.	4 is a factor.	No other whole numbers divide **evenly** into 16.

$16\overline{)16}$ 1 $2\overline{)16}$ 8 $4\overline{)16}$ 4 $3\overline{)16}$ $5\,R1$ $5\overline{)16}$ $3\,R1$ $6\overline{)16}$ $2\,R4$ $7\overline{)16}$ $2\,R2$ and so on.

The factors of 16 are 1, 2, 4, 8, and 16.

Ring the numbers that are factors of the first number given.

$9\overline{)9}$ yes $4\overline{)9}$ $\overset{R1}{}$ no

1. 9 ① 2 ③ 4 5 6 7 8 ⑨

2. 18 ① ② ③ 4 5 ⑥ 7 8 ⑨ 10 11 12 13 14 15 16 17 ⑱

3. 20 ① ② 3 ④ ⑤ 6 7 8 9 ⑩ 11 12 13 14 15 16 17 18 19 ⑳

4. 17 ① 2 3 4 5 6 7 8 9 10 11 12 13 14 15 16 ⑰

List all the factors of each number.

5. 6 _____ 1,2,3,6
6. 4 _____ 1,2,4
7. 17 _____ 1,17
8. 32 _____ 1,2,4,8,16,32
9. 26 _____ 1,2,13,26
10. 23 _____ 1,23
11. 75 _____ 1,3,5,15,25,75
12. 56 _____ 1,2,4,7,8,14,28,56
13. 54 _____ 1,2,3,6,9,18,27,54
14. 108 _____ 1,2,3,4,6,9,12,18,27 36,54,108

Use division to tell if the first number is a factor of the second number. Answer yes or no.

15. 9 333 _____ yes
16. 17 10,608 _____ yes
17. 28 2,774 _____ no

Does 9 divide evenly into 333?

18. 64 20,928 _____ yes
19. 27 15,687 _____ yes
20. 48 30,142 _____ no

Enrichment Supplement, page 48

Name _____   To follow text: page 165

Guess the Number

The seventh-grade Math Club played a game with numbers. Each member thought of a 1- or 2-digit number and then gave clues. The others tried to guess it.

Read each set of clues and guess the number.

1. Teresa's clues: This number is a factor of 18. It is divisible by 2 and by 3 but not by 4.
Teresa's number is ___6___

2. Harry's clues: This number is a multiple of 4. It is not a multiple of 5. It is a factor of 24 but not a factor of 16.
Harry's number is __12 or 24__

3. Amanda's clues: This number has 2 digits. It is divisible by 2 and by 3. The sum of its digits is 6 and the ones' digit is half the tens' digit.
Amanda's number is ___42___

4. Gwen's clues: This number has 2, 3, and 6 among its factors. The number is the square of one of the digits. The sum of the digits is 9.
Gwen's number is ___36___

5. Jack's clues: This number is a factor of 72. It is less than 72 and it has two digits. It is divisible by the sum of its digits but not the product of its digits.
Jack's number is ___18___

6. Pat's clues: This number is a factor of 36. The sum of the digits in its square equals the number itself.
Pat's number is ___9___

Practice Supplement, page 62

Name _____   To follow text: page 165

Factors

List all the factors of each number.

1.
45
1×45
3×15
5×9

1, 3, 5, 9, 15, 45

2.
32
1×32
2×16
4×8

1, 2, 4, 8, 16, 32

3.
56
1×56
2×28
4×14
7×8

1, 2, 4, 7, 8, 14, 28, 56

4. 36 _____ 1, 2, 3, 4, 6, 9, 12, 18, 36
5. 78 _____ 1, 2, 3, 6, 13, 26, 39, 78
6. 14 _____ 1, 2, 7, 14
7. 30 _____ 1, 2, 3, 5, 6, 10, 15, 30
8. 19 _____ 1, 19
9. 42 _____ 1, 2, 3, 6, 7, 14, 21, 42
10. 49 _____ 1, 7, 49
11. 64 _____ 1, 2, 4, 8, 16, 32, 64
12. 104 _____ 1, 2, 4, 8, 13, 26, 52, 104
13. 105 _____ 1, 3, 5, 7, 15, 21, 35, 105
14. 60 _____ 1, 2, 3, 4, 5, 6, 10, 12, 15, 20, 30, 60
15. 80 _____ 1, 2, 4, 5, 8, 10, 16, 20, 40, 80
16. 140 _____ 1, 2, 4, 5, 7, 10, 14, 20, 28, 35, 70, 140
17. 150 _____ 1, 2, 3, 5, 6, 10, 15, 25, 30, 50, 75, 150

Use division to answer each question.

18. Is 4 a factor of 54? ___no___
19. Is 3 a factor of 48? ___yes___
20. Is 7 a factor of 105? ___yes___
21. Is 9 a factor of 108? ___yes___
22. Is 8 a factor of 200? ___yes___
23. Is 11 a factor of 132? ___yes___
24. Is 36 a factor of 144? ___yes___
25. Is 45 a factor of 190? ___no___
26. Is 22 a factor of 444? ___no___
27. Is 75 a factor of 600? ___yes___

Quick Review Have students tell which differences are incorrect.
495.67 − 32.88 = 362.88 **Incorrect**   932.21 − 458.62 = 473.59
62.98 − 46.52 = 15.46   678.5 − 398.8 = 248.7 $20.00 − 17.98 = $2.02
Incorrect   **Incorrect**

Lesson Focus To use divisibility rules to decide if numbers are divisible by 2, 3, 5, 9 or 10

Ideas for Getting Started

To check if students are familiar with the simple divisibility tests for 2, 5, or 10, write these numbers on the chalkboard.

172   335   614   190

"Which numbers can be divided by 2 with zero remainder?" (172, 614, 190) Explain that this means these numbers have 2 as a factor. Repeat the question for 5 and 10. Ask students how they arrived at their answers. If they used a rule, have them state the rule in their own words.

Using Page 166

Motivational Problem After students read the problem at the top of the page, have them identify the question and the data. Point out that we could solve the problem by actually dividing, but in this case there is a rule we can use mentally to answer the question.

Lesson Development Discuss the steps for testing divisibility by 3. The sum of the digits is 6. Since 6 is divisible by 3, 141 is divisible by 3. Have students check the rule by actually dividing 141 by 3 to get a quotient of 47 with 0 remainder. Then show how to use the divisibility rule for 9. Help students see that it is similar to the divisibility rule for 3.

Other Examples Work through these examples with students. Point out that if a number is divisible by 9, it must also be divisible by 3 since 3 is a factor of 9. Similarly, if a number is divisible by 10, it is also divisible by 2 and 5.

Warm Up Provide an opportunity for students to check and discuss their answers before proceeding to page 167.

Divisibility Rules

Beth Ann has 141 newspapers for a paper route. Can she divide the papers into 3 piles with the same number in each pile?

She could divide to find out. However, Beth Ann knows a rule that she can use without dividing.

$141 \rightarrow 1 + 4 + 1 = 6$
6 is divisible by 3,
so 141 is divisible by 3.

3 Add the digits of the number. If the sum is divisible by 3, so is the number.

$2{,}916 \rightarrow 2 + 9 + 1 + 6 = 18$
18 is divisible by 9,
so 2,916 is divisible by 9.

9 The divisibility rule for 9 is like the divisibility rule for 3.

You may already know the divisibility rules for 2, 5, and 10.

2 The ones digit must be **even**; 0, 2, 4, 6, 8.

5 The ones digit must be 5 or 0.

10 The ones digit must be 0.

Other Examples

$672 \rightarrow 6 + 7 + 2 = 15$
672 is divisible by 2.
672 is divisible by 3.
672 is not divisible by 5, 9, or 10.

$3{,}105 \rightarrow 3 + 1 + 0 + 5 = 9$
3,105 is divisible by 5.
3,105 is divisible by 3 and 9.
3,105 is not divisible by 2 or 10.

Warm Up

Use the divisibility rules to decide if each number is divisible by 2, 3, 5, 9, 10, or none of these numbers.

1. 912 2, 3   2. 9,375 3, 5   3. 5,550 2, 3, 5, 10   4. 1,890 2, 3, 5, 9, 10

5. 2,331 3, 9   6. 283 none   7. 8,577 3, 9   8. 83,760 2, 3, 5, 10

166

Follow Up

Reteaching

Have students use the divisibility rules to complete the chart below and then use a calculator to check their work. An example is given.

Number	Divisible by				
	2	5	10	3	9
321	no	no	no	yes	no
9,117	no	no	no	yes	yes
5,205	no	yes	no	yes	no
7,710	yes	yes	yes	yes	no
18,162	yes	no	no	yes	yes
40,140	yes	yes	yes	yes	yes

Enrichment

Write this divisibility rule on the chalkboard: Any number is divisible by 4 if the last two digits are divisible by 4. Ask students to use the divisibility rule to determine if the following numbers are divisible by 4.

1. 9,344 **yes**   2. 16,422 **no**

3. 761,284 **yes**   4. 512,932 **yes**

5. 1,242,326 **no**   6. 6,200,904 **yes**

7. 129,215 **no**   8. 21,960 **yes**

Assignment Guide

	Minimum	Average	Extended
page 167		1–42	1–41 odd, 42, TM

State if each number is divisible by 3.

1. 213 yes   **2.** 624 yes   **3.** 115 no   **4.** 810 yes   **5.** 2,349 yes

6. 6,227 no   **7.** 111 yes   **8.** 1,011 yes   **9.** 726 yes   **10.** 555 yes

11. 4,281 yes   **12.** 57 yes   **13.** 1,089 yes   **14.** 4,431 yes   **15.** 111,012 yes

State if each number is divisible by 9.

16. 513 yes   **17.** 784 no   **18.** 396 yes   **19.** 405 yes   **20.** 267 no

21. 1,236 no   **22.** 6,021 yes   **23.** 108 yes   **24.** 656 no   **25.** 2,070 yes

26. 1,234 no   **27.** 6,669 yes   **28.** 42,723 yes   **29.** 56,725 no   **30.** 111,111,111 yes

State if each number is divisible by 2, 3, 5, 9, 10, or none of these numbers.

31. 714   **32.** 420   **33.** 9,125   **34.** 123   **35.** 3,150
2, 3   2, 3, 5, 10   5   3   2, 3, 5, 9, 10

36. 5,310   **37.** 666   **38.** 4,277   **39.** 23,634   **40.** 88,524
2, 3, 5, 9, 10   2, 3, 9   none   2, 3, 9   2, 3, 9

41. Jeremy must deliver 112 Sunday newspapers. Can he divide that number of newspapers into 9 stacks with the same number in each stack? no

42. Juan will deliver a number of newspapers that can be divided by 2, 3, 5, 9, and 10. What is the smallest number of papers he could deliver? 90

▌THINK MATH▐

Abundant Numbers

A number is **abundant** if the sum of its factors (other than the number itself) is greater than the given number.

Factors of 20: **1, 2, 4, 5, 10**

Sum of the factors: $1 + 2 + 4 + 5 + 10 = 22$

Since $22 > 20$, 20 is an **abundant number**.

What is the smallest abundant number? 12
Which numbers less than 50 are abundant numbers? 12, 18, 20, 24, 30, 36, 40, 42, 48

167

Using Page 167

Exercises 1–30 The divisibility rules for 3 and 9 have relatively simple algebraic proofs, but these are beyond the level of most students at this grade level. The rules can be made plausible by noting the patterns in the sum of the digits for the multiples of 3 or 9. For example, using multiples of 9 we have the following. In each case the sum of the digits is a multiple of 9.

9	99	999
18	108	1008
27	117	1017
36	126	1026
54	135	1035
·	·	·
·	·	·

Think Math This problem involves an understanding of the meaning of *abundant number* and the ability to list all factors of a number. To find abundant numbers students can guess and check.

Ideas that Work

Special Education

A game for stressing divisibility and factoring is "Factor Fun." To play the game, make a chart of the numbers 2 through 40 on the chalkboard or overhead projector. Divide the class into two groups. The first team crosses out one of the numbers on the chart, for example 12. That number is the team's score for the turn and may not be selected again. The second team now has a turn. If the number selected by the first team has any factors remaining on the chart, the second team must take all of them. In the present example, the second team crosses out 2, 3, 4, and 6. The sum of

these numbers is the second team's score for the turn.

```
 X  X  X  5  X  7  8  9  10
11 (X) 13 14 15 16 17 18 19 20
21 22 23 24 25 26 27 28 29 30
31 32 33 34 35 36 37 38 39 40
```

If the number selected by the first team does not have any factors remaining in the chart, the second team can select any number they wish.

Play continues in the same fashion until all numbers have been selected. When all numbers are crossed off, the team with the highest score wins.

Practice Supplement, page 63

Numbers and Numeration

Quick Review Read the following aloud and have students identify how many places and in what direction the decimal point must be shifted.

72.5 ÷ 100 **2, left**	4.789 × 100,000 **5, right**	3.32 × 0.1 **1, left**
364.3 ÷ 1,000 **3, left**	0.479 × 1,000 **3, right**	4.95 × 0.001 **3, left**

Lesson Focus To determine whether a number greater than 1 is prime or composite

Ideas for Getting Started

Review the meaning of factors of a number. "How many factors does the number 18 have?" (6 factors → 1, 2, 3, 6, 9, 18) "Can you find a number with 4 factors? with 3 factors? with 2 factors?" (Many answers are possible.) "What number has exactly 1 factor?" (1)

Using Page 168

Lesson Development Discuss *prime* and *composite* numbers. Point out that the numbers 0 and 1 are neither prime nor composite. Have students give examples to illustrate the idea that every number is a factor of 0. ($0 \cdot 0 = 0$, $0 \cdot 1 = 0$, $0 \cdot 2 = 0$, $0 \cdot 3 = 0$, . . .)

Warm Up Work through these exercises orally with the class. Have students tell why a number is prime or composite.

Prime and Composite Numbers

Jacqueline uses a computer to find the factors of some numbers. The computer screen shows the factors of the numbers. It also lists each number as **prime** or **composite**.

Prime numbers have exactly two factors.

Composite numbers have more than two factors.

The numbers 0 and 1 are neither prime nor composite.

1 has only one factor.
Every number is a factor of 0.

Warm Up

What would the computer screen show for numbers 11 through 20?

	Number	Factors	Prime or Composite
1.	11	1, 11	prime
2.	12	1, 2, 3, 4, 6, 12	composite
3.	13	1, 13	prime
4.	14	1, 2, 7, 14	composite
5.	15	1, 3, 5, 15	composite
6.	16	1, 2, 4, 8, 16	composite
7.	17	1, 17	prime
8.	18	1, 2, 3, 6, 9, 18	composite
9.	19	1, 19	prime
10.	20	1, 2, 4, 5, 10	composite

168

Follow Up

Reteaching

Use arrays to illustrate the ideas of prime and composite numbers. Form arrays for numbers 2 through 12 to show all the factors of each number. Focus students' attention on whether a number has exactly two factors or more than two factors. Use these ideas to discuss prime and composite. Have students summarize the findings in a table.

Enrichment

Let students work together to make a bulletin board chart of prime numbers following these steps.
1) Leave the first box of a large 10 by 10 grid blank and write the numbers 2 through 100 on the grid.
2) Circle the smallest prime number (2). Mark out all multiples of 2.
3) Circle the next number not marked out (3). Mark out all the multiples of 3.
4) Continue until all the numbers on the grid are circled or marked out. The circled numbers are the primes.

Assignment Guide	Minimum	Average	Extended
page 169	1–28	1–30, 33	1–27 odd, 28–33, TM

Write P (prime), C (composite), or N (neither) for each number.

1. 21 C **2.** 31 P **3.** 33 C **4.** 47 P **5.** 51 C

6. 0 N **7.** 23 P **8.** 99 C **9.** 81 C **10.** 91 C

11. 53 P **12.** 63 C **13.** 73 P **14.** 83 P **15.** 93 C

Find the prime number in each list.

16. 8, 9, 10, 11, 12 11

17. 0, 5, 10, 15, 20 5

18. 21, 23, 25, 27 23

19. 33, 35, 37, 39 37

20. 49, 50, 51, 52, 53 53

21. 81, 89, 91, 93 89

Find the composite number in each list. Find the factors of that number.

22. 11, 21, 31, 41 21; 1, 3, 7, 21

23. 23, 33, 43, 53 33; 1, 3, 11, 33

24. 17, 71, 16, 61 16; 1, 2, 4, 8, 16

25. 0, 1, 3, 100 100; 1, 2, 4, 5, 10, 20, 25, 50, 100

26. 89, 79, 69, 59 69; 1, 3, 23, 69

27. 7, 17, 49, 71 49; 1, 7, 49

28. Make a list of all the prime numbers less than 100. You should find 25 prime numbers.
See teaching notes.

29. Choose any two prime numbers. Find their product. Is the product a prime number or a composite number?
composite

30. What is the only even prime number? 2

31. How many composite numbers are less than 100? 73 (1 is not composite)

32. What are the only two consecutive prime numbers? (Their difference is 1.) 2, 3

33. Show that 413 is not a prime number. Find another factor of 413, other than 1 or 413, by dividing. 7 × 59 = 413

THINK MATH

Prime Number Patterns

The pattern at the right seems to always have sums that are prime numbers.

Write several more sums in the pattern.
41, 53, 67, 83, 101, 121
Find the first sum in the pattern that is not a prime number.
121

$11 + 0 = 11$ ← prime
$11 + 2 = 13$ ← prime
$13 + 4 = 17$ ← prime
$17 + 6 = 23$ ← prime
$23 + ? = 31$ ← ?
8   prime

More Practice, page 426, Set A

169

Using Page 169

Exercise 1–27 Students often think that numbers such as 39, 51, 57, 87, and 91 are prime because one of the factors of these numbers lies outside the range of factors of memorized products. Remind students that both quotient and divisor are factors of the dividend when the remainder is 0.

Exercise 28

Primes Less Than 100				
2	3	5	7	11
13	17	19	23	29
31	37	41	43	47
53	59	61	67	71
73	79	83	89	97

Exercise 33 Students may divide by consecutive whole numbers to find a factor. Point out that they only need to divide by consecutive prime numbers.

Think Math This problem involves a simple pattern and an understanding of prime numbers. Consecutive even numbers are added to each of the previously obtained sums. The pattern continues ten times but fails on the eleventh:
$101 + 20 = 121$. Since $121 = 11 \times 11$, 121 is not prime.

More Practice, page 426, Set A

Quick Review Have students tell whether angles with the following measures are acute, obtuse, right, or straight.

123°	90°	102°	15°	80°
180°	95°	18°	45°	89°

Lesson Focus To give the prime factorization of a composite number and to express the factorization using exponents

Ideas for Getting Started

Review the concept of prime numbers and factors of numbers. "What are the factors of 20?" (1, 2, 3, 4, 5, 10, 20) "Which of the factors of 20 are prime numbers?" (2, 5) "What are the factors of 30?" (1, 2, 3, 5, 6, 10, 15, 30) "Which of the factors are prime numbers?" (2, 3, 5)

Review the use of exponents for writing repeated factors. Have students give the exponent in each of the following.

$2 \times 2 \times 2 \times 2 = 2^{\square}$ $\qquad$ $7 \times 7 \times 7 = 7^{\square}$
$5 \times 5 \times 5 \times 5 \times 5 \times 5 = 5^{\square}$ $10 = 10^{\square}$

Have students give the standard numeral for each of the following powers.

3^3 $\qquad$ 2^4 $\qquad$ 6^2 $\qquad$ 10^3

2^3 $\qquad$ 7^2 $\qquad$ 5^4 $\qquad$ 10^5

Using Page 170

Lesson Development Have students read the material at the top of the page. Explain that this is an important theorem in mathematics called the *Fundamental Theorem of Arithmetic.* Direct students' attention to the factor tree. Point out that the numbers in each row of the factor tree have a product equal to the starting number, 48. The final row, containing only prime numbers, is the *prime factorization* of 48.

Show students that factor trees may grow up or down as illustrated in these examples.

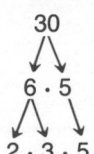 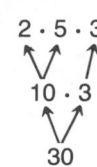

Use these examples to note that the numbers in a factor tree may vary depending upon the first factors chosen. The final row, however, contains the same prime numbers although the order of the factors may vary.

Warm Up Make certain students continue factoring until all of the factors are prime.

Prime Factorization

Each composite number can be expressed as a product of prime factors. This is the **prime factorization** of the composite number. Except for the order of the factors, there is only one prime factorization of a composite number.

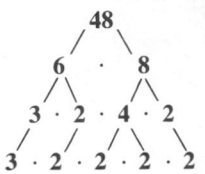

Number		Prime Factorization
30	=	$2 \cdot 3 \cdot 5$
24	=	$2 \cdot 2 \cdot 2 \cdot 3$
99	=	$3 \cdot 3 \cdot 11$
143	=	$11 \cdot 13$

To find the prime factors of a number, find any two factors. Then find the prime factors of these factors.

$60 = 6 \cdot 10$
$60 = 2 \cdot 3 \cdot 2 \cdot 5$
$\underbrace{}_{\text{prime factorization}}$

A **factor tree** may help to find the prime factors of a number. The lowest row of the tree contains only prime numbers.

```
         48
        /  \
      6  ·  8
     / \   / \
    3 · 2 · 4 · 2
         / \
    3 · 2 · 2 · 2 · 2
```

We can write prime factorizations using exponents.

$48 = 2 \cdot 2 \cdot 2 \cdot 2 \cdot 3$
$48 = 2^4 \cdot 3$

Other Examples

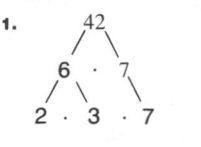
$63 = 9 \cdot 7$
$63 = 3 \cdot 3 \cdot 7$

$72 = 8 \cdot 9$
$72 = 2 \cdot 2 \cdot 2 \cdot 3 \cdot 3$

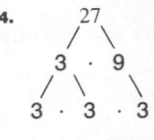
$120 = 10 \cdot 12$
$120 = 2 \cdot 5 \cdot 2 \cdot 2 \cdot 3$

Warm Up

Complete each factor tree. Give the prime factorization of each number.

1.
```
    42
   /  \
  6  · 7
 / \
2 · 3 · 7
```
$42 = 2 \cdot 3 \cdot 7$

2.
```
      36
     /  \
    9  · 4
   / \  / \
  3 · 3 · 2 · 2
```
$36 = 3 \cdot 3 \cdot 2 \cdot 2$

3.
```
   21
  /  \
 3 · 7
```
$21 = 3 \cdot 7$

4.
```
     27
    /  \
   3 · 9
      / \
  3 · 3 · 3
```
$27 = 3 \cdot 3 \cdot 3$

Give the prime factorization of each number using exponents.

5. 8 2^3
6. 24 $2^3 \cdot 3$
7. 63 $3^2 \cdot 7$
8. 50 $5^2 \cdot 2$

170

Follow Up

Reteaching

Show students the method for finding the prime factorization of a number described in Teaching Tips, p. 162 C. The example below shows the prime factorization of 36.

	1
3	3
3	9
2	18
2	36

$36 = 2 \cdot 2 \cdot 3 \cdot 3$

Have students use this method to find the prime factorizations of other numbers.

Enrichment

Have students show all the different factor trees for 100. There are six different factor trees. Two of them are shown below.

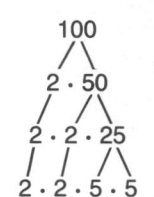 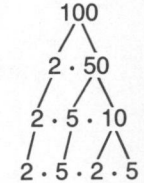

Assignment Guide			
	Minimum	Average	Extended
page 171	1–24	1–25, 27–30	1–25 odd, 26–30

Complete each factor tree. Give the prime factorization of each number.

1.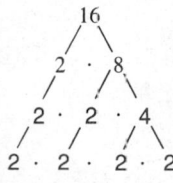
16
$16 = 2 \cdot 2 \cdot 2 \cdot 2$

2.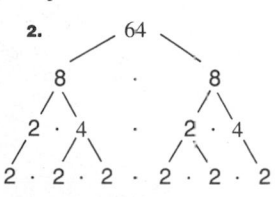
64
$64 = 2 \cdot 2 \cdot 2 \cdot 2 \cdot 2 \cdot 2$

3.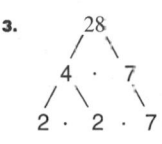
28
$28 = 2 \cdot 2 \cdot 7$

4.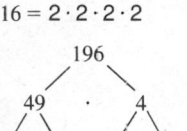
196
$196 = 7 \cdot 7 \cdot 2 \cdot 2$

5.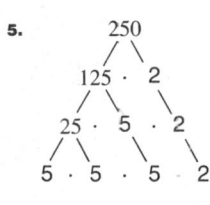
250
$250 = 5 \cdot 5 \cdot 5 \cdot 2$

6.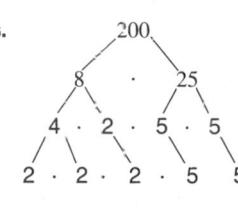
200
$200 = \quad 2 \cdot 2 \cdot 2 \cdot 5 \cdot 5$

Make a factor tree for each number. Give the prime factorization of the number.

7. 70 $2 \cdot 5 \cdot 7$
8. 84 $2 \cdot 2 \cdot 3 \cdot 7$
9. 80 $2 \cdot 2 \cdot 2 \cdot 2 \cdot 5$
10. 81 $3 \cdot 3 \cdot 3 \cdot 3$
11. 300 $3 \cdot 2 \cdot 5 \cdot 2 \cdot 5$
12. 120 $2 \cdot 2 \cdot 2 \cdot 3 \cdot 5$
13. 96 $2 \cdot 2 \cdot 2 \cdot 3 \cdot 2 \cdot 2$
14. 105 $5 \cdot 3 \cdot 7$
15. 72 $3 \cdot 3 \cdot 2 \cdot 2 \cdot 2$
16. 1,000 $2 \cdot 5 \cdot 2 \cdot 5 \cdot 2 \cdot 5$

Write the prime factorization of each number using exponents.

17. $968 = 2 \cdot 2 \cdot 2 \cdot 11 \cdot 11 \ 2^3 \cdot 11^2$

18. $1{,}125 = 3 \cdot 3 \cdot 5 \cdot 5 \cdot 5 \ 3^2 \cdot 5^3$

19. $162 = 2 \cdot 3 \cdot 3 \cdot 3 \cdot 3 \ 2 \cdot 3^4$

20. $1{,}372 = 2 \cdot 2 \cdot 7 \cdot 7 \cdot 7 \ 2^2 \cdot 7^3$

21. $18{,}865 = 5 \cdot 7 \cdot 7 \cdot 7 \cdot 11 \ 5 \cdot 7^3 \cdot 11$

22. $396 = 2 \cdot 2 \cdot 3 \cdot 3 \cdot 11 \ 2^2 \cdot 3^2 \cdot 11$

23. $900 = 2 \cdot 2 \cdot 3 \cdot 3 \cdot 5 \cdot 5 \ 2^2 \cdot 3^2 \cdot 5^2$

24. $300 = 2 \cdot 2 \cdot 3 \cdot 5 \cdot 5 \ 2^2 \cdot 3 \cdot 5^2$

25. Make a factor tree for 1 million. Give the prime factorization.
$2 \cdot 5 \cdot 2 \cdot 5 \cdot 2 \cdot 5 \cdot 2 \cdot 5 \cdot 2 \cdot 5 \cdot 2 \cdot 5; \ 2^6 \cdot 5^6$

★ 26. What are the next three numbers in this pattern? 2, 6, 30, 210, . . . Hint: What is the prime factorization of the numbers?
2,310; 30,030; 510,510

Give the prime factorizations. Each number below is the product of three of the prime numbers (one from each row in the table).

27. 27,178
$2 \times 107 \times 127$

28. 66,155
$5 \times 101 \times 131$

29. 42,051
$3 \times 107 \times 131$

30. 86,219
$7 \times 109 \times 113$

2	3	5	7
101	103	107	109
173	127	131	137

More Practice, page 426, Set B

171

Using Page 171

Exercises 7–16 Students may use different factors in their factor trees, but the final row will be the same. Every number has only one prime factorization.

Exercise 26 The hint will help most students see the pattern.

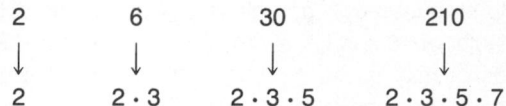

The next three numbers are
$2{,}310 = 2 \cdot 3 \cdot 5 \cdot 7 \cdot 11$
$30{,}030 = 2 \cdot 3 \cdot 5 \cdot 7 \cdot 11 \cdot 13$
$510{,}510 = 2 \cdot 3 \cdot 5 \cdot 7 \cdot 11 \cdot 13 \cdot 17$

More Practice, page 426, Set B

Reteaching Supplement, page 50

Enrichment Supplement, page 50

Practice Supplement, page 65

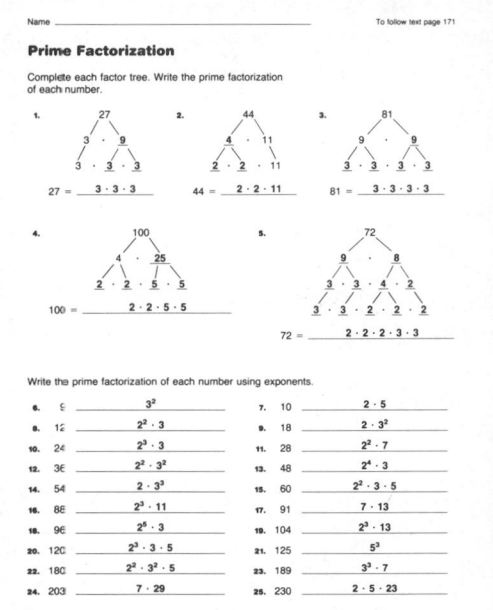

Lesson Focus To find the greatest common factor of two numbers

Ideas for Getting Started

Tell students they are going to play "Guess the Factor." Name pairs of numbers and select the greatest common factor of each pair for the factor to be guessed. "I am thinking of a number. It is a factor of 18 and 24. What is the number?" (6) Students may guess 1, 2, 3, or 6. If someone suggests a number such as 4 or 12, point out that it is not a factor of both numbers.

Repeat the game with pairs of numbers such as 12 and 16, 30 and 45, and 60 and 40 until students realize that you are always choosing the largest or greatest common factor of the two numbers.

Using Page 172

Motivational Problem Have students read the introductory problem. "What does the question ask you to find?" (the greatest possible length of the sides of squares to be cut from the material) "What data is given in the problem?" (The material is 54 in. wide and 126 in. long.) Point out that we cannot solve the problem by choosing a single operation.

Lesson Development Write out the factors of 54 and the factors of 126 on the chalkboard. Circle the factors common to both numbers. Then show that 18 is the *greatest common factor* or GCF. Note that the quilt would be cut into 3 rows of squares with 7 squares in each row since 3×18 = 54 and 7×18 = 126.

Work through finding the GCF of 54 and 126 using the prime factorizations. Only the prime factors common to each number are factors of the GCF.

Explain that every pair of numbers has 1 as a common factor. If 1 is the only common factor of the pair, the two numbers are *relatively prime,* as are any two different prime numbers.

Warm Up Some students may need to list all the factors of each number before giving the common factors and the GCF.

Greatest Common Factor (GCF)

Pat has a piece of material 54 in. wide and 126 in. long. Squares must be cut out that are as large as possible without wasting any material. What is the greatest possible length of each side of the squares?

To solve the problem, we need to find the largest number that is a factor of both 54 and 126.

Factors of 54:   **1, 2, 3, 6, 9, 18, 27, 54**

Factors of 126:   **1, 2, 3, 6, 7, 9, 14, 18, 21, 42, 63, 126**

Common factors: **1, 2, 3, 6, 9, 18**

The **greatest common factor** (GCF) is **18**.

Pat can cut the material into squares that are 18 in. on each side.

We can use the prime factorizations of two numbers to find the greatest common factor.

$54 = 2 \cdot 3 \cdot 3 \cdot 3$
$126 = 2 \cdot 3 \cdot 3 \cdot 7$
$GCF = 2 \cdot 3 \cdot 3 \quad = 18$

Two numbers are **relatively prime** if their GCF is 1.

Factors of 8: **1, 2, 4, 8**
Factors of 9: **1, 3, 9**
8 and 9 are relatively prime.

Other Examples

Find the GCF of 10 and 18.
10 : **1, 2, 5, 10**
18 : **1, 2, 3, 6, 9, 18**
GCF : **2**

Find the GCF of 40 and 50.
$40 = 2 \cdot 2 \cdot 2 \cdot 5$
$50 = \quad\quad 2 \cdot 5 \cdot 5$
$GCF = \quad\quad 2 \cdot 5 \quad = 10$

Warm Up

List the common factors of each pair of numbers. Give the GCF.

1. 4, 10 1, 2; 2   **2.** 22, 33 1, 11; 11   **3.** 5, 15 1, 5; 5   **4.** 45, 75 1, 3, 5, 15; 15

Give the GCF of each pair of numbers. State if they are relatively prime.

5. 3, 5   **6.** 8, 18   **7.** 9, 13   **8.** 7, 14
172   1; relatively prime   2   1; relatively prime   7

Follow Up

Reteaching

If students have difficulty finding the GCF of two numbers, stress the method of listing all factors of the numbers, finding the common factors, and selecting the greatest of these factors. The main skill involved in this method is the ability to list the factors of a number.

Work through an example with students, using this method.

32, 40

32: ①, ②, ④, ⑧, 16, 32
40: ①, ②, ④, 5, ⑧, 10, 20, 40
GCF = 8

Enrichment

Write the following table on the chalkboard. Have students find the GCF of each pair of numbers and complete the table.

GCF	6	10	12	18	24
2	2	2	2	2	2
3	3	1	3	3	3
6	6	2	6	6	6
9	3	1	3	9	3
12	6	2	12	6	12

You may wish to have students expand the table with additional numbers.

Assignment Guide			
	Minimum	Average	Extended
page 173	1–12, 25–33, SK	1–33, SK	1–33 odd, 34, SK

List the common factors of each pair of numbers. Give the GCF.

1. 3, 18
1, 3; 3

2. 14, 28
1, 2, 7; 7

3. 20, 50
1, 2, 5, 10; 10

4. 16, 32
1, 2, 4, 8, 16; 16

Find the GCF of each pair of numbers.

5. $4 = 2 \cdot 2$
$6 = 2 \cdot 3$ 2

6. $9 = 3 \cdot 3$
$45 = 3 \cdot 3 \cdot 5$ 9

7. $42 = 2 \cdot 3 \cdot 7$
$105 = 3 \cdot 5 \cdot 7$ 21

8. $90 = 2 \cdot 3 \cdot 3 \cdot 5$
$105 = 3 \cdot 5 \cdot 7$ 15

9. $12 = 2 \cdot 2 \cdot 3$
$60 = 2 \cdot 2 \cdot 3 \cdot 5$ 12

10. $42 = 2 \cdot 3 \cdot 7$
$28 = 2 \cdot 2 \cdot 7$ 14

11. $150 = 2 \cdot 3 \cdot 5 \cdot 5$
$105 = 3 \cdot 5 \cdot 7$ 15

12. $108 = 2 \cdot 2 \cdot 3 \cdot 3 \cdot 3$
$90 = 2 \cdot 3 \cdot 3 \cdot 5$ 18

Use prime factorizations of each pair of numbers to find the GCF.

13. $28 = 2 \cdot 2 \cdot 7$
$35 = 5 \cdot 7$ 7

14. $30 = 2 \cdot 3 \cdot 5$
$24 = 2 \cdot 3 \cdot 2 \cdot 2$ 6

15. $18 = 2 \cdot 3 \cdot 3$
$45 = 5 \cdot 3 \cdot 3$ 9

16. $36 = 2 \cdot 3 \cdot 2 \cdot 3$
$40 = 2 \cdot 2 \cdot 2 \cdot 5$ 4

Find the GCF of each pair of numbers.

17. 27, 36 9

18. 18, 24 6

19. 36, 42 6

20. 20, 45 5

21. 60, 18 6

22. 30, 105 15

23. 42, 90 6

24. 36, 24 12

25. 44, 36 4

26. 14, 90 2

27. 18, 42 6

28. 8, 15 1

29. 24, 25 1

30. 39, 65 13

31. 63, 56 7

32. 100, 350 50

33. Hua has a piece of material that is 45 in. wide and 75 in. long. He wants to cut it into the largest possible squares without wasting any material. What is the length of the sides of the largest possible squares? 15 in.

34. Janice is crocheting a tablecloth that will be 60 in. wide and 75 in. long. She wants to make the largest squares possible. How many squares will she have to make for the tablecloth? 20 squares

SKILLKEEPER

9.6	0.258	9.63	7.55	0.145
1. 5)48	**2.** 23)5.934	**3.** 13)125.19	**4.** 8)60.4	**5.** 14)2.03
6. $673 \div 0.01$	**7.** $97.2 \div 0.1$	**8.** $9,247 \div 0.001$	**9.** $0.592 \div 0.01$	**10.** $9.12 \div 0.001$
67,300	972	9,247,000	59.2	9,120
563	6.39	2.158	148	0.589
11. 0.05)28.15	**12.** 2.3)14.697	**13.** 54)116.532	**14.** 0.36)53.28	**15.** 5.8)3.4162

More Practice, page 426, Set C   173

More Practice, page 426, Set C

Using Page 173

Exercises 5–12 In these exercises the prime factorizations of the two numbers are given, so students should use the prime factorization method to find the GCF.

Skillkeeper This skill was originally taught in Chapter 5.

Reteaching Supplement, page 51   **Enrichment Supplement,** page 51   **Practice Supplement,** page 66

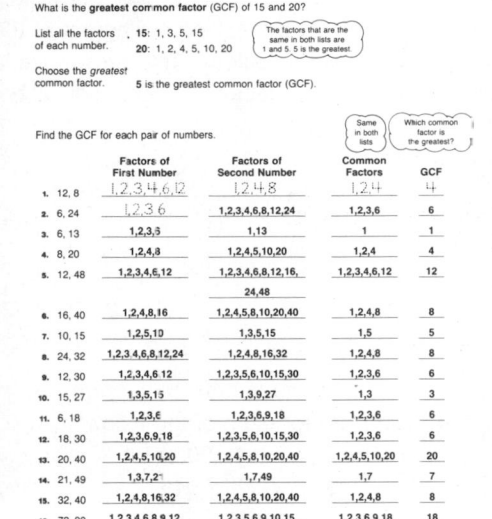

Quick Review Have students give the correct symbol, >, <, or =, for each of the following.

0.58 ⊙ 0.375	1.93 ⊙ 0.9	0.048 ⊙ 0.12
0.721 ⊙ 0.7205	2.900 ⊙ 2.9	15.703 ⊙ 15.73

Lesson Focus To find the least common multiple of two numbers

Ideas for Getting Started

Review the meaning of multiple of a number by writing the following sequences on the chalkboard. Have students give the next three multiples of each number.

3 → 0, 3, 6, 9, 12, . . . (15, 18, 21)
6 → 0, 6, 12, 18, 24, . . . (30, 36, 42)
10 → 0, 10, 20, 30, 40, . . . (50, 60, 70)

Next list the multiples of 8 and 12 that are less than 50.

8 → 0, 8, 16, 24, 32, 40, 48
12 → 0, 12, 24, 36, 48

Ask students to name the multiples common to both numbers. (0, 24, 48) Then have them find the smallest multiple, other than zero, that is common to both 8 and 12. (24)

Using Page 174

Motivational Problem Have students read the problem and identify the question and the data in the problem. Explain that one plan to solve the problem is to make a table of the skaters' times each time they cross the starting point, or complete a lap.

Lap	1	2	3	4	5	6	7	8	9	10
Skater A	60	120	180	240	300	360	420	480	540	600
Skater B	54	108	162	216	270	324	378	432	486	540

After students study the table, ask "How many laps has skater A completed at the end of 540 s?" (9) "How many laps has skater B completed at the end of 540 s?" (10) Point out that the skaters are together after 540 s and not earlier and that 540 is the *least common multiple* of 60 and 54.

Lesson Development On the chalkboard show how to use prime factorizations to find the LCM of 54 and 60. Stress that common factors are used only once because we want the smallest multiple of both numbers.

Other Examples In the first example, note that 4 and 15 are relatively prime, so the LCM is the product of the two numbers. The second example shows a method of finding the LCM mentally. Work through this example with students. Point out that it is easier to use multiples of the larger of the two numbers and then, as each multiple is listed, check to see if it is divisible by the smaller number.

Least Common Multiple (LCM)

Two skaters start at the same point on an oval rink. One skater takes exactly 60 s to go once around the rink. A faster skater takes only 54 s. How many seconds will it be until the skaters are together at the starting point?

We need to find the smallest multiple of both 54 and 60. This number is the **least common multiple** (**LCM**) of 54 and 60.

We can use prime factorization to find the LCM of 54 and 60.

$$54 = 2 \cdot 3 \cdot 3 \cdot 3$$
$$60 = 2 \cdot 2 \cdot 3 \cdot 5$$
$$LCM = 2 \cdot 2 \cdot 3 \cdot 3 \cdot 3 \cdot 5 = 540$$

The skaters will be together at the starting point after 540 s, or 9 min.

Other Examples

Find the LCM of 4 and 15.

$$4 = 2 \cdot 2$$
$$15 = 3 \cdot 5$$
$$LCM = 2 \cdot 2 \cdot 3 \cdot 5 = 60$$

Find the LCM of 6 and 8 mentally.

> Multiples of 8: 8, 16, 24
> 24 is a multiple of 6.
> LCM = 24

Warm Up

Find the LCM of each pair of numbers. Use the prime factorization method.

1. $9 = 3 \cdot 3$
   $12 = 2 \cdot 2 \cdot 3$ 36

2. $8 = 2 \cdot 2 \cdot 2$
   $10 = 2 \cdot 5$ 40

3. $10 = 2 \cdot 5$
   $15 = 3 \cdot 5$ 30

4. $7 = 1 \cdot 7$
   $21 = 3 \cdot 7$ 21

Find the LCM of each pair of numbers mentally.

5. 4, 6 12
6. 6, 10 30
7. 4, 5 20
8. 8, 12 24

174

Follow Up

Reteaching

Show students how to find the LCM of two numbers by listing the multiples of the larger number and then checking to see if it is a multiple of the smaller number. Explain that the first multiple of the larger number that is also a multiple of the smaller number is the LCM.

Example: 16, 20

Multiples of 20: 20, 40, 60, 80

1	2	3	5
16)20	16)40	16)60	16)80
16	32	48	80
4	8	12	0

LCM = 80

Enrichment

Show students how to find the LCM of 20 and 24 by making a diagram of their prime factorizations. The circles overlap when prime factors are common to both numbers.

20 = 2 · 2 · 5   24 = 2 · 2 · 2 · 3
LCM = 5 · 2 · 2 · 2 · 3

Ask students to draw a diagram and find the LCM for each of the following.

1. 36, 27   2. 30, 42   3. 60, 35
   108   210   420

Assignment Guide	Minimum	Average	Extended
page 175	1–24	1–30	9–31, TM

Use the prime factorizations of each pair of numbers to find the LCM.

1. $14 = 2 \cdot 7$ 70
$35 = 5 \cdot 7$

2. $18 = 2 \cdot 3 \cdot 3$ 72
$24 = 2 \cdot 2 \cdot 2 \cdot 3$

3. $30 = 2 \cdot 3 \cdot 5$ 60
$12 = 2 \cdot 2 \cdot 3$

4. $36 = 2 \cdot 3 \cdot 2 \cdot 3$ 252
$42 = 2 \cdot 3 \cdot 7$

5. $16 = 2 \cdot 2 \cdot 2 \cdot 2$ 32
$32 = 2 \cdot 2 \cdot 2 \cdot 2 \cdot 2$

6. $14 = 2 \cdot 7$ 210
$15 = 3 \cdot 5$

7. $15 = 3 \cdot 5$ 60
$20 = 2 \cdot 2 \cdot 5$

8. $75 = 3 \cdot 5 \cdot 5$ 525
$35 = 5 \cdot 7$

Find the LCM of each pair of numbers.

9. 4, 8 8 **10.** 10, 12 60 **11.** 9, 15 45 **12.** 6, 5 30

13. 8, 20 40 **14.** 18, 20 180 **15.** 21, 12 84 **16.** 6, 14 42

17. 6, 24 24 **18.** 15, 25 75 **19.** 24, 42 168 **20.** 21, 6 42

21. 11, 15 165 **22.** 20, 24 120 **23.** 48, 20 240 **24.** 12, 63 252

Copy and complete the table.

	Numbers	GCF	Product	Product ÷ GCF	LCM
	6, 10	2	$6 \times 10 = 60$	$60 \div 2 = 30$	30
25.	9, 15	3	$9 \times 15 = 135$	$135 \div 3 = 45$	45
26.	9, 12	3	$9 \times 12 = 108$	$108 \div 3 = 36$	36
27.	12, 18	6	$12 \times 18 = 216$	$216 \div 6 = 36$	36
28.	15, 20	5	$15 \times 20 = 300$	$300 \div 5 = 60$	60
29.	45, 30	15	$45 \times 30 = 1,350$	$1,350 \div 15 = 90$	90

Find the LCM of each pair of numbers.

30. $133,518 = 2 \cdot 3 \cdot 7 \cdot 11 \cdot 17^2$
$20,349 = 3^2 \cdot 7 \cdot 17 \cdot 19$ 7,610,526

31. $8,993 = 17 \cdot 23^2$
$154,037 = 13 \cdot 17^2 \cdot 41$ 81,485,573

THINK MATH

Mental Math

Use the table to find the products.

1. $2^3 \cdot 5^3 \cdot 139$
139,000

2. $2^4 \cdot 5^4 \cdot 1,103$
11,030,000

3. $2^2 \cdot 1,123 \cdot 5^2$
112,300

4. $2^5 \cdot 5^6 \cdot 7$
3,500,000

5. $2^6 \cdot 5^7 \cdot 11$
55,000,000

6. $2^6 \cdot 5^6 \cdot 18$
18,000,000

$2 \cdot 5 = 10$
$2^2 \cdot 5^2 = 100$
$2^3 \cdot 5^3 = 1,000$
$2^4 \cdot 5^4 = 10,000$
$2^5 \cdot 5^5 = 100,000$
$2^6 \cdot 5^6 = 1,000,000$

More Practice, page 426, Set D   175

Using Page 175

Exercises 9–24 Students should use the easiest method for them to find the LCM in these exercises. Some of the LCMs can be found mentally.

Exercises 25–29 In these exercises, students should see that if the product of the two numbers is divided by their GCF, the quotient is the LCM of the two numbers.

Think Math This problem involves multiplying by powers of 10 and seeing patterns. In part 3, the associative and commutative properties must be used.

$$2^2 \cdot (1,123 \cdot 5^2) = 2^2 \cdot (5^2 \cdot 1,123)$$
$$= (2^2 \cdot 5^2) \cdot 1,123$$

In part 4, students must see that
$$2^5 \cdot 5^6 \cdot 7 = (2^5 \cdot 5^5) \cdot 5 \cdot 7.$$

Part 5 is similar.
$$2^6 \cdot 5^7 \cdot 11 = (2^6 \cdot 5^6) \cdot 5 \cdot 11$$

More Practice, page 426, Set D

Reteaching Supplement, page 52

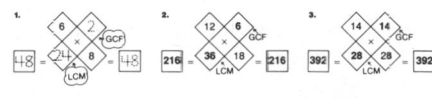

Enrichment Supplement, page 52

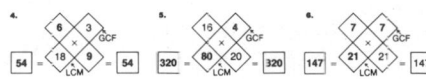

Practice Supplement, page 67

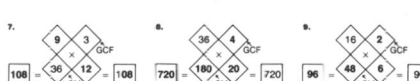

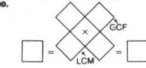
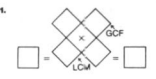

Numbers and Numeration

Lesson Focus To evaluate expressions for given replacements of the variable

Ideas for Getting Started

Draw a picture of a "Math Machine" on the chalkboard.

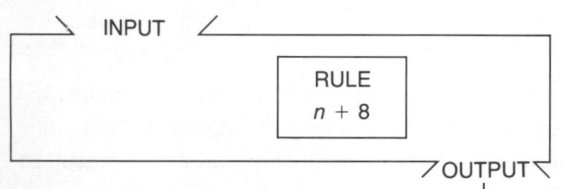

Explain that for each input number (n) the rule given by $n + 8$ tells the machine how to find the output. Have students give the output numbers for each of these input numbers.

6   10   16   25   100

Change the rule so that all 4 operations are used.

$x - 2$ $3 \times r$ $s \div 2$

Using Page 176

Lesson Development Have students read the material at the top of the page. Explain that although neither Dave's age nor Jean's age is known, we know how their ages are related. We can use any letter, or *variable,* to represent Dave's age. When we know Dave's age, the *expression* $d - 4$ tells what we must do to find Jean's age. Show how to evaluate $d - 4$ for $d = 10$, 13, and 20.

Direct students' attention to the examples in the table. Point out that the phrase "5 times t" can be written as $5 \times t$, $5 \cdot t$, or $5t$ and that $k \div 3$ can be written as $\frac{k}{3}$. In algebra, the latter form is used.

Warm Up Use these as oral exercises with students to check their understanding of variable and evaluating expressions.

Variables and Expressions

Jean is 4 years younger than her brother Dave. We can write an **expression** for Jean's age.

Let d = Dave's age.

$d - 4$ = Jean's age

The letter d is a **variable.** Any letter could be used as the variable.

To **evaluate an expression**, we substitute a number for the variable and perform the operations.

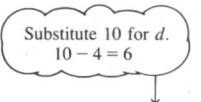
Substitute 10 for d.
$10 - 4 = 6$

Dave's Age	Jean's Age
10	6
13	9
20	16

If d is **10**, then $d - 4$ is **6**.

If d is **13**, then $d - 4$ is **9**.

If d is **20**, then $d - 4$ is **16**.

Study the examples in the table below.

Expression in words	Variable	Expression with a variable
5 times a number t	t	$5t$ or $5 \cdot t$
A number k divided by 3	k	$\frac{k}{3}$ or $k \div 3$
The sum of b and 7	b	$b + 7$
6 minus a number n	n	$6 - n$

Warm Up

Name the variable in each expression.

1. $n + 7$ n 2. $r - 6$ r 3. $9y$ y 4. $\frac{t}{7}$ t 5. $17z$ z

Evaluate each expression.

6. $5t$
if t is 7 **35**

7. $\frac{k}{3}$
if k is 24 **8**

8. $a + 7$
if a is 15 **22**

9. $14 - n$
if n is 9 **5**

10. $10z$
if z is 8 **80**

176

Follow Up

Reteaching

Write $\square$ + 8 on the chalkboard. Ask students to give a number for the $\square$ and find the sum. Have students repeat the activity using another number. Explain that instead of the box we can use a letter, or variable, as a placeholder for any number. Then write $n + 8$ on the chalkboard and tell students that we call this an expression.

Have students evaluate the following expressions if t is 10.

$6t$ $5 + t$ $\frac{t}{2}$ $t - 7$

Then have students choose another value for t and evaluate each expression.

Enrichment

Provide students with the chart below.

k	$k \cdot 2$	$(k \cdot 2) \div 4$	$(k \cdot 2) \div 4 + 8$
4	8	2	10
3	6	1.5	9.5
7	14	3.5	11.5
6	12	3	11
8	16	4	12
0	0	0	8

Have them use the given values for k to evaluate the expressions and complete the table.

Assignment Guide			
	Minimum	Average	Extended
page 177	1–27	1–35, TM	1–15 odd, 16–35, TM

Evaluate each expression.

1. $n + 11$
if n is 10 21

2. $8m$
if m is 7 56

3. $100 - s$
if s is 65 35

4. $\frac{h}{2}$
if h is 40 20

5. $13b$
if b is 4 52

Complete each sentence by evaluating the expression.

6. If t is 7, then $9t$ is ___?___. 63

7. If c is 11, then $9c$ is ___?___. 99

8. If x is 19, then $x - 12$ is ___?___. 7

9. If f is 1, then $f + 99$ is ___?___. 100

10. If m is 20, then $\frac{m}{5}$ is ___?___. 4

11. If p is 87, then $\frac{p}{3}$ is ___?___. 29

12. If y is 19, then $4y$ is ___?___. 76

13. If j is 47, then $100 - j$ is ___?___. 53

14. If x is 8, then $\frac{x}{8}$ is ___?___. 1

15. If h is 9, then $16 - h$ is ___?___. 7

Complete each table by evaluating the expressions.

	k	$k + 12$
16.	3	15
17.	9	21
18.	15	27
19.	38	50

	z	$4z$
20.	7	28
21.	10	40
22.	15	60
23.	25	100

	b	$17 - b$
24.	10	7
25.	9	8
26.	6	11
27.	1	16

Write an expression.

28. 4 times a number t $4t$

29. 8 less than a number x $x - 8$

30. a number z divided by 5 $\frac{z}{5}$

31. 20 decreased by a number q $20 - q$

32. 9 more than a number n $n + 9$

33. a number k divided by 7 $\frac{k}{7}$

34. the product of 8 and a number d $8d$

35. the sum of a number w and 11 $w + 11$

■ THINK MATH ■

Number Clues

In what year did Neil Armstrong walk on the moon? Substitute the correct numbers for the variables in the expression, and you will find out. 1969

$y + d + w + m$ 1492 + 365 + 52 + 60

y = year Columbus discovered America

d = days in a year that is not a leap year

w = weeks in a year

m = minutes in an hour

More Practice, page 427, Set A

Using Page 177

Exercises 1–27 As students work on these exercises, check to see that they are substituting correctly in the expressions.

Exercises 28–35 Make certain students are writing the correct expressions. For example, in exercise 29 students should write $x - 8$, and not $8 - x$.

Think Math This problem extends the ideas of the lesson to include several variables in an expression.

More Practice, page 427, Set A

Reteaching Supplement, page 53

Name _____ To follow text page 177

Variables and Expressions

Expression in Words	Expression with a Variable	Substitute 6 for the Variable and Evaluate
The sum of 7 and y	$7 + y$ (variable)	$7 + y = 7 + 6 = 13$ (Substitute 6 for y)
2 less than a number b	$b - 2$	$b - 2 = 6 - 2 = 4$
4 times a number z	$4z$	$4z = 4 \cdot 6 = 24$
12 divided by a number t	$\frac{12}{t}$ or $12 \div t$	$12 \div t = 12 \div 6 = 2$

Evaluate each expression.

1. $n - 7$ $n = 10$
$10 - 7 = \underline{3}$

2. $\frac{x}{3}$ $x = 9$
$\frac{9}{3} = \underline{3}$

3. $8t$ $t = 6$
$8 \cdot 6 = \underline{48}$

4. $p + 12$ $p = 5$
$5 + 12 = \underline{17}$

5. $\frac{n}{4}$ $n = 16$
$\frac{16}{4} = \underline{4}$

6. $20 - r$ $r = 3$
$20 - 3 = \underline{17}$

7. $\frac{21}{k}$ $k = 7$
$\frac{21}{7} = \underline{3}$

8. $x + 5$ $x = 6$
$6 + 5 = \underline{11}$

9. $17 - w$ $w = 15$
$17 - 15 = \underline{2}$

10.
m	$5m$
3	15
9	45
0	0
11	55

11.
x	$x + 10$
8	18
42	52
16	26
13	23

12.
c	$15 - c$
6	9
0	15
11	4
9	6

Write an expression for each.

13. 3 more than a number d $d + 3$

14. the product of 6 and a number x $6x$

15. a number m divided by 8 $\frac{m}{8}$

16. a number y increased by 3 $y + 3$

17. 4 times a number p $4p$

18. 20 divided by a number r $\frac{20}{r}$

Enrichment Supplement, page 53

Name _____ To follow text page 177

It's an Expression

Use the given expression to complete each table.

1. The expression $25 \cdot t$ tells us the number of times we blink in a given period of time.
(t = the number of minutes)

Time	t	1 minute	5 minutes	30 minutes	1 hour	8 hours
Number of blinks	$25 \cdot t$	25	125	750	1,500	12,000

2. The expression $\frac{34 - a}{2}$ tells us how many hours of sleep we need each night based on our age.
(a = age in years up to 18)

Age	a	2	4	6	8	10	12	14	16	18
Hours of sleep	$\frac{34-a}{2}$	16	15	14	13	12	11	10	9	8

3. The expression $\frac{c}{7} + 3$ tells us what the temperature is (in degrees Celsius) based on the number of chirps of a cricket.
(c = the number of chirps of a cricket in one minute)

Chirps/minute	c	49	63	70	91	112	161
Temperature (°C)	$\frac{c}{7} + 3$	10	12	13	16	19	26

Practice Supplement, page 68

Name _____ To follow text page 177

Variables and Expressions

Complete each table by evaluating the expressions.

1.
m	$m + 8$
6	14
9	17
12	20
22	30
64	72

2.
y	$y - 6$
9	3
15	9
24	18
32	26
47	41

3.
b	$3b$
5	15
10	30
13	39
21	63
35	105

4.
s	$\frac{s}{2}$
6	3
18	9
24	12
34	17
48	24

5.
n	$n + 12$
4	16
10	22
12	24
31	43
57	69

6.
x	$10x$
8	80
15	150
27	270
59	590
82	820

Write as expression.

7. 9 times a number d $9d$

8. 7 more than a number f $f + 7$

9. 2 less than a number j $j - 2$

10. 75 decreased by a number l $75 - l$

11. a number e divided by 6 $\frac{e}{6}$

12. 8 times a number k $8k$

13. the sum of a number p and 9 $p + 9$

14. 12 minus a number w $12 - w$

15. a number t times 30 $30t$

16. 18 more than a number c $c + 18$

17. 39 divided by a number u $\frac{39}{u}$

18. a number a minus 15 $a - 15$

19. 42 plus a number g $42 + g$

20. a number v plus 8 $v + 8$

21. a number r divided by 10 $\frac{r}{10}$

22. 57 minus a number q $57 - q$

Quick Review Read these exercises aloud and have students find the sums mentally.

$27 + 9$	$52 + 11$	$7 + 35$	$18 + 20$
$43 + 10$	$9 + 16$	$61 + 12$	$13 + 27$	$26 + 32$

Lesson Focus To solve equations by adding or subtracting the same number from each side of the equation

Ideas for Getting Started

Write these exercises on the chalkboard and have students perform the computation.

$12 + 4 - 4$ $20 - 8 + 8$
$263 - 49 + 49$ $2,793 + 1,664 - 1,664$
$x + 13 - 13$ $y - 9 + 9$

Elicit from students that adding a number and then subtracting the same number gives the starting number. Also, subtracting a number and then adding the same number gives the starting number.

Using Page 178

Motivational Problem After students read the introductory problem and examine the illustration, have them restate the question. Then ask students to give the data found in the statement of the problem and in the illustration. Explain that writing an equation can help us solve the problem.

Lesson Development Tell students that an equation is like a balance. The equal sign corresponds to the balance point or fulcrum on the balance. If we take 6 counters off one side of the scale, it will not balance unless we take 6 counters off the other side. Taking 6 counters off each side of the scale corresponds to subtracting 6 from each side of the equation.

On the chalkboard, work through each step of the example. Point out that we begin by labeling the variable. Explain that simplify means perform the arithmetical operations. In the last step we substitute 36 in the original equation to check if it is the solution. Then show students how to solve $y - 8 = 23$ by adding the same number to each side of the equation.

Addition and Subtraction Equations

The same number of counters are on each side of the balance scale. How many counters are in the container?

To find the number of counters, we can write and solve an **equation** for the problem.

Let x = the number of counters in the container.

Equation	$x + 6 = 42$
Subtract the same number from each side of the equation.	$x + 6 - 6 = 42 - 6$
Simplify.	$x = 36$
Substitute the number for the variable in the first equation.	$36 + 6 = 42$

It checks. The solution to the equation is 36.

There are 36 counters in the container.

To solve some equations, we may need to *add* the same number to each side.

Equation	$y - 8 = 23$
Add 8 to each side of the equation.	$y - 8 + 8 = 23 + 8$
Simplify.	$y = 31$
Substitute 31 for y in the first equation.	$31 - 8 = 23$

$x + 6$ counters   42 counters

x 36 counters

6   6

Warm Up

Solve each equation.

1. $x + 8 = 23$ $x = 15$ 2. $t + 11 = 30$ $t = 19$ 3. $k + 9 = 27$ $k = 18$ 4. $n + 15 = 40$ $n = 25$

5. $s - 7 = 16$ $s = 23$ 6. $q - 10 = 25$ $q = 35$ 7. $z - 6 = 14$ $z = 20$ 8. $m - 16 = 16$ $m = 32$

178

Follow Up

Reteaching

Write the following equations on the chalkboard. Have students describe the first step in solving each equation.

$n + 6 = 9$ (Subtract 6 from both sides.)
$y + 8 = 19$ (Subtract 8 from both sides.)
$s - 14 = 11$ (Add 14 to both sides.)
$h - 22 = 22$ (Add 22 to both sides.)

Then have students solve each equation at the chalkboard, writing out each step. If students cannot do the arithmetic mentally, have them write the addition or subtraction at the side.

Enrichment

Have students write an equation for each of the following sentences.

1. The sum of a number w and 7 is 29.
   $w + 7 = 29$
2. Six more than a number n is 15.
   $n + 6 = 15$
3. A number r decreased by 9 is 21.
   $r - 9 = 21$
4. Four less than a number y is 17.
   $y - 4 = 17$
5. Nine increased by a number s is 20.
   $9 + s = 20$

Assignment Guide			
	Minimum	Average	Extended
page 179	1–24	1–39	1–39 odd, TM

Solve each equation.

1. $x + 9 = 16$ $x = 7$
2. $n + 12 = 20$ $n = 8$
3. $y + 6 = 21$ $y = 15$

4. $a + 13 = 30$ $a = 17$
5. $w + 7 = 15$ $w = 8$
6. $m + 23 = 50$ $m = 27$

7. $k + 14 = 26$ $k = 12$
8. $g + 17 = 25$ $g = 8$
9. $h + 8 = 33$ $h = 25$

10. $q + 34 = 60$ $q = 26$
11. $z + 58 = 74$ $z = 16$
12. $s + 284 = 419$ $s = 135$

Solve each equation.

13. $t - 4 = 11$ $t = 15$
14. $r - 15 = 6$ $r = 21$
15. $z - 8 = 14$ $z = 22$

16. $j - 9 = 26$ $j = 35$
17. $p - 21 = 15$ $p = 36$
18. $f - 12 = 19$ $f = 31$

19. $n - 10 = 13$ $n = 23$
20. $x - 17 = 17$ $x = 34$
21. $k - 6 = 0$ $k = 6$

22. $s - 18 = 16$ $s = 34$
23. $v - 15 = 38$ $v = 53$
24. $z - 26 = 35$ $z = 61$

Solve each equation. You may have to add or subtract.

25. $m - 7 = 18$ $m = 25$
26. $w + 4 = 14$ $w = 10$
27. $b - 12 = 8$ $b = 20$

28. $x + 1 = 50$ $x = 49$
29. $h - 9 = 27$ $h = 36$
30. $j + 11 = 20$ $j = 9$

31. $c - 40 = 60$ $c = 100$
32. $g + 27 = 33$ $g = 6$
33. $n - 41 = 39$ $n = 80$

34. $x - 25 = 75$ $x = 100$
35. $n - 33 = 167$ $n = 200$
36. $g + 19 = 99$ $g = 80$

Solve each equation. 🖩

37. $m + 19,384 = 21,928$
$m = 2,544$
38. $k - 26,009 = 84,356$
$k = 110,365$
39. $w + 6,587 = 12,063$
$w = 5,476$

▌ THINK MATH ▐

Logical Reasoning

A quarter and a dime balance with three dimes. How many dimes would it take to balance four quarters? 8

More Practice, page 427, Set B   **179**

Using Page 179

Exercises 1–39 Some students may think that it is sufficient to give only the solution of the equation without showing any of the steps. Of course, in simple equations such as $x + 7 = 10$ this is quite easy to do. Point out that if the equation were $x + 2,976 = 6,041$, they probably could not find the solution in their heads. Omitting the steps could lead to errors such as the following:

$$x + 2,976 = 6,041 + 2,976$$

Think Math This problem involves logical reasoning and the idea that a scale will remain balanced if the same amount is taken off each side. If 1 dime is taken off each side of the balance, 1 quarter will balance with 2 dimes. Therefore, 4 quarters will balance with 8 dimes. (This is not the actual relationship between the weights of quarters and dimes, but it is approximate.)

More Practice, page 427, Set B

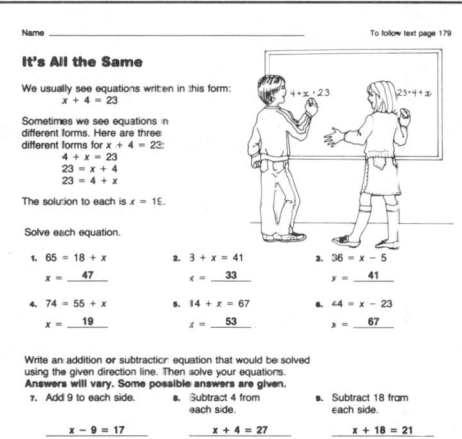

Reteaching Supplement, page 54

Name _____   To follow text page 179

Addition and Subtraction Equations

Addition Equation: $n + 9 = 23$
Subtract the same number from each side of the equation. $n + 9 - 9 = 23 - 9$
Simplify. $n = 14$
Substitute the number for the variable in the first equation. $14 + 9 = 23$

Subtraction Equation: $z - 5 = 28$
Add the same number to each side of the equation. $z - 5 + 5 = 28 + 5$
Simplify. $z = 33$
Substitute the number for the variable in the first equation. $33 - 5 = 28$

Solve the equations.

1. $r - 12 = 13$
$r - 12 + 12 = 13 + 12$
$r = 25$ (Equals zero, leaves r)
2. $t + 18 = 31$
$t + 18 - 18 = 31 - 18$
$t = 13$
3. $x - 24 = 52$
$x - 24 + 24 = 52 + 24$
$x = 76$ (Add 24 to each side)
4. $y + 10 = 43$
$y + 10 - 10 = 43 - 10$
$y = 76$
5. $z - 7 = 17$
$z - 7 + 7 = 17 + 7$
$z = 24$
6. $a + 12 = 25$
$a + 12 - 12 = 25 - 12$
$a = 13$
7. $b - 18 = 37$
$b - 18 + 18 = 37 + 18$
$b = 55$
8. $s - 24 = 56$
$s - 24 + 24 = 56 + 24$
$s = 80$
9. $l + 15 = 40$
$l + 15 - 15 = 40 - 15$
$l = 25$
10. $m + 9 = 27$
$m + 9 - 9 = 27 - 9$
$m = 18$
11. $z - 30 = 60$
$z - 30 + 30 = 60 + 30$
$z = 90$
12. $f - 21 = 21$
$f - 21 + 21 = 21 + 21$
$f = 42$
13. $w + 29 = 54$
$w + 29 - 29 = 54 - 29$
$w = 25$
14. $h - 43 = 8$
$h - 43 + 43 = 8 + 43$
$h = 51$
15. $k + 39 = 45$
$k + 39 - 39 = 45 - 39$
$k = 6$
16. $j - 10 = 84$
$j - 10 + 10 = 84 + 10$
$j = 94$
17. $c + 19 = 29$
$c + 19 - 19 = 29 - 19$
$c = 10$
18. $z + 321 = 445$
$z + 321 - 321 = 445 - 321$
$z = 124$

Enrichment Supplement, page 54

Name _____   To follow text page 179

It's All the Same

We usually see equations written in this form:
$x + 4 = 23$

Sometimes we see equations in different forms. Here are three different forms for $x + 4 = 23$:
$4 + x = 23$
$23 = x + 4$
$23 = 4 + x$

The solution to each is $x = 19$.

Solve each equation.

1. $65 = 18 + x$
$x = 47$
2. $3 + x = 41$
$x = 38$
3. $36 = x - 5$
$x = 41$
4. $74 = 55 + x$
$x = 19$
5. $14 + x = 67$
$x = 53$
6. $44 = x - 23$
$x = 67$

Write an addition or subtraction equation that would be solved using the given direction line. Then solve your equations.
Answers will vary. Some possible answers are given.

7. Add 9 to each side.
$x - 9 = 17$
$x = 26$
8. Subtract 4 from each side.
$x + 4 = 27$
$x = 23$
9. Subtract 18 from each side.
$x + 18 = 21$
$x = 3$

10. Add 40 to each side.
$x - 40 = 28$
$x = 68$
11. Add 100 to each side.
$x - 100 = 107$
$x = 207$
12. Subtract 82 from each side.
$x + 82 = 94$
$x = 12$

13. Add 27 to each side.
$x - 27 = 42$
$x = 69$
14. Subtract 53 from each side.
$x + 53 = 104$
$x = 51$
15. Subtract 19 from each side.
$x + 19 = 47$
$x = 28$

Practice Supplement, page 69

Name _____   To follow text page 179

Addition and Subtraction Equations

Solve each equation.

1. $f - 8 = 7$
$f - 8 + 8 = 7 + 8$
$f = 15$
2. $k + 6 = 13$
$k + 6 - 6 = 13 - 6$
$k = 7$
3. $c - 7 = 2$
$c - 7 + 7 = 2 + 7$
$c = 9$
4. $m + 8 = 18$
$m + 8 - 8 = 18 - 8$
$m = 10$
5. $j + 9 = 17$
$j + 9 - 9 = 17 - 9$
$j = 8$
6. $q - 5 = 7$
$q - 5 + 5 = 7 + 5$
$q = 12$
7. $s + 13 = 41$
$s + 13 - 13 = 41 - 13$
$s = 28$
8. $a - 16 = 38$
$a - 16 + 16 = 38 + 16$
$a = 54$
9. $g - 19 = 14$
$g - 19 + 19 = 14 + 19$
$g = 33$
10. $n + 36 = 40$
$n + 36 - 36 = 40 - 36$
$n = 4$
11. $r - 18 = 32$
$r - 18 + 18 = 32 + 18$
$r = 50$
12. $b + 46 = 74$
$b + 46 - 46 = 74 - 46$
$b = 28$
13. $d - 19 = 74$
$d - 19 + 19 = 74 + 19$
$d = 93$
14. $p + 28 = 61$
$p + 28 - 28 = 61 - 28$
$p = 33$
15. $h - 50 = 27$
$h - 50 + 50 = 27 + 50$
$h = 77$
16. $n + 38 = 38$
$n + 38 - 38 = 38 - 38$
$n = 0$
17. $l - 74 = 0$
$l - 74 + 74 = 0 + 74$
$l = 74$
18. $e + 92 = 100$
$e + 92 - 92 = 100 - 92$
$e = 8$

Equations

Quick Review Have students find the missing diameter or radius.
$d = 14.2$ cm, $r =$ <u>7.1 cm</u> $d = 15$ m, $r =$ <u>7.5 m</u> $d = 3$ mm, $r =$ <u>1.5 mm</u>
$r = 3.5$ m, $d =$ <u>7 m</u> $r = 7.27$ m, $d =$ <u>14.54 m</u> $r = 37.7$ cm, $d =$ <u>75.4 cm</u>

Lesson Focus To solve equations by multiplying or dividing each side of the equation by the same number

Ideas for Getting Started

Write these exercises on the chalkboard or overhead projector. Have students supply the missing numbers.

$12 \div 4 \times 4 =$ _____ $(6 \times 8) \div 6 =$ _____

$\frac{20}{5} \times 5 =$ _____ $7 \times \frac{35}{7} =$ _____

$2 \times n \div 2 =$ _____ $r \times 3 \div 3 =$ _____

Ask students to summarize the results of these exercises. Help them to see that if we divide by a number and multiply by the same number, the original number is obtained.

Using Page 180

Motivational Problem Have students read the introductory problem. "What does the question ask us to find?" (the number of counters in each container) "What data is needed to solve the problem?" (4 containers with the same number of counters balance with 48 counters) Point out that we can write and solve an equation to find the number of counters.

Lesson Development The balance scale is used again to illustrate the equation $4p = 48$. As you go through each step of the example with students, explain that since p is multiplied by 4, we should divide by 4 to get p alone. If we divide the left side of the equation by 4, we must then divide the right side by 4. Next show how the equation $\frac{n}{3} = 8$ can be solved by multiplying each side of the equation by 3.

Multiplication and Division Equations

Four containers each have the same number of counters. The containers balance with 48 counters. How many counters are in each container?

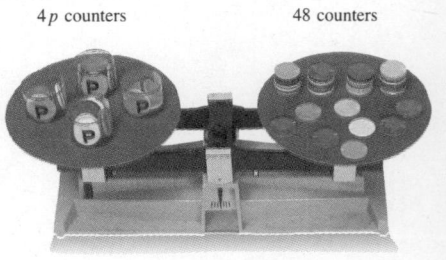

4p counters   48 counters

To find the number of counters, we can write and solve an equation.
Let $p =$ the number of counters in one container.

Equation $4p = 48$

Divide each side $\frac{4}{4}p = \frac{48}{4}$
of the equation
by the same number.

Simplify. $p = 12$

Substitute the number $4 \cdot 12 = 48$
for the variable in
the first equation.   *It checks. The solution to the equation is 12.*

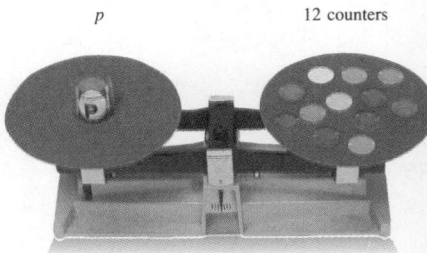

p 12 counters

There are 12 counters in each container.

To solve some equations, we may need to *multiply* each side of the equation by the same number.

$\frac{n}{3}$ means n divided by 3. $\frac{n}{3} = 8$
Multiply each side of $\frac{n}{3} \cdot 3 = 8 \cdot 3$
the equation by 3.

Simplify. $n = 24$

Substitute 24 for n in $\frac{24}{3} = 8$
the first equation.
It checks.

Warm Up

Solve each equation.

1. $7p = 56$ $p = 8$ 2. $8y = 24$ $y = 3$ 3. $10k = 70$ $k = 7$ 4. $9z = 54$ $z = 6$

5. $\frac{p}{5} = 30$ $p = 150$ 6. $\frac{n}{7} = 42$ $n = 294$ 7. $\frac{t}{9} = 9$ $t = 81$ 8. $\frac{b}{12} = 6$ $b = 72$

Follow Up

Reteaching

On the chalkboard, write equations like the following with the first step in solving partially completed. Have selected students tell what numbers are missing and then solve the equations at the chalkboard.

$6x = 42$

$\frac{6x}{\Box} = \frac{42}{\Box}$

$\frac{s}{7} = 14$

$\frac{s}{7} \cdot \Box = 14 \cdot \Box$

Enrichment

Have students write an equation for each of the following sentences.

1. Seven times a number c is 42.
   $7c = 42$

2. The product of 2 and a number n is 15. $2n = 15$

3. A number s divided by 8 is 3. $\frac{s}{8} = 3$

4. When a number t is divided by 9, the quotient is 7. $\frac{t}{9} = 7$

5. When 3 is multiplied by a number r, the product is 54. $3r = 54$

Assignment Guide			
	Minimum	Average	Extended
page 181	1–24, SK	1–39, SK	1–39 odd, SK

Solve each equation.

1. $3c = 27$ $c = 9$ **2.** $9n = 72$ $n = 8$ **3.** $5k = 50$ $k = 10$

4. $6m = 48$ $m = 8$ **5.** $12b = 12$ $b = 1$ **6.** $15t = 45$ $t = 3$

7. $7d = 0$ $d = 0$ **8.** $4x = 100$ $x = 25$ **9.** $19w = 19$ $w = 1$

10. $14k = 42$ $k = 3$ **11.** $17z = 170$ $z = 10$ **12.** $37h = 148$ $h = 4$

Solve each equation.

13. $\frac{h}{2} = 5$ $h = 20$ **14.** $\frac{j}{5} = 7$ $j = 35$ **15.** $\frac{z}{10} = 4$ $z = 40$

16. $\frac{x}{11} = 3$ $x = 33$ **17.** $\frac{p}{9} = 6$ $p = 54$ **18.** $\frac{q}{7} = 7$ $q = 49$

19. $\frac{s}{6} = 0$ $s = 0$ **20.** $\frac{n}{2} = 13$ $n = 26$ **21.** $\frac{t}{5} = 12$ $t = 60$

22. $\frac{m}{9} = 16$ $m = 144$ **23.** $\frac{b}{7} = 23$ $b = 161$ **24.** $\frac{g}{18} = 3$ $g = 54$

Solve each equation. You may have to multiply or divide.

25. $4r = 32$ $r = 8$ **26.** $\frac{h}{6} = 5$ $h = 30$ **27.** $\frac{g}{9} = 2$ $g = 18$

28. $\frac{n}{15} = 1$ $n = 15$ **29.** $7p = 84$ $p = 12$ **30.** $\frac{z}{4} = 25$ $z = 100$

31. $12m = 48$ $m = 4$ **32.** $3r = 51$ $r = 17$ **33.** $65x = 3,640$ $x = 56$

34. $18n = 36$ $n = 2$ **35.** $\frac{x}{7} = 14$ $x = 98$ **36.** $9r = 45$ $r = 5$

Solve each equation.

37. $27,500x = 110,000$
$x = 4$

38. $\frac{m}{19,392} = 671$
$m = 13,012,032$

39. $55,655n = 4,841,985$
$n = 87$

SKILLKEEPER

List all the factors of each number.

1. 10   1, 2, 5, 10   **2.** 35   1, 5, 7, 35   **3.** 17   1, 17   **4.** 60   1, 2, 3, 4, 5, 6, 10, 12, 15, 20, 30, 60   **5.** 23   1, 23

Write P (prime) or C (composite) for each number.

6. 43   P   **7.** 59   P   **8.** 27   C   **9.** 19   P   **10.** 51   C

Write the prime factorization of each number.

11. 54   **12.** 16   **13.** 48   **14.** 30   **15.** 21
$2 \cdot 3 \cdot 3 \cdot 3$ $2 \cdot 2 \cdot 2 \cdot 2$ $2 \cdot 2 \cdot 2 \cdot 2 \cdot 3$ $2 \cdot 3 \cdot 5$ $3 \cdot 7$

More Practice, page 427, Set C   **181**

Using Page 181

Exercises 1–39 Even though many of the equations can be solved by inspection, ask students to write out all the steps for the equations on this page. Stress the technique of solving an equation at this point, rather than the answer.

Skillkeeper This Skillkeeper reviews material taught in this chapter.

More Practice, page 427, Set C

Reteaching Supplement, page 55   **Enrichment Supplement,** page 55   **Practice Supplement,** page 70

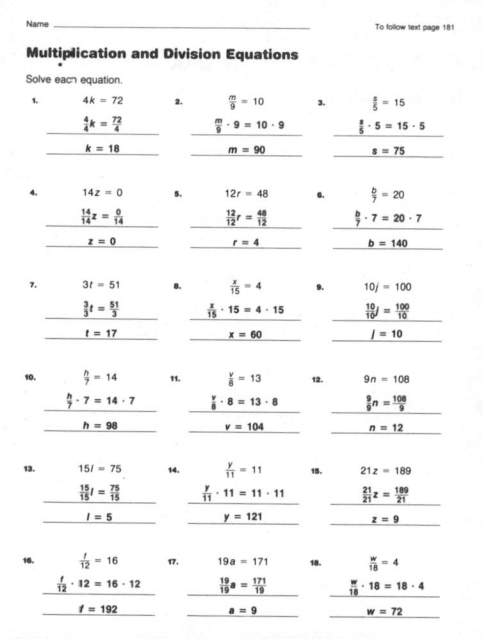

Applications

Lesson Focus To choose the correct equation for a word problem and solve the equation

Ideas for Getting Started

Write these sentences and equations on the chalkboard. Have students match the sentences with the correct equation. Then ask selected students to tell how they decided on the matches they made.

1. Eight times a certain number is 40.
2. If 8 is added to a number, the sum is 40.
3. When a certain number is divided by 8, the quotient is 40.
4. If a certain number is decreased by 8, the difference is 40.

A. $n + 8 = 40$
B. $8n = 40$
C. $n - 8 = 40$
D. $\frac{n}{8} = 40$

Notice with the students key words in the sentences such as times, difference, sum, and quotient that help match the sentences to the equations. Then have students solve each equation.

Using Page 182

Lesson Development Have students read the problem at the top of the page. Ask them to identify the question in the problem. Explain that since the problem asks for the number of boxes, we should let the variable represent this number. Stress the relationship between the question and the variable in the equation.

Have students identify the data in the problem and then find the equation that shows the correct relationship between the data. Explain that we multiply 24 times the number of boxes to get the total number of cans which is 1,800. Therefore, the correct equation is $24b = 1,800$. On the chalkboard, find the solution to the equation and state the answer to the problem.

Exercises 1–2 These problems may be used as further examples if needed.

PROBLEM SOLVING: Choosing the Right Equation

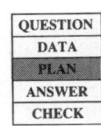

QUESTION
DATA
PLAN
ANSWER
CHECK

A case packer puts 24 cans of vegetables in a box and seals the box. How many boxes will be needed for 1,800 cans of vegetables?

An equation can be used to solve the problem. You need to choose an equation that uses the necessary data and the right operations. Which equation below can be used?

Let b = the number of boxes.

$b + 24 = 1,800$ $1,800\,b = 24$

$24\,b = 1,800$ $\frac{b}{24} = 1,800$

Since there are 24 cans in each box, 24 times the number of boxes needed must equal 1,800.

The correct equation is $24\,b = 1,800$.

$$24\,b = 1,800$$

$$\frac{24\,b}{24} = \frac{1,800}{24} \quad \text{Divide each side by 24.}$$

$$b = 75 \quad \text{Simplify.}$$

$$24 \times 75 = 1,800 \quad \text{It checks.}$$

The case packer will need 75 boxes.

Choose the equation that will solve the problem. Use the equation to find the answer.

1. The sum of a certain number and 15 is 63. What is the number?
   Let n = the number. $n = 48$
   (A) $n + 15 = 63$ **B** $15\,n = 63$
   C $n + 63 = 15$ **D** $n - 15 = 63$

2. When a certain number is multiplied by 21, the product is 315. What is the number?
   Let t = the number. $t = 15$
   A $315\,t = 21$ (B) $21\,t = 315$
   C $t + 21 = 315$ **D** $315 - t = 21$

Follow Up

Reteaching

Have students give a brief statement telling the relationship between the data in the problems on pages 182–183. Some examples are shown below.

Exercise 2:
  a number times 21 is 315

Exercise 8:
  downpayment + amount owed = cost

Exercise 10:
  number of letters × cost per letter = total cost

Enrichment

Display the following on the chalkboard. Have students solve each equation and write the variables above matching values.

$\frac{r}{3} = 9$ $14t = 70$ $\frac{a}{2} = 12$

$5p = 35$ $e - 27 = 23$

$s + 17 = 23$ $16u = 48$

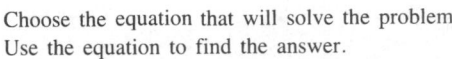

$\underset{6}{s}\ \underset{3}{u}\ \underset{7}{p}\ \underset{50}{e}\ \underset{27}{r}\ \underset{6}{s}\ \underset{5}{t}\ \underset{24}{a}\ \underset{27}{r}$

Assignment Guide			
	Minimum	Average	Extended
page 182–183	1–8	1–9, 12	1–12

3. When a certain number is divided by 16, the quotient is 34. What is the number?
Let d = the number. $d = 544$

  A $16\,d = 34$ **B** $16 + d = 34$

  C $\frac{d}{16} = 34$ **D** $d - 16 = 34$

4. If 35 is subtracted from a certain number, the difference is 77. What is the number?
Let b = the number. $b = 112$

  A $77 + b = 35$ **B** $35 - b = 77$

  C $35\,b = 77$ **D** $b - 35 = 77$

5. Curtis bought a 69¢ ballpoint pen and some paper. He spent $1.48 altogether. What was the cost of the paper?
Let p = the cost of the paper in cents.

  A $p + 69 = 148$ **B** $69\,p = 148$

  C $p - 69 = 148$ **D** $\frac{p}{69} = 148$ $p = 79$

6. Lisa earns $8 an hour. If Lisa earns $312, how many hours must she work?
Let h = the number of hours worked.

  A $312 - h = 8$ **B** $8\,h = 312$ $h = 39$

  C $h = 8 \times 312$ **D** $h + 8 = 312$

7. Leonard has collected 792 stamps. This is 6 times as many stamps as Diane has in her collection. How many stamps does Diane have in her collection?
Let s = the number of stamps Diane has. $s = 132$

  A $792 - s = 6$ **B** $s = 6 \times 792$

  C $6\,s = 792$ **D** $s + 6 = 792$

8. Mayeta buys a car that costs $6,779. She pays $2,150 down on the car. How much more does she owe?
Let n = the amount owed. $n = 4,629$

  A $n = 6,779 + 2,150$ **B** $n + 2,150 = 6,779$

  C $2,150\,n = 6,779$ **D** $n - 2,150 = 6,779$

9. A certain number of eggs are packed in cartons of 12 each. All together there are 52 cartons of eggs. How many eggs are packed?
Let e = the number of eggs. $e = 624$

  A $12\,e = 52$ **B** $52 - e = 12$

  C $e + 12 = 52$ **D** $\frac{e}{12} = 52$

10. Joan buys 3 cans of fruit for $2.07. What is the cost of each can?
Let c = the cost of one can of fruit in cents. $c = 69$

  A $c + 3 = 207$ **B** $3\,c = 207$

  C $207 - c = 3$ **D** $c = 3 \times 207$

11. A company paid $12 (1200¢) in postage to mail letters. Each letter cost 20¢ to mail. How many letters were mailed?
Let m = the number of letters. $m = 60$

  A $1,200\,m = 20$ **B** $\frac{m}{20} = 1,200$

  C $1,200 + m = 20$ **D** $20\,m = 1,200$

12. **Try This** Mountain View Swimming Pool uses chlorine that costs 40.9¢ per liter. Fairfield City Pool uses chlorine costing 34.9¢ per liter. The cities bought the same amount of chlorine, but Mountain View paid $120 more than Fairfield. How many liters did each city buy? Hint: Solve a simpler problem first. **2,000 L**

Using Page 183

Exercises 3–11 If students have difficulty choosing the correct equation, ask them to verbally describe the relationship between the data. Then help them see how to translate these words to symbols.

Try This A possible strategy, Solve a Simpler Problem, was taught on page 158.

Discussion Have students tell what the problem asks us to find. Then ask what is given in the problem and how the data is related. Call attention to the hint. Ask students to give a simpler problem. If they have difficulty thinking of a simpler problem, you may wish to use the following as an example.

Maury pays 40¢ per liter. Louise pays 30¢ per liter. They bought the same amount of gasoline, but Maury's gasoline cost $1.00 or 100¢ more. How many liters did they buy?

40¢ − 30¢ = 10¢ Maury pays 10¢ more per liter.
100¢ ÷ 10¢ = 10 They each bought 10 liters.

Solution:
40.9¢ − 34.9¢ = 6¢
$120 = 12,000¢
12,000¢ ÷ 6¢ = 2,000
They each bought 2,000 liters.

Ideas That Work

Math for the Gifted

On page 167, students learned about abundant numbers in the Think Math problem. Use the examples below to introduce *deficient* and *perfect* numbers.

Factors of 10: 1, 2, 5 (except 10)
1 + 2 + 5 = 8
Since 8 < 10, 10 is a deficient number.

Factors of 6: 1, 2, 3 (except 6)
1 + 2 + 3 = 6

Since 6 = 6, 6 is a perfect number. Have students tell what kind of numbers each of these are: abundant, deficient, or perfect.

1. 26 **deficient**   2. 28 **perfect**
3. 16 **deficient**   4. 18 **abundant**
5. 32 **deficient**   6. 45 **deficient**

Point out that the first two perfect numbers are 6 and 28. Challenge students to find the next greater perfect number.
496

Practice Supplement, page 71

Name _____   To follow text page 183

Problem Solving: Choosing the Right Equation

Ring the equation that will solve the problem.
Use the equation to find the answer.

1. When a certain number is multiplied by 12, the product is 120. What is the number? Let s = the number.
$12 + s = 120$ $s - 12 = 120$
$12s = 120$ $120s = 12$
$\frac{12}{12}s = \frac{120}{12}$ $s = 10$

2. The sum of a certain number and 18 is 59. What is the number? Let n = the number.
$n + 18 = 59$ $18n = 59$
$n + 59 = 13$ $59 - n = 18$
$n + 18 - 18 = 59 - 18$ $n = 41$

3. When a certain number is divided by 8, the quotient is 13. What is the number? Let m = the number.
$8m = 13$ $8 + m = 13$
$\frac{13}{m} = 8$ $\frac{m}{8} = 13$
$\frac{m}{8} \cdot 8 = 13 \cdot 8$ $m = 104$

4. If 41 is subtracted from a certain number, the difference is 16. What is the number? Let x = the number.
$41 - x = 16$ $x - 41 = 16$
$x + 41 = 16$ $41x = 16$
$x - 41 + 41 = 16 + 41$ $x = 57$

5. Wendy bought a $40 dress and a shirt. She spent $65 altogether. How much was the shirt? Let c = the cost of the shirt.
$65 + 40 = c$ $c - 65 = 40$
$c + 40 = 65$ $40\,c = 65$
$c + 40 - 40 = 65 - 40$ $c = 25

6. Bill earns $6 an hour. If he earns $126, how many hours must he work? Let w = the number of hours.
$6w = 126$ $\frac{w}{6} = 126$
$\frac{6}{w} = 126$ $6 + w = 126$
$\frac{6w}{6} = \frac{126}{6}$ $w = 21$

7. Elmer bought 4 pens for $1.96. What was the cost of each pen? Let p = the cost of each pen.
$\frac{p}{196} = 4$ $196 - 4 = p$
$4p = 196$ $196p = 4$
$\frac{4p}{4} = \frac{196}{4}$ $p = 49¢$

8. 9 boxes each have an equal number of cans in them. If there are 180 cans altogether, how many are in each box? Let v = the number of cans in each box.
$9v = 180$ $180 - v = 9$
$180 - 9 = v$ $180 + v = 9$
$\frac{9v}{9} = \frac{180}{9}$ $v = 20$

Applications

Quick Review Conduct an oral drill and have students perform operations mentally.

$(7 \times 9) + 6$ 69	$(54 \div 6) \times 3$ 27	$(5 \times 8) - 12$ 28	$(3 + 8) \times 5$ 55
$(72 \div 9) \times 7$ 56	$(15 - 8) \times 3$ 21	$(9 + 7) \div 4$ 4	$(42 \div 6) + 7$ 14

Lesson Focus To solve word problems by writing and solving an equation for the problem

Ideas for Getting Started

Write this problem on the chalkboard or overhead projector.

The highest point in Missouri is 539 m above sea level. This is 7.7 times the height of the lowest point in Missouri. What is the height of the lowest point?

Have students identify the question in the problem. Choose a variable for this number and write the variable and what it represents on the chalkboard. For example:

Let h = height of the lowest point.

Then ask students to give an equation using the variable and the data.

$$7.7h = 539$$

Have students explain the steps in the solution as you solve the equation on the chalkboard.

$$\frac{7.7h}{7.7} = \frac{539}{7.7}$$

$$h = 70$$

$$7.7 \cdot 70 = 539$$

The lowest point in Missouri is 70 m above sea level.

Using Page 184

Lesson Development Have students read the introductory problem. Explain that since the question asks us to find the height of Mt. Everest, we choose a variable to represent that height. Then we use the data and the variable to write the equation. On the chalkboard show the steps in solving the equation.

Exercises 1–2 You may wish to use these problems as additional examples. Note that a variable has been selected for the student in each of these problems. This is an important first step and should be associated with the question phase of the 5-Point Checklist.

PROBLEM SOLVING: Writing and Solving an Equation

QUESTION
DATA
PLAN
ANSWER
CHECK

James Fulton is a ranger in Mt. McKinley National Park. He knows that Mt. McKinley has a height of about 6,195 m. The height of Mt. McKinley is about 0.7 of the height of Mt. Everest. What is the height of Mt. Everest?

To solve this problem, you can write and solve an equation.

Choose a variable to represent the number you must find.	Let h = the height of Mt. Everest.	
Write an equation.	$0.7h = 6,195$	0.7 of the height of Mt. Everest equals the height of Mt. McKinley.
Solve the equation.	$\dfrac{0.7h}{0.7} = \dfrac{6,195}{0.7}$ $h = 8,850$ $0.7 \times 8,850 = 6,195.0$	Divide both sides by 0.7 and simplify. It checks.

Mt. Everest has a height of about 8,850 m.

Write and solve an equation for each problem.

1. Atlanta, Georgia is 336 m above sea level. This elevation is 0.21 of the elevation of Denver, Colorado. What is the elevation of Denver?
Let d = the elevation of Denver.
$0.21d = 336$; $d = 1,600$ m

2. If 339 m is subtracted from the elevation of Albuquerque, New Mexico, the result is the elevation of Salt Lake City. The elevation of Salt Lake City is 1,286 m. What is the elevation of Albuquerque?
Let h = the elevation of Albuquerque.
$h - 339 = 1,286$; $h = 1,625$ m

3. Mt. McKinley is 6,195 m in height. Mt. Logan in Yukon Territory is the highest mountain in Canada. If 144 m is added to the height of Mt. Logan, the sum is the height of Mt. McKinley. What is the height of Mt. Logan?
$h + 144 = 6,195$; $h = 6,051$ m

4. Gannett Peak, with a height of 4,207 m, is the highest point in Wyoming. This height is 7 times the height of Mt. Curwood, the highest point in Michigan. What is the height of Mt. Curwood?
$7h = 4,207$; $h = 601$ m

184

Follow Up

Reteaching

Discuss the meaning of addition, subtraction, multiplication, and division. Have students tell the kinds of problems that can be solved by each of the four operations. First ask for general descriptions. For example, subtraction problems involve 1) finding how much greater one number is than another; 2) finding how much more of one quantity is needed to make a certain amount; or 3) finding how much is left when a certain amount is taken away.

After general descriptions are given, have students make up problems and tell what operation can be used to solve them.

Enrichment

Challenge students with the following problem.

I'm a 2-digit prime and no more.
Subtract my digits, you'll get 4.
Their sum is not 10.
Try and find me then.
It's really not such a chore.

Assignment Guide			
	Minimum	Average	Extended
page 184–185	1–6	1–7, 9	1–10

Using Page 185

Data Hunt Provide an almanac or reference books for the Data Hunt problem on this page.

Try This A possible strategy, Work Backward, was taught on page 130.

Discussion Ask students to identify the question and the data. Have them tell how the data is related and make a flow chart showing the relationship.

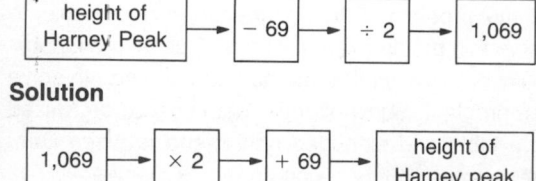

Solution

The height of Harney Peak is 2,207 m.

5. The highest point in Mississippi is Mt. Woodall with a height of 245 m. The highest point in Pennsylvania is Mt. Davis. If the height of Mt. Davis is divided by 4, the quotient is the height of Mt. Woodall. What is the height of Mt. Davis? $\frac{h}{4} = 245$; $h = 980$ m

6. When 586 m is subtracted from the height of Wheeler Peak in New Mexico, the result is the height of Mt. Hood in Oregon. Mt. Hood is 3,425 m in height. What is the height of Wheeler Peak? $h - 586 = 3,425$; $h = 4,011$ m

7. The highest point in California is Mt. Whitney with a height of about 4,410 m. This height is 42 times the height of the highest point in Florida. What is the height of the highest point in Florida? $42 h = 4,410$; $h = 105$ m

8. The highest point in Colorado is Mt. Ebert and the lowest point is 1,021 m. This is 3,379 m less than the height of Mt. Ebert. What is the height of Mt. Ebert? $h - 3,379 = 1,021$; $n = 4,400$ m

9. DATA HUNT What is the highest point in your state or province and a nearby state or province? Make up a problem about the data. Write and solve an equation for your problem.

10. Try This The highest point in South Dakota is Harney Peak. If 69 m is subtracted from its height and the difference is divided by 2, the quotient is 1,069 m. This is the height of White Butte, the highest point in North Dakota. What is the height of Harney Peak? Hint: Work backward. 2,207 m

185

Reteaching Supplement, page 56

Name _____   To follow text page 185

Problem Solving: Writing and Solving an Equation

The world's highest suspension bridge is over the Royal Gorge in Colorado. Its length, 268 m, is 53 m less than its height. What is its height?

Choose a variable to represent the number you must find. → Let h = height of the Royal Gorge Bridge

Write an equation. → $h - 53 = 268$

Solve the equation. → $h - 53 + 53 = 268 + 53$
$h = 321$
$321 - 53 = 268$ It checks.

Royal Gorge Bridge is 321 m high.

Write and solve an equation for each problem.

1. In Seattle, a bridge has a floating section which is 2,334 m long. The length of the floating section is 0.6 times the total length of the bridge. What is the total length?

3,840 m

l = total length
$0.6 \times l = 2,304$
$\frac{0.6 \times l}{0.6} = \frac{2,304}{0.6}$
$l = 3,840$

2. The San Francisco-Oakland Bay Bridge has 2 spans. The shorter span, about 423 m long, is 0.6 times as long as the longer span. What is the length of the longer span?

705 m

l = longer span
$l \times 0.6 = 423$
$\frac{l \times 0.6}{0.6} = \frac{423}{0.6}$
$l = 705$

Use a multiplication equation.

3. One of the widest bridges in the world is in Sydney, Australia. If you divide its length by 10, the quotient is about the same as its width, which is 50.3 m. What is the length of the bridge?

503 m

$\frac{l}{10} = 50.3$
$\frac{l}{10} \times 10 = 50.3 \times 10$
$l = 503$

4. The longest natural stone arch bridge in North America is 429 m shorter than the world's longest steel arch bridge which is 518 m long. How long is the natural stone arch bridge?

89 m

n = natural stone arch bridge
$n + 429 = 518$
$n + 429 - 429 = 518 - 429$
$n = 89$

56

Enrichment Supplement, page 56

Name _____   To follow text page 185

A Best Seller

Use the given theme to write a story problem that would be solved using the given equation. Then solve the equation to answer the problem. Your problems may involve money or measurement. **Story problems will vary.**

1. Record albums $4 \times n = 27.30$
$n = 6.95$

2. A vacation trip $425 - p = 180$
$p = 245$

3. A movie theater $\frac{t}{8} = 3.75$
$t = 30$

4. Department store sale $(q \times 4) - 5 = 23$
$q = 7$

5. Sales tax $a + (0.05 \times a) = 10.50$
$a = 10$

56

Problem Solving: Writing and Solving an Equation

Practice Supplement, page 72

Name _____   To follow text page 185

Problem Solving: Writing and Solving an Equation

Write and solve an equation for each problem.

1. Mount Whitney, the highest point in California, is 4,418 m in height. If 19 m is added to the height of Mount Elbert, the sum is the height of Mount Whitney. What is the height of Mount Elbert?
$e - 19 = 4,418$ $e = 4,399$ m

2. Gannett Peak, the highest point in Wyoming, is 4,206 m in height. This is 6 times the height of Eagle Mountain, the highest point in Minnesota. What is the height of Eagle Mountain?
$5e = 4,206$ $e = 701$ m

3. The highest point in Arkansas is Magazine Mountain with a height of 840 m. The height of Mauna Kea, the highest point in Hawaii, is divided by 5, the quotient is the height of Magazine Mountain. What is the height of Mauna Kea?
$\frac{k}{5} = 840$ $k = 4,200$ m

4. Mount Marcy, the highest point in New York, is 1,629 m in height. If 408 m is subtracted from the height of Mount Mitchell, the highest point in North Carolina, the difference is the height of Mount Marcy. What is the height of Mount Mitchell?
$m - 408 = 1,629$ $m = 2,037$ m

5. Wheeler Peak, the highest point in New Mexico, is 4,014 m in height. If the height of Mount Mansfield, the highest point in Vermont, is multiplied by 3, the product is the height of Wheeler Peak. What is the height of Mount Mansfield?
$3m = 4,014$ $m = 1,338$ m

6. Woodall Mountain, the highest point in Mississippi, is 245 m in height. If the height of Mount Davis, the highest point in Pennsylvania, is divided by 4, the quotient is the height of Woodall Mountain. What is the height of Mount Davis?
$\frac{d}{4} = 245$ $d = 980$ m

7. Backbone Mountain, the highest point in Maryland, is 1,024 m in height. If 40 m is subtracted from the height of Mount Greylock, the highest point in Massachusetts, the difference is the height of Backbone Mountain. What is the height of Mount Greylock?
$g - 40 = 1,024$ $g = 1,064$ m

8. Cheaha Mountain, the highest point in Alabama, is 734 m in height. If 262 m is added to the height of Campbell Hill, the highest point in Ohio, the sum is the height of Cheaha Mountain. What is the height of Campbell Hill?
$c + 262 = 734$ $c = 472$ m

72

Ideas for Getting Started

Write this problem on the chalkboard or overhead projector.

Denise is 12 years old and her mother is 3 times as old as Denise. How old will Denise be when her mother is only twice as old as Denise?

Have students identify the data and the question in the problem. Some students may be able to solve this problem quickly using Guess and Check. Point out that another method can be used to solve the problem. Show how the data can be organized in a table and extended until it shows when Denise's mother will be twice as old as Denise.

Denise's age	12	13	16	20	24
Mother's age	36	37	40	44	48

Tell students that the table shows Denise will be 24 when her mother is 48 or twice Denise's age.

Using Page 186

Motivational Problem Have students read the Try This problem at the top of the page. After the question and data have been identified, put the outline of the table on the chalkboard or overhead projector. Explain that a table can help us answer the question. Have a volunteer add the strategy Make a Table to the problem-solving bulletin board display.

Lesson Development Ask students to fill in the table for each successive year, increasing Eileen's salary by $3,000 and Karen's salary by $1,000 each year. Have students tell what year both women earn the same salary.

Exercises 1–2 Assign the two problems at the bottom of the page for individual work. Since construction of the outline of the table is a crucial part of the problem, you may need to help some students with this part of the problem.

Lesson Focus To make a table as a strategy for solving nonroutine word problems

---

PROBLEM SOLVING: Make a Table

QUESTION
DATA
PLAN
ANSWER
CHECK

Try This

In 1982 Eileen and Karen started new jobs. Eileen got $10,000 for the first year with a $3,000 raise each year after that. Karen got a starting salary of $16,000 a year with a $2,000 raise each year after that. In what year will Eileen and Karen be earning the same salary?

To solve some problems, you may need to use the same operation many times until you get the answer. To organize your work, it will help if you use the strategy **Make a Table**.

First make a table that shows the data in the problem.

Year	1982	1983	1984
Eileen	$10,000	$13,000	
Karen	$16,000	$18,000	

Now fill in the table for other years until you find the year when the salaries are the same.

Year	1982	1983	1984	1985	1986	1987	1988
Eileen	$10,000	$13,000	$16,000	$19,000	$22,000	$25,000	$28,000
Karen	$16,000	$18,000	$20,000	$22,000	$24,000	$26,000	$28,000

The salaries are the same in 1988.

Solve.

1. In 1980 Stella and Bob each started a job that paid $10,000 a year. Each year Stella got a raise of $5,000 and Bob got a raise of $2,000. In what year will Stella be earning twice as much as Bob? **1990**

2. In 1975 Johnny started working at a job that paid $8,500 the first year with a $1,000 raise each year. In the same year, Pearl started a job that paid $6,000 a year with a raise of $1,800 each year. How much more was Pearl earning in 1985 than Johnny? **$5,500**

Strategy Test Item

Optional Problem If you wish to assess students' ability to apply the strategy called Make a Table introduced in this chapter, provide them with the problem below.

The Cougars were leading the Lions 69 to 53 in a basketball game with 5 minutes to go. During the last 5 minutes the Cougars averaged 6 points per minute. The Lions averaged 9 points per minute. What was the final score? Who won?

Solution

Minutes	0	1	2	3	4	5
Cougars	69	75	81	87	93	99
Lions	53	62	71	80	89	98

Cougars won by 1 point, 99 to 98.

CHAPTER REVIEW/TEST

List all the factors of each number.

1. 10 1, 2, 5, 10   **2.** 23 1, 23   **3.** 15 1, 3, 5, 15   **4.** 24 1, 2, 3, 4, 6, 8, 12, 24

5. Which number is divisible by 9?

114   (2,718)   7,024

6. Which number is divisible by 3?

233   (87)   173

7. Which number is a prime number?

15, 27, 43, 57, or 81 43

8. Which number is a composite number?

7, 17, 27, 37, or 47 27

Find the prime factorization of each number.

9. 20 $2 \cdot 2 \cdot 5$ **10.** 75 $3 \cdot 5 \cdot 5$ **11.** 42 $2 \cdot 3 \cdot 7$

Find the greatest common factor (GCF) of each pair of numbers.

12. 20, 45 5   **13.** 12, 36 12   **14.** 18, 45 9

Find the least common multiple (LCM) of each pair of numbers.

15. 6, 8 24   **16.** 8, 12 24   **17.** 10, 15 30

Complete each table by evaluating the expressions.

	n	$4n$
18.	3	▦ 12
19.	5	▦ 20
20.	10	▦ 40

	x	$\frac{x}{5}$
21.	20	▦ 4
22.	45	▦ 9
23.	60	▦ 12

	y	$y + 9$
24.	17	▦ 26
25.	4	▦ 13
26.	21	▦ 30

Solve each equation.

27. $x - 4 = 16$ $x = 20$ **28.** $k + 12 = 23$ $k = 11$

29. $7n = 70$ $n = 10$ **30.** $\frac{b}{7} = 3$ $b = 21$

31. Write the equation for the problem. Solve the equation.

When 9 is subtracted from a certain number, the difference is 12. What is the number? Let x = the number.
$x - 9 = 12$; $x = 21$

32. Write and solve an equation for the problem.

Twelve times a certain number is 132. What is the number? Let k = the number.
$12k = 132$; $k = 11$

187

Using Page 187

The exercises in the Chapter Review/Test emphasize the major concepts and skills presented in this chapter. These exercises may be used as a review assignment or as a test, depending upon your needs.

Item Analysis The table below correlates the Chapter Review/Test items with objectives and with the student text pages on which the concepts or skills were taught. Please note that items 5–6 are derived from a lesson from which no "Minimum" assignment was suggested in the Assignment guide. Only those students who were assigned this lesson should be expected to complete the corresponding Chapter Review/Test items.

Items	Objectives	Related Text Pages
1–11	7.1	164–171
12–17	7.2	172–175
18–26	7.3	176–177
27–30	7.4	178–181
31–32	7.5	182–185

Assessment Options

If you use the Chapter Review/Test as a review assignment, you may wish to use the free-response test or the multiple-choice test to evaluate mastery of the chapter objectives. The items on these tests have one-to-one correspondence in terms of content and level difficulty. A correlation of test items to objectives and student text pages is provided in the Management Guide for Chapter 7. Note: Items 5–6 are derived from lessons for which no minimum assignment was suggested in the Assignment Guide.

Multiple-Choice Test, TRB pages 19–21
Free-Response Test, TRB pages 61–62

TRB Options

The following blackline masters are available for use with this chapter. If you have not already assigned these materials, you may wish to use them to close the chapter.

Recreation, TRB page 161
Consumer Applications, TRB page 179
Calculator Technology, TRB page 197
Computer Technology, TRB pages 212–214
Reading Math, TRB page 233
Family Involvement, TRB pages 257–258

Reteaching

Using Page 188

The exercises on this page are intended for those students who experienced difficulty with the Chapter Review/Test on page 187. Should students require reteaching of these key concepts and skills, please refer to the teaching notes below. Otherwise, the Another Look exercises can be assigned as independent work, with students using the accompanying sample problems and hints as guides.

Exercises 1–3 This skill was originally taught on pages 164–165. Remind students to think of pairs as they list all the factors of a number. The number itself and 1 should always be included.

Exercises 4–9 This skill was originally taught on pages 168–171. Have students study the examples in the display box. Ask them to give the meaning of prime and composite. Notice with students that the factors in each row of the factor tree have a product of 18.

Exercises 10–12 This skill was originally taught on pages 172–173. Direct students' attention to the example on the left. Explain that the prime factorization can be used to find the GCF of two numbers. Point out that the GCF contains only the prime factors common to both 12 and 30.

Exercises 13–15 This skill was originally taught on pages 174–175. Discuss the prime factorization method of finding the LCM. Explain that since we want the smallest multiple of both numbers, we do not want to include extra factors. Encourage students to align common factors so that the extra factors are not included.

Exercises 16–21 This skill was originally taught on pages 176–177. Have students examine the example in the display box. On the chalkboard, show how to substitute a number for the variable to evaluate an expression.

Exercises 22–29 This skill was originally taught on pages 178–181. On the chalkboard, work through each step in the examples. Point out that since 7 is subtracted from k, we should add 7 to get k alone. Review the analogy of an equation to a balance scale. Explain that if we add 7 to the left side of the equation, we must then add 7 to the right side.

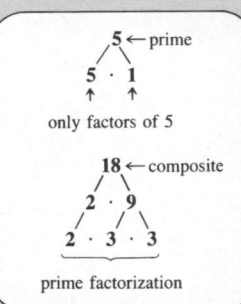

List all the factors of each number.

1. 12 1, 2, 3, 4, 6, 12   **2.** 40 1, 2, 4, 5, 8, 10, 20, 40   **3.** 35 1, 5, 7, 35

Write (P) prime or (C) composite for each number.

4. 21 C   **5.** 23 P   **6.** 99 C

Find the prime factorization of each number.

7. 30 $2 \cdot 3 \cdot 5$ **8.** 28 $2 \cdot 2 \cdot 7$ **9.** 54 $3 \cdot 3 \cdot 2 \cdot 3$

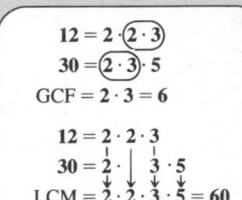

Find the greatest common factor (GCF) of each pair of numbers.

10. 8, 12 4   **11.** 9, 27 9   **12.** 30, 45 15

Find the least common multiple (LCM) of each pair of numbers.

13. 5, 6 30   **14.** 8, 24 24   **15.** 20, 30 60

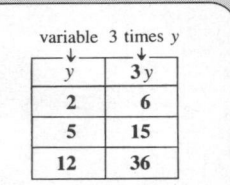

Complete each table by evaluating the expression.

	n	$8n$		x	$x - 3$
16.	4	▦ 32	**19.**	30	▦ 27
17.	7	▦ 56	**20.**	45	▦ 42
18.	10	▦ 80	**21.**	120	▦ 117

Solve each equation.

22. $x + 19 = 35$ $x = 16$ **23.** $7n = 56$ $n = 8$

24. $y - 13 = 9$ $y = 22$ **25.** $\frac{z}{6} = 13$ $z = 78$

26. $p + 75 = 125$ $p = 50$ **27.** $r - 17 = 29$ $r = 46$

28. $5b = 250$ $b = 50$ **29.** $\frac{s}{8} = 32$ $s = 256$

188

Just for Teachers

Pythagorean Number Lore

Numbers have always held some mystery for people. Even today certain numbers hold mysterious powers; 13 is considered such bad luck that many buildings do not have a 13th floor, but skip from 12 to 14.

Ancient Greeks were particularly interested in the concept that numbers are endowed with certain qualities or hold secrets of the universe. By 600 B.C. they had established colonies and trade routes throughout the Mediterranean, absorbing the practical mathematics of the Middle East and Asia refined over thousands of years. The Greeks—and the Hebrews—eventually used letters of their alphabet to represent numbers, removing mathematics even further from its practical base and giving rise to a whole new superstitious practice.

In its simplest form, Greek number lore borrowed from the Chinese and classified odd numbers as masculine and even numbers as feminine. The discovery by Pythagoras of the numeric relationships between the seven notes of their musical scale was applied to the seven heavenly bodies of their sky, the influence of numbers providing a "harmony of the spheres" existing throughout the universe.

ENRICHMENT

Number Relationships

Finding the greatest common factor of two large numbers can be difficult. The direction boxes below give a method that will make the problem easier. You may want to use a calculator.

What is the greatest common factor of 11,039 and 3,458?

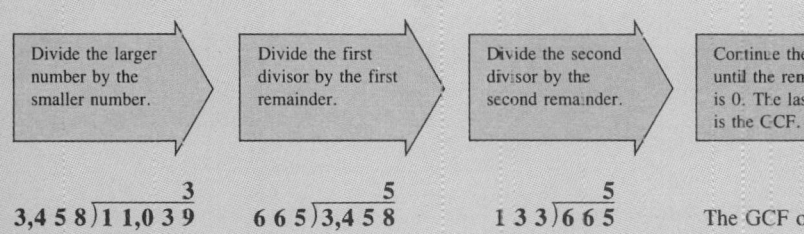

| Divide the larger number by the smaller number. | Divide the first divisor by the first remainder. | Divide the second divisor by the second remainder. | Continue the process until the remainder is 0. The last divisor is the GCF. |

$$3,458\overline{)11,039}$$
$$\underline{10374}$$
$$665$$
→ 3

$$665\overline{)3,458}$$
$$\underline{3325}$$
$$133$$
→ 5

$$133\overline{)665}$$
$$\underline{665}$$
$$0$$
→ 5

The GCF of 11,039 and 3,458 is 133.

Check:

$11,039 = 133 \times 83$
$3,458 = 133 \times 26$

The GCF of 83 and 26 is 1, therefore 133 is the GCF of 11,039 and 3,458.

Find the GCF of each pair of numbers.

1. 1,001 and 4,466   77

2. 2,813 and 5,771   29

3. 642 and 25,787   107

4. 5,585 and 65,903   1,117

5. 1,541 and 67,603   67

6. 531,389 and 13,606,507   1

7. Choose two large numbers and find their greatest common factor.

189

Using Page 189

This page is intended for those students who successfully completed the Chapter Review/Test on page 187. You may wish to assign this page as independent work while you use Another Look exercises to reteach the basic concepts and skills of the chapter. Or, you may decide that all students would benefit from exposure to this Enrichment activity.

Suggested Materials Calculators

Lesson Development The method for finding the greatest common factor of 2 numbers by the repeated division process shown in the lesson is sometimes called the Euclidean Algorithm after the Greek mathematician Euclid. You may want to demonstrate the algorithm with two small numbers before going through the example on the page. For instance, find the GCF of 308 and 84.

$$84\overline{)308}$$
$$\underline{252}$$
$$56$$
→ 3

$$56\overline{)84}$$
$$\underline{56}$$
$$28$$
→ 1

$$28\overline{)56}$$
$$\underline{56}$$
$$0$$
→ 2

The GCF of 308 and 84 is 28.
The division can be arranged in this form:

$$84\overline{)308} \quad 3$$
$$\underline{252} \quad 1$$
$$56\overline{)84}$$
$$\underline{56} \quad 2$$
$$28\overline{)56}$$
$$\underline{56}$$
$$0$$

Have students check their solutions by showing that the number they find for the GCF of the pair of numbers is a common factor of the numbers.

$$308 = 28 \cdot 11$$
$$84 = 28 \cdot 3$$

Since 3 and 11 are relatively prime, 28 is the GCF of 84 and 308.

The influence of the Orient is seen in another Pythagorean practice. The early Chinese had constructed Magic Squares, 3×3 or 4×4 arrangements of numbers such that vertical, horizontal, and diagonal rows added to the same sum. The Greeks investigated the makeup of numbers, i.e., prime numbers and the factors of composite numbers. In so doing, they discovered "amicable" and "perfect" numbers:

Amicable—220 and 284—the sum of all divisors of 220, except the number itself, equals 284 and vice-versa.

Perfect—6, 28, 496—the sum of all the divisors of the number, except the number itself, equals the number

Magic Squares, and finding prime numbers and amicable numbers provide mathematical challenges even today. Perfect numbers are a job for computers; after the series 6, 28, 496, and 8,128, there is not another perfect number until 33,550,336.

Lesson Focus
Lesson Focus To read and understand a computer program that uses an INPUT statement

Ideas for Getting Started

Display the following on the chalkboard. Tell students that line 30 is part of a computer program. Ask them to give values for A and B and record these in the chart. Next have students find the value for X in line 30. Write this value in the chart.

$30 \ X = 2 * (A+B)$

A	
B	
X	

Continue having students name values for A and B. Cross out the old values as the new ones are entered. With each entry of A and B, have students find the value for X in line 30.

Using page 190

Lesson Development Explain to students that each time the computer receives information, or input, it must store that information in its memory. Point out that variables name memory locations in the computer, and that these names or labels are necessary in order for information to be retrieved from the memory locations when needed. Tell students that only one piece of information can be stored in each location. If new information is directed to a location that already contains data, the original data will be lost.

Have students read the material at the top of the page. Explain that an INPUT statement in a program allows the person running the program to enter data. On the chalkboard, work through the program one step at a time. Tell students that when the computer gets to line 30 during the RUN, it will stop, print a "?", and wait to receive data. Emphasize that in a statement, INPUT is always followed by a variable that identifies the data and labels the storage location for later reference.

Write a chart with the variable names on the chalkboard and go through each step of the program with students. When you come to lines 30, 50, and 60, the values of the variables should be written in the chart. Then have students take turns "running" the program. When they get to lines 30 and 50, they should cross out the old data and write their input in the chart. Ask students what happens to the data already stored in the computer's memory in A, B, and C when the next person "runs" the program. (It is erased by the new data and lost.)

A	41
B	13
C	28

Using INPUT in a Computer Program

A computer program can be written so that the computer can ask questions and receive data. This data is called INPUT.

The INPUT may be numbers that are used to solve problems.

A pollster collects data that will be used with a computer to prepare a public opinion survey.

Program	Comments
10 REM DIFFERENCE OF AGES	REM (Remark) statements are
20 PRINT "GIVE YOUR MOTHER'S AGE."	ignored by the computer. Here, REM names the program.
30 INPUT A	INPUT is the number you
40 PRINT "WHAT IS YOUR AGE?"	choose.
50 INPUT B	Another INPUT number
60 C = A - B	C is the difference using
70 PRINT "YOUR MOTHER IS ";C	INPUT numbers.
80 PRINT "YEARS OLDER THAN YOU."	
90 END	

Here is an example RUN for the program.

```
RUN
GIVE YOUR MOTHER'S AGE.
?41
WHAT IS YOUR AGE?
?13
YOUR MOTHER IS 28
YEARS OLDER THAN YOU.
```

What would a RUN of this program be using your mother's age and your age?

190

Technology for Teachers

There are four main parts to a computer system: the input unit, the output unit, the central processing unit, and the memory. The *input* device transmits information to the computer. It is often designed like a typewriter keyboard. The *output* device gets information from the computer to the people using it. A common output device is a TV monitor, or CRT (*C*athode *R*ay *T*ube) display. Most manufacturers use the same coding scheme in their input and output devices. This code is called the *A*merican *S*tandard *C*ode for *I*nformation *I*nterchange, or ASCII.

The *central processing unit,* or CPU, is the "brain" of the computer. It is a complex set of electrical circuitry that executes the program. The CPU consists of two parts, the control unit and the arithmetic/logic unit. The control unit directs and coordinates the entire computer system in carrying out the stored program instructions. The arithmetic/logic unit controls all arithmetic operations and logical operations, such as addition, subtraction, multiplication, division, and comparing.

A fourth component of a computer system is *memory*. During operation, programs and data are stored in *R*andom *A*ccess *M*emory, or RAM. When the power to the computer is turned off, all data held in RAM is lost. RAM can be erased and repro-

Write a RUN for each program. Use the given INPUT numbers.

```
1. 10 REM MULTIPLYING NUMBERS
   20 PRINT "CHOOSE A NUMBER."
   30 INPUT A
   40 PRINT "CHOOSE ANOTHER
      NUMBER."
   50 INPUT B
   60 C = A * B
   70 PRINT "THE PRODUCT IS ";C
   80 END

   INPUT: A = 27, B = 35
```

```
2. 10 REM AVERAGE
   20 PRINT "CHOOSE 3 NUMBERS."
   30 INPUT A
   40 INPUT B
   50 INPUT C
   60 D = (A + B + C)/3
   70 PRINT "AVERAGE = ";D
   80 END

   INPUT: A = 3, B = 6, C = 21
```

```
3. 10 REM SQUARES AND CUBES
   20 PRINT "CHOOSE A NUMBER."
   30 INPUT A
   40 B = A * A
   50 C = A * A * A
   60 PRINT A;" SQUARED = ";B
   70 PRINT A;" CUBED = ";C
   80 END

   INPUT: A = 5
```

```
4. 10 REM YOUR AGE
   20 PRINT "WHAT IS THIS YEAR?"
   30 INPUT Y
   40 PRINT "WHAT IS YOUR
      BIRTH YEAR?"
   50 INPUT B
   60 A = Y - B
   70 PRINT "YOU ARE ";A
   80 END

   INPUT: Y = This year
          B = Your birth year
```

```
5. 10 REM ESTIMATING
   20 PRINT "HOW MANY SECONDS
      DOES"
   30 PRINT "IT TAKE TO WALK
      100 METERS?"
   40 INPUT S
   50 T = 10 * S/60
   60 PRINT "YOU CAN WALK 1 KM"
   70 PRINT "IN ";T;" MINUTES."
   80 END

   INPUT: S = 54
```

6. Write a RUN for the program in exercise 5 using your own INPUT number.

7. Write a computer program that will find the sum of three INPUT numbers. Write a RUN of the program using your own INPUT.

grammed by the operator as frequently as necessary. The amount of available RAM, measured in kilobytes (K), determines the "size" of the computer. Read Only Memory is programmed into the computer by the manufacturer. It cannot be erased or reprogrammed by usual computer operations. The ROM contains the system programs the CPU refers to as a program runs. The BASIC language is often provided in ROM on microcomputers.

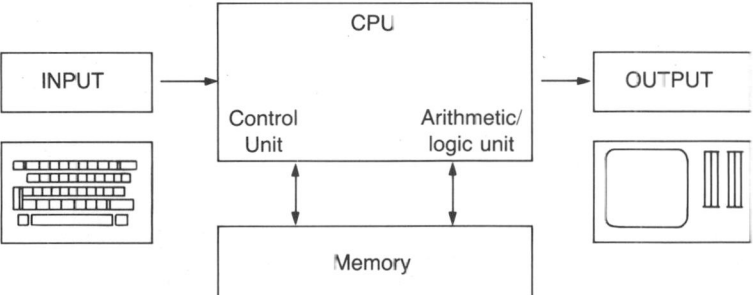

Using Page 192

The exercises on the page provide practice for maintaining cumulative skills. The emphasis in this Cumulative Review is on decimal multiplication (Chapter 4) and geometry problem-solving (Chapter 6).

Item Analysis The table below correlates the Cumulative Review items with objectives and with the student book pages on which the concepts or skills were taught.

Items	Objectives	Related Text Pages
1–3	4.2	92–95, 98–99
4	4.3	100
5	4.2	92–95, 98–99
6	4.4	102–103
7	6.1	138–139
8–9	6.2	140–145
10	6.3	146–147
11	6.1	136–137
12	6.1	138–139
13	6.2	140–145
14	7.5	182–185

CUMULATIVE REVIEW

Find the products.

1. $\begin{array}{r} 41.37 \\ \times \quad 12 \end{array}$ (A) 496.44   B 49.674
       C 49.644   D not given

2. $\begin{array}{r} 742 \\ \times 0.18 \end{array}$ A 135   B 134.37
       (C) 133.56   D not given

3. $\begin{array}{r} 0.004 \\ \times \quad 0.6 \end{array}$ A 0.00024   B 2.40
       C 0.024   (D) not given

4. Choose the best estimate.

    $\begin{array}{r} 6.82 \\ \times 2.05 \end{array}$ (A) 14   B 12
       C 18   D not given

5. Multiply.

    $0.7194 \times 1,000$ A 71.94
       B 7,194
       (C) 719.4
       D not given

6. What is the standard numeral for 3.9×10^5?

    A 3,900,000   B 39,000
    (C) 390,000   D not given

7. What kind of angle is $\angle ABC$?

    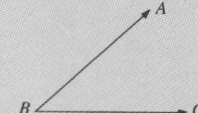

    (A) acute
    B right
    C straight
    D not given

8. What is the measure of the third angle?

    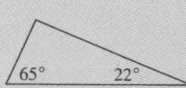

    A 90°
    B 87°
    (C) 93°
    D not given

9. What is the name of polygon $ABCDE$?

    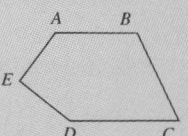

    A hexagon
    B quadrilateral
    (C) pentagon
    D not given

10. What is the name of the chord which passes through the center point of a circle?

    (A) diameter   B arc
    C radius   D not given

11. What is the symbol for ray AB?

    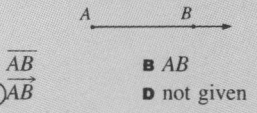

    A $\overline{AB}$ B AB
    (C) $\overrightarrow{AB}$ D not given

12. What is the measure of any right angle?

    A 360°   (B) 90°
    C 180°   D not given

13. How many sides does a hexagon have?

    A 9   B 11
    C 8   (D) not given

14. On a map, 1 cm represents 45.7 km. What distance would 7.9 cm represent?

    A 360 km   (B) 361.03 km
    C 36.103 km   D not given

Objectives

8.1 Find equivalent and lowest-terms fractions.

8.2 Write a number as an improper fraction or a mixed number.

8.3 Compare fractions and mixed numbers.

8.4 Find the sums and differences of fractions.

8.5 Find the sums and differences of mixed numbers.

8.6 Solve word problems using the 5-Point Checklist and cumulative computational skills.

Summary

This chapter is concerned with the meaning of fractions and developing skills necessary for the addition and subtraction of fractions. A review of equivalent fractions and of reducing fractions to lowest terms is presented. Students compare fractions, estimate fractions, and write numbers as improper fractions and mixed numbers. Addition and subtraction of fractions and mixed numbers is reviewed. Problem solving is extended to include addition and subtraction of fractions and mixed numbers.

Mathematical Background

Fraction Concepts A review of fractions begins with writing fractions for parts of regions or parts of sets. Fractions are then related to division as illustrated in the figure below.

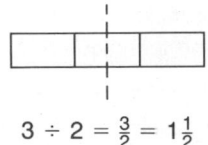

$$3 \div 2 = \frac{3}{2} = 1\frac{1}{2}$$

The idea that different fractions can be used to describe the same part of a region leads to the idea of equivalent fractions. Equivalent fractions can be generated by multiplying the numerator and denominator of a given fraction by the same nonzero number. This idea can be illustrated with a model.

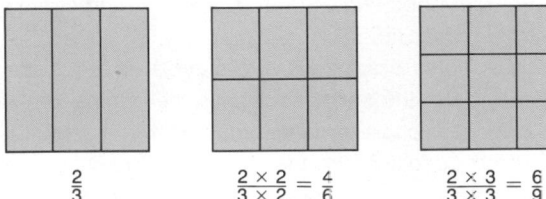

$$\frac{2}{3} \qquad \frac{2 \times 2}{3 \times 2} = \frac{4}{6} \qquad \frac{2 \times 3}{3 \times 3} = \frac{6}{9}$$

Equivalent fractions can also be formed by dividing the numerator and denominator of a fraction by the same nonzero number. If the numerator and denominator are divided by the greatest common factor, the fraction will be expressed in lowest terms.

Addition and Subtraction of Fractions The methods for adding and subtracting fractions use skills developed in earlier chapters. For example, to find the least common denominator, students will need to know how to find the least common multiple of two numbers. The skills involving equivalent fractions are also used in the algorithms for adding and subtracting fractions that have different denominators. These algorithms are then extended to adding and subtracting mixed numbers.

Renaming is perhaps the most difficult process students will encounter in this chapter. In addition of mixed numbers, renaming takes place after the computation is complete. It involves writing answers which are improper fractions as mixed numbers. In subtraction of mixed numbers, the renaming is done before the computation in much the same way that regrouping is handled with whole numbers. Pictorial examples of the renaming process may help students obtain a clearer understanding of the concepts involved.

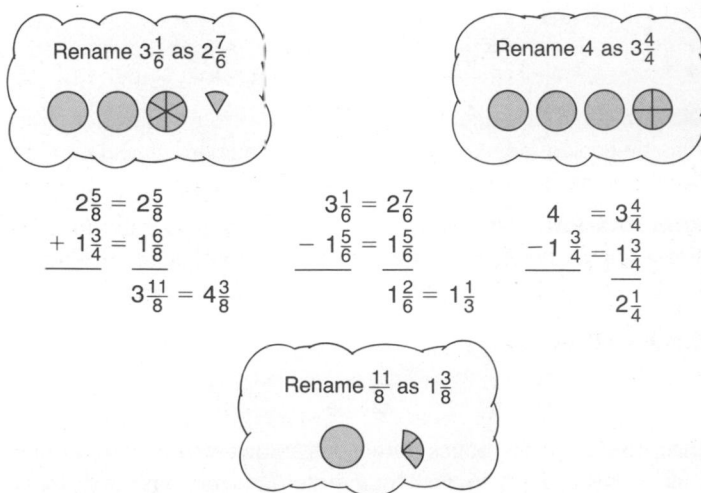

Problem Solving In this chapter, problem-solving skills are extended to include problems involving addition and subtraction of fractions as well as operations with numbers developed in earlier chapters. On page 205, the focus of the lesson is on using data from a table. A problem-solving lesson on page 217 provides practice solving standard single- and multiple-step problems. To solve these problems, students must apply computational skills and concepts learned in this chapter and in earlier ones. On page 218, students learn a new strategy, Choose the Operations, for solving nonroutine word problems.

Vocabulary

fraction	improper fraction
numerator	lowest-terms fraction
denominator	least common denominator
mixed number	

Error Analysis

This chapter reviews the meaning of a fraction and addition and subtraction of fractions. Although most topics in this chapter are review, many students traditionally find working with fractions difficult. Many student errors occur in the content taught in this chapter. Some common errors are listed below.

Error Pattern 1

$$\frac{1}{2} = \frac{3}{4} = \frac{5}{6} = \frac{7}{8} \qquad \frac{2}{3} = \frac{5}{6} = \frac{8}{9} = \frac{11}{12} \qquad \frac{1}{5} = \frac{6}{10} = \frac{11}{15} = \frac{16}{20}$$

Diagnosis The student has attempted to form equivalent fractions by adding the same amount to both numerator and denominator. The model used was $\frac{a}{b} = \frac{a+n}{b+n}$.

Remediation Manipulative materials should be used to show that $\frac{1}{2} \neq \frac{3}{4}$. Show through drawings of regions how to form equivalent fractions. Then move to the generalization, $\frac{a}{b} = \frac{a \times n}{b \times n}$.

Error Pattern 2

$$\frac{1\cancel{2}}{\cancel{2}9} = \frac{1}{9} \qquad \frac{2\cancel{4}}{3\cancel{2}} = \frac{4}{3} \qquad \frac{1\cancel{2}}{\cancel{2}4} = \frac{1}{4}$$

Diagnosis When reducing fractions to lowest terms, the student canceled like digits in both numerator and denominator. Place value was not considered. No knowledge of the concept of dividing by a common factor is shown.

Remediation Begin with an example such as $\frac{12}{24}$. Draw pictures to show that $\frac{12}{24} = \frac{1}{2}$, not $\frac{1}{4}$. Try to develop a symbolic procedure by encouraging the student to find factors common to both the denominator and numerator. For instance, ask students if 12 and 24 can be divided by 2. Then write $\frac{12}{24} = \frac{12 \div 2}{12 \div 2} = \frac{6}{12}$. Repeat the procedure until the fraction is in lowest terms.

Error Pattern 3

$$\begin{array}{r} \frac{3}{8} \\ + \frac{5}{8} \\ \hline \frac{8}{8} = 1 \end{array} \qquad \begin{array}{r} \frac{1}{4} \\ + \frac{3}{8} \\ \hline \frac{4}{12} = \frac{1}{3} \end{array} \qquad \begin{array}{r} \frac{2}{5} \\ + \frac{1}{2} \\ \hline \frac{3}{7} \end{array} \qquad \begin{array}{r} \frac{5}{6} \\ + \frac{3}{4} \\ \hline \frac{8}{10} = \frac{4}{5} \end{array}$$

Diagnosis In adding fractions with unlike denominators, the student added numerators and denominators. No attempt was made to write equivalent fractions with a common denominator.

Remediation Use a model to show that two fractions with unlike denominators can be added but there is no way to report the sum.

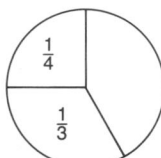

Explain that a common denominator must be found first and then we can add and give the sum.

Problem Solving

Extending a Problem-Solving Lesson

In the 5-Point Checklist, "checking back" is the final stage in solving a particular problem. It is important that problem-solving lessons do not end with the solution to a particular problem. Extend the problem-solving experience by helping students generalize what they did on a particular problem to what they know, in general, about problem solving. Here are four teaching actions you can use to extend your problem-solving lessons.

- *Show two solution strategies for a problem whenever possible.* Many students have the misconception that there is only one way to solve every math problem. Showing more than one solution strategy for a problem helps change this misconception. Also, when possible, show variations in the use of a particular solution strategy. For example, two students may both have used an organized list to solve a problem but may have organized their lists in different ways. Showing variations in the way a particular strategy is used to solve a given problem expands students' knowledge about the use of that strategy.

- *Name the strategy or strategies used.* The primary reason for having students name the problem-solving strategies is to make them aware of the techniques they have learned for solving problems. When students are aware of the strategies in their repertoire, they are better able to suggest possible solution strategies for a particular problem. Naming the solution strategy reinforces that the method the student used is an accepted problem-solving technique.

- *Relate the problem to similar problems.* Many students have difficulty recognizing problems that can be solved using the same solution strategy. Some students, for example, may think that two problems can be solved using the same solution strategy if both problems have the same setting—for example, if both are about cows—regardless of other characteristics of the problems. Discussing problems similar to the original one illustrates how a particular problem-solving strategy can be used in a variety of settings. Relating a problem to similar ones shows that problem-solving strategies are not problem specific.

- *Discuss or solve extensions of the problem.* Problem extensions may have the same setting as the original problem but differ in certain characteristics such as the size of the numbers or the conditions of the problem. Presenting problems that involve changes in problem characteristics helps students understand that certain conditions in a problem may affect the way one goes about finding the solution. Extensions may also have the effect of encouraging students to generalize using a particular solution strategy in situations similar to the original problem.

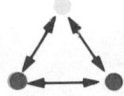 **Special Education**

This chapter reviews many fraction concepts and skills which typically present problems for students with memory, reasoning, and other learning difficulties. Special instructional approaches are often required in the treatment of these topics to fill gaps in learning created by problems students experienced during previous instruction. The ideas which follow may be helpful in teaching your special students the topics of the chapter.

Actively Involve Students

Throughout the chapter, it is important to model concepts being reviewed and to actively involve students in interpreting, or justifying, the procedures used. When discussing the procedures, provide opportunity for the special students in your class to work with the models. Whenever possible, invite them to describe in their own words the idea or procedure being focused upon. This last point is critical, since frequently these students will learn and retain only if they hear themselves speak.

Mixed Numbers and Improper Practices

Because there are so many numbers and operations to sort out in working with mixed numbers and improper fractions, the special students in your class may lose track of the sequence for dealing with them. Therefore, they may require a visual, hands-on review. For example, provide blank strips of fractional pieces and invite students to illustrate the renaming of selected examples.

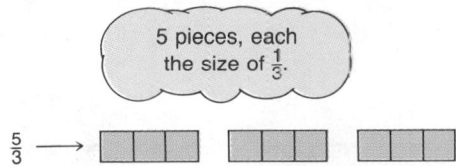

"How many whole strips can be filled?
How many pieces are left?" ($1\frac{2}{3}$)

Explain to students that the denominator (3) tells the number in each strip, so we can divide to get the same result.

$$\frac{5}{3} \longrightarrow 3\overline{)5}^{\,1\,R2} = 1\frac{2}{3} = 1\frac{2}{3}$$

The color coding which is illustrated can be used if needed. A similar procedure, in which wholes are traded for pieces, establishes the basis for the "multiply and add" procedure used to change mixed numbers to improper fractions.

Common Denominators

Students need to find common denominators when comparing, adding, and subtracting fractions in this chapter. Realizing that a common denominator is needed and being able to determine what that denominator should be are separate skills. Some of these students initially will need to write multiples of each denominator as an aid to thinking about them. Referring to a multiplication table and additional practice with oral skip counting will also help. From the list of written multiples, students can circle all those that are common to both lists, and then finger trace or otherwise mark the smallest of these. While any common multiple can be used as a common denominator, using the smallest minimizes errors which otherwise often appear in work with larger numbers.

As students become more comfortable with the idea of finding the lowest common multiple and more familiar with skip counting patterns, they will be able to mentally scan the multiples of the greater denominator and stop when they find one that also is a multiple of the other denominator.

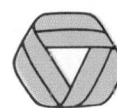 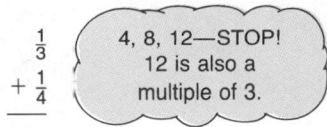

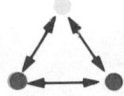 **Subject Integration**

Subject matter related to other areas of the curriculum has been integrated into the following lessons. This provides an opportunity to highlight the interaction between mathematics and other subjects.

Career Awareness Paramedic, page 194; pet store, pages 200–201; graphic artist, pages 206–207; plant store, pages 208–209; produce market clerk, page 218

Physical Education Cross-country skiing, pages 198–199; races, jumps, baseball, and football, page 217

Social Studies United Nations, pages 202–203

Consumer Awareness Making estimates, page 204; monthly sales, page 205

Industrial Arts Plumbing, pages 210–211; carpentry, pages 212–213

Computer Awareness Computer use, pages 214–215

Management Guide

Teaching Chapter 8				Meeting Individual Needs					
Objectives	Chapter Content	Pages	TRB Test Items	Lesson Assignments			Follow Up		
				Minimum	Average	Extended	Reteaching	Enrichment	Practice
	Chapter Opener	193							
8.1 Find equivalent and lowest-terms fractions.	Fractions	194–195	1–2	1–21	1–23	1–23			PS 73
	Equivalent Fractions	196–197	3–5	1–28	1–34	1–35 odd, TM	SE6 Ch 8 RS 57	ES 57	MP 428 PS 74
	Lowest-Terms Fractions	198–199	6–8	1–31, SK	1–31, 34, SK	1–31 odd, 32–34, SK	SE6 Ch 8 RS 58	ES 58	MP 428 PS 75
8.2 Write a number as an improper fraction or a mixed number.	Improper Fractions and Mixed Numbers	200–201	9–14	1–41	1–41, 46–49	1–39 odd, 41–52	SE6 Ch 8 RS 59	ES 59	MP 428 PS 76
8.3 Compare fractions and mixed numbers.	Comparing Fractions	202–203	15–17	1–16, 25–33	1–33, TM	2–34 even, TM	SE6 Ch 8 RS 60	ES 60	MP 429 PS 77
	Using Fractions in Estimation	204	18–19	1–8	1–10	1–10			PS 78
8.4 Find the sums and differences of fractions.	Adding Fractions	206–207	20–22	1–20, 26	1–26	1–25 odd, 26–29	SE6 Ch 8 RS 62	ES 62	MP 429 PS 79
	Subtracting Fractions	208–209	23–25	1–20 26, SK	1–26, SK	2–26, even 27, SK	SE6 Ch 8 RS 63	ES 63	MP 429 PS 80
8.5 Find the sums and differences of mixed numbers.	Adding Mixed Numbers	210–211	26–28	1–20, 26	1–26	2–26, even 27, TM	SE6 Ch 8 RS 64	ES 64	MP 430 PS 81
	Subtracting Mixed Numbers	212–213	29–31	1–22, 25	1–25, 28	1–25 odd, 26–28, TM	SE6 Ch 8 RS 65	ES 65	MP 430 PS 82
	Subtracting Mixed Numbers with Renaming	214–215	32–34	1–22, 25	1–25	1–25 odd, 26, TM	SE6 Ch 8 RS 66	ES 66	MP 430 PS 83
	Skills Practice	216		1–28	1–37	2–42 even			
8.6 Solve word problems using the 5-Point Checklist and cumulative computational skills.	Problem Solving: Using Data from a Table	205	35–38	1–7	1–10	4–12	RS 61	ES 61	
	Problem Solving: Practice	217		1–6	1–8	1–8			PS 84
	Problem Solving: Choose the Operations	218							
	Chapter Review/Test	219							
	Another Look/ Enrichment	220–221							

SE6   Student Edition, Book 6
RS   Reteaching Supplement
ES   Enrichment Supplement
PS   Practice Supplement
MP   More Practice
TM   Think Math
SK   Skillkeeper
TRB   Teacher's Resource Book

Masters for use

. . . before Chapter 8

Readiness
Improper Fractions — 118

Readiness
Writing Fractions — 117

. . . during Chapter 8

Calculator Technology
Pascal's Triangle — 198

Consumer Applications
Renting Vs. Buying — 180

Teaching Aids — 278, 279

Recreation
Mathword Jumble — 162

Activities That Count
Equivalent Fractions — 146

. . . after Chapter 8

Record Keeping — 303

Family Involvement
At-Home Activities — 260

Family Involvement
Key Math — 259

Reading Math
Fraction Concepts — 234

Chapter 8 Test
Free-Response Format — 63–64

Chapter 8 Test
Multiple-Choice Format — 22–24

Mid-Year Test — 81–84

Supplements

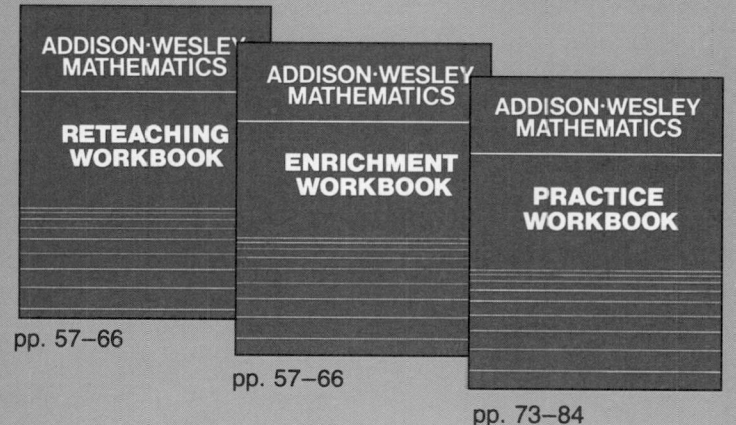

ADDISON-WESLEY MATHEMATICS RETEACHING WORKBOOK — pp. 57–66

ADDISON-WESLEY MATHEMATICS ENRICHMENT WORKBOOK — pp. 57–66

ADDISON-WESLEY MATHEMATICS PRACTICE WORKBOOK — pp. 73–84

Other Addison-Wesley Resources

Books and Kits

The Mad Minute pp. 171–175
General Mathematics: Making Practice Fun 31, 33 B, 43 A, B, 45 A, B, 46 A, B, 47 A, B, 48 A, B, 49
Arithmetic Primer pp. 114–121, 127–128, 139–166
Problem-Solving Experiences in Mathematics, Grade 7 Problems 72, 77, 92, 117, 128, 142

Technology

Computer Math Activities Volumes 2, 5
Computer Math Games Volumes 1, 3, 6

Activities That Count

Activities That Count are designed for use throughout this chapter and subsequent chapters. Before beginning Chapter 8 you may wish to review these activities and select the ones you consider appropriate for your class.

Equivalent Fractions   Game

Purpose To identify equivalent fractions

Materials Game sheet (TRB p. 146), paper clips for spinner, game markers

Activity In turn, players spin a number on each spinner and use the numbers to form a fraction. The fraction that is formed, or an equivalent fraction, is then covered on the game sheet. The first player to get four in a row vertically, horizontally, or diagonally wins.

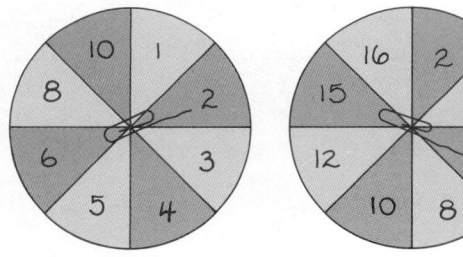

Fractions in History   Project

Purpose To read about and report on the history of fractions

Activity Have students read about the development of methods used for writing fractions. Ask them to find out whether there were other notations before the one we use of numerator over denominator. Have them write a report on their findings.

Tangram Fractions   Math Lab

Purpose To write fractions for parts of a region and express fractions in lowest terms

Materials Tangram puzzle (TRB p. 279)

Activity Explain to students that the tangram puzzle represents 1 unit. Have them tell what fraction is represented by each piece. Fractions should be given in lowest terms.

Next have students create figures with the puzzle pieces and give the fraction of the entire tangram puzzle that the pieces would cover. Examples are shown below.

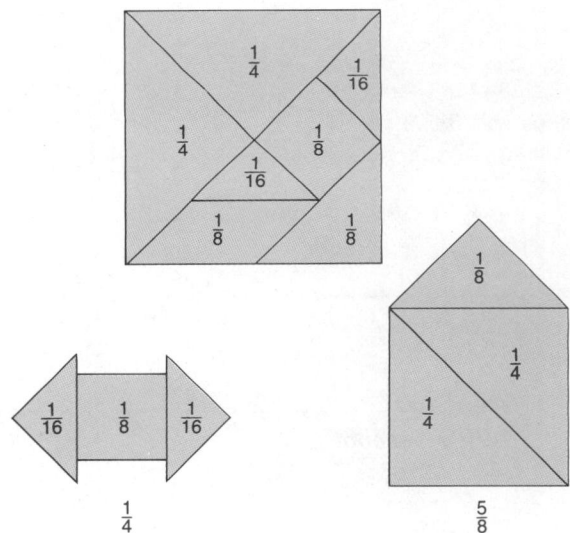

Fraction Addition   Game

Purpose To add and compare fractions

Materials 24 index cards labeled 1 through 12 (2 each)

Activity The object of the game is to make the greatest sum. Each player draws 4 cards and places them to form 2 fractions. The fractions are then added. The player with the greatest sum scores a point. The winner is the player with the highest score after 5 rounds. Variation: Players can subtract to make the greatest difference.

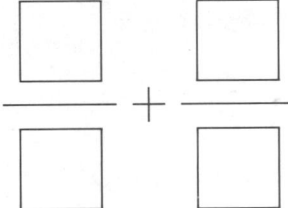

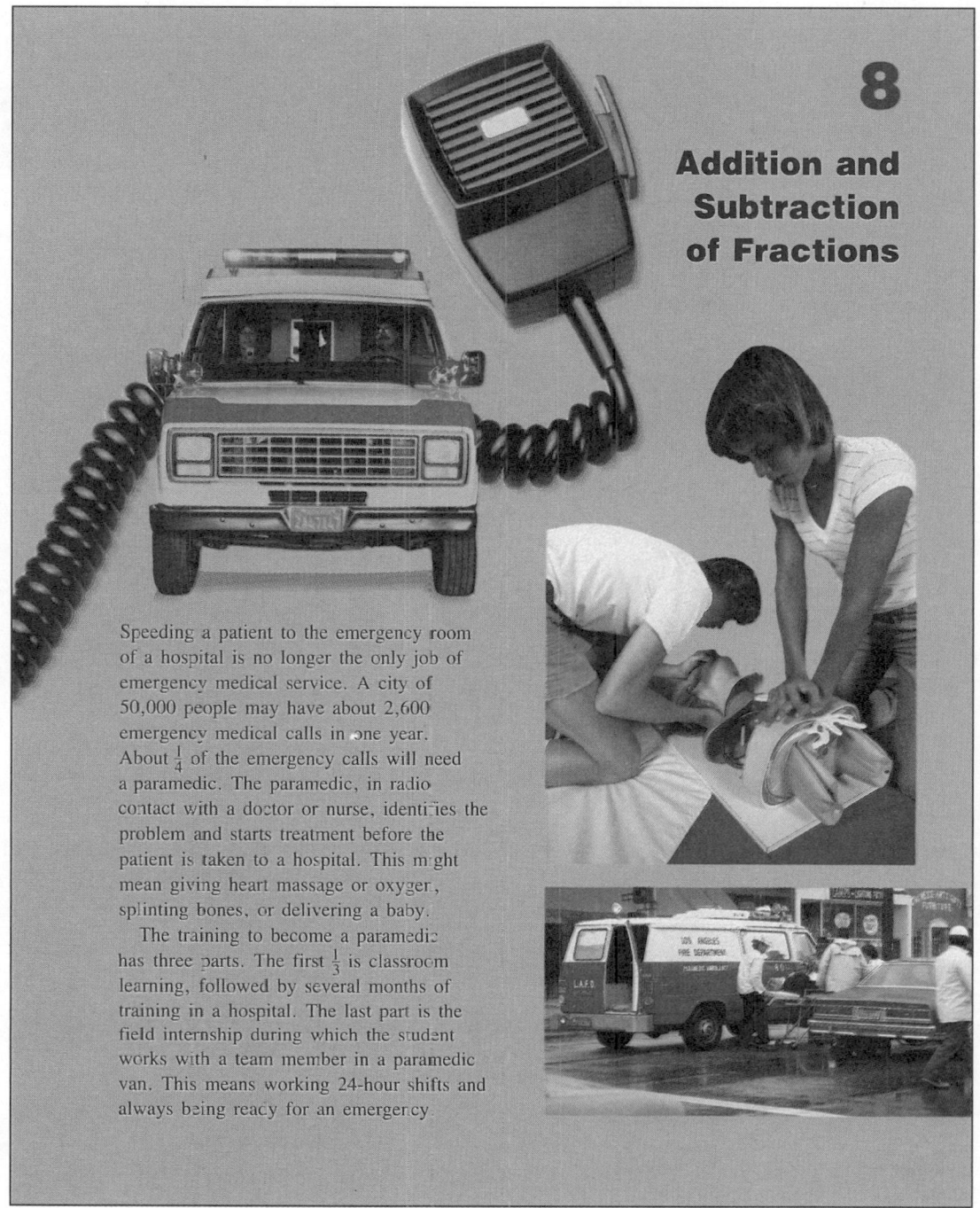

8

Addition and Subtraction of Fractions

Speeding a patient to the emergency room of a hospital is no longer the only job of emergency medical service. A city of 50,000 people may have about 2,600 emergency medical calls in one year. About $\frac{1}{4}$ of the emergency calls will need a paramedic. The paramedic, in radio contact with a doctor or nurse, identifies the problem and starts treatment before the patient is taken to a hospital. This might mean giving heart massage or oxygen, splinting bones, or delivering a baby.

The training to become a paramedic has three parts. The first $\frac{1}{3}$ is classroom learning, followed by several months of training in a hospital. The last part is the field internship during which the student works with a team member in a paramedic van. This means working 24-hour shifts and always being ready for an emergency.

Introducing the Chapter

Discussion Have students read the article about paramedics. Encourage discussion about the article and the accompanying pictures. Point out that Chapter 8 deals with the addition and subtraction of fractions. Ask students to identify the fractions in the article and tell what they represent.

Use this as an opportunity for students to create their own problems based on the data in the article. As you teach the chapter, you may wish to refer back to the article and pose the following questions.

Follow-Up Questions

After Page 199 In a city of about 50,000 people, there was a total of 2,590 medical calls in one year. Of these calls, 1,775 required first aid. What fraction of the calls required first aid? Write the answer in lowest terms. $\left(\frac{355}{518}\right)$

After Page 203 Out of a total of 2,150 medical calls, 675 required a paramedic. Did 1/3 or more of the calls require a paramedic? (No, $\frac{675}{2,150} < \frac{1}{3}$)

After Page 217 The average time it takes the paramedic van to respond is 5 minutes. After one call, a van's response time was $2\frac{7}{12}$ minutes. How much below the average was this time? ($2\frac{5}{12}$ minutes)

Quick Review Conduct an oral drill where students mentally find the product of three or more factors.

2 × 3 × 5 **30**   3 × 3 × 7 **63**   5 × 6 × 4 **120**   3 × 2 × 9 **54**
5 × 5 × 4 **100**   4 × 2 × 6 **48**   2 × 3 × 6 **36**

Lesson Focus To write fractions for parts of a region and parts of a set and to relate a fraction to division

Ideas for Getting Started

On the chalkboard, draw models such as the ones below. Ask students to name the fractional part that is shaded and to write the fraction on the chalkboard.

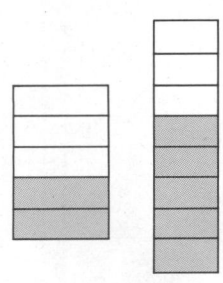

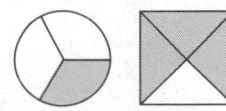

Then give students the names of fractions and have them draw models to illustrate the fractions.

Using Page 194

Lesson Development Have students read the material at the top of the page and examine the pictures. Point out that fractions can be used to show a part of a region, such as the part of the spinner that is blue, or a part of a set, such as the part of the markers that are yellow. Review with students the names for the terms of the fraction, the numerator and the denominator.

Direct students' attention to the middle of the page. Discuss the idea that a fraction can be related to division. Help students understand that 1 ÷ 3 means 1 unit divided into 3 parts. The answer, $\frac{1}{3}$, means that each part is $\frac{1}{3}$ of the whole unit. In the same way, if 2 units are divided into 3 parts, each part is $\frac{2}{3}$ of 1 whole unit.

Warm Up Have students give the answers to these exercises orally and assess their understanding of the basic concepts of fractions.

Fractions

We use fractions to describe a part of a region or a part of a set.

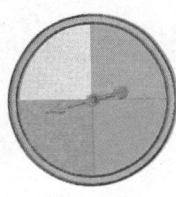

1 of **4** equal parts of the spinner is blue.

One fourth of the spinner is blue. $\frac{1}{4}$ ← numerator ← denominator

4 of the **7** markers are yellow.

Four sevenths of the markers are yellow. $\frac{4}{7}$ ← numerator ← denominator

A fraction can also be related to division.

1 whole unit is divided into **3** equal parts.

Each part is $\frac{1}{3}$ of **1** whole unit.

2 whole units can be divided into **3** equal parts.

Each part is $\frac{2}{3}$ of **1** whole unit.

1 ÷ 3   1 ÷ 3 = $\frac{1}{3}$ 2 ÷ 3   2 ÷ 3 = $\frac{2}{3}$

Warm Up

Name the fraction for the part of the region or set that is shaded.

1. 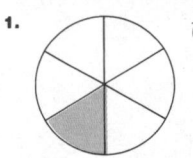 $\frac{1}{6}$

2. $\frac{3}{4}$

3. 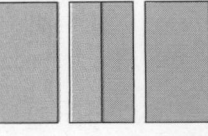 $\frac{2}{7}$

Give a fraction for each division exercise.

4. 1 ÷ 4 $\frac{1}{4}$ **5.** 2 ÷ 9 $\frac{2}{9}$ **6.** 1 ÷ 10 $\frac{1}{10}$

194

Follow Up

Reteaching

Fold strips of paper to illustrate fractions. To fold in thirds, loop the strip one and one half times and crease.

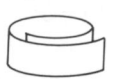

To fold in fifths, loop the strip two and one half times before creasing.

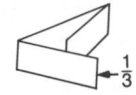

The strip can be folded into sixths by making 3 loops or by folding thirds and then halves.

Enrichment

Have students draw two equilateral triangles on isometric dot paper (TRB p. 282). Present the following problems.

1. Locate the midpoint of each side of a triangle. Draw three line segments to connect the three midpoints. What fractional part of the larger triangle is each small triangle? $\frac{1}{4}$

2. Find the midpoint of each side of the second triangle. Draw line segments from each vertex to the midpoint of the opposite side. What fractional part of the largest triangle is a small triangle? $\frac{1}{24}$

Assignment Guide			
	Minimum	Average	Extended
page 195	1–21	1–23	1–23

Write a fraction for the part of the region or set that is shaded.

1. 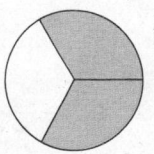 $\frac{2}{3}$

2. 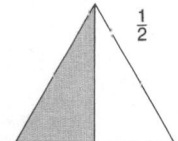 $\frac{1}{9}$

3. 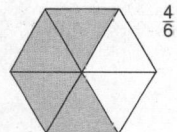 $\frac{1}{2}$

4. 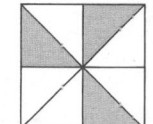 $\frac{4}{6}$

5. 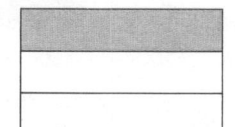 $\frac{3}{8}$

6.  $\frac{1}{3}$

7. 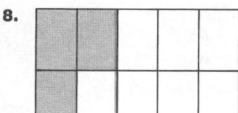 $\frac{4}{5}$

8. 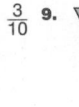 $\frac{3}{10}$

9. 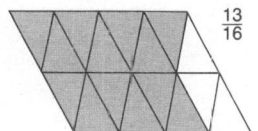 $\frac{13}{16}$

Write a fraction for each division exercise.

10. $2 \div 5$ $\frac{2}{5}$

11. 5 divided by 6 $\frac{5}{6}$

12. $9 \div 7$ $\frac{9}{7}$

13. 7 divided by 100 $\frac{7}{100}$

14. $8 \div 25$ $\frac{8}{25}$

15. $10 \div 16$ $\frac{10}{16}$

Write a division exercise for each fraction.

16. $\frac{5}{9}$ $5 \div 9$

17. $\frac{11}{12}$ $11 \div 12$

18. $\frac{5}{4}$ $5 \div 4$

19. $\frac{23}{100}$ $23 \div 100$

20. $\frac{7}{10}$ $7 \div 10$

21. $\frac{3}{2}$ $3 \div 2$

22. A game spinner is divided into 6 equal sections. What fractional part of the spinner is each section? $\frac{1}{6}$

23. There are 5 players. What fractional part of 8 game markers are left if each player picks 1 marker? $\frac{3}{8}$

24. Dana and Phil played 8 games and made a graph of the games they won. What fractional part of the games did Dana win? $\frac{5}{8}$

Games Won

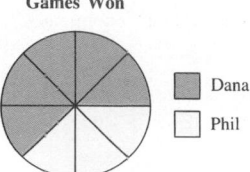

Dana
Phil

Using Page 195

Exercises 1–21 These exercises deal with basic concepts of fractions and should be review for most students. Assign the exercises as independent work and then conduct a class discussion concerning students' answers. Emphasize the idea brought out in exercises 10–21: a fraction can be thought of as the numerator divided by the denominator.

Ideas That Work

Special Education

Have students play "Fringo" to reinforce the basic fraction concepts reviewed in this lesson and provide practice in writing fractions. This latter goal particularly applies to the special students in your class who have weak motor or spatial organization skills. Students will need index cards labeled as shown, laminated game sheets with a fraction in each square, and crayons.

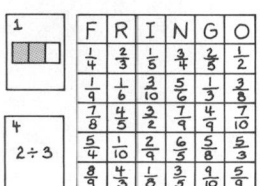

Students can work independently, in pairs, or in small groups. Each player in turn draws a card and states the fraction name. If the symbol is on their game sheets, players write over it with the crayon. The first player to mark four squares in a row, down, across, or diagonally wins.

Practice Supplement, page 73

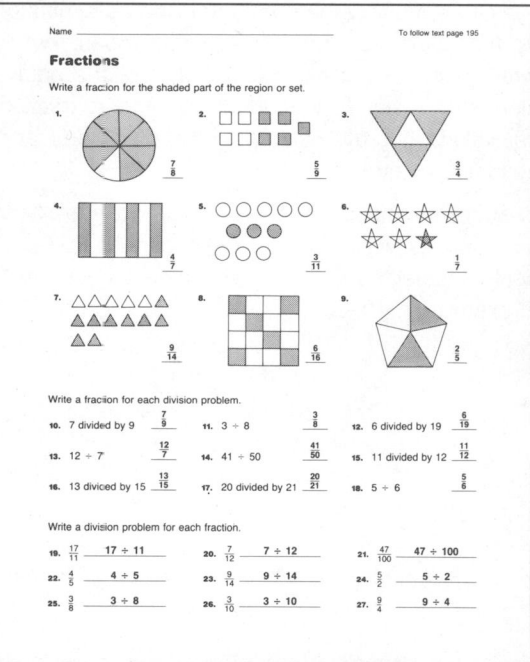

Lesson Focus To write fractions that are equivalent to a given fraction

Ideas for Getting Started

Introduce the idea of equivalent fractions by drawing these models on the chalkboard. Ask students what fraction is named by the shaded parts of each model.

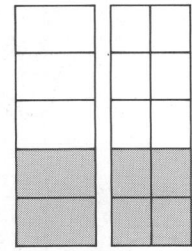

Notice with students that the same amount of each model is shaded. Explain that this shows that $\frac{2}{5}$ is equal to $\frac{4}{10}$.

Display the models below and ask students to name the fractions for each pair of pictures. Have them tell whether or not the fractions are equivalent.

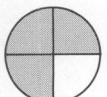 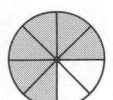 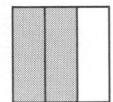 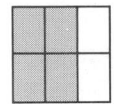

Using Page 196

Lesson Development After students read the material at the top of the page, direct their attention to the picture showing the cube's face. Point out that 6 out of 9 squares, or $\frac{6}{9}$, is *equivalent* to 2 out of 3 rows of squares, or $\frac{2}{3}$.

Next ask students to name two equivalent fractions to describe the part of the face that is not orange. They should observe that $\frac{3}{9}$ or $\frac{1}{3}$ of the face is not orange and that the fractions $\frac{3}{9}$ and $\frac{1}{3}$ are equivalent.

Show students that we can form equivalent fractions if we multiply the numerator and denominator by the same number. On the chalkboard, work through the examples, illustrating fractions equivalent to $\frac{2}{3}$. Then ask students to find a fraction equivalent to $\frac{2}{3}$ by multiplying the numerator and denominator by 5.

Warm Up These exercises can be done orally or assigned as written work. Make certain that students understand that the fractions are equivalent. In exercise 1, $\frac{5}{8} = \frac{15}{24}$.

Equivalent Fractions

Gordon is trying to make one face of the puzzle cube all orange. What part of the face is orange?

6 out of 9 squares are orange.

$\frac{6}{9}$ of the top face is orange.

2 out of 3 rows of squares are orange.

$\frac{2}{3}$ of the top face is orange.

Two fractions which name the same part of a region or the same part of a set are **equivalent fractions**.

$\frac{2}{3}$ and $\frac{6}{9}$ are equivalent fractions. $\frac{2}{3} = \frac{6}{9}$

Equivalent fractions can be formed by multiplying the numerator and denominator by the same number that is not zero.

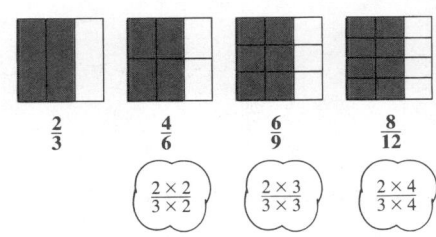

$$\frac{2}{3} \qquad \frac{4}{6} \qquad \frac{6}{9} \qquad \frac{8}{12}$$

$$\left(\frac{2 \times 2}{3 \times 2}\right) \quad \left(\frac{2 \times 3}{3 \times 3}\right) \quad \left(\frac{2 \times 4}{3 \times 4}\right)$$

Warm Up

Give the missing numerator or denominator.

1. $\frac{5 \times 3}{8 \times 3} = \frac{\text{⫿}}{24}$ **15**   2. $\frac{2 \times 4}{3 \times 4} = \frac{8}{\text{⫿}}$ **12**   3. $\frac{3 \times 10}{5 \times 10} = \frac{\text{⫿}}{50}$ **30**

Give the next two equivalent fractions.

4. $\frac{1}{2}, \frac{2}{4}, \frac{\text{⫿}}{\text{⫿}}, \frac{\text{⫿}}{\text{⫿}}$ **$\frac{3}{6}, \frac{4}{8}$**   5. $\frac{3}{4}, \frac{6}{8}, \frac{\text{⫿}}{\text{⫿}}, \frac{\text{⫿}}{\text{⫿}}$ **$\frac{9}{12}, \frac{12}{16}$**   6. $\frac{1}{3}, \frac{2}{6}, \frac{\text{⫿}}{\text{⫿}}, \frac{\text{⫿}}{\text{⫿}}$ **$\frac{3}{9}, \frac{4}{12}$**

196

Follow Up

Reteaching

Use drawings of fractional parts of regions to illustrate equivalent fractions. Ask students what part of the region is shaded. Then draw a line as shown and ask what part of the region is shaded.

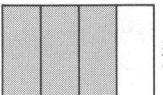 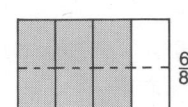

Emphasize there are 2 times as many parts and 2 times as many shaded parts. Show that an equivalent fraction is formed when the numerator and denominator are multiplied by the same number.

Enrichment

Write the following exercises on the chalkboard. Have students find the missing numerators and denominators.

1. $\frac{2}{3} = \frac{\boxed{4}}{6} = \frac{8}{\boxed{12}} = \frac{\boxed{16}}{24}$

2. $\frac{1}{6} = \frac{\boxed{2}}{12} = \frac{\boxed{4}}{24} = \frac{8}{\boxed{48}}$

3. $\frac{\boxed{3}}{5} = \frac{\boxed{9}}{15} = \frac{18}{30} = \frac{36}{\boxed{60}}$

4. $\frac{\boxed{3}}{5} = \frac{6}{\boxed{10}} = \frac{15}{25} = \frac{\boxed{18}}{30}$

Assignment Guide			
	Minimum	Average	Extended
page 197	1–28	1–34	1–35 odd, TM

Write the missing numerator or denominator.

1. $\frac{2 \times 4}{3 \times 4} = \frac{\text{\tiny▨}}{12}$ 8   2. $\frac{5 \times 5}{6 \times 5} = \frac{25}{\text{\tiny▨}}$ 30   3. $\frac{3 \times 6}{8 \times 6} = \frac{\text{\tiny▨}}{48}$ 18   4. $\frac{1 \times 9}{2 \times 9} = \frac{9}{\text{\tiny▨}}$ 18   5. $\frac{4 \times 6}{7 \times 6} = \frac{\text{\tiny▨}}{42}$ 24

6. $\frac{3}{4} = \frac{\text{\tiny▨}}{16}$ 12   7. $\frac{3}{5} = \frac{21}{\text{\tiny▨}}$ 35   8. $\frac{3}{10} = \frac{\text{\tiny▨}}{30}$ 9   9. $\frac{1}{4} = \frac{\text{\tiny▨}}{16}$ 4   10. $\frac{2}{9} = \frac{\text{\tiny▨}}{45}$ 10

11. $\frac{5}{12} = \frac{\text{\tiny▨}}{60}$ 25   12. $\frac{8}{9} = \frac{16}{\text{\tiny▨}}$ 18   13. $\frac{4}{15} = \frac{\text{\tiny▨}}{45}$ 12   14. $\frac{2}{7} = \frac{\text{\tiny▨}}{70}$ 20   15. $\frac{7}{12} = \frac{21}{\text{\tiny▨}}$ 36

16. $\frac{3}{4} = \frac{\text{\tiny▨}}{32}$ 24   17. $\frac{1}{3} = \frac{\text{\tiny▨}}{48}$ 16   18. $\frac{3}{16} = \frac{27}{\text{\tiny▨}}$ 144   19. $\frac{5}{8} = \frac{\text{\tiny▨}}{64}$ 40   20. $\frac{19}{20} = \frac{\text{\tiny▨}}{100}$ 95

Write the next three equivalent fractions.

21. $\frac{3}{8}, \frac{6}{16}, \frac{9}{24}, \frac{\text{\tiny▨}}{\text{\tiny▨}}, \frac{\text{\tiny▨}}{\text{\tiny▨}}, \frac{\text{\tiny▨}}{\text{\tiny▨}}$ $\frac{12}{32}, \frac{15}{40}, \frac{18}{48}$

22. $\frac{1}{10}, \frac{2}{20}, \frac{3}{30}, \frac{\text{\tiny▨}}{\text{\tiny▨}}, \frac{\text{\tiny▨}}{\text{\tiny▨}}, \frac{\text{\tiny▨}}{\text{\tiny▨}}$ $\frac{4}{40}, \frac{5}{50}, \frac{6}{60}$

23. $\frac{5}{6}, \frac{10}{12}, \frac{15}{18}, \frac{\text{\tiny▨}}{\text{\tiny▨}}, \frac{\text{\tiny▨}}{\text{\tiny▨}}, \frac{\text{\tiny▨}}{\text{\tiny▨}}$ $\frac{20}{24}, \frac{25}{30}, \frac{30}{36}$

Write an equivalent fraction with a denominator of 24 for each fraction.

24. $\frac{1}{2}$ $\frac{12}{24}$ 25. $\frac{3}{8}$ $\frac{9}{24}$ 26. $\frac{3}{4}$ $\frac{18}{24}$ 27. $\frac{5}{6}$ $\frac{20}{24}$ 28. $\frac{11}{12}$ $\frac{22}{24}$

Write an equivalent fraction with a denominator of 100 for each fraction.

29. $\frac{3}{5}$ $\frac{60}{100}$ 30. $\frac{9}{10}$ $\frac{90}{100}$ 31. $\frac{7}{20}$ $\frac{35}{100}$ 32. $\frac{3}{25}$ $\frac{12}{100}$ 33. $\frac{3}{2}$ $\frac{150}{100}$

34. Keiko made 3 of the 9 small squares on one face of the cube yellow. How many ninths of the face is yellow? $\frac{3}{9}$

35. One sixth of the small squares on the puzzle cube are orange. There are 54 small squares in all. How many 54ths of the small squares are orange? $\frac{9}{54}$

THINK MATH

Fraction Concepts

What part of the large square is shaded? $\frac{3}{8}$

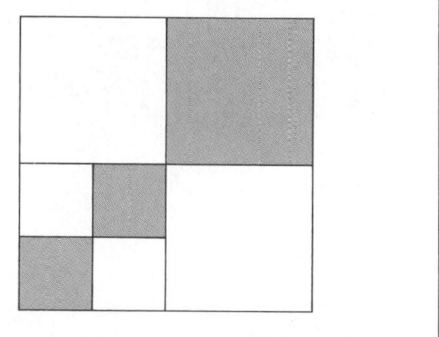

More Practice, page 428, Set A

Using Page 197

Exercises 6–20 Before assigning these exercises, work through an example with the class. Write $\frac{4}{6} = \frac{\text{\tiny—}}{18}$ on the chalkboard. Ask what we multiply times 6 to get 18. Remind students that the numerator and denominator must be multiplied by the same number. Since 6 was multiplied by 3 to get 18, 4 must be multiplied by 3 to get the missing numerator.

Think Math This problem can be solved by tracing the figure on paper and adding lines to determine what fractional part of the square is shaded. Once the square is divided into sixteenths, it is easy to see that $\frac{6}{16}$, or $\frac{3}{8}$, of the large square is shaded.

More Practice, page 428, Set A

Reteaching Supplement, page 57   **Enrichment Supplement,** page 57   **Practice Supplement,** page 74

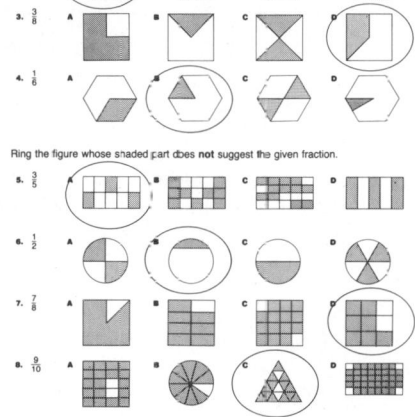

Quick Review Display the numbers below. Point to different combinations of three numbers and have students order them from least to greatest.

4,617   4,617.03   4,617.003   4,636.89   4,636.9

Lesson Focus To write a fraction in lowest terms

Ideas for Getting Started

To prepare students for this lesson, review how to find the GCF of two numbers. Have one student write all the factors of 12 on the chalkboard while another student writes all the factors of 18. Then have them circle the factors common to both numbers. Have the class name the greatest common factor.

Next have students illustrate equivalent fractions by folding paper. Ask them to show $\frac{2}{4}$ is the same as $\frac{1}{2}$, $\frac{2}{6}$ is the same as $\frac{1}{3}$, and $\frac{4}{8}$ is the same as $\frac{1}{2}$.

Using Page 198

Lesson Development After students read the material at the top of the page, discuss the meaning of lowest-terms fraction. Explain that a fraction is in lowest terms if 1 is the only number that will divide both the numerator and denominator with 0 remainder.

On the chalkboard, work through the steps shown to find the lowest-terms fraction for $\frac{24}{60}$. Point out that when this method is used, sometimes the numerator and denominator must be divided by more than one number to find the lowest-terms fraction. Show students that dividing the numerator and denominator by the GCF always gives the lowest-terms fraction. Ask students to compare the method used in this lesson to the method used in the previous lesson. They should observe that in the previous lesson both terms of the fraction were multiplied by the same number, while in this lesson both terms are divided by the same number to get equivalent fractions.

Other Examples In the third example, the numerator and denominator are relatively prime, so the fraction is in lowest terms.

Warm Up Use these exercises to assess students' understanding of lowest-terms fractions. Make sure students continue to divide by a common factor until the GCF of the numerator and denominator is 1.

Lowest-Terms Fractions

Renee skied a cross-country course in 24 min, or $\frac{24}{60}$ of an hour. What is the **lowest-terms fraction** for $\frac{24}{60}$?

A fraction is in lowest terms if the greatest common factor (GCF) of the numerator and denominator is 1.

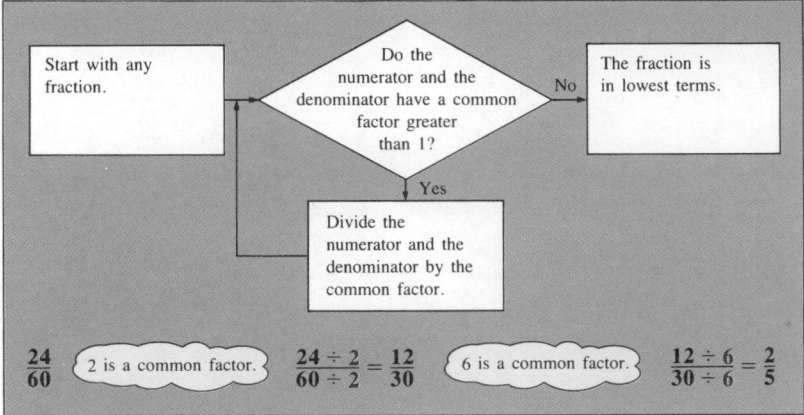

The lowest-terms fraction for $\frac{24}{60}$ is $\frac{2}{5}$.

Dividing by the GCF can save steps.

$$\frac{24}{60} = \frac{24 \div 12}{60 \div 12} = \frac{2}{5}$$

Other Examples

$$\frac{5}{15} = \frac{5 \div 5}{15 \div 5} = \frac{1}{3} \qquad \frac{18}{27} = \frac{18 \div 9}{27 \div 9} = \frac{2}{3} \qquad \frac{11}{12} \quad \boxed{GCF = 1} \quad \frac{11}{12} \text{ is in lowest terms.}$$

Warm Up

Give each fraction in lowest terms.

1. $\frac{6}{8}$ $\frac{3}{4}$ 2. $\frac{12}{18}$ $\frac{2}{3}$ 3. $\frac{35}{50}$ $\frac{7}{10}$ 4. $\frac{24}{28}$ $\frac{6}{7}$

5. $\frac{20}{100}$ $\frac{1}{5}$ 6. $\frac{8}{9}$ $\frac{8}{9}$ 7. $\frac{12}{16}$ $\frac{3}{4}$ 8. $\frac{56}{64}$ $\frac{7}{8}$

198

Follow Up

Reteaching

Begin with a fraction such as $\frac{12}{18}$. Ask students to find common factors. "Is 2 a factor of 12?" (yes) "Is 2 a factor of 18?" (yes) Write $\frac{12}{18} = \frac{12 \div 2}{18 \div 2} = \frac{6}{9}$.

Repeat the questions with 6 and 9. Since 2 is not a factor of 9, try the next prime number, 3. "Is 3 a factor of 6?" (yes) "Is 3 a factor of 9?" (yes) Write $\frac{6}{9} = \frac{6 \div 3}{9 \div 3} = \frac{2}{3}$.

Next focus on the factors of 12 and 18 and find the greatest common factor. Show that dividing by the GCF can save steps. Write $\frac{12}{18} = \frac{12 \div 6}{18 \div 6} = \frac{2}{3}$.

Enrichment

Write the following sets of four numbers on the chalkboard. Have students use pairs of numbers to write as many proper fractions in lowest terms as possible.

1. 4, 5, 8, 16 $\frac{4}{5}, \frac{5}{8}, \frac{5}{16}$
2. 2, 3, 4, 9 $\frac{2}{3}, \frac{3}{4}, \frac{2}{9}, \frac{4}{9}$
3. 2, 4, 5, 10 $\frac{2}{5}, \frac{4}{5}$
4. 2, 3, 5, 7 $\frac{2}{3}, \frac{2}{5}, \frac{3}{5}, \frac{2}{7}, \frac{3}{7}, \frac{5}{7}$

Assignment Guide			
	Minimum	Average	Extended
page 199	1–31, SK	1–31, 34, SK	1–31 odd, 32–34, SK

Write each fraction in lowest terms.

1. $\frac{5}{10}$ $\frac{1}{2}$　　2. $\frac{8}{12}$ $\frac{2}{3}$　　3. $\frac{3}{9}$ $\frac{1}{3}$　　4. $\frac{3}{12}$ $\frac{1}{4}$　　5. $\frac{10}{24}$ $\frac{5}{12}$

6. $\frac{8}{14}$ $\frac{4}{7}$　　7. $\frac{6}{15}$ $\frac{2}{5}$　　8. $\frac{25}{60}$ $\frac{5}{12}$　　9. $\frac{6}{18}$ $\frac{1}{3}$　　10. $\frac{18}{36}$ $\frac{1}{2}$

11. $\frac{6}{24}$ $\frac{1}{4}$　　12. $\frac{16}{30}$ $\frac{8}{15}$　　13. $\frac{32}{36}$ $\frac{8}{9}$　　14. $\frac{40}{60}$ $\frac{2}{3}$　　15. $\frac{75}{100}$ $\frac{3}{4}$

16. $\frac{15}{30}$ $\frac{1}{2}$　　17. $\frac{250}{1,000}$ $\frac{1}{4}$　　18. $\frac{2}{24}$ $\frac{1}{12}$　　19. $\frac{30}{100}$ $\frac{3}{10}$　　20. $\frac{8}{10}$ $\frac{4}{5}$

21. $\frac{750}{1,000}$ $\frac{3}{4}$　　22. $\frac{48}{100}$ $\frac{12}{25}$　　23. $\frac{20}{24}$ $\frac{5}{6}$　　24. $\frac{560}{1,000}$ $\frac{14}{25}$　　25. $\frac{15}{48}$ $\frac{5}{16}$

26. $\frac{27}{81}$ $\frac{1}{3}$　　27. $\frac{42}{48}$ $\frac{7}{8}$　　28. $\frac{120}{150}$ $\frac{4}{5}$　　29. $\frac{55}{75}$ $\frac{11}{15}$　　30. $\frac{48}{96}$ $\frac{1}{2}$

31. Marj skied 200 yards (yd) of a 400-yard course. What fraction of the course did she ski? $\frac{1}{2}$

32. Brent finished a race in 56 s. What fraction of one minute is this? $\frac{14}{15}$

33. A ski area was open for skiing 13 weeks one year. About what fractional part of the year was this? $\frac{1}{4}$

34. **DATA BANK** What was the time for the winner of the 500-meter speed skating competition in the 1964 Winter Olympics? What was the time as a fraction of a minute? (See page 415.) 45.0 s; $\frac{3}{4}$

SKILLKEEPER

Find the GCF of each pair of numbers.

1. 35, 18 1　　2. 24, 32 8　　3. 20, 30 10　　4. 30, 45 15　　5. 12, 18 6

6. 80, 200 40　　7. 51, 39 3　　8. 56, 38 2　　9. 48, 80 16　　10. 8, 27 1

Find the LCM of each pair of numbers.

11. 7, 10 70　　12. 16, 24 48　　13. 25, 10 50　　14. 36, 48 144　　15. 8, 12 24

16. 30, 45 90　　17. 40, 60 120　　18. 49, 21 147　　19. 8, 6 24　　20. 12, 15 60

More Practice, page 428, Set B

Using Page 199

Exercises 1–30 Make sure students understand that we can find the lowest-terms fraction by repeatedly dividing by a factor of both the numerator and denominator, or by finding the GCF and simply dividing both numerator and denominator by that number.

Skillkeeper These skills were originally taught in Chapter 7.

More Practice, page 428, Set B

Reteaching Supplement, page 58　　　**Enrichment Supplement,** page 58　　　**Practice Supplement,** page 75

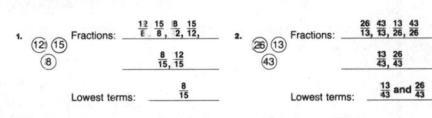

Quick Review Have students find the measure of the complement to each angle.

| 15° **75°** | 42° **48°** | 85° **5°** | 26° **64°** |
| 30° **60°** | 65° **25°** | 72° **18°** | 45° **45°** |

Ideas for Getting Started

To introduce the idea of improper fractions and mixed numbers, draw 7 half circles on the chalkboard. Ask students to tell how many circles could be formed.

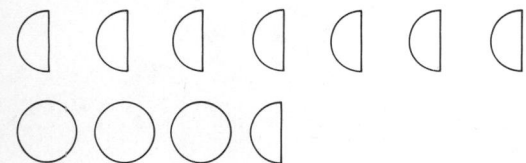

Point out that $\frac{7}{2}$ is another name for $3\frac{1}{2}$.

Ask how many fourths are in $2\frac{3}{4}$. Have a volunteer draw a picture to show the answer. Ask another student to draw a picture showing the number of thirds in $4\frac{1}{3}$.

Using Page 200

Lesson Development Have students read the material at the top of the page. Point out that 5 cans of food divided 3 ways is $\frac{5}{3}$. Explain that $\frac{5}{3}$ is an *improper fraction* because the numerator is larger than the denominator.

Introduce the term *mixed number*. On the chalkboard, work through the steps in the first set of direction boxes to show the process of changing an improper fraction to a mixed number. Identify the whole number part of the quotient. Tell students that the remainder is the number of thirds or the fraction part left after finding the whole number part.

With students, work through the second set of direction boxes showing the steps in changing a mixed number to an improper fraction. Note that the first step gives the number of fourths in 3 wholes. Explain that 1 more fourth is then added to get a total of $\frac{13}{4}$.

Other Examples The first and second examples show that sometimes an improper fraction forms a whole number. This is true when there is no remainder after dividing the numerator by the denominator. In the fourth example, the fraction part of the mixed number can be reduced.

Warm Up You may wish to require students to give their answers in lowest terms. The fractions in exercises 4 and 5 can be reduced either before or after finding the mixed number.

Improper Fractions and Mixed Numbers

Judy keeps a record of the food she feeds each animal in a pet store. She uses 5 cans of dog food to feed 3 puppies.

Since the amount is $5 \div 3$, she can write a fraction. $\frac{5}{3}$ is an **improper fraction**.

We can use the idea that $\frac{5}{3}$ means $5 \div 3$ to write $\frac{5}{3}$ as a **mixed number**.

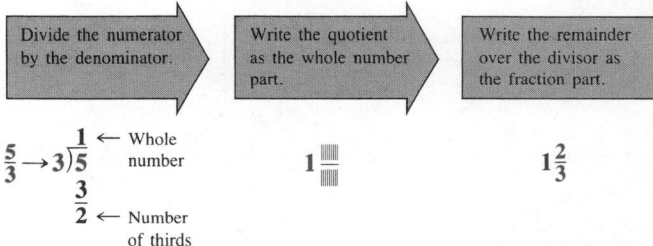

| Divide the numerator by the denominator. | Write the quotient as the whole number part. | Write the remainder over the divisor as the fraction part. |

$$\frac{5}{3} \rightarrow 3\overline{)5} \begin{array}{l} 1 \leftarrow \text{Whole} \\ \text{number} \\ 3 \\ \overline{2} \leftarrow \text{Number} \\ \text{of thirds} \end{array} \qquad 1\frac{\blacksquare}{\blacksquare} \qquad 1\frac{2}{3}$$

Mixed numbers like $3\frac{1}{4}$ can be written as improper fractions.

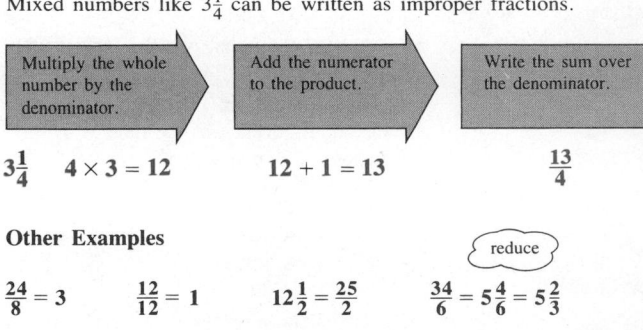

| Multiply the whole number by the denominator. | Add the numerator to the product. | Write the sum over the denominator. |

$$3\frac{1}{4} \qquad 4 \times 3 = 12 \qquad 12 + 1 = 13 \qquad \frac{13}{4}$$

Other Examples

$$\frac{24}{8} = 3 \qquad \frac{12}{12} = 1 \qquad 12\frac{1}{2} = \frac{25}{2} \qquad \frac{34}{6} = 5\frac{4}{6} = 5\frac{2}{3}$$ (reduce)

Warm Up

Write each improper fraction as a mixed number or a whole number.

1. $\frac{11}{3}$ $3\frac{2}{3}$ 2. $\frac{16}{4}$ 4   3. $\frac{23}{5}$ $4\frac{3}{5}$ 4. $\frac{22}{8}$ $2\frac{3}{4}$ 5. $\frac{40}{12}$ $3\frac{1}{3}$

Write each mixed number as an improper fraction.

6. $3\frac{5}{6}$ $\frac{23}{6}$ 7. $2\frac{1}{4}$ $\frac{9}{4}$ 8. $5\frac{2}{3}$ $\frac{17}{3}$ 9. $7\frac{5}{8}$ $\frac{61}{8}$ 10. $2\frac{3}{16}$ $\frac{35}{16}$

200

Follow Up

Reteaching

Show students that $\frac{11}{4}$ can be written as $\frac{4}{4} + \frac{4}{4} + \frac{3}{4} = 1 + 1 + \frac{3}{4} = 2\frac{3}{4}$. Use models to demonstrate the process.

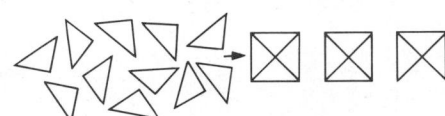

Explain that dividing by the denominator gives the same result.

$$11 \div 4 = 2 \text{ R3} \longrightarrow 2\frac{3}{4}$$

Present a similar demonstration of changing a mixed number to an improper fraction.

Enrichment

Display the number lines below and have students give the improper fractions that go with points A, B, C, D, E, and F.

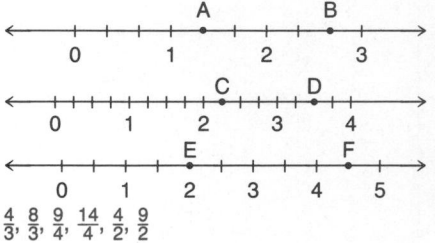

$$\frac{4}{3}, \frac{8}{3}, \frac{9}{4}, \frac{14}{4}, \frac{4}{2}, \frac{9}{2}$$

Assignment Guide			
	Minimum	Average	Extended
page 201	1–41	1–41, 46–49	1–39 odd, 41–52

Write each improper fraction as a mixed number or a whole number.

1. $\frac{7}{4}$ $1\frac{3}{4}$ 2. $\frac{9}{8}$ $1\frac{1}{8}$ 3. $\frac{13}{5}$ $2\frac{3}{5}$ 4. $\frac{14}{6}$ $2\frac{1}{3}$ 5. $\frac{6}{2}$ 3

6. $\frac{15}{8}$ $1\frac{7}{8}$ 7. $\frac{21}{3}$ 7 8. $\frac{18}{9}$ 2 9. $\frac{24}{5}$ $4\frac{4}{5}$ 10. $\frac{33}{12}$ $2\frac{3}{4}$

11. $\frac{60}{15}$ 4 12. $\frac{17}{4}$ $4\frac{1}{4}$ 13. $\frac{100}{100}$ 1 14. $\frac{56}{8}$ 7 15. $\frac{27}{3}$ 9

16. $\frac{80}{10}$ 8 17. $\frac{64}{10}$ $6\frac{2}{5}$ 18. $\frac{15}{4}$ $3\frac{3}{4}$ 19. $\frac{16}{12}$ $1\frac{1}{3}$ 20. $\frac{30}{15}$ 2

Write each mixed number as an improper fraction.

21. $2\frac{3}{4}$ $\frac{11}{4}$ 22. $7\frac{1}{3}$ $\frac{22}{3}$ 23. $9\frac{5}{8}$ $\frac{77}{8}$ 24. $10\frac{1}{8}$ $\frac{81}{8}$ 25. $6\frac{4}{5}$ $\frac{34}{5}$

26. $7\frac{3}{8}$ $\frac{59}{8}$ 27. $6\frac{5}{24}$ $\frac{149}{24}$ 28. $5\frac{7}{12}$ $\frac{67}{12}$ 29. $4\frac{3}{10}$ $\frac{43}{10}$ 30. $1\frac{1}{8}$ $\frac{9}{8}$

31. $12\frac{2}{3}$ $\frac{38}{3}$ 32. $3\frac{7}{100}$ $\frac{307}{100}$ 33. $2\frac{27}{100}$ $\frac{227}{100}$ 34. $3\frac{15}{16}$ $\frac{63}{16}$ 35. $6\frac{7}{12}$ $\frac{79}{12}$

36. $15\frac{23}{60}$ $\frac{923}{60}$ 37. $15\frac{3}{10}$ $\frac{153}{10}$ 38. $10\frac{2}{3}$ $\frac{32}{3}$ 39. $7\frac{7}{24}$ $\frac{175}{24}$ 40. $13\frac{2}{3}$ $\frac{41}{3}$

41. Judy used $3\frac{1}{2}$ bags of dog food. Write an improper fraction for this mixed number. $\frac{7}{2}$

42. How many cans of food were fed to each hamster? Write the answer as a mixed number. $1\frac{3}{4}$

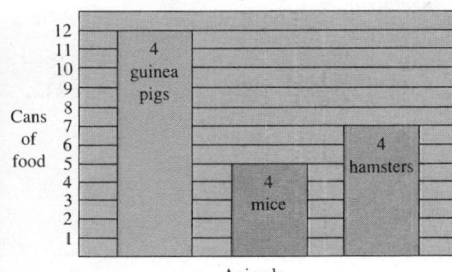

Animals

Write each mixed number as an improper fraction.

43. $27\frac{5}{8}$ $\frac{221}{8}$ 44. $176\frac{7}{16}$ $\frac{2,823}{16}$ 45. $92\frac{37}{64}$ $\frac{5,925}{64}$ 46. $101\frac{100}{101}$ $\frac{10,301}{101}$ 47. $2,974\frac{77}{127}$ $\frac{377,775}{127}$

Write each improper fraction as a mixed number or as a whole number.

48. $\frac{1,825}{175}$ $10\frac{3}{7}$ 49. $\frac{516}{387}$ $1\frac{1}{3}$ 50. $\frac{6,555}{228}$ $28\frac{3}{4}$ 51. $\frac{7,921}{801}$ $9\frac{8}{9}$ 52. $\frac{76,323}{5,871}$ 13

More Practice, page 428, Set C

Using Page 201

Exercises 1–52 Note that showing answers as lowest-terms fractions is not required, but you may wish to make that requirement, depending on the ability of students.

To answer the question in exercise 42, students need to obtain data from the graph. The graph shows that 7 cans of food were fed to 4 hamsters.

More Practice, page 428, Set C

Reteaching Supplement, page 59

Enrichment Supplement, page 59

Practice Supplement, page 76

Quick Review Have students write the standard numeral.

5.4×10^5 540,000 3.91×10^4 39,100 7.06×10^6 7,060,000

2.3×10^{10} 23,000,000,000 3.8×10^2 380 5.81×10^3 5,810

Lesson Focus To compare fractions

Ideas for Getting Started

Write these pairs of numbers on the chalkboard. Review how to find the least common multiple with these examples.

2, 3   6, 4   6, 9   5, 12

Provide students with the following exercises to practice finding equivalent fractions. Have them supply the missing numbers.

$\frac{2}{5} = \frac{}{15}$ $\frac{3}{4} = \frac{}{16}$ $\frac{2}{3} = \frac{}{9}$ $\frac{1}{6} = \frac{}{12}$

Using Page 202

Motivational Problem Read the introductory problem with students. Have them restate the question and identify the data needed to solve the problem. Point out that the resolution will pass if $\frac{5}{8}$ is equal to or greater than $\frac{2}{3}$, so our plan is to compare fractions.

Lesson Development On the chalkboard, work through the steps in the instruction boxes, comparing $\frac{5}{8}$ and $\frac{2}{3}$. Notice with students that in the second step the least common multiple of 8 and 3 is used for the common denominator. Explain that after writing equivalent fractions with a common denominator, we can compare the fractions by comparing numerators.

Other Examples In the second example, the common denominator is a denominator of one of the given fractions. In the third example, the given fractions have the same denominator. The last example shows how to compare mixed numbers.

Warm Up Have students work these exercises independently. Provide an opportunity for checking answers and discussing any difficulties that may have arisen.

Comparing Fractions

In the United Nations, a resolution will pass when at least $\frac{2}{3}$ of the nations present vote in favor of the resolution. If $\frac{5}{8}$ of the nations present vote in favor of a resolution, will the resolution pass?

The resolution will pass if $\frac{5}{8}$ is equal to or greater than $\frac{2}{3}$. We need to compare fractions.

Look at the denominators. →	Write equivalent fractions with a common denominator. →	Compare the numerators. →	The fractions compare the same way the numerators compare.
$\frac{5}{8}$ $\frac{2}{3}$ 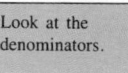 Unlike denominators	$\frac{5}{8} = \frac{15}{24}$ $\frac{2}{3} = \frac{16}{24}$	$15 < 16$	$\frac{15}{24} < \frac{16}{24}$ so $\frac{5}{8} < \frac{2}{3}$

Since $\frac{5}{8}$ is less than $\frac{2}{3}$, the resolution will not pass.

Other Examples

$\frac{7}{12} = \frac{14}{24}$
$\frac{5}{8} = \frac{15}{24}$ $\frac{5}{8} > \frac{7}{12}$

$\frac{1}{4} = \frac{4}{16}$
$\frac{5}{16} = \frac{5}{16}$ $\frac{1}{4} < \frac{5}{16}$

$\frac{11}{16} < \frac{13}{16}$
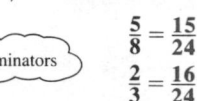 Same denominators

To compare mixed numbers, compare the whole numbers, then compare the fractions if necessary.

$3\frac{1}{2} > 2\frac{3}{4}$
$3 > 2$

$4\frac{2}{3} = 4\frac{8}{12}$
$4\frac{3}{4} = 4\frac{9}{12}$ } $4\frac{2}{3} < 4\frac{3}{4}$

Warm Up

Compare the numbers. Write $>$ or $<$ for each 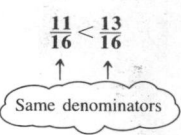.

1. $\frac{5}{8}$ ● $\frac{3}{4}$ $<$ 2. $\frac{3}{4}$ ● $\frac{9}{16}$ $>$ 3. $\frac{3}{5}$ ● $\frac{7}{12}$ $>$ 4. $\frac{7}{10}$ ● $\frac{11}{15}$ $<$

5. $2\frac{1}{3}$ ● $2\frac{1}{4}$ $>$ 6. $4\frac{1}{10}$ ● $3\frac{9}{10}$ $>$ 7. $1\frac{5}{6}$ ● $1\frac{4}{7}$ $>$ 8. $\frac{15}{16}$ ● 1 $<$

202

Follow Up

Reteaching

Ask students to tell which is greater, $\frac{1}{2}$ or $\frac{2}{3}$. Show how to determine the answer by using a region marked into sixths.

$\frac{1}{2} = \frac{3}{6}$

$\frac{2}{3} = \frac{4}{6}$

Explain that the fractions were changed to equivalent fractions with a common denominator. Point out that fractions having the same denominator can be compared by simply comparing numerators. Since $\frac{4}{6} > \frac{3}{6}$, $\frac{2}{3} > \frac{1}{2}$.

Enrichment

Display the following sets of fractions. Have students order the fractions from least to greatest.

1. $\frac{1}{16}, \frac{1}{8}, \frac{1}{2}, \frac{1}{4}, \frac{1}{16}, \frac{1}{8}, \frac{1}{4}, \frac{1}{2}$

2. $\frac{3}{16}, \frac{1}{8}, \frac{3}{4}, \frac{1}{2}, \frac{1}{8}, \frac{3}{16}, \frac{1}{2}, \frac{3}{4}$

3. $\frac{2}{3}, \frac{2}{5}, \frac{2}{9}, \frac{2}{7}, \frac{2}{9}, \frac{2}{7}, \frac{2}{5}, \frac{2}{3}$

4. $\frac{1}{5}, \frac{3}{10}, \frac{2}{3}, \frac{4}{5}, \frac{1}{5}, \frac{3}{10}, \frac{2}{3}, \frac{4}{5}$

5. $\frac{5}{7}, \frac{5}{9}, \frac{5}{3}, \frac{5}{8}, \frac{5}{9}, \frac{5}{8}, \frac{5}{7}, \frac{5}{3}$

Assignment Guide	Minimum	Average	Extended
page 203	1–16, 25–33	1–33, TM	2–34 even, TM

Compare the fractions. Write > or < for each ●.

1. $\frac{7}{8}$ ● $\frac{13}{16}$ >
2. $\frac{3}{7}$ ● $\frac{1}{2}$ <
3. $\frac{7}{9}$ ● $\frac{5}{6}$ <
4. $\frac{7}{12}$ ● $\frac{3}{4}$ <

5. $\frac{2}{15}$ ● $\frac{1}{5}$ <
6. $\frac{6}{7}$ ● $\frac{23}{28}$ >
7. $\frac{5}{12}$ ● $\frac{1}{2}$ <
8. $\frac{8}{15}$ ● $\frac{2}{5}$ >

9. $\frac{21}{24}$ ● $\frac{3}{4}$ >
10. $\frac{7}{20}$ ● $\frac{2}{5}$ <
11. $\frac{5}{16}$ ● $\frac{3}{8}$ <
12. $\frac{5}{8}$ ● $\frac{25}{50}$ >

13. $\frac{7}{34}$ ● $\frac{1}{6}$ >
14. $\frac{7}{10}$ ● $\frac{33}{38}$ <
15. $\frac{17}{100}$ ● $\frac{7}{36}$ <
16. $\frac{39}{100}$ ● $\frac{11}{36}$ >

17. $\frac{13}{16}$ ● $\frac{7}{9}$ >
18. $\frac{4}{7}$ ● $\frac{13}{20}$ <
19. $\frac{13}{47}$ ● $\frac{5}{12}$ <
20. $\frac{23}{32}$ ● $\frac{17}{21}$ <

21. $\frac{17}{49}$ ● $\frac{9}{28}$ >
22. $\frac{33}{98}$ ● $\frac{7}{24}$ >
23. $\frac{12}{83}$ ● $\frac{7}{30}$ <
24. $\frac{6}{51}$ ● $\frac{4}{39}$ >

Compare the mixed numbers. Write > or < for each ●.

25. $1\frac{4}{5}$ ● $1\frac{1}{2}$ >
26. $7\frac{1}{2}$ ● $5\frac{2}{3}$ >
27. $3\frac{1}{3}$ ● $3\frac{1}{4}$ >
28. $6\frac{9}{10}$ ● $6\frac{3}{4}$ >

29. 2 ● $2\frac{1}{10}$ <
30. $6\frac{7}{8}$ ● $6\frac{11}{12}$ <
31. $5\frac{3}{10}$ ● $5\frac{27}{100}$ >
32. $4\frac{4}{9}$ ● $4\frac{7}{15}$ <

33. If $\frac{7}{12}$ of the nations present voted to send aid to the victims of a flood, would the vote pass by a $\frac{2}{3}$ majority?

no, $\frac{7}{12} < \frac{2}{3}$

34.

Nations Present	Yes Vote	No Vote
19	12	5

Would the vote pass by a $\frac{2}{3}$ majority?

no, $\frac{12}{19} < \frac{2}{3}$

▓ THINK MATH ▓

Comparing Fractions

You can compare two fractions using a "cross-products" method.

first (4 ✕ 5) → $15 \times 5 = 75$
second (15 ✕ 18) → $4 \times 18 = 72$ $72 < 75$

The product for the first step is less than the product for the second step,

so $\frac{4}{15} < \frac{5}{18}$.

Use the cross-products method and a calculator to compare $\frac{267}{489}$ with each fraction below.

1. $\frac{578}{997}$

$\frac{267}{489} < \frac{578}{997}$

2. $\frac{754}{1,443}$

$\frac{267}{489} > \frac{754}{1,443}$

3. $\frac{2,103}{5,274}$

$\frac{267}{489} > \frac{2,103}{5,274}$

More Practice, page 429, Set A

Using Page 203

Exercises 12–24 You may wish to have students use calculators for these exercises.

Think Math This problem shows another way to compare fractions. With this method, we are actually comparing the numerators of 2 equivalent fractions that have a common denominator equal to the product of the two denominators.

More Practice, page 429, Set A

Reteaching Supplement, page 60

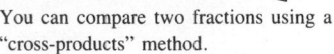

Enrichment Supplement, page 60

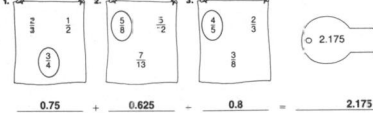
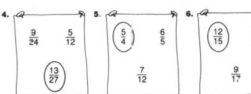

Practice Supplement, page 77

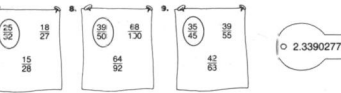

Quick Review Have students find the quotients to the nearest hundredth.

0.173 0.17

$23\overline{)4}$

1.411 1.41

$0.26\overline{)0.367}$

24.785 24.79

$14\overline{)347}$

Lesson Focus To estimate fractions; to solve problems using data from a table

Ideas for Getting Started

Draw a rectangle on the chalkboard similar to the one shown. Ask students to tell about what part of the rectangle is shaded. Then discuss how they arrived at their answers. Stress that several answers could be close.

"about $\frac{5}{6}$"

"about $\frac{6}{7}$"

Next present students with the following problem. It rained 6 out of 31 days in May. About what fraction of days did it rain? After students have had an opportunity to give their estimates, explain that the exact answer is $\frac{6}{31}$. Point out that by rounding 31 to 30, we can reduce the fraction to lower terms, $\frac{6}{30} = \frac{1}{5}$. In this way, we can estimate the number of days of rain to be about $\frac{1}{5}$.

Using Page 204

Exercises 1–10 Remind students that answers will not be exact. Encourage them to round the numerator or denominator in the fractions to make a simpler fraction whenever possible.

Using Fractions in Estimation

Make an estimate for each picture.

1. About what part of the glass is filled? $\frac{1}{4}$

2. About what part of the tank is full? $\frac{5}{8}$

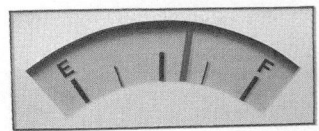

3. About what part of the notebook is green? $\frac{2}{3}$

4. About what part of the mosaic is finished? $\frac{3}{4}$

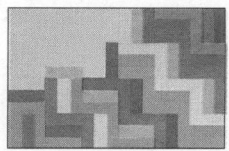

5. About what part of the pie is left? $\frac{3}{4}$

6. About how full is the bowl? $\frac{1}{2}$

7. The length of the short pencil is about what part of the length of the new pencil? $\frac{9}{10}$

8. Jonathan's score is about what part of Nancy's score? $\frac{5}{8}$

9. About what part of a minute is shown on the stop watch? $\frac{5}{6}$

10. About what part of an hour has passed since 8:00? $\frac{1}{6}$

Follow Up

Reteaching

Have students draw pictures to show each of the following.

1. a pie that is about $\frac{2}{3}$ eaten
2. a window that is about $\frac{1}{4}$ open
3. a bulletin board that is about $\frac{4}{5}$ covered
4. a pitcher that is about $\frac{3}{8}$ full
5. a wall that is $\frac{5}{6}$ painted

Enrichment

Have students draw a 4-inch line segment and mark the approximate location of $\frac{3}{8}$ in., $\frac{7}{16}$ in., $\frac{5}{4}$ in., $\frac{21}{8}$ in., $\frac{15}{4}$ in., and $\frac{64}{16}$ in.

Assignment Guide

	Minimum	Average	Extended
204	1–8	1–10	1–10
page 205	1–7	1–10	4–12

Applications

PROBLEM SOLVING: Using Data from a Table

QUESTION
DATA
PLAN
ANSWER
CHECK

Martha Hines owns a T-shirt store. She keeps records of the monthly sales. Use the table, if necessary, to solve the problems below.

	V-neck	Crew Neck	Total
Jan	75	450	525
Feb	200	475	675
Mar	275	600	875
April	270	650	920

1. What part of the January sales were V-neck shirts? Give the answer as a fraction in lowest terms. $\frac{1}{7}$

2. What part of the January sales were crew neck shirts? Give the answer as a fraction in lowest terms. $\frac{6}{7}$

3. What part of the March sales were V-neck shirts? $\frac{11}{35}$

4. What part of the March sales were crew neck shirts? $\frac{24}{35}$

5. What was the total number of T-shirts sold during the four months? 2,995

6. What was the average number of T-shirts sold per month during the four-month period? 748.75 (749)

7. Were the January sales above or below the average? below

8. What will be the total sales for May? Use the January through April sales to make a prediction. Predictions will vary.

9. In February the crew neck shirts were on sale for $9.00 each. The V-neck shirts sold for $10.99. What was the total number of dollars of sales for February? $6,473

10. How many more shirts were sold in April than in March? 45

11. The T-shirts in the store are either blue, yellow, or red. In February, 240 red shirts and 137 yellow shirts were sold. How many blue shirts were sold? 298

12. **Try This** In January a store sold 500 T-shirts and 150 tank tops. Each month after that the number of T-shirts sold decreased by 20 and the number of tank tops sold increased by 30. In what month did the number of tank tops sold equal the number of T-shirts sold? Hint: Make a table. August

Month	Jan	Feb	March
T-shirts	500	480	▦
Tank tops	150	180	▦

205

Using Page 205

Lesson Development Ask students to read the introductory material and study the table at the top of the page. Have students use the table to answer questions like the following. "How many crew neck shirts were sold in March?" (600) "What was the total number of shirts sold in January?" (525)

Work through the first problem on the chalkboard as an example. Ask students to restate the question and give the data needed to solve the problem. Explain that the total number of shirts sold in January is the denominator, and the number of V-neck shirts sold is the numerator. Ask students to reduce the fraction to lowest terms. $(\frac{75}{525} = \frac{1}{7})$

Exercise 8 Have students tell how they arrived at their predictions.

Try This A possible strategy, Make a Table, was taught on page 186.

Discussion Have students identify the question and the data in the problem. Then ask, "How many T-shirts were sold in March?" (460) "How many tank tops were sold in March?" (210) Explain that to solve the problem we can extend the table.

Solution

Month	Jan	Feb	Mar	Apr	May
T-shirts	500	480	460	440	420
Tank tops	150	180	210	240	270

Month	Jun	Jul	Aug
T-shirts	400	380	360
Tank tops	300	330	360

In August the number of tank tops sold was equal to the number of T-shirts sold.

Reteaching Supplement, page 61

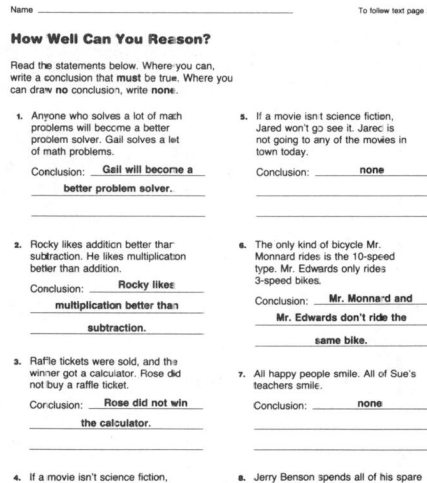

Name _____ To follow text page 205

Problem Solving: Using Data from a Table

Two surveys were taken to find out what kind of cereal is liked best.

Cereal Liked Best

	Corn cereal	Wheat cereal	Other	Total
January	64	20	16	100
June	59	18	13	90

59 out of 90 people liked corn cereal best.

Use the table to solve these problems.

1. What part of the 100 people surveyed in January liked corn cereal best? Write the answer as a lowest-terms fraction.
   liked corn cereal → $\frac{64}{100}$ = $\frac{16}{25}$ (Write in lowest terms.)
   total → 100

2. What part of the 90 people surveyed in June liked wheat cereal best? Write the answer as a lowest-terms fraction.
   $\frac{18}{90} = \frac{1}{5}$

3. What part of the 100 people surveyed in January liked wheat cereal the best? Write the answer as a lowest-terms fraction.
   $\frac{1}{5}$

4. What part of the 90 people surveyed in June liked corn cereal best? Write the answer as a lowest-terms fraction.
   $\frac{59}{90}$

5. How many of the people surveyed in January did not like corn cereal best?
   36

6. What part of the people surveyed in January did not like corn cereal best? Give the answer as a lowest-terms fraction.
   $\frac{36}{100} = \frac{9}{25}$

7. Did the number of people liking corn cereal best increase or decrease from January to June?
   decrease

8. Did the fraction of people liking corn cereal best increase or decrease from January to June?
   $\frac{64}{100} < \frac{59}{90}$ increase

Enrichment Supplement, page 61

Name _____ To follow text page 205

How Well Can You Reason?

Read the statements below. Where you can, write a conclusion that **must** be true. Where you can draw **no** conclusion, write **none**.

1. Anyone who solves a lot of math problems will become a better problem solver. Gail solves a lot of math problems.
   Conclusion: **Gail will become a better problem solver.**

2. Rocky likes addition better than subtraction. He likes multiplication better than addition.
   Conclusion: **Rocky likes multiplication better than subtraction.**

3. Raffle tickets were sold, and the winner got a calculator. Rose did not buy a raffle ticket.
   Conclusion: **Rose did not win the calculator.**

4. If a movie isn't science fiction, Jared won't go to see it. All of the movies in town this week are suspense thrillers.
   Conclusion: **Jared won't go to the movies this week.**

5. If a movie isn't science fiction, Jared won't go see it. Jared is not going to any of the movies in town today.
   Conclusion: **none**

6. The only kind of bicycle Mr. Monnard rides is the 10-speed type. Mr. Edwards only rides 3-speed bikes.
   Conclusion: **Mr. Monnard and Mr. Edwards don't ride the same bike.**

7. All happy people smile. All of Sue's teachers smile.
   Conclusion: **none**

8. Jerry Benson spends all of his spare time reading math books. He doesn't like sports. Mr. Schmidt is a teacher. On Tuesday nights, he plays basketball.
   Conclusion: **Jerry doesn't play basketball with Mr. Schmidt.**

Practice Supplement, page 78

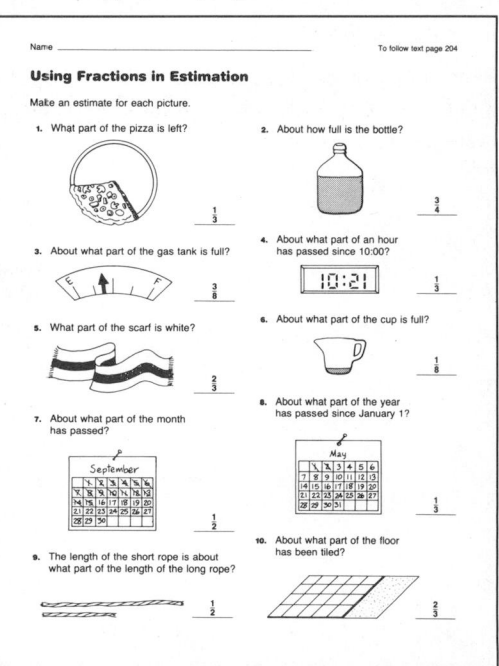

Name _____ To follow text page 204

Using Fractions in Estimation

Make an estimate for each picture.

1. What part of the pizza is left? $\frac{1}{3}$

2. About how full is the bottle? $\frac{3}{4}$

3. About what part of the gas tank is full? $\frac{3}{8}$

4. About what part of an hour has passed since 10:00? $\frac{1}{3}$

5. What part of the scarf is white? $\frac{2}{3}$

6. About what part of the cup is full? $\frac{1}{8}$

7. About what part of the month has passed? $\frac{1}{2}$

8. About what part of the year has passed since January 1? $\frac{1}{3}$

9. The length of the short rope is about what part of the length of the long rope? $\frac{1}{2}$

10. About what part of the floor has been tiled? $\frac{2}{3}$

Quick Review Have students decide which of the following are prime factorizations.

$20 = 2 \cdot 2 \cdot 5$ (circled) $54 = 9 \cdot 2 \cdot 3$ $42 = 2 \cdot 21$

$24 = 2 \cdot 2 \cdot 6$ $28 = 2 \cdot 2 \cdot 7$ (circled) $44 = 2 \cdot 2 \cdot 11$ (circled)

Lesson Focus To add fractions with like and unlike denominators

Ideas for Getting Started

On the chalkboard, draw a number line showing eighths. Use the number line to illustrate addition of fractions.

$$\frac{3}{8} + \frac{1}{8} = \frac{4}{8}$$

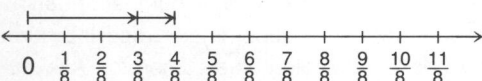

$$0 \quad \frac{1}{8} \quad \frac{2}{8} \quad \frac{3}{8} \quad \frac{4}{8} \quad \frac{5}{8} \quad \frac{6}{8} \quad \frac{7}{8} \quad \frac{8}{8} \quad \frac{9}{8} \quad \frac{10}{8} \quad \frac{11}{8}$$

Next review how to find the least common multiple. Write a pair of numbers on the chalkboard. Ask a volunteer to write the multiples of the larger number on the chalkboard. Then have the class determine when the least common multiple has been written.

Using Page 206

Motivational Problem After students read the problem at the top of the page, have them tell what the question asks us to find. "What data is needed to answer the question?" (advertisers have purchased $\frac{1}{4}$ and $\frac{1}{8}$ of a page) "What operation should we plan to use to find the part of the page the two advertisements cover?" (addition)

Lesson Development On the chalkboard, work the problem with students, following the steps shown. Point out that the least common multiple becomes the least common denominator in the second step. Stress that only the numerators are added. Show students that any common denominator gives us the same answer, but the least common denominator involves smaller numbers.

Other Examples In the first example, the answer can be reduced, $\frac{4}{10} = \frac{2}{5}$. The sum in the second example is an improper fraction. Notice with students that the addition of fractions can be written either horizontally or vertically.

Warm Up Have students work these exercises independently. Watch for students who add numerators and denominators to find the sum of the fractions.

Adding Fractions

A graphic artist is arranging advertisements on a magazine page. The advertisers have purchased $\frac{1}{4}$ of a page and $\frac{1}{8}$ of a page. What part of the page do the two advertisements cover?

To find the total part of the page, we add $\frac{1}{4}$ and $\frac{1}{8}$.

Look at the denominators.	Find the least common denominator (LCD).	Write equivalent fractions with this denominator.	Add the numerators. Write the sum over the common denominator.

$$\frac{1}{4}$$ $$+\frac{1}{8}$$ (Unlike denominators)

The LCD is the least common multiple of 4 and 8. The LCD is 8.

$$\frac{1}{4} = \frac{2}{8}$$
$$+\frac{1}{8} = \frac{1}{8}$$

$$\frac{1}{4} = \frac{2}{8}$$
$$+\frac{1}{8} = \frac{1}{8}$$
$$\frac{3}{8}$$

The two advertisements cover $\frac{3}{8}$ of a page.

Other Examples

$$\frac{3}{10} + \frac{1}{10} = \frac{4}{10} = \frac{2}{5}$$ (reduce)

$$\frac{6}{8} = \frac{18}{24}$$
$$+\frac{1}{3} = \frac{8}{24}$$
$$\frac{26}{24} = 1\frac{1}{12}$$ (rename)

$$\frac{4}{5} + \frac{7}{10} = \frac{8}{10} + \frac{7}{10} = \frac{15}{10} = 1\frac{1}{2}$$

$$\frac{3}{4} = \frac{9}{12}$$
$$\frac{1}{2} = \frac{6}{12}$$
$$+\frac{2}{3} = \frac{8}{12}$$
$$\frac{23}{12} = 1\frac{11}{12}$$

Warm Up

Add.

1. $\frac{4}{9} + \frac{2}{9}$ $\frac{2}{3}$

2. $\frac{3}{8} + \frac{2}{8}$ $\frac{5}{8}$

3. $\frac{1}{6} + \frac{2}{3}$ $\frac{5}{6}$

4. $\frac{5}{12} + \frac{1}{4}$ $\frac{2}{3}$

5. $\frac{1}{3}$
   $+\frac{3}{4}$
   $1\frac{1}{12}$

6. $\frac{2}{5}$
   $+\frac{3}{10}$
   $\frac{7}{10}$

7. $\frac{5}{8}$
   $+\frac{1}{3}$
   $\frac{23}{24}$

8. $\frac{1}{3}$
   $\frac{5}{6}$
   $+\frac{1}{2}$
   $1\frac{2}{3}$

206

Follow Up

Reteaching

Emphasize that addition of fractions involves finding common denominators. Write the following exercise on the chalkboard. Have students list multiples of the larger denominator, 5, and look for one that is also a multiple of 3.

$$\frac{2}{3}$$
$$+\frac{1}{5}$$ → 5, 10, 15   15 is also a multiple of 3

Then show how to write equivalent fractions with 15 as the common denominator. As you complete the exercise at the chalkboard, have students describe each step in their own words.

Enrichment

Show students the following method for finding sums of fractions. Point out that it does not include finding the least common denominator.

$$\frac{a}{b} + \frac{c}{d} = \frac{(a \cdot d) + (b \cdot c)}{b \cdot d}$$

$$\frac{3}{8} + \frac{3}{4} = \frac{12 + 24}{32} = \frac{36}{32} = 1\frac{1}{8}$$

Have students solve the exercises below using this method.

1. $\frac{5}{6} + \frac{2}{3}$ $1\frac{1}{2}$

2. $\frac{2}{3} + \frac{3}{4}$ $1\frac{5}{12}$

3. $\frac{5}{6} + \frac{3}{8}$ $1\frac{5}{24}$

4. $\frac{5}{8} + \frac{1}{2}$ $1\frac{1}{8}$

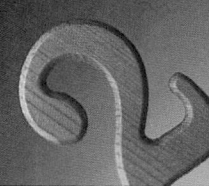

Add.

1. $\frac{3}{16} + \frac{5}{16}$ $\frac{1}{2}$

2. $\frac{1}{5} + \frac{3}{5}$ $\frac{4}{5}$

3. $\frac{5}{8} + \frac{3}{8}$ 1

4. $\frac{7}{12} + \frac{11}{12}$ $1\frac{1}{2}$

5. $\frac{5}{9} + \frac{2}{9}$ $\frac{7}{9}$

6. $\begin{array}{r} \frac{1}{10} \\ + \frac{3}{10} \\ \hline \frac{2}{5} \end{array}$

7. $\begin{array}{r} \frac{5}{24} \\ + \frac{7}{24} \\ \hline \frac{1}{2} \end{array}$

8. $\begin{array}{r} \frac{1}{4} \\ + \frac{1}{4} \\ \hline \frac{1}{2} \end{array}$

9. $\begin{array}{r} \frac{3}{16} \\ + \frac{15}{16} \\ \hline 1\frac{1}{8} \end{array}$

10. $\begin{array}{r} \frac{3}{4} \\ + \frac{2}{3} \\ \hline 1\frac{5}{12} \end{array}$

11. $\begin{array}{r} \frac{1}{2} \\ + \frac{2}{3} \\ \hline 1\frac{1}{6} \end{array}$

12. $\begin{array}{r} \frac{7}{8} \\ + \frac{1}{4} \\ \hline 1\frac{1}{8} \end{array}$

13. $\begin{array}{r} \frac{7}{10} \\ + \frac{1}{5} \\ \hline \frac{9}{10} \end{array}$

14. $\begin{array}{r} \frac{3}{4} \\ + \frac{1}{3} \\ \hline 1\frac{1}{12} \end{array}$

15. $\begin{array}{r} \frac{5}{6} \\ + \frac{1}{4} \\ \hline 1\frac{1}{12} \end{array}$

16. $\begin{array}{r} \frac{3}{8} \\ + \frac{1}{6} \\ \hline \frac{13}{24} \end{array}$

17. $\begin{array}{r} \frac{5}{12} \\ + \frac{1}{3} \\ \hline \frac{3}{4} \end{array}$

18. $\begin{array}{r} \frac{1}{2} \\ + \frac{5}{16} \\ \hline \frac{13}{16} \end{array}$

19. $\begin{array}{r} \frac{7}{8} \\ + \frac{1}{10} \\ \hline \frac{39}{40} \end{array}$

20. $\begin{array}{r} \frac{7}{100} \\ + \frac{7}{10} \\ \hline \frac{77}{100} \end{array}$

21. $\begin{array}{r} \frac{2}{3} \\ \frac{1}{4} \\ + \frac{1}{12} \\ \hline 1 \end{array}$

22. $\begin{array}{r} \frac{1}{2} \\ \frac{5}{6} \\ + \frac{7}{12} \\ \hline 1\frac{11}{12} \end{array}$

23. $\begin{array}{r} \frac{5}{8} \\ \frac{1}{2} \\ + \frac{1}{4} \\ \hline 1\frac{3}{8} \end{array}$

24. $\begin{array}{r} \frac{3}{100} \\ \frac{9}{10} \\ + \frac{1}{2} \\ \hline 1\frac{43}{100} \end{array}$

25. $\begin{array}{r} \frac{7}{8} \\ \frac{3}{4} \\ + \frac{5}{16} \\ \hline 1\frac{15}{16} \end{array}$

26. A shoe company bought a $\frac{1}{2}$ page advertisement and a $\frac{1}{6}$ page advertisement. What total part of a page did the shoe company buy? $\frac{2}{3}$

27. An advertisement for shoes took $\frac{1}{2}$ of a page, an advertisement for tires took $\frac{1}{3}$ of a page, and an advertisement for books took $\frac{1}{6}$ of a page. What part of the page was filled with advertisements? 1 (whole page)

28. Write and solve an addition problem for the drawings.

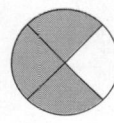 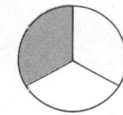 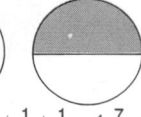

29. **DATA HUNT** Find a page in a magazine with two or more advertisements. What part of the page does each advertisement cover? Make an estimate. What part of the page do the combined advertisements cover? Make an estimate.

More Practice, page 429, Set B $\frac{3}{4} + \frac{1}{3} + \frac{1}{2} = 1\frac{7}{12}$ or $\frac{1}{4} + \frac{2}{3} + \frac{1}{2} = 1\frac{5}{12}$

Using Page 207

Exercises 1–27 Students are not required to give answers in simplest form. Depending on the abilities of your students, you may choose to require fractions to be changed to mixed numbers and reduced to lowest terms.

Data Hunt Students may find it interesting that ads are sold by the fraction of a page. It may be easier for students to estimate the fraction of a page if they cut out the advertisements and paste them on a blank sheet.

> A full page of practice, problem solving, and extension exercises allows for individualized assignments.

> Over 2,000 additional exercises are located in the appendix of each student book.

More Practice, page 429, Set B

Reteaching Supplement, page 62

Enrichment Supplement, page 62

Practice Supplement, page 79

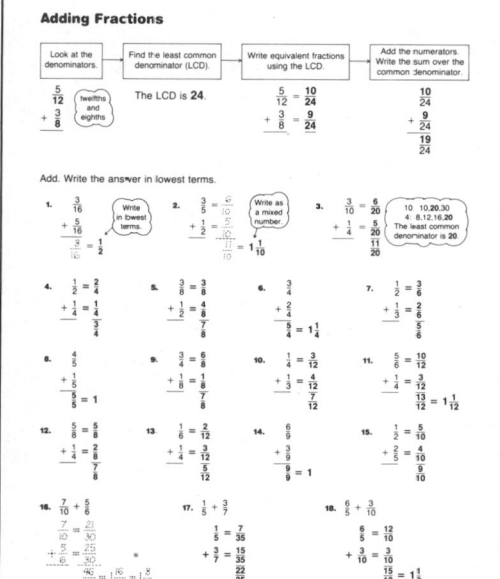

Fractions

Quick Review Display the numbers below. Point to a number and call out 0.1, 0.01, or 0.001. Have students find the product.

| 16.2 | 157 | 2,010 | 7.5 |
| 27 | 5 | 932 | 86.5 |

Lesson Focus To subtract fractions with like and unlike denominators

Ideas for Getting Started

Display a number line showing fractions in tenths. Use the number line to demonstrate subtracting fractions with like denominators.

$$\frac{9}{10} - \frac{6}{10} = \frac{3}{10}$$

0 $\frac{1}{10}$ $\frac{2}{10}$ $\frac{3}{10}$ $\frac{4}{10}$ $\frac{5}{10}$ $\frac{6}{10}$ $\frac{7}{10}$ $\frac{8}{10}$ $\frac{9}{10}$ $\frac{10}{10}$ $\frac{11}{10}$ $\frac{12}{10}$

Using Page 208

Motivational Problem Have students read the introductory problem. Ask them to identify the question and the data needed to solve the problem. Explain that since we need to find the amount of plant food left, our plan is to subtract.

Lesson Development Work through the problem on the chalkboard showing the steps in the instruction boxes. Make certain that students understand that we need to write equivalent fractions with a common denominator before we can subtract. Emphasize that only the numerators are subtracted.

Other Examples Notice with students that the difference in the first example can be reduced. In the second example, the common denominator is the denominator of one of the given fractions. Point out that we can write subtraction exercises either vertically or horizontally.

Subtracting Fractions

Seth works in a plant store. He needs $\frac{3}{8}$ cup (c) of plant food to feed all the plants in the store. He has $\frac{1}{2}$ c of plant food. What fraction of a cup will be left?

To find the amount left, we subtract. Since the fractions have unlike denominators, a common denominator must be found.

| Look at the denominators. | Find the least common denominator (LCD). | Write equivalent fractions with this denominator. | Subtract the numerators. Write the difference over the common denominator. |

$\frac{1}{2}$ (Unlike denominators)
$-\frac{3}{8}$

The LCD is 8.

$\frac{1}{2} = \frac{4}{8}$
$-\frac{3}{8} = \frac{3}{8}$

$\frac{1}{2} = \frac{4}{8}$
$-\frac{3}{8} = \frac{3}{8}$
$\frac{1}{8}$

There will be $\frac{1}{8}$ c of plant food left.

Other Examples

$\frac{5}{9} - \frac{2}{9} = \frac{3}{9} = \frac{1}{3}$ (reduce)

$\frac{5}{12} - \frac{1}{3} = \frac{5}{12} - \frac{4}{12} = \frac{1}{12}$

$\frac{3}{4} = \frac{15}{20}$
$-\frac{2}{5} = \frac{8}{20}$
$\frac{7}{20}$

Warm Up

Subtract.

1. $\frac{7}{8} - \frac{3}{8}$ $\frac{1}{2}$

2. $\frac{5}{16} - \frac{3}{16}$ $\frac{1}{8}$

3. $\frac{3}{4} - \frac{1}{4}$ $\frac{1}{2}$

4. $\frac{4}{5} - \frac{2}{6}$ $\frac{7}{15}$

5. $\frac{1}{2}$
$-\frac{1}{4}$
$\frac{1}{4}$

6. $\frac{5}{8}$
$-\frac{3}{16}$
$\frac{7}{16}$

7. $\frac{2}{3}$
$-\frac{1}{4}$
$\frac{5}{12}$

8. $\frac{6}{12}$
$-\frac{1}{3}$
$\frac{1}{6}$

208

Follow Up

Reteaching

Review with students how to find the LCD. Use an example such as $\frac{3}{4} - \frac{4}{5}$. Stress that before we can subtract, the fractions must be changed to equivalent fractions with like denominators. Discuss various ways to determine the LCD. For example, if both denominators are prime, simply multiply them. If one denominator is a multiple of the other, the LCD is the larger of the two.

Elicit from students that the denominators in the example are relatively prime, so the LCD is 4×5 or 20. On the chalkboard, work through each step to find the difference.

Enrichment

Write the following exercises on the chalkboard. Have students fill in the missing fractions.

1. $\frac{2}{3} - \frac{1}{2} = \frac{1}{6}$

2. $\frac{7}{8} - \frac{3}{4} = \frac{1}{8}$

3. $\frac{7}{8} - \frac{1}{24} = \frac{5}{6}$

4. $\frac{1}{3} - \frac{1}{5} = \frac{2}{15}$

Subtract.

1. $\frac{5}{6} - \frac{1}{6}$ $\frac{2}{3}$

2. $\frac{3}{5} - \frac{1}{5}$ $\frac{2}{5}$

3. $\frac{7}{10} - \frac{3}{5}$ $\frac{1}{10}$

4. $\frac{5}{8} - \frac{3}{8}$ $\frac{1}{4}$

5. $\frac{2}{3} - \frac{5}{9}$ $\frac{1}{9}$

6. $\frac{3}{4}$ $-\frac{1}{4}$ $\frac{1}{2}$

7. $\frac{5}{16}$ $-\frac{3}{16}$ $\frac{1}{8}$

8. $\frac{11}{12}$ $-\frac{5}{6}$ $\frac{1}{12}$

9. $\frac{2}{3}$ $-\frac{1}{2}$ $\frac{1}{6}$

10. $\frac{3}{4}$ $-\frac{1}{6}$ $\frac{7}{12}$

11. $\frac{2}{5}$ $-\frac{1}{10}$ $\frac{3}{10}$

12. $\frac{9}{10}$ $-\frac{3}{100}$ $\frac{87}{100}$

13. $\frac{1}{4}$ $-\frac{1}{5}$ $\frac{1}{20}$

14. $\frac{2}{3}$ $-\frac{1}{8}$ $\frac{13}{24}$

15. $\frac{3}{8}$ $-\frac{1}{3}$ $\frac{1}{24}$

16. $\frac{7}{10}$ $-\frac{1}{6}$ $\frac{8}{15}$

17. $\frac{5}{12}$ $-\frac{1}{4}$ $\frac{1}{6}$

18. $\frac{7}{16}$ $-\frac{3}{8}$ $\frac{1}{16}$

19. $\frac{7}{8}$ $-\frac{3}{16}$ $\frac{11}{16}$

20. $\frac{1}{3}$ $-\frac{3}{36}$ $\frac{1}{4}$

21. $\frac{8}{9}$ $-\frac{2}{3}$ $\frac{2}{9}$

22. $\frac{33}{100}$ $-\frac{1}{10}$ $\frac{23}{100}$

23. $\frac{11}{12}$ $-\frac{7}{8}$ $\frac{1}{24}$

24. $\frac{4}{5}$ $-\frac{1}{8}$ $\frac{27}{40}$

25. $\frac{7}{16}$ $-\frac{1}{4}$ $\frac{3}{16}$

26. Sue has $\frac{5}{8}$ c of potting mix. She uses $\frac{1}{2}$ c. What fraction of a cup of potting mix is left? $\frac{1}{8}$ c

27. Aaron is going to use a mixture of bone meal and potting soil. He needs $\frac{3}{4}$ c of mixture altogether. He uses $\frac{1}{3}$ c of bone meal. How much potting soil must he use? $\frac{5}{8}$ c

---

SKILLKEEPER

Write each fraction in lowest terms.

1. $\frac{12}{20}$ $\frac{3}{5}$

2. $\frac{8}{20}$ $\frac{2}{5}$

3. $\frac{24}{64}$ $\frac{3}{8}$

4. $\frac{15}{24}$ $\frac{5}{8}$

5. $\frac{28}{32}$ $\frac{7}{8}$

Write each improper fraction as a mixed number.

6. $\frac{22}{5}$ $4\frac{2}{5}$

7. $\frac{31}{3}$ $10\frac{1}{3}$

8. $\frac{23}{3}$ $7\frac{2}{3}$

9. $\frac{58}{7}$ $8\frac{2}{7}$

10. $\frac{43}{6}$ $7\frac{1}{6}$

Write each mixed number as an improper fraction.

11. $7\frac{1}{8}$ $\frac{57}{8}$

12. $6\frac{1}{9}$ $\frac{55}{9}$

13. $2\frac{5}{8}$ $\frac{21}{8}$

14. $5\frac{1}{7}$ $\frac{36}{7}$

15. $9\frac{1}{4}$ $\frac{37}{4}$

More Practice, page 429, Set C

209

Using Page 209

Exercises 1–27 Students should observe that the use of equivalent fractions in subtraction is the same as in addition.

Skillkeeper This Skillkeeper reviews material taught in this chapter.

More Practice, page 429, Set C

Reteaching Supplement, page 63

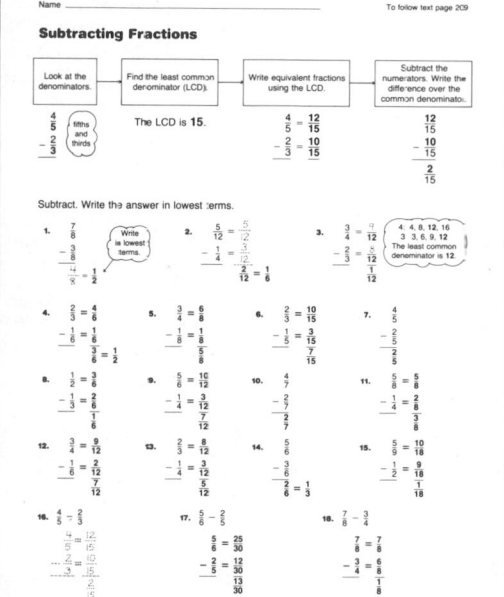

Enrichment Supplement, page 63

Practice Supplement, page 80

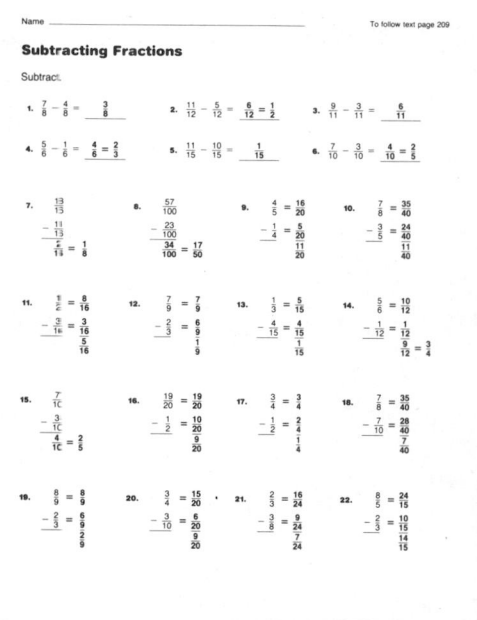

Quick Review Have students find the measure of the third angle of a triangle if two angles have the given measures.

42°, 60° **78°** 55°, 25° **100°** 90°, 37° **53°**
20°, 48° **112°** 32°, 102° **46°** 72°, 27° **81°**

Lesson Focus To add mixed numbers both with and without renaming

Ideas for Getting Started

Review with students how to change an improper fraction to a mixed or whole number. Use the following fractions as examples.

$$\frac{11}{8} \qquad \frac{16}{4} \qquad \frac{13}{5}$$

Next write numbers like the ones below and ask students to change the fractional part to a mixed number and then add the whole numbers.

$$5\frac{8}{5} \qquad 2\frac{5}{4} \qquad 6\frac{5}{2}$$

Using Page 210

Motivational Problem After students read the introductory problem, have them tell what the question asks us to find. "What data is needed to answer the question?" (the two pieces measure $15\frac{1}{2}$ in. and $8\frac{5}{8}$ in.) "What operation can we use to solve the problem?" (addition)

Lesson Development Display the problem on the chalkboard and work through each step. Notice with students that the common denominator is the denominator of one of the given fractions. Point out that the last step is to rename $23\frac{9}{8}$ as $24\frac{1}{8}$.

Other Examples In the first two examples renaming is not necessary. The second example shows the addition of a mixed number and a whole number. The third example shows the addition of a mixed number and a fraction.

Adding Mixed Numbers

A plumber used two pieces of pipe. One piece was $15\frac{1}{2}$ in. long. The other piece was $8\frac{5}{8}$ in. long. What was the total length of pipe used?

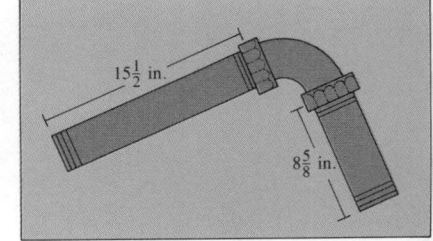

To find the total length, we add.

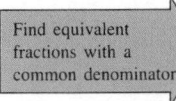

Find equivalent fractions with a common denominator. → Add the fractions. → Add the whole numbers.

$$15\frac{1}{2} = 15\frac{4}{8}$$
$$+\ 8\frac{5}{8} =\ 8\frac{5}{8}$$

$$15\frac{1}{2} = 15\frac{4}{8}$$
$$+\ 8\frac{5}{8} =\ 8\frac{5}{8}$$
$$\overline{\qquad \frac{9}{8}}$$

$$15\frac{1}{2} = 15\frac{4}{8}$$
$$+\ 8\frac{5}{8} =\ 8\frac{5}{8}$$
$$\overline{23\frac{9}{8} = 24\frac{1}{8}}$$

The total length of pipe used was $24\frac{1}{8}$ in.

rename

Other Examples

$$4\frac{1}{3} = 4\frac{4}{12}$$
$$+2\frac{1}{4} = 2\frac{3}{12}$$
$$\overline{6\frac{7}{12}}$$

$$4$$
$$+6\frac{7}{8}$$
$$\overline{10\frac{7}{8}}$$

$$3\frac{1}{2} = 3\frac{3}{6}$$
$$+\ \frac{2}{3} =\ \frac{4}{6}$$
$$\overline{3\frac{7}{6} = 4\frac{1}{6}}$$

Warm Up

Find the sums.

1. $7\frac{1}{8}$
    $+1\frac{3}{8}$
    $\overline{8\frac{1}{2}}$

2. 4
    $+5\frac{4}{5}$
    $\overline{9\frac{4}{5}}$

3. $2\frac{5}{8}$
    $+6\frac{3}{4}$
    $\overline{9\frac{3}{8}}$

4. $5\frac{2}{3}$
    $+2\frac{1}{6}$
    $\overline{7\frac{5}{6}}$

5. $1\frac{7}{8}$
    $+3\frac{1}{3}$
    $\overline{5\frac{5}{24}}$

6. 2
    $+4\frac{7}{10}$
    $\overline{6\frac{7}{10}}$

7. $3\frac{2}{3}$
    $+\ \frac{1}{9}$
    $\overline{3\frac{7}{9}}$

8. $12\frac{5}{16}$
    $+23\frac{3}{4}$
    $\overline{36\frac{1}{16}}$

210

Follow Up

Reteaching

Use models to demonstrate the addition of mixed numbers. As you work through examples, give students an opportunity to participate in each step.

$$1\frac{1}{2}$$
$$+2\frac{3}{4}$$

$$3\frac{5}{4} = 4\frac{1}{4}$$

Enrichment

Display the following on the chalkboard. Have students copy and complete the diagram.

$\left(1\frac{1}{2}\right) + \left(2\frac{3}{4}\right) + \left(1\frac{1}{4}\right) + \left(3\frac{1}{3}\right) = \left(8\frac{5}{6}\right)$

$\left(4\frac{1}{4}\right) + \left(4\right) + \left(4\frac{7}{12}\right) = \left(12\frac{5}{6}\right)$

$\left(8\frac{1}{4}\right) + \left(8\frac{7}{12}\right) = \left(16\frac{5}{6}\right)$

$\left(16\frac{5}{6}\right)$

Assignment Guide			
	Minimum	Average	Extended
page 211	1–20, 26	1–26	2–26 even, 27, TM

Add.

1. $6\frac{1}{2}$
$+3\frac{1}{4}$
$9\frac{3}{4}$

2. $6\frac{3}{10}$
$+10$
$16\frac{3}{10}$

3. $8\frac{3}{4}$
$+3\frac{1}{4}$
12

4. 15
$+9\frac{3}{16}$
$24\frac{3}{16}$

5. $7\frac{1}{2}$
$+\frac{3}{4}$
$8\frac{1}{4}$

6. $2\frac{8}{12}$
$+1\frac{1}{4}$
$3\frac{11}{12}$

7. $12\frac{1}{2}$
$+17\frac{1}{2}$
30

8. $9\frac{2}{3}$
$+8\frac{5}{6}$
$18\frac{1}{2}$

9. $\frac{1}{6}$
$+7\frac{3}{4}$
$7\frac{11}{12}$

10. $20\frac{1}{2}$
$+19\frac{3}{6}$
40

11. $7\frac{1}{2}$
$+4\frac{5}{6}$
$12\frac{1}{3}$

12. $12\frac{1}{3}$
$+\frac{3}{5}$
$12\frac{14}{15}$

13. $2\frac{3}{7}$
$+5\frac{1}{3}$
$7\frac{16}{21}$

14. $11\frac{3}{8}$
$+13\frac{5}{16}$
$24\frac{11}{16}$

15. $14\frac{7}{10}$
$+5\frac{3}{100}$
$19\frac{73}{100}$

16. $47\frac{4}{5}+16$
$63\frac{4}{5}$

17. $13\frac{5}{16}+20\frac{5}{8}$
$33\frac{15}{16}$

18. $16\frac{2}{3}+5\frac{7}{9}$
$22\frac{4}{9}$

19. $36\frac{2}{5}+17\frac{7}{10}$
$54\frac{1}{10}$

20. $\frac{7}{8}+28\frac{3}{4}$
$29\frac{5}{8}$

21. $4\frac{1}{2}$
$3\frac{1}{4}$
$-6\frac{1}{2}$
$14\frac{1}{4}$

22. $17\frac{1}{8}$
$11\frac{1}{4}$
$+13\frac{1}{2}$
$41\frac{7}{8}$

23. $6\frac{5}{12}$
$3\frac{1}{4}$
$+\frac{1}{3}$
10

24. $7\frac{5}{6}$
$2\frac{1}{8}$
$+1\frac{1}{2}$
$11\frac{11}{24}$

25. $57\frac{2}{3}$
$15\frac{5}{6}$
$+29\frac{1}{2}$
103

26. A plumber used pipes that were $29\frac{3}{4}$ in. long and $16\frac{7}{8}$ in. long. What was the total length of the pipe used? $46\frac{5}{8}$ in.

27. A plumber used two pieces of copper tubing. One piece was $26\frac{1}{2}$ in. long. The other piece was $3\frac{1}{2}$ in. longer than that. What was the total length of the two pieces? $56\frac{1}{2}$ in.

▰▰▰ THINK MATH ▰▰▰

Math History

Unit fractions, fractions with a numerator of one, were important in ancient Egyptian mathematics. All other fractions were written as the sum of unit fractions with different denominators.

$\frac{3}{5}$ became $\frac{1}{3}+\frac{1}{5}+\frac{1}{15}$ or $\frac{1}{2}+\frac{1}{10}$.

Write each fraction as the sum of unit fractions.

1. $\frac{2}{5}$ 2. $\frac{2}{3}$ 3. $\frac{2}{7}$ 4. $\frac{3}{7}$

See teaching notes.

More Practice, page 430, Set A   **211**

Using Page 211

Exercises 1–25 Horizontal and vertical formats are used in these exercises. A third addend is introduced in exercises 21–25. You may want to work through exercises such as these on the chalkboard before making the assignment.

Think Math In this problem, students are given an historical look at fractions. The problems can be solved by trial and error. Some students may discover a method such as the following to write unit fractions for fractions having a numerator of 2.

To find the denominator of the first unit fraction, add 1 to the original denominator, then divide by 2.

original fraction		first unit fraction
$\frac{2}{5}$	$\dfrac{1}{\frac{5+1}{2}}$ or	$\frac{1}{3}$

To find the denominator of the second unit fraction, multiply the original denominator by the denominator computed in step 1.

$$\text{second unit fraction}$$
$$\frac{1}{5 \cdot 3} \quad \text{or} \quad \frac{1}{15}$$

$$\frac{2}{5} = \frac{1}{3} + \frac{1}{15}$$

To find fractions with a numerator of 3 or more, use the method above and think of the fraction as the sum of two or more fractions with numerators of 1 or 2.

$$\frac{3}{5} = \frac{1}{5} + \frac{2}{5} \text{ so } \frac{3}{5} = \frac{1}{5} + \frac{1}{3} + \frac{1}{15}$$

Answers
1. $\frac{1}{3}+\frac{1}{15}$ 2. $\frac{1}{2}+\frac{1}{6}$
3. $\frac{1}{4}+\frac{1}{28}$ 4. $\frac{1}{7}+\frac{1}{4}+\frac{1}{28}$

More Practice, page 430, Set A

Reteaching Supplement, page 64

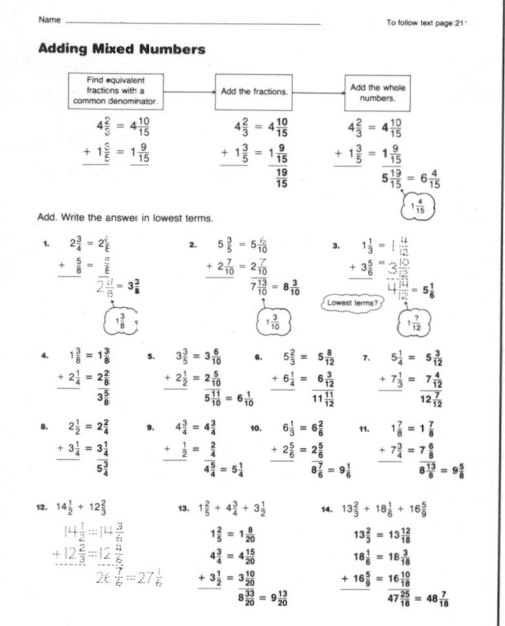

Enrichment Supplement, page 64

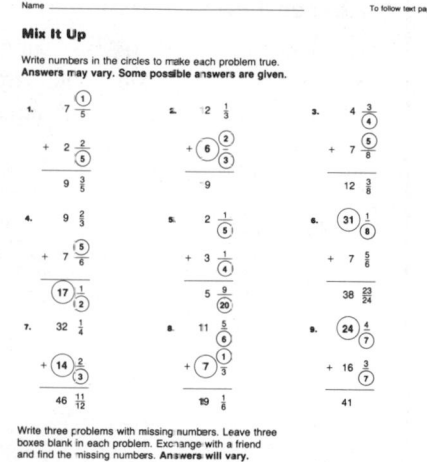

Practice Supplement, page 81

Quick Review Have students write zeros if necessary and place decimal points in the products.

$1.37 \times 0.07 = 0.0959$ $0.9 \times 0.024 = 0.0216$ $3.1 \times 0.72 = 2,232$
$4.14 \times 0.2 = 0.828$ $0.041 \times 0.23 = 0.00943$ $0.86 \times 1.42 = 1,2212$

Lesson Focus To subtract mixed numbers without renaming

Ideas for Getting Started

Review subtracting fractions by discussing these exercises with students.

$$\frac{1}{2} \qquad \frac{3}{4} \qquad \frac{9}{10}$$
$$-\frac{3}{8} \qquad -\frac{2}{5} \qquad -\frac{5}{6}$$

Then ask students to recall the steps needed to solve the following exercise.

$$2\frac{5}{12}$$
$$+3\frac{1}{6}$$

Using Page 212

Motivational Problem Call on a student to read the problem at the top of the page. Have students restate the question and give the data needed to solve the problem. Elicit from students the idea that since we want to determine how much longer the nail is than the first piece of wood, we should plan to subtract.

Lesson Development Work through the problem on the chalkboard according to the steps in the instruction boxes. Have students look for similarities to the process for adding mixed numbers. Ask students to check the answer by using addition.

$$1\frac{7}{16}$$
$$+1\frac{1}{16}$$
$$2\frac{8}{16} = 2\frac{1}{2}$$

Other Examples The second example shows a whole number subtracted from a mixed number. It is a simple exercise but some students may not realize how simple it is at first glance. The difference in the third example can be reduced.

Subtracting Mixed Numbers

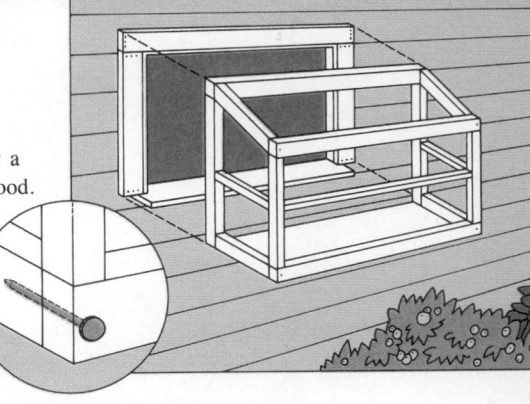

The plans for a greenhouse window show a $2\frac{1}{2}$-inch nail driven through $1\frac{7}{16}$ in. of wood. How far will the nail extend into the second piece of wood?

To find out how much longer the nail is than the first piece of wood, we subtract.

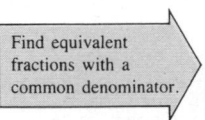

Find equivalent fractions with a common denominator.	Subtract the fractions.	Subtract the whole numbers.

$$2\frac{1}{2} = 2\frac{8}{16} \qquad 2\frac{1}{2} = 2\frac{8}{16} \qquad 2\frac{1}{2} = 2\frac{8}{16}$$
$$-1\frac{7}{16} = 1\frac{7}{16} \qquad -1\frac{7}{16} = 1\frac{7}{16} \qquad -1\frac{7}{16} = 1\frac{7}{16}$$
$$\frac{1}{16} \qquad\qquad\qquad 1\frac{1}{16}$$

The nail will extend $1\frac{1}{16}$ inches into the second piece of wood.

Other Examples

$$12\frac{1}{2} = 12\frac{5}{10} \qquad 8\frac{3}{4} \qquad 10\frac{5}{6} = 10\frac{5}{6}$$
$$-3\frac{2}{5} = 3\frac{4}{10} \qquad -3 \qquad -2\frac{1}{2} = 2\frac{3}{6}$$
$$9\frac{1}{10} \qquad\quad 5\frac{3}{4} \qquad\qquad 8\frac{2}{6} = 8\frac{1}{3}$$

Warm Up

Find the differences.

1. $5\frac{1}{2}$ 2. $8\frac{2}{3}$ 3. $12\frac{9}{10}$ 4. $20\frac{3}{4}$
   $-1\frac{1}{4}$ $-3\frac{1}{3}$ -6 $-9\frac{5}{8}$
   $4\frac{1}{4}$ $5\frac{1}{3}$ $6\frac{9}{10}$ $11\frac{1}{8}$

5. $87\frac{1}{2}$ 6. $99\frac{99}{100}$ 7. $66\frac{2}{3}$ 8. $5\frac{9}{10}$
   $-29\frac{1}{2}$ $-83\frac{3}{4}$ $-33\frac{1}{3}$ $-5\frac{3}{4}$
   58                   $16\frac{6}{25}$ $33\frac{1}{3}$ $\frac{3}{20}$

212

Follow Up

Reteaching

Draw diagrams to illustrate subtracting mixed numbers. On the chalkboard work through this example with students.

$$2\frac{5}{6} = 2\frac{5}{6}$$
$$-1\frac{1}{3} = 1\frac{2}{6}$$
$$1\frac{3}{6} = 1\frac{1}{2}$$

Enrichment

Write these equations on the chalkboard. Have students give the correct sign (+ or −) for each $\bigcirc$.

$$(2\frac{1}{2} \oplus 1\frac{1}{4}) \ominus 1\frac{3}{4} = 2$$
$$4\frac{2}{3} \ominus (4\frac{2}{3} \ominus 3\frac{1}{5}) = 3\frac{1}{5}$$
$$2\frac{1}{2} \ominus (2\frac{1}{3} \ominus 1\frac{1}{6}) = 1\frac{1}{3}$$

Assignment Guide

	Minimum	Average	Extended
page 213	1–22, 25	1–25, 28	1–25 odd, 26–28, TM

Subtract.

1. $7\frac{1}{2}$ $-3\frac{1}{8}$ $4\frac{3}{8}$

2. $16\frac{3}{5}$ -9 $7\frac{3}{5}$

3. $12\frac{3}{4}$ $-5\frac{5}{8}$ $7\frac{1}{8}$

4. $27\frac{2}{3}$ $-18\frac{1}{2}$ $9\frac{1}{6}$

5. $30\frac{7}{10}$ $-15\frac{1}{5}$ $15\frac{1}{2}$

6. $18\frac{5}{8}$ $-9\frac{5}{16}$ $9\frac{5}{16}$

7. $42\frac{1}{5}$ $-29\frac{13}{100}$ $13\frac{7}{100}$

8. $11\frac{15}{16}$ $-7\frac{1}{2}$ $4\frac{7}{16}$

9. $2\frac{4}{5}$ $-2\frac{1}{6}$ $\frac{19}{30}$

10. $21\frac{7}{16}$ $-13\frac{1}{4}$ $8\frac{3}{16}$

11. $33\frac{5}{8}$ -18 $15\frac{5}{8}$

12. $7\frac{11}{12}$ $-4\frac{2}{3}$ $3\frac{1}{4}$

13. $8\frac{5}{9}$ $-1\frac{1}{6}$ $7\frac{7}{18}$

14. $60\frac{1}{2}$ $-37\frac{1}{6}$ $23\frac{1}{3}$

15. $41\frac{3}{8}$ $-27\frac{3}{16}$ $14\frac{3}{16}$

16. $79\frac{3}{4}$ $-38\frac{3}{10}$ $41\frac{9}{20}$

17. $7\frac{1}{2}$ $-3\frac{1}{7}$ $4\frac{5}{14}$

18. $96\frac{5}{6}$ $-21\frac{1}{5}$ $75\frac{19}{30}$

19. $96\frac{1}{4}$ $-8\frac{1}{8}$ $88\frac{1}{8}$

20. $98\frac{1}{2}$ $-66\frac{1}{3}$ $32\frac{1}{6}$

21. $32\frac{3}{4} - 27\frac{1}{3}$ $5\frac{5}{12}$

22. $75\frac{2}{5} - 29\frac{1}{4}$ $46\frac{3}{20}$

23. $66\frac{2}{3} - 39$ $27\frac{2}{3}$

24. $98\frac{9}{16} - 75\frac{1}{4}$ $23\frac{5}{16}$

25. A nail is $2\frac{1}{4}$ in. long. A piece of wood is $1\frac{2}{16}$ in. thick. How much longer is the nail than the thickness of the wood? $1\frac{1}{8}$ in.

26. Mitch drove a nail $2\frac{1}{2}$ in. long into a piece of wood $2\frac{11}{16}$ in. thick. How close was the point of the nail to the other side of the wood? $\frac{3}{16}$ in.

27. Cesar had a piece of lumber that was $42\frac{15}{16}$ in. long. He sawed off $14\frac{1}{4}$ in. He then had to saw off $1\frac{1}{2}$ in. more. How long was the piece that was left? $27\frac{3}{16}$ in.

28. **DATA BANK** How many inches longer is a 16-penny nail than a 7-penny nail? (See page 413.) $1\frac{1}{4}$ in.

THINK MATH

Shape Perception

The 16 nails form 5 squares. Move only 3 of the nails to new positions so that just 4 squares are formed.
See teaching notes.

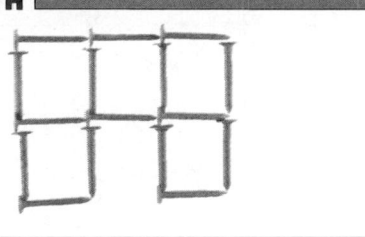

More Practice, page 430, Set B   213

Using Page 213

Exercises 21–24 These exercises are written horizontally. Students can rewrite them in vertical format before they are solved.

Data Bank Students may be interested to know that the name of the size of a nail comes from the original cost of that size nail per 100. Thus, a 7-penny nail cost 7¢ per 100.

Think Math This problem involves spatial visualization and logical reasoning. If students need a hint, tell them that the problem can be solved if they can find a way to eliminate 2 squares and form only 1 new square. The solution is shown below.

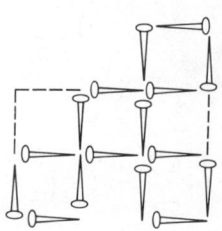

More Practice, page 430, Set B

Reteaching Supplement, page 65

Enrichment Supplement, page 65

Practice Supplement, page 82

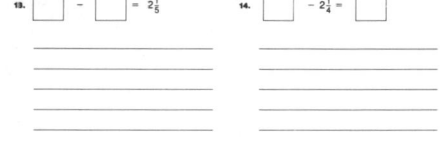

Quick Review Have students name a value for r and evaluate each expression. Repeat as time allows.

$r + 27$	$r - 16$	$5r$	$\frac{r}{2}$
$30 - r$	$8r$	$\frac{r}{10}$	$15 + r$

Lesson Focus To subtract mixed numbers with renaming

Ideas for Getting Started

To prepare students for the lesson, ask them to determine whether or not the following pairs of numbers are equivalent. Pictures can be used to help them decide.

$$1, \frac{6}{6} \qquad 2\frac{1}{3}, 1\frac{4}{3} \qquad 3\frac{3}{5}, 2\frac{8}{5}$$

Then ask students to use pictures to help them supply the missing numerators.

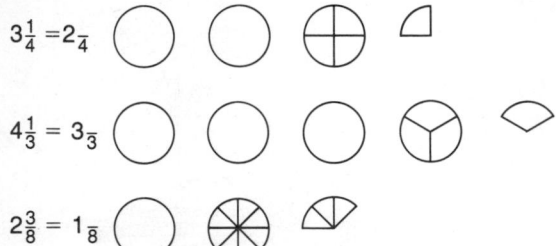

$$3\frac{1}{4} = 2\frac{}{4}$$

$$4\frac{1}{3} = 3\frac{}{3}$$

$$2\frac{3}{8} = 1\frac{}{8}$$

Using Page 214

Motivational Problem Have students read the introductory problem. "What does the question ask us to find?" (how long it took to complete the second assignment) "What data is needed to solve the problem?" (Two assignments took $5\frac{1}{2}$ h and the first assignment took $3\frac{3}{4}$ h.) Ask students to explain why the plan is to subtract the number of hours.

Lesson Development Work through each step of the problem on the chalkboard. Expect the second step to be difficult for students. You may wish to use pictures to help students understand this step. Show that the problem can be checked by using addition.

Other Examples Work through these examples on the chalkboard. Notice with students that the difference in the first example can be reduced. The second example involves subtraction from a whole number. Help students understand how to determine which fractional parts to use when renaming.

Subtracting Mixed Numbers with Renaming

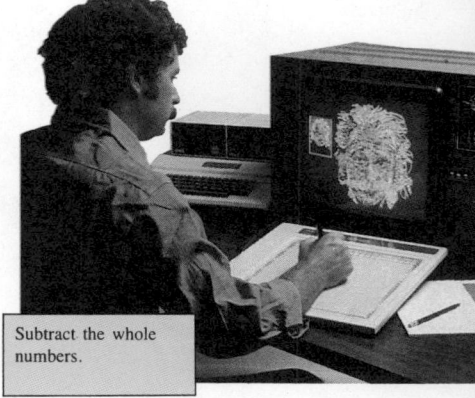

A computer science student used $5\frac{1}{2}$ hours (h) of computer time to complete two assignments. The first assignment took $3\frac{3}{4}$ h. How long did the second assignment take?

To find the amount of time for the second assignment, we can subtract.

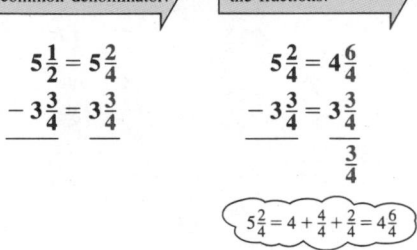

Find equivalent fractions with a common denominator. → Rename the fractions if necessary. Subtract the fractions. → Subtract the whole numbers.

$$
\begin{aligned}
5\frac{1}{2} &= 5\frac{2}{4} \\
-3\frac{3}{4} &= 3\frac{3}{4}
\end{aligned}
\qquad
\begin{aligned}
5\frac{2}{4} &= 4\frac{6}{4} \\
-3\frac{3}{4} &= 3\frac{3}{4} \\
\hline
&\quad\ \frac{3}{4}
\end{aligned}
\qquad
\begin{aligned}
5\frac{2}{4} &= 4\frac{6}{4} \\
-3\frac{3}{4} &= 3\frac{3}{4} \\
\hline
&\ 1\frac{3}{4}
\end{aligned}
$$

$$5\frac{2}{4} = 4 + \frac{4}{4} + \frac{2}{4} = 4\frac{6}{4}$$

The second assignment took $1\frac{3}{4}$ h.

Other Examples

$$
\begin{aligned}
3\frac{1}{10} &= 2\frac{11}{10} \\
-1\frac{7}{10} &= 1\frac{7}{10} \\
\hline
1\frac{4}{10} &= 1\frac{2}{5}
\end{aligned}
\qquad
\begin{aligned}
6 &= 5\frac{3}{3} \\
-2\frac{1}{3} &= 2\frac{1}{3} \\
\hline
3\frac{2}{3}
\end{aligned}
\qquad
\begin{aligned}
10\frac{1}{4} &= 10\frac{2}{8} = 9\frac{10}{8} \\
-\ \frac{5}{8} &= \ \frac{5}{8} = \ \frac{5}{8} \\
\hline
&\qquad\qquad 9\frac{5}{8}
\end{aligned}
$$

Warm Up

1.	2.	3.	4.
$3\frac{1}{4}$	4	6	$10\frac{1}{5}$
$-1\frac{3}{4}$	$-\frac{5}{6}$	$-3\frac{7}{10}$	$-2\frac{3}{5}$
$1\frac{1}{2}$	$3\frac{1}{6}$	$2\frac{3}{10}$	$7\frac{3}{5}$

5.	6.	7.	8.
$15\frac{1}{2}$	$9\frac{3}{8}$	$5\frac{3}{16}$	$7\frac{1}{3}$
$-3\frac{5}{6}$	$-8\frac{3}{4}$	$-2\frac{3}{4}$	$-2\frac{1}{2}$
214 $11\frac{2}{3}$	$\frac{5}{8}$	$2\frac{7}{16}$	$4\frac{5}{6}$

Follow Up

Reteaching

Give students exercises to practice renaming mixed numbers. Have them match each mixed number with a fraction in the column at the right.

1. $3\frac{1}{5}$	A. $4\frac{5}{3}$	1. D
2. $5\frac{2}{3}$	B. $2\frac{6}{4}$	2. A
3. $4\frac{3}{5}$	C. $3\frac{8}{6}$	3. F
4. $3\frac{1}{2}$	D. $2\frac{6}{5}$	4. B
5. $4\frac{1}{3}$	E. $2\frac{5}{4}$	5. C
6. $3\frac{1}{4}$	F. $3\frac{8}{5}$	6. E

Enrichment

Display these tables on the chalkboard. Have students substitute each value for n and complete the tables.

n	$n - \frac{1}{4}$
$\frac{1}{3}$	$\frac{1}{12}$
$\frac{3}{8}$	$\frac{1}{8}$
$2\frac{1}{2}$	$2\frac{1}{4}$
$1\frac{2}{5}$	$1\frac{3}{20}$
$3\frac{1}{8}$	$2\frac{7}{8}$

n	$n - 2\frac{1}{3}$
$2\frac{5}{6}$	$\frac{1}{2}$
$3\frac{3}{4}$	$1\frac{5}{12}$
$3\frac{1}{4}$	$\frac{11}{12}$
$5\frac{2}{3}$	$3\frac{1}{3}$
6	$3\frac{2}{3}$

Assignment Guide

	Minimum	Average	Extended
page 215	1–22, 25	1–25	1–25 odd, 26, TM

Subtract.

1. $4\frac{1}{5}$
$-2\frac{1}{3}$
$\overline{1\frac{13}{15}}$

2. $7\frac{1}{4}$
$-3\frac{3}{4}$
$\overline{3\frac{1}{2}}$

3. 13
$-5\frac{2}{3}$
$\overline{7\frac{1}{3}}$

4. $7\frac{5}{16}$
$-\frac{9}{16}$
$\overline{6\frac{3}{4}}$

5. 4
$-\frac{1}{2}$
$\overline{3\frac{1}{2}}$

6. $14\frac{1}{2}$
$-9\frac{9}{10}$
$\overline{4\frac{3}{5}}$

7. $9\frac{2}{5}$
$-1\frac{3}{4}$
$\overline{7\frac{13}{20}}$

8. 99
$-33\frac{1}{3}$
$\overline{65\frac{2}{3}}$

9. 13
$-6\frac{7}{8}$
$\overline{6\frac{1}{8}}$

10. $9\frac{1}{2}$
$-3\frac{2}{3}$
$\overline{5\frac{5}{6}}$

11. $6\frac{1}{4}$
$-1\frac{3}{4}$
$\overline{4\frac{1}{2}}$

12. 18
$-10\frac{9}{10}$
$\overline{7\frac{1}{10}}$

13. $2\frac{17}{100}$
$-\frac{1}{4}$
$\overline{1\frac{23}{25}}$

14. $10\frac{1}{5}$
$-3\frac{4}{5}$
$\overline{6\frac{2}{5}}$

15. $14\frac{3}{16}$
$-12\frac{7}{16}$
$\overline{1\frac{3}{4}}$

16. 8
$-2\frac{2}{3}$
$\overline{5\frac{1}{3}}$

17. $16\frac{1}{4}$
$-4\frac{1}{2}$
$\overline{11\frac{3}{4}}$

18. $12\frac{1}{4}$
$-10\frac{5}{8}$
$\overline{1\frac{5}{8}}$

19. 25
$-19\frac{11}{16}$
$\overline{5\frac{5}{16}}$

20. $17\frac{1}{3}$
$-11\frac{5}{8}$
$\overline{5\frac{17}{24}}$

21. $9\frac{2}{5}-1\frac{7}{10}$ $7\frac{7}{10}$

22. $17\frac{3}{4}-6\frac{7}{8}$ $10\frac{7}{8}$

23. $15-3\frac{3}{8}$ $11\frac{5}{8}$

24. $13\frac{2}{3}-8\frac{7}{8}$ $4\frac{19}{24}$

25. Ellen used the computer $4\frac{5}{6}$ h on Monday and $6\frac{1}{3}$ h on Tuesday. How much longer did she use the computer on Tuesday? $1\frac{1}{2}$ h

26. Brad used the computer a total of 9 h. He used the computer $2\frac{1}{4}$ h on Monday and $2\frac{1}{2}$ h on Tuesday. How many more hours did he use the computer? $4\frac{1}{4}$ h

---

▮ THINK MATH ▮

Logical Reasoning

Complete the Magic Square.

The magic sum is $4\frac{1}{2}$.

$1\frac{7}{20}$	$\frac{8}{10}$	$1\frac{1}{20}$	$1\frac{3}{10}$
$1\frac{1}{4}$	$1\frac{1}{10}$	$\frac{3}{4}$	$1\frac{2}{5}$
$\frac{9}{10}$	$1\frac{9}{20}$	$1\frac{1}{5}$	$\frac{19}{20}$
1	$1\frac{3}{20}$	$1\frac{1}{2}$	$\frac{17}{20}$

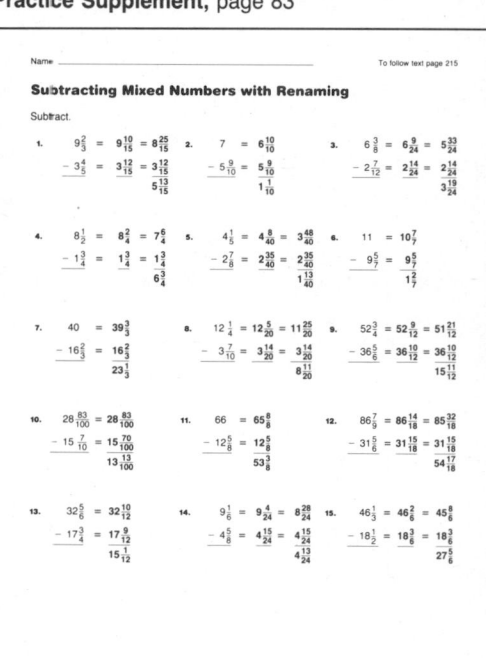

More Practice, page 430, Set C

215

Using Page 215

Exercises 1–24 Your treatment of these exercises will depend upon the success students had with the Warm Up exercises. You may want to work through one or more of these exercises as a class activity.

Think Math The key to completing the magic square lies in finding a row, column, or diagonal which has only one number missing. The first row is an example. To find the missing number in that row the student must add the other three numbers and subtract that sum from the magic sum, $4\frac{1}{2}$. Then students should find the next row, column, or diagonal where only one number is missing.

More Practice, page 430, Set C

Reteaching Supplement, page 66

Name _____

Subtracting Mixed Numbers with Renaming

Enrichment Supplement, page 66

Name _____

Mixed Numbers and Patterns

Complete the problems in the top half of the figure. Shade in each section if the answer is 3 or less. Draw lines in each section if the answer is greater than 3.

Then make up new problems for the bottom half so that the geometric pattern at the top is repeated. **Problems will vary.**

Practice Supplement, page 83

Name _____

Subtracting Mixed Numbers with Renaming

Fractions

Lesson Focus To practice adding and subtracting fractions and mixed numbers; to solve word problems using cumulative computational skills

Ideas for Getting Started

To introduce the problem-solving lesson on page 217, display the following problem on the chalkboard.

Joan lives $3\frac{1}{2}$ blocks from Pam. She ran $1\frac{3}{4}$ blocks and walked the rest of the way to Pam's house. How far did she walk?

After reading the problem with students, focus their attention on the 5-Point Checklist logo at the top of page 217. Ask students to describe the steps and then apply them to the problem on the chalkboard.

Using Page 216

Exercises 1–42 Assign these exercises as needed for strengthening skills in addition and subtraction of fractions. If any students have difficulty working these exercises, you may want to ask some of the more able students to work with them on a one-to-one basis. You can suggest that they review the appropriate lessons in the chapter and select various exercises to use as examples in their explanations.

Skills Practice

Add.

1. $\frac{6}{8}+\frac{1}{4}$ 1

2. $\frac{4}{5}+\frac{11}{25}$ $1\frac{6}{25}$

3. $\frac{5}{21}+\frac{1}{7}$ $\frac{8}{21}$

4. $\frac{1}{3}+\frac{4}{9}$ $\frac{7}{9}$

5. $\frac{4}{9}$ $+\frac{3}{4}$ $1\frac{7}{36}$

6. $\frac{5}{6}$ $+\frac{8}{9}$ $1\frac{13}{18}$

7. $\frac{2}{8}$ $+\frac{2}{3}$ $\frac{11}{12}$

8. $\frac{1}{3}$ $+\frac{3}{4}$ $1\frac{1}{12}$

9. $7\frac{1}{10}$ $+6\frac{9}{10}$ 14

10. $13\frac{5}{8}$ $+9\frac{2}{5}$ $23\frac{1}{40}$

11. $45\frac{6}{8}$ $+10\frac{6}{7}$ $56\frac{17}{28}$

12. $9\frac{4}{5}$ $+17\frac{1}{3}$ $27\frac{2}{15}$

13. $34\frac{3}{9}$ $+27\frac{2}{4}$ $61\frac{5}{6}$

14. $19\frac{3}{6}$ $+11\frac{2}{8}$ $30\frac{3}{4}$

Subtract.

15. $\frac{4}{8}-\frac{1}{4}$ $\frac{1}{4}$

16. $\frac{1}{2}-\frac{1}{3}$ $\frac{1}{6}$

17. $\frac{3}{4}-\frac{3}{10}$ $\frac{9}{20}$

18. $\frac{8}{9}-\frac{3}{4}$ $\frac{5}{36}$

19. $7\frac{3}{9}$ $-6\frac{2}{6}$ 1

20. 15 $-11\frac{1}{2}$ $3\frac{1}{2}$

21. $8\frac{3}{8}$ $-3\frac{1}{3}$ $5\frac{1}{24}$

22. $16\frac{4}{5}$ $-4\frac{2}{3}$ $12\frac{2}{15}$

23. $9\frac{2}{10}$ $-4\frac{1}{3}$ $4\frac{13}{15}$

24. $6\frac{1}{6}$ $-5\frac{3}{4}$ $\frac{5}{12}$

25. $17\frac{2}{5}$ $-8\frac{1}{2}$ $8\frac{9}{10}$

26. $33\frac{1}{5}$ $-13\frac{3}{8}$ $19\frac{33}{40}$

27. $14\frac{4}{16}$ $-13\frac{1}{4}$ 1

28. $28\frac{3}{7}$ $-26\frac{1}{2}$ $1\frac{13}{14}$

Add or subtract.

29. $\frac{3}{4}-\frac{1}{5}$ $\frac{11}{20}$

30. $\frac{1}{9}+\frac{4}{3}$ $1\frac{4}{9}$

31. $\frac{5}{7}+\frac{1}{3}$ $1\frac{1}{21}$

32. $\frac{1}{2}-\frac{1}{13}$ $\frac{11}{26}$

33. $5\frac{7}{8}$ $+10\frac{1}{6}$ $16\frac{1}{24}$

34. $9\frac{3}{16}$ $-8\frac{3}{4}$ $\frac{7}{16}$

35. $22\frac{3}{10}$ $-17\frac{4}{5}$ $4\frac{1}{2}$

36. $61\frac{2}{5}$ $-59\frac{3}{4}$ $1\frac{13}{20}$

37. 7 $-5\frac{8}{56}$ $1\frac{6}{7}$

38. $26\frac{1}{2}$ $8\frac{2}{8}$ $+14\frac{3}{4}$ $49\frac{1}{2}$

39. $10\frac{2}{3}$ $19\frac{4}{6}$ $+7\frac{1}{4}$ $37\frac{7}{12}$

40. $55\frac{1}{2}$ $37\frac{5}{9}$ $+81\frac{2}{6}$ $174\frac{7}{18}$

41. $22\frac{2}{3}$ $25\frac{3}{4}$ $+23\frac{1}{2}$ $71\frac{11}{12}$

42. $10\frac{4}{5}$ $19\frac{5}{6}$ $+1\frac{2}{3}$ $32\frac{3}{10}$

216

Follow Up

Reteaching

If students have difficulty solving the problems on page 217, suggest that they replace the fractions or decimals with whatever whole numbers they choose and solve the problems. Then have them rework the problems with the original numbers. Stress that the plan used to solve a problem is the same whether whole numbers, decimals, or fractions are involved.

Enrichment

Challenge students with the following problem.

A microbe colony with plenty of food doubles its population every three hours. At noon the colony had a billion microbes. When was the population 500 million? **9 a.m.**

Assignment Guide	Minimum	Average	Extended
page 216	1–28	1–37	2–42 even
page 217	1–6	1–8	1–8

217

Applications

PROBLEM SOLVING: Practice

QUESTION
DATA
PLAN
ANSWER
CHECK

Solve.

1. The school record for the standing broad jump was $20\frac{1}{2}$ ft. Bonnie made a jump of $18\frac{5}{6}$ ft. How much shorter than the school record was her jump? **$1\frac{2}{3}$ ft**

2. Franklin ran in a 2-mile race. He ran the first mile in $5\frac{1}{2}$ min. He ran the second mile in $6\frac{1}{10}$ min. What was his total time for the race? **$11\frac{3}{5}$ min**

3. In the high jump, Keith jumped $4\frac{3}{4}$ ft. The world record for the high jump was $6\frac{7}{12}$ ft. How much below that world record was Keith's jump? **$1\frac{5}{6}$ ft**

4. A baseball game lasted for 9 innings. Lefty McGuire pitched the first $6\frac{1}{3}$ innings. Roberto Macias pitched the next $1\frac{1}{3}$ innings. Bob Blazer finished the game as pitcher. How many innings did Bob pitch? **$1\frac{1}{3}$ innings**

5. Delia had times of 11.2 s, 10.8 s, 11.0 s, and 10.6 s for the 100-yard dash. Find the average time to the nearest tenth of a second. **10.9 s**

6. Halfback Rick Freeman had a total of 168 yards gained in carrying the ball 27 times. How many yards per carry did Rick average in the game? Round your answer to the nearest tenth. **6.2 yd**

7. The mile relay team ran its fastest race in 4 min 6 s. The four runners ran the next race in 59.6 s, 66.4 s, 60.2 s, and 59.5 s. What was their total time for the race? Did the team break their record? If so, by how much?
245.7 s or 4 min 5.7 s; yes; 0.3 s

8. Try This In the 880-yard run, Willie's time was 0.2 s faster than Carlton's. Mike's time for the race was 2 min 21.4 s. Ben was 0.9 s slower than Mike but 0.1 s faster than Willie. Jerome was 0.3 s behind Willie. What was the order of finish in the race and what was each person's time for the race? **See teaching notes.**

217

Using Page 217

Exercises 1–7 Encourage students to use the 5-Point Checklist to solve these problems. In exercise 7, three questions are asked. First students must determine the total time for the race, then compare their answer to the record time, and then subtract from the old record time to find the difference.

Try This A possible strategy, Draw a Picture, was taught on page 108.

Discussion Have students identify the question being asked and the data in the problem. They should see that the data is difficult to analyze in its current form. Explain that a picture can help organize the data. Have students suggest ways to draw the picture so that the relationship between data is clear.

Solution

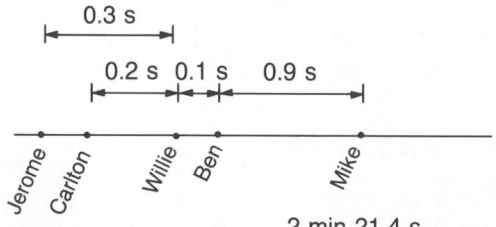

Mike's time	2 min 21.4 s
Ben's time	2 min 21.4 s + 0.9 s = 2 min 22.3 s
Willie's time	2 min 22.3 s + 0.1 s = 2 min 22.4 s
Carlton's time	2 min 22.4 s + 0.2 s = 2 min 22.6 s
Jerome's time	2 min 22.4 s + 0.3 s = 2 min 22.7 s

Ideas That Work

Special Education

To reinforce the skills practice of this lesson, let two or three students work together and play "Toss Up." Students will need two number cubes (TRB p. 278) labeled 1 through 6 and A through F, and a game sheet as shown.

	A	B	C	D	E	F
1						
2						
3						
4						
5						
6						

Have each group of students write exercises from page 216 in the squares of their game sheet. In turn, players roll the number cubes and work the problem indicated. The player obtaining the greatest number as an answer (if the answer is correct) earns 1 point. If both answers are the same, each player earns a point. The winner is the player who has the highest score when time is called.

Practice Supplement, page 84

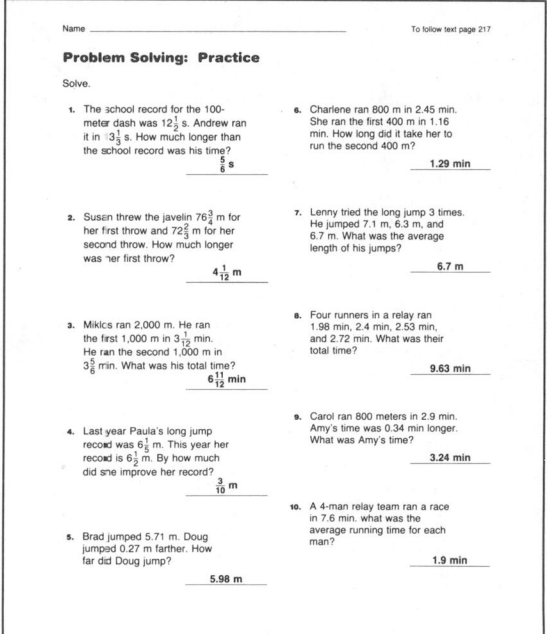

Lesson Focus
To choose the operations as a strategy for solving nonroutine word problems

Ideas for Getting Started

Provide students with the following problems. Ask them to solve each problem and tell which operation they used.

- A first snail traveled 6 m in 3 hours. How far did it travel in 1 hour?
- Dan pays $600 each month for rent. How much does he pay for rent in a year?
- Before Mr. Green started his trip, his odometer read 15,200 km. When he returned, it read 17,500 km. How far did he drive?
- Rita was 152 cm tall. She grew 2.5 cm during the summer. How tall was she at the end of the summer?

Lead a discussion about the meaning of addition, subtraction, multiplication and division. Ask students to describe the kinds of problems that can be solved by each operation.

Using Page 218

Motivational Problem Call on a student to read the Try This problem at the top of the page. Ask students to identify the question. Be certain students understand that the question does not ask for the number of bags filled but for the number of peaches left over after the bags were filled. Have students give the data needed to answer the question and tell which operation or operations they should plan to use to solve the problem.

Lesson Development On the chalkboard, work through the problem. Point out that it is sometimes helpful to label numbers in a problem as is shown in the first step of the solution. Ask students what the number 24 means in the second step. (24 bags can be filled) The remainder shows that there were 5 peaches left over. Have students check back in the problem to make sure the question has been answered and makes sense.

Exercises 1–2 Assign these exercises as independent work. Remind students to use the 5-Point Checklist.

PROBLEM SOLVING: Choose the Operations

| QUESTION |
| DATA |
| **PLAN** |
| ANSWER |
| CHECK |

Try This

Jennifer is a clerk in a produce market. She had a box with 214 peaches that she wanted to put into bags, 8 peaches to a bag. She had to throw away 17 peaches that were damaged. How many peaches were left after she had filled as many bags as possible?

When you try to solve a problem like the one above, you must decide which operations are needed and the order in which to use them. Sometimes you may find different ways to solve the same problem. We call this strategy **Choose the Operations**.

Addition +	**Subtraction −**	**Multiplication ×**	**Division ÷**
• Total • Combining • How many in all? • Sum	• How many more or less? • Compare • Take away • Difference	• Total of same size groups • Repeated addends • Product	• How many same size groups? • How many in each group? • How many times? • Quotient

Use this strategy to solve the problem above.

To find the number of peaches to be put in bags, you will need to subtract.

To find how many bags, you need to divide by the number of peaches per bag.

The remainder tells how many peaches are left over. This is the answer.

There were 5 peaches left over.

	Total peaches	Throw away	Peaches to be put into bags
	214	− 17	= 197

$$8\overline{)197} \quad \begin{array}{r} 24 \\ \underline{16} \\ 37 \\ \underline{32} \\ 5 \end{array} \leftarrow \text{remainder}$$

Solve.

1. Roland picked 85 cherries. He ate 9 cherries and shared the rest evenly with Maggie. She ate 12 cherries and shared the rest evenly with Amy. How many cherries did Amy get? 13

2. Niagara Falls moved upstream about 1.4 m each year between 1700 and 1900. The falls moved about half as far each year since 1900. How far did the falls move between 1700 and 1984? 338.8 m

218

Strategy Test Item

Optional Problem If you wish to assess students' ability to apply the strategy called Choose the Operations introduced in this chapter, provide them with the problem below.

> Larry bought a bicycle for $129.95. There was an additional $8.12 for sales tax. Larry paid $35.00 down and was going to pay the rest at $15.00 each week. How many weeks will it take for Larry to pay for the bicycle?

Solution

$129.95 + $8.12 = $138.07

$138.07 − $35.00 = $103.07

6 weeks at $15 per week

1 week − $13.07

$$15\overline{)103.07} \quad \begin{array}{r} 6. \\ \underline{90} \\ 13\ 07 \end{array}$$

It will take 7 weeks for Larry to pay for the bicycle.

CHAPTER REVIEW/TEST

Write a fraction for the part of the region or set that is shaded.

1.  $\frac{3}{5}$

2. 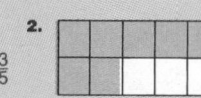 $\frac{7}{10}$

3.  $\frac{1}{3}$

4.  $\frac{7}{8}$

Write the missing numerator or denominator.

5. $\frac{2}{5} = \frac{}{20}$ 8

6. $\frac{8}{12} = \frac{}{3}$ 2

7. $\frac{5}{6} = \frac{}{60}$ 50

8. $\frac{3}{4} = \frac{27}{}$ 36

Write each fraction in lowest terms.

9. $\frac{4}{12}$ $\frac{1}{3}$

10. $\frac{20}{24}$ $\frac{5}{6}$

11. $\frac{15}{18}$ $\frac{5}{6}$

12. $\frac{24}{100}$ $\frac{6}{25}$

Write each improper fraction as a mixed number or a whole number.

13. $\frac{8}{3}$ $2\frac{2}{3}$

14. $\frac{22}{8}$ $2\frac{3}{4}$

15. $\frac{28}{7}$ 4

16. $\frac{38}{16}$ $2\frac{3}{8}$

Write each mixed number as an improper fraction.

17. $5\frac{2}{3}$ $\frac{17}{3}$

18. $3\frac{5}{8}$ $\frac{29}{8}$

19. $10\frac{2}{5}$ $\frac{52}{5}$

20. $2\frac{9}{10}$ $\frac{29}{10}$

Compare the fractions. Write > or < for each ●.

21. $\frac{5}{9} ● \frac{1}{2}$ >

22. $\frac{7}{12} ● \frac{3}{4}$ <

23. $\frac{3}{8} ● \frac{3}{10}$ >

24. $\frac{2}{3} ● \frac{11}{16}$ <

Add or subtract.

25. $\begin{array}{r} \frac{1}{8} \\ + \frac{5}{8} \\ \hline \frac{3}{4} \end{array}$

26. $\begin{array}{r} \frac{3}{4} \\ + \frac{7}{12} \\ \hline 1\frac{1}{3} \end{array}$

27. $\begin{array}{r} \frac{11}{12} \\ - \frac{5}{12} \\ \hline \frac{1}{2} \end{array}$

28. $\begin{array}{r} \frac{4}{5} \\ - \frac{3}{10} \\ \hline \frac{1}{2} \end{array}$

29. $\begin{array}{r} 4\frac{2}{3} \\ + 2\frac{3}{5} \\ \hline 7\frac{4}{15} \end{array}$

30. $\begin{array}{r} 6 \\ - 3\frac{2}{3} \\ \hline 2\frac{1}{3} \end{array}$

31. $\begin{array}{r} 23\frac{9}{10} \\ + 18\frac{1}{2} \\ \hline 42\frac{2}{5} \end{array}$

32. $\begin{array}{r} 10\frac{1}{3} \\ - 3\frac{5}{6} \\ \hline 6\frac{1}{2} \end{array}$

33. Megan ran a mile in $7\frac{3}{4}$ min. Then she took $8\frac{1}{2}$ min to run another mile. What was the total time for the two miles? $16\frac{1}{4}$ min

34. A recipe calls for $3\frac{1}{2}$ c of flour. Penny has only $2\frac{2}{3}$ c of flour. How much more flour does she need for the recipe? $\frac{5}{6}$ c

---

Using Page 219

The exercises in the Chapter Review/Test emphasize the major concepts and skills presented in this chapter. These exercises may be used as a review assignment or as a test, depending upon your needs.

Item Analysis The table below correlates the Chapter Review/Test items with objectives and with the student text pages on which the concepts or skills were taught.

Items	Objectives	Related Text Pages
1–12	8.1	194–199
13–20	8.2	200–201
21–24	8.3	202–204
25–28	8.4	206–209
29–32	8.5	210–215

Each chapter ends with a comprehensive review, reteaching opportunities, an enrichment activity, and a cumulative review. See the next three pages.

Assessment Options

If you use the Chapter Review/Test as a review assignment, you may wish to use the free-response test or the multiple-choice test to evaluate mastery of the chapter objectives. The items on these tests have a one-to-one correspondence in terms of content and level of difficulty. A correlation of test items to objectives and student text pages is provided in the Management Guide for Chapter 8.

Multiple-Choice Test, TRB pages 22–24
Free-Response Test, TRB pages 63–64

TRB Options

The following blackline masters are available for use with this chapter. If you have not already assigned these materials, you may wish to use them to close the chapter.

Recreation, TRB page 162
Consumer Applications, TRB page 180
Calculator Technology, TRB page 198
Reading Math, TRB page 234
Family Involvement, TRB pages 259–260

Reteaching

Using Page 220

The exercises on this page are intended for those students who experienced difficulty with the Chapter Review/Test on page 219. Should students require reteaching of these key concepts and skills, please refer to the teaching notes below. Otherwise, the Another Look exercises can be assigned as independent work, with students using the accompanying sample problems and hints as guides.

Exercises 1–3 This skill was originally taught on pages 196–197. Have students study the example in the display box. Point out that equivalent fractions can be formed by multiplying the numerator and denominator by the same number. Work through the first exercise on the chalkboard. Ask students what to multiply times 6 to get 12. Explain that since the denominator was multiplied by 2, the numerator is multiplied by 2.

Exercises 4–6 This skill was originally taught on pages 198–199. Review the steps in reducing a fraction to lowest terms, by working through the example on the chalkboard. Remind students that a fraction is in lowest terms when 1 is the only common factor of the numerator and denominator.

Exercises 7–18 This skill was originally taught on pages 200–201. Direct students' attention to the example in the display box. Point out that the picture shows $1\frac{1}{3}$ is the same as $\frac{4}{3}$. Explain that the denominator, 3, tells the number in each whole, so to change the improper fraction to a mixed number, we can divide by 3 to find the whole number part and write the remainder over the divisor as the fraction part. In the reversed process we multiply by the denominator, since there are 3 parts in each whole. Then the numerator is added to the product and the sum is written over the denominator.

Exercises 19–24 This skill was originally taught on pages 202–203. On the chalkboard, work through the example shown in the display box. Point out that when the fractions are written with a common denominator, the fractions compare the way the numerators compare.

Exercises 25–33 This skill was originally taught on pages 206–215. Display the addition example on the chalkboard and work through the steps to find the sum. Emphasize writing equivalent fractions with a common denominator. Point out that the sum, $7\frac{5}{4}$, can be renamed as $8\frac{1}{4}$.

Next work through the subtraction example with students. Stress that since $\frac{2}{3}$ cannot be subtracted from $\frac{1}{3}$, we must rename $2\frac{1}{3}$ as $1\frac{4}{3}$.

ANOTHER LOOK

$$\frac{2\times3}{3\times3}=\frac{6}{9}$$ Multiply to find equivalent fraction.

$$\frac{6\div3}{9\div3}=\frac{2}{3}$$ Divide to rewrite in lowest terms.

Write the missing numerator or denominator.

1. $\frac{4}{6}=\frac{}{12}$ 8

2. $\frac{2}{5}=\frac{}{25}$ 10

3. $\frac{1}{3}=\frac{7}{21}$ 21

Write each fraction in lowest terms.

4. $\frac{2}{6}$ $\frac{1}{3}$

5. $\frac{8}{24}$ $\frac{1}{3}$

6. $\frac{16}{100}$ $\frac{4}{25}$

$$1\frac{1}{3}=\frac{4}{3}$$
↑ ↑
mixed number / improper fraction

Write each improper fraction as a whole number or a mixed number.

7. $\frac{11}{3}$ $3\frac{2}{3}$

8. $\frac{21}{5}$ $4\frac{1}{5}$

9. $\frac{35}{8}$ $4\frac{3}{8}$

10. $\frac{23}{4}$ $5\frac{3}{4}$

11. $\frac{15}{12}$ $1\frac{1}{4}$

12. $\frac{36}{12}$ 3

Write each mixed number as an improper fraction.

13. $5\frac{5}{6}$ $\frac{35}{6}$

14. $3\frac{1}{8}$ $\frac{25}{8}$

15. $7\frac{2}{3}$ $\frac{23}{3}$

16. $1\frac{7}{12}$ $\frac{19}{12}$

17. $10\frac{2}{3}$ $\frac{32}{3}$

18. $6\frac{7}{8}$ $\frac{55}{8}$

Compare $\frac{2}{3}$ and $\frac{3}{5}$.

$\boxed{10>9}$

$\frac{10}{15}>\frac{9}{15}$
so
$\frac{2}{3}>\frac{3}{5}$

Compare the numbers. Write > or < for each ▨.

19. $\frac{9}{11}$ ▨ $\frac{4}{5}$ >

20. $\frac{5}{8}$ ▨ $\frac{7}{16}$ >

21. $\frac{3}{4}$ ▨ $\frac{20}{24}$ <

22. $3\frac{5}{8}$ ▨ $3\frac{7}{8}$ <

23. $1\frac{5}{6}$ ▨ $1\frac{1}{2}$ >

24. $6\frac{8}{15}$ ▨ $7\frac{5}{8}$ <

$$5\frac{3}{4}=5\frac{3}{4}$$
$$+2\frac{1}{2}=2\frac{2}{4}$$
$$\overline{7\frac{5}{4}=8\frac{1}{4}}$$

$$2\frac{1}{3}=1\frac{4}{3}$$
$$-1\frac{2}{3}=1\frac{2}{3}$$
$$\overline{\frac{2}{3}}$$

Add or subtract.

25. $\frac{5}{6}$ $+\frac{1}{3}$ $1\frac{1}{6}$

26. $\frac{11}{12}$ $-\frac{2}{3}$ $\frac{1}{4}$

27. $\frac{7}{10}$ $+\frac{2}{3}$ $1\frac{11}{30}$

28. $2\frac{1}{2}$ $+2\frac{7}{8}$ $5\frac{3}{8}$

29. 6 $-4\frac{5}{8}$ $1\frac{3}{8}$

30. $3\frac{3}{4}$ $-1\frac{5}{8}$ $2\frac{1}{8}$

31. $8\frac{7}{8}+5\frac{5}{6}$ $14\frac{17}{24}$

32. $4\frac{3}{8}-2\frac{3}{4}$ $1\frac{5}{8}$

33. $6\frac{2}{5}-3\frac{7}{10}$ $2\frac{7}{10}$

Just for Teachers

Hindu Development of Fractions

The *Lilavati* of Aryabhata, an early reference to Hindu mathematics dated about A.D. 470, indicates a level of sophistication equal to that of Alexandria before the fall of the Roman Empire. The value of *pi,* the laws of positives and negatives, and trigonometric tables corresponding to those formulated by Alexandrian scholars are cited in the *Lilavati.* One hundred fifty years later, the writings of other Hindu scholars reveal the establishment of a decimal positional notation system. Also found were rules for adding, subtracting, and multiplying with zero, and evidence of the fractional notation of numerator over denominator. By A.D. 850, rules for calculating with fractions were developed.

This development of the concept of fractions, like the concept of zero as a place holder, set Hindu mathematics apart by reflecting an entirely new attitude toward frac-

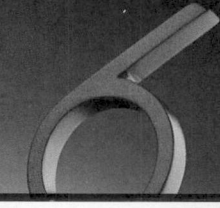

ENRICHMENT

Fractions

"Transjovian Pipeline"
Computer-generated
artwork by David Em
Copyright © 1979

Use the clues to name the mystery fractions.

1. My numerator is 1 less than my denominator. Both my numerator and denominator are prime. Which fraction am I? $\frac{2}{3}$

2. I am greater than 1 but less than 2. The sum of my numerator and denominator is 9. My denominator subtracted from my numerator is 1. Which fraction am I? $\frac{5}{4}$

3. I am greater than $\frac{1}{3}$ but less than $\frac{1}{2}$. My denominator is 12. Which fraction am I? $\frac{5}{12}$

4. I am greater than $\frac{1}{2}$ but less than $\frac{3}{4}$. My denominator is 8. Which fraction am I? $\frac{5}{8}$

5. My denominator is a prime number less than 10. My numerator is a perfect square. I am equal to the whole number 5. Which fraction am I? $\frac{25}{5}$

6. I am greater than 5 but less than 6. My numerator is a perfect square. The sum of my numerator and denominator is 19. Which fraction am I? $\frac{16}{3}$

7. I am greater than $\frac{1}{2}$ but less than $\frac{2}{3}$. The difference between my numerator and denominator is 5. The product of my numerator and denominator is 84. Which fraction am I? $\frac{7}{12}$

8. I am greater than 1 but less than $1\frac{1}{2}$. My numerator and denominator are prime numbers less than 20. The sum of my numerator and denominator is a multiple of 5. Which fraction am I? $\frac{17}{13}$

9. We are two fractions. Our sum is 1. Our difference is $\frac{1}{5}$. Who are we? $\frac{2}{5}$ and $\frac{3}{5}$

10. We are two numbers. Our sum is 2. Our difference is $\frac{1}{2}$. Who are we? $\frac{3}{4}$ and $1\frac{1}{4}$

221

Using Page 221

This page is intended for those students who successfully completed the Chapter Review/Test on page 219. You may wish to assign this page as independent work while you use Another Look exercises to reteach the basic concepts and skills of the chapter. Or, you may decide that all students would benefit from exposure to this Enrichment activity.

Lesson Development Review with students the meaning of prime number, multiple, and perfect square. Then tell students that they are going to play the game "Which Fraction Am I?" Give orally or write on the chalkboard this problem.

I am greater than 2 but less than 3. My denominator is the smallest prime number. Which fraction am I?

Some students will find the answer quickly. After most students appear to have the fraction $\frac{5}{2}$, have students explain how they arrived at their answers.

Exercises 1—10 Work through exercise 1 as a class activity and then assign the rest of the exercises as independent work. After students complete the assignment, you may wish to have them write puzzles for fractions and present them to the class.

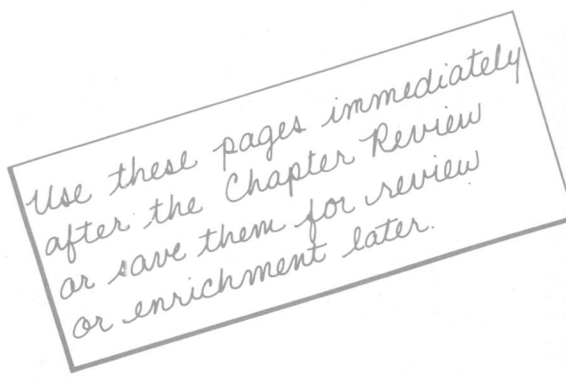

Use these pages immediately after the Chapter Review or save them for review or enrichment later.

---

tions. Mathematicians in antiquity had never devised a systematic method for handling them, though fractions have been found in early mathematical records.

The Hindus, along with the Arabs who inherited part of the crumbled Roman Empire, used fractions in their studies of astronomy. They were able to improve upon the Alexandrian trigonometric tables which were useful to celestial observation. Formulating these tables had involved the extraction of square roots, a tedious task on the abacus. Hindu-Arabic scholars, however, were "freed" from the abacus by the new numbers. Positional and fractional notations helped scholars find square roots to more precise values.

Using Page 222

The exercises on the page provide practice for maintaining cumulative skills. The emphasis in this Cumulative Review is on division of decimals (Chapter 5) and number relationships and equations (Chapter 7).

Item Analysis The table below correlates the Cumulative Review items with objectives and with the student book pages on which the concepts or skills were taught.

Items	Objectives	Related Text Pages
1–5	5.1	116–120
6	5.3	128
7	7.1	164–171
8	7.2	172–175
9–12	7.4	178–181
13	5.4	121–123; 126–127
14	7.5	182–185

CUMULATIVE REVIEW

Find the quotients.

1. $16\overline{)6.96}$

A 0.475 B 0.435 ✓
C 47.5 D not given

2. $226\overline{)33.9}$

A 0.15 ✓ B 1.5
C 0.20 D not given

Find each quotient to the nearest hundredth.

3. $29\overline{)24.7}$

A 0.86 B 0.851
C 0.85 ✓ D not given

4. $41\overline{)94.87}$

A 2.41 B 2.313
C 0.231 D not given ✓

5. Divide.

$7,297 \div 1,000$

A 729.7 B 72.97
C 7.297 ✓ D not given

6. Estimate the quotient.

$0.247\overline{)7.57}$

A 3.5 B 40 ✓
C 4 D not given

7. What is the prime factorization of 88?

A $2 \cdot 2 \cdot 2 \cdot 11$ ✓ B $2 \cdot 4 \cdot 11$
C $2 \cdot 2 \cdot 11$ D not given

8. What is the GCF of 24 and 180?

A 24 B 12 ✓
C 18 D not given

Solve each equation.

9. $x + 12 = 39$

A $x = 22$ B $x = 12$
C $x = 32$ D not given ✓

10. $5t = 125$

A $t = 25$ ✓ B $t = 55$
C $t = 625$ D not given

11. $\frac{y}{6} = 60$

A $y = 6$ B $y = 360$ ✓
C $y = 10$ D not given

12. $z - 2 = 63$

A $z = 65$ ✓ B $z = 61$
C $z = 62$ D not given

13. Natalie ran a 10 km race in 45.2 min. How long did it take her to run 1 km?

A 4.52 min ✓ B 4 min
C 45 s D not given

14. The same number of nickels are in each of 7 stacks. The stacks balance with 84 nickels. Which equation shows this situation?

A $7x = 84$ ✓ B $7 + x = 84$
C $\frac{7}{x} = 84$ D not given

Multiplication and Division of Fractions

Overview Chapter 9

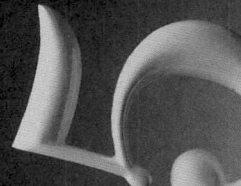

Objectives

9.1 Find the product of fractions or mixed numbers.

9.2 Find the reciprocal of a number.

9.3 Find the quotient of fractions or of mixed numbers.

9.4 Compare two fractions by comparing their decimal equivalents.

9.5 Solve word problems using the 5-Point Checklist and cumulative computational skills.

Summary

This chapter deals with multiplication and division of fractions. The multiplication lessons include finding a fraction of a number, multiplying fractions, and multiplying mixed numbers. The division section of the chapter presents lessons on reciprocals, dividing fractions, and dividing mixed numbers. These operations are related to problem situations which promote an understanding of fraction computational concepts.

In this chapter, the relationship between fractions and decimals is presented. Students find a decimal for a given fraction by dividing the numerator by the denominator. The decimal equivalents are then used to compare fractions. The problem-solving strand is extended in this chapter to include multiplication and division of fractions and mixed numbers.

Mathematical Background

Multiplication of Fractions The standard algorithm for multiplying fractions is introduced as well as the shortcut of dividing numerators and denominators by common factors. Prerequisite skills include writing whole and mixed numbers as fractions, writing fractions as whole or mixed numbers, and writing fractions in lowest terms. Models can be used to help students obtain a clearer understanding of fraction multiplication.

Fraction of a whole number

To find $\frac{2}{3}$ of 15, first divide 15 objects into thirds, or three groups. Then count the number of objects in two of the groups.

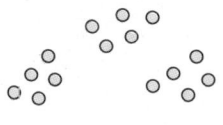 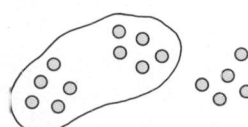

$$\frac{2}{3} \text{ of } 15 = 10$$

Fraction times a fraction

To find $\frac{2}{3} \times \frac{4}{5}$, shade $\frac{4}{5}$ of the region with one color. Then with a second color shade $\frac{2}{3}$ of the $\frac{4}{5}$.

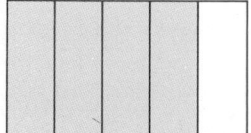 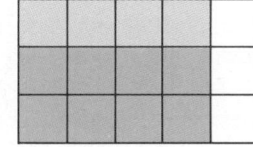

$$\frac{2}{3} \times \frac{4}{5} = \frac{8}{15}$$

Division of Fractions An intuitive grasp of the concept of division of fractional numbers can be given with a graphic illustration. The figures below show how many $\frac{3}{4}$ pieces are in $2\frac{1}{4}$.

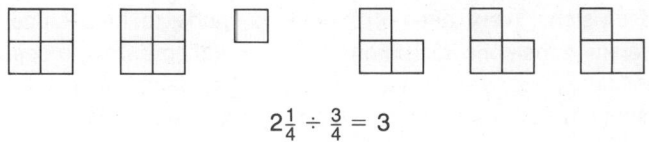

$$2\frac{1}{4} \div \frac{3}{4} = 3$$

The rule for dividing two fractions can be explained using the inverse relationship between multiplication and division and the idea that every nonzero number has a reciprocal. To find the quotient in the exercise $\frac{5}{8} \div \frac{3}{4} = n$, we must find a number n such that $n \times \frac{3}{4} = \frac{5}{8}$. Since $\frac{4}{3} \times \frac{3}{4} = 1$, n must be $\frac{5}{8}$ of $\frac{3}{4}$, or $\frac{5}{8} \times \frac{3}{4}$. Therefore, $\frac{5}{8} \div \frac{3}{4} = \frac{5}{8} \times \frac{4}{3}$. More generally, $\frac{a}{b} \div \frac{c}{d} = \frac{a}{b} \times \frac{d}{c}$ if $\frac{c}{d} \neq 0$.

Fractions and Decimals This chapter shows the relationship between decimal numbers and fractions. Every fractional number can be expressed as a repeating or terminating decimal. Conversely, every repeating decimal or terminating decimal represents a fractional number. In Book 8 of this series, students will learn that there are decimals which are neither terminating nor repeating. These are the *irrational numbers*. To find a decimal for a given fraction, the numerator is divided by the denominator. If a remainder of zero is reached, the resulting decimal terminates. In some cases a zero remainder is never reached, but the same remainder occurs twice. At this point, the digits in the quotient repeat.

$\frac{3}{8}$ is a terminating decimal

```
    0.375
8)3.000
  2 4
  ─────
    60
    56
  ─────
    40
    40
  ─────
     0
```

$\frac{5}{6}$ is a repeating decimal

```
    0.833 . . .
6)5.000
  4 8
  ─────
    20
    18
  ─────
    20
    18
  ─────
     2
```

Problem Solving In this chapter, problem solving is extended to include multiplication and division of fractions and mixed numbers. On pages 236 and 237, the lesson includes problems involving the use of electricity. The second step of the 5-Point Checklist is highlighted as the students use data from a table to solve problems. A new strategy for nonroutine problems, called Use Logical Reasoning, is taught on page 242. In this lesson, Venn diagrams are used to help students reason logically about problems.

Vocabulary

reciprocal   repeating decimal   terminating decimal

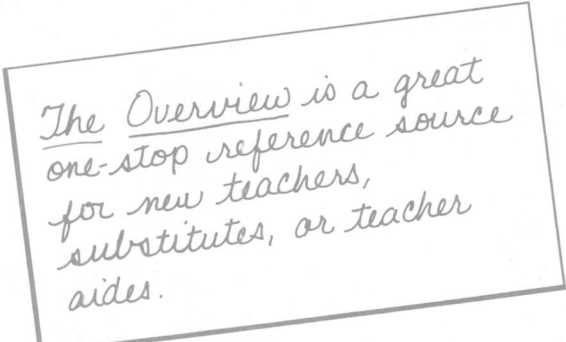

The Overview is a great one-stop reference source for new teachers, substitutes, or teacher aides.

Teaching Tips

Error Analysis

This chapter extends fraction operations to include multiplication and division. Every attempt should be made to help students understand the concepts before the computational work is begun. Traditionally, many error patterns occur in students' work with the content of this chapter. Some common errors are given below.

Error Pattern 1

$$\frac{1}{3} \times 3 = 9 \qquad \frac{1}{5} \times 6 = 30 \qquad \frac{1}{2} \times 8 = 16$$

Diagnosis The student has multiplied the denominator of the fraction times the whole number.

Remediation Begin with problems such as $\frac{1}{2} \times 8$. Read this as $\frac{1}{2}$ of 8 and represent this with objects. Have students take $\frac{1}{2}$ of the 8 objects and write the number. After the concept is clear to the student, move to the algorithm.

Error Pattern 2

$$\frac{2}{3} \times \frac{3}{5} = \frac{10}{9} \qquad \frac{4}{5} \times \frac{1}{2} = \frac{8}{5} \qquad \frac{3}{5} \times \frac{3}{8} = \frac{24}{15}$$

Diagnosis The student "cross-multiplied" to find the product.

Remediation Use an area model to develop the meaning of fraction multiplication. After the student works through several examples using models, focus on the algorithmic form $\frac{a}{b} \times \frac{c}{d} = \frac{a \times c}{b \times d}$.

Error Pattern 3

$$\frac{3}{4} \times \frac{2}{3} = \frac{\cancel{3}}{4} \times \frac{2}{\cancel{3}} = \frac{2}{4} \qquad \frac{3}{4} \times \frac{\cancel{4}}{5} = \frac{\cancel{4}}{4} \times \frac{3}{5} = \frac{1}{20}$$

$$\frac{6}{7} \times \frac{6}{1} = \frac{\cancel{6}}{7} \times \frac{\cancel{6}}{1} = \frac{1}{7} \qquad \frac{5}{8} \times \frac{1}{8} = \frac{5}{\cancel{8}} \times \frac{1}{\cancel{8}} = \frac{5}{1}$$

Diagnosis The student cancelled like numbers regardless of where they occurred. Cancelling has occurred in the numerators, denominators, or a mixture of both.

Remediation Use an area model to show an example such as $\frac{3}{4} \times \frac{2}{3}$. Discuss reducing to lowest terms and show that to reduce, the numerator and denominator must contain common factors. Explain that in an exercise such as $\frac{3}{4} \times \frac{3}{5}$, the numerators and denominators have no common factors. The product, $(\frac{9}{20})$ is in lowest terms.

Error Pattern 4

$$3\frac{1}{4} \times 2\frac{1}{3} = 6\frac{1}{12} \qquad 5\frac{2}{3} \times 4\frac{4}{5} = 20\frac{8}{15} \qquad 2\frac{7}{8} \times 5\frac{1}{3} = 10\frac{7}{24}$$

Diagnosis The student multiplied mixed numbers by multiplying the whole numbers and then multiplying the fractions.

Remediation Explain that the first step in multiplying mixed numbers is to change each mixed number to an improper fraction. Then multiply as with fractions. Work through an example with the student.

$$5\frac{2}{3} \times 4\frac{4}{5} = \frac{17}{3} \times \frac{24}{5} = \frac{17}{\cancel{3}_1} \times \frac{\cancel{24}^8}{5} = \frac{136}{5} = 27\frac{1}{5}$$

Error Pattern 5

$$\frac{2}{5} \div \frac{1}{8} = \frac{2}{5} \div \frac{1}{\cancel{8}_4} = \frac{1}{5} \div \frac{1}{4} = \frac{1}{5} \times \frac{4}{1} = \frac{4}{5}$$

$$\frac{6}{7} \div \frac{2}{7} = \frac{\cancel{6}^2}{7} \div \frac{2}{\cancel{9}_3} = \frac{2}{7} \div \frac{2}{3} = \frac{2}{7} \times \frac{3}{2} = \frac{6}{14}$$

Diagnosis The student used the multiplication shortcut before changing the exercise to multiplication.

Remediation Review the division algorithm with the student. Stress that the shortcut can be used only after the reciprocal of the divisor is found and the exercise is written as the dividend times the reciprocal of the divisor.

Problem Solving

Helping Students Read Mathematics Problems

A student's reading ability has some influence on whether that student becomes a successful problem solver. At the most basic level, a student must be able to recognize words and associate meaning with them. At a higher level, a student must be able to combine words into sentences and give meaning to the sentences. Research suggests, however, that the ability to read each word and sentence in a problem, and even the ability to explain the meaning of each sentence, does *not* guarantee that a student will *understand* a problem sufficiently well to select and implement an appropriate solution strategy. The teaching-tips discussion in Chapter 3, page 54 C, provides a list of ideas for helping students *understand* math problems. The ideas listed below for improving students' reading skills will also increase their skills in understanding problems and the area of understanding math problems may be necessary for your students.

- Make a bulletin board display of words that have special meanings in mathematics. Examples:

place value	difference	perimeter
sum	divisor	area
addend	meter	face

- Have students write sentences illustrating the different meanings of a word. Examples:

  Johnny's <u>face</u> is red.

  The <u>face</u> of a cube is a square.

- Have students rewrite number words as numerals. Example: Have students write two hundred twenty-five as 225.
- Give students opportunities to write their own word problems. See Chapter 11, page 268 C, for teaching tips to help students formulate problems.
- Have students first read problems silently, then reread the problems aloud and slowly.
- Have students substitute nouns for pronouns if the action in the problem is confusing.
- Have a mathematics dictionary available to students.

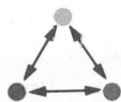 **Special Education**

As in previous chapters, the special students in your class will often need an intuitive development of concepts and skills before turning to the textbook reviews presented. Such a development usually is necessary in order to fill gaps in learning and to compensate for difficulties students have. The ideas that follow focus on ways to provide visual, verbal, and manipulative guidance as the basis for this development in important lessons of this chapter.

Filling Loops

To help students better picture multiplications such as $\frac{2}{3}$ of 12, give them a sheet like that of the figure. The sheet has three loops drawn on it, two of which are framed. For this example, students take 12 counters and place them, one by one, into the loops until all 12 are distributed. They then are asked to describe what they see. (8 of the 12, or $\frac{2}{3}$ are inside the frame.) Remind students that $\frac{2}{3}$ *of* 12 is written $\frac{2}{3} \times 12$.

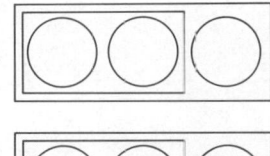
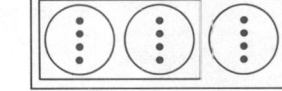

Shade It

Using construction paper models or worksheet pictures of geometric regions, have students shade $\frac{1}{3} \times 6$, $\frac{3}{4} \times 12$, and so on. Help them say and write equations which describe the shaded parts. This activity can be used later for examples like $\frac{2}{3} \times \frac{3}{4}$ and $\frac{7}{10} \times \frac{5}{6}$.

Look for Patterns

As students work with the models, retain a list of exercises with answers. Ask students if they see a pattern. (The same answers can be found by multiplying numerators, multiplying denominators.) Test this pattern on other problems before turning to the summary of this idea on page 226. For the special students in your class, it may be better to emphasize the general procedure for multiplying two fractions, including multiplication involving mixed numbers, before introducing the shortcut of page 227.

Dramatizing Division

"Snack bars" can help special students approach division of fractions meaningfully. Provide construction paper snack bars which are pre-marked into thirds, fourths, and sixths. Invite students to cut out bites and tell the total number of bites required to eat the bars. In the example below, there are 2 snack bars. With each bite, $\frac{1}{3}$ of the bar is eaten. It takes 6 bites to eat the bars.

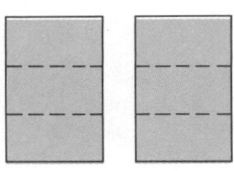 $\qquad 2 \div \frac{1}{3} = 6$

After students use the snack bars to illustrate several examples of division, elicit from them that we could get the same answer if we invert the divisor and multiply.

$$2 \div \frac{1}{3} = 2 \times \frac{3}{1} = 6$$

The One Step

Students may require isolated practice on particular steps for multiplying or dividing fractions. Two examples of steps which typically cause special students much difficulty are: 1) changing mixed numbers to improper fractions before multiplying or dividing, and 2) inverting the correct fraction in division. Exercises which require students to carry out just one step of several exercises, such as inverting, may be necessary. After this part of the exercise is checked, students can then work the exercises to completion.

 **Subject Integration**

Subject matter related to other areas of the curriculum has been integrated into the following lessons. This provides an opportunity to highlight the interaction between mathematics and other subjects.

Consumer Awareness Cosmetics, page 223; stock market prices, page 245
Fine Arts Gemstones, pages 224–225; fresco restoration, page 226; symphonies, page 241
Industrial Arts Models, pages 228–229
Physical Education Gymnastics, page 231; softball diamond, pages 234–235; health class, soccer, page 242
Science Aquarium, pages 232–233
Home Economics Electricity, pages 236–237

Management Guide

	Teaching Chapter 9				Meeting Individual Needs				
					Lesson Assignments			Follow Up		
Objectives	Chapter Content	Pages	TRB Test Items	Minimum	Average	Extended	Reteaching	Enrichment	Practice
	Chapter Opener	223							
9.1 Find the products of fractions or mixed numbers.	Finding a Fraction of a Whole Number	224–225	1–2	1–33	1–33	1–33 odd, 34	SE6 Ch 9 RS 67	ES 67	PS 85
	Multiplying Fractions	226	3–5	1–16, 21	1–21	1–21 odd, 22	SE6 Ch 9		
	Using a Multiplication Shortcut	227		1–16	1–24	1–23 odd	RS 68	ES 68	MP 431 PS 86
	Multiplying with Mixed Numbers	228–229	6–10	1–24, 29, SK	1–29, SK	1–29 odd, SK	RS 69	ES 69	MP 431 PS 87
	Skills Practice	230		1–24	1–36	2–36 even			
9.2 Find the reciprocal of a number.	Reciprocals	231	11–13	1–19	1–20	1–20			MP 431 PS 88
9.3 Find the quotient of fractions or of mixed numbers.	Dividing Fractions	232–233	14–17	1–21, 28	1–28, TM	2–28 even, 29, TM	SE6 Ch 9 RS 70	ES 70	MP 431 PS 89
	Dividing with Mixed Numbers	234–235	18–21	1–20, 29, SK	1–29, 32, SK	1–29 odd, 30–32, SK	SE6 Ch 9 RS 71	ES 71	MP 432 PS 90
9.4 Compare two fractions by comparing their decimal equivalents.	Fractions and Decimals	238–233	22–24	1–24, 35–45	1–45	1–45 odd, 46, TM	RS 73	ES 73	MP 432 PS 92
	Repeating and Terminating Decimals	241	25–28	1–18, 29–32	1–32	2–32 odd	RS 74	ES 74	MP 432 PS 93
	Skills Practice	240		1–32	1–44	2–52 even			
9.5 Solve word problems using the 5-Point Checklist and cumulative computational skills.	Problem Solving: Using Data from a Table	236–237	29–32	1–10, 13	1–14	5–15	RS 72	ES 72	PS 91
	Problem Solving: Use Logical Reasoning	242							
	Chapter Review/Test	243							
	Another Look/Enrichment	244–245							
	Cumulative Review	246							

SE6 Student Edition, Book 6
RS Reteaching Supplement
ES Enrichment Supplement
PS Practice Supplement
MP More Practice
TM Think Math
SK Skillkeeper
TRB Teacher's Resource Book

Masters for use

. . . before Chapter 9

Readiness Dividing with Fractions	120
Readiness Multiplying with Fractions	119

. . . after Chapter 9

Record Keeping	304
Family Involvement At-Home Activities	262
Family Involvement Key Math	261
Reading Math Fraction Operations	235
Chapter 9 Test Free-Response Format	65–66
Chapter 9 Test Multiple-Choice Format	25–27

. . . during Chapter 9

Calculator Technology Fraction Scramble	199
Consumer Applications Recipe Conversions	181
Teaching Aids	277, 283, 285
Recreation Number Puzzle	163
Activities That Count Magic Squares	147

Supplements

ADDISON·WESLEY MATHEMATICS
RETEACHING WORKBOOK
pp. 67–72

ADDISON·WESLEY MATHEMATICS
ENRICHMENT WORKBOOK
pp. 67–72

ADDISON·WESLEY MATHEMATICS
PRACTICE WORKBOOK
pp. 85–93

Other Addison-Wesley Resources

Books and Kits

General Mathematics: Making Practice Fun   pp. 37 A, B, 39 A, B, 40 A, B, 41 A, B

Arithmetic Primer   pp. 167–200

Problem-Solving Experiences in Mathematics, Grade 7
   Problems 33, 34, 35, 69, 70, 75, 80, 82, 87, 95, 98, 100, 102, 107, 109, 113, 118, 128, 133, 134, 143, 149

Technology

Computer Math Activities   Volume 4
Computer Math Games   Volume 1

Activities That Count

Activities That Count are designed for use throughout this chapter and subsequent chapters. Before beginning Chapter 9, you may wish to review these activities and select the ones you consider appropriate for your class.

Concentration Game

Purpose To recognize equivalent fractions and decimals

Materials 24 index cards labeled as shown below

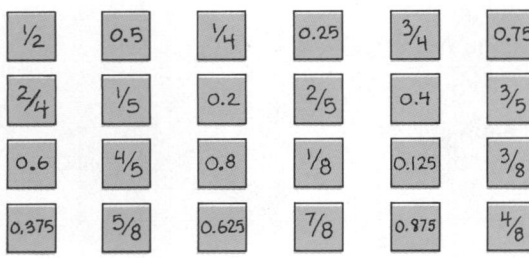

Activity Mix the cards and place them face down. In turn, each player turns over two cards, trying to match a decimal with a fraction. If they do not match, the player must turn cards face down again, and the next player takes a turn. Matching cards are taken off playing area and stacked in front of players. The player with the most cards at the end of the game is the winner.

Taking Stock Project

Purpose To solve problems involving fractions and decimals

Activity Have students choose a stock from a newspaper stock exchange report and pretend to have bought 100 shares at that day's closing price. Have students follow the stock daily, and determine how much they would gain or lose after one month.

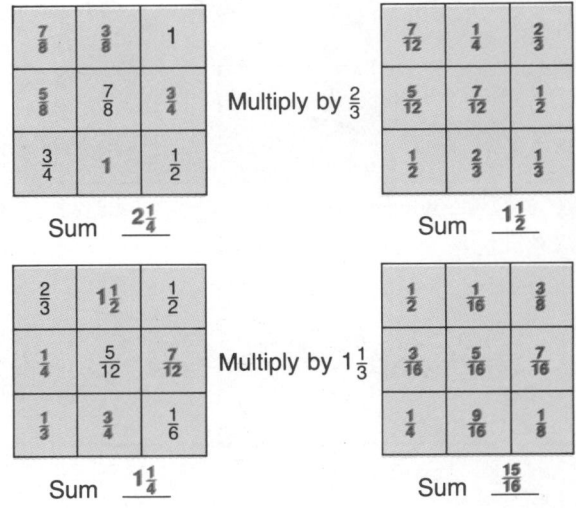

Magic Squares Game

Purpose To add, subtract, multiply, and divide fractions

Materials Game sheet (TRB p. 147)

Activity Students may be interested to know that magic squares date back to ancient times when people believed they held mystical powers because of their special properties. Have students complete each magic square and record the sums. Then have them form new squares by performing the given operation and recording answers in the squares at the right. Ask them to check if the new squares are magic squares. Challenge students to start with one of the squares on the sheet and create their own magic squares.

$\frac{7}{8}$	$\frac{3}{8}$	1
$\frac{5}{8}$	$\frac{7}{8}$	$\frac{3}{4}$
$\frac{3}{4}$	1	$\frac{1}{2}$

Sum $2\frac{1}{4}$

Multiply by $\frac{2}{3}$

$\frac{7}{12}$	$\frac{1}{4}$	$\frac{2}{3}$
$\frac{5}{12}$	$\frac{7}{12}$	$\frac{1}{2}$
$\frac{1}{2}$	$\frac{2}{3}$	$\frac{1}{3}$

Sum $1\frac{1}{2}$

$\frac{2}{3}$	$1\frac{1}{2}$	$\frac{1}{2}$
$\frac{1}{4}$	$\frac{5}{12}$	$\frac{7}{12}$
$\frac{1}{3}$	$\frac{3}{4}$	$\frac{1}{6}$

Multiply by $1\frac{1}{3}$

$\frac{1}{2}$	$\frac{1}{16}$	$\frac{3}{8}$
$\frac{3}{16}$	$\frac{5}{16}$	$\frac{7}{16}$
$\frac{1}{4}$	$\frac{9}{16}$	$\frac{1}{8}$

Sum $1\frac{1}{4}$

Sum $\frac{15}{16}$

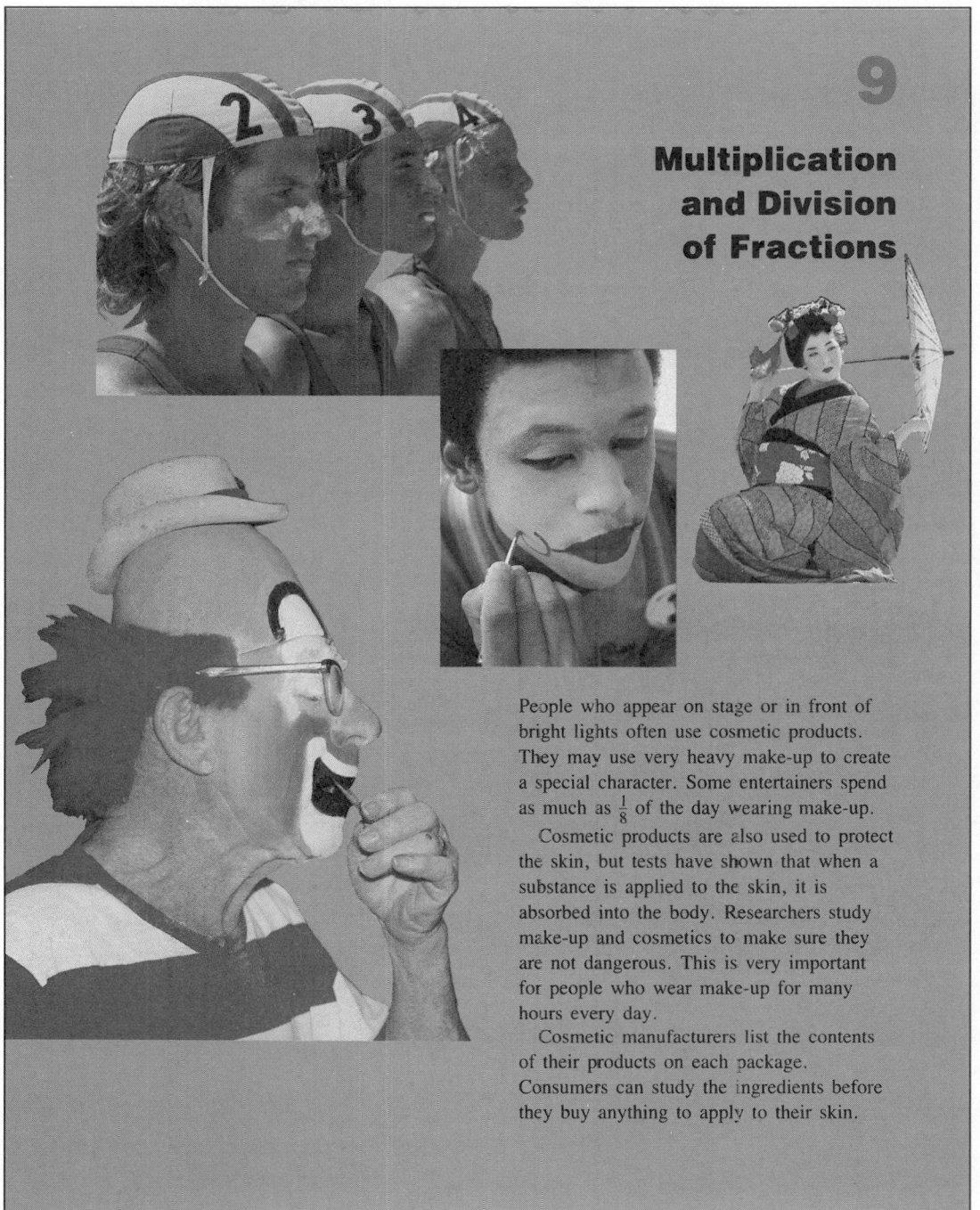

9

Multiplication and Division of Fractions

People who appear on stage or in front of bright lights often use cosmetic products. They may use very heavy make-up to create a special character. Some entertainers spend as much as $\frac{1}{8}$ of the day wearing make-up.

Cosmetic products are also used to protect the skin, but tests have shown that when a substance is applied to the skin, it is absorbed into the body. Researchers study make-up and cosmetics to make sure they are not dangerous. This is very important for people who wear make-up for many hours every day.

Cosmetic manufacturers list the contents of their products on each package. Consumers can study the ingredients before they buy anything to apply to their skin.

Introducing the Chapter

Discussion Have students read the article about cosmetics and examine the accompanying photographs. Encourage discussion about the data in the article, and use this as an opportunity for students to create problems based on this data.

As you teach the chapter, you may wish to refer back to this page and discuss the questions below. Briefly review the contents of the article before posing the questions.

Follow-Up Questions

After Page 225 According to the article, some entertainers spend $\frac{1}{8}$ of the day wearing make-up. How many hours do they wear make-up? (3 hours)

After Page 227 Suntan lotion can be made by using $\frac{1}{4}$ cup palm oil, $\frac{1}{4}$ cup coconut oil, and $\frac{1}{8}$ cup lanolin. If you doubled this recipe, how much of each ingredient would you need? ($\frac{1}{2}$ cup palm oil, $\frac{1}{2}$ cup coconut oil, and $\frac{1}{4}$ cup lanolin) How many cups of lotion would you have? ($1\frac{1}{4}$ cups)

After Page 229 Oil from the endangered sperm whale was used for many years in the manufacture of cosmetics, but a substitute has been found. Oil is extracted from seeds of the jojoba bush. One Apache tribe in Arizona made $100,000 from jojoba production in 1979. In 1980, their intake was $1\frac{1}{2}$ times greater. How much money did they make in 1980? ($150,000)

Fractions

Quick Review Have students find the greatest common factor of each pair of numbers.

12, 18	6	35, 42	7	6, 8	2	45, 60	15
60, 48	12	7, 8	1	27, 30	3	10, 25	5

Lesson Focus To multiply a fraction and a whole number

Ideas for Getting Started

On the chalkboard, display arrays of dots to review finding a fraction of a whole number. Ask students to solve these exercises using the arrays.

$\frac{1}{2}$ of 8 $\frac{1}{3}$ of 12 $\frac{1}{6}$ of 12

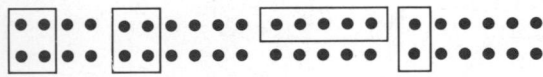

Using Page 224

Motivational Problem Read the introductory problem with students. "What does the question ask us to find?" (the number of turquoise gemstones) "What data is needed to solve the problem?" ($\frac{1}{3}$ of the 12 gemstones are turquoise) Elicit from students that $\frac{1}{3}$ of a number can be found by dividing by 3.

Lesson Development On the chalkboard, show students how to find $\frac{1}{3}$ of 12. Discuss the idea that $\frac{1}{3}$ of 12 means $\frac{1}{3} \times 12$. Then show students how to find $\frac{2}{3}$ of a number. Help them understand that since $\frac{1}{3}$ of 12 is 4, $\frac{2}{3}$ of 12 should be twice as much, or 8.

Other Examples Work through these examples on the chalkboard giving students the opportunity to participate in each step.

Warm Up Use the pictures to help students see that multiplying by $\frac{1}{3}$ is the same as dividing by 3, or multiplying by $\frac{1}{4}$ is the same as dividing by 4. Have students complete the exercises independently.

Finding a Fraction of a Whole Number

Jack tumble-polished 12 gemstones in a machine. He saw that $\frac{1}{3}$ of the gemstones were turquoise. How many gemstones were turquoise?

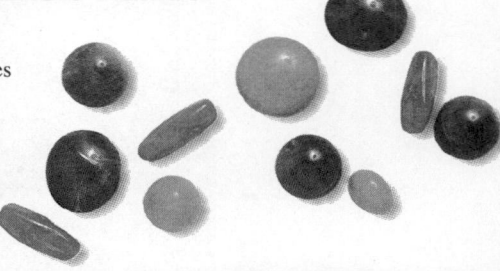

To find $\frac{1}{3}$ of a number, divide the number by 3.	To find $\frac{2}{3}$ of a number, find $\frac{1}{3}$ of the number, then multiply by 2.

We think: $\frac{1}{3}$ of **12** is **4**.
We write: $\frac{1}{3} \times 12 = 4$.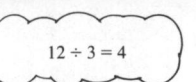

There were 4 turquoise gemstones.

We think: $\frac{2}{3}$ of **12** is **8**.
We write: $\frac{2}{3} \times 12 = 8$.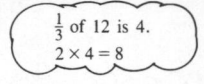

There were 8 gemstones that were not turquoise.

Other Examples

$\frac{1}{4}$ of **16** is **4**. $\frac{1}{4} \times 16 = 4$ $\frac{1}{8}$ of **24** is **3**. $\frac{3}{8} \times 24 = 9$

$\frac{3}{4} \times 16 = 12$ $\frac{5}{8} \times 24 = 15$

Warm Up

Find the fraction of the number.

1. $\frac{1}{3}$ of 9 3   **2.** $\frac{1}{4}$ of 8 2   **3.** $\frac{2}{3}$ of 6 4

   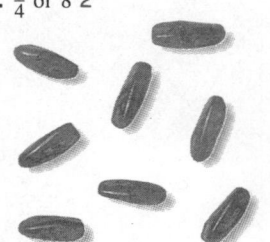   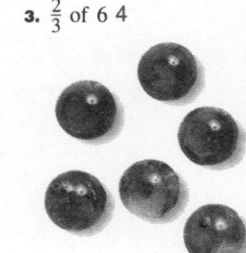

4. $\frac{1}{3} \times 9$ 3   **5.** $\frac{1}{7} \times 14$ 2   **6.** $\frac{9}{10} \times 10$ 9

224

Follow Up

Reteaching

Discuss what is meant by taking a fractional part of a number. Use counters to illustrate examples, such as $\frac{1}{3}$ of 15. Separate the counters into 3 groups. Explain that we can think "15 ÷ 3." Since there are 5 counters in each group, $\frac{1}{3}$ of 15 is 5. On the chalkboard, write the equation: $\frac{1}{3} \times 15 = 5$.

Have students use counters to show other examples.

Enrichment

Have students replace each ◯ with >, <, or =.

1. $\frac{1}{2} \times 10$ ⊙ $\frac{2}{3} \times 6$

2. $\frac{1}{4} \times 12$ ⊜ $\frac{1}{3} \times 9$

3. $\frac{3}{8} \times 16$ ⊙ $\frac{2}{5} \times 10$

4. $\frac{3}{4} \times 12$ ⊙ $\frac{5}{8} \times 16$

5. $\frac{5}{6} \times 54$ ⊙ $\frac{2}{3} \times 60$

6. $\frac{5}{12} \times 36$ ⊙ $\frac{7}{8} \times 24$

Assignment Guide			
	Minimum	Average	Extended
page 225	1–33	1–33	1–33 odd, 34

Find the fraction of the number.

1. $\frac{2}{3}$ of 9 6

2. $\frac{4}{5}$ of 10 8

3. $\frac{1}{6}$ of 12 2

4. $\frac{5}{6}$ of 12 10

5. $\frac{1}{2} \times 6$ 3

6. $\frac{2}{5} \times 20$ 8

7. $\frac{3}{8} \times 8$ 3

8. $\frac{5}{6} \times 18$ 15

9. $\frac{5}{8} \times 32$ 20

10. $\frac{1}{7} \times 28$ 4

11. $\frac{5}{9} \times 27$ 15

12. $\frac{1}{4} \times 40$ 10

13. $\frac{9}{10} \times 30$ 27

14. $\frac{1}{3} \times 27$ 9

15. $\frac{1}{8} \times 56$ 7

16. $\frac{2}{3} \times 18$ 12

17. $\frac{1}{4} \times 100$ 25

18. $\frac{3}{4} \times 80$ 60

19. $\frac{1}{16} \times 32$ 2

20. $\frac{5}{12} \times 24$ 10

21. $\frac{6}{7} \times 21$ 18

22. $\frac{3}{4} \times 60$ 45

23. $\frac{5}{8} \times 48$ 30

24. $\frac{7}{10} \times 50$ 35

25. $\frac{1}{100} \times 500$ 5

26. $\frac{1}{16} \times 64$ 4

27. $\frac{2}{3} \times 300$ 200

28. $\frac{9}{10} \times 10$ 9

29. $\frac{5}{8} \times 80$ 50

30. $\frac{1}{6} \times 126$ 21

31. $\frac{3}{20} \times 80$ 12

32. $\frac{5}{6} \times 84$ 70

33. Ernie bought a sack of 30 round flint rocks called geodes. He found that $\frac{2}{15}$ of them contained fossils. How many of the geodes contained fossils? 4

34. Simona bought $\frac{5}{6}$ of a dozen geodes that were to have purple quartz inside and $\frac{1}{2}$ of a dozen geodes that were to have a brown flint inside. How many geodes did she buy? 16

Using Page 225

Exercises 1–32 Students should realize that $\frac{2}{3}$ of a number is 2 times as much as $\frac{1}{3}$ of that number, and $\frac{4}{5}$ of a number is 4 times as much as $\frac{1}{5}$ of that number. Encourage the use of pictures or objects if students have difficulty with these exercises.

Reteaching Supplement, page 67

Enrichment Supplement, page 67

Practice Supplement, page 85

Quick Review Have students identify those fractions that are not in lowest terms and then write them in lowest terms.

$\frac{7}{21}$ $\frac{1}{3}$ $\frac{10}{35}$ $\frac{2}{7}$ $\frac{7}{16}$ $\frac{21}{30}$ $\frac{7}{10}$

$\frac{36}{43}$ $\frac{9}{39}$ $\frac{3}{13}$ $\frac{8}{33}$

Lesson Focus To multiply fractions

Ideas for Getting Started

Introduce students to the idea of multiplying fractions by drawing a rectangle on the chalkboard and dividing it in fourths as shown below. Ask students to find $\frac{1}{2}$ of $\frac{1}{4}$.

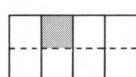

"Which operation is used in finding $\frac{1}{2}$ of another number?" (multiplication) Have students draw diagrams on the chalkboard to represent these equations.

$\frac{1}{3}$ of $\frac{1}{2}$ $\frac{1}{4}$ of $\frac{1}{2}$ $\frac{1}{2}$ of $\frac{2}{3}$

Some students may recognize that the answer can also be found by multiplying numerators and multiplying denominators.

Using Page 226

Motivational Problem Ask students to read the introductory problem and restate the question. Have them give the data needed to solve the problem. Then ask, "What operation can be used to find $\frac{3}{4}$ of $\frac{1}{2}$?" (multiplication)

Lesson Development Work through the problem on the chalkboard, using the steps in the instruction boxes. Ask students to reread the problem to see if the answer makes sense.

Other Examples Notice with students that the product in the first example can be reduced. Point out that the last two examples have whole number factors which can be written as fractions with a denominator of 1.

Exercises 1–22 Have students complete these exercises independently and then check and discuss their work. You may want to require students to write answers in lowest terms and rename improper fractions.

Multiplying Fractions

Gary is restoring a fresco for a museum of ancient art. He began work on $\frac{1}{2}$ of the fresco. During the past month he has restored $\frac{3}{4}$ of the $\frac{1}{2}$ section. What fractional part of the whole fresco has he restored?

Since we want to find $\frac{3}{4}$ of $\frac{1}{2}$, we can multiply.

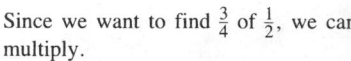

| Multiply the numerators. | Multiply the denominators. |

$\frac{3}{4} \times \frac{1}{2} = \frac{3}{\rule{1cm}{0.15cm}}$ $\frac{3}{4} \times \frac{1}{2} = \frac{3}{8}$

Gary has restored $\frac{3}{8}$ of the whole fresco.

Other Examples

$\frac{2}{5} \times \frac{3}{8} = \frac{6}{40} = \frac{3}{20}$ $\frac{3}{4} \times 12 = \frac{3}{4} \times \frac{12}{1} = \frac{36}{4} = 9$ $7 \times \frac{1}{2} = \frac{7}{1} \times \frac{1}{2} = \frac{7}{2} = 3\frac{1}{2}$

Multiply.

1. $\frac{1}{5} \times \frac{2}{3}$ $\frac{2}{15}$ 2. $\frac{3}{5} \times \frac{3}{4}$ $\frac{9}{20}$ 3. $\frac{1}{2} \times \frac{1}{2}$ $\frac{1}{4}$ 4. $\frac{3}{4} \times \frac{1}{6}$ $\frac{1}{8}$

5. $6 \times \frac{1}{4}$ $1\frac{1}{2}$ 6. $\frac{9}{10} \times \frac{1}{3}$ $\frac{3}{10}$ 7. $8 \times \frac{2}{3}$ $5\frac{1}{3}$ 8. $\frac{1}{3} \times 10$ $3\frac{1}{3}$

9. $\frac{5}{8} \times \frac{3}{5}$ $\frac{3}{8}$ 10. $\frac{1}{6} \times \frac{4}{5}$ $\frac{2}{15}$ 11. $\frac{7}{10} \times \frac{5}{6}$ $\frac{7}{12}$ 12. $\frac{3}{8} \times \frac{2}{9}$ $\frac{1}{12}$

13. $\frac{3}{2} \times \frac{2}{3}$ 1 14. $\frac{3}{4} \times 5$ $3\frac{3}{4}$ 15. $\frac{1}{2} \times \frac{5}{8}$ $\frac{5}{16}$ 16. $\frac{3}{10} \times 16$ $4\frac{4}{5}$

17. $\frac{8}{10} \times \frac{5}{6}$ $\frac{2}{3}$ 18. $\frac{2}{3} \times \frac{1}{6}$ $\frac{1}{9}$ 19. $\frac{1}{8} \times \frac{8}{3}$ $\frac{1}{3}$ 20. $\frac{5}{9} \times \frac{3}{10}$ $\frac{1}{6}$

21. Gary had $\frac{3}{4}$ of a can of paint. He used $\frac{2}{3}$ of it. What fractional part of a can of paint did he use? $\frac{1}{2}$

22. Gary had a box of 24 brushes. He used $\frac{5}{6}$ of them. How many brushes did he use? 20

226

Follow Up

Reteaching

Illustrate multiplication of fractions by using arrays drawn on dot paper. Have students draw loops to solve multiplication exercises.

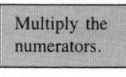

$\frac{1}{4} \times \frac{2}{3}$ $\frac{3}{5} \times \frac{1}{3}$

$\frac{2}{12}$ or $\frac{1}{6}$ $\frac{3}{15}$ or $\frac{1}{5}$

$\frac{3}{5} \times \frac{3}{4}$

$\frac{9}{20}$

Enrichment

Have students use the basic properties of multiplication to help them replace each $\square$ with a fraction.

1. $\frac{2}{3} \times \frac{5}{8} = \frac{5}{8} \times \square$ $\frac{2}{3}$

2. $(\frac{2}{5} \times \frac{1}{4}) \times \frac{5}{8} = \frac{2}{5} \times (\square \times \frac{5}{8})$ $\frac{1}{4}$

3. $\square \times 1 = \frac{4}{5}$ $\frac{4}{5}$

4. $\frac{3}{8} \times (7 + \frac{1}{2}) = (\frac{3}{8} \times 7) + (\frac{3}{8} \times \square)$ $\frac{1}{2}$

5. $\frac{9}{10} \times \square = \frac{5}{6} \times \frac{9}{10}$ $\frac{5}{6}$

6. $\square \times (\frac{1}{5} + \frac{1}{6}) = (\frac{2}{3} \times \frac{1}{5}) + (\frac{2}{3} \times \frac{1}{6})$ $\frac{2}{3}$

Assignment Guide

	Minimum	Average	Extended
page 226	1–16, 21	1–21	1–21 odd, 22
page 227	1–16	1–24	1–23 odd

Using a Multiplication Shortcut

Jean and Al were asked to find $\frac{3}{4}$ of $\frac{5}{12}$, and to give the answer in lowest terms.

Jean's Method

Al's Shortcut

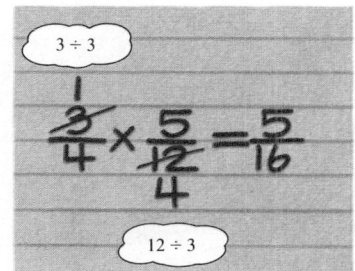

Jean divided the numerator and denominator of $\frac{15}{48}$ by 3 **after multiplying**.

Al divided a numerator by 3 and a denominator by 3 **before multiplying**.

The product, in lowest terms, is the same by either method.

Other Examples

$$\frac{\cancel{5}^{1}}{\cancel{8}_{2}} \times \frac{\cancel{4}^{1}}{\cancel{25}_{5}} = \frac{1}{10} \qquad \frac{\cancel{3}^{1}}{\cancel{10}_{2}} \times \frac{\cancel{2}^{1}}{\cancel{9}_{3}} \times \frac{\cancel{5}^{1}}{\cancel{8}_{4}} = \frac{1}{24}$$

Find the products. Use the shortcut when possible.

1. $\frac{2}{7} \times \frac{5}{8}$ **$\frac{5}{28}$**
2. $\frac{1}{8} \times \frac{4}{9}$ **$\frac{1}{18}$**
3. $\frac{3}{4} \times \frac{1}{6}$ **$\frac{1}{8}$**
4. $\frac{3}{8} \times \frac{2}{15}$ **$\frac{1}{20}$**

5. $\frac{5}{12} \times \frac{4}{5}$ **$\frac{1}{3}$**
6. $\frac{5}{16} \times \frac{2}{10}$ **$\frac{1}{16}$**
7. $\frac{2}{3} \times \frac{5}{6}$ **$\frac{5}{9}$**
8. $\frac{3}{10} \times \frac{5}{6}$ **$\frac{1}{4}$**

9. $\frac{3}{2} \times \frac{8}{9}$ **$1\frac{1}{3}$**
10. $\frac{3}{10} \times \frac{4}{7}$ **$\frac{6}{35}$**
11. $\frac{3}{4} \times \frac{8}{15}$ **$\frac{2}{5}$**
12. $\frac{2}{3} \times \frac{2}{3}$ **$\frac{4}{9}$**

13. $\frac{5}{8} \times \frac{4}{5} \times \frac{1}{2}$ **$\frac{1}{4}$**
14. $\frac{7}{16} \times \frac{4}{7} \times \frac{2}{3}$ **$\frac{1}{6}$**
15. $\frac{1}{2} \times \frac{2}{3} \times \frac{3}{4}$ **$\frac{1}{4}$**
16. $\frac{5}{12} \times \frac{9}{20} \times \frac{4}{15}$ **$\frac{1}{20}$**

17. $\frac{9}{10} \times \frac{5}{3} \times \frac{3}{8}$ **$\frac{9}{16}$**
18. $\frac{1}{2} \times \frac{1}{3} \times \frac{2}{5}$ **$\frac{1}{15}$**
19. $\frac{7}{8} \times \frac{2}{7} \times \frac{4}{9}$ **$\frac{1}{9}$**
20. $\frac{15}{16} \times \frac{4}{5} \times \frac{1}{3}$ **$\frac{1}{4}$**

21. $\frac{21}{30} \times \frac{3}{4} \times \frac{5}{7}$ **$\frac{3}{8}$**
22. $\frac{9}{20} \times \frac{5}{12} \times \frac{4}{15}$ **$\frac{1}{20}$**
23. $\frac{3}{16} \times \frac{4}{27} \times \frac{9}{12}$ **$\frac{1}{48}$**
24. $\frac{3}{2} \times \frac{2}{3} \times \frac{5}{5}$ **1**

More Practice, page 431, Set A

227

Using Page 227

Lesson Development Have students study Jean's and Al's methods for multiplying fractions. Ask them to explain why the answers are the same. Elicit from them the idea that Jean divided the numerator and denominator of the answer by 3 to get a lowest-terms fraction while Al divided a numerator and denominator before multiplying. Point out that Al's method is considered to be a shortcut because the numbers involved are smaller and therefore easier to work with.

Other Examples On the chalkboard, work through the two examples. Notice with students that the multiplication shortcut is used more than once in these examples.

Exercises 1–24 Watch for students who overlook factors after using the shortcut, as shown below.

$$\frac{1}{\cancel{2}} \times \frac{5}{\cancel{8}} = \frac{5}{7} \qquad \frac{\cancel{21}^{3}}{\cancel{30}_{10}^{2}} \times \frac{\cancel{3}^{1}}{4} \times \frac{1}{\cancel{8}_{1}} = \frac{3}{2}$$

More Practice, page 431, Set A

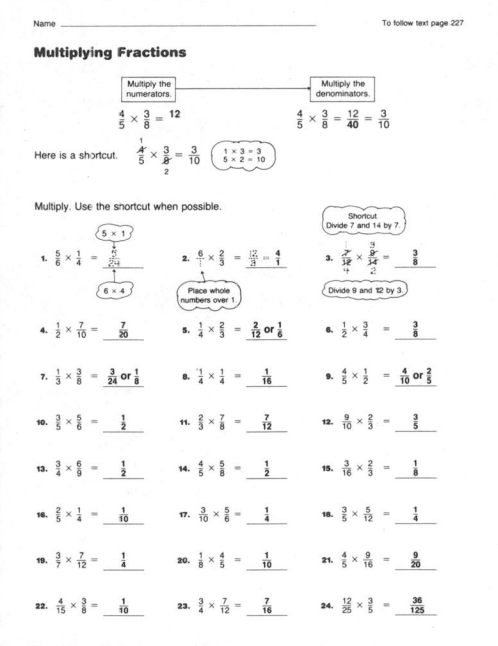
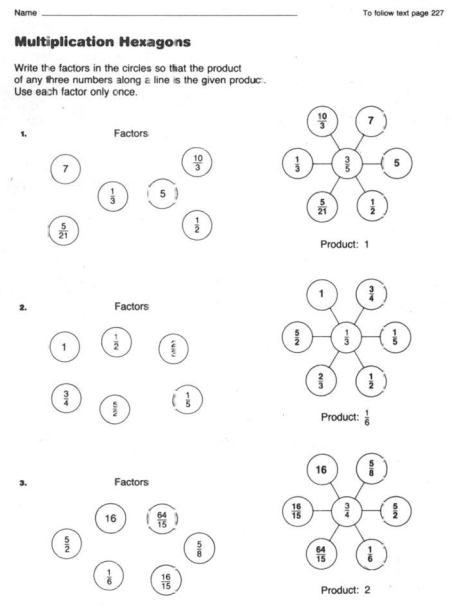

Fractions

Quick Review Have students estimate the sums and differences. Answers may vary.

42.51 + 74.22 110	87.24 − 81.5 10	32.8 + 48.9 80
75.67 − 42.81 40	62.4 − 38.5 20	18.76 + 52.09 70

Lesson Focus To multiply mixed numbers

Ideas for Getting Started

Write the following numbers on the chalkboard and ask students to write each mixed number as an improper fraction.

$$2\frac{2}{3} \qquad 5\frac{1}{8} \qquad 3\frac{2}{5} \qquad 1\frac{5}{12}$$

Write these improper fractions on the chalkboard and ask students to write each as a mixed or whole number.

$$\frac{11}{8} \qquad \frac{9}{4} \qquad \frac{3}{3} \qquad \frac{10}{3}$$

Review the previous lesson by working through the following exercises with students. Emphasize using the multiplication shortcut.

$$\frac{5}{8} \times \frac{2}{3} \qquad \frac{3}{5} \times \frac{1}{10} \qquad \frac{5}{6} \times \frac{4}{5}$$

Using Page 228

Motivational Problem Ask students to read the problem at the top of the page. Have them tell what question is being asked and what data is needed to solve the problem. Observe with students that since the actual model is $3\frac{1}{2}$ times as long as the picture, we multiply the length of the picture by $3\frac{1}{2}$.

Lesson Development Have students study the instruction boxes. Explain that by changing the mixed numbers to improper fractions, we can use the method of multiplying fractions learned in the previous lesson. On the chalkboard, work through the exercise one step at a time. Ask students to check to see if the answer is reasonable.

Other Examples Work the examples on the chalkboard, discussing each step. Be sure students realize that the multiplication shortcut of dividing by common factors applies to multiplying with mixed numbers.

Multiplying with Mixed Numbers

The reduced picture of a model airplane is $2\frac{3}{4}$ in. long. The actual model is $3\frac{1}{2}$ times as long as the picture. How long is the model?

|← —— $2\frac{3}{4}$ in. —— →|

To find the actual length of the model, we multiply $3\frac{1}{2}$ times $2\frac{3}{4}$.

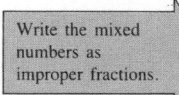

Write the mixed numbers as improper fractions. → Multiply the fractions.

$$3\frac{1}{2} \times 2\frac{3}{4} = \frac{7}{2} \times \frac{11}{4} \qquad \frac{7}{2} \times \frac{11}{4} = \frac{77}{8} = 9\frac{5}{8}$$

The model is $9\frac{5}{8}$ in. long.

Other Examples

Dividing by common factors before multiplying may make the work easier.

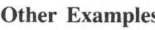

$$6 \times 3\frac{3}{8} = \frac{\overset{3}{6}}{1} \times \frac{27}{\underset{4}{8}} = \frac{81}{4} = 20\frac{1}{4} \qquad 2\frac{2}{3} \times 15 = \frac{8}{\underset{1}{3}} \times \frac{\overset{5}{15}}{1} = \frac{40}{1} = 40$$

Warm Up

Find the products.

1. $2\frac{2}{3} \times 1\frac{4}{6}$ $4\frac{4}{9}$
2. $3\frac{2}{5} \times 1\frac{3}{10}$ $4\frac{21}{50}$
3. $6\frac{1}{4} \times 8$ 50
4. $3\frac{5}{8} \times \frac{4}{5}$ $2\frac{9}{10}$
5. $7\frac{1}{2} \times 3\frac{2}{3}$ $27\frac{1}{2}$
6. $8 \times 2\frac{1}{6}$ $17\frac{1}{3}$
7. $1\frac{7}{12} \times \frac{2}{3}$ $1\frac{1}{18}$
8. $2\frac{1}{12} \times 5\frac{2}{6}$ $11\frac{1}{9}$

228

Follow Up

Reteaching

To successfully multiply mixed numbers, students must be able to write mixed numbers as improper fractions and find the product of two fractions. Review these skills with students. Stress that mixed numbers should be changed to improper fractions before multiplying.

Have students work exercises at the chalkboard. Encourage them to divide numerators and denominators by common factors before they multiply. Work individually with students having difficulty with any part of the process.

Enrichment

Show students the following shortcut method of multiplying certain mixed numbers by whole numbers.

$$10 \times 4\frac{1}{5} = (10 \times 4) + (10 \times \frac{1}{5})$$
$$= 40 + 2$$
$$= 42$$

Have students use these exercises to practice the shortcut.

1. $12 \times 3\frac{1}{4}$ 39
2. $9 \times 2\frac{2}{3}$ 24
3. $8 \times 4\frac{1}{2}$ 36
4. $9 \times 5\frac{1}{3}$ 48
5. $15 \times 3\frac{2}{5}$ 51
6. $6 \times 4\frac{1}{3}$ 26
7. $10 \times 3\frac{7}{10}$ 37
8. $12 \times 2\frac{3}{4}$ 33

Assignment Guide			
	Minimum	Average	Extended
page 229	1–24, 29, SK	1–29, SK	1–29 odd, SK

Find the products.

1. $1\frac{2}{3} \times 2\frac{3}{4}$ $4\frac{7}{12}$
2. $6 \times 4\frac{1}{3}$ 26
3. $6\frac{1}{3} \times \frac{3}{8}$ $2\frac{3}{8}$
4. $\frac{4}{5} \times 2\frac{3}{4}$ $2\frac{1}{5}$

5. $1\frac{1}{3} \times 2\frac{1}{4}$ 3
6. $\frac{2}{3} \times 1\frac{1}{2}$ 1
7. $5 \times 7\frac{1}{2}$ $37\frac{1}{2}$
8. $4\frac{1}{8} \times 2\frac{2}{3}$ 11

9. $\frac{2}{5} \times 2\frac{1}{2}$ 1
10. $6\frac{5}{12} \times 1\frac{6}{9}$ $10\frac{25}{36}$
11. $5\frac{2}{3} \times 2\frac{1}{10}$ $11\frac{9}{10}$
12. $3\frac{2}{10} \times 1\frac{1}{10}$ $3\frac{13}{25}$

13. $1\frac{2}{3} \times 1\frac{4}{5}$ 3
14. $1\frac{1}{3} \times \frac{3}{5}$ $\frac{4}{5}$
15. $8 \times \frac{11}{8}$ 11
16. $3\frac{3}{4} \times 2\frac{2}{5}$ 9

17. $3\frac{1}{2} \times 2\frac{1}{4}$ $7\frac{7}{8}$
18. $\frac{2}{3} \times 4\frac{1}{5}$ $2\frac{4}{5}$
19. $2\frac{3}{8} \times 4$ $9\frac{1}{2}$
20. $5 \times 3\frac{1}{3}$ $16\frac{2}{3}$

21. $\frac{3}{5} \times 3\frac{1}{3}$ 2
22. $5\frac{3}{5} \times 2\frac{1}{6}$ $12\frac{2}{15}$
23. $6\frac{2}{3} \times 1\frac{1}{9}$ $7\frac{11}{27}$
24. $\frac{6}{7} \times 2\frac{2}{6}$ 2

25. $10\frac{1}{2} \times 1\frac{5}{7}$ 18
26. $2\frac{3}{4} \times 2\frac{3}{4}$ $7\frac{9}{16}$
27. $6 \times 2\frac{1}{12}$ $12\frac{1}{2}$
28. $4\frac{2}{3} \times \frac{1}{14}$ $\frac{1}{3}$

29. A model ship is $6\frac{1}{2}$ times as long as the picture. How long is the actual model? $12\frac{3}{16}$ in.

$1\frac{7}{8}$ in.

30. The length of a model spaceship is $\frac{1}{4}$ of an inch less than 3 times the length shown in the picture. What is the actual length of the model? $7\frac{5}{8}$ in.

$2\frac{5}{8}$ in.

SKILLKEEPER

1. $\frac{5}{6} + \frac{1}{6}$ 1
2. $\frac{3}{4} + \frac{5}{6}$ $1\frac{7}{12}$
3. $\frac{4}{5} + \frac{9}{10}$ $1\frac{7}{10}$
4. $\frac{2}{3} + \frac{5}{12}$ $1\frac{1}{12}$
5. $\frac{1}{4} + \frac{5}{6}$ $1\frac{1}{12}$

6. $5\frac{1}{3}$ $+ 6\frac{1}{3}$ $11\frac{2}{3}$
7. $4\frac{1}{2}$ $+ 7\frac{1}{2}$ 12
8. $4\frac{1}{2}$ $+ 2\frac{1}{10}$ $6\frac{3}{5}$
9. $3\frac{1}{5}$ $+ 7\frac{4}{5}$ 11
10. $5\frac{3}{4}$ $+ 7\frac{1}{2}$ $13\frac{1}{4}$

11. $\frac{3}{4} - \frac{2}{3}$ $\frac{1}{12}$
12. $\frac{4}{5} - \frac{1}{4}$ $\frac{11}{20}$
13. $\frac{2}{3} - \frac{5}{8}$ $\frac{1}{24}$
14. $\frac{8}{9} - \frac{1}{2}$ $\frac{7}{18}$
15. $\frac{1}{3} - \frac{1}{4}$ $\frac{1}{12}$

16. 8 $- 5\frac{3}{5}$ $2\frac{2}{5}$
17. $6\frac{1}{2}$ $- 5\frac{2}{3}$ $\frac{5}{6}$
18. $4\frac{1}{4}$ $- 2\frac{1}{2}$ $1\frac{3}{4}$
19. $18\frac{1}{2}$ $- 9\frac{7}{12}$ $8\frac{11}{12}$
20. $15\frac{1}{2}$ $- 8\frac{1}{8}$ $7\frac{3}{8}$

More Practice, page 431, Set B

229

Using Page 229

Exercises 1–28 Encourage students to use the multiplication shortcut of dividing by common factors. You might want to require students to express the answers to the exercises as lowest-terms fractions or mixed numbers.

Skillkeeper These skills were originally taught in Chapter 8.

More Practice, page 431, Set B

Reteaching Supplement, page 69

Name _____ To follow text page 229

Multiplying with Mixed Numbers

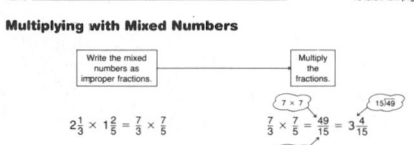

Enrichment Supplement, page 69

Name _____ To follow text page 229

Estimating Products

Practice Supplement, page 87

Name _____ To follow text page 229

Multiplying with Mixed Numbers

Find the products.

Fractions

Quick Review Have students write the name for the polygon with the given number of sides.

3 triangle   6 hexagon   8 octagon

5 pentagon   4 quadrilateral

Lesson Focus To practice adding, subtracting, and multiplying fractions; to find the reciprocal of a number

Ideas for Getting Started

To introduce the lesson on page 231, write the following pairs of exercises on the chalkboard. Have selected students go to the chalkboard and work the exercises while other students check the work at their desks.

$6 \times \frac{1}{2}$	$12 \times \frac{1}{3}$	$2 \times \frac{1}{3}$	$8 \times \frac{1}{4}$
$6 \div 2$	$12 \div 3$	$2 \div 3$	$8 \div 4$

Conduct a class discussion about reasons why the answers are the same for each pair of exercises.

Using Page 230

Exercises 1–36 The work on this page provides students with an opportunity to review their work with the computation of fractions presented thus far. Students' performances on this page will enable you to identify those areas in which reteaching or practice is needed.

Skills Practice

Add.

1. $\frac{3}{4} + \frac{1}{2}$ $1\frac{1}{4}$
2. $\frac{1}{2} + \frac{1}{5}$ $\frac{7}{10}$
3. $\frac{3}{8} + \frac{3}{4}$ $1\frac{1}{8}$
4. $\frac{9}{16} + \frac{1}{4}$ $\frac{13}{16}$

5. $\frac{1}{4}$
   $+\frac{2}{5}$
   $\frac{13}{20}$

6. $\frac{2}{3}$
   $+\frac{1}{2}$
   $1\frac{1}{6}$

7. $\frac{4}{6}$
   $+\frac{2}{4}$
   $1\frac{1}{6}$

8. $\frac{6}{8}$
   $+\frac{1}{3}$
   $1\frac{1}{12}$

9. $3\frac{1}{3}$
   $+7\frac{2}{3}$
   11

10. $12\frac{3}{4}$
    $+27\frac{1}{2}$
    $40\frac{1}{4}$

11. $12\frac{3}{10}$
    $15\frac{1}{2}$
    $+\ 9\frac{4}{5}$
    $37\frac{3}{5}$

12. $27\frac{1}{2}$
    $9\frac{3}{4}$
    $+56\frac{5}{8}$
    $93\frac{7}{8}$

Subtract.

13. $\frac{2}{3} - \frac{1}{2}$ $\frac{1}{6}$
14. $\frac{9}{10} - \frac{1}{2}$ $\frac{2}{5}$
15. $\frac{7}{8} - \frac{3}{4}$ $\frac{1}{8}$
16. $\frac{9}{10} - \frac{3}{4}$ $\frac{3}{20}$

17. 12
    $-\ 3\frac{1}{2}$
    $8\frac{1}{2}$

18. $9\frac{3}{4}$
    $-2\frac{1}{3}$
    $7\frac{5}{12}$

19. $21\frac{1}{2}$
    $-16\frac{3}{4}$
    $4\frac{3}{4}$

20. $9\frac{3}{10}$
    $-3\frac{4}{5}$
    $5\frac{1}{2}$

21. $20\frac{1}{4}$
    -17
    $3\frac{1}{4}$

22. $17\frac{2}{5}$
    $-13\frac{1}{3}$
    $4\frac{1}{15}$

23. $7\frac{5}{16}$
    $-3\frac{3}{4}$
    $3\frac{9}{16}$

24. $28\frac{3}{10}$
    $-26\frac{1}{3}$
    $1\frac{29}{30}$

Multiply.

25. $\frac{7}{10} \times \frac{2}{3}$ $\frac{7}{15}$
26. $\frac{3}{8} \times \frac{4}{5}$ $\frac{3}{10}$
27. $10 \times \frac{1}{5}$ 2
28. $\frac{3}{4} \times 8$ 6

29. $4 \times 2\frac{1}{2}$ 10
30. $\frac{1}{6} \times 30$ 5
31. $2\frac{1}{8} \times 1\frac{1}{2}$ $3\frac{3}{16}$
32. $\frac{8}{3} \times \frac{3}{16}$ $\frac{1}{2}$

33. $4\frac{1}{4} \times \frac{4}{5}$ $3\frac{2}{5}$
34. $2\frac{2}{3} \times 4\frac{1}{2}$ 12
35. $10 \times 1\frac{1}{10}$ 11
36. $2\frac{1}{4} \times \frac{8}{9}$ 2

Follow Up

Reteaching

Use the exercises below to help students understand that multiplying a number by its reciprocal gives a product of 1. Have students replace each ☐ with a fraction.

1. $\frac{2}{3} \times \frac{3}{2} = ☐ = 1$
2. $\frac{3}{8} \times \frac{8}{3} = ☐ = 1$
3. $4 \times \frac{1}{4} = ☐ = 1$
4. $\frac{5}{4} \times \frac{4}{5} = ☐ = 1$
5. $\frac{2}{5} \times ☐ = \frac{10}{10} = 1$
6. $\frac{1}{3} \times ☐ = \frac{3}{3} = 1$
7. $\frac{5}{6} \times ☐ = \frac{30}{30} = 1$
8. $\frac{4}{3} \times ☐ = \frac{12}{12} = 1$

Enrichment

Have students write the reciprocal for each number below:

1. $3\frac{1}{5}$ $\frac{5}{16}$
2. $9\frac{2}{3}$ $\frac{3}{29}$
3. $8\frac{1}{9}$ $\frac{9}{73}$
4. $10\frac{1}{3}$ $\frac{3}{31}$
5. $2\frac{7}{16}$ $\frac{16}{39}$
6. $11\frac{1}{4}$ $\frac{4}{45}$
7. $1\frac{1}{2}$ $\frac{2}{3}$
8. $5\frac{3}{5}$ $\frac{5}{28}$

Assignment Guide			
	Minimum	Average	Extended
page 230	1–24	1–36	2–36 even
page 231	1–19	1–20	1–20

231
Fractions

Reciprocals

There are 24 students on a gymnastics team. They are divided into 6 groups to work out on the gymnastics equipment. How can we find the number of students in each group?

To find the number of students in each group, divide 24 by 6 or multiply 24 times $\frac{1}{6}$.

Dividing a number by 6 gives the same answer as multiplying the number by $\frac{1}{6}$.

$24 \times \frac{1}{6} = \frac{24}{6} = 4$ $24 \div 6 = 4$

Two numbers are **reciprocals** if their product is 1.
$6 \times \frac{1}{6} = 1$ 6 and $\frac{1}{6}$ are reciprocals.

Other Examples

$\frac{3}{4} \times \frac{4}{3} = 1$ $2\frac{1}{2} \times \frac{2}{5} = \frac{5}{2} \times \frac{2}{5} = 1$ $0 \times ? = 1$

$\frac{3}{4}$ and $\frac{4}{3}$ are reciprocals. $2\frac{1}{2}$ and $\frac{2}{5}$ are reciprocals.   Zero has no reciprocal.

Give the reciprocal of each number.

1. $\frac{1}{2}$ 2
2. $\frac{2}{3}$ $\frac{3}{2}$
3. $\frac{5}{8}$ $\frac{8}{5}$
4. $\frac{7}{2}$ $\frac{2}{7}$
5. $\frac{1}{10}$ 10

6. 9 $\frac{1}{9}$
7. $1\frac{1}{2}$ $\frac{2}{3}$
8. $1\frac{1}{1}$
9. $2\frac{1}{4}$ $\frac{4}{9}$
10. $\frac{9}{10}$ $\frac{10}{9}$

Give the number for n in each equation.

11. $\frac{3}{5} \times n = 1$ $n = \frac{5}{3}$
12. $n \times \frac{7}{8} = 1$ $n = \frac{8}{7}$
13. $1\frac{1}{3} \times n = 1$ $n = \frac{3}{4}$
14. $4 \times n = 1$ $n = \frac{1}{4}$

15. $2\frac{1}{6} \times \frac{6}{13} = n$ $n = 1$
16. $\frac{3}{8} \times n = 1$ $n = \frac{8}{3}$
17. $n \times 3\frac{1}{4} = 1$ $n = \frac{4}{13}$
18. $1\frac{7}{9} \times \frac{9}{16} = n$ $n = 1$

19. There are 36 gymnasts training in 4 groups. How many gymnasts are in each group? Solve the problem using both multiplication and division.
$36 \div 4 = 9$
$36 \times \frac{1}{4} = 9$

20. There are 35 gymnasts on a team. If 5 are absent, how many groups of 5 can be formed? 6

More Practice, page 431, Set C

231

Using Page 231

Lesson Development Read the introductory material with students. Point out that there are two ways to find the number of students in each group. Introduce the definition of reciprocals. Stress that reciprocals express a relationship between two factors. Each factor is the reciprocal of the other factor.

Other Examples Direct students' attention to the first example. Ask if anyone can give a simple rule to find the reciprocal of a given fraction. Expect answers given in informal language, such as "Turn the fraction over."
The second example shows that to find the reciprocal of a mixed number, we first write it as an improper fraction.
The third example shows that since no number can be multiplied times 0 to equal 1, 0 has no reciprocal.

Exercises 1–10 To check answers in these exercises, have students multiply to see that the product is 1.

Exercises 11–18 Have students check their solutions by substituting them back in the original equations.

More Practice, page 431, Set C

Ideas That Work

Special Education

Let students work in pairs to play "Fric Frac Fro." They will need a game sheet as shown, 24 index cards with exercises similar to those of this lesson and numbered for easy reference to an answer key, and distinguishable game markers.
Students mix the cards and place 9 of them face up on the game sheet. In turn, each player chooses a space. At "go," both players write the answer to their exercise card. If correct, the cards are turned over and players place their markers on the space. An answer key can be used to check. The first player to get three in a row wins the round. Cards are mixed and players begin another round. The winner of the game is the player who has won the most rounds when time is called.

Fric	Frac	Fro

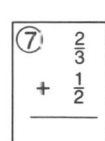

① 12
− $3\frac{1}{2}$

⑦ $\frac{2}{3}$
+ $\frac{1}{2}$

Quick Review Have students rename each of these fractions.

$16\frac{4}{3}$ $17\frac{1}{3}$ $10\frac{16}{11}$ $11\frac{5}{11}$ $26\frac{49}{49}$ 27 $12\frac{12}{8}$ $13\frac{1}{2}$

$38\frac{17}{9}$ $39\frac{8}{9}$ $14\frac{37}{24}$ $15\frac{13}{24}$ $27\frac{12}{10}$ $28\frac{1}{5}$

Lesson Focus To divide fractions

Ideas for Getting Started

Ask students the following questions to develop an intuitive idea of dividing by fractions. After students answer each question, write the corresponding equation on the chalkboard.

"How many fourths are in one?" $(1 \div \frac{1}{4} = 4)$

"How many halves are in three?" $(3 \div \frac{1}{2} = 6)$

"How many fourths are in one half?" $(\frac{1}{2} \div \frac{1}{4} = 2)$

Using Page 232

Motivational Problem Have students read the introductory problem and restate the question. Ask students to give the data needed to find how long it will take to fill the pool $\frac{9}{10}$ full. Discuss why we can divide to find the answer.

Lesson Development Work through the exercise on the chalkboard and show the steps one at a time. Stress the importance of identifying the divisor and finding the reciprocal of the divisor. Have students check the answer by using multiplication.

Other Examples Have students work through these examples on the chalkboard. Remind students that the whole numbers in the last two examples can be written as fractions with denominators of 1.

Warm Up Use these exercises to diagnose any difficulty students may have with the steps in dividing fractions.

Dividing Fractions

The dolphin tank at a city aquarium was emptied and is to be refilled until it is $\frac{9}{10}$ full. It takes 1 h to fill $\frac{1}{5}$ of the pool. How long will it take to fill the pool $\frac{9}{10}$ full?

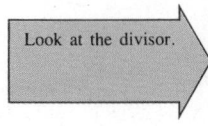

We need to find the number of fifths in $\frac{9}{10}$. To do this, we divide $\frac{9}{10}$ by $\frac{1}{5}$.

Dividing by a number gives the same answer as multiplying by the reciprocal of the number.

Look at the divisor.	Find the reciprocal of the divisor.	Multiply the dividend by the reciprocal of the divisor.

$\frac{9}{10} \div \frac{1}{5} \leftarrow$ divisor

dividend

$\frac{5}{1}$

$\frac{9}{10} \times \frac{\overset{1}{\cancel{5}}}{1} = \frac{9}{2} = 4\frac{1}{2} \leftarrow$ quotient

To check the problem, multiply the quotient by the divisor.

$4\frac{1}{2} \times \frac{1}{5} = \frac{9}{2} \times \frac{1}{5} = \frac{9}{10}$ It checks.

It will take $4\frac{1}{2}$ h to fill the tank $\frac{9}{10}$ full.

Other Examples

$\frac{1}{2} \div \frac{3}{4} = \frac{1}{\cancel{2}} \times \frac{\overset{2}{\cancel{4}}}{3} = \frac{2}{3}$ $\frac{3}{5} \div 6 = \frac{\cancel{3}}{5} \times \frac{1}{\cancel{6}} = \frac{1}{10}$ $4 \div \frac{3}{8} = \frac{4}{1} \times \frac{8}{3} = \frac{32}{3} = 10\frac{2}{3}$

Warm Up

Find the quotients.

1. $\frac{3}{5} \div \frac{2}{3}$ $\frac{9}{10}$ 2. $\frac{5}{8} \div \frac{1}{6}$ $3\frac{3}{4}$ 3. $\frac{3}{16} \div \frac{1}{4}$ $\frac{3}{4}$ 4. $\frac{7}{10} \div \frac{5}{16}$ $2\frac{6}{25}$

5. $3 \div \frac{1}{2}$ 6 6. $\frac{7}{8} \div \frac{3}{8}$ $2\frac{1}{3}$ 7. $\frac{3}{4} \div \frac{1}{2}$ $1\frac{1}{2}$ 8. $\frac{2}{3} \div 4$ $\frac{1}{6}$

232

Follow Up

Reteaching

Display the following on the chalkboard. Ask students to tell how many sixths are in $1\frac{1}{3}$. (8)

Write the division equation on the chalkboard: $1\frac{1}{3} \div \frac{1}{6} = 8$. Have students check by multiplying. $(\frac{1}{6} \times 8 = 1\frac{1}{3})$ Show that we could write the exercises as $1\frac{1}{3} \times 6 = 8$. Work through other examples in the same way.

Enrichment

Have students match the division to the multiplication exercises and write the correct letter in each blank below.

1. $\frac{3}{4} \div \frac{1}{6}$ A. $\frac{4}{1} \times \frac{3}{2}$

2. $\frac{1}{2} \div \frac{2}{3}$ C. $\frac{3}{4} \times \frac{1}{3}$

3. $\frac{4}{8} \div \frac{1}{2}$ F. $\frac{1}{2} \times \frac{3}{2}$

4. $\frac{1}{9} \div \frac{5}{6}$ I. $\frac{4}{8} \times \frac{2}{1}$

5. $4 \div \frac{2}{3}$ N. $\frac{4}{6} \times \frac{2}{1}$

6. $\frac{4}{6} \div \frac{1}{2}$ O. $\frac{1}{9} \times \frac{6}{5}$

7. $\frac{3}{4} \div 3$ R. $\frac{7}{10} \times \frac{5}{1}$

8. $\frac{7}{10} \div \frac{1}{5}$ T. $\frac{3}{4} \times \frac{6}{1}$

F R A C T I O N

2 8 5 7 1 3 4 6

A C T I O N

5 7 1 3 4 6

Assignment Guide			
	Minimum	Average	Extended
page 233	1–21, 28	1–28, TM	2–28 even, 29, TM

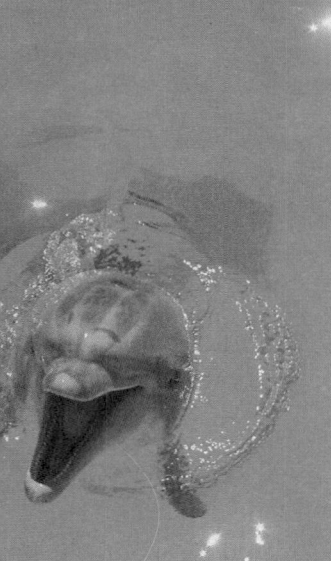

Find the quotients.

1. $\frac{3}{4} \div \frac{1}{5}$ $3\frac{3}{4}$

2. $\frac{4}{5} \div \frac{1}{2}$ $1\frac{3}{5}$

3. $\frac{5}{9} \div \frac{2}{3}$ $\frac{5}{6}$

4. $\frac{3}{8} \div \frac{2}{3}$ $\frac{9}{16}$

5. $\frac{3}{8} \div 3$ $\frac{1}{8}$

6. $\frac{3}{4} \div \frac{2}{5}$ $1\frac{7}{8}$

7. $\frac{5}{12} \div \frac{3}{8}$ $1\frac{1}{9}$

8. $\frac{7}{10} \div 5$ $\frac{7}{50}$

9. $\frac{7}{8} \div \frac{3}{16}$ $4\frac{2}{3}$

10. $\frac{1}{2} \div 7$ $\frac{1}{14}$

11. $\frac{5}{8} \div \frac{1}{16}$ 10

12. $\frac{2}{3} \div \frac{1}{6}$ 4

13. $6 \div \frac{2}{3}$ 9

14. $\frac{7}{12} \div \frac{3}{15}$ $2\frac{11}{12}$

15. $\frac{3}{5} \div \frac{3}{8}$ $1\frac{3}{5}$

16. $\frac{11}{12} \div \frac{3}{4}$ $1\frac{2}{9}$

17. $\frac{1}{12} \div \frac{1}{4}$ $\frac{1}{3}$

18. $3 \div \frac{7}{10}$ $4\frac{2}{7}$

19. $\frac{1}{4} \div 5$ $\frac{1}{20}$

20. $\frac{5}{16} \div \frac{2}{3}$ $\frac{15}{32}$

21. $16 \div \frac{4}{5}$ 20

22. $\frac{3}{8} \div \frac{3}{16}$ 2

23. $\frac{7}{12} \div \frac{5}{6}$ $\frac{7}{10}$

24. $\frac{9}{10} \div 10$ $\frac{9}{100}$

25. $\frac{3}{7} \div \frac{7}{12}$ $\frac{36}{49}$

26. $1 \div \frac{5}{8}$ $1\frac{3}{5}$

27. $\frac{4}{5} \div \frac{2}{5}$ 2

28. A class aquarium is to be filled $\frac{2}{3}$ full of water. It takes 1 min to fill $\frac{1}{4}$ of it. How long will it take to fill the aquarium $\frac{2}{3}$ full? $2\frac{2}{3}$ min

29. An aquarium tide pool is to be filled $\frac{7}{8}$ full of water. It takes 5 min to fill the tide pool $\frac{1}{4}$ full. How many minutes will it take to fill the tide pool $\frac{7}{8}$ full? $17\frac{1}{2}$ min

THINK MATH

Guess and Check

Fill in the six circles with the fractions $\frac{1}{8}$, $\frac{2}{8}$, $\frac{3}{8}$, $\frac{4}{8}$, $\frac{5}{8}$, and $\frac{6}{8}$ so that the sum of the three fractions on each side of the triangle is the same.

There is more than one way to do this. Find as many ways as you can.

Sums may be $\frac{9}{8}$, $\frac{10}{8}$, $\frac{11}{8}$, or $\frac{12}{8}$.

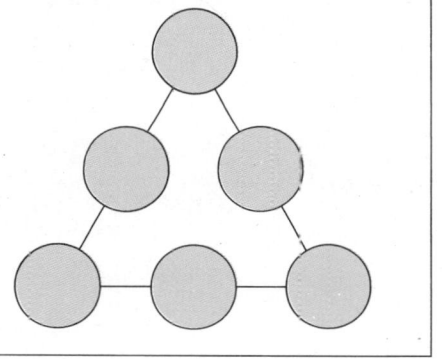

More Practice, page 431, Set D

233

Using Page 233

Exercise 29 This exercise involves two steps. First, students should find how many $\frac{1}{4}$s are in $\frac{7}{8}$.

$$\frac{7}{8} \div \frac{1}{4} = \frac{7}{\underset{2}{8}} \times \frac{\overset{1}{4}}{1} = \frac{7}{2}$$

Then $\frac{7}{2}$ is multiplied by 5 to find the number of minutes it will take to fill the pool $\frac{7}{8}$ full.

$$\frac{7}{2} \times \frac{5}{1} = \frac{35}{2} = 17\frac{1}{2}$$

Think Math This problem involves Guess and Check and addition of fractions. The solutions are shown below.

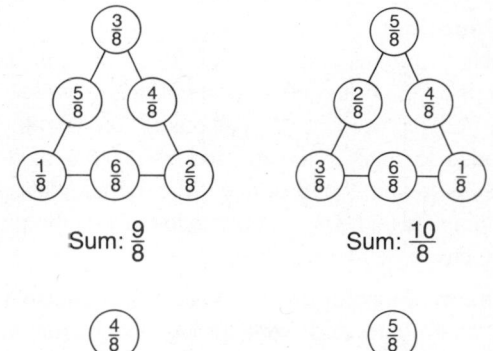

Sum: $\frac{9}{8}$ Sum: $\frac{10}{8}$

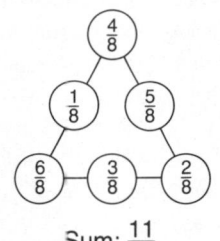   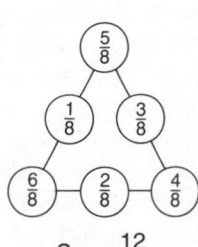

Sum: $\frac{11}{8}$ Sum: $\frac{12}{8}$

More Practice, page 431, Set D

Reteaching Supplement, page 70

Name _____ To follow text page 233

Dividing Fractions

Enrichment Supplement, page 70

Name _____ To follow text page 233

Complex Fractions

Practice Supplement, page 89

Name _____ To follow text page 233

Dividing Fractions

Lesson Focus To divide mixed numbers

Ideas for Getting Started

Write the following pairs of numbers on the chalkboard. Ask students to tell which of the number pairs are reciprocals.

$\frac{3}{5}$ and $1\frac{2}{3}$ $2\frac{3}{8}$ and $\frac{19}{8}$ $\frac{2}{7}$ and $3\frac{1}{2}$

Remind students that mixed numbers can be written as improper fractions and then "inverted" to make the reciprocal.

Using Page 234

Motivational Problem Read the introductory problem with students. "What does the question ask us to find?" (the number of strides Polly took to run from home plate to first base) "What data is needed to answer the question?" (Polly's strides are $3\frac{1}{3}$ ft and the distance from home plate to first base is 60 ft.) Ask students to tell why the plan is to divide.

Lesson Development Write the exercise on the chalkboard and work through each step according to the instruction boxes. Notice with students that after writing the mixed or whole numbers as improper fractions, we simply multiply by the reciprocal of the divisor. Ask students if the answer makes sense. "Can the answer be checked by multiplication?" (yes)

$$18 \times 3\frac{1}{3} = \overset{6}{\cancel{18}}{1} \times \frac{10}{\cancel{3}} = 60$$

Other Examples Work through the examples on the chalkboard, giving students the opportunity to participate in each step.

Warm Up Watch for students who forget to give the reciprocal of the divisor or give the reciprocal of the dividend. After students complete the exercises, provide time for checking answers and discussing any difficulties before proceeding to page 235.

Dividing with Mixed Numbers

It is 60 ft from home plate to first base on a softball diamond. Polly ran this distance taking strides of about $3\frac{1}{3}$ ft each. About how many strides did she take to run from home plate to first base?

To find how many strides of $3\frac{1}{3}$ ft are in 60 ft, we divide 60 by $3\frac{1}{3}$.

Write mixed numbers or whole numbers as improper fractions.	Divide the fractions.

$$60 \div 3\frac{1}{3} = \frac{60}{1} \div \frac{10}{3} \qquad \overset{6}{\cancel{\frac{60}{1}}} \times \frac{3}{\cancel{10}} = \frac{18}{1} = 18$$

Polly took about 18 strides to run from home plate to first base.

Other Examples

$$6\frac{2}{3} \div 5\frac{1}{3} = \frac{20}{3} \div \frac{16}{3} = \overset{5}{\cancel{\frac{20}{\cancel{3}}}} \times \overset{1}{\frac{\cancel{3}}{\cancel{16}}}_{4} = \frac{5}{4} = 1\frac{1}{4}$$

$$3\frac{1}{4} \div 2 = \frac{13}{4} \div \frac{2}{1} = \frac{13}{4} \times \frac{1}{2} = \frac{13}{8} = 1\frac{5}{8}$$

$$2\frac{2}{5} \div \frac{5}{6} = \frac{12}{5} \div \frac{5}{6} = \frac{12}{5} \times \frac{6}{5} = \frac{72}{25} = 2\frac{22}{25}$$

Warm Up

Find the quotients.

1. $5\frac{2}{3} \div 1\frac{1}{4}$ $4\frac{8}{15}$
2. $1\frac{3}{4} \div 4\frac{1}{2}$ $\frac{7}{18}$
3. $5\frac{1}{2} \div \frac{4}{5}$ $6\frac{7}{8}$
4. $4 \div 1\frac{1}{9}$ $3\frac{3}{5}$
5. $8\frac{1}{6} \div \frac{6}{7}$ $9\frac{19}{36}$
6. $2\frac{3}{4} \div 6$ $\frac{11}{24}$
7. $4\frac{1}{3} \div 2\frac{1}{2}$ $1\frac{11}{15}$
8. $5 \div 3\frac{5}{8}$ $1\frac{11}{29}$

234

Follow Up

Reteaching

Review with students the following skills: 1) changing a mixed number to an improper fraction, 2) writing the reciprocal of a fraction, and 3) writing a division exercise as a multiplication exercise with the dividend times the reciprocal of the divisor.

Have students apply these skills to the following exercises.

1. $1\frac{1}{3} \div 2\frac{1}{2}$ $\frac{8}{15}$
2. $4\frac{1}{2} \div 2\frac{7}{10}$ $1\frac{2}{3}$
3. $6\frac{1}{2} \div 1\frac{1}{4}$ $5\frac{1}{5}$

Enrichment

Display the following and have students complete the path.

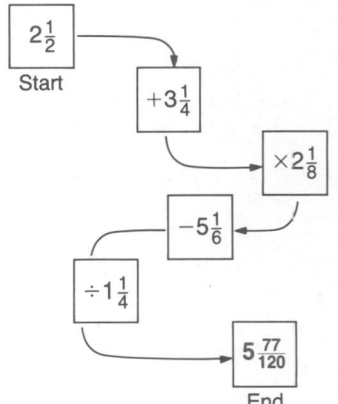

Find the quotients.

1. $2\frac{7}{8} \div 1\frac{1}{4}$ $2\frac{3}{10}$

2. $2 \div 7\frac{1}{2}$ $\frac{4}{15}$

3. $6\frac{1}{2} \div 2\frac{2}{3}$ $2\frac{7}{16}$

4. $1\frac{2}{5} \div \frac{2}{5}$ $3\frac{1}{2}$

5. $9 \div 1\frac{1}{2}$ 6

6. $\frac{2}{3} \div 1\frac{1}{5}$ $\frac{5}{9}$

7. $1\frac{3}{10} \div 2\frac{1}{2}$ $\frac{13}{25}$

8. $5\frac{1}{3} \div 2\frac{2}{3}$ 2

9. $1\frac{7}{8} \div 5\frac{1}{4}$ $\frac{5}{14}$

10. $1\frac{3}{16} \div 1\frac{1}{3}$ $\frac{57}{64}$

11. $3\frac{3}{8} \div 4$ $\frac{27}{32}$

12. $3\frac{2}{9} \div \frac{2}{3}$ $4\frac{5}{6}$

13. $2\frac{5}{12} \div \frac{3}{8}$ $6\frac{4}{9}$

14. $6\frac{1}{2} \div 7$ $\frac{13}{14}$

15. $3\frac{7}{8} \div 7\frac{1}{2}$ $\frac{31}{60}$

16. $7\frac{2}{3} \div 3\frac{1}{4}$ $2\frac{14}{39}$

17. $6 \div 1\frac{3}{16}$ $5\frac{1}{19}$

18. $\frac{5}{8} \div 3\frac{1}{3}$ $\frac{3}{16}$

19. $3\frac{1}{12} \div 2\frac{2}{3}$ $1\frac{5}{32}$

20. $1\frac{5}{9} - 3$ $\frac{14}{27}$

21. $2\frac{3}{8} \div 2\frac{1}{4}$ $1\frac{1}{18}$

22. $4\frac{1}{6} \div 1\frac{4}{9}$ $2\frac{23}{26}$

23. $12 \div 5\frac{1}{3}$ $2\frac{1}{4}$

24. $\frac{5}{6} \div 2\frac{3}{4}$ $\frac{10}{33}$

25. $\frac{2}{3} \div 2\frac{2}{5}$ $\frac{5}{18}$

26. $7\frac{1}{3} \div 3\frac{2}{3}$ 2

27. $\frac{5}{16} \div 1\frac{5}{8}$ $\frac{5}{26}$

28. $1\frac{9}{12} \div 1\frac{4}{5}$ $\frac{35}{36}$

29. Mick ran 60 ft from first base to second base. Each stride was about $3\frac{3}{4}$ ft long. About how many strides did he take? 16

30. Chuy hit a home run in baseball. It is 90 ft between the bases. If each stride was about $4\frac{1}{6}$ ft long, how many strides was it around all the bases? $86\frac{2}{5}$

31. One mile is 5,280 ft. About how many strides would it take to walk a mile if each stride was about $2\frac{7}{10}$ ft long? about 1,956

32. **DATA HUNT** Measure the length of one of your strides. About how many strides would you take to walk one mile?

SKILLKEEPER

Find the fraction of the number.

1. $\frac{1}{5}$ of 25 5

2. $\frac{4}{5}$ of 10 8

3. $\frac{2}{3}$ of 15 10

4. $\frac{3}{5}$ of 25 15

5. $\frac{1}{5}$ of 60 12

6. $\frac{2}{3} \times 24$ 16

7. $\frac{5}{6} \times 30$ 25

8. $\frac{7}{8} \times 48$ 42

9. $\frac{3}{4} \times 32$ 24

10. $\frac{3}{10} \times 50$ 15

Multiply.

11. $\frac{1}{8} \times \frac{1}{2}$ $\frac{1}{16}$

12. $\frac{2}{3} \times \frac{1}{4}$ $\frac{1}{6}$

13. $\frac{3}{4} \times \frac{2}{3}$ $\frac{1}{2}$

14. $\frac{5}{12} \times \frac{1}{2}$ $\frac{5}{24}$

15. $\frac{7}{8} \times \frac{2}{7}$ $\frac{1}{4}$

16. $\frac{1}{10} \times \frac{5}{12}$ $\frac{1}{24}$

17. $\frac{2}{3} \times \frac{5}{8}$ $\frac{5}{12}$

18. $\frac{7}{8} \times \frac{4}{5}$ $\frac{7}{10}$

19. $\frac{8}{15} \times \frac{5}{9}$ $\frac{8}{27}$

20. $\frac{9}{10} \times \frac{5}{6}$ $\frac{3}{4}$

More Practice, page 432, Set A

235

Using Page 235

Exercises 1–28 You may want to require students to give answers in lowest terms and write improper fractions as mixed or whole numbers.

Data Hunt Provide students with a tape measure or yard stick to measure the lengths of their strides.

Skillkeeper This Skillkeeper reviews material taught in this chapter.

More Practice, page 432, Set A

Reteaching Supplement, page 71

Enrichment Supplement, page 71

Practice Supplement, page 90

236
Applications

Quick Review Display the following equations. Call on students to state what operation should be used to solve the equation.

$x - 54 = 32$ addition $17\,y = 85$ division $\frac{r}{7} = 14$ multiplication

$12\,t = 36$ division $n + 35 = 70$ subtraction

Lesson Focus To solve word problems using data from a table

Ideas for Getting Started

Ask students to tell which of the following appliances they think uses the most and the least electricity per hour: color TV, frying pan, oven, clothes dryer, or vacuum cleaner. Write the responses on the chalkboard. Have students compare their responses to the data in the table on page 236.

Using Page 236

Lesson Development Have students read the material at the top of the page. Ask them to give the amount of electricity used by these appliances in one hour.

Color TV ($\frac{3}{20}$ kWh)   Hair dryer ($1\frac{1}{4}$ kWh)
Stove oven ($1\frac{1}{3}$ kWh)   Steam iron ($\frac{1}{3}$ kWh)

Read the introductory problem with students. Have them identify the question and the necessary data. Point out to students that since the broiler uses the same amount of electricity each hour, we can multiply to find the answer.

Exercises 1–8 You may wish to work through one or more of these problems as a class activity. Before making the assignment, tell students that some of the problems require more than one step to solve.

PROBLEM SOLVING: Using Data from a Table

| QUESTION |
| DATA |
| PLAN |
| ANSWER |
| CHECK |

Electricity is used in homes for lighting, cooking, heating, and for electrical appliances. The amount of electricity we use is measured in kilowatt-hours (kWh). The table shows the amount of electricity certain appliances use in one hour.

A broiler was used for $\frac{3}{4}$ of an hour. How much electricity did it use?

$$\frac{3}{4} \times 1\frac{1}{2} = \frac{3}{4} \times \frac{3}{2} = \frac{9}{8} = 1\frac{1}{8}$$

The broiler used $1\frac{1}{8}$ kWh of electricity.

Appliance	Electricity (kWh) used per hour
Broiler, portable	$1\frac{1}{2}$
Color TV	$\frac{3}{20}$
Clothes dryer	$2\frac{4}{5}$
Frying pan	$\frac{1}{2}$
Hair dryer	$1\frac{1}{4}$
Stove oven	$1\frac{1}{3}$
Stove burners	$1\frac{1}{4}$
Steam iron	$\frac{1}{3}$
Vacuum cleaner	$\frac{3}{4}$

Use the table to solve these problems.

1. It took $2\frac{1}{2}$ h to roast a small turkey in an oven. How many kilowatt-hours of electricity were used? $3\frac{1}{3}$ kWh

2. Carey used the stove burners $\frac{1}{2}$ h at breakfast. How many kilowatt-hours of electricity did she use? $\frac{5}{8}$ kWh

3. Sanjay used the vacuum cleaner, the oven, and the clothes dryer each for 1 h. How much electricity did he use in all? $4\frac{53}{60}$ kWh

4. An electric company estimated that an electric hot water heater will use 6,935 kWh of electricity per year to heat water for a household. About how many kilowatt-hours is that per day? 19 kWh

5. Debbie estimated that she uses about 30 kWh of electricity each month with her electric stove burners. About how many hours does she use the burners? 24 h

6. A color TV set was used for 5 h. How much did it cost for the electricity if each kilowatt-hour cost 8¢? 6¢

7. How many color TV sets, each running for 1 h, would it take to use the same amount of electricity it takes to use a clothes dryer for 1 h? $18\frac{2}{3}$

8. An oven and burners were each used for 3 h. How much more electricity was used by the oven than by the burners? $\frac{1}{4}$ kWh

236

Follow Up

Reteaching

Have students write problems based on the data given in the recipe below and present them to the class to solve.

Chicken Casserole (Serves 4)

$1\frac{1}{4}$ cups uncooked macaroni

$\frac{3}{4}$ cup shredded cheddar cheese

$1\frac{1}{2}$ cups diced cooked chicken

1 can cream of chicken soup

$\frac{3}{4}$ cup milk

$\frac{1}{2}$ tsp salt

Enrichment

Ask students to bring to class a recipe for one of their favorite dishes. Then have them figure out and list the amount of each ingredient they would use to make enough of the dish for the entire class.

Assignment Guide			
	Minimum	Average	Extended
pages 236–237	1–10, 13	1–14	5–15

Using Page 237

Exercise 12 This problem has two questions. Be sure that students answer both of them.

Try This A possible strategy, Choose the Operations, was taught on page 218.

Discussion After students read the problem, have them state the question in their own words. Make sure students understand that the question asks for the total cost for the year. Have students give the data needed to solve the problem. Some students may not realize there is data which must be obtained from the table on page 236.

Solution Cost of dryer per week:
$$4 \times 2\frac{4}{5} \times 8¢ = 89\frac{3}{5}¢$$
Cost of dryer per year:
$$89\frac{3}{5} \times 52 = 4,659\frac{1}{5}¢ = \$46.59$$
Cost of burner per day:
$$2 \times 1\frac{1}{4} = 2\frac{1}{2}¢ \times 8¢ = 20¢$$
Cost of burner per year:
$$20¢ \times 365 = 7,300¢ = \$73.00$$
Total cost:
$$\$46.59 + \$73.00 = \$119.59$$
The total cost of electricity per year is $119.59.

9. A family uses their clothes dryer 15 h each month. Their electricity costs 9¢ per kilowatt-hour. What is the cost per month for drying clothes? $3.78

10. It cost a family $564 a year to heat water by electricity. They changed to a natural gas water heater which cost $207 a year to heat their water. How much money did they save a year on water heating? $357

11. How much electricity would be used if the frying pan, the steam iron, and the vacuum cleaner were all used for 2 h each? $3\frac{1}{6}$ kWh

12. How many hours would a clothes dryer be in service to use 70 kWh of electricity? What is the cost of this amount of electricity at 9¢ per kilowatt-hour?
25 h ; $2.25

13. **DATA HUNT** What is the average cost per kilowatt-hour for electricity in your area? Find the amount of a home electric bill for one month. Divide by the number of kilowatt-hours used to find the average cost per kilowatt-hour.

14. **DATA BANK** What would be the total cost of using a broiler and a frying pan for 1 h each in San Juan, Puerto Rico? (See page 415.) $0.08 or 8¢

15. **Try This** The Hinson family uses their electric clothes dryer 4 h a week. They use their stove burners 2 h a day. They pay 8¢ per kilowatt-hour for electricity. What is the total cost (to the nearest cent) of electricity per year for the stove burners and clothes dryer?
Hint: Choose the operations. $119.59

237

Reteaching Supplement, page 72

Name _____

To follow text page 237

Problem Solving: Using Data from a Table

This table shows the number of hours each horse was ridden during the week.

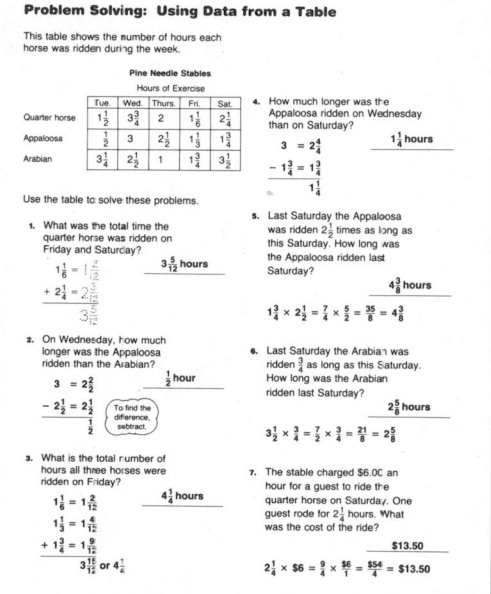

Pine Needle Stables

Hours of Exercise

	Tue.	Wed.	Thurs.	Fri.	Sat.
Quarter horse	$1\frac{1}{2}$	$3\frac{3}{4}$	2	$1\frac{1}{8}$	$2\frac{1}{4}$
Appaloosa	$\frac{1}{2}$	3	$2\frac{1}{2}$	$1\frac{1}{3}$	$1\frac{3}{4}$
Arabian	$3\frac{1}{4}$	$2\frac{1}{2}$	1	$1\frac{3}{4}$	$3\frac{1}{2}$

Use the table to solve these problems.

1. What was the total time the quarter horse was ridden on Friday and Saturday?
$$1\frac{1}{8} = 1\frac{1}{8}$$
$$+ 2\frac{1}{4} = 2\frac{2}{8}$$
$$3\frac{3}{8}$$
$3\frac{5}{12}$ hours

2. On Wednesday, how much longer was the Appaloosa ridden than the Arabian?
$$3 = 2\frac{2}{2}$$
$$- 2\frac{1}{2} = 2\frac{1}{2}$$
$$\frac{1}{2}$$
To find the difference, subtract.
$\frac{1}{2}$ hour

3. What is the total number of hours all three horses were ridden on Friday?
$$1\frac{1}{8} = 1\frac{3}{24}$$
$$1\frac{1}{3} = 1\frac{8}{24}$$
$$+ 1\frac{3}{4} = 1\frac{18}{24}$$
$$3\frac{29}{24}$$
$4\frac{1}{4}$ hours

4. How much longer was the Appaloosa ridden on Wednesday than on Saturday?
$$3 = 2\frac{4}{4}$$
$$- 1\frac{3}{4} = 1\frac{3}{4}$$
$$1\frac{1}{4}$$
$1\frac{1}{4}$ hours

5. Last Saturday the Appaloosa was ridden $2\frac{1}{2}$ times as long as this Saturday. How long was the Appaloosa ridden last Saturday?
$$1\frac{3}{4} \times 2\frac{1}{2} = \frac{7}{4} \times \frac{5}{2} = \frac{35}{8} = 4\frac{3}{8}$$
$4\frac{3}{8}$ hours

6. Last Saturday the Arabian was ridden $\frac{3}{4}$ as long as this Saturday. How long was the Arabian ridden last Saturday?
$$3\frac{1}{2} \times \frac{3}{4} = \frac{7}{2} \times \frac{3}{4} = \frac{21}{8} = 2\frac{5}{8}$$
$2\frac{5}{8}$ hours

7. The stable charged $6.00 an hour for a guest to ride the quarter horse on Saturday. One guest rode for $2\frac{1}{4}$ hours. What was the cost of the ride?
$$2\frac{1}{4} \times \$6 = \frac{9}{4} \times \frac{\$6}{1} = \frac{\$54}{4} = \$13.50$$
$13.50

Enrichment Supplement, page 72

Name _____

To follow text page 237

What Are You Asking Me?

Write a question you can answer using the data in each story. Exchange with a friend and answer each other's questions. **Answers will vary.**

1. This week Joan worked $4\frac{1}{2}$ h on Monday, $6\frac{1}{2}$ h on Tuesday, 5 h on Wednesday, and $7\frac{1}{2}$ h on Thursday. Last week she worked a total of 15 h at a salary of $3.50 per hour. This week she earned $4.00 per hour.

Answer: _____

2. Tina bought a blouse, shoes, and jeans on sale. The blouse was $6.50 off the regular price of $19.95. The shoes were $5.50 off the regular price of $29.75. The $18.00 jeans were on sale for $15.50.

Answer: _____

3. Dave has a $20 bill. He bought 2 records for $4.55 each and a poster for $2.95. Sandwiches at a restaurant cost $1.75 and $2.00.

Answer: _____

4. The Canterbury Hotel has five meeting rooms. Two rooms can hold between 75 and 125 people. Two other rooms can hold between 125 and 200 people. The large meeting room can hold 450 people.

Answer: _____

5. Greg is taking a two-day business trip. His air fare is $90.00 round trip. His car rental is $24.50 per day plus an $8.00 insurance fee. Greg estimated his travel expenses to be about $62.00 per day if he drove his own car.

Answer: _____

6. John and Jennifer bought the refreshments for a party. They bought 2 large bottles of juice at $3.15 each, a bag of apples for $0.79, and 3 bags of peanuts at $0.65 each.

Answer: _____

Practice Supplement, page 91

Name _____

To follow text page 237

Problem Solving: Using Data from a Table

Cities	Driving Time (h)
Johnstown to Owensville	$1\frac{1}{2}$
Owensville to Fleming	$\frac{3}{4}$
Fleming to Cypress	$\frac{1}{2}$
Cypress to Johnstown	$1\frac{2}{3}$
Johnstown to Fleming	$2\frac{1}{12}$
Owensville to Cypress	$1\frac{1}{6}$

Use the table to solve these problems.

1. Terry drove from Owensville to Fleming and then from Fleming to Cypress. What was his driving time?
$1\frac{1}{4}$ h

2. There is a fruit stand $\frac{2}{3}$ of the way between Fleming and Cypress. How long does it take to get to the fruit stand from Fleming?
$\frac{1}{3}$ h

3. How much longer does it take to drive from Johnstown to Owensville than it takes to drive from Owensville to Fleming?
$\frac{3}{4}$ h

4. Oscar and Mandy are going to share driving from Cypress to Johnstown. How long should each person drive?
$\frac{5}{6}$ h

5. How much longer does it take to drive from Fleming to Cypress to Johnstown than to drive directly from Fleming to Johnstown?
$\frac{1}{12}$ h

6. Alice drove from Cypress to Johnstown and then returned to Cypress. What was her driving time?
$3\frac{1}{3}$ h

7. Bill is on his way to Cypress from Owensville. He has driven $\frac{3}{4}$ hour. How much longer must he drive to get to Cypress?
$\frac{5}{12}$ h

8. Frank drove from Cypress to Johnstown and from Johnstown to Fleming. What was his driving time?
$3\frac{3}{4}$ h

Quick Review Display the numbers below. Point randomly to digits and have students give the place value of those digits.

507.0932   67.21596   13.32176

4,328.975   417.62381

Lesson Focus To write a fraction for a decimal and to write a decimal for a fraction by finding an equivalent fraction with a denominator of 10, 100, or 1,000

Ideas for Getting Started

Write the following fractions on the chalkboard. Ask students to tell what the fractions have in common. They should realize that none of the fractions are in lowest terms.

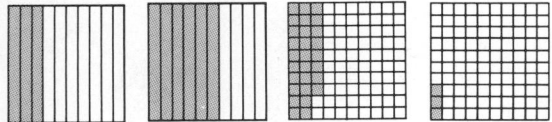

$$\frac{8}{12} \quad \frac{3}{9} \quad \frac{16}{100} \quad \frac{5}{15} \quad \frac{6}{10}$$

Have selected students go to the chalkboard and reduce the fractions.

Display the following models on the chalkboard. Ask students to give a decimal that represents the part that is shaded in each.

Using Page 238

Motivational Problem Have students read the problem at the top of the page. Ask them to restate the question and give the data needed to answer the question. Point out that there are different ways to write the answer.

Lesson Development Observe with students that 8 tenths can be written as a decimal or a fraction. Note that $\frac{8}{10}$ written in lowest terms is $\frac{4}{5}$. Point out that although many fractions name the same number, there is only one lowest-terms fraction for a given number.

Other Examples Have students study the examples. Discuss the idea that the clue to writing a fraction for a decimal lies in being able to read the decimal. For example, 0.125 is read "one hundred twenty-five thousandths" and the fraction is written $\frac{125}{1,000}$. Then the fraction can be reduced.

On the chalkboard, work through the last four examples showing how to write decimals for some fractions by finding equivalent fractions with denominators that are powers of 10.

Fractions and Decimals

There are 10 cars on a roller coaster. The seats are taken in 8 of the 10 cars. What part of the cars are filled?

8 **tenths** of the cars are filled.

We can write 8 tenths as a decimal or a fraction.

$$8 \text{ tenths} = \underset{\underset{\text{Decimal}}{\downarrow}}{0.8} = \underset{\underset{\text{Fraction}}{\downarrow}}{\frac{8}{10}} = \underset{\underset{\substack{\text{Lowest-terms} \\ \text{fraction}}}{\downarrow}}{\frac{4}{5}}$$

Other Examples

$36 \text{ hundredths} = 0.36 = \frac{36}{100} = \frac{9}{25}$ $125 \text{ thousandths} = 0.125 = \frac{125}{1,000} = \frac{1}{8}$

$2 \text{ and } 3 \text{ tenths} = 2.3 = 2\frac{3}{10}$ $4 \text{ and } 75 \text{ hundredths} = 4.75 = 4\frac{75}{100} = 4\frac{3}{4}$

We can write decimals for some fractions by finding equivalent fractions with denominators that are 10, 100, 1,000, and so on.

$\frac{1}{2} = \frac{1 \times 5}{2 \times 5} = \frac{5}{10} = 0.5$ $\frac{3}{4} = \frac{3 \times 25}{4 \times 25} = \frac{75}{100} = 0.75$

$\frac{11}{20} = \frac{11 \times 5}{20 \times 5} = \frac{55}{100} = 0.55$ $\frac{7}{25} = \frac{7 \times 4}{25 \times 4} = \frac{28}{100} = 0.28$

Warm Up

Write each number as a decimal and as a lowest-terms fraction or a mixed number.

1. 4 tenths
0.4; $\frac{2}{5}$

2. 35 hundredths
0.35; $\frac{7}{20}$

3. 1 and 6 tenths
1.6; $1\frac{3}{5}$

4. 408 thousandths
0.408; $\frac{51}{125}$

Write each decimal as a lowest-terms fraction.

5. 0.28
$\frac{7}{25}$

6. 0.2
$\frac{1}{5}$

7. 0.060
$\frac{3}{50}$

8. 2.25
$2\frac{1}{4}$

Write each fraction or mixed number as a decimal.

9. $\frac{4}{5}$ 0.8

10. $\frac{37}{50}$ 0.74

11. $2\frac{3}{4}$ 2.75

12. $\frac{117}{250}$ 0.468

238

Follow Up

Reteaching

Have students write decimals in a place-value chart (TRB p. 277) and name the value of the place occupied by the last digit. Explain that this number can be used as the denominator of the equivalent fraction.

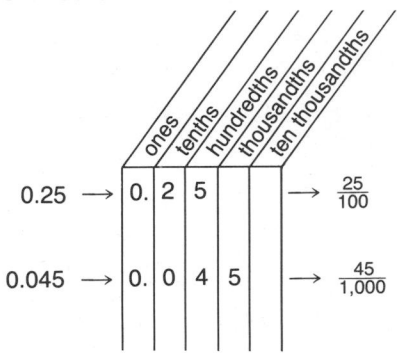

$0.25 \rightarrow \; 0. \; 2 \; 5 \; \rightarrow \frac{25}{100}$

$0.045 \rightarrow \; 0. \; 0 \; 4 \; 5 \; \rightarrow \frac{45}{1,000}$

Enrichment

Provide students with the puzzle below. Have them write the letter of each fraction above the matching decimal.

A. $\frac{3}{4}$ I. $\frac{1}{5}$ P. $\frac{1}{25}$ C. $\frac{1}{8}$

L. $\frac{7}{50}$ S. $\frac{3}{10}$ D. $\frac{7}{10}$ M. $\frac{3}{8}$

T. $\frac{4}{5}$ E. $\frac{7}{20}$ N. $\frac{3}{5}$ V. $\frac{1}{1,000}$

H. $\frac{1}{4}$ O. $\frac{7}{25}$

D	E	C	I	M	A	L	S
0.7	0.35	0.125	0.2	0.375	0.75	0.14	0.3

H	A	V	E	A
0.25	0.75	0.001	0.35	0.75

P	O	I	N	T
0.04	0.28	0.2	0.6	0.8

Assignment Guide			
	Minimum	Average	Extended
page 239	1–24, 35–45	1–45	1–45 odc, 46, TM

Write each number as a decimal and as a lowest-terms fraction or a mixed number.

1. 6 tenths 0.6; $\frac{3}{5}$ **2.** 2 and 5 tenths 2.5; $2\frac{1}{2}$ **3.** 24 hundredths 0.24; $\frac{6}{25}$

4. 50 hundredths 0.50; $\frac{1}{2}$ **5.** 250 thousandths 0.250; $\frac{1}{4}$ **6.** 3 and 36 hundredths 3.36; $3\frac{9}{25}$

7. 75 thousandths 0.075; $\frac{3}{40}$ **8.** 10 and 8 tenths 10.8; $10\frac{4}{5}$ **9.** 125 ten-thousandths 0.0125; $\frac{1}{80}$

Write each decimal as a lowest-terms fraction or a mixed number.

10. 0.4 $\frac{2}{5}$ **11.** 0.14 $\frac{7}{50}$ **12.** 0.06 $\frac{3}{50}$ **13.** 0.48 $\frac{12}{25}$ **14.** 0.1 $\frac{1}{10}$

15. 0.04 $\frac{1}{25}$ **16.** 3.28 $3\frac{7}{25}$ **17.** 5.7 $5\frac{7}{10}$ **18.** 0.355 $\frac{71}{200}$ **19.** 0.80 $\frac{4}{5}$

20. 8.12 $8\frac{3}{25}$ **21.** 12.5 $12\frac{1}{2}$ **22.** 0.006 $\frac{3}{500}$ **23.** 7.64 $7\frac{16}{25}$ **24.** 8.45 $8\frac{9}{20}$

25. 24.2 $24\frac{1}{5}$ **26.** 0.0008 $\frac{1}{1,250}$ **27.** 0.125 $\frac{1}{8}$ **28.** 5.55 $5\frac{11}{20}$ **29.** 0.00001 $\frac{1}{100,000}$

Write each fraction as a decimal.

30. $\frac{1}{4}$ 0.25 **31.** $\frac{8}{10}$ 0.8 **32.** $\frac{3}{4}$ 0.75 **33.** $3\frac{1}{4}$ 3.25 **34.** $\frac{3}{5}$ 0.6

35. $\frac{7}{20}$ 0.35 **36.** $2\frac{3}{4}$ 2.75 **37.** $\frac{13}{25}$ 0.52 **38.** $\frac{37}{100}$ 0.37 **39.** $\frac{33}{50}$ 0.66

40. $\frac{9}{10}$ 0.9 **41.** $5\frac{4}{5}$ 5.8 **42.** $\frac{327}{1,000}$ 0.327 **43.** $25\frac{7}{10}$ 25.7 **44.** $15\frac{3}{4}$ 15.75

45. A waiting line for an amusement park ride had 100 spaces. The line had only 0.64 of the spaces filled. What fraction of the spaces were filled? $\frac{16}{25}$

46. A large parking lot was completely filled with 1,000 cars. Then 200 cars left the lot. What part of the parking spaces were now filled? Give the answer as a decimal and as a lowest-terms fraction. $\frac{4}{5}$; 0.8

THINK MATH

Fraction Patterns

Find the sums. Do you see a pattern for the sums?
See teaching notes.

What would the sum be if the last addend were $\frac{1}{99 \times 100}$? $\frac{99}{100}$

1. $\frac{1}{1 \times 2} + \frac{1}{2 \times 3}$ $\frac{2}{3}$

2. $\frac{1}{1 \times 2} + \frac{1}{2 \times 3} + \frac{1}{3 \times 4}$ $\frac{3}{4}$

3. $\frac{1}{1 \times 2} + \frac{1}{2 \times 3} + \frac{1}{3 \times 4} + \frac{1}{4 \times 5}$ $\frac{4}{5}$

4. $\frac{1}{1 \times 2} + \frac{1}{2 \times 3} + \frac{1}{3 \times 4} + \frac{1}{4 \times 5} + \frac{1}{5 \times 6}$ $\frac{5}{6}$

More Practice, page 432, Set B

239

Using Page 239

Exercises 1–29 If students have difficulty reducing fractions to lowest terms, remind them that powers of 10 have only 2 and 5 as prime factors. The denominators of these fractions are powers of 10, so the only possible prime factors that could be common to the numerator and denominator are 2 and 5.

Think Math The pattern for the formation of the fractions is easy to see. Each additional fraction has a numerator of 1, and the denominator is formed by writing the last factor in the denominator of the previous fraction times the next consecutive whole number. The pattern is $\frac{1}{1 \times 2} + \frac{1}{2 \times 3} + \frac{1}{3 \times 4} + \ldots + \frac{1}{n(n+1)}$, where n is the number of fractions in the series. The first few examples show that the sums are of the form $\frac{1}{n+1}$. If the last addend in the series is $\frac{1}{99 \times 100}$, the sum of the series is $\frac{99}{100}$.

More Practice, page 432, Set B

Reteaching Supplement, page 73

Enrichment Supplement, page 73

Practice Supplement, page 92

Fractions

Lesson Focus To practice addition, subtraction, multiplication, and division of fractions; to write a terminating or repeating decimal for a given fraction.

Ideas for Getting Started

Write these division exercises on the chalkboard and ask students to find the quotients.

$8\overline{)3.000}$ $6\overline{)5.000}$ $7\overline{)3.000}$

Review with students the three uses of fractions introduced in Chapter 8. A fraction can express part of a region, part of a set, or division. Illustrate each meaning with a model as shown below.

1 divided by 3

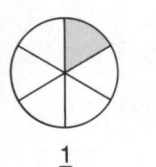  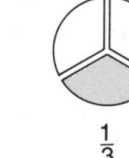

$\frac{1}{6}$ $\frac{3}{5}$ $\frac{1}{3}$

Using Page 240

Exercises 1–52 These exercises provide an opportunity for students to review adding, subtracting, multiplying, and dividing with fractions and mixed numbers. Use the exercises to assess students' understanding of fraction computation. Observe whether any students are having difficulty. If so, work with them individually or in small groups and reteach the appropriate lessons.

Skills Practice

Find the quotients.

1. $\frac{2}{5} \div \frac{1}{8}$ $3\frac{1}{5}$
2. $\frac{5}{11} \div 5$ $\frac{1}{11}$
3. $\frac{4}{9} \div \frac{1}{3}$ $1\frac{1}{3}$
4. $\frac{4}{6} \div \frac{2}{9}$ 3

5. $10 \div \frac{15}{17}$ $11\frac{1}{3}$
6. $2\frac{1}{3} \div 4\frac{1}{5}$ $\frac{5}{9}$
7. $4\frac{2}{4} \div 5\frac{1}{3}$ $\frac{27}{32}$
8. $8\frac{1}{4} \div 1\frac{3}{8}$ 6

9. $5\frac{2}{6} \div \frac{1}{3}$ 16
10. $1\frac{4}{12} \div \frac{8}{11}$ $1\frac{5}{6}$
11. $5\frac{5}{7} \div 1\frac{1}{14}$ $5\frac{1}{3}$
12. $\frac{1}{10} \div 2\frac{2}{8}$ $\frac{2}{45}$

Divide.

13. $9\frac{2}{6} \div \frac{2}{3}$ 14
14. $11\frac{4}{7} \div 4\frac{1}{2}$ $2\frac{4}{7}$
15. $12\frac{1}{4} \div 10\frac{1}{2}$ $1\frac{1}{6}$
16. $14\frac{2}{5} \div \frac{9}{10}$ 16

17. $5\frac{1}{3} \div \frac{4}{5}$ $6\frac{2}{3}$
18. $10\frac{2}{4} \div 11\frac{2}{3}$ $\frac{9}{10}$
19. $12\frac{4}{5} \div 13\frac{1}{3}$ $\frac{24}{25}$
20. $2\frac{8}{14} \div 2\frac{4}{7}$ 1

21. $5\frac{8}{11} \div 1\frac{4}{5}$ $3\frac{2}{11}$
22. $1\frac{1}{8} \div 18$ $\frac{1}{16}$
23. $9\frac{1}{3} \div 1\frac{2}{5}$ $6\frac{2}{3}$
24. $9\frac{3}{5} \div \frac{6}{10}$ 16

Add, subtract, multiply, or divide.

25. $1\frac{3}{5} \times 2\frac{1}{16}$ $3\frac{3}{10}$
26. $2\frac{1}{3} + 4\frac{6}{8}$ $7\frac{1}{12}$
27. $4 - \frac{4}{10}$ $3\frac{3}{5}$
28. $1\frac{3}{10} \times 2\frac{1}{2}$ $3\frac{1}{4}$

29. $1\frac{7}{8} \div 1\frac{1}{4}$ $1\frac{1}{2}$
30. $4\frac{6}{7} \times \frac{8}{17}$ $2\frac{2}{7}$
31. $11\frac{6}{8} + 3\frac{1}{5}$ $14\frac{19}{20}$
32. $2\frac{9}{12} \div \frac{11}{48}$ 12

33. $36 - \frac{10}{52}$ $35\frac{21}{26}$
34. $1\frac{1}{5} - \frac{4}{10}$ $\frac{4}{5}$
35. $6\frac{5}{6} + 7\frac{1}{5}$ $14\frac{1}{30}$
36. $1\frac{1}{36} \div \frac{5}{18}$ $3\frac{7}{10}$

37. $42\frac{8}{9} + 52\frac{5}{6}$ $95\frac{13}{18}$
38. $1\frac{1}{11} \div 8\frac{4}{7}$ $\frac{7}{55}$
39. $72\frac{1}{9} - 69\frac{3}{4}$ $2\frac{13}{36}$
40. $1\frac{2}{8} \times 3\frac{1}{5}$ 4

Solve.

41. $22\frac{5}{8} - 21\frac{2}{3}$ $\frac{23}{24}$
42. $11\frac{4}{5} + 10\frac{2}{3}$ $22\frac{7}{15}$
43. $\frac{8}{9} \div 14\frac{2}{5}$ $\frac{5}{81}$
44. $1\frac{1}{10} \times \frac{3}{22}$ $\frac{3}{20}$

45. $3\frac{3}{5} \div \frac{9}{13}$ $5\frac{1}{5}$
46. $3\frac{9}{11} \times \frac{5}{6}$ $3\frac{2}{11}$
47. $40\frac{1}{8} + 63\frac{2}{7}$ $103\frac{23}{56}$
48. $29\frac{1}{8} - 13\frac{5}{6}$ $15\frac{7}{24}$

49. $1\frac{13}{20} \times 3\frac{2}{11}$ $5\frac{1}{4}$
50. $\frac{6}{25} \div \frac{7}{30}$ $1\frac{1}{35}$
51. $5\frac{1}{3} - 4\frac{4}{18}$ $1\frac{1}{9}$
52. $18\frac{2}{5} + 1\frac{11}{15}$ $20\frac{2}{15}$

Follow Up

Reteaching

Write the fractions below on the chalkboard. Have students mark off 10 by 10 squares on graph paper (TRB p. 284). Tell them to write the fractions as decimals and check their answers by shading the appropriate regions of the squares.

Example: $\frac{1}{4}$ $\begin{array}{r} 0.25 \\ 4\overline{)1.00} \end{array}$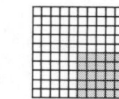

$\frac{3}{4}$ $\frac{2}{10}$ $\frac{1}{20}$ $\frac{2}{5}$ $\frac{8}{25}$ $\frac{7}{10}$ $\frac{5}{2}$

Enrichment

Explain to students that if the denominator of a fraction has only 2 or 5 or both as prime factors, it can be written as a terminating decimal. Ask students to find all the unit fractions with a denominator of 100 or less that can be written as terminating decimals.

$\frac{1}{2}, \frac{1}{4}, \frac{1}{5}, \frac{1}{8}, \frac{1}{10}, \frac{1}{16}, \frac{1}{20}, \frac{1}{25}, \frac{1}{32}, \frac{1}{40}, \frac{1}{50},$

$\frac{1}{64}, \frac{1}{80}, \frac{1}{100}$

Assignment Guide			
	Minimum	Average	Extended
page 240	1–32	1–44	2–52 even
page 241	1–18, 29–32	1–32	2–32 even

Terminating and Repeating Decimals

The Riverside Symphony has played $\frac{7}{8}$ of its concerts.

$$\frac{7}{8} \rightarrow 8\overline{)7.000} \quad \begin{array}{l} 0.875 \leftarrow \text{Terminating} \\ \text{decimal} \end{array}$$

$$\begin{array}{r} 64 \\ \hline 60 \\ 56 \\ \hline 40 \\ 40 \\ \hline 0 \leftarrow \text{Zero remainder} \end{array}$$

The Lincoln Philharmonic has played $\frac{5}{6}$ of its concerts.

$$\frac{5}{6} \rightarrow 6\overline{)5.000} \quad \begin{array}{l} 0.833\ldots \leftarrow \text{Repeating} \\ \text{decimal} \end{array}$$

$$\begin{array}{r} 48 \\ \hline 20 \\ 18 \\ \hline 20 \\ 18 \\ \hline 2 \leftarrow \text{Remainder is never zero.} \end{array}$$

Every fractional number can be written as a **terminating decimal** or a **repeating decimal**.

To show a repeating decimal, place a bar over the digits that repeat.

$$\frac{5}{6} = 0.833\ldots = 0.8\overline{3}$$

$$\frac{4}{33} = 0.1212\ldots = 0.\overline{12}$$

Write each repeating decimal using a bar.

1. 0.434343...
0.$\overline{43}$

2. 1.077077...
1.$\overline{077}$

3. 0.0575757...
0.0$\overline{57}$

4. 20.55555...
20.$\overline{5}$

5. 2.345345...
2.$\overline{345}$

6. 0.81188118...
0.$\overline{8118}$

7. 0.231231231...
0.$\overline{231}$

8. 3.27276666...
3.2727$\overline{6}$

Find the decimal for each fraction. Use a bar to show repeating decimals.

9. $\frac{5}{9}$ 0.$\overline{5}$

10. $\frac{1}{6}$ 0.1$\overline{6}$

11. $\frac{23}{25}$ 0.92

12. $\frac{7}{12}$ 0.58$\overline{3}$

13. $\frac{2}{3}$ 0.$\overline{6}$

14. $\frac{8}{15}$ 0.5$\overline{3}$

15. $\frac{9}{8}$ 1.125

16. $\frac{21}{28}$ 0.75

17. $\frac{4}{27}$ 0.$\overline{148}$

18. $\frac{29}{50}$ 0.58

19. $\frac{5}{3}$ 1.$\overline{6}$

20. $\frac{7}{22}$ 0.31$\overline{8}$

21. $\frac{11}{12}$ 0.91$\overline{6}$

22. $\frac{9}{18}$ 0.5

23. $\frac{13}{5}$ 2.6

24. $\frac{55}{33}$ 1.$\overline{6}$

25. $\frac{19}{20}$ 0.95

26. $\frac{17}{68}$ 0.25

27. $\frac{13}{15}$ 0.8$\overline{6}$

28. $\frac{13}{18}$ 0.7$\overline{2}$

Compare the two fractions by comparing their decimals. Use > or <. 🖩

29. $\frac{11}{15}$ ⬤ $\frac{7}{12}$

30. $\frac{11}{27}$ ⬤ $\frac{26}{64}$

31. $\frac{11}{12}$ ⬤ $\frac{89}{90}$

32. $\frac{37}{80}$ ⬤ $\frac{127}{275}$

More Practice, page 432, Set C
0.$\overline{407}$ > 0.40625
0.91$\overline{6}$ < 0.9$\overline{8}$
0.4625 > 0.461$\overline{8}$ **241**
0.7$\overline{3}$ > 0.58$\overline{3}$

Using Page 241

Lesson Development Have students study the material at the top of the page. Point out that the first example shows a remainder of 0 and a *terminating decimal.* In the second example, the digits in the quotient repeat to form a *repeating decimal.* Show how a bar can be used to indicate that digits repeat.

Exercises 9–27 Before making the assignment, you may want to work through one or more of these exercises on the chalkboard. Explain that students should carry out the division until the remainder is 0 or the digits in the quotient repeat.

Exercises 29–32 Students can use a calculator to find the decimal equivalents and then compare the decimals.

More Practice, page 432, Set C

Reteaching Supplement, page 74

Enrichment Supplement, page 74

Practice Supplement, page 93

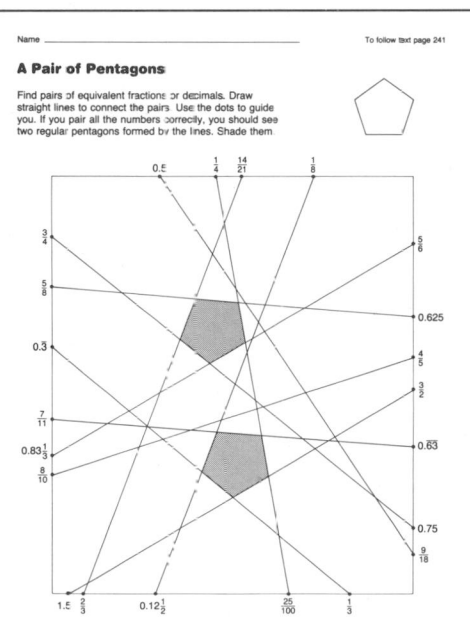

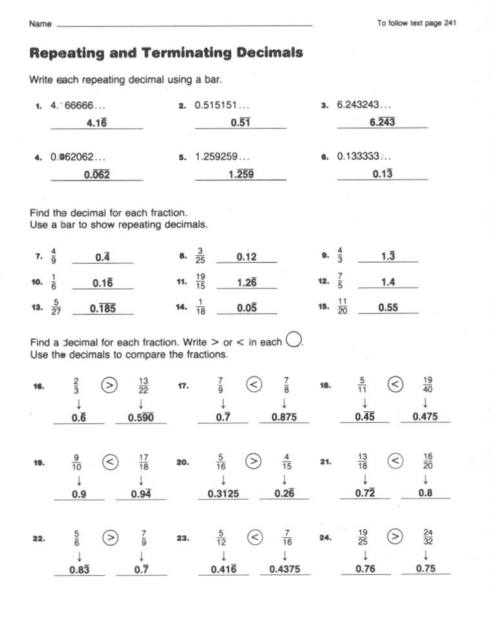

Ideas for Getting Started

Lesson Focus To use logical reasoning as a strategy to solve nonroutine word problems

Display the following problem on the chalkboard.

There are 26 students in the room. 10 are in the band. 9 are in the chorus. 11 are not in either band or chorus.
Next draw a *Venn diagram* to show these facts.

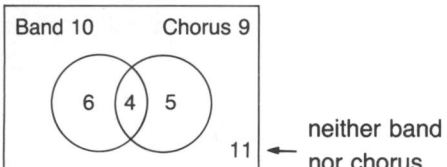

Ask students to explain why some students must be in both the band and the chorus. Point out that there are only 26 students and 10 + 9 + 11 = 30, so 4 students must be in both band and chorus.

Complete the diagram, showing the number of students in each region: 4 in both band and chorus, 6 in only the band, and 5 in only the chorus.

Using Page 242

Motivational Problem Have students read the Try This problem at the top of the page. Ask them to identify the question and the data needed to solve the problem. Explain that a Venn diagram can help us show the data and to reason logically about the problem.

Lesson Development Draw a diagram on the chalkboard. Have students explain how to label each region with the appropriate data. Ask them to tell how many students voted for either carrots or spinach. (24 − 7 = 17) Explain that since there were 11 votes for carrots and 9 votes for spinach, 3 students must have voted for both. (11 + 9 = 20, 20 − 17 = 3)

Some students might add 11 + 9 + 7 to get 27. This is 3 more than the total number of students, so 3 students voted for both vegetables. A Venn diagram can be used to check the answer.

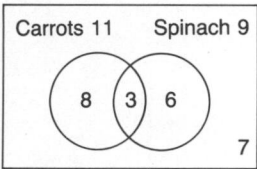

Exercises 1–2 Assign these exercises for independent or group work. Have students show their diagrams and discuss their reasoning for each problem.

PROBLEM SOLVING: Use Logical Reasoning

| QUESTION |
| DATA |
| PLAN |
| ANSWER |
| CHECK |

Try This

A health-class teacher asked her students to raise their hands if they liked carrots. 11 students raised their hands. There were 9 students who raised their hands as liking spinach. There were 7 students who did not like either of the vegetables. All 24 students in the class voted. How many students like both carrots and spinach?

With some problems it may be difficult to organize the data or to decide what to do. To solve such problems, it may be helpful to use a strategy called **Use Logical Reasoning**.

To help you reason logically, you can draw a special diagram called a **Venn diagram**.

Draw and label a diagram that shows how all the data in the problem are related.

Use the diagram to help you think logically about the problem.

There were **24 − 7 = 17** students who voted for either spinach or carrots.

Since **11 + 9 = 20**, there must have been **20 − 17 = 3** students that voted for both vegetables.

All 24 students

(Venn diagram showing: Carrots 11, Carrots and spinach, Spinach 9, Neither carrots nor spinach 7)

Solve.

1. In a class of 30 students, 18 students play soccer. There are 15 students that play softball. There are 9 students that play neither soccer nor softball. How many students play both soccer and softball? 12

2. Margarita made a list of 25 numbers. There were 10 numbers that were not divisible by 2 or by 3. There were 12 numbers that were divisible by 2 and among these 12 numbers, 8 were divisible by 2 and by 3. How many of the numbers were divisible by 3 but not by 2? 3

242

Strategy Test Item

Optional Problem If you wish to assess students' ability to apply the strategy called Use Logical Reasoning introduced in this chapter, provide them with the problem below.

There were 40 people at a party. 29 persons were 25 years of age or younger. 23 persons were 16 years of age or older. How many persons were between the ages of 16 and 25?

Solution

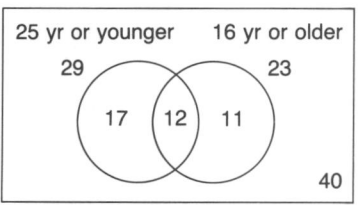

12 persons were between the ages of 16 and 25.

CHAPTER REVIEW/TEST

Find the fraction of the number.

1. $\frac{1}{4}$ of 20 5 2. $\frac{1}{5}$ of 35 7 3. $\frac{2}{3}$ of 12 8 4. $\frac{3}{4}$ of 16 12

Multiply.

5. $\frac{1}{2} \times \frac{2}{3}$ $\frac{1}{3}$ 6. $\frac{5}{8} \times \frac{2}{3}$ $\frac{5}{12}$ 7. $\frac{7}{16} \times \frac{4}{3}$ $\frac{7}{12}$ 8. $\frac{9}{10} \times \frac{5}{12}$ $\frac{3}{8}$

9. $2\frac{2}{3} \times 2\frac{1}{2}$ $6\frac{2}{3}$ 10. $8 \times 4\frac{3}{4}$ 38 11. $10 \times 2\frac{2}{3}$ $26\frac{2}{3}$ 12. $1\frac{7}{8} \times 3\frac{3}{4}$ $7\frac{1}{32}$

13. $\frac{3}{4} \times 3\frac{1}{2}$ $2\frac{5}{8}$ 14. $\frac{4}{3} \times \frac{3}{4}$ 1 15. $1\frac{1}{3} \times 18$ 24 16. $6\frac{1}{4} \times \frac{1}{2}$ $3\frac{1}{8}$

Give the reciprocal of each number.

17. $\frac{7}{8}$ $\frac{8}{7}$ 18. $\frac{5}{2}$ $\frac{2}{5}$ 19. $1\frac{3}{4}$ $\frac{4}{7}$ 20. 6 $\frac{1}{6}$

Divide.

21. $\frac{2}{3} \div \frac{5}{6}$ $\frac{4}{5}$ 22. $\frac{7}{12} \div \frac{3}{4}$ $\frac{7}{9}$ 23. $3 \div \frac{1}{2}$ 6 24. $\frac{3}{4} \div 2$ $\frac{3}{8}$

25. $2\frac{2}{3} \div \frac{8}{9}$ 3 26. $5\frac{1}{4} \div \frac{7}{10}$ $7\frac{1}{2}$ 27. $16 \div 3\frac{1}{5}$ 5 28. $5\frac{1}{2} \div 2\frac{1}{2}$ $2\frac{1}{5}$

29. $1 \div \frac{1}{4}$ 4 30. $\frac{5}{8} \div \frac{5}{8}$ 1 31. $3\frac{1}{4} \div 2\frac{1}{2}$ $1\frac{3}{10}$ 32. $12\frac{1}{2} \div 5$ $2\frac{1}{2}$

Write each decimal as a lowest-terms fraction.

33. 0.5 $\frac{1}{2}$ 34. 0.24 $\frac{6}{25}$ 35. 0.025 $\frac{1}{40}$ 36. 0.375 $\frac{3}{8}$

Write each fraction as a repeating or terminating decimal.

37. $\frac{13}{15}$ $0.8\overline{6}$ 38. $\frac{7}{9}$ $0.\overline{7}$ 39. $\frac{4}{15}$ $0.2\overline{6}$ 40. $1\frac{1}{3}$ $1.\overline{3}$

41. An oven uses $1\frac{1}{3}$ kWh of electricity each hour. How much electricity would it use for a roast that cooked $2\frac{1}{2}$ h? $3\frac{1}{3}$ kWh

42. Bill ran with a stride that measured $3\frac{3}{4}$ ft. How many strides would he take while running 120 ft? 32

243

Using Page 243

The exercises in the Chapter Review/Test emphasize the major concepts and skills presented in this chapter. These exercises may be used as a review assignment or as a test, depending upon your needs.

Item Analysis The table below correlates the Chapter Review/Test items with objectives and with the student text pages on which the concepts or skills were taught.

Items	Objectives	Related Text Pages
1–16	9.1	224–280
17–20	9.2	231
21–32	9.3	232–235
33–40	9.4	238–241
41–42	9.5	236–237

Assessment Options

If you use the Chapter Review/Test as a review assignment, you may wish to use the free-response test or the multiple-choice text to evaluate mastery of the chapter objectives. The items on these tests have a one-to-one correspondence in terms of content and level of difficulty. A correlation of test items to objectives and student text pages is provided in the Management Guide for Chapter 9.

Multiple-Choice Test, TRB page 25–27
Free-Response Test, TRB pages 65–66

TRB Options

The following blackline masters are available for use with this chapter. If you have not already assigned these materials, you may wish to use them to close the chapter.

Recreation, TRB page 163
Consumer Applications, TRB page 181
Calculator Technology, TRB page 199
Reading Math, TRB page 235
Family Involvement, TRB pages 261–262

Using Page 244

The exercises on this page are intended for those students who experienced difficulty with the Chapter Review/Test on page 243. Should students require reteaching of these key concepts and skills, please refer to the teaching notes below. Otherwise, the Another Look exercises can be assigned as independent work, with students using the accompanying sample problems and hints as guides.

Exercises 1–6 This skill was originally taught on pages 224–225. Have students study the example in the display box on the left. Explain how an array can be used to find the fraction of a number. Work through the multiplication exercise on the chalkboard. Emphasize the multiplication shortcut.

Exercises 7–15 This skill was originally taught on pages 226–229. On the chalkboard, work through the example in the display box one step at a time. Stress that we can divide out factors common to numerators and denominators before multiplying. You may wish to work through an example of multiplying with mixed numbers. Make sure students understand that before multiplying, mixed numbers should be written as improper fractions.

Exercises 16–24 This skill was originally taught on pages 231–235. On the chalkboard, work through the example with students. Point out that to divide, we always find the reciprocal of the divisor and then write the exercise as the dividend times the reciprocal. You may wish to show students an example of dividing with mixed numbers. Emphasize writing mixed numbers as improper fractions and finding the reciprocal of the divisor. Be sure students understand that the shortcut can be used after writing the exercise as multiplication.

Exercises 25–33 This skill was originally taught on page 241. Remind students that a fraction can be thought of in terms of division. Work through the examples in the display box with students. Stress that the division should be carried out until the remainder is 0 or until digits in the quotient repeat.

ANOTHER LOOK

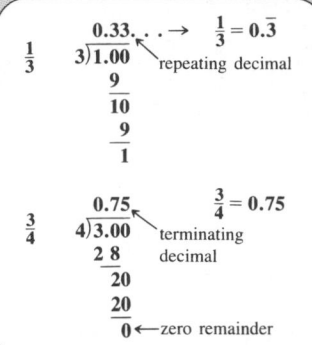

Find the fraction of the number.

1. $\frac{1}{5}$ of 10 2

2. $\frac{1}{4}$ of 24 6

3. $\frac{1}{8}$ of 40 5

4. $\frac{3}{4}$ of 12 9

5. $\frac{2}{3}$ of 9 6

6. $\frac{9}{10}$ of 20 18

Multiply.

7. $\frac{1}{2} \times \frac{1}{5}$ $\frac{1}{10}$

8. $\frac{3}{4} \times \frac{8}{9}$ $\frac{2}{3}$

9. $\frac{5}{6} \times \frac{9}{10}$ $\frac{3}{4}$

10. $2\frac{1}{4} \times 4$ 9

11. $1\frac{7}{8} \times \frac{7}{15}$ $\frac{7}{8}$

12. $1\frac{2}{3} \times 1\frac{2}{3}$ $2\frac{7}{9}$

13. $20 \times 1\frac{3}{4}$ 35

14. $\frac{1}{2} \times 3\frac{3}{4}$ $1\frac{7}{8}$

15. $5 \times 3\frac{3}{5}$ 18

Divide.

16. $\frac{2}{3} \div \frac{2}{5}$ $1\frac{2}{3}$

17. $\frac{15}{16} \div \frac{5}{4}$ $\frac{3}{4}$

18. $3 \div \frac{3}{4}$ 4

19. $1\frac{1}{2} \div 2$ $\frac{3}{4}$

20. $2 \div 1\frac{1}{2}$ $1\frac{1}{3}$

21. $6 \div \frac{2}{3}$ 9

22. $8\frac{3}{4} \div 3\frac{3}{4}$ $2\frac{1}{3}$

23. $10 \div \frac{1}{3}$ 30

24. $15 \div 1\frac{1}{4}$ 12

Write a repeating decimal or a terminating decimal for each fraction.

25. $\frac{2}{3}$ $0.\overline{6}$

26. $\frac{11}{25}$ 0.44

27. $\frac{1}{8}$ 0.125

28. $\frac{5}{6}$ $0.8\overline{3}$

29. $\frac{8}{15}$ $0.53\overline{3}$

30. $\frac{7}{3}$ $2.\overline{3}$

31. $1\frac{1}{2}$ 1.5

32. $\frac{7}{8}$ 0.875

33. $\frac{4}{6}$ $0.\overline{6}$

244

Just for Teachers

Music and Mathematics

Perhaps no art form is as dependent upon mathematics for its composition and expression as music. As early as 2500 B.C., the Chinese understood that the musical tone of a bamboo reed was a function of its length, but it was not until 500 B.C. that the underlying mathematical structure of music was discovered.

Pythagoras, experimenting with the length of a plucked string, found that whole number relationships existed between the tones of the scale but this discovery did not significantly affect musical expression. Until about A.D. 900, when polyphony was introduced, Western music was usually a single line of notes, sometimes augmented by an identical line an octave above or below. Musical form then rapidly evolved, employing both harmony and rhythm, and involving new instruments.

While artistic innovation expanded the acceptable limits of form and expression, scientific inquiry consolidated knowledge of sound properties. DaVinci conceived of sound as a "percussion of the air." Newton postulated that sound travelled through a

This page is intended for those students who successfully completed the Chapter Review/Test on page 243. You may wish to assign this page as independent work while you use Another Look exercises to reteach the basic concepts and skills of the chapter. Or, you may decide that all students would benefit from exposure to this Enrichment activity.

Lesson Development Have students study the table at the top of the page. Explain that stock prices are expressed in fractions of a dollar. Today's high for a share of AMRO stock was $35.50. Point out that the "change" column indicates the difference between the closing price yesterday and today.

Ask students the following questions. "What was today's closing price for a share of AMRO?" ($29.75) "What was today's low for a share of New Gas?" ($47.25) "How would $36.50 be written in the stock market column?" ($36\frac{1}{2}$)

Exercises 1–7 You may wish to have students use calculators to work these problems or to check their answers.

ENRICHMENT

Converting Fractions to Decimals

Stock	Today's high	Today's low	Today's close	Change
AMRO	$34\frac{1}{2}$	$28\frac{1}{2}$	$29\frac{3}{4}$	$-\frac{3}{4}$
Betins	59	$51\frac{1}{2}$	$54\frac{1}{2}$	$-1\frac{3}{8}$
Computer	$13\frac{5}{8}$	$13\frac{1}{2}$	$13\frac{1}{2}$	$+\frac{1}{2}$
ITE	$26\frac{1}{2}$	$14\frac{1}{2}$	26	$+\frac{1}{4}$
New Gas	$47\frac{3}{4}$	$47\frac{1}{4}$	$47\frac{1}{2}$	$-1\frac{1}{4}$
PITT	$26\frac{7}{8}$	$26\frac{5}{8}$	$26\frac{3}{4}$	$+\frac{1}{8}$
Servco	31	$29\frac{1}{2}$	$29\frac{3}{4}$	$-1\frac{5}{8}$

A newspaper reports stock prices in fractions of a dollar. A price of $24\frac{3}{4}$ means $24.75.

Use a calculator to do these problems. Record the answers as decimals.

1. What is the difference between today's high and low for each of the following stocks?

PITT	Betins	Computer	Servco
$0.25	$7.50	$0.125	$1.50

2. What is the cost of buying 100 shares of each of the following stocks at today's closing price?

Computer	ITE	AMRO	New Gas
$1,350	$2,600	$2,975	$4,750

3. The "change" column indicates the difference between the closing price yesterday and today. A plus sign means a gain in price and a minus sign means a loss in price. What was the closing price yesterday for each of these stocks?

PITT	Servco	AMRO	Betins
$26.625	$31.375	$30.50	$55.875

4. Suppose you sell 10 shares of ITE stock and 10 shares of AMRO stock at today's low. How many dollars do you receive? $430

5. Suppose you sell 200 shares of Computer stock and 100 shares of Betins stock at today's closing price. How much money do you receive? $8,150

6. Each share of New Gas stock is worth $1\frac{1}{4}$ dollars less at today's closing price than yesterday's closing price. How much less is 100 shares of New Gas stock worth at today's closing price than yesterday's closing price? $125

7. What is the total cost of buying 50 shares each of PITT, AMRO, and Betins at today's low? $5,331.25

245

---

medium in waves which alternately compressed and expanded it. The basic laws of pitch, relating a string's vibration to its length, weight, and tension, were articulated in 1636 by the French mathematician Marin Mersenne.

Throughout history, the number of tones in a scale has varied. The ancient Greeks had a seven-tone scale, the Chinese a five-tone, and the Hindus a complex 22-tone. By 1700, Europe had standardized the diatonic scale based on natural frequency ratios. While precisely mathematical, the diatonic scale was not practical because it required too many fractionally different tones. Transposing from one key to another was virtually impossible unless each octave were divided into an impractically large number of tones. The "equal temperament" scale was thus developed. By slightly lowering the vibrational frequency of each fifth interval on the keyboard, an octave of 12 equal semi-tones, reproduceable in any key, was created.

Using Page 246

The exercises on the page provide practice for maintaining cumulative skills. The emphasis in this Cumulative Review is on geometry (Chapter 6) and operations with fractions (Chapter 8).

Item Analysis The table below correlates the Cumulative Review items with objectives and with the student book pages on which the concepts or skills were taught.

Items	Objectives	Related Text Pages
1	6.1	136–137
2–3	6.2	138–139
4–5	6.3	141–145
6	6.5	148–151
7	6.4	146–147
8	8.1	194–199
9	8.2	200–201
10	8.3	202–204
11	8.4	206–209
12–13	8.5	210–215
14	8.6	205, 217

CUMULATIVE REVIEW

1. What is the symbol for segment AB?

   A •————————• B

   A $\overrightarrow{AB}$ **B** $\overleftrightarrow{AB}$
   Ⓒ AB **D** not given

2. What kind of angle is $\angle CED$?

   A acute
   Ⓑ obtuse
   C right
   D not given

3. What is the measure of an angle that is complementary to $\angle XOY$?

   Ⓐ 55°
   B 50°
   C 145°
   D not given

4. What kind of quadrilateral is figure $QRST$?

   A triangle
   Ⓑ trapezoid
   C rectangle
   D not given

5. What is the sum of the measures of the angles in any triangle?

   A 360°   Ⓑ 180°
   C 90°   **D** not given

6. How many lines of symmetry does a square have?

   Ⓐ 4   **B** 8
   C 2   **D** not given

7. If the length of a radius of a circle is 2.4 cm, what is the length of the diameter?

   A 6.9   **B** 1.2
   Ⓒ 4.8   **D** not given

8. What is $\frac{18}{20}$ in lowest terms?

   A $\frac{8}{10}$ Ⓑ $\frac{9}{10}$
   C $\frac{2}{5}$ **D** not given

9. What is the mixed number for $\frac{28}{5}$?

   A $4\frac{5}{8}$ Ⓑ $5\frac{3}{5}$
   C $5\frac{2}{5}$ **D** not given

10. Which is correct?

    A $\frac{5}{8} > \frac{2}{3}$ **B** $\frac{3}{4} > \frac{4}{5}$
    Ⓒ $\frac{2}{5} < \frac{5}{8}$ **D** not given

Add or subtract.

11. $\frac{1}{8}$
       $+\frac{1}{2}$

    A $\frac{3}{4}$ **B** $\frac{3}{16}$
    Ⓒ $\frac{5}{8}$ **D** not given

12. $3\frac{1}{2}$
       $+8\frac{3}{8}$

    A $11\frac{3}{4}$ Ⓑ $11\frac{7}{8}$
    C $12\frac{1}{8}$ **D** not given

13. $7\frac{1}{2}$
       $-5\frac{3}{4}$

    A $2\frac{3}{4}$ **B** $1\frac{1}{4}$
    C $2\frac{1}{2}$ Ⓓ not given

14. Elinor has $\frac{3}{4}$ c of flour. She uses $\frac{5}{8}$ c. What fraction of a cup of flour is left?

    Ⓐ $\frac{1}{8}$ c   **B** $\frac{1}{4}$ c
    C $\frac{1}{2}$ c   **D** not given

Measurement: Metric Units

Overview Chapter 10

Objectives

10.1 Express metric units of length in larger or smaller metric units.

10.2 Find the perimeter and area of a simple polygon and the surface area of a rectangular prism.

10.3 Find the volume of a prism.

10.4 Choose appropriate metric units of capacity and weight and express in larger or smaller units; read Celsius temperatures.

10.5 Solve word problems using the 5-Point Checklist and cumulative computational skills.

Summary

This chapter has two main goals: 1) To review and extend metric units of measurement, and 2) to solve practical word problems related to measurement. Although students at this grade level should have had considerable experience with metric units, the basic relationships between units are carefully reviewed. The concepts of area and volume are reviewed, and area and volume formulas are used to find area of plane figures and volume of prisms. Metric units of capacity and weight are introduced. The relationship between capacity and weight is presented by showing that a liter of water has a weight of one kilogram, or 1 milliliter of water has a weight of 1 gram. At appropriate intervals in the chapter, students solve problems that are related to the measurement concepts that have been presented.

Mathematical Background

Metric Units of Measurement The metric units, prefixes, and symbols used in this series are those adopted by the International System of Units, more commonly called SI units. The meter, the basic unit of length in this system, is one of the seven SI *base units.*

The names of the multiples and submultiples of the base units of the SI system are given below.

Prefix	Symbol	Multiplying Factor
tera	T	$10^{12} = 1,000,000,000,000$
giga	G	$10^{9} = 1,000,000,000$
mega	M	$10^{6} = 1,000,000$
kilo	k	$10^{3} = 1,000$
hecto	h	$10^{2} = 100$
deka	da	$10^{1} = 10$
deci	d	$10^{-1} = 0.1$
centi	c	$10^{-2} = 0.01$
milli	m	$10^{-3} = 0.001$
micro	μ	$10^{-6} = 0.0000001$
nano	η	$10^{-9} = 0.0000000001$
pico	p	$10^{-12} = 0.0000000000001$

In the SI system, area is not considered to be a base unit. Area is a unit derived by multiplying base units of length.

The SI system is designed so that for practical purposes, 1 kg of water will fill a container with a volume of 1 $dm^3 = 1,000$ cm^3, or a capacity of 1 liter. From these relationships, we can find that

1 g of water has a volume of 1 cm^3 or a capacity of 1 mL.

The SI unit of temperature is the kelvin (K). The lowest possible temperature, absolute zero, is 0 K. Water freezes at 373.15 K. Throughout most of the world, however, the Celsius temperature scale is used for the ordinary range of temperatures. Celsius temperatures may be obtained by subtracting 273.15 from the given kelvin temperature.

Area and Volume To find the area of a plane region, there are three essential steps: 1) select a unit of measure, usually a unit square, 2) divide the region into unit squares, and 3) count the number of units. The area of the region is the number of unit squares that cover the region.

To develop formulas for certain polygons, a basic concept is that the number of units for the area of a polygon is not changed if the region is cut apart and reassembled into another shape.

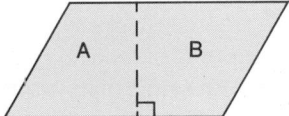 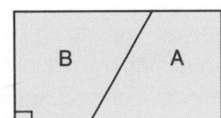

If the region shown above is cut into regions A and B and reassembled to form a rectangle, then the area of the original region is equal to the area of the rectangle. Thus, the formula for the area of a parallelogram is derived from the area of a rectangle. In a similar way, the area formulas for triangles and trapezoids are derived from the formula for a parallelogram.

The volume of a space figure is the number of unit cubes that it takes to fill the figure. The steps for finding the volume of any space figure are basically the same as for area: 1) select a unit, usually a unit cube, 2) divide the region into unit cubes, and 3) count the number of units.

The volume of a rectangular prism is the basis for developing volume formulas. The volume of a rectangular prism is simply the product of its length, width, and height. Since lw = area of the base, the formula for the volume of any prism can be $V = Bh$ where B is the area of the base and h is the height.

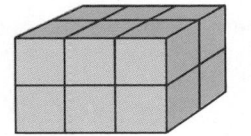

$$V = lwh$$
$$V = Bh$$

Problem Solving The problem-solving sets in this chapter deal with practical applications of measurement. On pages 255 and 259, students solve problems dealing with area and surface area. The problem-solving practice on page 263 is concerned with capacity. In a lesson on page 265, students use data from a table to solve problems concerning weight. The problem-solving practice on page 267 deals with temperature. On page 268, the nine strategies for solving nonroutine problems which were introduced in previous chapters, are reviewed.

Vocabulary

meter	centi-	surface area	weight
kilo-	milli-	volume	gram
hecto-	perimeter	capacity	temperature
deci-	area	liter	Celsius

Error Analysis

This chapter provides practice with the units of the metric system and emphasizes relationships among these units. Many concepts are involved in the content of this chapter. Error patterns that occur will most likely reflect lack of knowledge of the meaning of concepts, lack of knowledge of relationships between units, or the inability to apply these concepts in measurement situations. Obviously, computational skill is needed to complete most exercises, but when analyzing error patterns, look for computational error and for evidence of misunderstanding of the underlying concepts. Some possible error patterns are given below.

Error Pattern 1

$$50 \text{ cm} = 500 \text{ dm} \qquad 3.2 \text{ mm} = 32 \text{ cm}$$
$$536 \text{ dm} = 5{,}360 \text{ cm} \qquad 0.8 \text{ hm} = 8 \text{ km}$$

Diagnosis The student has changed from a smaller unit to the next largest unit by multiplying by 10 instead of dividing by 10. This error reflects incorrect knowledge of how metric units are related.

Remediation Begin with a meter stick or a 150-cm tape measure. Show the various metric units of length. Focus on the relative size of these units. Work through examples with the student to show how the units are related. Explain that in changing from a smaller unit to a larger unit, the number of units will get smaller so division is the operation to use.

Error Pattern 2

$$A = lw = 5 \times 3 = 15 \text{ cm} \qquad A = lw = 1.3 \times 4.6 = 5.98 \text{ m}$$

Diagnosis The student formed the product correctly but did not use the appropriate unit for area. The student may have confused area with perimeter or may not realize why the answer should be in square units.

Remediation Illustrate the meaning of area by covering a rectangular region with square units. Emphasize that square units are the units for area.

Error Pattern 3

8 m

9 m

12 m

$$A = \tfrac{1}{2}(b_1 + b_2)h$$
$$= (6 + 8) \times 9$$
$$= 126$$

Diagnosis The student multiplied $\frac{1}{2}$ times one of the bases instead of times the sum of the bases. The numbers were substituted correctly, but the operations were not performed in the correct order.

Remediation Review the meaning of parentheses. Stress that operations inside parentheses are performed first. Work through an example of using the formula to find the area of a trapezoid. Emphasize the order of operations.

Problem Solving

Working with Small Groups

Many teachers find that using small groups can be a valuable way to organize the classroom for teaching problem solving. One of the most important things a teacher of problem solving can do is to move around the room observing and questioning students while they solve problems. If there are 25 students in a class, it is difficult to give much attention to any one student. When small groups are formed, most teachers find it easier to monitor and assess their students' problem-solving performance.

In addition to helping in the management of instruction, there are other benefits of using small groups. Students who have not had much experience with problem solving may have considerable problem-solving anxiety. The use of small groups is one way to reduce the pressure on the individual student. In problem-solving groups, progress and success on a problem are the responsibility of the group, not the individual. Another benefit of small-group instruction is in eliciting behaviors that promote the improvement of problem-solving performance. For example, students are often required to justify their ideas, evaluate the ideas of others, and deal with contradictions. Here are other guidelines for using small groups.

- Limit the group size to 3 or 4 students.
- Accept a higher noise level in the classroom.
- Do not interrupt a group that is working well. If a group appears to be floundering, however, ask a student to tell what the group is discussing or which part of the problem is giving them difficulty.
- Ask discussion questions, rather than telling a group what to do.
- Try different grouping patterns—homogeneous, heterogeneous, teacher-selected groups, student-selected groups, for example—to find what works best for your students.

When small groups are used, it is important to keep every student involved in the problem-solving task. Here are some ideas.

- Identify a group captain for the day. This person is responsible for explaining the group's work that day.
- Identify a recorder to write all of the group's work.
- Require that students ask for your help only when everyone in the group has the same question.
- Require that everyone in the group agree on one answer.
- Question students who appear not to be involved in the group's work. Try to determine whether the students do not understand the problem or whether they are not participating.

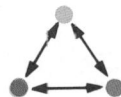 **Special Education**

Many of the topics in this chapter are extensions of topics students have already encountered in earlier grades. Much of the focus of the material will be on consolidating and strengthening student understanding and skills. The following activities and approaches may assist you in directing your instruction to meet the needs of the special students in your class.

Building Ties to Numeration Skills

Changing measurements of length from one metric unit to another is extended in this chapter to include all of the metric units of length from the millimeter through the kilometer. The conversion of units can be accomplished by using the method shown in the text or by placing the measurement on the metric measurement chart and then moving the decimal according to the following procedure. Suppose you wish to change 34.17 m to mm. First place the measurement of 34.17 m on the metric measurement chart as shown.

km	hm	dam	m	dm	cm	mm
		3	4	1	7	

To change the measurement to mm, we need to shift the decimal point to the space following the mm column. This necessitates adding a zero to fill out the column.

km	hm	dam	m	dm	cm	mm
		3	4	1	7	0.

After several measurements are changed in this fashion, students are more prepared for shifting the decimal according to the rules related to multiplying by or dividing by powers of 10.

Minimizing Memorization Requirements

Memorization of measurement formulas for perimeter and area can pose real problems for students who have inadequate memorization skill. For this reason, the number of formulas to be learned and applied should be kept to a minimum. Instead of requiring special students to memorize formulas, have them write each formula and draw the appropriate figure on an index card for ready reference. The cards can then be used to help students decide which formula to apply to an exercise.

Selecting Reasonable Units

A final suggestion for working with the special needs student is to give extra practice in selecting the type of measurements needed and the best unit of that type of measurement for the situation. This can be done verbally in class by describing a situation and then asking what type of measurement is needed (length, area, volume, capacity, weight, or temperature). When this has been decided, have students tell the unit of that type of measure which would best fit the job at hand. Finally, ask them to give a mental estimate of the answer to the problem described.

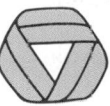 **Subject Integration**

Subject matter related to other areas of the curriculum has been integrated into the following lessons. This provides an opportunity to highlight the interaction between mathematics and other subjects.

Physical Education Outdoor adventures, pages 247, 254; bowling, page 264
Science Biology, page 250; Celsius temperature, pages 266–267; Archimedes' Principle, page 271
History Greek Parthenon, page 252
Consumer Awareness Landscaping, page 255
Home Economics Sewing, page 258; capacity, pages 262–263

Management Guide

Teaching Chapter 10				Meeting Individual Needs					
Objectives	Chapter Content	Pages	TRB Test Items	Lesson Assignments			Follow Up		
				Minimum	Average	Extended	Reteaching	Enrichment	Practice
	Chapter Opener	247							
10.1 Express metric units of length in larger or smaller metric units.	Units of Length	248–249	1–8	1–25	1–32	1–33	SE6 Ch7 RS 75	ES 75	PS 94
	Changing Units of Length	250–251		1–50	1–50, TM	1–49 odd, 50, TM			PS 95
10.2 Find the perimeter and area of a simple polygon and the surface area of a rectangular prism.	Perimeter	252–253	9–10	1–13, SK	1–14, SK	1–15, SK			MP 433 PS 96
	Area of Rectangles and Parallelograms	254	11–13	1–16	1–16	2–16 even	RS 76	ES 76	MP 433 PS 97
	Area of Triangles and Trapezoids	256–257	14–17	1–6	1–13	1–13 odd, 14, 15, TM	RS 77	ES 77	MP 433 PS 98
	Surface Area	258	18–19	1–6	1–9	1–9			PS 99
10.3 Find the volume of a prism.	Volume	260–261	20–22	1–13, SK	1–14, 16, SK	1–13 odd, 14–16, SK	RS 78	ES 78	MP 433 PS 100
10.4 Choose appropriate metric units of capacity and weight, and express in larger and smaller units; read Celsius temperatures.	Capacity	262	23–25	1–8	1–8	1–8	SE6 Ch 7 RS 79	ES 79	PS 101
	Units of Weight	264	26–28	1–20	1–20	1–20	SE6 Ch 7 RS 80	ES 80	PS 102
	Celsius Temperature	266	29–30	1–6	1–6	1–6	SE6 Ch 7		PS 103
10.5 Solve word problems using the 5-Point Checklist and cumulative computational skills.	Problem Solving: Practice	255	31–35	1–6	1–8	1–9			
	Problem Solving: Practice	259		1–5	1–6, 9	1–9			
	Problem Solving: Practice	263		1–8	1–9, 12	4–12			
	Problem Solving: Using Data from a Table	265		1–6	1–8, 11	1–11			
	Problem Solving: Practice	267		1–6, 9	1–7, 9–10	4–10			
	Problem Solving: Using the Strategies	268							
	Chapter Review/Test	269							
	Another Look/ Enrichment	270–271							
	Technology	272–273							
	Cumulative Review	274							

SE6 Student Edition, Book 6
RS Reteaching Supplement
ES Enrichment Supplement
PS Practice Supplement
MP More Practice
TM Think Math
SK Skillkeeper
TRB Teacher's Resource Book

Masters for use

. . . before Chapter 10

Readiness Volume and Capacity	122
Readiness Length and Area	121

. . . during Chapter 10

Calculator Technology Measuring Up	200
Consumer Applications Cost Comparisons	182
Teaching Aids	280, 283, 284
Recreation Paper Folding	164
Activities That Count Estimating Areas	148

. . . after Chapter 10

Record Keeping	305
Family Involvement At-Home Activities	264
Family Involvement Key Math	263
Reading Math Metric Vocabulary	236
Computer Technology Decisions	217
Computer Technology Computers and the Work World	216
Computer Technology Flowcharts and Programs	215
Chapter 10 Test Free-Response Format	67–68
Chapter 10 Test Multiple-Choice Format	28–30

Supplements

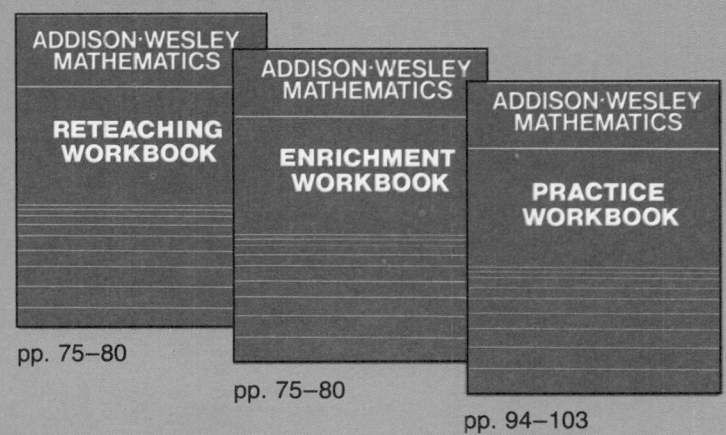

ADDISON·WESLEY MATHEMATICS **RETEACHING WORKBOOK**
pp. 75–80

ADDISON·WESLEY MATHEMATICS **ENRICHMENT WORKBOOK**
pp. 75–80

ADDISON·WESLEY MATHEMATICS **PRACTICE WORKBOOK**
pp. 94–103

Other Addison-Wesley Resources

Books and Kits

A New Twist   pp. 55, 57, 58

General Mathematics: Making Practice Fun   62, 63, 67A, B, 69A, B, 70A, B, 72, 73A

Arithmetic Primer   pp. 208–209, 240

Problem-Solving Experiences in Mathematics, Grade 7   Problems 53, 112

Technology

Computer Math Activities   Volume 1

Activities That Count

Activities That Count are designed for use throughout this chapter and subsequent chapters. Before beginning Chapter 10, you may wish to review these activities and select the ones you consider appropriate for your class.

Estimating Area   Math Lab

Purpose To estimate and find areas of polygons

Materials Activity sheet (TRB p. 148)

Activity Have students fold the bottom half of their game sheets under the top half. They must choose and circle the best estimate for the area of each polygon. Then students should unfold the paper and use the measures given to find the area for each polygon.

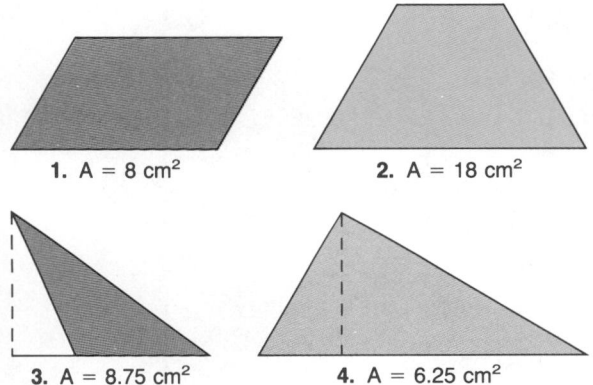

1. $A = 8$ cm^2 2. $A = 18$ cm^2

3. $A = 8.75$ cm^2 4. $A = 6.25$ cm^2

Territorial Claims   Game

Purpose To recognize polygons with a given area, and to develop shape perception

Materials Number cube labeled 1 through 6, centimeter graph paper (TRB p. 278), tagboard

Activity Have students cut out several tagboard shapes having areas of 1 cm^2, 2 cm^2, ..., 6 cm^2 as shown below. Centimeter graph paper can be used to make patterns. Paste a 10 by 10 centimeter grid on tagboard for the game board.

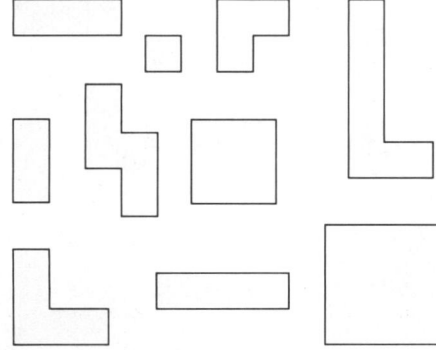

In turn, a player rolls the number cube and places a shape on the game board that has an area equal to the number on the cube. A player must pass if the number of square units on the game board is less than the number rolled, or if a shape would overlap any shape already on the board. The player who fits the last piece on the board is the winner.

Trundle Wheel   Project

Purpose To make a trundle wheel and use it to measure distances

Materials Heavy cardboard, wooden stick for handle, nut and bolt, colored marker

Activity Have students make a metric trundle wheel using heavy cardboard or plywood. The radius of the wheel should be 15.9 cm (which means the circumference is about 1 meter). With the colored marker, a line should be drawn which can be used to count revolutions of the wheel. A handle can be attached with a small nut and bolt through the center of the circle.

Have students estimate distances of 10, 20, 50, or 100 meters. Then have them use the trundle to measure and check their estimates.

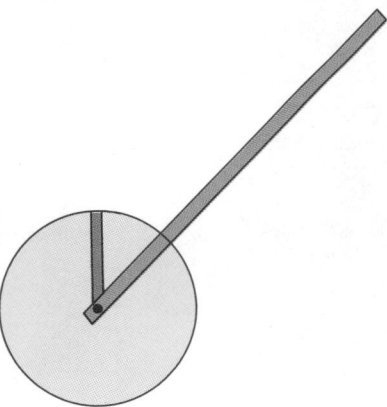

Concentration   Game

Adapt the activity described on page 223 F for matching equivalent measures.

10

Measurement: Metric Units

Outdoor clubs and groups often organize programs that give young people experience in an outdoor adventure that is hard physically and mentally. The experience may be a one-day orienteering event in which a compass and map are used for a timed cross-country competition. The experience could also be learning how to survive when in the water, climbing a mountain, or staying overnight in extreme temperatures of −15°C.

The necessary survival skills are taught by experienced instructors. Before actually climbing a mountain, groups are taught how to use the 46 m ropes for climbing and safety. Strength and endurance must also be built as young people prepare for hikes of 80 km with backpacks that weigh 14 kg.

Outdoor adventures can mean taking responsibility for other people and relying on them for survival. Most young people say they gain both physical strength and self-confidence.

Introducing the Chapter

Discussion Point out to students that Chapter 10 concerns measurement and metric units. Suggest that as they read the article, they note the differents ways metric measurements are used. Encourage students to share with the class any outdoor adventures they may have experienced. Use this as an opportunity for students to create their own problems based on the data in the article.

As you teach this chapter, you may wish to refer back to this page and discuss the questions below. Review briefly the contents of the page before asking the questions.

Follow-Up Questions

After Page 251 A hike may be 80 km long. How many meters is this? (80,000 m) Ropes used for climbing are 46 m. How many centimeters is this? (4,600 cm)

After Page 255 Some hikers make rectangular platforms out of snow for their sleeping bags. One rectangle was 1.8 m wide and 9 m long. What was the perimeter of the rectangle? (21.6 m)

After Page 263 What unit of capacity would best measure the amount of water a hiker carries on a 2 day hike? (liter)

After Page 267 The temperature at the start of an uphill hike was 12°C. Hikers spent that night on a glacier where the temperature was −1°C. How much colder was it on the glacier than at the start of the hike? (13°)

Quick Review Display the numbers below. Point to a number and call out 10, 100, or 1,000 as a divisor. Have students find the quotient.

123	45.75	2,545	10.375
7	13.2		8.5

Lesson Focus To review metric units of length from kilometer to millimeter

Suggested Materials Metersticks, metric rulers (TRB p. 280)

Ideas for Getting Started

On the chalkboard, draw and label segments that are 1 meter, 1 decimeter, and 1 centimeter in length. Have students name objects in the room that are about these lengths. Have them check their answers by measuring the objects.

Illustrate dekameter, hectometer, and kilometer by having students estimate distances for these measures. Some examples that could be used are the length of a classroom for 1 dekameter, the length of a football field for 1 hectometer, and three or four city blocks for 1 kilometer.

Have students use their rulers to draw line segments of these lengths.

3 cm	4.5 cm	15 mm
2 dm	0.5 dm	3.9 cm

Using Page 248

Lesson Development Review with students the meaning of the metric prefixes. Write the following on the chalkboard.

kilo - one thousand   deci - one tenth of

hecto - one hundred   centi - one hundredth of

deka - ten   milli - one thousandth of

Ask students to read and study the information on the page. Stress that metric units are related by tens. Students should know how the units are related in size; that is, centimeters are smaller than meters, millimeters are smaller than decimeters, and so on.

Warm Up These exercises can be completed as an oral activity or assigned as written work.

Units of Length

The kite is about 1 **meter (m)** long.

The basic unit of length in the metric system is the meter.

Other units are related to the meter.

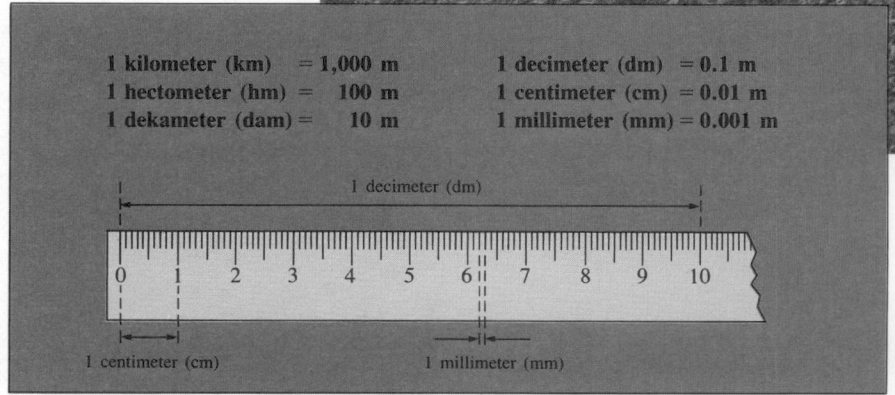

1 kilometer (km)	= 1,000 m	1 decimeter (dm)	= 0.1 m
1 hectometer (hm)	= 100 m	1 centimeter (cm)	= 0.01 m
1 dekameter (dam)	= 10 m	1 millimeter (mm)	= 0.001 m

Warm Up

1. How many millimeters are in a centimeter? **10**

2. How many centimeters are in a decimeter? **10**

3. How many millimeters are in a meter? **1,000**

4. How many decimeters are in a meter? **10**

5. How many centimeters are in a meter? **100**

6. A centimeter is what decimal part of a meter? **0.01 m**

7. A meter is what decimal part of a kilometer? **0.001 km**

8. A millimeter is what decimal part of a meter? **0.001 m**

248

Follow Up

Reteaching

To provide a variety of measurement opportunities for students, give them a worksheet like the one below. List classroom objects whose lengths are to be measured and recorded in millimeters, centimeters, and meters.

Object	mm	cm	m
Desk width			
Pencil			
Door height			
Table length			
Eraser			

Enrichment

Let students work in pairs and play "Estimation Golf." Have pairs of students go around the room, choose an object, each make an estimate of its length in metric units, and record the estimates on a score card. Then students should measure the object and find their score by taking the difference between the estimate and the measure. Tell students to do this with nine objects. The player with the lowest score wins.

Estimate the length.

1. The height of a door

   A 2 dm   **B** 2 m

   c 2 cm   **D** 2 km

2. The height of a basketball goal

   A 3 m   **B** 3 dm

   c 3 km   **D** 3 hm

3. The flying altitude for a large jet airplane

   A 10 m   **B** 10 km

   c 10 cm   **D** 10 hm

4. The length of a baseball bat

   A 100 m   **B** 100 km

   c 100 mm   **D** 100 cm

5. The diameter of a penny

   A 2 cm   **B** 2 dm

   c 2 mm   **D** 2 m

6. The thickness of a dime

   A 1 mm   **B** 10 mm

   c 1,000 mm   **D** 1 dm

7. The height of the seat of a chair from the floor

   A 45 m   **B** 45 mm

   c 45 dm   **D** 45 cm

8. The distance from Detroit, Michigan to Memphis, Tennessee

   A 1,000 dm   **B** 1,000 hm

   c 1,000 dam   **D** 1,000 km

9. The length of a swimming pool

   A 25 km   **B** 25 m

   c 25 cm   **D** 25 dm

10. The length of a compact car

   A 4,900 mm   **B** 4,900 hm

   c 4,900 m   **D** 4,900 dam

Write the missing units.

11. 1 cm = 10 ▓ mm

12. 100 ▓ = 1 m cm

13. 10 dm = 1 ▓ m

14. 1,000 m = 1 ▓ km

15. 0.1 m = 1 ▓ dm

16. 0.01 m = 1 ▓ cm

17. 100 m = 1 ▓ hm

18. 0.001 km = 1 ▓ m

19. 0.001 m = 1 ▓ mm

Write the missing numbers.

20. 1 m = ▓ cm 100

21. 1 cm = ▓ mm 10

22. 1 hm = ▓ m 100

23. 1 dam = ▓ m 10

24. 1 km = ▓ dam 100

25. 1 cm = ▓ m 0.01

26. ▓ mm = 1 cm 10

27. 1,000 mm = ▓ m 1

28. ▓ cm = 1 m 100

29. ▓ m = 1 km 1,000

30. 1 cm = ▓ dm 0.1

31. 10 dm = ▓ m 1

32. Which metric unit would you use to measure the distance between two cities?
kilometer

33. How many meters more than 1 km is 1,011 m? 11 m

Using Page 249

Exercises 1–10 These exercises emphasize estimation and reasonableness of answers.

Exercises 11–31 In completing these exercises, students should refer to the table and picture on page 248 or use their rulers (TRB p. 280) to check relationships between the various units.

Reteaching Supplement, page 75

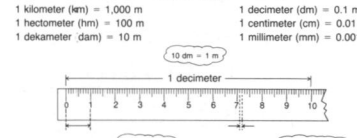

Enrichment Supplement, page 75

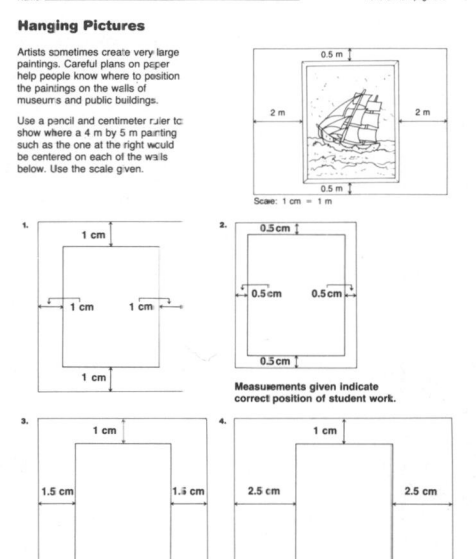

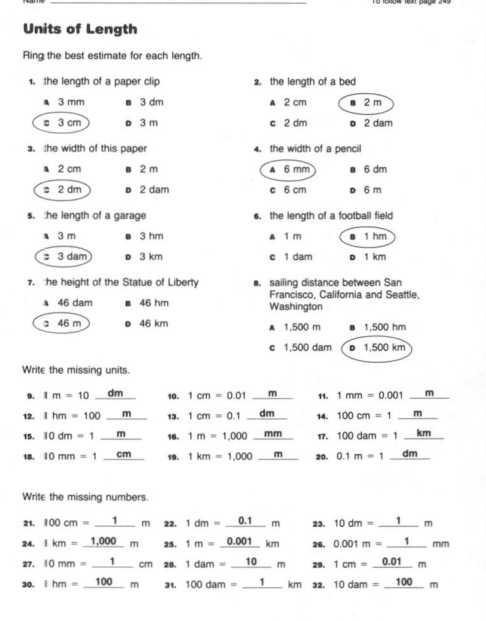

Practice Supplement, page 94

Quick Review Display the numbers below. Have students multiply by 100 and then by 0.01.

48.21	3.15	105.3	0.235
	78.2	58.45	0.02

Lesson Focus To express metric units of length in larger or smaller units

Ideas for Getting Started

Write these words on the chalkboard in the following order. Have students arrange the units in order of size from largest to smallest.

centimeter   hectometer   millimeter   meter

kilometer   decimeter   dekameter

Using Page 250

Lesson Development Have students read the example at the top of the page. "What was done to express 7 mm as centimeters?" (7 was divided by 10 or multipled by 0.1) "What was done to express 7 mm as decimeters?" (7 was divided by 100 or multiplied by 0.01) "What was done to express 7 mm as meters?" (7 was divided by 1,000 or multiplied by 0.001)

Write the metric unit table on the chalkboard.

km	hm	dam	m	dm	cm	mm

Review the idea that a centimeter is ten times as large as a millimeter, a decimeter is ten times as large as a centimeter, and so on. Work through the example showing how the metric table can be used to help place the decimal point when changing to larger or smaller metric units. Notice with students that zero must be annexed in some cases to place the decimal point correctly.

Changing Units of Length

A biology teacher asked students to measure the length of a ladybug. They found that it was 7 mm long.

7 mm = 0.7 cm
7 mm = 0.07 dm
7 mm = 0.007 m

To change from one unit to another in the metric system, we shift the position of the decimal point in the measure. This is because each unit in the table is 10 times as large as the unit on its right.

km	hm	dam	m	dm	cm	mm

Change kilometers to meters.

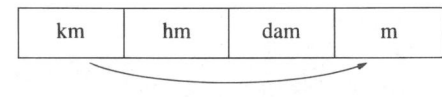

1.827 km = **1,827** m

shift 3 places right

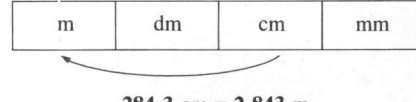

284.3 cm = **2.843** m

shift 2 places left

Change meters to millimeters.

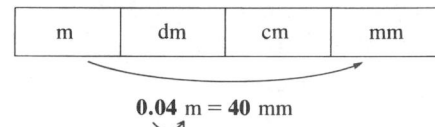

0.04 m = **40** mm

shift 3 places right

Change meters to kilometers.

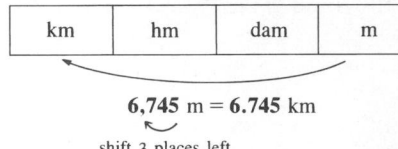

6,745 m = **6.745** km

shift 3 places left

Warm Up

1. Change 2,745 m to kilometers. 2.745 km
2. Change 3.587 m to centimeters. 358.7 cm
3. Change 32.7 cm to meters. 0.327 m
4. Change 3.5 dm to centimeters. 35 cm
5. Change 0.184 km to meters. 184 m
6. Change 2,354 mm to meters. 2.354 m
7. Change 54,000 cm to kilometers. 0.54 km
8. Change 838 cm to meters. 8.38 m

250

Follow Up

Reteaching

Display this diagram on the chalkboard and show students how to use it to change to larger or smaller metric units. Explain that when changing from a larger to a smaller unit, we multiply. When changing from a smaller to a larger unit, we divide.

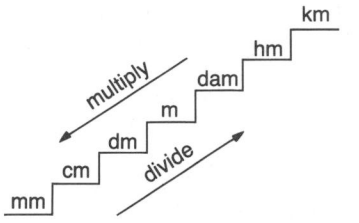

Enrichment

Write the following pairs of measurements on the chalkboard. Have students indicate the larger measurement.

1. <u>75 m</u> 750 cm
2. 2.5 dm <u>250 cm</u>
3. <u>15 km</u> 1,500 m
4. <u>70 hm</u> 72,000 mm
5. <u>3.75 mm</u> 0.3 cm
6. 400 m <u>5 hm</u>

Change each length to meters.

1. 163 cm 1.63 m
2. 38.4 dm 3.84 m
3. 5 km 5,000 m
4. 6,388 mm 6.388 m
5. 93.5 cm 0.935 m
6. 2.85 dam 28.5 m
7. 18.42 hm 1,842 m
8. 0.754 km 754 m
9. 2 km 2,000 m
10. 2.5 km 2,500 m
11. 500 cm 5.00 m
12. 2,500 mm 2.5 m

Change each length to centimeters.

13. 2.53 m 253 cm
14. 29 mm 2.9 cm
15. 8.1 dm 81 cm
16. 0.75 m 75 cm
17. 2.73 km 273,000 cm
18. 0.06 m 6 cm
19. 0.2 dm 2 cm
20. 484 mm 48.4 cm
21. 2 m 200 cm
22. 5 dm 50 cm
23. 1 km 100,000 cm
24. 65 mm 6.5 cm

Change each length to kilometers.

25. 2,000 m 2 km
26. 2,135 m 2.135 km
27. 23,000 cm 0.23 km
28. 807 m 0.807 km
29. 1,000,000 mm 1 km
30. 9,800 dm 0.98 km
31. 54 hm 5.4 km
32. 200 dam 2 km
33. 750 m 0.75 km
34. 58.5 m 0.0585 km
35. 20,000 m 20 km
36. 150,000 m 150 km

Change each length to millimeters.

37. 3 cm 30 mm
38. 1.7 cm 17 mm
39. 0.6 cm 6 mm
40. 0.01 cm 0.1 mm
41. 0.05 m 50 mm
42. 25 cm 250 mm
43. 2 dm 200 mm
44. 3 m 3,000 mm
45. 0.002 m 2 mm
46. 0.95 cm 9.5 mm
47. 6.2 cm 62 mm
48. 0.06 dm 6 mm

49. A measurement is 35 mm. What is it in centimeters, decimeters, and meters? 3.5 cm; 0.35 dm; 0.035 m

50. **DATA HUNT** What is your height in each of the six metric units in this lesson? Find your height to the nearest centimeter. Change the centimeter measurement to each of the other units.

━━ THINK MATH ━━

Using Metric Prefixes

Suppose that metric prefixes were used for money, with the dollar as the unit. A decidollar would be one tenth of a dollar or 10 cents. How much money would each of the following be?

1. 1 centidollar $0.01
2. 1 dekadollar $10
3. 1 hectodollar $100
4. 1 kilodollar $1,000
5. 3 decidollars $0.30
6. 56 centidollars $0.56
7. 2.5 decidollars $0.25
8. 2,000 millidollars $2

251

Using Page 251

Exercises 1–48 Your treatment of the exercises on this page will depend upon the success students had with the Warm Up exercises on page 250. You may wish to work through one or two exercises in each set as an oral class activity. Emphasize checking to see if answers are reasonable. In changing 163 cm to meters, students should realize that the change is from a smaller unit to a larger unit, so the number of meters should be smaller than the number of centimeters.

163 cm = 1.63 m   reasonable
163 cm = 16,300   not reasonable

Similarly, changing from a larger unit to a smaller unit gives a greater number of units.

3 cm = 30 mm   reasonable
3 cm = 0.3 mm   not reasonable

Data Hunt Encourage as many students as possible to try the Data Hunt. Metersticks should be available for students who do not know their height in centimeters.

Think Math This problem involves an understanding of the meaning of metric prefixes and applies them to our money system.

Ideas That Work

Special Education

To reinforce expressing metric measurements in larger or smaller units, have students play "Metric Match." Students will need a set of index cards with pairs of equivalent metric measures. Have two to four students distribute the cards among themselves, pairing any equivalent metric measures they have in hand. In turn, players draw from the student at their right. If the card drawn completes a pair, the player continues to draw until the card drawn does not complete a pair. Then it is the next player's turn. The object of the game is to match all cards.

A metric Olympics activity can also help students master metric measurement conversion. Students can be divided into teams and participate in the length, area, volume, capacity, mass, or temperature "divisions." In each division there can be questions about exact conversions, appropriate units, or estimates.

Practice Supplement, page 95

Name _____   To follow text page 251

Changing Units of Length

Change each length to meters.

1. 217 cm = **2.17** m
2. 46.1 dm = **4.61** m
3. 17.4 cm = **0.174** m
4. 6.21 dam = **62.1** m
5. 8 km = **8,000** m
6. 53.22 hm = **5,322** m
7. 1,438 mm = **1.438** m
8. 0.666 km = **666** m

Change each length to centimeters.

9. 92 mm = **9.2** cm
10. 6 m = **600** cm
11. 0.01 m = **1** cm
12. 4 km = **400,000** cm
13. 318 mm = **31.8** cm
14. 8.93 km = **893,000** cm
15. 8 dm = **80** cm
16. 0.9 dm = **9** cm

Change each length to kilometers.

17. 820 m = **0.82** km
18. 31.4 m = **0.0314** km
19. 70,000 m = **70** km
20. 4,000 mm = **0.004** km
21. 2,600 dm = **0.26** km
22. 53 hm = **5.3** km
23. 6,000 m = **6** km
24. 7,414 m = **7.414** km

Change each length to millimeters.

25. 0.08 dm = **8** mm
26. 8.5 cm = **85** mm
27. 0.07 m = **70** mm
28. 5 m = **5,000** mm
29. 4 cm = **400** mm
30. 0.005 m = **5** mm
31. 0.09 cm = **0.9** mm
32. 0.3 cm = **3** mm

Quick Review Have students orally round each number to the nearest hundred and then to the nearest thousand.

| 33,952 | | 152,432 | | 85,461 | | 142,725 |
| | 38,046 | | 100,922 | | 6,850 | |

Lesson Focus To find the perimeter of a polygon

Suggested Materials metersticks

Ideas for Getting Started

Draw a rectangle on the chalkboard. Remind students that perimeter is the distance around a geometric figure. Have a volunteer use a meterstick to measure the lengths of the sides of the rectangle. Ask students to find the perimeter by adding the lengths of the four sides.

Repeat this activity with a triangle and with an irregularly shaped quadrilateral.

Using Page 252

Motivational Problem After students read the introductory problem, have them identify the question and the data needed to solve the problem. Then ask students what plan can be used to answer the question.

Lesson Development On the chalkboard, show that the perimeter can be found by adding the lengths of the four sides. Point out that in this addition, 72 and 34 were added twice. Instead of adding the four numbers, we could just add 72 and 34 and then multiply by 2.

Explain that since the opposite sides of rectangles have the same length, the following formula can be used to find the perimeter of rectangles.

Perimeter = 2 × (length + width) or
$$P = 2(l + w)$$

Make certain that students understand that the 2 followed by parentheses indicates multiplication.

Work through finding the perimeter of the triangle on the chalkboard. Notice with students that the lengths of the sides of the triangle are given in different units. Point out that all measures could be expressed in centimeters.

$$1.27 \text{ m} = 127 \text{ cm}$$
$$P = 127 + 84 + 63$$
$$P = 274$$

The perimeter of the triangle is 274 cm.

Perimeter

The base of the Parthenon in Greece is a rectangle. The length is 72 m and the width is 34 m. What is the distance around the base of the Parthenon?

The **perimeter** of a geometric figure is the distance around the figure.

We could find the perimeter by adding the lengths of the sides:

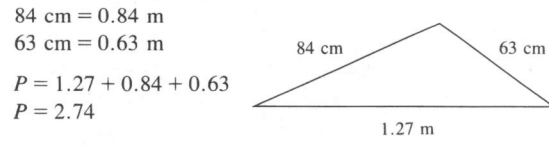

```
   34
   72
   34
 + 72
 ─────
  212
```
$l = 72$ m, $w = 34$ m

For rectangles we can also use a perimeter formula.

Perimeter = **2** × (**length** + **width**)
$$P = 2(l + w)$$
$$P = 2(72 + 34)$$
$$P = 2 \times 106$$
$$P = 212$$

The perimeter of the Parthenon is 212 m.

What is the perimeter of the triangle in meters?

84 cm = 0.84 m
63 cm = 0.63 m

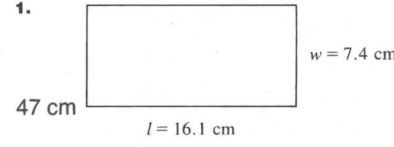

84 cm   63 cm
1.27 m

$$P = 1.27 + 0.84 + 0.63$$
$$P = 2.74$$

> When adding or subtracting measures, all measures must be expressed in the same unit.

The perimeter of the triangle is 2.74 m.

Warm Up

Find the perimeter of each figure.

1.
$w = 7.4$ cm
47 cm
$l = 16.1$ cm

2.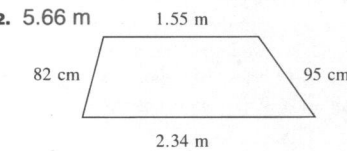
5.66 m   1.55 m
82 cm   95 cm
2.34 m

252

Follow Up

Reteaching

Have students use a metric trundle wheel to find the length and width of the room. On the chalkboard, work through finding the perimeter of the room with students participating in each step. Then have students check the answer by using the trundle wheel to find the distance around the room.

Enrichment

Ask students to find as many polygons as possible with different shapes and a perimeter of 10 units. The polygons should be recorded on graph paper. (TRB p. 284) The length of each side must be a whole number.

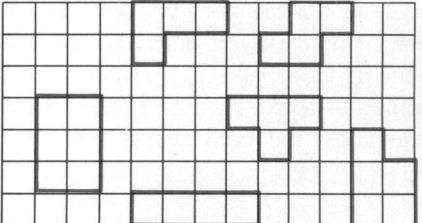

Assignment Guide			
	Minimum	Average	Extended
page 253	1–13, SK	1–14, SK	1–15, SK

Find the perimeter of each figure.

1. 17 m
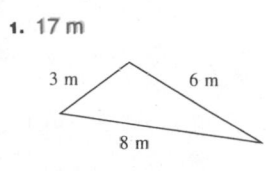
3 m 6 m 8 m

2. 58 cm
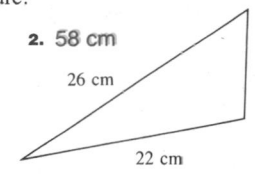
26 cm 10 cm 22 cm

3.
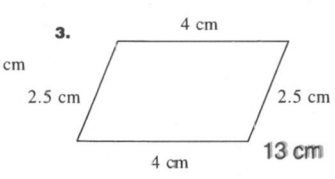
4 cm 2.5 cm 2.5 cm 4 cm 13 cm

4.
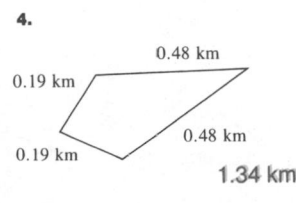
0.48 km 0.19 km 0.19 km 0.48 km 1.34 km

5.
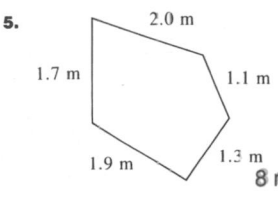
2.0 m 1.7 m 1.1 m 1.9 m 1.3 m

6. 22.5 m
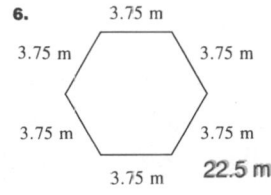
3.75 m 3.75 m 3.75 m 3.75 m 3.75 m 8 m 3.75 m

Find the perimeter of each rectangle.

7. $l = 120$ cm
$w = 36$ cm **312 cm**

8. $l = 4$ m
$w = 4$ m **16 m**

9. $l = 273$ km
$w = 139$ km **824 km**

10. $l = 64$ mm
$w = 35$ mm **198 mm**

11. $l = 100$ m
$w = 25$ m **250 m**

12. $l = 83$ dm
$w = 75$ dm **316 dm**

13. What is the perimeter of a window frame that is 91 cm wide and 208 cm high? **598 cm**

14. What is the total length of weather stripping needed for 12 windows that each measure 90 cm by 120 cm? **5,040 cm**

★ **15.** How long is the piece of tape if it goes completely around the box? Write the answer in centimeters. **84 cm**
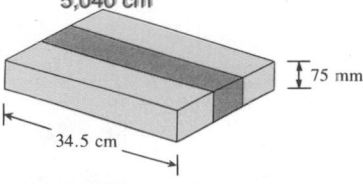
75 mm 34.5 cm

SKILLKEEPER

1. $\frac{1}{8} \times 24$ 3
2. $\frac{2}{3} \times 6$ 4
3. $\frac{1}{2} \times \frac{5}{6}$ $\frac{5}{12}$
4. $\frac{3}{4} \times 1\frac{1}{3}$ 1
5. $\frac{2}{3} \times \frac{9}{10}$ $\frac{3}{5}$

6. $1\frac{6}{7} \times 3$ $5\frac{4}{7}$
7. $6\frac{2}{3} \times 2$ $13\frac{1}{3}$
8. $9 \times 1\frac{2}{3}$ 15
9. $\frac{3}{5} \times 1\frac{3}{4}$ $1\frac{1}{20}$
10. $3\frac{3}{8} \times 3\frac{1}{3}$ $11\frac{1}{4}$

11. $\frac{4}{9} \div \frac{2}{3}$ $\frac{2}{3}$
12. $\frac{1}{10} \div \frac{2}{5}$ $\frac{1}{4}$
13. $1\frac{1}{3} \div \frac{3}{4}$ $1\frac{7}{9}$
14. $3\frac{5}{6} \div 3$ $1\frac{5}{18}$
15. $3\frac{1}{3} \div \frac{1}{10}$ $33\frac{1}{3}$

More Practice, page 433, Set A

Using Page 253

Exercises 7–12 The perimeter of the rectangles in these exercises can be found with the perimeter formula. Some students may simply add the lengths of the four sides. You may want students using this method to check their answers by using the formula.

Exercise 15 This exercise involves measurements having different units as well as space perception of a 3-dimensional object.

Skillkeeper These skills were originally taught in Chapter 9.

More Practice, page 433, Set A

Ideas That Work

Chalk It Up

Display the following on the chalkboard.

1. 25 mm	A. 40 mm
2. 2.5 m	C. 4 hm
3. 4 km	D. 500 cm
4. 5 m	E. 1 km
5. 40 dm	H. 0.002 m
6. 500 mm	L. 2.5 cm
7. 400 m	M. 5 km
8. 1,000 cm	N. 50 cm
9. 10 hm	O. 4,000 m
10. 20 km	P. 250 cm
11. 2 mm	T. 400 cm
	U. 10 m
	W. 20,000 m

Have students match each measure to an equivalent measure in the column at the right. Then have them decode the message by writing the correct letters in the blanks below.

"P E O P L E   W H O
2 9 3 2 1 9 10 11 3

D O N ' T   C O U N T
4 3 6 5 7 3 8 6 5

W O N ' T   C O U N T"
10 3 6 5 7 3 8 6 5

Anatole France

Practice Supplement, page 96

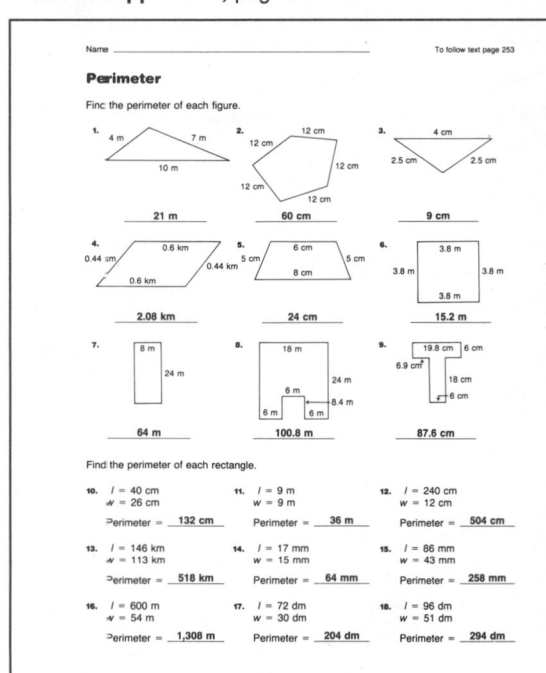

Measurement

Lesson Focus To find the area of a rectangle and a parallelogram; to solve word problems related to areas of rectangles and parallelograms

Suggested Materials Tagboard

Ideas for Getting Started

To review the concept of area, draw some rectangles on the chalkboard. Show a tagboard square and ask students to estimate how many it would take to cover each rectangle. Then ask a student to go to the chalkboard and draw around the square until the rectangle is filled. Have students count the squares and parts of squares and compare the numbers to the estimates.

Most students will be familiar with the formula for the area of a rectangle. Demonstrate that the formula simply gives a way of finding the number of squares to cover a region without counting.

Using Page 254

Motivational Problem Read the problem at the top of the page with students. Ask them to restate the question and identify the data necessary to solve the problem. Explain that the formula for the area of a rectangle can be used to answer the question.

Lesson Development Find the area of the rectangle with students. Point out that area is expressed in square units, in this case square meters.

To make the formula for the area of a parallelogram more meaningful to students, demonstrate how to transform a parallelogram into a rectangle. Cut out a region of a parallelogram from tagboard. Cut off the triangular region from one end and reassemble the pieces to form a rectangle.

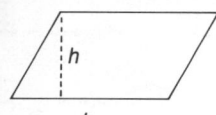 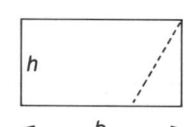

Exercises 1–16 Assign these exercises as independent written work. Check to see that students label their answers with the correct units of area.

Area of Rectangles and Parallelograms

The floor in a tent is a rectangle 6.0 m long and 5.4 m wide. What is the **area** of the floor?

The **area** of a region is the number of unit squares it takes to cover the region.

Area of a rectangle = **length** × **width**

$A = lw$
$A = 6.0 \times 5.4$
$A = 32.40$

The area is 32.40 square meters (m²).

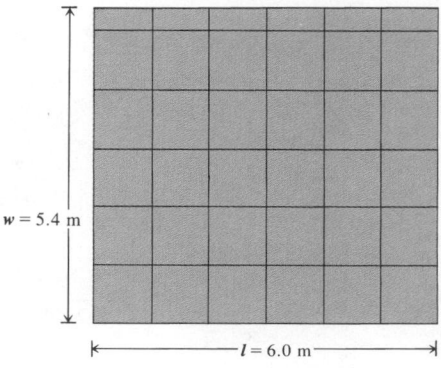

$w = 5.4$ m
$l = 6.0$ m

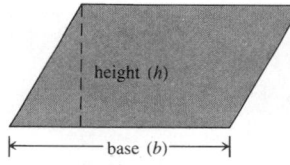 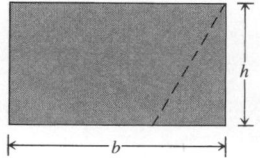

height (h) base (b) h b

The area of the parallelogram = the area of the rectangle.

Area of a parallelogram = **base** × **height**
$A = bh$

Find the area of each rectangle.

1. $l = 12$ cm
   $w = 8$ cm **96 cm²**

2. $l = 25$ m
   $w = 10$ m **250 m²**

3. $l = 3.8$ m
   $w = 2.0$ m **7.6 m²**

4. $l = 22$ mm
   $w = 9$ mm **198 mm²**

5. $l = 6.5$ cm
   $w = 2.8$ cm
   18.2 cm²

6. $l = 30$ cm
   $w = 30$ cm
   900 cm²

7. $l = 7.4$ m
   $w = 0.5$ m
   3.7 m²

8. $l = 2.8$ km
   $w = 1.6$ km
   4.48 km²

Find the area of each parallelogram.

9. $b = 15$ cm
   $h = 8$ cm **120 cm²**

10. $b = 24$ cm
    $h = 12$ cm **288 cm²**

11. $b = 3.1$ m
    $h = 2.0$ m **6.2 m²**

12. $b = 32$ m
    $h = 9$ m **288 m²**

13. $b = 4.9$ cm
    $h = 3.0$ cm
    14.7 cm²

14. $b = 16.8$ m
    $h = 5.2$ m
    87.36 m²

15. $b = 18$ cm
    $h = 12$ cm
    216 cm²

16. $b = 32.5$ m
    $h = 11.7$ m **380.25 m²**

254

More Practice, page 433, Set B

Follow Up

Reteaching

Have students draw several rectangles and parallelograms of different sizes on graph paper (TRB p. 284). Ask them to count the number of units of length and width for each rectangle, and base and height for each parallelogram. Then have them use the formulas to find the area of each figure. Encourage them to check their answers by counting the total number of square units in each rectangle or parallelogram.

Enrichment

Provide students with centimeter graph paper (TRB p. 284) and ask them to draw one rectangle and one parallelogram with each of the following areas.

7 cm²   6 cm²   14 cm²   2 cm²
10 cm²   25 cm²   15 cm²

Assignment Guide			
	Minimum	Average	Extended
page 254	1–16	1–16	2–16 even
page 255	1–6	1–8	1–9

Applications

PROBLEM SOLVING: Practice

QUESTION
DATA
PLAN
ANSWER
CHECK

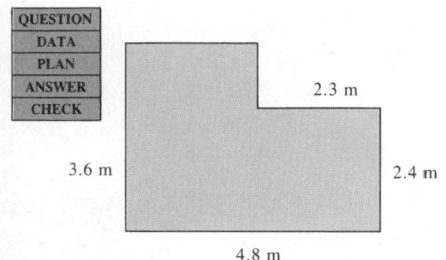

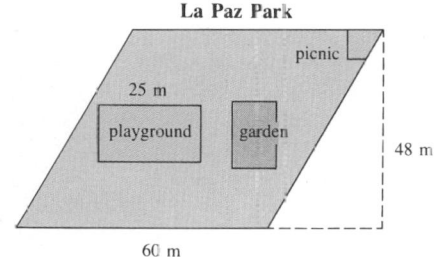

La Paz Park

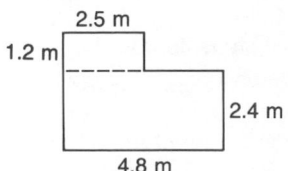

Use the figure above for problems 1–4.

1. A drawing was made of a part of a park lawn that needed new sod. What was the area of sod needed? 14.52 m²

2. The city bought 20 m² of sod for the lawn. The cost of the sod was $3.98 per square meter. What was the total cost of the sod? $79.60

3. How many square meters of sod were left over? 5.48 m²

4. About what was the cost of the leftover sod? $21.81

Use the figure above for problems 5–8.

5. The park is on a lot in the shape of a parallelogram with a base of 60 m and a height of 48 m. What is the area of the lot? 2,880 m²

6. A playground in the park is rectangular and is 25 m long. If the area of the rectangle is 350 m², what is the width of the playground? 14 m

7. A garden in the park covers 160 m² and a picnic area covers 42 m². What is the total area covered by the garden, the picnic area, and the playground? 552 m²

8. What is the area of the park that is not covered by the garden, the picnic area, and the playground? 2,328 m²

9. Try This Dee Lewis bought 30 m² of carpeting at $22.50 per square meter. The carpet was used to cover a rectangular floor 5.3 m long and 4.1 m wide. Dee was able to return 4 m² of the carpeting for a full refund. What was the cost (to the nearest cent) of the remainder of the carpet that was not returned and was not used on the floor? $96.08

255

Using Page 255

Exercises 1–8 Problems 1–4 are related as are problems 5–8. In problem 1, the area of the park can be found by dividing the figure into two rectangles as shown below.

A second method of solving problem 1 is to find the area of a 3.6 m by 4.8 m rectangle, and then subtract the area of the cut out rectangular region in the upper corner.

Try This A possible strategy, Choose the Operations, was taught on page 218.

Discussion After students read the problem, have them tell what the question asks us to find. Then have them list the data given in the problem. "What operations will we need to use?" (multiplication and subtraction) "What would be a good place to start?" (find the area of the room)

Solution

$5.3 \times 4.1 = 21.73$ m²	area of the room
$30 - 4 = 26$ m²	amount of carpet kept after refund
$26 - 21.73 = 4.27$ m²	amount kept less amount used
$4.27 \times 22.50 = 96.075$ = $96.08	cost of carpet not used

The cost of carpet that was not returned and not used on the floor was $96.08.

More Practice, page 433, Set B

Reteaching Supplement, page 76   **Enrichment Supplement,** page 76   **Practice Supplement,** page 97

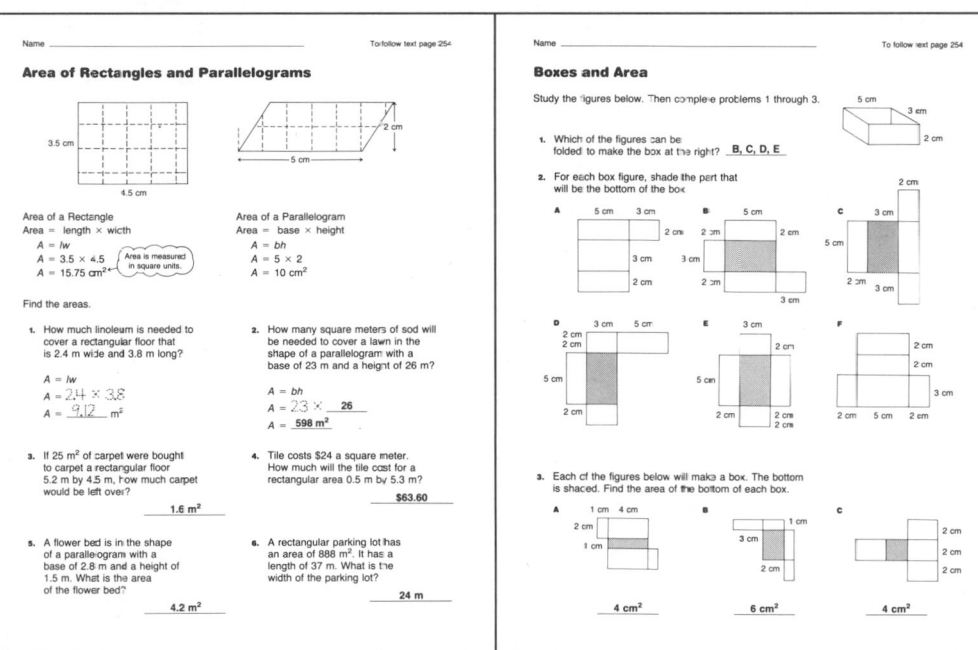

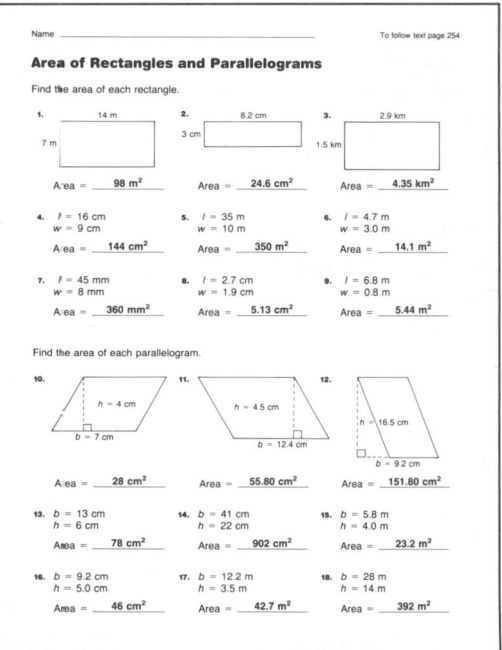

Quick Review Have students unscramble these geometry terms. Then have them give an example of an object that suggests each idea.

topin	point	lapelarl	parallel	nepal	plane
strenicte	intersect	stemgen	segment	eiln	line

Lesson Focus To find the area of a triangle and a trapezoid

Suggested Materials Tagboard

Ideas for Getting Started

Display a region of a parallelogram made from tagboard. Tell students that the area of the region is 100 square units. Cut the region along the diagonal and show that the two triangles are congruent by placing one on top of the other.

Parallelogram

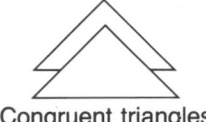
Congruent triangles

Ask students to find the area of each triangle. Point out that each triangle has $\frac{1}{2}$ the area of the parallelogram, or 50 square units.

Using Page 256

Motivational Problem Have students read the introductory problem. Ask them to identify the question and the data in the problem. Point out that the area of a parallelogram can be used to help us find a formula for the area of a triangle.

Lesson Development On the chalkboard, work through finding the area of a triangle by using the formula. Explain that any side of a triangle can be used as the *base*. The *height* of the triangle is in reference to the chosen base. Show these examples of the way heights of triangles can be pictured.

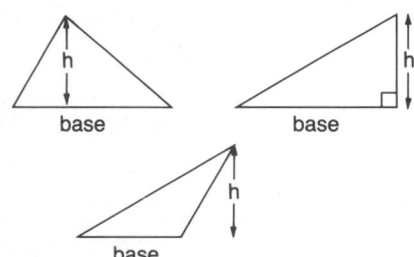

Draw a trapezoid on the chalkboard. Explain that the bases are the two parallel sides and the height is the perpendicular distance between them. Work through the example of finding the area of a trapezoid with students.

Warm Up Watch for students who multiply $\frac{1}{2}$ times both the base and the height to find the area of a triangle or those who multiply $\frac{1}{2}$ times both the sum of the bases and the height to find the area of a trapezoid.

Area of Triangles and Trapezoids

The jib, a triangular sail on a sailboat, has a **base** of 6.6 m and a **height** of 2.1 m. What is the area of the jib?

We need to find the area of a triangle.

The area of $\triangle ABC$ is $\frac{1}{2}$ the area of parallelogram $ABCD$.

Area of parallelogram $ABCD = bh$
Area of $\triangle ABC = \frac{1}{2}bh$

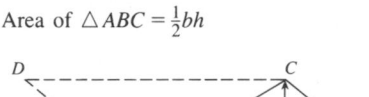

$A = \frac{1}{2}bh$
$A = \frac{1}{2} \times 6.6 \times 2.1$
$A = 6.93$

The area of the jib is 6.93 m².

Area of a trapezoid $= \frac{1}{2}$ the area of a parallelogram

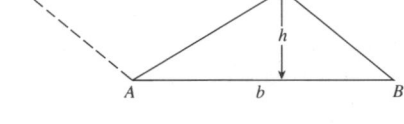

$A = \frac{1}{2}(b_1 + b_2)h$
$A = \frac{1}{2}(3.6 + 2.4)2.8$
$A = \frac{1}{2} \times 6 \times 2.8$
$A = 8.4$ cm²

b_1 (b sub 1) and b_2 (b sub 2) are the upper and lower bases of the trapezoid.

The area of the trapezoid is 8.4 cm².

Warm Up

1. Find the area of the triangle. 10.8 cm²

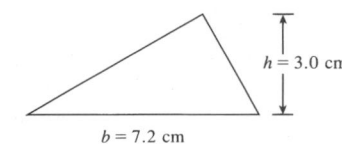

2. Find the area of the trapezoid. 13 cm²

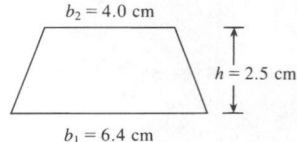

256

Follow Up

Reteaching

Have students make a parallelogram with a diagonal on a geoboard or dot paper (TRB p. 283). By matching areas, show students that the area of each triangle formed equals one half of the area of the parallelogram. Help students understand that since the area of the original parallelogram was $A = bh$, the area of each triangle is $A = \frac{1}{2}bh$.

Next have students make triangles on the geoboard or dot paper and find the area of each.

Enrichment

Display the figure below. Challenge students to find the area of the shaded region.

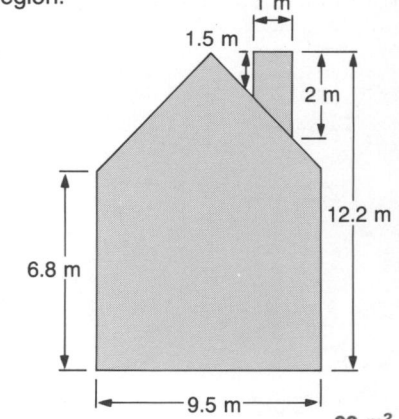

92 m²

Find the area of each triangle.

1. 35.55 cm²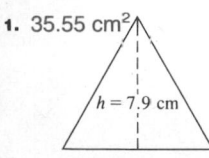
$h = 7.9$ cm
$b = 9$ cm

2. 37.2 cm²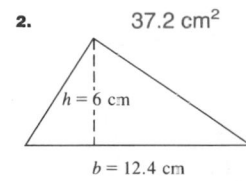
$h = 6$ cm
$b = 12.4$ cm

3. 135 cm²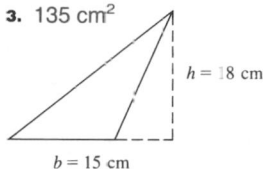
$h = 18$ cm
$b = 15$ cm

4. $b = 2.7$ cm, $h = 0.08$ cm
0.108 cm²

5. $b = 2$ m, $h = 1$ m
1 m²

6. $b = 25$ m, $h = 10$ m
125 m²

Find the area of each trapezoid.

7.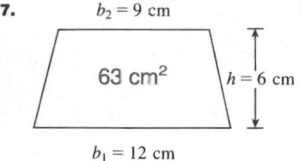
$b_2 = 9$ cm
63 cm² $h = 6$ cm
$b_1 = 12$ cm

8.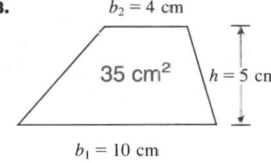
$b_2 = 4$ cm
35 cm² $h = 5$ cm
$b_1 = 10$ cm

9.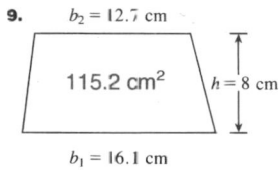
$b_2 = 12.7$ cm
115.2 cm² $h = 8$ cm
$b_1 = 16.1$ cm

10. $b_1 = 20$ dm, $b_2 = 14$ dm, $h = 10$ dm 170 dm²

11. $b_1 = 5.7$ km, $b_2 = 1.3$ km, $h = 2.0$ km 7 km²

12. $b_1 = 80$ m, $b_2 = 60$ m, $h = 10.5$ m 735 m²

13. What is the area of a triangle with a base of 5 m and a height of 4 m? 10 m²

14. Find the height of a triangle with a base of 12 cm and an area of 18 cm². 3 cm

★ 15. Find the area of the path around the flowerbed. 26 m²

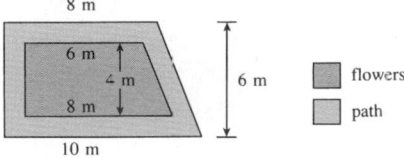

8 m
6 m
4 m
8 m
6 m
10 m
■ flowers
□ path

■ THINK MATH ■

Shape Perception

Each small square is 1 square unit.

How many square units of area does the shaded triangular region cover?

14 square units

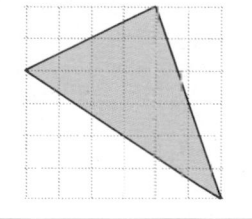

More Practice, page 433, Set C

Using Page 257

Exercises 1–15 You may wish to show students that the formulas for area can be written in two forms.

$$A = \tfrac{1}{2} bh \text{ or } \tfrac{bh}{2}$$

$$A = \tfrac{1}{2} h(b_1 + b_2) \text{ or } \tfrac{h(b_1 + b_2)}{2}$$

These formulas reflect the fact that multiplying by $\tfrac{1}{2}$ is equivalent to dividing by 2.

Exercise 15 This exercise involves multiple steps with the trapezoid area formula.

Think Math The Think Math involves shape perception and area concepts. Some students may try to find the area by counting and estimating parts of square units. Another method is to subtract the areas of the three triangles around the shaded region from the area of the 6 by 6 square.

More Practice, page 433, Set C

Reteaching Supplement, page 77

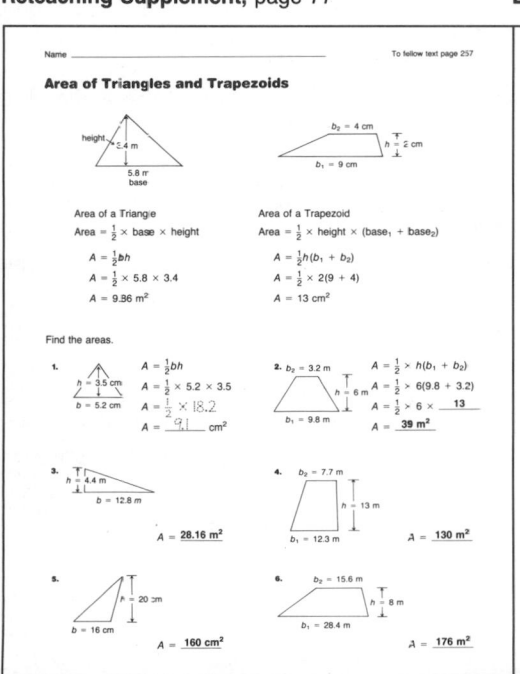

Enrichment Supplement, page 77

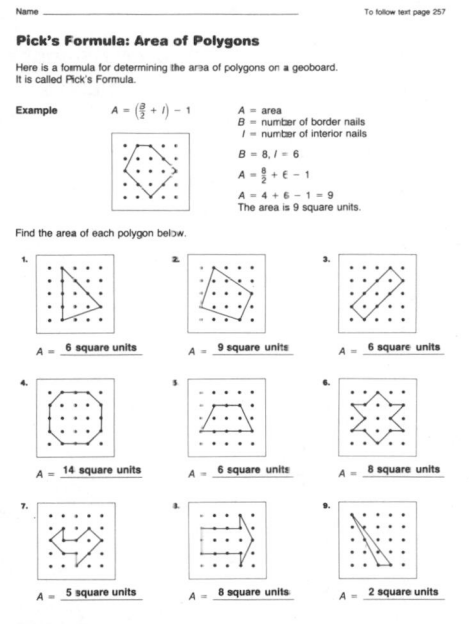

Practice Supplement, page 98

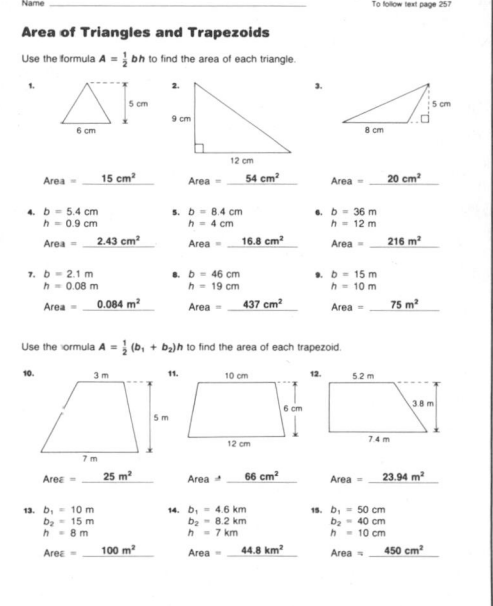

Quick Review Have students find the fraction of the number.

$\frac{4}{5} \times 25$ 20 $\frac{1}{4} \times 28$ 7 $\frac{6}{7} \times 21$ 18 $\frac{1}{6} \times 48$ 8

$\frac{9}{10} \times 200$ 180 $\frac{1}{3} \times 15$ 5 $\frac{3}{4} \times 32$ 24

Lesson Focus To find the surface area of a rectangular prism; to solve word problems related to surface area

Suggested Materials Models of rectangular prisms

Ideas for Getting Started

Display a model of a rectangular prism. Review with students the ideas of face, edge, and vertex. Place the prism so that one face is flat on the chalkboard and draw around it. Turn the prism so that an adjoining face is on the chalkboard and draw around it. Continue in this way until a complete pattern of the prism is formed. Label each face of the pattern.

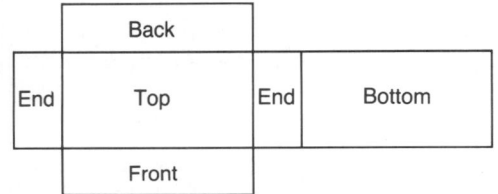

Explain that the surface area of the prism is the total area of the six rectangular faces.

Using Page 258

Motivational Problem Have students read the introductory problem and examine the accompanying photograph. "What does the question ask us to find?" (the surface area of the box) "What data is needed to solve the problem?" ($h = 10$ cm, $l = 30$ cm, $w = 12$ cm) Tell students that we could find the surface area by finding the sum of the areas of all the faces of the box, or we could use a formula.

Lesson Development Show students how the surface area formula is developed by using the area formula for rectangles. Point out that opposite faces have the same area, so we can find the area of the top, front, and one end and then multiply by 2. On the chalkboard, work through finding the surface area of the box.

It is not necessary for all students to memorize the formula. The area of each face of a prism can be found and then the total surface area can be computed.

Exercises 1–9 Work through one or more of these exercises as a class activity. Assign the rest of the exercises as independent work.

Surface Area

A sewing box has the shape of a rectangular prism. What is the total surface area of the box?

The **surface area** of the box is the sum of the areas of all faces of the box. Since the opposite faces have the same area, we can find the area of the front, top, and one end and then multiply their sum by 2.

Area of front $= lh$

Area of top $= lw$

Area of end $= wh$

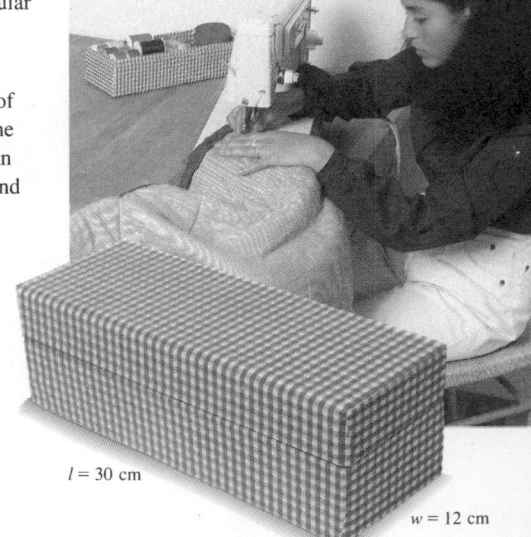

$h = 10$ cm

$l = 30$ cm

$w = 12$ cm

Surface area $= 2(lh + lw + wh)$

$A = 2(30 \times 10 + 30 \times 12 + 12 \times 10)$

$A = 2(300 + 360 + 120)$

$A = 2(780) = 1{,}560$

The total surface area is 1,560 cm^2.

Find the total surface area of each box or rectangular prism.

1. 114 cm^2

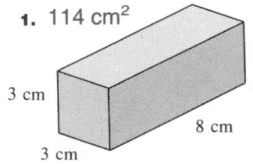

3 cm

3 cm

8 cm

2. 127 cm^2

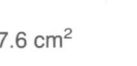

10 cm

0.9 cm

5 cm

3. 426 cm^2

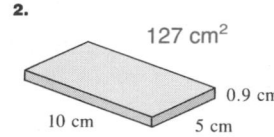

5 cm

12 cm

9 cm

4. $l = 9$ cm   217.6 cm^2
   $w = 5.6$ cm
   $h = 4$ cm

5. $l = 2$ m   11.6 m^2
   $w = 1.5$ m
   $h = 0.8$ m

6. $l = 2.7$ cm   23.96 cm^2
   $w = 2$ cm
   $h = 1.4$ cm

7. $l = 25$ cm   3,250 cm^2
   $w = 25$ cm
   $h = 20$ cm

8. $l = 4.5$ m   59.6 m^2
   $w = 3.2$ m
   $h = 2.0$ m

9. $l = 0.8$ cm   2.36 cm^2
   $w = 0.6$ cm
   $h = 0.5$ cm

258

Follow Up

Reteaching

Cut the shape below out of graph paper (TRB p. 284). Show students the figure and have them count the number of square units. (32) Then fold and tape the model to form a rectangular prism. Have students record the dimensions and find the surface area. Ask students if their answer is the same as the number of squares counted.

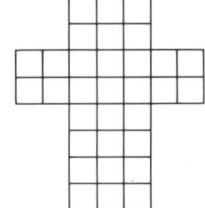

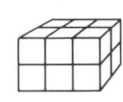

Enrichment

Challenge students to solve the problems below.

1. The base of a triangle is 12 cm and its area is 42 cm^2. What is the height? **7 cm**

2. One base of a trapezoid is 15 cm and the other base is 25 cm. What is the height if the area is 200 cm^2? **10 cm**

3. The base and height of a triangle have the same measures. The area of the triangle is 18 m^2. Find the base and height. **6m, 6m**

Assignment Guide			
	Minimum	Average	Extended
page 258	1–6	1–9	1–9
page 259	1–5	1–6, 9	1–9

Applications

PROBLEM SOLVING: Practice

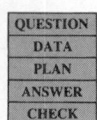

Solve.

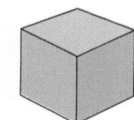

1. One face of a cube has an area of 12.25 cm². What is the total surface area of the cube? 73.5 cm²

2. The total surface area of a cube is 2,400 cm². What is the length of each edge of the cube? 20 cm

3. What is the total surface area of a rectangular prism with a length of 2.5 m, a width of 1.5 m, and a height of 3 m? 31.5 m²

4. A box in the shape of a rectangular prism has a length of 0.5 m, a width of 0.4 m, and a height of 0.3 m. Can all sides of the box be covered with 1 m² of contact paper? How much contact paper will be left over or how much more is needed?
yes; 0.06 m² over

5. Joseph Carillo estimates that a large building has 330 m² of area to be painted. A can of paint covers about 15 m² and costs $10.95. What will be the cost of the paint for the building? $240.90

6. A rectangular room has a length of 7 m and a width of 4 m. The height of the wall is 2.5 m. A door and two windows are about 8 m² of area. What is the remaining area of the four walls of the room? 47 m²

★ 7. A carpenter cut out this shape from a piece of wood. What is the total surface area of the shape? 1,090 cm²

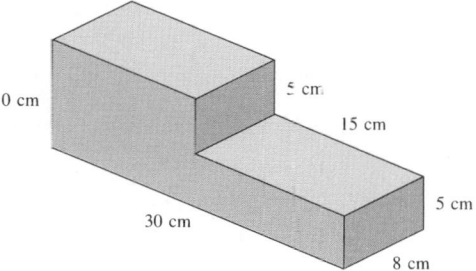

★ 8. A solid rectangular block of wood, 10 cm by 8 cm by 5 cm, has a square 2-cm groove cut in the top face as shown in the figure. How much greater is the total surface area of the grooved block than the original block? 32 cm²

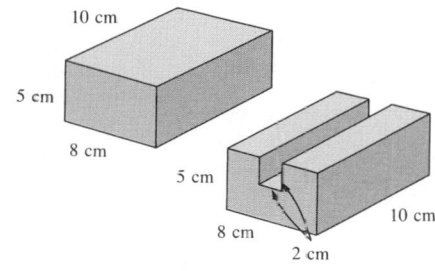

9. **Try This** The total number of dots on opposite faces of a die is always 7. Lonnie tossed 3 dice and a 3, 5, and 2 came up on top. What is the total number of dots on the 12 faces that were not on the top or bottom of Lonnie's dice? Hint: Use logical reasoning. 42

Using Page 259

Exercise 7 The surface area can be found by finding the area of each face separately. It will be necessary to divide the L-shaped faces into two rectangles. Some students may discover some shortcuts in solving the problem.

Exercise 8 Notice that the area of the bottom of the 2 cm by 2 cm groove is the same as the area lost from the top of the face. The two vertical sides of the groove increase the surface area of the original block by 2 × (2 × 10) cm² or 40 cm². But 8 cm² are lost from the front and back sides of the block when the groove is cut. Hence, the total surface area is increased by (40 − 8) cm² = 32 cm².

Try This A possible strategy, Use Logical Reasoning, was taught on page 242.

Discussion After students read the problem, discuss the question to make sure that everyone understands what the question asks us to find. Have students identify the data in the problem. Then ask "How many pairs of faces are not on the top or bottom of one die?" (2 pairs) "What is the sum of dots on these faces?" (2 × 7 = 14) Help students to see that 3 dice have 6 pairs of faces that are not on the top or bottom, and each pair has a sum of 7 dots.

Solution 6 × 7 = 42
The total number of dots on the 12 faces is 42.

Ideas That Work

Special Education

The topic of surface area is a difficult topic for many special-needs students to visualize. In order that they can better deal with this concept, you might consider the following activities.

Allow students to make models of space figures from patterns so that they can see the shape of each face. The opposite activity can also be carried out; students can cut various paper models apart to examine the shapes that make up the models. As another activity, you might have students cut out rectangular pieces of paper and cover a given solid surface. These activities strengthen the student's ability to work with space figures.

After students understand the concept of surface area, the rectangle formula for area can be used over and over again to find the necessary surface areas.

Practice Supplement, page 99

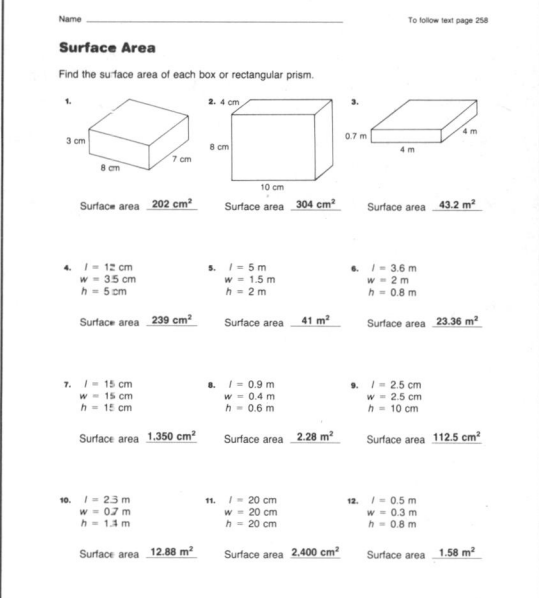

Measurement

Quick Review Have students list all the factors of each number and identify those factors that are prime.

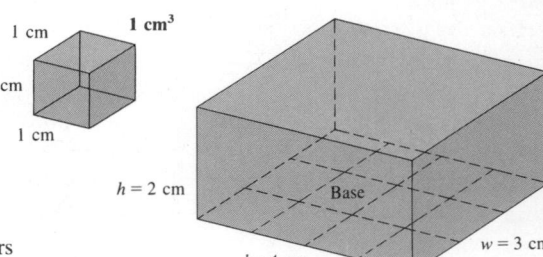

24 1, 2, 3, 4, 6, 8, 12, 24   33 1, 3, 11, 33   25 1, 5, 25
28 1, 2, 4, 7, 14, 28   30 1, 2, 3, 5, 6, 10, 15, 30

Lesson Focus To find the volume of a prism

Suggested Materials Models of prisms, open-top box, unit cubes

Ideas for Getting Started

Show students the open box and the cubes. Explain that the cubes are unit-cubes, or 1 unit on each side. Ask students to estimate how many cubes it will take to fill the box. Then have students count the number of cubes it takes to fill the box and compare this number to their estimates. Explain that this number of cubes is the *volume* of the box.

Display a picture of a box filled with cubes on the chalkboard or overhead projector. Have students tell how many cubes are in the box.

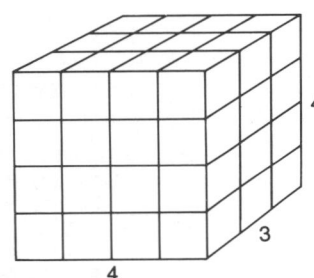

Help students to realize that the number of cubes can be found by multiplying $4 \times 3 \times 4$.

Using Page 260

Lesson Development Have students read the material at the top of the page and study the illustration. The formula, $V = lwh$, will be review for many students. Stress the exponential notation used for a unit of volume. Point out that when using the formula, the measurements for l, w, and h must be in the same unit. Then the unit of volume is the cube of that unit.

Direct students' attention to the second formula given for volume. Point out that since $l \times w$ is the area of the base, we can also write the formula for volume as $V = $ Area of Base $\times$ height.

Other Examples On the chalkboard, work through the examples of finding the volume of a triangular prism and a hexagonal prism. Be sure that students understand that $V = Bh$ is a general formula that applies to all prisms, while the formula $V = lwh$ applies only to rectangular prisms.

Warm Up Use these exercises to assess students' understanding of finding the volume of a prism. Exercise 3 shows a triangular prism oriented so that the prism does not rest on its base. Remind students that the bases of a prism are congruent polygons in parallel planes.

Volume

Volume is the measure of a region of space. A unit for volume is a cube which has 1 unit on each edge. To find volume, we count the number of **cubic units**.

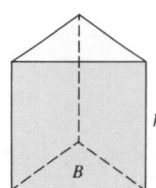

The box will hold 2 layers of 12 cubes or 24 cubic centimeters (cm^3). The volume is 24 cm^3.

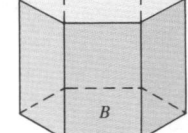

The volume of any rectangular prism can be found by using a formula.

Volume = *length* $\times$ *width* $\times$ *height*

$V = lwh$
$V = 4 \times 3 \times 2 = 24$
$V = 24$ cm^3

Since $l \times w = $ area of the base, the volume formula is also

Volume = Area of *Base* $\times$ *height*

$V = Bh$
$V = 12 \times 2 = 24$
$V = 24$ cm^3

Other Examples

The formula $V = Bh$ can be used to find the volume of any prism.

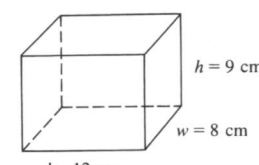

$B = 30$ cm^2
$h = 10$ cm

$V = Bh$
$V = 30 \times 10 = 300$
$V = 300$ cm^3

Triangular prism

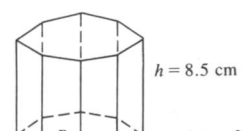

$B = 40.5$ cm^2
$h = 12$ cm

$V = Bh$
$V = 40.5 \times 12 = 486.0$
$V = 486.0$ cm^3

Hexagonal prism

Warm Up

1. Find the volume. 864 cm^3 Use $V = lwh$.

2. Find the volume. 714 cm^3 Use $V = Bh$.

3. Find the volume. 294 cm^3 Use $V = Bh$.

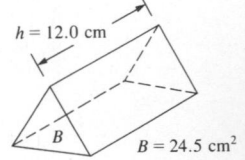

$h = 12.0$ cm

$B = 24.5$ cm^2

$h = 9$ cm
$w = 8$ cm
$l = 12$ cm

$h = 8.5$ cm
$B = 84$ cm^2

Follow Up

Reteaching

Make models of rectangular prisms out of graph paper (TRB p. 284). Have students find the volume of a prism by counting the number of cubes in one layer and then multiplying that number times the height.

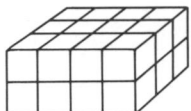 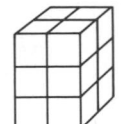

Show students that the same answer will be found by using $V = lwh$

Enrichment

Challenge students with the following problem.

The Carrico's have an A-frame house. To buy the right air conditioner, they need to find the volume. The height of the house is 8 m, the width is 6 m, and the length is 12 m. What is the volume of the house? **288 m^3**

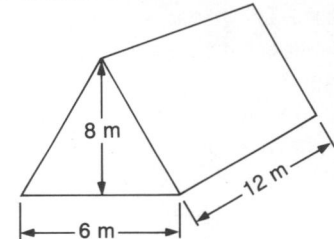

8 m
12 m
6 m

Find the volume of each rectangular prism.

1. $l = 11$ cm
$w = 8$ cm
$h = 6$ cm
528 cm³

2. $l = 20$ cm
$w = 20$ cm
$h = 12$ cm
4,800 cm³

3. $l = 2$ m
$w = 1.5$ m
$h = 0.8$ m
2.4 m³

4. $l = 7$ mm
$w = 6$ mm
$h = 5$ mm
210 mm³

5. $l = 8.5$ cm
$w = 5.4$ cm
$h = 4.0$ cm
183.6 cm³

6. $l = 4$ dm
$w = 3$ dm
$h = 3$ dm
36 dm³

7. $l = 25$ km
$w = 10$ km
$h = 4$ km
1,000 km³

8. $l = 0.8$ m
$w = 0.8$ m
$h = 0.4$ m
0.256 m³

Find the volume of each prism.

9.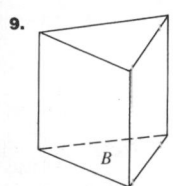
$B = 18$ cm²
$h = 10$ cm
180 cm³

10.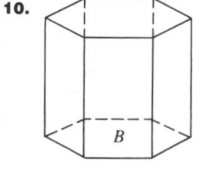
$B = 56$ cm²
$h = 7$ cm
392 cm³

11.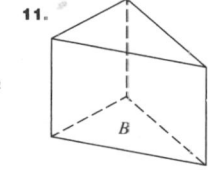
$B = 20.0$ cm²
$h = 6.5$ cm
130 cm³

12.
$B = 4.5$ cm²
$h = 4.8$ cm
21.6 cm³

13. What is the volume of concrete needed for a patio in the shape of a rectangle 9.7 m long, 7.3 m, wide, and 0.15 m thick? 10.6215 m³

14. The cost to excavate the dirt for a pool that will be a rectangular prism 25 m by 15 m, and 4 m deep, is $4,125. What is the cost per cubic meter? $2.75

★ **15.** Which has the greater volume, two boxes the same size or one box with double the dimensions of the two boxes?
One box with double dimensions.

16. **DATA HUNT** What is the volume of your classroom? Measure the length, the width, and the height of the room to the nearest tenth of a meter.

SKILLKEEPER

Write the missing numbers.

1. 92 cm = ▦ m
0.92

2. 6.25 mm = ▦ cm
0.625

3. 23 km = ▦ m
23,000

4. 1,956 m = ▦ km
1.956

5. 5 m = ▦ dm
50

6. 72,600 dm = ▦ km
7.26

7. 2,592 m = ▦ km
2.592

8. 912 m = ▦ mm
912,000

9. 0.05 hm = ▦ km
0.005

10. 257 m = ▦ km
0.257

11. 9,240 dm = ▦ km
0.924

12. 29.6 km = ▦ m
29,600

More Practice, page 433, Set D

Using Page 261

Exercise 13 Suggest that students draw a figure for this exercise.

Exercise 14 Calculators should be available for this problem.

Exercise 15 Students might think of an example to answer the question.

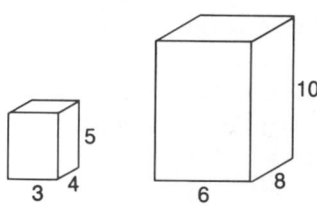

$V = 3 \times 4 \times 5 = 60$ cubic units
$V = 6 \times 8 \times 10 = 480$ cubic units

2 boxes: 120 cubic units

An algebraic explanation is given below.

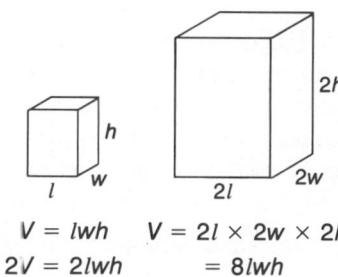

$V = lwh$ $V = 2l \times 2w \times 2h$
$2V = 2lwh$ $= 8lwh$

Skillkeeper This Skillkeeper reviews material taught in this chapter.

More Practice, page 433, Set D

Reteaching Supplement, page 78

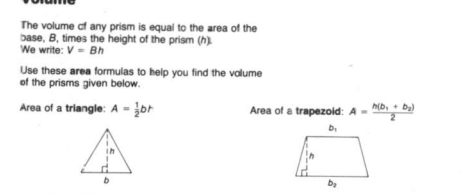

Name _____ To follow text page 261

Volume

Volume of a Rectangular Prism
Volume = length × width × height
$V = lwh$
$V = 12 \times 3 \times 4.5$
$V = 162$ cm³ — Volume is measured in cubic units.

Volume of any Prism
Volume = Base × height
$V = Bh$
$V = 53 \times 21$
$V = 1,113$ cm³

Find the volume of each prism.

1. $V = lwh$
$V = 20 \times 4 \times 15$
$V = 1200$ cm³

2. $V = Bh$
$B = 67.5$ cm²
$V = 67.5 \times 3$
$V = 202.5$ cm³

3. $B = 52$ cm²
$V = 624$ cm³

4. $V = 144$ m³

5. $V = 800$ cm³

6. $B = 53$ cm²
$V = 277.2$ cm³

7. $B = 71.6$ cm²
$V = 730.32$ cm³

8. $V = 60$ cm³

Enrichment Supplement, page 78

Name _____ To follow text page 261

Volume

The volume of any prism is equal to the area of the base, B, times the height of the prism (h).
We write: $V = Bh$

Use these area formulas to help you find the volume of the prisms given below.

Area of a triangle: $A = \frac{1}{2}bh$

Area of a trapezoid: $A = \frac{h(b_1 + b_2)}{2}$

Area of a parallelogram: $A = b \times h$

Area of a regular hexagon: A is approximately 0.072 p^2 (p is the perimeter of the hexagon)

Find the volume. The dark lines show the base of each figure.

1. Area of base = 36 cm²
Volume of prism = 216 cm³

2. Area of base = 6 cm²
Volume of prism = 30 cm³

3. Area of base = 61.2 cm²
Volume of prism = 195.84 cm³

4. Area of base = 41.472 cm²
Volume of prism = 514.2528 cm³

Practice Supplement, page 100

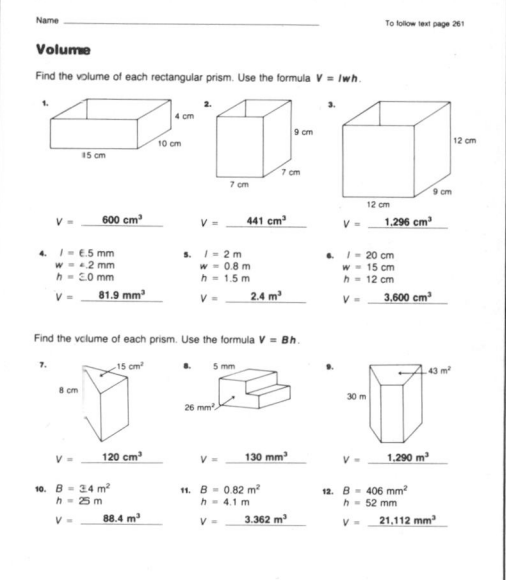

Name _____ To follow text page 261

Volume

Find the volume of each rectangular prism. Use the formula $V = lwh$.

1. $V = 600$ cm³

2. $V = 441$ cm³

3. $V = 1,296$ cm³

4. $l = 6.5$ mm
$w = 4.2$ mm
$h = 3.0$ mm
$V = 81.9$ mm³

5. $l = 2$ m
$w = 0.8$ m
$h = 1.5$ m
$V = 2.4$ m³

6. $l = 20$ cm
$w = 15$ cm
$h = 12$ cm
$V = 3,600$ cm³

Find the volume of each prism. Use the formula $V = Bh$.

7. $V = 120$ cm³

8. $V = 130$ mm³

9. $V = 1,290$ m³

10. $B = 3.4$ m²
$h = 25$ m
$V = 88.4$ m³

11. $B = 0.82$ m²
$h = 4.1$ m
$V = 3.362$ m³

12. $B = 406$ mm²
$h = 52$ mm
$V = 21,112$ mm³

Quick Review Have students estimate to determine which of the following quotients are incorrect.

$3,672 \div 51 = 7$ **incorrect** $966 \div 23 = 42$ $2,812 \div 38 = 74$

$774 \div 86 = 90$ **incorrect** $900 \div 18 = 5$ **incorrect**

Lesson Focus To review units of capacity; to solve word problems related to capacity and volume

Suggested Materials Standard metric containers for measuring liters and milliliters, various containers such as bottles and cans

Ideas for Getting Started

Display a liter container. Then show other containers and have students estimate the capacity of these containers in liters. If possible, check the estimates by filling the containers from a calibrated metric container.

Using Page 262

Lesson Development Have students read the material at the top of the page and study the relationship between metric units of capacity. Only liters, kiloliters, and milliliters are discussed in this lesson since they are the most frequently used units.

Discuss with students the relationship between units of volume and units of capacity. Point out that cubic centimeters and milliliters are both measures of volume. In practice, however, volume of liquids is expressed in milliliters, liters, and kiloliters, so we refer to them as units of capacity.

Exercises 1–8 Use these exercises as an oral class activity.

Capacity

Mario has some mugs that each hold 200 **milliliters (mL)** of hot chocolate. Milliliters are units of liquid measure, or **capacity**.

1 **kiloliter (kL)** = **1,000 liters (L)**
1 **liter (L)**   = **1,000 milliliters (mL)**

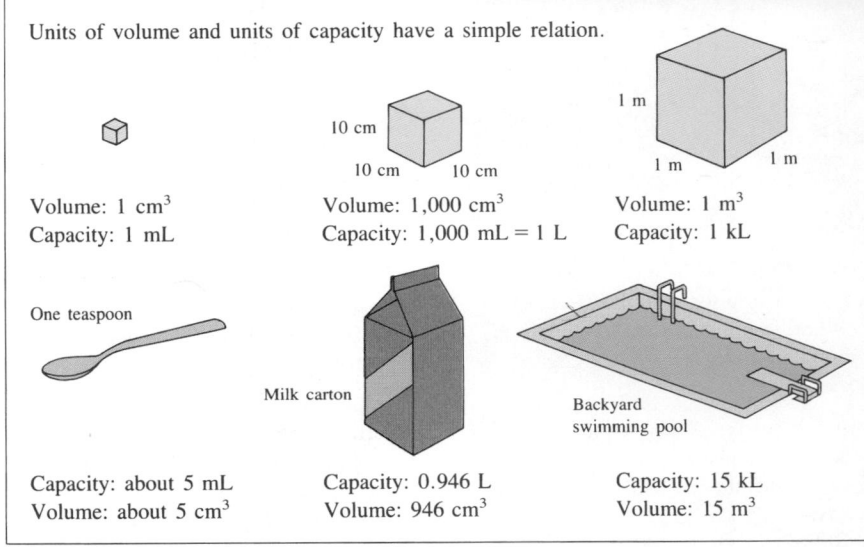

Units of volume and units of capacity have a simple relation.

Volume: 1 cm³
Capacity: 1 mL

Volume: 1,000 cm³
Capacity: 1,000 mL = 1 L

Volume: 1 m³
Capacity: 1 kL

One teaspoon

Capacity: about 5 mL
Volume: about 5 cm³

Milk carton

Capacity: 0.946 L
Volume: 946 cm³

Backyard swimming pool

Capacity: 15 kL
Volume: 15 m³

Give the missing numbers.

1. Juice jug: 1,500 cm³
   Capacity: ▓ mL   1,500

2. Can of paint: 873 cm³
   Capacity: ▓ mL   873

Which unit of capacity (mL, L, or kL) would you use to measure the capacity of each?

3. A juice glass   mL

4. Home hot water heater   L

5. The amount of water in Lake Michigan   kL

6. The amount of water you drink each day   L

7. The fuel tank of an automobile   L

8. The amount of liquid in an eyedropper   mL

262

Follow Up

Reteaching

Provide students with liquid containers of various sizes and ask them to estimate and then measure the capacity of the containers in milliliters and liters. Label each container A, B, C, and so on, and have students record their estimates and measures.

Enrichment

Let students construct a cubic decimeter, or box that holds 1 liter. Have them cut out five tagboard squares each 10 cm by 10 cm. Next have them paste centimeter graph paper (TRB p. 284) on each square and tape the squares together to form a box as shown.

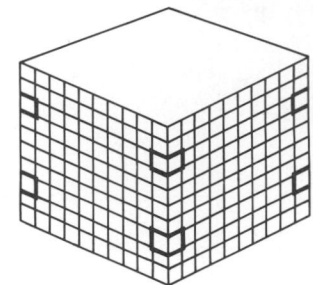

Applications

PROBLEM SOLVING: Practice

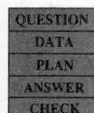

QUESTION
DATA
PLAN
ANSWER
CHECK

Solve.

1. A large milk carton holds 3.46 L of milk. How many milliliters does it hold? **3,460 mL**

2. The sun evaporated about 0.8 kL of water from a swimming pool each day. How many liters of water evaporated? **800 L**

3. A jug of apple juice holds 1.75 L. What is the capacity of the jug in milliliters? **1,750 mL**

4. There are 2 L of fruit punch. If 20 servings of 72 mL each are served, about how many servings will be left? **about 8**

5. A hummingbird feeder holds 475 mL of liquid. The hummingbirds drink about 75 mL each day. The feeder was last filled on Tuesday morning. When will it need to be filled again? **Monday morning**

6. A small can of frozen orange juice has a capacity of 175 mL. There are 48 cans in a case of juice. How many liters of juice are there in a case? **8.4 L**

7. A can of frozen lemonade has a capacity of 468 mL. To make lemonade, the directions say to add 3 full cans of water. How many milliliters of lemonade would this make? How many liters is that? **1,827 mL; 1.827 L**

8. Leone bought 1.89 L of low-fat milk, 0.95 L of non-fat milk, and 0.47 L of whipping cream. What was the total amount of milk and cream? **3.31 L**

9. A can of condensed soup has a capacity of 325 mL. To make the soup, a full can of milk must be added to the condensed soup. What is the total amount of soup that can be made from 3 cans of condensed soup? **1,950 mL**

★ **10.** How high will the water level be in this aquarium if it is filled with 16 L of water? **12.5 cm**

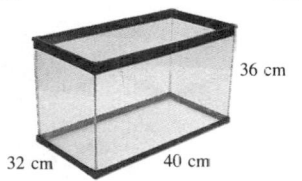

36 cm

32 cm   40 cm

11. A 1.89-liter carton of milk costs $1.08. What is the cost of 1 liter of milk? Round your answer to the nearest cent. **$0.57**

12. Try This A glass holds 120 mL. A faucet starts dripping water into the glass. The first minute it drips 1 mL. The second minute it drips 2 mL, the third minute it drips 3 mL, and so on. How many minutes will it be until the glass is filled with water? **15 min**

263

Using Page 263

Exercise 10 This exercise is a multiple-step problem.

$$16 \text{ L} = 16,000 \text{ mL} = 16,000 \text{ cm}^3$$
$$40 \times 32 = 1,280$$
$$16,000 \div 1,280 = 12.5 \text{ cm}$$

Try This A possible strategy, Make a Table, was taught on page 186.

Discussion After students read the problem, have them restate the question and identify the data given in the problem. Ask students to tell how to make a table that shows the data.

Solution

Time	1	2	3	4		13	14	15
mL	1	2	3	4		13	14	15
Total	1	3	6	10		91	105	120

The glass is filled with water after 15 minutes.

Extension Mrs. Palgutta hired Ed to bring in her mail for the 10 days she was away on vacation. For bringing in the mail on the first day, Ed was paid 1 nickel. For bringing in the mail the second day, he was paid 5 nickels. For the third day, he was paid 14 nickels, and for the fourth day he was paid 30 nickels. This pattern continued for 10 days. How much did Mrs. Palgutta pay Ed for all 10 days? ($60.50)

Reteaching Supplement, page 79

Name _____ To follow text page 262

Capacity

Capacity Units

A thimble holds about 5 milliliters (mL).

A saucepan holds about 3 liters (L).

A large waterbed mattress holds about 1 kiloliter (kL).

Metric Relationships

1 liter (L) = 1,000 milliliters (mL)

1 kiloliter (kL) = 1,000 liters (L)

1 cubic centimeter — has a capacity of → 1 milliliter

1,000 cubic centimeters — have a capacity of → 1 liter

1 cubic meter — has a capacity of → 1 kiloliter

Write the unit of capacity (mL, L, or kL) you would use to measure the capacity of each.

1. a small fish tank ___L___
2. a measuring cup ___mL___
3. a swimming pool ___kL___

4. a juice glass ___mL___
5. a bucket ___L___
6. a small vase ___mL___

Complete.

7. A box with a volume of 283 cm³ has a capacity of __283__ mL. (1 cm³ = 1 mL)

8. A tank with a capacity of 18 kL has a volume of __18__ m³.

9. A bottle with a capacity of 3 L has a volume of __3,000__ cm³. (1 L = 1,000 cm³)

10. A box with a volume of 9,000 cm³ has a capacity of __9__ L.

Solve.

11. A can of juice has a volume of 1,400 cm³. What is the capacity of the can in liters? __1.4 L__

12. A punch recipe calls for 500 mL of lemonade, 750 mL of orange juice, 750 mL of pineapple juice, and 2 L of ginger ale. How many liters of punch does the recipe make? __4 L__

Enrichment Supplement, page 79

Name _____ To follow text page 262

Converting Capacity

Draw a ring around the measurement that is equal to the given measurement.

1. 4 kL 200 L
A. 204 L
B. 4,200 L ⟲
C. 600 L

2. 7 L 200 mL
A. 7.2 L ⟲
B. 720 mL
C. 720 L

3. 240 L 240 mL
A. 480 mL
B. 240,240 L
C. 240,240 mL ⟲

4. 1 kL 1 L
A. 101 L
B. 1,001 L ⟲
C. 1.01 kL

5. 2 kL 2 mL
A. 22 kL
B. 202 kL
C. 2,000.002 mL ⟲

6. 14 kL 95 L
A. 14.95 kL
B. 1,495 kL
C. 14.095 kL ⟲

7. 67 L 4 mL
A. 674 L
B. 67,004 m ⟲
C. 67.004 mL

8. 999 L 1 mL
A. 999,001 mL ⟲
B. 999 kL
C. 1 kL

9. 42 L 42 mL
A. 4,242 L
B. 42,042 mL ⟲
C. 420.42 L

Write two measurements equal to the given measurement. Answers will vary. Some possible answers are given.

10. 9 L 425 mL
__9,425 mL__
__9.425 L__

11. 4 kL 88 L
__4,088 L__
__4.088 kL__

12. 7 L 745 mL
__7,000.745 L__
__7,000.745 mL__

13. 140 L 623 mL
__140.623 L__
__140,623 mL__

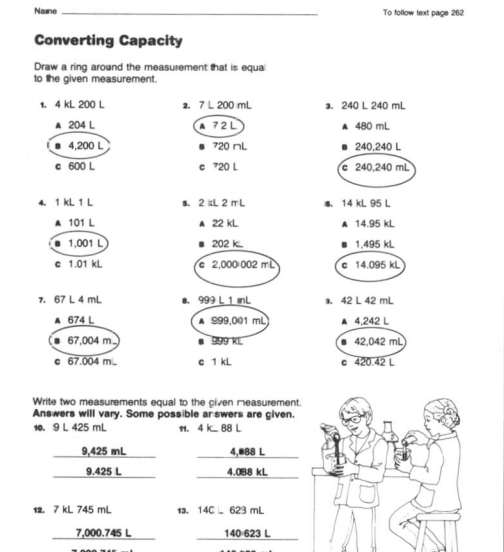

Practice Supplement, page 101

Name _____ To follow text page 262

Capacity

Write the volume of each container in cubic centimeters. Then write the capacity in milliliters (mL).

1. 3 cm, 5 cm, 4 cm
Volume = __60 cm³__
Capacity = __60 mL__

2. 6 cm, 8 cm, 10 cm
Volume = __480 cm³__
Capacity = __480 mL__

3. 5 cm, 15 cm, cm
Volume = __300 cm³__
Capacity = __300 mL__

Write the volume of each container in cubic meters. Then write the capacity in kiloliters (kL).

4. 10 m, 10 m, 20 m
Volume = __2,000 m³__
Capacity = __2,000 kL__

5. h = 8 m, B = 240 m
Volume = __1,920 m³__
Capacity = __1,920 kL__

6. 5 m, 6 m, 10 m
Volume = __300 m³__
Capacity = __300 kL__

Which unit would you use to measure the capacity of each? Choose mL, L, or kL.

7. a cup __mL__
8. a spoon __mL__
9. a bucket __L__
10. a barrel __L__
11. a pond __kL__
12. a bathtub __L__
13. a thimble __mL__
14. a sugar bowl __mL__

Quick Review Have students solve each equation.

$d - 13 = 6$ **19** $12p = 48$ **4** $r + 32 = 42$ **10**
$6s = 36$ **6** $\frac{b}{14} = 2$ **28** $t - 37 = 12$ **49**

Lesson Focus To express measurements of weight in milligrams, grams, kilograms, or metric tons; to solve word problems using data from a table

Suggested Materials Metric scales, standard metric weights

Ideas for Getting Started

Show students a standard 1-kg weight. Let students hold the weight and compare it to the weight of other objects in the room.

Demonstrate that the weight of 1 L of water is 1 kg. First find the weight of an empty container and then find the weight of that container with 1 L of water in it.

Ask students to visualize a tank in the form of a cube that measures one meter on each edge. Explain that this tank would hold 1,000 L or 1 kL. The water would weigh 1,000 kg or 1 metric ton.

Using Page 264

Lesson Development Have students read the material at the top of the page and study the relationship between metric units of weight. This lesson is concerned with the units of milligram, gram, kilogram, and ton. Other metric units of weight are seldom used.

Emphasize that 1 L of water weighs 1 kg and that 1 mL or 1 cm³ of water weighs 1 g.

Exercises 1–2 Assign these exercises as independent written work. Remind students to check the reasonableness of their answers. They should remember that changing from a larger unit to a smaller unit gives a greater number of units, while changing from a smaller unit to a larger unit gives a smaller number of units.

Units of Weight

Adrian Bishop likes to bowl. His bowling ball has a **weight** of a little more than 7 **kilograms (kg)**. A kilogram is a unit of weight.

1 metric ton (t) = 1,000 kilograms (kg)
1 kilogram (kg) = 1,000 grams (g)
1 gram (g)   = 1,000 milligrams (mg)

One drop of water	Nickel	Large book	School bus

About 50 mg	About 5 g	About 6 kg	About 5 t

There is a simple relation between the volume of pure water and the weight of the water.

1 L of water has a weight of 1 kg.

1 mL of water has a weight of 1 g.

Give the unit (mg, g, kg, t) that would be used to measure the weight of each object.

1. A penny **g**   **2.** A person **kg**   **3.** A truck **t**   **4.** A drop of oil **mg**

Give the weight of each amount of water.

5. 3 L **3 kg**   **6.** 500 mL **500 g**   **7.** 1.5 L **1.5 kg**   **8.** 27 mL **27 g**

Give the missing numbers.

9. 2,000 g = ▓ kg **2**   **10.** 3,174 g = ▓ kg **3.174**   **11.** 5 kg = ▓ g **5,000**
12. 1.8 kg = ▓ g **1,800**   **13.** 0.001 kg = ▓ g **1**   **14.** 0.001 g = ▓ mg **1**
15. 2 g = ▓ mg **2,000**   **16.** 500 mg = ▓ g **0.5**   **17.** 0.454 kg = ▓ g **454**
18. 0.7 kg = ▓ g **700**   **19.** 7,200 mg = ▓ g **7.2**   **20.** 2.938 kg = ▓ g **2,938**

264

Follow Up

Reteaching

Provide an opportunity for students to estimate and then find the weight of a variety of objects, using metric scales or balances. Display a collection of objects on a table. Have students lift each object and write an estimate of its weight. Students can then use a metric scale to check the actual weight.

Enrichment

Have students tell what unit they would use to measure each of the following.

1. weight of a grain of sand **mg**
2. width of a paper clip **mm**
3. height of a pine tree **m**
4. weight of a dog **kg**
5. capacity of a fish tank **L**
6. distance between 2 cities **km**
7. weight of a pen **g**
8. capacity of an eye dropper **mL**

Assignment Guide			
	Minimum	Average	Extended
page 264	1–20	1–20	1–20
page 265	1–6	1–8, 11	1–11

PROBLEM SOLVING: Using Data from a Table

QUESTION
DATA
PLAN
ANSWER
CHECK

King-size Hamburger Ingredients

Roll	28 g	Onions	14 g
Patty	113 g	Pickles	12 g
Tomatoes	22 g	Ketchup	8 g
Mayonnaise	3 g	Lettuce	20 g

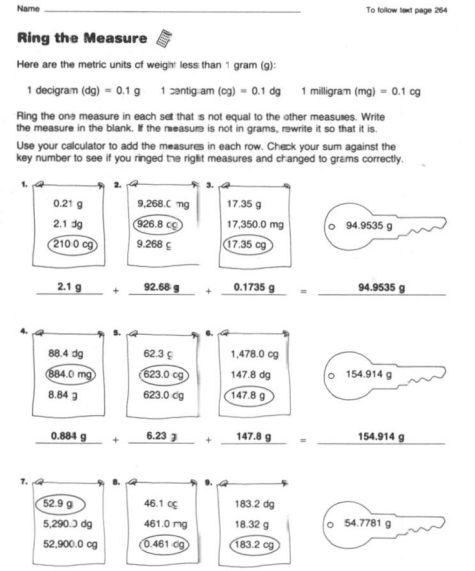

Solve.

1. About how many hamburger patties does it take to equal 1 kg? Round your answer to the nearest whole number. **9**

2. The rolls come in packages of 12. What is the weight of a package of rolls? **336 g**

3. What is the total weight of all the ingredients in one king-size hamburger? **220 g**

4. Sal ate two king-size hamburgers and a fruit drink. The fruit drink had a weight of 350 g. How much less than a kilogram did Sal eat? **210 g**

5. Wakenda ordered a king-size hamburger without mayonnaise, onions, or tomatoes. What was the weight of her hamburger? **181 g**

6. Robbie ordered a king-size hamburger, onion rings (weight 188 g), and a small fruit drink (weight 240 g). What was the total weight of Robbie's order? **648 g**

7. The weight of ketchup in a full bottle is 336 g. How many king-size hamburgers could be served with one bottle of ketchup? **42**

8. A head of lettuce has a weight of about 500 g. How many portions of lettuce for king-size hamburgers can be made from one head of lettuce? **25**

9. On Saturday 250 king-size hamburgers were sold. How many kilograms of patties is this? **28.25 kg**

10. A large jar of mayonnaise has a weight of 1,560 g. About how many hamburgers could be served with this amount of mayonnaise? **520**

11. **Try This** Doug ordered an avocado sandwich, a fruit drink, and some carrot sticks. The fruit drink cost 25¢ more than the carrot sticks. The sandwich cost 50¢ more than the fruit drink. Doug paid for his meal with a $5 bill and got $1.75 back in change. How much did each kind of food cost? **carrot sticks, 75¢; fruit drink, $1.00; sandwich, $1.50**

265

Using Page 265

Exercises 1–10 Students will need to use data from the table to solve these problems.

Try This A possible strategy, Guess and Check, was taught on page 24.

Discussion After students read the problem, have them identify the questions and the data. Ask them to find the amount Doug paid for his meal. ($5 − $1.75 = $3.25) Then elicit from students a strategy that could be used to solve the problem.

Solution

Guess: Carrot sticks $0.75
        Fruit drink   1.00
        Sandwich   1.50

Check: $0.75 + $1.00 + $1.50 = $3.25

The carrot sticks cost $0.75, the fruit drink cost $1.00, and the sandwich cost $1.50.

Reteaching Supplement, page 80

Name _____   To follow text page 254

Units of Weight

Weight Units

A tiny seed weighs about 25 milligrams (mg).

A paper clip weighs about 4 grams (g).

A 2 L carton of milk weighs about 2 kilograms (kg).

A small whale weighs about 30 metric tons (t).

Metric Relationships

1 gram (g) = 1,000 milligrams (mg)
1 kilogram = 1,000 grams (g)
1 metric ton (t) = 1,000 kilograms
1 liter of water —weighs→ 1 kilogram
1 milliliter of water —weighs→ 1 gram

Write the unit of weight (mg, g, kg, t) you would use to measure the weight of each.

1. a car   **t**   2. a grain of salt   **mg**   3. a chair   **kg**   4. a class ring   **g**

Give the weight of each amount of water.

5. 525 mL (1 mL → 1 g)   **525** g   6. 5 L (1 L → 1 kg)   **5** kg   7. 3.7 L   **3.7** kg   8. 78 mL   **78** g

Complete.

(3 × 1,000 = ?)   (25 ÷ 1,000 = ?)   (0.75 × 1,000 = ?)

9. 3 kg = **3,000** g   10. 25 g = **0.025**   11. 0.75 kg = **750** g
12. 6 kg = **6,000** g   13. 124 g = **0.124** kg   14. 287 g = **0.287** kg

Solve.

15. Ann feeds her cat 275 g of food each day. How many kilograms of food does the cat eat in one week? **1.925 kg**

16. Jose feeds his dog 3 kg of food a week. How many grams does the dog eat per day? **429 g**

Enrichment Supplement, page 80

Name _____   To follow text page 264

Ring the Measure ✎

Here are the metric units of weight less than 1 gram (g):

1 decigram (dg) = 0.1 g   1 centigram (cg) = 0.1 dg   1 milligram (mg) = 0.1 cg

Ring the one measure in each set that is not equal to the other measures. Write the measure in the blank. If the measure is not in grams, rewrite it so that it is.

Use your calculator to add the measures in each row. Check your sum against the key number to see if you ringed the right measures and changed to grams correctly.

1.
0.21 g
2.1 dg
(210.0 cg)

2.
9,268.0 mg
(926.8 cg)
9.268 g

3.
17.35 g
17,350.0 mg
(17.35 cg)

○ 94.9535 g

2.1 g + 92.68 g + 0.1735 g = 94.9535 g

4.
88.4 dg
(884.0 mg)
8.84 g

5.
62.3 g
623.0 cg
623.0 g

6.
1,478.0 cg
147.8 dg
(147.8)

○ 154.914 g

0.884 g + 6.23 g + 147.8 g = 154.914 g

7.
52.9 g
5,290.0 dg
52,900.0 mg

8.
46.1 cg
461.0 mg
(0.461 g)

9.
183.2 dg
18.32 g
(183.2 cg)

○ 54.7781 g

52.9 g + 0.0461 g + 1.832 g = 54.7781 g

Practice Supplement, page 102

Name _____   To follow text page 264

Units of Weight

Write **mg, g, kg,** or **t** to tell which unit you would use to measure the weight of each object.

1. a pen   **g**   2. a dog   **kg**
3. a truck   **t**   4. a man   **kg**
5. an apple   **g**   6. an ant   **mg**
7. a dime   **g**   8. a chair   **kg**
9. a house   **t**   10. a blueberry   **mg**

Write the weight of each amount of water.

11. 25 mL   **25** g   12. 2 L   **2 kg**
13. 46 mL   **46** g   14. 375 mL   **375** g
15. 15 L   **15** kg   16. 600 mL   **600** g
17. 6.4 L   **6.4** kg   18. 2 mL   **2** g
19. 3.9 L   **3.9** kg   20. 5 L   **5** kg

Write the missing numbers.

21. 4,000 g = **4** kg   22. 7 kg = **7,000** g
23. 3.6 kg = **3,600** g   24. 2,746 g = **2.746** kg
25. 0.004 kg = **4** g   26. 0.002 g = **2** mg
27. 400 mg = **0.4** g   28. 0.827 kg = **827** g
29. 6 g = **6,000** mg   30. 5.536 kg = **5,536** g
31. 4,500 mg = **4.5** g   32. 0.9 kg = **900** g

Quick Review Have students write each fraction as a decimal.

$\frac{1}{2}$ 0.5 $\frac{7}{10}$ 0.7 $\frac{3}{50}$ 0.06 $\frac{1}{4}$ 0.25

$\frac{9}{100}$ 0.09 $\frac{4}{5}$ 0.8 $\frac{3}{20}$ 0.15

Lesson Focus To review Celsius temperature; to solve word problems related to Celsius temperature

Suggested Materials Celsius thermometer

Ideas for Getting Started

Display the thermometer. Ask selected students to give the reading on the thermometer. If possible, immerse the thermometer in cold water and then have a student give the reading. Hold the bulb in your hand a minute and notice with students the rise in temperature.

Using Page 266

Lesson Development Have students read the material at the top of the page. The freezing and boiling temperatures of water should be learned by all students. These temperatures serve as good reference points for estimating other temperatures.

The use of negative numbers for temperatures should be familiar to most students. Emphasize the use of the raised minus sign to denote negative temperatures.

Discuss the table of common Celsius temperatures. These temperatures provide other convenient reference points for Celsius temperature.

Exercises 1–6 These exercises give practice in reading the scale on a thermometer. After students read the thermometer, have them use the table to help them describe something that might have that temperature.

Celsius Temperature

The thermometer shows a room temperature of 20 **degrees Celsius** (20°C).

On a Celsius scale, water freezes at 0°C and boils at 100°C.

A temperature of $^-8$°C means 8 degrees "below zero." We can read $^-8$ as "minus 8" or "negative 8."

Common Celsius Temperatures			
Water freezes	0°C	Very hot day	40°C
Water boils	100°C	Very cold day	$^-30$°C
Room temperature	20°C	Refrigerator	5°C
Body temperature	37°C	Freezer	$^-6$°C
Moderate oven	175°C	Hot oven	250°C

Give the temperature on each Celsius scale.

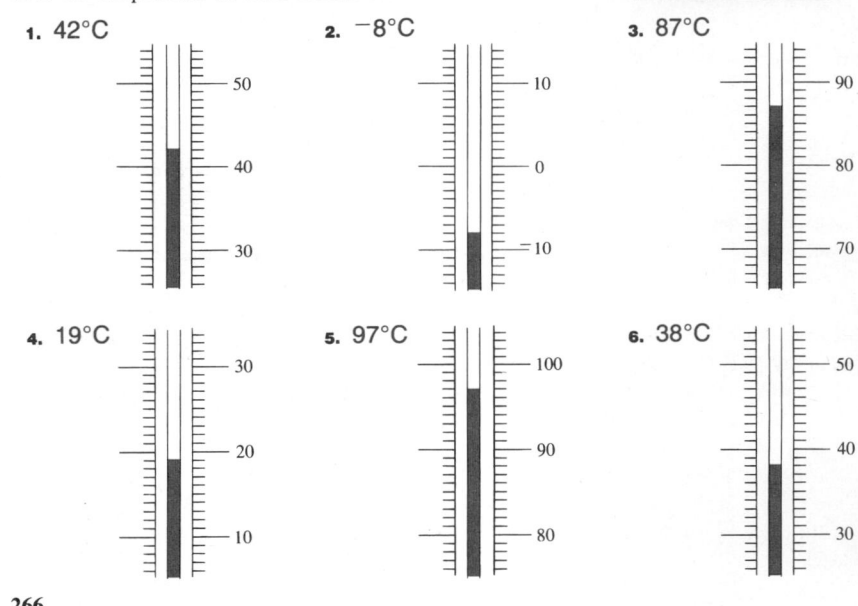

1. 42°C   2. $^-8$°C   3. 87°C

4. 19°C   5. 97°C   6. 38°C

266

Follow Up

Reteaching

Have students find the high temperature for a recent day in several cities around the country. Then have them draw a thermometer showing these temperatures and label each temperature with the appropriate city.

Enrichment

Have students make a bulletin board of significant Celsius temperatures. An assortment of pictures, either drawn or cut from old magazines, can be placed on the bulletin board and labeled with appropriate temperatures.

Assignment Guide			
	Minimum	Average	Extended
page 266	1–6	1–6	1–6
page 267	1–6, 9	1–7, 9–10	4–10

Applications

PROBLEM SOLVING: Practice

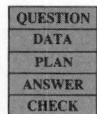

Solve.

1. The oven temperature for fruit cobbler should start at 215°C. After 15 min, the temperature should be lowered 35°C. What is the lower temperature? 180°C

2. Butter will melt at about 31°C. Paraffin will melt at about 55°C. How much higher is the melting temperature of paraffin? 24°C

3. Pure iron melts at 1,535°C. Pure gold will melt at a temperature that is 473°C lower. What is the melting temperature of gold? 1,062°C

4. The normal body temperature of a spiny anteater is 23.2°C. How much lower than normal human body temperature is this? 13.8°C

5. The normal body temperature of a songbird is about 13°C higher than the normal body temperature of a human. What is the normal body temperature of a songbird? 50°C

6. Lead will melt at about 327°C. The melting point of aluminum is 6°C higher than twice the melting temperature of lead. What is the melting temperature of aluminum? 660°C

7. Silver will boil at a temperature of 1,950°C. It will become solid at a temperature which is 15°C less than one half its boiling temperature. What is the temperature at which silver becomes solid? 960°C

★ 8. The coldest recorded weather temperature on earth was 88°C below zero, or ⁻88°C. The highest temperature ever recorded on earth was 58°C. How many degrees would the temperature have to rise from ⁻88°C to reach 58°C? 146°C

9. **DATA BANK** Find the lowest recorded temperatures in Bismarck, North Dakota and Honolulu, Hawaii. How many degrees difference is there between the two temperatures? (See page 416.) 54°

10. **Try This** The temperature went up 3°C per hour from 6:00 a.m. to 1:00 p.m. At 1:00 p.m. the temperature was 7°C. What was the temperature at 6 a.m.? ⁻14°C

267

Using Page 267

Exercises 1–7 Before assigning these exercises, direct students' attention to the problem-solving logo at the top of the page. Remind students to use the 5-Point Checklist to help them solve the problems.

Exercise 8 This is a starred exercise because it involves both positive and negative numbers. Students can reason that the temperature must rise to 88° to get to 0°C. Then it must rise 58° more. The total is 88° + 58° = 146°.

Try This Possible strategies, Make a Table and Work Backward, were taught on pages 186 and 130.

Discussion After students read the problem, have them identify the question and the data given in the problem. Point out that we know the temperature at the end of the interval of time. Elicit from students that the strategy Work Backward can be used. Explain that we can organize the data in a table.

Solution

Time	1 p.m.	12 noon	11 a.m.	10 a.m.
Temperature	7°C	4°C	1°C	⁻2°C
Time	9 a.m.	8 a.m.	7 a.m.	6 a.m.
Temperature	⁻5°C	⁻8°C	⁻11°C	⁻14°C

The temperature at 6 a.m. was ⁻14°C.

Ideas That Work

Calculator Bonus

Present students with the following problem.

Which is the greater amount of money?

1. A bag of dimes with the same weight as yourself. (A dime has a weight of 2 g.)
2. 50¢ a day for every day you have lived since you were born.

Have students estimate first and then calculate each amount.

Practice Supplement, page 103

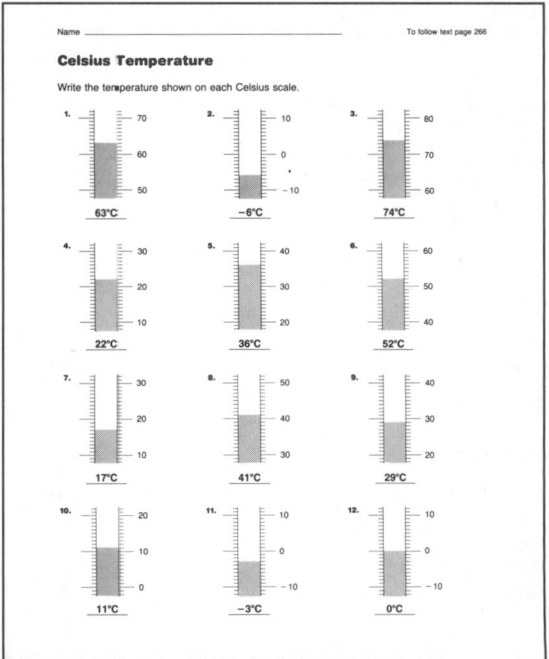

Name _____ To follow text page 266

Celsius Temperature

Write the temperature shown on each Celsius scale.

1. 63°C 2. ⁻6°C 3. 74°C
4. 22°C 5. 36°C 6. 52°C
7. 17°C 8. 41°C 9. 29°C
10. 11°C 11. ⁻3°C 12. 0°C

Lesson Focus To apply the strategies to solve nonroutine word problems

Ideas for Getting Started

Choose problems at random from text pages 24, 50, 108, 130, 158, 186, 218, and 242. After reading a problem aloud to the class, have students name the strategy they might plan to use to solve the problem. If students suggest strategies that differ from those on the pages, have them explain how they would use the strategy. Then ask other students to name a strategy they might use to solve the problem. Emphasize that different strategies can be used to solve the same problem.

Using Page 268

Lesson Development Ask students to name the nine strategies they have learned. On the chalkboard, list the strategies as the students name them. Then compare the students' list to the list of strategies in the text.

Exercise 1 A possible strategy, Make an Organized List, was introduced on page 50. Suggest that students use the first letter of each name to make the list simpler.

AF	VF	FM
AV	VM	
AM		

Exercise 2 A possible strategy, Work Backward, was introduced on page 130.

$$52 \rightarrow \boxed{\times 2} \rightarrow \boxed{+30} \rightarrow \boxed{\times 2} \rightarrow 268$$

Exercise 3 A possible strategy, Guess and Check, was introduced on page 24.

Guess: Joshua ($3.65) Ben ($6.35)

Check: $3.65 + $6.35 = $10.00

Exercise 4 A possible strategy, Draw a Picture, was introduced on page 108. Elicit from students the idea that a picture can be used to show the relationship between the data in the problem.

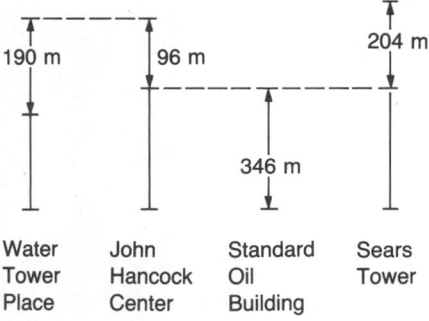

Sears Tower	346 + 204 = 550 m
John Hancock Center	346 + 96 = 442 m
Water Tower Place	442 − 190 = 252 m

PROBLEM SOLVING: Using the Strategies

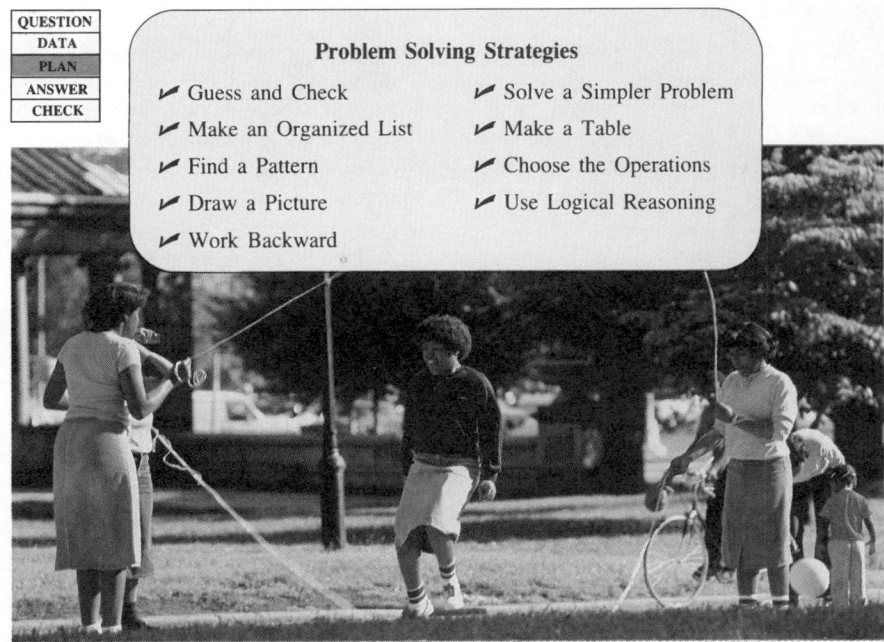

QUESTION
DATA
PLAN
ANSWER
CHECK

Problem Solving Strategies

- Guess and Check
- Make an Organized List
- Find a Pattern
- Draw a Picture
- Work Backward
- Solve a Simpler Problem
- Make a Table
- Choose the Operations
- Use Logical Reasoning

The problems on this page can be solved with the help of one or more of the different strategies you have learned.

1. Amy, Vicki, Francine, and Magdalena have a double-Dutch rope jumping team. While two girls turn the rope, two other girls jump as partners. How many different combinations of partners could jump? 6

2. Paul is making a wooden window box to start seedlings. He cut a long board into two pieces of equal length. He cut 30 cm off one of the pieces and then cut the same piece into two more pieces of equal length of 52 cm. How long was the original board? 268 cm

3. While riding the bus to a natural history museum, Ben and Joshua discover they have exactly $10.00. Ben has $2.70 more than Joshua. How much does each person have?
Ben, $6.35; Joshua, $3.65

4. Water Tower Place has a height of 190 m less than the John Hancock Center. The Sears Tower is 204 m higher than the Standard Oil Building. The John Hancock Center is 96 m taller than the Standard Oil Building, which is 346 m tall. What are the heights of the other three buildings? Water Tower Place, 252 m; John Hancock Center, 442 m; Sears Tower, 550 m

268

CHAPTER REVIEW/TEST

Write the missing numbers.

1. 1 cm = ▧ mm 10

2. 1 m = ▧ cm 100

3. 1,000 mm = ▧ m 1

4. 1 km = ▧ m 1,000

5. 2,000 m = ▧ km 2

6. 0.1 m = ▧ dm 1

Change each length to centimeters.

7. 2.75 m 275 cm

8. 68 mm 6.8 cm

9. 0.53 m 53 cm

Change each length to meters.

10. 384 cm 3.84 m

11. 3.5 km 3,500 m

12. 27 dm 2.7 m

Find the perimeter and the area of each figure.

13.

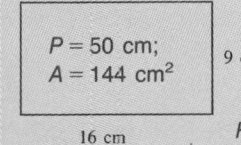

$P = 50$ cm;
$A = 144$ cm^2

16 cm

14.

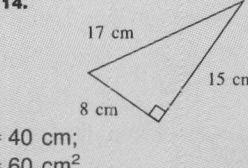

17 cm

9 cm

15 cm

8 cm

$P = 40$ cm;
$A = 60$ cm^2

15.

$b_2 = 16$ cm

13 cm $h = 12$ cm   13 cm

$P = 64$ cm; $b_1 = 22$ cm
$A = 228$ cm^2

16. Find the total surface area.

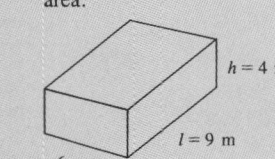

$h = 4$ m

$l = 9$ m

$w = 6$ m

228 m^2

17. Find the volume.

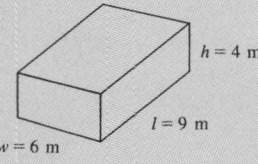

$h = 8$ cm

$l = 20$ cm

$w = 15$ cm

2,400 cm^3

18. Find the volume.

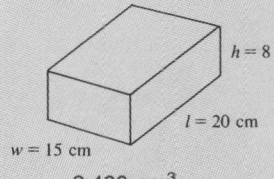

$h = 18$ cm

$B = 215$ cm^2

3,870 cm^3

Write the missing numbers.

19. 42 L = ▧ mL 42,000

20. 220 cm^3 = ▧ mL 220

21. 6,252 cm^3 = ▧ L 6.252

22. 2.5 kg = ▧ g 2,500

23. 600 mg = ▧ g 0.6

24. 5,249 g = ▧ kg 5.249

25. A can of frozen orange juice concentrate has a capacity of 175 mL. If 3 cans of water are added to the frozen juice, how many milliliters of juice will be made? 700 mL

26. A pie was baked for 10 min at 225°C. Then the temperature was lowered 38°C. What was the new baking temperature? 187°C

Reteaching

Using Page 270

The exercises on this page are intended for those students who experienced difficulty with the Chapter Review/Test on page 269. Should students require reteaching of these key concepts and skills, please refer to the teaching notes below. Otherwise, the Another Look exercises can be assigned as independent work, with students using the accompanying sample problems and hints as guides.

Exercises 1–4 This skill was originally taught on pages 248–251. Direct students' attention to the example in the display box. Explain that since there are 100 cm in 1 m, we need to multiply by 100 to change from meters to centimeters. Remind students that the shortcut for multiplying by 100 is shifting the decimal point two places to the right.

Exercises 5–8 This skill was originally taught on pages 252–253. Have students study the example in the display box. Elicit from students that the perimeter of a polygon is found by adding the lengths of its sides.

Exercises 9–12 This skill was originally taught on pages 254–257. Review with students the formulas for area shown in the display box. On the chalkboard, draw the figures below. Remind students that the area of a triangle or trapezoid is one half the area of the parallelogram.

Exercises 13–14 This skill was originally taught on pages 260–261. Have students study the formulas in the display box. Remind students that the formula $V = lwh$, can only be used to find the volume of a rectangular prism. The formula $V = Bh$ can be used to find the volume of any prism, where B represents the area of the base.

Exercises 15–16 This skill was originally taught on pages 262–263. After students study the information in the display box, ask them to give the relationship between a liter and a milliliter. Explain that since there are 1,000 milliliters in one liter, we divide the number of milliliters by 1,000 to change to liters.

---

m	dm	cm	mm

2.75 m = 275 cm
shift 2 places right

Write the missing numbers.

1. 185 cm = ▨ m 1.85

2. 67 mm = ▨ cm 6.7

3. 3,000 m = ▨ km 3

4. 0.9 cm = ▨ mm 9

Perimeter is the distance around a figure.

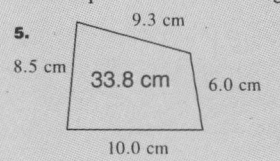

$P = 3 + 7 + 8 = 18$
$P = 18$ cm

Find the perimeter of each figure.

5. 8.5 cm, 9.3 cm, 6.0 cm, 10.0 cm 33.8 cm

6. 82 cm, 14 cm, 27 cm

7. A triangle with sides 2.3 mm, 6.9 mm, and 1.6 mm 10.8 mm

8. A parallelogram with sides 2.7 cm, 6.8 cm, 2.7 cm, and 6.8 cm 19 cm

---

Area formulas:
Rectangle: $A = lw$
Parallelogram: $A = bh$
Triangle: $A = \frac{1}{2}bh$
Trapezoid: $A = \frac{1}{2}h(b_1 + b_2)$

Find the area of each figure.

9. $h = 10$ cm, $b = 19$ cm 95 cm²

10. $b_2 = 8$ cm, $h = 6$ cm, $b_1 = 12$ cm 60 cm²

11. A rectangle with length 8.5 cm and width 2.4 cm 20.4 cm²

12. A parallelogram with base 16 m and height 7 m 112 m²

Volume of a
rectangular prism: $V = lwh$
Volume of a prism: $V = Bh$

Find the volume of each prism.

13. 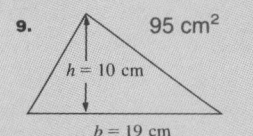 $h = 12$ cm, $B = 25$ cm² 300 cm³

14. 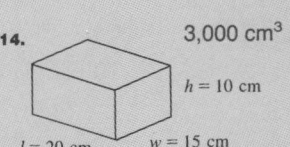 $h = 10$ cm, $l = 20$ cm, $w = 15$ cm 3,000 cm³

1,000 mL = 1 L

1 cm³ has a capacity of 1 mL.

Write the capacity in liters.

15. 1,750 mL 1.750 L

16. 3,200 cm³ 3.2 L

Just for Teachers

Practical Applications of "Pure" Mathematics

"Pure" mathematics is a kind of art. To the layperson, it can appear as representational as a circle or a cube, or as abstract as $\sqrt{-1}$. "Pure" mathematics has invariably satisfied the practical needs of civilization by providing solutions to problems in astronomy and geography, construction and engineering, warfare and navigation, to name only a few. Alexandrians applied measurement to classic Greek theorems to devise star charts and lines of latitude and longitude useful to navigators. They also discovered the laws of pulleys, water displacement, and center of gravity, fundamental to the coining of money, the engineering of bridges, and the design of skyscrapers. Perhaps the most famous Greek abstraction of all, the Pythagorean right-triangle theorem (actually discovered centuries earlier by the Babylonians and independently proved by the Chinese at about the same time as Pythagoras), has been used by countless builders to ensure perfect rectangularity of rooms.

ENRICHMENT

Measurement

Archimedes (287–212 B.C.) discovered the principle that an object floating on water displaces a weight of water equal to the weight of the floating object.

Here is a way you can repeat the experiment for the discovery made by Archimedes.

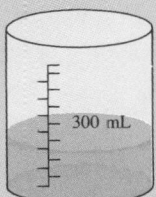

300 mL

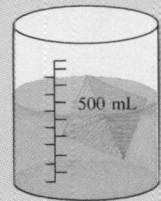

500 mL

Put water in a metric container level to some mark.

Put in an object that floats in the water.

Find the amount of water displaced.

$$\begin{array}{r} 500 \text{ mL} \\ - 300 \text{ mL} \\ \hline 200 \text{ mL} \end{array}$$

200 mL of water has a weight of 200 g. The weight of the floating object is 200 g.

What is the weight of each floating object?
The amount of water in each container at the start was 300 mL.

1.
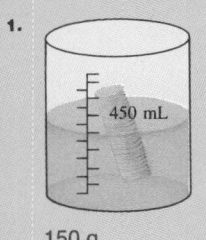
450 mL

150 g

2.
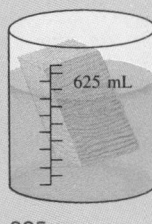
625 mL

325 g

3.
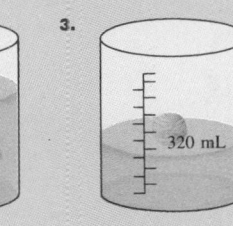
320 mL

20 g

4.
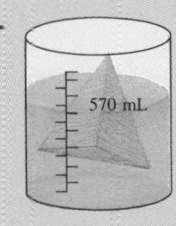
570 mL

270 g   **271**

Using Page 271

This page is intended for those students who successfully completed the Chapter/Review Test on page 269. You may wish to assign this page as independent work while you use Another Look exercises to reteach the basic concepts and skills of the chapter. Or, you may decide that all students would benefit from exposure to this Enrichment activity.

Lesson Development If materials are available, perform a demonstration similar to the one suggested on the page. After the weight of the floating object has been determined by Archimedes' method, check the result by finding the mass using a scale.

Exercises 1–4 Have students work the exercises independently. If time permits, allow students to find weights of some floating objects using the calibrated container of water.

Throughout the Dark Ages, the Middle Ages, and the Renaissance, "pure" abstractions found their way into practical life. Mathematics rapidly grew, adding the branches of calculus and number theory. Regardless of how abstract the concepts were, they had practical applications in everyday life. For instance, French mathematician Sophie Germain used the calculus of variations to solve a problem relating to the physics of a vibrating elastic surface. Her resulting fourth-order partial differential equation is an abstract and cryptic mathematical sentence. The calculus of variations, nevertheless, could be appreciated by anyone faced with the problem of shoveling snow between various points in a yard, because it can be used to determine the minimum amount of necessary work.

Lesson Focus To read and interpret computer programs that contain IF ...THEN statements

Ideas for Getting Started

Display this flowchart on the chalkboard.

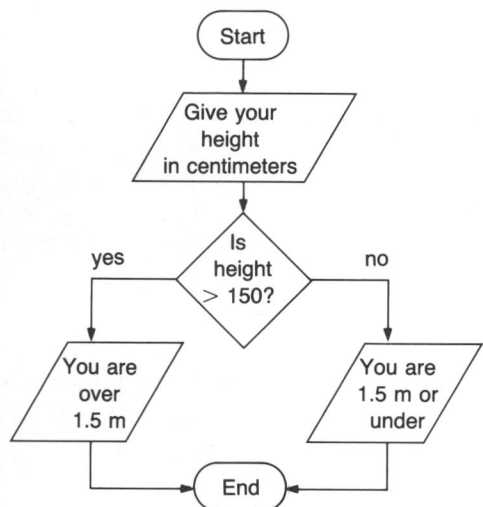

Explain that the diamond in the flowchart is used to indicate a decision point in the program. Work through the flowchart with students, using a variety of input values. Emphasize that the decision box shows two paths or branches that we can take, depending on the answer to the question.

Using Page 272

Lesson Development Have students read the material at the top of the page and study the flowchart. Discuss the relationship between the flowchart and the program written to carry out the idea in the chart. For example, the first parallelogram corresponds to lines 10 and 20 in the program. Make certain that students understand how the IF...THEN statement affects the direction of flow through the program. Explain that when the "IF part" is true, the "THEN part" follows. When the "IF part" is false, the computer drops down to the next statement ignoring the "THEN part."

Point out that the GOTO statement in line 60 also affects the flow of the program. Whenever a GOTO statement is encountered, the computer jumps to the specified line number.

Have students work through the program trying a variety of input values.

Computer Decisions

A computer can be given a program so that it can make a **decision** about INPUT data.

This program instructs the computer to make a decision about the voting age of a person.

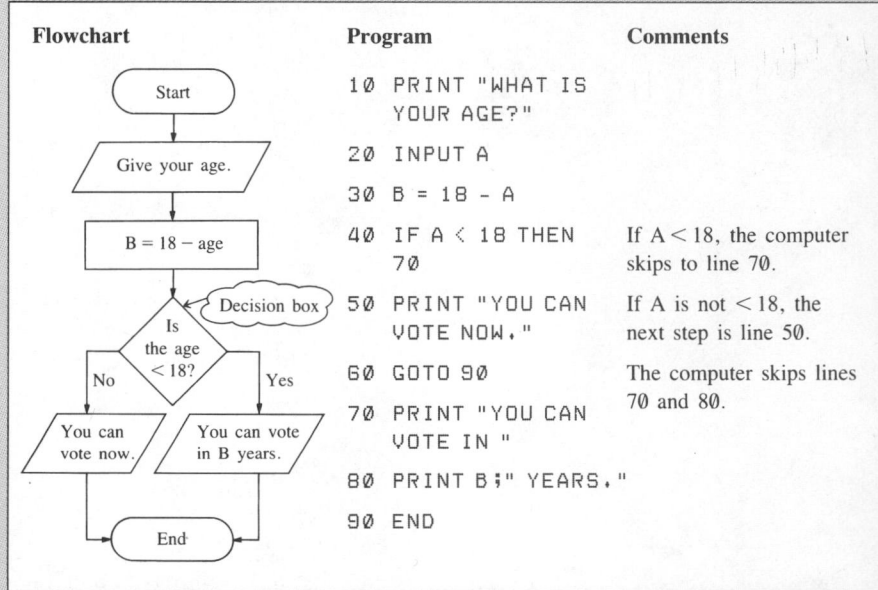

Compare each RUN of the program below.

```
RUN
WHAT IS YOUR AGE?
?11   INPUT: Age = 11
YOU CAN VOTE IN
7 YEARS.
```

```
RUN
WHAT IS YOUR AGE?
?23   INPUT: Age = 23
YOU CAN VOTE NOW.
```

What would a RUN of this program be if you used your own age as INPUT A?

272

Technology for Teachers

Computers are usually thought of as very complex mechanisms. Actually, these machines understand only two states which make up machine language. This two-state system is called the *binary system*. It uses a base of two and the two digits, 0 and 1. These digits are called *bits* for *b*inary dig*its*. Within the computer, each bit is represented by two different voltages, usually called "high" (1) and "low" (0).

The bit is the basic unit for storing data in the internal memory of a computer. Bits by themselves cannot store all the numbers, letters, and special characters used by the computer, so they are usually organized in groups of eight, called *bytes*. Each byte of information occupies one memory location.

The American Standard Code for Information Interchange is one of the most commonly used codes. When a key on the ASCII keyboard is pressed, a seven-bit

See teaching notes for answers to exercises 1–4.
Write the RUN for each program. Use the given INPUT numbers.

1.
```
10    PRINT "DOLLARS IN YOUR
      ACCOUNT?"
20    INPUT A
30    PRINT "AMOUNT TO
      WITHDRAW?"
40    INPUT B
50    C = A - B
60    IF A < B THEN 90
70    PRINT "YOUR BALANCE IS
      $";C
80    GOTO 100
90    PRINT "YOU DON'T HAVE
      ENOUGH MONEY."
100   END
```
A INPUT A = $549.12
   INPUT B = $277.95
B INPUT A = $549.12
   INPUT B = $549.15

2.
```
10  PRINT "GUESS A NUMBER
    < 20."
20    INPUT A
30    N = 12
40    IF A = N THEN 100
50    IF A < N THEN 80
60    PRINT "TOO LARGE!"
70    GOTO 10
80    PRINT "TOO SMALL!"
90    GOTO 10
100   PRINT "THAT'S IT!"
110   END
```
A INPUT A = 7
B INPUT A = 15
C INPUT A = 12

3.
```
10    PRINT "WHAT NUMBER
      TIMES"
20    PRINT "8 EQUALS 296?"
30    INPUT A
40    B = 296/8
50    IF A = B THEN 80
60    PRINT "TRY AGAIN."
70    GOTO 10
80    PRINT "THAT'S RIGHT!"
90    END
```
A INPUT A = 32
B INPUT A = 37

4.
```
10    PRINT "SOLVE THE
      EQUATION."
20    PRINT "7N = 112."
30    PRINT "N = ?"
40    INPUT A
50    N = 112/7
60    IF A = N THEN 90
70    PRINT "TRY AGAIN."
80    GOTO 20
90    PRINT "RIGHT! N = ";A
100   END
```
A INPUT A = 13
B INPUT A = 16

5. Write a program similar to the one in exercise 4. Choose your own equation. Give a RUN of your program.

6. Write a computer program which uses an IF . . . THEN statement and GOTO commands. Give a RUN of your program.

273

Using Page 273

Exercises 1–5 You may wish to have students enter these programs on a computer. In exercise 1, caution students not to type the dollar sign when they enter the INPUT numbers.

1.
```
DOLLARS IN YOUR ACCOUNT?
?549.12
AMOUNT TO WITHDRAW?
?277.95
YOUR BALANCE IS $271.17

DOLLARS IN YOUR ACCOUNT?
?549.12
AMOUNT TO WITHDRAW?
?549.15
YOU DON'T HAVE ENOUGH MONEY.
```

2.
```
GUESS A NUMBER < 20.
?7
TOO SMALL!
GUESS A NUMBER < 20.
?15
TOO LARGE!
GUESS A NUMBER < 20.
?12
THAT'S IT!
```

3.
```
WHAT NUMBER TIMES
8 EQUALS 296?
?32
TRY AGAIN.
WHAT NUMBER TIMES
8 EQUALS 296?
?37
THAT'S RIGHT!
```

4.
```
SOLVE THE EQUATION.
7N = 112
N = ?
?13
TRY AGAIN.
7N = 112
N = ?
?16
RIGHT! N = 16
```

character is sent to the computer, as well as a signal that indicates a key has been pressed. Each character in ASCII has a unique seven-bit code. Some examples are shown below.

Character	ASCII Code
A	1000001
8	0111000
?	0111111

The size of a computer's memory, or capacity of storage, is expressed in terms of the letter K. Normally, K means 1,000 but in computer work it means 2^{10} or 1,024. A kilobyte is K bytes, so a computer with 32K memory can hold $32 \times 1,024 = 32,768$ bytes.

Using Page 274

The exercises on the page provide practice for maintaining cumulative skills. The emphasis in this Cumulative Review is on number relationships (Chapter 7) and multiplication and division of fractions (Chapter 9).

Item Analysis The table below correlates the Cumulative Review items with objectives and with the student book pages on which the concepts or skills were taught.

Items	Objectives	Related Text Pages
1	7.1	164–171
2–3	7.2	172–175
4–6	7.4	178–181
7–8	9.1	224–230
9	9.2	231
10	9.3	232–235
11–12	9.4	238–241
13	7.5	182–185
14	9.5	236–237

CUMULATIVE REVIEW

1. What is the prime factorization of 144?

(A) $2^4 \cdot 3^2$ B $2^2 \cdot 6^2$
C $2^3 \cdot 3^2$ D not given

2. What is the GCF of 25 and 150?

A 5 B 10
(C) 25 D not given

3. What is the LCM of 11 and 15?

A 11 (B) 165
C 55 D not given

Solve each equation.

4. $5a = 75$

A $a = 20$ B $a = 80$
C $a = 375$ (D) not given

5. $\frac{h}{9} = 54$

A $h = 6$ B $h = 63$
(C) $h = 486$ D not given

6. $z - 17 = 62$

A $z = 36$ (B) $z = 79$
C $z = 45$ D not given

Multiply.

7. $\frac{3}{8} \times \frac{4}{5}$

(A) $\frac{3}{10}$ B $1\frac{1}{2}$
C $\frac{12}{35}$ D not given

8. $6\frac{1}{8} \times 10$

A $\frac{3}{40}$ (B) $61\frac{1}{4}$
C 60 D not given

9. Solve.

$n \times 2\frac{2}{3} = 1$

(A) $n = \frac{3}{8}$ B $n = \frac{7}{2}$
C $n = \frac{2}{7}$ D not given

10. Find the quotient.

$\frac{5}{6} \div \frac{3}{8}$

A 3 (B) $2\frac{2}{9}$
C $2\frac{1}{9}$ D not given

11. What is the lowest-terms fraction for 0.56?

(A) $\frac{14}{25}$ B $\frac{28}{50}$
C $\frac{7}{5}$ D not given

12. What is the decimal for $\frac{17}{20}$?

(A) 0.85 B 1.176
C 11.76 D not given

13. The sum of a certain number and 27 is 95. What is the number?

A 122 B 70
C 40 (D) not given

14. A small movie theater can seat 200 people. Only 0.35 of the theater was filled. What fraction of the theater was filled?

(A) $\frac{7}{20}$ B $\frac{12}{25}$
C $\frac{1}{2}$ D not given

Objectives

11.1 Write a ratio as a fraction in lowest terms and use cross products to determine if two ratios are equal.

11.2 Write and solve proportions.

11.3 Use proportions to find the length of a side given a pair of similar figures.

11.4 Solve word problems using the 5-Point Checklist and cumulative computational skills.

Summary

The concepts of ratio and proportion are introduced in this chapter. Students also learn to solve a proportion for an unknown quantity using the method of cross products. After learning the skill of solving a simple proportion, students use the skill in problems involving practical applications, such as scale drawings. The topics presented in this chapter rely on previously taught skills and concepts, particularly those concerning fractions and equations.

Mathematical Background

Ratio A ratio is a way of comparing two numbers. The ratio of the dark circles to the light circles shown below is 3 to 8.

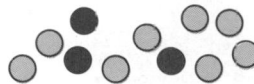

The first lesson in this chapter presents three notations for ratio: 3 to 8, 3:8, $\frac{3}{8}$.

A rate is a special form of ratio which compares two unlike units. Some examples of rate are 25 kilograms for $10, 3 tickets for $5, and 3 eggs for every 2 persons. Sometimes rates are stated as a quantity per unit. For example, 120 kilometers in 2 hours is a rate that could be expressed as $\frac{60 \text{ km}}{1 \text{ h}}$ or 60 km/h.

A ratio is often used to compare the relative sizes of two sets. The numbers of X's to O's below can be stated in two ways: 4 to 8 or 1 to 2. The ratio in simplest form is written 1 to 2 or $\frac{1}{2}$. Notice the similarity between expressing a ratio in simplest form and a fraction in lowest terms.

X	X	X	X
OO	OO	OO	OO

Proportions A proportion is a statement that two ratios are equal. The cross products of equal ratios are equal as shown below.

$$\frac{a}{b} = \frac{c}{d} \qquad a \times d = b \times c$$

The idea of cross products can be used to find an unknown in a proportion.

$$\frac{3}{5} = \frac{9}{n}$$

$$3 \times n = 5 \times 9$$

$$n = 15$$

The ability to solve proportions has a wide range of applications and should be considered a key part of the chapter.

One such application found in this chapter involves finding missing lengths in similar triangles. Two triangles are similar if their vertices can be matched so that the ratios of the lengths of corresponding sides are equal and the matching angles are congruent. We can think of triangles being similar when they have the same shape, but not necessarily the same size. Since the sides of similar triangles are proportional, the length of a missing side can be found by solving a proportion.

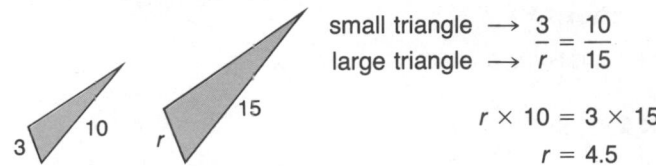

small triangle $\longrightarrow$ $\dfrac{3}{r} = \dfrac{10}{15}$
large triangle $\longrightarrow$

$$r \times 10 = 3 \times 15$$
$$r = 4.5$$

Problem Solving The problem solving in this chapter focuses on problems that can be solved using proportions. The first problem-solving lesson on pages 282 and 283 features the use of the 5-Point Checklist which is emphasized throughout this text for helping students learn key aspects of the problem-solving process. In this lesson, problems involve solving proportions as well as using operations presented in previous chapters. On page 286, the lesson concerns using scales in maps to determine distances. The third problem-solving lesson on page 287 shows students how to estimate answers to work problems involving proportions. In the last problem-solving lesson of the chapter on page 288, students use the strategies taught in previous chapters.

Vocabulary

ratio	proportion	similar triangles
rate	cross products	scale drawing

Teaching Tips

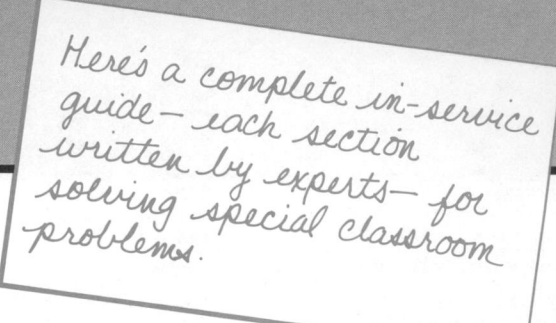
Here's a complete in-service guide—each section written by experts—for solving special classroom problems.

Error Analysis

This chapter introduces the very important concepts of ratio and proportion. The knowledge of these concepts and related skills are basic for the study of advanced mathematics and they have a variety of practical applications. The content of this chapter contains material that is often misunderstood. This misunderstanding is reflected in various error patterns. Some error patterns are given below.

Error Pattern 1

"Write each ratio as a fraction in lowest terms."

8 to 9 $\quad \frac{9}{8}$ $\qquad$ 5 to 12 $\quad \frac{5}{12}$ $\qquad$ 3 out of 4 $\quad \frac{4}{3}$

Diagnosis The student has written fractions with no regard to the order of comparison. Sometimes the fraction reflects the ratio, but in other cases the numerator and denominator are reversed.

Remediation Review the three ways to write a ratio.

8 to 9 $\qquad$ 8:9 $\qquad$ $\frac{8}{9}$

Explain that the numbers are compared in a certain order. Stress that when writing a fraction for a ratio, the first number is always the numerator.

Error Pattern 2

$$\frac{5}{7} = \frac{x}{35}$$
$$5\,x = 7 \cdot 35$$
$$\frac{5}{5}x = \frac{245}{5}$$
$$x = 49$$

$$\frac{1}{3} = \frac{5}{x}$$
$$\frac{5}{3} = \frac{3x}{3}$$
$$\frac{5}{3} = x$$

Diagnosis The student attempted to solve the proportion but began incorrectly. Instead of finding the cross products, the student multiplied numerator times numerator and denominator times denominator.

Remediation Begin with sets of objects or drawings to show two equal ratios. For example, the diagram below shows 3 circles to 6 squares or 1 circle for 2 squares.

Explain that since the ratios are equal we can write the proportion, $\frac{3}{6} = \frac{1}{2}$. Next show that the cross products are equal and that the product of the numerators is not equal to the product of the denominators.

 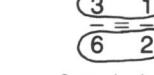

$3 \times 2 = 6 \times 1$ $\qquad$ $3 \times 1 \neq 6 \times 2$

Then work through an example showing how to solve a proportion. Emphasize that the first step is to find the cross products.

Error Pattern 3

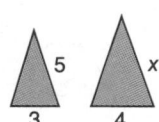 $\qquad \frac{3}{4} = \frac{x}{5}$ $\qquad$ 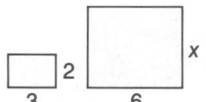 $\qquad \frac{2}{3} = \frac{6}{x}$

Diagnosis The student used the concept of ratio and proportion with similar figures. But in doing this, the student did not write ratios reflecting the same comparison.

Remediation Review how a proportion is used in solving problems with similar figures. Show the following example.

 $\qquad\qquad$

short side → $\dfrac{2}{3}$ $=$ $\dfrac{x}{4}$ ← short side
long side → $\quad$ ← long side

Emphasize that the ratios must compare the same thing.

Problem Solving

Teaching Students to Formulate Problems

The most important element in improving students' problem-solving performance is solving and discussing many problems. However, improving performance in problem solving involves more than simply doing a task over and over again. Formulating problems, a valuable component in an elementary school problem-solving program, focuses the student's attention on particular parts of the problem-solving process in isolation from the solution itself. Some of the skills needed in formulating problems are:

- asking a question that makes sense,
- incorporating all relevant data in a story,
- incorporating action in a story appropriate for the operation(s) needed to find a solution.

The following two examples are situations in which students are asked to formulate a problem.

"Make up a story you could solve using the equation 45 + 26 = ?"

"Make up a story that this picture would help you to solve."

Numerous opportunities to formulate problems can facilitate the improvement of a student's problem-solving performance. Many such opportunities are included in this program. These experiences require little teaching time, provide success experiences for most students, and are easy to generate. They should be given to students on a regular basis. For example, three days each week, the Quick Review in the Teacher's Edition could be followed by a "formulating-a-problem" activity. Providing frequent experiences in formulating problems can be a valuable addition to a problem-solving program.

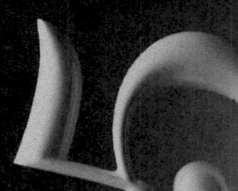

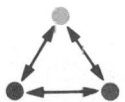 **Special Education**

The topics discussed in this chapter provide a basis for work with percent in Chapter 12 and for future applications in geometry and other school subjects. The understanding of ratios and proportion, combined with the ability to solve a proportion when three of the numbers involved are known, comprises the critical content of the chapter.

Visualizing the Ratio Concept

One method to help students visualize the ratio concept is to use paper folding. Have students fold a piece of paper in half from top to bottom. Have them shade in one half of the page. The ratio of shaded regions to the number of total regions is 1 to 2. Repeated foldings give rise to ratios such as 2 to 4, 4 to 8, and 8 to 16. The doubling pattern can be investigated in order to see the role of multiplying both the number of shaded regions by 2 and the number of total regions by 2 with each fold.

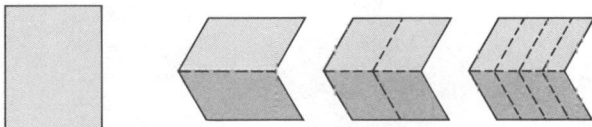

Using Color Cues

Chips can be used to show the equivalence of various ratios. Consider the ratio of 6 to 8 shown below. The white chips show the 8 parts, and the 6 red chips on top of the white chips indicate that 6 of the 8 have been covered with another chip. The ratio of red chips to white chips can be written as 6 to 8. The model can also be split into groups of two. In this case the white chips in three of the four groups have been covered with red chips, or the ratio of red chips to white chips can be written as 3 to 4.

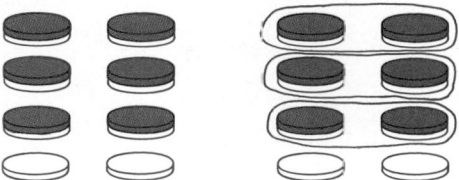

Creating the Questions to Ask in Ratio Situations

In working with ratios, students need to learn which questions to consider, as well as the sequence of those questions, in order to adequately prepare for percent concepts and other ratio situations. The major ideas that need to be mastered are the idea of the comparison groups (part and whole) and the direction of the comparison. When faced with a comparison setting, the student must learn to ask these questions.

"What is being compared?"
"What is the order of the comparison?"
"What are the numbers in the first group and what are the numbers for the second group?"

The student should then be ready to write the ratio.

Making Scale Drawings

Another activity for the chapter is to have students make their own scale drawings after completing the material covered on page 286. The project of creating a scale drawing of the room can make the topic of scale and ratio more realistic for special-needs students. This activity provides a review of all of the major concepts in the chapter, as well as providing transfer skills to other areas of the junior high curriculum.

 **Subject Integration**

Subject matter related to other areas of the curriculum has been integrated into the following lessons. This provides an opportunity to highlight the interaction between mathematics and other subjects.

History Benjamin Banneker, page 275; golden ratio, page 291
Science Nature hike, pages 276–277
Consumer Awareness Grocery store, pages 278–279
Industrial Arts Machines, pages 280–281
Fine Arts Tapes and records, pages 282–283
Language Arts Photographs in books, pages 284–285
Social Studies Map distance, page 286

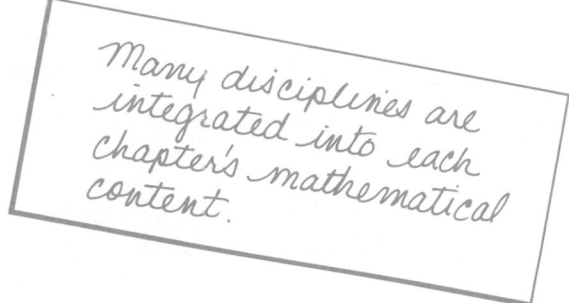

Many disciplines are integrated into each chapter's mathematical content.

Management Guide

Teaching Chapter 11				Meeting Individual Needs					
Objectives	Chapter Content	Pages	TRB Test Items	Lesson Assignments			Follow Up		
				Minimum	Average	Extended	Reteaching	Enrichment	Practice
	Chapter Opener	275							
11.1 Write a ratio as a fraction in lowest terms and use cross products to determine if two ratios are equal.	Ratio	276–277	1–20	1–27	1–29	1–29, TM	SE6 Ch 11		PS 104
	Equal Ratios	278–279		1–33, SK	1–35, SK	1–33 odd, 34–36, SK	SE6 Ch 11 RS 81	ES 81	MP 434 PS 105
11.2 Write and solve proportions.	Solving Proportions	280–281	21–25	1–12	1–14, TM	1–14, TM	SE6 Ch 11 RS 82	ES 82	MP 434 PS 106
11.3 Use proportions to find the length of a side given a pair of similar figures.	Similar Figures	284–285	26–29	1–7, SK	1–8, SK	1–8, SK	SE6 Ch 11 RS 84	ES 84	PS 108
11.4 Solve word problems using the 5-Point Checklist and cumulative computational skills.	Problem Solving: Using the 5-Point Checklist	282–283	30–33	1–7, 11	1–11	1–12	RS 83	ES 83	PS 107
	Problem Solving: Using Data from a Map	286		1–5	1–7	1–7			
	Problem Solving: Using Estimation	287		1–5	1–6	1–7	RS 85	ES 85	PS 109
	Problem Solving: Using the Strategies	288							
	Chapter Review/Test	289							
	Another Look/ Enrichment	290–291							
	Cumulative Review	292							

SE6 Student Edition, Book 6
RS Reteaching Supplement
ES Enrichment Supplement
PS Practice Supplement
MP More Practice
TM Think Math
SK Skillkeeper
TRB Teacher's Resource Book

Masters for use

. . . before Chapter 11

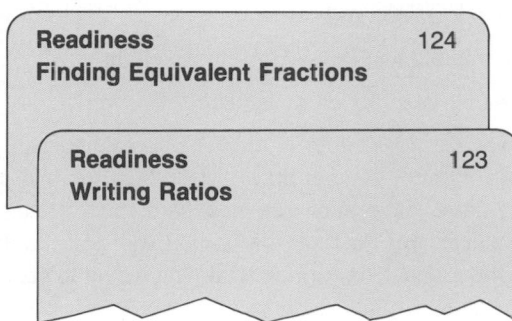

| Readiness Finding Equivalent Fractions | 124 |
| Readiness Writing Ratios | 123 |

. . . during Chapter 11

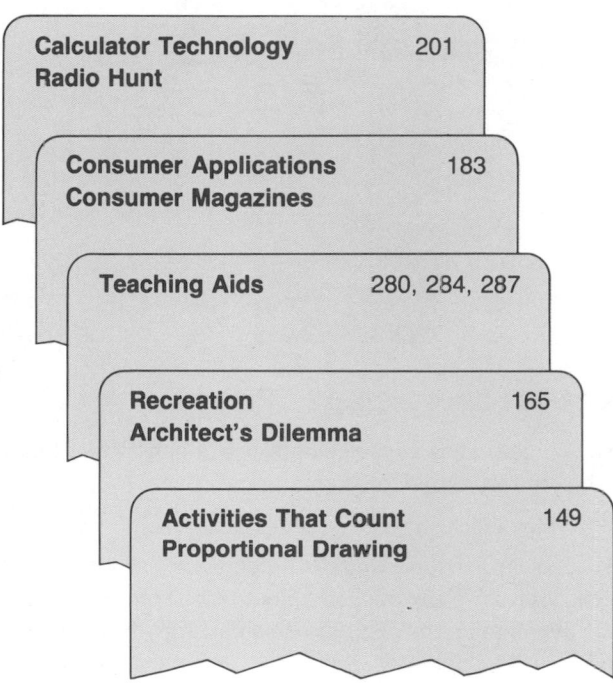

Calculator Technology Radio Hunt	201
Consumer Applications Consumer Magazines	183
Teaching Aids	280, 284, 287
Recreation Architect's Dilemma	165
Activities That Count Proportional Drawing	149

. . . after Chapter 11

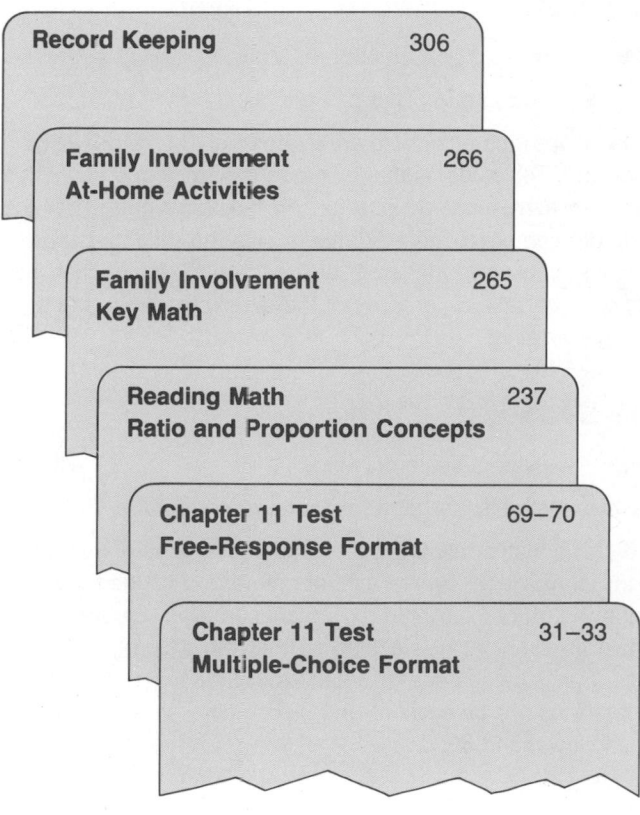

Record Keeping	306
Family Involvement At-Home Activities	266
Family Involvement Key Math	265
Reading Math Ratio and Proportion Concepts	237
Chapter 11 Test Free-Response Format	69–70
Chapter 11 Test Multiple-Choice Format	31–33

Supplements

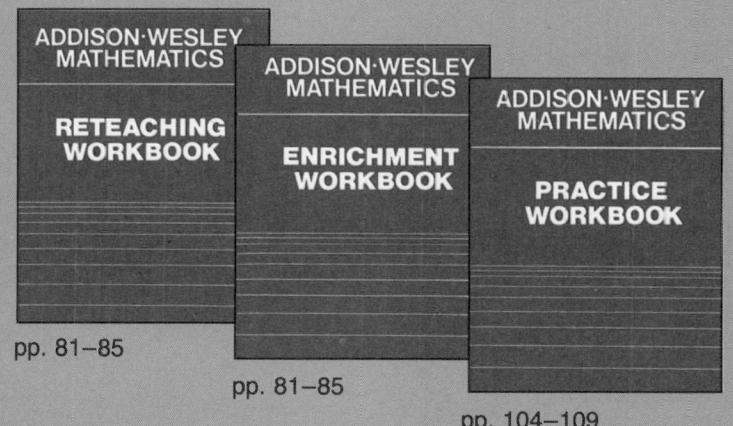

ADDISON-WESLEY MATHEMATICS
RETEACHING WORKBOOK
pp. 81–85

ADDISON-WESLEY MATHEMATICS
ENRICHMENT WORKBOOK
pp. 81–85

ADDISON-WESLEY MATHEMATICS
PRACTICE WORKBOOK
pp. 104–109

Other Addison-Wesley Resources

Books and Kits

The Mad Minute pp. 171–175
General Mathematics: Making Practice Fun 50, 51A, 51 B, 52, 53

Activities That Count are designed for use throughout this chapter and subsequent chapters. Before beginning Chapter 11 you may wish to review these activities and select the ones you consider appropriate for your class.

Proportional Drawing   Math Lab

Purpose To make a proportional drawing

Materials Drawing grid (TRB p. 149)

Activity Have students make an enlargement of the drawing on the small grid. Tell students that a line on the small grid should be drawn in the corresponding position on the large grid. After the drawings are complete, ask students to give the ratio of the width of the small drawing to the width of the large drawing. Then ask them to give the ratio of the area of the small drawing to the area of the large drawing.

Scale Drawing   Project

Purpose To make a scale drawing

Materials Meterstick or tape measure, metric ruler

Activity Have students find the actual dimensions of the classroom, the playground, or the school cafeteria and then make a scale drawing of the floor plan for the chosen area. Students may need help in planning their scales so that the drawing will fit on the paper that is being used. Have them include in the drawing as many details as are practical for the given scale—such as chairs, tables, windows, and doors.

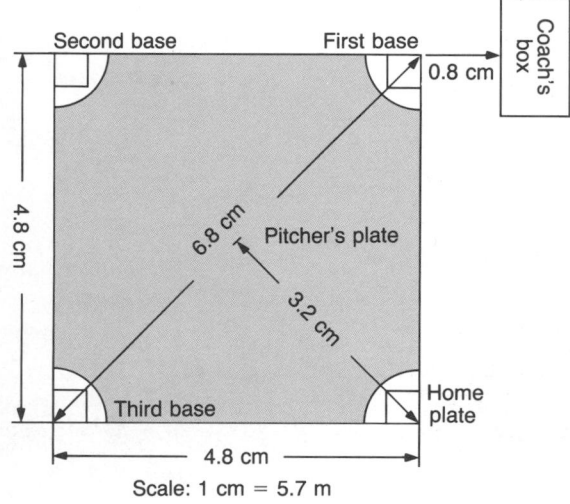

Build a Proportion   Game

Purpose To determine if two ratios form a proportion

Materials Three sets of index cards labeled 1 through 10

Activity Each player is dealt four cards. The remaining cards are placed in a pile. In turn, players draw a card from the pile or the top discarded card. After each draw, a card must be discarded. The first player who forms a proportion with four cards scores a point for the round. The winner is the first player to score 5 points.

Indirect Measurement   Project

Purpose To use ratios of matching sides of similar triangles to solve indirect measurement problems

Materials Meterstick

Activity Explain to students how proportions can be used to find the height of objects by measurement of their shadows. At the same time any day, the ratios of the heights of any two objects to their shadows are equal.

Let students go outside on a sunny day and set up ratio problems. Have them measure their shadow and the shadow of an object such as a tree, a flag pole, or the school building. Then have them write a proportion and find the unknown height.

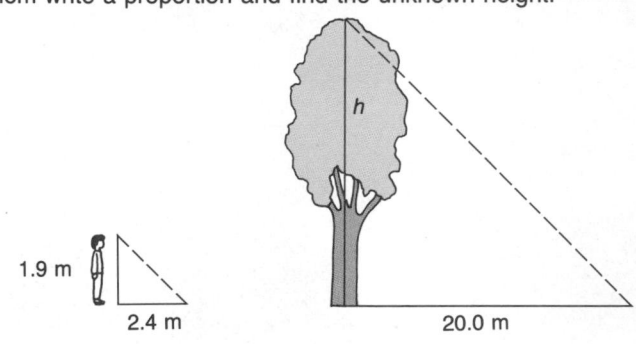

1.9 m   2.4 m   20.0 m h

$$\frac{1.9}{2.4} = \frac{h}{20.0}$$

11

Ratio and Proportion

Benjamin Banneker was born in 1731 in Maryland. He attended school until he was 15 years old. Once he was out of school, he had to work hard on a farm. He continued to study, however, and mathematics became his greatest interest.

Through a variety of accomplishments, Benjamin Banneker became well-known for his brilliant mind. By studying the series of connected gear wheels in a tiny watch, he learned the ratio of the number of teeth on each gear wheel to the circumference of the gear wheels. He used the ratios to make larger gear wheels and built the first clock made entirely of American parts. Banneker observed nature and published almanacs which became popular and useful throughout America. Thomas Jefferson appointed Banneker to a commission to plan the city of Washington, D.C.

Introducing the Chapter

Discussion Have students read the article about Benjamin Banneker and examine the accompanying pictures. Encourage discussion and comment. This is an opportunity for students to generate questions based on the data in the article. As you teach the chapter, you may wish to refer back to this page and discuss the questions below.

Follow-Up Questions

After Page 279 The spur gear is designed so that the teeth of one gear fit into the teeth of another. When the first gear turns, the second gear turns with it. The gear ratio can be found either from the number of turns or from the number of teeth of the gears. A large gear has 30 teeth and the small gear has 12 teeth. Write the gear ratio as a fraction in lowest terms. ($\frac{30}{12} = \frac{5}{2}$)

After Page 283 The ratio of the large gear teeth to the small gear teeth is the same as the ratio of the small gear turns to the large gear turns. While a large gear makes 1 complete turn, a small gear makes 3 complete turns. The small gear has 9 teeth. Find the number of teeth in the large gear. ($\frac{3}{1} = \frac{x}{9}$, x = 27)

Lesson Focus To write a ratio for a comparison or rate

Ideas for Getting Started

Display each of the following comparisons on the chalkboard and ask the corresponding questions.

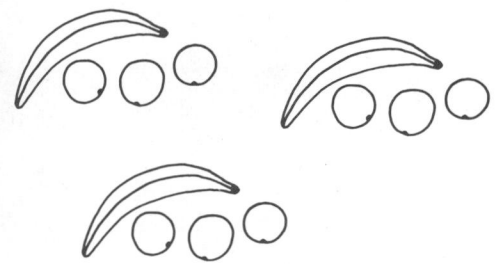

"How many oranges are there for every banana?" (3)

"3 out of 5 flowers are daisies. How many out of 5 flowers are tulips?" (2)

Discuss with students several situations involving ratios that are readily apparent in the classroom, for example, the number of students compared to the number of desks. Then ask students to suggest comparisons of other classroom objects.

Using Page 276

Lesson Development Have students read the material at the top of the page. Ask them to compare the number of sparrow hawks to the number of birds in all. Introduce the term *ratio*. Have students examine the three ways to write a ratio. Notice with students that one of the ways to write a ratio is as a fraction.

Explain that a *rate* is a ratio which compares different kinds of units. Discuss with students the examples that show rates written as ratios. Point out that $\frac{6 \text{ km}}{3 \text{ h}}$ can be reduced to $\frac{2 \text{ km}}{1 \text{ h}}$, and written as 2 km/h.

Ratio

On a nature hike, species of birds were identified. There were 2 sparrow hawks, 1 barn owl, and 6 gray partridges. The students observed 9 birds in all.

We can use a **ratio** to compare the numbers.

2 out of 9 birds were sparrow hawks.

2 to 9, 2:9, or $\frac{2}{9}$ (Read: "2 to 9")

A **rate** is a ratio which compares different kinds of units.

A field guidebook of American birds costs $8.

Ratio: $\frac{\text{Dollars} \rightarrow}{\text{Books} \rightarrow}$ $\frac{\$8}{1}$ or $8 per guide

It took 3 hours to walk 6 km.

Ratio: $\frac{\text{Km} \rightarrow}{\text{Hours} \rightarrow}$ $\frac{6}{3}$ or 2 km/h

Sparrow hawk

Barn owl

Gray partridge

Warm Up

Write each ratio as a fraction.

1. 3 to 8 $\frac{3}{8}$
2. 1:7 $\frac{1}{7}$
3. 4 out of 5 $\frac{4}{5}$
4. 7 to 10 $\frac{7}{10}$
5. 40 m to 5 s $\frac{40 \text{ m}}{5 \text{ s}}$ or 8 m/s
6. $24 in 3 h $\frac{\$24}{3\text{h}}$ or $8/h
7. 100 L in 4 min $\frac{100 \text{ L}}{4 \text{ min}}$ or 25 L/min
8. $6 for 2 L $\frac{\$6}{2\text{ L}}$ or $3/L

276

Follow Up

Reteaching

Have students find the following ratios and express them in three ways.

1. The number of people in the room who wear glasses to the total number of people in the room.
2. The number of windows in the room to the number of doors in the room.
3. The number of letters in your first name to the number of letters in your last name.
4. The number of chairs in the room to the number of desks in the room.

Enrichment

Display a calendar for the current month and have students list as many ratios involving the data from the calendar as they can. Some possibilities are:

- Number of Mondays to number of days in the month.
- Number of weekdays to number of days in the month.
- Number of 1-digit dates to number of 2-digit dates.
- Number of odd-number dates to number of even-number dates.
- Number of prime-number dates to number of nonprime-number dates.

Assignment Guide			
	Minimum	Average	Extended
page 277	1-27	1-29	1-29, TM

Write each ratio as a fraction.

1. 8 to 9 $\frac{8}{9}$　　**2.** 5:11 $\frac{5}{11}$　　**3.** 3 out of 4 $\frac{3}{4}$　　**4.** 9 to 7 $\frac{9}{7}$

5. 5 to 12 $\frac{5}{12}$　　**6.** 4 out of 12 $\frac{4}{12}$　　**7.** 16:6 $\frac{16}{6}$　　**8.** 2 out of 6 $\frac{2}{6}$

9. 4 out of 7 $\frac{4}{7}$　　**10.** 1.2 to 4.3 $\frac{1.2}{4.3}$　　**11.** 0.76 to 1.34 $\frac{0.76}{1.34}$　　**12.** 1 out of 8 $\frac{1}{8}$

13. 10 to 1 $\frac{10}{1}$　　**14.** 2.5 to 7 $\frac{2.5}{7}$　　**15.** 9:100 $\frac{9}{100}$　　**16.** 1:1,000 $\frac{1}{1,000}$

Write each rate as a fraction.

17. 24 m in 6 s $\frac{24\text{ m}}{6\text{ s}}$ or 4 m/s

18. \$8.00 for 50 L $\frac{\$8.00}{50\text{ L}}$ or \$0.16/L

19. 8 cups in 2 L $\frac{8\text{ c}}{2\text{ L}}$ or 4 c/L

20. 66 words per min $\frac{66\text{ words}}{1\text{ min}}$ or 66 words/min

21. 85 km in 1 h $\frac{85\text{ km}}{1\text{ h}}$ or 85 km/h

22. 3 tickets for \$9.75 $\frac{\$9.75}{3\text{ tickets}}$ or \$3.25/ticket

23. \$225 for 4 tires $\frac{\$225}{4\text{ tires}}$ or \$56.25/tire

24. 3 c flour for 2 eggs $\frac{3\text{ c}}{2\text{ eggs}}$

25. 1,400 km in 2 h $\frac{1,400\text{ km}}{2\text{ h}}$ or 700 km/h

26. \$105 for 7 days $\frac{\$105}{7\text{ days}}$ or \$15/day

27. What is the ratio of swamp sparrows to king rails? $\frac{3}{1}$ or 3:1

28. What is the ratio of king rails to total birds identified? $\frac{1}{6}$ or 1:6

29. Tommy identified 4 American kestrels, 1 barn owl, and 12 gray partridges. What was the ratio of American kestrels to gray partridges? $\frac{4}{12}$ or $\frac{1}{3}$

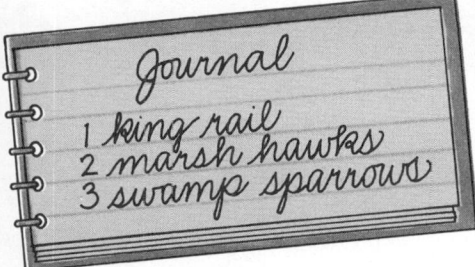

Journal
1 king rail
2 marsh hawks
3 swamp sparrows

◼ THINK MATH ◼

Estimation

John won a contest which awarded him a prize of \$1,000 a week for life. Estimate how many years it will take John to collect \$1,000,000. Then calculate the total number of years and weeks. Use 52 weeks for 1 year. about 20 years; 19 years 12 weeks

Using Page 277

Exercises 27–28 Students will need to use data from the illustration to solve these problems.

Think Math Students should first estimate the number of years. They might multiply 52 times \$1,000 to get \$52,000 per year. This could be rounded to \$50,000. By dividing \$1,000,000 by \$50,000, we arrive at the estimate of 20 years. To calculate the exact number of years, divide \$1,000,000 by \$52,000 to get 19 with a remainder of \$12,000. This would be 19 years and 12 weeks.

Ideas That Work

Math for the Gifted

Challenge students with the following problem.

Suppose that you have two containers, one that will hold 4 liters and one that will hold 9 liters. There are no markings on either container to indicate smaller quantities. How can you measure out 6 liters of water using only these two containers?

The necessary steps are these:

1) Fill the 9 L container. Fill the 4 L container from the 9 L container.

2) Dump out the water in the 4 L container. Refill it with water from the 9 L container. There is 1 L left in the 9 L container.

3) Dump out the water in the 4 L container. Pour the 1 L of water from the 9 L container into the 4 L container.

4) Fill the 9 L container. Pour enough water into the 4 L container to fill it. This is 3 L, so 6 L remain in the 9 L container.

Practice Supplement, page 104

Name			To follow text page 277

Ratio

Write each ratio as a fraction.

1. 7 to 11 $\frac{7}{11}$　　**2.** 3:8 $\frac{3}{8}$　　**3.** 5 out of 9 $\frac{5}{9}$

4. 15 to 13 $\frac{15}{13}$　　**5.** 6 to 10 $\frac{6}{10}$　　**6.** 9 out of 14 $\frac{9}{14}$

7. 13:5 $\frac{13}{5}$　　**8.** 7 out of 15 $\frac{7}{15}$　　**9.** 3 out of 7 $\frac{3}{7}$

10. 3.4 to 5.7 $\frac{3.4}{5.7}$　　**11.** 9:17 $\frac{9}{17}$　　**12.** 0.17 to 1.22 $\frac{0.17}{1.22}$

13. 5 out of 10 $\frac{5}{10}$　　**14.** 3:100 $\frac{3}{100}$　　**15.** 7:1,000 $\frac{7}{1,000}$

Write each rate as a fraction.

16. 2 for \$5 $\frac{\$5}{2}$　　**17.** 15 m in 7 s $\frac{15\text{ m}}{7\text{ s}}$

18. 80 km in 2 h $\frac{80\text{ km}}{2\text{ h}}$　　**19.** 40¢ for 3 m $\frac{40\text{ ¢}}{3\text{ m}}$

20. 200 km/h $\frac{200\text{ km}}{1\text{ h}}$　　**21.** 3 boys to 2 chairs $\frac{3\text{ boys}}{2\text{ chairs}}$

22. 4 pages in 3 min $\frac{4\text{ pages}}{3\text{ min}}$　　**23.** \$66 for 12 books $\frac{\$66}{12\text{ books}}$

24. 2 tacks for 1 paper $\frac{2\text{ tacks}}{1\text{ paper}}$　　**25.** 15 tickets for 5 people $\frac{15\text{ tickets}}{5\text{ people}}$

26. 200 m in 25 s $\frac{200\text{ m}}{25\text{ s}} = 8$ m/s　　**27.** 5 eggs in 1 nest $\frac{5\text{ eggs}}{1\text{ nest}}$

28. 17 birds in 2 trees $\frac{17\text{ birds}}{2\text{ trees}}$　　**29.** \$17 for 2 records $\frac{\$17}{2\text{ records}}$

30. 12 hits out of 20 free throws $\frac{12\text{ hits}}{20\text{ free throws}}$　　**31.** 5 km for 1 cm $\frac{5\text{ km}}{1\text{ cm}}$

32. 22 people to 6 cars $\frac{22\text{ people}}{6\text{ cars}}$　　**33.** 52 weeks in 1 year $\frac{52\text{ weeks}}{1\text{ year}}$

Ratio

Quick Review Have students find the GCF and LCM of each pair of numbers.

3,7 1;21   4,8 4;8   4,14 2;28

15,40 5;80   6,21 3;42   8,20 4;40   5,7 1;35

Lesson Focus To determine if two ratios form a proportion

Ideas for Getting Started

Display the drawing on the chalkboard and ask students to fill in the blanks for each ratio.

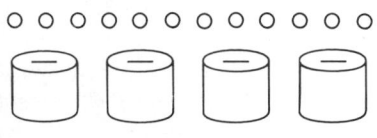

_____ coins for 4 banks

_____ coins for 1 bank

_____ coins for 2 banks

Next display the drawing below and ask students to name two ratios.

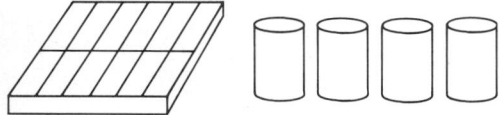

Using Page 278

Motivational Problem After students read the introductory problem, ask them these questions. "What does the problem ask us to find?" (the ratio of white eggs to brown eggs) "What data is given in the problem?" (2 cartons of white eggs, 2 cartons of brown eggs, 12 eggs per carton) Point out that the ratio can be written as a fraction.

Lesson Development Explain that the ratio of white eggs to brown eggs can be written in two ways. The ratio $\frac{24}{36}$ means that there are 24 white eggs to 36 brown eggs, while the ratio $\frac{2}{3}$ means that there are 2 cartons of white eggs to 3 cartons of brown eggs. Notice with students that $\frac{24}{36}$ written in lowest terms is $\frac{2}{3}$. Thus, $\frac{24}{36}$ and $\frac{2}{3}$ are *equal ratios.*

Call on a student to read the rule for determining if two ratios are equal, found in the box under the illustration. Make sure students understand the term "cross product." Then introduce the idea that if two ratios are equal, they form a *proportion.*

Other Examples Work through these examples as a class activity. The first two examples show how to write a ratio as a lowest-terms fraction.

Equal Ratios

Ken saw 2 cartons of white eggs and 3 cartons of brown eggs on the grocery shelf. Each carton had 12 eggs. What is the ratio of white eggs to brown eggs?

White eggs → $\frac{24}{36} = \frac{24 \div 12}{36 \div 12} = \frac{2}{3}$ ← Brown eggs

The ratio is $\frac{24}{36}$. In **lowest terms** it is $\frac{2}{3}$.

Both ratios give the same comparison of white eggs to brown eggs. They are **equal ratios**. $\frac{24}{36} = \frac{2}{3}$

A statement that two ratios are equal is called a **proportion**. $\frac{24}{36} = \frac{2}{3}$ is a proportion.

> If two ratios are equal, then their "cross products" are equal. If the cross products are equal, then the ratios are equal.
>
> $\frac{24}{36} \times \frac{2}{3}$ → $36 \times 2 = 72$
>
> → $24 \times 3 = 72$

Other Examples

$\frac{3}{4} = \frac{9}{12}$ because $\begin{array}{l} 4 \times 9 = 36 \\ 3 \times 12 = 36 \end{array}$

The cross products are equal.

The ratio 8 to 10 as a fraction in lowest terms is $\frac{4}{5}$.

$\frac{8}{10} = \frac{8 \div 2}{10 \div 2} = \frac{4}{5}$

means "is not equal to"

$\frac{1}{3} \neq \frac{3}{10}$ because $\begin{array}{l} 3 \times 3 = 9 \\ 1 \times 10 = 10 \end{array}$

The cross products are not equal.

The ratio 30:10 as a fraction in lowest terms is $\frac{3}{1}$.

$\frac{30}{10} = \frac{3}{1}$

Warm Up

Write = or ≠ for each ⬤. Use cross products to decide.

1. $\frac{8}{3}$ ⬤ $\frac{16}{6}$ =

2. $\frac{3}{8}$ ⬤ $\frac{4}{10}$ ≠

3. $\frac{14}{5}$ ⬤ $\frac{28}{10}$ =

4. $\frac{7}{8}$ ⬤ $\frac{12}{15}$ ≠

Write each ratio as a fraction in lowest terms.

5. 10:15 $\frac{2}{3}$

6. 8:6 $\frac{4}{3}$

7. $\frac{125}{100}$ $\frac{5}{4}$

8. $\frac{18}{20}$ $\frac{9}{10}$

278

Follow Up

Reteaching

Have students write sets of equivalent fractions for the lowest-terms fractions $\frac{1}{2}$, $\frac{2}{3}$, and $\frac{3}{4}$. Then ask them to select pairs of fractions from each set and use them to write proportions. For example, they might select $\frac{2}{4}$ and $\frac{5}{10}$ and write the proportion $\frac{2}{4} = \frac{5}{10}$.

After students write a proportion, have them find the cross products. If they write $\frac{4}{6} = \frac{10}{15}$, they should then show $4 \times 15 = 6 \times 10$, or $60 = 60$.

Enrichment

Give students several sets of four numbers and have them use the four numbers to write a proportion. Cross products can be used to show that the ratios are equal.

1. 2, 64, 16, 8 $\frac{2}{16} = \frac{8}{64}$

2. 1, 51, 3, 17 $\frac{1}{3} = \frac{17}{51}$

3. 6, 8, 2, 24 $\frac{2}{6} = \frac{8}{24}$

4. 6, 12, 9, 8 $\frac{6}{9} = \frac{8}{12}$

5. 3, 3, 1, 9 $\frac{1}{3} = \frac{3}{9}$

6. 7, 24, 8, 21 $\frac{7}{8} = \frac{21}{24}$

More than one proportion can be written for each set of four numbers.

Write = or ≠ for each   Use cross products to decide.

1. $\frac{2}{5}$ $\frac{4}{10}$ =

2. $\frac{4}{8}$ $\frac{4}{16}$ ≠

3. $\frac{8}{12}$ $\frac{2}{3}$ =

4. $\frac{16}{8}$ $\frac{8}{3}$ ≠

5. $\frac{1}{3}$ $\frac{3}{9}$ =

6. $\frac{2}{7}$ $\frac{6}{21}$ =

7. $\frac{3}{5}$ $\frac{5}{9}$ ≠

8. $\frac{4}{10}$ $\frac{8}{25}$ ≠

9. $\frac{6}{10}$ $\frac{5}{9}$ ≠

10. $\frac{5}{2}$ $\frac{40}{16}$ =

11. $\frac{3}{7}$ $\frac{4}{9}$ ≠

12. $\frac{20}{16}$ $\frac{5}{4}$ =

13. $\frac{1}{3}$ $\frac{4}{11}$ ≠

14. $\frac{3}{21}$ $\frac{1}{7}$ =

15. $\frac{2}{3}$ $\frac{6}{12}$ ≠

16. $\frac{7}{8}$ $\frac{6}{7}$ ≠

Write each ratio as a fraction in lowest terms.

17. 4 to 6 $\frac{2}{3}$

18. 10 to 2 $\frac{5}{1}$

19. 12:16 $\frac{3}{4}$

20. 18:20 $\frac{9}{10}$

21. 6 out of 15 $\frac{2}{5}$

22. 20 out of 25 $\frac{4}{5}$

23. 9:3 $\frac{3}{1}$

24. 50:200 $\frac{1}{4}$

25. $\frac{16}{32}$ $\frac{1}{2}$

26. $\frac{75}{100}$ $\frac{3}{4}$

27. $\frac{40}{15}$ $\frac{8}{3}$

28. $\frac{36}{60}$ $\frac{3}{5}$

29. $\frac{10}{45}$ $\frac{2}{9}$

30. $\frac{18}{60}$ $\frac{3}{10}$

31. $\frac{15}{24}$ $\frac{5}{8}$

32. $\frac{20}{28}$ $\frac{5}{7}$

33. Cans of tomato paste were priced at 3 cans for 87¢. Another store had the same tomato paste priced at 1 can for 29¢. Are the ratios $\frac{87¢}{3}$ and $\frac{29¢}{1}$ equal? yes

34. Apples were priced at 96¢ for a dozen in one store. The same size apples were priced at 4 for 35¢ in another store. Are the ratios equal? At which price are the apples cheaper? no; 96¢ for a dozen

35. Three of the four ratios are equal. Which one does not belong with the equal ratios? Check the cross products.

A $\frac{7.8}{13}$ (B) $\frac{19.2}{28.9}$ C $\frac{2.7}{4.5}$ D $\frac{0.45}{0.75}$

36. **DATA HUNT** Write ratios for the prices of loose potatoes and large bags of potatoes. Which price is more economical?

More Practice, page 434, Set A

Using Page 279

Exercises 1–33 Students should be able to complete these exercises independently.

Exercise 34 By checking cross products, students will find that $\frac{96}{12} \ne \frac{35}{4}$ since $\frac{35 \times 3}{4 \times 3} = \frac{105}{12}$, and the cheaper price is 96¢ for a dozen.

Exercise 35 Another way to determine if the ratios are equal is to change each to a decimal.

$\frac{7.8}{13} = 0.6$ $\frac{19.2}{28.9} = 0.6643..$ $\frac{2.7}{4.5} = 0.6$ $\frac{0.45}{0.75} = 0.6$

Skillkeeper This skill was originally taught in Chapter 7.

More Practice, page 434, Set A

Ratio

Quick Review Have students find the sums and differences

$\frac{1}{2} + \frac{1}{3}$ $\frac{5}{6}$ $\frac{2}{5} - \frac{1}{10}$ $\frac{3}{10}$ $\frac{3}{8} + \frac{1}{2}$ $\frac{7}{8}$

$\frac{5}{6} - \frac{5}{12}$ $\frac{5}{12}$ $\frac{2}{5} + \frac{1}{4}$ $\frac{13}{20}$

Lesson Focus To solve proportions and to write and solve proportions for word problems

Ideas for Getting Started

Present these equations for students to solve. Have them show each step on the chalkboard.

$6n = 36$ $13t = 39$ $28 = 7x$ $14c = 98$

Ask students to recall how to determine if two ratios form a proportion. Use examples like those below in the discussion.

$\frac{5}{8}$ and $\frac{20}{32}$ $\frac{16}{3}$ and $\frac{96}{18}$

Using Page 280

Motivational Problem Have students read the introductory problem and restate the question in their own words. Then have them give the data needed to solve the problem. Explain that a plan to solve the problem can involve equal ratios.

Lesson Development In order to write equal ratios for the data in the problem, we can let a variable represent the number of bottles capped in 60s. Emphasize how the proportion is written in the first step. The top number of each ratio refers to the number of bottles, while the bottom number of each ratio refers to the number of seconds. On the chalkboard, work through each step in solving the proportion. Have students check to see if the answer is reasonable.

Other Examples Work through these examples as a class activity. Point out that the variable may appear on either side of the equation and in either the top or bottom part of the ratio.

Warm Up Assign these exercises as independent written work. Make sure students find the cross-product equation as the first step. Allow time for students to check and discuss their work.

Solving Proportions

A bottle capping machine is set to cap 6 bottles every 5 s.

At this rate, how many bottles would the machine cap in 60 s, or 1 min?

Since the rate of capping stays the same, we can use equal ratios to write a proportion.

Let b = the number of bottles capped in 60 s.

Write the proportion.

Bottles $\rightarrow$ $\frac{6}{5} = \frac{b}{60}$ $\leftarrow$ Seconds

Find the cross-product equation.

$$5\,b = 6 \cdot 60$$
$$5\,b = 360$$

Solve the equation.

$$\frac{5\,b}{5} = \frac{360}{5}$$
$$b = 72$$

The machine would cap 72 bottles in 60 s.

Other Examples

$\frac{4}{x} = \frac{18}{27}$ $\frac{3}{8} = \frac{15}{t}$ $\frac{n}{42} = \frac{15}{18}$

$18x = 27 \cdot 4$ $3t = 8 \cdot 15$ $18n = 15 \cdot 42$

$18x = 108$ $3t = 120$ $18n = 630$

$x = 6$ $t = 40$ $n = 35$

Warm Up

Solve each proportion.

1. $\frac{2}{x} = \frac{6}{9}$ $x = 3$ 2. $\frac{5}{6} = \frac{15}{x}$ $x = 18$ 3. $\frac{x}{10} = \frac{9}{30}$ $x = 3$ 4. $\frac{20}{6} = \frac{x}{15}$ $x = 50$

280

Follow Up

Reteaching

Discuss the similarity of working with equal ratios and equivalent fractions. Point out that some problems may be solved by finding the number by which the numerator and denominator were multiplied.

Show students examples of proportions that can be solved both ways.

$\frac{8}{15} = \frac{n}{45}$ $\frac{8}{15} = \frac{n}{45}$

$\frac{8 \times 3}{15 \times 3} = \frac{24}{45}$ $15n = 8 \cdot 45$

$n = 24$ $\frac{15n}{15} = \frac{360}{15}$

$n = 24$

Enrichment

Display the following exercises on the chalkboard. Have students solve the proportions and write the letters of matching values in the blanks below.

$\frac{e}{5} = \frac{14}{35}$ $\frac{5}{o} = \frac{23}{69}$ $\frac{t}{40} = \frac{3}{12}$

$\frac{h}{9} = \frac{14}{6}$ $\frac{10}{30} = \frac{p}{12}$ $\frac{50}{w} = \frac{20}{14}$

$\frac{6}{n} = \frac{4}{6}$ $\frac{10}{15} = \frac{18}{r}$ $\frac{x}{60} = \frac{24}{18}$

$\underset{4}{\text{P}}\ \underset{15}{\text{O}}\ \underset{35}{\text{W}}\ \underset{2}{\text{E}}\ \underset{27}{\text{R}}$ $\underset{10}{\text{T}}\ \underset{15}{\text{O}}$ $\underset{10}{\text{T}}\ \underset{21}{\text{H}}\ \underset{2}{\text{E}}$

$\underset{2}{\text{E}}\ \underset{80}{\text{X}}\ \underset{4}{\text{P}}\ \underset{15}{\text{O}}\ \underset{9}{\text{N}}\ \underset{2}{\text{E}}\ \underset{9}{\text{N}}\ \underset{10}{\text{T}}$

Assignment Guide			
	Minimum	Average	Extended
page 281	1–12	1–14, TM	1–14, TM

Solve each proportion.

1. $\frac{1}{3} = \frac{x}{18}$ $x = 6$ **2.** $\frac{5}{6} = \frac{x}{24}$ $x = 20$ **3.** $\frac{2}{3} = \frac{8}{x}$ $x = 12$ **4.** $\frac{10}{16} = \frac{15}{x}$ $x = 24$

5. $\frac{15}{3} = \frac{x}{8}$ $x = 40$ **6.** $\frac{10}{x} = \frac{4}{8}$ $x = 20$ **7.** $\frac{2}{5} = \frac{x}{250}$ $x = 100$ **8.** $\frac{15}{1} = \frac{x}{4}$ $x = 60$

Read the problem. Then solve the proportion.

9. A machine can seal 12 bottles in 45 s. How long would it take the machine to seal 60 bottles?
Let t = the number of seconds to seal 60 bottles.

Bottles → $\frac{12}{45} = \frac{60}{t}$ $t = 225$
Seconds →

10. If 1 out of 80 bottles had a defect, how many defective bottles were in a shipment of 1,200 bottles?
Let b = the number of defective bottles in 1,200 bottles.

Defective bottles → $\frac{1}{80} = \frac{t}{1,200}$ $b = 15$
All bottles →

Complete and solve the proportion for each problem.

11. A machine put labels on cans at a rate of 7 labels every 4 s. How many cans could the machine label in 28 s?
Let n = the number of cans labeled in 28 s.

Labels → $\frac{7}{4} = \frac{\blacksquare}{\blacksquare}$ $\frac{7}{4} = \frac{n}{28}$; $n = 49$
Seconds →

12. A movable belt for a can-labeling machine travels 115 cm in 5 s. How far does a point on the belt move in 1 s?
Let d = the distance the point moves in 1 s.

Centimeters → $\frac{\blacksquare}{\blacksquare} = \frac{\blacksquare}{\blacksquare}$ $\frac{115}{5} = \frac{d}{1}$; $d = 23$
Seconds →

Write and solve a proportion for each problem.

13. A machine can fill 3 bottles in 8 s. At this rate, how long will it take to fill 48 bottles?
Let t = the time to fill 48 bottles.
$\frac{3}{8} = \frac{48}{t}$; $t = 128$

14. A machine sealed 225 boxes in 3 h. At this rate, how many boxes would be sealed in an 8-hour shift?
Let b = the number of boxes sealed in 8 h.
$\frac{225}{3} = \frac{b}{8}$; $b = 600$

THINK MATH

Guess and Check

How many proportions can you make using only these numbers? Each number can be used only once in each proportion.

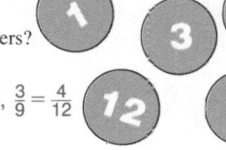

$8; \frac{1}{3} = \frac{4}{12}, \frac{3}{1} = \frac{12}{4}, \frac{4}{1} = \frac{12}{3}, \frac{1}{4} = \frac{3}{12}, \frac{3}{4} = \frac{9}{12}, \frac{4}{3} = \frac{12}{9}, \frac{9}{3} = \frac{12}{4}, \frac{3}{9} = \frac{4}{12}$

More Practice, page 434, Set B

281

Using Page 281

Exercises 1–14 Before making the assignment, direct students' attention to exercise 9. Point out that each ratio in a proportion must compare things in the same way. In the proportion given, each ratio compares bottles to seconds. The same problem could be solved using this proportion: $\frac{45}{12} = \frac{t}{60}$. Each ratio in this proportion compares seconds to bottles. The answer will be the same when either proportion is used.

Caution students that exercise 9 cannot be solved using $\frac{12}{45} = \frac{t}{60}$, since one ratio compares bottles to seconds and the other ratio compares seconds to bottles.

Think Math Students are asked to form as many proportions as possible using only the five numbers given. Be sure they realize that each number can be used only once in each proportion.

More Practice, page 434, Set B.

Reteaching Supplement, Page 82

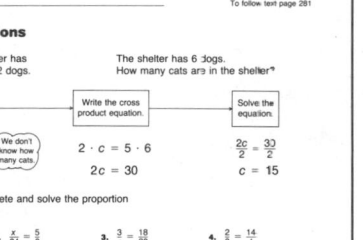

Enrichment Supplement, page 82

It's All to Scale

Practice Supplement, page 106

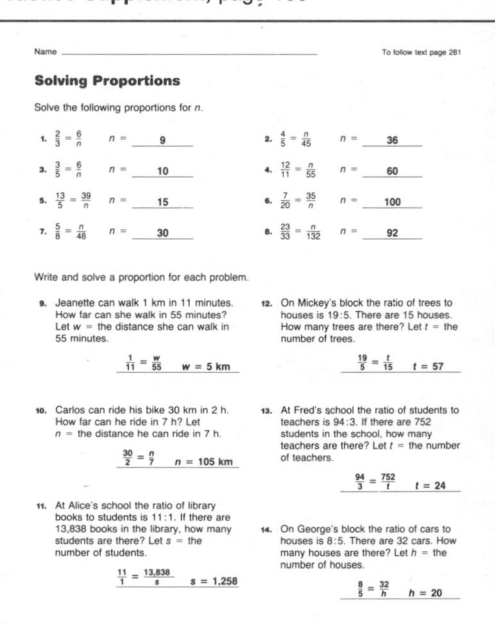

Quick Review Have students estimate the products orally. Then have them do the multiplication.

482 × 209	**100,738**	784 × 356	**279,104**
591 × 328	**193,848**	618 × 681	**420,858**

Lesson Focus To use the 5-Point Checklist to solve word problems involving proportions and other operations

Ideas for Getting Started

Review with students the steps used to write a proportion. Emphasize the idea that each ratio in the proportion must be written in the same way. Remind students that there is more than one way to write a proportion.

Display the following on the chalkboard and ask which proportion is incorrect.

3 teachers for 45 students
5 teachers for x students

$$\frac{45}{x} = \frac{3}{5} \qquad \frac{3}{45} = \frac{5}{x} \qquad \frac{3}{45} = \frac{x}{5} \text{ (incorrect)}$$

On the chalkboard, solve the two correct proportions to show that even though the proportions look different, the answers are the same.

Using Page 282

Lesson Development Conduct a brief discussion of the steps in the 5-Point Checklist. Then read the introductory problem with students. You may wish to have students complete the Problem Solving Worksheet (TRB p. 287) as you discuss each of the 5 points. Point out that one way to organize the data for a proportion problem is to write it in a table.

Tell students that a key part of the plan is to let a variable represent the answer we are trying to find. Then we write and solve the proportion. Notice with students that the answer in a proportion problem can be checked by determining if cross products are equal.

PROBLEM SOLVING: Using the 5-Point Checklist

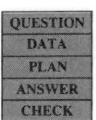

To Solve a Problem
1. Understand the QUESTION   4. Find the ANSWER
2. Find the needed DATA   5. CHECK back
3. PLAN what to do

Review the 5-Point Checklist for solving problems. Then study the problem below and its solution.

A tape recording of 42 min used 1,464 ft of tape. How many feet of tape were used to record a song that lasted 14 min?

1. **Understand the QUESTION**
   How many feet of tape are needed for 14 min of taping?

2. **Find the needed DATA**

minutes	42	14
feet	1,464	?

3. **PLAN what to do**
   Let $n =$ the number of feet of tape needed for 14 min of taping. Write a proportion using the data and n.

   $$\frac{42}{1,464} = \frac{14}{n}$$

4. **Find the ANSWER**
   Solve the proportion for n.

   $$\frac{42}{1,464} = \frac{14}{n}$$
   $$42 \cdot n = 20,496$$
   $$n = 488$$

   488 ft of tape were used.

5. **CHECK back**
   The answer seems reasonable.

   $\frac{42}{1,464} = \frac{14}{488}$ because
   $14 \cdot 1,464 = 42 \cdot 488 = 20,496$

282

Follow Up

Reteaching

Present students with these short story problems. Have them write and solve a proportion for each.

1. 6 mi in 15 min
   How many miles in 30 min? **12 mi**
2. 3 tapes for $5
   How many tapes for $15? **9 tapes**
3. 2 laps in 8 min
   How many laps in 12 min? **3 laps**
4. 2 hits for 7 times at bat
   How many hits for 210 times at bat?
   60 hits

Enrichment

Challenge students with the following problem.
The ratio of boys to girls in a group of students was 3 to 5. Then 24 girls left the group and 24 more boys joined it. The ratio of boys to girls became 5 to 3. How many boys and girls were in the original group?

36 boys, 60 girls

Assignment Guide			
	Minimum	Average	Extended
page 283	1–7, 11	1–11	1–12

Solve. Use the 5-Point Checklist.

1. At a recording company, 2 out of every 7 employees are technicians. The company employs 21 people. How many are technicians? 6

2. A popular jazz group has averaged 2 hit singles for every 15 singles recorded. They have recorded 45 singles. How many were hits? 6

3. A group of musicians worked in a recording studio 6 h a day for 46 days to make an album. The studio charged $135 an hour. What was the total cost of using the studio? $37,260

4. In January, the ratio of records sold to the number of tapes sold was 5 to 2. There were 2,235 records sold. How many tapes were sold? 894

5. A 16-track tape uses 15 in. of tape per second. How many inches of tape are used to record a 7-minute song? 6,300 in.

6. A salesperson sells about 11 record albums per hour. If he works 8 h a day, about how many record albums does he sell in 5 days? 440

7. To make a record, each singer and instrument is recorded on a different track of 24-track tape. The 24 tracks are then mixed into 2 tracks. A 35-minute recording takes about 300 h to mix. How long will it take to mix a 14-minute recording? 120 h

8. What fraction of the business was radio and TV advertisements? $\frac{5}{12}$

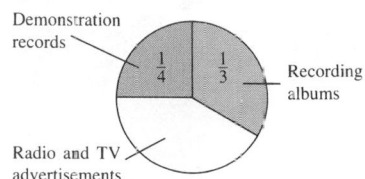
Demonstration records — $\frac{1}{4}$ — $\frac{1}{3}$ — Recording albums — Radio and TV advertisements

9. Lametra bought 3 cassette tapes that cost $2.79 each. She bought 2 eight-track tapes that cost $9.95 each. She paid for them with two $20 bills. How much money did she get back? $11.73

10. A pop band receives 78¢ in royalties for every album sold. Use the table to compute their royalties. What is the total amount they received? $284,805.30

Country	Number of Albums Sold
Japan	86,534
Germany	64,287
Australia	91,064
United States	123,250

11. **DATA BANK** If the same orchestra is heard on 3 out of 5 FM stations in Utah, how many FM stations is this? (See page 413.) 12

12. **Try This** The drummer in a band received her paycheck on Wednesday. She spent $\frac{1}{4}$ of it that day. She spent $\frac{1}{2}$ of what was left on Thursday, and still had $48. How much was the paycheck before any money was spent? $128

Using Page 283

Exercises 1–11 Remind students to use the 5-Point Checklist. Caution students that not all problems involve writing and solving proportions. Have a calculator available for exercise 10.

Try This A possible strategy, Work Backward, was taught on page 130.

Discussion After students read the problem, have them restate the question in their own words. Ask them to identify the data needed to solve the problem. Help students see that since we know the amount of money the drummer had left, we can work backward to find the original amount.

Solution

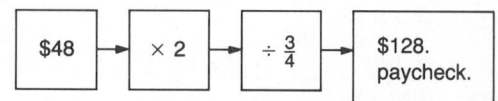

$48 → × 2 → ÷ $\frac{3}{4}$ → $128. paycheck.

The paycheck was $128.

Extension One year frost killed 20 rose bushes in Eileen's garden. To replace the bushes, she bought just as many as she had left. Then she divided all of the bushes evenly among herself and 3 friends. Eileen got 25 bushes. How many bushes did Eileen have before the frost? (70 bushes)

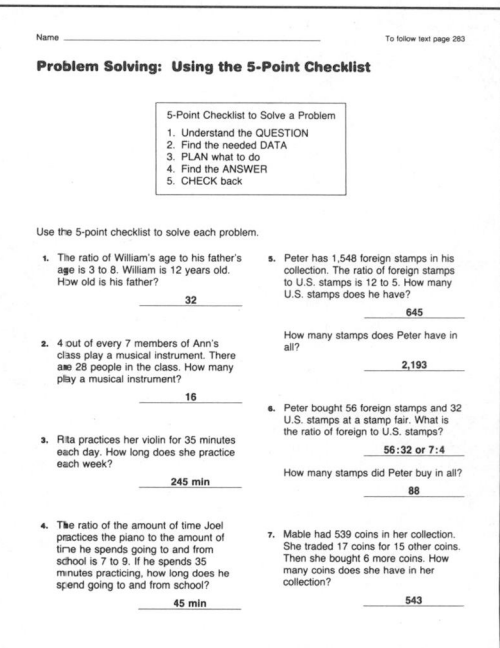

Reteaching Supplement, page 83

Enrichment Supplement, page 83

Practice Supplement, page 107

Quick Review Have students write each fraction as a decimal.

$\frac{3}{4}$ 0.75 $\frac{1}{8}$ 0.125 $\frac{2}{9}$ $0.\overline{2}$ $\frac{3}{5}$ 0.6

$\frac{2}{3}$ $0.\overline{6}$ $\frac{7}{8}$ 0.875 $\frac{1}{6}$ $0.1\overline{6}$

Lesson Focus To use proportions to find the missing lengths of the corresponding sides of similar figures

Ideas for Getting Started

Draw some figures on the chalkboard. For each figure, have a student draw another figure which has the same shape but is larger or smaller than the original figure.

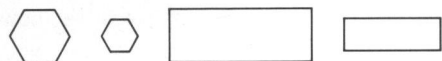

Review with students the method for solving proportions. On the chalkboard, solve these proportions as a class activity.

$$\frac{14}{x} = \frac{3}{126} \qquad \frac{5}{130} = \frac{6}{x}$$

Using Page 284

Motivational Problem Have students read the introductory problem and examine the accompanying photographs. Ask students to identify the question and the data in the problem. Explain that since the ratios of the corresponding sides are equal, we can plan to write a proportion to find the missing height.

Lesson Development Introduce the name for figures which have the same shape but different sizes, *similar figures*. Tell students that similar figures have a special relationship, that is, the lengths of their corresponding sides have the same ratio. Illustrate the meaning of corresponding sides by using examples of figures on the chalkboard.

Work through writing and solving a proportion for the introductory problem one step at a time. Give students the opportunity to participate in each step. Have them check the answer by using cross products.

Similar Figures

A photograph for use in a book is 25 cm wide and 20 cm in height. A lithographer must make a reduced photograph that will be only 10 cm wide to fit the space in the book. What will be the height of the reduced photograph?

Original photograph

25 cm

20 cm

The two photographs are examples of a pair of **similar figures**. Similar figures have the same shape.

The lengths of the corresponding sides of similar figures have equal ratios. We can use these ratios to form a proportion.

Reduced photograph

10 cm

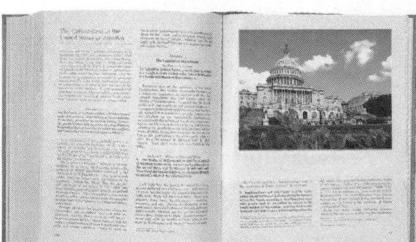

Let h = the height of the reduced photograph.

Original → $\dfrac{25}{10} = \dfrac{20}{h}$ ← Reduced

$25 \cdot h = 200$

$h = 8$

The reduced photograph will have a height of 8 cm.

Warm Up

1. The two triangles are similar. Find the length x.

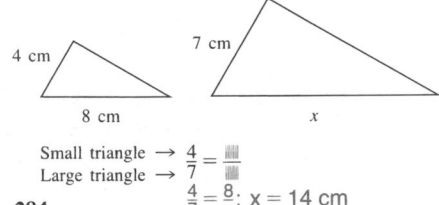

4 cm   7 cm

8 cm x

Small triangle → $\dfrac{4}{7} = \dfrac{\blacksquare}{\blacksquare}$

Large triangle → $\dfrac{4}{7} = \dfrac{8}{x}$; $x = 14$ cm

284

2. The two parallelograms are similar. Find the length x.

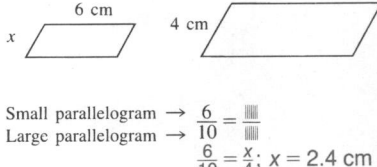

10 cm

6 cm   4 cm

x

Small parallelogram → $\dfrac{6}{10} = \dfrac{\blacksquare}{\blacksquare}$

Large parallelogram → $\dfrac{6}{10} = \dfrac{x}{4}$; $x = 2.4$ cm

Follow Up

Reteaching

Have students cut similar figures out of colored paper and display the figures on a bulletin board. Under each pair of figures, they should write a proportion showing that lengths of corresponding sides have the same ratio.

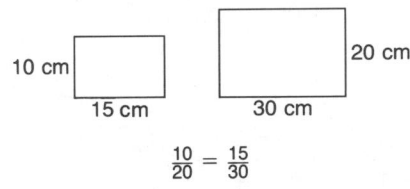

10 cm   20 cm

15 cm   30 cm

$\dfrac{10}{20} = \dfrac{15}{30}$

Enrichment

Have students use a protractor and ruler to copy the figures below. Then have them measure the other sides and show that lengths of corresponding sides have equal ratios.

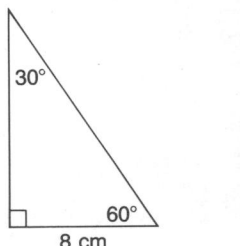

30°   60°

8 cm

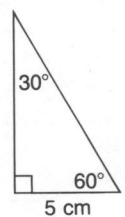

30°   60°

5 cm

	Assignment Guide		
	Minimum	Average	Extended
page 285	1–7, SK	1–8, SK	1–8, SK

Find the length x for each pair of similar figures.

1. $x = 24$ cm
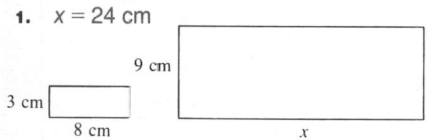
9 cm

3 cm

8 cm x

2. $x = 3$ m
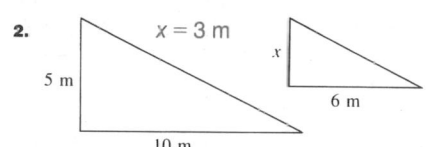
5 m x
6 m
10 m

3. $x = 16$ cm
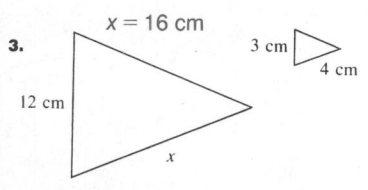
3 cm
4 cm
12 cm
x

4. $x = 6$ mm
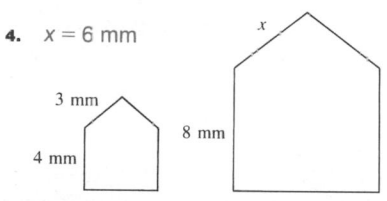
x
3 mm
8 mm
4 mm

5. $x = 84$ m
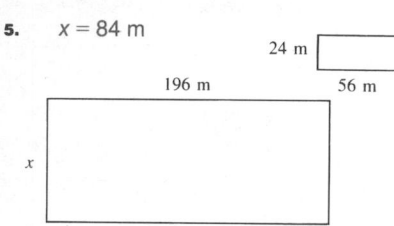
24 m
196 m   56 m
x

6. $x = 468$ mm
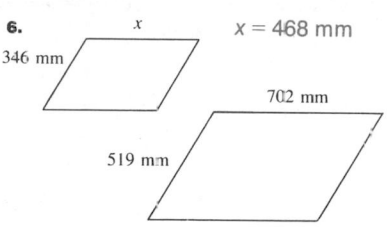
x
346 mm
702 mm
519 mm

7. A small wallet-sized photograph is 4 cm wide and 5 cm in height. An enlarged copy of the photograph will be 12 cm wide. What will be the height of the enlarged photograph? 15 cm

8. A rectangular picture that was 15 cm wide and 9 cm high was reduced to fit a space 5 cm wide and 3 cm high. What is the ratio of the lengths of the sides of the large picture to the small picture? Give the ratio in lowest terms. $\frac{3}{1}$

SKILLKEEPER

Give each ratio as a fraction in lowest terms.

1. 7 to 8 $\frac{7}{8}$

2. 2 to 6 $\frac{1}{3}$

3. 18:3 $\frac{6}{1}$

4. 6:10 $\frac{3}{5}$

5. 1:7 $\frac{1}{7}$

6. 12 to 1 $\frac{12}{1}$

7. 17:2 $\frac{17}{2}$

8. 14:7 $\frac{2}{1}$

9. 23 to 56 $\frac{23}{56}$

10. 4 to 12 $\frac{1}{3}$

11. 6 out of 12 $\frac{1}{2}$

12. 9 out of 45 $\frac{1}{5}$

13. 100 out of 10 $\frac{10}{1}$

14. 72 to 9 $\frac{8}{1}$

15. 8:100 $\frac{2}{25}$

16. 3 out of 33 $\frac{1}{11}$

285

Using Page 285

Exercises 1–8 You may wish to write the proportion for the first exercise as a class activity. Emphasize that proportions should be written so that the ratios reflect the same comparison. Remind students to check their answers using cross products.

Reteaching Supplement, page 84

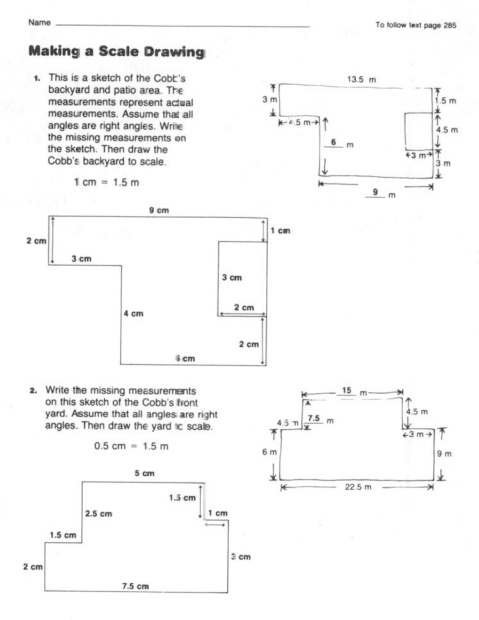

Enrichment Supplement, page 84

Practice Supplement, page 108

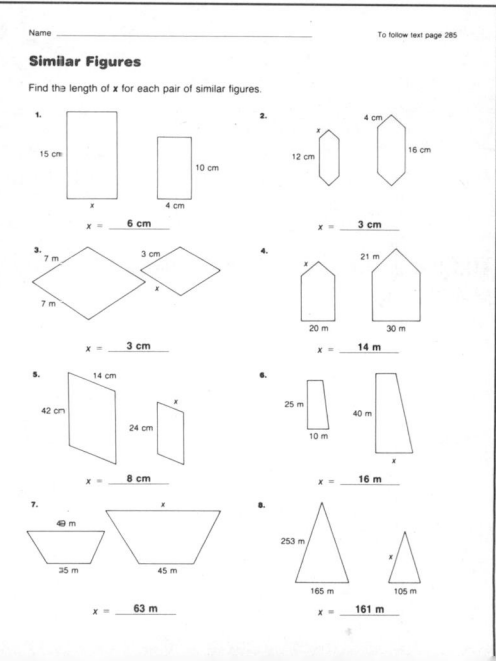

Lesson Focus To solve word problems using scale drawings; to solve word problems involving proportions using estimation

Suggested Materials Maps

Ideas for Getting Started

Provide several maps for students to examine. Conduct a discussion centering on the map scales. Explain that the scale on a map is a ratio comparing the distance on the map to the actual distance.

Using Page 286

Lesson Development Ask students to read the introductory problem and study the map of Oahu. Have them restate the question in their own words. Then have them give the data necessary to solve the problem. Notice with students that the data is found partly in the problem and partly on the map scale. Point out that the map scale is a ratio stating that for every centimeter on the map, the actual distance is 7 kilometers. Observe with students that the plan is to let a variable represent the unknown distance, and to write a proportion comparing the map distances to the actual distances.

On the chalkboard, work through solving the proportion one step at a time. Have students check the answer by using cross products.

Exercises 1–6 These problems give practice using a scale to solve problems.

Try This A possible strategy, Use Logical Reasoning, was taught on page 242.

Discussion After students read the problem, have them identify the question and the data needed to solve the problem. Remind students that Venn diagrams help us to reason logically about the data. Ask students to tell how a Venn diagram could be drawn for this problem.

Solution

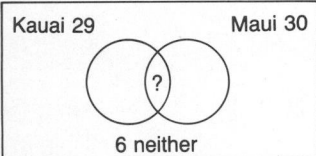

$$44 - 6 = 38$$
$$29 + 30 = 59$$
$$59 - 38 = 21$$

The number of people who visited both Kauai and Maui is 21.

PROBLEM SOLVING: Using Data from a Map

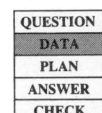
QUESTION
DATA
PLAN
ANSWER
CHECK

On this map of the island of Oahu, Hawaii, it is about 1.5 cm from Diamond Head to Koko Head. What is the actual distance in kilometers?

The map is a **scale drawing**. The **scale** gives the ratio of the map distance to the actual distance.

Map distance $\;\rightarrow\;\dfrac{1}{7}$ cm
Actual distance $\;\rightarrow\;\phantom{\dfrac{1}{7}}$ km

You can use this ratio to write and solve a proportion for the problem.

Let d = the actual distance from Diamond Head to Koko Head.

$$\frac{1}{7} = \frac{1.5}{d}$$
$$1 \cdot d = 7 \cdot 1.5$$
$$d = 10.5$$

The actual distance is about 10.5 km.

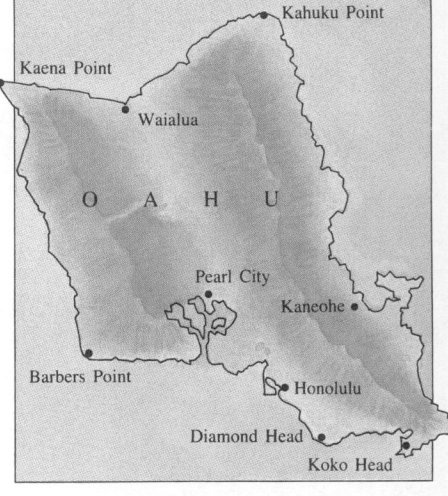

Scale: 1 cm : 7 km
↑ ↑
Map   Actual
distance   distance

Solve. Find all distances to the nearest tenth.

1. The map distance from Koko Head to Pearl City is 4.3 cm. What is the actual distance? 30.1 km

2. The map distance from Barbers Point to Kaena Point is about 5 cm. How many kilometers is the actual distance? 35 km

3. The distance from Honolulu to Barbers Point is 24 km. What is the map distance in centimeters? 3.4 cm

4. On the map, it is 7.9 cm from Koko Head to Kahuku Point. How many kilometers is the actual distance? 55.3 km

5. The map distance from Honolulu to Kahuku Point is about 6.5 cm. The sailing distance is about twice this straight line distance. What is the actual sailing distance? 91 km

6. The map distance between Kaneohe and Waialua is 5.2 cm. What is the actual round-trip distance? 72.8 km

7. **Try This** Of 44 people on a sightseeing trip, 29 people had visited the island of Kauai, 30 had visited the island of Maui, and 6 had not visited either of these islands. How many people had visited both Kauai and Maui? Hint: Use logical reasoning. 21

286

Follow Up

Reteaching

Provide students with maps for some additional activities with scale drawings. Allow students to work in pairs. Have them measure the distance between various points and use the map scale to determine the actual distance.

Enrichment

Have students look in resource books to find an example of a scale drawing that is an enlargement rather than a reduction. Have them make a copy of the drawing and find the actual size of the object in the drawing.

Example:

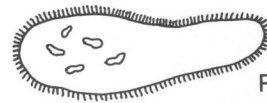

Paramecium
Scale: 200 times
actual size

Assignment Guide			
	Minimum	Average	Extended
page 286	1–5	1–7	1–7
page 287	1–5	1–6	1–7

Applications

PROBLEM SOLVING: Using Estimation

QUESTION
DATA
PLAN
ANSWER
CHECK

Choose an estimate for the answer. Then solve the problem. Compare your answer with your estimate.

1. At a marine park, about three out of four people visiting the park see the performing porpoises and whales. One day 2,416 people visited the park. How many persons saw the porpoises and whales? Hint: round 2,416 to 2,400.

A 600　**B** 800　Ⓒ1,800
1,812

2. The 10 porpoises at the park eat 140 kg of fish each day. The park got 2 more porpoises. How many kilograms of fish are needed each day to feed the porpoises now?

A 28 kg　**B** 100 kg　Ⓒ170 kg
168 kg

3. A porpoise swam 114 km in 3 h. At this rate, what distance would the porpoise swim in 7 h?

A 300 km　**B** 700 km　Ⓒ210 km
266 km

4. The ratio of the length of a common porpoise to the largest dolphin, called a killer whale, is 1 to 5. The length of a common porpoise is 1.8 m. What is the length of a killer whale?

Ⓐ10 m　**B** 15 m　**C** 20 m
9 m

5. The ratio of the length of a bowhead whale's head to its total length is 2 to 5. Its head is 6.2 m long. What is its total length?

A 10 m　Ⓑ15 m　**C** 20 m
15.5 m

6. DATA BANK What is the ratio of the length of a Baird's beaked whale to the length of a black right whale? (See page 416.) $\frac{12}{18}$ or $\frac{2}{3}$

7. Try This There are 25 animals that perform at the park. The park has a morning show in which 13 animals perform. There are 14 animals in the afternoon show. Six animals are in training and do not appear in either show. How many animals perform in both shows? 8

287

Using Page 287

Lesson Development Display the following on the chalkboard and have students choose the best estimate for *x*. Elicit from them the idea that 394 can be rounded to 400 in order to make the estimate

$$\frac{3}{8} = \frac{x}{394}$$

a) *x* = 50
b) *x* = 100
c) *x* = 150

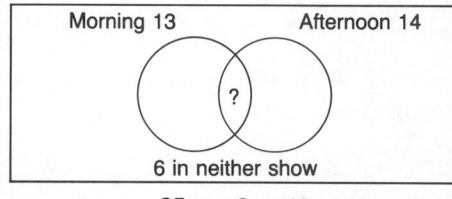

$$\frac{3 \cdot 50}{8 \cdot 50} = \frac{}{400}$$

Exercises 1–5 Tell students that these problems require them to make estimates.

Try This A possible strategy, Use Logical Reasoning, was taught on page 242.

Discussion Have students restate the question and identify the data needed to solve the problem. Ask students if they have solved problems similar to this one. (This problem is similar to the Try This on page 286). Elicit from students that a Venn diagram will help to reason logically about the data.

Solution

Morning 13　　Afternoon 14

?

6 in neither show

$$25 - 6 = 19$$
$$14 + 13 = 27$$
$$27 - 19 = 8$$

There are 8 animals performing in both shows.

Reteaching Supplement, page 85

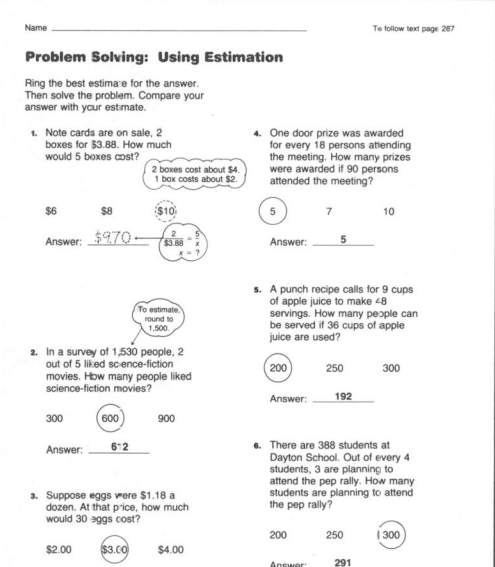

Enrichment Supplement, page 85

Camping Equipment Sale

Practice Supplement, page 109

Problem Solving: Using Estimation

Strategies

Lesson Focus To apply the strategies to solve nonroutine word problems

Ideas for Getting Started

To review the strategies, turn to pages 24, 50, 82, 108, 130, 158, 186, 218, and 242, and randomly select problems to read to the class. Have students name a strategy they might use to solve each problem.

Using Page 288

Lesson Development Tell students that nine strategies have been introduced in previous chapters. Have selected students write the names of strategies on the chalkboard.

Exercise 1 A possible strategy, Draw a Picture, was introduced on page 108.

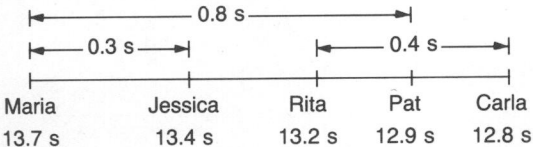

Maria	Jessica	Rita	Pat	Carla
13.7 s	13.4 s	13.2 s	12.9 s	12.8 s

Exercise 2 A possible strategy, Make a Table, was introduced on page 186.

		1	2	3	4	5	6	7	8
Ann	$100	108	116	124	132	140	148	156	164
Sid	$ 60	70	80	90	100	110	120	130	140

9	10	11	12	13	14	15	16	17	18	19	20
172	180	188	196	204	212	220	228	236	244	252	260
150	160	170	180	190	200	210	220	230	240	250	260

Exercise 3 A possible strategy, Make an Organized List, was introduced on page 50.

AB	BC	CD	DE	EF
AC	BD	CE	DF	
AD	BE	CF		
AE	BF			
AF				

There are 15 matches to be played in the tournament.

Exercise 4 A possible strategy, Work Backward, was taught on page 130.

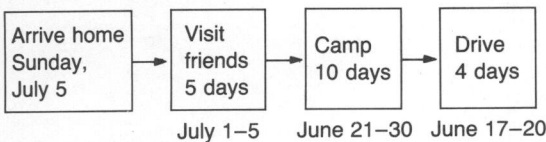

The Loportos must start on their trip June 17. Since July 5, June 28, and June 21 are Sundays, June 17 is a Wednesday.

PROBLEM SOLVING: Using the Strategies

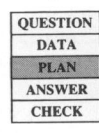

QUESTION
DATA
PLAN
ANSWER
CHECK

Problem Solving Strategies

- Guess and Check
- Make an Organized List
- Find a Pattern
- Draw a Picture
- Work Backward
- Solve a Simpler Problem
- Make a Table
- Choose the Operations
- Use Logical Reasoning

Choose one or more of the strategies to solve each problem below.

1. Rita ran the 100-meter dash in 13.2 s. Jessica's time was 0.3 s less than Maria's. Carla beat Rita by 0.4 s. Pat's time of 12.9 s was 0.8 s less than Maria's time. What was the order in which the five girls finished the race? What was the time for each girl? Carla, 12.8 s; Pat, 12.9 s; Rita, 13.2 s; Jessica, 13.4 s; Maria, 13.7 s

2. Ann has $100 in a savings account and puts in $8 each week. Sid has $60 in his savings account but puts $10 each week into his account. How many weeks will it be until Sid and Ann have the same amount in their savings accounts? 20 weeks

3. A group of 6 tennis players are going to play in a "round robin" tournament. Each player must play 1 match with each of the other players. How many matches will be played in the tournament? 15

4. The Loporto family is planning a trip. They know they have to get back from their vacation on Sunday, July 5. They plan 10 days for camping in a national park. They want to spend 5 days visiting friends. They know it will take 4 days of driving in addition to the other days. What date and day of the week should they start on their trip? June 17, Wednesday

CHAPTER REVIEW/TEST

Write each ratio as a fraction.

1. 4 out of 11 $\frac{4}{11}$ **2.** \$21 for 2 $\frac{\$21}{2}$ **3.** 3 to 16 $\frac{3}{16}$ **4.** 7:10 $\frac{7}{10}$

Write each ratio as a fraction in lowest terms.

5. 5 to 15 $\frac{1}{3}$ **6.** 8:16 $\frac{1}{2}$ **7.** 16 out of 24 $\frac{2}{3}$ **8.** 20:15 $\frac{4}{3}$

Write = or ≠ for each ⬤. Use cross products to decide.

9. $\frac{3}{2}$ ⬤ $\frac{12}{8}$ = **10.** $\frac{2}{15}$ ⬤ $\frac{6}{40}$ ≠ **11.** $\frac{3}{15}$ ⬤ $\frac{15}{75}$ = **12.** $\frac{4}{3}$ ⬤ $\frac{20}{12}$ ≠

Solve each proportion.

13. $\frac{5}{9} = \frac{20}{x}$ $x = 36$ **14.** $\frac{12}{18} = \frac{x}{21}$ $x = 14$ **15.** $\frac{x}{12} = \frac{14}{6}$ $x = 28$ **16.** $\frac{3}{7} = \frac{x}{35}$ $x = 15$

Find the length x for each pair of similar figures.

17. $x = 2$ mm

18. $x = 8$ cm

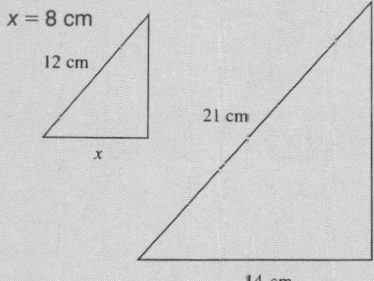

19. The scale on a map is 1 cm: 25 km. The distance between Hampton and Bellville on the map is 5 cm. What is the actual distance between the two towns? 125 km

20. The distance between two cities is 180 km. They are shown on a map with a scale of 1 cm representing 40 km. What is the map distance in centimeters? 4.5 cm

21. There are 3 books for every 4 students. How many books are there for 24 students? 18

22. Kinuko drove 170 km in 2 h. At this rate, how far will she drive in 3 h? 255 km

289

Using Page 289

The exercises in the Chapter Review/Test emphasize the major concepts and skills presented in this chapter. These exercises may be used as a review assignment or as a test, depending upon your needs.

Item Analysis The table below correlates the Chapter Review/Test items with objectives and with the students text pages on which the concepts or skills were taught.

Items	Objectives	Related Text Pages
1–12	11.1	276–279
13–16	11.2	280–281
17–18	11.3	284–285
19–22	11.4	282–283, 286–287

Assessment Options

If you use the Chapter Review/Test as a review assignment, you may wish to use the free-response test or the multiple-choice test to evaluate mastery of the chapter objectives. The items on these tests have a one-to-one correspondence in terms of content and level of difficulty. A correlation of test items to objectives and student text pages is provided in the Management Guide for Chapter 11.

Multiple-Choice Test, TRB pages 31–33
Free-Response Test, TRB pages 69–70

TRB Options

The following blackline masters are available for use with this chapter. If you have not already assigned these materials, you may wish to use them to close the chapter.

Recreation, TRB page 165
Consumer Applications, TRB page 183
Calculator Technology, TRB page 201
Reading Math, TRB page 237
Family Involvement, TRB pages 265–266

Using Page 290

The exercises on this page are intended for those students who experienced difficulty with the Chapter Review/Test on page 289. Should students require reteaching of these key concepts and skills, please refer to the teaching notes below. Otherwise, the Another Look exercises can be assigned as independent work, with students using the accompanying sample problems and hints as guides.

Exercises 1–6 This skill was originally taught on pages 276–277. Direct students' attention to the examples in the display box. Notice with students that the first ratio compares 8 to 12, while the second ratio compares 12 to 8. Point out that ratios can be written as fractions.

Exercises 7–12 This skill was originally taught on pages 278–279. Have students study the example in the display box. Then write two ratios on the chalkboard, such as $\frac{9}{6}$ and $\frac{12}{8}$. Ask students to find the cross products and tell whether or not the ratios are equal.

Exercises 13–18 This skill was originally taught on pages 280–281. On the chalkboard, work through the example one step at a time. Stress that the first step in solving a proportion is finding the cross products.

Exercises 19–22 This skill was originally taught on pages 284–285. Have students examine the similar figures in the display box. Ask them to give the lengths of the two pairs of corresponding sides (9 and x, 6 and 2). Work through the example with students. Emphasize that in writing the proportion, the ratios must show the same comparison.

| ANOTHER LOOK |

8 to 12 → $\frac{8}{12}$

12 to 8 → $\frac{12}{8}$

Write each ratio as a fraction.

1. 6 to 4 $\frac{6}{4}$ **2.** 3 out of 5 $\frac{3}{5}$ **3.** 9:7 $\frac{9}{7}$

4. 3 for \$15 $\frac{\$15}{3}$ **5.** 5.4 to 1.8 $\frac{5.4}{1.8}$ **6.** 174 to 560 $\frac{174}{560}$

Ratios are equal if cross products are equal.

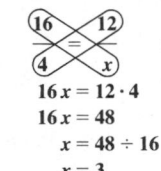

$12 = 12$

Write = or ≠ for each ⬤. Use cross products to decide.

7. $\frac{1}{2}$ ⬤ $\frac{2}{4}$ =   **8.** $\frac{4}{16}$ ⬤ $\frac{2}{8}$ =   **9.** $\frac{3}{5}$ ⬤ $\frac{4}{7}$ ≠

10. $\frac{9}{10}$ ⬤ $\frac{7}{8}$ ≠   **11.** $\frac{2}{3}$ ⬤ $\frac{4}{6}$ =   **12.** $\frac{7}{6}$ ⬤ $\frac{4}{3}$ ≠

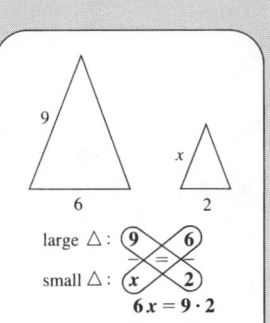

$16x = 12 \cdot 4$

$16x = 48$

$x = 48 \div 16$

$x = 3$

Solve each proportion. $x = 48$

13. $\frac{x}{32} = \frac{5}{8}$ $x = 20$ **14.** $\frac{12}{18} = \frac{x}{6}$ $x = 4$ **15.** $\frac{6}{16} = \frac{18}{x}$

16. $\frac{x}{24} = \frac{2}{3}$ $x = 16$ **17.** $\frac{21}{x} = \frac{7}{8}$ $x = 24$ **18.** $\frac{15}{20} = \frac{x}{12}$

    $x = 9$

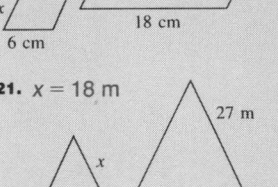

large △ : $\frac{9}{x}$ ⨯ $\frac{6}{2}$

small △ :

$6x = 9 \cdot 2$

$6x = 18$

$x = 3$

Find the missing lengths in each pair of similar figures.

19. $x = 5$ cm

15 cm

x 18 cm

6 cm

20. $x = 2$ m

6 m

4 m

x 3 m

21. $x = 18$ m

27 m

x

12 m   18 m

22.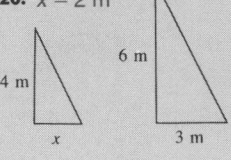

4 cm

x $x = 12$ cm

27 cm

9 cm

290

Just for Teachers

Identifying the Mathematically Gifted Student

An exciting challenge to teachers is to provide for the special needs of students gifted in mathematics. In order to foster and stimulate the development of the gifted and talented, teachers must be able to identify the specific abilities that distinguish these students from their peers. Educators must consider the special students' learning characteristics and modes of thinking when developing and evaluating special programs.

Certain behavior patterns characterize students who are gifted in mathematics. This student often exhibits a swiftness in thought processes and omits seemingly necessary steps when reasoning. Because of this tendency to combine several steps, gifted students may find it difficult to explain how they arrive at an answer.

A talented student is inclined to generalize mathematical relationships. When gifted students are given a problem, they focus on the mathematical structure and interpret the problem in abstract terms with disregard for the concrete data. In fact, a gifted stu-

ENRICHMENT

Finding the Golden Ratio

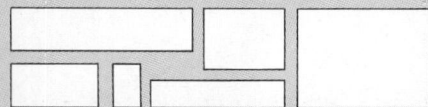

Which rectangle do you like best?

Some rectangles appear more pleasing to the eye than others.

The ancient Greeks believed that a certain shape of rectangle, called a **golden rectangle**, was the best shape. Golden rectangles have been found in Greek art and architecture and are still in use today.

The Erechtheion

Use graph paper and follow the steps below to make a golden rectangle.

1. Draw square *ABCD*.

2. Mark *M*, the midpoint of $\overline{AB}$, and draw $\overline{MC}$.

3. With a compass point at *M*, draw $\overset{\frown}{CP}$.

4. Draw $\overline{PN}$ and complete the rectangle *APND*.

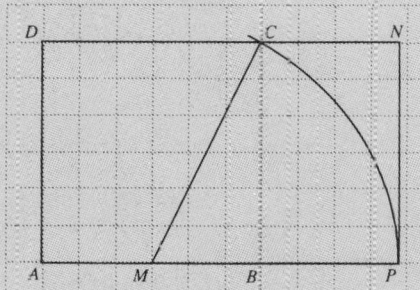

Rectangle *APND* is a golden rectangle. The **golden ratio** is the ratio of the length divided by the width of a golden rectangle.

What is the golden ratio of your golden rectangle? Give the ratio as a decimal rounded to the hundredths place.

A spiral drawn in a golden rectangle resembles the spiral seen in the shell of the nautilus.

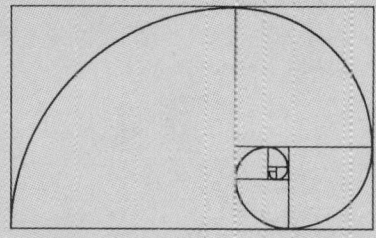

291

Using Page 291

This page is intended for those students who successfully completed the Chapter Review/Test on page 289. You may wish to assign this page as independent work while you use Another Look exercises to reteach the basic concepts and skills of the chapter. Or, you may decide that all students would benefit from exposure to this Enrichment activity.

Suggested Materials Straightedge, compass, graph paper (TRB p. 284)

Lesson Development Direct students' attention to the six rectangles shown at the top of the page. Designate them by a number or letter and ask students to vote for the rectangle that they feel is most pleasing in shape. You may expect a variation in choices, but some rectangles will probably be selected more often than others.

Tell students that ancient Greek mathematicians named a rectangle with a certain shape a golden rectangle because they believed it had a shape most pleasing to the eye. Point out the golden rectangle that appears in the photograph of the Erechtheion. The rectangle is defined by the two corner and center statues. Have students use graph paper, compass, and straightedge to make a golden rectangle. The graph paper will help students to make the construction quickly and easily. Regardless of the original size of the square *ABCD*, the ratio of the length to the width should be the same for all rectangles constructed by students. Have students find the golden ratio and express it as a decimal to the nearest hundredth. Write several of the ratios found by students on the chalkboard for comparison.

Mathematically, the golden ratio is expressed as $\frac{l}{w} = \frac{1 + \sqrt{5}}{2} \approx 1.618$. Most of the ratios found by students should be near 1.6.

dent may solve a problem on a general level and neglect to answer the original question.

In searching for solutions to problems, gifted students will diversify their methods and switch easily from one approach to another. They often use nonstandard methods and see alternative or simpler strategies for solving problems. Flexiblity of thinking and divergent thinking are characteristic of gifted students. They are able to approach situations from different perspectives. Gifted students may delay solving a problem because they are able to see multiple interpretations or alternate solutions.

The teacher who is able to recognize the characteristics of the gifted student is better prepared to develop that student's full potential by providing the necessary challenge.

Using Page 292

The exercises on the page provide practice for maintaining cumulative skills. The emphasis in this Cumulative Review is on addition and subtraction of fractions (Chapter 8) and metric measurement (Chapter 10).

Item Analysis The table below correlates the Cumulative Review items with objectives and with the student book pages on which the concepts or skills were taught.

Items	Objectives	Related Text pages
1	8.3	202–204
2–3	8.1	194–199
4	8.2	200–201
5	8.4	206–209
6	8.5	210–215
7	8.4	206–209
8–9	10.1	248–251
10–11	10.2	252–258
12	10.3	260–261
13	8.6	205
14	10.5	255, 259, 263, 265

CUMULATIVE REVIEW

1. Which is correct?

   Ⓐ $1\frac{1}{2} > 1\frac{1}{3}$ **B** $5\frac{3}{4} < 5\frac{2}{3}$

   c $2\frac{3}{4} > 2\frac{7}{8}$ **D** not given

2. Find the missing number.

   $\frac{12}{14} = \frac{\blacksquare}{28}$ **A** 12   **B** 6

             Ⓒ 24   **D** not given

3. What is $\frac{9}{54}$ in lowest terms?

   A $\frac{1}{8}$ Ⓑ $\frac{1}{6}$

   c $\frac{3}{5}$ **D** not given

4. What is the mixed number for $\frac{52}{9}$?

   A $6\frac{1}{9}$ **B** $5\frac{8}{9}$

   Ⓒ $5\frac{7}{9}$ **D** not given

Add.

5. $\frac{9}{16} + \frac{5}{8}$ **A** $\frac{7}{8}$ **B** $1\frac{3}{4}$

                  Ⓒ $\frac{19}{16}$ **D** not given

6. $\begin{aligned}12\frac{3}{4}\\+\ 5\frac{7}{8}\end{aligned}$ **A** $17\frac{5}{8}$ Ⓑ $18\frac{5}{8}$

                  c $18\frac{1}{2}$ **D** not given

7. Subtract.

   $\frac{3}{4} - \frac{7}{12}$ Ⓐ $\frac{1}{6}$ **B** $\frac{1}{12}$

                  c $\frac{1}{4}$ **D** not given

Change each measurement to millimeters.

8. 124 cm   **A** 0.124 mm   **B** 12.4 mm

                  Ⓒ 1,240 mm   **D** not given

9. 9.2 m   Ⓐ 9,200 mm   **B** 0.092 mm

                c 920 mm   **D** not given

10. What is the perimeter?

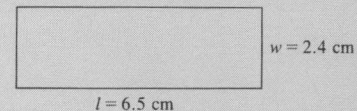

   A 11.3 cm   Ⓑ 17.8 cm

   c 15.6 cm   **D** not given

11. What is the area?

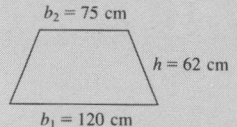

   A 319 cm²   **B** 159.5 cm²

   c 257 cm²   Ⓓ not given

12. What is the volume?

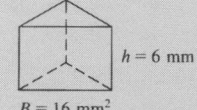

   Ⓐ 96 mm³   **B** 28 mm³

   c 192 mm³   **D** not given

13. A nail is $2\frac{3}{8}$ in. long. A piece of wood is $1\frac{1}{4}$ in. thick. How much longer is the nail than the thickness of the wood?

   A $1\frac{1}{4}$ in.   Ⓑ $1\frac{1}{8}$ in.

   c $1\frac{3}{4}$ in.   **D** not given

14. What is the total length of molding needed for 18 windows that each measure 85 cm by 105 cm?

   Ⓐ 6,840 cm   **B** 3,420 cm

   c 8,925 cm   **D** not given

Percent

Objectives

12.1 Express ratios, fractions, and decimals as percents, and percents as fractions and decimals.

12.2 Find a percent of a number.

12.3 Find the percent one number is of another.

12.4 Find a number when a percent of it is known.

12.5 Write and solve a proportion for a percent problem.

12.6 Solve word problems using the 5-Point Checklist and cumulative computational skills.

Summary

This chapter begins with a review of the basic concept of percent as a special language that compares a number to 100. While the language of percent is quite helpful in describing many practical kinds of problems, percent notation in its usual form is not used for calculating or for solving problems. Instead, the percent is written as an equivalent decimal or fraction. Therefore, students are given considerable practice in converting decimals and fractions to percent and vice versa. Estimating percents, rounding percents, and applying percents are also emphasized.

Mathematical Background

Percent Concepts A percent is used to compare a number to 100. One percent means 1 out of 100, $\frac{1}{100}$, or 0.01. In general, if n is any number, $n\%$ means the ratio of n to 100 and can be written as the fraction $\frac{n}{100}$ or the decimal $0.01n$. This basic definition of percent allows us to work interchangeably with equivalent percents, fractions, or decimals.

Percent problems are sometimes taught stressing the basic relationship, Percentage = Base × Rate. While this relationship can be used to unify all cases of percent, in practice, many students have difficulty distinguishing between percentage, base, and rate. By stressing the basic concept of percent, each application of percent is presented in a way that is meaningful to students.

Applying Percent This chapter explores the applications of percent in three types of problems:

1) Finding a percent of a number.
(What is 30% of 500?)

2) Finding what percent one number is of another.
(What percent of 24 is 16?)

3) Finding a number when a percent of it is known.
(8 is 4% of what number?)

In previous chapters, students have used multiplication to find a decimal part of a number or a fraction of a number. This idea is extended to percents in this chapter. To find a percent of a number, we simply change the percent to a decimal and multiply.

To find what percent one number is of another, the idea of ratio is used. After the ratio is written, it is changed to a percent. When ratios are simple fractions with denominators that are factors of 100, the following method is used to change to a percent.

$$\frac{6}{25} \longrightarrow \frac{6 \times 4}{25 \times 4} = \frac{24}{100} = 24\%$$

In other instances, division is used to write the ratio as a decimal and then as a percent.

$$\frac{1}{8} \longrightarrow \begin{array}{r} 0.125 = 12.5\% \\ 8\overline{)1.000} \end{array}$$

An equation can be used to solve the third type of percent problem: find a number when the percent of it is known. The idea of multiplying to find the percent of a number helps us write the equation, as shown below.

$$15\% \text{ of what number is } 24?$$
$$\text{Let } n = \text{the number}$$
$$15\% \times n = 24$$
$$0.15 \times n = 24$$
$$\frac{0.15}{0.15} \times n = \frac{24}{0.15}$$
$$n = 160$$

Percent concepts are closely related to ideas of ratio and proportion. In one lesson we summarize the cases of percent and show that each of the cases can be solved by writing and solving a proportion.

Problem Solving The problem-solving sets in this chapter extend problem-solving skills to word problems involving percents. The simple interest formula, $I = PRT$, and the formula for the amount, $A = P + I$, are presented on pages 304 and 305. The ideas underlying simple interest are prerequisite to more advanced interest concepts such as compound interest.

A problem-solving lesson on pages 308 and 309 deals with the familiar school application of test scores as percents. Sales prices and discounts as percents are familiar to all newspaper readers. On page 313, a lesson covering this important topic is presented and should be taught carefully. The last problem-solving lesson of the chapter on page 316 focuses on applied problem solving. In this lesson, students make a decision about a real-world problem based on the data given.

Vocabulary

percent	principal	regular price
interest	amount	sale price
interest rate	discount	

Teaching Tips

 ## Error Analysis

In this chapter, the concept of percent is presented and related to ratios, fractions, and decimals. Percents are often used in everyday situations and can be applied to a variety of problem-solving settings.

Several skills are involved in developing a working knowledge of percent. A lack of understanding of any of these skills could result in error patterns with percent. Some common errors are given below.

Error Pattern 1

$$\frac{50}{100} = .50\% \qquad \frac{2}{100} = .02\% \qquad \frac{42}{100} = .42\%$$

Diagnosis The student changed the fraction to a decimal but did not change the decimal to a percent. A percent sign was simply written after the decimal.

Remediation Review the meaning of a percent as the number per hundred. Use drawings to illustrate an example such as 78%. Stress that $\frac{78}{100}$, 0.78, and 78% are three ways of expressing the same number. Show with drawings that .50% and 50% are different values.

Error Pattern 2

$$0.237 = 237\% \qquad 0.005 = 5\% \qquad 1.5 = 15\%$$

Diagnosis The student changed the decimals to percents by moving the decimal point to the right of the last digit and then writing the percent sign. The number of places the decimal point was moved had no significance to the student.

Remediation Emphasize that percent means per hundred. Discuss an example. Since 0.26 means $\frac{26}{100}$, 0.26 = 26%. Observe with the student that when a decimal is written as a percent the decimal point moves two places to the right. Another example is: 1.5 means $\frac{15}{10}$ or $\frac{150}{100}$, so 1.5 = 150%.

Work through writing other decimals as percents, noting that in each case the decimal point moves two places to the right.

Error Pattern 3

$$15\% \text{ of } 200 = 15 \times 200 \qquad 6\% \text{ of } 75 = 6 \times 75$$
$$= 3,000 \qquad\qquad = 450$$

Diagnosis The student multiplied by the percent. He or she did not change the percent to a fraction or a decimal.

Remediation Point out that 15% means $\frac{15}{100}$ or 0.15. If a number is multiplied by a factor less than one, the product is less than the original number. Emphasize that to find a percent of a number, the percent should be changed to a decimal before multiplying.

 ## Problem Solving

Adjusting Instruction for Low Achievers

The problem-solving experiences in this program are appropriate for the wide range of achievement levels found in most classrooms. The types of experiences and the organization of these experiences described in the teaching notes provide the flexibility and assistance necessary to meet the needs of a wide range of students. However, the instructional techniques used for teaching mathematics to low achievers must take into consideration their special needs. This is true for nearly every mathematics topic we teach, including problem solving. Below are some of the ways your problem-solving instruction can be adjusted to meet the needs of low achievers.

- Regularly use the tips for helping students understand problems. (See the Teaching Tips in Chapter 3.)
- Provide frequent opportunities to formulate problems. (See Chapter 11, page 275 C.)
- Discuss problems by relating students' work to each step in the 5-Point Checklist.
- Encourage students to act out problems.
- Encourage students to use objects to model a problem.
- Encourage students to draw pictures.
- Use hints that are problem-specific rather than general.
- Recognize and reinforce behaviors beyond getting correct answers, such as willingness, perseverance, or using the strategies, particularly at the beginning of the year.

All students, regardless of their achievement level, need to be competent problem solvers. The problem-solving experiences provided in this program, together with these teaching tips, will promote the improvement of problem-solving performance for all students.

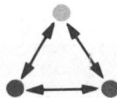 ## Special Education

The topic of percent is one of the most frequently used topics developed in the junior high school years. Percents are widely used in newspapers, in legal papers, and in advertisements of all kinds. There is a variety of consumer applications of percent. Therefore, it is important for the special-needs student to gain an understanding of percent and be able to apply it to problem-solving situations.

Building Concepts

Since percent means per hundred or hundredths, physical models having one hundred units can be used in teaching percent concepts. These include models such as a 10 by 10 square grid, a pegboard with a 10 by 10 array of pegs, a meter stick, a hundred-square from place-value blocks, and a dollar bill.

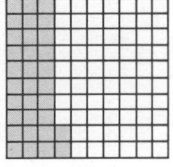 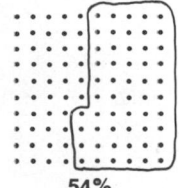

| 32% | 54% |

Money is a familiar model which can be used to illustrate the relationship between fractions, decimals, and percents. For example, a quarter is 25 cents, $0.25, or 25% of a dollar.

Thinking Percents

The work with verbal questions for writing ratios should be extended in this chapter. Students need to learn which questions to consider in situations where a part of a group is being compared to the whole group. After a ratio is written, it is converted into an equal ratio in which the second component is 100. Problems can be examined in light of "part to whole" as "percent to 100." When students can identify these components in a percent problem, they are well on their way to mastering percent skills.

Using the Calculator

The solution of percent problems in real-world applications sometimes involves difficult calculations beyond the skill level of a special needs-student. To overcome this difficulty and help the student develop daily living skills, work with the calculator should be integrated into the class during this chapter. This is especially important in the completion of the material on interest rates and on sale prices.

 ## Subject Integration

Subject matter related to other areas of the curriculum has been integrated into the following lessons. This provides an opportunity to highlight the interaction between mathematics and other subjects.

History Women in law, page 293; illiteracy, page 298
Home Economics Fabrics, pages 296–297
Career Awareness Meteorologist, pages 300–301
Fine Arts Musical instruments, pages 302–303
Consumer Awareness Savings account, pages 304–305; discounts, pages 212–213
Physical Education Camping, pages 306–307
Science Volcanoes, canyons, pages 310–311
Social Studies Rural and urban population, page 299; census, page 319

Teaching Chapter 12				Meeting Individual Needs					
				Lesson Assignments			Follow Up		
Objectives	Chapter Content	Pages	TRB Test Items	Minimum	Average	Extended	Reteaching	Enrichment	Practice
	Chapter Opener	293							
12.1 Express ratios, fractions, and decimals as percents, and percents as fractions and decimals.	Percent	294–295	1–4	1–26	1–27	1–27	SE6 Ch 12		PS 110
	Percents and Fractions	296–297	5–9	1–33	1–34, 36	1–33 odd, 34–36, TM	SE6 Ch 12 RS 86	ES 86	MP 434 PS 111
	Percents and Decimals	298	10–13	1–30	1–30	2–30 even	SE6 Ch 12 RS 87	ES 87	MP 435 PS 112
	Estimating Percents	299		1–4	1–8	1–8			
	Finding Percents for Other Fractions	300–301	14–16	1–27, SK	1–27, 30, SK	1–19 odd, 21–30, SK	RS 88	ES 88	MP 435 PS 113
12.2 Find a percent of a number.	Finding a Percent of a Number	302–303	17–22	1–24, 41	1–41, 44	1–41 odd, 42–44	SE6 Ch 12 RS 89	ES 89	MP 435 PS 114
	Finding Simple Interest	304	23–24	1–6	1–6	1–6	RS 90	ES 90	PS 115
12.3 Find the percent one number is of the other.	Finding the Percent One Number is of Another	306–307	25–28	1–8, 15–21	1–21, TM	1–21 odd, 22, TM	RS 91	ES 91	MP 436 PS 116
12.4 Find a number when a percent of it is known.	Finding a Number When a Percent of It Is Known	310–311	29–32	1–16, 24–30, SK	1–30, SK	2–30 even, 31, SK	RS 92	ES 92	MP 436 PS 118
	Discounts and Sales Prices	313	33–34	1–6	1–7	1–8	RS 93	ES 93	PS 119
	Skills Practice	312		1–30, 41–60	1–64	1–64 even			
12.5 Write and solve a proportion for a percent problem.	Proportions and Percents	314–315	35–36		1–16, 20	1–20, TM			MP 436 PS 120
12.6 Solve word problems using the 5-Point Checklist and cumulative computational skills.	Problem Solving: Using Simple Interest Formulas	305	37–40	1–6	1–9	1–11			
	Problem Solving: Using Percents for Test Scores	308–309		1–10	1–12, 16	4–16			PS 117
	Applied Problem Solving	316							
	Chapter Review/Test	317							
	Another Look/ Enrichment	318–319							
	Cumulative Review	320							

SE6 Student Edition, Book 6
RS Reteaching Supplement
ES Enrichment Supplement
PS Practice Supplement
MP More Practice
TM Think Math
SK Skillkeeper
TRB Teacher's Resource Book

Masters for use

. . . before Chapter 12

| Readiness Percent Expressions | 126 |
| Readiness Percent | 125 |

. . . during Chapter 12

Calculator Technology Sale Prices	202
Consumer Applications Health Insurance	184
Teaching Aids	278, 279, 285
Recreation The Long and Short of It	166
Activities That Count Commission	150

. . . after Chapter 12

Record Keeping	307
Family Involvement At-Home Activities	268
Family Involvement Key Math	267
Reading Math Vocabulary	238
Chapter 12 Test Free-Response Format	71–72
Chapter 12 Test Multiple-Choice Format	34–36

Supplements

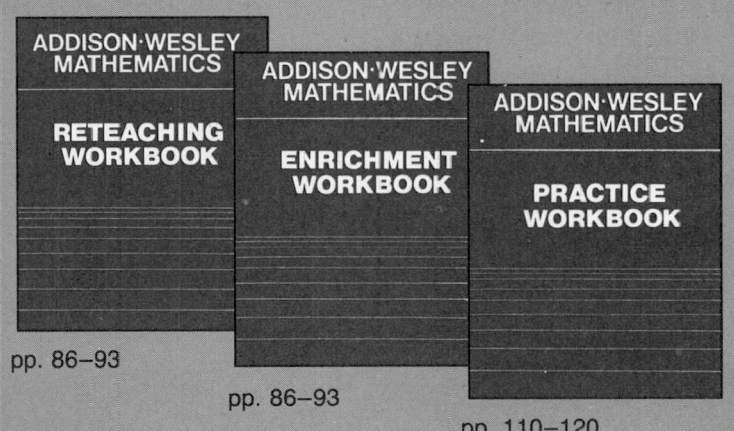

ADDISON-WESLEY MATHEMATICS RETEACHING WORKBOOK pp. 86–93

ADDISON-WESLEY MATHEMATICS ENRICHMENT WORKBOOK pp. 86–93

ADDISON-WESLEY MATHEMATICS PRACTICE WORKBOOK pp. 110–120

Other Addison-Wesley Resources

Books and Kits

Baseball: A Game of Numbers pp. 98–139
Skillseekers III (%) 1–4
The Mad Minute pp. 176–190
General Mathematics: Making Practice Fun 54, 55, 56, 57 A, B, 58 A, B, 59 60
Problem-Solving Experiences in Mathematics, Grade 7 Problems 108, 122, 137, 138

Technology

Computer Math Activities Volume 4
Computer Math Games Volume 1

Activities That Count

Activities That Count are designed for use throughout this chapter and subsequent chapters. Before beginning Chapter 12, you may wish to review these activities and select the ones you consider appropriate for your class.

Commission   Game

Purpose To solve percent problems involving commission

Materials Game board (TRB p. 150), two number cubes (TRB p. 278), one labeled 1 through 6 and the other labeled 1%, 2%, 5%, 7.5%, 12%, and 20%, game markers

Activity In turn, players roll the number cubes. One cube indicates the number of spaces to move and the other indicates the rate of commission. After moving the number of spaces indicated, players determine the commission on the sale shown in their space. Each player should keep a running total of the money they make on commissions. The winner is the player with the highest total when time is called.

Sales Tax   Project

Purpose To use a sales tax table

Activity Have students obtain a copy of a state sales tax table for your state. Local business firms or district tax offices can provide the tables. Have students show how a table is used to determine sales tax.

Percent Chart   Math Lab

Purpose To make a chart and use it to check percent problems

Materials Graph paper (TRB p. 284), string

Activity Have students use a 10 by 10 grid to make a percent chart. The grid should be labeled as shown below and a string attached through a hole at the zero mark in the upper left-hand corner.

Display the following examples and explain to students how the chart can be used to estimate or check answers to percent problems. To find 60% of 50, the string is stretched to 50 on the base scale, and a line is drawn from 60 on the percent scale to the string. A vertical line is then drawn from the string to the answer, 30. A similar process is used to find what percent 30 is of 50. In this case, the answer is found by drawing a vertical line from the string to the percent scale.

If 40% of a number is 30, the number can be found by drawing a horizontal line from 40 on the percent scale and a vertical line from 30 on the base scale. Mark a point where the lines intersect and stretch a string to the point of intersection. Extend the string in a straight line to the base scale for the answer, 75.

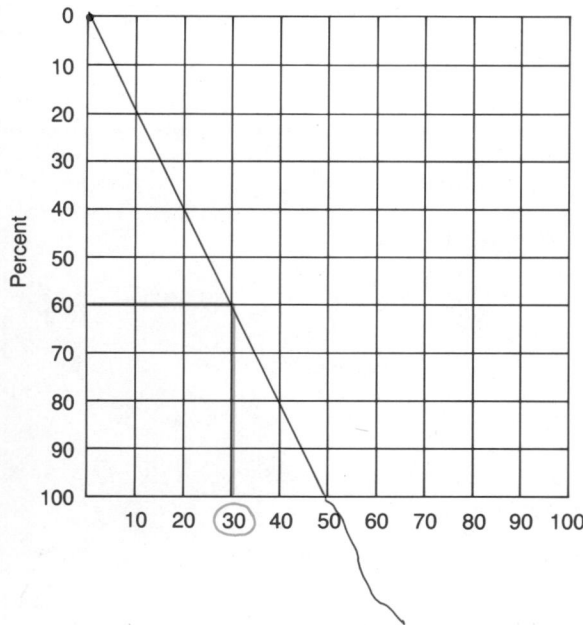

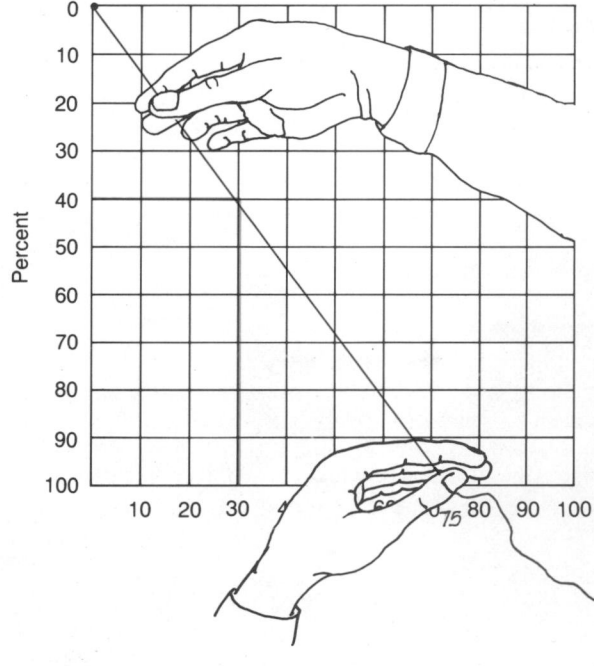

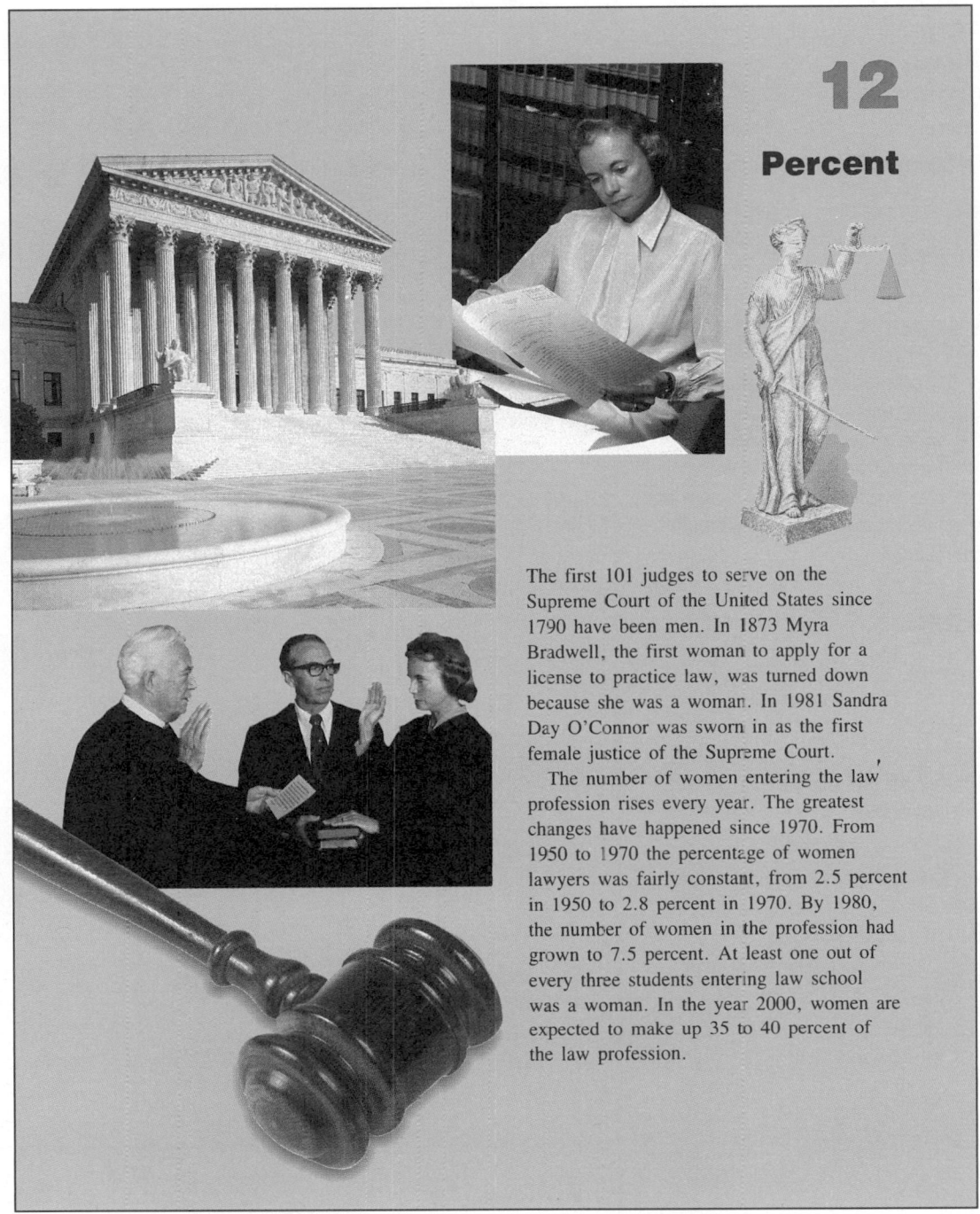

12

Percent

The first 101 judges to serve on the Supreme Court of the United States since 1790 have been men. In 1873 Myra Bradwell, the first woman to apply for a license to practice law, was turned down because she was a woman. In 1981 Sandra Day O'Connor was sworn in as the first female justice of the Supreme Court.

The number of women entering the law profession rises every year. The greatest changes have happened since 1970. From 1950 to 1970 the percentage of women lawyers was fairly constant, from 2.5 percent in 1950 to 2.8 percent in 1970. By 1980, the number of women in the profession had grown to 7.5 percent. At least one out of every three students entering law school was a woman. In the year 2000, women are expected to make up 35 to 40 percent of the law profession.

Introducing the Chapter

Discussion After students have had an opportunity to read the article and examine the photographs, discuss the data given. "What percent of lawyers were women in 1970?" (2.8 percent) "In 1980, what percent of lawyers were women?" (7.5 percent) "What was the ratio of women entering law school to students entering law school in 1980?" (1 out of 3)

Use this as an opportunity for students to create their own questions based on data in the article. As you teach the chapter, you may wish to refer back to this page and have students solve the following problems.

Follow-Up Questions

After Page 297 In 1980, 50% of the women lawyers were 32 years old or younger. Express this percent as a fraction. ($\frac{1}{2}$) In a 1980 survey of the 50 largest law firms in the U.S., $\frac{1}{50}$ of the law partners were women. What percent is this? (2%)

After Page 298 What percent of lawyers were women in 1950? (2.5%) Express the percent as a decimal. (0.025) It is predicted that by 1990, the percent of women lawyers may be as high as 25%. Write this percent as a decimal. (0.25)

After Page 303 In 1970 there were 324,800 lawyers. About how many lawyers were women? (9,094) In 1980 there were 535,000 lawyers. How many lawyers were women? (40,125)

After Page 307 What percent of the students entering law school in 1980 were women? ($33\frac{1}{3}$%)

Quick Review Have students estimate the products.

| 6.8 × 3.4 | **21** | 12.2 × 1.8 | **24** | 7.9 × 8.3 | **64** | 9.8 × 9.7 | **100** |
| 5.46 × 3.21 | **15** | 6.82 × 7.34 | **49** | 4.82 × 5.74 | **30** | | |

Lesson Focus To compare a number to 100 by means of a ratio, fraction, decimal, or percent

Suggested Materials 10 by 10 grid transparency for the overhead projector

Ideas for Getting Started

Have students compare a certain number of cents to 100¢ or a dollar. Ask students, "What part of a dollar is a penny?" ($\frac{1}{100}$ or 0.01) "What part of a dollar is a nickel?" ($\frac{5}{100}$ or 0.05) Repeat the questions for a dime, quarter, or other amounts of money.

Display a 10 by 10 grid on the overhead projector. Shade 3 squares and ask students what fractional part of the large square is shaded. Write the fraction $\frac{3}{100}$ and the decimal 0.03 on the chalkboard. Tell students that another way to describe the shaded part is by a percent. Write "3 percent" and "3%" on the chalkboard.

Using Page 294

Lesson Development Have students read the material at the top of the page. Discuss the meaning of *percent*. Stress that it means *per hundred*. Display some simple percents on the chalkboard. Have selected students shade in the appropriate part of the grid and write the shaded part of the grid as a decimal, fraction, and percent.

Other Examples Discuss these examples with students. Point out that in the last example the entire square is shaded, illustrating 100%.

Percent

A full sheet of postage stamps had 100 stamps. There are 78 stamps left.

We can describe the part of the sheet of stamps in several ways.

Ratio: **78** out of **100** stamps are left.
Fraction: $\frac{78}{100}$ of the stamps are left.
Decimal: **0.78** of the stamps are left.

We can also use a **percent**. **Percent** means **per hundred**. The symbol for percent is **%**. 78 percent or 78% of the stamps are left.

What part of the large square is shaded?

There are 25 squares out of 100 squares shaded.

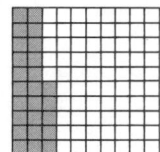

Fraction: $\frac{25}{100}$
Decimal: **0.25**
Percent: **25%**

Other Examples

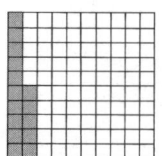

Fraction: $\frac{15}{100}$
Decimal: **0.15**
Percent: **15%**

294

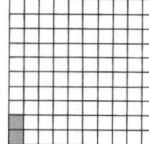

Fraction: $\frac{2}{100}$
Decimal: **0.02**
Percent: **2%**

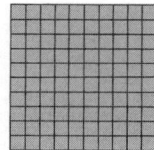

Fraction: $\frac{100}{100}$
Decimal: **1.00**
Percent: **100%**

Follow Up

Reteaching

Use place-value models to illustrate percents. Let the hundred-square represent 1 unit or 100%. Then 0.01 is represented by the unit-cube and 0.1 is represented by the ten-stick. Call out an amount, for example 32%. Ask students to think of the percent as $\frac{32}{100}$ or 32 out of 100 and then show that amount with models. Continue with other examples.

Enrichment

Have students make a set of "Percent Concentration" cards by labeling index cards with common percents. For each percent that is written, a fractional or decimal equivalent should be written on another card.

Cards should be placed face down. The object of the game is to turn over two matching cards. If the cards match, the student keeps the two cards. If the cards do not match, they are turned face down and it is the next student's turn. The winner is the student with the most cards after all matches are made.

What percent of each square is shaded?

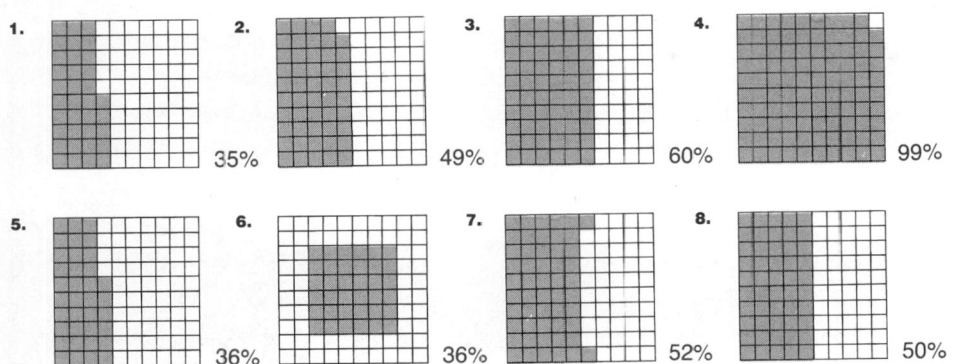

1. 35% 2. 49% 3. 60% 4. 99%

5. 36% 6. 36% 7. 52% 8. 50%

One dollar is 100 cents. What percent of a dollar is each amount?
Example: 35¢ is 35% of a dollar.

9. 15¢ 15%   10. 1¢ 1%   11. 50¢ 50%   12. 95¢ 95%   13. 38¢ 38%

14. $0.25 25%   15. $0.64 64%   16. $0.08 8%   17. $0.41 41%   18. $0.03 3%

Copy and complete the table.

	Ratio	Fraction	Decimal	Percent
19.	8 to 100	$\frac{8}{100}$	0.08	8%
20.	17 to 100	$\frac{17}{100}$	0.17	17%
21.	6 per hundred	$\frac{6}{100}$	0.06	6%
22.	37 out of 100	$\frac{37}{100}$	0.37	37%
23.	39 to 100	$\frac{39}{100}$	0.39	39%
24.	95 to 100	$\frac{95}{100}$	0.95	95%
25.	100 to 100	$\frac{100}{100}$	1.0	100%

26. A sheet of 100 stamps had 39 stamps left. What percent of the stamps were left? 39%

27. A sheet of 100 stamps had 27 stamps left. Then 18 of these stamps were used. What percent of 100 stamps are there now? 9%

295

Using Page 295

Exercises 9–18 These exercises relate money and percent. Remind students that to write each amount as a percent of a dollar, they need to compare the amount to 100¢.

Exercises 19–25 In these exercises, it is not necessary for students to express the fractions in lowest terms. In fact, doing so may cause some confusion to students.

Ideas That Work

Special Education

Present the activity "Made in the Shade" to strengthen percent recognition. Provide graph paper (TRB p. 285) and have students outline several 10 by 10 grids. In an envelope, place index cards with a percent written on the front, and a grid illustration on the back of each, as shown.

A student selects a card from the envelope, reads the front, and then must correctly shade his or her 10 by 10 grid to illustrate that percent. The student can then turn the card over to check the answer.

This activity can be done in reverse order with the student selecting a card, "reading" the illustration, and writing the appropriate percent. The student can again check the answer by turning the card over.

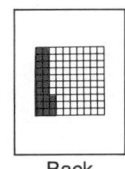

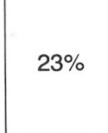

Back   Front

23%

Practice Supplement, page 110

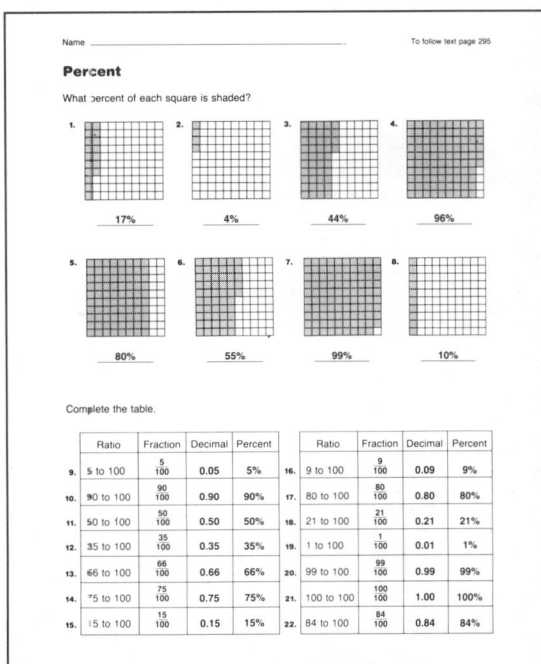

Quick Review Have students multiply and express their answers in lowest terms.

$\frac{1}{5} \times \frac{1}{6}$ $\frac{1}{30}$ $\frac{4}{9} \times \frac{3}{4}$ $\frac{1}{3}$ $\frac{5}{8} \times \frac{2}{3}$ $\frac{5}{12}$

$\frac{1}{12} \times \frac{4}{7}$ $\frac{1}{21}$ $\frac{2}{5} \times \frac{10}{13}$ $\frac{4}{13}$ $\frac{5}{6} \times \frac{3}{10}$ $\frac{1}{4}$ $\frac{2}{9} \times \frac{3}{4}$ $\frac{1}{6}$

Lesson Focus To write lowest-terms fractions for percents and to express fractions whose denominators are factors of 100 as percents

Ideas for Getting Started

Use the following examples to review finding lowest-terms fractions.

$\frac{20}{100}$ $\frac{75}{100}$ $\frac{25}{100}$ $\frac{24}{100}$ $\frac{8}{10}$

$\frac{96}{100}$ $\frac{20}{40}$ $\frac{6}{10}$ $\frac{5}{50}$ $\frac{40}{100}$

Then have students write each of the following fractions with a denominator of 100.

$\frac{1}{4}$ $\frac{2}{5}$ $\frac{1}{2}$ $\frac{3}{4}$ $\frac{4}{25}$

$\frac{3}{10}$ $\frac{7}{20}$ $\frac{6}{5}$ $\frac{9}{10}$ $\frac{4}{2}$

Using Page 296

Motivational Problem After students read the introductory problem, have them identify the question and the data needed to solve the problem. Elicit from students the idea that since percent means per hundred, 80% can be written as a fraction with a denominator of 100.

Lesson Development On the chalkboard, show how to write 80% as a fraction in lowest terms. Remind students that a fraction is in lowest terms when the only factor common to the numerator and denominator is 1. Next show how to write $\frac{1}{4}$ as a percent. Ask students what 4 can be multiplied by to get 100. On the chalkboard, multiply the numerator and denominator by 25 to get $\frac{25}{100}$ or 25%.

Other Examples Work through these examples as a class activity.

Percents and Fractions

A pullover is 80% cotton. What fractional part of the material in the pullover is cotton? Give the part as a lowest-terms fraction.

$$80\% = \frac{80}{100} = \frac{80 \div 20}{100 \div 20} = \frac{4}{5}$$

The lowest-terms fraction for 80% is $\frac{4}{5}$.

The pullover is $\frac{4}{5}$ cotton.

The pullover is marked "$\frac{1}{4}$ off." Give the fraction as a percent.

$$\frac{1}{4} = \frac{1 \times 25}{4 \times 25} = \frac{25}{100} = 25\%$$

The pullover is marked 25% off.

SALE! $\frac{1}{4}$ off price marked!

Other Examples

Percents to fractions

$45\% = \frac{45}{100} = \frac{9}{20}$

$125\% = \frac{125}{100} = \frac{5}{4}$

Fractions to percents

$\frac{2}{5} = \frac{2 \times 20}{5 \times 20} = \frac{40}{100} = 40\%$

$3 = \frac{3}{1} = \frac{300}{100} = 300\%$

Warm Up

Give the lowest-terms fraction for each percent.

1. 5% $\frac{1}{20}$
2. 16% $\frac{4}{25}$
3. 8% $\frac{2}{25}$
4. 20% $\frac{1}{5}$
5. 50% $\frac{1}{2}$
6. 84% $\frac{21}{25}$
7. 60% $\frac{3}{5}$
8. 2% $\frac{1}{50}$
9. 33% $\frac{33}{100}$
10. 85% $\frac{17}{20}$

Give the percent for each fraction.

11. $\frac{1}{10}$ 10%
12. $\frac{3}{4}$ 75%
13. $\frac{3}{20}$ 15%
14. $\frac{4}{5}$ 80%
15. $\frac{1}{100}$ 1%
16. $\frac{5}{20}$ 25%
17. $\frac{99}{100}$ 99%
18. $\frac{7}{1}$ 700%
19. $\frac{8}{10}$ 80%
20. $\frac{3}{2}$ 150%

296

Follow Up

Reteaching

Focus on the meaning of percent as a ratio or comparison to 100. Review with students the idea of equal ratios and how to solve a proportion. Show students how to find a percent for a fraction by writing a proportion.

$$\frac{3}{20} = \frac{n}{100}$$

$$20\,n = 3 \times 100$$

$$\frac{20\,n}{20} = \frac{300}{20}$$

$$n = 15$$

Enrichment

Have students copy and complete the following table.

Lowest-Terms Fractions	Decimal	Percent
$\frac{3}{10}$	**0.3**	**30%**
$\frac{3}{25}$	**0.12**	12%
$\frac{9}{20}$	0.45	**45%**
$\frac{9}{50}$	**0.18**	18%
$\frac{3}{2}$	1.5	**150%**
$\frac{1}{20}$	**0.05**	**5%**

Assignment Guide			
	Minimum	Average	Extended
page 297	1–33	1–34, 36	1–33 odd, 34–36, TM

Write the lowest-terms fraction for each percent.

	%	Fraction			%	Fraction			%	Fraction	
1.	10%		$\frac{1}{10}$	5.	40%		$\frac{2}{5}$	9.	75%		$\frac{3}{4}$
2.	20%		$\frac{1}{5}$	6.	50%		$\frac{1}{2}$	10.	80%		$\frac{4}{5}$
3.	25%		$\frac{1}{4}$	7.	60%		$\frac{3}{5}$	11.	90%		$\frac{9}{10}$
4.	30%		$\frac{3}{10}$	8.	70%		$\frac{7}{10}$	12.	100%		1

Write each fraction as a percent.

13. $\frac{8}{25}$ 32% 14. $\frac{9}{1}$ 900% 15. $\frac{4}{20}$ 20% 16. $\frac{39}{100}$ 39% 17. $\frac{8}{5}$ 160%

18. $\frac{13}{50}$ 26% 19. $\frac{3}{25}$ 12% 20. $\frac{11}{25}$ 44% 21. $\frac{5}{4}$ 125% 22. $\frac{10}{1}$ 1,000%

Write each fraction in lowest terms. Then write the percent for the fraction.

23. $\frac{9}{12}$ $\frac{3}{4}$; 75% 24. $\frac{7}{14}$ $\frac{1}{2}$; 50% 25. $\frac{9}{36}$ $\frac{1}{4}$; 25% 26. $\frac{21}{30}$ $\frac{7}{10}$; 70% 27. $\frac{18}{40}$ $\frac{9}{20}$; 45%

28. $\frac{36}{60}$ $\frac{3}{5}$; 60% 29. $\frac{99}{198}$ $\frac{1}{2}$; 50% 30. $\frac{36}{18}$ 2; 200% 31. $\frac{29}{116}$ $\frac{1}{4}$; 25% 32. $\frac{144}{1,600}$ $\frac{9}{100}$; 9%

33. A suit is 5% silk. What is the lowest-terms fraction for the part of the suit that is silk? $\frac{1}{20}$

34. A dress is 60% polyester, 25% cotton, and the rest is silk. What percent of the dress is silk? What is the lowest-terms fraction for the part that is silk? 15%; $\frac{3}{20}$

35. A coat is $\frac{4}{5}$ wool, $\frac{1}{10}$ linen, and the rest is polyester. What percent of the coat is made of linen and wool together? 90%

36. **DATA HUNT** Find an article of clothing that is made of different materials. Find the percent of each material. What is the fraction in lowest terms for each percent?

THINK MATH

Guess and Check

What is the greatest amount of money you can have (using pennies, nickels, dimes, quarters, and half dollars) and still not be able to give someone change for a dollar? $1.19; See teaching notes.

More Practice, page 434, Set C

297

Using Page 297

Exercises 1–12 These exercises deal with percents related to fractions in halves, fourths, fifths, or tenths. Most students should be familiar with these percents and commit them to memory.

Data Hunt Have students check fabric content labels on their sweaters or jackets for percents.

Think Math This problem can be solved using the Guess and Check strategy. Some students may think 99¢ in coins is the solution. However, it is possible to have $1.19 in change and still not be able to give change for a dollar. The $1.19 can be formed in several ways:

- 3 quarters, 4 dimes, and 4 pennies
- 1 half dollar, 1 quarter, 4 dimes, and 4 pennies
- 9 dimes, 1 quarter, and 4 pennies

More Practice, page 434, Set C

Percent

Quick Review Have students change each measurement to centimeters.
1,400 mm   **140 cm**   80 m   **8,000 cm**   15.6 dm   **156 cm**
0.41 m   **41 cm**   35 mm   **3.5 cm**

Lesson Focus To write percents as decimals and decimals as percents; to estimate a percent of a region using a picture

Ideas for Getting Started

Review with students the shortcuts for multiplying and dividing decimals by powers of 10.

Have students multiply each of these numbers by 100.

    0.26   0.375   0.4   0.06

Then have students divide these numbers by 100.

    46   9   46.7   150

Using Page 298

Lesson Development Read the introductory material with students. Stress that percent means per hundred, so to write a percent as a decimal we divide by 100 and drop the percent sign. Discuss with students the examples showing how to write percents as decimals.

Explain that writing a decimal as a percent is just a reversal of the process above. We move the decimal point 2 places to the right and write the percent sign. This shortcut can be justified mathematically as follows:

$$0.287 = 0.287 \times \frac{100}{100} = \frac{28.7}{100} = 28.7\%$$

With students, work through the examples of writing a percent for a decimal.

Exercises 1–30 Have students complete these exercises independently. Provide ample time for them to check their work and discuss any area of difficulty.

Percents and Decimals

To use percents in problem solving, we must often write a decimal for a percent.

What is the decimal for 13.3%? What is the decimal for 10.7%? Remember that percent means per hundred.

$$13.3\% = \frac{13.3}{100} = 0.133$$
$$10.7\% = \frac{10.7}{100} = 0.107$$

Dividing by 100 shifts the decimal point 2 places to the left. This is a shortcut.

26.7% = 0.267	125% = 1.25
7.8% = 0.078	0.5% = 0.005
63% = 0.63	200% = 2.00

To write a percent for a decimal, shift the decimal 2 places to the right.

0.287 = 28.7%	1.33 = 133%
0.033 = 3.3%	0.008 = 0.8%
0.07 = 7%	5.00 = 500%

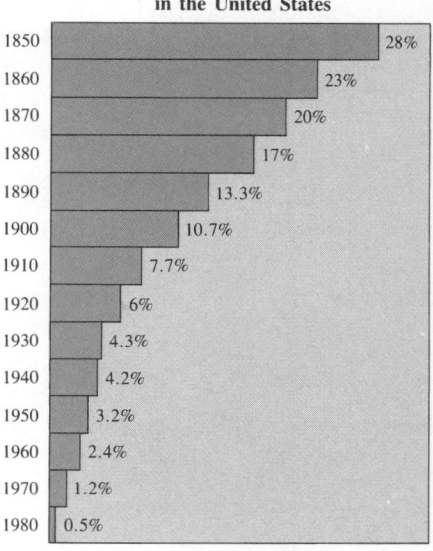

The Decreasing Percent of Illiteracy in the United States

Year	Percent of illiteracy
1850	28%
1860	23%
1870	20%
1880	17%
1890	13.3%
1900	10.7%
1910	7.7%
1920	6%
1930	4.3%
1940	4.2%
1950	3.2%
1960	2.4%
1970	1.2%
1980	0.5%

Percent of illiteracy

Write each percent as a decimal.

1. 38% 0.38   2. 16% 0.16   3. 8% 0.08   4. 79% 0.79   5. 11% 0.11

6. 23.5% 0.235   7. 12.8% 0.128   8. 9.6% 0.096   9. 10.2% 0.102   10. 18.45% 0.1845

11. 0.6% 0.006   12. 105% 1.05   13. 325% 3.25   14. 1.55% 0.0155   15. 100% 1.0

Write each decimal as a percent.

16. 0.48 48%   17. 0.95 95%   18. 0.09 9%   19. 0.19 19%   20. 0.02 2%

21. 0.064 6.4%   22. 0.1667 16.67%   23. 0.028 2.8%   24. 0.505 50.5%   25. 0.0975 9.75%

26. 1.36 136%   27. 3 300%   28. 0.0025 0.25%   29. 10.00 1,000%   30. 0.0125 1.25%

       More Practice, page 435, Set A

Follow Up

Reteaching

Set up a chart as shown below. Emphasize the meaning of percent as per hundred. Have students help complete the chart.

Percent	Fraction	Decimal
35%	$\frac{35}{100}$	0.35
8%		
18%		
175%		

After the chart is complete, elicit from students a shortcut for writing a decimal for a percent: move the decimal point two places to the left.

Enrichment

Have students find examples of the use of percent in newspapers. Then have them write these percents as decimals and as fractions. You may wish to display the newspaper clippings along with the equivalent fractions, decimals, and percents on a bulletin board.

Assignment Guide			
	Minimum	Average	Extended
page 298	1–30	1–30	2–30, even
page 299	1–4	1–8	1–8

Estimating Percents

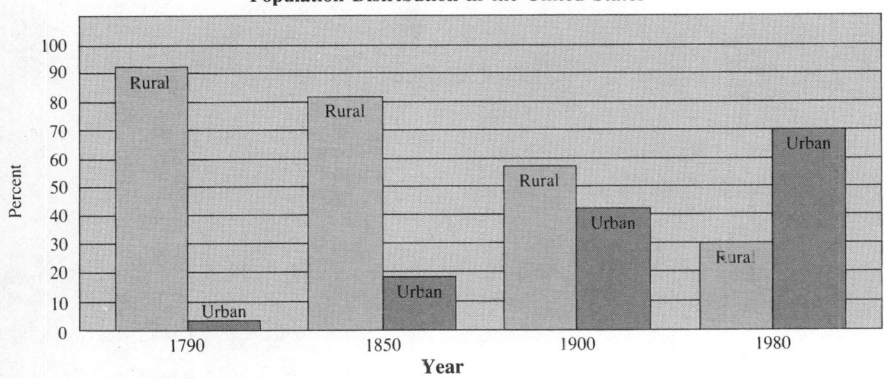

Population Distribution in the United States

What is an estimate of the percent of the population in 1790 that was rural?

The graph shows more than 90% but less than 95%.

Estimate: About 93% of the population was rural.

Estimate the percents. Answers may vary.

1. What percent of the population in 1850 was urban? What percent was rural?
18%; 82%

2. What percent of the population in 1900 was urban? What percent was rural?
43%; 57%

3. What percent of the population in 1980 was urban? What percent was rural?
70%; 30%

4. What was the increase of the percent of urban population from 1790 to 1980?
66%

Andrew made a circle graph showing how he uses his leisure time.
Use the circle graph to estimate each percent.

5. About what percent of the leisure time does the graph show for using the computer? 25%

6. About what percent of the time is shown for sports? 45%

7. About what percent of the time is shown for reading? 10%

8. About what percent of the time is shown for club activities? 20%

Use of Leisure Time

299

Using Page 299

Lesson Development Point out that the bar graph at the top of the page shows the percent of the population that was rural and the percent that was urban in various years. After students have had an opportunity to study the graph, direct their attention to the bar representing the rural population in 1790. Explain that the graph shows the population to be more than 90% but less than 95% rural. A good estimate would be 93%. Ask students to estimate the percent of the population that was urban in 1790. (4%)

Tell students that thinking of a fraction can be helpful in making percent estimations. Before assigning the exercises, you may wish to review with students the percents for simple fractions.

Exercises 5–8 These exercises deal with a circle graph. Most students at this grade level will be familiar with this type of graph. Little interpretation of the graph is needed to answer the questions, other than what fractional part of the circular region is shaded for each activity.

More Practice, page 435, Set A

Reteaching Supplement, page 87

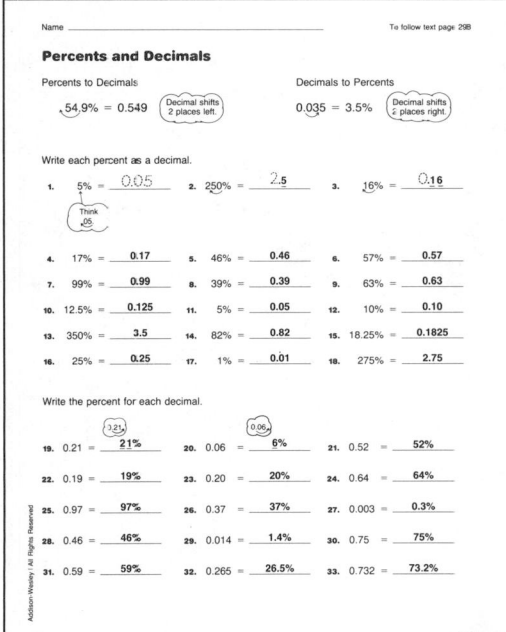

Enrichment Supplement, page 87

Practice Supplement, page 112

Quick Review Have students find the LCD of each pair of fractions and find the equivalent fractions with that denominator.

$\frac{2}{5}, \frac{7}{15}$ $\frac{6}{15}, \frac{7}{15}$ $\frac{3}{8}, \frac{2}{3}$ $\frac{9}{24}, \frac{16}{24}$ $\frac{7}{6}, \frac{3}{4}$ $\frac{14}{12}, \frac{9}{12}$

$\frac{1}{6}, \frac{1}{10}$ $\frac{5}{30}, \frac{3}{30}$ $\frac{4}{9}, \frac{4}{27}$ $\frac{12}{27}, \frac{4}{27}$

Lesson Focus To find a percent for a fraction by dividing, and to round percents to the nearest whole percent

Ideas for Getting Started

Write these mixed numbers on the chalkboard and have students round each to the nearest whole number. Explain that if the fraction part is $\frac{1}{2}$ or more, they should add 1 to the whole number. If the fraction part is less than $\frac{1}{2}$, it is simply dropped.

$9\frac{2}{3}$ $16\frac{3}{4}$ $6\frac{3}{10}$ $42\frac{1}{8}$

$10\frac{1}{2}$ $66\frac{5}{8}$ $87\frac{1}{6}$ $3\frac{7}{10}$

Using Page 300

Motivational Problem Have students read the problem at the top of the page. Ask them to restate the question in their own words and to identify the needed data. Explain that to write 7 out of 30 as a percent, we can first write $\frac{7}{30}$ as a decimal by dividing.

Lesson Development On the chalkboard, work through finding the percent for 7 out of 30. Point out that the division is carried out to the hundredths place and the remainder is expressed as a lowest-terms fraction. Remind students that to change a decimal to a percent, we multiply by 100 or move the decimal point 2 places to the right and write a percent sign.

Discuss the process of rounding to the nearest whole percent. Explain to students that a shortcut can be used to find the nearest whole percent. If the remainder is $\frac{1}{2}$ or more of the divisor, add 1 to the quotient. If the remainder is less than $\frac{1}{2}$ of the divisor, the quotient remains the same.

Other Examples Work through these examples as a class activity. Explain that in the first example, we round to 86% since 5 is more than $\frac{1}{2}$ of 7. The second example shows that a percent can be expressed as a decimal or a mixed decimal. In this case, $\frac{1}{8}$ can be written as 12.5% or $12\frac{1}{2}$%.

Finding Percents for Other Fractions

Serena Miller is a meteorologist. She found that in 7 out of 30 days of June it had rained. What percent of the days in June had it rained?

To find the percent for 7 out of 30, we can find a decimal for $\frac{7}{30}$ by dividing. Then we can write a percent for the decimal.

$$\begin{array}{r} 0.2\,3\ \frac{10}{30} \\ 30\overline{)7.0\,0} \\ \underline{6\,0} \\ 1\,0\,0 \\ \underline{9\,0} \\ 1\,0 \end{array} = 0.23\frac{1}{3} = 23\frac{1}{3}\%$$

It rained on $23\frac{1}{3}$% of the days.

Sometimes percents are rounded to the **nearest whole percent**. $23\frac{1}{3}$% rounded to the nearest whole percent is 23%.

Other Examples

What percent is $\frac{6}{7}$?

$$\begin{array}{r} 0.8\,5\ \frac{5}{7} \\ 7\overline{)6.0\,0} \\ \underline{5\,6} \\ 4\,0 \\ \underline{3\,5} \\ 5 \end{array}$$ $\frac{6}{7} = 85\frac{5}{7}\%$

To the nearest whole percent, this is 86%.

What percent is $\frac{1}{8}$?

$$\begin{array}{r} 0.1\,2\,5 \\ 8\overline{)1.0\,0\,0} \\ \underline{8} \\ 2\,0 \\ \underline{1\,6} \\ 4\,0 \\ \underline{4\,0} \\ 0 \end{array} = 12.5\%$$ $\frac{1}{8} = 12.5\% = 12\frac{1}{2}\%$

To the nearest whole percent, this is 13%.

Warm Up

Give the percent for each fraction. Round to the nearest whole percent.

1. $\frac{1}{3}$ 33%   2. $\frac{3}{8}$ 38%   3. $\frac{1}{6}$ 17%   4. $\frac{7}{8}$ 88%   5. $\frac{5}{8}$ 63%

6. $\frac{5}{9}$ 56%   7. $\frac{1}{8}$ 13%   8. $\frac{5}{12}$ 42%   9. $\frac{9}{16}$ 56%   10. $\frac{7}{12}$ 58%

300

Follow Up

Reteaching

In order to find percents for the fractions in this lesson, students must be able to 1) write a decimal for a fraction, and 2) write a percent for a decimal. Review these skills with students. Then have them write percents for the following fractions at the chalkboard.

$\frac{3}{16}$ $18\frac{3}{4}$% $\frac{21}{34}$ $61\frac{13}{17}$%

$\frac{1}{12}$ $8\frac{1}{3}$% $\frac{8}{9}$ $88\frac{8}{9}$%

Enrichment

Have students use estimation to write the correct symbol, $>$, $<$, or $=$ in the $\bigcirc$.

1. 55% of 200 $\bigcirc{>}$ 95
2. 39% of 70 $\bigcirc{<}$ 35
3. 16% of 10 $\bigcirc{<}$ 6
4. 47% of 92 $\bigcirc{>}$ 20
5. 50% of 120 $\bigcirc{=}$ 60
6. 48% of 52 $\bigcirc{<}$ 27
7. 120% of 70 $\bigcirc{>}$ 65
8. 150% of 84 $\bigcirc{>}$ 90

Find the percent for each fraction. Round to the nearest whole percent.

1. $\frac{5}{6}$ 83% **2.** $\frac{8}{12}$ 67% **3.** $\frac{9}{11}$ 82% **4.** $\frac{8}{9}$ 89% **5.** $\frac{5}{11}$ 45%

6. $\frac{11}{16}$ 69% **7.** $\frac{10}{17}$ 59% **8.** $\frac{5}{18}$ 28% **9.** $\frac{11}{12}$ 92% **10.** $\frac{13}{16}$ 81%

11. $\frac{6}{9}$ 67% **12.** $\frac{13}{18}$ 72% **13.** $\frac{17}{24}$ 71% **14.** $\frac{33}{40}$ 83% **15.** $\frac{19}{35}$ 54%

16. $\frac{26}{27}$ 96% **17.** $\frac{17}{29}$ 59% **18.** $\frac{5}{18}$ 28% **19.** $\frac{29}{60}$ 48% **20.** $\frac{35}{45}$ 78%

The decimal for each fraction has been found using a calculator.
Write each decimal as a percent rounded to the nearest tenth.

Example: $\frac{84}{152} = 0.5526316$ 55.26316% rounded to the nearest tenth is 55.3%

21. $\frac{75}{160} = 0.46875$ 46.9% **22.** $\frac{33}{111} = 0.2972972$ 29.7% **23.** $\frac{71}{90} = 0.7888889$ 78.9%

24. $\frac{133}{87} = 1.5287356$ 152.9% **25.** $\frac{110}{245} = 0.4489795$ 44.9% **26.** $\frac{1,475}{1,525} = 0.9672131$ 96.7%

27. In Cleveland, Ohio, 212 out of 365 days were cloudy. What percent of the days were cloudy? Round the percent to the nearest whole percent. 58%

28. In Albuquerque, New Mexico, only 84 out of 365 days were cloudy. What percent of the days were not cloudy? Round the percent to the nearest tenth of a percent. 77%

★ **29.** In Bridge City, about 66% of the days are cloudy. Estimate how many days a year are cloudy. about 240–255 days

30. DATA BANK How many days of precipitation does Miami, Florida average during the month of August? What is the percent of days in August with precipitation? Round the percent to the nearest whole percent. (See page 414.) 17; 55%

SKILLKEEPER

Find the area of each triangle. Use $A = \frac{1}{2}bh$.

1. $b = 20$ cm
$h = 12$ cm
120 cm²

2. $b = 32$ m
$h = 16$ m
256 m²

3. $b = 4.5$ cm
$h = 2.6$ cm
5.85 cm²

4. $b = 80$ m
$h = 62$ m
2,480 m²

5. $b = 2.6$ cm
$h = 0.8$ cm
1.04 cm²

Find the volume of each prism. Use $V = Bh$.

6. $B = 16$ cm²
$h = 10$ cm
160 cm³

7. $B = 12.2$ cm²
$h = 5.9$ cm
71.98 cm³

8. $B = 6$ cm²
$h = 1.9$ cm
11.4 cm³

9. $B = 295$ mm²
$h = 27$ mm
7,965 mm³

10. $B = 0.92$ m²
$h = 0.002$ m
0.00184 m³

More Practice, page 435, Set B

301

Using Page 301

Exercises 21–26 Use a calculator to demonstrate exercises similar to these to the class. Explain that although changing a decimal to a percent is simply a matter of moving the decimal point, it is often more practical to round a decimal than to use the decimal with several places.

Exercises 27–28 You may wish to have students use a calculator to solve these problems.

Exercise 29 Students may reason that 66% is about 0.7 and then estimate 0.7 of 365. Or they may think of 66% as close to $\frac{2}{3}$ and estimate $\frac{2}{3}$ of 365.

More Practice, page 435, Set B

Reteaching Supplement, page 88   Enrichment Supplement, page 88   Practice Supplement, page 113

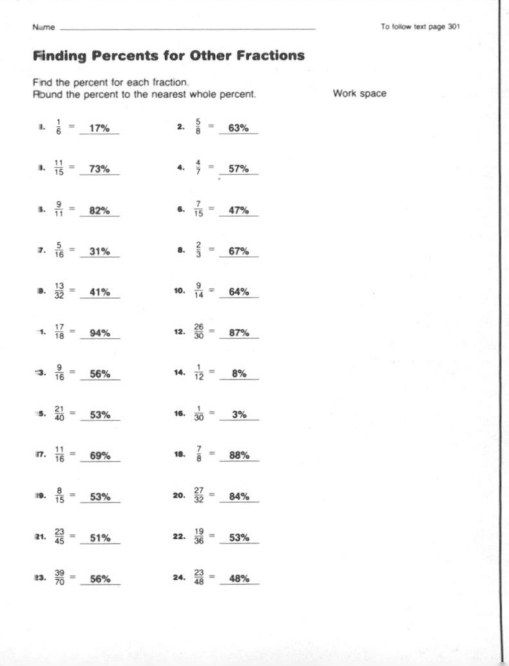

Quick Review Have students subtract and write answers in lowest terms.

$17\frac{7}{12} - 8\frac{1}{4}$ $9\frac{1}{3}$ $34\frac{5}{6} - 20\frac{1}{2}$ $14\frac{1}{3}$ $9\frac{8}{9} - 4\frac{2}{9}$ $5\frac{2}{3}$

$27\frac{7}{10} - 12\frac{3}{5}$ $15\frac{1}{10}$ $15\frac{2}{5} - 11\frac{1}{3}$ $4\frac{1}{15}$

Lesson Focus To find a percent of a number

Ideas for Getting Started

To prepare students for the lesson, give a brief review of writing fractions or decimals for percents. Then have them write each of the following as a fraction and a decimal.

50%	20%	25%	80%	10%
1%	75%	$33\frac{1}{3}$%	60%	90%

Using Page 302

Motivational Problem Have students read the introductory problem. Ask them to identify the question and the data needed to answer the question. Explain that 24% of 25 means 24% times 25, so our plan is to multiply.

Lesson Development On the chalkboard, work through the computation to solve the problem. Emphasize that the percent is written as a decimal before multiplying. Have students check the answer by showing that the ratio of 6 to 25 is the same as 24 to 100 or 24%.

Other Examples Work through these examples with students. Point out that if a percent has a simple fractional equivalent, as in the first example, it may be easier to use the fraction than a decimal. Observe with students that in the last example the product is greater than 240, since 150% is greater than 1.

Warm Up Assign these exercises as independent written work. Make certain students write a fraction or decimal for the percents before multiplying. In exercises 1–6, encourage students to use the multiplication shortcut.

Finding a Percent of a Number

In a class of 25 students, 24% of the students play a musical instrument. How many students play a musical instrument?

Since 24% of 25 means 24% × 25, we can change the percent to a decimal and multiply.

$24\% = 0.24$

$$\begin{array}{r} 2\,5 \\ \times\,0.2\,4 \\ \hline 1\,0\,0 \\ 5\,0 \\ \hline 6.0\,0 \end{array}$$

There are 6 students who play a musical instrument.

Other Examples

Find 20% of 60.	What is 7% of 85?	Find 150% of 240.
Since 20% = $\frac{1}{5}$, it is easy to use the fraction for the percent.	$\begin{array}{r} 8\,5 \\ \times\,0.0\,7 \\ \hline 5.9\,5 \end{array}$	$\begin{array}{r} 2\,4\,0 \\ \times\,1.5\,0 \\ \hline 1\,2\,0\,0\,0 \\ 2\,4\,0 \\ \hline 3\,6\,0.0\,0 \end{array}$
$\frac{1}{5} \times 60 = 12$		

Warm Up

Give the percent of each number. Use a lowest-terms fraction for the percent.

1. 10% of 80 8
2. 50% of 38 19
3. 75% of 28 21
4. $33\frac{1}{3}$% of 15 5
5. 80% of 30 24
6. 25% of 108 27

Give the percent of each number. Use a decimal for the percent.

7. 37% of 26 9.62
8. 77% of 125 96.25
9. 67% of 130 87.10
10. 8.5% of 200 17
11. 123% of 94 115.62
12. 0.5% of 700 3.5

302

Follow Up

Reteaching

Review writing fractions and decimals as percents, such as $\frac{1}{2}$ = 0.50 = 50% and $\frac{3}{4}$ = 0.75 = 75%. Next discuss finding a fraction of a number. Emphasize that the word "of" means times.

Work through examples such as $\frac{1}{2}$ of 10 and 0.06 of 15, and relate these exercises to finding a percent of a number. Explain that to find a percent of a number we can write the percent as a fraction or decimal and multiply.

Enrichment

Give students this cross-number puzzle to solve.

^{1}2	2	^{2}4	
1		^{3}9	^{4}6
^{5}9	^{6}2		9
	^{7}1	0	3

Across	Down
1. 64% of 350	1. 25% of 876
3. 48% of 200	2. 20% of 245
5. 92% of 100	4. 33% of 2,100
7. 50% of 206	6. 20% of 105

Assignment Guide

page 303	Minimum	Average	Extended
	1–24, 41	1–41, 44	1–41 odd, 42–44

Find the percent of each number. Use a lowest-terms fraction for each number.

1. 25% of 80 20   **2.** 50% of 62 31   **3.** 80% of 75 60   **4.** 10% of 250 25

5. 30% of 30 9   **6.** 75% of 36 27   **7.** 40% of 45 18   **8.** 90% of 300 270

Find the percent of each number. Use a decimal for the percent.

9. 21% of 54 11.34   **10.** 18% of 325 58.50   **11.** 95% of 700 665   **12.** 3% of 66 1.98

13. 150% of 48 72   **14.** 110% of 60 66   **15.** 6.5% of 200 13   **16.** 12.5% of 124 15.5

Find the percent of each number.

17. 24% of 84 20.16   **18.** 50% of 214 107   **19.** 10.3% of 78 8.034   **20.** 25% of 200 50

21. 75% of 60 45   **22.** 13% of 620 80.6   **23.** 45% of 250 112.5   **24.** 200% of 800 1,600

Find 1% of each number.

Example: 1% of 800 = 0.01 × 800 = 8.00

25. 400 4   **26.** 1,000 10   **27.** 750 7.5   **28.** 80 0.8

29. 2,500 25   **30.** 260 2.6   **31.** 2,860 28.6   **32.** 50,000 500

Find 10% of each number.

Example: 10% of 450 = 0.1 × 450 = 45.0

33. 300 30   **34.** 870 87   **35.** 1,600 160   **36.** 25 2.5

37. 2,000 200   **38.** 8,000 800   **39.** 60,000 6,000   **40.** 1,000,000 100,000

41. In a class of 25 students, 8% of the students play the piano. How many students play the piano? 2

42. In a school of 1,640 students, 10% of the students either sing in the chorus or play in the band. There are 73 students in the chorus. How many students are in the band? 91

43. A school has a total enrollment of 480 students. One day 97.5% of the students were in school. How many students were in school? How many students were absent? 468; 12

44. Make up a problem about finding the percent of a number. Use real data from your school or your class. Solve the problem.

More Practice, page 435, Set C

Using Page 303

Exercises 17–24 In these exercises, students must decide whether to use a decimal or a fraction for the percent.

Exercises 25–40 Shortcuts are suggested for finding 1% and 10% of a number. Encourage better students to do the multiplication mentally and record only the answers to these problems.

Exercise 43 Although this is a calculator problem, students can use paper and pencil. Note that two questions must be answered.

Exercise 44 Encourage students to be creative and write their own problems as suggested. Display some of the problems on a bulletin board or use them as test questions.

More Practice, page 435, Set C

Reteaching Supplement, page 89

Enrichment Supplement, page 89

Practice Supplement, page 114

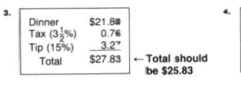
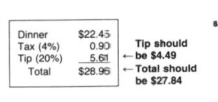

Lesson Focus To find simple interest using interest formulas; to solve word problems involving interest

Suggested Materials Newspaper advertisements of bank interest rates

Ideas for Getting Started

Display an advertisement that shows interest as a percent and conduct a class discussion about the meaning of *interest*. Emphasize that interest is the charge for the use of money. Explain that banks charge interest on money they loan, while they pay interest on money loaned to them—that is, money in savings accounts.

Using Page 304

Motivational Problem Have students read the information in the box at the top of the page. You may want to emphasize this information by writing it on the chalkboard. Read the introductory problem with students, and have them restate the questions. Note that there are two questions. We are to find the interest and the amount. Ask students to identify the data in the problem. Explain that formulas can be used to solve the problem.

Lesson Development Tell students that by using the interest formula, $I = PRT$, we can find the interest. Point out that the interest rate is per year and the time is in years. The interest rate can be given in terms of days, months, weeks, or years. The time must be given in the same unit as the rate.

On the chalkboard, write the interest formula, substitute the values for P, R, and T, and find the interest. Then find the amount using the formula $A = P + I$.

Other Examples Work through the example on the chalkboard, giving students an opportunity to participate in each step.

Exercises 1–6 Make certain students are applying the formulas correctly. Suggest that they identify P, R, and T in writing before using the formula.

Finding Simple Interest

Darlene Fields put $800 in a savings account that will earn **interest** at a **rate** of 9% per year. She plans to keep the money in the savings account for 3 years. How much interest will be earned? What will be the **amount** after 3 years?

To find the interest, we can use the interest formula $I = PRT$.

$P = \$800,\ R = 9\%,\ T = 3$ **years**
$I = \$800 \times 0.09 \times 3$
$I = \$216.00$

The interest is $216.

To find the amount after 3 years, we add the **principal** to the interest.

$A = P + I$
$P = \$800,\ I = \$216$
$A = \$800 + \$216 = \$1{,}016$

The amount is $1,016.

Principal (*P*):	Amount loaned or borrowed
Interest (*I*):	Charge for the use of money
Rate (*R*):	A percent of the principal charged as interest
Time (*T*):	Length of time the principal is loaned or borrowed
Amount (*A*):	Principal plus interest

Interest = Principal · Rate · Time
$$I = PRT$$
Amount = Principal + Interest
$$A = P + I$$

Other Examples

Find the interest and amount on a principal of $2,000 at 10% per year for 18 months.

$P = \$2{,}000$ $I = PRT$ $A = P + I$
$R = 10\% = 0.10$ $I = \$2{,}000 \times 0.10 \times 1.5 = \$300$ $A = \$2{,}000 + \$300 = \$2{,}300$
$T = 18$ months $= 1.5$ years

The interest is $300. The amount is $2,300.

Find the interest.

1. $P = \$3{,}000$
   $R = 12\%$ per year
   $T = 2$ years
   $720

2. $P = \$20{,}000$
   $R = 16\%$ per year
   $T = 6$ months
   (Use 0.5 year.) $1,600

3. $P = \$2{,}500$
   $R = 1.5\%$ per month
   $T = 5$ months
   $187.50

Find the amount.

4. $P = \$650$
   $I = \$26$
   $676

5. $P = \$1{,}800$
   $R = 10\%$ per year
   $T = 5$ years
   $2,700

6. $P = \$9{,}000$
   $R = 18\%$ per year
   $T = 2.5$ years
   $13,050

304

Follow Up

Reteaching

Allow students to work in pairs. Have students take turns making up and solving problems involving interest.

Enrichment

Provide students with information about various kinds of savings accounts and bank interest. You may wish to obtain brochures from your local banks.

Have students choose an amount of money to save and decide the length of time they wish to leave their money in the bank. Considering these factors, students should select the type of savings account they want to have. Then students should find the amount of interest they will receive at the end of the given time.

Assignment Guide			
	Minimum	Average	Extended
page 304	1–6	1–6	1–6
page 305	1–6	1–9	1–11

305

Applications

PROBLEM SOLVING: Using Simple Interest Formulas

QUESTION
DATA
PLAN
ANSWER
CHECK

Solve.

1. If a rate of 8% per year were paid on a principal of $500, what would be the interest at the end of 1 year? **$40**

2. If a rate of 15% per year were paid on a principal of $6,600, what would be the interest for 3 months? (Use 0.25 of a year.) **$247.50**

3. Will Maxon borrowed $500 for 1 year. The rate was 19% per year. What was the interest on the principal? **$95**

4. Gwen Masoni put $5,000 into a savings account that paid an interest rate of 12% per year. What is the amount she will have at the end of 6 years? **$8,600**

5. Isabelle Wilson put $3,600 into a money-market fund that paid a 14% rate of interest per year. How much interest would the principal earn in 2 months? (Use $\frac{1}{6}$ year for 2 months.) **$84**

6. Kevin Hough had $600 in a savings account that paid an interest rate of 6% per year. At the end of 4 months Kevin decided to draw out all his money, including the interest. What was the total amount? **$612**

7. Janalee Hughes bought a used car. She borrowed $3,800 for 4 years at a rate of 17% per year. What was the amount that she had to repay? **$6,384**

8. Calvin Wong borrowed $2,000 for 1 year. At the end of the year he repaid his loan with $2,300. How much was the interest? What was the interest rate? **$300; 15%**

9. A business borrowed $32,000 for 1 year at an interest rate of 18%. What is the amount that must be repaid in 1 year? **$37,760**

★ **10.** Sylvia can earn up to $2,000 tax-free interest in 1 year. How much principal must she invest at an interest rate of 16% per year in order to earn $2,000 interest? **$12,500**

11. Try This A bank has checkbook covers that are either pocket- or desk-size. The covers are orange, black, red, or tan. The customer's name will be stamped on the cover in gold or silver. How many different combinations of covers are possible? Hint: Make an organized list. **16**

305

Using Page 305

Exercises 1–9 Before assigning these exercises, you may wish to discuss one or more of the problems and have students identify the values for P, R, and T.

Exercise 10 This problem is starred because students must find the principal instead of the interest. Have students identify the various data in writing and then substitute in the interest formula.

$$I = \$2,000 \qquad R = 16\% = 0.16 \qquad T = 1$$
$$I = PRT$$
$$\$2,000 = P \times 0.16 \times 1$$
$$\$2,000 = 0.16\,P$$
$$P = \$2,000 \div 0.16$$
$$P = \$12,500$$

Try This A possible strategy, Make an Organized List, was taught on page 50.

Discussion After students read the problem, have them identify the question and the data. Ask them to name one possible combination of covers. Elicit from students that the strategy, Make an Organized List, can be used to solve the problem.

Solution

POG	POS	DOG	DOS
PBG	PBS	DBG	DBS
PRG	PRS	DRG	DRS
PTG	PTS	DTG	DTS

There are 16 combinations of covers.

Reteaching Supplement, page 90

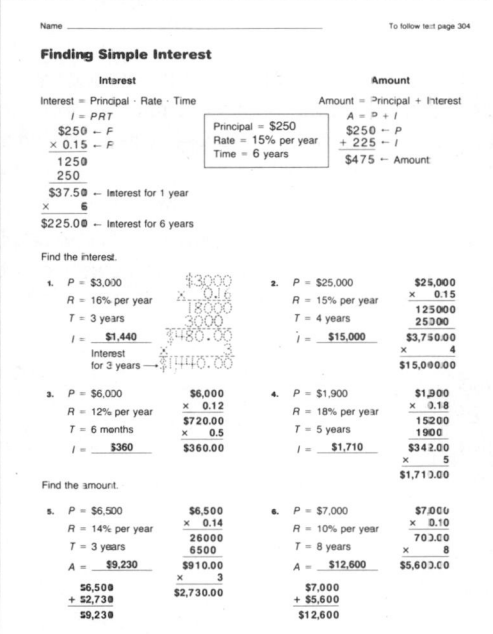

Enrichment Supplement, page 90

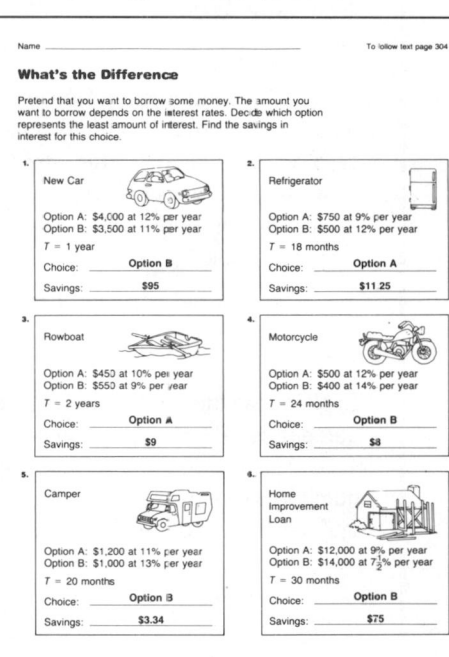

Practice Supplement, page 115

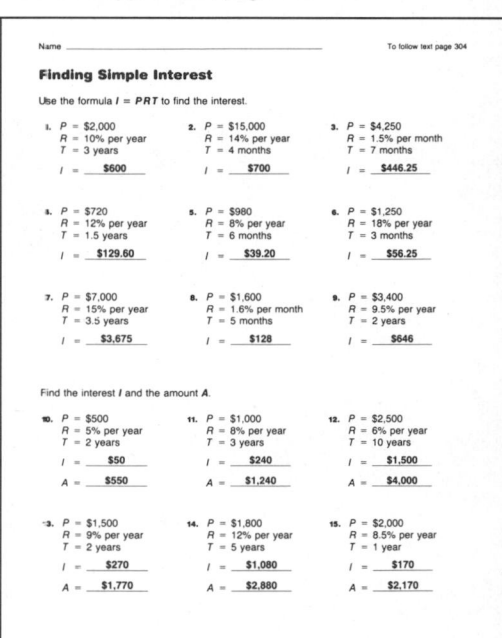

Quick Review Have students estimate the quotients.

21.92 ÷ 0.52	**40**	0.359 ÷ 7.7	**0.05**
29.462 ÷ 0.06	**500**	1.895 ÷ 2.87	**0.6**

Lesson Focus To find the percent one number is of another number

Ideas for Getting Started

Review with students how to find a percent for a fraction. Then have them write the following fractions as percents.

$$\frac{8}{10} \qquad \frac{3}{5} \qquad \frac{24}{25} \qquad \frac{1}{8} \qquad \frac{15}{10} \qquad \frac{6}{3}$$

Using Page 306

Motivational Problem Have students read the problem and restate the question in their own words. Ask them to identify the data that is given. Elicit from students that a plan for solving the problem is to write the percent for the ratio, 52 out of 80.

Lesson Development On the chalkboard, write the ratio, $\frac{52}{80}$, and discuss with students how to express it as a percent. Some students may notice that the fraction can be reduced to $\frac{13}{20}$ and then written as $\frac{65}{100}$ or 65%. Other students will recall the division process:

$$\begin{array}{r} 0.65 = 65\% \\ 80\overline{)52.00} \end{array}$$

Have students multiply to check if 65% of 80 is 52.

Other Examples Work through these examples as a class activity.

Warm Up Assign these exercises as independent written work. Watch for students who write an incorrect ratio, especially when the ratio is greater than 1, as in exercises 2 and 4.

Finding the Percent One Number Is of Another

A campground has 80 camping spaces. One night, 52 of the spaces were in use. The manager had to record the percent of spaces in use. What percent of the spaces were in use?

To solve the problem, we can find the percent for the ratio of the two numbers.

Ratio: **52** out of **80** spaces → $\frac{52}{80}$

Percent: $\frac{52}{80} = 0.65 = 65\%$

65% of the spaces were in use.

Check: 65% of 80 = 0.65 × 80 = 52

Other Examples

What percent of 20 is 16?

Ratio: $\frac{16}{20}$

Percent: $\frac{16}{20} = 0.80 = 80\%$

12 is what percent of 8?

Ratio: $\frac{12}{8}$

Percent: $\frac{12}{8} = 1.50 = 150\%$

What percent is 9 out of 15?

Ratio: $\frac{9}{15}$

Percent: $\frac{9}{15} = 0.60 = 60\%$

What percent of 4 is 12?

Ratio: $\frac{12}{4}$

Percent: $\frac{12}{4} = 3.00 = 300\%$

Warm Up

1. What percent of 12 is 6? **50%**

2. What percent of 8 is 20? **250%**

3. 3 is what percent of 30? **10%**

4. What percent of 4 is 6? **150%**

5. What percent of 16 is 4? **25%**

6. 18 is what percent of 24? **75%**

306

Follow Up

Reteaching

If some students have difficulty deciding on the proper ratio to use for the kind of problem presented in this lesson, suggest that they write the ratio so that the "is number" is over the "of number," as in this example.

"19 is what percent *of 40?"*

$$\frac{19}{40} = 47\tfrac{1}{2}\%$$

Explain that this method works because percent is always the number out of 100. The "of number" is always the number which represents 100% of the unit being considered.

Enrichment

Have students conduct a survey and collect data on a topic such as the clubs or extracurricular activities in which members of the class participate. They should then report the results to the class in terms of percent. For example, 30% of the students in the class may be members of the band.

Assignment Guide			
	Minimum	Average	Extended
page 307	1–8, 15–21	1–21, TM	1–21 odd, 22, TM

Find the percents.

1. 12 is what percent of 60? **20%**

2. What percent is 8 out of 25? **32%**

3. 30 is what percent of 40? **75%**

4. What percent of 72 is 18? **25%**

5. What percent is 9 out of 12? **75%**

6. 24 is what percent of 12? **200%**

7. 3 is what percent of 8? **37.5%**

8. What percent of 15 is 45? **300%**

9. What percent of 35 is 14? **40%**

10. 8 is what percent of 400? **2%**

11. What percent of 2 is 5? **250%**

12. What percent is 20 out of 25? **80%**

Find the percents. Round each percent to the nearest whole percent.

Example: 2 out of 3 is what percent?

$\frac{2}{3} = 0.66\frac{2}{3} = 66\frac{2}{3}\%$ or 67%, rounded to the nearest whole percent.

13. What percent is 11 out of 33? **33%**

14. 18 is what percent of 66? **27%**

15. What percent of 9 is 12? **133%**

16. 15 is what percent of 16? **94%**

17. What percent is 21 out of 78? **27%**

18. What percent of 360 is 6? **2%**

19. 216 is what percent of 512? **42%**

20. What percent is 475 out of 1,800? **26%**

21. A campground had only 24 out of 80 camping spaces filled. What percent of the camping spaces were filled? **30%**

22. There were 120 requests for 80 camping spaces. To the nearest whole percent, what percent of the 120 requests could not be given a camping space? **33%**

THINK MATH

Magic Square Percents

Find the percent for each ratio. Write the percent in the matching square. The correct answers in the squares will form a Magic Square. The sum in each row, column, and diagonal should be the same.

A 63 to 175   **D** 3.875 to 12.5   **G** 0.4 to 1.25

B 7.25 ÷ 25   **E** 2,211 : 6,700   **H** $\frac{29 + 45}{2^3 \cdot 5^2}$

C $\frac{153}{450}$ **F** 91 out of 260   **I** $\frac{100 - 67}{4,267 - 4,157}$

What is the magic sum? **99%**

A 36%	**B** 29%	**C** 34%
D 31%	**E** 33%	**F** 35%
G 32%	**H** 37%	**I** 30%

More Practice, page 436, Set A

Using Page 307

Exercises 13–20 You may wish to review rounding percents to the nearest whole percent before making the assignment. Point out that in using the division process, students need to find the quotient only through hundredths. If there is a remainder, it can be expressed as a fraction or used to round to the nearest whole percent.

Think Math A calculator can be used for this problem. The memory key will be helpful in parts H and I.

More Practice, page 436, Set A

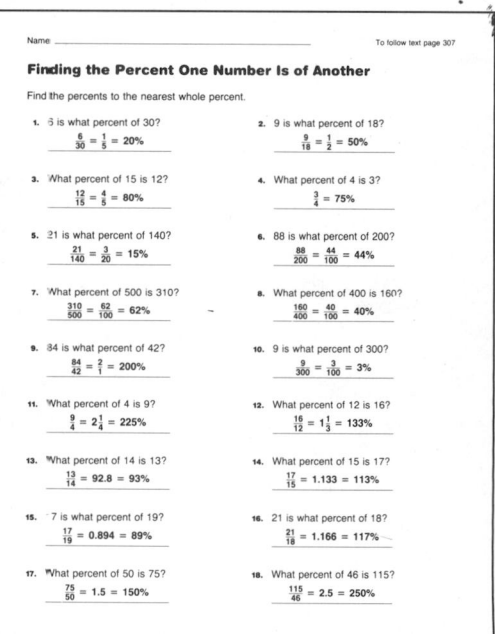

Reteaching Supplement, page 91

Enrichment Supplement, page 91

Practice Supplement, page 116

Quick Review Have students determine whether each statement is a proportion by using cross products.

$\frac{5}{9} = \frac{15}{10}$ no $\frac{3}{5} = \frac{12}{20}$ yes $\frac{3}{8} = \frac{6}{16}$ yes $\frac{11}{5} = \frac{10}{22}$ no

$\frac{7}{3} = \frac{21}{9}$ yes $\frac{4}{7} = \frac{12}{14}$ no $\frac{9}{2} = \frac{45}{10}$ yes

Lesson Focus To solve word problems involving percent

Ideas for Getting Started

Write these ratios on the chalkboard. Have students find the percents for the ratios.

$$\frac{8}{10} \qquad \frac{9}{12} \qquad \frac{14}{20} \qquad \frac{20}{30} \qquad \frac{40}{50}$$

Review the meaning of percent scores on tests. Explain that the ratio of the number of correct test items to the total number of test items is expressed as a percent.

Using Page 308

Lesson Development Read the introductory problem with students. Have them identify the question and the data in the problem. Then ask students to suggest a plan for solving the problem.

Observe with students that $\frac{27}{30}$ was reduced to $\frac{9}{10}$. Since the denominator is now 10, it is easy to write the fraction as a decimal and as a percent. Ask students if 90% is a reasonable answer. They can check by finding 90% of 30.

Work through the second example with students. Remind students that if division is carried out to the hundredths place, it is easy to write the decimal as a percent. Notice with students that the example shows rounding to the nearest whole percent. This may often be the case with test scores.

Exercises 1–6 These problems involve finding the percent of a number and finding what percent one number is of another. Remind students to think carefully about the question that is used.

PROBLEM SOLVING: Using Percents for Test Scores

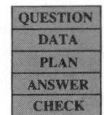
QUESTION
DATA
PLAN
ANSWER
CHECK

Beverly got 27 out of 30 problems correct on a math test. What percent of the problems did she get correct?

Since you want to find a percent for a ratio, you can find a decimal and then a percent for the ratio.

Number correct $\rightarrow$
Total number $\rightarrow$ $\dfrac{27}{30} = \dfrac{9}{10} = 0.90 = 90\%$

Beverly got 90% of the problems correct. Her test score was 90%.

Jake got 25 out of 30 problems correct on a spelling test. What was his percent score?

$$\frac{25}{30} = 0.83\frac{1}{3} = 83\frac{1}{3}\%$$

Jake's test score was $83\frac{1}{3}\%$. His score to the nearest whole percent is 83%.

Solve. Round all percents to the nearest whole percent.

1. Tish got 19 out of 20 questions correct on a science test. What was her test score? 95%

2. Bud took a multiple-choice test. There were 100 items on the test. His test score was 83%. How many items did he answer correctly? 83

3. The lowest passing score for a test was 70%. Elise got 2 out of every 3 problems correct. What was her test score? Was it a passing score? 67%; no

4. A teacher said that 68% would be the lowest passing test score. Kanisha got 19 out of 28 problems correct. What was her test score? Was it a passing score? 68%; yes

5. Akira got 48 out of 50 spelling words correct on a spelling test. What was his test score? 96%

6. Valerie's teacher told her that her test score was 85%. If there were 40 problems on the test, how many problems did Valerie get correct? 34

308

Follow Up

Reteaching

Review the meaning of ratio as the comparison of two sets. Emphasize that the percent on a test is based on the ratio of the number of items correct to the total number of items.

Discuss how to use a calculator to find the percent one number is of another. Then have students use a calculator to find the percent scored on each of the following tests.

Math: 14 correct out of 15 **93%**

English: 42 correct out of 48 **88%**

Science: 58 correct out of 64 **91%**

Health: 17 correct out of 20 **85%**

Enrichment

Instruct students to label their Tangram puzzles (TRB p. 279) as shown. Have them answer the following questions.

1. What percent of the large square is each piece? **A 25%, B 25%, C $12\frac{1}{2}$%, D $6\frac{1}{4}$%, E $12\frac{1}{2}$%, F $12\frac{1}{2}$%, G $6\frac{1}{4}$%**

2. Which pieces can be used to form a square that is 50% the size of the large square? **A and B; A, D, G, and E; C, D, E, F, and G**

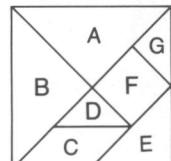

Assignment Guide			
	Minimum	Average	Extended
pages 308–309	1–10	1–12, 16	4–16

7. Elliot's test score on a true-false test of 60 questions was 90%. How many questions did Elliot miss? 6

8. Ryan got 27 out of 32 questions correct on a social studies test. What was his test score? 84%

9. Marquita got 17 out of 20 problems correct on Monday's quiz. She got 13 out of 15 problems correct on Wednesday's quiz. What was her test score for each quiz? On which day was her score the highest?
85%; 87%; Wednesday

10. On a semester test, Hanna got 65 out of 75 problems correct. What was her test score? 87%

11. On a true-false quiz of 50 questions, Randy was sure he knew the correct answers to 36 of the questions. He guessed at the rest of the questions, expecting to get one half of them correct. What test score does Randy think he should make? 86%

12. A driver's license test has 40 questions. To pass the test, no more than 6 questions can be missed. What is the lowest passing score? 85%

13. Monica got 9 out of 10 problems correct for 90% on one test. She got 16 out of 20 problems correct for 80% on another test. What percent of the problems on both tests did she get correct? Is this the same as the average of 90% and 80%? 83%; no

14. A passing grade on a test with 45 true-false questions is 72%. Gil got 36 questions correct. Is this a passing grade? yes; 80%

15. Check your answers to problems 1–14. What percent of the problems did you answer correctly?

16. **Try This** A class of 35 students took a math test and a science test. 12 students got 100% on the math test. 9 students got 100% on the science test. There were 19 students who made less than 100% on both tests. How many students made 100% on both tests? 5

309

Using Page 309

Exercises 7–15 Several of these exercises are multiple-step problems. In some problems, more than one question is asked. You may want to discuss exercise 13 with students. On both tests Monica got 25 out of 30 problems correct or $83\frac{1}{3}$%, while the average of the two scores is 85%. This problem illustrates the danger of averaging percents.

Try This A possible strategy, Use Logical Reasoning, was taught on page 242.

Discussion After students read the problem, have them tell what the question asks us to find. Next have them identify the data given in the problem. Ask students what strategy they might use to answer the question. Point out that a Venn diagram can help in reasoning logically about the problem.

Solution

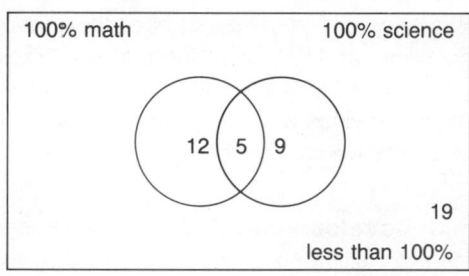

35 − 19 = 16 students scoring 100% on a test. Since 12 + 9 = 21, there must be 5 students who made 100 on both tests.

Ideas That Work

Math for the Gifted

Discuss the meaning of *compound interest* as interest paid on interest. Explain that some banks pay one quarter of the annual interest four times a year, instead of just once a year. The interest is compounded quarterly. Work through the following example with students.

    Annual interest rate: 8%

    Deposit: $1,000

    Interest compounded quarterly.

$$I = PRT$$

1st quarter: $I = \$1,000 \times 0.08 \times 0.25$

      = $20

2nd quarter: $I = \$1,020 \times 0.08 \times 0.25$

      = $20.40

Have students find the interest for the third and fourth quarters as well as the total interest for the year. ($20.81, $21.22, $82.43)

Then have them find the interest on $1,000 at 8% from a bank that compounds annually. ($80)

Ask students to explain why a bank that compounds quarterly pays more interest than a bank that compounds annually. (A bank that compounds quarterly pays interest on the interest after the first quarter.)

Practice Supplement, page 117

Name _____ To follow text page 309

Problem Solving: Using Percents for Test Scores

Solve. Round all percents to the nearest whole percent.

1. Carl got 17 out of 25 correct on a biology test. What was his test score? 68%

2. Sandy took a French test. There were 50 items on the test. Her score was 88%. How many items did she answer correctly? 44

3. Edgar got 35 out of 40 items correct on a test. What was his test score? 88%

4. Sylvia's test score was 90%. If there were 80 items on the test, how many did she answer correctly? 72

5. Brian's test score on an English test was 80%. If there were 45 items on the test, how many did he miss? 9

6. Gloria got 17 out of 19 questions correct on a math test. What was her test score? 89%

7. On a quiz Harry got 12 out of 15 items correct. What was his quiz score? 80%

8. Rhonda's test score was 75%. It there were 48 items on the test, how many did she answer correctly? 36

9. Stan's test score was 60% on a science test. If there were 35 items on the test, how many did Stan miss? 14

10. Tom got 18 out of 25 items correct on an anatomy exam. What was his test score? 72%

Quick Review Challenge students to give at least three equivalent fractions for each fraction below.

$\frac{4}{7}$ $\frac{2}{3}$ $\frac{3}{5}$ $\frac{5}{14}$ $\frac{7}{9}$

$\frac{1}{6}$ $\frac{3}{8}$ $\frac{6}{11}$

Lesson Focus To find a number when a percent of it is known

Ideas for Getting Started

Write these equations on the chalkboard. Review how to solve the equations by dividing each side by the same number.

$0.3\,n = 12$ $0.05\,n = 6$ $0.16\,n = 4.8$

$n = \frac{12}{0.3}$ $n = \frac{6}{0.05}$ $n = \frac{4.8}{0.16}$

$n = 40$ $n = 120$ $n = 30$

Next have students write a decimal for each of the following percents.

4%	18%	66%	200%
25%	95%	150%	5.2%

Using Page 310

Motivational Problem After students read the problem at the top of the page, have them identify the question and the data in the problem. Explain that the plan is to write and solve an equation. Point out that since we want to find the height before eruption, we choose the variable to represent this number.

Lesson Development Explain to students that the idea of multiplying to find a percent of a number can be used to help us write an equation. On the chalkboard, write and solve the equation one step at a time. Give students an opportunity to participate in each step. You may want to have a student use a calculator to find the quotient, $\frac{8,419}{0.87} = 9,677.0115$. Since it would not make sense to expect this measurement to be to the nearest ten-thousandth of a meter, we round the answer to the nearest whole number.

Other Examples Work through these examples with students. In each case $n =$ the number.

Warm Up Assign these exercises as independent written work. Make certain that students write the percent as a decimal before dividing.

Finding a Number when a Percent of It Is Known

The volcano in Washington called Mount St. Helens erupted in 1980 and blew off part of its peak. It then had a height of 8,419 ft. This is only about 87% of its height before the eruption. What was its height before the eruption?

To find the height before eruption, we can write an equation.

Let $h =$ the height before eruption.

Percent equation	$87\% \times h = 8,419$
Write the percent as a decimal.	$0.87 \times h = 8,419$
Divide both sides by 0.87.	$\frac{0.87}{0.87} \times h = \frac{8,419}{0.87}$
Simplify and round to the nearest whole number.	$h = 9,677$

The height before the eruption was about 9,677 ft.

Other Examples

15% of what number is 24?

$15\% \times n = 24$
$0.15 \times n = 24$
$\frac{0.15}{0.15} \times n = \frac{24}{0.15}$
$n = 160$

40% of what number is 1.8?

$40\% \times n = 1.8$
$0.40 \times n = 1.8$
$\frac{0.40}{0.40} \times n = \frac{1.8}{0.40}$
$n = 4.5$

Warm Up

Solve.

1. $8\% \times n = 4$ $n = 50$
2. $50\% \times n = 52$ $n = 104$
3. $1\% \times n = 19$ $n = 1,900$
4. $13\% \times n = 52$ $n = 400$
5. $200\% \times n = 84$ $n = 42$
6. $80\% \times n = 15$ $n = 18.75$

310

Follow Up

Reteaching

A diagram like the one below may help students to understand percent problems. Work through the following problem with students, using the diagram.

40% of what number is 12?

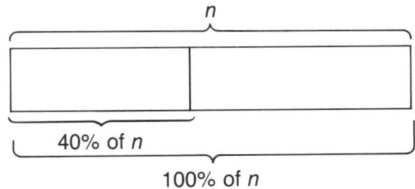

$40\% \times n = 12$

$\frac{0.40}{0.40} \times n = \frac{12}{0.40}$

$n = 30$

Enrichment

Display the following exercises. Have students estimate the number and then use a calculator to check their estimates.

You may wish to discuss some estimation techniques. One useful technique is to use a simple fraction for the percent. For example, in the first exercise, 23% is about $\frac{1}{4}$. Round 17.5 to 20. Since $\frac{1}{4} \times n = 20$, n is about 80.

1. 23% of $n = 17.5$ 2. 9% of $n = 5.8$
3. 7.5% of $n = 29$ 4. 67% of $n = 1.5$
5. 161% of $n = 31.5$ 6. 12% of $n = 9$

Solve.

1. $5\% \times n = 20$ $n = 400$ 　**2.** $16\% \times n = 40$ $n = 250$ 　**3.** $10\% \times n = 6$ $n = 60$

4. $50\% \times n = 22$ $n = 44$ 　**5.** $6\% \times n = 21$ $n = 350$ 　**6.** $75\% \times n = 15$ $n = 20$

7. $9\% \times n = 63$ $n = 700$ 　**8.** $12\% \times n = 3.6$ $n = 30$ 　**9.** $100\% \times n = 83$ $n = 83$

10. $7\% \times n = 84$ $n = 1,200$ 　**11.** $17\% \times n = 136$ $n = 800$ 　**12.** $15\% \times n = 2.10$ $n = 14$

Write and solve an equation for each question.

13. 20% of what number is 18?
$20\% \times n = 18$; $n = 90$

14. 45% of what number is 36?
$45\% \times n = 36$; $n = 80$

15. 56% of what number is 42?
$56\% \times n = 42$; $n = 75$

16. 99% of what number is 495?
$99\% \times n = 495$; $n = 500$

17. 9% of what number is 2.7?
$9\% \times n = 2.7$; $n = 30$

18. 60% of what number is 333?
$60\% \times n = 333$; $n = 555$

19. 150% of what number is 9?
$150\% \times n = 9$; $n = 6$

20. 15% of what number is 48?
$15\% \times n = 48$; $n = 320$

Find the number.

21. 31% of $n = 4.65$ $n = 15$ 　**22.** $57\% \times n = 17.1$ $n = 30$ 　**23.** $9\% \times n = 33.48$ $n = 372$

24. $67\% \times n = 548.73$ $n = 819$ 　**25.** $2.5\% \times n = 4.70$ $n = 188$ 　**26.** $106\% \times n = 97.52$ $n = 92$

27. $29\% \times n = 104.4$ $n = 360$ 　**28.** $72\% \times n = 45.36$ $n = 63$ 　**29.** $6.3\% \times n = 6224.4$ $n = 98,800$

30. At one time Mt. Mazama, the mountain of Crater Lake, Oregon, was about 12,000 ft high. This is about 150% of its present height. What is the height of Mt. Mazama today? **8,000 ft**

31. About $4\frac{1}{2}$ million years ago, the Grand Canyon may have been about 3,960 ft deep. This is about 75% of its depth today. What is the depth of the Grand Canyon today? **5,280 ft**

SKILLKEEPER

Write each fraction as a percent.
Round to the nearest whole percent.

1. $\frac{7}{15}$ 47% 　**2.** $\frac{10}{12}$ 84% 　**3.** $\frac{5}{16}$ 31% 　**4.** $\frac{9}{14}$ 64% 　**5.** $\frac{2}{9}$ 22%

6. $\frac{7}{32}$ 22% 　**7.** $\frac{17}{20}$ 85% 　**8.** $\frac{9}{40}$ 23% 　**9.** $\frac{5}{11}$ 45% 　**10.** $\frac{12}{27}$ 44%

11. $\frac{7}{25}$ 28% 　**12.** $\frac{8}{22}$ 36% 　**13.** $\frac{45}{48}$ 94% 　**14.** $\frac{9}{20}$ 45% 　**15.** $\frac{32}{40}$ 80%

More Practice, page 436, Set B

Using Page 311

Exercises 1–20 Note the sequencing of these exercises. The percent equations are given in exercises 1–12. Students must write and solve equations in exercises 13–20. If students have difficulty with these exercises, a diagram like the one shown below may help them write equations from the questions.

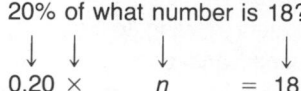

20% of what number is 18?

0.20 ×　　　n　　= 18

Skillkeeper This Skillkeeper reviews material taught in this chapter.

More Practice, page 436, Set B

Reteaching Supplement, page 92　　　**Enrichment Supplement,** page 92　　　**Practice Supplement,** page 118

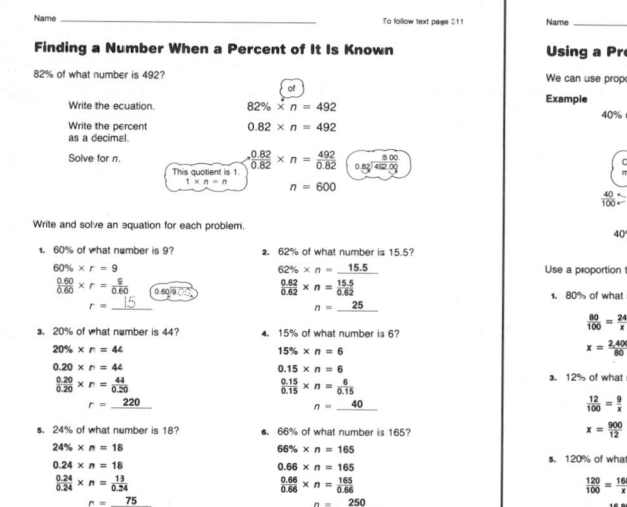

Quick Review Have students find the measure of the fourth angle in a quadrilateral with the given three angles.

100°, 50°, 40° **170°**   70°, 70°, 110° **110°**

90°, 140°, 45° **85°**   40°, 150°, 110° **60°**   58°, 104°, 96° **102°**

Lesson Focus To practice skills with percents; to find amounts of discounts and sale prices

Suggested Materials Newspaper sales advertisements giving percent discounts

Ideas for Getting Started

Introduce the lesson on page 313 by displaying newspaper sales advertisements. Discuss data from the advertisement relating to regular prices, sale prices, discounts, and percent of discount. Point out that discounts are often described as so many dollars off; "save $20" and "20% off" refer to discounts. Explain that the percent of discount may be given as a percent but often is given as a simple fraction such as "$\frac{1}{3}$ off." Ask students to name percents for these fractions.

$$\frac{1}{3} \qquad \frac{1}{2} \qquad \frac{1}{4}$$

Using Page 312

Exercises 1–64 The exercises on this page give students an opportunity to review skills with percents. Students' performances on this page will enable you to identify those areas in which reteaching or practice is needed.

Skills Practice

Write each percent as a decimal.

1. 15% 0.15　　2. 39% 0.39　　3. 75% 0.75　　4. 8% 0.08　　5. 20% 0.20

6. 3% 0.03　　7. 400% 4　　8. 33% 0.33　　9. 62% 0.62　　10. 125% 1.25

Write each decimal as a percent.

11. 0.35 35%　　12. 0.18 18%　　13. 0.39 39%　　14. 0.50 50%　　15. 0.07 7%

16. 2.50 250%　　17. 0.01 1%　　18. 0.99 99%　　19. 0.002 0.2%　　20. 6.8 680%

Find the percent for each fraction. Round to the nearest tenth of a percent.

21. $\frac{3}{5}$ 60%　　22. $\frac{6}{10}$ 60%　　23. $\frac{3}{4}$ 75%　　24. $\frac{7}{20}$ 35%　　25. $\frac{11}{25}$ 44%

26. $\frac{3}{8}$ 37.5%　　27. $\frac{79}{100}$ 79%　　28. $\frac{3}{2}$ 150%　　29. $\frac{1}{3}$ 33.3%　　30. $\frac{5}{6}$ 83.3%

31. $\frac{9}{10}$ 90%　　32. $\frac{4}{9}$ 44.4%　　33. $\frac{11}{12}$ 91.7%　　34. $\frac{4}{15}$ 26.7%　　35. $\frac{8}{5}$ 160%

Find the lowest-terms fraction for each percent.

36. 25% $\frac{1}{4}$　　37. 10% $\frac{1}{10}$　　38. 80% $\frac{4}{5}$　　39. 15% $\frac{3}{20}$　　40. 4% $\frac{1}{25}$

41. 16% $\frac{4}{25}$　　42. 45% $\frac{9}{20}$　　43. 17% $\frac{17}{100}$　　44. 28% $\frac{7}{25}$　　45. 96% $\frac{24}{25}$

46. 150% $1\frac{1}{2}$　　47. 200% 2　　48. 76% $\frac{19}{25}$　　49. 55% $\frac{11}{20}$　　50. 125% $1\frac{1}{4}$

Find the percent of each number.

51. 50% of 48 24　　52. 10% of 300 30　　53. 5% of 80 4

54. 18% of 2,500 450　　55. 108% of 300 324　　56. 6% of 75 4.5

Find the percents.

57. 7 is what percent of 10? 70%　　58. 16 is what percent of 20? 30%

59. 9 is what percent of 15? 60%　　60. 45 is what percent of 150? 30%

Find the numbers.

61. 10% of a number is 8. 80　　62. 25% of a number is 40. 160

63. 90% of a number is 315. 350　　64. 64% of a number is 16. 25

312

Follow Up

Reteaching

Provide students with the chart below. Calculators can be used to help them complete the chart. They should round answers to the nearest cent.

Item	Original Price	Rate of Discount	Discount Price
Radio	$ 30.00	35%	$ 19.50
Bicycle	$160.00	2.5%	$156.00
Clock	$ 15.95	10%	$ 14.35
Shoes	$ 25.99	20%	$ 20.79

Enrichment

Have students write problems involving discounts based on the data from newspaper advertisements. They should then solve their own problems. You may wish to duplicate a selection of these problems for the rest of the students to solve.

Discounts and Sale Prices

A garden shop reduced the price of a lawnmower by 20%. The regular price was $350. What was the sale price?

The amount that the price was reduced is called the **discount**. The **percent of discount** is 20%.

The diagram shows the relation between the regular price, the sale price, and the percent of discount.

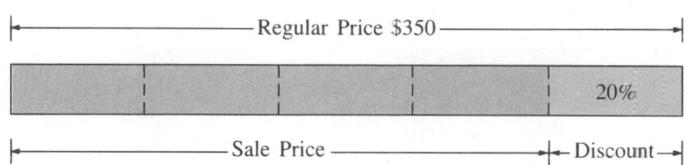

|← Regular Price $350 →|
| 20% |
|← Sale Price →|← Discount →|

Discount percent × regular price = discount

20% × $350 = discount
0.20 × $350 = **$70**
The discount is $70.

Regular price − discount = sale price

$350 − $70 = sale price
$350 − $70 = **$280**
The sale price is $280.

Find the discount and the sale price.

1. Regular Price: $60
   Discount Percent: 15% $9; $51

2. Regular Price: $75
   Discount Percent: 50% $37.50; $37.50

3. Regular Price: $240
   Discount Percent: 20% $48; $192

4. Regular Price: $27.50
   Discount Percent: 10% $2.75; $24.75

5. Regular Price: $12.50
   Discount Percent: 40% $5.00; $7.50

6. Regular Price: $6,500
   Discount Percent: 8% $520; $5,980

Solve.

7. Potted citrus trees had a regular price of $16.00. They were put on sale at 30% off. What was the discount? What was the sale price? $4.80; $11.20

8. Peat moss was regularly priced at $10 a bale. It was put on sale at $7.50 a bale. What was the discount? What was the discount percent? $2.50; 25%

313

Using Page 313

Motivational Problem Have students read the problem at the top of the page. Ask them to identify the question and the data given in the problem. Display the diagram showing the relationship between sale price, discount, and regular price. Explain that the diagram can help to make a plan to solve the problem.

Lesson Development Point out that there are two steps in finding the sale price. First the amount of discount is found, and then the discount is subtracted from the regular price. Work through the steps in the solution on the chalkboard. Give students an opportunity to participate in each step.

An alternate method of finding the sale price without actually computing the amount of discount is to subtract the discount percent from 100% and multiply the regular price by the difference. In the motivational problem, the sale price is 80% of the regular price. 80% of $350 is $280. This method is not presented here since we want to emphasize finding both discount and sale price.

Exercise 8 Note that this problem asks for the discount percent.

Reteaching Supplement, page 93

Name _____   To follow text page 313

Discounts and Sale Prices

Find the discount and the sale price of the typewriter.

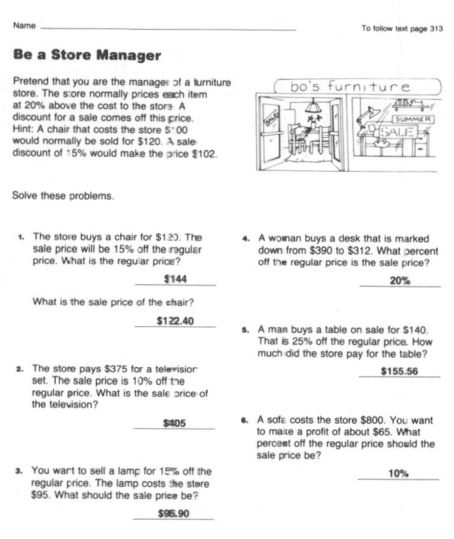

Discount
Discount Percent × Regular Price = Discount
15% × $460 = Discount
0.15 × $460 = $69
The **discount** is $69.

Sale Price
Regular Price − Discount = Sale Price
$460 − $69 = Sale Price
$460 − $69 = $391
The **sale price** is $391.

Find the discount and the sale price for each item.

		Discount	Sale Price
1.	Regular Price: $80 Discount Percent: 30%	30% of $80 = Discount 0.30 × $80 = $24	Discount $80 − $24 = $56
2.	Regular Price: $65 Discount Percent: 20%	20% of $65 = Discount 0.20 × $65 = $13	$65 − $13 = $52
3.	Regular Price: $50 Discount Percent: 30%	30% of $50 = Discount 0.30 × $50 = $15	$50 − $15 = $35
4.	Regular Price: $90 Discount Percent: 40%	40% of $90 = Discount 0.40 × $90 = $36	$90 − $36 = $54
5.	Regular Price: $75 Discount Percent: 28%	28% of $75 = Discount 0.28 × $75 = $21	$75 − $21 = $54
6.	Regular Price: $250 Discount Percent: 50%	50% of $250 = Discount 0.50 × $250 = $125	$250 − $125 = $125
7.	Regular Price: $10.50 Discount Percent: 20%	20% of $10.50 = Discount 0.20 × $10.50 = $2.10	$10.50 − $2.10 = $8.40
8.	Regular Price: $3,200 Discount Percent: 50%	50% of $3,200 = Discount 0.50 × $3,200 = $1,600	$3,200 − $1,600 = $1,600

Enrichment Supplement, page 93

Name _____   To follow text page 313

Be a Store Manager

Pretend that you are the manager of a furniture store. The store normally prices each item at 20% above the cost to the store. A discount for a sale comes off this price. Hint: A chair that costs the store $100 would normally be sold for $120. A sale discount of 15% would make the price $102.

Solve these problems.

1. The store buys a chair for $120. The sale price will be 15% off the regular price. What is the regular price? **$144**

   What is the sale price of the chair? **$122.40**

2. The store pays $375 for a television set. The sale price is 10% off the regular price. What is the sale price of the television? **$405**

3. You want to sell a lamp for 15% off the regular price. The lamp costs the store $95. What should the sale price be? **$95.90**

4. A woman buys a desk that is marked down from $390 to $312. What percent off the regular price is the sale price? **20%**

5. A man buys a table on sale for $140. That is 25% off the regular price. How much did the store pay for the table? **$155.56**

6. A sofa costs the store $800. You want to make a profit of about $65. What percent off the regular price should the sale price be? **10%**

Practice Supplement, page 119

Name _____   To follow text page 313

Discounts and Sale Prices

Find the amount of the discount and the sale price.

1. Regular Price: $52
   Discount Percent: 25%
   Discount: **$13**
   Sale Price: **$39**

2. Regular Price: $90
   Discount Percent: 15%
   Discount: **$13.50**
   Sale Price: **$76.50**

3. Regular Price: $80
   Discount Percent: 20%
   Discount: **$16**
   Sale Price: **$64**

4. Regular Price: $1,200
   Discount Percent: 12%
   Discount: **$144**
   Sale Price: **$1,056**

5. Regular Price: $36.50
   Discount Percent: 40%
   Discount: **$14.60**
   Sale Price: **$21.90**

6. Regular Price: $70
   Discount Percent: 30%
   Discount: **$21**
   Sale Price: **$49**

7. Regular Price: $17.80
   Discount Percent: 10%
   Discount: **$1.78**
   Sale Price: **$16.02**

8. Regular Price: $120
   Discount Percent: 15%
   Discount: **$18**
   Sale Price: **$102**

9. Regular Price: $250
   Discount Percent: 18%
   Discount: **$45**
   Sale Price: **$205**

10. Regular Price: $16.50
    Discount Percent: 50%
    Discount: **$8.25**
    Sale Price: **$8.25**

Percent

Quick Review Have students find the area of a rectangle with the given length and width.

$l = 15$ cm, $w = 8$ cm **120 cm²** $l = 5$ m, $w = 2.7$ m **13.5 m²**

$l = 6$ cm, $w = 0.8$ cm **4.8 cm²** $l = 37$ mm, $w = 22$ mm **814 mm²**

Lesson Focus To solve percent problems by writing and solving proportion

Ideas for Getting Started

Have students write each percent as a fraction with a denominator of 100.

8%   23%   2%   12.5%

Use the following examples to review solving proportions.

$$\frac{n}{16} = \frac{5}{100} \qquad \frac{25}{100} = \frac{40}{n}$$

Using Page 314

Lesson Development Explain to students that the first example shows how to use proportions to find a percent of a number. The diagram can be used to identify each *part* and each *whole* used to write the proportion. Complete the steps in the solution with students.

Point out that the second example uses a proportion to find what percent one number is of another number. Have students use the diagram to identify each part and each whole in the proportion. On the chalkboard, show the steps in solving the proportion.

Direct students' attention to the last example showing how to use a proportion to find a number when the percent is known. Work through the solution one step at a time.

Warm Up Assign these exercises as independent written work. When students finish, have them present their solutions at the chalkboard.

Proportions and Percents

Percent problems can be solved by writing and solving a **proportion**. Each ratio in the proportion compares a **part** to a **whole**.

Find 15% of 80.

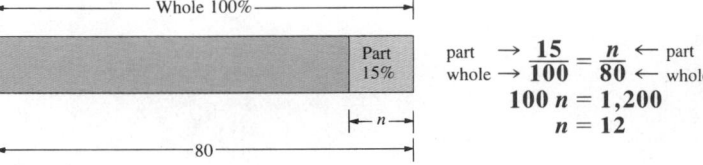

part → $\dfrac{15}{100} = \dfrac{n}{80}$ ← part
whole →   ← whole

$100\,n = 1{,}200$
$n = 12$

15% of 80 is 12.

30 is what percent of 50?

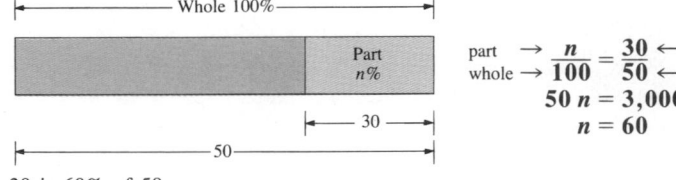

part → $\dfrac{n}{100} = \dfrac{30}{50}$ ← part
whole →   ← whole

$50\,n = 3{,}000$
$n = 60$

30 is 60% of 50.

25% of a number is 8. What is the number?

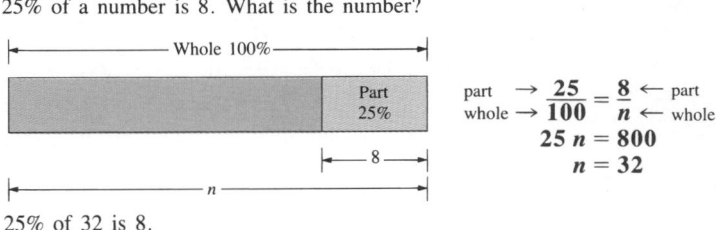

part → $\dfrac{25}{100} = \dfrac{8}{n}$ ← part
whole →   ← whole

$25\,n = 800$
$n = 32$

25% of 32 is 8.

Warm Up

Write and solve a proportion for each question.

1. What is 60% of 35?
   $\frac{60}{100} = \frac{n}{35}$; **n = 21**

2. 20% of a number is 12. What is the number? $\frac{20}{100} = \frac{12}{n}$; **n = 60**

3. 24 is what percent of 60? $\frac{n}{100} = \frac{24}{60}$; **n = 40**

4. What is 65% of 300? $\frac{65}{100} = \frac{n}{300}$; **n = 195**

5. 16 is what percent of 20?
   $\frac{n}{100} = \frac{16}{20}$; **n = 80**

6. 64% of a number is 16. What is the number? $\frac{64}{100} = \frac{16}{n}$; **n = 25**

Follow Up

Reteaching

Discuss the exercises in this lesson in terms of part to whole and percent to 100. Have students identify these parts in the exercises below, and write a proportion for each.

Example: 24 is what percent of 60?

part   percent   whole

$\frac{24}{60} = \frac{n}{100}$

1. 15% of what number is 32? $\frac{15}{100} = \frac{32}{n}$

2. What is 27% of 40? $\frac{n}{40} = \frac{27}{100}$

3. 16 is what percent of 50? $\frac{16}{50} = \frac{n}{100}$

Enrichment

Have students write proportions to solve the following problems.

1. A team won 9 out of 21 games. To the nearest percent, what percent of the games were won? **43%**

2. Rent accounted for 36% of one family's monthly income. What was their monthly income if they paid $540 in rent? **$1,500**

3. In a school of 450 students, 12% of them were absent one day last week. How many were absent? **54**

4. A coat was on sale for 20% off the regular price. If the sale price is $86, what was the regular price? **$107.50**

Write and solve a proportion for each question.

1. What is 48% of 75?
$\frac{48}{100} = \frac{n}{75}$; $n = 36$

2. 10% of a number is 24. What is the number? $\frac{10}{100} = \frac{24}{n}$; $n = 240$

3. 20 is what percent of 25?
$\frac{n}{100} = \frac{20}{25}$; $n = 80$

4. What percent of 50 is 37?
$\frac{n}{100} = \frac{37}{50}$; $n = 74$

5. What is 36% of 200?
$\frac{36}{100} = \frac{n}{200}$; $n = 72$

6. 75% of a number is 45. What is the number? $\frac{75}{100} = \frac{45}{n}$; $n = 60$

7. What is 90% of 330?
$\frac{90}{100} = \frac{n}{330}$; $n = 297$

8. What is 66% of 800?
$\frac{66}{100} = \frac{n}{800}$; $n = 528$

9. 12.5% of a number is 18. What is the number? $\frac{12.5}{100} = \frac{18}{n}$; $n = 144$

10. 17 is what percent of 68?
$\frac{n}{100} = \frac{17}{68}$; $n = 25$

11. What is 125% of 88?
$\frac{125}{100} = \frac{n}{88}$; $n = 110$

12. What is 13% of 56?
$\frac{13}{100} = \frac{n}{56}$; $n = 7.28$

13. 60% of a number is 213. What is the number? $\frac{60}{100} = \frac{213}{n}$; $n = 355$

14. 85% of a number is 17. What is the number? $\frac{85}{100} = \frac{17}{n}$; $n = 20$

15. 28 is what percent of 56?
$\frac{n}{100} = \frac{28}{56}$; $n = 50$

16. What percent of 80 is 48?
$\frac{n}{100} = \frac{48}{80}$; $n = 60$

17. Janelle is 144 cm tall. This is 90% of Kimberly's height. How tall is Kimberly? 160 cm

18. Carlene is 171 cm tall. Justin is 190 cm tall. Carlene's height is what percent of Justin's height? 90%

19. Lawan is 170 cm tall. Andy's height is 85% of Lawan's height. What is Andy's height? 144.5 cm

20. **DATA HUNT** Find your height. Find a classmate's height. Your height is what percent of your classmate's height?

■ THINK MATH ■

Space Perception

An exercise course in a park is on both sides of a stream and on two small islands in the stream. There are seven bridges that cross the stream and connect the islands. Is it possible to go through each exercise station and cross each bridge exactly one time? no

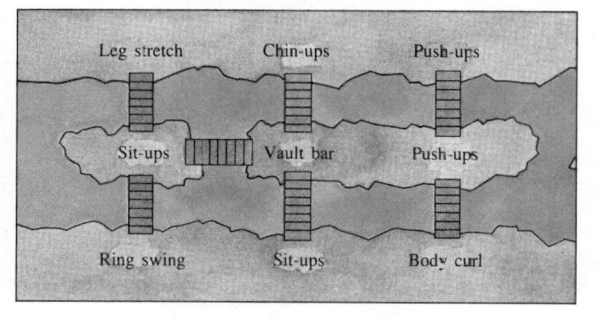

More Practice, page 436, Set C

315

Using Page 315

Exercises 1–19 Have students compare these exercises to the sample problem on page 314 to help them make diagrams or set up proportions.

Think Math This problem involves visual perception. Students should soon discover that it is impossible to go through each exercise station and cross each bridge exactly once.

More Practice, page 436, Set C

Ideas That Work

Calculator Bonus

Distribute classified ads from local newspapers to students for use in the following activities. You may wish to discuss the use of the percent key on a calculator and have students use this key to solve the problems below.

1. Have students select a car from the advertisements. Ask them to find the amount of a 25% down payment on the total price. Next have them determine the balance, and find the amount of interest paid if the balance were borrowed for 1 year at 15%. Then ask students to find the total amount paid for the car.

2. Explain that real-estate agents earn a *commission* for selling a house. The commission is a certain percent of the sale price. Ask students to choose some houses from the ads and find the commission charge for selling each house if the rate of commission is 6%.

Practice Supplement, page 120

Name _____ To follow text page 315

Proportions and Percents

Write and solve a proportion for each problem.

1. What is 56% of 50?
$\frac{56}{100} = \frac{n}{50}$ $n = 28$

2. What percent of 36 is 27?
$\frac{n}{100} = \frac{27}{36}$ $n = 75\%$

3. 15% of a number is 12. What is the number?
$\frac{15}{100} = \frac{12}{n}$ $n = 80$

4. 95% of a number is 38. What is the number?
$\frac{95}{100} = \frac{38}{n}$ $n = 40$

5. What percent of 25 is 16?
$\frac{n}{100} = \frac{16}{25}$ $n = 64$

6. What is 150% of 72?
$\frac{150}{100} = \frac{n}{72}$ $n = 108$

7. What is 80% of 45?
$\frac{80}{100} = \frac{n}{45}$ $n = 36$

8. What percent of 60 is 24?
$\frac{n}{100} = \frac{24}{60}$ $n = 40\%$

9. 42% of a number is 21. What is the number?
$\frac{42}{100} = \frac{21}{n}$ $n = 50$

10. 75% of a number is 63. What is the number?
$\frac{75}{100} = \frac{63}{n}$ $n = 84$

11. What is 125% of 120?
$\frac{125}{100} = \frac{n}{120}$ $n = 150$

12. What is 300% of 18?
$\frac{300}{100} = \frac{n}{18}$ $n = 54$

13. What percent of 68 is 51?
$\frac{n}{100} = \frac{51}{68}$ $n = 75\%$

14. 45 is what percent of 50?
$\frac{n}{100} = \frac{45}{50}$ $n = 90\%$

15. 19 is what percent of 76?
$\frac{n}{100} = \frac{19}{76}$ $n = 25\%$

16. What percent of 400 is 96?
$\frac{n}{100} = \frac{96}{400}$ $n = 24\%$

Applications

Lesson Focus To interpret, organize, and use data to make a decision about a real-world problem

Suggested Materials Newspaper advertisements from several supermarkets or grocery stores

Ideas for Getting Started

Display the advertisements and lead a class discussion about supermarket "specials." Explain that some markets may advertise items which are sold near to actual cost or slightly below cost to attract customers. These items are sometimes called "loss leaders."

Using Page 316

Lesson Development After students read the material at the top of the page, direct their attention to the list of groceries and their prices. Then read with students "Some Things to Consider." Explain that these are conditions that wilm affect students' decisions in the lesson. Point out that in real-life situations, there may be more conditions than have been listed here.

To help students begin thinking about the problem, ask the following questions. "Which market sells eggs for the lowest price?" (Broadway Food Store) "Does it make a difference where cat food is puchased?" (no) "Which store sells laundry soap at the lowest price?" (Main Market)

Have the students work through "Some Questions to Answer." Remind them to refer back to the data in the price list and the conditions in "Some Things to Consider" as they answer the questions. Then discuss answers students give for "What Is Your Decision." While it is true that the Broadway Food Store is the single store with the lowest total price for the groceries, one could save even more by shopping at all three stores. Discuss the fact that shopping at all three stores might involve additional time and additional expense for transportation which might offset the savings obtained. Discuss other factors that might affect the choice of markets such as cleanliness, freshness of merchandise, business hours, proximity to home, carry-out help, and so on.

As an extension of this problem, choose two more grocery stores in your community. Have students do a price comparison of groceries such as those suggested on this page, and have them decide which is the best place for a family of four to buy their groceries.

APPLIED PROBLEM SOLVING

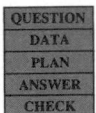

You have a neighbor who is unable to go out to shop for groceries. You have volunteered to do the shopping. Your neighbor gave you a grocery list. You need to decide where you will do the shopping.

Grocery List	Main Market	Lesso's Super	Broadway Food Store
1 dozen eggs	$0.77	$0.79	$0.69
laundry soap	$1.69	$1.78	$1.73
2 lb chicken *or*	$0.99 / lb	$0.79 / lb	$0.89 / lb
1 lb ground beef	$1.99 / lb	$1.89 / lb	$1.69 / lb
cat food	$0.99	$0.99	$0.99
loaf of bread	$0.79	$0.95	$0.69
$\frac{1}{2}$ gal milk	$1.05	$1.04	$1.05
1 lb apples	$0.59	$0.69	$0.49
cereal	$2.29	$2.33	$2.19

Some Things to Consider

- You can shop at any one of three stores.
- You can use the newspaper advertisements to compare prices at the three stores.
- Your neighbor gave you $10 to buy the groceries.
- Your neighbor is on a strict budget and wants to save as much money as possible.

Some Questions to Answer

1. What is the most expensive item on the list? cereal

2. What is the price of 2 lb of chicken at each store? How do these prices compare with the price of 1 lb of ground beef at each store? Main Market: $1.98 (C); $1.99 (GB) Lesso's: $1.58 (C); $1.89 (GB) Broadway: $1.78 (C); $1.69 (GB)

3. Will you have enough money to do all your shopping at Main Market? no; $10.15 with chicken, $10.16 with ground beef

4. Will you have enough money to do all your shopping at Broadway Food Store? yes; $9.61 with chicken, $9.52 with ground beef

5. Will you have enough money to do all your shopping at Lesso's Super? no; $10.15 with chicken, $10.46 with ground beef

What Is Your Decision?

In which store will you buy the groceries on the list? Broadway Food Store. To save the most, shop at all three stores. Minimum cost: $9.36.

CHAPTER REVIEW/TEST

Write each ratio or number as a percent.

1. 7 to 100 7%   **2.** 45 out of 100 45%   **3.** $\frac{3}{100}$ 3%   **4.** 0.17 17%

Write each fraction as a percent.

5. $\frac{1}{4}$ 25%   **6.** $\frac{3}{20}$ 15%   **7.** $\frac{5}{50}$ 10%   **8.** $\frac{3}{5}$ 60%

Write each percent as a lowest-terms fraction.

9. 10% $\frac{1}{10}$ **10.** 75% $\frac{3}{4}$ **11.** 16% $\frac{4}{25}$ **12.** 90% $\frac{9}{10}$

Write each decimal or fraction as a percent.

13. 0.1886 18.86%   **14.** 0.0251 2.51%   **15.** $\frac{3}{8}$ 37.5%   **16.** $\frac{7}{8}$ 87.5%

17. Find 25% of 74. 18.5   **18.** Find 40% of 90. 36

19. Find 13.7% of 300. 41.1   **20.** 15 is what percent of 60? 25%

21. What percent is 18 of 48? 37.5%   **22.** What percent of 80 is 15? 18.75%

23. 90 is 3% of what number? 3,000   **24.** 75% of what number is 30? 40

Write and solve a proportion for each question.

25. What is 42% of 80? $\frac{42}{100} = \frac{n}{80}$; $n = 33.6$

26. 20% of a number is 24. What is the number? $\frac{20}{100} = \frac{24}{n}$; $n = 120$

27. 30 is what percent of 60? $\frac{n}{100} = \frac{30}{60}$; $n = 50$

Solve.

28. June has 30 days. During that month, 40% of the days were sunny. How many days were sunny? 12

29. In one class, 9 out of 30 students play musical instruments. What percent of the class plays musical instruments? 30%

317

Using Page 317

The exercises in the Chapter Review/Test emphasize the major concepts and skills presented in this chapter. These exercises may be used as a review assignment or as a test, depending upon your needs.

Item Analysis The table below correlates the Chapter Review/Test items with objectives and with the student text pages on which the concepts or skills were taught. Please note that items 25–27 are derived from a lesson from which no "Minimum" assignment was suggested in the Assignment Guide. Only those students who were assigned this lesson should be expected to complete the corresponding Chapter Review/Test items.

Items	Objectives	Related Text Pages
1–16	12.1	294–301
17–19	12.2	302–304
20–22	12.3	306–307
23–24	12.4	310–312
25–27	12.5	314–315
28–29	12.6	305, 308–309, 313

Assessment Options

If you use the Chapter Review/Test review assignment, you may wish to use the free-response test or the multiple-choice test to evaluate mastery of the chapter objectives. The items on these tests have a one-to-one correspondence in terms of content and level of difficulty. A correlation of test items to objectives and student text pages is provided in the Management Guide for Chapter 12. Note: Items 35–36 are derived from lessons for which no minimum assignment was suggested in the Assignment Guide.

Multiple-Choice Test, TRB pages 34–36
Free-Response Test, TRB pages 71–72

TRB Options

The following blackline masters are available for use with this chapter. If you have not already assigned these materials, you may wish to use them to close the chapter.

Recreation, TRB page 166
Consumer Applications, TRB page 184
Calculator Technology, TRB page 202
Reading Math, TRB page 238
Family Involvement, TRB pages 267–268

Reteaching

Using Page 318

The exercises on this page are intended for those students who experienced difficulty with the Chapter Review/Test on page 317. Should students require reteaching of these key concepts and skills, please refer to the teaching notes below. Otherwise, the Another Look exercises can be assigned as independent work, with students using the accompanying sample problems and hints as guides.

Exercises 1–10 This skill was originally taught on pages 294–297. Have students study the examples in the display box. Remind them that percent means per hundred. Explain that since 75 squares out of 100 squares are shaded, we can write this as 75%. On the chalkboard, work through an example of writing a fraction, such as $\frac{7}{10}$, as a percent. Elicit from students that the numerator and denominator should be multiplied by 10. Next show how to write a lowest-terms fraction for a percent.

Exercises 11–18 This skill was originally taught on page 298. Have students study the examples in the display box. Point out that since percent means per hundred, we divide by 100 to change a percent to a decimal. Review the shortcut for dividing a decimal by 100. To write a decimal as a percent, the process is simply reversed.

Exercises 19–22 This skill was originally taught on pages 300–301. On the chalkboard work through the example of writing $\frac{5}{6}$ as a percent by dividing.

Exercises 23–24 This skill was originally taught on pages 302–303. Direct students' attention to the example in the display box. Remind students that the word "of" means "times" in an exercise such as 5% of 80. Emphasize that before multiplying, the percent should be written as a decimal.

Exercises 25–26 This skill was originally taught on pages 306–307. On the chalkboard, work through the example of writing a percent for 3 out of 5. Stress that a percent is a ratio or the number out of 100.

Exercises 27–28 This skill was originally taught on pages 310–311. Show students how to write an equation for "20% of a number is 24." Emphasize that 20% of a number means 20% times a number. Work through the steps of solving the equation on the chalkboard.

ANOTHER LOOK

100 squares 75 shaded

$$\frac{75}{100} = \frac{3}{4} \leftarrow \text{fraction}$$

$$\frac{75}{100} = 0.75 \leftarrow \text{decimal}$$

$$\frac{75}{100} = 75\% \leftarrow \text{percent}$$

What percent of each square is shaded?

1. 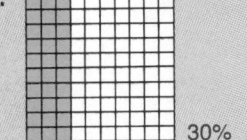 30%

2. 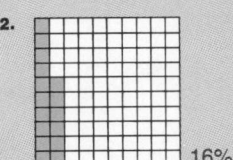 16%

Write each fraction as a percent.

3. $\frac{27}{100}$ 27% **4.** $\frac{3}{10}$ 30% **5.** $\frac{4}{5}$ 80% **6.** $\frac{17}{25}$ 68%

Write the lowest-terms fraction for each percent.

7. 20% $\frac{1}{5}$ **8.** 50% $\frac{1}{2}$ **9.** 44% $\frac{11}{25}$ **10.** 65% $\frac{13}{20}$

$$57.3\% = 0.573$$

shift 2 places left

$$0.333 = 33.3\%$$

shift 2 places right

Write each percent as a decimal.

11. 28% **12.** 160% **13.** 62.5% **14.** 9%
     0.28   1.6   0.625   0.09

Write each decimal as a percent.

15. 0.23 23% **16.** 0.06 6% **17.** 0.315 **18.** 1.80
                                        31.5%   180%

$$\frac{5}{6} = 6\overline{)5.00} \quad 0.833 \rightarrow 83\%$$

Find the percent for each fraction. Round to the nearest whole percent.

19. $\frac{3}{8}$ 38% **20.** $\frac{2}{3}$ 67% **21.** $\frac{11}{17}$ 65% **22.** $\frac{7}{12}$ 58%

5% of 80
$0.05 \times 80 = 4.00$

3 out of 5
$\frac{3}{5} = \frac{60}{100} = 60\%$

20% of $n = 10$
$n = \frac{10}{0.20} = 50$

23. Find 20% of 250. 50 **24.** Find 7% of 900. 63

25. What percent is 12 out of 20? 60% **26.** What percent of 25 is 15? 60%

27. 80% of a number is 24. What is the number? 30 **28.** 5% of a number is 30. What is the number? 600

318

Just for Teachers

Money and Banking

King Croesus established the western world's first imperial coinage in Lydia, a region in northwest Turkey. In 550 B.C., Lydia was known for rich deposits of gold, and the discovery there of the touchstone two centuries earlier had given rise to the production of gold coins whose worth could be certified by scratching them on the touchstone. Soon a number of cities and states were coining money, and trade increased as the concept of coins as an acceptable exchange for goods and services spread.

Increased commerce meant increased bookkeeping. Accurate bookkeeping had become important since the development of agriculture and settled communities. Scribes, nr bookkeepers, were respected members of Egyptian society and were depicted in artworks tallying accounts and levying and collecting taxes. These fiscal responsibilities were handled by similar officials in cultures the world over. In varying degrees of sophistication, the abacus had developed as the bookkeepers' "calculator." The Chinese are credited with the refinement of its present form to moveable beads on rods.

ENRICHMENT

Calculating Percents

1980 Census Data on Metropolitan Growth

Standard Metropolitan Area	1970 Population	1980 Population	Percent Change
Fort Lauderdale-Hollywood, FL	620,000	1,005,000	62
Phoenix, AZ	971,000	1,505,000	55
Tampa-Saint Petersburg, FL	1,013,000	1,552,000	53
Houston, TX	1,985,000	2,887,000	45
Atlanta, GA	1,390,000	2,004,000	44
Riverside-San Bernardino-Ontario, CA	1,139,000	1,537,000	35
Denver-Boulder, CO	1,228,000	1,613,000	31
Dallas-Fort Worth, TX	2,318,000	2,961,000	28
Knoxville, TN	409,000	477,000	17
Portland, OR	1,007,000	1,236,000	23
Tulsa, OK	549,000	690,000	26
San Jose, CA	1,065,000	1,283,000	20

The Fort Lauderdale-Hollywood area increased in population by 62% between 1970 and 1980. You can use a calculator to find the percent of change in population for the other areas. Follow the steps shown below for Fort Lauderdale-Hollywood.

	Enter	Press	Read
Find the difference between the 1980 and 1970 populations.	1,005,000	−	1005000
	620,000	÷	385000
Divide by the 1970 population. Round to the nearest hundredth. Write a percent for the decimal.	620,000	=	0.6209677 0.62 62%

1. Find the percent of change for each of the other areas in the chart.

2. Find the percent of change in population between 1970 and 1980 for your metropolitan area or for your local community.

319

In India after the collapse of the Roman Empire, the Hindus developed the most efficient "aid" to computation until the invention of the computer—positional notation with nine numbers and zero. Soon after the introduction of positional notation to the trade community in Europe around A.D. 1200, double-entry bookkeeping developed in Italy.

Italian financiers devised the bill of exchange, a note of credit drawn for a specific amount and payable to a particular party which tradesmen could carry instead of gold. These notes of credit were redeemed at money lenders' exchange tables, called *bancas.* This was the beginning of the banking industry. Modern times have also witnessed changes in "money"—the revolutionary 20th Century inventions of the computer and plastic may eventually do away with both coins and paper as "legal tender."

Using Page 319

This page is intended for those students who successfully completed the Chapter Review/Test on page 317. You may wish to assign this page as independent work while you use Another Look exercises to reteach the basic concepts and skills of the chapter. Or, you may decide that all students would benefit from exposure to this Enrichment activity.

Lesson Development After students have had an opportunity to study the table, write the information given for the Fort Lauderdale-Hollywood area on the chalkboard. Show students how to find the percent of change. Explain that first the difference between populations is found, and then it is expressed as a percent of the original (1970) population.

$$1,005,000 - 620,000 = 385,000$$

$$\frac{385,000}{620,000} \rightarrow 385,000 \div 620,000 = 0.6209677$$

$$0.62 = 62\%$$

Direct students' attention to the box with the calculator codes. Notice with students that the codes show the same method for finding percent change. Have students work through these steps with their calculators.

Note: There are two logic systems used by calculators, arithmetic logic and algebraic logic.

Most students will have calculators with arithmetic logic, but if a calculator with algebraic logic is used, the = key should be pressed after subtracting:

Enter	Press	Read
1,005,000	−	1005000
620,000	=	385000
	÷	385000
620,000	=	0.6209677

Exercise 1 Have students use their calculators to complete the table. You may wish to point out that the use of memory keys makes it possible to enter the 1970 population once and use it both as a subtrahend and as a divisor. The calculator code for this method is shown below.

Enter	Press	Read
1,005,000	−	1005000
620,000	M+	620000
	÷	385000
	MR	620000
	=	0.6209677

Exercise 2 To solve this problem students will need to collect data regarding the population of your community.

Using Page 320

The exercises on the page provide practice for maintaining cumulative skills. The emphasis in this Cumulative Review is on multiplication and division of fractions (Chapter 9) and metric measurement (Chapter 10).

Item Analysis The table below correlates the Cumulative Review items with objectives and with the student book pages on which the concepts or skills were taught.

Items	Objectives	Related Text Pages
1–3	9.1	224–230
4	9.3	232–235
5–6	9.4	238–241
7–8	10.1	248–251
9–10	10.4	264
11–12	10.2	252–254, 256–258
13	9.5	236–237
14	10.5	255, 259, 263, 265

CUMULATIVE REVIEW

1. What is $\frac{7}{8}$ of 72?

   A 67   B 63
   c 56   D not given

Find the products.

2. $6 \times \frac{5}{6}$ A 41   B 40
   C 5   D not given

3. $4\frac{2}{3} \times \frac{3}{7}$ A 12   B $2\frac{2}{7}$
   C 2   D not given

4. Find the quotient.

   $1\frac{5}{6} \div 3\frac{1}{2}$

   A $\frac{11}{21}$ B $\frac{11}{12}$
   c $\frac{5}{21}$ D not given

5. What is the decimal for $\frac{6}{17}$?

   A 0.36   B 0.32
   c 0.28   D not given

6. What is the lowest-terms fraction for 0.68?

   A $\frac{17}{25}$ B $\frac{12}{25}$
   c $\frac{24}{50}$ D not given

Find the missing numbers.

7. 60 km = 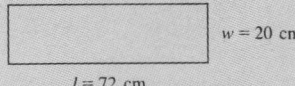 m

   A 6,000   B 60,000
   c 600   D not given

8. 1,675 cm = 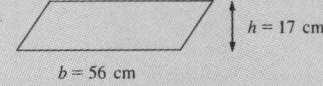 m

   A 0.1675   B 167.5
   C 16.75   D not given

9. 0.967 kg = ▨ g

   A 967   B 9.67
   c 9,670   D not given

10. 720 mg = ▨ g

    A 7,200   B 0.72
    c 7.2   D not given

11. What is the perimeter?

    $w = 20$ cm
    $l = 72$ cm

    A 92 cm   B 184 cm
    c 1,440 cm   D not given

12. What is the area?

    $h = 17$ cm
    $b = 56$ cm

    A 952 cm^2 B 9,520 cm^2
    c 146 cm^2 D not given

13. There were 39 players trying out for a field hockey team. The coach chose $\frac{1}{3}$ of the players for the team. How many players did she choose?

    A 13   B 11
    c 16   D not given

14. One face of a cube has an area of 16.24 cm^2. What is the surface area of the cube?

    A 129.92 cm^2 B 64.96 cm^2
    C 97.44 cm^2 D not given

Circles and Cylinders

Objectives

13.1 Find the circumference of a circle.

13.2 Find the area of a circle.

13.3 Find the lateral area and total surface area of a cylinder.

13.4 Find the volume of a cylinder.

13.5 Identify the cross-section view of a space figure.

13.6 Solve word problems using the 5-Point Checklist and cumulative computational skills.

Summary

The main emphasis of this chapter is on measurement of circles and cylinders. The nonmetric aspects of circles and cylinders were studied in Chapter 6. The concepts of circumference of a circle and area of a circle are basic. The formulas for area and circumference of circles are presented in the early lessons in the chapter. This is followed by a lesson on lateral and total surface area of cylinders and a lesson dealing with the volume of cylinders.

Several problem-solving sets require that students apply problem-solving skills to problems related to circles and cylinders. One lesson introduces the concept of a cross section of a space region. This lesson shows a relationship between plane regions and space regions and is designed to strengthen the space perception of students.

Mathematical Background

Circles In formal geometry courses, the circumference of a circle is defined as the limit of the perimeters of the inscribed regular polygons.

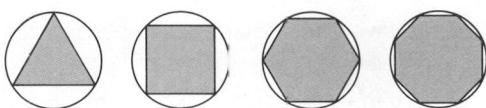

As the number of sides of the inscribed polygons increases, their perimeters increase but have an upper bound. The least upper bound of the perimeters is the circumference of the circle. In this chapter the description of circumference as "the distance around a circle" is intuitive, but easily understood by students at this grade level.

Of equal importance in the study of circles is the idea that the ratio of the circumference to the diameter is the same number in every circle. This statement can be made plausible by actual measurement of several objects, computing the ratio $\frac{C}{d}$ and observing that it is about 3.1. This constant ratio is denoted by the Greek letter π (pi). Since $\frac{C}{d} = \pi$, the formula for the circumference of a circle is immediately seen to be $C = \pi d$.

The area of a circle is presented intuitively as the number of square units needed to cover the interior of a circle. We do not attempt to prove or justify the area formula, $A = \pi r^2$.

Cylinders The circumference and area concepts and formulas for circles are prerequisite for the work with area and volume of cylinders. The formula for lateral area of a cylinder can be derived from the area of a rectangle. The lateral area of a cylinder is the same as the area of a rectangle with a length of $2\pi r$ and a width equal to h.

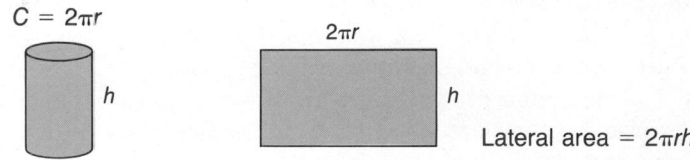

Lateral area $= 2\pi rh$

To find the total surface area, the area of the two bases is added to the lateral area.

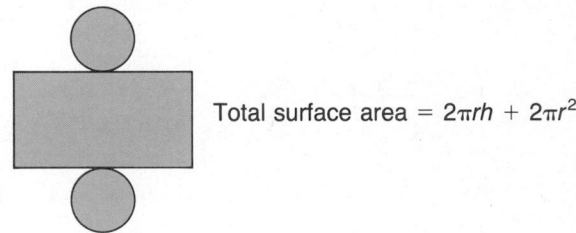

Total surface area $= 2\pi rh + 2\pi r^2$

The formula for the volume of a cylinder is developed by showing that if a prism and a cylinder have equal heights and bases of equal area, they must have equal volumes. Since the basic volume formula for a prism is $V = Bh$, where B is the area of the base and h is the height, we can use the same formula for a cylinder. In a cylinder $B = \pi r^2$, so the formula for the volume of a circular cylinder is $V = \pi r^2 h$.

Problem Solving The word problems in this chapter apply the measurement formulas for circles and cylinders. There are also problems that review skills developed in previous chapters. The problem-solving practice on pages 326–327 and 332–333 emphasize all parts of the 5-Point Checklist.

In the applied problem-solving lesson on page 336, students make decisions about whether it is more advantageous to sell an old TV set or trade it in for the new one.

Vocabulary

circumference π (pi)   cross section

Error Analysis

This chapter extends the measurement ideas of previous chapters to the study of circles and cylinders. New concepts are introduced, and ideas previously developed such as lateral and total surface area are applied to circles and cylinders. Because of the many formulas and computations required, student errors are common. Some of these errors are listed below.

Error Pattern 1

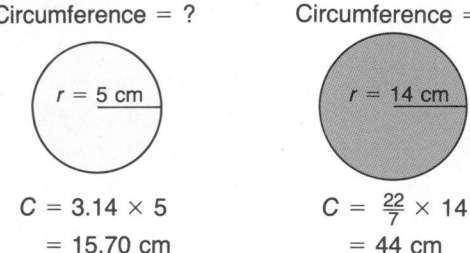

Circumference = ?   Circumference = ?

$r = 5$ cm $r = 14$ cm

$C = 3.14 \times 5$ $C = \frac{22}{7} \times 14$

$= 15.70$ cm $= 44$ cm

Diagnosis The student used the radius times π to find the circumference.

Remediation Review with the student the relationship between the circumference and the diameter, and between the radius and the diameter. Use circular objects and string to illustrate the relationship. Show that the circumference is a little more than three times greater than the diameter. Emphasize that to find the circumference we must multiply $3.14 \times d$ or $3.14 \times 2r$.

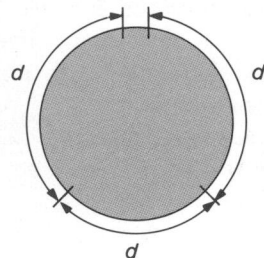

Error Pattern 2

Area = ?   Area = ?

$r = 4$ cm $r = 10$ cm

$A = \pi r^2$ $A = \pi r^2$

$= 3.14 \times 4^2$ $= 3.14 \times 10^2$

$= 12.56^2$ $= 314^2$

$= 157.7536$ cm^2 $= 98{,}596$ cm^2

Diagnosis The student used the correct formula and substituted correctly, but simplified incorrectly. He or she multiplied the radius times 3.14 and then found the square of the product.

Remediation Explain to the student that the formula means $A = \pi \times (r \times r)$. The exponent indicates that the radius is used as a factor two times. Emphasize that we multiply times π after the radius is squared. In general, powers are found before performing other operations.

Error Pattern 3

Volume = ?

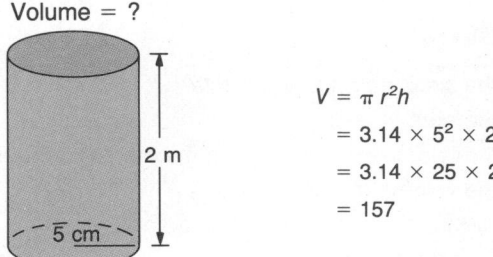

2 m

5 cm

$V = \pi r^2 h$

$= 3.14 \times 5^2 \times 2$

$= 3.14 \times 25 \times 2$

$= 157$

Diagnosis The student substituted measures of different units in the formula for volume. He or she used a radius in cm and a height in m.

Remediation Discuss the concept of volume as the number of unit-cubes in a figure. Explain that if the radius is in cm, the area of the base of the cylinder will be in cm^2. To find the number of cm^3 in the cylinder, the height must be given in cm.

Problem Solving

A Problem-of-the-Week Bulletin Board

One way to introduce problem-solving experiences in the classroom is through the use of a "problem-of-the-week" bulletin board. This approach to teaching problem solving allows you to provide students with challenging math problems without impinging on your teaching time. Many students enjoy problems that they can work at for a time, leave, and then return to.

The bulletin board design below is useful for a problem-of-the-week. The bulletin board can be entitled, "Have You Tried This?" and consists of four parts.

- *The Problem*—a statement of the problem
- *Will This Help?*—questions and ideas related to the problem
- *What Others Have Tried*—samples of possible methods for solving the problem
- *What I Have Tried*—a space for students to display their own attempts at solving the problem

The problem statement is always visible, but other sections of the board are designed so that only one piece of information can be seen at a time. For example, each question for "Will This Help?" is printed on a separate sheet of paper so that to read more than one question it is necessary to flip to the next sheet.

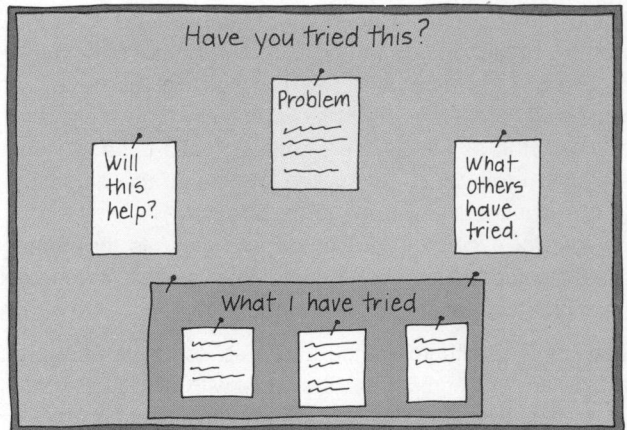

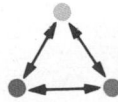

Special Education

The chapter deals with circles and cylinders. Students are presented with measurement situations in which some of the measures are along curves rather than segments. This type of measurement needs careful introduction for understanding and retention. The following suggestions may help you meet the needs of your special students.

Developing the Concept of π

The development of the concept of π can provide a review of the earlier work with ratios, as well as a real-world model for students to use in future measurement situations. The equipment needed in order to carry out the activity is metric tape measures or string, rulers, calculators and data sheets as shown. Students should measure circular objects found in the school or classroom. The circumference of these objects can be measured with the tape measure or string and ruler. The diameters can be measured with a cardboard caliper, similar to the one shown below. After the measurements are made, the ratio of the circumference to the diameter of each object should be found using the calculator. When the worksheets are complete, the pattern that the ratios follow can be discussed. This provides a good review of terminology and emphasizes the relationship between the circumference and diameter of a circle and π.

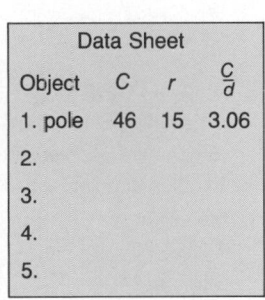

Data Sheet			
Object	C	r	$\frac{C}{d}$
1. pole	46	15	3.06
2.			
3.			
4.			
5.			

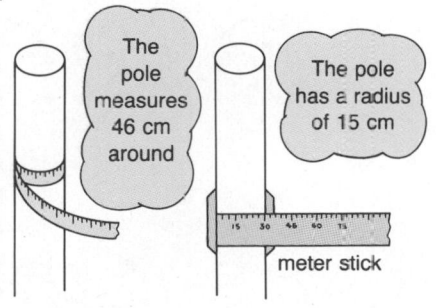

The pole measures 46 cm around

The pole has a radius of 15 cm

meter stick

Checking Prerequisite Skills

Before beginning the work with cylinders on page 328, you may need to review cylinders and surface area of a space figure. Working with models such as tin cans and cardboard tubes will help students visualize the concepts.

Minimizing Memorization Requirements

Memorization of measurement formulas for area and volume can pose problems for students who have difficulty with memorization. For this reason, the number of formulas to be learned and applied should be kept to a minimum. Instead of requiring special students to memorize formulas, you may wish to have them write each formula and draw the appropriate figure on an index card for ready reference. The cards can then be used to help students decide which formula to apply to an exercise.

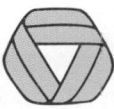

Subject Integration

Subject matter related to other areas of the curriculum has been integrated into the following lessons. This provides an opportunity to highlight the interaction between mathematics and other subjects.

Science Lasers, page 321

Career Awareness Minerologist, pages 322–323; drafting, page 334

Consumer Awareness Rug pricing, page 324; decision making, page 336

Physical Education Bicycles, pages 326–327

Industrial Arts Wood, pages 332–333

Computer Awareness Hex numeration system, page 339

Management Guide

Teaching Chapter 13				Meeting Individual Needs					
				Lesson Assignments			Follow Up		
Objectives	Chapter Content	Pages	TRB Test Items	Minimum	Average	Extended	Reteaching	Enrichment	Practice
	Chapter Opener	321							
13.1 Find the circumference of a circle.	Circumference	322–323	1–6	1–12, 19	1–19, 22	1–22	SE6 Ch 14 RS 94	ES 94	MP 437 PS 121
13.2 Find the area of a circle.	Area of Circles	324–325	7–9	1–12, SK	1–17, SK	1–17, SK	SE6 Ch 14 RS 95	ES 95	MP 437 PS 122
13.3 Find the lateral area and total surface area of a cylinder.	Area of Cylinders	328–329	10–13	1–6, 11–17	1–17, 20	1–15 odd, 17–20, TM			MP 437 PS 124
13.4 Find the volume of a cylinder.	Volume of Cylinders	330–331	14–15	1–6, SK	1–7, SK	1–8, SK	RS 96	ES 96	MP 437 PS 125
13.5 Identify the cross-section view of a space figure.	Cross Sections	334–335	16–17		1–9	1–9, TM			PS 127
13.6 Solve word problems using the 5-Point Checklist and cumulative computational skills.	Problem Solving: Practice	326–327	18–20	1–7	1–8, 12	1–12			PS 123
	Problem Solving: Practice	332–333		1–7	1–8, 11–12	1–12			PS 126
	Applied Problem Solving	336							
	Chapter Review/Test	337							
	Another Look/ Enrichment	338–339							
	Technology	340–341							
	Cumulative Review	342							

SE6 Student Edition, Book 6
RS Reteaching Supplement
ES Enrichment Supplement
PS Practice Supplement
MP More Practice
TM Think Math
SK Skillkeeper
TRB Teacher's Resource Book

Masters for use

. . . before Chapter 13

Readiness
Perimeter and Area — 128

Readiness
Measuring Circles — 127

. . . during Chapter 13

Calculator Technology
Going in Circles — 203

Consumer Applications
Meal Ticket — 185

Teaching Aids — 278, 281, 284

Recreation
Multicultural Number Problems — 167

Activities That Count
Flowchart Game — 151

. . . after Chapter 13

Record Keeping — 308

Family Involvement
At-Home Activities — 270

Family Involvement
Key Math — 269

Reading Math
Circle and Cylinder Concepts — 239

Computer Technology
Decision Loops — 220

Computer Technology
Computer Tables — 219

Computer Technology
Area and Volume — 218

Chapter 13 Test
Free-Response Format — 73–74

Chapter 13 Test
Multiple-Choice Format — 37–38

Supplements

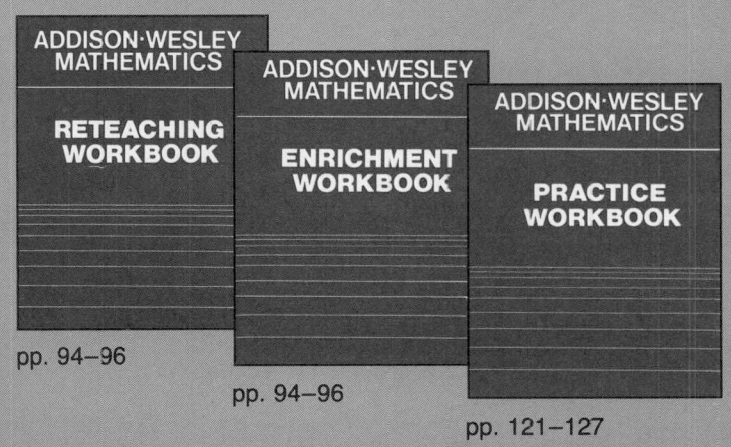

ADDISON·WESLEY MATHEMATICS
RETEACHING WORKBOOK
pp. 94–96

ADDISON·WESLEY MATHEMATICS
ENRICHMENT WORKBOOK
pp. 94–96

ADDISON·WESLEY MATHEMATICS
PRACTICE WORKBOOK
pp. 121–127

Other Addison-Wesley Resources

Books and Kits

Making Practice Fun 68 A, B, 73 B

Activities That Count are designed for use throughout this chapter and subsequent chapters. Before beginning Chapter 13 you may wish to review these activities and select the ones you consider appropriate for your class.

Curves of Constant Width   Math Lab

Purpose To construct a curve of constant width

Materials Compass

Activity You may wish to introduce this activity by discussing the Wankel engine. This is an innovative design of an internal combustion engine that uses a rotary piston instead of the usual cylindrical one. The rotor is a modified curve of constant width.

Explain that a circle is an example of a curve of constant width. This means that a circle of diameter d can roll between two parallel lines which are 2 units apart, touching both lines continuously. Tell students that there are other curves besides circles that have this same property and that they can construct such a curve by following these steps:

Step 1

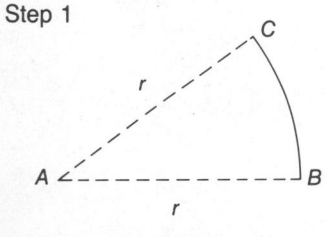

Draw arc BC with
radius r and center A.

Step 2

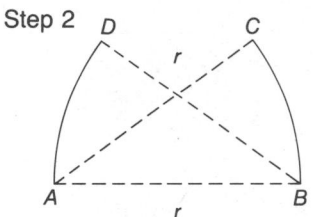

Draw arc AD with
radius r and center B.

Step 3

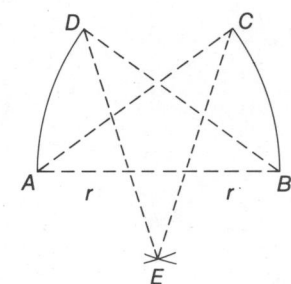

Locate point E which is
the intersection of arcs
with radius r and centers
at D and C.

Step 4

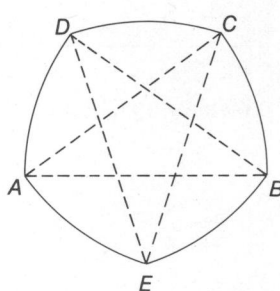

Draw arc AE with center C.
Draw arc DC with center E.
Draw arc BE with center D.

The closed curve $AEBCD$ is a curve of constant width. It will roll between two parallel lines which are r units apart and will always be touching both lines.

Some students may be interested in using a piece of cardboard and constructing a large copy of the curve. They can cut out the curve and test its properties.

Discovery of π Project

Purpose To read and report on the history of π

Activity Have students research the history of π, values used for π over the centuries, and various methods used to approximate π. Students should report their findings to the class.

Flowcharts   Game

Purpose To use a flowchart

Materials Game board (TRB p. 151), game markers, two number cubes (TRB p. 278) labeled 1 through 6, a spinner (TRB p. 281) numbered 1 through 10

Activity Students place their markers on Start and in turn follow instructions in the rectangles, moving according to flow lines. When a player reaches the next rectangle in a turn, he or she follows those instructions on the next turn. The first player to reach End wins.

Circles and Cylinders

A laser beam has special characteristics. It is narrow and spreads out very little, so it can travel much farther than ordinary light. When a laser beam was bounced off the moon, the pencil-thin beam of light spread out only about 3 km in diameter after traveling for approximately 380,000 km. The light of a laser is only one color and it is much brighter than sunlight.

Lasers are used in industry to drill tiny holes and cut thick steel. Surgeons can use lasers because the laser light can be focused down to a spot 0.0005 mm in diameter. This narrow beam of light becomes a laser knife that can seal off blood vessels as it cuts. With the help of lasers, photographers can take three-dimensional pictures and scientists can measure pollution in the air. The storage capacity of computers has been greatly increased using laser technology. Television broadcasting companies hope to one day use laser beams as transmitters.

Light from a flashlight spreads out in all directions.

The narrow beam of laser light has sides that are nearly parallel.

Introducing the Chapter

Discussion Give students the opportunity to read the article and examine the accompanying pictures. Discuss the data in the article and use this as an opportunity for students to form their own questions using the data.

As you teach the chapter, you may wish to refer back to this page and discuss the following problems. Review the contents of the article before asking the questions.

Follow-Up Questions

After Page 323 It would take hours by ordinary methods to drill a hole in an industrial diamond, but in $2\frac{1}{2}$ minutes a hole 0.16 mm in diameter can be drilled by a laser. What is the circumference of the hole? (0.5024 mm) What is the circumference of the spot of laser light a surgeon may use as a tiny scalpel? (0.00157 mm)

After Page 325 What was the approximate area of the spot of laser light that was bounced off the moon? (7.065 km²)

After Page 329 Theodore Maiman built the first laser. It was called a ruby laser because it worked by exciting the atoms in an artificial ruby crystal. The ruby was a tiny cylinder about 4 cm high and 0.5 cm in diameter. What was the surface area of the ruby cylinder? (6.6725 cm²)

Quick Review Display these figures and have students find the perimeters.

4 m   7 m   8 m   **19 m**   1.9 m   1.8 m   0.5 m   1 m   2 m   **7.2 m**   8.1 cm   15.8 cm   **47.8 cm**

Lesson Focus To find the circumference of a circle

Suggested Materials Circular objects such as empty cans, centimeter rulers (TRB p. 280), string, calculators

Ideas for Getting Started

Review with students the meaning of radius and diameter of a circle. Write the word *circumference* on the chalkboard. Explain that the distance around a circle is the circumference.

Have students measure the diameter and circumference of circular objects to the nearest tenth of a centimeter. The circumference can be measured by wrapping a string around the object and then measuring the length of the string, or by rolling the circular object one revolution along a centimeter ruler. On the chalkboard, record the circumference and diameter of each circle. Then have students express the ratio $\frac{C}{d}$ as a decimal to the nearest tenth.

Using Page 322

Lesson Development Have students read the material at the top of the page. They should understand that the ratio $\frac{C}{d}$ is the same number for all circles. Show that the formulas $C = \pi d$ and $C = 2\pi r$ are derived from the definition of the ratio, $\pi = \frac{C}{d}$.

Observe with students that the decimal for π does not terminate or repeat. It is an irrational number. Explain that the numbers 3.14 and $\frac{22}{7}$ are approximations of π that are useful in most practical measurement problems.

Other Examples Point out that we use an approximate value for π, so calculations using π are approximations. In the examples the symbol $\approx$ is used to indicate "is approximately equal to."

Warm Up Have students use the formula $C = \pi d$ and work these exercises independently.

Circumference

Maurice Thompson is a mineralogist. He measured the **diameter** (*d*) of some petrified logs and then measured the distance around the logs. The distance around a circle is called the **circumference** (*C*).

Diameter (*d*)	Circumference (*C*)	$\frac{C}{d}$
0.8 m	2.5 m	3.1
2.1 m	6.6 m	3.1
1.4 m	4.4 m	3.1
1.6 m	5.0 m	3.1

For every circle, the ratio $\frac{C}{d}$ $\left(\frac{\text{Circumference}}{\text{diameter}}\right)$ is the same number. We use the Greek letter π (**pi**) for this ratio. The decimal for π is unending and does not repeat.

$\pi = 3.14159265358979323846264 3 \ldots$

We will use 3.14 or $\frac{22}{7}$ for π.

Circumference = $\pi \times$ **diameter**
$C = \pi d$ or $C = 2\pi r$

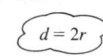
$d = 2r$

Other Examples

Find *C* if *d* = 8 cm. Use 3.14 for π.

$C = \pi d$
$C \approx 3.14 \times 8$
$C \approx 25.12$ cm
$\approx$ means "is approximately equal to"

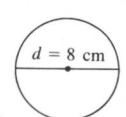
d = 8 cm

Find *C* if *r* = 14 cm. Use $\frac{22}{7}$ for π.

$C = 2\pi r$
$C \approx 2 \times \frac{22}{7} \times 14$
$C \approx 88$ cm

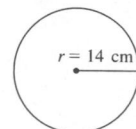
r = 14 cm

Warm Up

Find the circumference of each circle.

Use 3.14 for π.

1. *d* = 3 cm   9.42 cm

2. *d* = 0.75 m   2.355 m

Use $\frac{22}{7}$ for π.

3. *d* = 42 cm   132 cm

4. *d* = 70 m   220 m

322

Follow Up

Reteaching

Review the idea of perimeter of polygons and relate this concept to the circumference of a circle. Have students draw circles of various sizes with a compass. Then have them cut pieces of string equal to the diameter of the circle and find how many pieces of string this length are needed to go completely around the circle. (a little more than 3)

On the chalkboard, write $C = \pi d$. Explain that π stands for the number that is a little more than 3, approximately 3.14. Then show how the formula can be used to find the circumference of a circle.

Enrichment

Have students find the decimal approximation for $\frac{22}{7}$. Ask them to tell which approximation, $\frac{22}{7}$ or 3.14, is closer to the actual value of π. ($\frac{22}{7}$ is closer to the actual value of π)

Assignment Guide			
	Minimum	Average	Extended
page 323	1–12, 19	1–19, 22	1–22

Find the circumference of each circle. Use 3.14 for π.

1.
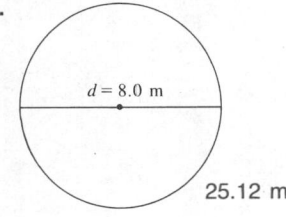
$d = 8.0$ m
25.12 m

2.
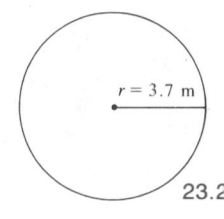
$r = 3.7$ m
23.236 m

3.
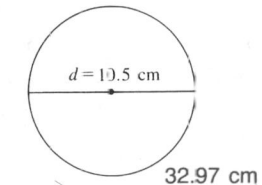
$d = 10.5$ cm
32.97 cm

4. $r = 3.6$ m 22.608 m   **5.** $d = 6.0$ cm 18.84 cm   **6.** $r = 15$ km 94.2 km

Find the circumference of each circle. Use $\frac{22}{7}$ for π.

7. $d = 21$ mm 66 mm   **8.** $r = 7$ m 44 m   **9.** $d = 10.5$ m 33 m

10. $r = 0.7$ m 4.4 m   **11.** $r = 28$ cm 176 cm   **12.** $d = 3.5$ km 11 km

Since $C = \pi d$, $d = \frac{C}{\pi}$. Use this formula to find the diameter of each circle with the given circumference. Use 3.14 for π.

13. $C = 18.84$ cm 6 cm   **14.** $C = 28.26$ m 9 m   **15.** $C = 37.68$ mm 12 mm

16. $C = 4.71$ m 1.5 m   **17.** $C = 25.12$ cm 8 cm   **18.** $C = 78.5$ m 25 m

19. A petrified conifer has a diameter of 3.4 m. What is the circumference of the petrified tree? 10.676 m

20. A petrified tree found in Michigan has a diameter of 1.2 m. How much greater is the circumference of a petrified tree with a diameter of 2.9 m? 5.338 m

★ **21.** The "Queen Tree," a petrified tree in Calistoga, California, has a circumference of 11.46 m. What is the radius of the tree, to the nearest tenth of a meter? 1.8 m

22. Find a decimal for the fraction $\frac{355}{113}$. To what decimal place is this a correct value for π? 3.1415929; millionths

More Practice, page 437, Set A

Using Page 323

Exercises 1–12 Note that in some exercises the diameters of the circles are given, while in others the radii of the circles are given. In exercises 1–6, students use 3.14 for π. The fraction for π, $\frac{22}{7}$, is used in exercises 7–12.

Exercises 13–18 In these exercises students use the formula $d = \frac{C}{\pi}$ to find the diameter of a circle given the circumference.

Exercise 21 Students could use the formula $d = \frac{C}{\pi}$ to find the diameter and then take half of the diameter to find the radius. Some students may realize that $r = \frac{C}{2\pi}$.

Exercise 22 Have students compare the decimal value of $\frac{355}{113}$ to the decimal value of π given on page 322.

More Practice, page 437, Set A

Reteaching Supplement, page 94

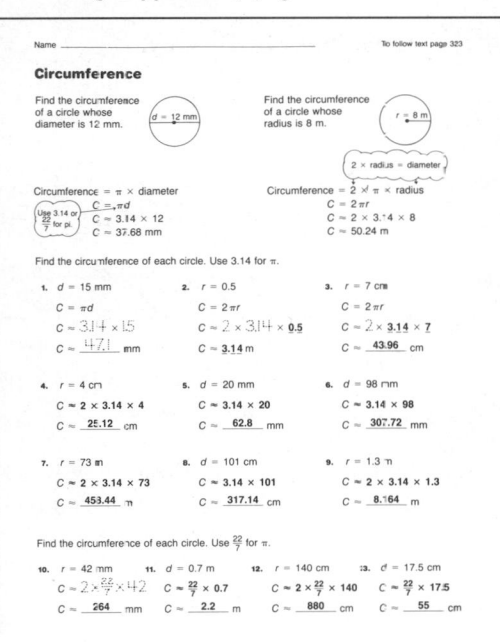

Enrichment Supplement, page 94

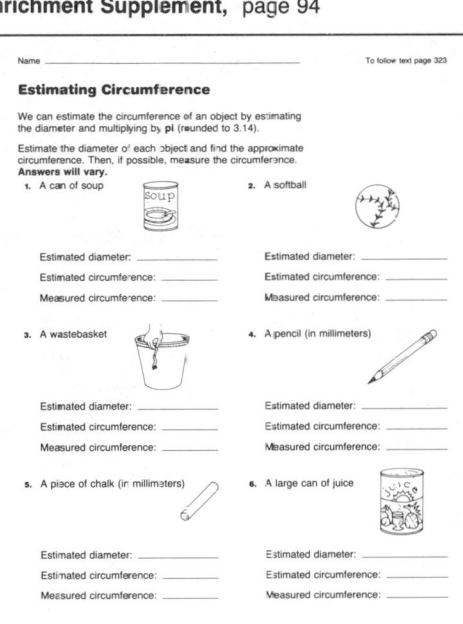

Practice Supplement, page 121

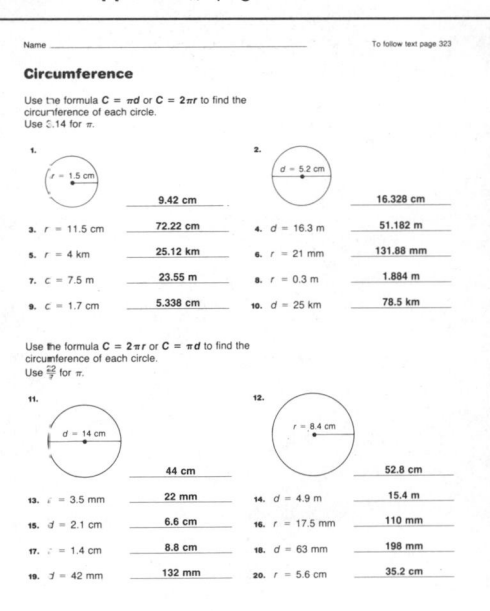

Quick Review Have students write the improper fractions as mixed numbers or whole numbers.

$\frac{12}{5}$ $2\frac{2}{5}$		$\frac{72}{9}$ 8		$\frac{28}{15}$ $1\frac{13}{15}$		$\frac{24}{9}$ $2\frac{2}{3}$	
$\frac{11}{2}$ $5\frac{1}{2}$	$\frac{26}{3}$ $8\frac{2}{3}$		$\frac{24}{6}$ 4		$\frac{30}{6}$ 5		$\frac{11}{7}$ $1\frac{4}{7}$

Lesson Focus To find the area of a circle

Suggested Materials Square grid transparency for the overhead projector

Ideas for Getting Started

Review with students the concept of area as the number of square units needed to cover a region. Next draw several circles on the transparency grid. Have students estimate the number of squares in the interior of the circles by counting the whole squares and estimating parts of squares. Record the estimates. Explain that in the lesson, students will find out how to check their estimates.

Using Page 324

Motivational Problem Read the introductory problem with students. Have them identify the question and the data given in the problem. Explain that we can plan to find the area by estimation and then use a formula to check the estimate.

Lesson Development Write the formula for the area of a circle on the chalkboard and show how it is used to find area. Point out that before multiplying by 3.14 we square the radius. Notice with students that the unit of area is the square of the unit of length used for the radius.

Other Examples Work through the examples as a class activity. The second example shows the extra step that is needed when the diameter of a circle is given. We must divide the diameter by 2 to get the radius.

Warm Up Watch for students who multiply the radius by two instead of squaring it. Provide an opportunity for students to discuss any difficulties before assigning exercises on page 325.

Area of Circles

A department store prices its rugs according to the area of the rugs. What is the area of a large circular rug that has a radius of 2 m?

We can estimate the area by counting the squares and parts of squares inside the circle on the grid below.

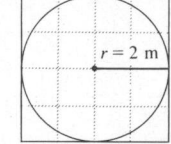

Whole squares → **4**
Estimated part squares → **+8**
Total squares → **12**

We can use multiplication to find area.

Area of a circle = $\pi \times$ square of radius
$A = \pi r^2$

Use 3.14 for π.
$A \approx 3.14 \times 2^2$
$A \approx 3.14 \times 4$
$A \approx 12.56$

The area of the rug is about 12.56 m².

Other Examples

Find A if $r = 5$ cm.

$A = \pi r^2$
$A \approx 3.14 \times 5^2$
$A \approx 3.14 \times 25$
$A \approx 78.50$

The area is about 78.50 cm².

Find A if $d = 2.4$ m.

$A = \pi r^2$
$r = 2.4 \div 2 = 1.2$
$A \approx 3.14 \times (1.2)^2$
$A \approx 3.14 \times 1.44$
$A \approx 4.5216$

The area is about 4.5216 m².

Warm Up

Find the area of each circle. Use 3.14 for π.

1. $r = 10$ cm 314 cm²
2. $d = 18$ m 254.34 m²
3. $r = 2.4$ m 18.0864 m²
4. $d = 40$ cm 1,256 cm²
5. $r = 0.5$ m 0.785 m²
6. $r = 7$ mm 153.86 mm²

324

Follow Up

Reteaching

Have students draw several circles on graph paper (TRB p 284). Ask them to count the squares inside the circle and estimate the parts of circles to determine the approximate area.

Next have students find the length of the radius and use the formula $A = \pi r^2$ to compute the area. They should then compare their estimates to the area found by using the formula.

Enrichment

Have students complete the chart and answer the questions below.

Radius	Circumference	Area
1 cm	6.28 cm	3.14 cm²
2 cm	12.56 cm	12.56 cm²
3 cm	18.84 cm	28.26 cm²
4 cm	25.12 cm	50.24 cm²

1. Tell what number the circumference is multiplied by if the radius is multiplied by   a) 2 2 b) 3 3 c) 4 4
2. Tell what number the area is multipled by if the radius is multiplied by a) 2 4 b) 3 9 c) 4 16

Assignment Guide			
	Minimum	Average	Extended
Page 325	1–12, SK	1–17, SK	1–17, SK

Find the area of each circle. Use 3.14 for π.

1.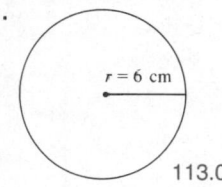
$r = 6$ cm

113.04 cm²

2.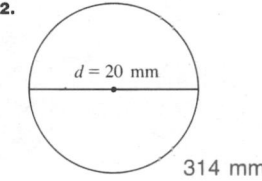
$d = 20$ mm

314 mm²

3.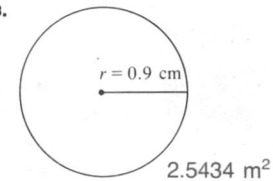
$r = 0.9$ cm

2.5434 m²

4. $r = 12$ cm 452.16 cm²

5. $d = 100$ m 7,850 m²

6. $r = 0.1$ cm 0.0314 cm²

7. $r = 2$ cm 12.56 cm²

8. $d = 8$ cm 50.24 cm²

9. $r = 11$ cm 379.94 cm²

10. $r = 1$ m 3.14 m²

11. $r = 1.5$ m 7.065 m²

12. $d = 4.4$ m 15.1976 m²

13. $d = 0.6$ cm 0.2826 cm²

14. $r = 75$ cm 17,662.5 cm²

15. $d = 9$ cm 63.585 cm²

16. A small circular throw rug has a radius of 0.4 m. What is the area of the rug, to the nearest tenth of a square meter?
0.5 m²

17. One circular throw rug has a diameter of 1 m. Another circular rug has a diameter of 2 m. Is the area of the larger rug 2 times or 4 times the area of the smaller rug? 4 times

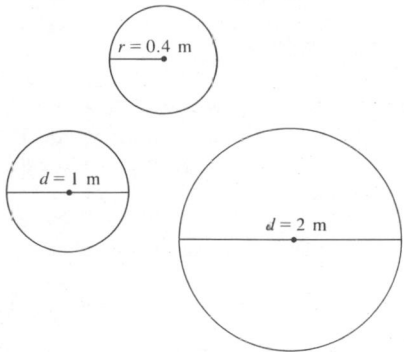
$r = 0.4$ m
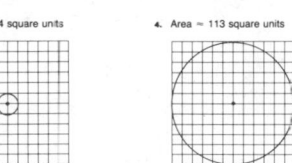
$d = 1$ m
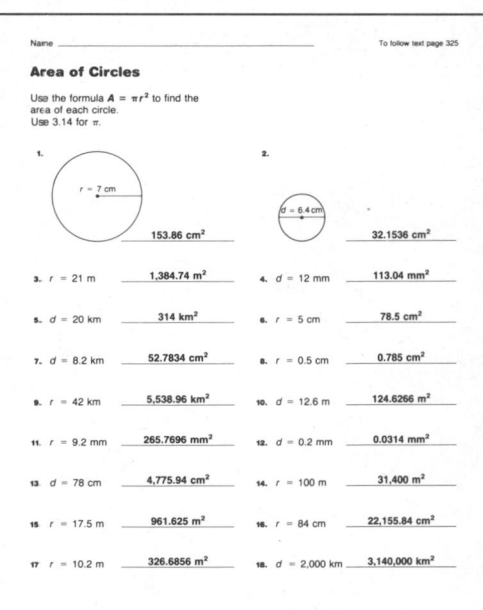
$d = 2$ m

SKILLKEEPER

Write each percent as a decimal.

1. 29% 0.29 **2.** 12.6% 0.126 **3.** 2.3% 0.023 **4.** 16.5% 0.165 **5.** 0.7% 0.007

6. 125% 1.25 **7.** 19.96% 0.1996 **8.** 2% 0.02 **9.** 1.16% 0.0116 **10.** 179% 1.79

Find the percent of each number.

11. 30% of 52 15.6
12. 95% of 41 38.95
13. 45% of 200 90
14. 80% of 23 18.4
15. 5% of 45 2.25

16. 35% of 26 9.1
17. 75% of 41 30.75
18. 50% of 15 7.5
19. 7% of 100 7
20. 40% of 81 32.4

More Practice, page 437, Set B

325

Using Page 325

Exercises 1–15 In these exercises either the radius or the diameter of each circle is given. Caution students that when the diameter is given, they must divide by 2 to find the radius.

Exercise 17 This exercise shows that doubling the diameter of a circle quadruples the area. You may wish to extend the problem by asking students to find what happens if the diameter is multiplied by 3. (The area is multiplied by 3², or 9.)

Skillkeeper These skills were originally taught in Chapter 12.

More Practice, page 437, Set B

Reteaching Supplement, page 95

Name _____ To follow text page 325

Area of Circles

Find the area of a circle whose radius is 3 cm.
$r = 3$ cm

Area = $\pi \times$ radius squared
$A = \pi r^2$
$A \approx 3.14 \times 3^2$ ($\pi \approx 3.14$)
$A \approx 3.14 \times 9$
$A \approx 28.26$ cm²

Find the area of each circle.

1. $r = 0.6$ m
$A = \pi r^2$
$A \approx 3.14 \times (0.6)^2$
$A \approx 3.14 \times 0.36$
$A \approx 1.1304$ m²

2. $d = 16$ mm (Divide 16 mm by 2)
$r = 8$ mm
$A = \pi r^2$
$A \approx 3.14 \times 8^2$
$A \approx 200.96$ mm²

3. $d = 6.8$ m
$r = 3.4$
$A = \pi r^2$
$A \approx 3.14 \times 3.4^2$
$A \approx 36.2984$ m²

4. 1 cm
$A \approx$ 3.14 cm²

5. 2.8 cm
$A \approx$ 6.1544 cm²

6. 7 m
$A \approx$ 153.86 m²

7. $r = 2$ cm
$A \approx$ 12.56 cm²

8. $d = 40$ mm
$A \approx$ 1,256 mm²

9. $r = 0.8$ m
$A \approx$ 2.0096 m²

10. $d = 10$ cm
$A \approx$ 78.5 cm²

11. $r = 30$ m
$A \approx$ 2,826 m²

12. $d = 22$ mm
$A \approx$ 379.94 mm²

13. $r = 15$ m
$A \approx$ 706.5 m²

14. $d = 5.6$ cm
$A \approx$ 24.6176 cm²

15. $r = 29$ cm
$A \approx$ 2,640.74 cm²

Enrichment Supplement, page 95

Name _____ To follow text page 325

Circles

Use a compass to make a circle with an area that is approximately ($\approx$) the given number.

1. Area ≈ 28 square units

2. Area ≈ 79 square units

3. Area ≈ 3.14 square units

4. Area ≈ 113 square units

5. Area ≈ 13 square units

6. Area ≈ 50 square units

Practice Supplement, page 122

Name _____ To follow text page 325

Area of Circles

Use the formula $A = \pi r^2$ to find the area of each circle. Use 3.14 for π.

1. $r = 7$ cm 153.86 cm²

2. $d = 6.4$ cm 32.1536 cm²

3. $r = 21$ m 1,384.74 m²

4. $d = 12$ mm 113.04 mm²

5. $d = 20$ km 314 km²

6. $r = 5$ cm 78.5 cm²

7. $d = 8.2$ km 52.7834 cm²

8. $r = 0.5$ cm 0.785 cm²

9. $r = 42$ km 5,538.96 km²

10. $d = 12.6$ m 124.6266 m²

11. $r = 9.2$ mm 265.7696 mm²

12. $d = 0.2$ mm 0.0314 mm²

13. $d = 78$ cm 4,775.94 cm²

14. $r = 100$ m 31,400 m²

15. $r = 17.5$ m 961.625 m²

16. $r = 84$ cm 22,155.84 cm²

17. $r = 10.2$ m 326.6856 m²

18. $d = 2,000$ km 3,140,000 km²

Quick Review Have students give the missing numbers.
5 m = __500__ cm   35 cm = __0.35__ m   7 km = __7,000__ m
          75 m = __0.075__ km   25 mm = __2.5__ cm

Lesson Focus To solve word problems involving area and circumference and to solve multiple-step problems

Ideas for Getting Started

Review with students the circumference and area formulas for circles.

$C = \pi d$ $C = 2\pi r$ $A = \pi r^2$

Using Page 326

Lesson Development Help students understand that a wheel rolling along a flat surface will travel a distance equal to the circumference of the circle in one revolution of the wheel.

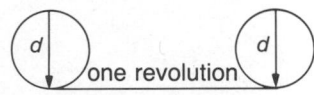

one revolution

|←——circumference——→|

Exercises 1–7 Remind students to think about the 5-Point Checklist as they solve these problems.

PROBLEM SOLVING: Practice

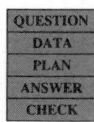
QUESTION
DATA
PLAN
ANSWER
CHECK   Solve. Use 3.14 for π.

1. Robin's bicycle wheels each have a radius of 33 cm. For each revolution of a wheel, the bicycle will roll forward the circumference of the wheel. What is this distance? **207.24 cm**

2. Giles estimated that his bicycle travels about 2 m for each revolution of the wheels. How many revolutions would one of the wheels make in traveling 5 km? **2,500**

3. Alvin bought a new bicycle tire for $8.99 and a bicycle light for $6.50. If he paid for these items with a $20 bill, how much change should he get back? **$4.51**

4. On a bicycle trip, Charity and three friends traveled 54 km in 2.5 h. How many kilometers did they average in 1 h? **21.6 km**

5. A reflector lens on Nora's bicycle has a radius of 4 cm. What is the area of the reflector lens? **50.24 cm²**

6. The circular headlight lens on Tom's bicycle has a diameter of 6 cm. What is the area of the lens? **28.26 cm²**

7. A bicycle store has an antique "high-wheeler" bicycle on display. The front wheel of the bicycle has a diameter of 1.5 m. What is the circumference of the front wheel? **4.71 m**

326

Follow Up

Reteaching

Emphasize the strategy of drawing a picture for problems involving area and circumference. Work through the following example with students.

If a record has a circumference of 94 cm and a diameter of 30 cm, what is its area?

Draw a picture to help students identify the needed data. Then show students how to apply the formula.

$C = 94$ cm

$d = 30$ cm

$A = \pi r^2$
$= 3.14 \times 15^2$
$= 3.14 \div 225$
$= 706.5$ cm²

Enrichment

Present students with the following problem.

A circular flower bed is surrounded by a circular walk 2 meters wide. The diameter of the flower bed is 20 meters. What is the area of the walk?

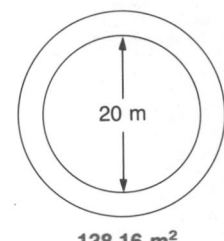

20 m

138.16 m²

Assignment Guide			
	Minimum	Average	Extended
pages 326–327	1–7	1–8, 12	1–12

8. The back wheel of the high-wheeler has a diameter of 0.4 m. What is the circumference of the back wheel? 1.256 m

9. How many times would the back wheel of the high-wheeler have to turn while the front wheel is making one complete turn? 3.75

10. Molly would like to buy a new bicycle that costs $188. She has already saved $60 and is planning to save $8 a week until she has enough money to pay for the bicycle. How many weeks must she plan to save $8 a week? 16

11. Carlotta rode her bicycle for 1.5 hours, averaging 32 km/h. She has 9 more kilometers to ride. How far will she ride in all? 57 km

12. **Try This** Ralph rode his bicycle from his house to a state park. He rode $\frac{1}{2}$ of the way in the first half-hour. In the next half-hour he rode $\frac{2}{5}$ of the distance. At this point he was still 3 km from the park. What is the total distance from Ralph's house to the park? Hint: Choose the operations. 30 km

327

Using Page 327

Exercise 9 Data from exercises 7 and 8 is needed to solve this problem.

Try This A possible strategy, Choose the Operations, was taught on page 218.

Discussion After students read the problem, have them identify the question and the data. Then ask "How can we find what part of the total distance Ralph traveled after riding an hour?" ($\frac{1}{2} + \frac{2}{5}$) "What was the remaining distance?" (3 km)
   Help students to understand that once they find what fractional part 3 km is of the total distance, they can find the total distance by multiplying.

Solution

$\frac{1}{2} + \frac{2}{5} = \frac{5}{10} + \frac{4}{10} = \frac{9}{10}$ Fraction of distance he rode in the first hour

3 km $1 - \frac{9}{10} = \frac{1}{10}$ Distance remaining

$3 \times 10 = 30$ km   Total distance

The total distance from Ralph's house to the park is 30 km.

Extension Derek has 3 times as many records as Barbara. Barbara has $\frac{2}{3}$ as many records as Sean. If Sean has 27 records, how many records does Derek have? (54)

Ideas That Work

Chalk It Up

Display these problems on the chalkboard. Have students select the correct circumference for each exercise. Answers are rounded to the nearest tenth.

1. $r = 7$ cm   **A.** 62.8 m
2. $r = 10$ m   **C.** 6.3 m
3. $r = 2.5$ cm   **E.** 22.0 cm
4. $d = 2$ m   **I.** 15.7 cm
5. $d = 7$ cm   **L.** 44.0 cm
6. $d = 1.7$ cm   **P.** 5.3 cm

Students should select the correct area for each of the following. Answers are rounded to the nearest hundredth.

7. $r = 2$ cm   **R.** 22.0 m²
8. $r = 3$ cm   **S.** 12.6 cm²
9. $d = 7$ m   **W.** 153.9 m²
              Y. 18.8 cm²

After students find the answers, have them decode the message by writing the correct letters in the blanks below.

C	I	R	C	L	E	S
4.	3.	9.	4.	1.	5.	7.

A	R	E	E	A	S	Y
2.	9.	5.	5.	2.	7.	8.

A	S	P	I
2.	7.	6.	3.

Practice Supplement, page 123

Name _____ To follow text page 327

Problem Solving: Practice

Solve. Use 3.14 for π.

1. Mr. Black has a car with tires that have a radius of 23 cm. What is the circumference of each tire?
   144.44 cm

2. Mr. Phillips estimates that his car travels 1.5 m for every revolution of the wheels. How many revolutions does each tire make in 3 km?
   2,000

3. Ms. Winston bought gas for $16.60 and a can of oil for $1.50. If she paid with a $20 bill, how much change should she receive?
   $1.90

4. Mr. Baker traveled 280 km in 3.5 h. How many kilometers did he average per hour?
   80 km

5. A wheel cover on Ms. Graham's car has a diameter of 36 cm. What is the area of the wheel cover?
   1,017.36 cm²

6. Mr. Yates wants to buy $339 seat covers for his car. He has $129 and plans to save $30 a week until he has enough money to buy the seat covers. How long before he can buy the seat covers?
   7 weeks

7. Ms. Varella's steering wheel has a diameter of 32 cm. What is the circumference of her steering wheel?
   100.48 cm

8. Mr. Hughes drove for $1\frac{3}{4}$ h averaging 60 km per hour. How far did he drive?
   105 km

9. The dials on Ms. Lempka's car radio have a radius of 1.5 cm. What is the area of each dial?
   7.065 cm²

10. Mr. Sendejas is driving from Morse City to Andersonville, a distance of 287 km. He has already driven 193 km. How much farther is Andersonville?
   94 km

Quick Review Have students add and write answers in lowest terms.

$5\frac{2}{3} + 4\frac{2}{3}$ $10\frac{1}{3}$ $16\frac{2}{5} + 38\frac{3}{4}$ $55\frac{3}{20}$ $40\frac{5}{8} + 18\frac{1}{4}$ $58\frac{7}{8}$

$28\frac{1}{3} + 36\frac{1}{9}$ $64\frac{4}{9}$ $12\frac{5}{6} + 21\frac{3}{8}$ $34\frac{5}{24}$

Lesson Focus To find the lateral area and total surface area of a cylinder

Suggested Materials Models of cylinders, empty cans

Ideas for Getting Started

Prepare a rectangular piece of paper that will just cover the lateral area of a model of a cylinder. Tape it around the cylinder.

Show the cylinder to students. Point out the circular bases of the cylinder and the lateral area. Then remove the paper covering the cylinder and ask students how to find the area. Since it is a rectangle, students should realize that the area is length × width. Demonstrate that the length of the paper is the circumference of the cylinder which is 2 πr. Explain that if h is the height, then the area is 2πrh.

Using Page 328

Motivational Problem Have students read the introductory problem and examine the illustration. Ask them to identify the question and the data needed to solve the problem. Elicit from students that the plan is to multiply length × width to find the area of the rectangle.

Lesson Development Write the formula for lateral area on the chalkboard and work through the solution of the problem. Then show how the total surface area is found by adding the area of the two bases to the lateral area. A formula for the total area is not presented although one could be developed.

$$\text{Total surface area} = 2\pi rh + 2\pi r^2$$

Warm Up Assign these exercises for individual work or for practice at the chalkboard.

Area of Cylinders

Moriko covered the curved part of a can with a rectangular piece of paper. The area of this part of a cylinder is called the **lateral area**. What is the lateral area of the can?

To find the lateral area, we can find the area of the rectangle.

Length = circumference of the cylinder ($2\pi r$)
Width = height of the cylinder (h)
Area = circumference × height

Lateral area = circumference × height
$A = 2\pi rh$

$A \approx 2 \times 3.14 \times 4 \times 15$
$A \approx 376.8$

The lateral area of the can is about 376.8 cm².

To find the **total surface area** of the cylinder, we must add the area of the top and bottom circular bases to the lateral area.

Area of each base: $A \approx 3.14 \times 4^2 = 50.24$
Lateral area: $A \approx 376.8$
Total surface area: $\approx 376.8 + 50.24 + 50.24$
≈ 477.28

The total surface area is about 477.28 cm².

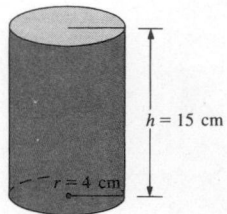
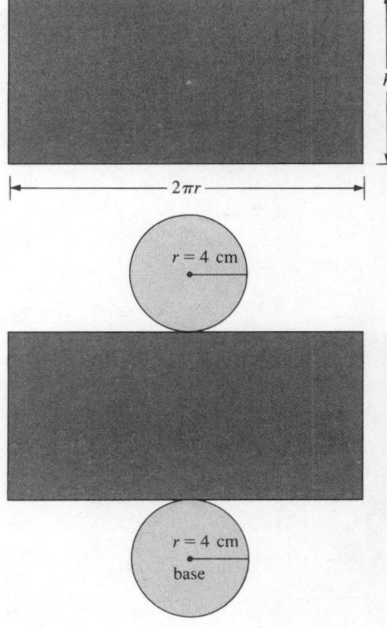

Warm Up

Find the lateral area of each cylinder. Use 3.14 for π.

1. $r = 10$ cm
$h = 12$ cm   753.6 cm²

2. $r = 1$ cm
$h = 15$ cm   94.2 cm²

3. $r = 5$ cm
$h = 7$ cm   219.8 cm²

Find the total area of each cylinder. Use 3.14 for π.

4. $r = 3$ cm
$h = 5$ cm   150.72 cm²

5. $r = 2$ cm
$h = 4$ cm   75.36 cm²

6. $r = 0.5$ cm
$h = 5$ cm   17.27 cm²

328

Follow Up

Reteaching

Give students models of cylinders that are labeled with measures of the radius and height. Have them cut out rectangular pieces of paper that will cover (with no overlap) the lateral surface of each model. Then ask students to find the areas of the rectangles by using the given values for r and h.

Enrichment

Challenge students with the following problem.

Which figure has the greater surface area, a rectangular prism with $l = 5$ cm, $w = 4$ cm, $h = 6$ cm, or a cylinder with $r = 3$ and $h = 6$?   **cylinder (169.56 cm²)**

Find the lateral area of each cylinder. Use 3.14 for π.

1.
$r = 3.3$ cm
$h = 4$ cm
82.896 cm²

2.
$r = 4$ cm
$h = 10$ cm
251.2 cm²

3.
$r = 3.3$ cm
$h = 7$ cm
145.068 cm²

4.
$r = 2.8$ cm
$h = 13.5$ cm
237.384 cm²

5. $r = 5$ cm
$h = 10$ cm
314 cm²

6. $r = 6.4$ cm
$h = 12$ cm
482.304 cm²

7. $r = 10$ cm
$h = 15$ cm
942 cm²

8. $r = 0.3$ cm
$h = 8$ cm
15 072 cm²

Find the total surface area of each cylinder. Use 3.14 for π.

9. $r = 2$ m
$h = 5$ m
87.92 m²

10. $r = 2$ mm
$h = 10$ mm
150.72 mm²

11. $r = 9$ cm
$h = 3$ cm
678.24 cm²

12. $r = 0.8$ m
$h = 2.5$ m
16.5792 m²

13. $r = 1$ cm
$h = 1$ cm
12.56 cm²

14. $r = 6$ cm
$h = 4.5$ cm
395.64 cm²

15. $r = 10$ m
$h = 1$ m
690.8 m²

16. $r = 11$ cm
$h = 20$ cm
2,141.48 cm²

17. A rolled-oats carton is a cylinder with a radius of 5 cm and a height of 18 cm. What is the area of the label around the carton? 565.2 cm²

18. A container of salt is a cylinder with a radius of 4 cm and a height of 13.5 cm. What is the total surface area of the container? 439.6 cm²

19. Use this information to write and solve your own problem.
Cylinder: $r = 12$ cm
$h = 30$ cm

20. **DATA HUNT** Measure the radius and height of a cylinder, such as a can of food. What is the lateral area and the total surface area of the can?

THINK MATH

Guess and Check

Dave has only $7.00. Which choice below will give him the most pizza for his money?

Two 24 cm pizzas 904.32 cm²
One 24 cm and one 32 cm pizza 1,256 cm²
One 40 cm pizza 1,256 cm²

Diameter	Cost	
24 cm pizza	$3.00	452.16 cm²
32 cm pizza	$4.00	803.84 cm²
40 cm pizza	$6.00	1,256 cm²

Guess which is the best choice, then find the area of each pizza to check your guess.
One 40 cm pizza

More Practice, page 437, Set C

Using Page 329

Exercises 1–18 You may wish to have students use a calculator for these exercises. If calculators have a memory key and 3.14 is stored in memory, students can compute surface area quite easily.

Think Math This problem involves area of a circle and logical reasoning. The measurements given for the pizzas refer to the diameters. One 40 cm pizza is the best choice because it gives the same amount of pizza as one 24 cm and one 32 cm pizza, but costs $1 less.

More Practice, page 437, Set C

Ideas That Work

Special Education

Have students participate in an "Estimation Fair" to reinforce the concepts of lateral area and total surface area.

To prepare for the activity, arrange a set of cylinders as shown and ask students to rank them in order from largest to smallest in terms of both lateral surface area and total surface area. To emphasize some of the relationships, include two cans having the same size base but with different heights. Also include two cans with the same height but with bases of different size. After students make their estimates, provide them with a worksheet giving the actual dimensions of the cans and have them find the various areas and check their estimates.

As a readiness activity for the next lesson, you may wish to repeat the process using the volume of the cylinders.

Practice Supplement, page 124

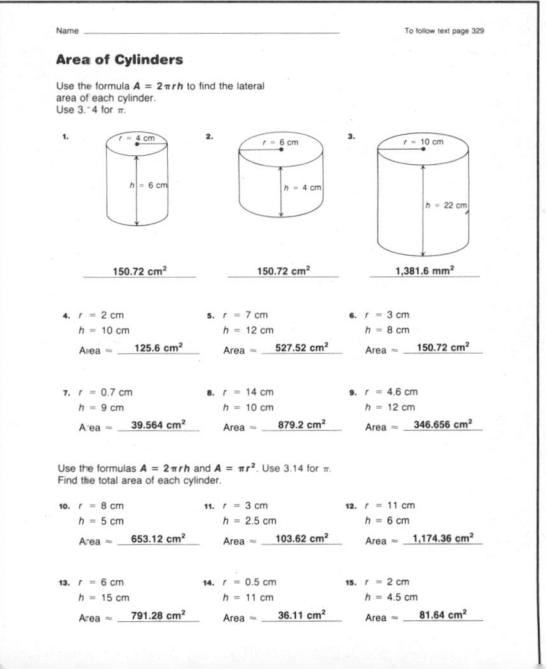

Quick Review Have students find the incorrect quotients.
$25.92 \div 4.8 = 0.54$ **incorrect** $2.834 \div .065 = 43.6$ $7.956 \div 0.39 = 20.4$
$0.473 \div 8.4 = 0.563$ **incorrect** $36.408 \div 0.37 = 89.9$ **incorrect**

Lesson Focus To find the volume of a cylinder

Suggested Materials Models of a cylinder and a rectangular prism having equal heights and bases of equal area, rice or sand

Ideas for Getting Started

Display the models described above. Explain that the cylinder and prism have equal heights and bases of equal area. Fill the cylinder with rice or sand. Next pour out the contents of the cylinder into the prism and show that the prism is full. Elicit from students that the area of the prism can be found by multiplying the area of the base times the height. ($V = Bh$) Then point out that this formula must also apply to the cylinder.

Using Page 330

Lesson Development Have students read the material at the top of the page. Demonstrate how the formula $V = \pi r^2 h$ is derived form the basic volume formula, $V = Bh$. Then find the volume of the cylinder in the illustration as a class activity.

Other Examples Work through the examples with students. Point out that the radius and height must be in the same unit of measure and that the volume is in the cube of the unit.

Volume of Cylinders

If a cylinder and a prism have equal heights and the areas of their bases are equal, then their volumes are equal.

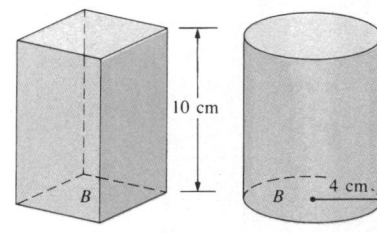

To find the volume of a cylinder, we can use this formula.

Volume = area of Base × height
$V = Bh$ or $V = \pi r^2 h$

If $r = 4$ cm and $h = 10$ cm, then
$V \approx 3.14 \times 4^2 \times 10$ Use 3.14 for π.
$V \approx 3.14 \times 16 \times 10$
$V \approx 502.40$

The volume of the cylinder is about 502.40 cm³.

Other Examples

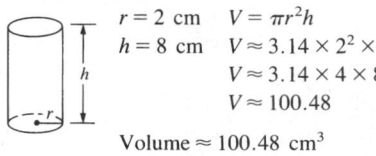

$r = 2$ cm $V = \pi r^2 h$
$h = 8$ cm $V \approx 3.14 \times 2^2 \times 8$
              $V \approx 3.14 \times 4 \times 8$
              $V \approx 100.48$

Volume ≈ 100.48 cm³

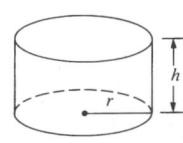

$r = 6$ m $V = \pi r^2 h$
$h = 6$ m $V \approx 3.14 \times 6^2 \times 6$
             $V \approx 3.14 \times 36 \times 6$
             $V \approx 678.24$

Volume ≈ 678.24 m³

Warm Up

Find the volume of each cylinder. Use 3.14 for π.

1. $r = 10$ cm
$h = 20$ cm
330 6,280 cm³

2. $r = 8$ dm
$h = 12$ dm
2,411.52 dm³

3. $r = 20.8$ cm
$h = 4$ cm
5,433.9584 cm³

4. $r = 2$ m
$h = 6$ m
75.36 m³

Follow Up

Reteaching

Work through the example below with students. Then have them copy and complete the chart.

	Area of Base $A = \pi r^2$	Volume of Cylinder $V = Bh$
$r = 2$ cm $h = 5$ cm	$3.14 \times 2^2 =$ 12.56 cm²	$12.56 \times 5 =$ 62.80 cm³
$r = 3$ cm $h = 8$ cm	28.26 cm²	226.08 cm³
$r = 2.5$ cm $h = 10$ cm	19.625 cm²	196.25 cm³
$r = 1$ m $h = 5$ m	3.14 m²	15.7 m³

Enrichment

Have students complete the following table, and answer the questions below.

Radius	Height	Volume
1 cm	10 cm	**31.4 cm³**
2 cm	10 cm	**125.6 cm³**
3 cm	10 cm	**282.6 cm²**
4 cm	10 cm	**502.4 cm²**

1. If the radius is doubled, the volume is multiplied by what number? **4**
2. If the radius is tripled, the volume is multiplied by what number? **9**
3. If the radius is quadrupled, the volume is multiplied by what number? **16**

Find the volume of each cylinder. Use 3.14 for π.

1.
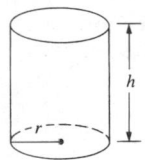
$r = 5$ cm
$h = 12$ cm **942 cm³**

2.
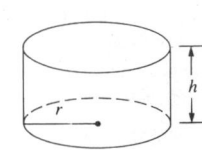
$r = 7$ dm
$h = 10$ dm **1,538.6 dm³**

3.
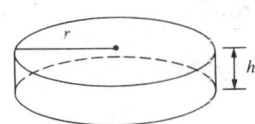
$r = 10$ cm
$h = 4$ cm **1,256 cm³**

4.
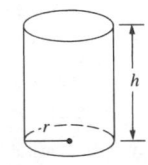
$r = 6$ mm
$h = 16$ mm **1,808.64 mm³**

5.
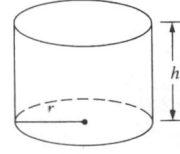
$r = 3$ m
$h = 5$ m **141.3 m³**

6.
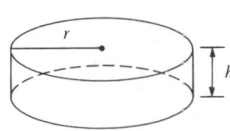
$r = 4$ m
$h = 2.5$ m **125.6 m³**

7. Which has the greater volume, the rectangular prism or the cylinder? How much greater is the volume? **rectangular prism; 46.44 cm³**

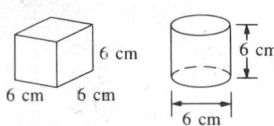
6 cm   6 cm   6 cm
6 cm

8. A mug has a base with an area of 44 cm². The height of the mug is 7.5 cm. How high should it be filled so that it contains 250 cm³ or 250 mL of water? Round your answer to the nearest tenth. **5.7 cm**

SKILLKEEPER

Find the circumference of each circle. Use 3.14 for π.

1. $r = 2.5$ cm
15.7 cm

2. $r = 17.2$ mm
108.016 mm

3. $d = 19$ m
59.66 m

4. $d = 0.6$ mm
1.884 mm

5. $r = 32$ cm
200.96 cm

6. $d = 607$ mm
1,905.98 mm

7. $r = 20.25$ cm
127.17 cm

8. $d = 66$ m
207.24 m

9. $r = 2.5$ km
15.7 km

10. $r = 0.008$ mm
0.05024 mm

Find the area of each circle. Use 3.14 for π.

11. $r = 29$ km
2,640.74 km²

12. $d = 15$ cm
176.625 cm²

13. $d = 12$ mm
113.04 mm²

14. $r = 0.12$ cm
0.045216 cm²

15. $d = 2.4$ mm
4.5216 mm²

16. $r = 62$ cm
12,070.16 cm²

17. $r = 2.6$ mm
21.2264 mm²

18. $d = 24$ km
452.16 km²

19. $d = 12.2$ mm
116.8394 mm²

20. $d = 0.3$ cm
0.07065 cm²

More Practice, page 437, Set D

Using Page 331

Exercises 1–6 Students should be able to complete these exercises without additional instruction.

Exercise 7 The volume of the rectangular prism is 216 cm³, while the volume of the cylinder is 169.56 cm³.

Exercise 8 A picture may help students see the relationship between data given in the problem.

$V = Bh$
$250 = 44h$
$h = \dfrac{250}{44}$
$h = 5.7$

7.5 h

Area of base: 44 cm²

Skillkeeper This Skillkeeper reviews skills taught in this chapter.

More Practice, page 437, Set D

Reteaching Supplement, page 96

Enrichment Supplement, page 96

Practice Supplement, page 125

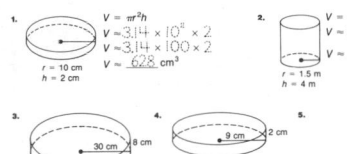

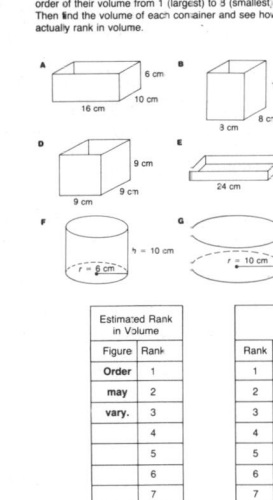

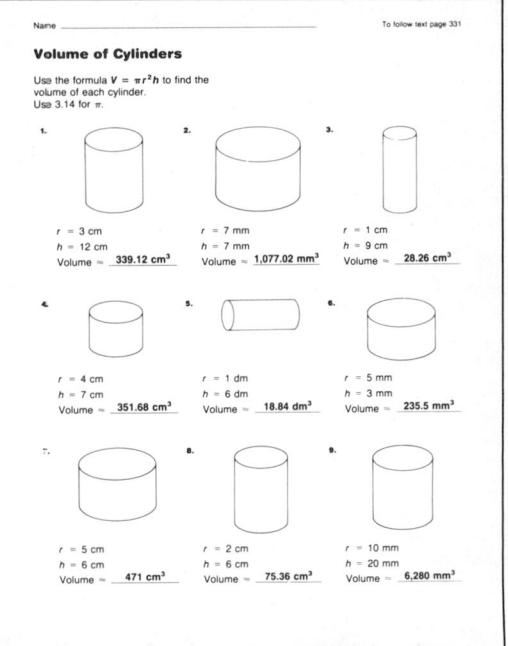

Quick Review Have students write each fraction as a percent.

$\frac{12}{15}$ 80% $\frac{1}{2}$ 50% $\frac{9}{10}$ 90% $\frac{3}{4}$ 75%

$\frac{49}{100}$ 49% $\frac{3}{2}$ 150% $\frac{1}{3}$ $33\frac{1}{3}\%$

Lesson Focus To solve word problems involving circumference and area of circles and area and volume of cylinders

Ideas for Getting Started

Review the formulas for area and circumference of circles. Have students find the area and circumference of the circles with the following radii.

$r = 6$ m $r = 10$ m $r = 0.5$ m

Review the formulas for lateral area and volume of cylinders. Have students find the lateral area and volume of these cylinders.

$r = 8$ cm $r = 4$ m
$h = 10$ cm $h = 3$ m

Using Page 332

Lesson Development Have students read the introductory paragraphs and observe the accompanying photograph. Discuss the data given about wood and wood products. Work through the first problem as a class activity. Give students an opportunity to participate in each step. Remind them to think of the 5-Point Checklist as they solve the problems in this lesson.

Exercise 2 Note that this problem contains more information than is needed for a solution.

PROBLEM SOLVING: Practice

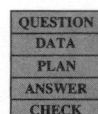

QUESTION
DATA
PLAN
ANSWER
CHECK

Wood is a valuable resource. Wood and wood products are used in many different ways. Much of the wood milled in the United States is used to make paper. Each person in this country uses about 300 kg of paper each year.

Modern sawmills are careful not to waste wood. Some of them use computers to help decide how to cut a log so that it will yield the greatest amount of lumber.

Solve. Use 3.14 for π.

1. A large redwood log has the shape of a cylinder. The log is 12 m long and has a radius of 1 m. What is the volume of the log in cubic meters? 37.68 m³

2. A sawmill uses water under high pressure to remove bark from logs. The machine uses 3,700 L of water per minute. The water travels at a rate of 8 km/min. How many liters of water does the machine use per hour? 222,000 L

332

Follow Up

Reteaching

Give students models of rectangular prisms and cylinders and have them determine the volume of each. Allow students to discuss the methods they used. Elicit from them the similarity between finding the volume of a cylinder and finding the volume of a prism.

Enrichment

Explain to students that the volume of a cone is one third the volume of a cylinder having the same base and height. Then have them find the volume of each cone.

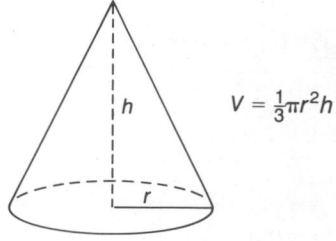

$V = \frac{1}{3}\pi r^2 h$

1. $r = 1$ m, $h = 1$ m 1.05 cm³
2. $r = 5$ cm, $h = 10$ cm 261.7 cm³
3. $r = 2.5$ cm, $h = 4$ cm 26.2 cm³

Assignment Guide

	Minimum	Average	Extended
page 333	1–7	1–8, 11–12	1–12

3. During a 16-hour period, a machine removed the bark from 600 logs. About how many minutes per log does it take to remove the bark? 1.6 min/log

4. To record the diameter of a log which is not exactly round, a sawmill worker makes two measurements of the diameter. The **recorded diameter** is the average of the two measurements. For one log, the first measurement was 92 cm and the second measurement was 74 cm. What was the recorded diameter of the log? 83 cm

5. A water-storage tank at a sawmill has the shape of a cylinder. The radius of the tank is 2 m and the height is 5 m. What is the volume of the storage tank? 62.8 m³

6. A painting contractor must find the lateral area of the water tank in order to estimate the cost of painting the tank. What is the lateral area? 62.8 m²

7. In a wooded area, a forest worker counted 18 Douglas firs, 30 western hemlocks, and 12 Sitka spruces. What percent of the total number of trees were Douglas firs? 30%

8. The diameter of a log was 1.8 m. After the bark was removed, the diameter was 1.6 m. How much less was the circumference of the log after the bark was removed? 0.628 m

9. A log had a diameter of 1 m and was 6 m long. A large square post, 70 cm on each side and 6 m long, was sawed from the log. What was the volume of the square post? What was the volume of the part of the log that was sawed off to form the post? 2.94 m³; 1.77 m³

10. A log had a diameter of 1.5 m and was 8 m long. Which measurement is not needed to find the circumference of the log? 8 m

11. The dogwood tree is native to 76% of the states in the United States. The dogwood is native to how many states? 38

12. **Try This** A tree was 48 m tall. During a storm it was broken off, and the part broken off was 3 times as long as the part that remained standing. What were the lengths of each part? 12 m; 36 m

333

Using Page 333

Exercise 8 This is a multiple-step problem. First find the circumference of the log with bark and the circumference of the log without bark. Then find the difference.

$C = 1.8 \times 3.14$ $\qquad\qquad$ $C = 1.6 \times 3.14$
$C = 5.652$ $\qquad\qquad\qquad$ $C = 5.024$

$$5.652 \text{ m} - 5.024 \text{ m} = 0.628 \text{ m}$$

Some students may solve the problem by finding the difference between the diameters and multiplying the difference times 3.14.

$$1.8 \text{ m} - 1.6 \text{ m} = 0.2 \text{ m}$$
$$3.14 \times 0.2 \text{ m} = 0.628 \text{ m}$$

Exercise 9 Two questions are asked in this problem. Note that the sides of the square post are given in centimeters while the length is given in meters. To compute the volume, the same units must be used.

Try This A possible strategy, Draw a Picture, was taught on page 108.

Discussion After students read the problem, have them state the question in their own words. Ask them to identify the data given in the problem and tell how it is related. Elicit from students that a picture will help show the relationship between data.

Solution

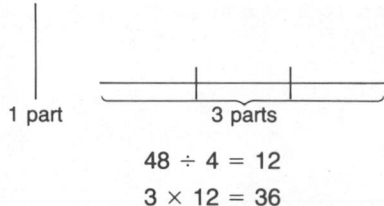

1 part   3 parts

$$48 \div 4 = 12$$
$$3 \times 12 = 36$$

The part of the tree that remained standing was 12 m and the part broken off was 36 m.

Ideas That Work

Calculator Bonus

Challenge students with the following problem.

If the smallest possible square were drawn around 4 touching nickels, what would be the area of the square in mm²? (1,764 mm²) Approximately what percent of the square would be covered by nickels? The diameter of a nickel is 21 mm. (About 78.5%)

You may wish to display the following information as well.

Area of a circle = πr^2

Area of a square = s^2 where s is the length of the side.

Practice Supplement, page 126

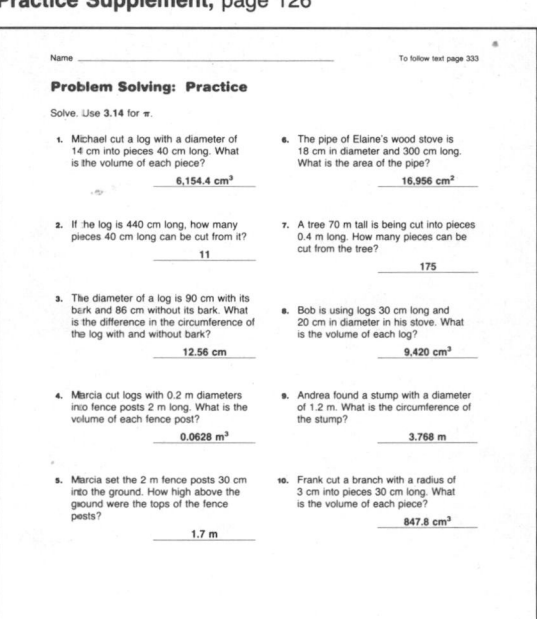

Name _____   To follow text page 333

Problem Solving: Practice

Solve. Use **3.14** for π.

1. Michael cut a log with a diameter of 14 cm into pieces 40 cm long. What is the volume of each piece? 6,154.4 cm³

2. If the log is 440 cm long, how many pieces 40 cm long can be cut from it? 11

3. The diameter of a log is 90 cm with its bark and 86 cm without its bark. What is the difference in the circumference of the log with and without bark? 12.56 cm

4. Marcia cut logs with 0.2 m diameters into fence posts 2 m long. What is the volume of each fence post? 0.0628 m³

5. Marcia set the 2 m fence posts 30 cm into the ground. How high above the ground were the tops of the fence posts? 1.7 m

6. The pipe of Elaine's wood stove is 18 cm in diameter and 300 cm long. What is the area of the pipe? 16,956 cm²

7. A tree 70 m tall is being cut into pieces 0.4 m long. How many pieces can be cut from the tree? 175

8. Bob is using logs 30 cm long and 20 cm in diameter in his stove. What is the volume of each log? 9,420 cm³

9. Andrea found a stump with a diameter of 1.2 m. What is the circumference of the stump? 3.768 m

10. Frank cut a branch with a radius of 3 cm into pieces 30 cm long. What is the volume of each piece? 847.8 cm³

Quick Review Remind students that the formula for area of a triangle is $A = \frac{1}{2}bh$. Then have them find the area of each triangle.

$b = 20$ cm $b = 15$ mm $b = 30$ dm $b = 12$ m

$h = 10$ cm   **100 cm²** $h = 8$ mm   **60 mm²** $h = 18$dm   **270 dm²** $h = 20$ m   **120 m²**

Lesson Focus To sketch cross-section views of space figures

Ideas for Getting Started

Sketch these figures on the chalkboard. Tell students that the pictures represent familiar objects that have been sliced by a straight cut. Have students try to identify the objects.

(apple)   (pencil)   (loaf of bread)

Explain that the pictures are *cross sections* of figures.

Using Page 334

Lesson Development Have students read the material at the top of the page. Point out that the machine part has two holes drilled completely through it. Observe with students that the cross section shows the holes as two rectangles. The boundary of the section is L-shaped.

Direct students' attention to the two examples in the middle of the page. These examples show that the cross section of a given space figure depends upon the orientation of the cutting plane.

Exercises 1–2 Use these exercises as an oral class activity.

Cross Sections

Linda Wahnee works in the drafting department of a company that makes machine parts. Linda makes blueprints that sometimes show **cross sections** of parts.

Linda thinks of a plane cutting the figure with a straight cut. The cross section is the intersection of the cutting plane and the figure.

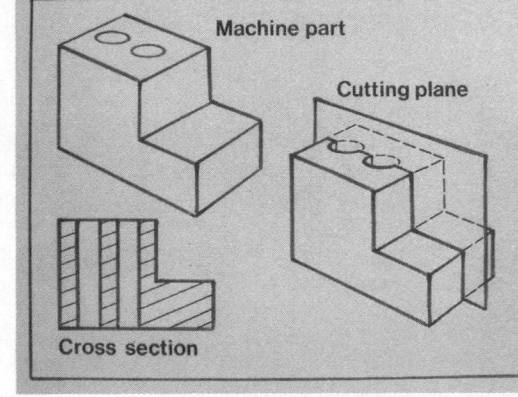

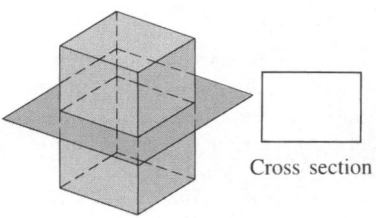

Cross section

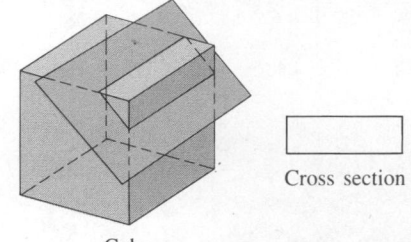

Cross section

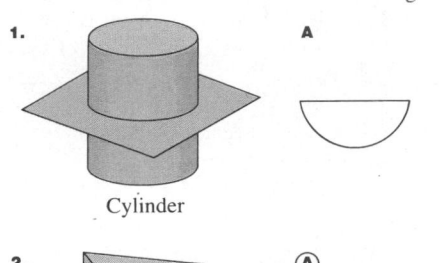

Cross section

Cube

Cross section

Choose the correct cross section for each figure.

1.

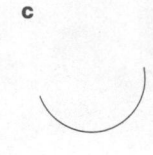

Cylinder

A   B   C

2.

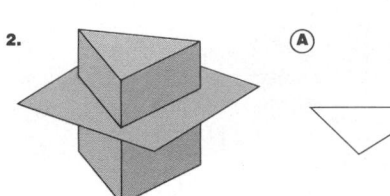

Triangular prism

A   B   C

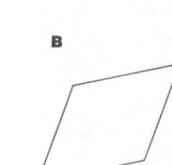 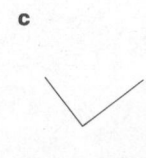

334

Follow Up

Reteaching

If students have difficulty visualizing the cross sections, have them use modeling clay to make the figures in the lesson. They can then slice the models to see the cross sections.

Enrichment

Provide students with modeling clay and ask them to find as many shapes as possible by taking cross sections of a cube. After they have had an opportunity to investigate, discuss their discoveries and why it is impossible to find a cross section with 7 or more sides. (The cube only has 6 faces.)

Students may also wish to investigate the cross sections of cylinders, cones, and pyramids.

Draw a picture of each cross-section view.

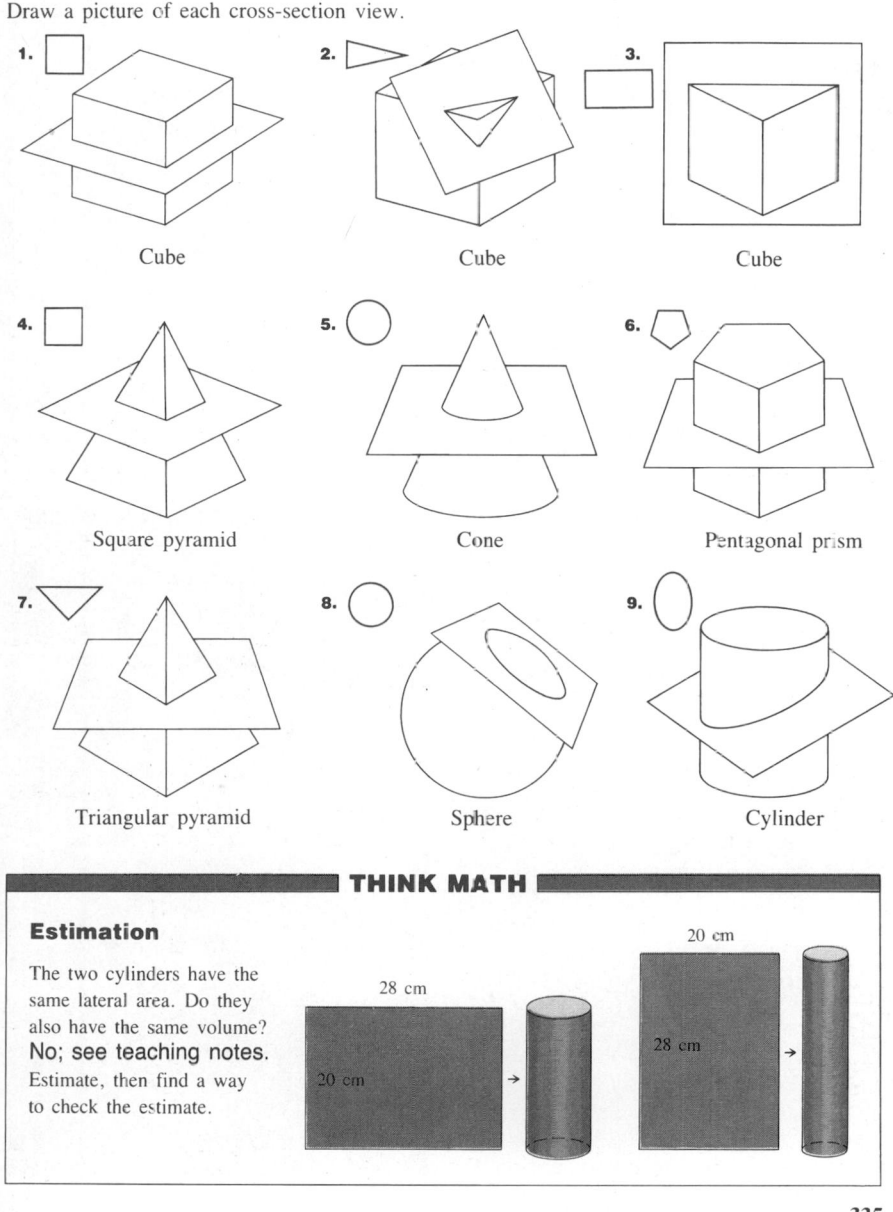

1. Cube

2. Cube

3. Cube

4. Square pyramid

5. Cone

6. Pentagonal prism

7. Triangular pyramid

8. Sphere

9. Cylinder

▌ THINK MATH ▐

Estimation

The two cylinders have the same lateral area. Do they also have the same volume?
No; see teaching notes.
Estimate, then find a way to check the estimate.

28 cm

20 cm

20 cm

28 cm

335

Using Page 335

Exercises 1–9 You may want to find methods of demonstrating some of the cross sections. One technique is to cut holes of the approximate size and shape in pieces of tagboard. Each hole represents a cross section of a figure. The tagboard can be placed over models of space figures to illustrate the cutting plane.

Think Math It is quite likely that some students will estimate that the two cylinders have the same volume. To show this is not true, make models of the two cylinders using two pieces of tagboard, 20 cm by 28 cm. Tape a base on each cylinder. Fill the taller cylinder with dry material. Next pour the contents into the shorter cylinder. The shorter cylinder will not be filled, which shows it has a greater volume.

The radii of the two cylinders can be determined and then the actual volumes computed.

Shorter cylinder: $r_1 = \dfrac{28}{2(3.14)} = 4.46$ cm

$$V_1 = 1{,}249.2 \text{ cm}^3$$

Taller cylinder: $r_2 = \dfrac{20}{2(3.14)} = 3.18$ cm

$$V_2 = 889 \text{ cm}^3$$

The cylinder with the larger radius has the larger volume.

Ideas That Work

Math for the Gifted

Display the following figures. Have students find the area of the shaded regions.

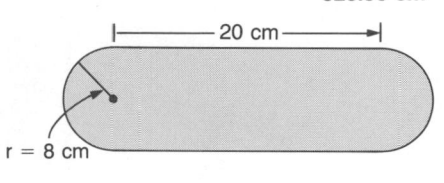

520.96 cm²

├── 20 cm ──┤

r = 8 cm

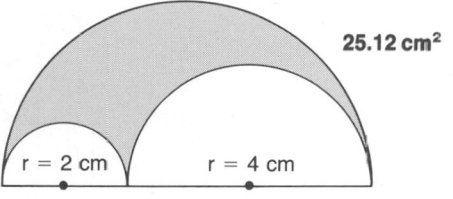

25.12 cm²

r = 2 cm   r = 4 cm

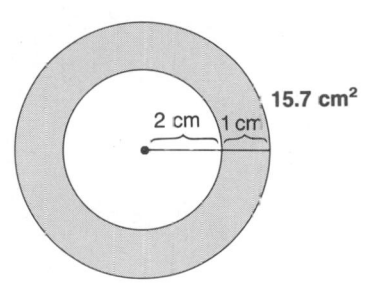

15.7 cm²

2 cm 1 cm

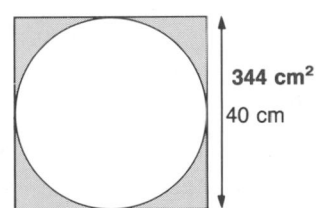

344 cm²

40 cm

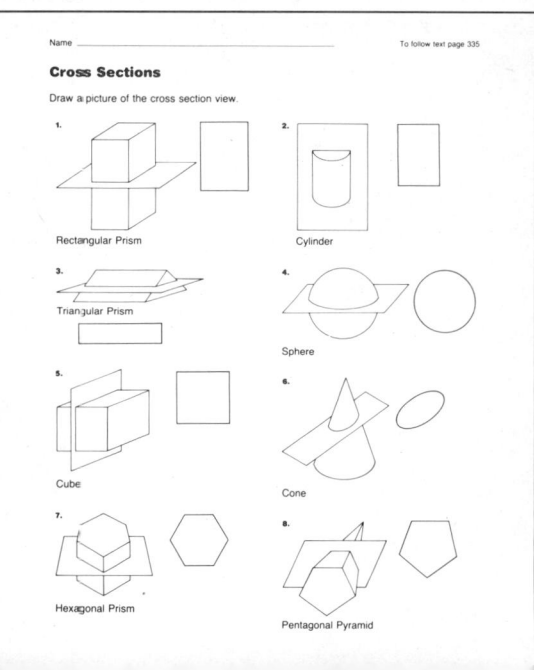

Name _____ To follow text page 335

Cross Sections

Draw a picture of the cross section view.

1. Rectangular Prism
2. Cylinder
3. Triangular Prism
4. Sphere
5. Cube
6. Cone
7. Hexagonal Prism
8. Pentagonal Pyramid

Lesson Focus To interpret, organize, and use data to make a decision about a real-world problem

Ideas for Getting Started

Discuss with students some of the concerns associated with buying a major item when you still have a usable old item. For example, students might want to buy a new bicycle while they have an old bicycle that still works. Have students suggest options that might be available.

- Sell the old bike to a friend.
- Advertise the old bike in a newspaper.
- Trade in the old bike on a new one.
- Keep the old bike.
- Discard the old bike.

Be sure that students understand the meaning of trading in the old bike on a new one. Point out that the dealer accepts the old bicycle and reduces the price of the new one. In doing so, the dealer is likely to make the trade-in value of the old bicycle slightly less than what the dealer expects to get for it when it is sold.

Using Page 336

Lesson Development Have students read the problem at the top of the page and restate the two options for disposing of the old TV set. Read with students "Some Things to Consider." The numerical data in this section will be used to answer the questions that follow.

You may wish to use "Some Questions to Answer" as an oral class activity. Then discuss the decisions students make.

Students may respond to the decision in different ways. Some may feel that it is easier to just trade in the old TV set on the new one. Others may think that it would be more profitable to sell the TV set by advertisement. Point out that since 9 days of advertising cost $24.75 and the trade-in value is $25, it would not pay to advertise for more than 9 days.

APPLIED PROBLEM SOLVING

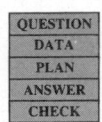

QUESTION
DATA
PLAN
ANSWER
CHECK

You have an old TV set and you want to buy a new one. You could try to sell the old set through a newspaper advertisement before you buy a new TV set, or you could trade in your old set on a new set.

Some Things to Consider

- The old TV set is in fairly good condition.
- You want to get a new TV set within two weeks.
- A newspaper advertisement costs $2.75 a day.
- You expect to sell the old set for $50.
- A new TV set costs $389.
- You can trade in your old set on a new set and get $25 off the cost of the new set.

Some Questions to Answer

1. How much money will you have to pay for the new TV set with a trade-in? $364

2. What is the cost of an advertisement for one week? What is the cost of an advertisement for two weeks? $19.25; $38.50

3. If the old TV does not sell after the advertisement runs for two weeks, you must use the old TV as a trade-in. What is the total cost of the new TV set and the advertisement? $402.50

4. How much money must you pay for the new TV set if someone buys the old TV after only one day? $341.75

What Is Your Decision?

How will you plan to use your old TV set to help you buy a new TV set? Answers may vary. If the old set is sold within 9 days, it is better to sell it than to trade it in. To sell the set after 9 days will cost more than to use it for a trade-in.

336

CHAPTER REVIEW/TEST

Find the circumference of each circle. Use 3.14 for π.

1. 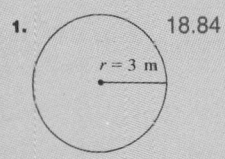 18.84 m   **2.** 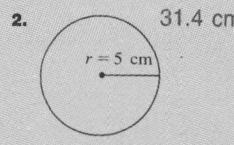 31.4 cm   **3.** 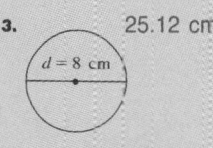 25.12 cm

4. $r = 2.5$ m   15.7 m   **5.** $d = 20$ km   62.8 km   **6.** $d = 12$ mm   37.68 mm

Find the circumference of each circle. Use $\frac{22}{7}$ for π.

7. $r = 28$ cm   176 cm   **8.** $r = 21$ m   132 m   **9.** $d = 98$ cm   308 cm

Find the area of each circle. Use 3.14 for π.

10. $r = 4$ cm   50.24 cm^2 **11.** $r = 7$ cm   153.86 cm^2 **12.** $d = 2$ cm   3.14 cm^2

13. $r = 10$ km   314 km^2 **14.** $d = 4$ m   12.56 m^2 **15.** $d = 30$ m   706.5 m^2

Find the lateral area and the total surface area of each cylinder. Use 3.14 for π.

16. $r = 2$ cm   125.6 cm^2;   **17.** $r = 5$ cm   785 cm^2;   **18.** $r = 3$ cm   150.72 cm^2;
     $h = 10$ cm   150.72 cm^2 $h = 25$ cm   942 cm^2 $h = 8$ cm   207.24 cm^2

Find the volume of each cylinder.

19. $r = 1$ cm   6.28 cm^3 **20.** $r = 3$ cm   141.3 cm^3 **21.** $r = 5$ cm   157 cm^3
     $h = 2$ cm $h = 5$ cm $h = 2$ cm

Draw a picture of each cross-section view.

22.    **23.**    **24.**

25. An irrigated field is a circle with a radius of 80 m. What is the area of the field? 20,096 m^2

26. An irrigation tank is a cylinder with a diameter of 8 m and a depth of 2 m. What is the volume of the tank? 100.48 m^3

337

Using Page 337

The exercises in the Chapter Review/Test emphasize the major concepts and skills presented in this chapter. These exercises may be used as a review assignment or as a test, depending upon your needs.

Item Analysis The table below correlates the Chapter Review/Test items with objectives and with student text pages on which the concepts or skills were taught. Please note that items 22–24 are derived from a lesson for which no "Minimum" assignment was suggested in the Assignment Guide. Only those students who were assigned this lesson should be expected to complete the corresponding Chapter Review/Test items.

Items	Objectives	Related Text Pages
1–9	13.1	322–323
10–15	13.2	324–325
16–18	13.3	328–329
19–21	13.4	330–331
22–24	13.5	334–335
25–26	13.6	326–332

Assessment Options

If you use the Chapter Review/Test as a review assignment, you may wish to use the free-response test or the multiple-choice test to evaluate mastery of the chapter objectives. The items on these tests have a one-to-one correspondence in terms of content and level of difficulty. A correlation of test items to objectives and student text pages is provided in the Management Guide for Chapter 13. Note: Items 16–17 are derived from lessons for which no minimum assignment was suggested in the Assignment Guide.

Multiple-Choice Test, TRB pages 37–38
Free-Response Test, TRB pages 73–74

TRB Options

The following blackline masters are available for use with this chapter. If you have not already assigned these materials, you may wish to use them to close the chapter.

Recreation, TRB page 167
Consumer Applications, TRB page 187
Computer Technology, TRB pages 218–220
Calculator Technology, TRB page 203
Reading Math, TRB page 239
Family Involvement, TRB pages 269–270

Using Page 338

The exercises on this page are intended for those students who experienced difficulty with the Chapter Review/Test on page 337. Should students require reteaching of these key concepts and skills, please refer to the teaching notes below. Otherwise, the Another Look exercises can be assigned as independent work, with students using the accompanying sample problems and hints as guides.

Exercises 1–4 This skill was originally taught on pages 322–323. Have students study the information in the display box. With students, work through examples of finding the circumference of a circle by applying the formulas. Remind students that if they are given the radius of a circle, they must multiply by 2 and by π.

Exercises 5–8 This skill was originally taught on pages 324–325. On the chalkboard, work through the examples in the display box. Emphasize that before multiplying times 3.14, we must square the radius.

Exercises 9–12 This skill was originally taught on pages 328–329. Have students study the material in the display box. Discuss the relationship between the lateral area and total surface area of a cylinder. With students, work through an example of finding the lateral area of a cylinder. Give students an opportunity to participate in each step. Then show how to find the total surface area by adding the area of the two bases.

Exercises 13–14 This skill was taught on pages 330–331. Write the general formula for the volume of a prism on the chalkboard and show how to derive the formula for the volume of a cylinder.

$$B = \pi r^2 \text{ and } V = Bh$$
$$\text{Therefore, } V = \pi r^2 h$$

Work through an example of finding the volume of a cylinder one step at a time.

ANOTHER LOOK

Circumference is the distance around a circle.

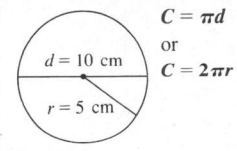

$$C = \pi d$$
or
$$C = 2\pi r$$

$d = 10$ cm
$r = 5$ cm

Use 3.14 or $\frac{22}{7}$ for π.

Find the circumference of each circle. Use 3.14 for π.

1. $d = 20$ m 62.8 m   2. $r = 8$ cm 50.24 cm

Find the circumference of each circle. Use $\frac{22}{7}$ for π.

3. $d = 35$ m 110 m   4. $r = 10.5$ m 66 m

$$A = \pi r^2 = \pi \times r \times r$$

$r = 3$ cm

$$A \approx 3.14 \times 3 \times 3 \approx 3.14 \times 9$$
$$A \approx 28.26 \text{ cm}^2$$

Find the area of each circle. Use 3.14 for π.

5. $r = 5$ cm   6. $r = 2$ km

$r = 5$ cm 78.5 cm² $r = 2$ km 12.56 km²

7. $r = 0.8$ cm 2.0096 cm²   8. $r = 30$ cm 2,826 cm²

Lateral area of a cylinder equals circumference of the base times the height.

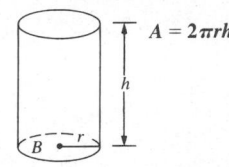

$$A = 2\pi rh$$

h
B r

Total surface area = lateral area + area of two bases

Find the lateral area of each cylinder.

9. $r = 2$ cm   10. $r = 10$ cm
$h = 6$ cm 75.36 cm² $h = 15$ cm 942 cm²

Find the total surface area of each cylinder.

11. $r = 1$ cm   12. $r = 4$ cm
$h = 2$ cm 18.84 cm² $h = 5$ cm 226.08 cm²

Volume $= Bh$
$$V = \pi r^2 h$$

Find the volume of each cylinder.

13. $r = 3$ cm   14. $r = 2.5$ mm
$h = 9$ cm 254.34 cm³ $h = 4$ mm 78.5 mm³

Just for Teachers

Determining π

Finding an exact value for π has occurred mathematicians throughout history. An Egyptian papyrus scroll dating to 1850 B.C. shows a method of calculating the volume of a pyramid. A ratio of 256:81, or in decimal notation about 3.16, was used for π. In the 3rd Century B.C., Archimedes determined that π lay between $3\frac{10}{71}$ and $3\frac{1}{7}$ (about 3.141 and 3.142). By A.D. 500 a Chinese irrigation engineer, Tsu Ch'ung Chih, placed π between 3.1415926 and 3.1415927. Al Kashi of Samarkand computed the value of π beyond nine decimal places about A.D. 1430 Two hundred years later, π was computed to 35 decimal places, and today, with the help of a computer, it has been stretched to 100,000 decimal places. An absolute value will never be found.

The Japanese of about A.D. 1700 had determined a value for π correct to fifty places in decimal notation. Their calculation was based upon superimposing two sets of rectangles of equal width upon a circle. By repeating this procedure with rectangles of smaller and smaller width, they were able to use the concept of *series* to state in

Hex Numeration System

Some computers and microcomputers use a numeration system based on sixteen instead of base ten.

This system is called a **hexadecimal**, or **hex**, numeration system. The hex system has sixteen digits.

Hex	0	1	2	3	4	5	6	7	8	9	A	B	C	D	E	F
Base ten	0	1	2	3	4	5	6	7	8	9	10	11	12	13	14	15

To use the hex system, we must think about grouping by **sixteens** instead of by tens.

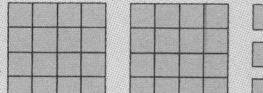

2 sixteens and 3 ones
We write: 23_{hex}
We read: "two three base hex"

Since 2 sixteens and 3 ones in base ten is 35, we can write $23_{hex} = 35_{ten}$.

We can use the expanded notation of a hex numeral to find the base-ten numeral.

$A8_{hex} = 10 \cdot 16 + 8 = 160 + 8 = 168_{ten}$

$13C_{hex} = 1 \cdot 16^2 + 3 \cdot 16 + 12 = 256 + 48 + 12 = 316_{ten}$

$3FD_{hex} = 3 \cdot 16^2 + 15 \cdot 16 + 13 = 768 + 240 + 13 = 1,021_{ten}$

Write a hex numeral for each figure.

1. 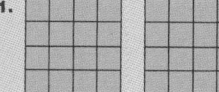 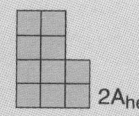 $2A_{hex}$
2. 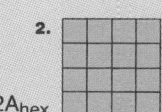 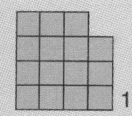 $1F_{hex}$
3. 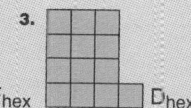 D_{hex}

Write a base-ten numeral for each hex numeral.

4. 21_{hex} 33
5. $2B_{hex}$ 43
6. 89_{hex} 137
7. AA_{hex} 170

8. $5C_{hex}$ 92
9. $A2_{hex}$ 162
10. $E0_{hex}$ 224
11. FF_{hex} 255

12. 111_{hex} 273
13. $1AB_{hex}$ 427
14. $20D_{hex}$ 525
15. 615_{hex} 1,557

16. ACE_{hex} 2,766
17. $B0B_{hex}$ 2,827
18. FED_{hex} 4,077
19. DAB_{hex} 3,499

339

Using Page 339

This page is intended for those students who successfully complete the Chapter Review/Test on page 337. You may wish to assign this page as independent work while you use Another Look exercises to reteach the basic concepts and skills of the chapter. Or, you may decide that all students would benefit from exposure to this activity.

Lesson Development Draw 25 X's on the chalkboard. Show that when we group the X's by tens, we get 2 tens and 5 ones.

```
X  X    X  X    X
X  X    X  X    X
X  X    X  X    X      2 tens  5 ones
X  X    X  X    X         25_ten
X  X    X  X    X
```

Next mark another set of 25 X's on the chalkboard. Show that if we group these X's by sixteens, we get 1 sixteen and 9 ones. Then write the hex numeral, 19_{hex}.

```
X  X  X  X  X
X  X  X  X  X
X  X  X  X  X      1 sixteen  9 ones
X  X  X  X  X          19_hex
X  X  X  X  X
```

Display the following chart and show how we can use expanded notation for the hex numeral below to find the corresponding base-ten numeral.

$(sixteen)^2$	sixteen	ones
256	16	1

$$2AD_{hex} = 2 \cdot 16^2 + 10 \cdot 16 + 13$$
$$= 512 + 160 + 13 = 685_{ten}$$

Exercises 1–19 Have students work these exercises independently.

general terms a formula to narrow the limits of the value of π.

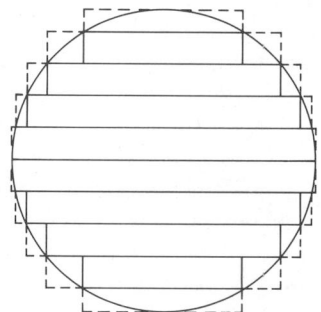

In the illustration, one set of rectangles lies inside the circle, the other set outside. Given a radius of 1 unit, the value for π will lie between the sum of the areas of the inner rectangles and the sum of the areas of the outer rectangles.

Lesson Focus
To read and understand a computer program that uses a decision loop and a counter

Ideas for Getting Started

Write this program and chart on the chalkboard. Work through the program one step at a time and have students give values for R, S, and T. Record these as well as the value for A in the chart.

```
10 INPUT R, S, T
20 A = (R + S + T)/3
30 PRINT A
40 GOTO 10
50 END
```

R	
S	
T	
A	

Continue to have students give new INPUT numbers. After working through three or four values for A, ask students when the program will end. They should see that it will never reach line 50. Explain that when a group of statements is repeated in a program, it is called a loop. Tell students that in this lesson they will learn a way to control looping in a program.

Using Page 340

Lesson Development Explain to students that in BASIC the equal sign (=) has a meaning different from the meaning it has in mathemtics. The equal sign in BASIC means "replace the value on the left by the value of the number or expression on the right." Write these statements on the chalkboard. Point out that in mathematics there are no equations like those in lines 20 and 40, since there is no value of A that will make the equation A = A + 1 true.

```
10 A =1
20 A = A +1
30 N = A
40 N = N +2
```

"What is the value of A in line 10?" (1)
"What is the new value of A in line 20?" (2)
"What is the value of N in line 30?" (2)
"What is the new value of N in line 40?" (4)

Have students read the material at the top of the page and study the flowchart. On the chalkboard, work through each step of the program recording values for N and the numbers in the output. Point out that statement 50 is a test that will finally make the program stop. This statement controls the number of times the computer executes the loop. Notice with students that "<=" is used in line 50. Explain that this is the BASIC symbol for "is less than or equal to." In mathematics, the comparable symbol is ≤.

Loops in Computer Programs

A computer can be programmed to keep track of items by counting. To do this, the computer must be told how far to count. In the program below, the computer is told to count and print the first five multiples of 3. The program uses a **loop**. A loop is a command that causes the computer to go back to an earlier step in the program and repeat the step.

A Universal Product Code symbol

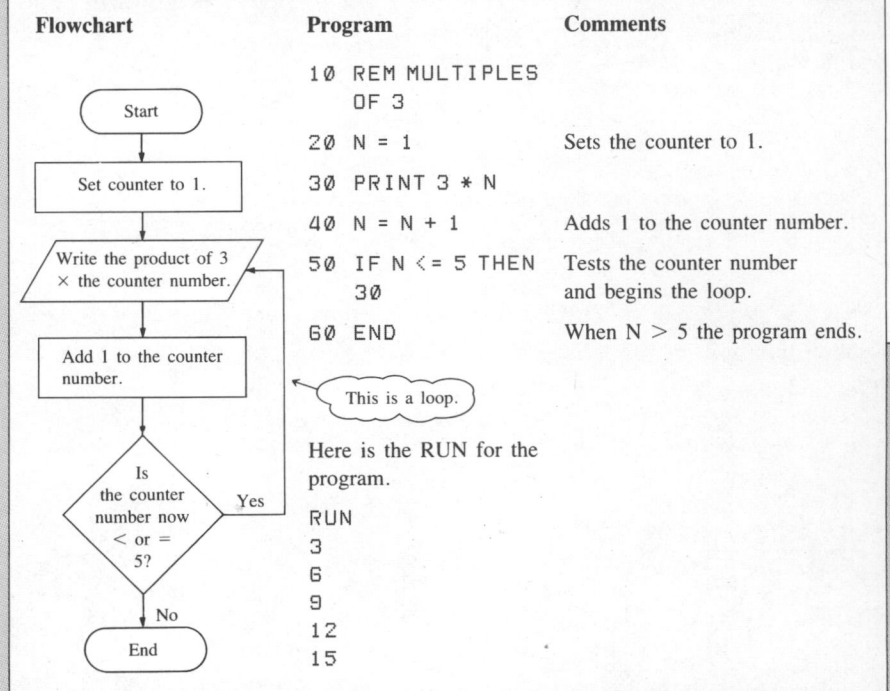

Flowchart	Program	Comments
	10 REM MULTIPLES OF 3	
	20 N = 1	Sets the counter to 1.
	30 PRINT 3 * N	
	40 N = N + 1	Adds 1 to the counter number.
	50 IF N <= 5 THEN 30	Tests the counter number and begins the loop.
	60 END	When N > 5 the program ends.

Here is the RUN for the program.

```
RUN
3
6
9
12
15
```

1. How could the program be changed so that the RUN would be the first ten multiples of 3? Change line 50 to:
   50 IF N <= 10 THEN 30

2. How could the program be changed so that the RUN would be multiples of 4? Change line 30 to: 30 PRINT 4 * N

Technology for Teachers

BASIC is only one of more than one hundred fifty computer languages now in existence. It was originally written in 1963 at Dartmouth College to help students with no background in programming to learn to use the computer. Today the language is used by professionals for a wide variety of applications.

PILOT and Logo are other languages you and your students may want to learn about. PILOT was first written as a language for teachers writing instructional material for use on computers. Rather than common English words, PILOT commands are initials representing English words. For example, "T" represents the command to Type or print on the screen. "A" stands for Accept and is most like the INPUT statements in BASIC. "M" means to Match and is one of the commands that makes the language especially good for instructional material, since you can give the computer several possible answers that would be acceptable responses. "J" represents Jump and is

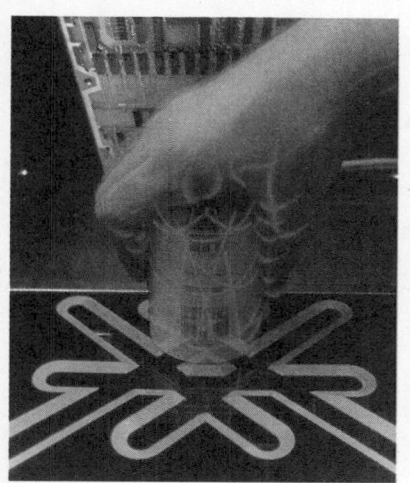

The bar code scanner used in supermarkets reads the Universal Product Code symbols to give an accurate tally of purchases and manages the store inventory.

Write a RUN for each program.

```
1. 10  REM COUNT TO 10      RUN
   20  N = 1                1
   30  PRINT N              2
   40  N = N + 1            3
   50  IF N <= 10 THEN 30   4
   60  END                  5
                            6
                            7
                            8
                            9
                            10
```

```
2. 10  REM ODD NUMBERS      RUN
   20  N = 0                1
   30  PRINT 2 * N + 1      3
   40  N = N + 1            5
   50  IF N <= 5 THEN 30    7
   60  END                  9
                            11
```

```
3. 10  REM COUNTING BACKWARD  RUN
   20  N = 6                  6
   30  PRINT N                5
   40  N = N - 1              4
   50  IF N > 0 THEN 30       3
   60  END                    2
                              1
```

```
4. 10  REM NUMBER PATTERN
   20  N = 1                       RUN
   30  B = 4 * N - 3               1
   40  PRINT B                     5
   50  N = N + 1                   9
   60  IF N <= 6 THEN 30           13
   70  PRINT "FIND MORE NUMBERS"   17
   80  PRINT "IN THIS PATTERN."    21
   90  END            FIND MORE NUMBERS
                      IN THIS PATTERN.
```

```
5. 10  REM SUM OF 10 NUMBERS  RUN
   20  N = 1                   55
   30  T = 0
   40  T = T + N
   50  N = N + 1
   60  IF N <= 10 THEN 40
   70  PRINT T
   80  END
```

6. Write a computer program that has a loop in it. Write a RUN of your program.

Using Page 341

Exercise 6 You may wish to show students another way a decision loop can be used in a program. In the program shown below, the user controls whether or not the loop is executed by giving the answer yes or no. Usually, "1" is used for yes and "0" is used for no.

```
10 REM AVERAGE
20 PRINT "CHOOSE 3 NUMBERS."
30 INPUT A, B, C
40 D = (A + B + C)/3
50 PRINT "AVERAGE ="; D
60 PRINT "DO YOU HAVE 3 MORE
     NUMBERS?"
70 PRINT "TYPE 1 FOR YES AND 0 FOR NO."
80 INPUT Q
90 IF Q = 1 THEN 20
100 END
```

The test statement is in line 90. If the user enters 0 for no, the program ends.

somewhat like a GOTO in BASIC. Since the commands are single letters, some versions of PILOT are useful as introductory programming language for children.

Logo is best known for the part of the language called Turtle Graphics. The Logo language was developed in the Artificial Intelligence department at MIT to study the actual learning process. Turtle Graphics provides students with an opportunity to explore the relationship between lines, angles, shapes, distance, and direction. Turtle Graphics can be especially useful in exploring many fundamental geometric concepts. Unlike most other computer languages, you can write your own language in Logo, naming your procedures as you develop them. In this way, students can "invent" their own version of the language. The Technology lesson in Chapter 16 gives students an opportunity to work with Logo.

Using Page 342

The exercises on the page provide practice for maintaining cumulative skills. The emphasis in this Cumulative Review is on metric measurement (Chapter 10) and percent (Chapter 12).

Item Analysis The table below correlates the Cumulative Review items with objectives and with the student book pages on which the concepts or skills were taught.

Items	Objectives	Related Text Pages
1–2	10.1	248–251
3–4	10.2	252–254, 256–258
5	10.3	260–261
6	10.4	262, 264, 266
7–10	12.1	294–301
11	12.2	302–304
12	12.3	306–307
13	10.5	255, 259, 263, 265
14	12.6	305, 308–309, 313

CUMULATIVE REVIEW

Find the missing numbers.

1. 12.5 cm = ▨ m

   A 1.25   **B** 125
   © 0.125   **D** not given

2. 6,250 m = ▨ km

   Ⓐ 6.250   **B** 625
   c 62.50   **D** not given

3. What is the perimeter?

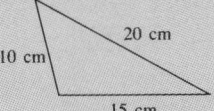

   A 40 cm
   Ⓑ 45 cm
   c 3,750 cm
   D not given

4. What is the area?

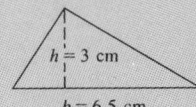

   Ⓐ 9.75 cm²
   B 9.5 cm²
   c 19.5 cm²
   D not given

5. What is the volume?

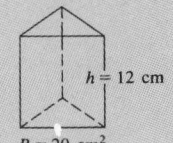

   A 64 cm³
   Ⓑ 240 cm³
   c 52 cm³
   D not given

6. What is the capacity?

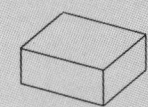

Volume: 6 cm³

   A 12 mL
   B 36 mL
   c 24 mL
   Ⓓ not given

7. What is the percent for $\frac{3}{5}$?

   A 16%   **Ⓑ** 60%
   c 35%   **D** not given

8. What is the decimal for 129%?

   Ⓐ 1.29   **B** 12.9
   c 0.129   **D** not given

9. What is the percent for 0.076?

   A 76%   **B** 760%
   © 7.6%   **D** not given

10. What is the lowest-terms fraction for 18%?

   A $\frac{3}{25}$ **B** $\frac{9}{25}$
   c $\frac{6}{50}$ **Ⓓ** not given

11. What is 25% of 9?

   Ⓐ 2.25   **B** 3.2
   c 4   **D** not given

12. What percent of 5 is 9?

   Ⓐ 180%   **B** 55%
   c 18%   **D** not given

13. Which metric unit would you use to measure the length of a pencil?

   A meter   **B** kilometer
   © centimeter **D** not given

14. If $500 earns 6% interest per year, how much interest will be earned in 7 years?

   A $350   **Ⓑ** $210
   c $30   **D** not given

Probability, Statistics, and Graphs

Objectives

14.1 Find the probability of a particular outcome given several equally likely outcomes.

14.2 Find the probability of an event when the outcomes are ordered pairs.

14.3 Identify the frequency of an event and find the range, mode, arithmetic mean, and median of a set of numerical data.

14.4 Read, interpret, and make bar graphs, line segment graphs, pictographs, and circle graphs.

14.5 Solve word problems using the 5-Point Checklist and cumulative computational skills.

Summary

There are three closely related strands of content in this chapter. In the first part of the chapter, simple probability concepts and notation are developed. The next part of the chapter deals with statistics. The topics covered are frequency, range, mode, median, and arithmetic mean. The last part of the chapter reviews and extends work with graphs. Bar graphs, line segment graphs, pictographs, and circle graphs are presented. While the emphasis is on reading and interpreting graphs, there are also opportunities for students to construct graphs. As in previous chapters, there are several word problem sets. In this chapter, the problems are related to probability and statistics.

Mathematical Background

Probability When a penny is tossed there are 2 equally likely outcomes: heads and tails. There is 1 chance in 2 that the penny will come up heads. Thus, the probability of tossing heads with a penny is $\frac{1}{2}$. In general, if an experiment has n equally likely outcomes, the probability of each outcome is $\frac{1}{n}$. The probability of any outcome is always a number from 0 to 1. A probability of 1 indicates that the outcome is certain while a probability of 0 indicates that the outcome is impossible.

In certain experiments, outcomes can be expressed as ordered pairs. For example, if two dice are tossed, a possible outcome is (4, 5). A grid can be used to show that there are 36 ordered-pair outcomes.

To give the probability of rolling a sum of 9, we must find the number of outcomes with a sum of 9. Since there are 4 such outcomes, the probability of rolling a sum of 9 is $\frac{4}{36}$ or $\frac{1}{9}$.

$$P(\text{sum of } 9) = \frac{4}{36} \begin{array}{l} \leftarrow \text{ Number of outcomes with sum of 9} \\ \leftarrow \text{ Total number of outcomes} \end{array}$$
$$= \frac{1}{9}$$

Statistics The subject of statistics is concerned with ways of organizing and presenting numerical data so that interpretation and use of the data is easier. The use of tables and graphs to show statistical data is important. This chapter reviews and extends work with bar graphs, line segment graphs, pictographs, and circle graphs.

Associated with lists of numerical data are certain measures or statistics called measures of central tendency. In this chapter, the statistics presented include frequency, range, mode, arithmetic mean, and median. These measures of a list of numerical data describe the distribution of the data. The frequency gives the number of times a bit of data is repeated. The range is the difference between the smallest and largest numbers in the list. The mode is the most frequently occurring number in the set, if there is one. Some lists of numbers can have more than one mode. The arithmetic mean or average is the sum of the numbers in the list divided by the number of addends. The median is the middle number or the average of the two middle numbers when the numbers of the list are ordered in size.

Problem Solving The problem-solving sets in this chapter incorporate the content of the chapter. On pages 350 and 351, problems are concerned with using probability to predict the expected number of outcomes. Students use data from a table on page 355 to solve problems dealing with measures of central tendency. On pages 360 and 361, students use data from graphs to solve problems. In the applied problem-solving lesson on page 362, students use the idea of a sample to make a decision about a real-world problem.

Vocabulary

outcome	mode	bar graph
equally likely outcomes	median	histogram
probability	arithmetic mean	pictograph
frequency	line segment graph	circle graph
range		

Error Analysis

In this chapter the idea of probability is developed, and statistics and graphs are presented as ways of organizing and displaying data. As in previous chapters, the errors students make in their computation will reflect a misunderstanding of the underlying concepts and/or the ability to carry out basic computation covered in previous chapters. Some possible errors are given below.

Error Pattern 1

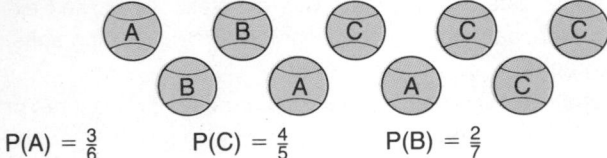

$P(A) = \frac{3}{6}$ $\qquad$ $P(C) = \frac{4}{5}$ $\qquad$ $P(B) = \frac{2}{7}$

Diagnosis The student found the probability by comparing the number of possible outcomes for a given letter to the number of outcomes remaining. The total number of equally likely outcomes was not used.

Remediation Review the concept of the probability of an event. Stress the definition of $P(A)$:

$$P(A) = \frac{\text{Number of A}}{\text{Number of equally likely outcomes.}}$$

Try examples and focus on this relationship.

Error Pattern 2

32, 64, 47, 64, 36, 18, 18, 64	Mean = 64
19, 81, 17, 39, 19, 26	Mean = 19
103, 57, 84, 93, 87, 57	Mean = 57

Diagnosis The student selected the most frequently occurring value for the mean. This shows a misunderstanding of terms mean and mode.

Remediation Begin with two numbers and review the concept of "finding an average." Discuss the procedure to be followed: divide the sum by the number of values added. Extend this idea to more than two numbers.

Error Pattern 3

15, 23, 32, 39, 47, 98, 99	Median = 39
35, 43, 46, 54, 92, 98	Median = 46, 54
22, 23, 25, 28, 31, 34, 46, 91	Median = 28, 31

Diagnosis The student correctly selected the middle number when an odd number of terms was given. However, when an even number of terms was given, the student named the two middle numbers, rather than finding their mean.

Remediation Explain that the median is the middle number in a set of numbers. There is an equal number of values above and below the median. Use an example of an even number of terms and show how the median is found.

```
    2 numbers            2 numbers
   ⌒⌒⌒⌒⌒             ⌒⌒⌒⌒⌒
 20     22    27     30    33     39
        (27 + 30) ÷ 2 = 28.5
```

Problem Solving

Starting a Problem-Solving Resource Center

In the previous chapter, a "problem-of-the-week" bulletin board was suggested as one way to provide students with challenging math problems without the time limitations inherent in most teaching schedules. A problem-solving resource center is a second way. This resource center should be more than a collection of challenging problems. A good resource center is one where students can get assistance (without asking the teacher) when they become stymied on a problem and one where students can extend their work on a similar problem.

To set up a resource center with these characteristics, use three problem-solving file boxes labeled as shown below.

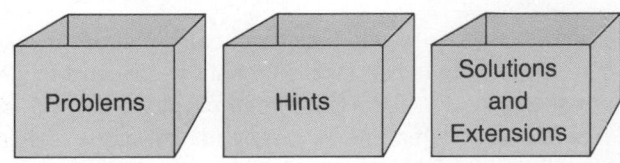

The "Problems" box contains a collection of problems. One problem should be on each numbered card. The cards could be grouped by levels of difficulty or by chapter to correspond with the strategies developed in the student book. The "Hints" box contains cards numbered to correspond to the problem cards. One side of each card lists questions which, if answered correctly, would help students find a solution. On the other side of the card are answers to the questions.

In the "Solutions and Extensions" box, one side of each card shows one or two solutions to the problem. The other side has a problem that is an extension of the original problem. These cards can also be numbered to correspond to the numbers on the "Problems" and "Hints" cards.

The strategy lessons and Try This problems in the student book, together with the teacher notes for these lessons, can provide useful models for the types of problems, hints, and extensions to be used in the resource center.

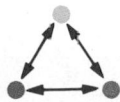

Special Education

This chapter contains a wealth of material for students to investigate and master. Many of the skills developed are basic skills needed in everyday life. The idea of probabilities is with us whenever we think about the weather report or choose to take one route over another. Graphs and statistics confront us every time we open a newspaper or news magazine. To help our special-needs students master the necessary skills, we need to provide them with alternate approaches and additional models.

Considering Types of Outcomes

The notion of an equally likely outcome takes on significance when one has had an opportunity to look at outcomes which are not equally likely. This can be done through experiments in the classroom. One of these is the rolling of a die shaped like the one pictured below. While rolling each number is not equally likely, we could ask if some of the numbers are equally likely outcomes. An investigation of several rolls using a frequency chart would show that the numbers 1 and 6 are equally likely outcomes as are the numbers 2 through 5. The discussion of outcomes which are not equally likely should be extended to situations dealing with weather, sports results, and similar events.

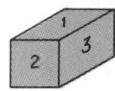

Perceptual Problems

Some of the difficulties students have in dealing with probability are tied to perceptual problems or thinking fixations. For example, a student who has difficulty determining if two segments or regions are congruent may have difficulty determining the probability of an outcome in a physical experiment. Other students may fix on a color in an experiment with a spinner and feel that the spinner will land on their favorite color even though it has the least probability of happening. Care must be taken to help the special student learn the difference between wishes and probability.

Graphing with the Sliding Scale

One of the difficulties that many special students have is reading data from a graph. To ease this problem, we can make a sliding scale out of a piece of cardboard, or paper, to slide across the graph. This sliding scale is shown below. A similar piece of paper can be used to help read data from a frequency chart by using it to block out extra information while lining up the desired data.

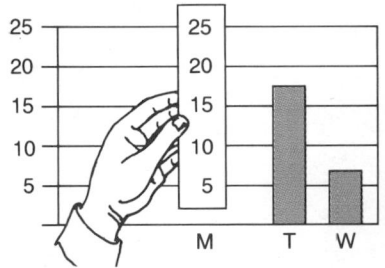

Age	Number
16	5
17	2
18	9
19	16
20	18
21	14

Checking Out Prerequisite Skills

The construction of circle graphs will require students to use skills presented in Chapter 6 and Chapter 12. These topics will need review, as will the actual use of a protractor in constructing the central angles for the graphs. Students will need to be introduced to the shifting of the protractor to each new angle for marking off a portion of the graph.

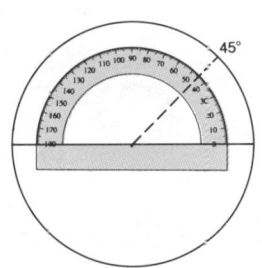 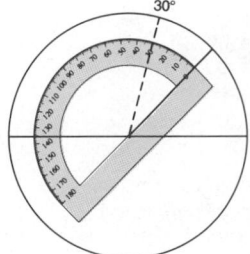

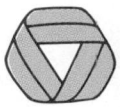

Subject Integration

Subject matter related to other areas of the curriculum has been integrated into the following lessons. This provides an opportunity to highlight the interaction between mathematics and other subjects.

Science Bald eagles, page 343; weather records, page 350
Physical Education Tennis, page 344; exercise machine, page 357
Fine Arts Records, pages 346–347
Career Awareness Part-time work, pages 352–353
Social Studies U.S. Farms, page 358; land use, page 359

Management Guide

Teaching Chapter 14				Meeting Individual Needs					
				Lesson Assignments			Follow Up		
Objectives	Chapter Content	Pages	TRB Test Items	Minimum	Average	Extended	Reteaching	Enrichment	Practice
	Chapter Opener	343							
14.1 Find the probability of a particular outcome given several equally likely outcomes.	Equally Likely Outcomes	344–345	1–4	1–9	1–12	1–12			PS 128
	Chances and Probability	346–347		1–18, 22, SK	1–19, 22, SK	1–22, SK	SE6 Ch 13 RS 97	ES 97	PS 129
14.2 Find the probability of an event when the outcomes are ordered pairs.	Ordered Pairs in Probability	348–349	5–7	1–7	1–10	1–10, TM	RS 98	ES 98	PS 130
14.3 Identify the frequency of an event and find the range, mode, arithmetic mean, and median of a set of numerical data.	Frequency, Range, and Mode	352–353	8–11	1–9, SK	1–9, SK	1–10, SK	SE6 Ch 13		MP 438 PS 132
	Arithmetic Mean and Median	354		1–8	1–8	1–8	SE6 Ch 13 RS 99	ES 99	MP 438 PS 133
14.4 Read, interpret, and make bar graphs, line segment graphs, pictographs, and circle graphs.	Bar Graphs	356	12–23	1–9	1–10	1–10	SE6 Ch 13		
	Line Segment Graphs	357		1–10	1–11	1–11	SE6 Ch 13 RS 100	ES 100	PS 134
	Pictographs	358		1–9	1–10	1–10	SE6 Ch 13		
	Circle Graphs	359		1–8	1–10, TM	1–10			PS 135
14.5 Solve word problems using the 5-Point Checklist and cumulative computational skills.	Problem Solving: Practice	350–351	24–25	1–10	1–11, 14	1–14			PS 131
	Problem Solving: Using Data from a Table	355		1–8	1–10	1–11			
	Problem Solving: Using Data from a Graph	360–361		1–8	1–10	1–10	RS 101	ES 101	PS 136
	Applied Problem Solving	362							
	Chapter Review/Test	363							
	Another Look/ Enrichment	364–365							
	Cumulative Review	366							

SE6 Student Edition, Book 6
RS Reteaching Supplement
ES Enrichment Supplement
PS Practice Supplement
MP More Practice
TM Think Math
SK Skillkeeper
TRB Teacher's Resource Book

Masters for use

. . . before Chapter 14

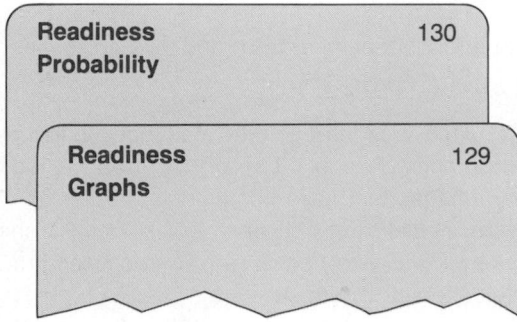

Readiness Probability	130
Readiness Graphs	129

. . . during Chapter 14

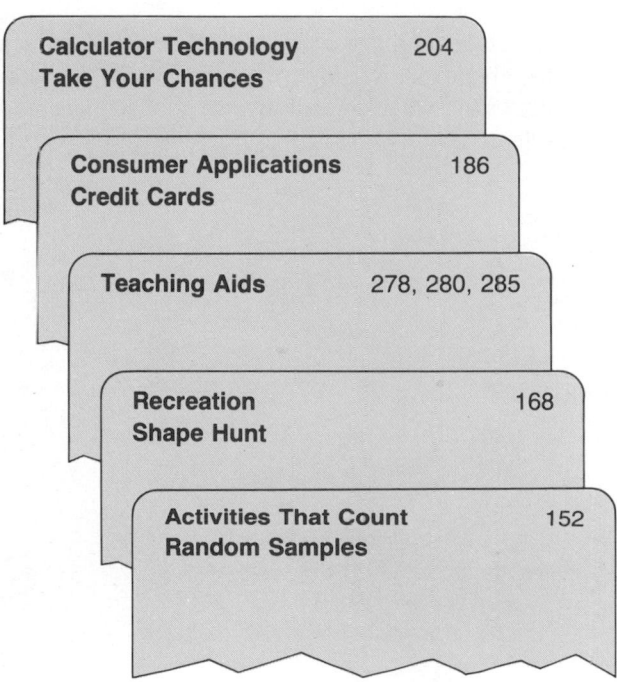

Calculator Technology Take Your Chances	204
Consumer Applications Credit Cards	186
Teaching Aids	278, 280, 285
Recreation Shape Hunt	168
Activities That Count Random Samples	152

. . . after Chapter 14

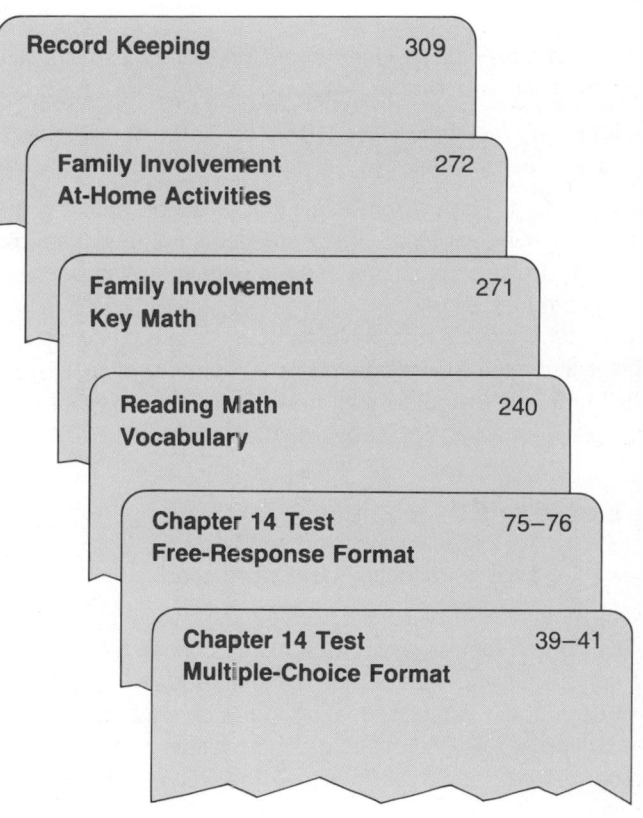

Record Keeping	309
Family Involvement At-Home Activities	272
Family Involvement Key Math	271
Reading Math Vocabulary	240
Chapter 14 Test Free-Response Format	75–76
Chapter 14 Test Multiple-Choice Format	39–41

Supplements

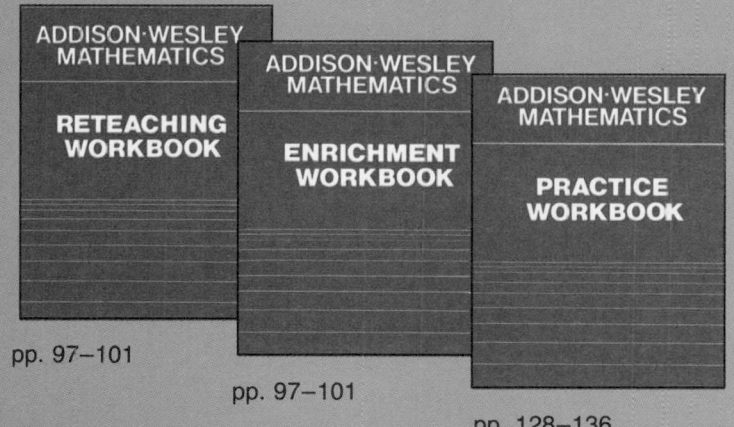

ADDISON·WESLEY MATHEMATICS
RETEACHING WORKBOOK

ADDISON·WESLEY MATHEMATICS
ENRICHMENT WORKBOOK

ADDISON·WESLEY MATHEMATICS
PRACTICE WORKBOOK

pp. 97–101

pp. 97–101

pp. 128–136

Other Addison-Wesley Resources

Books and Kits

Baseball: A Game of Numbers   pp. 141–176

General Mathematics: Making Practice Fun   77–78, 79 A, B, 80, 81

Activities That Count

Activities That Count are designed for use throughout this chapter and subsequent chapters. Before beginning Chapter 14 you may wish to review these activities and select the ones you consider appropriate for your class.

Chance It   Game

Purpose To use intuitive ideas about probability and practice adding and multiplying

Materials Two number cubes (TRB p. 278), one labeled 0 through 5 and the other labeled 6 through 11

Activity In turn, players roll both number cubes and find the product of the numbers rolled. If the product is not 0, players get that number of points. Then they may roll again or stop and add those points to their score.

On each turn, players may have as many rolls as they choose until they either roll a 0 or decide to stop. When 0 is rolled, players lose their turn and any points they may have earned on that turn. The first player to score 500 or over is the winner.

The Letter "E"   Project

Purpose To make a frequency distribution chart

Activity The letter "e" is said to be the most frequently used letter in the English language. Have students choose a paragraph from a newspaper or magazine and make a frequency distribution chart of each of the letters appearing in the paragraph. After the chart is complete, ask students to order the letters of the alphabet according to what they think might be the frequency of use of each letter.

> Four scor⊚ and s⊚v⊚n y⊚ars ago our
> fath⊚rs brought forth on this contin⊚nt
> a n⊚w nation, conc⊚iv⊚d in Lib⊚rty and
> d⊚dicat⊚d to th⊚ proposition that all
> m⊚n ar⊚ cr⊚at⊚d ⊚qual . . .

Random Sample   Math Lab

Purpose To use a random number table and take a sample

Materials Activity sheet (TRB p. 152)

Activity Have students look through their math book to find pages that have photographs of people. Explain that if we wanted to know the number of pages that have photographs of people, we could use a sample to make an estimate. Ask students if they think it would make a difference how a sample is chosen. Then have them complete the activity sheet.

Budget Graph   Project

Purpose To make a circle graph

Activity Have students make a circle graph to show the way they budget their money for a month. They should record their expenses and determine what percent of their monthly income is used for each item.

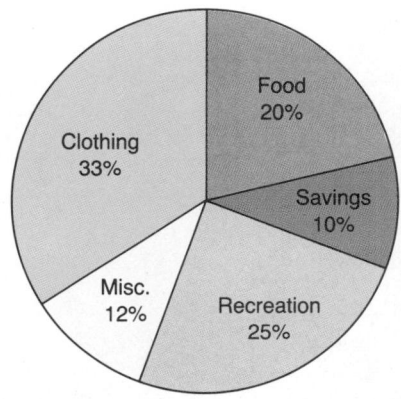

14

Probability, Statistics, and Graphs

The bald eagle was chosen as the national bird of the United States in 1782. The eagle has long been thought of as a symbol of strength and bravery.

In the wild, eagles generally live from 20 to 30 years. The nests of bald eagles are built near water in tall trees. Eagles first breed when they are about four years old. Bald eagles do not defend a large territory. There may be an average of three nests within 1.6 km of each other.

Bald eagles are not actually bald. Their heads are covered with white feathers. The length of bald eagles ranges from 76 cm to 89 cm. Their weights range from about 3.6 kg to 6 kg. Their wingspans measure from 1.8 m to 2.3 m.

At one time bald eagles were found throughout North America. Today there are less than 15,000 bald eagles in the United States, and all but about 5,000 of them are in Alaska. Federal laws and wildlife refuges now protect the bald eagle.

Introducing the Chapter

Discussion Give students an opportunity to read the article and enjoy the photographs. Discuss the data given in the article. Ask students questions such as, "What is the length of a bald eagle?" (The length ranges from 76 cm to 89 cm.) "What percent of the bald eagles in the United States are in Alaska?" (33%)

Use this as an opportunity for students to create their own problems based on the data in the article. As you teach the chapter, you may wish to refer to this page and ask students the following questions.

Follow-Up Questions

After Page 353 Display this frequency chart showing the age of eaglets when they leave the nest. Ask students to find the mode and the range of the ages. (mode: 83 days; range: 7 days)

Age in days	Number
78	2
80	4
82	4
83	5
85	3

After Page 355 Display this table. What is the median wingspan of the five birds? (1.9 m) What is the mean of the wingspans? (2.02 m) Which bird has a wingspan nearest the mean? (golden eagle)

Wingspan (m)	
Bald eagle	2.2
Golden eagle	1.9
Harpy eagle	1.8
Black vulture	1.4
California condor	2.7

Probability

Quick Review Conduct an oral drill on percents and decimals. Call out the percent and ask students to give the decimal.

| 41% | 0.41 | 30% | 0.3 | 6% | 0.06 |
| 150% | 1.5 | 12.5% | 0.125 | 17% | 0.17 |

Lesson Focus To identify outcomes of an experiment and tell whether or not the outcomes are equally likely

Suggested Materials Coin, cube (TRB p. 278)

Ideas for Getting Started

Print the letter A on three faces of the cube, print B on two faces of the cube, and print C on the remaining face. Show students the cube. Then ask "If I drop the cube on the floor, is it just as likely that A will be the letter on top as C?" (no) "Which letter is most likely to be on top?" (A) "Which letter is least likely to be on top?" (C)

Drop the cube several times and keep a tally of the results. Explain that the letters A, B, and C are the *outcomes*. A is the most likely outcome and B is the least likely.

Show students a coin. Then ask "If I toss the coin on the floor, what are the possible outcomes?" (heads, tails) "Is one of the outcomes more likely than the other?" (No, they are equally likely.)

Using Page 344

Lesson Development Have students read the material at the top of the page. Explain that tennis players often use the method of spinning a racket to see which player or team starts serving first. If possible, demonstrate this with a tennis racket. Stress that "up" and "down" are the only two outcomes and that they are *equally likely*. Give students the following intuitive explanation of equally likely outcomes: If you were to spin a racket 100 times, you would expect that the number of "up" spins would be about equal to the number of "down" spins.

Discuss the experiment with the tennis ball can. Point out that there are three outcomes and that in this case they are not equally likely.

Warm Up Discuss the four experiments in the Warm Up exercises. In exercise 4, the spinner landing on a line is not an outcome. If this were to happen, the person would spin again.

Equally Likely Outcomes

Before playing a game of tennis, Christy spun her tennis racquet to see who would serve first.

The letter U on the racquet handle could come "Up" or "Down." These are the only possible **outcomes**.

Each outcome is **equally likely** to happen.

If a tennis ball can were dropped, there would be three possible outcomes.

These three outcomes are **not equally likely**. The can is most likely to fall on the side.

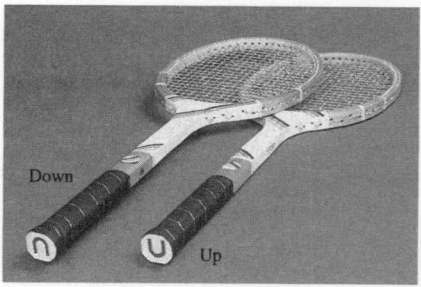

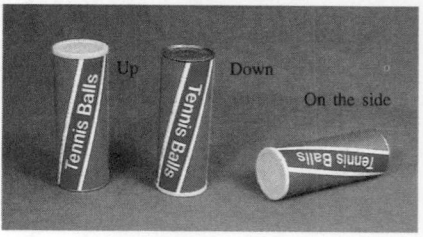

Warm Up

For each experiment, state if the outcomes are equally likely or not equally likely. If the outcomes are not equally likely, state which outcome is most likely.

1. Toss a coin.
Outcomes: Heads, Tails
equally likely

2. Roll a die.
Outcomes: 1,2,3,4,5,6
equally likely

3. Draw a ball from the box while blindfolded.
Outcomes:
Red ball,
Green ball,
Blue ball
equally
likely

4. Spin the spinner.
Outcomes: Yellow, Green not equally likely; yellow

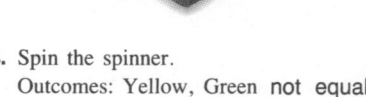

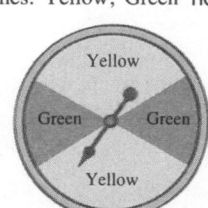

344

Follow Up

Reteaching

Place five squares of red paper and five squares of green paper in an envelope. Ask students to tell what they might expect to draw. (red square or green square) Explain that these draws are called possible outcomes. Then ask students whether the outcomes are equally likely if one square is removed. Vary the ratio of red squares to green squares and continue to ask if the outcomes are equally likely.

Enrichment

Have students choose about 100 telephone numbers at random from a directory and record the last digit of each number. Ask them to determine by the experiment if each of the ten digits (0, 1, 2, 3, 4, 5, 6, 7, 8, 9) is equally likely to occur.

Assignment Guide			
	Minimum	Average	Extended
page 345	1–9	1–12	1–12

List all of the possible outcomes for each experiment.
State if the outcomes are equally likely or not equally likely.

1. Spin the spinner. A, B, C, D; equally likely

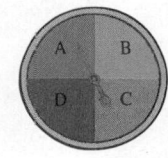

2. Draw a name from the hat while blindfolded.

Leo, Bess, Pam, Roy; equally likely

3. Spin the spinner. orange, blue, white; not equally likely

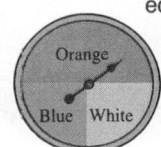

4. Roll a cube with faces lettered **A,B,C,D,E**, and **F**. A,B,C,D,E,F; equally likely

5. Drop a plastic cup on the floor. up, down, side; not equally likely

6. Drop a thumbtack on a hard floor. side, head; not equally likely

Write the number of possible outcomes for each experiment.
State if the outcomes are equally likely or not equally likely.

7. Spin the spinner. 3; not equally likely

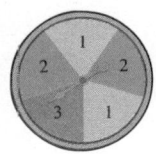

8. Spin the spinner. 5; equally likely

9. Guess the answer to a multiple-choice question. 4; equally likely

A 16.2   **B** 1.62
C 0.162   **D** not given

10. Pick one of the days of June without looking. 30; equally likely

11. Turn up a card from a deck of playing cards. 52; equally likely

12. Draw a door-prize ticket from tickets numbered 1 to 100. 100; equally likely

345

Using Page 345

Exercises 1–12 Several of these experiments could be used as activities for students. Have them perform an experiment and keep a tally of the number of times each outcome occurs.

In exercise 6, students may have difficulty deciding if the two possible outcomes are equally likely or not. For most thumbtacks the outcomes are not equally likely.

Ideas That Work

Math for the Gifted

In the Enrichment lesson on page 339, students learned about the hex numeration system. Briefly review with students the idea of grouping by sixteens. Then show them how to write a hex numeral for a base-ten numeral. Use the following examples.

$$83_{ten} \quad \frac{5}{16)\overline{83}} \quad \text{5 sixteens 3 ones} \rightarrow 53_{hex}$$
$$\frac{80}{3}$$

$$45_{ten} \quad \frac{2}{16)\overline{45}} \quad \text{2 sixteens 13 ones} \rightarrow 2D_{hex}$$
$$\frac{32}{13}$$

Have students find hex numerals for these base-ten numerals.

1. 37_{ten}
25_{hex}

2. 63_{ten}
$3F_{hex}$

3. 257_{ten}
101_{hex}

4. 100_{ten}
64_{hex}

5. 294_{ten}
126_{hex}

6. 450_{ten}
$1C2_{hex}$

Practice Supplement, page 128

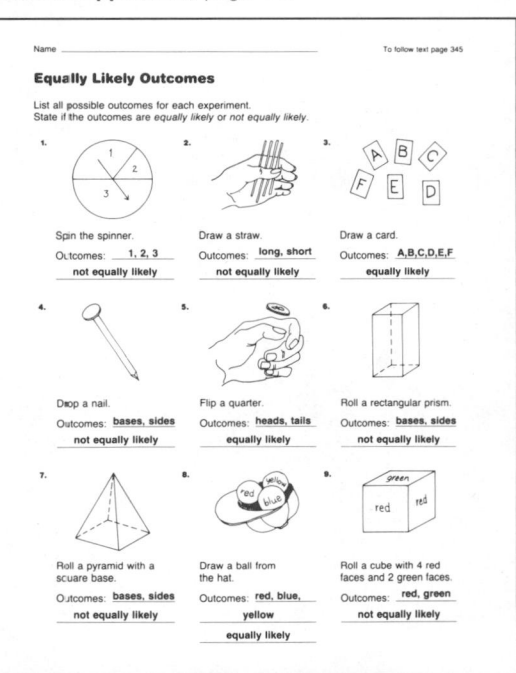

Quick Review Have students compare the fractions and write $>$, $<$, or $=$ for each $\bigcirc$.

$\frac{2}{3} \bigcirc \frac{1}{2}$ $\frac{7}{10} \bigcirc \frac{4}{5}$ $\frac{1}{4} \bigcirc \frac{1}{5}$ $\frac{3}{4} \bigcirc \frac{5}{8}$

$\frac{8}{12} \bigcirc \frac{2}{3}$ $\frac{5}{9} \bigcirc \frac{5}{6}$ $\frac{3}{5} \bigcirc \frac{9}{15}$

Lesson Focus To find the probability of an outcome

Ideas for Getting Started

Use questions like these to help students develop an intuitive understanding of the probabilities of an outcome.

"If you toss a coin several times, about what part of the tosses should result in tails?" $\left(\frac{1}{2}\right)$

"If you toss a number cube labeled 1 through 6, about what part of the tosses will result in 6?" $\left(\frac{1}{6}\right)$

"If you toss the same number cube, about what part of the tosses will be greater than 1?" $\left(\frac{5}{6}\right)$

Using Page 346

Lesson Development Read the material at the top of the page with students. Explain that "3 chances in 5" means that the probability is $\frac{3}{5}$. Point out that the denominator of a probability fraction of an event is the total number of equally likely outcomes. The numerator is the number of "favorable outcomes" in the event. Because there are 3 vocal records out of a total of 5 records, the probability of choosing a vocal recording is $\frac{3}{5}$.

Be sure that students understand the meaning of the probabilities 0 and 1. Use the example of a number cube labeled 1 through 6 and ask students these questions. "What is the probability of getting an 8?" (0) "What is the probability of getting a number greater than 0 and less than 10?" (1)

Warm Up Use these exercises as an oral class activity. Point out the notation used for the probability of an event.

Chance and Probability

Sid has a stack of 5 records. There are vocal recordings (V) on 3 records and there is band music (B) on 2 records. Sid chose a record without looking and put it on the record player. What is the probability that it is a vocal recording?

Each of the 5 records is equally likely to be chosen.

There are **3 chances in 5** that Sid chose a vocal recording.

The **probability** that it is a vocal recording is $\frac{3}{5}$.

We write: $P(\text{V}) = \dfrac{3}{5}$ ← Vocal records
                                    ← Total records

There are **2** chances in **5** that Sid chose a band record.

The probability of it being a band record is $\frac{2}{5}$.

         $P(\text{B}) = \dfrac{2}{5}$ ← Band records
                            ← Total records

If an **outcome** cannot occur, its probability is 0.

    $P(\text{jazz record}) = \dfrac{0}{5}$ ← Jazz records
                                     ← Total records

If an **outcome** is certain, its probability is 1.

$P(\text{non-jazz record}) = \dfrac{5}{5}$ ← Non-jazz records
                                             ← Total records

Warm Up

Give the missing numbers. Then give the probability.

1. Toss a coin. There is 1 chance in ▦ it will be heads.   2
$P(\text{heads}) = ▦$ $\frac{1}{2}$

2. Spin the spinner. There are 2 chances in ▦ it will be even.   5
$P(\text{even number}) = ▦$ $\frac{2}{5}$

346

Follow Up

Reteaching

Write the numbers 1 through 10 on slips of paper. Ask students what number they might expect to draw. "Are all numbers equally likely to be drawn?" (yes) "How many numbers, or outcomes, are there?" (10) Explain that since there is 1 chance in 10 that a 3 is drawn, the probability of choosing a 3 is 1 of 10.

Write the notation for probability on the chalkboard: $P(3) = \frac{1}{10}$. Elicit from students that the numerator tells the number of 3s in the group, and the 10 tells the number of equally likely outcomes.

Enrichment

Design a spinner which has several outcomes that are not equally likely. Have students spin the spinner many times and record the outcomes. Ask students to use the results of the experiment and estimate the probability of each outcome.

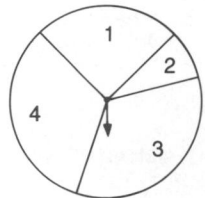

Give each probability for a spinner with the numbers **1**, **2**, **3**, **4**, **5**, **6**, **7**, and **8**.

1. $P(2)$ $\frac{1}{8}$ **2.** $P(6)$ $\frac{1}{8}$

3. $P(4)$ $\frac{1}{8}$ **4.** $P(\text{an odd number})$ $\frac{4}{8}$ or $\frac{1}{2}$

5. $P(\text{a number less than 6})$ $\frac{5}{8}$ **6.** $P(\text{a prime number})$ $\frac{4}{8}$ or $\frac{1}{2}$

7. $P(\text{a number greater than 10})$ 0   **8.** $P(\text{a number less than 8})$ $\frac{7}{8}$

9. $P(\text{a number less than 1})$ 0   **10.** $P(\text{a number less than 3})$ $\frac{2}{8}$ or $\frac{1}{4}$

Give each probability for a die with the numbers **1**, **2**, **3**, **4**, **5**, and **6**.

11. $P(4)$ $\frac{1}{6}$ **12.** $P(1)$ $\frac{1}{6}$

13. $P(7)$ 0   **14.** $P(\text{a number greater than 4})$ $\frac{2}{6}$ or $\frac{1}{3}$

15. $P(\text{a number less than 1})$ 0   **16.** $P(\text{a prime number})$ $\frac{3}{6}$ or $\frac{1}{2}$

17. $P(2)$ $\frac{1}{6}$ **18.** $P(\text{a number less than 7})$ 1

19. Laurie put a record on the stereo without looking to see if it was side 1 or side 2. What is $P(\text{side 2})$? $\frac{1}{2}$

20. Yuki has 3 classical records, 4 jazz records, and 1 rock'n'roll record. What kind of record has a probability of $\frac{1}{2}$ of being selected? jazz record

21. Write and solve a word problem for this data. $P(\text{an outcome}) = \frac{4}{9}$

22. **DATA HUNT** Toss a coin 100 times. Keep a tally of the results. Find $P(\text{heads})$. Is it about $\frac{1}{2}$?

SKILLKEEPER

Find the volume of each prism. Use $V = lwh$.

1. $l = 7$ m   **2.** $l = 25$ cm   **3.** $l = 15$ cm   **4.** $l = 13$ m   **5.** $l = 7$ m
$w = 4.5$ m $w = 20$ cm $w = 12$ cm $w = 9.5$ m $w = 4.5$ m
$h = 9$ m $h = 30$ cm $h = 20$ cm $h = 4$ m $h = 9$ m
283.5 m³   15,000 cm³   3,600 cm³   494 m³   283.5 m³

Find the volume of each prism. Use $V = Bh$.

6. $B = 42$ m²   **7.** $B = 135.9$ cm²   **8.** $B = 150$ m²   **9.** $B = 12$ m²   **10.** $B = 1,959$ cm²
$h = 1.5$ m $h = 9.5$ cm $h = 4$ m $h = 9$ m $h = 14$ cm
63 m³   1,291.05 cm³   600 m³   108 m³   27,426 cm³

Using Page 347

Exercises 1–18 Students may need some help with these exercises because of difficulty with the concept or the notation for probability. To help students arrive at the answer for exercise 6, ask these questions.

"What is the total number of possible outcomes?" (8)

"Is each outcome equally likely?" (yes)

"Which numbers on the spinner are prime numbers?" (2, 3, 5, 7)

"What is the ratio of prime numbers to all the numbers?" ($\frac{4}{8}$ or $\frac{1}{2}$)

Data Hunt Have students work in pairs or small groups. Post the results of the experiments on the chalkboard or bulletin board. You may wish to combine all the results and find the experimental ratio, number of heads to total number of tosses.

Skillkeeper These skills were originally taught in Chapter 10.

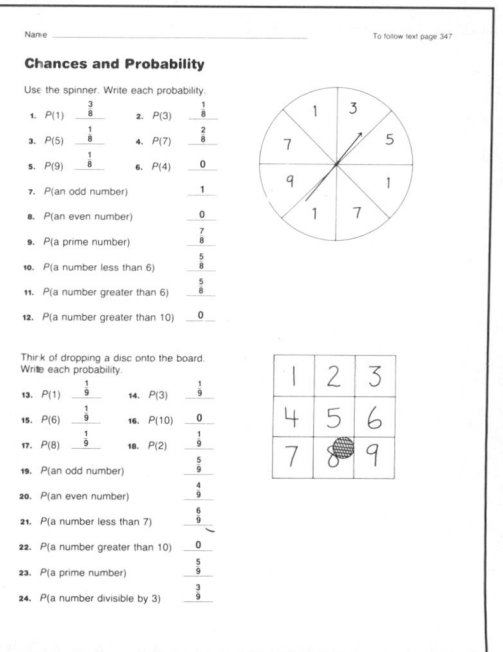

Reteaching Supplement, page 97

Chance and Probability

Spin the spinner.

Chance		Probability
There are 3 chances in 8 of stopping on red.	→	Probability of red = $\frac{3}{8}$ $P(\text{red}) = \frac{3}{8}$
There are 2 chances in 8 of stopping on green.	→	$P(\text{green}) = \frac{2}{8} = \frac{1}{4}$
There are 0 chances in 8 of stopping on yellow.	→	$P(\text{yellow}) = \frac{0}{8} = 0$

Write each probability.

One of these names is to be drawn from a hat.

Mary | Jenny | Bob | Marilyn | Bill | Jack | Jerry | Tina | Connie | Joe

1. $P(\text{3-letter name}) = \frac{3}{10}$

2. $P(\text{4-letter name}) = \frac{4}{10} = \frac{2}{5}$ **3.** $P(\text{name starting with B}) = \frac{2}{10} = \frac{1}{5}$

4. $P(\text{name starting with T}) = \frac{1}{10}$ **5.** $P(\text{7-letter name}) = \frac{1}{10}$

6. $P(\text{name starting with S}) = \frac{0}{10}$ **7.** $P(\text{name ending with Y}) = \frac{3}{10}$

One of these cards will be drawn without looking.

10 | 4 | 7 | J | S | 9 | 10 | 2 | M | 5 | 4 | J

8. $P(2) = \frac{1}{12}$

9. $P(5) = \frac{1}{12}$ **10.** $P(J) = \frac{2}{12} = \frac{1}{6}$ **11.** $P(\text{a number}) = \frac{8}{12} = \frac{2}{3}$

12. $P(4) = \frac{2}{12} = \frac{1}{6}$ **13.** $P(T) = \frac{0}{12}$ **14.** $P(\text{a letter}) = \frac{4}{12} = \frac{1}{3}$

Enrichment Supplement, page 97

Sampling and Prediction

What is the most common word length in the first passage of The Declaration of Independence? To predict the answer to this question, you can count the number of letters in each word of a sample.

The Declaration of Independence

Lines
1   When in the Course of human events, it becomes
2   necessary for one people to dissolve the political
3   bands which have connected them with another, and
4   to assume among the powers of the earth, the separate
5   and equal station to which the Laws of Nature and
6   of Nature's God entitle them, a decent respect to
7   the opinions of mankind requires that they should
8   declare the causes which impel them to the separation.

To collect a sample, select one line and count the letters in each word in the line. Record the number of one-letter words, two-letter words, and so on. Do the same for a three-line sample and a five-line sample.

Word length (number of letters)	1	2	3	4	5	6	7	8	9	10
One-line sample (line 1)	0	3	1	1	2	1	0	0	0	
Three-line sample (lines 1, 3, and 5)	0	5	5	5	3	3	0	1	0	
Five-line sample (lines 1, 2, 3, 5, and 7)	0	7	9	7	5	5	4	3	3	0

1. What would you predict the most common word length to be based on the one-line sample? 2 letters three-line sample? 2, 3, 4, or 5 letters

five-line sample? 3 letters

2. Which sample do you think is the most accurate prediction? the five-line sample

Why? because the sample is the largest of the three

3. Now find the number of letters in every word in the given passage.

Word length	1	2	3	4	5	6	7	8	9	10
Entire passage	1	12	15	9	9	9	8	4	3	1

Was the five-line sample an accurate prediction? yes

Practice Supplement, page 129

Chances and Probability

Use the spinner. Write each probability.

1. $P(1)$ $\frac{1}{8}$ **2.** $P(3)$ $\frac{1}{8}$

3. $P(5)$ $\frac{1}{8}$ **4.** $P(7)$ $\frac{1}{8}$

5. $P(9)$ $\frac{1}{8}$ **6.** $P(4)$ $\frac{0}{8}$

7. $P(\text{an odd number})$ $\frac{1}{1}$

8. $P(\text{an even number})$ $\frac{0}{1}$

9. $P(\text{a prime number})$ $\frac{7}{8}$

10. $P(\text{a number less than 6})$ $\frac{5}{8}$

11. $P(\text{a number greater than 6})$ $\frac{5}{8}$

12. $P(\text{a number greater than 10})$ 0

Think of dropping a disc onto the board. Write each probability.

13. $P(1)$ $\frac{1}{9}$ **14.** $P(3)$ $\frac{1}{9}$

15. $P(6)$ $\frac{1}{9}$ **16.** $P(10)$ 0

17. $P(8)$ $\frac{1}{9}$ **18.** $P(2)$ $\frac{1}{9}$

19. $P(\text{an odd number})$ $\frac{5}{9}$

20. $P(\text{an even number})$ $\frac{4}{9}$

21. $P(\text{a number less than 7})$ $\frac{6}{9}$

22. $P(\text{a number greater than 10})$ 0

23. $P(\text{a prime number})$ $\frac{5}{9}$

24. $P(\text{a number divisible by 3})$ $\frac{3}{9}$

1	2	3
4	5	6
7	8	9

Quick Review Have students write expressions, choose a value for each variable, and evaluate the expressions.

8 more than a number x   x + 8   a number y decreased by 5   y – 5

10 times a number w   10w   a number a divided by 2 $\frac{a}{2}$

Lesson Focus To find the probability of an event when the outcomes are ordered pairs of numbers

Suggested Materials Two dice of different colors

Ideas for Getting Started

Show students the dice. Toss the dice and record the outcomes and sum. If one die lands on 3 and the other on 5, write 3, 5, and 8 on the chalkboard. Ask students "How many other ways could the dice show a sum of 8?" (4) Make a chart to show the ways.

Red	Green	Sum
3	5	8
4	4	8
2	6	8
5	3	8
6	2	8

Repeat the activity with other numbers. Students should find that there is only one way to obtain a sum of 2 or 12.

Using Page 348

Lesson Development After students read the material at the top of the page, draw a 6 by 6 grid on the chalkboard. Explain how each dot represents an ordered pair of numbers that shows the outcome for a toss of the dice.

Have students come to the chalkboard and identify points on the grid that show a certain sum of the numbers on the dice. For example, the pairs (6,3), (5,4), (4,5), and (3,6) show a sum of 9. Since 4 of the outcomes have a sum of 9, there are 4 chances in 36 of rolling a sum of 9. The probability is $\frac{1}{9}$.

Other Examples For each of the examples, have students identify the dots on the grid and name the possible outcomes.

Ordered Pairs in Probability

Using a red die and a green die from a game of backgammon, what is the probability of rolling a sum of 10?

Each outcome is an **ordered pair** of numbers: the number on the red die first and the number on the green die second.

We must find the total number of outcomes *and* the number of outcomes which have a sum of 10.

The grid shows there are 36 ordered-pair outcomes.

Only 3 of the outcomes have a sum of 10.

$$P(\text{sum of } 10) = \frac{3}{36} = \frac{1}{12}$$

There are 3 chances in 36 or 1 chance in 12 of rolling a sum of 10. The probability is $\frac{1}{12}$.

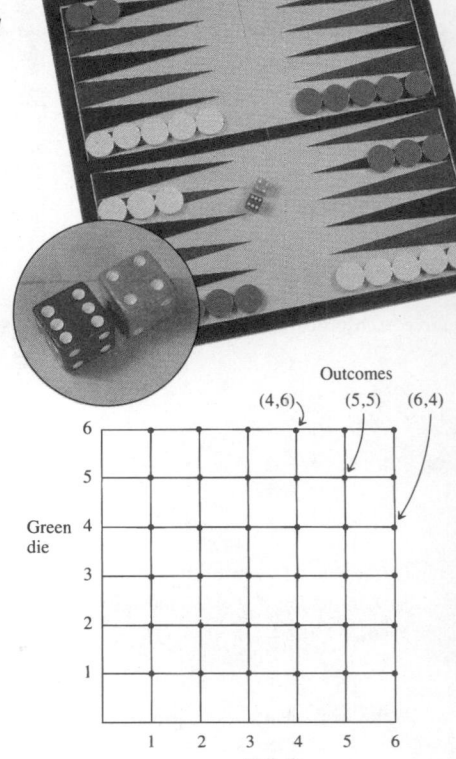

Outcomes
(4,6) (5,5) (6,4)

Green die (vertical axis), Red die (horizontal axis)

Other Examples

$P(2,4) = \frac{1}{36}$ $P(\text{sum of } 11) = \frac{2}{36} = \frac{1}{18}$ $P(\text{sum} < 5) = \frac{6}{36} = \frac{1}{6}$

The outcomes are **(5,6)** and **(6,5)**.

The outcomes are **(1,1),(1,2),(2,1), (3,1),(2,2),(1,3)**.

Warm Up

1. Use the grid above and list the ordered pairs that have a sum of 4. What is $P(\text{sum of } 4)$? (3,1), (2,2), (1,3); $\frac{1}{12}$

2. Use the grid above and list the ordered pairs that have a sum of 9. What is $P(\text{sum of } 9)$? (6,3), (3,6), (5,4), (4,5); $\frac{1}{9}$

3. $P(\text{sum of } 8)$ $\frac{5}{36}$

4. $P(\text{sum of } 7)$ $\frac{1}{6}$

5. $P(\text{sum of } 6)$ $\frac{5}{36}$

6. $P(\text{sum} > 10)$ $\frac{1}{12}$

7. $P(1,1)$ $\frac{1}{36}$

8. $P(\text{sum} < 7)$ $\frac{5}{12}$

348

Follow Up

Reteaching

Have students perform the two experiments described on page 349. Assist them in devising a system for recording their data so that it can be analyzed after the desired number of trials. Have them compare their results to the probability of each outcome.

Enrichment

Tell students that the slips of paper labeled as shown are placed in a hat. Have them give each probability below if one slip is drawn.

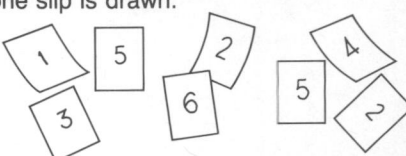

1   5   2   4
3   6   5   2

1. P(2) $\frac{1}{4}$

2. P(6) $\frac{1}{8}$

3. P(not 5) $\frac{3}{4}$

4. P(7) **0**

5. P(even number) $\frac{1}{2}$

6. P(1 or 2) $\frac{3}{8}$

7. P(2 or 5) $\frac{1}{2}$

8. P(not prime) $\frac{3}{8}$

9. P(factor of 8) $\frac{1}{2}$

10. P(6 or 8) $\frac{1}{8}$

Assignment Guide			
	Minimum	Average	Extended
page 349	1–7	1–10, TM	1–10, TM

Give each probability for tossing a penny and a nickel.

1. List the possible outcomes as ordered pairs. How many outcomes are possible? (H,H),(H,T),(T,H),(T,T); 4

2. What is P(H,T)? $\frac{1}{4}$

3. What is P(H,H)? $\frac{1}{4}$

4. What is P(T,T)? $\frac{1}{4}$

5. Which probability is greater, that both coins will be the same or that they will be different? Neither, the probabilities are the same.

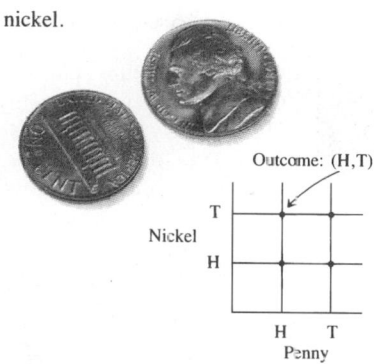

Give each probability for a coin with heads (H) and tails (T) and a spinner with the numbers **1, 2, 3, 4,** and **5.**

6. List the possible outcomes as ordered pairs. How many outcomes are possible? (H,1),(H,2),(H,3),(H,4),(H,5), (T,1),(T,2),(T,3),(T,4),(T,5); 10

7. What is P(T,5)? $\frac{1}{10}$

8. What is the probability of getting heads and a number greater than 3? $\frac{1}{5}$

9. What is the probability of getting tails and an odd number? $\frac{3}{10}$

10. What is the probability of getting heads and an even number? $\frac{1}{5}$

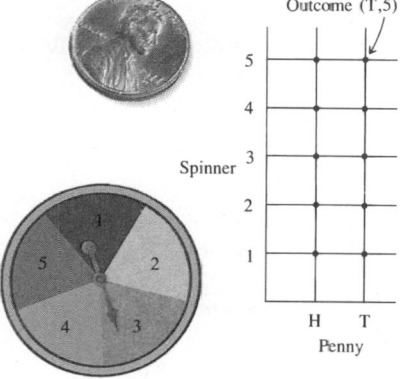

THINK MATH

Estimating Probability

Can you estimate how many times out of 25 you would get 3 heads if you tossed 3 coins at once? Make an estimate. Then try the experiment and record the results. See teaching notes.

Tally Sheet

3H	2H,1T	1H,2T	3T
I	III	IIII	II

349

Using Page 349

Exercises 1–10 Be sure that students understand the notation used for outcomes and for probability. Before assigning these exercises, you may need to discuss this notation.

Think Math This problem involves estimating and determining probability by experimental methods. Most students will not be able to make a close estimate of the number of times the 3 coins will come up heads. The theoretical probability is $\frac{1}{8}$. In 25 tosses of 3 coins, we should find that we get 3 heads about 3 times. Help students understand the probability of $\frac{1}{8}$ by listing the 8 different and equally likely outcomes.

1st coin	2nd coin	3rd coin
H	H	H
H	H	T
H	T	H
T	H	H
H	T	T
T	H	T
T	T	H
T	T	T

Reteaching Supplement, page 98

Enrichment Supplement, page 98

Practice Supplement, page 130

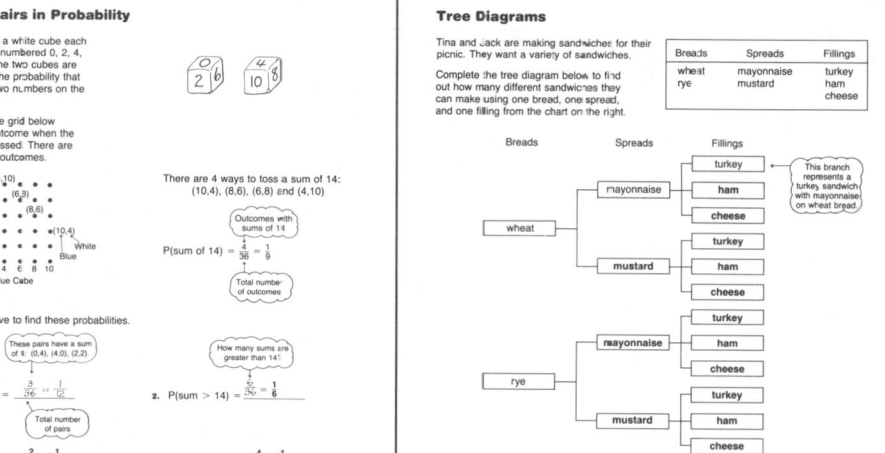

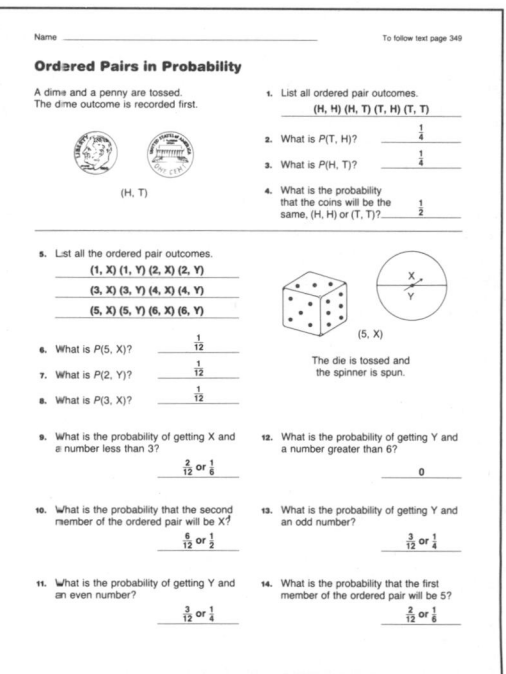

Lesson Focus To solve word problems related to probability experiments

Suggested Materials Coin, die

Ideas for Getting Started

Show students a coin. Ask "What is the probability of getting heads when the coin is tossed?" ($\frac{1}{2}$) "If the coin is tossed 50 times, about how many times should we expect to get heads?" (25) "Do you think we would get heads exactly 25 times?" (no)

Show students the die. Ask "What is the probability of rolling a 6 with the die?" ($\frac{1}{6}$) "If we roll the die 30 times, about how many times should we get 6? (5) "Do you think we would get 6 exactly 5 times?" (no)

Using Page 350

Lesson Development Have students read the problem at the top of the page. Ask them to identify the question and the data in the problem. Point out that to find the expected number of rainy days, we write the percent as a fraction and multiply. Explain that probabilities are often expressed as percents and that when computing with probability, either the fraction or decimal form is used.

Emphasize that expected results may be quite different from the actual results.

Exercises 1–6 You may wish to work through one or more of these problems on the chalkboard as a class activity.

PROBLEM SOLVING: Practice

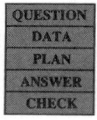

Weather records for New York City show that the probability of rain on any day in June is $33\frac{1}{3}$% or $\frac{1}{3}$. About how many rainy days can be expected in New York City during the month of June?

There are 30 days in June. Since $P(\text{rain}) = 33\frac{1}{3}$% or $\frac{1}{3}$, this means that 1 day in every 3 days is expected to be a rainy day.

Expected rainy days = $P(\textbf{rain}) \times$ **number of days**
$$= \frac{1}{3} \times 30 = 10$$

About 10 rainy days are expected in June.

Remember, if 10 rainy days are expected, this does not mean that 10 rainy days will occur. There may be more or less than 10 rainy days.

Solve.

1. A meteorologist said the probability of snow in the mountains on any of the next 30 days was 30%. How many snowy days were expected? **9**

2. The probability of a cloudy day in Phoenix, Arizona is about 14%. About how many cloudy days are expected in Phoenix during the year? About how many non-cloudy days a year are expected? **51; 314**

3. An air traffic controller knew that the probability of a clear day in Juneau, Alaska is 32%. About how many clear days a year are expected in Juneau? **about 117**

4. A travel agent read that the probability of rain for any day of the year in San Juan, Puerto Rico is about 55%. About how many rainy days a year are expected in San Juan? **201**

5. Weather records in Reno, Nevada show that there was rainfall on 51 days out of 365 days over a period of several years. What is the probability of rainfall in Reno? Write the probability as a percent to the nearest whole percent. **14%**

6. The probability of rainfall in Los Angeles for any day in a year is about 9%. How many days with rainfall would be expected in Los Angeles during a year? **33**

350

Follow Up

Reteaching

Ask students to make a prediction about which sum is most likely to occur when two dice are rolled. Have students roll the dice 50 times, recording the sum each time. Then have students compare their predictions with the actual outcomes.

Enrichment

Have students give the probability of the following situations.

1. Getting an even product when multiplying an even number by an odd number. (1)

2. Getting an even product when multiplying two odd numbers. (0)

3. Getting an even sum when adding two odd numbers. (1)

4. Getting an even sum when adding an even number and an odd number. (0)

5. Getting an odd product when multiplying an even number of odd numbers. (1)

10. If Danielle tosses a penny and a nickel 20 times, about how many times should both coins be expected to come up heads? Hint: What is $P(H,H)$ when two coins are tossed? **5**

11. Luis tossed two coins 100 times. He got an outcome of "one head, one tail" 57 times. How close was this to the expected number of outcomes? **7 more than expected**

12. Holly made two spinners like the ones below. She spun both spinners and recorded the pairs of letters for an outcome. About how many times should the outcome (B,B) be expected in 60 trials? **5**

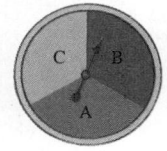 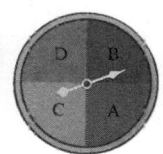

13. The probability of guessing the correct answer on a true-false test without reading the question is $\frac{1}{2}$. On a true-false test with 40 questions, students must answer 28 questions correctly to pass the test. About how many questions might a student who guesses without reading the questions get right? Would this be a passing score? **20; no**

7. Milly tossed a coin 150 times and kept a tally of the heads and tails. About how many times should heads be expected to come up? **75**

8. Fayetta plans to toss a die with numbers from one to six 30 times and to keep a tally of the outcomes. About how many times can she expect to get an outcome of 5? **5**

9. Casey tossed a pair of dice 180 times. About how many times did he get a sum of 7? Hint: What is P(sum of 7) with two dice? **30**

14. Try This Tim, Ada, Carol, and Betsy each used a different coin for a probability experiment. They used a penny, a nickel, a dime, and a quarter. Ada's coin had Lincoln's face on the heads side. Carol did not use a quarter. Betsy's coin had Monticello on the tails side. Which coin did each person use? **Tim, quarter; Ada, penny; Carol, dime; Betsy, nickel**

351

Using Page 351

Exercises 7–13 Several of these problems involve two steps. First, the probability must be found and then the expected number of occurrences is computed.

Try This A possible strategy, Use Logical Reasoning, was taught on page 242.

Discussion Have students read the problem and restate the question in their own words. Explain to students that a chart can help us organize the data and think logically about the problem.

Display the following chart on the chalkboard. Ask students to give the data in the problem. Show them how the data can be recorded in the chart and used to eliminate possibilities. For example, since Ada's coin had Lincoln's face on the head's side, Ada has a penny and the data is recorded as follows:

	Tim	Ada	Carol	Betsy
Penny	no	yes	no	no
Nickel		no		
Dime		no		
Quarter		no		

Help students record the rest of the data in the chart. Note that Monticello is on the tail's side of a nickel.

Solution Ada has the penny, Betsy has the nickel, Carol has the dime, and Tim has the quarter.

Ideas That Work

Chalk It up

Display the following on the chalkboard. Have the students place operation signs $+$, $-$, $\times$, or $\div$, between the sixes so that each equation will be correct. Use parentheses where necessary. Answers may vary.

1. $(6 + 6) \div 6 + 6 = 8$
2. $(6 + 6) + (6 \div 6) = 13$
3. $(6 \times 6) \times 6 - 6 = 210$
4. $(6 \times 6) + 6 + 6 = 48$
5. $(6 \div 6) \times (6 \div 6) = 1$
6. $(6 + 6 + 6) \div 6 = 3$

Practice Supplement, page 131

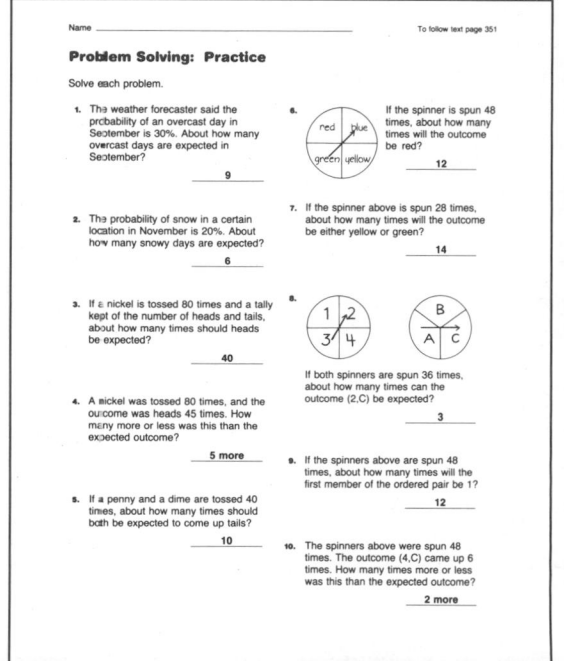

Quick Review Have students give the missing numbers.
200 mg = <u>0.2</u> g   0.5 kg = <u>500</u> g   0.4 g = <u>400</u> mg
575 g = <u>0.575</u> kg   7 g = <u>7,000</u> mg

Lesson Focus To find the frequency, range, and mode of a set of data

Ideas for Getting Started

Write this set of data on the chalkboard.

Kilometers driven per day			
25	40	23	32
15	27	25	29
23	25	20	25

Ask students to describe the data. Encourage them to identify such things as the largest number, the smallest number, and the number that occurs most often.

Using Page 352

Lesson Development Have students read the material in the middle of the page and study the chart. Then ask these questions about the data in the chart. "What is the age of the youngest part-time employee?" (16 years) "What is the age of the oldest part-time employee?" (23 years) "How many part-time employees are there?" (50) "Which age group in the chart has the greatest number?" (17 years)

Emphasize that the *mode* is the most frequently occurring number in the set, and the *range* is the difference between the largest number and the smallest number in the data.

Warm Up Use these exercises as an oral class activity. Notice with students that in exercise 2 there are two modes.

Frequency, Range, and Mode

The city of Bridgeport has some young people working part time.

The employment manager made this **frequency chart** to show the number of people of each age that work for the city.

The **mode** is the age that occurs most often. Twelve people are 17 years old. The mode of the ages is 17 years. Some data may have more than one mode.

The ages of the part-time employees are listed from 16 years to 23 years. The **range** is the difference between the greatest number of years and the least number of years.

Range = **23 − 16 = 7**

The range of ages is 7 years.

Part-time Employees	
Age in years	Number
16	6
17	12
18	10
19	7
20	5
21	4
22	3
23	3
	Total 50

Warm Up

1. What is the mode of this list of ages of senior citizens? What is the range?

   72, 74, 74, 78, 78, 78,
   83, 85, 85, 90, 92, 96 78; 24

2. This list of ages has more than one mode. What are the modes? What is the range?

   68, 70, 72, 80, 82, 82, 82, 82, 85,
   87, 87, 87, 87, 93, 94, 94, 96, 98
   82, 87; 30

352

Follow Up

Reteaching

Have students organize this data in a frequency chart. Then have them give the range and mode. (range: 7, mode: 1)

Number of Brothers and Sisters				
0	2	2	4	2
1	1	0	3	7
3	1	1	0	1
5	2	1	1	2

Enrichment

Have students choose a topic and make a survey of students in the school. Results should be recorded in a frequency chart and the range and mode determined. Possible topics include:

- How many hours a day do you watch TV?
- How long does it take to get to school?
- How many letters are in your last name?
- How many hours a week do you exercise?

Assignment Guide			
	Minimum	Average	Extended
page 353	1–9, SK	1–9, SK	1–10, SK

Use the frequency chart at the right to answer questions 1–5.

1. How many people worked 15 h per week? 11

2. What is the mode of the hours worked per week? 10

3. What is the range of hours worked per week? 12

4. How many employees are shown in the frequency chart? 61

Hours Worked by Part-time Employees

Hours worked per week	Number of employees
3	1
5	4
6	5
8	10
10	16
12	14
15	11

5. Which group worked the greatest total number of hours during the week, the 14 employees who worked 12 h each or the 11 employees who worked 15 h each? 14 who worked 12 h each

Use the frequency chart at the right to answer questions 6–10.

6. How many employees earned $45 a week? 9

7. How many people earned $20 per week? 5

8. What is the mode of the earnings? $30

9. What is the range of the earnings? $35

10. What are the total earnings of the 50 employees? $1,479

Earnings per Week by Part-time Employees

Earnings per week	Number of employees
$10	2
$15	4
$20	5
$24	8
$30	15
$36	7
$45	9

---SKILLKEEPER---

Give each probability for tossing a die with numbers from **1** to **6**.

1. $P(5)$ $\frac{1}{6}$ 2. $P(2)$ $\frac{1}{6}$ 3. $P(7)$ 0   4. $P(6)$ $\frac{1}{6}$ 5. $P(4)$ $\frac{1}{6}$

6. P(a number less than 4) $\frac{1}{2}$ 7. P(a number greater than 5) $\frac{1}{6}$

8. P(an odd number) $\frac{1}{2}$ 9. P(an even number) $\frac{1}{2}$

10. P(a prime number) $\frac{1}{2}$ 11. P(a number less than 6) $\frac{5}{6}$

More Practice, page 438, Set A

Using Page 353

Exercises 1–10 Students will need to use data from the tables for these exercises. A calculator is recommended for exercise 10, although the exercise may be answered by using paper and pencil.

Skillkeeper This Skillkeeper reviews material taught in this chapter.

More Practice, page 438, Set A

Ideas That Work

Special Education

The topics of frequency, range, mode, mean, and median introduced in this and following lessons can form the basis for a project. Have students select a research topic with an outcome that can be tallied in a frequency chart. The topic might be one where students conduct interviews or one where they obtain data from reference materials.

Some topics include points scored in a season by a particular player, inches of snow (or rain) your locale has had each year for the past 40 years, or the class sizes in your school for the past 10 years. When the data has been collected, students should write up their findings and present graphs displaying the data they found.

Prior to the start of the project, discuss with students the differences in using each type of graph and measure of central tendency (mean, median, mode). Help students understand that certain situations may be best described by one type of situation rather than another. For example, if a situation has an outcome of "yes" or "no," the mean offers little information while the mode will describe the results.

Practice Supplement, page 132

Name _____   To follow text page 353

Frequency, Range, and Mode

Use the frequency chart to answer each question.

Test Scores

Score	Number of People
98	3
92	5
85	11
80	12
77	10
72	6
68	4

1. How many people scored 80? 12

2. How many people scored 68? 4

3. What is the mode of the scores? 80

4. What is the range of the scores? 30

5. How many people's scores are given on the frequency chart? 51

Use the frequency chart to answer each question.

Amount Saved per Week

Amount per Week	Number of People
$2	5
$5	11
$10	15
$15	8
$20	4
$30	2
$50	1

6. How many people saved $50 per week? 1

7. How many people saved $2 per week? 5

8. What is the mode of the amount saved per week? $10

9. What is the range of the amount saved per week? $48

10. Which amount is saved least frequently? $50

Quick Review Have students subtract and write answers in lowest terms.

$15 - 6\frac{2}{3}$ $8\frac{1}{3}$ $36\frac{1}{4} - 18\frac{1}{2}$ $17\frac{3}{4}$

$10\frac{5}{8} - 4\frac{7}{8}$ $5\frac{3}{4}$ $42\frac{1}{2} - 21\frac{5}{9}$ $20\frac{17}{18}$

Lesson Focus To find the arithmetic mean and median of a set of data

Ideas for Getting Started

Write these test scores on the chalkboard: 96, 92, 90, 88, 84, 80, 80. Ask students to give the range of scores and the mode (16, 80). Review how to find the average. Then ask students to find the average of these scores. (87.14)

Test Scores
96
92
90
88
84
80
80

Ask students to name the middle score. (88) Point out that it is not necessarily the same as the average score.

Using Page 354

Lesson Development Have students read the material at the top of the page and examine the chart. Finding the average of a list of numbers is a review but the alternate name, *arithmetic mean,* is a new term.

Discuss the meaning of *median* as the middle number of a list that is arranged in order of size. Direct students' attention to the example of the list with six numbers. Since there is not one middle number, the average of the two middle numbers is the median.

Exercises 1–8 Assign these exercises as independent written work.

Arithmetic Mean and Median

Freshwater fish are a valuable food source and are also caught for recreational sport.

The table shows the adult length of some common freshwater fish.

The **arithmetic mean** or **average** of the lengths of the 5 fish is the sum of their lengths divided by the number of fish.

Freshwater Fish Adult length (cm)	
Catfish	75
Walleye	66
Bass	50
Yellow perch	30
Bluegill	20

Sum = **75 + 66 + 50 + 30 + 20 = 241**

Arithmetic mean = **241 ÷ 5 = 48.2**

The average length is 48.2 cm.

The **median** is the middle number in a list of numbers given in order.

Median length = **50 cm**

When there are two middle numbers, find the mean of those middle numbers.

22, 23, 25, 28, 33, 37

middle numbers

Median = $\frac{25 + 28}{2} = \frac{53}{2} = 26.5$

Find the arithmetic mean and median of each list of numbers.

1. 18		**2.** 30		**3.** 93		**4.** 1.8	
28		30		104		2.7	
41 29; 28		40		109		4.5 3; 2.7	
		80 45; 35		110 104; 106.5			

Find the arithmetic mean and median of each list of numbers. Round to the nearest tenth if necessary.

5. 78, 78, 82, 88, 90 83.2; 82   **6.** 22, 23, 28, 31, 35, 37 29.3; 29.5   **7.** 7, 29, 18, 11, 16, 20, 14 16.4; 16   **8.** 320, 195, 222, 307 261; 264.5

354   More Practice, page 438, Set B

Follow Up

Reteaching

Display these steps on the chalkboard and have students follow them to find the median and the mean of each list of numbers below.

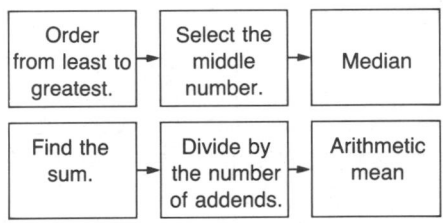

1. 55, 60, 57, 68, 47 **57, 57.4**
2. 29, 19, 30, 27, 18, 30, 22 **27, 25**
3. 17.9, 15.2, 22.4 **17.9, 18.5**

Enrichment

Have students use data from the last five school days to determine the arithmetic mean and median for class attendance, temperature, or other topics they may choose.

Assignment Guide			
	Minimum	Average	Extended
page 354	1–8	1–8	1–8
page 355	1–8	1–10	1–11

PROBLEM SOLVING: Using Data from a Table

QUESTION
DATA
PLAN
ANSWER
CHECK

Solve. Use the table of tropical fish for exercises 1–4.

1. List the lengths of the fish in the table from greatest to least. 18, 15, 13, 11, 10, 5, 5

2. What is the median length of the seven fish? Which fish has the median length? 11 cm; flamefish

3. What is the arithmetic mean of the lengths of the fish? 11 cm

4. Which fish is nearest the mean length? How much more or less than the mean length is it? flamefish; same

Use the table of freshwater fish for exercises 5–9.

5. List the lengths of the eight freshwater fish in order from greatest to least. What are the two middle lengths? 250, 140, 130, 125, 110, 100, 65, 30; 125 cm, 110 cm

6. What is the median length of the freshwater fish? 117.5 cm

7. What is the arithmetic mean (to the nearest tenth) of the lengths of the fish? 118.8 cm

8. Which fish is nearest the mean length? How much more or less than the mean length is it? inconnu; 6.2 cm more

9. How many adult sunfish would it take to have a total length equal to the length of an alligator gar? about 8.3

Tropical Fish
Adult length (cm)

Clown anemone	5
Bluehead	15
Butterfly	13
Flamefish	11
Moorish idol	18
Neon goby	5
Trunkfish	10

Freshwater Fish
Adult length (cm)

Alligator gar	250
Carp	100
Chinook salmon	130
Sunfish	30
Drum	65
Inconnu	125
Lake sturgeon	140
Muskellunge	110

10. DATA BANK Four kinds of trout are the rainbow, the lake, the cutthroat, and the brook. What is their mean adult length to the nearest tenth of a centimeter? Which kind of trout is nearest the mean length? (See page 413.) 80.3 cm; cutthroat

11. Try This Mara caught three catfish. The first two fish were the same length. The other fish was 12 cm shorter than the combined length of the first two fish. The total length of all three fish was 124 cm. What was the length of each fish? 34 cm, 34 cm, 56 cm

355

Using page 355

Lesson Development Direct students' attention to the table of Tropical Fish. Ask students to name the shortest fish and give its length. (The clown anemone and neon goby are both 5 cm.) "What fish is the longest? What is its length?" (moorish idol, 18 cm) "What is the range of the lengths of the fish?" (13 cm)

Exercises 1–9 In exercises 1–4 students must use data from the table of Tropical Fish. The table of Freshwater Fish should be used for exercises 5–9.

Try This A possible strategy, Guess and Check, was taught on page 24.

Discussion After students read the problem, have them identify the question and the data. Ask students if they can solve the problem directly by using computation. Elicit from them possible strategies to use. Suggest that they use Guess and Check if they do not name that strategy.

Solution

Guess: First fish (34)   Second fish (34)
       Third fish (56)

Check: (34 × 2) + 56 = 124

The first two fish were 34 cm and the third fish was 56 cm.

More Practice, page 438, Set B

Reteaching Supplement, page 99

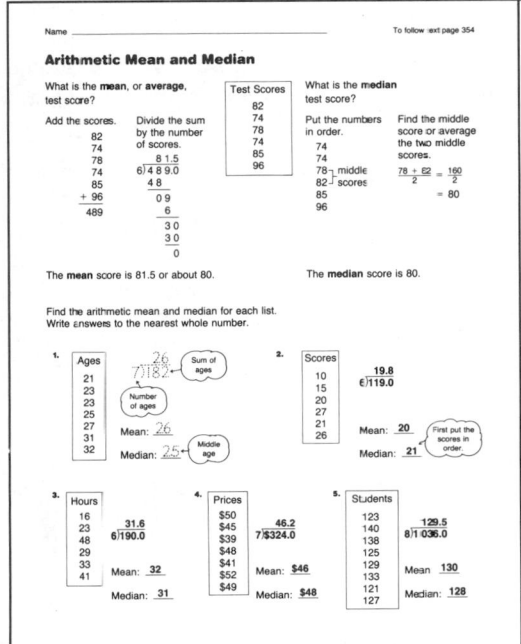

Enrichment Supplement, page 99

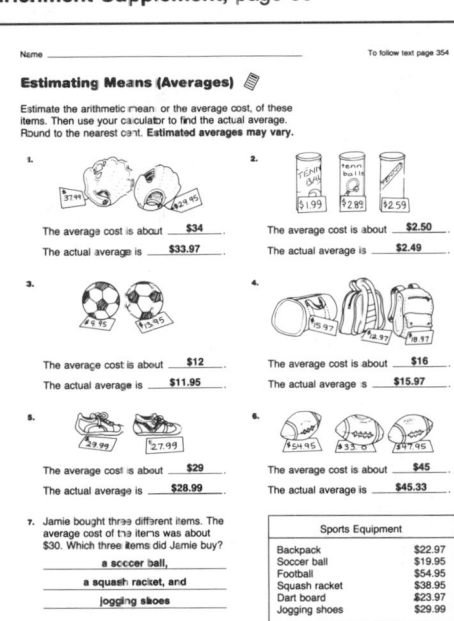

Practice Supplement, page 133

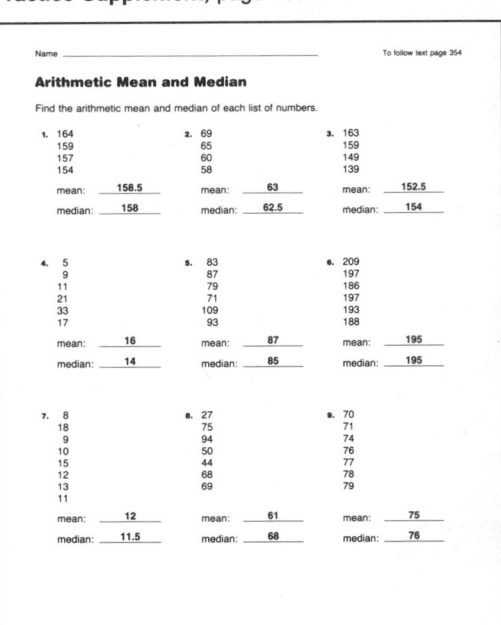

Graphs

Quick Review Have students write each fraction as a decimal and as a percent.

$\frac{7}{10}$ 0.7, 70% $\frac{3}{4}$ 0.75, 75% $\frac{37}{100}$ 0.37, 37%

$\frac{2}{5}$ 0.4, 40% $\frac{3}{50}$ 0.06, 6% $\frac{1}{8}$ 0.125, 12.5%

Lesson Focus To read and make bar graphs and line segment graphs

Suggested Materials Bar graphs and line segment graphs from newspapers or magazines, graph paper (TRB p. 284)

Ideas for Getting Started

Explain that the previous lessons dealt with data in tables. In this lesson two familiar kinds of graphs are used to show data. Point out that newspapers and magazines often show graphs. If possible, show students some examples.

Using Page 356

Lesson Development Before assigning the exercises, discuss the structure of the *double bar graph*. Ask "What do the two bars above each person's name show?" (number of heads and number of tails) "Which outcome occurred most often for Lina?" (tails)

Direct students' attention to the *histogram* at the bottom of the page. Explain that histograms are bar graphs that show frequency distributions. Ask "How many tosses gave a sum of 3 on the dice?" (5) "What is the total number of tosses that gave a sum of 4 or less?" (16)

Exercise 10 You may wish to have students make the histogram on graph paper.

Bar Graphs

This **double bar graph** shows data from a coin-tossing experiment.

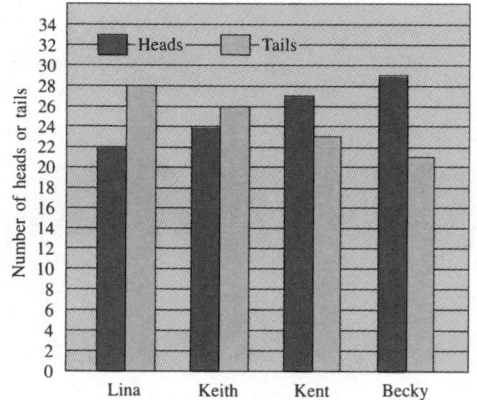

Penny Tossing Experiment

1. How many heads did Lina get? How many tails did she get? 22; 28

2. How many tosses did Lina make in all? 50

3. Which person got the least number of tails? How many was this? Becky, 21

4. What is the total number of tosses made by all four people? 200

5. How many of the total tosses were heads? How many were tails? 102; 98

This **histogram**, or bar graph of frequencies, shows the outcomes for tossing a pair of dice.

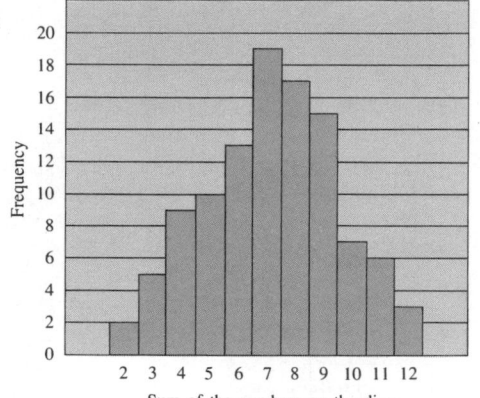

Dice Tossing Experiment

6. Which outcome had the greatest frequency? What was its frequency? 7; 19

7. Which outcome had the least frequency? What was its frequency? 2; 2

8. What is the total number of tosses shown by the graph? 106

9. What percent of the total number of tosses had the outcome of 7? Round your answer to the nearest whole percent. 18%

10. Make a histogram that will show the data in the table for tossing four coins at a time. The histogram should reflect the data given in the table.

Coin Toss

Outcome	4H	3H,1T	2H,2T	1H,3T	4T
Frequency	3	17	24	15	5

356

Follow Up

Reteaching

Have students find bar graphs and line segment graphs in newspapers and magazines. They should study the graphs and then report to the class the information given in the graphs.

Enrichment

Have students make two line segment graphs, using the same set of data: Week 1, 75; Week 2, 76; Week 3, 78; Week 4, 79; Week 5, 81. One graph should show increments of five and the other graph should show increments of one. After the graphs are complete, ask students why the graphs look so different.

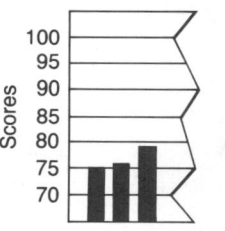
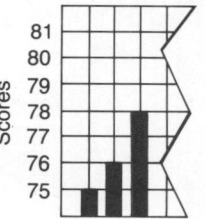

Assignment Guide			
	Minimum	Average	Extended
page 356	1–9	1–10	1–10
page 357	1–10	1–11	1–11

Line Segment Graphs

An exercise machine records pulse rates and the amount of time the machine is used. This **line segment graph** shows the results.

1. What was the pulse rate at the start? **70**

2. How much did the pulse rate rise by the end of the first 2 min of exercise? **40**

3. Estimate the highest pulse rate shown by the line graph. After how many minutes did this rate occur? **about 125; 5 min**

4. What was the pulse rate at the end of 10 min? **100**

5. What is the range of the pulse rates? **about 55**

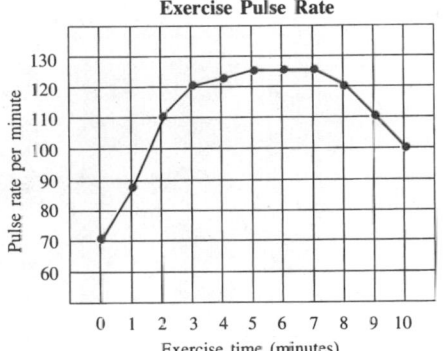

Exercise Pulse Rate

A record of pulse rates after stopping an exercise is shown on this line segment graph.

6. What was the pulse rate at 0 min? **130**

7. How much did the pulse rate drop after 1 min? **20**

8. Estimate the pulse rate at the end of 2 min. **about 98**

9. Estimate the pulse rate at the end of 8 min. **about 72**

10. What is the range of the pulse rates? **about 58**

Pulse Rate After Exercise

11. Make a line segment graph of the data in the table. **The line graph should reflect the data given in the table.**

Exercise Pulse Rate

Time (minutes)	0	1	2	3	4	5	6
Pulse beats per minute	60	75	90	120	115	95	80

357

Using Page 357

Lesson Development Discuss what the line segment graphs show. Then ask these questions to make certain that students can read the graphs correctly. "How many minutes of exercise did it take for the pulse rate to rise to 120 beats per minute?" (3 minutes) "Estimate the pulse rate after $1\frac{1}{2}$ minutes of exercise." (100) "How much did the pulse rise by the end of the first 3 minutes of exercise?" (50)

Exercise 11 You may wish to provide graph paper for students to use in this exercise.

Reteaching Supplement, page 100

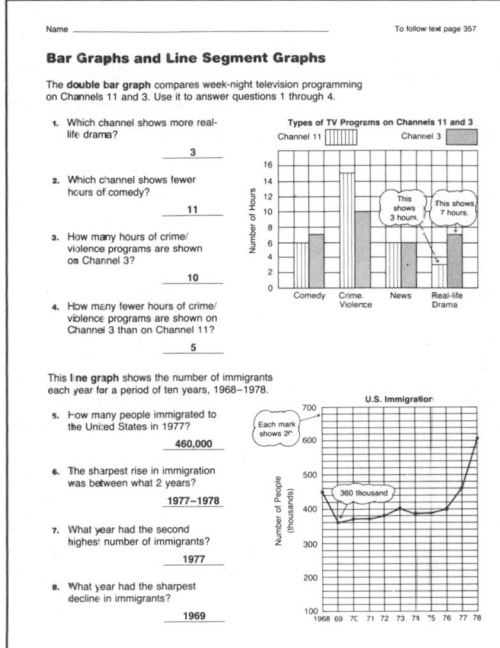

Enrichment Supplement, page 100

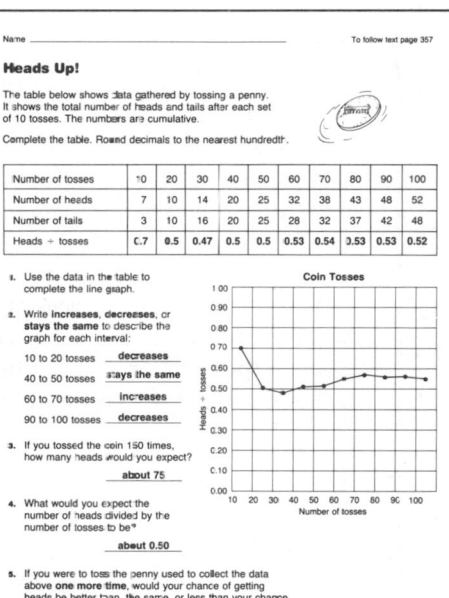

Practice Supplement, page 134

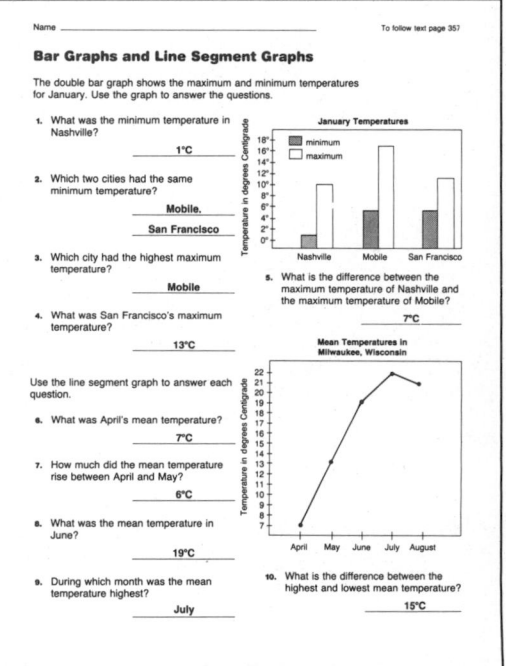

No materials are required for this daily skills maintenance program.

Quick Review Have students find the surface area of boxes with these dimensions.

$l = 4$ cm	$l = 1.2$ m	$l = 0.8$ m
$w = 6$ cm	$w = 1.2$ m	$w = 0.5$ m
$h = 4$ cm 148 cm²	$h = 1.2$ m 8.64 m²	$h = 1.2$ m 3.92 m²

Lesson Focus To read and make pictographs and circle graphs

Suggested Materials Pictographs and circle graphs from newspapers or magazines, protractors (TRB p. 280), compasses

Ideas for Getting Started

Display a pictograph and ask students to tell what data they can read from the graph. Discuss the idea that most of the data that can be read from pictographs is approximate rather than exact.

Display a circle graph and ask students to describe the data that is represented. Point out that circle graphs are used when we wish to show how some unit is divided into parts.

Review finding a percent of a number. Use the following examples.

8% of 250	15% of 300
32% of 360	45% of 18

Using Page 358

Lesson Development The pictographs on this page should be relatively easy for most students to interpret. Point out that some estimation is involved when half of a picture is shown. If 1 picture represents 1 million farms, then $\frac{1}{2}$ of the picture represents 500,000 farms.

Exercise 10 In making the pictograph for this exercise, students must decide what symbol to use to denote a number of acres. For example, a small square ☐ could represent 50 acres. Then 9 such squares would be needed to show the average size of farms for 1980.

Explain to students that an acre is a customary unit of land measure. One acre = 43,560 ft². A football field is about 1.3 acres.

Pictographs

This **pictograph** or **picture graph** shows the number of farms in the United States from 1940 to 1980.

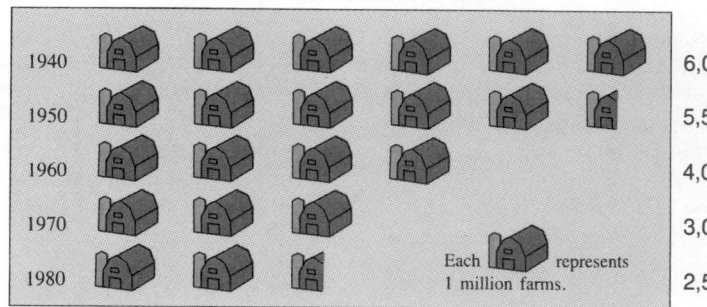

Number of U.S. Farms 1940–1980

1. Each 🏠 represents how many farms? 1,000,000

2. How many farms does the symbol 🏠 represent? 500,000

3. Give the number of farms for each year shown by the pictograph. See graph.

4. How many fewer farms were there in 1980 than in 1940? 3,500,000

This pictograph shows how the farm population has changed from 1940 to 1980.

5. Each figure represents how many people? 2,000,000

6. What was the farm population in 1940? 30,000,000

7. What was the farm population in 1950? 24,000,000

8. What was the farm population in 1960, in 1970, and in 1980? 15,000,000; 10,000,000; 7,000,000

9. How much less was the farm population in 1980 than in 1940? 23,000,000

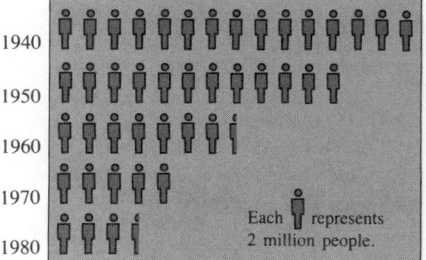

U.S. Farm Population 1940–1980

10. Make a pictograph that shows the average size of farms for the years shown in the table. The pictograph should reflect the data given in the table.

Farm Size in the U.S.

Year	1940	1950	1960	1970	1980
Number of acres	167	213	297	374	450

358

Follow Up

Reteaching

Have students search through news magazines, almanacs, and other resource books to find examples of pictographs and circle graphs. Ask them to keep a list of the various uses of each type of graph.

Have them choose one circle graph and one pictograph and write questions about the information presented in the graphs. These questions can be given to the rest of the students to answer.

Enrichment

Have students select a stock from the New York Stock Exchange and graph the closing price over a period of several days. Tell them to think carefully about the type of graph they choose to use.

Assignment Guide			
	Minimum	Average	Extended
page 358	1–9	1–10	1–10
page 359	1–8	1–10	1–10

Circle Graphs

This circle graph shows how land in the United States is used.

The sector for grazing represents 30% of the 9 million km².

$$0.30 \times 9 = 2.70$$

The graph shows 2.70 million km² of land for grazing.

The central angle for the grazing sector is 30% of 360°.

$$0.30 \times 360° = 108°$$

Use the circle graph to answer these questions.

1. How many square kilometers does the graph show for forests?
2.88 million km²

2. What is the central angle of the sector for forests? 115.2°

3. How many square kilometers does the graph show for crops? 1.53 million km²

4. What is the central angle of the sector for crops? 61.2°

5. How many more square kilometers of land are used for grazing than for crops? 1.17 million km²

6. How many square kilometers does the graph show for deserts and mountains? 1.17 million km²

7. What is the central angle of the sector for deserts and mountains? 46.8°

8. How many square kilometers does the graph show for parks? 0.72 million km²

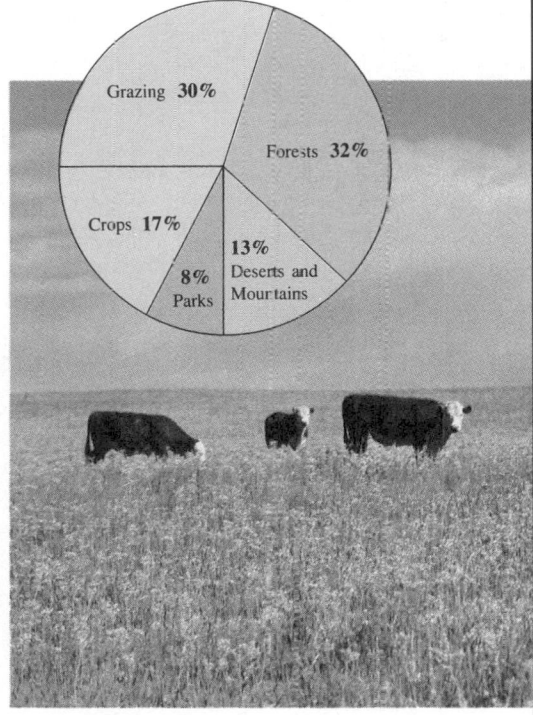

Land Use in the U.S.
Total: 9 million km²

Grazing 30%
Forests 32%
Crops 17%
13% Deserts and Mountains
8% Parks

9. What is the central angle of the sector for parks? 28.8°

10. Make a circle graph using the data in the table below.

Kinds of Farms in U.S.
Total: 1,700,000 farms

Grain	34%	Cotton and tobacco	7%
Livestock	29%	Poultry	3%
Dairy	12%		
Fruit and vegetable	4%	Other	11%

The circle graph should reflect the data given in the table.

359

Using Page 359

Lesson Development Read the material at the top of the page with students. On the chalkboard, work through the examples showing how to find the amount of land for grazing and the number of degrees in the central angle. Have students use their protractors to check the measure of the central angle for the grazing sector.

Exercise 10 Students can use a compass to draw the circle for the graph in exercise 10. Protractors are needed to draw the appropriate central angles.

Ideas That Work offer optional activities to meet individual needs.

Ideas That Work

Calculator Bonus

Display the following information about baseball statistics. Then have students solve the problems below.

Batting Average	=	Total Hits	÷	Total Times at bat

Slugging Average	=	Total Bases	÷	Times at bat

(Both averages are usually rounded to the nearest thousandth.)

1. Lou Gehrig was named the American League's Most Valuable Player in 1927. That year he had 218 hits and 584 times at bat. What was his batting average? **.373**

2. In 1941, Ted Williams had 185 hits in 456 times at bat. He was the last major league player to have a batting average over .400. What was William's batting average for 1941? **.406**

3. In 1971, Hank Aaron had the highest slugging average for the major leagues. He had 331 bases in 495 times at bat. What was his slugging average for 1971? **.669**

4. Babe Ruth holds the record for the highest slugging average for a single season. In 1920, Ruth had 388 total bases in 458 times at bat. What was his slugging average? **.847**

Practice Supplement, page 135

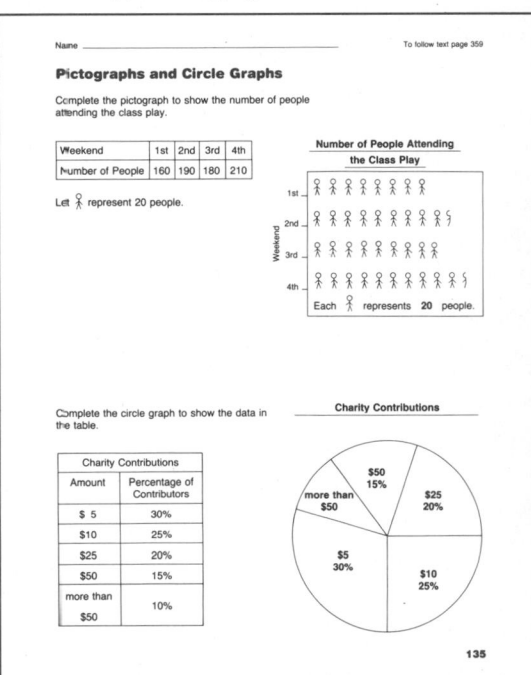

Name _____ To follow text page 359

Pictographs and Circle Graphs

Complete the pictograph to show the number of people attending the class play.

Weekend	1st	2nd	3rd	4th
Number of People	160	190	180	210

Let 👤 represent 20 people.

Number of People Attending the Class Play

Each 👤 represents **20** people.

Complete the circle graph to show the data in the table.

Charity Contributions

Amount	Percentage of Contributors
$ 5	30%
$10	25%
$25	20%
$50	15%
more than $50	10%

Charity Contributions

$50 15%
$25 20%
more than $50
$5 30%
$10 25%

135

Quick Review Have students divide. Tell them to write answers in lowest terms.

$\frac{4}{5} \div \frac{4}{9}$ $1\frac{4}{5}$ $\frac{7}{8} \div 2$ $\frac{7}{16}$ $8 \div \frac{8}{9}$ 9

$\frac{1}{2} \div \frac{1}{3}$ $1\frac{1}{2}$ $\frac{5}{8} \div \frac{1}{4}$ $2\frac{1}{2}$

Lesson Focus To solve word problems using data from graphs

Ideas for Getting Started

Review the kinds of graphs that have been studied in this chapter: bar graph, line segment graph, pictograph, and circle graph. Discuss the meaning of range, arithmetic mean, and median of a list of numbers. Write the following list of numbers on the chalkboard.

36, 39, 45, 46, 50, 56, 57

Have students find the arithmetic mean (47), median (46), and range (21).

Using page 360

Lesson Development Direct students' attention to the graph at the top of the page. Discuss what the graph shows. Ask "What is the lowest elevation in Illinois?" (85 m) "Which state has the highest elevation?" (Iowa) "What is the range of elevations for Indiana?" (287 m)

Next have students tell what the histogram shows. Ask the following questions. "How many tosses had an outcome of 4 heads?" (5) "How many tosses had an outcome of 2 heads and 2 tails?" (33) "Which outcome had a higher frequency, 3 heads and 1 tail or 1 head and 3 tails?" (1 head, 3 tails)

Exercises 1–10 Students should be able to proceed on their own with these problems.

PROBLEM SOLVING: Using Data from a Graph

QUESTION
DATA
PLAN
ANSWER
CHECK

Use the double bar graph for questions 1–5.

1. What is the range of elevations for the state of Ohio? 340 m

2. What is the arithmetic mean of the highest and lowest elevations in Ohio? 302 m

3. What is the median of the highest elevations of the four states? 427.5 m

4. What is the median of the lowest elevations of the four states? 114 m

5. Which state has the greatest range of elevations? Iowa

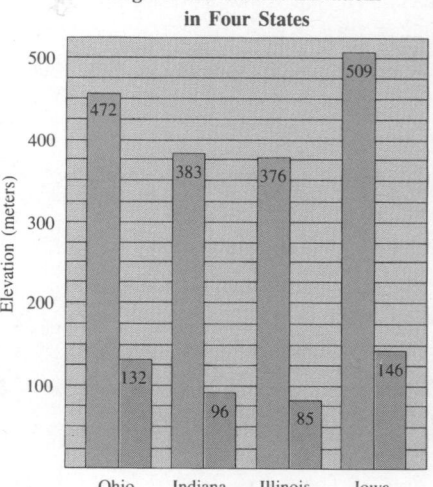

Highest and Lowest Elevations in Four States

Michael tossed four coins at a time and recorded how many coins came up heads and how many coins came up tails. The graph shows the frequency of the outcomes.

6. What is the total number of tosses shown by the graph? 80

7. What fractional part of the tosses resulted in an outcome of 4 heads? $\frac{1}{16}$

8. What fractional part of the tosses resulted in 3 heads, 1 tail? $\frac{9}{40}$

9. Did more than $\frac{1}{2}$ of the tosses result in 2 heads, 2 tails? How much more or less than $\frac{1}{2}$ of the tosses gave this outcome? no; 7 less

10. Michael found that the probability of tossing 3 heads, 1 tail with four coins was $\frac{1}{4}$. About how many times should Michael expect this outcome in 80 tosses? 20

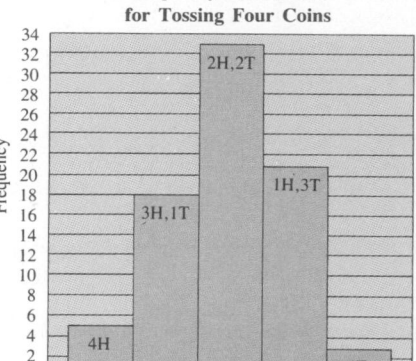

Frequency Distribution for Tossing Four Coins

360

Follow Up

Reteaching

Display graphs from newspapers and news magazines. Present problems to students based on the data in these graphs.

Enrichment

Have students use this data to make four kinds of graphs: bar graph, line segment graph, pictograph, and circle graph.

Money earned	
Monday	$5
Tuesday	$15
Wednesday	$10
Thursday	$12
Friday	$18

After students have completed the graphs, discuss reasons for having different graphs.

Use the line segment graph for problems 11–15.

11. Which day had the greatest range of temperatures? What was the range? Tuesday; 18°

12. Which day had the smallest range of temperatures? What was the range? Sunday; 9°

13. The **mean daily temperature** is the average of the daily high and low temperatures. What was the mean daily temperature for Saturday? 18°

14. List the daily high temperatures from lowest to highest. What is the median of the daily high temperatures? 17°, 18°, 19°, 20°, 22°, 22°, 24°; 20°

15. What is the median of the low temperatures? 8°

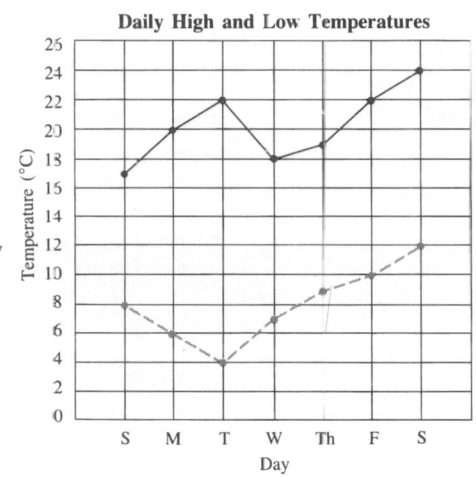

Daily High and Low Temperatures

Yolanda made a circle graph to show how she uses her time.

16. How many hours for school are shown by the graph? 6 h

17. How many more hours are shown for sleep than for school? 3 h

18. What percent of the circular region is "Hobbies?" 14.5%

19. If 37.5% of each day for a year is spent sleeping, how many hours is this? How many days is this? 3,285 h; 136.875 days

20. **Try This** In 24 h, Arthur sleeps 30% of the time, works 35% of the time, eats for 2 h, and spends half as much time for exercise as for sleeping. How many hours does Arthur have left for all other activities during one day? 2.8 h

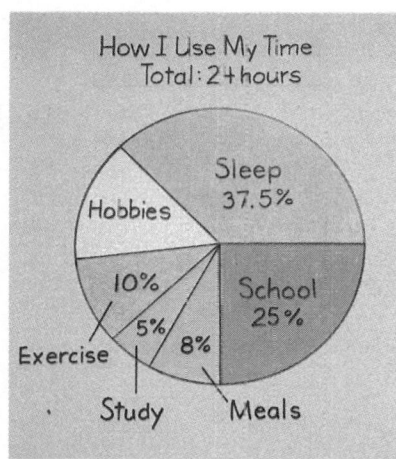

How I Use My Time
Total: 24 hours
Sleep 37.5%
Hobbies
10%
5% 8%
Exercise
School 25%
Study
Meals

361

Using Page 361

Exercises 11–15 Point out that the solid line in the line segment graph shows the daily high temperatures, while the dotted line shows the daily low temperatures.

Exercises 16–18 Students should use the data in the circle graph for these problems.

Try This A possible stragegy, Choose the Operations, was taught on page 218.

Discussion After students read the problem have them restate the question and identify the data. Then ask "How can you find the percent of a number?" (Write the percent as a decimal and multiply.) "Can you use this method to find the number of hours Arthur sleeps and works?" (yes) "How is the time for exercise related to the time for sleeping?" (half of time for sleeping) "How can you find the amount of time left for other activities?" (Subtract the total from 24.)

Solution

$$30\% \times 24 = 7.20 \text{ h sleep}$$
$$35\% \times 24 = 8.41 \text{ h work}$$
$$2.00 \text{ h meals}$$
$$\tfrac{1}{2} \times 7.2 = 3.60 \text{ h exercise}$$
$$21.20 \text{ h total}$$

$$24 - 21.2 \text{ h} = 2.8 \text{ h other activities}$$

Arthur has 2.8 h left for other activities.

Extension Have students show the results of the problem in a circle graph.

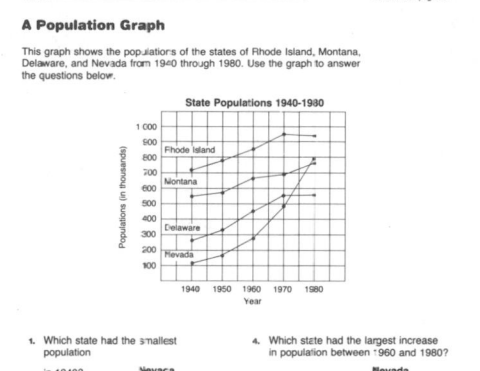

Lesson Focus To interpret, organize, and use data to make a decision about a real-world problem

Ideas for Getting Started

Discuss the idea of a sample and the way samples can be used to make predictions about large sets of data. Use the following example of students in the class as a sample of all students in the school. "Suppose 2 out of 25 students in the class are left-handed. Then among the 400 students in the school, we would predict that about 32 students are left-handed." Explain that we expect the same ratio of left-handed students for the whole school as in the sample. $(\frac{2}{25} = \frac{32}{400})$ Point out that when an exact answer to a problem is not necessary or when it would be costly or time consuming to survey a large number of cases, it is useful to use a sample.

Using Page 362

Lesson Development Have students read the problem and "Some Things to Consider." Ask students what decision must be made. (whether or not there is enough food for the herd of 150 deer in the forest) Point out that the data for the problem consists of the size of the herd (150), the data in the table concerning the number of acorns in sample plots, and the data that is given in "Some Things to Consider."

Assign "Some Questions to Answer" as independent written work. In exercise 1, some students may think that there are 4,000 m² in the forest. Remind them that 1 km² = 1,000 m × 1,000 m, or 1,000,000 m².

After students complete exercises 1–5, discuss their answers. Then ask for the students' decisions. If the result from exercise 5 was used, the total number of acorns is 4.5 × 4,000,000 = 18,000,000. The weight of the acorns is 90,000 kg. This amount will feed 90,000 ÷ 450 = 200 deer. Therefore, it appears that there might be enough food for the herd. If a decision is made on the basis of samples B, D, F, or G, then there would not be enough food for the herd.

APPLIED PROBLEM SOLVING

| QUESTION |
| DATA |
| PLAN |
| ANSWER |
| CHECK |

There are about 150 deer who get much of their food from the acorns of an oak forest that they inhabit. You are helping a naturalist who needs to decide if there is enough food for the deer. To find the amount of acorns available, you take several samples from plots of one square meter and count the acorns in these samples.

Sample Plots (1 m²)	Number of Acorns
A	4
B	1
C	10
D	3
E	7
F	0
G	2
H	9

Some Things to Consider

- The oak forest covers about 4 km².
- About 450 kg of acorns are needed for each deer.
- Acorns weigh about 5 g each.
- The oak trees are fairly evenly distributed throughout the forest.

Some Questions to Answer

1. What is the number of square meters in the oak forest? 4,000,000 m²

2. Which sample plot has the greatest number of acorns? Which sample plot has the least number of acorns? C; F

3. Use sample plot D to estimate the number of acorns in the forest. Number of acorns = number in sample × area of forest in square meters.
3 × 4,000,000 = 12,000,000

12,000,000 × 5 = 60,000,000 g; 60,000 kg; 60,000 ÷ 450 = 133.3 deer

4. Using sample plot D, about how many grams of acorns are there in the forest? How many deer would this feed?

5. What is the average number of acorns in all 8 samples? total 36 ÷ 8 = 4.5 acorns

What Is Your Decision?

Are there enough acorns in the forest for the deer population, or should some of the deer be resettled in other areas where there is a better supply of food? Yes, there should be enough acorns, since the average of the sample plots is 4.5 acorns per square meter. This is enough to feed 200 deer.

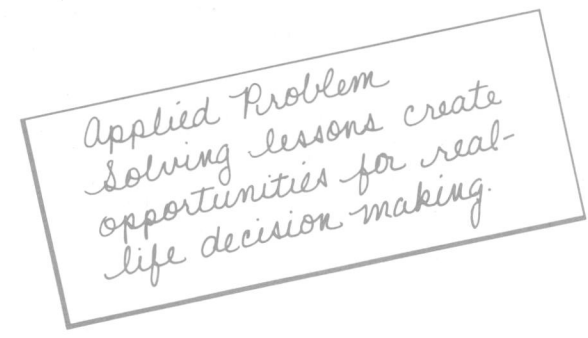

Applied Problem Solving lessons create opportunities for real-life decision making.

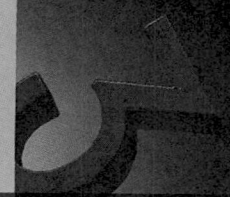

Assessment

CHAPTER REVIEW/TEST

Give the probability of each outcome when a die with faces numbered **1, 2, 3, 4, 5**, and **6** is tossed.

1. What is $P(3)$? $\frac{1}{6}$

2. What is P(odd number)? $\frac{1}{2}$

3. What is P(a number less than 4)? $\frac{1}{2}$

Give each probability for a penny and a dime tossed together.

4. List all possible outcomes as ordered pairs of heads and tails. (H,H), (H,T), (T,T), (T,H)

5. What is the probability of getting a head with the penny and a tail with the dime? $\frac{1}{4}$

6. What is the probability of getting one head and one tail? $\frac{1}{2}$

7. What is the probability of getting two heads? $\frac{1}{4}$

Use the line segment graph to answer questions 8–12.

8. How many days had a low temperature of 6°C? 3

9. What is the range of temperatures? 9°

10. What is the mode of the temperatures? 6°C

11. What is the median temperature? 6°C

12. Find the arithmetic mean of the temperatures. 5°C

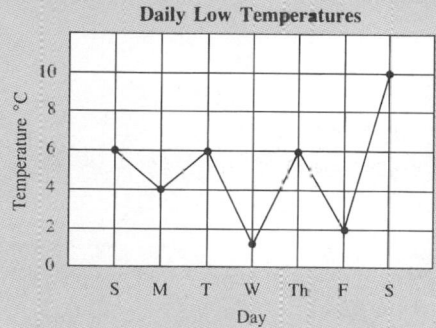

Daily Low Temperatures

Use the circle graph to answer questions 13–17.

13. How many hours are shown for school? 6 h

14. How many hours are shown for sleep? 10.08 h

15. How many hours are shown for recreation? 4.08 h

16. What is the central angle of the sector for meals? 28.8°

17. How many more hours are shown for sleep than for school? 4.08 h

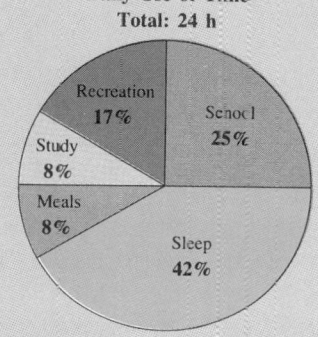

Daily Use of Time
Total: 24 h

363

Using Page 363

The exercises in the Chapter Review/Test emphasize the major concepts and skills presented in this chapter. These exercises may be used as a review assignment or as a test, depending upon your needs.

Item Analysis The table below correlates the Chapter Review/Test items with objectives and with the student text pages on which the concepts or skills were taught.

Items	Objectives	Related Text Pages
1–3	14.1	344–347
4–7	14.2	348–349
8–12	14.3	352–355
13–16	14.4	356–359
17	14.5	360–361

Assessment Options

If you use the Chapter Review/Test as a review assignment, you may wish to use the free-response test or the multiple-choice test to evaluate mastery of the chapter objectives. The items on these tests have a one-to-one correspondence in terms of content and level of difficulty. A correlation of test items to objectives and student text pages is provided in the Management Guide for Chapter 14.

Multiple-Choice Test, TRB pages 39–41
Free-Response Test, TRB pages 75–76

TRB Options

The following blackline masters are available for use with this chapter. If you have not already assigned these materials, you may wish to use them to close the chapter.

Recreation, TRB page 168
Consumer Applications, TRB page 186
Calculator Technology, TRB page 204
Reading Math, TRB page 240
Family Involvement, TRB pages 271–272

Using Page 364

The exercises on this page are intended for those students who experienced difficulty with the Chapter Review/Test on page 363. Should students require reteaching of these key concepts and skills, please refer to the teaching notes below. Otherwise, the Another Look exercises can be assigned as independent work, with students using the accompanying sample problems and hints as guides.

Exercises 1–4 This skill was originally taught on pages 344–347. Have students study the example in the display box. Remind students that the numerator of a probability fraction is the number of favorable outcomes and the denominator is the total number of equally likely outcomes. Since there is 1 chance of getting a 3, and there are 4 possible outcomes, the probability of getting a 3 is $\frac{1}{4}$. Review the notation, P(3).

Exercises 5–7 This skill was originally taught on pages 348–349. Read the material in the display box with students. Discuss the meaning of the probability fraction explained above. Review the notation used for ordered pairs in probability. In exercise 7, explain that since (C,4) is not a possible outcome, the probability of (C,4) occurring is 0.

Exercises 8–10 This skill was originally taught on pages 352–354. After students study the material in the display box, write this list of numbers on the chalkboard: 70, 74, 81, 85, 99. Ask students to find the range (29), the mode (85), the median (83), and the mean ($82\frac{1}{3}$).

Exercises 11–12 This skill was originally taught on page 359. Discuss the example in the display box. Remind students that when computing with percents, they should be written as decimals or fractions. Ask students how to find the amount of money spent for food. (0.25 × $1,200) Then work through the problem on the chalkboard.

ANOTHER LOOK

> There is 1 **chance** in 4 that the spinner will land on 3. The **probability** of getting 3 is $\frac{1}{4}$.
>
> $P(3) = \frac{1}{4}$

Think of spinning the spinner. (4),(1),(2),(3)

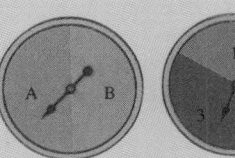

1. List all of the possible outcomes.

2. Is each outcome equally likely? yes

3. What is $P(1)$? $\frac{1}{4}$

4. What is $P(\text{even number})$? $\frac{1}{2}$

> The outcome shown is (A,3). There is 1 chance in 6 that this outcome will occur.
>
> $P(A,3) = \frac{1}{6}$

Think of spinning both spinners.

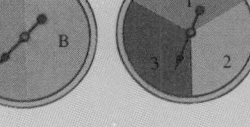

5. List all of the possible outcomes. (A,1),(A,2), (A,3),(B,1),(B,2),(B,3)

6. What is $P(A,1)$? $\frac{1}{6}$

7. What is $P(C,4)$? 0

> Range = highest–lowest
> Median = middle
> Mode = most often
> Mean = average

Use the table to answer questions 8–10.

Daily Temperature (°C)

28	22	30	34	28	31	25
S	M	T	W	Th	F	S

8. Give the highest and lowest temperatures and the range of temperatures. 34°C, 22°C; 12°

9. Give the mode and the median of the temperatures. 28°C; 28°C

10. Find the mean temperature to the nearest whole degree. 28°C

> 8% for clothing
> percent × total
>
> 8% × $1,200 = 0.08 × 1,200
> = $96.00

Use the circle graph to answer questions 11 and 12.

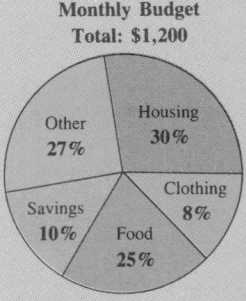

Monthly Budget
Total: $1,200

11. How much money is shown for housing? $360

12. How much more money is shown for food than for savings? $180

364

Just for Teachers

Polling Methods

Polls are taken to obtain information or opinions from a large number of people. Even though the population represented may include millions of people, only a small number of them may actually be questioned. The interviews from the sample are used to make predictions about the whole population.

There are two methods of selecting a sample: 1) random, or probability, sampling and 2) quota sampling. In probability sampling, the people to be interviewed are chosen entirely by chance. The probability of selecting each person in the population is the same. Quota sampling selects people to be interviewed because they represent a certain segment of the population.

In 1948, polls based on quota samples predicted that Thomas Dewey would get 49.5% of the vote to defeat Harry Truman. The polls were inaccurate for two reasons: the polls were taken ten to twelve days before the votes were cast, and many voters

ENRICHMENT

Probability

You can find an approximate value of $\pi = 3.14159\ldots$ by doing this experiment.

You will need a penny and a large grid of squares drawn on paper or posterboard.

Make the sides of each square of the grid the same length as the diameter of a penny (1.8 cm).

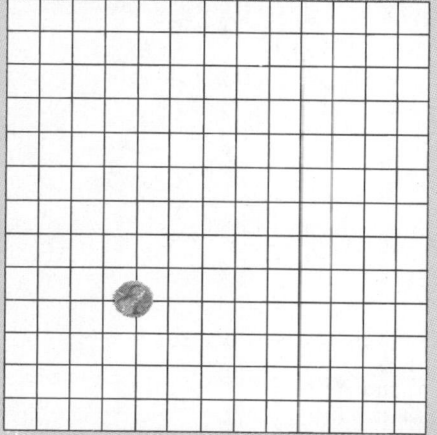

Toss a penny on the grid. The outcome is a "hit" if the penny covers a point of intersection on the grid. Otherwise, it is a "miss."

Toss a penny on the grid 100 times. Keep a tally of the number of hits and misses.

Tosses = hits + misses

Use this formula to compute an approximate value for π.

$$\pi \approx \frac{4 \times \text{number of hits}}{\text{number of tosses}}$$

Combine your numbers of hits and misses with those of several classmates. Use the formula for π again to see if the combined results are a better approximation of π.

365

Using Page 365

This page is intended for those students who successfully completed the Chapter Review/Test on page 363. You may wish to assign this page as independent work while you use Another Look exercises to reteach the basic concepts and skills of the chapter. Or, you may decide that all students would benefit from exposure to this Enrichment activity.

Suggested Materials Centimeter graph paper (TRB p. 284)

Lesson Development If possible prepare a 1.8 cm grid in advance of the activity and provide grids for student use. Four copies made from a duplication master could be taped together by students to make a large grid. If a soft mat is placed under the grid, the penny will not be as likely to bounce off the grid.

Have students follow the instructions and compute the value for π. Results can be combined to make a class tally. Students can check to see if a better approximation of π is obtained by using the combined results. An explanation of the experiment can be made as follows.

Let P be any intersection of the grid and r represent the radius of the penny. The penny will cover the point P if its center lies within the circle of radius r. It will miss P if the center lies in the shaded portion of the square with sides $2r$ and center at P.

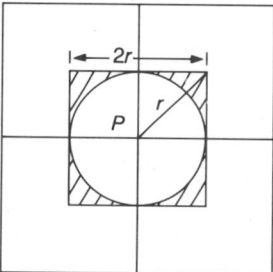

Therefore, the ratio of hits to total tosses should be about the same as the ratio of the area of the circle to the area of the square with sides of $2r$.

$$\frac{\text{hits}}{\text{tosses}} \approx \frac{\pi r^2}{(2r)^2} = \frac{\pi r^2}{4r^2} = \frac{\pi}{4}$$

Thus, $\dfrac{4 \times \text{hits}}{\text{tosses}} \approx \dfrac{4 \times \pi}{4} = \pi$

Do not expect great accuracy in this experiment. An actual experiment might yield 75 hits in 100 tosses so that $\pi \approx \frac{4 \times 75}{100} = \frac{300}{100} = 3.00$. Combining the results of several students' experiments may give better approximations of π.

changed their minds; secondly, the samples were not representative of the voting population.

After 1948, most polling organizations began to use probability sampling. In this method, the area to be surveyed is divided into major geographic regions. Then specific areas are selected by chance and various neighborhoods within each area are also selected by chance. Several people in each neighborhood are randomly chosen to be interviewed.

The reliability of a poll is determined mainly by the size of the sample and the procedures used in drawing the sample. National polls usually involve 1,500 interviews. When scientific methods are used in selecting the sample, the sampling error can be determined. Sampling error is the probability that the sample is not representative and is expressed as a range of percentage points above or below the findings of the poll.

Using Page 366

The exercises on the page provide practice for maintaining cumulative skills. The emphasis in this Cumulative Review is on ratios and proportion (Chapter 11) and circles and cylinders (Chapter 13).

Item Analysis The table below correlates the Cumulative Review items with objectives and with the student book pages on which the concepts or skills were taught.

Items	Objectives	Related Text Pages
1–2	11.1	276–279
3–5	11.2	280–281
6	11.3	284–285
7	13.1	322–323
8–9	13.2	324–325
10–11	13.3	328–329
12	13.4	330–331
13	13.6	326, 332
14	11.4	282–283, 286–287

CUMULATIVE REVIEW

1. Which proportion is correct?

   A $\frac{7}{10} = \frac{14}{22}$ **B** $\frac{2}{3} = \frac{1}{6}$

   © $\frac{3}{8} = \frac{6}{16}$ **D** not given

2. What is 12 to 20 as a fraction in lowest terms?

   A $\frac{6}{5}$ **®** $\frac{3}{5}$

   c $\frac{6}{10}$ **D** not given

Solve each proportion.

3. $\frac{3}{12} = \frac{x}{28}$ **A** $x = 7$ **B** $x = 19$

   c $x = 2$ **D** not given

4. $\frac{6}{10} = \frac{x}{15}$ **A** $x = 4$ **®** $x = 9$

   c $x = 5$ **D** not given

5. $\frac{15}{20} = \frac{21}{x}$ **A** $x = 40$ **B** $x = 26$

   c $x = 14$ **®** not given

6. The rectangles are similar. What is length x?

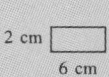

   2 cm ▭
   6 cm   24 cm

   A $x = 12$ **B** $x = 7$

   © $x = 8$ **D** not given

For 7–13, use 3.14 for π.

7. What is the circumference?

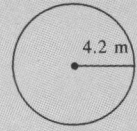

   4.2 m

   Ⓐ 26.376 m
   B 8.4 m
   c 13.188 m
   D not given

Find the area of each circle.

8. $r = 0.7$ m **A** 4.396 m² **B** 2.198 m²
   © 1.5386 m² **D** not given

9. $d = 5$ cm **A** 15.7 cm² **®** 19.625 cm²
   c 8.5 cm² **D** not given

10. What is the lateral area of a cylinder with $r = 0.2$ cm and $h = 6$ cm?

    A 1.2 cm² **®** 7.536 cm²
    c 3.768 cm² **D** not given

11. What is the total surface area of a cylinder with $r = 4$ cm and $h = 11$ cm?

    A 276.32 cm² **B** 1,532.32 cm²
    c 2,788.32 cm² **®** not given

12. What is the volume of a cylinder with $r = 0.4$ cm and $h = 6$ cm?

    A 6.0286 cm³ **B** 15.072 cm³
    c 7.536 cm³ **®** not given

13. A mug has a base with an area of 35 cm². The height of the mug is 6.5 cm. About how much liquid will the mug hold?

    A 210 mL **B** 113.75 mL
    © 227.5 mL **D** not given

14. A case packer can pack 16 boxes in 8 min. How long would it take the machine to pack 12 boxes?

    A 5 min **®** 6 min
    c 4.7 min **D** not given

Objectives

15.1 Read, write, and compare integers.

15.2 Find the sum of two or more integers.

15.3 Find the difference of two integers.

15.4 Find the product of two or more integers and find the quotient of two integers.

15.5 Give integer coordinates of points in a coordinate plane and graph an equation using integer coordinates.

15.6 Solve word problems using the 5-Point Checklist and cumulative computational skills.

Summary

This chapter introduces positive and negative integers and the notation for these numbers. The models for integers are drawn from experiences familiar to students, such as distances measured above or below sea level, and temperatures above and below zero.

Addition of integers is presented by thinking of distances traveled along a straight street or road. The street is then replaced by the more abstract number line as the basic tool for students to use. Subtraction of integers is related to addition of integers and the familiar shortcut rule is developed for subtracting integers. The rules for multiplying two integers are developed from a physical model and then division of integers is presented as finding a missing factor in a multiplication problem. The integers are used in a coordinate system to locate points in the plane. Problem-solving skills are extended in this chapter to include solving problems with integers.

Mathematical Background

Integers Formal studies of integers often begin by creating the set of negative integers ($^-1$, $^-2$, $^-3$, ...) as the solution of the set of equations, $x + 1 = 0$, $x + 2 = 0$, $x + 3 = 0$, and so on. The negative integers are then joined with the positive integers and 0 to form the complete set of integers. In this set of integers, each number has an additive inverse or opposite. The usual properties of associativity, commutativity, and distributivity hold true and the identity elements are 0 and 1. By using these basic properties, the usual computational rules for addition, subtraction, multiplication, and division can be proved.

The approach to integers in this chapter is more intuitive. Appropriate models for the integers are used and the idea that each integer has an opposite is introduced. The computational rules for integers are derived by using a number line. We can observe that our rules are in agreement with the usual basic properties. For example, using the number line model for addition we find that $^-4 + 3 = ^-1$ and that $3 + ^-4 = ^-1$.

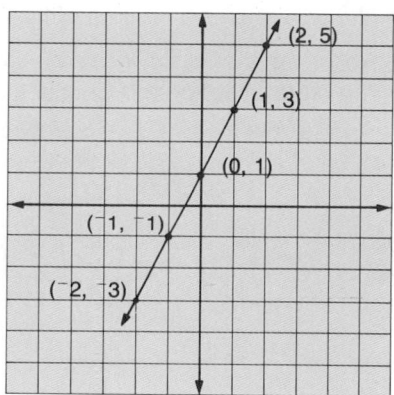

This is in agreement with the basic property of commutativity of addition, $^-4 + 3 = 3 + ^-4$, or more generally $a + b = b + a$ for every pair of integers a and b.

Integer Coordinates In this chapter, students are introduced to graphing points in a plane with integer coordinates. It is generally agreed that in graphing the ordered pair (a, b), a is located on the horizontal axis and b is located on the vertical axis. The point (a, b) is the intersection of a vertical line through a and a horizontal line through b:

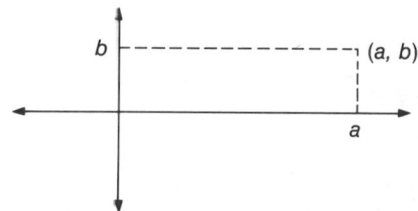

Negative numbers may also be used as values for a and b.

An optional lesson treats the idea of graphing equations. An equation of the form $y = ax + b$ produces a straight line graph. To graph the equation, a table is completed by choosing a value for x and finding the corresponding value for y. The ordered pairs thus formed are located in the coordinate plane and the points are connected.

Equation: $y = 2x + 1$

x	2	1	0	$^-1$	$^-2$
y	5	3	1	$^-1$	$^-3$
(x, y)	(2, 5)	(1, 3)	(0, 1)	($^-1$, $^-1$)	($^-2$, $^-3$)

The coordinates of every point on the line will satisfy the equation. Hence, the line is the graph of the equation.

Problem Solving This chapter extends problem solving to include work with integers. On page 378, students use data from a graph to solve problems about wind speed, temperature, and the chill factor. Meteorology is also the theme of a problem-solving practice set on page 379. An applied problem-solving lesson on page 388 asks students to make a decision about a real-world problem.

Vocabulary

positive integer	opposite	coordinates
negative integer	opposites property	origin

Error Analysis

This chapter introduces the concept of integer and operations with integers. Integer operations are introduced through "moves on a number line." Many misconceptions are possible as students progress through this chapter. Some errors commonly made are given below.

Error Pattern 1

$$9 > 6 \qquad ^-7 > ^-2 \qquad ^-5 > 1 \qquad ^-15 > 7$$

Diagnosis The student compared the numbers without regard to the negative signs. Because 7 is greater than 2, $^-7$ is greater than $^-2$. The student does not understand the concept of negative number.

Remediation Go back to the number line and show positive and negative integers. Explain that numbers become smaller as you move to the left. Put the numbers into some context, such as money paid out and money received.

$ Paid out ←——+——+——+——+——+——+——+——+——+——+——→ $ Received
　　　　　　$^-5$ $^-4$ $^-3$ $^-2$ $^-1$ 0 1 2 3 4 5

Error Pattern 2

$$^-4 + ^-3 = ^-7 \qquad ^-6 + ^-1 = ^-7 \qquad 6 + ^-8 = 14$$
$$^-4 + 5 = ^-9 \qquad 8 + ^-3 = 11 \qquad ^-4 + 13 = ^-17$$

Diagnosis The student added the numbers disregarding negative signs. He or she gave the sum the sign of the first addend.

Remediation Return to the basic ideas of adding integers. Draw a number line on the chalkboard. Explain that the positive and negative signs suggest a direction on the number line. Use an example such as $^-4 + 7$.

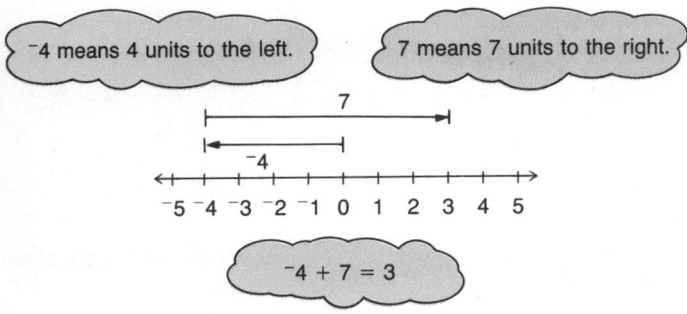

$^-4$ means 4 units to the left.　7 means 7 units to the right.

$^-4 + 7 = 3$

Error Pattern 3

$$^-3 - ^+5 = ^+2 \qquad ^-6 - ^-4 = ^-2$$
$$^-8 - ^+2 = ^-6 \qquad ^-7 - ^+4 = ^-3$$

Diagnosis The student subtracted the smaller number (in absolute value) from the larger and affixed the sign of the larger to the answer.

Remediation Rewrite subtraction exercises as missing addend problems. For example, $^-3 - 5 = \underline{\ ?\ }$　$\underline{\ ?\ } + 5 = ^-3$. After the student completes the subtraction, show that the same result is obtained by adding the opposite. Emphasize that subtracting an integer is the same as adding its opposite.

Error Pattern 4

$$5 \cdot 6 = 30 \qquad ^-8 \cdot ^-5 = ^-40$$
$$^-6 \cdot ^-9 = ^-54 \qquad 7 \cdot 8 = 56$$

Diagnosis The student multiplied two negative integers and got a negative product. He or she may have reasoned that since a positive times a positive yields a positive, a negative times a negative yields a negative.

Remediation Use a pattern to help the student see that the product of two negative integers is positive. Show the student the following:

$^-3$	$^-3$	$^-3$	$^-3$	$^-3$	$^-3$
$\times 3$	$\times 2$	$\times 1$	$\times 0$	$\times ^-1$	$\times ^-2$
$^-9$	$^-6$	$^-3$	0	$?$	$?$

Ask the student to describe the pattern. Then ask the student what the next two numbers should be. Point out that this means $^-3 \times ^-1 = 3$ and that $^-3 \times ^-2 = 6$. Explain that when a negative integer is multiplied by a negative integer, the product is always positive.

 ## Problem Solving

Writing Problem Extensions

In Chapter 8, problem extensions (posing another problem similar to the original problem) were identified as an excellent way to help students better understand the problem-solving process in general, and the use of specific problem-solving strategies in particular. In that chapter, it was suggested that the teacher provide students with extensions of the problem. Another technique for improving problem-solving performance is to encourage students to write their own problem extensions. There are many ways to extend a given problem. Below is a problem and three extensions of that problem.

Some chickens and cows are in a barnyard. Altogether there are 10 animals and 28 legs. How many chickens and how many cows are in the barnyard?

Extension 1:　Change the numbers in the problem.

Some chickens and cows are in a barnyard. Altogether there are 16 animals and 50 legs. How many chickens and how many cows are in the barnyard?

Extension 2:　Change the conditions of the problem.

(The condition that there were more than 10 chickens was added in this example.)
Some chickens and cows are in a barnyard. Altogether there are 28 legs and there are more than 10 chickens. How many chickens and how many cows are in the barnyard?

Extension 3:   Reverse the given and wanted in the problem.

> Some chickens and cows are in a barnyard. There are 7 chickens and 5 cows. Altogether how many animal legs are in the barnyard?

In your early work with students on writing problem extensions, tell them the particular way you want them to extend a given problem. Later, allow them to decide how to extend a problem. Also, encourage students to find their own ways to extend problems. Following are additional ways in which students might extend problems: (a) add unnecessary data; (b) change the data source (e.g., place the data from a story in a chart or picture); (c) write another question that could be answered wth the given data; and (d) use combinations of all of the above.

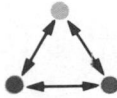

Special Education

This chapter reviews integers in a realistic setting and gradually introduces the number line for comparing, adding, and multiplying integers. Ideas to supplement the presentations of this chapter for subtraction and several additional comments to help the special students in your class are given below.

Different Sequence

If a student has reasoning difficulties, refer to the Teaching Tips of Chapter 5 before beginning subtraction of integers. The "Different Approaches" suggestions in the Special Education section provide general guidelines for helping these students with the page 376 lesson.

Add Its Opposite

For other students, the "add its opposite" rule might be informally introduced as follows. Present a problem like $^-10 - {}^-2$. Starting at $^-2$ on the numberline, students find that they must take 8 steps in a negative direction to get to $^-10$. This result should be charted along with others obtained in this manner.

$^-10 - {}^-2 = {}^-8$

> Start at $^-2$. How many units to $^-10$? 8 to the left.

$^-8$

$^-10\ ^-9\ ^-8\ ^-7\ ^-6\ ^-5\ ^-4\ ^-3\ ^-2\ ^-1\ 0\ 1$

Then group like exercises as shown, and help students note the pattern. Before reading the rule from page 376, have them state the "add its opposite" rule in their own words, and use the number line to verify the equivalence of like pairs.

$^-10 - {}^-2 = {}^-8$	$3 - 9 = {}^-6$	$^-3 - {}^-8 = 5$
$^-10 + 2 = {}^-8$	$3 + {}^-9 = {}^-6$	$^-3 + 8 = 5$

Match

Design worksheets or card-sort activities in which students solve and then match an integer subtraction exercise to an equivalent addition exercise. When all matches are made, the students should be required to use a number line to verify the equivalence of selected matches.

The One Step

Next, give students integer subtraction exercises and instruct them to carry out just the first step of each, rewriting the equivalent addition exercise.

$$\begin{array}{cc} 7 & 7 \\ -\ ^-3 & +\ ^+3 \end{array}$$

Different Approaches

If students have persistent difficulty with the above sequence, try the idea suggested in the figure. This approach allows students to remain very concrete in their thinking.

$$8 - {}^-2 = \square$$
"What number added to $^-2$ gives 8?"

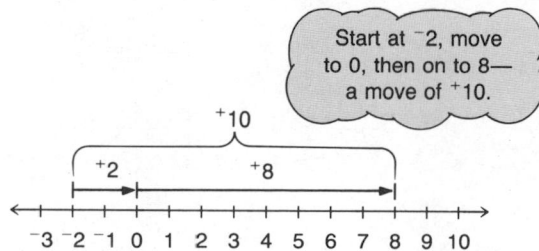

> Start at $^-2$, move to 0, then on to 8— a move of $^+10$.

The method is based on the addition-subtraction relationship, but does not use the traditional "add the opposite" rule. Students are encouraged to picture number line moves to a target number. If the move crosses the zero point, it is recorded in two steps as illustrated.

Subject Integration

Subject matter related to other areas of the curriculum has been integrated into the following lessons. This provides an opportunity to highlight the interaction between mathematics and other subjects.

Science Cryogenics, page 367; wind chill factor, page 378
Physical Education Bicycles, page 370–371
Consumer Awareness Wind-powered generator, page 379
Social Studies Yellowstone National Park, page 384

Management Guide

Teaching Chapter 15				Meeting Individual Needs					
				Lesson Assignments			Follow Up		
Objectives	Chapter Content	Pages	TRB Test Items	Minimum	Average	Extended	Reteaching	Enrichment	Practice
	Chapter Opener	367							
15.1 Read, write and compare integers.	Positive and Negative Integers	368–369	1–6	1–21	1–25	1–25	SE6 Ch 15		MP 438 PS 137
15.2 Find the sum of two or more integers.	Basic Properties for Integers	370–371		1–30	1–30	1–30, TM	SE6 Ch 15		MP 439 PS 138
	Adding Integers	372–373	7–15	1–28, 38–39, SK	1–39, SK	1–23 even, 25–41, SK	SE6 Ch 15 RS 103	ES 103	MP 439 PS 139
	Adding Positive and Negative Integers	374–375		1–20, 30	1–30, TM	1–19 odd, 21–31, TM	SE6 Ch 15 RS 102	ES 102	MP 439 PS 140
15.3 Find the difference of two integers.	Subtracting Integers	376–377	16–24	1–30	1–37	1–35 odd, 37–40, TM	SE6 Ch 15 RS 104	ES 104	MP 440 PS 141
15.4 Find the product of two or more integers and find the quotient of two integers.	Multiplying Integers	380–381	25–32	1–32	1–41	1–31 odd, 35–50, TM	RS 105	ES 105	MP 440 PS 143
	Dividing Integers	382–383	33–42	1–28, SK	1–36, SK	2–28 even, 33–40, SK	RS 106	ES 106	MP 440 PS 144
15.5 Give integer co-ordinates of points in a coordinate plane and graph an equation using integer coordinates.	Integer Coordinates	384–385	43–45	1–19	1–25	1–25, TM	RS 107	ES 107	PS 145
	Graphing Equations	386–387	46–47		1–6, 12	1–12	SE6 Ch 15		PS 146
15.6 Solve word problems using the 5-Point Checklist and cumulative computational skills.	Problem Solving: Using Data from a Graph	378	48–50	1–4, 7	1–7	1–8			PS 142
	Problem Solving: Practice	379		1–5	1–6	1–7			
	Applied Problem Solving	388							
	Chapter Review/Test	389							
	Another Look/ Enrichment	390–391							
	Cumulative Review	392							

SE6   Student Edition, Book 6
RS   Reteaching Supplement
ES   Enrichment Supplement
PS   Practice Supplement
MP   More Practice
TM   Think Math
SK   Skillkeeper
TRB   Teacher's Resource Book

For each chapter, the objectives, lessons, assignments, test items, and follow up options are organized and cross-referenced in the management guide.

In Addison-Wesley mathematics, all of the supplemental materials are unique. Each is designed to fill an individual classroom need.

Masters for use

. . . before Chapter 15

Readiness Addition of Integers	132
Readiness Integers	131

. . . during Chapter 15

Calculator Technology Calculator Puzzles	205
Consumer Applications Budgeting	187
Teaching Aids	281, 284, 286
Recreation Fraction Pattern	169
Activities That Count Add/Sub Slide Rule	153

. . . after Chapter 15

Record Keeping	310
Family Involvement At-Home Activities	274
Family Involvement Key Math	273
Reading Math Integer Concepts	241
Chapter 15 Test Free-Response Format	77–78
Chapter 15 Test Multiple-Choice Format	42–44

Supplements

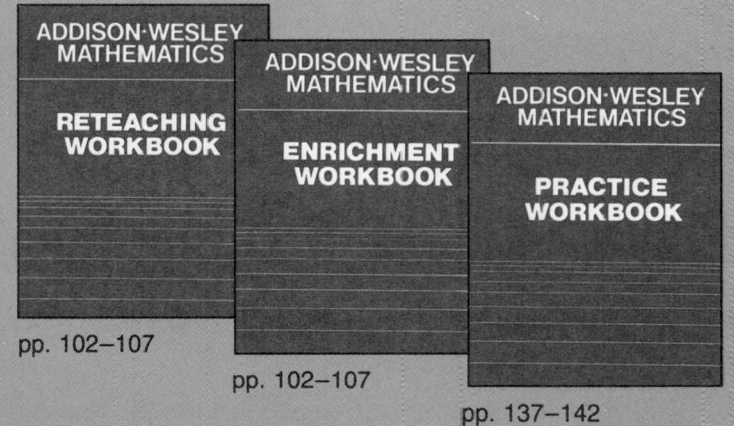

ADDISON-WESLEY MATHEMATICS
RETEACHING WORKBOOK
pp. 102–107

ADDISON-WESLEY MATHEMATICS
ENRICHMENT WORKBOOK
pp. 102–107

ADDISON-WESLEY MATHEMATICS
PRACTICE WORKBOOK
pp. 137–142

Other Addison-Wesley Resources

Books and Kits

Dice and Dots pp. 43–47

A New Twist pp. 55, 57, 85

General Mathematics: Making Practice Fun pp. 65, 69 A, B, 70 A, B, 73 A

Technology

Computer Math Activities Volumes 1–5

Computer Math Games Volumes 1, 2, 3, 6

Activities That Count

Activities That Count are designed for use throughout this chapter and subsequent chapters. Before beginning Chapter 15 you may wish to review these activities and select the ones you consider appropriate for your class.

Integer Number Line   Game

Purpose To use the number line to add integers

Materials Spinner labeled ⁻3 through 3 (TRB p. 281), game markers, number line from ⁻10 to 10

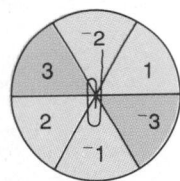

Activity In turn, players place their markers on zero, spin the spinner, and move according to the number on the spinner. If the arrow lands on a positive integer, a player moves the counter to the right the indicated number of units. If the arrow lands on a negative integer, the player moves the counter to the left.

The player who reaches 10 or ⁻10 first wins the game.

Negative Numbers   Project

Purpose To read about and report on negative numbers

Activity Have students read about negative numbers in an encyclopedia or math history book. Suggest that they try to find how long negative numbers have been used, how they were invented, and what kinds of symbols have been used to denote negative numbers. Have students report their findings to the class.

Add/Sub Slide Rule   Math Lab

Purpose To use a number line slide rule to find the sum or difference of two integers

Materials Activity sheet (TRB p. 153)

Activity Have students add and subtract integers using a number line slide rule. Explain that to add two integers, we align zero on the bottom rule with the first addend on the top rule. Then the second addend is located on the bottom rule. The sum is the integer above the second addend. The example below shows $3 + {}^-5 = {}^-2$.

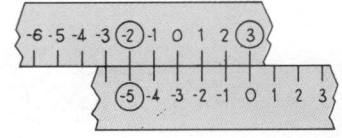

The number lines can also be used for subtraction. For example, to subtract ⁻7 from ⁻4, align ⁻7 on the top rule with zero on the bottom rule. Then locate ⁻4 on the top rule. The difference is the integer below ⁻4.

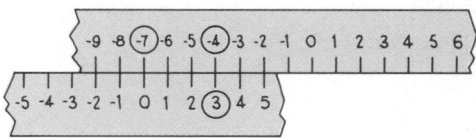

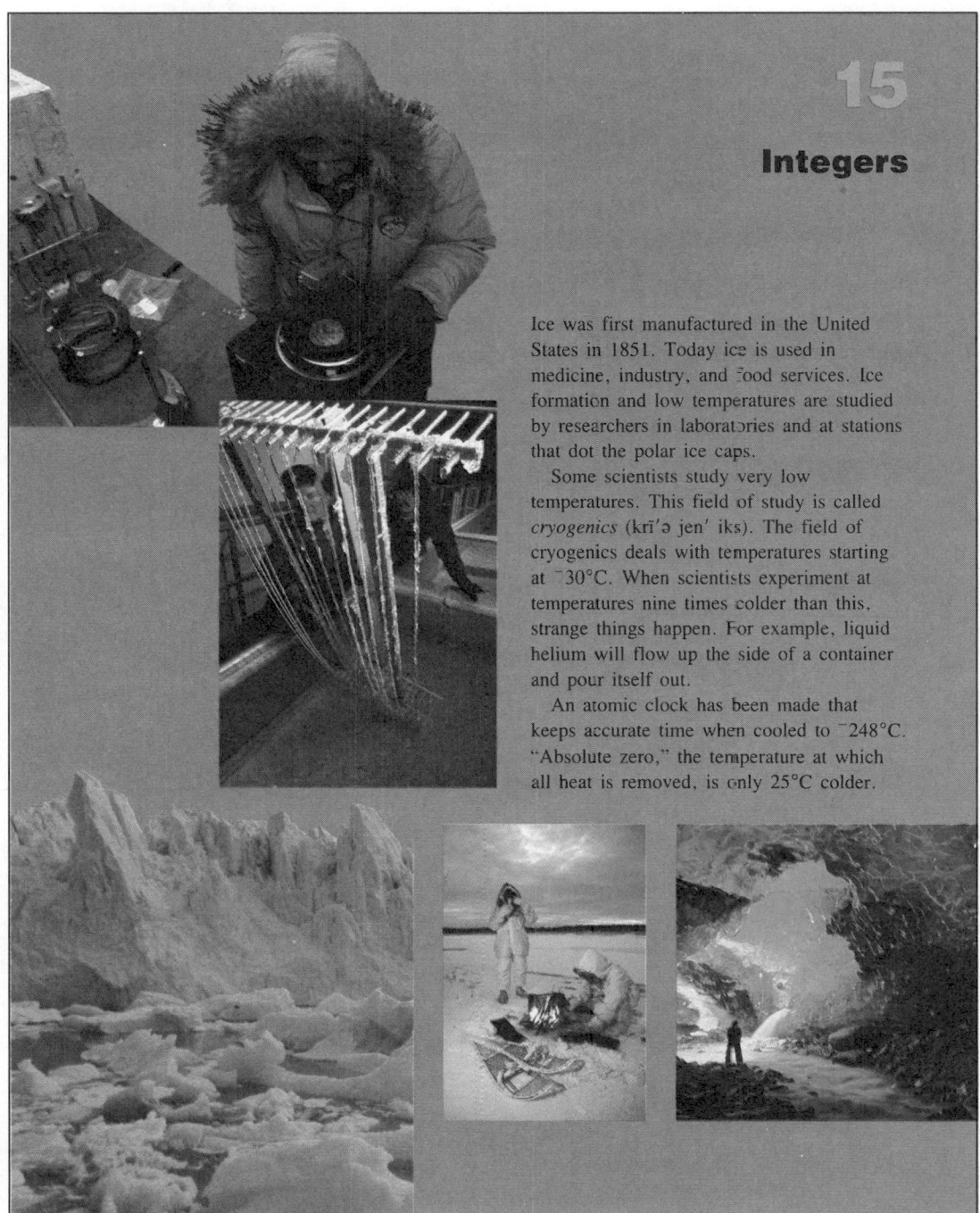

15

Integers

Ice was first manufactured in the United States in 1851. Today ice is used in medicine, industry, and food services. Ice formation and low temperatures are studied by researchers in laboratories and at stations that dot the polar ice caps.

Some scientists study very low temperatures. This field of study is called *cryogenics* (krī'ə jen' iks). The field of cryogenics deals with temperatures starting at ⁻30°C. When scientists experiment at temperatures nine times colder than this, strange things happen. For example, liquid helium will flow up the side of a container and pour itself out.

An atomic clock has been made that keeps accurate time when cooled to ⁻248°C. "Absolute zero," the temperature at which all heat is removed, is only 25°C colder.

Introducing the Chapter

Discussion Have students read the article and examine the accompanying photographs. Encourage discussion and comment. Use this as an opportunity for students to formulate questions based on the data in the article.

As you teach the chapter you may wish to refer back to this page and ask students the questions below. Briefly review the contents of the article before asking the questions.

Follow-Up Questions

After Page 369 Mercury is a fluid used in some thermometers. It freezes at 40° below 0 on the Celsius scale. Represent this temperature with an integer. (⁻40°C) Ethyl alcohol freezes at ⁻130°C. Which fluid freezes at the higher temperature, ethyl alcohol or mercury? (mercury)

After Page 375 A mixture of equal parts of water and ethylene glycol freezes at ⁻37°C. Pure ethylene glycol freezes at a temperature that is 24° higher. At what temperature does ethylene glycol freeze? (⁻13°C)

After Page 377 What is absolute zero on the Celsius scale? (⁻273°C)

After Page 381 At about what temperature does liquid helium flow up the side of a container? (⁻270°C)

Quick Review Have students use cross products to see which pairs of ratios are equal.

$\frac{9}{48} \stackrel{=}{\bigcirc} \frac{6}{32}$ $\frac{10}{15} \stackrel{\neq}{\bigcirc} \frac{17}{16}$ $\frac{14}{20} \stackrel{=}{\bigcirc} \frac{70}{100}$ $\frac{8}{20} \stackrel{=}{\bigcirc} \frac{12}{30}$

Lesson Focus To use integers to describe real-world situations and to compare integers

Ideas for Getting Started

Ask students to describe some situations where negative numbers would be used. Temperatures below zero and distances below sea level are likely to be mentioned. Other suggestions might be the amount of decrease in stock prices, the count of seconds before liftoff of a space vehicle, and the amount of money owed.

Using Page 368

Lesson Development Read through the introductory sentences with students. Point out that the raised plus and minus signs are used in order that they will not be confused with the plus and minus signs used for addition and subtraction. Direct students' attention to the picture with the vertical number scale. Explain that distances above sea level are denoted by positive integers while distances below sea level are denoted by negative integers. Ask students to give the location of the kite (70 m above sea level) and the location of the shark (50 m below sea level).

Discuss the meaning of the *opposite* of an integer. This is an important concept and will be used later in the chapter.

Exercises 1–18 Use these exercises to help summarize the lesson. Exercises 1–9 should be discussed orally. Ask students to write the symbols for the integers in exercises 10–18.

Positive and Negative Integers

To describe distances **above** and **below** sea level, we can use **positive** and **negative integers**.

$$\ldots \;\; ^-3, \; ^-2, \; ^-1, \; 0, \; ^+1, \; ^+2, \; ^+3 \;\; \ldots$$

$\underbrace{\qquad\qquad\qquad}_{\text{Negative integers}}$ $\underbrace{\qquad\qquad\qquad}_{\text{Positive integers}}$

The integer 0 is neither positive nor negative.

$^+2$ is read "**positive** two."
$^-7$ is read "**negative** seven."

Object	Location	Integer
Boat	At sea level	0
Bird	40 m **above** sea level	$^+40$
Diver	10 m **below** sea level	$^-10$
Kite	70 m **above** sea level	$^+70$
Treasure	100 m **below** sea level	$^-100$

Each integer has an **opposite**.

The **opposite** of $^+3$ is $^-3$.
The **opposite** of $^-6$ is $^+6$.
The **opposite** of 0 is 0.

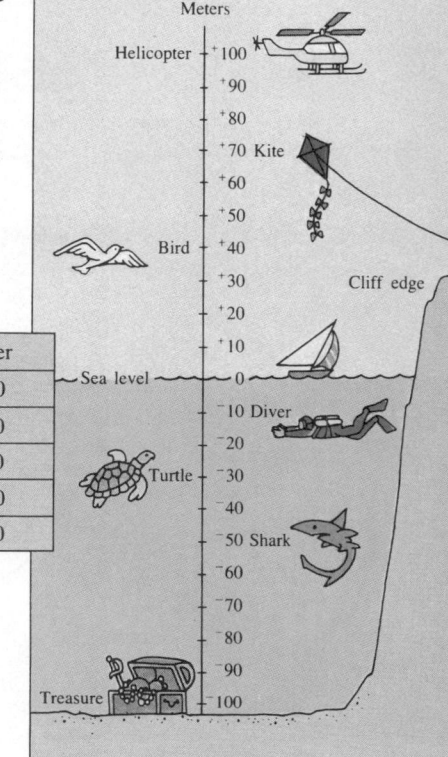

Give an integer for the location of each object.

1. Turtle $^-30$ **2.** Cliff height $^+30$ **3.** Helicopter $^+100$

State if each integer is positive or negative.

4. $^+7$ positive **5.** $^-8$ negative **6.** $^+15$ positive **7.** $^-100$ negative **8.** 0 neither **9.** $^+1$ positive

Give the opposite of each integer.

10. $^+10$ $^-10$ **11.** $^-1$ $^+1$ **12.** $^-19$ $^+19$ **13.** 0 0 **14.** $^+20$ $^-20$ **15.** $^+8$ $^-8$

Write each integer.

16. Positive six $^+6$ **17.** Negative four $^-4$ **18.** Negative eighteen $^-18$

368

Follow Up

Reteaching

Have students use a 30-cm strip of tagboard to make their own integer number line. Points should be marked at each centimeter and the center point should be labeled 0.

Ask students questions like the following and have them use the number lines to find the answers. "What integer is 4 units to the left of 0?" ($^-4$) "What integer is 6 units to the right of 0?" (6) "What integer is 1 unit to the left of $^-2$?" ($^-3$)

Enrichment

Display this number line on the chalkboard. Have students find the letter that is above each of the following integers. To find the message, they should write the correct letters in the blanks.

T ON I   YE PG   UH
←+++++++++++++++++++++++++++++→
          $^-5$ 0

$\underset{^-2}{Y}$ $\underset{^-9}{O}$ $\underset{5}{U}$ $\underset{2}{G}$ $\underset{^-1}{E}$ $\underset{^-11}{T}$

$\underset{^-11}{T}$ $\underset{6}{H}$ $\underset{^-1}{E}$ $\underset{1}{P}$ $\underset{^-9}{O}$ $\underset{^-7}{I}$ $\underset{8}{N}$ $\underset{^-11}{T}$

Assignment Guide			
	Minimum	Average	Extended
page 368	10–18	10–18	10–18
page 369	1–21	1–25	1–25

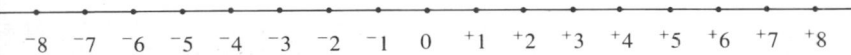

$$^-8 \quad ^-7 \quad ^-6 \quad ^-5 \quad ^-4 \quad ^-3 \quad ^-2 \quad ^-1 \quad 0 \quad ^+1 \quad ^+2 \quad ^+3 \quad ^+4 \quad ^+5 \quad ^+6 \quad ^+7 \quad ^+8$$

We can use the horizontal number line above to help think of the order of integers and to compare two integers.

The integers increase in size from left to right on the number line.

$^-2$ **is less than** $^+7$	$^-2 < ^+7$
$^-1$ **is greater than** $^-4$	$^-1 > ^-4$
$^-2$ **is less than** $^+1$	$^-2 < ^+1$
0 **is greater than** $^-5$	$0 > ^-5$

Write < or > for each ●.

1. $^+8$ ● $^-2$ >
2. $^-4$ ● $^+4$ <
3. $^-1$ ● 0 <
4. $^-3$ ● $^-7$ >
5. $^+10$ ● $^-10$ >
6. $^+9$ ● $^+19$ <
7. 0 ● $^-8$ >
8. $^-5$ ● $^-6$ >
9. $^+1$ ● $^-100$ >
10. $^-6$ ● $^-5$ <
11. $^+12$ ● $^+1$ >
12. $^-13$ ● 0 <
13. $^-7$ ● 8 <
14. $^+9$ ● $^-10$ >
15. $^-32$ ● $^-20$ <

Write the missing integers.

16. 10 degrees above zero is $^+10°$C.
   15 degrees below zero is ▦. $^-15°$C

17. A loss of 25¢ is $^-25$¢.
   A gain of 50¢ is ▦ $^+50$¢

18. Six seconds before liftoff is $^-6$ s.
   Five seconds after liftoff is ▦. $^+5$ s

19. 3 km north is $^+3$ km.
   2 km south is ▦. $^-2$ km

20. Four years from now is $^+4$ years.
   Two years ago is ▦. $^-2$ years

21. 8 km east is $^+8$ km.
   6 km west is ▦. $^-6$ km

22. Write the integers in order from least to greatest.
   $^-7, ^-3, ^-10, ^+2, ^-5$
   $^-10, ^-7, ^-5, ^-3, ^+2$

23. Write the integers in order from greatest to least.
   $^-11, 0, 7, ^-5, ^-3$
   $7, 0, ^-3, ^-5, ^-11$

24. List all the negative integers that are greater than $^-5$. $^-4, ^-3, ^-2, ^-1$

25. List all the integers that are less than $^-2$ but greater than $^-7$.
   $^-3, ^-4, ^-5, ^-6$

More Practice, page 438, Set C

Ideas That Work

Special Education

To practice comparing integers, let students play "Cross Over." Each pair of students will need a game sheet as pictured, a die marked with > and <, and game markers.

CROSS OVER						
0	8	$^-13$	26	$^-41$	5	0
0	$^-2$	17	$^-7$	Free	6	0
0	$^-19$	$^-4$	Free	10	$^-13$	0
0	6	$^-31$	12	$^-42$	18	0

Player A's game markers here. → ← Player B's game markers here.

Players place their markers in the "0" spaces of one of the end columns. In turn, they roll the die. For <, a marker is moved to any adjacent number less than the one it covers. For >, a marker is moved to an adjacent number that is greater than the one it covers. The free spaces may be occupied any time. If an opponent's marker is in a space, a player may jump over it. Players pass if no move is possible. The first to move four markers to the opponent's "0" row wins the round. The player who has won the most rounds when time is called is the winner.

Using Page 369

Exercises 1–15 Before assigning these exercises, draw a number line on the chalkboard. Explain that the numbers increase in size moving from left to right. This means that every positive number is greater than any negative number.

Exercises 16–21 These exercises show students simple applications of integers. The exercises also illustrate that in certain applications we must make agreements about the use of integers. For example, if distances east of a certain point in a road are considered positive, then distances west of the point would be considered negative.

More Practice, page 438, Set C

Practice Supplement, page 137

Name _____ To follow text page 369

Positive and Negative Integers

Write the opposite of each integer.

1. $^-3$ $^+3$
2. 5 $^+5$
3. 7 $^-7$
4. $^-9$ $^+9$
5. $^-6$ $^+6$
6. 0 0
7. $^-4$ $^+4$
8. 1 $^+1$
9. $^-8$ $^+8$
10. $^-2$ $^+2$
11. $^-15$ $^+15$
13. 13 $^+13$

Use the number line to compare the integers.
Write > or < for each ○.

$^-10\ ^-9\ ^-8\ ^-7\ ^-6\ ^-5\ ^-4\ ^-3\ ^-2\ ^-1\ 0\ ^+1\ ^+2\ ^+3\ ^+4\ ^+5\ ^+6\ ^+7\ ^+8\ ^+9\ ^+10$

13. $^-6 > ^-6$
14. $7 < 4$
15. $^-9 < ^-5$
16. $^-7 > ^-2$
17. $^-3 > ^-5$
18. $^-1 > 1$
19. $^-7 < ^-3$
20. $2 < 0$
21. $0 < ^-4$
22. $^-6 > 4$
23. $7 < 3$
24. $^-2 > 1$
25. $^-4 < ^-3$
26. $0 > ^-5$
27. $1 > 8$
28. $^-6 < ^-4$
29. $^-4 > 7$
30. $3 > 1$
31. $^-5 > ^-2$
32. $^-3 > 4$
33. $1 < 0$
34. $^-4 < ^-4$
35. $3 < 9$
36. $^-7 > 8$
37. $^-5 > 7$
38. $1 > 4$
39. $2 < 1$

Quick Review Have students choose the best estimate of the Celsius temperature.

inside a refrigerator ‾10°C, **2°C**, 15°C   high fever 22°C, **39°C**, 54°C

hot summer day **35°C**, 80°C, 100°C   indoor temperature **20°C**, 40°C, 60°C

Lesson Focus To use the basic properties for integers

Ideas for Getting Started

Review with students the commutative, associative, distributive, one, and zero properties for whole numbers. Have them use these properties to give the missing numbers in these equations.

$2 \cdot \square = 6 \cdot 2$ $(5 + 2) + 8 = 5 + (\square + 8)$

$12 \cdot \square = 12$ $2(3 + 7) = (2 \cdot 3) + (\square \cdot 7)$

$\square + 0 = 15$ $(4 \cdot 5) \cdot \square = 4 \cdot (5 \cdot 3)$

Ask students what the result would be if they scored 10 points and lost 10 points; if they received $20 and spent $20; if they traveled 3 km east and 3 km west. Elicit from them that in each case they will end up with zero or at the point where they started.

Using Page 370

Lesson Development Have students study the chart showing the basic properties for integers. Draw a number line on the chalkboard and illustrate the opposites property. Show students that if we move 7 units to the right and then 7 units to the left, we end up at 0.

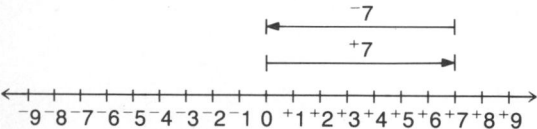

Point out that the basic properties for whole numbers also hold true for integers. Notice with students that we can group or order addends and factors any way we choose because of the commutative and associative properties. Parentheses can be omitted when only one operation is used.

Warm Up Use these exercises as an oral class activity.

Basic Properties for Integers

Opposites Property	The sum of any integer and its opposite is zero.	$^+7 + {}^-7 = 0$
Zero Property	For every integer n, $n + 0 = n$	$^-6 + 0 = {}^-6$
One Property	For every integer n, $n \cdot {}^+1 = n$	$^-3 \cdot {}^+1 = {}^-3$
Commutative Properties	For any integers x and y, $x + y = y + x$ and $x \cdot y = y \cdot x$	$^-10 + {}^+4 = {}^+4 + {}^-10$ $^+9 \cdot {}^-3 = {}^-3 \cdot {}^+9$
Associative Properties	For any three integers, x, y, and z, $(x + y) + z = x + (y + z)$ and $(x \cdot y) \cdot z = x \cdot (y \cdot z)$	$(^+2 + {}^+3) + {}^-4 = {}^+2 + ({}^+3 + {}^-4)$ $(^-5 \cdot {}^+2) \cdot {}^+6 = {}^-5 \cdot ({}^+2 \cdot {}^+6)$
Distributive Property	For any three integers, x, y, and z, $x \cdot (y + z) = x \cdot y + x \cdot z$	$^+4 \cdot ({}^-5 + {}^+7) = {}^+4 \cdot {}^-5 + {}^+4 \cdot {}^+7$

Because of the commutative and associative properties for addition and multiplication, we can *group* or *order* addends or factors any way we choose. When only one operation is used, we can omit the parentheses.

$(^+5 + {}^-2) + {}^-3 = {}^+5 + {}^-2 + {}^-3$ $^+8 \cdot ({}^-10 \cdot {}^+2) = {}^+8 \cdot {}^-10 \cdot {}^+2$

Warm Up

Name the property used.

1. $^-5 \cdot {}^+1 = {}^-5$ One
2. $^+7 \cdot {}^+6 = {}^+6 \cdot {}^+7$ Commutative
3. $^-2 + {}^-8 = {}^-8 + {}^-2$ Commutative
4. $(^+6 + {}^+4) + {}^-4 = {}^+6 + ({}^+4 + {}^-4)$ Associative
5. $^+10 \cdot ({}^+5 + {}^-1) = {}^+10 \cdot {}^+5 + {}^+10 \cdot {}^-1$ Distributive
6. $^+23 + 0 = {}^+23$ Zero
7. $(^-4 \cdot {}^-7) \cdot {}^-3 = {}^-4 \cdot ({}^-7 \cdot {}^-3)$ Associative
8. $^-26 + {}^+26 = 0$ Opposites

370

Follow Up

Reteaching

Review the basic properties for whole numbers. Remind students that commute means to move from one place to another, associate means to group together, and distribute means to spread out or allot to several. Point out that the property of opposites is a new property. Illustrate the opposite property by using examples of situations that can be represented as adding opposites. For instance:

· Win 7 points, then lose 7 points.
· Deposit $25, withdraw $25.
· Lose 2 pounds, gain 2 pounds.

Enrichment

Have students complete these statements:

1. The opposite of a positive integer is a **negative** integer.
2. The opposite of a negative integer is a **positive** integer.
3. If the opposite of a number is a positive integer, the number must be a **negative** integer.
4. If the opposite of a number is a negative integer, the number must be a **positive** integer.
5. The opposite of the opposite of the opposite of ‾4 is **4**.

Assignment Guide			
	Minimum	Average	Extended
page 371	1–30	1–30	1–30, TM

371

Use the opposites property to find the missing integers.

1. $^+4 + {}^-4 = $ ▨ 0 **2.** $^-14 + {}^+14 = $ ▨ 0 **3.** $^+50 + {}^-50 = $ ▨ 0

4. $^+2 + $ ▨ $= 0$ $^-2$ **5.** $^-11 + $ ▨ $= 0$ $^+11$ **6.** ▨ $+ {}^+15 = 0$ $^-15$

Use the zero property or the one property to find the missing integers.

7. $^+12 + 0 = $ ▨ $^+12$ **8.** $^-3 + 0 = $ ▨ $^-3$ **9.** $^+16 \cdot {}^+1 = $ ▨ $^+16$

10. $^-4 + $ ▨ $= {}^-4$ 0 **11.** ▨ $\cdot {}^+1 = {}^-18$ $^-18$ **12.** $^-25 \cdot$ ▨ $= {}^-25$ $^+1$

13. ▨ $+ {}^-7 = {}^-7$ 0 **14.** ▨ $\cdot {}^-9 = {}^-9$ $^+1$ **15.** $0 + $ ▨ $= {}^+64$ $^+64$

Use the commutative properties to write the addends or factors in a different way.

16. $^+7 \cdot {}^+3$ $^+3 \cdot {}^+7$ **17.** $^-6 \cdot {}^+6$ $^+6 \cdot {}^-6$ **18.** $^-7 + {}^-1$ $^-1 + {}^-7$

19. $^+24 \cdot {}^-1$ $^-1 \cdot {}^+24$ **20.** $0 + {}^+11$ $^+11 + 0$ **21.** $^-3 \cdot {}^-27$ $^-27 \cdot {}^-3$

Use the associative properties to write the addends or factors in a different way.

22. $(^+9 + {}^+7) + {}^-7$ **23.** $^-1 \cdot ({}^-1 \cdot {}^-5)$ **24.** $^+12 + ({}^-12 - {}^+19)$
   $9 + ({}^+7 + {}^-7)$ $({}^-1 \cdot {}^-1) + {}^+5$ $({}^+12 + {}^-12) + {}^+19$

25. $(^-3 \cdot {}^-2) \cdot {}^+2$ **26.** $(^-7 + 0) + {}^+7$ **27.** $^-24 \cdot ({}^-5 \cdot {}^+5)$
   $^-3 \cdot ({}^-2 \cdot {}^+2)$ $^-7 + (0 + {}^+7)$ $({}^-24 \cdot {}^-5) \cdot {}^+5$

Use the distributive property to write the addends or factors in a different way.

28. $^+4 \cdot ({}^+2 + {}^+3)$ **29.** $^+3 \cdot {}^+5 + {}^+3 \cdot {}^-5$ **30.** $^-8 \cdot ({}^+4 + {}^+6)$
   $^+4 \cdot {}^+2 + {}^+4 \cdot {}^+3$ $^+3 \cdot ({}^+5 + {}^-5)$ $^-8 \cdot {}^+4 + {}^-8 \cdot {}^+6$

━━━ **THINK MATH** ━━━

Logical Reasoning

Find the missing integers. Use the basic properties.

1. $^+8 + ({}^+5 + $ ▨ $) = {}^+8$ $^-5$ **2.** $^-6 + ({}^-3 + $ ▨ $) = {}^-6$ $^+3$

3. $^+10 + ($ ▨ $+ {}^-2) = {}^-2$ $^-10$ **4.** $^-4 \cdot ({}^+1 + $ ▨ $) = {}^-4$ 0

5. $^-2 \cdot ($ ▨ $+ {}^-8) = 0$ $^+8$ **6.** ▨ $\cdot (0 + {}^+1) = {}^+5$ $^+5$

More Practice, page 439, Set A

371

Using Page 371

Exercises 1–30 Assign these exercises as independent written work.

Think Math These problems involve using logical reasoning and the basic properties for integers. For example in exercise 1, $^+8 + ({}^-5 + \square) = {}^+8$, so $({}^-5 + \square) = 0$. (zero property) If $({}^-5 + \square) = 0$, then +5 must be the missing number. (opposites property)

More Practice, page 439, Set A

Ideas That Work

Chalk It Up

Display these sequences on the chalkboard. Have students find the pattern and give the next three integers.

1. $^-1, 1, {}^-3, 3, {}^-5, 5, \ldots$
   $^-7, 7, {}^-9$

2. $^-2, {}^-4, {}^-6, {}^-8, {}^-10, {}^-12, \ldots$
   $^-14, {}^-16, {}^-18$

3. $5, {}^-10, 15, {}^-20, 25, {}^-30, \ldots$
   $35, {}^-40, 45$

4. $28, 24, 20, 16, 12, 8, \ldots$
   $4, 0, {}^-4$

5. $0, {}^-1, {}^-3, {}^-6, {}^-10, {}^-15, \ldots$
   $^-21, {}^-28, {}^-36$

6. $^-20, {}^-17, {}^-14, {}^-11, {}^-9, {}^-6, \ldots$
   $^-3, 0, 3$

7. $^-20, {}^-19, {}^-17, {}^-14, {}^-10, {}^-5, \ldots$
   $1, 8, 16$

8. $2, {}^-1, 4, {}^-2, 6, {}^-3, \ldots$
   $8, {}^-4, 10$

Practice Supplement, page 138

Name _____   To follow text page 371

Basic Properties for Integers

Use the opposites property to find the missing integers.

1. $^+6 + {}^-6 = $ __0__   2. __$^+3$__ $+ {}^-3 = 0$

3. $^-4 + $ __$^+4$__ $= 0$ 4. $^-21 + $ __$^+21$__ $= 0$

5. $^+17 + {}^-17 = $ __0__   6. $^+8 + {}^-8 = $ __0__

Use the zero or the one property to find the missing integers.

7. $^+8 + 0 = $ __$^+8$__   8. $^-7 + 0 = $ __$^-7$__

9. $^+9 \cdot$ __$^+1$__ $= {}^+9$ 10. $^-3 \cdot {}^+1 = $ __$^-3$__

11. $^+16 + $ __0__ $= {}^+16$ 12. $^+11 \cdot$ __$^+1$__ $= {}^+11$

Use the commutative properties to write the addends or factors in a different way.

13. $^-4 \cdot {}^+2$ __$^+2 \cdot {}^-4$__   14. $^-5 + {}^+10$ __$^+10 + {}^-5$__

15. $^+8 - {}^+9$ __$^+9 + {}^+8$__   16. $^+12 \cdot {}^-3$ __$^-3 \cdot {}^+12$__

Use the associative properties to write the addends or factors in a different way.

17. $(^+5 + {}^+2) + {}^+3$ __$^+5 + ({}^+2 + {}^+3)$__   18. $^-8 + ({}^-8 + {}^+3)$ __$({}^-8 + {}^-8) + {}^+3$__

19. $^+6 \cdot ({}^-8 \cdot {}^+4)$ __$({}^+6 \cdot {}^-8) \cdot {}^+4$__   20. $(^+12 \cdot {}^-3) \cdot {}^+2$ __$^+12 \cdot ({}^-3 \cdot {}^+2)$__

Use the distributive property to write the addends or factors in a different way.

21. $^+3 \cdot ({}^+4 + {}^+6)$ __$^+3 \cdot {}^+4 + {}^+3 \cdot {}^+6$__   22. $^+2 \cdot {}^+5 + {}^+2 \cdot {}^-3$ __$^+2 \cdot ({}^+5 + {}^-3)$__

23. $^-6 \cdot ({}^+8 + {}^+3)$ __$^-6 \cdot {}^+8 + {}^-6 \cdot {}^+3$__   24. $^-7 \cdot {}^-8 + {}^-7 \cdot {}^-2$ __$^-7 \cdot ({}^+8 + {}^-2)$__

Quick Review Have students tell whether each number is prime, composite, or neither.

93 **composite**	31 **prime**	1 **neither**
34 **composite**	51 **composite**	2 **prime**

Lesson Focus To find the sum of two positive integers or the sum of two negative integers

Ideas for Getting Started

On the chalkboard draw a number line and illustrate the addition of $^+4 + {}^+2$.

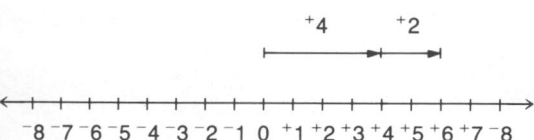

"What is the sum of $^+4$ and $^+2$?" ($^+6$) "How could we show the addition of $^-4$ and $^-2$?" Have a volunteer show the arrows for the exercise and determine that the sum is $^-6$. Repeat the activity for other examples. Use addends that are both positive or both negative.

Using Page 372

Motivational Problem Have students read the problem at the top of the page. Ask them to identify the question and the data in the problem. Explain that the number line can be used to show the answer.

Lesson Development Draw a number line on the chalkboard. Students should understand that distances east are positive and distances west are negative. Ask a volunteer to show the arrows that represent the addition of $^-3$ and $^-2$. Explain that since the sum is $^-5$, Eric was 5 km west of his home.

Discuss the next example. Point out that positive integers are the same as whole numbers greater than 0, and that we can omit the raised plus sign when writing them.

Other Examples Work through these examples with students using the number line.

Adding Integers

Eric rode his bicycle 3 km west from his home. Then he rode 2 km farther west. How far and in what direction was he from his home?

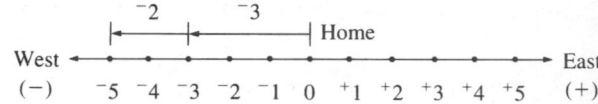

We can use the number line above to add the integers.

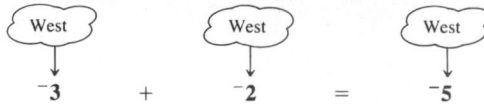

Eric was 5 km west of his home.

The number line below shows the addition of two positive integers.

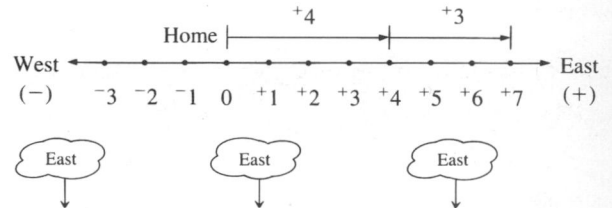

Positive integers are the same as whole numbers greater than 0. From now on we will omit the raised plus sign ($^+$) for positive integers.

Other Examples

$4 + 5 = 9$	$^-3 + {}^-3 = {}^-6$	$^-4 + {}^-5 + {}^-3 = {}^-12$

Warm Up

Add.

1. $^-2 + {}^-2$ $^-4$	2. $2 + 4$ 6	3. $^-3 + {}^-5 + {}^-6$ $^-14$
4. $^-4 + {}^-1$ $^-5$	5. $5 + 2$ 7	6. $7 + 8 + 3$ 18

372

Follow Up

Reteaching

Use colored counters or dots to represent integers. Explain to students that red counters will represent negative integers and blue counters will represent positive integers. Then illustrate finding sums as indicated below.

$4 + 2 = 6$ $^-3 + {}^-5 = {}^-8$

Enrichment

Have students use the properties of integers to solve these exercises without computing.

1. $^-4 + 2 + {}^-2 + 7 + 4$	7
2. $^-6 + 11 + 9 + {}^-9 + {}^-11 + 6$	0
3. $^-3 + 9 + {}^-7 + 3 + 7 + {}^-2 + {}^-9$	$^-2$
4. $8 + {}^-4 + 6 + {}^-6 + 4 + 6 + {}^-8$	6

Assignment Guide			
	Minimum	Average	Extended
page 373	1–28, 38–39, SK	1–39, SK	1–23 odd, 25–41, SK

Find the sums.

1. ⁻2 + ⁻3 ⁻5
2. 4 + 6 10
3. ⁻5 + ⁻4 ⁻9
4. ⁻1 + ⁻9 ⁻10
5. 4 + 3 7
6. ⁻8 + ⁻1 ⁻9
7. ⁻3 + ⁻7 ⁻10
8. 5 + 3 8
9. ⁻8 + ⁻4 ⁻12
10. ⁻5 + ⁻5 ⁻10
11. 4 + 1 5
12. ⁻6 + ⁻2 ⁻8
13. 2 + 6 8
14. ⁻2 + ⁻1 ⁻3
15. 7 + 2 9
16. 6 + 6 12
17. ⁻3 + ⁻8 ⁻11
18. ⁻1 + ⁻1 ⁻2
19. 6 + 7 13
20. ⁻5 + ⁻9 ⁻14
21. ⁻9 + ⁻9 ⁻18
22. 8 + 5 13
23. ⁻4 + ⁻7 ⁻11
24. ⁻9 + ⁻6 ⁻15

25. Negative four plus negative two ⁻6
26. Positive seven plus positive three 10
27. Negative 8 plus negative 6 ⁻14
28. Positive 3 plus positive 9 12

Find the sums. Add the numbers inside the parentheses first.

29. (2 + 3) + 4 9
30. (⁻4 + ⁻1) + ⁻2 ⁻7
31. (⁻5 + ⁻3) + ⁻3 ⁻11
32. ⁻7 + (⁻2 + ⁻4) ⁻13
33. ⁻6 + (⁻8 + ⁻4) ⁻18
34. 9 + (2 + 5) 16
35. (⁻1 + ⁻2) + ⁻3 ⁻6
36. ⁻5 + (⁻5 + ⁻5) ⁻15
37. (6 + 8) + 2 16

38. Is the sum of two positive integers a positive integer or a negative integer?
positive

39. Is the sum of two negative integers a positive integer or a negative integer?
negative

40. Dora rode her bike 7 km west from her home. Then she rode 4 km farther west. How far and in what direction was she from her home? 11 km west

41. Clarence rode his bike 12 km east in one hour. The second hour he rode 9 km farther east. The third hour he rode 5 km east. How far and in what direction was he from his starting point?
26 km east

SKILLKEEPER

Find the arithmetic mean and the median of each list of numbers. Round the answers to the nearest tenth if necessary.

1. 25, 29, 32, 36, 37, 39, 42 34.3; 36
2. 5, 12, 16, 25, 7, 20 14.2; 14
3. 16, 20, 25, 40 25.3; 22.5
4. 252, 275, 310, 325, 350 302.4; 310
5. 46, 19, 65, 22, 73 45; 46
6. 172, 179, 185, 187, 195, 200 186.3; 186
7. 2, 7, 12, 52, 3, 16, 25, 42, 49 23.1; 16
8. 39, 45, 53, 65, 72, 84, 92 64.3; 65

Using Page 373

Exercises 25–28 These exercises are stated in words. Students should write the addends and the sum in standard integer notation.

Exercises 38–39 Two important generalizations are made in these exercises about the sum of two positive or two negative integers.

Skillkeeper These skills were originally taught in Chapter 14.

More Practice, page 439, Set B

Reteaching Supplement, page 102

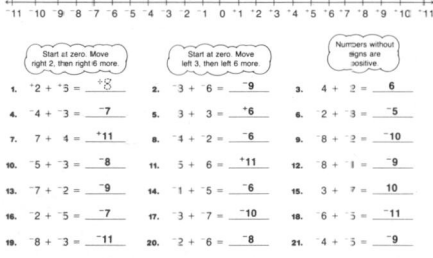

Enrichment Supplement, page 102

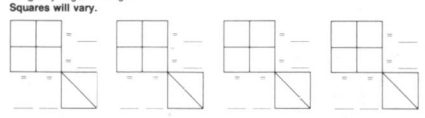

Practice Supplement, page 139

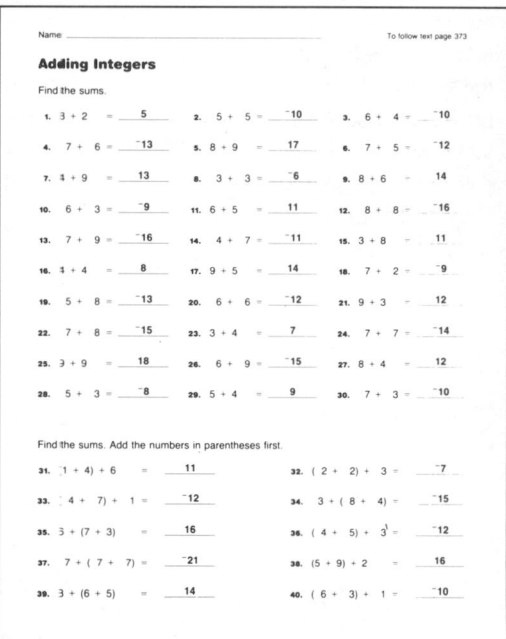

Quick Review Have students change to improper fractions and multiply.

$3\frac{1}{2} \times 2\frac{1}{2}$ $8\frac{3}{4}$ $4\frac{3}{8} \times 1\frac{4}{7}$ $6\frac{7}{8}$ $5\frac{2}{3} \times 1\frac{3}{4}$ $9\frac{11}{12}$

$6\frac{2}{7} \times 3\frac{3}{11}$ $20\frac{4}{7}$ $2\frac{8}{9} \times 1\frac{1}{2}$ $4\frac{1}{3}$

Ideas for Getting Started

Lesson Focus To find the sum of a positive integer and a negative integer

On the chalkboard, draw a number line like the one below.

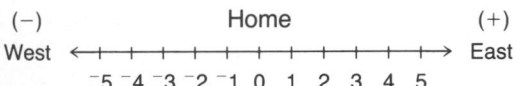

(−)   Home   (+)
West ←+—+—+—+—+—+—+—+—+—+—+→ East
       ⁻5 ⁻4 ⁻3 ⁻2 ⁻1 0 1 2 3 4 5

Home

Tell students to think of each unit as a city block and give them oral problems like these. In each case, they should start at home or 0.

"Walk 4 blocks east, then 2 blocks west. Where are you?" (2 blocks east)

"Walk 3 blocks west, then 2 blocks east. Where are you?" (1 block west)

"Walk 4 blocks west, then 7 blocks east. Where are you?" (3 blocks east)

Using Page 374

Motivational Problem After students read the introductory problem, have them state the question in their own words. Ask them to identify the data and suggest a plan they can use to solve the problem.

Lesson Development Draw a number line from ⁻10 to 10 on the chalkboard. Have students tell how the number line can be used to illustrate the distance traveled in the problem. On the chalkboard, write the addition exercise showing the addends and the sum.

$$\begin{array}{ccc} ^-4 & + 6 & = 2 \\ \uparrow & \uparrow & \uparrow \\ \text{Addends} & & \text{Sum} \end{array}$$

Some students may have difficulty understanding the idea that the sum is smaller than one of the addends. Point out that the sum is interpreted as the result of combining two distances that are opposite in direction and that the sum gives the distance and the direction from the starting point.

Work through the next example with students. Give additional examples as needed.

Adding Positive and Negative Integers

Ricardo rode the train 4 km west from his home. Then he rode a return train 6 km east. How far and in what direction was he from his home?

We can use the number line to help think about the problem.

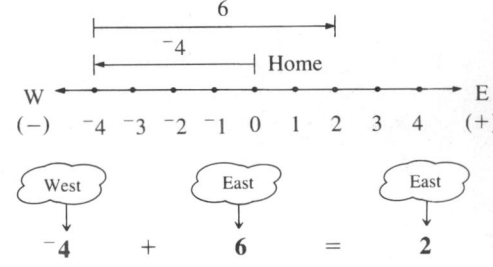

$$^-4 + 6 = 2$$
West   East   East

Ricardo was 2 km east of his home.

The number line below shows the addition of a positive integer and a negative integer.

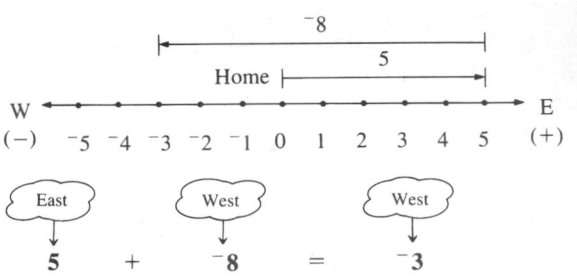

$$5 + {}^-8 = {}^-3$$
East   West   West

Warm Up

Add. Use a number line if necessary.

1. ⁻4 + 9 5   2. 6 + ⁻6 0   3. ⁻2 + ⁻2 ⁻4   4. ⁻3 + 0 ⁻3
5. 4 + ⁻7 ⁻3   6. ⁻8 + 6 ⁻2   7. 10 + ⁻1 9   8. 5 + 11 16

374

Follow Up

Reteaching

Illustrate adding integers by using colored counters as described on p. 372. Tell students to think of each red dot as cancelling out a blue dot. Work through the following examples with students.

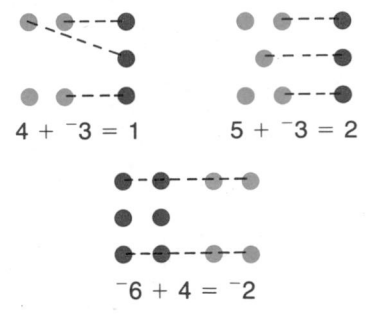

$$4 + {}^-3 = 1 \qquad 5 + {}^-3 = 2$$

$$^-6 + 4 = {}^-2$$

Enrichment

Have students complete the magic squares.

3	⁻2	⁻1
⁻4	0	4
1	2	⁻3

5	⁻6	⁻5	8
0	3	2	⁻3
4	⁻1	⁻2	1
⁻7	6	7	⁻4

Assignment Guide			
	Minimum	Average	Extended
page 375	1–20, 30	1–30, TM	1–19 odd, 21–31 TM

Find the sums. Use the number line if necessary.

```
 ̄10        ̄5         0          5         10
```

1. $ ̄4 + 7$ 3
2. $6 + ̄4$ 2
3. $ ̄5 + ̄6$ $ ̄1$
4. $9 - ̄7$ 2

5. $ ̄10 + 2$ $ ̄8$
6. $1 + ̄9$ $ ̄8$
7. $3 + ̄3$ 0
8. $ ̄7 + 3$ $ ̄4$

9. $ ̄8 + 1$ $ ̄7$
10. $ ̄7 + ̄12$ $ ̄19$
11. $8 + ̄15$ $ ̄7$
12. $ ̄5 + 10$ 5

13. $ ̄10 + 14$ 4
14. $6 + ̄8$ $ ̄2$
15. $ ̄9 + 9$ 0
16. $ ̄4 + ̄7$ $ ̄11$

17. $2 + ̄6$ $ ̄4$
18. $ ̄8 + 16$ 8
19. $ ̄5 + ̄2$ $ ̄7$
20. $ ̄4 + 13$ 9

Find the sums. Add the integers inside the parentheses first.

21. $(4 + ̄2) + ̄5$ $ ̄3$
22. $ ̄1 + (̄3 + 5)$ 1
23. $(2 + 5) + ̄4$ 3

24. $6 + (̄8 + 2)$ 0
25. $(̄3 + ̄4) + 5$ $ ̄2$
26. $6 + (̄7 + ̄6)$ $ ̄7$

27. $(̄2 + ̄3) + ̄4$ $ ̄9$
28. $9 + (̄6 + ̄4)$ $ ̄1$
29. $(̄8 + 10) + ̄7$ $ ̄5$

30. Marcia rode 8 km east. Then she rode 13 km west. How far and in what direction was she from her starting point? Write an integer addition equation.
$8 + ̄13 = ̄5$; 5 km west

31. Rob rode 9 km west. Then he rode 6 km east, and 5 km west. How far and in what direction was he from his starting point? Write an integer equation.
$(̄9 + 6) + ̄5 = ̄8$; 8 km west

▌ THINK MATH ▌

Using a Calculator

The $\boxed{+/-}$ key on a calculator can be used to add integers. Enter any number, then press the $\boxed{+/-}$ key. This enters the opposite of the number. To find $ ̄6 + 4$ on the calculator, follow these steps.

$\boxed{6}$ $\boxed{+/-}$ $\boxed{+}$ $\boxed{4}$ $\boxed{=}$

The answer displayed should be $ ̄2$.

Find each of these sums on a calculator.

1. $ ̄10 + 7$ $ ̄3$
2. $ ̄8 + ̄9$ $ ̄17$
3. $15 + ̄25$ $ ̄10$
4. $ ̄31 + 19$ $ ̄12$
5. $57 + ̄75$ $ ̄18$
6. $ ̄94 + 165$ 71
7. $ ̄53 + ̄49$ $ ̄102$
8. $ ̄217 + 528$ 311
9. $537 + ̄880$ $ ̄343$
10. $ ̄2,647 + 1,999$ $ ̄648$
11. $1,000 + ̄3,775$ $ ̄2,775$
12. $ ̄2,364 + ̄5,938$ $ ̄8,302$

More Practice, page 439, Set C

375

More Practice, page 439, Set C

Using Page 375

Exercises 1–31 Students are expected to use the number line as an aid in finding the sums. Some students may develop their own methods for finding the sums without the use of the number line. Some of the exercises involve adding two negative or two positive integers. This is a review from the previous lesson.

Think Math Many calculators are able to add integers. Some of these have a $\boxed{+/-}$ key, while others simply use the addition and subtraction keys.

Reteaching Supplement, page 103

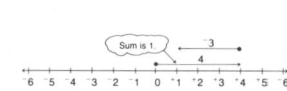

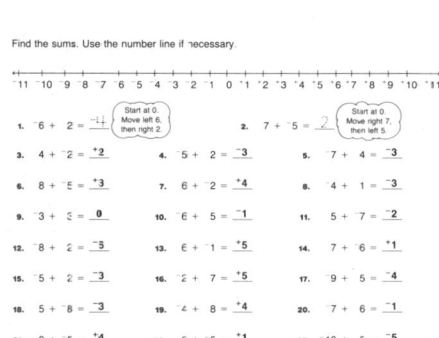

Enrichment Supplement, page 103

Practice Supplement, page 140

Quick Review Have students find the range, mode, median, and arithmetic mean of this list of numbers: 24, 30, 35, 41, 41, 45.

range 21, mode 41, median 38, mean 36

Lesson Focus To find the difference of two integers

Ideas for Getting Started

Review the relationship between addition and subtraction. Show examples of using addition to check subtraction.

$$10 - 6 = 4 \text{ because } 4 + 6 = 10$$
$$16 - 9 = 7 \text{ because } 7 + 9 = 16$$

Next write: $^-8 - 2 = \underline{\ ?\ }$ because $\underline{\ ?\ } + 2 = {}^-8$. Ask "What integer is added to 2 to give a sum of $^-8$?" When students respond $^-10$, write $^-10$ in the blanks. Use other examples such as these.

$$5 - {}^-10 = \underline{\ ?\ } \text{ because } \underline{\ ?\ } + {}^-10 = 5$$
$$2 - 6 = \underline{\ ?\ } \text{ because } \underline{\ ?\ } + 6 = 2$$

Using Page 376

Motivational Problem Read the introductory problem with students. Have them identify the question and the data needed to solve the problem. Elicit from students that since we are looking for the difference, the plan is to subtract.

Lesson Development On the chalkboard write $2 - {}^-10 = \underline{\ ?\ }$ because $\underline{\ ?\ } + {}^-10 = 2$. Ask students what number is added to $^-10$ to give 2. When they answer 12, write 12 in the blanks. Point out that $2 - {}^-10 = 12$ and that $2 + 10 = 12$. Elicit from students the idea that subtracting $^-10$ is the same as adding the opposite of $^-10$.

Other Examples Work through these examples, emphasizing that subtracting an integer is the same as adding its opposite.

Warm Up Assign these exercises as independent written work. Suggest that students write each subtraction problem as an addition problem by adding the opposite of the integer that is subtracted.

Subtracting Integers

The air temperature outside a plane was $^-10°C$ at an altitude of 1,500 m. The temperature at ground level was 2°C. What is the difference between the ground level temperature and the temperature at 1,500 m?

To find the difference, we subtract.

$$2 - {}^-10 \quad \text{(What number added to } ^-10 \text{ equals 2?)}$$

Since $12 + {}^-10 = 2$, then $2 - {}^-10 = 12$.

The difference in the temperature is 12°C.

To *subtract* any integer, we *add* its *opposite*.

$$2 - {}^-10 = 2 + 10 = 12$$
(opposites)

$$3 - 8 = 3 + {}^-8 = {}^-5$$
(opposites)

Other Examples

$$0 - {}^-6 = 0 + 6 = 6$$ (opposites) $\qquad$ $$3 - 5 = 3 + {}^-5 = {}^-2$$ (opposites) $\qquad$ $$^-1 - {}^-3 = {}^-1 + 3 = 2$$ (opposites)

Warm Up

Subtract.

1. $9 - 2$ 7   2. $8 - {}^-3$ 11   3. $^-1 - 3$ $^-4$ 4. $^-6 - {}^-2$ $^-4$

5. $5 - 3$ 2   6. $0 - {}^-4$ 4   7. $^-2 - {}^-5$ 3   8. $^-4 - {}^-4$ 0

9. $^-11 - 4$ $^-15$ 10. $1 - {}^-1$ 2   11. $5 - {}^-6$ 11   12. $1 - {}^-5$ 6

376

Follow Up

Reteaching

Display the following on the chalkboard. Ask students to start at $^-2$ and to tell how many units they must move to get to $^-7$.

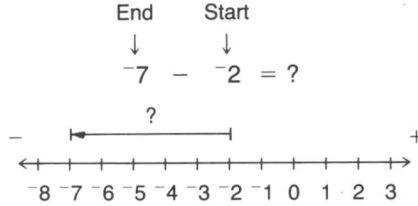

End   Start
↓   ↓
$^-7 \ - \ {}^-2 \ = \ ?$

$-$? $+$

$^-8\ ^-7\ ^-6\ ^-5\ ^-4\ ^-3\ ^-2\ ^-1\ 0\ 1\ 2\ 3$

Explain that since it takes a move of 5 units in the negative direction to get to $^-7$, the difference is $^-5$.

Enrichment

Have students replace the ☐ with an integer to complete each equation.

1. $^-6 + \boxed{11} = 5$ 6. $\boxed{3} - 4 = {}^-1$

2. $\boxed{^-6} + 4 = {}^-2$ 7. $^-8 - \boxed{^-3} = {}^-5$

3. $^-7 + {}^-3 = \boxed{^-10}$ 8. $2 - 9 = \boxed{^-7}$

4. $5 + \boxed{^-8} = {}^-3$ 9. $\boxed{^-5} - {}^-8 = 3$

5. $\boxed{9} + {}^-1 = 8$ 10. $^-4 - \boxed{3} = {}^-7$

Assignment Guide			
	Minimum	Average	Extended
page 377	1–30	1–37	1–35 odd, 37–40, TM

Subtract.

1. ⁻6 − 2 ⁻8
2. 2 − ⁻7 9
3. 0 − 4 ⁻4
4. 5 − ⁻2 7
5. 2 − 8 ⁻6
6. ⁻5 − 8 ⁻13
7. ⁻7 − ⁻9 2
8. ⁻7 − ⁻1 ⁻6
9. 14 − ⁻6 20
10. ⁻7 − 13 ⁻20
11. ⁻9 − 3 ⁻12
12. ⁻4 − 10 ⁻14
13. 0 − ⁻5 5
14. ⁻6 − ⁻8 2
15. ⁻11 − ⁻6 ⁻5
16. 8 − 12 ⁻4
17. 12 − ⁻4 16
18. 17 − ⁻8 25
19. 4 − ⁻11 15
20. ⁻8 − ⁻10 2
21. ⁻4 − 5 ⁻9
22. ⁻3 − 7 ⁻10
23. 15 − ⁻6 21
24. 2 − 8 ⁻6
25. ⁻8 − 2 ⁻10
26. ⁻2 − 8 ⁻10
27. 5 − ⁻3 8
28. ⁻6 − 9 ⁻15
29. ⁻8 − 12 ⁻20
30. ⁻3 − ⁻5 2
31. 4 − 0 4
32. 27 − ⁻5 32
33. 19 − ⁻4 23
34. ⁻17 − ⁻17 0
35. ⁻10 − ⁻9 ⁻1
36. 27 − 27 0

37. When negative 4 is subtracted from positive 7, what is the difference? 11

38. If positive 10 is subtracted from negative 8, what is the difference? ⁻18

39. The temperature at 2,000 m is ⁻15°C. At ground level the temperature is 3°C. What is the difference between the temperature at ground level and the temperature at 2,000 m? 3 − ⁻15 = 18

40. The outside air temperature at an altitude of 6,100 m was ⁻26°C. When a pilot increased his altitude to 9,100 m, the temperature dropped to ⁻44°C. What is the difference between the temperatures at 6,100 m and 9,100 m? ⁻26 − ⁻44 = 18

THINK MATH

Guess and Check

Place the nine integers 4, 3, 2, 1, 0, ⁻1, ⁻2, ⁻3, ⁻4 in the circles so that the sum of the four integers along each side of the triangle is 0.

Then try to get a sum of ⁻1 along each side of the triangle. See teaching notes.

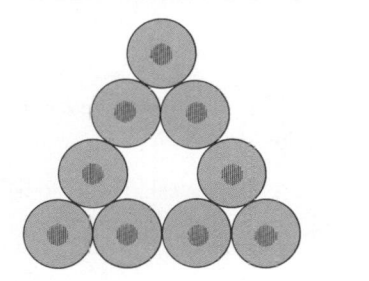

More Practice, page 440, Set A

377

Using Page 377

Exercises 1–36 You may wish to have students show a check of the first few exercises. In exercise 1, ⁻6 − 2 = ⁻8 because ⁻8 + 2 = ⁻6. If students need to rewrite these exercises as adding the opposite, they should continue to do so. However, have them work toward making this a mental step.

Think Math This problem involves the Guess and Check strategy, logical reasoning, and addition of integers. Possible solutions are shown below.

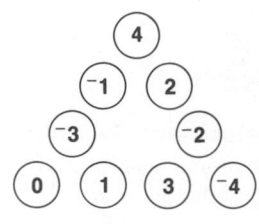

Sum: 0

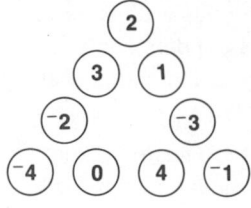

Sum: ⁻1

More Practice, page 440, Set A

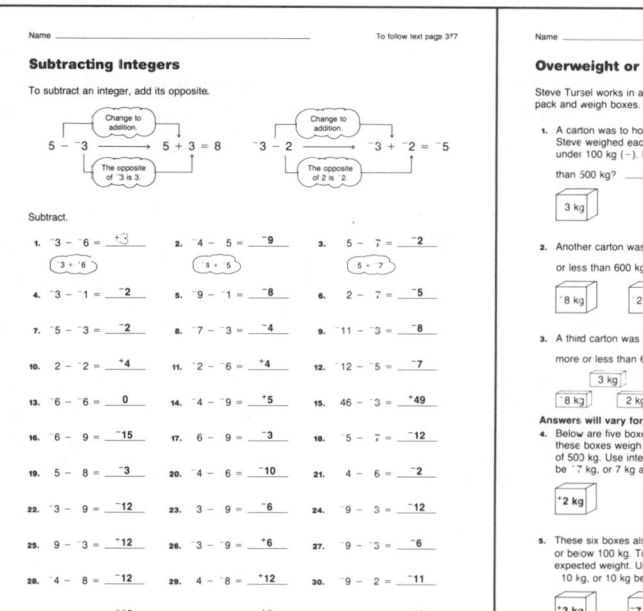
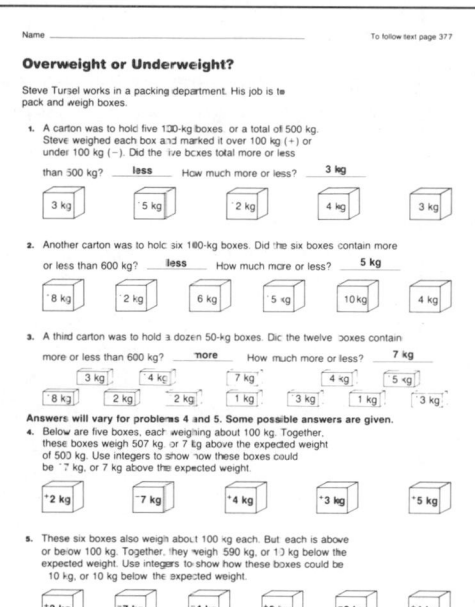

Applications

Quick Review Have students find the percent of each number.
30% of 50 **15**   42% of 75 **31.5**   24% of 82 **19.68**
15% of 24 **3.6**   65% of 52 **33.8**

Lesson Focus To solve word problems using integers and data from a graph; to solve word problems using cumulative skills

Ideas for Getting Started

Ask students if they have heard a meteorologist on a TV weather forecast speak of the *chill factor* of the wind. Explain that meteorologists have made studies about wind chill that tell how much colder air feels to us with wind than it does when the air is calm. The chill factor is the difference between the temperature of still air and the way it feels when wind is blowing.

Using Page 378

Lesson Development Read the introductory material with students and have them study the graph at the top of the page. Ask "What is the wind speed if the apparent temperature is ⁻9°C?" (8 km/h) "What is the apparent temperature when the wind is blowing at 18 km/h?" (⁻19°C) "What is the chill factor for this wind speed?" (12°)

When students understand the meaning of chill factor and can read the graph, assign the problems as independent work.

Exercises 1–6 These problems ask two questions. Remind students that both the questions must be answered.

Data Bank The chill factor is the difference between the still air and the apparent temperature: ⁻24° − ⁻32° = 8°.

Try This A possible strategy, Draw a Picture, was taught on page 108.

Discussion Have students identify the question and the data in the problem. Ask them to describe how the data is related. Elicit from students the idea that a picture helps to show the relationship between data.

Solution 8°   2°   4°

Bill's guess

Lee's guess

Cynthia's guess

Actual temperature

⁻10°C

⁻18°C

⁻20°C

⁻24°C

The actual temperature was ⁻24°C.

PROBLEM SOLVING: Using Data from a Graph

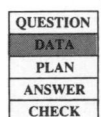

QUESTION
DATA
PLAN
ANSWER
CHECK

The difference between the temperature of still air and the **apparent temperature** when the wind blows is called the **chill factor** of the wind.

The graph shows the chill factors for a still-air temperature of ⁻7°C.

When the wind speed is 24 km/h, the apparent temperature is ⁻23°C. The chill factor is 16°. The air feels 16° colder than if the air were still.

Chill Factor for Still-Air Temperature of ⁻7°C

(graph: Apparent temperature °C vs Wind speed km/h)

☐ Chill factor

Solve. Use the data from the graph.

1. The still-air temperature is ⁻7°. What is the apparent temperature when the wind speed is 10 km/h? What is the chill factor? **⁻11°C; 4°**

2. What is the wind speed when the apparent temperature is ⁻22°C? What is the chill factor for this wind speed? **22 km/h; 15°**

3. What is the apparent temperature when the wind speed is 12 km/h? What is the chill factor for this wind speed? **⁻13°C; 6°**

4. What is the wind speed when the chill factor is about 8°? What is the apparent temperature? **14 km/h; ⁻15°C**

5. How much does the chill factor increase when the wind speed increases from 8 km/h to 16 km/h? Is this chill factor more or less than when the wind speed increases from 0 to 8 km/h? **8°; more**

6. Estimate the wind speed when the chill factor of the wind is about 10°C. What is the apparent air temperature at this wind speed? **16 km/h; ⁻17°C**

7. **DATA BANK** If the lowest temperature of record for Wichita, Kansas was the still-air temperature and the apparent temperature was ⁻32°C, what was the chill factor? (See page 416.) **8°**

8. **Try This** Cynthia, Lee, and Bill guessed at the temperature on a cold winter morning. Cynthia's guess was 4° too high. Bill guessed ⁻10°C. Lee's guess was 8° below Bill's guess and 2° above Cynthia's guess. What was the actual temperature? Hint: Draw a picture. **⁻24°C**

378

Follow Up

Reteaching

Review adding and subtracting integers with students, and elicit from them these ideas.

- The sum of two positive integers is positive.
- The sum of two negative integers is negative.
- The sum of a positive and a negative integer may be either negative or positive depending on the numbers involved.
- The difference of two integers can be rewritten as a sum; to subtract an integer, add its opposite.

Enrichment

Have students write and solve an equation for each of the following.

1. When ⁻9 is added to a certain number, the sum is 3. What is the number? **n + ⁻9 = 3, n = 12**

2. What number added to ⁻6 will give a sum of ⁻14? **⁻6 + n = ⁻14, n = ⁻8**

3. When 5 is subtracted from a certain number, the difference is ⁻2. What is the number? **n − 5 = ⁻2, n = 3**

4. During a certain winter day, the temperature rose 12° to reach a high of 8° above zero. What was the low temperature of the day? **n + 12° = 8°, n = ⁻4°**

Assignment Guide	Minimum	Average	Extended
page 379	1–5	1–6	1–7
page 378	1–4, 7	1–7	1–8

379

Applications

PROBLEM SOLVING: Practice

QUESTION
DATA
PLAN
ANSWER
CHECK

Solve.

1. An **anemometer** is a device that is used to measure wind speed. In 2.5 h, the cups on an anemometer made 1,500 revolutions. How many revolutions is this per minute? **10**

2. When the wind blows at a speed of 16 km/h, an anemometer will turn 600 times in 1 h. How many revolutions would the anemometer make in 1 h in a 20 km/h wind? **750**

Anemometer

3. A wind-powered generator that is 9 m high produces about 125 kWh of electricity per month. If the generator were twice as tall, the electricity produced would increase by about 40% per month. What would be the increase? What would be the total amount of electricity produced? **50 kWh; 175 kWh**

Windpowered generator

4. John Herrington's yearly electricity costs were about $1,100 per year. With a windpowered generator, he now produces about 90% of the electricity he uses. How much money does he save per year on electricity? **$990**

5. A windmill with a blade diameter of 1.5 m produces 24 kWh of electricity per month. A windmill with a blade diameter of 4.5 m would produce about 6.5 times as much electricity per month. How much electricity would this be? **156 kWh**

6. A jet stream of wind had a speed that was 204 km/h. This is about 0.17 of the speed of a supersonic wind. What is the speed of a supersonic wind? **1,200 km/h**

7. **Try This** In a certain location, the air temperature at ground level was 20°C. The air temperature dropped about 6.4° for each 1,000 m above ground. What would be the temperature outside an airplane flying at 10,000 m? **⁻44°C**

379

Using Page 379

Exercises 1–6 These problems involve a variety of operations with whole numbers, decimals, and percents.

Try This A possible strategy, Choose the Operations, was taught on page 218.

Discussion After students read the problem, have them restate the question in their own words. Ask them to identify the data needed to solve the problem. Help students understand that to find the difference between ground temperature and the temperature outside the airplane, they need to find the number of thousands in 10 thousand and multiply this times the number of degrees the temperature drops each thousand meters.

Solution
Number of 1,000 m above ground:
$$10,000 \div 1,000 = 10$$
Difference between temperature outside the airplane and ground temperature:
$$10 \times 6.4° = 64°$$
Temperature outside airplane:
$$20° - 64° = {}^-44°$$

The temperature outside an airplane flying at 10,000 m is ⁻44°C.

Ideas That Work

Math for the Gifted

Discuss the meaning of the symbols $>$, $<$, $\geq$, $\leq$. Explain to students that mathematical sentences that contain these symbols are *inequalities*. Tell students that if we let n stand for any integer, the inequality $n < {}^-2$ has many solutions. In fact, every integer less than ⁻2 is a solution.

Discuss *compound inequalities* such as ⁻2 $< n \leq$ 3. This inequality says two things: ⁻2 $< n$ and $n \leq$ 3. Show students the graph of the solution to ⁻2 $< n$ $\leq$ 3.

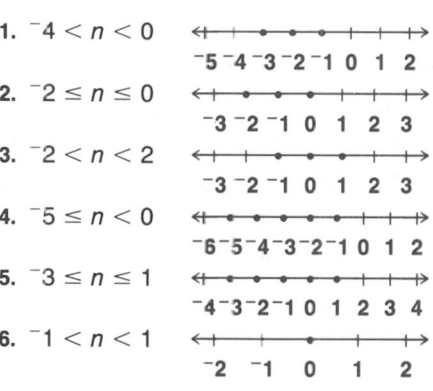

Have students draw number lines and graph the solution of each inequality.

1. ⁻4 $< n <$ 0

⁻5 ⁻4 ⁻3 ⁻2 ⁻1 0 1 2

2. ⁻2 $\leq n \leq$ 0

⁻3 ⁻2 ⁻1 0 1 2 3

3. ⁻2 $< n <$ 2

⁻3 ⁻2 ⁻1 0 1 2 3

4. ⁻5 $\leq n <$ 0

⁻6 ⁻5 ⁻4 ⁻3 ⁻2 ⁻1 0 1 2

5. ⁻3 $\leq n \leq$ 1

⁻4 ⁻3 ⁻2 ⁻1 0 1 2 3 4

6. ⁻1 $< n <$ 1

⁻2 ⁻1 0 1 2

Practice Supplement, page 142

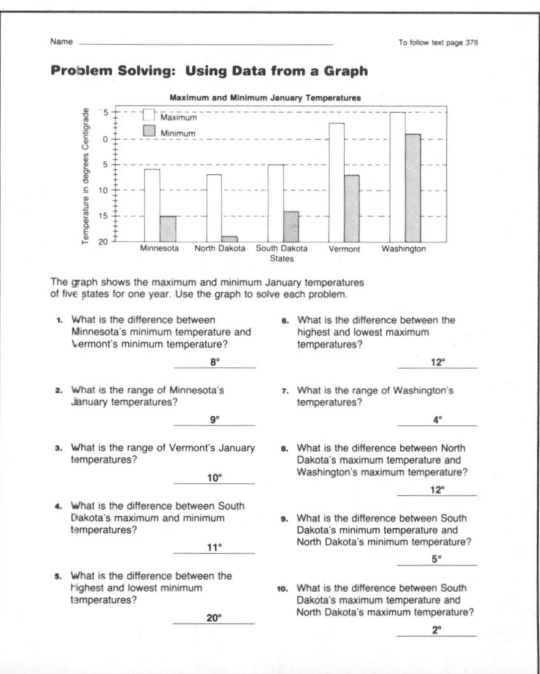

Quick Review Have students find the circumference of each circle.

d = 10 cm   **31.4 cm**   r = 10 cm   **62.8 cm**   r = 5 m   **31.4 m**

d = 27 mm   **84.78 mm**   r = 2 m   **12.56 m**

Lesson Focus To find the product of two integers

Ideas for Getting Started

Display $^-2 + ^-2 + ^-2 + ^-2$ on the chalkboard. Ask students to give the sum. ($^-10$) Explain that since the addend, $^-2$, is repeated, we can write the addition exercise as multiplication. Have students give the multiplication equation. ($5 \times ^-2 = ^-10$)

Next ask students to find $^-2 \times 5$. Most should agree that since the factors are simply reversed, the product is still $^-10$. Finally, ask students what they think is the product of $^-5 \times ^-2$. Students may have different ideas about the product. Tell them that in this lesson we will develop some simple rules for finding the product of two integers.

Using Page 380

Lesson Development Draw a number line on the chalkboard like the one on this page. Tell students that we will use the following rules.

- Rates walking east are positive.
- Rates walking west are negative.
- Hours from now are positive.
- Hours ago are negative.
- Distances east are positive.
- Distances west are negative.

Work through each of the four cases of multiplying integers. The last example of multiplying a negative integer times a negative integer to get a positive product is the most difficult for students to accept. Use the number line and other examples to strengthen students' understanding of multiplication of integers. Summarize the page by writing the rules for multiplying integers on the chalkboard.

Warm Up Use these exercises as an oral class activity.

Multiplying Integers

We can use the number line to help understand the rules we use for multiplication of integers.

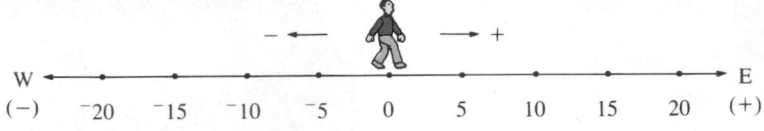

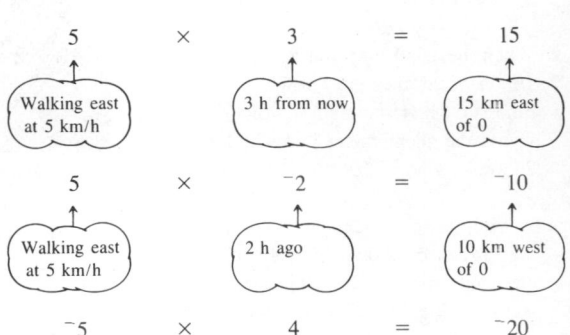

You are now at 0 walking **east** at 5 km/h. Where will you be **3 h from now**?   5   ×   3   =   15
(Walking east at 5 km/h)   (3 h from now)   (15 km east of 0)

You are now at 0 walking **east** at 5 km/h. Where were you **2 h ago**?   5   × $^-2$ = $^-10$
(Walking east at 5 km/h)   (2 h ago)   (10 km west of 0)

You are now at 0 walking **west** at 5 km/h. Where will you be **4 h from now**? $^-5$ ×   4   = $^-20$
(Walking west at 5 km/h)   (4 h from now)   (20 km west of 0)

You are now at 0 walking **west** at 5 km/h. Where were you **3 h ago**? $^-5$ × $^-3$ =   15
(Walking west at 5 km/h)   (3 h ago)   (15 km east of 0)

The product of a **positive integer** and a **negative integer** is a **negative integer**.

The product of **two positive integers** or **two negative integers** is a **positive integer**.

Warm Up

Multiply.

1. $4 \cdot ^-4$ $^-16$ 2. $^-7 \cdot ^-1$ 7   3. $0 \cdot ^-8$ 0   4. $21 \cdot 4$ 84

5. $(^-2 \cdot 4) \cdot 3$ $^-24$ 6. $5 \cdot (^-5 \cdot ^-5)$ 125   7. $^-2 \cdot (3 \cdot ^-1)$ 6   8. $4 \cdot (8 \cdot 4)$ 128

380

Follow Up

Reteaching

Display these sets of multiplication equations on the chalkboard. Have students study the patterns and complete the equations in each set. Then have them summarize the rules for multiplying integers by filling out the chart below.

$^-2 \times 2 = ^-4$ $3 \times 1 = 3$
$^-2 \times 1 = ^-2$ $3 \times 0 = 0$
$^-2 \times 0 = 0$ $3 \times ^-1 = ^-3$
$^-2 \times ^-1 = 2$ $3 \times ^-2 = ^-6$
$^-2 \times ^-2 = 4$ $3 \times ^-3 = ^-9$
$^-2 \times ^-3 = 6$ $3 \times ^-4 = ^-12$

×	+	−
+	+	−
−	−	+

Enrichment

Have students copy and complete these charts.

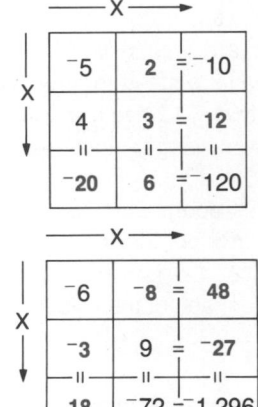

Assignment Guide			
	Minimum	Average	Extended
page 381	1–32	1–41	1–31 odd, 33–50, TM

Multiply.

1. $7 \cdot {}^-6$ $^-42$
2. $^-5 \cdot 4$ $^-20$
3. $^-4 \cdot 3$ $^-12$
4. $8 \cdot 7$ 56

5. $^-9 \cdot 6$ $^-54$
6. $7 \cdot {}^-8$ $^-56$
7. $^-6 \cdot {}^-4$ 24
8. $9 \cdot {}^-9$ $^-81$

9. $^-8 \cdot 6$ $^-48$
10. $4 \cdot {}^-9$ $^-36$
11. $^-8 \cdot {}^-5$ 40
12. $^-7 \cdot 3$ $^-21$

13. $6 \cdot {}^-10$ $^-60$
14. $^-7 \cdot 0$ 0
15. $^-6 \cdot {}^-8$ 48
16. $^-8 \cdot 1$ $^-8$

17. $^-18 \cdot 6$ $^-108$
18. $7 \cdot 13$ 91
19. $^-12 \cdot 3$ $^-36$
20. $^-24 \cdot {}^-4$ 96

21. $^-7 \cdot 15$ $^-105$
22. $42 \cdot {}^-9$ $^-378$
23. $^-21 \cdot {}^-5$ 105
24. $^-36 \cdot {}^-4$ 144

25. $^-95 \cdot {}^-4$ 380
26. $^-46 \cdot {}^-2$ 92
27. $^-9 \cdot {}^-28$ 252
28. $^-54 \cdot 3$ $^-162$

29. $12 \cdot {}^-9$ $^-108$
30. $^-15 \cdot 11$ $^-165$
31. $^-8 \cdot 25$ $^-200$
32. $^-10 \cdot {}^-20$ 200

Find the products.

33. $(^-2 \cdot 3) \cdot {}^-2$ 12
34. $^-4 \cdot (^-1 \cdot {}^-5)$ $^-20$
35. $(6 \cdot {}^-2) \cdot {}^-3$ 36

36. $8 \cdot (^-5 \cdot {}^-2)$ 80
37. $(^-8 \cdot {}^-3) \cdot {}^-1$ $^-24$
38. $(^-2 \cdot {}^-2) \cdot {}^-2$ $^-8$

39. $(10 \cdot 10) \cdot {}^-10$ $^-1{,}000$
40. $^-5 \cdot (^-4 \cdot 5)$ 100
41. $^-7 \cdot (^-2 \cdot {}^-7)$ $^-98$

Solve.

42. $5 \cdot (2 + {}^-3)$ $^-5$
43. $(^-4 \cdot 2) + (^-4 \cdot {}^-5)$ 12
44. $(3 \cdot 7) + (3 \cdot {}^-4)$ 9

45. $^-6 + (3 \cdot {}^-4)$ $^-18$
46. $^-2 \cdot (6 - 10)$ 8
47. $(5 \cdot {}^-2) - {}^-3$ $^-7$

48. $(^-1 \cdot {}^-5) - 7$ $^-2$
49. $^-6 \cdot (^-9 + 5)$ 24
50. $^-10 - (^-8 \cdot {}^-2)$ $^-26$

THINK MATH

Integer Patterns

Find the pattern for each sequence of integers.
Give the next three integers in the sequence.

1. $1, {}^-1, 3, {}^-3, 5, {}^-5, \quad , \quad$
   $7, {}^-7, 9$
2. $2, {}^-4, 8, {}^-16, 32, \quad , \quad$
   $^-64, 128, {}^-256$
3. $10, 7, 4, 1, {}^-2, \quad , \quad$
   $^-5, {}^-8, {}^-11$
4. $^-2, {}^-3, {}^-5, {}^-9, {}^-17, \quad . \quad$
   $^-33, {}^-65, {}^-129$

More Practice, page 440, Set B

381

Using Page 381

Exercises 42–50 These exercises involve addition, subtraction, and multiplication. Before assigning them, you may wish to work through examples of exercises similar to these. Remind students to do the operations in parentheses first.

Think Math These problems involve integer patterns. The patterns for each sequence are described below.

1. Odd positive and negative integers.
2. Successive terms are multiplied by $^-2$.
3. Successive terms are decreased by 3.
4. Double each term and add 1 to get the next term.

More Practice, page 440, Set B

Quick Review Have students choose the better measure of capacity for each of the following.

coffee mug   250 L,   <u>250 mL</u>   automobile gas tank 6L,   <u>60L</u>

juice can   <u>450 mL</u>,   45L   eyedropper   200 mL,   <u>2mL</u>   teaspoon   150 mL,   <u>15 mL</u>

Lesson Focus To find the quotient of two integers

Ideas for Getting Started

Review the relationship between multiplication and division of whole numbers. Ask students to give two division facts for the multiplication equation, $6 \times 4 = 24$. Next write these equations on the chalkboard and have students write two division facts for each.

$4 \times {}^-5 = {}^-20$ ${}^-2 \times 3 = {}^-6$ ${}^-4 \times {}^-3 = 12$

Using Page 382

Motivational Problem Have students read the introductory problem. Ask them to identify the question and the necessary data. Elicit from them that the plan to solve the problem is to divide.

Lesson Development As you work through the division exercises, remind students that finding a quotient means finding a missing factor. Point out the similarity of the rules for dividing integers to the rules for multiplying integers. Show students some other division notation.

$\frac{{}^-10}{2} = {}^-5$ $\frac{{}^-8}{={}^-2} = 4$ $9\overline{){}^-36}^{\ {}^-4}$ $8\overline{){}^-40}^{\ {}^-5}$

Dividing Integers

A clock lost 20 min in 5 h. How many minutes per hour did it lose?

To find the number of minutes per hour, we need to divide. To find a quotient, we can use the relation between multiplication and division.

${}^-20 \div 5 = ?$ Since ${}^-4 \cdot 5 = {}^-20$, then ${}^-20 \div 5 = {}^-4$.

The clock lost 4 min per hour.

$12 \div {}^-4 = ?$ Since ${}^-3 \cdot {}^-4 = 12$, then $12 \div {}^-4 = {}^-3$.

${}^-14 \div {}^-2 = ?$ Since $7 \cdot {}^-2 = {}^-14$, then ${}^-14 \div {}^-2 = 7$.

$15 \div 3 = ?$ Since $5 \cdot 3 = 15$, then $15 \div 3 = 5$.

The table at the right shows the kind of quotients we will get by using positive or negative dividends and divisors.

Remember, we cannot divide by 0.

Dividend	÷	Divisor	=	Quotient
+	÷	+	=	+
+	÷	−	=	−
−	÷	−	=	+
−	÷	+	=	−

Warm Up

Use the related multiplication fact to find the quotients.

1. $6 \cdot {}^-3 = {}^-18$
${}^-18 \div 6 = \blacksquare\ {}^-3$
${}^-18 \div {}^-3 = \blacksquare\ 6$

2. ${}^-8 \cdot 5 = {}^-40$
${}^-40 \div 8 = \blacksquare\ {}^-5$
${}^-40 \div {}^-8 = \blacksquare\ 5$

3. ${}^-7 \cdot {}^-1 = 7$
$7 \div {}^-7 = \blacksquare\ {}^-1$
$7 \div {}^-1 = \blacksquare\ {}^-7$

Divide.

4. $\frac{48}{={}^-6}\ {}^-8$ **5.** $\frac{{}^-72}{={}^-9}\ 8$ **6.** $\frac{{}^-21}{3}\ {}^-7$

7. ${}^-10\overline{)70}^{\ {}^-7}$ **8.** $12\overline{){}^-108}$ **9.** ${}^-15\overline{){}^-300}^{\ 20}$

Follow Up

Reteaching

Have students work in pairs and make basic-fact cards using integers. They should use all four operations. After the cards are complete, students can test each other with the cards.

Enrichment

Have students solve equations like those below.

1. $n \div {}^-7 = {}^-6$ $n = 42$
2. $11 \div n = {}^-1$ $n = {}^-11$
3. ${}^-80 \div n = 5$ $n = {}^-16$
4. $(5 \cdot n) \div 2 = {}^-10$ $n = {}^-4$
5. ${}^-48 \div ({}^-6 + 2) = n$ $n = 12$
6. $({}^-24 \div {}^-6) \div n = 2$ $n = 2$
7. $n \div ({}^-10 + 2) = 5$ $n = {}^-40$
8. $({}^-10 + {}^-18) \div (10 + {}^-3) = n$
$n = {}^-4$

Assignment Guide			
	Minimum	Average	Extended
page 383	1–28, SK	1–36, SK	2–28 even, 33–40, SK

Find the quotients.

1. 81 ÷ ⁻9 ⁻9
2. 28 ÷ ⁻4 ⁻7
3. 54 ÷ ⁻6 ⁻9
4. 24 ÷ ⁻8 ⁻3
5. ⁻21 ÷ ⁻7 3
6. ⁻24 ÷ 8 ⁻3
7. 56 ÷ ⁻7 ⁻8
8. 72 ÷ ⁻9 ⁻8
9. 63 ÷ 9 7
10. ⁻28 ÷ 4 ⁻7
11. 21 ÷ ⁻7 ⁻3
12. 45 ÷ ⁻5 ⁻9
13. ⁻9 ÷ ⁻9 1
14. 49 ÷ ⁻7 ⁻7
15. ⁻72 ÷ 8 ⁻9
16. 63 ÷ ⁻9 ⁻7

Divide.

17. $\frac{⁻35}{7}$ ⁻5
18. $\frac{⁻40}{8}$ ⁻5
19. $\frac{⁻18}{⁻3}$ 6
20. $\frac{⁻42}{⁻7}$ 6
21. $\frac{⁻64}{8}$ ⁻8
22. $\frac{48}{8}$ 6
23. $\frac{⁻12}{⁻12}$ 1
24. $\frac{⁻9}{⁻1}$ 9
25. $\frac{⁻27}{9}$ ⁻3
26. $\frac{⁻40}{⁻8}$ 5
27. $\frac{48}{6}$ 8
28. $\frac{⁻1}{1}$ ⁻1

29. 19)⁻285 ⁻15
30. ⁻74)⁻1,998 27
31. ⁻27)729 ⁻27
32. ⁻52)⁻1,976 38

33. Divide ⁻27 by ⁻3. 9
34. Divide 54 by the opposite of 9. ⁻6
35. Divide the opposite of 70 by ⁻10. 7
36. Divide the opposite of ⁻24 by the opposite of 6. ⁻4

Solve.

37. (⁻24 ÷ ⁻6) ÷ 2 2
38. ⁻24 ÷ (⁻6 ÷ 2) 8
39. (⁻36 + 24) ÷ ⁻4 3
40. (⁻36 ÷ ⁻4) + (24 ÷ ⁻4) 3

SKILLKEEPER

Add.

1. 17 + ⁻6 11
2. 5 + ⁻1 4
3. ⁻5 + 2 ⁻3
4. 25 + ⁻9 16
5. ⁻12 + 7 ⁻5
6. ⁻7 + 23 16
7. 6 + ⁻16 ⁻10
8. ⁻3 + ⁻2 ⁻5
9. ⁻11 + 9 ⁻2
10. ⁻5 + ⁻6 ⁻11
11. 12 + ⁻8 4
12. ⁻17 + 6 ⁻11
13. 8 + ⁻5 3
14. 19 + ⁻4 15
15. ⁻15 + 7 ⁻8

Subtract.

16. 0 − ⁻3 3
17. ⁻12 − ⁻8 ⁻4
18. ⁻4 − 7 ⁻11
19. ⁻8 − ⁻3 ⁻5
20. ⁻11 − 2 ⁻13
21. ⁻6 − 7 ⁻13
22. 9 − 14 ⁻5
23. ⁻12 − ⁻15 3
24. 4 − 9 ⁻5
25. ⁻6 − ⁻2 ⁻4
26. ⁻5 − 8 ⁻13
27. 4 − ⁻11 15
28. 14 − ⁻6 20
29. ⁻9 − 3 ⁻12
30. 12 − ⁻4 16

More Practice, page 440, Set C

383

Using Page 383

Exercises 1–36 Note that these exercises appear in four different forms.

Exercises 37–40 Students may need to be reminded to perform operations inside parentheses first.

Exercises 37–38 These exercises show that division of integers is not associative.

Exercises 39–40 These exercises show that dividing the sum of two integers by an integer gives the same result as dividing each addend by the integer and then adding the two quotients.

Skillkeeper This Skillkeeper reviews skills taught in this chapter.

More Practice, page 440, Set C

Reteaching Supplement, page 106

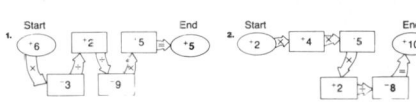

Enrichment Supplement, page 106

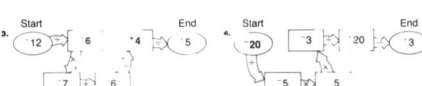

Practice Supplement, page 144

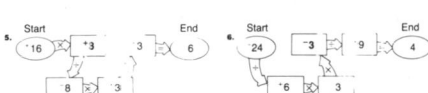

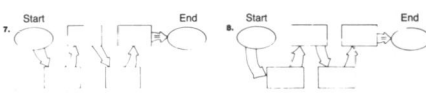

Quick Review Have students find the volume of each rectangular prism.

$l = 4$ m $l = 0.8$ m $l = 12.4$ cm

$w = 5$ m   120 m³ $w = 1.8$ m   3.168 m³ $w = 15$ cm   3,757.2 cm³

$h = 6$ m $h = 2.2$ m $h = 20.2$ cm

Lesson Focus To use ordered pairs of integers to locate points in the coordinate plane and to graph ordered pairs of integers

Suggested Materials Coordinate grid transparencies (TRB p. 286)

Ideas for Getting Started

Use a coordinate grid on the overhead projector or draw a grid on the chalkboard. Identify the two axes as the horizontal axis and the vertical axis. The intersection of the two axes is the *origin*. Mark a point on the grid and show how to read the ordered pair of integers for the point. Stress that the number from the horizontal axis is read first.

Reverse the process above. Write an ordered pair of numbers such as (⁻3, 2). Show how to find the point corresponding to these numbers. Write the word *coordinates* on the chalkboard. Explain that the coordinates of a point are the ordered pair of integers that name the point. Have students come to the grid and locate points as you name ordered pairs. Also have them give the coordinates for points that you indicate on the grid.

Using Page 384

Lesson Development Ask students to study the map at the top of the page and the coordinate system superimposed on the map. Have them locate the Fishing Bridge at the origin (0, 0). Name some of the places on the map and have students give the coordinates of these points.

Exercises 1–18 Use these exercises as an oral class activity. Note that in exercises 13–18, estimates of the coordinates must be made since the points do not fall at the intersections of the coordinate grid.

Integer Coordinates

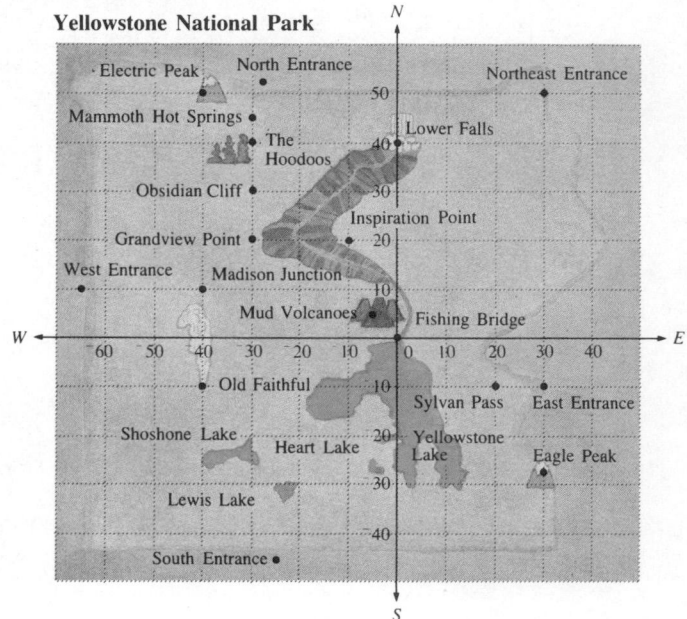

Yellowstone National Park

Locations on the map of Yellowstone Park can be given by ordered pairs of numbers called the **coordinates** of the points.

Fishing Bridge is at the **origin** (0,0).

East Entrance is 30 km east and 10 km south of Fishing Bridge. The coordinates of East Entrance are (30, ⁻10).

Give the coordinates of each location.

1. Lower Falls (0,40)   2. Madison Junction (⁻40,10)   3. Electric Peak (⁻40,50)

4. West Entrance (⁻65,10)   5. Grandview Point (⁻30,20)   6. Sylvan Pass (20,⁻10)

7. Northeast Entrance (30,50) 8. Obsidian Cliff (⁻30,30)   9. Inspiration Point (⁻10,20)

10. Mammoth Hot Springs   11. The Hoodoos (⁻30,40)   12. Old Faithful (⁻40,⁻10)
(⁻30,45)

Estimate the coordinates of each location. Estimates will vary.

13. South Entrance (⁻25,⁻45)   14. Mud Volcanoes (⁻5,5)   15. Eagle Peak (30,⁻28)

16. North Entrance (⁻29,52)   17. Lewis Lake (⁻25,⁻30)   18. Heart Lake (⁻5,⁻27)

384

Follow Up

Reteaching

Have students graph and label each point on a coordinate grid (TRB p. 286). Then have them draw line segments to connect the points in order.

A(3, 3) B(2, 2) C(0, 2) D(⁻1, 3)
E(⁻1,1) F(0, ⁻1) G(⁻2, ⁻4) H(⁻2, ⁻6)
I(1, ⁻7) J(4, ⁻6) K(4, ⁻4) L(2, ⁻1)
M(3, 1) A(3, 3)

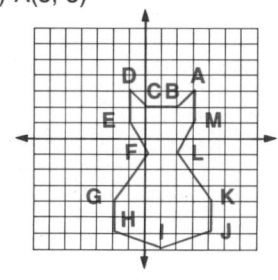

Enrichment

Ask students to draw a simple picture on a coordinate grid (TRB p. 286). In groups of two, have one student give the coordinates, in order, to the other. The classmate should then graph the coordinates and draw the picture. Pictures might be basic geometric figures or outlines of items (such as a paper cup, a vase, or a lamp shade) that can be drawn by connecting points in order.

Assignment Guide			
	Minimum	Average	Extended
page 385	1–19	1–25	1–25, TM

Give the coordinates of each point.

1. A (⁻2,4)   **2.** B (1,⁻4)   **3.** C (1,2)

4. D (0,4)   **5.** E (⁻4,4)   **6.** F (⁻2,1)

7. G (3,⁻2)   **8.** H (0,⁻2)   **9.** I (⁻3,⁻4)

10. J (4,0)   **11.** K (⁻5,⁻2)   **12.** L (⁻5,2)

13. M (3,2)   **14.** N (5,⁻4)   **15.** P (0,0)

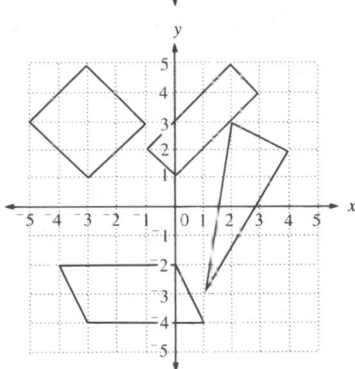

16. Give the coordinates of the three
vertices of the triangle.
(1,⁻3), (4,2), (2,3)

17. Give the coordinates of the four vertices
of the square.
(⁻3,1), (⁻1,3), (⁻3,5), (⁻5,3)

18. Give the coordinates of the four vertices
of the parallelogram.
(⁻3,⁻4), (1,⁻4), (0,⁻2), (⁻4,⁻2)

19. Give the coordinates of the four vertices
of the rectangle.
(0,1), (3,4), (2,5), (⁻1,2)

The coordinates of the vertices of six polygons are given below.
Graph the points and then draw each polygon. Name each polygon.

The graphs should show the given coordinates.

20. (⁻4,4), (2,4), (2,⁻2) triangle

21. (1,2), (⁻3,3), (⁻4,⁻1), (0,⁻2) square

22. (⁻2,⁻3), (2,⁻3), (4,0), (2,3), (⁻2,3), (⁻4,0) hexagon

23. (4,0), (0,3), (⁻4,0), (⁻2,⁻3), (2,⁻3) pentagon

24. (0,0), (⁻2,⁻1), (⁻3,⁻4), (3,⁻1) trapezoid

25. (3,4), (⁻3,3), (⁻4,⁻3), (2,⁻2) parallelogram

================ THINK MATH ================

Logical Reasoning

Graciela said, "I was 12 years old 2 days ago, but
next year I will be 15!" What is the date of
Graciela's birthday?   December 31

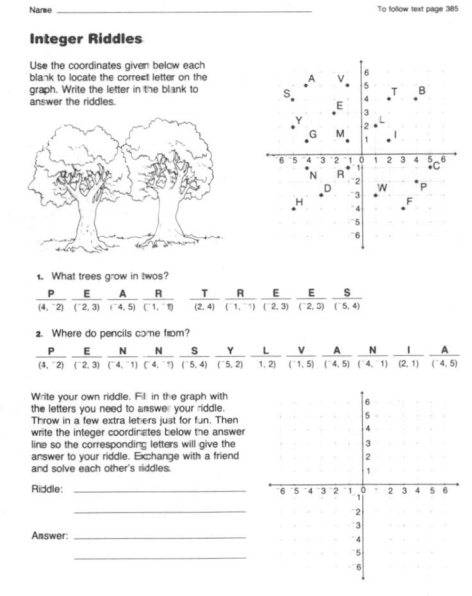

385

Using Page 385

Exercises 20–25 A coordinate grid (TRB p.286)
should be used for these exercises.

Think Math This problem involves logical
reasoning and knowledge of calendar dates. On
January 1st, Graciela could make the statement
given in the problem. Two days ago (Dec. 30th)
she was still 12 years old. One day ago (Dec. 31)
she became 13 years old. She will be 14 years old
Dec. 31 of this year since it is already Jan. 1 of this
year. Then she will be 15 years old next year.

Reteaching Supplement, page 107

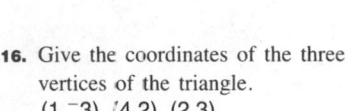

Enrichment Supplement, page 107

Practice Supplement, page 145

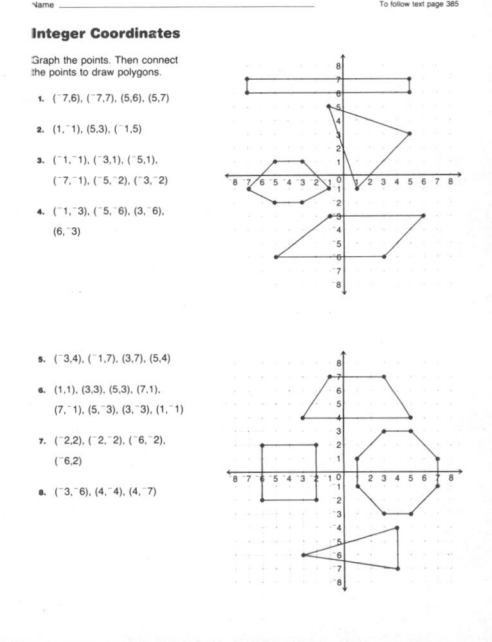

Equations

Quick Review Have students give the probability of selecting each of the following if there are 3 yellow, 5 red, and 8 green marbles in a bag.

P(red) $\frac{5}{16}$ P(green) $\frac{1}{2}$ P(yellow) $\frac{3}{16}$ P(black)   0

Lesson Focus To complete a table for a given equation and graph the equation

Suggested Materials Coordinate grid (TRB p. 286)

Ideas for Getting Started

Write these expressions on the chalkboard. Have students choose a value for x and evaluate each expression.

$x + 3$ $8 - x$ $\frac{1}{2}x$ $2x - 1$

Repeat the activity as time permits.

Using Page 386

Motivational Problem Have students read the introductory problem. Ask them to identify the question and the data. Explain that to graph the equation we can make a table of ordered pairs.

Lesson Development Display the table on the chalkboard and work through the steps to find a set of ordered pairs. Explain that we can choose any number for x and evaluate the expression $2x + 1$, to find the corresponding value for y. After a set of ordered pairs is found, locate the points for the ordered pairs on the grid and draw a line to connect the points. Point out that the line is the graph of the equation.

Warm Up Assign these exercises as independent written work. Have students correct and discuss their work before proceeding to page 387.

Graphing Equations

The points on a road on this map have coordinates given by the equation $y = 2x + 1$. What is the graph of the equation?

To graph the equation, first make a table of values for x and y.

Then choose any number for x. Multiply by 2 and add 1 to find the corresponding value for y.

Mark the points for the ordered pairs (x,y) found in the table, and connect the points.

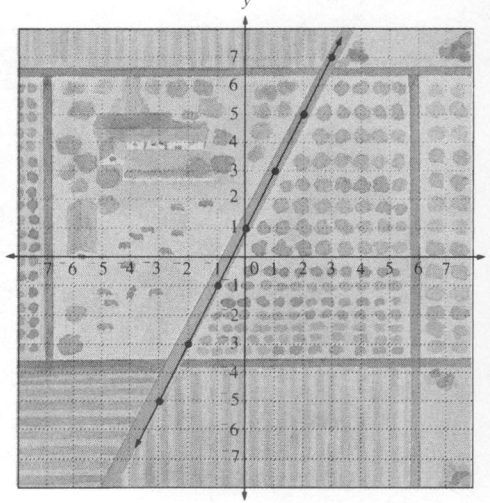

Table of values for the equation $y = 2x + 1$

x	3	2	1	0	$^-1$	$^-2$	$^-3$
$2x + 1$	$2 \cdot 3 + 1$	$2 \cdot 2 + 1$	$2 \cdot 1 + 1$	$2 \cdot 0 + 1$	$2 \cdot {}^-1 + 1$	$2 \cdot {}^-2 + 1$	$2 \cdot {}^-3 + 1$
y	7	5	3	1	$^-1$	$^-3$	$^-5$
(x, y)	(3,7)	(2,5)	(1,3)	(0,1)	($^-1,^-1$)	($^-2,^-3$)	($^-3,^-5$)

Warm Up

1. Copy and complete the table of values for the equation $y = x + 3$.

x	$^-5$	$^-3$	$^-1$	0	1	3	5
y	$^-2$	0	2	3	4	6	8
(x,y)	($^-5,^-2$)	($^-3,0$)	($^-1,2$)	(0,3)	(1,4)	(3,6)	(5,8)

2. Use the table of values from exercise 1.
   Graph the equation $y = x + 3$.
   The graph should reflect the values given in the table.

Follow Up

Reteaching

Have students make a table of values and graph the equation, $y = 3x - 2$. Remind them that multiplication is done before subtraction.

Students who have difficulty working with integers should always write out the step for adding the opposite in subtraction problems. For example, when $x = {}^-1$ in the equation above, they should write $3 \cdot {}^-1 + {}^-2 = {}^-3 + {}^-2 = {}^-5$. After completing the table, students should graph the ordered pairs.

Enrichment

Challenge students to graph these equations. Have them use both negative and positive values for x. They should join the points by curves rather than line segments.

1. $y = x^2 + 2$ 2. $y = x^3$

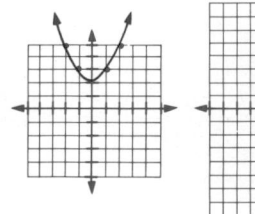
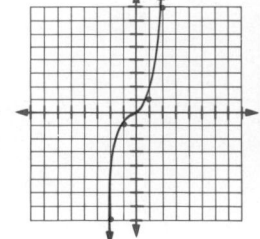

Assignment Guide			
	Minimum	Average	Extended
page 387		1–6, 12	1–12

Copy and complete each table of values. Then draw the graph of the equation.

1. Equation: $y = 5 - x$

x	8	5	3	1	$^-1$	$^-3$
y	$^-3$	0	2	4	6	8
(x,y)	$(8,^-3)$	$(5,0)$	$(3,2)$	$(1,4)$	$(^-1,6)$	$(^-3,8)$

2. Equation: $y = \frac{1}{2}x$

x	8	4	2	0	$^-2$	$^-4$	$^-8$
y	4	2	1	0	$^-1$	$^-2$	$^-4$
(x,y)	$(8,4)$	$(4,2)$	$(2,1)$	$(0,0)$	$(^-2,^-1)$	$(^-4,^-2)$	$(^-8,^-4)$

3. Equation: $y = x - 4$

x	7	5	3	1	$^-2$	$^-4$
y	3	1	$^-1$	$^-3$	$^-6$	$^-8$
(x,y)	$(7,3)$	$(5,1)$	$(3,^-1)$	$(1,^-3)$	$(^-2,^-6)$	$(^-4,^-8)$

4. Equation: $y = 2x - 2$

x	5	3	1	$^-1$	$^-3$
y	8	4	0	$^-4$	$^-8$
(x,y)	$(5,8)$	$(3,4)$	$(1,0)$	$(^-1,^-4)$	$(^-3,^-8)$

Make a table of values for each equation. Then draw the graph of each equation.

5. $y = x + 1$

6. $y = 3x - 1$

7. $y = 7 - x$

8. $y = x$

9. $y = \frac{1}{4}x + 2$

10. $y = 2x - 4$

Tables may vary. The graphs should reflect ordered pairs in the tables.

11. On the same coordinate grid, draw the graphs of the equations $y = 3 - x$ and $y = 2x - 3$. What are the coordinates of the point where the two graphs meet?
(2,1)

12. DATA HUNT What are the coordinates of your town or city? Use more than one map. Report the different ways the coordinates are labeled.

387

Using Page 387

Exercises 1–11 A coordinate grid should be used for these exercises. In exercises 5–11, suggest that students include some negative integers for x as well as some positive integers. Tell students that each of these equations should produce straight line graphs. If the graph of one of the ordered pairs is not in line with the others, they should check their computation.

Ideas That Work

Calculator Bonus

Show students the following example.

Example:
$$x^2 = 16$$
$$4 \cdot 4 = 16$$
$$^-4 \cdot {}^-4 = 16$$
$$x = 4 \text{ or } x = {}^-4$$

Next have them find two values, one negative and one positive, for each equation. They should make an estimate of the factors and then use the calculator to multiply and check. If calculators have a *square root* key, $\boxed{\sqrt{x}}$, some students may realize they can use it to find the solutions directly.

1. $y^2 = 81$ $y = 9$ or $^-9$
2. $b^2 = 169$ $b = 13$ or $^-13$
3. $c^2 = 3,025$ $c = 55$ or $^-55$
4. $t^2 = 2,116$ $t = 46$ or $^-46$
5. $a^2 = 144$ $a = 12$ or $^-12$
6. $r^2 = 1,089$ $r = 33$ or $^-33$
7. $s^2 = 4,356$ $s = 66$ or $^-66$
8. $w^2 = 15,625$ $2 = 125$ or $^-125$

Practice Supplement, page 146

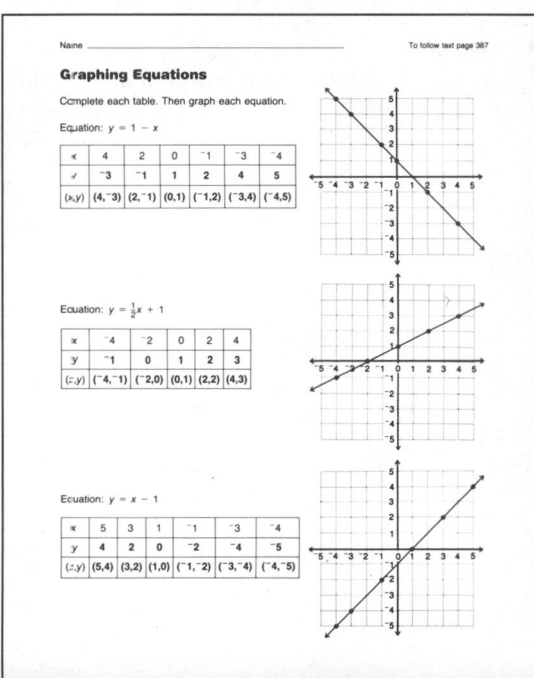

Name _____ To follow text page 387

Graphing Equations

Complete each table. Then graph each equation.

Equation: $y = 1 - x$

x	4	2	0	$^-1$	$^-3$	$^-4$
y	$^-3$	$^-1$	1	2	4	5
(x,y)	$(4,^-3)$	$(2,^-1)$	$(0,1)$	$(^-1,2)$	$(^-3,4)$	$(^-4,5)$

Equation: $y = \frac{1}{2}x + 1$

x	$^-4$	$^-2$	0	2	4
y	$^-1$	0	1	2	3
(x,y)	$(^-4,^-1)$	$(^-2,0)$	$(0,1)$	$(2,2)$	$(4,3)$

Equation: $y = x - 1$

x	5	3	1	$^-1$	$^-3$	$^-4$
y	4	2	0	$^-2$	$^-4$	$^-5$
(x,y)	$(5,4)$	$(3,2)$	$(1,0)$	$(^-1,^-2)$	$(^-3,^-4)$	$(^-4,^-5)$

Applications

Ideas for Getting Started

Lesson Focus To interpret, organize, and use data to make a decision about a real-world problem

Take a survey of students in your class to find out the following information.

- How many students can play a musical instrument?
- How many play in a school band, orchestra or other musical group?
- How many students own their own musical instrument?
- What was the approximate cost of the instrument?
- What is an estimate of the total cost of their music lessons?

Discuss with students the idea that many musical instrument stores have various plans to buy or rent instruments.

Using Page 388

Lesson Development After students read the introductory sentences ask the two conditions that must be met to play in the band. (have your own musical instrument and have at least 24 hours of lessons on the instrument) Read with students "Some Things to Consider." Discuss the three plans for buying or renting an instrument. In both the Rental Plan and the Rent-to-Buy Plan, there is a $45.00 charge for the 3-month period. Explain that one reason for this charge is that many beginning students find by the end of 3 months they do not want the instrument or they would like a different instrument. With these plans the music store gets paid for the use of the instrument and the student is not obligated beyond the first 3 months.

Assign "Some Questions to Answer" for independent written work. Allow time for students to correct and discuss these exercises.

Give students an opportunity to discuss their decisions. In the long run, buying the instrument may seem to be better than other plans. If at some later time the instrument is not used, it might be sold to recoup some of the cost. If the rental plan is continued past a year, the cost for playing the instrument continues to grow.

APPLIED PROBLEM SOLVING

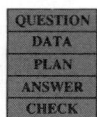

QUESTION
DATA
PLAN
ANSWER
CHECK

You want to learn to play the clarinet and become a member of the school band. To play in the band, you must have your own musical instrument and at least 24 hours of lessons.

Some Things to Consider

- You cannot pay cash for the clarinet.
- Music lessons are given once a week at $9 per hour.
- A music store sells new clarinets for $376 cash. They have three other plans for buying or renting instruments.

12-month Installment Plan to Buy	Rental Plan	Rent-to-Buy Plan
$34.50 per month	$45.00 for the first 3 months $27.00 per month thereafter	$45.00 for the first 3 months $41.00 per month for 9 months thereafter if you decide to buy

Some Questions to Answer

1. Using the 12-month installment plan, what is the cost of the clarinet? How much more is this than the cash price? $414; $38
2. What does it cost to rent a clarinet for 12 months? How much more or less is the rental price for 12 months than the intallment price to buy a clarinet? $288; $126 less

3. What is the cost of 24 hours of music lessons? $216

4. If you rent a clarinet while you are taking the lessons, what is the total amount you will spend by the time you finish the lessons? $342

5. If you use the rent-to-buy plan, how much will you pay for the instrument? $414

What Is Your Decision

What plan will you choose to be able to play a clarinet in the band? Answers will vary. The rental plan is cheaper per month, but students may choose owning the instrument as a better value. The rent-to-buy and installment plans have the same total. The rent-to-buy plan costs less for the first 3 months but has greater payments for the last 9 months.

388

CHAPTER REVIEW/TEST

Write < or > for each ◯.

1. ⁻3 ◯ 1 <
2. ⁻7 ◯ ⁻9 >
3. 0 ◯ ⁻6 >
4. 7 ◯ ⁻50 >

Add.

5. ⁻7 + ⁻3 ⁻10
6. ⁻6 + ⁻8 ⁻14
7. 2 + 10 12
8. ⁻4 + ⁻4 ⁻8
9. ⁻16 + 7 ⁻9
10. 3 + ⁻10 ⁻7
11. ⁻9 + 9 0
12. 14 + ⁻17 ⁻3

Subtract.

13. 8 − ⁻5 13
14. ⁻1 − 6 ⁻7
15. 7 − 12 ⁻5
16. ⁻9 − ⁻3 ⁻6
17. ⁻4 − ⁻6 2
18. 0 − ⁻5 5
19. ⁻6 − 2 ⁻8
20. 12 − 7 5

Multiply.

21. 3 · ⁻8 ⁻24
22. ⁻7 · ⁻4 28
23. ⁻6 · ⁻6 36
24. ⁻9 · 5 ⁻45
25. 8 · ⁻7 ⁻56
26. ⁻6 · ⁻9 54
27. ⁻1 · 10 ⁻10
28. ⁻2 · 15 ⁻30

Divide.

29. 42 ÷ ⁻6 ⁻7
30. ⁻28 ÷ 7 ⁻4
31. ⁻18 ÷ ⁻3 6
32. ⁻45 ÷ 9 ⁻5
33. ⁻60 ÷ ⁻10 6
34. 36 ÷ ⁻3 ⁻12
35. ⁻54 ÷ ⁻6 9
36. 32 ÷ ⁻4 ⁻8

Give the coordinates of each point.

37. A (2, ⁻2)
38. B (1,1)
39. C (⁻2,2)
40. D (⁻2,⁻1)
41. E (3,3)
42. F (1,⁻3)

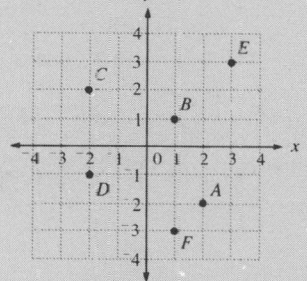

43. The temperature at ground level is 5°C. It is 20° colder at an altitude of 2,500 m. What is the temperature at 2,500 m? **⁻15°C**

44. The temperature due to the chill factor is ⁻13°C. In still air, the temperature would be 8° higher. What is the still-air temperature? **⁻5°C**

389

Using Page 389

The exercises in the Chapter Review/Test emphasize the major concepts and skills presented in this chapter. These exercises may be used as a review assignment or as a test, depending upon your needs.

Item Analysis The table below correlates the Chapter Review/Test items with objectives and with the student text pages on which the concepts or skills were taught.

Items	Objectives	Related Text Pages
1–4	15.1	368–369
5–12	15.2	370–375
13–20	15.3	376–377
21–36	15.4	380–383
37–42	15.5	384–387
43–44	15.6	378–379

Assessment Options

If you use the Chapter Review/Test as a review assignment, you may wish to use the free-response test or the multiple-choice test to evaluate mastery of the chapter objectives. The items on these tests have a one-to-one correspondence in terms of content and level of difficulty. A correlation of test items to objectives and student text pages is provided in the Management Guide for Chapter 15. Note: Items 46–47 are derived from lessons for which no minimum assignment was suggested in the Assignment Guide.

Multiple-Choice Test, TRB page 42–44
Free-Response Test, TRB pages 77–78

TRB Options

The following blackline masters are available for use with this chapter. If you have not already assigned these materials, you may wish to use them to close the chapter.

Recreation, TRB page 169
Consumer Applications, TRB page 187
Calculator Technology, TRB page 205
Reading Math, TRB page 241
Family Involvement, TRB pages 273–274

390

Reteaching

Using Page 390

The exercises on this page are intended for those students who experienced difficulty with the Chapter Review/Test on page 389. Should students require reteaching of these key concepts and skills, please refer to the teaching notes below. Otherwise, the Another Look exercises can be assigned as independent work, with students using the accompanying sample problems and hints as guides.

Exercises 1–6 This skill was originally taught on pages 368–369. Have students study the examples in the display box. Remind them that as you move from left to right on the number line the numbers get larger.

Exercises 7–15 This skill was originally taught on pages 372–375. On the chalkboard, draw a number line from ⁻10 to 10 and show students how to draw arrows to illustrate addition exercises. Then call on volunteers to draw the arrows as you work through other examples.

Exercises 16–24 This skill was originally taught on pages 376–377. Have students study the example in the display box. If students have difficulty subtracting integers, encourage them to write out each step and show the addition exercise for each problem. Emphasize that subtracting an integer is the same as adding its opposite.

Exercise 25–33 This skill was originally taught on pages 380–381. Read with students the rules for multiplying integers. Write some multiplication exercises on the chalkboard and have students apply the rules and give the products.

Exercises 34–42 This skill was originally taught on pages 382–383. After students read the rules for dividing integers, notice with them the similarity to the rules for multiplying integers. Work through several examples with students and have them apply the rules.

ANOTHER LOOK

⁻3 ⁻2 ⁻1 0 1 2 3
⁻3 is to the left of ⁻2.
⁻3 < ⁻2
2 is to the right of ⁻2.
2 > ⁻2

Write < or > for each ▦.
1. 6 ▦ ⁻4 > 2. ⁻10 ▦ ⁻4 < 3. 0 ▦ ⁻7 >
4. ⁻3 ▦ ⁻1 < 5. ⁻4 ▦ 0 < 6. ⁻8 ▦ ⁻9 >

+6 / ⁻4
⁻4 ⁻3 ⁻2 ⁻1 0 1 2
⁻4 + 6 = 2

Add.
7. ⁻3 + ⁻4 ⁻7   8. 7 + ⁻5 2   9. ⁻8 + 4 ⁻4
10. ⁻11 + ⁻3 ⁻14 11. 4 + ⁻9 ⁻5 12. 0 + ⁻6 ⁻6
13. ⁻6 + ⁻5 ⁻11 14. ⁻7 + 10 3 15. ⁻8 + ⁻7 ⁻15

7 − ⁻3 = 7 + 3 = 10
To subtract, *add* the opposite.
⁻9 − 4 = ⁻9 + ⁻4 = ⁻13

Subtract.
16. 6 − ⁻2 8   17. ⁻9 − 2 ⁻11 18. ⁻4 − ⁻7 3
19. 8 − 4 4   20. 10 − 12 ⁻2 21. ⁻1 − ⁻6 5
22. 9 − 15 ⁻6 23. ⁻4 − ⁻4 0 24. 0 − 8 ⁻8

negative × positive = negative
positive × negative = negative
negative × negative = positive
positive × positive = positive

Multiply.
25. ⁻7 · 2 ⁻14 26. 8 · ⁻3 ⁻24 27. ⁻5 · ⁻2 10
28. 6 · 3 18 29. ⁻4 · ⁻5 20 30. 9 · ⁻8 ⁻72
31. ⁻1 · ⁻1 1 32. 6 · ⁻8 ⁻48 33. ⁻7 · ⁻6 42

negative ÷ positive = negative
positive ÷ negative = negative
negative ÷ negative = positive
positive ÷ positive = positive

Divide.
34. ⁻8 ÷ 2 ⁻4 35. ⁻9 ÷ ⁻3 3 36. 21 ÷ ⁻7 ⁻3
37. ⁻40 ÷ 5 ⁻8 38. ⁻16 ÷ ⁻8 2 39. 36 ÷ ⁻4 ⁻9
40. ⁻24 ÷ ⁻6 4 41. 10 ÷ ⁻10 ⁻1 42. ⁻56 ÷ ⁻8 7

390

Just for Teachers

An Historical Look at the Negative

While the operation of subtraction is as ancient as mathematics itself, the minus symbol (−) first appeared in print only 500 years ago in Johann Widman's *Commercial Arithmetic,* published in Leipzig, Germany, where Widman taught arithmetic and algebra. The minus symbol to signify subtraction was derived from the Medieval practice of marking shipments of deficient weight with a bar to indicate shortage. Nearly a century elapsed before Widman's symbol became commonplace.

A negative number, however, represented an elusive concept that was avoided or ignored for much of history. The Hindus were aware of negative numbers and even formulated the laws of signs—"like" signs multiplied make positives, unlike signs multiplied make negatives. But while many Hindu-Arabic mathematicians grasped the *fact* that an equation could have a negative number for a solution, they had difficulty grasping the *idea* of that number. They had no thermometer or checking account overdrafts to which they could relate it.

The Italian Fibonacci (Leonardo da Pisa, c1170–1250) discovered a model for

ENRICHMENT

Function Rules

This machine operates on **input numbers** using a **rule** to give **output numbers**.

Rule: Multiply by 2 and add 1.

Input n	Output 2 · n + 1
5	11
3	7
⁻2	⁻3
⁻5	⁻9

Give the output numbers for each table.

1. Rule: Subtract 2 and multiply by 3.

Input n	Output (n − 2) · 3	
4		6
2		0
0		⁻6
⁻1		⁻9
⁻3		⁻15

2. Rule: Divide by 3, then add 1.

Input n	Output (n ÷ 3) + 1	
18		7
6		3
0		1
⁻3		0
⁻15		⁻4

3. Rule: Add ⁻10, then double.

Input n	Output (n + ⁻10) · 2	
20		20
10		0
5		⁻10
⁻5		⁻30
⁻10		⁻40

Give the rule for finding the output numbers in each table.

4. Rule: ? Subtract 4.

Input n	Output ?	
5	1	n − 4
4	0	
3	⁻1	
2	⁻2	
1	⁻3	

5. Rule: ? Multiply by ⁻5.

Input n	Output ?	
3	⁻15	n · ⁻5
2	⁻10	
7	⁻35	
⁻1	5	
⁻8	40	

6. Rule: ? Multiply the number by itself.

Input n	Output ?	
2	4	n · n
3	9	
⁻6	36	
5	25	
⁻10	100	

Using Page 391

This page is intended for those students who successfully completed the Chapter/Review Test on page 389. You may wish to assign this page as independent work while you use Another Look exercises to reteach the basic concepts and skills of the chapter. Or, you may decide that all students would benefit from exposure to this Enrichment activity.

Lesson Development Explain to students that the function rule tells how to find the output number for a given input number. On the chalkboard display the table with input numbers and function rule, 2 · n + 1. Have students use the rule to find the output numbers. Make sure students realize that each input number and rule determine a unique output number. Next play "Guess the Function Rule." Think of a rule and call on students to name input numbers. For example, use the rule "multiply by ⁻2." If a student names 3, you would say ⁻6. If a student names ⁻5, you would say 10. Continue in this way until someone guesses the correct rule. This student should then think of a function rule and respond with the output numbers for each input number given by other students. Repeat the activity as time permits.

Exercises 1–6 Assign the exercises as independent written work. Note that exercises 1–3 give practice in finding output numbers while exercises 4–6 require students to find the rule.

the abstract concept of negative numbers. Working with a financial problem, he saw that it could only be solved by assuming that there had been a debt to begin with. Still, mathematicians hesitated to accept negative numbers as a legitimate mathematical concept until the Renaissance saw new inquiry and the first significant advances in the field of algebra since the death of Diophantus, the Alexandrian "father of algebra", more than 1,000 years earlier.

Part of this inquiry centered on finding general solutions to cubic and quartic equations—those involving x^3 and x^4, respectively. Ultimately, the cubic was solved by Tartaglia, the quartic by Ferrari, and the work of both men was published in 1545 by Cardano in *Ars Magna,* a significant contribution to mathematical literature. Cardano not only provided a full treatment of negative numbers and their behavior in arithmetical and algebraic operations, he also "invented" the square root of a negative number, which we call an imaginary number.

Using Page 392

The exercises on the page provide practice for maintaining cumulative skills. The emphasis in this Cumulative Review is on percents (Chapter 12) and probabilities (Chapter 14).

Item Analysis The table below correlates the Cumulative Review items with objectives and with the student book pages on which the concepts or skills were taught.

Items	Objectives	Related Text Pages
1–2	12.1	294–301
3	12.2	302–304
4	12.3	306–307
5	12.4	310–311
6	12.2	304–306
7–8	14.1	344–347
11	14.3	352–355
12	14.4	352–355
13	12.6	305, 308–309, 313
14	14.5	350, 355, 360–361

1. What is the percent for $\frac{7}{8}$?

   (A) 87.5% B 56%
   c 114% D not given

2. What is the lowest-terms fraction for 72%?

   A $\frac{7}{25}$ B $\frac{35}{50}$
   (C) $\frac{18}{25}$ D not given

3. What is 12% of 27?

   A 5.4 (B) 3.24
   c 6.2 D not given

4. What percent of 16 is 5?

   A 3.2% B 1.2%
   (C) 31.25% D not given

5. 20% of what number is 17?

   A 54 B 340
   (C) 85 D not given

6. What would be the amount of interest charged on a $700 loan for 3 years at 12%?

   (A) $252 B $84
   c $168 D not given

7. What is $P(4)$?

   A $\frac{1}{2}$ B $\frac{1}{5}$
   (C) $\frac{1}{4}$ D not given

8. What is P(odd number)?

   (A) $\frac{1}{2}$ B $\frac{1}{4}$
   c $\frac{1}{3}$ D not given

9. What is the arithmetic mean of 23, 32, 41, 56, and 63?

   A 54.25 B 41
   c 43.4 (D) not given

10. What is the median of 2, 4, 5, 7, 9, 12, 13, and 14?

    A 7.5 (B) 8
    c 8.5 D not given

11. What is the mode of 23, 24, 25, 27, 28, 28, 28, 30, 32, 34, 34?

    A 28.5 B 34
    (C) 28 D not given

12. What is the name of a graph that uses drawings to report information?

    (A) pictograph B line segment graph
    c circle graph D not given

13. Justine got 27 out of 30 problems correct on a spelling test. What was her percent score?

    A 85% B 89%
    c 81% (D) not given

14. Steve has 4 pencils—red, green, yellow, and black—in his desk drawer. If he reaches into the drawer without looking, what is the probability of getting the green pencil?

    (A) $\frac{1}{4}$ B $\frac{1}{3}$
    c $\frac{1}{2}$ D not given

Objectives

16.1 Express customary units of length in larger or smaller customary units, and add and subtract inches, feet, and yards.

16.2 Find the area of a polygon in customary units.

16.3 Find the volume of a rectangular prism and a cylinder in customary units.

16.4 Express customary units of capacity and weight in larger or smaller customary units; estimate customary units of weight and temperature in degrees Fahrenheit.

16.5 Solve word problems using the 5-Point Checklist and cumulative computational skills.

Summary

In this chapter students review the customary units for measuring length, area, volume, liquid measure, weight, and Fahrenheit temperature.

Since the basic ideas for measurement were presented in Chapter 10, the units and the relationships between the units in customary measurement are the main points of emphasis. Area formulas for rectangles and circles, and volume formulas for prisms and cylinders, are the same as used in the metric measurement chapter.

Mathematical Background

Customary Units Although most countries in the world use only the metric system of measurement, the United States continues to use both the metric system and customary units of measure. Metric units of measure have long been used in the field of science, and in recent years have been increasingly used in business and industry. Packages of familiar grocery items often have measurements given in both metric and customary units. Gasoline is sold by the liter or by the gallon, depending upon the metering device installed in the gasoline pump. It appears that for some time to come, both metric and customary units will be used throughout the United States.

In teaching customary units, it is helpful to relate the units to familiar objects. A yard is approximately the distance from a person's nose to the tip of an outstretched arm. A foot is about the length of an adult's shoe, and an inch is about the width of a thumb. Familiar containers can be used to illustrate measures of capacity such as the cup, pint, quart, and gallon. One pint of water weighs about 1 pound. A baseball weighs about 5 ounces, and a bowling ball weighs a maximum of 16 pounds.

In addition to the material in the text, students should be given an opportunity to measure objects with devices scaled in customary units. Rulers scaled in inches and yardsticks should be available for use, as well as measures for capacity, weight, and Fahrenheit temperature.

Problem Solving The problem-solving sets in this chapter are related to customary units of measure and involve a variety of operations in single or multiple steps. On page 401, the problem-solving practice deals with customary units of liquid measure. A

problem-solving lesson on pages 404 and 405 involves computing unit prices of grocery items with the units including pounds, ounces, quarts, and gallons. An applied problem-solving lesson on page 406 also deals with unit pricing and making a decision about which item to buy.

Vocabulary

inch	cup	fluid ounce	Fahrenheit
foot	pint	ounce	unit price
yard	quart	pound	
mile	gallon	ton	

Error Analysis

This chapter deals with customary units of measure. The basic concepts of measurement are reviewed and relationships between customary units are presented. Errors in computation involving measurement often reflect a misunderstanding of relationships between units. Some common errors are given below.

Error Pattern 1

3 ft 6 in.	8 ft 9 in.
+ 5 ft 9 in.	+ 3 ft 9 in.
9 ft 5 in.	11 ft 8 in.

Diagnosis The student added like units but regrouped as if 1 ft = 10 in. The student followed the algorithm for addition of whole numbers.

Remediation Review the relationship between feet and inches. Have the student apply the relationship to exercises, such as 9 in. + 6 in. Ask "How many feet in 15 in.?" Explain that since 1 ft = 12 in., 15 in. = 12 in. + 3 in., or 1 ft 3 in.

Error Pattern 2

10 ft	→	9 ft 10 in.
− 2 ft 4 in.		− 2 ft 4 in.
		7 ft 6 in.

1 yd 1 ft 8 in.	→	0 yd 10 ft 18 in.
− 2 ft 11 in.		− 2 ft 11 in.
		8 ft 7 in.

Diagnosis The student regrouped as if 1 ft = 10 in. and 1 yd = 10 ft.

Remediation Use actual measuring situations to review the meaning of yards, feet, and inches. Have the student record the relationship of one unit to another on index cards and refer to the cards when necessary.

 ## Problem Solving

Using the Hand-Held Calculator

The solution to many problem-solving situations involves the use of computational skills. As a result, many problem-solving experiences are viewed as an opportunity for students to review computational skills. However, an overemphasis on computational skills during problem solving can shift attention away from what should be the major focus of problem solving—namely, understanding problems and selecting and carrying out appropriate solution strategies. There are many problem-solving situations where students could be allowed to use a hand-held calculator in order to reduce the time needed with paper and pencil calculations and to increase the time spent *thinking* about problems. In the following situations students could be allowed to use a calculator.

- The use of the Guess and Check strategy can be encouraged by the use of a calculator since the time required to check each guess is minimized.
- Possible number patterns can be tested rapidly with the aid of the calculator.
- Many problems involving the strategies Work Backward or Choose the Operations require several computational steps. The use of a calculator for these problems allows students to focus on how the action in the story suggests the operations needed to find a solution.
- Numerous problem-solving lessons in this program focus on estimation. In many of the lessons, the calculator can be used to find the exact answer after the student has completed the estimate.

Using a calculator during problem solving will instill enthusiasm in students. Many students will view the use of a calculator in school as a novelty and as a result will be enthusiastic about being allowed to use it. And, perhaps most important of all, the calculator may be the only vehicle by which students who are poor at computation can participate in problem-solving experiences. Problem-solving experiences for students with computational deficiencies should *not* be delayed until those deficiencies are remedied.

The calculator as a tool for problem solving has strong support for the "real world" where problems in business, industry, and science, for example, are solved with the aid of the calculator. Thus, the use of the calculator in problem solving gives students experience in a realistic and practical problem-solving mode.

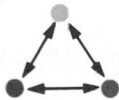 # Special Education

This chapter reviews some of the measurement concepts presented in earlier chapters. In addition, relationships between customary units of length, capacity, and weight are introduced. Converting to larger or smaller units of measure can cause difficulties for the special-needs student. The following suggestions will assist you in meeting the needs of the special students in your class.

Handling Regrouping

Changing to larger or smaller customary units requires that students have the ratios between units well in mind. To help students with this, give them regrouping exercises. For the special student this may mean using physical materials as they think through the exercises. They might trade 12-in. strips for a 1-ft ruler and 3 rulers for 1 yardstick. In working with liquid measure, provide students with sets of containers of standard measure. These can aid students in developing an understanding of the various units.

Building Models and Scaling Recipes

Activities that can bring together many of the skills covered in this book are drawing a scale model or decreasing or enlarging a given recipe. These activities will require converting units and writing ratios involving measures. Either activity will relate directly to the common use of these skills in students' everyday lives.

Practicing Conversion Skills

Two card games which are helpful in motivating students to practice conversion skills with customary measurements are "Match Me" and "Line Up."

Match Me is played by giving each student a customary measurement written on an index card. Students then look at the measurements given on the cards of their classmates and try to find the other student whose measurement is equal to theirs. If there is an odd number of students in the class, there will have to be one measurement which is given in three forms.

Line Up is played by giving each student a different linear measurement and having them decide on the correct ordering of the measures from smallest to largest. Students will have to compare their measures with each of the other students in the classroom as they line up in order. You will need to establish some reference points, such as one foot and ten feet, in order for students to start to determine where they should stand in lining up.

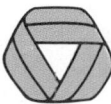 # Subject Integration

Subject matter related to other areas of the curriculum has been integrated into the following lessons. This provides an opportunity to highlight the interaction between mathematics and other subjects.

Physical Education Sailing, page 393
Industrial Arts Carpentry, pages 394–395
Home Economics Liquid measure, pages 400–401
Science Fahrenheit temperature, page 403
Consumer Awareness Unit prices, pages 404–405

Management Guide

Teaching Chapter 16				Meeting Individual Needs					
				Lesson Assignments			Follow Up		
Objectives	Chapter Content	Pages	TRB Test Items	Minimum	Average	Extended	Reteaching	Enrichment	Practice
	Chapter Opener	393							
16.1 Express customary units of length in larger or smaller customary units, and add and subtract, inches, feet, and yards.	Units of length	394–395	1–12	1–12 1–17, SK	1–14 1–17, 19, SK	1–16 1–20, SK	SE6 Ch 16 RS 108	ES 108	MP 441 PS 147
16.2 Find the area of a polygon in customary units.	Area	396–397	13–15	1–10	1–11	1–12	RS 109	ES 109	MP 441 PS 148
16.3 Find the volume of a rectangular prism and a cylinder in customary units.	Volume	398–399	16–18	1–13	1–14	1–14, TM	RS 110	ES 110	MP 441 PS 149
16.4 Express customary units of capacity and weight in larger or smaller customary units; estimate customary units of weight and temperature in degrees Fahrenheit.	Liquid Measure	400	19–22	1–12	1–14	1–14	RS 111	ES 111	PS 150
	Units of Weight	402	23–26	1–18	1–20	1–20	SE6 Ch 16		PS 151
	Fahrenheit Temperature	403	27–29	1–9, SK	1–11, SK	1–11, SK	RS 112	ES 112	
16.5 Solve word problems using the 5-Point Checklist and cumulative computational skills.	Problem Solving: Practice	401	30–35	1–9	1–10 13–14	5–14			
	Problem Solving: Using a Calculator	404–405		1–9	1–11, 14	4–14			PS 152
	Applied Problem Solving	406							
	Chapter Review/Test	407							
	Another Look/ Enrichment	408–409							
	Technology	410–411							
	Cumulative Review	412							

SE6 Student Edition, Book 6
RS Reteaching Supplement
ES Enrichment Supplement
PS Practice Supplement
MP More Practice
TM Think Math
SK Skillkeeper
TRB Teacher's Resource Book

Masters for use

. . . before Chapter 16

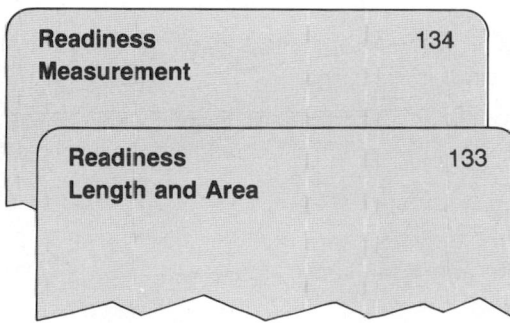

Readiness Measurement	134
Readiness Length and Area	133

. . . during Chapter 16

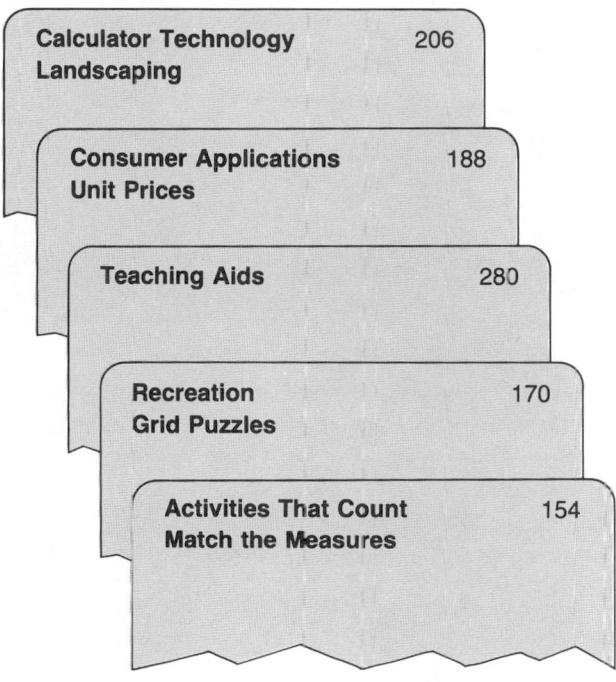

Calculator Technology Landscaping	206
Consumer Applications Unit Prices	188
Teaching Aids	280
Recreation Grid Puzzles	170
Activities That Count Match the Measures	154

. . . after Chapter 16

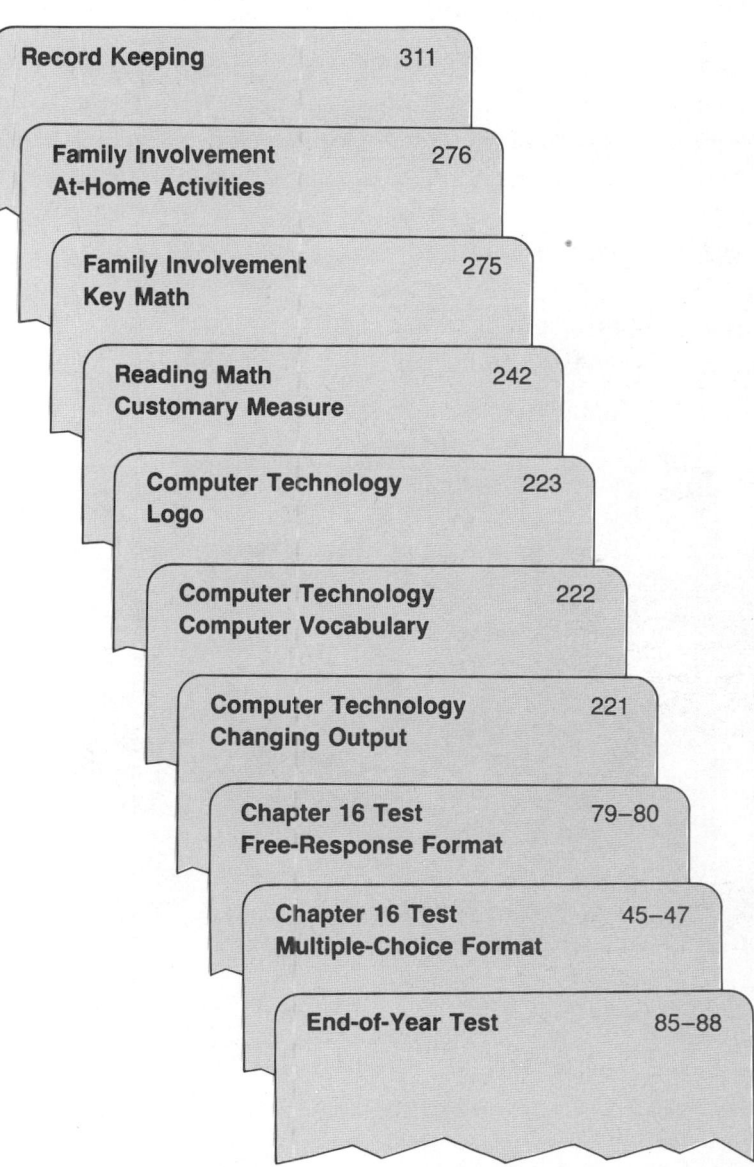

Record Keeping	311
Family Involvement At-Home Activities	276
Family Involvement Key Math	275
Reading Math Customary Measure	242
Computer Technology Logo	223
Computer Technology Computer Vocabulary	222
Computer Technology Changing Output	221
Chapter 16 Test Free-Response Format	79–80
Chapter 16 Test Multiple-Choice Format	45–47
End-of-Year Test	85–88

Supplements

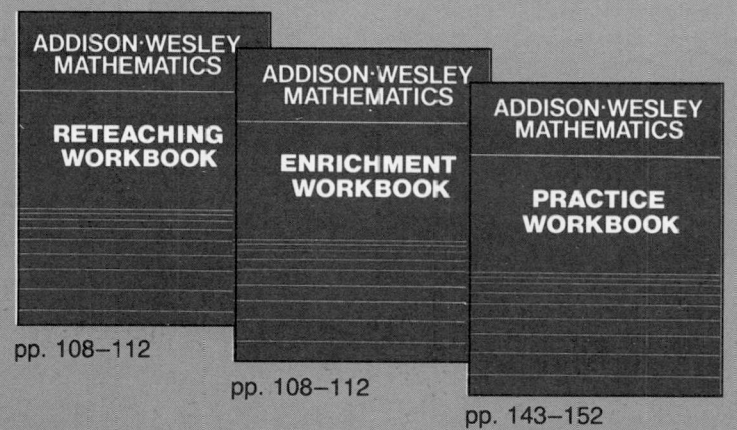

ADDISON·WESLEY MATHEMATICS
RETEACHING WORKBOOK
pp. 108–112

ADDISON·WESLEY MATHEMATICS
ENRICHMENT WORKBOOK
pp. 108–112

ADDISON·WESLEY MATHEMATICS
PRACTICE WORKBOOK
pp. 143–152

Other Addison-Wesley Resources

Books and Kits

Dice and Dots pp. 43–47
A New Twist pp. 55, 57, 85
General Mathematics: Making Practice Fun 65
Problem-Solving Experiences in Mathematics, Grade 7
   Problems 73, 78, 88, 97, 117, 123, 132

Activities That Count are designed for use throughout this chapter and subsequent chapters. Before beginning Chapter 16 you may wish to review these activites and select the ones you consider appropriate for your class.

Match the Measures   Math Lab

Purpose To find equivalent measures of length, weight, or capacity

Materials Activity sheet (TRB p. 154), scissors

Activity After students cut out the sixteen squares, have them form a 4 by 4 square so that matching sides name the same measure. The solution is shown below.

60 in.	5 ft	4 qt	1 gal	2 yd	6 ft	
2 pt	48 in.		1 lb		9 yd	
1 qt	4 ft		16 oz		27 ft	
2 gal	32 c	8 c	2 qt	48 oz	3 lb	
1,760 yd	16 fl oz		32 fl oz		30 in.	
1 mi	2 c		1 qt		$2\frac{1}{2}$ ft	
24 oz	$1\frac{1}{2}$ lb	1 T	2,000 lb	8 c	4 pt	
6 qt	2 yd		5,280 ft		16 fl oz	
12 pt	72 in.		1 mi		1 pt	
10 yd	30 ft	5 c	$2\frac{1}{2}$ pt	$1\frac{1}{2}$ ft	18 in.	

Size Wise   Project

Purpose To determine area by measuring and computing

Activity Have students find the dimensions of each room in their home and then determine the number of square feet of living space.

Measurement   Game

Purpose To find the area and perimeter of a rectangle, triangle, parallelogram, or circle in customary units

Materials Index cards with geometric figures, measures, and area; each figure should have 3 or 4 related cards to make sets

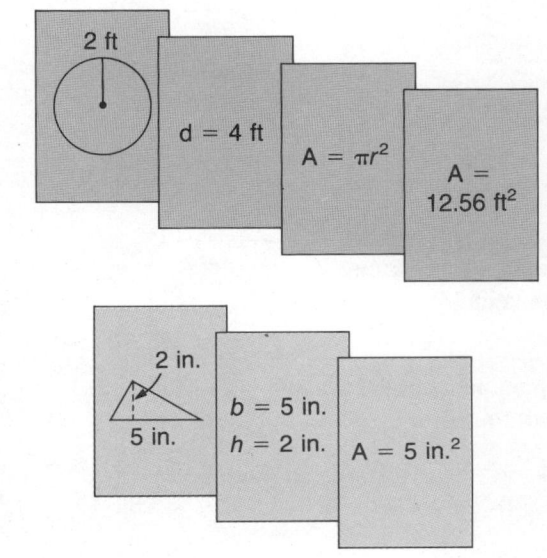

Activity After the cards are shuffled each player is given 7 cards. The remaining cards are placed in a pile and the top card is turned face up. In turn, players draw a card from the pile or the card that is face up. Players display as many pairs or triples of equivalents as possible and then discard one card. During a player's turn, single cards may be laid down to match the sets of other players.

Play continues until one player goes out by playing all cards in hand. Scores are determined by counting 5 points for each card that has been laid down. For each card that a player has left in hand, 5 points are deducted. The winner is the player with the highest score when time is called.

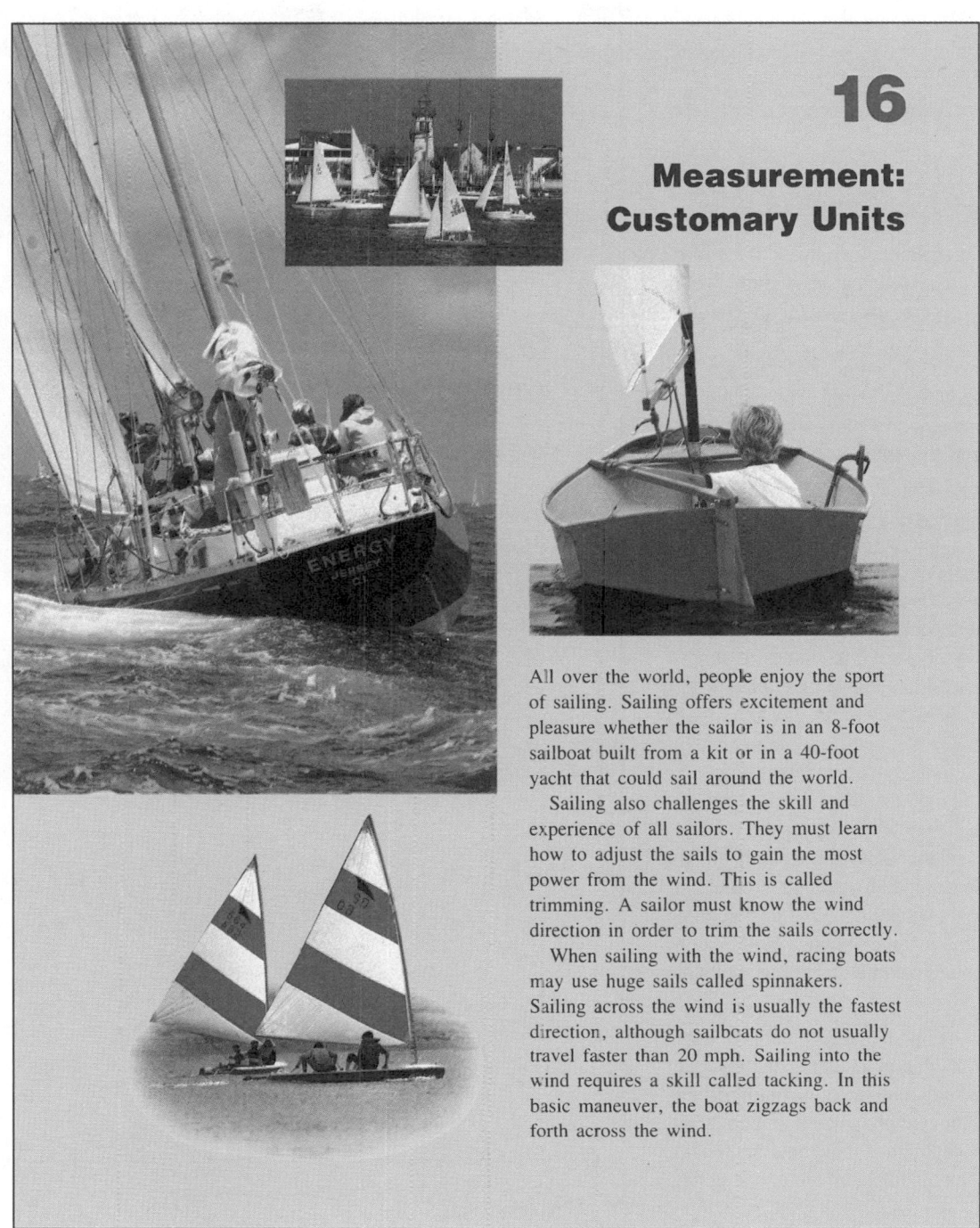

16

**Measurement:
Customary Units**

All over the world, people enjoy the sport of sailing. Sailing offers excitement and pleasure whether the sailor is in an 8-foot sailboat built from a kit or in a 40-foot yacht that could sail around the world.

Sailing also challenges the skill and experience of all sailors. They must learn how to adjust the sails to gain the most power from the wind. This is called trimming. A sailor must know the wind direction in order to trim the sails correctly.

When sailing with the wind, racing boats may use huge sails called spinnakers. Sailing across the wind is usually the fastest direction, although sailboats do not usually travel faster than 20 mph. Sailing into the wind requires a skill called tacking. In this basic maneuver, the boat zigzags back and forth across the wind.

Introducing the Chapter

Discussion Point out to students that Chapter 16 concerns measurement with customary units. Suggest that as they read the article, they look for different ways measurement is used. Ask students if they have had any experience with sailing. Encourage discussion and comment about the data in the article. This is an opportunity for students to formulate problems based on the data. As you teach the chapter you may wish to refer back to this page and ask students to solve the following problems.

Follow-Up Questions

After Page 395 What is the length in yards of a 40-foot yacht? ($13\frac{1}{3}$ yd) A certain sailboat can anchor in water no deeper than 15 yards. How many feet is this? (45 ft)

After Page 401 For a month's sea voyage the sailors brought along four 70-gallon tanks and four 5-gallon jugs. How many quarts of water is this altogether? (300 qt)

After Page 402 The world's largest sailing ship was the *Preussen,* a German vessel built in 1902. It could carry a cargo of 8,000 tons. How many pounds is this? (16,000,000 lb)

Quick Review Have students replace each ◯ with the correct symbol, > or <.

$^-1$ ⬤< 2 $^-2$ ⬤> $^-4$ $^-16$ ⬤< 1 $^-27$ ⬤> $^-30$

$^-22$ ⬤< 19   18 ⬤> $^-19$ 0 ⬤> $^-10$

Lesson Focus To express customary units of length in larger or smaller units and to add and subtract inches, feet, and yards

Suggested Materials Yardsticks and 12-inch rulers (TRB p. 280)

Ideas for Getting Started

Draw several line segments on the chalkboard. Have students find the lengths in inches. Then have them record some measurements in feet and inches.

Ask students to estimate some distances in the classroom in inches, feet, or yards. Then have selected students measure the distances and compare the measures to the estimates.

Using page 394

Lesson Development After students read the introductory problem, have them identify the question and the data needed to solve the problem. Ask them to examine the diagram and name the length of the smallest division on the inch ruler. ($\frac{1}{16}$ in.) Then have students give the length of each nail in the picture.

Direct students' attention to the tables showing commonly used units of length. Discuss the relationships between units. For the larger units of yard and mile, you might relate these units to the length of football fields or the distance around the school track. The oval tracks on athletic fields are often 440 yards or $\frac{1}{4}$ of a mile in length. Work through the examples of changing the units of length.

Exercises 1–16 These exercises may be used as other examples of changing units, or they may be assigned as written work. Note that periods are not used in symbols for length. An exception is the symbol for inch. In order that the word "in" is not confused with the symbol for inch, we use a period after the latter (in.).

Units of Length

Stephanie is building a planter box. She needs a nail that is $1\frac{7}{8}$ in. long. Which nail has this length?

Nail B has a length of $1\frac{7}{8}$ in.

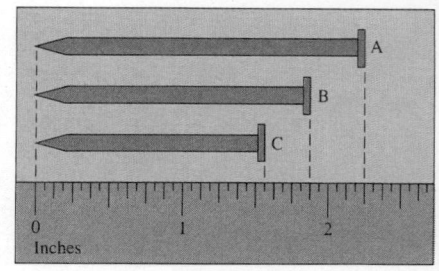

The tables below show some commonly used units of length.

Unit	Symbol
inch	in. or ″
foot	ft or ′
yard	yd
mile	mi

Relations Between Units
12 in. = 1 ft
3 ft = 1 yd
1,760 yd = 1 mi
5,280 ft = 1 mi

How many inches are there in 5 ft 7 in.?
There are 12 inches in 1 ft.

$5 \times 12 = 60$ $60 + 7 = 67$

5 ft 7 in. = 67 in.

$1\frac{1}{4}$ ft is how many inches?

$1\frac{1}{4} \times 12 = \frac{5}{4} \times 12 = 15$

$1\frac{1}{4}$ ft = 15 in.

How many yards are there in 27 ft?
There are 3 ft in 1 yd.

$27 \div 3 = 9$

27 ft = 9 yd

52 in. is how many feet?

$52 \div 12 = 4\frac{4}{12} = 4\frac{1}{3}$

52 in. = $4\frac{1}{3}$ ft

Give the missing numbers.

1. 2 ft = ___ in. 24
2. 5 yd = ___ ft 15
3. 60 in. = ___ ft 5
4. 2 mi = ___ yd 3,520
5. 1 ft 6 in. = ___ in. 18
6. 2 yd 1 ft = ___ ft 7
7. 1 yd = ___ in. 36
8. $2\frac{1}{4}$ ft = ___ in. 27
9. $1\frac{1}{3}$ yd = ___ ft 4
10. $\frac{1}{3}$ ft = ___ in. 4
11. 2.5 mi = ___ ft 13,200
12. 1 mi = ___ in. 63,360
13. How many yards are there in $\frac{1}{4}$ mi? 440 yd
14. How many yards are there in 3 mi? 5,280 yd
15. How many inches are there in $3\frac{1}{4}$ ft? 39 in.
16. Jeff is $58\frac{1}{4}$ in. tall. What is Jeff's height in feet and inches? 4 ft $10\frac{1}{4}$ in.

394

Follow Up

Reteaching

Give students an opportunity to participate in some measurement activities using customary units. Have them complete a worksheet like the one below listing classroom objects whose lengths are to be measured and recorded in inches, feet, and yards.

Object	in.	ft	yd
Desk width			
Door height			
Table length			
Pencil length			

Enrichment

Let students work in pairs and play "Estimation Golf" as described on page 248. Have them use customary units of length.

When measures of length are added or subtracted, we may need to regroup.

$$\begin{array}{r} \overset{1}{}7 \text{ ft } 9 \text{ in.} \\ +\ 3 \text{ ft } 6 \text{ in.} \\ \hline 11 \text{ ft } 3 \text{ in.} \end{array}$$

9 in. + 6 in. = 15 in.
15 in. = 1 ft 3 in.

$$\begin{array}{r} \overset{2}{\cancel{3}} \text{ yd } \overset{\overset{3}{\cancel{4}}}{\cancel{1}} \text{ ft } \overset{16}{\cancel{4}} \text{ in.} \\ -\ 1 \text{ yd } 2 \text{ ft } 7 \text{ in.} \\ \hline 1 \text{ yd } 1 \text{ ft } 9 \text{ in.} \end{array}$$

Add the lengths.

1. 2 ft 7 in.
 + 5 ft 4 in.
 7 ft 11 in.

2. 4 ft 10 in.
 + 2 ft 8 in.
 7 ft 6 in.

3. 4 yd 2 ft
 + 3 yd 2 ft
 8 yd 1 ft

4. 12 ft 11 in.
 + 9 ft 5 in.
 22 ft 4 in.

5. 4 ft 8 in.
 + 3 ft 9 in.
 8 ft 5 in.

6. 1 yd 1 ft 7 in.
 + 3 yd 2 ft 6 in.
 5 yd 1 ft 1 in.

7. 1 yd 2 ft 10 in.
 + _____ 11 in.
 2 yd 9 in.

8. 1 ft 7$\frac{1}{2}$ in.
 + 1 ft 9$\frac{1}{4}$ in.
 3 ft 4$\frac{3}{4}$ in.
 or 1 yd 4$\frac{3}{4}$ in.

Subtract the lengths.

9. 6 ft 9 in.
 − 1 ft 7 in.
 5 ft 2 in.

10. 5 ft 6 in.
 − 2 ft 8 in.
 2 ft 10 in.

11. 10 ft
 − 2 ft 4 in.
 7 ft 8 in.

12. 2 yd
 − 1 yd 2 ft
 1 ft

13. 2 ft
 − _____ 10 in.
 1 ft 2 in.

14. 6 ft 5 in.
 − 3 ft 9 in.
 2 ft 8 in.

15. 8 yd 1 ft 1 in.
 − 2 yd 2 ft 2 in.
 5 yd 1 ft 11 in.

16. 1 yd 1 ft 8 in.
 − _____ 2 ft 11 in.
 1 ft 9 in.

17. How much longer is a nail that is 2$\frac{1}{4}$ in. long than a nail that is 1$\frac{7}{8}$ in. long?
$\frac{3}{8}$ in.

18. Two boards of equal thickness are put on top of each other. A nail that is 2$\frac{1}{2}$″ long is nailed through the boards. There is $\frac{1}{4}$″ of the nail sticking through the boards. How thick is each board? 1$\frac{1}{8}$″

19. DATA HUNT The **cubit** is an ancient unit of length. What is your height in cubits?

20. DATA BANK How many **rods** are there in one mile? (See page 414.) **320 rods**

SKILLKEEPER

1. ⁻7 × 2 ⁻14 **2.** 7 × ⁻7 ⁻49 **3.** 12 × ⁻3 ⁻36 **4.** 9 × ⁻6 ⁻54 **5.** 2 × ⁻5 ⁻10

6. ⁻4 × ⁻9 36 **7.** 0 × ⁻4 0 **8.** ⁻9 × 7 ⁻63 **9.** ⁻10 × ⁻2 20 **10.** ⁻6 × 5 ⁻30

11. 12 ÷ ⁻4 ⁻3 **12.** 30 ÷ ⁻5 ⁻6 **13.** 20 ÷ ⁻4 ⁻5 **14.** ⁻14 ÷ ⁻2 7 **15.** ⁻24 ÷ 8 ⁻3

16. 35 ÷ ⁻5 ⁻7 **17.** ⁻18 ÷ 6 3 **18.** 81 ÷ ⁻9 ⁻9 **19.** ⁻15 ÷ ⁻3 5 **20.** ⁻9 ÷ 3 ⁻3

More Practice. page 441, Set A

Using Page 395

Exercises 1–16 Before assigning the exercises, use the example at the top of the page to show students how to add or subtract units of length. Be sure students understand the regrouping process.

Data Hunt This problem gives students the opportunity to work with a nonstandard unit of length. A cubit is the length of the arm from the tip of the middle finger to the elbow.

Skillkeeper These skills were originally taught in Chapter 15.

More Practice, page 441, Set A

Reteaching Supplement, page 108

Name _____   To follow text page 395

Units of Length

1 foot (ft) = 12 inches (in.)	1 mile (mi) = 1,760 yards
1 yard (yd) = 3 feet	1 mile = 5,280 feet
1 yard = 36 inches	

Multiply to change from a larger unit to a smaller unit.

6 ft = __?__ in. $\frac{1}{4}$ ft = __?__ in.
1 ft = 12 in.
6 × 12 = 72 in. $\frac{1}{4}$ × 12 = 3 in.

Divide to change from a smaller unit to a larger unit.

17 ft = __?__ yd   78 in. = __?__ yd
1 yd = 3 ft   1 yd = 36 in.
17 ÷ 3 = 5$\frac{2}{3}$ yd   78 ÷ 36 = 2$\frac{1}{6}$ yd

Complete.

1. 96 in. = __8__ ft   (Divide by 12.)
2. 3 mi = __5,280__ yd   (Multiply by 1,760.)
3. 3 ft 4 in. = __40__ in. (3 × 12 = 36, 36 + 4 = 40)
4. 83 in. = __6$\frac{11}{12}$__ ft
5. $\frac{1}{3}$ yd = __12__ in.
6. 45 in. = __1$\frac{1}{4}$__ yd
7. 2$\frac{2}{3}$ yd = __8__ ft
8. 3 mi = __15,840__ ft
9. 5 ft 9 in. = __69__ in.

Add or subtract the lengths.

10. 3$\frac{1}{3}$ ft 7 in.
 + 2 ft 7 in. (7 in. + 7 in. = 14 in. = 1 ft 2 in.)
 6 ft 2 in.

11. 5$\frac{6}{12}$ ft $\frac{4}{4}$ in.
 − 2 ft 6 in. (1 less foot 12 more inches)
 4 ft 10 in.

12. 1 yd 2 ft 6 in.
 + 3 yd 1 ft 3 in. (3 ft = 1 yd Regroup!)
 5 yd 9 in.

13. 7 ft 11 in.
 + 5 ft 9 in.
 13 ft 8 in.

14. 5 ft 6 in.
 + 4 ft 10 in.
 10 ft 4 in.

15. 5 ft 3 in.
 − 1 ft 9 in.
 3 ft 6 in.

16. 16 ft 7 in.
 − 5 ft 10 in.
 10 ft 9 in.

17. 4 ft
 − 2 ft 5 in.
 1 ft 7 in.

Enrichment Supplement, page 108

Name _____   To follow text page 395

That's About Right

Write an estimate for the measurement in each problem. Then find the actual measurement to the unit or part of a unit given.

Compare your estimate with a friend's estimate. The person whose estimate is closer to the actual measurement scores one point. See how many points you can score. **Answers will vary.**

1. Height of the doorknob (nearest inch)
Estimate: _____ Actual: _____

2. Width of your room (nearest foot)
Estimate: _____ Actual: _____

3. Length of your shoe (nearest $\frac{1}{2}$ in.)
Estimate: _____ Actual: _____

4. Length of your pencil (nearest $\frac{1}{4}$ in.)
Estimate: _____ Actual: _____

5. Width of a sheet of paper (nearest $\frac{1}{4}$ in.)
Estimate: _____ Actual: _____

6. Length of your math book (nearest $\frac{1}{2}$ in.)
Estimate: _____ Actual: _____

7. Length of a dollar bill (nearest $\frac{1}{8}$ in.)
Estimate: _____ Actual: _____

8. Length of a chalkboard (nearest inch)
Estimate: _____ Actual: _____

9. Height of the door (nearest inch)
Estimate: _____ Actual: _____

10. Width of a penny (nearest $\frac{1}{8}$ in.)
Estimate: _____ Actual: _____

11. Height of your desk (nearest inch)
Estimate: _____ Actual: _____

12. Width of a hallway (nearest inch)
Estimate: _____ Actual: _____

13. Thickness of your math book (nearest $\frac{1}{8}$ in.)
Estimate: _____ Actual: _____

14. Length of your school building (nearest yard)
Estimate: _____ Actual: _____

Practice Supplement, page 147

Name _____   To follow text page 395

Units of Length

Write the missing numbers.

1. 48 in. = __4__ ft
2. 1$\frac{3}{4}$ ft = __21__ in.
3. $\frac{1}{2}$ mi = __880__ yd
4. 2 ft 4 in. = __28__ in.
5. 2 yd 2 ft = __8__ ft
6. $\frac{2}{3}$ ft = __8__ in.
7. 1$\frac{2}{3}$ yd = __5__ ft
8. $\frac{1}{4}$ ft = __3__ in.
9. $\frac{1}{4}$ mi = __1,320__ ft
10. 7 yd = __21__ ft
11. 18 ft = __6__ yd
12. 1 yd 9 in. = __45__ in.

Add the lengths.

13. 7 ft 4 in.
 + 3 ft 7 in.
 10 ft 11 in.

14. 6 ft 11 in.
 + 4 ft 10 in.
 11 ft 9 in.

15. 5 yd 2 ft
 + 3 yd 2 ft
 9 yd 1 ft

16. 3 ft 6$\frac{1}{4}$ in.
 + 1 ft 2$\frac{3}{4}$ in.
 4 ft 9 in.

17. 2 yd 1 ft 6 in.
 + 3 yd 2 ft 7 in.
 6 yd 1 ft 1 in.

18. 1 yd 2 ft 3 in.
 + 1 yd 1 ft 6 in.
 3 yd 9 in.

Subtract the lengths.

19. 7 ft 8 in.
 − 3 ft 6 in.
 4 ft 2 in.

20. 4 ft 3 in.
 − 2 ft 6 in.
 1 ft 9 in.

21. 12 ft
 − 8 ft 4 in.
 3 ft 8 in.

22. 3 yd
 − 1 yd 1 ft
 1 yd 2 ft

23. 6 yd 2 ft 3 in.
 − 1 yd 1 ft 7 in.
 5 yd 8 in.

24. 3 yd 1 ft 5 in.
 − 2 ft 6 in.
 2 yd 1 ft 11 in.

Quick Review Have students divide. Tell them to give answers in lowest terms.

$5\frac{1}{3} \div 8$ $\frac{2}{3}$ $1\frac{7}{8} \div 3\frac{3}{4}$ $\frac{1}{2}$ $9\frac{1}{3} \div 2\frac{1}{3}$ 4

$6 \div 2\frac{2}{5}$ $2\frac{1}{2}$ $4\frac{1}{5} \div 3\frac{1}{2}$ $1\frac{1}{5}$

Lesson Focus To find the area of a rectangle and a circle in customary units

Suggested Materials Tagboard model of one square foot

Ideas for Getting Started

On the square foot made of tagboard, make a grid of one-inch squares to show that 144 in.^{2} = 1 ft^2. Use the square foot to find the area of the chalkboard by drawing around the square and then counting the number of squares needed to cover the chalkboard. Review the formulas for area of a rectangle and area of a circle.

$$A = lw \qquad\qquad A = \pi r^2$$

Using Page 396

Motivational Problem Have students read the problem at the top of the page and explain what the question asks us to find. Next have them identify the data needed to solve the problem. Elicit from students a plan for finding the answer.

Lesson Development The formula $A = lw$, should be familiar to all students. Be sure that the notation for square feet (ft^2) is understood by students. The second example shows how square feet can be expressed in the larger unit, square yards. The third example reviews area of a circle. Since the diameter of the circle is given in the problem, the radius must be found before using the formula $A = \pi r^2$.

Area

A rectangular section of a parade float is 16 ft long and 3 ft wide. What is the **area** of the section?

To find the area of a rectangle, we can use the formula for the area of a rectangle.

$A = lw$
  $l = 16$ ft $w = 3$ ft
$A = 3 \times 16 = 48$

The area is 48 square feet (ft^2).

Area is often given in square yards (yd^2). How many square yards are there in 48 ft^2?

1 yd^2 contains 9 ft^2.

$$48 \div 9 = 5\frac{1}{3}$$

There are $5\frac{1}{3}$ yd^2 in 48 ft^2.

A circular section of a float has a diameter of 16 in. What is the area of that section?

To find the area, we can use the formula for the area of a circle.

$A = \pi r^2$
  $r = 8$ in. $\pi \approx 3.14$
$A \approx 3.14 \times 8^2$
$A \approx 3.14 \times 64$
$A \approx 200.96$

The area is about 200.96 in.^{2}.

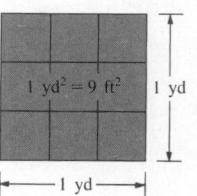
1 yd^2 = 9 ft^2 1 yd

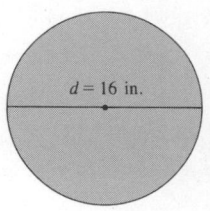
$d = 16$ in.

Warm Up

Give the area of each rectangle.

1. $l = 10$ in.	**2.** $l = 6.5$ ft	**3.** $l = 3\frac{1}{2}$ in.	**4.** $l = 3.1$ mi
$w = 8$ in.	$w = 4$ ft	$w = 1\frac{1}{2}$ in.	$w = 1.8$ mi
80 in.^{2}	26 ft^2	$5\frac{1}{4}$ in.^{2}	5.58 mi^2

Give the area of each circle. Use 3.14 for π.

5. $r = 10$ ft	**6.** $d = 8$ in.	**7.** $r = 2.5$ in.	**8.** $r = 0.5$ mi
396 314 ft^2	50.24 in.^{2}	19.625 in.^{2}	0.785 mi^2

Follow Up

Reteaching

Draw rectangles and circles on index cards and provide each student with a card. Have students measure the figure on their card and find the area in customary units. Students can then trade cards and compare answers.

Enrichment

Have students draw one rectangle and one circle with each of the following areas. They can use Guess and Check to determine the length and width of the rectangle or radius of the circle.

$1\frac{3}{4}$ in.^{2} 3 in.^{2} 7 in.^{2} $12\frac{1}{2}$ in.^{2}

Assignment Guide			
	Minimum	Average	Extended
page 397		1–11	1–12

Find the area of each shaded region.

1. 198 in.²

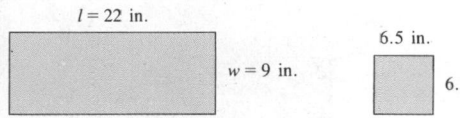
l = 22 in.
w = 9 in.

2. 42.25 in.²

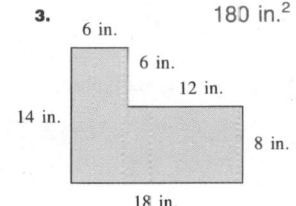
6.5 in.
6.5 in.

3. 180 in.²

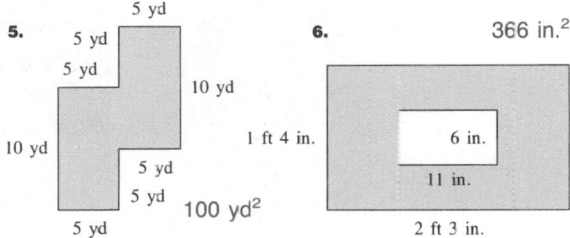
6 in.
6 in.
12 in.
14 in.
8 in.
18 in.

4. 205 in.²

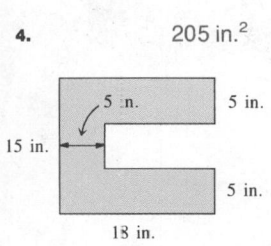
5 in.
5 in.
15 in.
5 in.
18 in.

5.

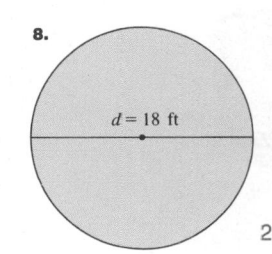
5 yd
5 yd
5 yd
10 yd
10 yd
5 yd
5 yd
5 yd
100 yd²

6. 366 in.²

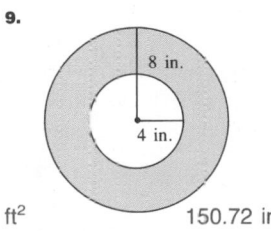
1 ft 4 in.
6 in.
11 in.
2 ft 3 in.

7.

r = 6 ft

113.04 ft²

8.

d = 18 ft

254.34 ft²

9.

8 in.
4 in.

150.72 in.²

10. Find the area of a rectangle that is 12 ft long and 9 ft wide. 108 ft²

11. Find the area of a rectangle that is 15 ft long and 12 ft wide. Give the area in square yards. 20 yd²

★ **12.** A stairway is 36 in. wide. Each step is 12 in. deep and each riser is 6 in. high. There are 8 steps in all. What would it cost to cover the stairway with carpet costing $18.95 per square yard? $75.80

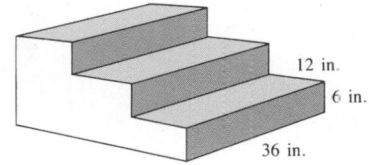
12 in.
6 in.
36 in.

More Practice, page 441, Set B

397

Using Page 397

Exercises 3–6 In these exercises, the area formulas need to be applied more than once. Students may use different but equivalent methods of finding the areas. For example, in exercise 3 the figure can be divided into two rectangles and the sum of the areas found.

$$(8 \times 18) + (6 \times 6) = 144 + 36$$
$$= 180 \text{ in.}^2$$

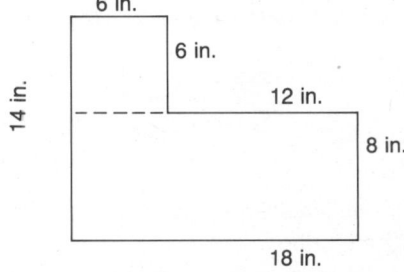
6 in.
6 in.
12 in.
14 in.
8 in.
18 in.

Another method is to think of the figures as a 14 in. by 18 in. rectangle with a 6 in. by 12 in. rectangle removed from one corner.

$$14 \times 18) - (6 \times 12) = 252 - 72$$
$$= 180 \text{ in.}^2$$

6 in.
6 in.
12 in.
14 in.
8 in.

Exercise 12 Each step requires 36 in. × 18 in. = 1 yd. × $\frac{1}{2}$ yd, or $\frac{1}{2}$ yd² of carpeting. Therefore, the 8 steps require $8 \times \frac{1}{2} = 4$ yd².

More Practice, page 441, Set B

Reteaching Supplement, page 109

Area

Rectangles	Circles
Area = length × width	Area = π × radius squared
A = lw	A = πr²
A = 3 × 1½	A = 3.14 × 5²
A = $\frac{7}{2}$ × $\frac{3}{2}$	A = 3.14 × 25
A = $\frac{9}{2}$ = 4½ ft²	A ≈ 78.5 in.²

Find the area of each region.

1. A = l × w, A = 3¼ × 2, A = $\frac{13}{4}$ × $\frac{2}{1}$, A = 6½ in.

2. Hint: Subtract the smaller area from the larger area. A = 72 in.² (of shaded region)

3. A = 51 ft² **4.** A = 82 in.² **5.** A = 200.96 ft²

6. A = 95 in.² (of unshaded region) **7.** A = 113.04 in.² **8.** A ≈ 103.62 ft² (of shaded region)

Enrichment Supplement, page 109

Lawn Mower Challenge

Solve the problem.

1. Randy and his sister agreed that they would each mow ½ the lawn. The lawn is a 40 ft by 80 ft rectangle. How many square feet should each mow? 1,600 ft²

2. The lawn mower cuts a path 2 ft wide. If Randy starts at one corner and mows a path completely around the outside, how many times around should he go to mow ½ the lawn? about 3¾ times, or 3 laps plus 84 ft

Note: Ways of solving this problem include:
▶ finding the area of the lawn remaining to be mowed after each lap; or
▶ finding the linear distance each child needs to walk in order to cut ½ the lawn.

Practice Supplement, page 148

Area

Use 3.14 for π when needed.
Find the area of each shaded region.

1. 12 in. 12 in. Area = 144 in.²
2. 15.5 in. 7.5 in. Area = 116.25 in.²
3. 9 in. 6 in. 3 in. Area = 45 in.²

4. 1 in. 8 in. 2 in. 5 in. Area = 47 in.²
5. 2 in. 2 in. 3 in. 7 in. 5 in. Area = 54 in.²
6. 11 in. 4 in. 6 in. 8 in. 5 in. Area = 84 in.²

7. 12 ft 8 ft 15 ft 5 ft 3 ft 15 ft 10 ft Area = 225 ft²
8. 40 ft 40 ft 30 ft 8 ft 2 ft Area = 1,540 ft²
9. 10 ft 5 ft 10 ft Area = 21.5 ft²

10. d = 16 ft Area = 200.96 ft²
11. 20 ft 4 ft r = 20 ft Area = 1,176 ft²
12. 3 in. 3 in. 3 in. 3 in. 3 in. 3 in. 3 in. Area = 45 in.²

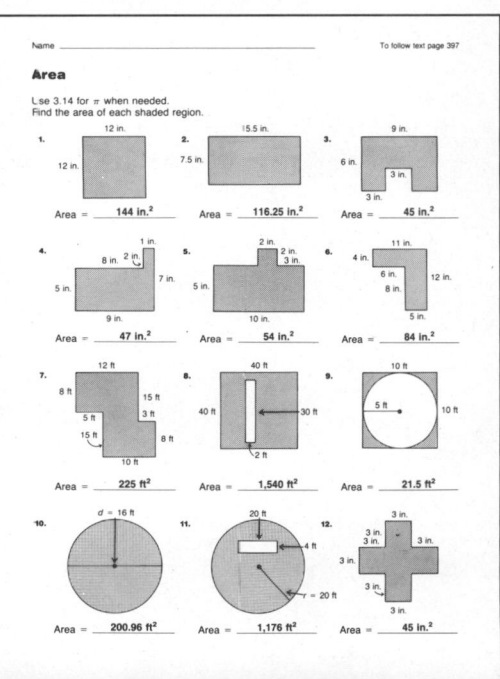

Lesson Focus To find the volume of a rectangular prism and a cylinder in customary units

Suggested Materials One-inch cubes

Ideas for Getting Started

Display one of the cubes. Tell students that it is 1 inch on each edge and that it is 1 cubic inch (in.³).

On the chalkboard draw a picture of a box, 4 in. by 3 in. by 2 in. Ask students to give the number of cubes it would take to fill the box. (24)

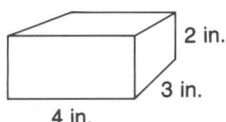

Then ask students if they can give the formula for the volume of a box.

Using Page 398

Motivational Problem After students read the introductory problem ask them to restate the question. Have them give the needed data and suggest a plan to solve the problem. Elicit from students that the formual for volume, $V = lwh$, can be used.

Lesson Development Point out that one side of the box is given in feet and inches, so we must change the measurement to inches in order to find the volume in cubic inches.

The second example reviews the volume of a cylinder. Since the diameter is given, the radius must be found before applying the volume formula $V = \pi r^2 h$.

Volume

A book company packs books in a box 1 ft 4 in. long, 10.5 in. wide, and 8 in. high. What is the **volume** of the box?

Use the volume formula $V = lwh$. All the measurements for l, w, and h must be in the same unit.

$l = 1$ ft 4 in. = 16 in.
$w = 10.5$ in.
$h = 8$ in.

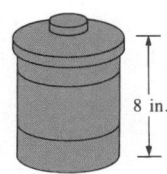

$V = 16 \times 10.5 \times 8 = 1{,}344.0$

The volume is 1,344 cubic inches (in.³).

A kitchen canister is a cylinder 8 inches in height with a diameter of 6 in. What is the volume of the canister?

Use the formula $V = \pi r^2 h$.

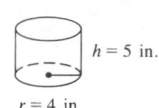

$\pi \approx 3.14$ $V \approx 3.14 \times 3^2 \times 8$
$r = 3$ in. $V \approx 3.14 \times 9 \times 8$
$h = 8$ in. $V \approx 226.08$

The volume is about 226.08 in.³.

Warm Up

Give the volume of each figure. Use 3.14 for π.

1. 280 in.³

2. 1,120 in.³

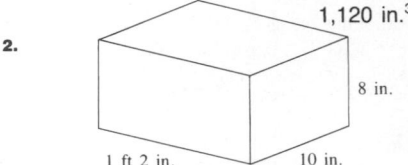

3. 251.2 in.³

$h = 5$ in.
$r = 4$ in.

4. 251.2 in.³

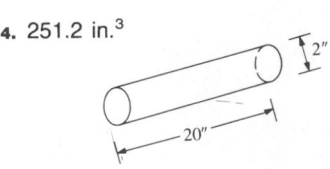

398

Follow Up

Reteaching

Help students estimate the volume of several boxes. Then ask them to measure the length, width, and height of each box and determine the volume. Have them compare the estimate with the computed volume.

Enrichment

Discuss the relationship between cubic units:

1 yd³ = 27 ft³   1 ft³ = 1,728 in.³

Then have students solve these problems.

1. The volume of a box is 2,592 in.³, what is the volume in cubic feet? **$1\frac{1}{2}$ ft³**

2. If the volume of a carton is 243 ft³, what is its volume in cubic yards? **9 yd³**

3. The volume of a box is $2\frac{1}{2}$ ft³. What is the volume in cubic inches? **4,320 in.³**

Assignment Guide			
	Minimum	Average	Extended
page 399		1–14	1–14, TM

Find the volume of each rectangular prism. Use $V = lwh$.

1. 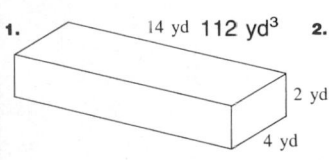 14 yd **112 yd³**

2. 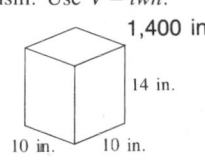 **1,400 in.³** 14 in. 10 in. 10 in.

3. 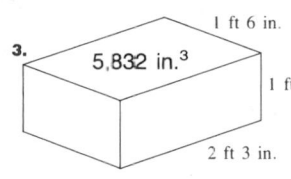 1 ft 6 in. **5,832 in.³** 1 ft 2 ft 3 in.

2 yd 4 yd

4. $l = 4$ in.
$w = 4$ in.
$h = 11$ in. **176 in.³**

5. $l = 10$ in.
$w = 8\frac{1}{2}$ in.
$h = 1\frac{3}{4}$ in. **148$\frac{3}{4}$ in.³**

6. $l = 1$ ft 7 in.
$w = 1$ ft 2 in.
$h = 8$ in. **2,128 in.³**

Find the volume of each cylinder. Use the formula $V = \pi r^2 h$. Use 3.14 for π

7. **502.4 in.³**
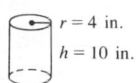 $r = 4$ in.
$h = 10$ in.

8. **56.52 ft³**
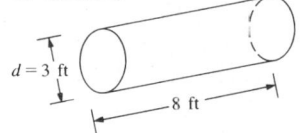 $d = 3$ ft 8 ft

9. **28.26 yd³**
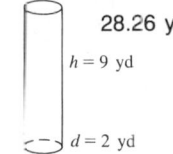 $h = 9$ yd $d = 2$ yd

10. $r = 10$ ft
$h = 10$ ft
3,140 ft³

11. $d = 24$ in.
$h = 1$ ft 3 in.
6,782.4 in.³

12. $d = 18$ in.
$h = 5$ in.
1,271.7 in.³

13. A cubic foot is a cube that measures 1 ft on each edge. What is the volume of a cubic foot in cubic inches?
1,728 in.³

★ **14.** What is the volume of this building?
3,530.4 ft³
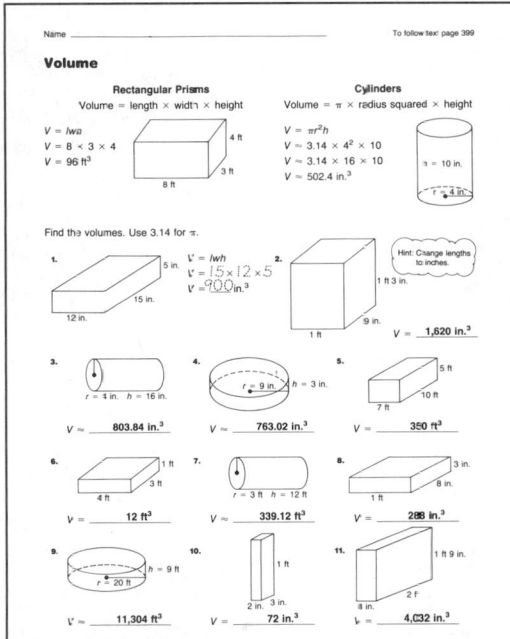 $r = 6$ ft 10 ft 12 ft 20 ft

---

THINK MATH

Guess and Check

A cube has a volume of 29,791 in.³. How long is each edge?

Guess the length, then use a calculator to check your guess. **31 in.**

$V = e \cdot e \cdot e$

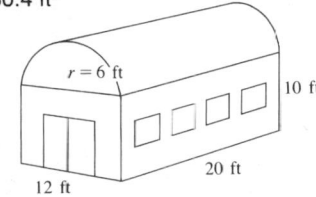 e e e

More Practice, page 441, Set C

399

Using Page 399

Exercises 1–12 Remind students to make certain that measurements are expressed in the same units before using the numbers in the volume formulas.

Exercise 14 Some students may need help to see that the volume can be found by thinking of the lower part of the building as a rectangular prism, 12 ft by 20 ft by 10 ft, and the upper part of the building as one-half of a cylinder. The cylinder has a radius of 6 ft and a height of 20 ft.

Think Math This problem can be solved by using the Guess and Check strategy. A calculator will help students check their guess quickly.

More Practice, page 441, Set C

Reteaching Supplement, page 110

Enrichment Supplement, page 110

Practice Supplement, page 149

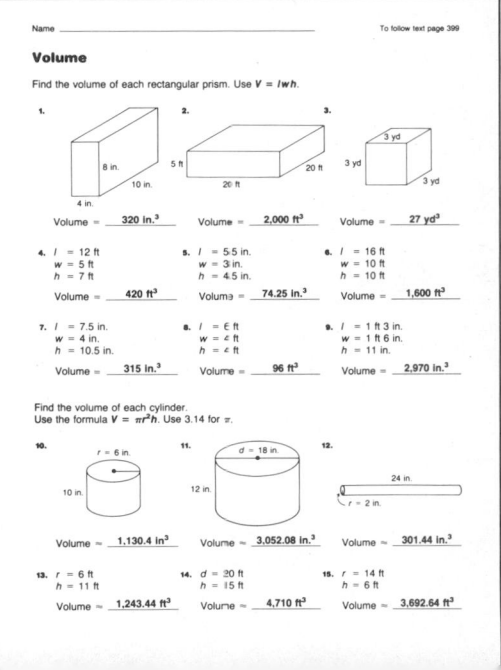

Quick Review Have students find the percents.
What percent is 8 out of 25? 32%   25 is what percent of 20? 125%
What percent is 14 out of 35? 40%

Lesson Focus To express customary units of liquid measure in larger or smaller units; to solve word problems related to liquid measure

Suggested Materials Containers with capacities of a cup, pint, quart, and gallon

Ideas for Getting Started

Display the various container. Ask students to compare the measures. "How many pints in a quart?" (2) "How many quarts in a gallon?" (4) "How many cups in a pint?" (2) "How many pints in a gallon?" (8)

Using Page 400

Lesson Development After students study the table and pictures at the top fo the page, have them read the introductory problem. Ask them to identify the question and the data in the problem. Explain that since there are 8 ounces in a cup, George will make 24 ÷ 8 or 3 cups of juice.

Other Examples Work through these examples with students, showing them how to use the information in the table to express each measure in different units.

Exercises 1–13 Assign these exercises as written work. You may need to give individual help to students who have had little experience with these units of liquid measure.

Liquid Measure

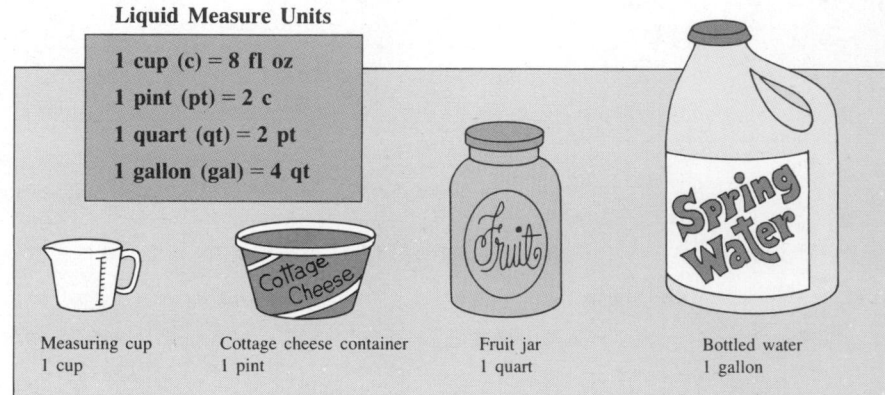

Liquid Measure Units

1 cup (c) = 8 fl oz
1 pint (pt) = 2 c
1 quart (qt) = 2 pt
1 gallon (gal) = 4 qt

Measuring cup 1 cup   Cottage cheese container 1 pint   Fruit jar 1 quart   Bottled water 1 gallon

George is making orange juice. He will make 24 fluid ounces (fl oz) of juice. How many cups of juice will this be?

There are 8 fl oz in 1 c.
24 ÷ 8 = 3

George will make 3 c of orange juice.

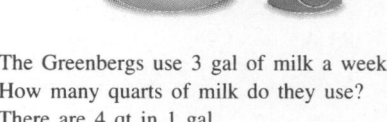

Other Examples

Lydia's car needs $1\frac{1}{2}$ qt of oil. How many pints of oil is this? There are 2 pt in 1 qt.

$2 \times 1\frac{1}{2} = 3$

The car needs 3 pt of oil.

The Greenbergs use 3 gal of milk a week. How many quarts of milk do they use? There are 4 qt in 1 gal.

$4 \times 3 = 12$

The Greenbergs use 12 qt of milk a week.

Give the missing numbers.

1. 16 fl oz =   c 2
2. 2 pt =   c 4
3. 2 gal =   qt 8
4. 1 gal =   pt 8
5. 1 qt =   fl oz 32
6. 6 pt =   qt 3
7. 10 gal =   qt 40
8. 4 fl oz =   c $\frac{1}{2}$
9. 1 pt =   qt $\frac{1}{2}$
10. 32 fl oz =   pt 2
11. 24 pt =   gal 3
12. 6 gal =   qt 24
13. How many fluid ounces are there in $2\frac{3}{4}$ c?
14. How many cups are there in $2\frac{1}{4}$ qt? 9 c

400   22 fl oz

Follow Up

Reteaching

Ratio tables can help students understand the relationships between units. Have students complete the tables below.

Pints	1	2	3	4	6	8
Cups	2	4	6	8	12	16

Cups	1	3	4	6	8	10
Ounces	8	24	32	48	64	80

Quarts	1	2	4	5	6	8
Gallons	4	8	16	20	24	32

Enrichment

Present students with these problems.

1. To paint a den, 3 gal of paint are needed. If you have 6 quart cans, how much more paint will you need? $1\frac{1}{2}$ **gal or 6 qt**

2. An aquarium holds 6 gal and 3 quart of water. There are now 5 gal and 1 pt of water in the aquarium. How much more water will it hold? **1 gal 2 qt 1 pt**

3. A restaurant had $9\frac{1}{2}$ gal of milk before lunchtime. During lunch, 3 gal 3 qt were used. How much milk was left? **5 gal 3 qt**

Assignment Guide			
	Minimum	Average	Extended
page 400	1–12	1–14	1–14
page 401	1–9	1–10, 13, 14	5–14

PROBLEM SOLVING: Practice

QUESTION
DATA
PLAN
ANSWER
CHECK

Solve.

1. Rachel made 2 gal of orange juice. How many quarts is this? **8 qt**

2. Joyce bought 3 qt of milk. How many fluid ounces of milk is this? **96 fl oz**

3. Todd made 3 qt of lemonade. How many 1-c servings is this? **12**

4. The gasoline tank in Nina's car has a capacity of 16 gal. Nina filled her tank with 11.5 gal. How much gasoline was already in the tank? **4.5 gal**

5. One bottle of shampoo held 10 fl oz. Another bottle held $\frac{3}{4}$ pt. Which amount is greater? How much greater? $\frac{3}{4}$ **pt; 2 fl oz greater**

6. Raul drank $\frac{1}{2}$ pt of milk with his lunch. How many fluid ounces of milk did Raul drink? **8 fl oz**

7. A recipe for 10 pancakes calls for 2 c of pancake mix and $1\frac{1}{3}$ c of milk. How much milk will be needed for 6 c of pancake mix? **4 c**

8. How much more expensive is salad dressing at 99¢ a quart than at 93¢ for 32 fl oz? **6¢**

9. Lemon juice is on sale at 89¢ for 16 fl oz. What would 1 qt of lemon juice cost at this rate? **$1.78**

10. A 48-fl oz can of tomato juice was on sale for 75¢. How many quarts is this? $1\frac{1}{2}$ **qt**

11. The answer to a certain question is, "The total cost is $4." Using liquid measurements, make up a problem that will have this answer.

12. One day Celeste drank 6 fl oz of orange juice at breakfast, 8 fl oz of milk at lunch, and 10 fl oz of water at dinner. How many pints of liquid did she drink that day? $1\frac{1}{2}$ **pt**

13. Gasoline costs $1.549 per gal. What is the cost (to the nearest cent) of 16.7 gal of gasoline? **$25.87**

14. Try This Helen filled the gasoline tank of her car and bought 1 qt of oil. The gasoline cost 10 times as much as the oil. The total cost was $19.25. What was the cost of the oil? What was the cost of the gasoline? **$1.75; $17.50**

401

Using Page 401

Exercises 1–13 Tell students that they may need to refer to the table of units on page 400 for data regarding the units. Remind them to use the 5-Point Checklist as they solve the problems.

Try This A possible strategy, Guess and Check, was taught on page 24.

Discussion After students read the problem, have them restate the question and identify the data. Ask "How much would the gasoline cost if the oil cost $1?" ($10) "What is the total cost?" ($11) "Is this enough?" (no) "What would be a good guess for the cost of the oil?" After students understand how to guess and check, have them complete the problem independently.

Solution

Guess: Oil ($1.75)   Gas ($17.50)
Check: $1.75 + $17.50 = $19.25

Reteaching Supplement, page 111

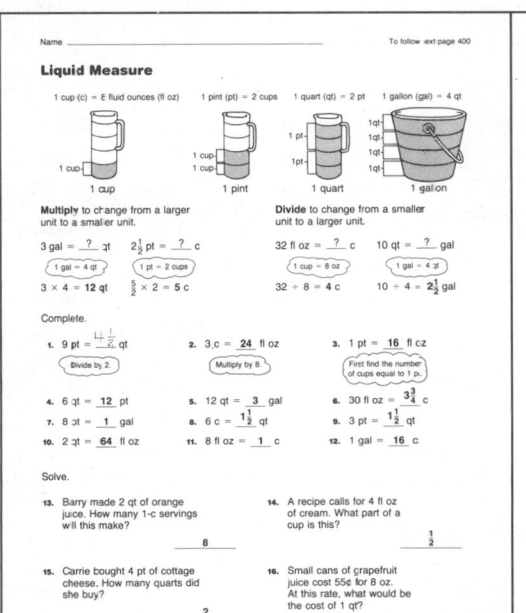

Enrichment Supplement, page 111

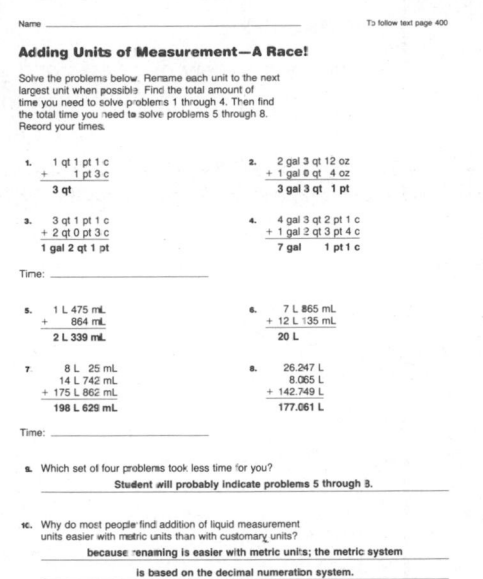

Practice Supplement, page 150

Quick Review Have students find the product or quotient.

$^-7 \cdot 4$	$^-28$	$16 \div ^-2$	$^-8$	$^-8 \cdot ^-7$	56	$^-27 \div 9$	$^-3$
$63 \div 9$	7	$12 \cdot ^-3$	$^-4$	$42 \div ^-7$	$^-6$		

Lesson Focus To estimate customary units of weight and express weight in larger or smaller units; to estimate Fahrenheit temperature

Ideas for Getting Started

Ask students to name some objects that weigh approximately 1 pound, 1 ounce, and 1 ton. Review the symbol for pound (lb). The symbol comes from the Latin word, *libra*, meaning scales.

Using Page 402

Lesson Development Discuss the examples at the top of the page for 1 ton, 1 pound, and 1 ounce. Point out the table that relates these units. On the chalkboard work through some examples of changing to larger or smaller units.

$$4 \text{ lb} = 4 \times 16 \text{ oz} = 64 \text{ oz}$$
$$1\tfrac{1}{2} \text{ lb} = 1\tfrac{1}{2} \times 16 \text{ oz} = 24 \text{ oz}$$
$$5,000 \text{ lb} = 5,000 \div 2,000 = 2\tfrac{1}{2} \text{ T}$$

Exercises 1–20 Discuss exercises 1–6 as a class activity and assign exercises 7–20 as individual work.

Units of Weight

Units of Weight
16 ounces (oz) = 1 pound (lb)
2,000 lb = 1 ton (T)

Clydesdale horse
1 ton

Kitten
1 pound

Tropical fish
1 ounce

Choose the best estimate of weight.

1. A compact car
   Ⓐ 2 T   **B** 20 T   **c** 20 lb

2. A textbook
   A 2 oz   Ⓑ 2 lb   **c** 2 T

3. An orange
   Ⓐ 6 oz   **B** 6 lb   **c** 60 lb

4. A bowling ball
   A 16 T   **B** 16 oz   Ⓒ 16 lb

5. A hippopotamus
   Ⓐ 2 T   **B** 20 lb   **c** 200 T

6. A hamburger patty
   A 400 oz   Ⓑ 4 oz   **c** 40 oz

Give the missing numbers.

7. 2 lb =   oz **32**

8. 48 oz =   lb **3**

9. 2 T =   lb **4,000**

10. 5 lb =   oz **80**

11. 1 lb 4 oz =   oz **20**

12. 2 lb 8 oz =   oz **40**

13. 128 oz =   lb **8**

14. 9 T =   lb **18,000**

15. $2\tfrac{1}{2}$ lb =   oz **40**

16. 10,000 lb =   T **5**

17. $1\tfrac{1}{4}$ T =   lb **2,500**

18. $\tfrac{3}{4}$ lb =   oz **12**

19. One package of frying chicken weighs 3 lb 4 oz. A second package weighs 2 lb 11 oz. How many more ounces are in the first package? **9 oz**

20. Mr. Liu is driving a truck with a total weight of 17,250 lb. A bridge has a load limit of 8 T. How much over the load limit is the total weight of the truck? **1,250 lb**

402

Follow Up

Reteaching

Display a variety of objects and a scale that measures pounds and ounces. Have students lift each object and estimate its weight. Have them record their estimates and then weigh the objects on the scale.

Enrichment

Have students find the number of :

1. Ounces in 1 T — **32,000 oz**
2. Pounds in 6 T — **12,000 lb**
3. Cups in 1 gal — **16 c**
4. Fluid ounces in 4 qt — **128 fl oz**
5. Gallons in 2,880 fl oz — **22.5 gal**
6. Inches in 1 mi — **63,360 in.**
7. Miles in 31,680 ft — **6 mi**
8. Yards in 60 mi — **105,600 yd**

Assignment Guide			
	Minimum	Average	Extended
page 402	1–18	1–20	1–20
page 403	1–9, SK	1–11, SK	1–11, SK

Fahrenheit Temperature

Weather temperatures and cooking temperatures are often given in **degrees Fahrenheit** (°F). Water freezes at 32°F and boils at 212°F.

Choose the best estimate of temperature.

1. A warm summer day
   A 8°F   B 28°F   Ⓒ 80°F

2. A snowy winter day
   A 50°F   B 40°F   Ⓒ 30°F

3. Moderate oven temperature
   A 150°F   Ⓑ 350°F   c 500°F

4. Water in a mountain stream
   Ⓐ 40°F   B 70°F   c 100°F

5. A cup of hot chocolate
   Ⓐ 150°F   B 250°F   c 50°F

Water boils 212°F →

Normal body temperature 98.6°F →
Room temperature 68°F →

Water freezes 32°F →

240, 220, 200, 180, 160, 140, 120, 100, 80, 60, 40, 20, 0

Fahrenheit

Estimate each temperature shown.

6. Oven gauge 325°F

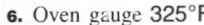

7. House thermostat 62°F

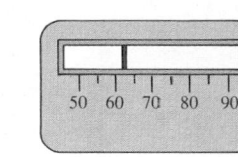

8. Meat thermometer 178°F

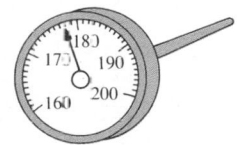

Solve.

9. Cooking instructions: Cook at 400°F for 10 min, then reduce temperature to 325°F. By how much should the temperature be reduced? **75°**

10. The high temperature on a summer day was 92°F. The low temperature was 64°F. What was the mean or average temperature for the day? **78°F**

SKILLKEEPER

1.	2.	3.	4.
2 ft 5 in. + 6 ft 7 in. **9 ft**	3 ft 3 in. + 7 ft 13 in. **11 ft 4 in.**	7 ft 8 in. + 6 ft 5 in. **14 ft 1 in.**	1 ft 3 in. + 5 ft 14 in. **7 ft 5 in.**
5. 3 yd 2 ft − 1 yd **2 yd 2 ft**	**6.** 7 ft − 4 in. **6 ft 8 in.**	**7.** 6 yd 3 ft − 4 yd 4 ft **1 yd 2 ft**	**8.** 12 ft 1 in. − 7 ft 3 in. **4 ft 10 in.**

Using Page 403

Lesson Development Draw a thermometer on the chalkboard. Put a mark at 32°F for the freezing point and at 212°F for the boiling point of water. Explain that the Fahrenheit scale is named after the German physicist who devised the scale. Ask students to estimate temperatures, such as room temperature and outdoor temperature, and have them mark their estimates on the scale.

Exercises 1–11 You may wish to use exercises 1–5 as an oral class activitiy. Exercises 7–11 should be assigned as independent written work.

Skillkeeper This Skillkeeper reviews material taught in this chapter.

Reteaching Supplement, page 112

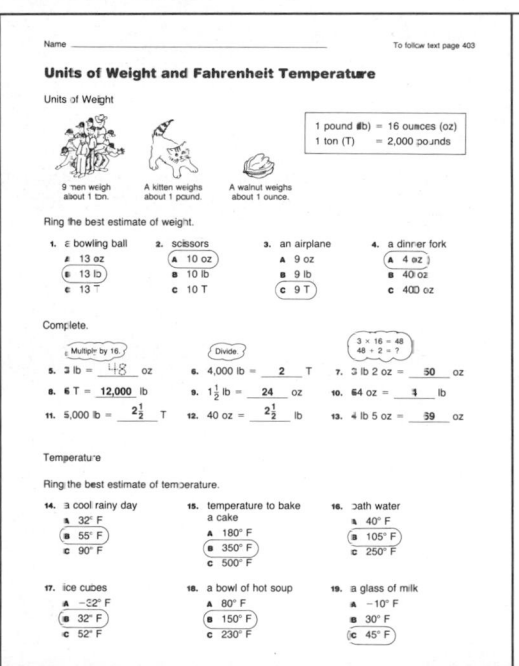

Enrichment Supplement, page 112

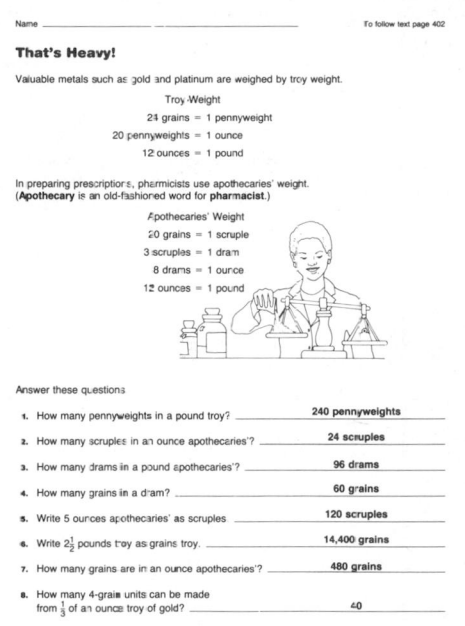

Practice Supplement, page 151

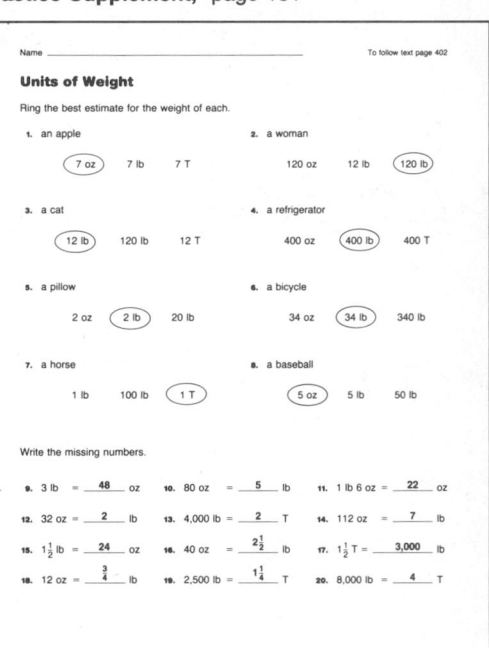

Quick Review Have students write an ordered pair for each description. Directions are from the origin (0,0).

left 5	right 2	right 6	left 3
up 3 (⁻5,3)	up 1 (2,1)	down 4 (6,⁻4)	down 2 (⁻3,⁻2)

Lesson Focus To solve word problems involving unit price

Suggested Materials Calculator

Ideas for Getting Started

Conduct an oral drill using price per unit and price for a number of articles. Use problems like the following. "A can of orange juice costs 50¢. What will 10 cans cost?" ($5) "The cost of 12 eggs is $1.20. What does 1 egg cost?" (12¢) "A beef roast costs $3.00 per pound. How many pounds can you buy for $12?" (4) "If 5 pounds of sugar costs $5, what is the cost of 1 pound?" ($1)

Ask students if they know what is meant by *unit price*. Explain that grocery stores may sell different sizes of the same article at different prices. For example, 10 pounds of potatoes may cost $1.80, while 5 pounds of potatoes may cost $1.05. Point out that we can compare the two prices by using the cost per pound or unit price. The unit price of the 10-pound bag is 18¢ per pound, while the unit price of the 5-pound bag is 21¢ per pound.

Using Page 404

Lesson Development Read the introductory problem with students. Have them identify the question and the data. Explain that to find the unit price, we divide the total cost by the number of units. In this case, the unit is pounds.

Exercises 1–6 You might encourage students to use calculators for the computation in this lesson.

PROBLEM SOLVING: Using a Calculator

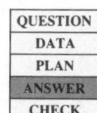

QUESTION
DATA
PLAN
ANSWER
CHECK

Mrs. Ramberg shops at a store that shows unit prices on all grocery items. What is the unit price on a 7-lb bag of pancake mix that sells for $3.92?

To find the unit price, divide the total cost by the number of units. Use a calculator.

$$\text{Unit price} = \frac{\text{total cost}}{\text{number of units}} \leftarrow \text{pounds}$$

$$\text{Unit price} = \frac{\$3.92}{7} = \$0.56$$

The unit price is 56¢ per pound.

$$\text{Unit price} \times \text{number of units} = \text{total cost}$$
$$4.9¢ \text{ per fl oz} \times 32 \text{ fl oz} = 156.8¢$$
$$= \$1.57$$

Rounded to the nearest cent.

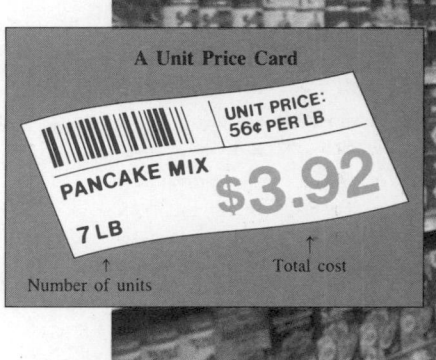

A Unit Price Card

UNIT PRICE: 56¢ PER LB

PANCAKE MIX

$3.92

7 LB

↑ Number of units

↑ Total cost

Solve.

1. Val bought a 2-lb box of crackers for $1.35. What is the unit price to the nearest tenth of a cent? $0.675

2. The unit price on a 12-oz can of peanuts is 18.6¢ per oz. What is the cost of this can of peanuts? $2.23

3. Jody bought 4 lb of spaghetti for $1.49. What is the unit price of the spaghetti? $0.3725

4. A 42-oz box of oatmeal is priced at $1.24. What is the unit price (to the nearest tenth of a cent) of the oatmeal? 3.0¢

5. The unit price on a 32-oz bottle of catsup is 3.71¢ per oz. What is the cost of the catsup? $1.18

6. A 14-oz bottle of catsup has a unit price of 4.86¢ per oz. What is the cost of the catsup? 68¢

404

Follow Up

Reteaching

Provide students with advertisements from local grocery stores. Have them find the unit prices of similar items and compare the costs.

Enrichment

Have students find the missing prices.

Net weight (pounds)	This package	Price per lb.
0.96	$2.29	**$2.39**
3.05	$4.85	**$1.59**
6.17	**$10.12**	$1.64
2.5	$7.23	**$2.89**
0.86	**$3.11**	$3.62

Assignment Guide	Minimum	Average	Extended
page 404–405	1–9	1–11, 14	4–14

7. Blair saw a box of 8 waffles for 97¢ and a box of 10 waffles for $1.09. Which size box has the lower unit price? Find each unit price to the nearest tenth of a cent. 10 for $1.09; 12.1¢; 10.9¢

8. A 2-lb box of flour has a price of $1.39. Write the unit price of the flour in cents per ounce. 0.0434375¢/oz

9. Kathleen chose a 22-oz bottle of liquid detergent. The price was not on the bottle but the unit price shown was 6.5¢ per oz. Kathleen used her calculator to find the price of the detergent. What is the price of the detergent? $1.43

10. Pam Fleetdeer checked the sizes and prices of baby shampoo: 7 oz for $1.99, 11 oz for $2.79, 16 oz for $3.29. Which size has the lowest unit price? Find the unit price (to the nearest hundredth of a cent) for each size. 16 oz; 28.43¢; 25.36¢; 20.56¢

11. Cole paid 54¢ for a quart of non-fat milk. He could have bought $\frac{1}{2}$ gal for $1.08. Find the cost per gallon for each. Is the unit price of one less than the unit price of the other? $2.16/gal; no

12. Katie bought a 48-oz can of vegetable juice that had a unit price of 2.09¢ per oz. She also had a coupon for 25¢ off the price of the juice. To the nearest cent, what did she have to pay for the can of juice? 75¢

13. A 6-oz can of frozen orange juice concentrate costs 54¢. What is the unit price of the concentrate? When the concentrate is mixed with water, it makes 24 oz of orange juice. Not including the price of water, what is the unit price of the orange juice? 9¢ per oz; 2.25¢

14. **Try This** A package of dried spaghetti and a can of spaghetti sauce cost $2.58. The spaghetti sauce cost $1.00 more than the dried spaghetti. How much did each item cost? dried spaghetti, $0.79; sauce, $1.79

405

Using Page 405

Exercises 7–13 Most of these exercises are mutliple-step problems. Exercises 7, 10, 11, and 13 have more than one answer.

Try This A possible strategy, Guess and Check, was taught on page 24.

Discussion After students read the problem, have them identify the question and the data. Ask students if they can solve this problem directly by computation. Some students may see that they can subtract $1.00 from the total cost and then divide by 2 to find the cost of the dried spaghetti. However, most students will probably suggest using the strategy, Guess and Check.

Solution

Guess: Spaghetti ($0.79)   Sauce ($1.79)

Check: $0.79 + $1.79 = $2.58

Ideas That Work

Special Education

An activity that will help students develop skills in unit pricing is "Price File." Give students a folder filled with a set of cards illustrating the labels and price markings from two related containers of food or other merchandise. Also give students a worksheet to record the answers.

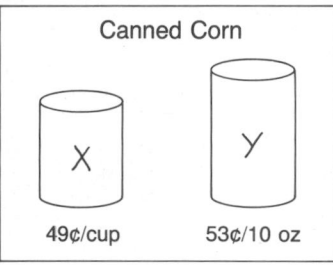

Canned Corn

49¢/cup   53¢/10 oz

Price Sheet			
	x	y	Best Buy
Corn	__ oz	__ oz	__
Beans	__ oz	__ oz	__
Bread	__ lb	__ lb	__
Ice Cream	__ gal	__ gal	__
Beef	__ lb	__ lb	__

Students should use calculators to find the unit price of each item on the card and then indicate which of the items is the better buy. Discuss the concept of "better buy" with special students. Discuss the difference between "quality" and "quantity."

Ideas for Getting Started

Lesson Focus To interpret, organize, and use data to make a decision about a real-world problem

Ideas for Getting Started

Review the meaning and use of unit prices. (See page 404.)

$$\text{Unit price} = \frac{\text{total cost}}{\text{number of units}}$$

Have students compute these unit prices.

- One dozen eggs for 84 ¢ (7 ¢/egg)
- 10 gal gasoline for $12.90 ($1.29 per gal)
- 12 oz soda for 60 ¢ (5 ¢/oz)

Using Page 406

Lesson Development Tell students that this lesson deals with the familiar consumer problem of deciding which one of several sizes of an item is the most economical. Explain that while larger sizes tend to be more economical, special sales or discount coupons can make smaller sizes a better buy. Point out that the word generic refers to a product that is sold without a name brand.

Have students read the information at the top of the page and "Some Things to Consider." Then have them answer the questions. Students should be encouraged to use calculators to compute the unit prices for these questions. The unit prices given in the annotated answers were found using a calculator. If students compute the answers with pencil and paper, suggest that the answers be worked out to at least the nearest tenth of a cent. In exercise 5, the "most economical buy" means the size with the smaller unit price. The small size toothpaste costs the least but is not the most economical.

Give students an opportunity to discuss their decisions. While generic toothpaste has the smallest unit price, some people may prefer buying a brand name toothpaste. One advantage of the brand name is that if the customer finds the item defective or unusable, the brand name manufacturer can be contacted for refund or replacement. This might be more difficult to do with generic items.

APPLIED PROBLEM SOLVING

| QUESTION |
| DATA |
| PLAN |
| ANSWER |
| CHECK |

You are in a supermarket. You need to decide which one of several different sizes of tubes of toothpaste would be most economical to buy.

50¢ off
Awake Toothpaste economy size

25¢ off
Awake Toothpaste small or regular size

Awake Toothpaste		
small	1.4 oz	$0.65
regular	4.6 oz	$1.39
family	6 oz	$1.75
economy	8.2 oz	$1.95
Generic	6.4 oz	$0.84

Some Things to Consider

- You have enough money to buy any size tube of toothpaste you wish.
- The supermarket does not have unit prices displayed.
- You want to buy only one tube of toothpaste.
- You have coupons for 25¢ off the small or regular size, and 50¢ off the economy size.

Some Questions to Answer

1. What is the price of the small size if you use the coupon? $0.40

2. What is the unit price for the small size if you use the coupon? $0.2857/oz

3. What is the price of the regular size if you use the coupon? $1.14

4. What is the unit price of the regular size if you use the coupon? $0.2478/oz

5. Which size is more economical to buy, the small or the regular size? regular

6. What are the unit prices for the family and generic sizes? family, $0.2916/oz; generic, $0.1312/oz

What Is Your Decision?

Which of the five sizes of tubes of toothpaste will you buy? The generic is most economical. Economy size with coupon is most economical of Awake sizes.

▌ CHAPTER REVIEW/TEST ▐

Write the missing numbers.

1. 2 yd = ▩ ft 6

2. 5,280 ft = ▩ mi 1

3. 48 in. = ▩ ft 4

4. 30 ft = ▩ yd 10

5. 5 ft = ▩ in. 60

6. 2 ft 9 in. = ▩ in. 33

Add or subtract.

7.
```
  3 ft  7 in.
+ 1 ft  9 in.
  5 ft  4 in.
```

8.
```
  4 ft 10 in.
- 1 ft  6 in.
  3 ft  4 in.
```

9.
```
  6 ft  6 in.
- 2 ft 11 in.
  3 ft  7 in.
```

10.
```
  2 ft  8 in.
+ 5 ft  9 in.
  8 ft  5 in.
```

11.
```
  8 ft
- 3 ft  9 in.
  4 ft  3 in.
```

12.
```
  2 yd 2 ft  9 in.
+        1 ft  6 in.
  3 yd 1 ft  3 in.
```

Find the area. Use 3.14 for π when necessary.

13. 240 in.^{2}

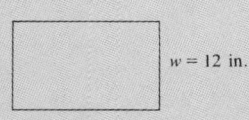
$w = 12$ in.
$l = 20$ in.

14. 270 in.^{2}

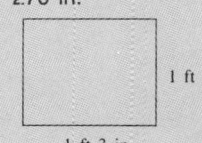
1 ft 6 in.
1 ft 3 in.

15. 113.04 in.^{2}

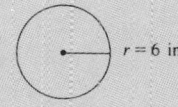
$r = 6$ in.

Find the volume. Use 3.14 for π when necessary.

16. 270 in.^{3}

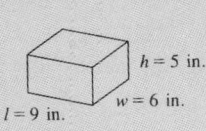
$h = 5$ in.
$w = 6$ in.
$l = 9$ in.

17.

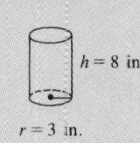
2.4 ft^3
1 ft
2 ft
1.2 ft

18. 226.08 in.^{3}

$h = 8$ in.
$r = 3$ in.

Write the missing numbers.

19. 2 pt = ▩ c 4

20. 1 gal = ▩ qt 4

21. 16 pt = ▩ gal 2

22. 32 oz = ▩ lb 2

23. 2 T = ▩ lb 4,000

24. 5 lb = ▩ oz 80

25. A 32-oz package of popcorn costs $1.92. What is the unit cost in cents per ounce? 6¢/oz

26. Normal body temperature is 98.6°F. How many degrees Fahrenheit is this above the freezing temperature of water? 66.6°

407

Using Page 407

The exercises in the Chapter Review/Test emphasize the major concepts and skills presented in this chapter. These exercises may be used as a review assignment or as a test, depending upon your needs.

Item Analysis The table below correlates the Chapter Review/Test items with objectives and with the students text pages on which the concepts or skills were taught. Please note that items 13–18 are derived from a lesson from which no "Minimum" assignment was suggested in the Assignment Guide. Only those students who were assigned this lesson should be expected to complete the corresponding Chapter Review/Test items.

Items	Objectives	Related Text Pages
1–12	16.1	394–395
13–15	16.2	396–397
16–18	16.3	398–399
19–24	16.4	400, 402–403
25–26	16.5	401, 404–405

Assessment Options

If you use the Chapter Review/Test as a review assignment, you may wish to use the free-response test or the multiple-choice test to evaluate mastery of the chapter objectives. The items on these tests have a one-to-one correspondence in terms of content and level of difficulty. A correlation of test items to objectives and student text pages is provided in the Management Guide for Chapter 16. Note: Items 13–18 are derived from lessons for which no minimum assignment was suggested in the Assignment Guide.

Multiple-Choice Test, TRB pages 45–47
Free-Response Test, TRB pages 79–80
End-of-Year Test, TRB pages 85–88

TRB Options

The following blackline masters are available for use with this chapter. If you have not already assigned these materials, you may wish to use them to close the chapter.

Recreation, TRB page 170
Consumer Applications, TRB page 188
Calculator Technology, TRB page 206
Computer Technology, TRB pages 221–223
Reading Math, TRB page 242
Family Involvement, TRB pages 275–276

Using Page 408

The exercises on this page are intended for those students who experienced difficulty with the Chapter Review/Test on page 407. Should students require reteaching of these key concepts and skills, please refer to the teaching notes below. Otherwise, the Another Look exercises can be assigned as independent work, with students using the accompanying sample problems and hints as guides.

Exercises 1–6 This skill was originally taught on page 394. On the chalkboard, work through an example of changing units of length, such as 22 in. = __?__ ft __?__ in. Ask students how the units are related. Explain that since there are 12 in. in 1 ft, we divide. Give students an opportunity to participate as you work through the examples.

Exercises 7–12 This skill was originally taught on page 395. Discuss the example in the display box. Emphasize the regrouping process and point out that we are not grouping by tens. Then work through an example of subtracting feet and inches on the chalkboard.

Exercises 13–21 This skill was originally taught on pages 400 and 402. Discuss the customary units of liquid measure and weight. Emphasize the relationships between units. Work through examples of changing units on the chalkboard. Have students give the necessary data from the display box regarding the relationship of units in each example.

Exercises 22–25 This skill was originally taught on page 403. Draw a temperature scale on the chalkboard. Have students locate the boiling point and the freezing point on the scale. Show how the drawing can be used to help students solve problems such as these.

ANOTHER LOOK

> 12 in. = 1 ft
> 3 ft = 1 yd
> 5,280 ft = 1 mi

Write the missing numbers.

1. 2 ft = ▓ in.
   24
2. 3 yd = ▓ ft
   9
3. 3 mi = ▓ ft
   15,840
4. 10 ft = ▓ yd ▓ ft
   3   1
5. 16 in. = ▓ ft ▓ in.
   1   4
6. 15 ft = ▓ yd
   5

> $\overset{1}{4}$ ft **7** in.
> + **3** ft **9** in.
> 8 ft 4 in.
>
> 9 in. + 7 in. = 16 in.
>   16 in. = 1 ft 4 in.

Add or subtract.

7.   2 ft 10 in.
   + 3 ft 8 in.
   ─────────────
     6 ft 6 in.

8.   4 ft 4 in.
   − 2 ft 9 in.
   ─────────────
     1 ft 7 in.

9.   2 yd 1 ft 9 in.
   + 3 yd 2 ft 3 in.
   ─────────────────
     6 yd 1 ft

10.   5 yd 1 ft 1 in.
    −   3 ft 4 in.
   ─────────────────
      4 yd   9 in.

11.   3 yd 1 ft 9 in.
    − 1 yd 3 ft 5 in.
   ─────────────────
      1 yd 1 ft 4 in.

12.   16 yd 12 ft
    + 12 yd 5 ft
   ─────────────
     33 yd 2 ft

> 1 c = 8 fl oz
> 1 pt = 2 c
> 1 qt = 2 pt
> 1 gal = 4 qt
>
> 16 oz = 1 lb
> 2,000 lb = 1 T

Write the missing numbers.

13. 4 c = ▓ pt 2
14. 2 gal = ▓ qt 8
15. 10 pt = ▓ qt 5
16. 12 qt = ▓ gal 3
17. 8 fl oz = ▓ c 1
18. 5 gal = ▓ qt 20
19. 2 lb = ▓ oz
    32
20. 6,000 lb = ▓ T
    3
21. 64 oz = ▓ lb
    4

> Water boils at 212°F.
> Water freezes at 32°F.

Write the temperatures.

22. 3° below the boiling point of water 209°
23. 10° below the freezing point of water 22°
24. Room temperature is 68°F. How much above the freezing temperature of water is this? 36°
25. Moderate oven temperature is 350°F. How much above the boiling temperature of water is this? 138°

408

Just for Teachers

$a^2 + b^2 = c^2$

"The square of the length of the hypotenuse of a right-angled triangle is equal to the sum of the squares of the lengths of the other two sides." This rule was known in Asia Minor for centuries before Pythogoras first proved it in the 6th Century B.C. In Eygpt and Mesopotamia, it was part of the practical mathematics used to construct temples and tombs, and it is thought that architects may have used a device for constructing a right angle.

Pythagoras is credited with the first proof that this rule holds true for all right triangles. However, mathematical historians believe that it was proven in China about the same time as in Greece. Oral tradition was recorded in the book of *Chou Pei Suan King* about A.D. 40, which includes an early Chinese proof of the right triangle rule.

Other Number Systems

The problems on this page use a new kind of arithmetic
called an eight-clock arithmetic. There are only eight numbers
in this arithmetic. You can think of these eight numbers
spaced equally around a clock face.

Study the examples below to see how to add and subtract
these eight-clock numbers.

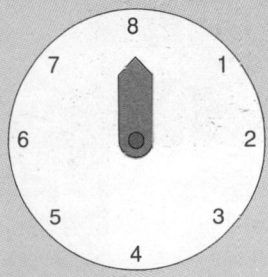 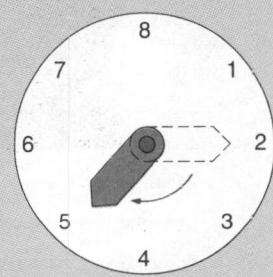 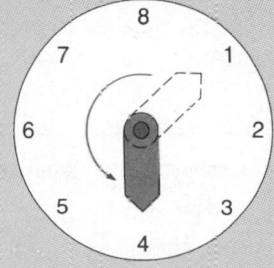

$2 + 3 = 5$ $\qquad\qquad$ $1 - 5 = 4$

To add, start at 2, $\qquad$ To subtract, start at 1,
then count 3 spaces $\qquad$ then count 5 spaces
clockwise to get to 5. $\qquad$ **counterclockwise** to get to 4.

Find the sums and differences using eight-clock arithmetic.

1. $4 + 2 = g$ $g = 6$	**2.** $4 + 3 = x$ $x = 7$	**3.** $4 + 4 = b$ $b = 8$
4. $4 + 5 = c$ $c = 1$	**5.** $4 + 6 = l$ $l = 2$	**6.** $4 + 7 = s$ $s = 3$
7. $4 + 8 = m$ $m = 4$	**8.** $5 + 8 = a$ $a = 5$	**9.** $6 + 8 = i$ $i = 6$
10. $5 - 2 = q$ $q = 3$	**11.** $5 - 3 = p$ $p = 2$	**12.** $5 - 4 = k$ $k = 1$
13. $5 - 5 = w$ $w = 8$	**14.** $5 - 6 = e$ $e = 7$	**15.** $5 - 7 = t$ $t = 6$
16. $5 - 8 = f$ $f = 5$	**17.** $6 - 8 = r$ $r = 6$	**18.** $7 - 8 = h$ $h = 7$
19. $8 - 8 = n$ $n = 8$	**20.** $1 - 8 = j$ $j = 1$	**21.** $3 - 8 = y$ $y = 3$

Decide how you would multiply in eight-clock arithmetic.
Make up and solve some multiplication problems.

409

Using Page 409

This page is intended for those students who successfully completed the Chapter Review/Test on
page 407. You may wish to assign this page as independent work while you use Another Look exercises to reteach the basic concepts and skills of
the chapter. Or, you may decide that all students
would benefit from exposure to this Enrichment
activity.

Lesson Development Most students will be
able to complete this page without additional instruction. If students have difficulty, have them
think of a 12-hour clock. On a 12-hour clock, we
could think of $10 + 3 = 1$; that is, 3 hours after 10
o'clock is 1 o'clock. Similarly, in 8-clock arithmetic,
$6 + 3 = 1$. Subtraction may be thought of as
counting backwards the number of hours to be
subtracted.

Multiplication can be thought of as repeated
addition.

$3 \times 5 = 5 + 5 + 5$ (1 complete turn + 7)
$5 \times 7 = 7 + 7 + 7 + 7 + 7$ (4 complete turns + 3)
$6 \times 4 = 4 + 4 + 4 + 4 + 4 + 4$ (3 complete turns)

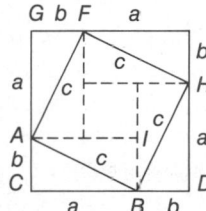

1) $\text{Area } (\triangle ABC)$ $\quad = \frac{1}{2} \text{ Area } (\square AIBC)$
$\qquad\qquad\qquad\qquad = \frac{1}{2} ab$

2) $\text{Area } (\square\ CDEG) = \text{Area } (\square ABHF) + 4 \text{ Area } (\triangle ABC)$
$\qquad\qquad\qquad\qquad = c^2 + 2ab$

3) $\text{Area } (\square\ CDEG) = (a + b)^2$
$\qquad\qquad\qquad\qquad = a^2 + 2ab + b^2$

Since equations 2 and 3 are two expressions for the area of square $CDEG$, $a^2 +$
$2ab + b^2 = c^2 + 2ab$. Subtracting $2ab$ from each side gives $a^2 + b^2 = c^2$.

Lesson Focus To use the Logo language to describe geometric figures

Ideas for Getting Started

On the chalkboard, display these words: Forward, Back, Right, and Left. Ask students to direct you to draw a square on the chalkboard, using only the four words above. Tell students that when the words "forward" or "back" are used, the number of units to move must be specified also. Explain that "right" and "left" will indicate turns. When these words are used, the number of degrees in the turn must be specified.

Call on selected students to give the directions. One possible set of directions for a square is shown below. The units used for "forward" and "back" moves may be any convenient length.

Forward 10
Right 90
Forward 10
Right 90
Forward 10
Right 90
Forward 10

Tell students that in this lesson they will learn about a programming language that uses these words to draw geometric shapes.

Using Page 410

Lesson Development Read the introductory material with students. Have them study the information in the box concerning Logo commands. On the chalkboard, work through the parallelogram program one step at a time. For example, after the statement, FD 30 RT 60, draw a segment 30 units long and then turn 60° clockwise.

To demonstrate the REPEAT command, you can use a parallelogram cut from tagboard. Place the parallelogram on the chalkboard and trace around it. The Logo statement tells us to "REPEAT 6 [RT 60 PARALLELOGRAM]," so place a pencil tip on a vertex of the parallelogram and turn (rotate) it 60°. Trace around the parallelogram and repeat the process until you have traced 6 parallelograms.

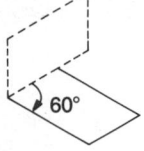

Computer Graphics

Logo is a special programming language that can be used to draw geometric shapes on a computer screen.

A small triangle, called a **turtle** ($\triangle$), acts like a pencil point in drawing figures. The point of the turtle shows the direction in which lines will be drawn.

The table below shows four simple Logo commands. Using just these four commands, a variety of geometric figures can be drawn.

Command	Short Form	Meaning
Forward 20	FD 20	Draws a line forward 20 units.
Back 20	BK 20	Draws a line backward 20 units.
Right 60	RT 60	Turns the turtle 60° clockwise.
Left 60	LT 60	Turns the turtle 60° counterclockwise.

This is a program for drawing a parallelogram.

```
TO PARALLELOGRAM
FD 30 RT 60
FD 50 RT 120
FD 30 RT 60
FD 50 RT 120
END
```

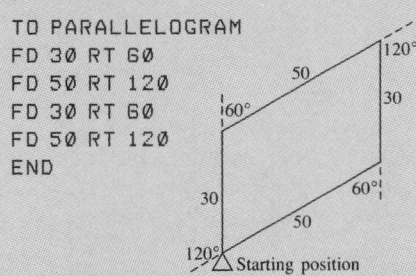

Now when you type PARALLELOGRAM the computer draws the parallelogram.

With the PARALLELOGRAM program stored in the computer's memory, we can use the command REPEAT for the PARALLELOGRAM to draw other shapes.

```
REPEAT 6 [RT 60 PARALLELOGRAM]
```

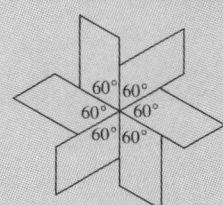

This tells the computer to show six parallelograms each rotated 60° from the starting point of the turtle.

410

Technology for Teachers

Logo was created in 1968 by Seymour Papert and a team of researchers whose major interest was the process of learning. Logo's designers saw the computer as an educational tool that could create new types of learning environments in which children could structure their own knowledge. The language can be learned through investigative activities, many of which are self-initiated. Logo lends itself to endless exploration and discovery.

Turtle graphics is the best known Logo feature. It is often used to introduce the basic ideas of Logo programming, as well as basic geometric concepts. Commands such as FORWARD, BACK, RIGHT, and LEFT are "built into" the language and called primitives. One special aspect of Logo is that the user can define new words and these words can become part of the computer's vocabulary. The definition of a new word is called a procedure.

1. Fill in the missing numbers in the
   program for the right triangle shown.

```
TO TRIANGLE
FD 20 RT 120
FD ▮ RT ▮ 40    150
FD ▮ RT ▮ 34.64 90
END
```

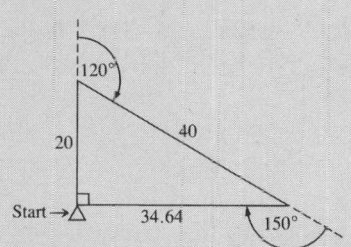

2. Complete the program for the rhombus.

```
TO RHOMBUS
FD 40 RT 72
FD ▮ RT ▮ 40  108
FD ▮ RT ▮ 40  72
FD ▮ RT ▮ 40  108
END
```

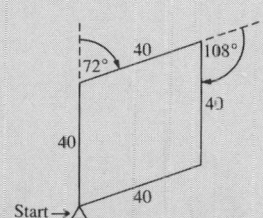

3. Using the rhombus program from
   exercise 2 and the REPEAT command,
   the figure at the right can be drawn.
   What are the two missing numbers in
   the program?

```
REPEAT ▮ [RT ▮ RHOMBUS]
        5      72
```

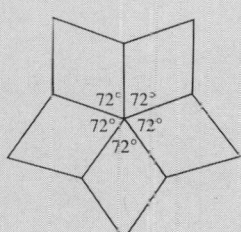

4. Write a program for drawing the
   SQUARESPIRAL at the right.

```
TO SQUARESPIRAL
REPEAT 2 [FD 5 RT 90]
REPEAT 2 [FD 10 RT 90]
REPEAT 2 [FD 15 RT 90]
REPEAT 2 [FD 20 RT 90]
REPEAT 2 [FD 25 RT 90]
END
```

5. Write a Logo program of your own
   for a geometric figure. Make a sketch
   of the figure for your program.

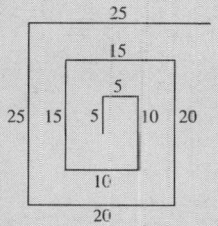

The following set of commands is a program to draw a parallelogram.

```
FD 30 RT 60
FD 50 RT 120
FD 30 RT 60
FD 50 RT 120
```

The word "parallelogram" can become part of the computer's vocabulary if it is defined as a procedure. This is accomplished by adding a title line, TO PARALLEL-OGRAM, to the set of commands and the word, END, to indicate that this is the end of the definition. Once PARALLELOGRAM is defined as a procedure, a parallelogram is drawn whenever PARALLELOGRAM is typed on the computer, and it can be used in further definitions.

The philosophy behind Logo and a detailed description of its development can be found in *Mindstorms: Children, Computers and Powerful Ideas,* by Papert.

Using Page 411

Exercises 1–5 Students can determine the missing numbers by examining the figures in exercises 1–3. In exercise 4, students are asked to write a program for the SQUARESPIRAL. One such program, using REPEAT, is shown in the annotated answers. A less efficient, but correct, program can be written without the REPEAT command. In exercise 5, students are asked to write a Logo program of their own for a geometric figure. Tell students that in thinking through the steps of a program, it helps to imagine walking the line that is drawn. When you come to a corner, think about the turn you would make to continue walking on the sides of the figure.

If you have access to the Logo language on a microcomputer, have students enter and run the programs on pages 410 and 411 as well as the programs they have written.

Using Page 412

The exercises on the page provide practice for maintaining cumulative skills. The emphasis in this Cumulative Review is on integers (Chapter 15) and customary measurement (Chapter 16).

Item Analysis The table below correlates the Cumulative Review items with objectives and with the student book pages on which the concepts or skills were taught.

Items	Objectives	Related Text Pages
1–2	15.1	367–369
3	15.2	370–375
4	15.3	376–377
5	15.4	380–381
6	15.5	382–383
7	16.1	394–395
8–9	16.4	400, 402–403
10	16.2	396–397
11	16.3	398–399
12	16.5	401, 404–405
13	15.7	378–379

CUMULATIVE REVIEW

1. What is the opposite of $^-7$?

   A $^-14$ B 0

   Ⓒ 7   D not given

2. Which is correct?

   A $^-12 > ^-5$ Ⓑ $^-2 > ^-5$

   C $7 < ^-4$ D not given

3. Find the sum.

   $^-8 + ^-25$

   A $^-17$ Ⓑ $^-33$

   C 17   D not given

4. Find the difference.

   $^-20 - ^-7$

   A $^-27$ B 27

   Ⓒ $^-13$ D not given

5. Multiply.

   $^-12 \times ^-4$

   Ⓐ 48   B $^-16$

   C $^-48$ D not given

6. Divide.

   $25 \div ^-5$

   A 20   Ⓑ $^-5$

   C 5   D not given

Find the missing numbers.

7. 5 ft = ▮ in.

   A 62   B 15

   C 45   Ⓓ not given

8. 4 pt = ▮ c

   A 2   Ⓑ 8

   C 4   D not given

9. 48 oz = ▮ lb

   A 4   B 12

   Ⓒ 3   D not given

10. 32 gal = ▮ qt

    A 16   B 8

    C 12.8   Ⓓ not given

11. Add.

    3 ft 7 in.
    + 4 ft 9 in.

    Ⓐ 8 ft 4 in.   B 8 ft 16 in.

    C 7 ft 4 in.   D not given

12. Subtract.

    12 yd 3 ft
    − 4 yd 4 ft

    A 7 yd 9 ft   Ⓑ 7 yd 2 ft

    C 8 yd 2 ft   D not given

13. The low temperature for the month of January was 12°F. The high temperature that month was 22°F. What was the mean or average temperature that month?

    A 10°F   B 34°F

    Ⓒ 17°F   D not given

14. If positive 12 is subtracted from negative 10, what is the difference?

    A 2   Ⓑ $^-22$

    C $^-2$ D not given

Appendix

DATA BANK

No. 884.	Commercial Broadcast Stations—States and Other Areas						
STATE	AM	FM	TV	STATE	AM	FM	TV
Ala	140	74	17	Mont	45	24	12
Alaska	22	11	7	Nbr	49	37	14
Ariz	61	31	13	Nev	22	12	8
Ark	90	54	9	N.H.	28	15	2
Calif	232	204	54	N.J.	39	34	5
Colo	72	51	12	N. Mex	57	29	9
Conn	39	25	5	N.Y.	161	119	30
Del	10	7	—	N.C.	211	88	19
D C.	7	9	5	N. Dak	26	10	11
Fla	199	115	31	Ohio	123	128	24
Ga	186	90	19	Okla	67	53	12
Hawaii	26	7	10	Oreg	80	35	12
Idaho	44	23	8	Pa	177	124	27
Ill	127	132	23	R.I.	15	7	2
Ind	86	95	20	S.C.	108	56	11
Iowa	76	75	13	S. Dak	33	18	11
Kans	59	45	12	Tenn	158	80	19
Ky	121	87	11	Tex	289	197	58
La	95	64	15	Utah	35	20	4
Maine	37	33	7	Vt	19	12	2
Md	50	37	6	Va	137	72	16
Mass	66	39	12	Wash	92	47	14
Mich	128	117	24	W. Va	63	34	9
Minn	93	69	12	Wis	102	92	17
Miss	106	72	10	Wyo	30	10	5
Mo	111	78	24	P. Rico	54	34	8
				Guam, V. Is.	7	5	3

Nail Chart

Size (Penny)	Length in inches
2	1
3	$1\frac{1}{4}$
4	$1\frac{1}{2}$
5	$1\frac{3}{4}$
6	2
7	$2\frac{1}{4}$
8	$2\frac{1}{2}$
9	$2\frac{3}{4}$
10	3
12	$3\frac{1}{4}$
16	$3\frac{1}{2}$
20	4
30	$4\frac{1}{2}$
40	5
50	$5\frac{1}{2}$
60	6

Adult Trout Length

Arctic trout
Salvelinus alpinus.................. 30 cm

Brook trout
Salvelinus fontinalis .... 45 cm

Brown trout
Salmo trutta..................... 25 cm

Cutthroat trout
Salmo clarki..................... 76 cm

Golden trout
Salmo aquabonita.................. 25 cm

Lake trout
Salvelinus namaycush.............. 90 cm

Rainbow trout
Salmo gairdneri.................. 110 cm

Sunapee trout
Salvelinus aureolus................ 50 cm

DATA BANK

Unusual or Old Units of Length

Cubit Length of the forearm from the elbow to the tip of the middle finger; about 18 in.

Hand Unit used in measuring the height of horses; about 4 in.

Fathom Unit used for measuring the depth of water; length of outstretched arms; about 6 ft

League An old unit of distance that varies from country to country; 3 mi

Rod 16.5 ft

Nautical mile Unit of distance used in sea or air navigation; 6,076.115 ft

Barleycorn An old unit of length; about ⅓ in. Three grains of barley were about 1 inch in length.

Pitchers of the Past

PITCHER	CAREER	YEARS	GAMES
Grover Cleveland Alexander	1911–1930	20	696
Mordecai Brown	1903–1916	12	411
Stan Coveleski	1912–1925	14	450
Bob Feller	1936–1956	18	570
Vernon Gomez	1930–1942	14	368
Sandy Koufax	1955–1966	12	397
Eppa Rixey	1912–1933	21	692
Charles Ruffing	1924–1947	22	624
Warren Spahn	1940–1967	21	750
Early Wynn	1939–1963	23	691
Denton Young	1890–1911	22	906

No. 289. Average Number of Days with Precipitation of 0.01 Inch or More—Selected Cities

State	Station	Length of record (yr.)	Jan	Feb	Mar	Apr	May	Jun	Jul	Aug	Sep	Oct	Nov	Dec	Annual
AL	Mobile	37	11	10	11	7	8	11	17	14	11	6	8	11	125
AK	Juneau	35	18	17	18	17	17	16	17	18	20	24	19	21	222
AZ	Phoenix	39	4	4	3	2	1	1	4	5	3	3	2	4	36
AR	Little Rock ..	36	10	9	10	10	10	8	9	7	7	6	8	9	103
CA	Los Angeles	43	6	6	5	3	1	1	1	(Z)	1	2	3	5	34
	Sacramento	39	10	9	8	6	3	1	(Z)	(Z)	1	3	7	9	57
	San Francisco	51	11	10	9	6	3	1	(Z)	1	1	4	7	10	63
CO	Denver	44	6	6	8	9	10	9	9	8	6	5	5	5	86
CT	Hartford	24	11	11	11	11	12	12	10	10	10	8	11	12	129
DE	Wilmington ..	31	11	9	11	11	12	9	9	9	8	7	10	10	116
DC	Washington	37	11	8	11	10	11	9	10	9	8	7	8	9	111
FL	Jacksonville	37	8	8	8	6	8	12	15	15	13	9	6	8	116
	Miami	36	7	6	6	6	11	15	16	17	17	15	8	7	131
GA	Atlanta	44	11	10	12	9	9	10	12	9	7	6	8	10	113
HI	Honolulu	29	10	9	9	9	7	6	8	7	7	9	10	10	101
ID	Boise	39	12	10	9	8	8	6	2	3	4	6	10	11	89
IL	Chicago	20	11	10	13	12	11	10	10	8	10	9	10	11	125
	Peoria	39	9	8	11	12	12	10	9	3	9	7	9	10	114
IN	Indianapolis	39	12	10	13	12	12	10	9	8	8	8	10	12	124
IA	Des Moines	39	7	7	10	10	11	11	9	9	9	7	7	8	105
KS	Wichita	25	5	5	7	8	11	9	8	7	8	6	5	6	85
KY	Louisville	31	12	11	13	12	11	10	11	8	8	7	10	11	124
LA	New Orleans	30	10	9	9	7	7	10	15	13	10	5	7	10	112

Z: Less than ½ day

Winter Olympics (Women) Gold Medalists

500-meter Speed Skating			*Time*
1960	Helga Haase	Germany	45.9 s
1964	Lydia Skoblikova	U.S.S.R.	45.0 s
1968	Ludmilla Titova	U.S.S.R.	46.1 s
1972	Anne Henning	U.S.A.	43.4 s
1976	Sheila Young	U.S.A.	42.8 s

Alpine Skiing			
Downhill	1948	Hedy Schlunegger	Switzerland
Giant Slalom	1952	Andrea Mead Lawrence	U.S.A.
Slalom	1948	Gretchen Frazer	U.S.A.

Nordic Skiing			
5 km	1964	Klaudia Boyerskikh	U.S.S.R.
10 km	1952	Lydia Wideman	Finland

Free Throw Percentage

PLAYER	ATTEMPT	FT	PERCENT
Rick Barry	4,090	3,675	0.899
Calvin Murphy	3,087	2,730	0.884
Bill Sharman	3,557	3,143	0.884
Mike Newlin	2,428	2,098	0.864
Fred Brown	1,581	1,364	0.863
Larry Siegfried	1,945	1,662	0.854
Flynn Robinson	1,881	1,597	0.849
Dolph Schayes	8,273	6,979	0.844
Jack Marin	2,852	2,405	0.843
Larry Costello	2,891	2,432	0.841

Distances of Planets from the Sun

Planet	Distance in million km	Distance in astronomical units
Mercury	57.9	0.387
Venus	108	0.723
Earth	149.6	1
Mars	227.9	1.524
Jupiter	778.3	5.203
Saturn	1,427	9.539
Uranus	2,869	19.18
Neptune	4,494	30.04
Pluto	5,900	39.44

The Cost of a Kilowatt-Hour of Electricity

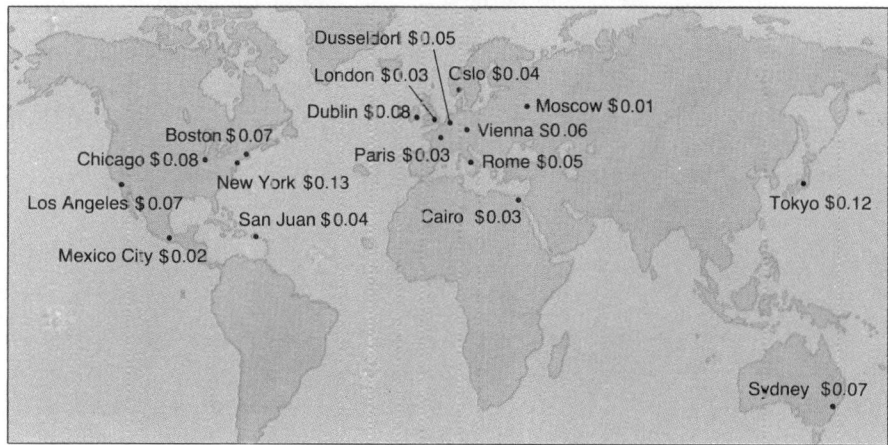

Dusseldorf $0.05
London $0.03
Oslo $0.04
Dublin $0.08
Moscow $0.01
Boston $0.07
Vienna $0.06
Chicago $0.08
Paris $0.03
Rome $0.05
New York $0.13
Los Angeles $0.07
San Juan $0.04
Cairo $0.03
Tokyo $0.12
Mexico City $0.02
Sydney $0.07

DATA BANK

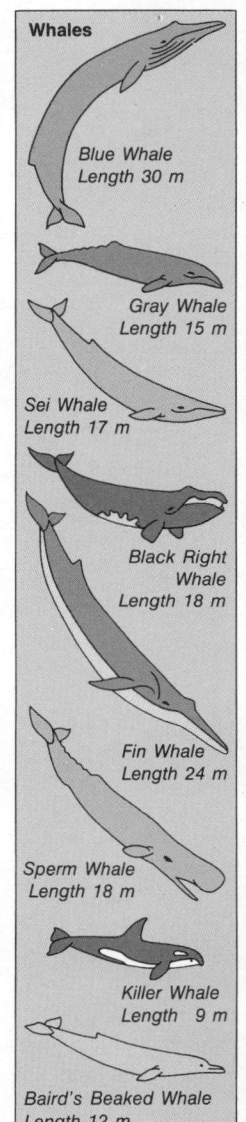

Whales

Blue Whale
Length 30 m

Gray Whale
Length 15 m

Sei Whale
Length 17 m

Black Right
Whale
Length 18 m

Fin Whale
Length 24 m

Sperm Whale
Length 18 m

Killer Whale
Length 9 m

Baird's Beaked Whale
Length 12 m

No. 737 Lowest Annual Temperature of Record—Selected Cities

State	Station	Temp. in degrees C	State	Station	Temp. in degrees C
AL	Mobile	−14	MT	Great Falls	−42
AK	Juneau	−30	NE	Omaha	−30
AZ	Phoenix	−8	NV	Reno	−27
AR	Little Rock	−21	NH	Concord	−38
CA	Sacramento	−7	NJ	Atlantic City	−24
CO	Denver	−34	NM	Albuquerque	−27
CT	Hartford	−32	NY	Albany	−33
DE	Wilmington	−21	NC	Charlotte	−19
DC	Washington	−17	ND	Bismarck	−42
FL	Jacksonville	−11	OH	Cincinnati	−32
GA	Atlanta	−19	OK	Oklahoma City	−20
HI	Honolulu	12	OR	Portland	−19
ID	Boise	−31	PA	Pittsburgh	−28
IL	Peoria	−32	RI	Providence	−25
IN	Indianapolis	−29	SC	Columbia	−16
IA	Des Moines	−31	SD	Sioux Falls	−38
KS	Wichita	−24	TN	Nashville	−26
KY	Louisville	−29	TX	El Paso	−22
LA	New Orleans	−10	UT	Salt Lake City	−34
ME	Portland	−39	VT	Burlington	−34
MD	Baltimore	−22	VA	Richmond	−24
MA	Boston	−24	WA	Spokane	−32
MI	Sault Ste. Marie	−37	WV	Charleston	−24
MN	Duluth	−39	WI	Milwaukee	−31
MS	Jackson	−14	WY	Cheyenne	−37
MO	St. Louis	−26	PR	San Juan	16

Daily Diet of Some Zoo Animals

	Elephant	Giraffe	Gorilla	Hippopotamus
Hay	25 kg	7 kg	—	18 kg
Grain	23 kg	0.5 kg	—	—
Fruit and vegetables	23 kg	—	8 kg	2 kg
Pellets	—	0.5 kg	—	7 kg
Leaves	—	0.5 kg	2 kg	—
Bread	12 kg	—	—	—

MORE PRACTICE

Set A   For use after page 7

Write > or < for each ●.

1. 2,046 ● 2,048 <
2. 3,642 ● 3,462 >
3. 24,500 ● 24,400 >
4. 620,000 ● 62,000 >
5. 785,610 ● 785,611 <
6. 409,111 ● 409,011 >
7. 3,460,014 ● 3,460,104 <
8. 47,000,000 ● 49,000 >
9. 51,866 ● 8,651 >
10. 92,567,402 ● 92,436,402 >

Set B   For use after page 9

Round to the nearest ten thousand.

1. 34,500 → 30,000
2. 29,600 → 30,000
3. 89,499 → 90,000
4. 45,500 → 50,000
5. 109,000 → 110,000
6. 325,444 → 330,000
7. 186,785 → 190,000
8. 404,651 → 400,000
9. 209,087 → 210,000
10. 335,460 → 340,000

Round to the nearest hundred thousand.

11. 484,085 → 500,000
12. 249,000 → 200,000
13. 857,066 → 900,000
14. 308,500 → 300,000
15. 967,068 → 1,000,000
16. 4,087,611 → 4,100,000
17. 6,554,300 → 6,600,000
18. 2,904,855 → 2,900,000
19. 197,366 → 200,000
20. 1,856,592 → 1,900,000

Set C   For use after page 11

Estimate each sum by rounding to the nearest thousand.

1. 24,411 + 36,270 → 60,000
2. 94,115 + 20,641 → 115,000
3. 180,270 + 365,590 → 546,000
4. 4,182 + 3,570 → 8,000
5. 4,061 + 6,506 → 11,000
6. 7,214 + 3,017 + 5,512 → 16,000
7. 23,805 + 16,457 → 40,000
8. 64,805 + 17,667 → 83,000
9. 627,512 + 139,815 → 768,000

Set A   For use after page 13

Add.

1. 29 + 98 = 127
2. 738 + 195 = 933
3. 603 + 397 = 1,000
4. 1,284 + 7,671 = 8,955
5. 3,046 + 6,359 = 9,405
6. 21,186 + 84,398 = 105,584
7. 66,434 + 29,607 = 96,041
8. 35,419 + 66,334 = 101,753
9. 14,016 + 24,495 = 38,511
10. 64,324 + 60,089 = 124,413
11. 61 + 3,447 + 209 = 3,717
12. 8,604 + 5,250 + 1,153 = 15,007
13. 76,408 + 3,215 + 4,479 = 84,102
14. 61,420 + 33,271 + 98,493 = 193,184
15. 78,447 + 36,110 + 43,408 + 92,173 = 250,138

Set B   For use after page 15

Subtract.

1. 408 − 59 = 349
2. 336 − 147 = 189
3. 98 − 49 = 49
4. 445 − 188 = 257
5. 2,615 − 1,108 = 1,207
6. 4,671 − 3,260 = 1,411
7. 9,700 − 6,833 = 2,867
8. 2,704 − 897 = 1,807
9. 3,145 − 1,846 = 1,299
10. 2,928 − 967 = 1,961
11. 8,400 − 5,291 = 3,109
12. 5,462 − 1,924 = 3,538
13. 3,000 − 1,280 = 1,720
14. 9,430 − 6,986 = 2,444
15. 4,000 − 3,294 = 706

Set C   For use after page 19

Add or subtract the hours and minutes.

1. 3 h 45 min + 7 h 20 min = 11 h 5 min
2. 12 h 15 min − 10 h 40 min = 1 h 35 min
3. 9 h − 3 h 15 min = 5 h 45 min
4. 14 h 17 min − 7 h 19 min = 6 h 58 min
5. 9 h 29 min + 5 h 48 min = 15 h 17 min
6. 24 h 48 min + 50 min = 25 h 38 min

Set A For use after page 37

Write <, =, or > for each ●.

1. 0.03 ● 0.30 <
2. 0.6 ● 6.0 <
3. 0.607 ● 0.067 >
4. 64.48 ● 64.488 <
5. 3.00 ● 3 =
6. 0.095 ● 0.099 <
7. 0.001 ● 0.0009 >
8. 5.020 ● 5.02 =
9. 3.664 ● 3.646 >

Set B For use after page 39

Round to the nearest thousandth.

1. 0.0418 → 0.042
2. 10.9945 → 10.995
3. 31.3546720 → 31.355
4. 1.14121356 → 1.141
5. 0.0008 → 0.001
6. 12.50109 → 12.501
7. 0.883914 → 0.884
8. 0.60982 → 0.610

Round to the nearest whole number.

9. 0.85 → 1
10. 25.09 → 25
11. 369.943 → 370
12. 26.554 → 27
13. 3,252.8376 → 3,253
14. 99.9 → 100
15. 1.14121356 → 1
16. 20.08 → 20

Round to 1-digit accuracy.

17. 4.9860 → 5
18. 0.00734 → 0.007
19. 0.108 → 0.1
20. 265.412 → 300
21. 0.0000564 → 0.00006
22. 0.986004 → 1
23. 19.9 → 20
24. 0.002912 → 0.003

Set C For use after page 41

Add.

1. 3.04 + 1.99 = 5.03
2. 18.057 + 3.96 = 22.017
3. 0.1040 + 0.7794 = 0.8834
4. 12.632 + 0.889 = 13.521
5. 0.7785 + 9.0323 = 9.8108
6. 3.216 + 4.805 + 6.664 = 14.685
7. 0.42 + 0.08 + 0.91 = 1.41
8. 35.412 + 7.68 + 16.004 = 59.096
9. 62.487 + 26.113 + 51.857 = 140.457
10. 35.016 + 9.931 + 74.073 = 119.020
11. $33.04 + 17.56 + 2.38 = $52.98
12. $0.62 + 0.38 + 0.90 = $1.90
13. $368.44 + 270.81 + 450.00 = $1,089.25
14. $32.54 + 0.71 + 0.68 + 17.44 = $51.37
15. $11.11 + 81.00 + 16.43 + 59.98 = $168.52

Set A For use after page 43

Subtract.

1. 68.1 − 37.5 = 30.6
2. 108.04 − 67.16 = 40.88
3. 0.406 − 0.198 = 0.208
4. 2.44 − 1.87 = 0.57
5. 53.446 − 18.971 = 34.475
6. 90.00 − 26.48 = 63.52
7. 3.001 − 1.942 = 1.059
8. 206.4 − 9.9 = 196.5
9. 1.048 − 0.019 = 1.029
10. 3.401 − 1.267 = 2.134
11. $26.00 − 5.49 = $20.51
12. $13.46 − 8.51 = $4.95
13. $100.00 − 0.35 = $99.65
14. $345.40 − 208.91 = $136.49
15. $1.46 − 0.88 = $0.58

Set B For use after page 45

Estimate each sum or difference by rounding to the nearest tenth.

1. 0.44 + 0.65 + 0.91 + 0.04 = 2.00
2. 12.09 + 8.40 + 19.67 + 11.54 = 51.70
3. 0.12 + 0.69 + 0.48 + 0.32 = 1.60
4. 6.14 + 3.27 + 8.49 + 4.50 = 22.40
5. 22.62 + 14.08 + 12.36 + 56.79 = 105.90
6. 64.27 − 35.75 = 28.50
7. 0.64 − 0.23 = 0.40
8. 2,306.50 − 1,174.88 = 1,131.60
9. 407.54 − 322.89 = 84.60
10. 66.22 − 35.57 = 30.60

Estimate each sum by rounding to the nearest dollar.

11. $1.08 + 4.35 + 6.67 + 9.49 = $21
12. $4.18 + 5.49 + 8.12 + 6.50 = $24
13. $0.86 + 1.19 + 4.85 + 6.31 = $13
14. $2.45 + 3.12 + 8.29 + 9.50 = $23
15. $6.06 + 1.57 + 2.39 + 4.50 = $15

Set C For use after page 59

Estimate each product by rounding to 1-digit accuracy.

1. 14 × 31 = 300
2. 2,704 × 95 = 300,000
3. 1,078 × 424 = 400,000
4. 8,234 × 375 = 3,200,000
5. 2,319 × 548 = 1,000,000
6. 2,927 × 3,389 = 9,000,000
7. 1,989 × 844 = 1,600,000
8. 15,018 × 4,299 = 80,000,000
9. 981 × 422 = 400,000
10. 692 × 731 = 490,000

Set A For use after page 61

Multiply.

1. $39 \times 4 = 156$
2. $63 \times 5 = 315$
3. $916 \times 5 = 4{,}580$
4. $322 \times 7 = 2{,}254$
5. $489 \times 4 = 1{,}956$
6. $2{,}904 \times 6 = 17{,}424$
7. $9{,}118 \times 4 = 36{,}472$
8. $3{,}470 \times 5 = 17{,}350$
9. $4{,}429 \times 7 = 31{,}003$
10. $3{,}008 \times 4 = 12{,}032$
11. $36 \times 7 = 252$
12. $408 \times 3 = 1{,}224$
13. $9{,}114 \times 5 = 45{,}570$
14. $7{,}541 \times 4 = 30{,}164$
15. $3{,}143 \times 6 = 18{,}858$

Set B For use after page 63

Multiply.

1. $42 \times 18 = 756$
2. $65 \times 48 = 3{,}120$
3. $17 \times 29 = 493$
4. $362 \times 41 = 14{,}842$
5. $804 \times 16 = 12{,}864$
6. $774 \times 29 = 22{,}446$
7. $220 \times 53 = 11{,}660$
8. $4{,}047 \times 36 = 145{,}692$
9. $2{,}951 \times 48 = 141{,}648$
10. $3{,}117 \times 45 = 140{,}265$
11. $6{,}497 \times 22 = 142{,}934$
12. $5{,}432 \times 84 = 456{,}288$
13. $6{,}224 \times 53 = 329{,}872$
14. $7{,}914 \times 68 = 538{,}152$
15. $5{,}901 \times 92 = 542{,}892$

Set C For use after page 65

Multiply.

1. $436 \times 873 = 380{,}628$
2. $240 \times 577 = 138{,}480$
3. $179 \times 432 = 77{,}328$
4. $344 \times 563 = 193{,}672$
5. $243 \times 774 = 188{,}082$
6. $3{,}432 \times 262 = 899{,}184$
7. $7{,}442 \times 450 = 3{,}348{,}900$
8. $6{,}322 \times 418 = 2{,}642{,}596$
9. $4{,}441 \times 226 = 1{,}003{,}666$
10. $5{,}626 \times 300 = 1{,}687{,}800$
11. $743 \times 288 = 213{,}984$
12. $9{,}244 \times 301 = 2{,}782{,}444$
13. $7{,}432 \times 227 = 1{,}687{,}064$
14. $1{,}040 \times 519 = 539{,}760$
15. $294 \times 176 = 51{,}744$

421

Set A For use after page 67

Write the factors for each number and find the products.

1. 4^3 $4 \cdot 4 \cdot 4 = 64$
2. 5^2 $5 \cdot 5 = 25$
3. 7^3 $7 \cdot 7 \cdot 7 = 343$
4. 8^2 $8 \cdot 8 = 64$
5. 6^3 $6 \cdot 6 \cdot 6 = 216$
6. 11^2 $11 \cdot 11 = 121$
7. 3^3 $3 \cdot 3 \cdot 3 = 27$
8. 8^3 $8 \cdot 8 \cdot 8 = 512$
9. 4^4 $4 \cdot 4 \cdot 4 \cdot 4 = 256$
10. 2^6 $2 \cdot 2 \cdot 2 \cdot 2 \cdot 2 \cdot 2 = 64$

Write in exponential notation.

11. $6 \cdot 6 \cdot 6$ 6^3
12. $15 \cdot 15$ 15^2
13. $9 \cdot 9$ 9^2
14. $4 \cdot 4 \cdot 4 \cdot 4$ 4^4
15. $5 \cdot 5$ 5^2
16. $3 \cdot 3 \cdot 3 \cdot 3 \cdot 3$ 3^5
17. $2 \cdot 2 \cdot 2 \cdot 2$ 2^4
18. $25 \cdot 25$ 25^2
19. $10 \cdot 10 \cdot 10$ 10^3
20. $7 \cdot 7 \cdot 7 \cdot 7$ 7^4

Set B For use after page 71

Estimate each quotient by rounding to 1-digit accuracy.

1. $529 \div 18$ 25
2. $431 \div 21$ 20
3. $948 \div 291$ 3
4. $598 \div 192$ 3
5. $1{,}900 \div 514$ 4
6. $\frac{4{,}388}{1{,}209}$ 4
7. $\frac{19{,}301}{5{,}299}$ 4
8. $\frac{21{,}494}{988}$ 20
9. $\frac{11{,}201}{488}$ 20
10. $\frac{3{,}901}{429}$ 10
11. $221\overline{)788}$ 4
12. $79\overline{)1{,}648}$ 25
13. $18\overline{)556}$ 30
14. $581\overline{)3{,}397}$ 5
15. $66\overline{)6{,}821}$ 100

Set C For use after page 72

Find the quotients and remainders.

1. $4\overline{)657}$ 164 R1
2. $9\overline{)408}$ 45 R3
3. $5\overline{)380}$ 76
4. $7\overline{)641}$ 91 R4
5. $3\overline{)904}$ 301 R1
6. $4\overline{)881}$ 220 R1
7. $8\overline{)5{,}427}$ 678 R3
8. $9\overline{)6{,}402}$ 711 R3
9. $7\overline{)4{,}907}$ 701
10. $5\overline{)3{,}229}$ 645 R4
11. $6\overline{)5{,}397}$ 899 R3
12. $2\overline{)1{,}895}$ 947 R1
13. $4\overline{)8{,}498}$ 2,124 R2
14. $6\overline{)3{,}320}$ 553 R2
15. $8\overline{)4{,}420}$ 552 R4

422

More Practice

Set A For use after page 73

Find the quotients and remainders. Use the short division method.

142 R1	13 R5	162 R1	328 R1	148
1. 3)427	2. 8)109	3. 6)973	4. 2)657	5. 3)444
57 R3	1,230 R4	223 R3	1,431 R5	326 R
6. 8)459	7. 7)8,614	8. 9)2,010	9. 6)8,591	10. 5)1,632
560 R5	875 R1	643 R1	502 R5	722 R
11. 6)3,365	12. 7)6,126	13. 4)2,573	14. 8)4,021	15. 3)2,168

16. $175 \div 3$ 58 R1
17. $3,044 \div 6$ 507 R2
18. $4,258 \div 7$ 608 R2
19. $2,107 \div 5$ 421 R2

Set B For use after page 75

Find the quotients and remainders.

56 R7	6 R29	19 R19	5	18 R7
1. 12)679	2. 45)299	3. 38)741	4. 92)460	5. 43)781
12 R36	5 R83	4 R3	285 R20	72 R84
6. 67)840	7. 92)543	8. 86)347	9. 32)9,140	10. 88)6,420
472 R56	696 R28	524 R36	927 R6	444 R51
11. 91)43,008	12. 77)53,620	13. 51)26,760	14. 14)12,984	15. 81)36,015

16. $2,209 \div 81$ 27 R22
17. $19,148 \div 88$ 217 R52
18. $23,762 \div 32$ 742 R18
19. $26,805 \div 31$ 864 R21

Set C For use after page 77

Find the quotients and remainders.

21 R117	2 R833	18 R281	38 R298	186 R94
1. 147)3,204	2. 914)2,661	3. 436)8,129	4. 369)14,320	5. 269)50,128
56 R145	379 R159	55 R187	349 R31	510 R2!
6. 770)43,265	7. 219)83,160	8. 644)35,607	9. 104)36,327	10. 912)465,377
505 R239	220 R120	451 R376	49 R678	114 R73
11. 244)123,459	12. 186)41,040	13. 982)443,258	14. 725)36,203	15. 446)50,917

16. $186,577 \div 324$ 575 R277
17. $113,245 \div 673$ 168 R181
18. $23,406 \div 189$ 123 R159
19. $436,970 \div 847$ 515 R765

Set A For use after page 93

Find the products.

1. 4.3 × 1.4 6.02	2. 6.9 × 3.5 24.15	3. 0.6 × 0.4 0.24	4. 1.42 × 1.5 2.13	5. 3.17 × 43 136.31
6. 9.26 × 0.08 0.7408	7. 72.4 × 6.8 492.32	8. 1.7 × 3.9 6.63	9. 12.44 × 0.08 0.9952	10. 2.227 × 1.59 3.54093

Set B For use after page 95

Find the products.

1. 0.0064 × 0.82 0.005248	2. 0.43 × 0.08 0.0344	3. 24 × 0.09 2.16	4. 3.3 × 0.0008 0.00264	5. 0.0038 × 0.26 0.000988
6. 4.3 × 0.02 0.086	7. 0.003 × 0.21 0.00063	8. 0.4 × 0.04 0.016	9. 5.08 × 0.61 3.0988	10. 0.077 × 0.042 0.003234

Set C For use after page 100

Estimate each product.

1. 6.2 × 2.4 12	2. 1.43 × 9.1 9	3. 91.34 × 32.06 2,700	4. 0.45 × 1.6 1	5. 0.143 × 0.018 0.002
6. $6.08 × 0.37 $2.40	7. $12.00 × 1.8 $20.00	8. $0.45 × 1.27 $0.50	9. $3.66 × 0.27 $1.20	10. $19.38 × 18 $400.00

Set D For use after page 103

Write each number in scientific notation.

1. 60,000,000 6×10^7
2. 690,000 6.9×10^5
3. 365,000,000 3.65×10^8
4. 64,000 6.4×10^4
5. 3,500,000,000 3.5×10^9
6. 923,000,000,000 9.23×10^{11}
7. 370 3.7×10^2
8. 6,750,000 6.75×10^6

Write the standard numeral.

9. 4.8×10^6 4,800,000
10. 2.2×10^2 220
11. 3.9×10^{12} 3,900,000,000,000
12. 8×10^5 800,000
13. 1.6×10^4 16,000
14. 7.53×10^9 7,530,000,000
15. 9.3×10^1 93
16. 9.08×10^3 9,080
17. 4.95×10^{10} 49,500,000,000

Set A For use after page 117

Find the quotients.

1. 3)20.1 → 6.7
2. 6)43.8 → 7.3
3. 7)1.68 → 0.24
4. 3)15.9 → 5.3
5. 9)72.9 → 8.1
6. 62)241.8 → 3.9
7. 85)81.6 → 0.96
8. 33)178.2 → 5.4
9. 12)0.624 → 0.052
10. 99)366.3 → 3.7

11. 507.78 ÷ 63   8.06
12. 2.436 ÷ 29   0.084
13. 249.48 ÷ 77   3.24
14. 58.5 ÷ 9   6.5
15. 37.95 ÷ 55   0.69

Set B For use after page 119

Find the quotients. Round to the nearest hundredth.

1. 7)12 → 1.71
2. 4)15 → 3.75
3. 3)12.4 → 4.13
4. 7)29 → 4.14
5. 16)3.7 → 0.23
6. 3)$26.45 → $8.82
7. 14)$25.00 → $1.79
8. 12)$6.98 → $0.58
9. 35)$438.20 → $12.52
10. 5)$11.03 → $2.21

Set C For use after page 125

Find the quotients to the nearest hundredth.

1. 9.1)46.21 → 5.08
2. 0.42)1.08 → 2.57
3. 6.2)3.74 → 0.6
4. 0.32)0.851 → 2.66
5. 1.8)0.643 → 0.36
6. 11)9 → 0.82
7. 0.5)1.374 → 2.75
8. 0.41)0.904 → 2.2
9. 1.3)0.04 → 0.03
10. 2.7)0.8923 → 0.33

Set D For use after page 129

Estimate each quotient.

1. 4.26)35.03 → 10
2. 0.32)0.2977 → 1
3. 0.37)26.41 → 75
4. 9.3)0.4374 → 0.04
5. 2.3)0.914 → 0.45
6. 4.03)22.94 → 5
7. 0.429)1.48 → 2.5
8. 2.7)0.3364 → 0.1
9. 17.201)256.73 → 15
10. 0.045)8.3 → 160

Set A For use after page 169

Write P (prime), C (composite), or N (neither) for each number.

1. 29 P
2. 48 C
3. 37 P
4. 43 P
5. 49 C
6. 77 C
7. 61 P
8. 1 N
9. 59 P
10. 87 C

Find the composite number in each list. Find the factors of that number.

11. 19, 29, 39, 59   39: 1, 3, 13, 39
12. 3, 7, 9, 11   9: 1, 3, 9
13. 17, 27, 37, 47   27: 1, 3, 9, 27
14. 19, 91, 17, 71   91: 1, 7, 13, 91
15. 57, 97, 41, 13   57: 1, 3, 19, 57
16. 33, 42, 90, 102   33: 1, 3, 11, 33

Set B For use after page 171

Give the prime factorization of each number.

1. 98 $2 \cdot 7 \cdot 7$
2. 56 $2 \cdot 2 \cdot 2 \cdot 7$
3. 68 $2 \cdot 2 \cdot 17$
4. 150 $2 \cdot 3 \cdot 5 \cdot 5$
5. 220 $2 \cdot 2 \cdot 5 \cdot 11$
6. 90 $2 \cdot 3 \cdot 3 \cdot 5$
7. 160 $2 \cdot 2 \cdot 2 \cdot 2 \cdot 2 \cdot 5$
8. 180 $2 \cdot 2 \cdot 3 \cdot 3 \cdot 5$
9. 210 $2 \cdot 3 \cdot 5 \cdot 7$
10. 60 $2 \cdot 2 \cdot 3 \cdot 5$
11. 360 $2 \cdot 2 \cdot 2 \cdot 3 \cdot 3 \cdot 5$
12. 7,350 $2 \cdot 3 \cdot 5 \cdot 5 \cdot 7 \cdot 7$
13. 405 $3 \cdot 3 \cdot 3 \cdot 3 \cdot 5$
14. 280 $2 \cdot 2 \cdot 2 \cdot 5 \cdot 7$
15. 750 $2 \cdot 3 \cdot 5 \cdot 5 \cdot 5$

Set C For use after page 173

Find the GCF of each pair of numbers.

1. 30, 135   15
2. 28, 20   4
3. 35, 42   7
4. 25, 36   1
5. 200, 75   25
6. 63, 42   21
7. 12, 30   6
8. 17, 34   17
9. 18, 35   1
10. 64, 80   16
11. 42, 63   21
12. 45, 42   3
13. 100, 98   2
14. 108, 81   12
16. 200, 64   8

Set D For use after page 175

Find the LCM of each pair of numbers.

1. 4, 10   20
2. 6, 9   18
3. 15, 10   30
4. 14, 4   28
5. 7, 6   42
6. 25, 10   50
7. 18, 45   90
8. 11, 6   66
9. 36, 45   180
10. 42, 12   84
11. 10, 14   70
12. 48, 96   96
13. 6, 15   30
14. 7, 15   105
15. 22, 33   66

Set A For use after page 177

Copy and complete each table by evaluating the expressions.

x	x+3
1. 0	■
2. 1	■
3. 8	■
4. 17	■

m	8m
5. 1	■
6. 5	■
7. 10	■
8. 11	■

t	$\frac{t}{2}$
9. 4	■
10. 10	■
11. 8	■
12. 12	■

Write an expression.

13. 9 less than a number p $p - 9$
14. 5 more than a number w $w + 5$
15. A number k multiplied by 10 $10k$
16. 15 divided by a number n $\frac{15}{n}$
17. A number r divided by 3 $\frac{r}{3}$
18. 17 decreased by a number h $17 - h$

Set B For use after page 179

Solve.

1. $x + 9 = 25$ $x = 16$
2. $s + 12 = 40$ $s = 28$
3. $t + 14 = 24$ $t = 10$
4. $m + 3 = 15$ $m = 12$
5. $x - 3 = 8$ $x = 11$
6. $z - 20 = 40$ $z = 60$
7. $x - 9 = 18$ $x = 27$
8. $k - 28 = 19$ $k = 47$
9. $y + 4 = 10$ $y = 6$
10. $l - 8 = 9$ $l = 17$
11. $t - 11 = 22$ $t = 33$
12. $x + 5 = 28$ $x = 23$

Set C For use after page 181

Solve.

1. $6x = 54$ $x = 9$
2. $10y = 80$ $y = 8$
3. $7p = 49$ $p = 7$
4. $2n = 32$ $n = 16$
5. $\frac{t}{8} = 9$ $t = 72$
6. $\frac{x}{13} = 2$ $x = 26$
7. $\frac{b}{6} = 6$ $b = 36$
8. $\frac{m}{5} = 100$ $m = 500$
9. $\frac{n}{18} = 1$ $n = 18$
10. $18z = 180$ $z = 10$
11. $8r = 88$ $r = 11$
12. $\frac{x}{4} = 13$ $x = 52$

Set A For use after page 197

Write the missing numerator or denominator.

1. $\frac{1}{4} = \frac{\blacksquare}{8}$ 2
2. $\frac{2}{3} = \frac{4}{\blacksquare}$ 6
3. $\frac{4}{9} = \frac{12}{\blacksquare}$ 27
4. $\frac{3}{5} = \frac{15}{\blacksquare}$ 25
5. $\frac{3}{11} = \frac{\blacksquare}{33}$ 9
6. $\frac{3}{4} = \frac{15}{\blacksquare}$ 20
7. $\frac{3}{8} = \frac{9}{\blacksquare}$ 24
8. $\frac{1}{7} = \frac{\blacksquare}{49}$ 7
9. $\frac{7}{10} = \frac{28}{\blacksquare}$ 40
10. $\frac{5}{12} = \frac{\blacksquare}{36}$ 15
11. $\frac{6}{7} = \frac{18}{\blacksquare}$ 21
12. $\frac{5}{8} = \frac{25}{\blacksquare}$ 40
13. $\frac{2}{9} = \frac{10}{\blacksquare}$ 45
14. $\frac{2}{13} = \frac{4}{\blacksquare}$ 26
15. $\frac{7}{15} = \frac{21}{\blacksquare}$ 45

Set B For use after page 199

Write each fraction in lowest terms.

1. $\frac{6}{10}$ $\frac{3}{5}$
2. $\frac{9}{27}$ $\frac{1}{3}$
3. $\frac{80}{100}$ $\frac{4}{5}$
4. $\frac{22}{44}$ $\frac{1}{2}$
5. $\frac{14}{30}$ $\frac{7}{15}$
6. $\frac{18}{24}$ $\frac{3}{4}$
7. $\frac{15}{36}$ $\frac{5}{12}$
8. $\frac{10}{50}$ $\frac{1}{5}$
9. $\frac{9}{12}$ $\frac{3}{4}$
10. $\frac{12}{16}$ $\frac{3}{4}$
11. $\frac{5}{9}$ $\frac{5}{9}$
12. $\frac{16}{40}$ $\frac{2}{5}$
13. $\frac{14}{21}$ $\frac{2}{3}$
14. $\frac{14}{70}$ $\frac{1}{5}$
15. $\frac{480}{1,000}$ $\frac{12}{25}$
16. $\frac{10}{36}$ $\frac{5}{18}$
17. $\frac{64}{100}$ $\frac{16}{25}$
18. $\frac{18}{42}$ $\frac{3}{7}$
19. $\frac{25}{60}$ $\frac{5}{12}$
20. $\frac{48}{80}$ $\frac{3}{5}$
21. $\frac{27}{36}$ $\frac{3}{4}$
22. $\frac{40}{100}$ $\frac{2}{5}$
23. $\frac{14}{42}$ $\frac{1}{3}$
24. $\frac{360}{1,000}$ $\frac{9}{25}$

Set C For use after page 201

Write each improper fraction as a mixed number or a whole number.

1. $\frac{9}{7}$ $1\frac{2}{7}$
2. $\frac{36}{12}$ 3
3. $\frac{10}{4}$ $2\frac{1}{2}$
4. $\frac{14}{5}$ $2\frac{4}{5}$
5. $\frac{30}{5}$ 6
6. $\frac{15}{4}$ $3\frac{3}{4}$
7. $\frac{15}{10}$ $1\frac{1}{2}$
8. $\frac{10}{3}$ $3\frac{1}{3}$
9. $\frac{14}{7}$ 2
10. $\frac{11}{5}$ $2\frac{1}{5}$
11. $\frac{26}{8}$ $3\frac{1}{4}$
12. $\frac{17}{9}$ $1\frac{8}{9}$
13. $\frac{37}{7}$ $5\frac{2}{7}$
14. $\frac{14}{6}$ $2\frac{1}{3}$
15. $\frac{27}{9}$ 3
16. $\frac{45}{45}$ 1
17. $\frac{100}{25}$ 4
18. $\frac{19}{3}$ $6\frac{1}{3}$

Write each mixed number as an improper fraction.

19. $1\frac{5}{8}$ $\frac{13}{8}$
20. $3\frac{3}{4}$ $\frac{15}{4}$
21. $1\frac{1}{9}$ $\frac{10}{9}$
22. $3\frac{3}{7}$ $\frac{24}{7}$
23. $8\frac{2}{3}$ $\frac{26}{3}$
24. $6\frac{2}{5}$ $\frac{32}{5}$
25. $8\frac{1}{4}$ $\frac{33}{4}$
26. $1\frac{7}{15}$ $\frac{22}{15}$
27. 12 $\frac{61}{5}$
28. $6\frac{3}{8}$ $\frac{51}{8}$
29. $12\frac{1}{5}$ $\frac{61}{5}$
30. $8\frac{1}{2}$ $\frac{17}{2}$
31. $33\frac{1}{3}$ $\frac{100}{3}$
32. $9\frac{1}{2}$ $\frac{19}{2}$
33. $49\frac{1}{2}$ $\frac{99}{2}$
34. $4\frac{3}{7}$ $\frac{31}{7}$
35. $6\frac{1}{4}$ $\frac{25}{4}$
36. $2\frac{3}{100}$ $\frac{203}{100}$

Set A For use after page 203

Compare the fractions. Write > or < for each ●.

1. $\frac{7}{12}$ ● $\frac{5}{8}$ <
2. $\frac{2}{3}$ ● $\frac{5}{9}$ >
3. $\frac{3}{8}$ ● $\frac{1}{3}$ >
4. $\frac{1}{6}$ ● $\frac{2}{9}$ <

5. $\frac{2}{3}$ ● $\frac{3}{4}$ <
6. $\frac{1}{2}$ ● $\frac{3}{8}$ >
7. $\frac{6}{7}$ ● $\frac{2}{3}$ >
8. $\frac{5}{7}$ ● $\frac{9}{14}$ >

9. $\frac{1}{2}$ ● $\frac{5}{16}$ >
10. $\frac{1}{3}$ ● $\frac{2}{9}$ >
11. $\frac{3}{5}$ ● $\frac{8}{15}$ >
12. $\frac{11}{24}$ ● $\frac{5}{12}$ >

Set B For use after page 207

Add.

1. $\frac{5}{6} + \frac{1}{6}$ 1
2. $\frac{2}{9} + \frac{1}{9}$ $\frac{1}{3}$
3. $\frac{5}{12} + \frac{5}{12}$ $\frac{5}{6}$
4. $\frac{7}{10} + \frac{7}{10}$ $1\frac{2}{5}$
5. $\frac{3}{16} + \frac{5}{16}$ $\frac{1}{2}$

6. $\frac{3}{8}$
$+ \frac{3}{4}$
$1\frac{1}{8}$

7. $\frac{3}{7}$
$+ \frac{5}{14}$
$\frac{11}{14}$

8. $\frac{5}{9}$
$+ \frac{5}{6}$
$1\frac{7}{18}$

9. $\frac{5}{6}$
$+ \frac{3}{4}$
$1\frac{7}{12}$

10. $\frac{1}{5}$
$+ \frac{7}{10}$
$\frac{9}{10}$

11. $\frac{3}{8}$
$+ \frac{3}{16}$
$\frac{9}{16}$

12. $\frac{1}{5}$
$+ \frac{7}{15}$
$\frac{2}{3}$

13. $\frac{5}{12}$
$+ \frac{5}{6}$
$1\frac{1}{4}$

14. $\frac{1}{10}$
$+ \frac{3}{20}$
$\frac{1}{4}$

15. $\frac{5}{9}$
$+ \frac{2}{3}$
$1\frac{2}{9}$

Set C For use after page 209

Subtract.

1. $\frac{7}{8} - \frac{5}{8}$ $\frac{1}{4}$
2. $\frac{7}{9} - \frac{4}{9}$ $\frac{1}{3}$
3. $\frac{11}{12} - \frac{5}{12}$ $\frac{1}{2}$
4. $\frac{9}{10} - \frac{3}{10}$ $\frac{3}{5}$
5. $\frac{5}{8} - \frac{1}{8}$ $\frac{1}{2}$

6. $\frac{5}{6}$
$- \frac{1}{3}$
$\frac{1}{2}$

7. $\frac{7}{8}$
$- \frac{1}{4}$
$\frac{5}{8}$

8. $\frac{3}{4}$
$- \frac{1}{3}$
$\frac{5}{12}$

9. $\frac{9}{10}$
$- \frac{3}{5}$
$\frac{3}{10}$

10. $\frac{3}{5}$
$- \frac{1}{2}$
$\frac{1}{10}$

11. $\frac{5}{12}$
$- \frac{3}{8}$
$\frac{1}{24}$

12. $\frac{5}{6}$
$- \frac{3}{5}$
$\frac{7}{30}$

13. $\frac{7}{10}$
$- \frac{1}{4}$
$\frac{9}{20}$

14. $\frac{2}{3}$
$- \frac{2}{5}$
$\frac{4}{15}$

15. $\frac{7}{9}$
$- \frac{2}{3}$
$\frac{1}{9}$

Set A For use after page 211

Add.

1. $3 + 7\frac{1}{4}$ $10\frac{1}{4}$
2. $6 + 6\frac{1}{2}$ $12\frac{1}{2}$
3. $8\frac{5}{9} + 9$ $17\frac{5}{9}$
4. $13 + 7\frac{3}{8}$ $20\frac{3}{8}$
5. $3\frac{1}{2} + 3\frac{1}{2}$ 7

6. $3\frac{5}{9}$
$+ 4\frac{1}{6}$
$7\frac{13}{18}$

7. $4\frac{3}{5}$
$+ 5\frac{11}{15}$
$10\frac{1}{3}$

8. $6\frac{1}{7}$
$+ 6\frac{2}{3}$
$12\frac{17}{21}$

9. $2\frac{2}{3}$
$+ 6\frac{5}{6}$
$9\frac{1}{2}$

10. $14\frac{7}{8}$
$+ 3\frac{1}{8}$
18

Set B For use after page 213

Subtract.

1. $7\frac{1}{4} - 3\frac{1}{8}$ $4\frac{1}{8}$
2. $9\frac{10}{12} - 3\frac{2}{3}$ $6\frac{1}{3}$
3. $2\frac{2}{4} - 1\frac{1}{9}$ $1\frac{7}{18}$
4. $3\frac{2}{3} - 1\frac{1}{7}$ $2\frac{11}{21}$
5. $8\frac{2}{3} - 2\frac{4}{5}$ $\frac{4}{15}$

6. $8\frac{1}{2}$
$- 4\frac{2}{3}$
$3\frac{5}{6}$

7. $4\frac{2}{8}$
$- 3\frac{1}{2}$
$\frac{3}{4}$

8. $7\frac{1}{10}$
$- 4\frac{3}{5}$
$2\frac{1}{2}$

9. $5\frac{3}{9}$
$- 1\frac{10}{12}$
$3\frac{1}{2}$

10. $6\frac{3}{4}$
$- 2\frac{12}{16}$
4

11. $15\frac{9}{14}$
$- 9\frac{3}{7}$
$6\frac{3}{14}$

12. $21\frac{2}{4}$
$- 7\frac{1}{3}$
$14\frac{1}{6}$

13. $40\frac{4}{9}$
$- 8\frac{2}{6}$
$32\frac{2}{9}$

14. $17\frac{4}{12}$
$- 4\frac{2}{12}$
$13\frac{1}{6}$

15. $82\frac{1}{3}$
$- 19\frac{1}{5}$
$63\frac{2}{15}$

Set C For use after page 215

Subtract.

1. $1 - \frac{4}{9}$ $\frac{5}{9}$
2. $6\frac{1}{8} - \frac{7}{10}$ $\frac{1}{2}$
3. $4\frac{1}{4} - 1\frac{1}{2}$ $2\frac{3}{4}$
4. $2\frac{2}{9} - \frac{10}{18}$ $\frac{3}{5}$
5. $7 - 2\frac{1}{2}$ $4\frac{1}{2}$

6. $5\frac{1}{3}$
$- 4\frac{4}{8}$
$\frac{5}{6}$

7. $2\frac{1}{9}$
$- \frac{5}{9}$
$1\frac{5}{9}$

8. $10\frac{1}{7}$
$- 8\frac{6}{7}$
$1\frac{2}{17}$

9. $12\frac{1}{3}$
$- 10\frac{1}{2}$
$1\frac{5}{6}$

10. $8\frac{7}{8}$
$- 7\frac{1}{2}$
$1\frac{3}{8}$

11. $1\frac{1}{8}$
$- \frac{4}{6}$
$\frac{11}{24}$

12. $73\frac{1}{2}$
$- 70\frac{3}{4}$
$2\frac{3}{4}$

13. $51\frac{3}{9}$
$- 48$
$3\frac{1}{3}$

14. $11\frac{1}{3}$
$- 10\frac{3}{9}$
1

15. 24
$- \frac{9}{10}$
$23\frac{1}{10}$

More Practice

Set A For use after page 227

Find the products.

1. $\frac{3}{5} \times \frac{1}{9}$ $\frac{1}{15}$
2. $\frac{1}{2} \times \frac{4}{5}$ $\frac{2}{5}$
3. $\frac{3}{4} \times \frac{2}{3}$ $\frac{1}{2}$
4. $\frac{5}{12} \times \frac{3}{10}$ $\frac{1}{8}$
5. $\frac{3}{7} \times \frac{14}{27}$ $\frac{2}{9}$
6. $\frac{2}{3} \times \frac{5}{6}$ $\frac{5}{9}$
7. $\frac{5}{12} \times \frac{8}{9}$ $\frac{2}{15}$
8. $\frac{1}{3} \times \frac{9}{10}$ $\frac{3}{10}$
9. $\frac{3}{4} \times \frac{1}{6}$ $\frac{1}{8}$
10. $\frac{5}{9} \times \frac{9}{10}$ $\frac{1}{2}$
11. $\frac{7}{12} \times \frac{2}{3}$ $\frac{7}{}$
12. $\frac{1}{12} \times \frac{8}{9}$ $\frac{2}{27}$
13. $\frac{3}{5} \times \frac{5}{6}$ $\frac{1}{2}$
14. $\frac{2}{5} \times \frac{1}{7}$ $\frac{2}{35}$
15. $\frac{1}{6} \times \frac{9}{10}$ $\frac{3}{20}$

Set B For use after page 229

Find the products.

1. $3\frac{1}{3} \times 1\frac{1}{2}$ $1\frac{1}{3}$
2. $2\frac{1}{2} \times 1\frac{1}{3}$ $3\frac{1}{3}$
3. $3\frac{1}{5} \times 1\frac{1}{4}$ 4
4. $1\frac{7}{8} \times 2\frac{2}{5}$ $4\frac{1}{2}$
5. $2\frac{1}{4} \times 5\frac{1}{3}$ 12
6. $1\frac{5}{6} \times 2\frac{2}{5}$ $4\frac{2}{5}$
7. $1\frac{1}{7} \times 2\frac{4}{5}$ $2\frac{2}{5}$
8. $2\frac{3}{8} \times 5\frac{1}{2}$ 13
9. $5\frac{1}{4} \times 1\frac{1}{7}$ 6
10. $4\frac{1}{5} \times 1\frac{9}{19}$ $4\frac{2}{5}$
11. $6 \times 2\frac{3}{4}$ $16\frac{1}{2}$
12. $3\frac{1}{2} \times 4\frac{2}{3}$ $16\frac{1}{3}$
13. $2\frac{7}{10} \times 5\frac{2}{6}$ $2\frac{1}{4}$
14. $4\frac{4}{5} \times 2\frac{3}{7}$ $10\frac{1}{5}$
15. $3\frac{1}{9} \times 2\frac{5}{8}$ $8\frac{1}{6}$

Set C For use after page 231

Give the reciprocal of each number.

1. $1\frac{4}{1}$
2. $6\frac{8}{8}$
3. $7\frac{1}{7}$
4. $5\frac{3}{5}$
5. $\frac{1}{6}$
6. $3\frac{1}{5}$
7. $1\frac{1}{3}$
8. $24\frac{1}{24}$
9. $2\frac{7}{7}$
10. $2\frac{10}{12}$

Set D For use after page 233

Find the quotients.

1. $2\frac{1}{3} \div 5\frac{1}{3}$
2. $\frac{3}{5} \div \frac{2}{5}$ $\frac{9}{10}$
3. $\frac{7}{8} \div \frac{1}{4}$ $3\frac{1}{2}$
4. $\frac{3}{10} \div \frac{2}{5}$ $\frac{3}{4}$
5. $\frac{1}{4} \div \frac{1}{4}$ $3\frac{1}{2}$
6. $\frac{3}{5} \div \frac{6}{10}$
7. $\frac{7}{7} \div \frac{4}{5}$ $\frac{3}{7}$
8. $\frac{3}{8} \div \frac{1}{4}$ $1\frac{3}{2}$
9. $\frac{4}{9} \div \frac{2}{2}$ $1\frac{3}{3}$
10. $\frac{1}{5} \div \frac{1}{10}$ $\frac{2}{3}$
11. $\frac{5}{8} \div \frac{3}{16}$ $3\frac{1}{5}$
12. $\frac{2}{5} \div \frac{6}{15}$ 1
13. $\frac{4}{5} \div \frac{1}{4}$ $2\frac{3}{4}$
14. $\frac{5}{16} \div \frac{8}{6}$ $2\frac{3}{6}$
15. $\frac{3}{10} \div \frac{2}{5}$ $\frac{3}{4}$

Set A For use after page 235

Find the quotients.

1. $3\frac{1}{3} \div 2\frac{2}{3}$ $1\frac{1}{4}$
2. $4\frac{2}{3} \div 2\frac{1}{3}$ 2
3. $3\frac{3}{4} \div 3$ $1\frac{1}{4}$
4. $\frac{5}{6} \div 1\frac{2}{3}$ $\frac{1}{2}$
5. $4\frac{1}{2} \div 1\frac{5}{8}$ $2\frac{10}{13}$
6. $9 \div 2\frac{2}{3}$ $3\frac{3}{8}$
7. $1\frac{4}{5} \div 2\frac{1}{10}$ $\frac{6}{7}$
8. $7\frac{1}{2} \div 3\frac{3}{4}$ 2
9. $2 \div 1\frac{1}{3}$ $1\frac{1}{6}$
10. $7\frac{1}{3} \div 1\frac{1}{3}$ 8
11. $4\frac{2}{5} \div 5\frac{1}{3}$ $\frac{33}{40}$
12. $2\frac{1}{16} \div 3\frac{1}{4}$ $\frac{7}{12}$
13. $9 \div 2\frac{2}{5}$ $3\frac{3}{4}$
14. $4\frac{1}{3} \div 5\frac{1}{4}$ $\frac{13}{16}$
15. $\frac{5}{7} \div 1\frac{2}{3}$ $\frac{3}{7}$

Set B For use after page 239

Write each decimal as a lowest-terms fraction or a mixed number.

1. 0.8 $\frac{4}{5}$
2. 0.3 $\frac{3}{10}$
3. 0.09 $\frac{9}{100}$
4. 0.03 $\frac{3}{100}$
5. 0.12 $\frac{3}{25}$
6. 3.04 $3\frac{1}{25}$
7. 17.017 $17\frac{17}{1,000}$
8. 3.95 $3\frac{19}{20}$
9. 2.125 $2\frac{1}{8}$
10. 14.75 $14\frac{3}{4}$

Write each fraction as a decimal.

11. $\frac{3}{5}$ 0.6
12. $\frac{27}{4}$ 6.75
13. $\frac{15}{16}$ 0.9375
14. $\frac{7}{25}$ 0.28
15. $\frac{1}{5}$ 0.2
16. $\frac{9}{16}$ 0.5625
17. $\frac{15}{30}$ 0.5
18. $\frac{25}{100}$ 0.25
19. $\frac{3}{4}$ 0.75
20. $\frac{80}{100}$ 0.8

Set C For use after page 241

Write the decimal for each fraction. Use a bar to show repeating decimals.

1. $\frac{3}{5}$ 0.6
2. $\frac{7}{9}$ $0.\overline{7}$
3. $\frac{5}{30}$ $0.1\overline{6}$
4. $\frac{4}{5}$ 0.8
5. $\frac{6}{9}$ $0.\overline{6}$
6. $\frac{3}{9}$ $0.\overline{3}$
7. $\frac{3}{8}$ 0.375
8. $\frac{10}{22}$ $0.4\overline{5}$
9. $\frac{14}{15}$ $0.9\overline{3}$
10. $\frac{68}{5}$ 13.6

Compare the fractions by comparing their decimals. Use > or <.

11. $\frac{4}{8}$ ● $\frac{5}{8}$ <
12. $\frac{4}{25}$ ● $\frac{7}{28}$ <
13. $\frac{3}{5}$ ● $\frac{2}{3}$ <
14. $\frac{4}{7}$ ● $\frac{2}{21}$ >
15. $\frac{4}{18}$ ● $\frac{3}{15}$ >
16. $\frac{5}{17}$ ● $\frac{2}{7}$ >
17. $\frac{3}{21}$ ● $\frac{4}{29}$ >
18. $\frac{3}{28}$ ● $\frac{4}{32}$ <
19. $\frac{36}{40}$ ● $\frac{17}{19}$ <
20. $\frac{1}{9}$ ● $\frac{3}{26}$ <

Set A   For use after page 253

Find the perimeter of each rectangle.

1. $l = 6.2$ m
   $w = 2.7$ m
   17.8 m

2. $l = 31.6$ cm
   $w = 7.2$ cm
   77.6 cm

3. $l = 8.1$ km
   $w = 3.53$ km
   23.26 km

4. $l = 4.96$ dm
   $w = 2.42$ dm
   14.76 dm

5. $l = 6.05$ m
   $w = 4.78$ m
   21.66 m

6. $l = 11.66$ km
   $w = 8.12$ km
   39.56 km

7. $l = 9.5$ dm
   $w = 6.38$ dm
   31.76 dm

8. $l = 27.9$ m
   $w = 6.4$ m
   68.6 m

9. $l = 8.62$ hm
   $w = 2.1$ hm
   21.44 hm

10. $l = 13.7$ mm
    $w = 4.6$ mm
    36.6 mm

Set B   For use after page 254

Find the area of each rectangle.

1. $l = 26.8$ cm
   $w = 8.3$ cm
   222.44 cm²

2. $l = 84$ km
   $w = 30$ km
   2,520 km²

3. $l = 51.4$ m
   $w = 12$ m
   616.8 m²

4. $l = 16.7$ dm
   $w = 1.9$ dm
   31.73 dm²

5. $l = 70$ mm
   $w = 33$ mm
   2,310 mm²

6. $l = 54$ m
   $w = 32$ m
   1,728 m²

7. $l = 10.6$ mm
   $w = 8.3$ mm
   87.98 mm²

8. $l = 71.5$ cm
   $w = 26.2$ cm
   1,873.3 cm²

9. $l = 8.9$ m
   $w = 4.6$ m
   40.94 m²

10. $l = 18$ km
    $w = 9$ km
    162 km²

Set C   For use after page 257

Find the area of each triangle.

1. $b = 47$ km
   $h = 5$ km
   117.5 km²

2. $b = 25$ cm
   $h = 7$ cm
   87.5 cm²

3. $b = 43$ m
   $h = 6$ m
   129 m²

4. $b = 57$ mm
   $h = 41$ mm
   1,168.5 mm²

5. $b = 68$ dm
   $h = 53$ dm
   1,802 dm²

6. $b = 20$ mm
   $h = 6$ mm
   60 mm²

7. $b = 61$ dm
   $h = 33$ dm
   1,006.5 dm²

8. $b = 27$ cm
   $h = 8$ cm
   108 cm²

9. $b = 59$ km
   $h = 13$ km
   383.5 km²

10. $b = 108$ m
    $h = 42$ m
    2,268 m²

Set D   For use after page 261

Find the volume of each rectangular prism.

1. $l = 12$ cm
   $w = 9$ cm
   $h = 7$ cm
   756 cm³

2. $l = 9$ dm
   $w = 6$ dm
   $h = 5$ dm
   270 dm³

3. $l = 3$ m
   $w = 2.1$ m
   $h = 0.7$ m
   4.41 m³

4. $l = 8$ mm
   $w = 7$ mm
   $h = 3$ mm
   168 mm³

5. $l = 7.6$ km
   $w = 3.8$ km
   $h = 4.2$ km
   121.296 km³

6. $l = 30$ m
   $w = 20$ m
   $h = 14$ m
   8,400 m³

7. $l = 0.6$ cm
   $w = 0.5$ cm
   $h = 0.3$ cm
   0.09 cm³

8. $l = 25$ dm
   $w = 11$ dm
   $h = 2$ dm
   550 dm³

Set A   For use after page 279

Write = or ≠ for each ●.

1. $\frac{2}{6}$ ● $\frac{5}{15}$ =
2. $\frac{3}{4}$ ● $\frac{9}{10}$ ≠
3. $\frac{6}{12}$ ● $\frac{5}{10}$ =
4. $\frac{3}{5}$ ● $\frac{4}{7}$ ≠
5. $\frac{1}{8}$ ● $\frac{4}{32}$ =

6. $\frac{2}{9}$ ● $\frac{3}{10}$ ≠
7. $\frac{1}{7}$ ● $\frac{4}{25}$ ≠
8. $\frac{15}{6}$ ● $\frac{5}{2}$ =
9. $\frac{4}{9}$ ● $\frac{7}{5}$ ≠
10. $\frac{8}{12}$ ● $\frac{6}{9}$ =

Write each ratio as a fraction in lowest terms.

11. 3 out of 18 $\frac{1}{6}$
12. 8:12 $\frac{2}{3}$
13. 10 to 35 $\frac{2}{7}$
14. 9 out of 24 $\frac{3}{8}$
15. 6 to 14 $\frac{3}{7}$

16. 60:20 3
17. 25 out of 100 $\frac{1}{4}$
18. 60:80 $\frac{3}{4}$
19. $\frac{45}{60}$ $\frac{3}{4}$
20. $\frac{80}{100}$ $\frac{4}{5}$

Set B   For use after page 281

Solve the proportions.

1. $\frac{2}{5} = \frac{4}{x}$ 10
2. $\frac{70}{100} = \frac{x}{10}$ 7
3. $\frac{9}{3} = \frac{12}{x}$ 4
4. $\frac{7}{14} = \frac{2}{x}$ 4
5. $\frac{3}{25} = \frac{9}{x}$ 75

6. $\frac{5}{4} = \frac{40}{x}$ 32
7. $\frac{4}{8} = \frac{5}{x}$ 10
8. $\frac{3}{15} = \frac{x}{10}$ 2
9. $\frac{x}{12} = \frac{4}{6}$ 8
10. $\frac{12}{x} = \frac{30}{5}$ 2

Set C   For use after page 297

Write the lowest-terms fraction for each percent.

1. 35% $\frac{7}{20}$
2. 90% $\frac{9}{10}$
3. 12% $\frac{3}{25}$
4. 150% $\frac{3}{2}$
5. 75% $\frac{3}{4}$

6. 80% $\frac{4}{5}$
7. 16% $\frac{4}{25}$
8. 32% $\frac{8}{25}$
9. 4% $\frac{1}{25}$
10. 250% $\frac{5}{2}$

Write the percent for each fraction.

11. $\frac{16}{50}$ 32%
12. $\frac{3}{20}$ 15%
13. $\frac{8}{10}$ 80%
14. $\frac{47}{100}$ 47%
15. $\frac{7}{4}$ 175%

16. $\frac{2}{25}$ 8%
17. $\frac{3}{5}$ 60%
18. $\frac{34}{50}$ 68%
19. $\frac{20}{10}$ 200%
20. $\frac{17}{25}$ 68%

Write each fraction in lowest terms. Then write the percent for the fraction.

21. $\frac{3}{6}$ 50%
22. $\frac{6}{15}$ 40%
23. $\frac{12}{48}$ 25%
24. $\frac{18}{30}$ 60%
25. $\frac{21}{7}$ 300%

26. $\frac{12}{75}$ 16%
27. $\frac{12}{120}$ 10%
28. $\frac{16}{800}$ 2%
29. $\frac{66}{275}$ 24%
30. $\frac{120}{48}$ 250%

Set A For use after page 298

Write each percent as a decimal.

1. 67% 0.67 2. 150% 1.50 3. 6.5% 0.065 4. 74% 0.74 5. 3% 0.03
6. 0.18% 0.0018 7. 63.4% 0.634 8. 500% 5.00 9. 18% 0.18 10. 0.25% 0.0025
11. 10.35% 0.1035 12. 0.6% 0.006 13. 6.75% 0.0675 14. 95% 0.95 15. 10% 0.10

Write each decimal as a percent.

16. 1.75 175% 17. 0.33 33% 18. 0.012 1.2% 19. 0.0099 0.99% 20. 0.0377 3.77%
21. 0.6 60% 22. 7.5 750% 23. 0.18 18% 24. 0.301 30.1% 25. 0.003 0.3%
26. 0.038 3.8% 27. 0.903 90.3% 28. 0.2 20% 29. 5.00 500% 30. 0.1227 12.27%

Set B For use after page 301

Find the percent for each fraction. Round the percent to the nearest whole percent.

1. $\frac{3}{7}$ 43% 2. $\frac{4}{9}$ 44% 3. $\frac{5}{6}$ 83% 4. $\frac{1}{16}$ 6% 5. $\frac{3}{11}$ 27%
6. $\frac{5}{12}$ 42% 7. $\frac{2}{3}$ 67% 8. $\frac{7}{9}$ 78% 9. $\frac{4}{15}$ 27% 10. $\frac{7}{24}$ 29%
11. $\frac{13}{16}$ 81% 12. $\frac{8}{9}$ 89% 13. $\frac{11}{13}$ 85% 14. $\frac{6}{7}$ 86% 15. $\frac{5}{14}$ 36%
16. $\frac{9}{11}$ 82% 17. $\frac{14}{17}$ 82% 18. $\frac{5}{18}$ 28% 19. $\frac{19}{27}$ 70% 20. $\frac{23}{45}$ 51%

Set C For use after page 303

Find the percent of each number.

1. $33\frac{1}{3}$% of 81 27 2. 25% of 64 16 3. 40% of 250 100 4. 75% of 28 21
5. 90% of 60 54 6. 20% of 10 2 7. 50% of 900 450 8. 60% of 75 45
9. 16% of 52 8.32 10. 99% of 25 24.75 11. 250% of 120 300 12. 5.5% of 66 3.63
13. 7% of 115 8.05 14. 85% of 150 127.5 15. 10.5% of 76 7.98 16. 110% of 3 3.3

Set A For use after page 307

Find the percents.

1. 35 is what percent of 70? 50% 2. What percent of 4 is 6? 150%
3. What percent of 20 is 8? 40% 4. What percent of 32 is 24? 75%
5. 18 is what percent of 30? 60% 6. 45 is what percent of 36? 125%
7. What percent is 14 out of 20? 70% 8. What percent is 11 out of 44? 25%
9. What percent of 6 is 15? 250% 10. What percent is 6 out of 150? 4%

Find the percents. Round each percent to the nearest whole percent.

11. 15 is what percent of 95? 16% 12. What percent of 150 is 175? 117%
13. What percent is 6 out of 14? 43% 14. 135 is what percent of 1,080? 13%
15. What percent is 10 out of 12? 83% 16. 98 is what percent of 40? 245%
17. What percent of 75 is 325? 433% 18. 312 is what percent of 400? 78%

Set B For use after page 311

Solve.

1. 75% × n = 12 16 2. 36% × n = 27 75 3. 16% × n = 8 50
4. 30% × n = 18 60 5. 72% × n = 36 50 6. 80% × n = 12 15
7. 38% × n = 19 50 8. 50% × n = 28 56 9. 15% × n = 21 140
10. 6% × n = 27 450 11. 55% × n = 11 20 12. 20% × n = 120 600
13. 18% × n = 9 50 14. 40% × n = 28 70 15. 48% × n = 12 25

Set C For use after page 315

Write and solve a proportion for each question.

1. What is 8% of 300? 24 2. 9 is 20% of what number? 45
3. What percent of 60 is 12? 20% 4. What is 82% of 450? 369
5. 75 is 150% of what number? 50 6. What percent of 350 is 14? 4%
7. What percent of 250 is 55? 22% 8. 90 is 120% of what number? 75

Set A   For use after page 323

Find the circumference of each circle. Use 3.14 for π.

1. $r = 5$ cm — 31.4 cm
2. $d = 13$ m — 40.82 m
3. $r = 60$ km — 376.8 km
4. $r = 25$ mm — 157 mm
5. $d = 5.6$ dm — 17.584 dm
6. $d = 32$ mm — 100.48 mm
7. $r = 0.4$ cm — 2.512 cm
8. $r = 7$ m — 43.96 m
9. $d = 0.3$ km — 0.942 km
10. $d = 10$ m — 31.4 m
11. $r = .08$ dm — 0.5024 dm
12. $r = 6$ km — 37.68 km
13. $d = 11$ cm — 34.54 cm
14. $r = 30$ mm — 188.4 mm
15. $d = 33.4$ m — 104.876 m

Set B   For use after page 325

Find the area of each circle. Use 3.14 for π.

1. $r = 5$ m — 78.5 m²
2. $d = 3.2$ mm — 8.0384 mm²
3. $r = 0.7$ cm — 1.5386 cm²
4. $d = 14$ mm — 153.86 mm²
5. $r = 1.4$ cm — 6.1544 cm²
6. $d = 28$ mm — 615.44 mm²
7. $d = 50$ cm — 1,962.5 cm²
8. $d = 6.6$ m — 34.1946 m²
9. $r = 5.4$ cm — 91.5624 cm²
10. $r = 0.8$ mm — 2.0096 mm²
11. $d = 200$ mm — 31,400 mm²
12. $r = 30$ m — 2,826 m²
13. $d = 2.2$ m — 3.7994 m²
14. $r = 6$ m — 113.04 m²
15. $r = 19$ m — 1,133.54 m²

Set C   For use after page 329

Find the total surface area of each cylinder. Use 3.14 for π.

1. $r = 40$ mm, $h = 71$ mm — 27,883.2 mm²
2. $r = 2.9$ m, $h = 5.1$ m — 145.696 m²
3. $r = 0.8$ m, $h = 1.3$ m — 10.5504 m²
4. $r = 6$ mm, $h = 1$ mm — 263.76 mm²
5. $r = 4$ cm, $h = 6$ cm — 251.2 cm²
6. $r = 7$ m, $h = 8$ m — 659.4 m²
7. $r = 2$ mm, $h = 30$ mm — 401.92 mm²
8. $r = 3$ cm, $h = 5$ cm — 150.72 cm²
9. $r = 11$ m, $h = 3$ m — 967.12 m²
10. $r = 1$ m, $h = 19$ m — 125.6 m²

Set D   For use after page 331

Find the volume of each cylinder. Use π for 3.14.

11. $r = 9$ cm, $h = 10$ cm — 2,543.4 cm³
12. $r = 7$ m, $h = 5$ m — 769.3 m³
13. $r = 30$ dm, $h = 20$ dm — 56,520 dm³
14. $r = 1.2$ mm, $h = 10$ mm — 45.216 mm³
15. $r = 8$ dm, $h = 3$ dm — 602.88 dm³
16. $r = 5$ m, $h = 3.6$ m — 282.6 m³
17. $r = 7$ mm, $h = 6$ mm — 923.16 mm³
18. $r = 8$ cm, $h = 0.1$ cm — 20.096 cm³
19. $r = 2$ km, $h = 3$ km — 37.68 km³
20. $r = 20$ m, $h = 9$ m — 11,304 m³

Set A   For use after page 353

Find the mode and range of each list of numbers.

1. 37, 14, 43, 38, 29, 14, 15, 34, 19, 14   14; 29
2. 1, 3, 7, 9, 12, 8, 7, 6, 8, 7, 10, 11   7; 11
3. 21, 42, 55, 23, 17, 21, 40, 35, 21, 18   21; 38
4. 17, 17, 13, 18, 14, 15, 16, 10   17; 8
5. 98, 92, 95, 92, 95, 89, 90, 91, 92   92; 9
6. 73, 73, 74, 78, 77, 89, 70, 71   73; 19
7. 102, 94, 96, 98, 99, 80, 99, 98   98; 99; 22
8. 3, 3, 6, 6, 7, 8, 1, 2, 3, 9   3; 8

Set B   For use after page 354

Find the arithmetic mean and the median of each list of numbers.

1. 36, 42, 57   45; 42
2. 130, 150, 200   160; 150
3. 97, 111, 173   127; 111
4. 6.3, 8.1, 10.8   8.4; 8.1
5. 0.009, 0.052, 0.161   0.074; 0.052
6. 18, 21, 26, 39, 40   28.8; 26
7. 42, 47, 51, 52, 60, 72   54; 51.5
8. 408, 113, 310, 225   264; 267.5
9. 12, 7, 3, 24, 4, 10   10; 8.5
10. 1.1, 2.3, 2.1, 1.7   1.8; 1.9
11. 0.12, 1.34, 2.4, 0.09, 1.05, 0.2   0.86; 0.625
12. 43.1, 42.4, 40, 38.9, 36.4, 41, 42.1, 40   40.4875; 40.5

Set C   For use after page 369

Write < or > for each ●.

1. $^+4$ ● $^-5$ >
2. $^-3$ ● $^-2$ <
3. $^+8$ ● $^-8$ >
4. $^+4$ ● 0 >
5. $^+16$ ● $^-18$ >
6. $^-8$ ● $^+8$ <
7. $^-16$ ● $^-17$ >
8. $^-32$ ● $^-15$ <
9. $^+9$ ● $^+8$ >
10. $^+1$ ● $^-10$ >
11. $^-3$ ● $^-4$ >
12. 0 ● $^-16$ >
13. $^+24$ ● $^+23$ >
14. $^+1$ ● $^-1$ >
15. $^+17$ ● $^-16$ >
16. $^+18$ ● $^-42$ >

Set A For use after page 371

Find the missing integers.

1. $^{+}5 + {}^{-}5 = \blacksquare$ 0
2. $^{-}3 + {}^{+}3 = \blacksquare$ 0
3. $^{+}10 + 0 = \blacksquare$ $^{+}10$
4. $^{+}4 + \blacksquare = 0$ $^{-}4$
5. $\blacksquare + {}^{-}6 = {}^{-}6$ 0
6. $^{-}7 + {}^{+}7 = \blacksquare$ 0
7. $^{+}8 + {}^{-}8 = 0$ 0
8. $^{-}20 + \blacksquare = 0$ $^{+}20$
9. $0 + \blacksquare = {}^{+}70$ $^{+}70$
10. $^{+}18 + \blacksquare = 0$ $^{-}18$
11. $\blacksquare + {}^{+}9 = 0$ $^{-}9$
12. $\blacksquare + {}^{+}11 = {}^{+}11$ 0
13. $^{-}12 + \blacksquare = {}^{-}12$ 0
14. $^{+}32 + {}^{-}32 = \blacksquare$ 0
15. $^{+}63 + {}^{-}63 = \blacksquare$ 0
16. $\blacksquare + 0 = {}^{+}18$ $^{+}18$
17. $\blacksquare + {}^{+}48 = 0$ $^{-}48$
18. $\blacksquare + {}^{-}13 = 0$ $^{+}13$

Set B For use after page 373

Find the sums.

1. $^{-}3 + {}^{-}1$ $^{-}4$
2. $^{-}7 + {}^{-}2$ $^{-}9$
3. $1 + 6$ 7
4. $^{-}3 + {}^{-}8$ $^{-}11$
5. $9 + 5$ 14
6. $^{-}7 + {}^{-}5$ $^{-}12$
7. $^{-}8 + {}^{-}8$ $^{-}16$
8. $7 + 9$ 16
9. $^{-}5 + {}^{-}5$ $^{-}10$
10. $^{-}6 + {}^{-}2$ $^{-}8$
11. $^{-}5 + {}^{-}9$ $^{-}14$
12. $^{-}1 + {}^{-}1$ $^{-}2$
13. $^{-}6 + {}^{-}7$ $^{-}13$
14. $^{-}4 + {}^{-}8$ $^{-}12$
15. $7 + 7$ 14
16. $^{-}4 + {}^{-}6$ $^{-}10$
17. $^{-}1 + {}^{-}3$ $^{-}4$
18. $8 + 2$ 10
19. $^{-}5 + {}^{-}1$ $^{-}6$
20. $^{-}8 + {}^{-}7$ $^{-}15$
21. $^{-}4 + {}^{-}5$ $^{-}9$
22. $^{-}7 + {}^{-}7$ $^{-}14$
23. $5 + 2$ 7
24. $^{-}1 + {}^{-}8$ $^{-}9$

Set C For use after page 375

Find the sums.

1. $1 + {}^{-}3$ $^{-}2$
2. $4 + {}^{-}4$ 0
3. $^{-}3 + 1$ $^{-}2$
4. $^{-}8 + {}^{-}2$ $^{-}10$
5. $6 + {}^{-}7$ $^{-}1$
6. $^{-}2 + 3$ 1
7. $4 + {}^{-}5$ $^{-}1$
8. $^{-}6 + 6$ 0
9. $8 + {}^{-}7$ 1
10. $^{-}4 + {}^{-}3$ $^{-}7$
11. $^{-}8 + 5$ $^{-}3$
12. $^{-}3 + 8$ 5
13. $10 + {}^{-}12$ $^{-}2$
14. $^{-}8 + 12$ 4
15. $^{-}6 + 11$ 5
16. $^{-}8 + 8$ 0
17. $5 + {}^{-}9$ $^{-}4$
18. $^{-}7 + 14$ 7
19. $^{-}6 + {}^{-}3$ $^{-}9$
20. $8 + {}^{-}12$ $^{-}4$
21. $6 + {}^{-}14$ $^{-}8$
22. $^{-}10 + 16$ 6
23. $^{-}4 + {}^{-}8$ $^{-}12$
24. $7 + {}^{-}15$ $^{-}8$

Set A For use after page 377

Subtract.

1. $^{-}5 - {}^{-}1$ $^{-}4$
2. $6 - {}^{-}3$ 9
3. $^{-}8 - 5$ $^{-}13$
4. $6 - {}^{-}4$ 10
5. $^{-}3 - {}^{-}3$ 0
6. $8 - 14$ $^{-}6$
7. $3 - {}^{-}1$ 4
8. $^{-}10 - {}^{-}10$ 0
9. $6 - {}^{-}9$ 15
10. $^{-}5 - 3$ $^{-}8$
11. $^{-}6 - 0$ $^{-}6$
12. $4 - 9$ $^{-}5$
13. $6 - {}^{-}6$ 12
14. $4 - 8$ $^{-}4$
15. $7 - {}^{-}5$ 12
16. $^{-}8 - 3$ $^{-}11$
17. $2 - 9$ $^{-}7$
18. $^{-}9 - {}^{-}5$ $^{-}4$
19. $^{-}8 - 8$ $^{-}16$
20. $17 - 8$ 9
21. $4 - {}^{-}6$ 10
22. $^{-}7 - 7$ $^{-}14$
23. $^{-}12 - {}^{-}6$ $^{-}6$
24. $7 - {}^{-}9$ 16

Set B For use after page 381

Multiply.

1. $7 \cdot {}^{-}3$ $^{-}21$
2. $^{-}6 \cdot 1$ $^{-}6$
3. $5 \cdot {}^{-}3$ $^{-}15$
4. $^{-}9 \cdot {}^{-}5$ 45
5. $3 \cdot 9$ 27
6. $^{-}6 \cdot {}^{-}5$ 30
7. $3 \cdot {}^{-}7$ $^{-}21$
8. $^{-}3 \cdot {}^{-}3$ 9
9. $^{-}5 \cdot 0$ 0
10. $^{-}8 \cdot 6$ $^{-}48$
11. $6 \cdot {}^{-}9$ $^{-}54$
12. $^{-}5 \cdot {}^{-}4$ 20
13. $12 \cdot 8$ 96
14. $20 \cdot {}^{-}3$ $^{-}60$
15. $26 \cdot {}^{-}5$ $^{-}130$
16. $^{-}17 \cdot {}^{-}3$ 51
17. $^{-}3 \cdot 5$ $^{-}15$
18. $6 \cdot ({}^{-}5 \cdot {}^{-}2)$ 60
19. $^{-}3 \cdot (4 \cdot 0)$ 0
20. $({}^{-}2 \cdot 2) \cdot 7$ $^{-}28$
21. $({}^{-}6 \cdot 1) \cdot 6$ $^{-}36$
22. $3 \cdot (3 \cdot 3)$ 27
23. $({}^{-}4 \cdot 2) \cdot {}^{-}7$ 56
24. $({}^{-}5 \cdot {}^{-}5) \cdot {}^{-}5$ $^{-}125$

Set C For use after page 383

Find the quotients.

1. $14 \div {}^{-}2$ $^{-}7$
2. $^{-}30 \div {}^{-}6$ 5
3. $45 \div {}^{-}9$ $^{-}5$
4. $64 \div {}^{-}8$ $^{-}8$
5. $^{-}35 \div 7$ $^{-}5$
6. $^{-}9 \div 3$ $^{-}3$
7. $21 \div {}^{-}7$ $^{-}3$
8. $^{-}2 \div 2$ $^{-}1$
9. $48 \div {}^{-}6$ $^{-}8$
10. $^{-}24 \div {}^{-}3$ 8
11. $^{-}18 \div 9$ $^{-}2$
12. $^{-}25 \div {}^{-}5$ 5
13. $40 \div {}^{-}8$ $^{-}5$
14. $12 \div 2$ 6
15. $32 \div {}^{-}8$ $^{-}4$
16. $^{-}16 \div 2$ $^{-}8$

Set A   For use after page 395

Add the lengths.

1. 3 ft 3 in.
    + 5 ft 9 in.
    _____
    9 ft

2. 6 ft 11 in.
    + 4 ft 9 in.
    _____
    11 ft 8 in.

3. 2 yd 2 ft
    + 6 yd 1 ft
    _____
    9 yd

4. 13 ft 10 in.
    + 9 ft 6 in.
    _____
    23 ft 4 in.

Subtract the lengths.

5. 7 ft 4 in.
    − 5 ft 2 in.
    _____
    2 ft 2 in.

6. 6 ft 2 in.
    − 3 ft 8 in.
    _____
    2 ft 6 in.

7. 4 ft
    − 2 ft 9 in.
    _____
    1 ft 3 in.

8. 9 yd
    − 5 yd 2 ft
    _____
    3 yd 1 ft

Set B   For use after page 397

Find the area of each rectangle.

1. $l = 30$ in.
    $w = 9$ in.
    270 in.²

2. $l = 8.6$ ft
    $w = 5$ ft
    43 ft²

3. $l = 4\frac{1}{2}$ in.
    $w = 2\frac{1}{2}$ in.
    11.25 in.²

4. $l = 7.4$ mi
    $w = 2.1$ mi
    15.54 mi²

Find the area of each circle. Use 3.14 for π.

5. $r = 4$ in.
    50.24 in.²

6. $r = 3.5$ ft
    38.465 ft²

7. $r = 7$ mi
    153.86 mi²

8. $d = 0.6$ ft
    0.2826 ft²

Set C   For use after page 399

Find the volume of each rectangular prism. Use $V = lwh$.

1. $l = 5$ in.
    $w = 4$ in.
    $h = 10$ in.
    200 in.³

2. $l = 3.5$ ft
    $w = 2$ ft
    $h = 4.5$ ft
    31.5 ft³

3. $l = 6\frac{1}{2}$ in.
    $w = 3\frac{1}{2}$ in.
    $h = 6$ in.
    136.5 in.³

4. $l = 2$ ft 3 in.
    $w = 2$ ft 1 in.
    $h = 6$ in.
    4,050 in.³

Find the volume of each cylinder. Use $V = \pi r^2 h$. Use 3.14 for π.

5. $r = 10$ in.
    $h = 5$ in.
    1,570 in.³

6. $r = 4$ ft
    $h = 13$ ft
    653.12 ft³

7. $r = 6$ in.
    $h = 1$ ft 3 in.
    1,695.6 in.³

8. $r = 7$ ft
    $h = 2$ ft
    307.72 ft³

TABLE OF MEASURES

Metric System		Customary System	

Length

1 meter (m)	1,000 millimeters (mm) 100 centimeters (cm) 10 decimeters (dm)	1 foot (ft)	12 inches (in.)
		1 yard (yd)	36 inches (in.) 3 feet (ft)
1 kilometer (km)	1,000 meters (m)		
1 hectometer (hm)	100 meters (m)	1 mile (mi)	5,280 feet (ft) 1,760 yards (yd)
1 dekameter (dam)	10 meters (m)		
1 decimeter (dm)	0.1 meter (m)	1 nautical mile	6,076 feet (ft) 1,852 meters (m)
1 centimeter (cm)	0.01 meter (m)		
1 millimeter (mm)	0.001 meter (m)		

Area

1 square meter (m^2)	100 square decimeters (dm^2) 10,000 square centimeters (cm^2)	1 square foot (ft^2)	144 square inches ($in.^2$)
1 hectare (ha)	0.01 square kilometer (km^2) 10,000 square meters (m^2)	1 square yard (yd^2)	9 square feet (ft^2) 1,296 square inches ($in.^2$)
1 square kilometer (km^2)	1,000,000 square meters (m^2) 100 hectares (ha)	1 acre (a.)	43,560 square feet (ft^2) 4,840 square yards (yd^2)
		1 square mile (mi^2)	640 acres (a.)

Volume

| 1 cubic decimeter (dm^3) | 0.001 cubic meter (m^3)
1,000 cubic centimeters (cm^3)
1 liter (L) | 1 cubic foot (ft^3) | 1,728 cubic inches ($in.^3$) |
| 1 cubic meter (m^3) | 1,000,000 cubic centimeters (cm^3)
1,000 cubic decimeters (dm^3) | 1 cubic yard (yd^3) | 27 cubic feet (ft^3)
46,656 cubic inches ($in.^3$) |

Capacity

1 teaspoon	5 milliliters (mL)	1 cup (c)	8 fluid ounces (fl oz)
1 tablespoon	12.5 milliliters (mL)	1 pint (pt)	16 fluid ounces (fl oz) 2 cups (c)
1 liter (L)	1,000 milliliters (mL) 1,000 cubic centimeters (cm^3) 1 cubic decimeter (dm^3) 4 metric cups	1 quart (qt)	32 fluid ounces (fl oz) 4 cups (c) 2 pints (pt)
1 kiloliter (kL)	1,000 liters (L)	1 gallon (gal)	128 fluid ounces (fl oz) 16 cups (c) 8 pints (pt) 4 quarts (qt)

Weight

1 gram (g)	1,000 milligrams (mg)	1 pound (lb)	16 ounces (oz)
1 kilogram (kg)	1,000 grams (g)	1 ton (T)	2,000 pounds (lb)
1 metric ton (t)	1,000 kilograms (kg)		

MATHEMATICAL SYMBOLS

$=$	Is equal to	$\overleftrightarrow{AB}$	Line through points A and B
$\neq$	Is not equal to	$\overrightarrow{AB}$	Ray AB
$>$	Is greater than	$\overline{AB}$	Segment with endpoints A and B
$<$	Is less than	$\angle ABC$	Angle ABC
$\geq$	Is greater than or equal to	$m\angle ABC$	Measure of angle ABC
$\leq$	Is less than or equal to	$\triangle ABC$	Triangle ABC
$\approx$	Is approximately equal to	$\overset{\frown}{RS}$	Arc with endpoints R and S
$\cong$	Is congruent to	$\overleftrightarrow{AB} \perp \overleftrightarrow{CD}$	Line AB perpendicular to line CD
$\sim$	Is similar to	$\overleftrightarrow{AB} \parallel \overleftrightarrow{CD}$	Line AB is parallel to line CD
$\%$	Percent	$35°$	Thirty-five *degrees*
π	Pi		
$0.\overline{6}$	Repeating decimal		

METRIC SYSTEM PREFIXES

tera	T	one trillion	deci	d	one tenth
giga	G	one billion	centi	c	one hundredth
mega	M	one million	milli	m	one thousandth
kilo	k	one thousand	micro	μ	one millionth
hecto	h	one hundred	nano	n	one billionth
deka	da	ten	pico	p	one trillionth

FORMULAS

$P = a + b + c$	Perimeter of triangle	$C = \pi d$	Circumference of circle
$P = 2(l + w)$	Perimeter of rectangle	$A = \pi r^2$	Area of circle
$A = lw$	Area of rectangle	$A = 2\pi rh$	Lateral area of cylinder
$A = bh$	Area of parallelogram	$A = 2\pi r^2 + 2\pi rh$	Surface area of cylinder
$A = \frac{1}{2}(b_1 + b_2)h$	Area of trapezoid	$A = 2(lh + lw + wh)$	Surface area of rectangular prism
$A = \frac{1}{2}bh$	Area of triangle	$V = \pi r^2 h$	Volume of cylinder
$V = lwh$	Volume of rectangular prism		
$V = Bh$	Volume of prism (B = base area)		

GLOSSARY

abundant number   Any number for which the sum of its factors (other than the number itself) is greater than the given number.

acute angle   An angle that has a measure less than 90°.

acute triangle   A triangle in which each angle has a measure less than 90°.

addend   A number that is added.

angle   Two rays with a single endpoint, called the vertex of the angle.

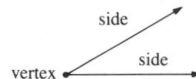

arc   A part of a circle.

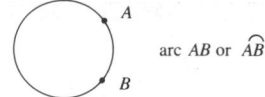

arc *AB* or $\overset{\frown}{AB}$

area   The measure of a plane region in terms of square units.

arithmetic mean   The quotient obtained when the sum of two or more numbers is divided by the number of addends.

associative property   The sum (or product) of three or more numbers is the same regardless of grouping:
$(a + b) + c = a + (b + c)$ or
$(a \cdot b) \cdot c = a \cdot (b \cdot c)$

average   See *arithmetic mean.*

base (in numeration)   The type of grouping involved in a system of numeration. In base eight, 346 means 3 sixty-fours, 4 eights, and 6.

base (of a polygon)   Any side of a polygon may be referred to as a base.

Base (of a space figure)   See examples below.

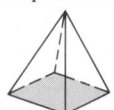

Bases of a cylinder   Base of a cone   Base of a pyramid

444

BASIC   A simple programming language.

binary   A base-two system of numeration.

bisect   To divide into two congruent parts.

bit   Binary digit, 0 or 1.

byte   String of bits whose length is the smallest accessible unit in computer memory.

capacity   The volume of a space figure given in terms of liquid measurement.

centimeter (cm)   A metric unit of length. One hundredth of a meter.

central angle   An angle that has its vertex at the center of a circle.

chord   A segment with both endpoints on a circle.

circle   All the points in a plane that are the same distance from one point called the center.

circumference   The distance around a circle.

commutative property   The sum (or product) of any two numbers is the same regardless of the order in which they are added (or multiplied):
$a + b = b + a$ or $a \cdot b = b \cdot a$

complementary angles   Two angles whose measures have a sum of 90°.

composite number   A number greater than 0 with more than two different factors.

cone   A space figure with a base that is a circular region and one vertex that is not in the same plane as the base.

congruent   Two geometric figures are congruent if they have the same size and shape.

coordinate axes Two intersecting perpendicular number lines used for graphing ordered number pairs.

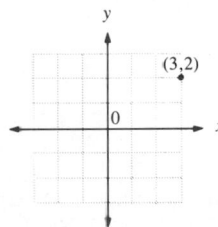

coordinates An ordered number pair matched with a point in the coordinate plane. See figure for *coordinate axes*.

cross products In the equation $\frac{a}{b} = \frac{c}{d}$, the products ad and bc are called cross products. Two ratios $\frac{a}{b} = \frac{c}{d}$ are equal if and only if $ad = bc$.

cross section The intersection of a space figure and a plane.

cube (numeration) A number raised to the third power. 8 is the cube of 2 because $2^3 = 8$. Also, to raise a number to the third power

cube (space figure) A prism whose faces are all congruent squares.

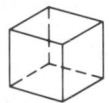

customary units Units of the system of measurement often used in the United States: pounds, ounces, tons, cups, pints, quarts, gallons, inches, feet, yards, miles, are customary units.

cylinder A space figure with two congruent bases that are circular regions in parallel planes, and a curved face.

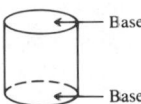

data A collection of unorganized facts that have not yet been processed into information.

decagon A polygon that has ten sides.

decimal (numeral) Any base-ten numeral written using a decimal point.

decimeter (dm) A metric unit of measurement of length equal to 0.1 m.

degree (°) A unit of measure for angles, $\frac{1}{90}$ of a right angle.

degree Celsius (°C) Unit for measuring temperature. On the Celsius scale, water freezes at 0°C and boils at 100°C.

degree Fahrenheit (°F) Unit for measuring temperature. On the Fahrenheit scale, water freezes at 32°F and boils at 212°F.

dekameter (dam) A metric unit of measurement of length equal to 10 m.

denominator For each fraction $\frac{a}{b}$, b is the denominator.

diagonal A segment connecting two non-consecutive vertices of a polygon.

diameter A chord that contains the center of a circle.

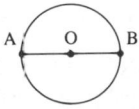

difference The number resulting from subtraction.

digits The basic symbols used in a place-value system of numeration. In base ten, the symbols are *0, 1, 2, 3, 4, 5, 6, 7, 8,* and *9.*

distributive property Connects addition and multiplication when both operations are involved.

$a(b + c) = a \cdot b + a \cdot c$

dividend The number to be divided in a division problem.

```
                    3  ← Quotient
Divisor →      5)17  ← Dividend
                   15
                   ‾‾
                    2  ← Remainder
```

445

divisible A given number is divisible by a second number if the remainder is zero.

divisor See *dividend*.

dodecahedron A polyhedron with twelve faces.

Regular dodecahedron

edge One of the segments making up any of the faces of a space figure.

equally likely outcomes Outcomes that have the same chance of occurring.

equal ratios Ratios that give the same comparison. $\frac{9}{27}$ and $\frac{1}{3}$ are equal ratios.

equation A mathematical sentence using the equality symbol ($=$).
$x - 27 = 102$ is an equation.

equilateral triangle A triangle with all three sides the same length.

equivalent fractions Fractions that represent the same number, such as $\frac{1}{3}$, $\frac{2}{6}$, and $\frac{3}{9}$.

estimate An approximation for a given number. Often used in the sense of a rough calculation.

expanded numeral Representations of numbers as a sum of multiples of 10 such as:

$4,325 = 4,000 + 300 + 20 + 5$ or

$4 \times 10^3 + 3 \times 10^2 + 2 \times 10 + 5$

exponent A number that tells how many times another number is to be used as a factor.

$$5 \cdot 5 \cdot 5 = 5^3 \quad \overset{\text{Exponent}}{\underset{\text{Base}}{}}$$

exponential notation A system of representing a number using an exponent.

expression (algebraic) Symbols or the combination of symbols, such as numerals, letters, operation symbols, and parentheses used to name a number.

face Any one of the bounding polygonal regions of a space figure.

446

factors Numbers that are to be multiplied.

factor tree A diagram suggestive of a tree showing the prime factorization of a number.

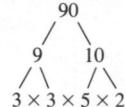

$3 \times 3 \times 5 \times 2$

flowchart A diagram that gives instructions in a logical order.

formula A general fact or rule expressed by using symbols. For example, the area (A) of any parallelogram with base b and height h is given by the formula $A = bh$.

fraction A number in the form $\frac{a}{b}$ when $b \neq 0$.

frequency The number of times a given item occurs in a set of data.

gallon (gal) A customary unit of liquid measure equal to 4 quarts or 16 cups.

gram (g) The basic unit of measurement of weight in the metric system.

greatest common factor (GCF) The greatest number that is a factor of each of two or more numbers.

hectometer (hm) A unit of measurement of length that is equal to 100 m.

heptagon A seven-sided polygon.

hexagon A six-sided polygon.

histogram A bar graph showing frequencies.

icosahedron A space figure with twenty faces.

Regular icosahedron

improper fraction A fraction whose numerator is greater than or equal to its denominator.

integer Any whole number or its opposite, and zero.

intersecting lines Lines that have one common point.

inverse (operation) Two operations that are opposite in effect. Adding 5 is the inverse of subtracting 5.

isosceles triangle A triangle with at least two congruent sides.

kilogram (kg) A metric unit of measurement of weight equal to 1,000 g.

kiloliter (kL) A metric unit of measurement of capacity equal to 1,000 L.

kilometer (km) A metric unit of measurement of length equal to 1,000 m.

least common denominator (LCD) The least common multiple of the denominators of two or more fractions. For example, the least common denominator of $\frac{5}{6}$ and $\frac{3}{4}$ is 12.

least common multiple (LCM) The smallest non-zero number that is a multiple of each of two or more given numbers. The LCM of 4 and 6 is 12.

line A straight path of points that goes on endlessly.

$$
\begin{array}{cc}
A & B \\
\bullet & \bullet
\end{array}
\qquad \text{Line } AB \text{ or } \overleftrightarrow{AB}
$$

line of symmetry A line on which a figure can be folded so that the two parts fit exactly.

liter (L) The basic unit of capacity in the metric system equal to 1,000 cm³.

loop A command that causes a computer to go back to an earlier step in the program and repeat it.

lowest-terms fraction A fraction for which the greatest common factor (GCF) of the numerator and denominator is 1.

median The middle number of a set of numbers that are arranged in order.

meter (m) The basic unit of measurement of length in the metric system.

metric ton (t) A unit of weight measurement equal to 1,000 kg.

microsecond One millionth of a second.

midpoint A point that divides a segment into two congruent segments.

milligram (mg) A metric unit of measurement of weight equal to 0.001 g.

milliliter (mL) A metric unit of measurement of capacity equal to 0.001 L.

millimiter (mm) A metric unit of measurement of length equal to 0.001 m.

mixed number A number such as $4\frac{2}{3}$ that has a whole number part and a fractional part.

mode In a list of data the mode is the number or item that occurs most often. There may be more than one mode.

multiple A number that is the product of a given number and a whole number.

$3 \cdot 8 = 24$ 24 is a multiple of 3.

negative integer The numbers less than zero that are opposites of natural numbers.

$\{^{-}1, \ ^{-}2, \ ^{-}3, \ \ldots\}$

nonagon A nine-sided polygon.

numeral A symbol for a number.

numerator For each fraction $\frac{a}{b}$, a is the numerator.

obtuse angle An angle with a measure greater than 90° and less than 180°.

obtuse triangle A triangle with one angle measuring more than 90°.

octagon An eight-sided polygon.

octahedron A space figure with eight faces.

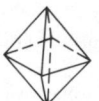 Regular octahedron

opposites property The sum of any number and its opposite is zero. $n + {}^{-}n = 0$

ordered pair A number pair arranged in order so there is a first number and a second number. The coordinates of a point in a plane such as (2,7) is an ordered pair of numbers.

447

ounce (oz) A customary unit of weight measurement. 16 ounces equal 1 pound.

outcome A possible result in a probability experiment.

parallel lines Lines in the same plane that do not intersect.

parallelogram A quadrilateral whose opposite sides are parallel.

pentagon A five-sided polygon.

percent (%) Literally, "per hundred." A way to compare a number with 100.

perimeter The sum of the length of the sides of a polygon.

period Each group of three digits starting with the ones digit is a period.

perpendicular bisector A line that bisects a segment and is perpendicular to it.

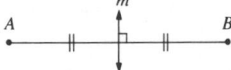

$m \perp$ bis $\overline{AB}$

perpendicular lines Two intersecting lines that form right angles.

pi (π) The ratio of the circumference of a circle to its diameter. The decimal for π is unending and does not repeat.
$\pi = 3.141592\ldots$

pint (pt) A customary unit of liquid measure equal to 2 cups.

place value The value given to the place a digit may occupy in a numeral. In the decimal numeration system, each place of a numeral has ten times the value of the place to its right.

polygon A closed plane figure formed by segments.

polyhedron A closed space figure whose faces are polygonal regions.

positive integer An integer greater than zero $\{1, 2, 3, \ldots\}$.

pound (lb) A customary unit of weight measurement.

prime factorization The expression of a composite number as the product of prime factors.
$36 = 2^2 \cdot 3^2$

prime number A whole number, greater than 1, whose only factors are itself and 1.

prism A space figure whose bases are congruent polygonal regions in parallel planes and whose faces are parallelograms.

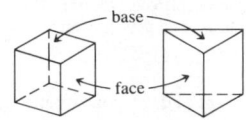

probability The ratio of the number of times a certain outcome can occur to the number of total possible outcomes.

product The number that results when two numbers are multiplied.

program Step-by-step instruction that directs the computer to perform operations.

property of one Any number multiplied by 1 will equal the number:
$a \times 1 = a$ or $a \div 1 = a$

property of zero For every integer a, $a + 0 = a$.

proportion An equation stating that two ratios are equal:
$\frac{3}{18} = \frac{1}{6}$

protractor An instrument for measuring the number of degrees (°) in an angle.

pyramid A space figure with a polygonal base and triangular faces with a common vertex.

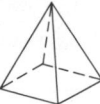

quadrilateral A four-sided polygon.

quart (qt) A customary unit of liquid measure equal to 2 pints or 4 cups.

quotient See *dividend*.

radius A segment or length of a segment from the center of a circle to a point on the circle.

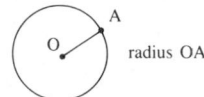

radius OA

range The difference between the greatest number and the least number in a set of data.

rate A ratio that compares different kinds of units.

ratio The ratio of two numbers a and b is their quotient, $\frac{a}{b}$.

ray A part of a line that has one endpoint and extends endlessly in one direction.

A ————————— B

Ray AB or $\overrightarrow{AB}$

reciprocals Two numbers are reciprocals if their product is 1. 7 and $\frac{1}{7}$ are reciprocals.

rectangle A parallelogram with four right angles.

region All the points in the part of a plane bounded by a simple closed curve.

regular polygon A polygon with all sides the same length and all angles the same measure.

relatively prime Two numbers with a greatest common factor (GCF) of 1 are relatively prime to each other. 8 and 27 are relatively prime numbers.

repeating decimal A decimal whose digits from some point on repeat endlessly. 6.2835835 . . . and 0.3333333 . . . are repeating decimals. They may also be written as $6.28\overline{35}$ and $0.\overline{3}$ respectively.

rhombus A parallelogram whose sides all have the same length.

right angle An angle that measures 90°.

right triangle A triangle with a right angle.

Roman numerals The numerals I, V, X, L, C, D, M, and combinations of these numerals, used in the Roman numeration system.

scale drawing A drawing made so that distances in the drawing are proportional to actual distances. A scale of 1:10 indicates that distances in the drawing are $\frac{1}{10}$ of the actual distances.

scalene triangle A triangle with all three sides having different measures.

scientific notation A system of writing a number as the product of a power of 10 and a number between 1 and 10.
$2,300,000 = 2.3 \times 10^6$

segment Two points and all points between them.

A ————————— B

Segment AB or $\overline{AB}$

similar figures Two or more figures with the same shape but not necessarily the same size.

space figures A (three-dimensional) geometric figure whose points do not all lie in the same plane.

sphere The set of all points in space at a fixed distance from a given point.

square (geometry) A quadrilateral with four right angles and all sides the same length.

square (numeration) A number raised to the second power. 9 is the square of 3. Also, to raise a number to the second power. $3^2 = 9$.

statistics Facts or data of a numerical kind.

straight angle An angle that has a measure of 180°.

string variables Locations in a computer that store data of any kind. A letter and the $ symbol form string variables. A$, B$, etc.

sum The result of the addition operation.

449

supplementary angles Two angles whose measures have a sum of 180°.

surface area The sum of the areas of all the faces of a space figure.

terminating decimal A decimal that represents the quotient of a whole number and a power of 10.

$$0.5 = \frac{5}{10} \qquad 1.28 = \frac{128}{10^2} \qquad 0.0307 = \frac{307}{10^4}$$

tetrahedron A polyhedron with four triangular faces.

ton (T) A customary unit of weight measurement equal to 2,000 pounds.

trapezoid A quadrilateral with one pair of parallel sides.

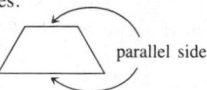

parallel sides

triangle A three-sided polygon.

unit An amount or quantity used as a standard of measurement.

variable A symbol, usually a letter, used to represent a number in an expression or an equation.

vertex (vertices) A point that two rays of an angle have in common. Also, the common point of any two sides of a polygon or the common point of intersection of three or more faces of a polyhedron.

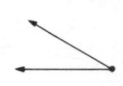 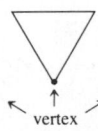 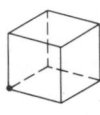

vertex

volume The measure of a space figure in terms of a chosen unit, usually a unit cube.

Venn diagram A special diagram using overlapping circles showing how data are related.

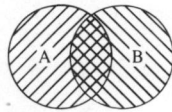

whole number Any number in the set {0, 1, 2, 3, . . .}.

zero property See *property of zero*.

Materials

This list is helpful in gathering and organizing materials that could be used for activities in each chapter.

Useful Materials for Book 7	Chapter															
	1	2	3	4	5	6	7	8	9	10	11	12	13	14	15	16
balance scale							√			√						
compass, chalkboard						√										
compasses						√					√		√	√	√	
containers (cup, pint, quart, gallon)																√
containers (milliliter, liter)										√						
coordinate grids*														√		
cubes, centimeter										√						
cubes, inch																√
cubes, number*		√		√		√	√	√				√	√	√	√	
decimal models			√	√	√								√			
dot paper*	√					√			√	√						
geoboards						√				√						
geometric models						√			√				√			√
graph paper, centimeter*		√	√	√						√	√		√			
graph paper, $\frac{1}{4}$-inch*				√		√			√				√	√		
grids, 10 × 10*		√					√						√			
hundred charts							√									
interlocking cubes	√	√	√	√	√											
isometric dot paper*						√		√								
meterstick											√	√	√			
place-value charts*		√							√							
place-value models	√	√	√	√	√								√			
probability devices													√			
protractors*						√					√			√		
ruler, centimeter*						√				√	√		√			
ruler, inch*																√
scale, customary																√
scale, metric										√						
spinners*														√	√	√
tangrams*						√		√					√			
thermometer, Celsius										√						
thermometer, Fahrenheit																√
trundle wheel										√						
weights, metric										√						
yardstick										√						√

*A form of this material is available in the Teaching Aids section of the Teacher's Resource Book.

Two courses of instruction help in pacing lessons throughout the school year.

Long-Range Planning Chart

Chapter	Minimum Course	Maximum Course
1 Addition and Subtraction of Whole Numbers	11 days pp. 1–23, 25–27, 30	10 days pp. 1–30
2 Addition and Subtraction of Decimals	9 days pp. 31–47, 51–54	7 days pp. 31–54
3 Multiplication and Division of Whole Numbers	12 days pp. 55–81, 83–86	10 days pp. 55–86
4 Multiplication	11 days pp. 87–107, 109–111, 114	10 days pp. 87–114
5 Division of Decimals	8 days pp. 115–129, 131–134	6 days pp. 115–134
6 Geometry	8 days pp. 135–151, 156–157, 159–162	10 days pp. 135–162
7 Number Relationships and Equations	12 days pp. 163–165, 168–185, 187–189, 192	14 days pp. 163–192
8 Addition and Subtraction of Fractions	12 days pp. 193–217, 219–222	11 days pp. 193–222
Mid-Year Review	3 days	2 days
9 Multiplication and Division of Fractions	10 days pp. 223–241, 243–246	8 days pp. 223–246
10 Measurement: Metric Units	11 days pp. 247–267, 269–271, 274	12 days pp. 247–274
11 Ratio and Proportion	7 days pp. 275–287, 289–292	8 days pp. 275–292
12 Percent	11 days pp. 293–313, 316–320	12 days pp. 293–320
13 Circles	8 days pp. 321–333, 337–339, 342	9 days pp. 321–342
14 Probability, Statistics, and Graphs	9 days pp. 343–361, 363–366	10 days pp. 343–366
15 Integers	10 days pp. 367–385, 389–392	12 days pp. 367–392
16 Measurement: Customary Units	5 days pp. 393–395, 400–405, 407–409, 412	7 days pp. 393–412
End-of-Year Review	3 days	2 days
Total:	160 days	160 days

Bibliography

Books for the Teacher

Adams, Sam, Leslie C. Ellis, and B. F. Beeson. *Teaching Mathematics with Emphasis on the Diagnostic Approach.* New York: Harper & Row, 1977.

Ashlock, Robert B. *Error Patterns in Computation: A Semi-Programmed Approach,* 3rd ed. Columbus, OH: Merrill, 1982.

Averbach, Bonnie, and Orin Chein. *Mathematics: Problem Solving Through Recreational Mathematics,* San Francisco Mathematical Sciences Series: Freeman, 1980.

Billstein, Richard, Schlomo Libeskind, and Johnny W. Lott. *A Problem Solving Approach to Mathematics for Elementary School Teachers.* Menlo Park, CA: Benjamin/Cummings, 1981.

Buxton, Laurie. *Do You Panic About Maths? Coping with Maths Anxiety.* Exeter, NH: Heinemann Educational Books, 1981.

Caravella, Joseph R. *Minicalculators in the Classroom.* Reston, VA: National Council of Teachers of Mathematics, 1977.

Charles, R.I., et al. *Problem-Solving Experiences in Mathematics.* Menlo Park, CA: Addison-Wesley, 1984.

Charles, R.I., and Frank Lester. *Problem Solving: What, Why, and How.* Palo Alto, CA: Dale Seymour, 1982.

Chayo, R. *General Mathematics: Making Practice Fun.* Reading, MA: Addison-Wesley, 1980.

Dolan, Daniel T., and James Williamson. *Teaching Problem Solving Strategies.* Menlo Park, CA: Addison-Wesley, 1983.

Dwyer, Thomas, and Margot Critchfield. *BASIC and the Personal Computer.* Reading, MA: Addison-Wesley, 1978.

Easterday, Kenneth E., Loren L. Henry, and F. Morgan Simpson. *Activities for Junior High School and Middle School Mathematics: Readings from the Arithmetic Teacher and the Mathematics Teacher.* Reston, VA: National Council of Teachers of Mathematics, 1981.

Fisher, Lyle, and William Medigovich. *Problem of the Week.* Palo Alto, CA: Dale Seymour, 1981.

Greenes, Carole, John Gregory, and Dale Seymour. *Successful Problem Solving Techniques.* Palo Alto, CA: Creative Publications, 1977.

Heimer, Ralph T., and Cecil R. Trueblood. *Strategies for Teaching Children Mathematics.* Reading, MA: Addison-Wesley, 1977.

Immerzeel, George, and Bob Willes. *Ideas from the Arithmetic Teacher.* Reston, VA: National Council of Teachers of Mathematics, 1979.

Jacobs, Harold R. *Mathematics—A Human Endeavor.* San Francisco: Freeman, 1970.

Krulik, Stephen, and Jesse A. Rudnick. *Problem-Solving: A Handbook for Teachers.* Rockleigh, NJ: Allyn and Bacon, 1980.

Kurtz, V. Ray. *Teaching Metric Awareness.* St. Louis: Mosby, 1976.

Lichtenberg, B. K., and A. P. Troutman, eds. *Fostering Creativity through Mathematics.* Tampa: Florida Council of Teachers of Mathematics, 1974.

Litwiller, Bonnie, and David Duncan. *Activities for the Maintenance of Computational Skills and the Discovery of Patterns.* Reston, VA: National Council of Teachers of Mathematics, 1980.

Lund, Chuck, and Margaret A. Smart. *Focus on Calculator Math.* Hayward, CA: Activity Resources, 1979.

Maletsky, Evan, and Christian Hirsch. *Activities from the Mathematics Teacher.* Reston, VA: National Council of Teachers of Mathematics, 1981.

National Council of Teachers of Mathematics. *Teaching Statistics and Probability: 1981 Yearbook.* Reston, VA: National Council of Teachers of Mathematics, 1981.

———, *Developing Computational Skills: 1978 Yearbook.* Reston, VA: National Council of Teachers of Mathematics, 1982.

———, *Problem Solving in School Mathematics: 1980 Yearbook.* Reston, VA: National Council of Teachers of Mathematics, 1980.

O'Daffer, P., and S. Clemens. *Geometry: An Investigative Approach.* Menlo Park, CA: Addison-Wesley, 1976.

O'Daffer, P., and S. Clemens. *Metric Measurement for Teachers: An Activity Approach.* Menlo Park, CA: Addison-Wesley, 1976.

Papert, Seymour. *Mindstorms: Children, Computers, and Powerful Ideas.* New York: Basic Books, 1980.

Pederson, Jean, and F. Armbruster. *A New Twist: Developing Arithmetic Skills Through Problem-Solving.* Menlo Park, CA: Addison-Wesley, 1978.

Ploutz, Paul F. *The Metric System: Content and Methods.* 2nd ed. Columbus, OH: Merrill, 1977.

Posamentier, Alfred S., and Gordon Sheridan. *Math Motivators: Investigations in Pre-Algebra.* Menlo Park, CA: Addison-Wesley, 1982.

Sentilovitz, M., and J. Thelen. *Baseball: A Game of Numbers.* Menlo Park, CA: Addison-Wesley, 1977.

———, and M. Trivisone. *Dice and Dots: A Book of Mathematical Games.* Menlo Park, CA: Addison-Wesley, 1979.

Shoecraft, Paul. *The Arithmetic Primer: Blueprint for Success.* Menlo Park, CA: Addison-Wesley, 1979.

Skolnick, Joan, Carol Langbort, and Lucille Day. *How To Encourage Girls in Math and Science: Strategies for Parents and Educators.* Englewood Cliffs, NJ: Prentice-Hall, 1982.

Thornburg, David D. *Picture This! An Introduction to Computer Graphics for Kids of All Ages.* Menlo Park, CA: Addison-Wesley, 1982.

———. *Picture This Too! An Introduction to Computer Graphics for Kids of All Ages.* Menlo Park, CA: Addison-Wesley, 1982.

Thornton, Carol A., et al. *Teaching Mathematics to Children with Special Needs.* Menlo Park, CA: Addison-Wesley, 1982.

Wheeler, Margariete M., and Clarence E. Hardgrove. *Mathematics Library—Elementary and Junior High School.* Reston, VA: National Council of Teachers of Mathematics, 1978.

Woodward, Dolores M. *Mainstreaming the Learning Disabled Adolescent: A Manual of Strategies and Materials.* Rockville, MD: Aspen Systems, 1981.

Recommended Periodicals

Arithmetic Teacher. Reston, VA: National Council of Teachers of Mathematics.

Instructor. New York: Instructor Publications, Inc.

Mathematics Teacher. Reston, VA: National Council of Teachers of Mathematics.

Books for the Student

Adler, David. *3, 2, 1 Number Fun.* New York: Doubleday, 1981.

Armstrong, Louise. *How to Turn Lemons into Money.* New York: Harcourt Brace Jovanovich, 1976.

Baird, Eva-Lee, and Rose Wyler. *Going Metric the Fun Way.* New York: Doubleday, 1980.

Barnett, Carne. *Metric Ease.* Palo Alto, CA: Creative Publications, 1975.

Barson, Alan. *Motivational Games for Mathematics.* Warrington, PA: Fabmath, 1981.

Benson, William H., and Oswald Jacoby. *New Recreations with Magic Squares.* New York: Dover, 1976.

Bitter, Gary G., and Thomas H. Metos. *Exploring with Pocket Calculators.* New York: Messner, 1977.

Brandes, Louis Grant. *Selected Cross-Number Puzzles.* Portland, ME: J. Weston Walch, 1976.

Burns, Marilyn. *The Book of Think (Or How to Solve a Problem Twice Your Size).* Little, Brown, 1976.

———. *The I Hate Mathematics! Book.* Boston: Little, Brown, 1975.

Carl, Iris M. *Computing with the Tangram.* Englewood Cliffs, NJ: Prentice-Hall, 1977.

Doty, Roy, and Leonard Maar. *How Much Does America Cost?* New York: Doubleday, 1979.

Evans, Larry. *Three-Dimensional Mazes.* San Francisco: Troubadour Press, 1976.

Fair, Jan. *Handy Math: Focus on Earning Money.* Palo Alto, CA: Creative Publications, 1981.

———. *Handy Math: Focus on Managing Money.* Palo Alto, CA: Creative Publications, 1981.

Fisher, David E. *The Ideas of Einstein.* New York: Holt, Rinehart & Winston, 1980.

Fraser, Don. *Newspaper Math.* New York: Collier/Macmillan, 1980.

Froman, Robert. *The Greatest Guessing Game.* New York: Thomas Y. Crowell, 1978.

Gregory, John, and Dale Seymour. *Limerick Number Puzzles.* Palo Alto, CA: Creative Publications, 1978.

Humphrey, Henry, and Dierdre O'Meara-Humphrey. *When Is Now? Experiments with Time and Timekeeping Devices.* New York: Doubleday, 1980.

Hunter, J. A. H., and Joseph S. Madachy. *Mathematical Diversions.* New York: Dover, 1975.

James, Elizabeth, and Carol Barkin. *What Do You Mean by "Average"? Means, Medians, and Modes.* New York: Lothrop, 1978.

Jespersen, James, and Jane Fitz-Randolph. *Time and Clocks for the Space Age.* New York: Atheneum, 1979.

King, Carol. *Buying with Sense,* Pacemaker Practical Arithmetic Series. Belmont, CA: Pitman Learning, 1980.

Mitchell, Merle. *Mathematical History: Activities, Puzzles, Stories and Games.* Reston, VA: National Council of Teachers of Mathematics, 1978.

Murphy, Elaine C. *Developing Skills with Tables and Graphs,* Book B. Palo Alto, CA: Dale Seymour, 1981.

O'Connor, Vincent F. *Mathematics on the Playground.* Milwaukee, WI: Raintree, 1978.

Peter, Rozsa. *Playing with Infinity: Mathematical Explorations and Excursions.* New York: Dover, 1976.

Polis, A. Richard, Earl Beard, and Fred Donatucci. *Magic Squares and Arrays.* Warrington, PA: Fabmath, 1980.

Porter, Richard D. *Project-A-Puzzle.* Reston, VA: National Council of Teachers of Mathematics, 1978.

Rice, Jean. *My Friend the Computer.* Minneapolis: Dennison, 1981.

Riedel, Manfred G. *Odds and Chances for Kids: A Look at Probability.* Englewood Cliffs, NJ: Prentice-Hall, 1979.

———. *Winning with Numbers: A Kid's Guide to Statistics.* Englewood Cliffs, NJ: Prentice-Hall, 1978.

Seymour, Dale. *Developing Skills in Estimation,* Books A and B. Palo Alto, CA: Dale Seymour, 1981.

Sitomer, Mindel, and Harry Sitomer. *Circles.* New York: Thomas Y. Crowell, 1971.

———. *Lines, Segments, Polygons.* New York: Thomas Y. Crowell, 1972.

———. *Zero Is Not Nothing.* New York: Thomas Y. Crowell, 1978.

Smith, David Eugene. *Number Stories of Long Ago,* Classics in Mathematics Education Series, Vol. 2. Reston, VA: National Council of Teachers of Mathematics, 1973.

Sohns, Marvin L., and Audrey V. Buffington. *The Measurement Book.* San Jose, CA: Enrich/Ohaus, 1977.

Spencer, Donald D. *Exploring the World of Computers.* Ormond Beach, FL: Camelot, 1982.

Srivastava, Jane Jonas. *Number Families.* New York: Thomas Y. Crowell, 1980.

Stern, David P. *Math Squared: Graph Paper Activities for Fun and Fundamentals.* New York: Teachers College Press, 1981.

Wallach, Paul J. *Meet the Metric System.* Belmont, CA: Pitman Learning, 1980.

Weiss, Malcolm E. *Six Hundred and Sixty-Six Jellybeans! All That? An Introduction to Algebra,* Young Math Series. New York: Harper & Row, 1976.

———. *Solomon Grundy, Born on Oneday,* Young Math Series. New York: Harper & Row, 1977.

Zaslavsky, Claudia. *Count on Your Fingers, African Style.* New York: Thomas Y. Crowell, 1980.

Software

Battling Bugs/Concentration (Apple II Plus, Atari). St. Louis: Milliken.

Bumble Plot (Apple). Menlo Park, CA: The Learning Company.

Computer Math Activities (Apple). Menlo Park, CA: Addison-Wesley.

Computer Math Games (Apple). Menlo Park, CA: Addison-Wesley.

Delta Drawing (Apple, Atari, IBM). Cambridge, MA: Spinnaker.

Golf Classic/Compubar (Apple II Plus, Atari). St. Louis: Milliken.

Teachers' references are in italics.

A

Abundant numbers, 167
Acute triangle, 140–141
Addition
  of decimals, 40–41
  equations, 178–179
  of fractions, 206–207, 233
  of integers, 370ff.
  basic properties, 370–371
  of mixed numbers, 210–211
  of units of time, 18–19
  of whole numbers, 12ff.
Angles, 138–139
Applied problem solving, 316, 336, 362,
  388, 406
Arc, 146–147
Area
  of circle(s), 324–325, 329, 396–397
  of cylinder(s), 328–329
  of parallelogram(s), 254, 396
  of rectangle(s), 254, 396
  surface, 258
  of trapezoid(s), 256–257
  of triangle(s), 256–257
Associative property
  of addition, 370
  of multiplication, 56
Average, 126–127, 354
Axis, 384ff.

B

Base (geometry), 156, 254, 260
Base (numeration)
  two, 53
  sixteen, 339
BASIC, *340–341*
Basic properties, 56, 370–371
Binary numbers, 53
Binary system, *272*
Bisect, 154–155
Bit, *272*
Bytes, *272*

C

Calculator activities, 28–29, 37, 77, 319,
  375, 404
Calculator logic, *28*
Capacity
  customary units, 400
  displacement, 271
  metric units, 262
Career awareness
  agriculture, 358, 359

art and entertainment, 115, 163, 226,
  241, 282–283
business services, 23, 81, 105, 206, 245
education, 78, 250, 308
environmental control, 64, 72, 73, 117,
  255, 319, 322, 332–333, 343, 358–359,
  362, 367
food service, 16–17, 76, 265
health and public service, 18, 55, 166,
  184, 193, 352, 362
law and government, 293
marketing, 1, 10, 182, 200, 205, 208,
  218, 313, 340
science and technical service, 31, 34, 38,
  55, 87, 92, 98, 112–113, 163, 210, 284,
  300, 332–333, 334, 350
sports, 74–75, 121, 150
transportation, 21, 29, 48–49, 78–79,
  135, 158, 376
Casting out nines, 111
Celsius scale, 266
Centimeter, 248–249
Circle, 146–147
  area, 324–325, 329, 396–397
  central angle, 146–147
  chord, 146–147
  circumference, 322–323
  diameter, 322–323
  minor arc, *146*
Commutative property, 56
Comparing, 6, 36, 202, 368
Compass, 152–156
Complementary angle, 138–139
Composite numbers, 168–169
Computer literacy
  BASIC, 67, 75, 112–113
  INPUT, 190–191
  Decisions, 272–273
  Loops, 340–341
  Graphics, 410–411
Cone, 156–157
Congruent figures, 148–149
Consumer applications
  see also Applied problem solving
  area, 255, 324–325
  average, 126–127
  customary units, 123, 126–127, 401, 402
  decimal numbers, 40–41, 44–45, 47, 76–
    77, 94–95, 101, 118–119, 122–123,
    124–125, 326–327
  estimation, 58–59, 129
  equations, 183, 255, 263, 283, 305
  fractions, 205, 236–237, 245
  metric units, 76–77, 101, 116–117, 121,
    263, 265
  percent, 296–297, 304, 305, 313
  rate, 122–123, 236–237, 316, 336, 404–
    405, 406
  ratio, 278–279, 282–283

time, 96–97
whole numbers, 8–9, 10–11, 14–15, 16–
  17, 23, 68–69
Coordinate(s), 384–385
Coplanar, *136*
CPU, *190*
Cross products, 278–279
Cross sections, 334–335
Cubic units, 260ff., 330, 398
Customary units of measure, 394ff.
Cylinder(s), 156–157
  area of, 328–329
  volume of, 330–331, 398

D

Data bank, 23, 413–416
Decagon, 144–145
Decimal(s), 32ff.
  adding, 40–41
  comparing and ordering, 36–37
  dividing, 116ff.
  estimation with, 44–45, 90–91, 100, 129
  fractions and, 238–239, 245
  multiplication of, 88ff.
  numeration system, 4–5, 34
  percent(s) and, 294–295, 298
  place value, 34–35
  repeating, 241
  rounding, 38–39, 44–45, 90–91, 100,
    118, 129
  subtraction of, 42–43
  terminating, 241
Decimeter, 248–249
Decision box, 272–273
Deficient numbers, *183*
Degree (angle measure), 138–139
Dekameter, 248–249
Diameter, 146–147, 322
Discount prices and percent, 313
Distributive property, *56*
Divisibility, 166–167
Division
  of decimals, 116ff.
  by a power of ten, 70, 120
  equations, 180–181
  estimation, 71
  of fractions, 232–235
  of integers, 382–383
  of mixed numbers, 234–235
  short division, 73
  of whole numbers, 70ff.

E

Equal ratios, 278–279
Equation(s), 178ff.
  addition, 178–179
  division, 180–181

graphing of, 386–387
multiplication, 180–181
subtraction, 178–179
Equilateral triangle(s), 140–141, 144–145
Equivalent fractions, 196–197
Error analysis, *1B, 31B, 55B, 87B, 115B,*
135B, 163B, 193B, 223B, 247B, 275B,
293B, 321B, 343B, 367B, 393B
Estimating
differences, 10–11, 44–45
fractional parts, 204
measurements, 249, 262, 264, 402, 403
percent(s), 299
products, 58–59, 90–91, 100
quotients, 71, 277
sums, 10–11, 44–45
volume, 335
Euclidian algorithm, *189*
Even number, *4*
Expanded notation, 4–5
Exponent(s), 66–67
Expression(s), 176–177

F

Factor(s), 164ff.
common, 172–173
greatest common, 172–173
prime, 170–171
tree, 170–171
Fahrenheit scale, 403
Fibonnaci sequence, 27
Foot, 394–395
Fraction(s), 194ff.
addition, 206–207, 210–211, 233
basic concepts, 194–195
comparing, 202–203
decimals and, 238–239, 245
division, 232–233, 234–235
equivalent, 196–197
estimation, 204
improper, 200–201
lowest-terms, 198–199
mixed numbers, 200–201
multiplication, 224–229
of a whole number, 224–225
percents and, 296–297, 300–301
reciprocals, 231
subtraction, 208–209, 212ff.
unit, 211
Frequency, 352–353

G

Gallon, 400
Games
Build a Number, *1F*
Build a Proportion, *275F*
Chance It, *343F*
Commission, *293F*
Concentration, *223F, 247F*
Decimal Race, *31F, 115F*
Digit Exchange, *31F*
The Dot Connection, *1F*
Equivalent Fractions, *193F*
Flow Charts, *321F*
Fraction Addition, *193F*
Guess My Numbers, *24*
Guess the Factor, *172*
Integer Number Line, *367F*
Magic Squares, *223F*
Measurement Rummy, *393F*
Missing Factor, *87F*
Prime Number, *163F*
Target Quotient, *115F*
Territorial Claims, *247F*
Quintet, *55F*
Unlucky 13, *135F*
Gifted students, activities for, *3, 107, 183,*
277, 290–291, 309, 335, 345, 379
Glide ratio, 78
Gram, 264
Graph(s)
bar, 356
circle, 359
coordinate, 384–385
double bar, *356*
histogram, *356*
of equations, 286–287
line segment, 357
making, 356–359
pictograph, 358
Greatest common factor (GCF), 172–173,
189, 198–199

H

Hectometer, 248–249
Heptagon, 144–145
Hexagon, 144–145
History of mathematics, *26–27, 52–53, 84–*
85, 110–111, 188–189, 220–221, 244–
245, 270–271, 318–319, 338–339,
390–391, 408–409

I

Icosahedron, 156–157
Identity element, *56*
Inch, 394–395
Inequalities, *379*
compound, *379*
INPUT, 190–191
Integer(s), 368ff.
addition, 372ff.
basic properties, 370–371
coordinate graph(s) and, 384–385
division, 382–383
multiplication, 380–381
negative, 368–369, 372–373
opposites, 368–369, 376–377
positive, 368–369, 372–373
subtraction, 376–377
Interest, compound, *309*
Interest, simple, 304
International System of Units (SI), *247A*

K

Kilogram, 264
Kiloliter, 262
Kilometer, 248–249
Kilowatts, *88*

L

Least common denominator (LCD), 206
Least common multiple (LCM), 174–175,
206
Length
customary units of, 394–395
metric units of, 248ff.
Line(s)
intersecting, 136–137
parallel, 136–137, 152–153
perpendicular, 152–153
of symmetry, 150–151
Liquid volume, *see* Capacity
Liter, 262
Logical reasoning, 43, 99, 179, 215, 385
problem-solving strategy, 242
Logo, 410–411
Loop, 340–341

M

Magic square(s), 43, 215, 307
Magic triangle(s), 233, 377
Math anxiety, *132–133*
Math Lab, *1F, 31F, 55F, 87F, 115F, 135F,*
163F, 193F, 247F, 275F, 293F, 321F,
343F, 367F, 393F
Mathematics history, 2–3, 85, 111, 133,
211, 271, 275
Mean, *see* Average
Measures, *see* Customary units, Metric
units
Median, 354
Memory, 28–29
Mental math
column addition, 13
decimal products, 98–99
division, 70, 120
products, 57, 175
subtraction, 19
Meter, 248–249
Metric units of measure, 248ff.

area and, 254, 256–257
changing units of length, 250–251
estimation, 249, 262, 264
prefixes, 251
surface area, 258
units of capacity, 262
units of length, 248ff.
units of weight, 264
volume, 260–261
Metric ton, 264
Mile, 394–395
Milligram, 264
Milliliter, 262
Millimeter, 248–249
Minuend, *14*
Mixed numbers, 200ff.
addition of, 210–211
comparing, 202–203
division of, 234–235
multiplication of, 228–229
subtraction of, 212ff.
Mode, 352–353
Modular arithmetic, 409
Multiplication
basic properties, 56, 370
by 10 and powers of 10, 57
integers, 380–381
of decimals, 88, 89, 92ff., 98–99
equations, 180–181
estimation, 58–59, 90–91,100
of fractions, 224–227
of integers, 380–381
of mixed numbers, 228–229
patterns, 175
of whole numbers, 56ff.

N

Napier's rods (Bones), 85
Negative integers, 368–369
Network(s), 315
Nonagon, 144–145
Number theory, 111, 164ff.
abundant numbers, 167
composite numbers, 168–169
divisibility, 166–167
factors, 164ff.
Fibonnaci, 27
greatest common factor (GCF), 172–173, 189
least common multiple (LCM), 174–175
palindromic, 65
prime factorization, 170ff.
prime numbers, 168–169
square, 11, 117
triangular, 11
Numerals
base-sixteen, 339
base-two (binary), 53

Chinese, 2
decimal numeration system, 4–5, 34–35
Egyptian, 2–3
Kamba counting, 2
Mayan, 2–3
Roman, 2–3

O

Obtuse angle, 138–139
Obtuse triangle, 140–141
Octagon, 144–145
Octahedron, 156–157
Odd number, 4
One, property of, 56, 370
Opposite(s), 368–369, 376–377
Opposites property, 370
Ordered pairs, 348–349
Ordinal number, *2*
Ounce, 402
Outcome(s), 344–345

P

Palindromic numbers, 65
Parallel lines, 136–137, 152–153
Parallelogram(s), 142–143
area of, 254, 396–397
Patterns, 7, 11, 65, 117, 169, 239, 375, 381
Pentagon(s), 144–145
Percent(s), 294ff.
decimals and, 294–295, 298
discounts and, 313
estimation of, 299
finding a number when a percent of it is known, 310–311
fractions and, 294ff., 300–301
interest, 304
of change, 319
one number is of another, 306–307
proportion and, 314–315
ratio and, 294–295, 306–307, 314–315
of a whole number, 302–303
Perfect numbers, *183*
Perimeter, 252–253
Period(s), 4
Perpendicular lines, 152–153
Perpendicular bisector, 154
Pi (π), 322–323, 365, 396
PILOT, *340–341*
Pint, 400
Place value
of decimals, 34–35
of whole numbers, 4–5, 53, 339
Plane, 136–137
Platonic solids, 161
Point(s), 136–137
Polling methods, *364–365*

Polygon(s), 144–145
concave and convex, *135A*
Polyhedrons, regular, 161
Positive integers, 368–369
Pound, 402
Power of, *55A*
Prediction, 205, 336, 334–351, 362
Prime factorization, 170–171
Prime numbers, 168–169
Prism, 156–157
volume of, 260–261, 390–391
Probability, 344ff.
chance and, 346–347
equally likely outcomes, 344–345
estimation of, 349
experiment, 365
graphs and, 356
ordered pairs, 348–349
outcome(s), 344–345
Problem solving
see also Applied problem-solving, Problem-solving applications, Problem-solving data sources, Problem-solving strategies
answering the question, 21
choosing the operations, 78–79
choosing equations, 182–183
finding averages, 126–127
finding unit prices, 404–405
practice, 68–69, 106–107, 121, 217, 255, 259, 263, 267, 326–327, 332–333, 350–351, 379, 401
understanding questions, 20
using a calculator, 28–29, 404–405
using data from an advertisement, 47
using a data bank, 23
using a graph, 360–361, 378
using a map, 48–49, 286
using a table, 96–97, 105, 122–123, 205, 236–237, 265, 355
using estimation, 101
using the 5-Point Checklist, 16–17, 282–283
using percent(s), 308–309
using simple interest, 305
writing questions, 20
writing and solving equations, 184–185
Problem-solving applications
area, 255, 259, 326, 333, 362
averages, 126–127, 135, 362
circumference, 326–327, 333
capacity, 263, 401
chill factor, *378*
commission, *315*
customary units, 78–79, 122–123, 127, 217, 282–283, 401, 404–405
decimal numbers, 46, 47, 69, 79, 96–97, 101, 105, 106–107, 121, 122–123, 126–127, 217, 316, 336, 379

equations, 182–183, 184–185
estimation, 101, 129, 287, 362
fractions, 205, 216, 217, 236–237, 360
graphs, 360–361, 378
interest, 305
integers, 378
metric units, 20, 121, 255, 259, 263, 265, 278, 332–333, 267, 286, 326–327, 355, 362
money, 47, 68–69, 96–97, 105, 122–123, 255, 297, 305, 313, 316, 336, 388, 404, 406
percent, 305, 308–309, 313, 333, 350–351, 361
probability, 350–351
ratio, 78, 282–283, 286–287
statistics, 350–351, 355, 358–359, 360–361
surface area, 3, 259
temperature, 267, 361, 378, 379
time, 20, 48–49, 69, 81, 96–97, 121, 217, 332, 336, 388
unit prices, 404–405, 406
volume, 263, 332–333
weight, 265
whole numbers, 16–17, 20, 21, 23, 68–69, 78–79, 126–127, 360, 362
Problem-solving data sources
advertisement, 47
data bank, 23, 413–416
drawing, 78, 255, 259
graph, 283, 360–361, 378
map, 48–49, 286, 415
menu, 16–17
table, 80, 96–97, 104–105, 122–123, 205, 236–237, 265, 355
Problem-solving strategies
choose the operations, 218
draw a picture, 108
find a pattern, 82
guess and check, 24
make an organized list, 50
make a table, 186
solve a simpler problem, 158
use logical reasoning, 242
using the strategies, 268, 288
work backward, 130
Problem-solving, teaching, 1B, 31B, 55B, 87B, 115B, 135B, 163B, 193B, 223B, 247B, 275B, 293B, 321B, 343B, 367B, 393B
Programs, computer, 112–113, 190–191, 272–273, 340–341, 410–411
Projects, 1F, 31F, 55F, 87F, 115F, 135F, 163F, 193F, 223F, 247F, 275F, 293F, 321F, 343F, 367F, 393F
Properties
for integers, 370–371

for whole numbers, 56
Proportion(s), 278ff.
percent and, 314–315
Protractor, 138–139
Puzzle, 93, 221
Pyramid(s), 156–157

Q

Quadrilateral(s), 142ff.
Quart, 400

R

Radius, 146–147, 396ff.
RAM, 190
Range (statistics), 352–353
Rate, 96–97, 276ff.
Ratio(s), 276ff.
cross products and, 278–279
equal, 278–279
golden, 291
percent and, 306–307
proportion, 278ff.
rate, 276
Ray, 136–137
Reciprocals, 231
Rectangle(s), 142–143
area of, 254, 396–397
Regular polygon(s), 144–145
Regular polyhedron(s), 161
Repeated factor, 66
Repeating decimal(s), 241
Rhombus, 142–143
Right angle, 138–139
Right triangle, 140–141
ROM, 190
Roman numerals, 2–3
Rounding
decimals, 38–39, 44–45, 90–91, 118–119
decimal quotients, 118–119
to estimate decimal quotients, 129
to estimate differences, 10–11
to estimate products, 58–59, 90–91
to estimate quotients, 71
to estimate sums, 10–11
whole numbers, 8ff.
RUN, 112–113
REM, 190–191

S

Scale drawing, 286
Scalene triangle, 140–141
Scientific notation, 102–103
Segment(s), line, 136–137, 154–155
Shape perception, 143, 145, 149, 155, 157, 213
Short division, 73

Similar figures, 284–285
Simple interest, 304
Skew, 136
Space figures, 156–157
Space perception, 161, 314
cross sections, 334–335
Special Education, 1C, 17, 23, 31C, 33, 55C, 69, 81, 87C, 91, 115C, 135C, 149, 155, 163C, 167, 193C, 195, 217, 223C, 231, 247C, 250, 259, 275C, 293C, 295, 321C, 329, 343C, 353, 367C, 369, 393C, 405
Sphere, 156–157
Square(s), 142ff.
Square numbers, 11, 117
Standard numerals, 4–5, 66–67, 102–103
Statistics
average, 354
frequency, 352–353
graphs and, 356ff.
median, 354
mode, 352–353
range, 352–353
sample, 362
tally sheet, 349
Subtraction
of decimals, 42–43
equations, 178–179
of fractions, 208–209
of integers, 376–377
of mixed numbers, 212ff.
of units of time, 18–19
of whole numbers, 14–15
Subtrahend, 14
Surface area, 258

T

Tax, 94–95
Technology, see also Calculator activities, Computer literacy, 28–29, 67, 75, 77, 85, 112–113, 190–191, 272, 273, 310–311, 340–341
Temperature
Celsius scale, 266
Fahrenheit scale, 403
Terminating decimals, 241
Time, adding and subtracting units of, 18–19, 48–49
Time zones, 48–49
Ton, 402
Topology, 160–161
Trapezoid(s), 142–143
area of, 256–257
Triangle(s), 140–141
area of, 256–257
Triangular numbers, 11
Turtle, 410

Index

U

Unit fractions, 211
Universal product code, 340–341

V

Variable(s), 176–177
Venn diagram, 242
Vertex (vertices), 138–139, 157
Volume
  and customary units, 398–399
  of cylinder(s), 330–331, 335, 398–399
  and metric units, 260–261
  of prism(s), 260–261, 398–399

W

Weight
  customary units of, 402
  metric units of, 264
Whole numbers
  addition of, 12–13
  comparing and ordering, 6–7
  division of, 72ff.
  finding a fraction of a, 224–225
  finding a percent of a, 302–303
  multiplication, 56ff.
  rounding, 8ff.
  subtraction, 14–15

Y

Yard, 394–395

Z

Zero(s)
  annexing, 40ff., 118–119
  in products, 94–95
  property of, 370–371

Illustrations

by courtesy of **Bay Area Rapid Transit District:** 374 bottom
Lisa French: 402
Linda Harris-Sweezy: 12, 38, 44
Tom Hickey: 18, 48
Masami Miyamoto: 135, 250, 262, 264, 321, 368, 380, 400, 403, 416
Sandra Popovich: 11, 17, 32, 58, 59, 72, 96, 98, 127, 278, 329, 334, 400
Valerie Randall: 59, 78, 102, 142, 150, 210, 212, 227, 277, 299
Cynthia Swann-Brodi: 29, 47, 271, 286, 384, 386
Margaret Tisdale: 27
Susan Wollum: 2, 3
from **The World Book Encyclopedia,** © 1982 **World Book-Childcraft International, Inc.:** 107

Photographs

Jeff Albertson/Stock, Boston: 313
Erik Anderson/Stock, Boston: 60 right
© 1979 **Jim Anderson/Woodfin Camp & Associates:** 101
© **Mark Antman/Stock, Boston:** 379 bottom
© 1980 **Craig Aurness/Woodfin Camp & Associates:** 393 top right
© **Craig Aurness/West Light:** 396
© 1976 **Craig Aurness/West Light:** 234
David Austen/Stock, Boston: 223 top left
© 1980 **Frank Balthis:** 362
John Barnett: 115 top left
Julian Baum/Bruce Coleman Inc.: 326–327, 372
Tom Bean/Tom Stack & Associates: 367 bottom right
© 1980 **C. Walsh Bellville/Photo Library:** 206
© 1981 **Nathan Benn/Woodfinn Camp & Associates:** 117
The Bettmann Archive, Inc.: 31 top right, 85, 271, 293 top right
© **John Blaustein/Woodfin Camp & Associates:** 23
Elihu Blotnick*: 322
© 1980 **Dennis Brack/Black Star:** 293 top left
Tom Brakefield/Bruce Coleman Inc.: 276 left
© 1982 **Sisse Brimberg/Woodfin Camp, Inc.:** 354
Alexander Cameron/Tandem Computers, Inc.: 113
© **Alan Clifton/After-Image:** 40
© **Stuart Cohen/Stock, Boston:** 255
Lois and George Cox/Bruce Coleman, Inc.: 323
Culver Pictures: 31 top left, 74, 133, 275 bottom right
© 1982 **Doris DeWitt/Atoz Images:** 130
© **Donald Dietz/Stock, Boston:** 264
David Em, artist; computer software written by **Dr. James F. Blinn:** 221
Milton Feinberg/Stock, Boston: 241, 256
© **Patricia Lanza Field/Bruce Coleman Inc.:** 410
© 1981 **Frank Fisher/After-Image:** 245
© **Jeff Foott/Bruce Coleman Inc.:** 144, 332–333, 343 top left
Lee Foster/Bruce Coleman Inc.: 78-79, 122
George B. Fry III*: 31 bottom left, 60 left, 62, 115 top right, center right, bottom left and bottom right, 129, 168
© **Paul Fusco/Magnum Photos:** 247 center right, 393 bottom left
© **Peter Garfield/After-Image:** 367 bottom center
© **Kenneth Garrett/Woodfin Camp, Inc.:** 275 center right
© **Burt Glinn/Magnum Photos:** 280
© 1979 **Luise Graff/Atoz Images:** 263 top

M. W. Grosnick/Bruce Coleman Inc.: 184–185
© 1980 **Gerhard Gscheidle/Peter Arnold, Inc.:** 190
© 1980 **George Hall/Woodfin Camp & Associates:** 68–69
© **Charles Harbutt/Archive Pictures:** 135 (both)
© **Erich Hartmann/Magnum Photos:** 148
© **Michal Heron/Woodfin Camp & Associates:** 232–233
© **D. P. Hershkowitz/Bruce Coleman Inc.:** 268
J. R. Holland/Stock, Boston: 120
© **Thomas Hopker/Woodfin Camp & Associates:** 121
© 1980 **Richard Howard/Black Star:** 367 top left and center left
© **Manfred Kage/Peter Arnold, Inc.:** 140
Stanley King Collection: 24 (all)
© **Pierre Kopp/West Light:** 393 center right
Larry Lee/West Light: 284 (both)
Wayland Lee*/Addison-Wesley Publishing Company: 1 bottom right, 2 (all), 4, 10 left and center, 14, 16, 17, 20, 31 bottom right, 44 left, 45, 50, 58 (both), 59 (both), 64, 66, 72, 73, 82, 92, 94, 95, 96, 98, 100 left, 102 bottom, 103, 118, 124, 127, 167, 172, 178 (both), 179, 180 (both), 194 (both), 196, 204 (all), 205, 213, 224 (all), 225 (all), 227, 228 left, 229 (both), 258 bottom, 262, 263 bottom, 265, 278, 293 bottom left, 294, 296, 297, 299, 329, 344 (all), 345 (all), 346 bottom left and bottom right, 347 (both), 348 (both), 349 (all), 351 left and right, 361, 364 (all), 365 (all), 375, 385, 388, 391, 398 (both), 400
Library of Congress: 1 top left
Lowell Observatory Photograph: 87 (all)
© 1982 **Jeff Lowenthal/Woodfin Camp & Associates:** 238
© 1982 **David Madison/Bruce Coleman Inc.:** 198, 214
Steven Mangold*: 1 top right, 44 right, 70, 71, 81, 88, 90
© 1980 **James Mason/Black Star:** 310
Mike Mazzaschi/Stock, Boston: 164
Coco McCoy/Rainbow: 27
© **Dan McCoy/Rainbow:** 10 right, 34 right, 55 top left, 215, 300, 321 bottom right
© 1980 **Wally McNamee/Woodfin Camp & Associates:** 150
Peter Menzel: 137 left
© 1981 **Peter Menzel:** 182
© **J. Messerschmidt/Bruce Coleman Inc.:** 291
Gary Millburn/Tom Stack & Associates: 136 right, 367 bottom left
© **Kurt Mitchell/Photo Library:** 174, 247 right
© **A. Moldvay/After-Image:** 202
© **Linda Moore/Rainbow:** 223 center, 308–309
Hank Morgan/Rainbow: 223 bottom left
NASA: 6, 102 top
National Semiconductor Corporation: 341
Nelson-Atkins Museum of Art; Kansas City, Missouri (Nelson Fund): 146
Mark Newman/Tom Stack & Associates: 343 center right
The New York Public Library; Astor, Lenox and Tilden Foundations: 1 bottom left, Prints Division; 275 top left; 275 top center, Rare Book Division
D. J. Palke/Atoz Images: 116
Brian Parker/Tom Stack & Associates: 379 top
Maryanne Pendergast, Department of Anatomy, University of North Carolina Medical Center: 34 left
© 1982 **Stacy Pick/Stock, Boston:** 226
Rod Planck/Tom Stack & Associates: 137 right
© 1982 **Marc Pokempner/Black Star:** 282
© **Hans Reinhard/Bruce Coleman Inc.:** 201, 276 bottom right
L. L. T. Rhodes/Atoz Images: 306

Editorial and Design Staff

Project Manager Rosalie Whitlock

Student Edition Editors Roger Kincaid, Wendy Earl

Teacher's Edition Editors Jean Carlson, Karen Gulliver, Rochelle Blair

Project Designer Don Taka

Student Edition Designer Victoria Philp, Margaret Tisdale

Project Photo Editor Karen Koppel